AF716885

PEOPLE'S CHINA AND INTERNATIONAL LAW

STUDIES IN EAST ASIAN LAW
Harvard University

VOLUME 1

PEOPLE'S CHINA and INTERNATIONAL LAW

A Documentary Study

JEROME ALAN COHEN and HUNGDAH CHIU

PRINCETON UNIVERSITY PRESS
Princeton, New Jersey

The Harvard Law School, in cooperation with Harvard's East Asian Research Center, the Harvard-Yenching Institute, and scholars from other institutions, has initiated a program of training and research designed to further scholarly understanding of the legal systems of China, Japan, Korea, and adjacent areas. A series of publications has been established in conjunction with this program. A list of the *Studies in East Asian Law* appears at the back of this book.

Copyright © 1974 by Princeton University Press
All Rights Reserved
LCC: 73–2475
ISBN: 0–691–09229–X
This book has been composed in Linotype Times Roman with headings in Linotype Bodoni Book by Port City Press, Baltimore, Md.

Library of Congress Cataloging in Publication Data will be found on the last printed page of this book.
Printed in the United States of America.

For our fathers —
Philip Cohen (1896-1949)
and
Han-ping Chiu,
lawyers from different traditions—
with hopes for a more lawful world.

On that grave day, you and your comrades put up a heroic resistance when the reactionaries attacked the Chinese Embassy, violating international law and diplomatic immunity.
So cowardly were those reactionaries as to open fire! You were the first to be hit, struck by a bullet in the right chest.
But you and your comrades unflinchingly continued to resist, forcing those cowards to flee in panic and disarray.
Barehanded, you repulsed the reactionaries' armed attack,
With your valour, you have set a fine example of self-defence!
A fine example! An example for all!
Said the reactionaries after the attack: Those Chinese are really amazing, all skilled in boxing.
Our reply is: We are not skilled in boxing. We only rely on friendship between peoples and on Mao Tse-tung's great thinking.
Your courage and the reactionaries' faint-heartedness made a sharp contrast. I congratulate you all on your great victory.
The Chinese people are not to be trifled with!
The people of the world are not to be trifled with!
Taking orders from US imperialism and relying on its aid, the reactionaries of all countries will come to no good end!

Lu Hsun, the great Chinese writer said:
Blood debts must be repaid with blood!
You should ponder this carefully, US imperialists and reactionaries!
The friendship between the Chinese and other Asian, African and Latin American peoples is stronger than the Great Wall.
If you doubt this, come for another trial of strength
And you will be buried, one and all!

Poem by the late Vice-Premier and Foreign Minister Ch'en Yi, written in 1967 to commemorate the heroism of Chao Hsiao-shou, staff member of the Chinese Embassy in Indonesia. "Chao Hsiao-shou—A Revolutionary Fighter on the Diplomatic Front," Peking Review *9.19:36 (May 6, 1966).*

Contents

Preface

In the autumn of 1971, after more than two decades of struggle for international acceptance, the People's Republic of China (PRC) was seated in the United Nations (UN) as the sole legitimate representative of the state of China. Moreover, in the period immediately preceding and following the UN decision, a large number of previously reluctant states recognized the PRC and established bilateral diplomatic relations with it. The world community has come to believe that the cooperation of the government that controls almost one-quarter of humanity is indispensable to the achievement of the most important tasks confronting mankind, ranging from arms control to protection of the environment.

Yet relatively little is known about the extent to which the People's Republic accepts the rules, institutions, and procedures of the world community. Governments unfriendly to the PRC have frequently asserted that it has violated international law.[1] Certain scholars have argued that "the series of domestic and international crimes committed by the Mao regime in the last twenty years must effectively relegate it to the status of an outlaw vis-à-vis international society." [2] And foreigners who have visited China have occasionally claimed that Chinese officials have informally expressed their scorn for international law as a foreign product that is inapplicable to China.[3]

The purpose of this study is to indicate the extent to which the People's Republic pays at least lip service to public international law. We have sought to make available in convenient form the PRC's views on the entire spectrum of questions ordinarily encompassed by that subject. These views are highly controversial and have often been subject to distortion; therefore, rather than package them in predigested form we have allowed the PRC to speak for itself.

The PRC, like other states, speaks with many voices. Thus, the materials presented range from official acts or statements of the Chinese government and its leaders to editorials and major articles in the *People's Daily* (*Jen-min jih-pao* [*JMJP*], the newspaper of the Chinese Communist Party) and dispatches of the New China News Agency and other government media. We have also included the writings of Chinese scholars although we realize that they cannot always be equated with official PRC positions, even in a country where no publication can be considered completely unofficial.

As background for this study, our Introduction summarizes the development of China's attitudes toward international law prior to the national triumph of communism in 1949, the nature of the PRC's domestic system of public order and the evolution of PRC foreign policy. We resort to explanatory Notes when the significance of materials is not apparent or when necessary to summarize pertinent information.

Where possible, we present illustrations of state practice. Yet it would be premature at this stage of our research to attempt a comprehensive analysis of the extent to which the PRC's practice conforms to the legal theories it has expressed. Efforts have recently been made to study Peking's actions regarding some of the principal aspects of international law.[4] Case studies of many other topics are also badly needed, but this will require a substantial allocation of scholarly resources and a considerable period of time. One should also recognize that, as so often occurs in world politics, many disputes involving contemporary China reflect differing perceptions of the facts rather than disagreement over the applicable legal principles, and it is frequently difficult for scholars to become sufficiently well informed to make accurate judgments about factual disputes between governments. To the extent that sources are available, we have presented the position of other governments concerning their disputes with the PRC. We have also included the written and oral accounts of persons who have been involved in some of these controversies.

Although this study is merely an introductory survey, the materials presented offer some insight into a number of related questions concerning contemporary Chinese attitudes toward international law. To what extent does Peking evaluate events in terms of familiar legal doctrines? What has been the impact of Chairman Mao's universalistic ideology of world revolution? To what extent do Peking's views reflect a consideration of China's national interests, and how do its views differ from those of previous Chinese governments? On any particular problem do these views accord more with those of non-Communist states, other Communist states (especially the Soviet Union) or the newly developing countries? Have PRC positions on various issues been consistent or have they shifted as it became expedient? To what extent have changes in the regime's foreign policy affected its attitude toward international law? Finally, do the answers to such questions add up to a distinctively Chinese Communist perception of international law?

Because of the importance of the work of academic specialists in the development of international law, the role of legal scholars in the PRC is of more than academic interest. The materials in this study illustrate the extent to which Peking's "academic workers" reiterate official positions, elaborate upon the government's legal arguments, or express disagreement with them. The materials also suggest the degree of controversy that has been permitted to emerge within the academic community and the intellectual currents that have influenced scholarly writing.

It is our hope that this study will constitute a helpful sourcebook for scholars of international law and politics, Communist affairs and modern China. It may also prove useful to officials of international organizations and national governments, journalists and others who seek to understand the outlook and conduct of the People's Republic. For five years, earlier drafts of these volumes have served as readings for the course in "Chinese Attitudes Toward International Law" at the Harvard Law School, and they benefitted from the comments of students. Perhaps the published work may supplement the teaching materials already in use at the many other law schools and universities that offer courses in international and comparative law.

Our study is divided into ten parts, each of which contains a number of chapters. Where existing English translations of Chinese language sources are adequate, we have drawn upon them. But we have had to translate many Chinese documents ourselves, and, unless the caption or footnote to an extract indicates otherwise, the translation is ours. The literalness of the translated texts represents a deliberate attempt to render the documents as close to the original as possible and to recapture the spirit in which they were written. Minor changes in capitalization and punctuation were adopted only to achieve a degree of consistency in style, and changes in phrasing have been enclosed in brackets. When a significant portion of a single paragraph or several paragraphs have been omitted, this is indicated by a series of four dots (. . . .).

Alphabetical footnotes found throughout the documents appeared in the original sources. They have been supplemented, when possible, with full bibliographic data. Numbered notes for each part contain our own references and appear at the end of the volume in which the part appears.

Material quoted from the *New York Times* is usually taken from the city edition, but, unless otherwise indicated, references to the *New York Times* contained in the numbered notes are to the late city edition, which is available on microfilm. Page numbers have been given whenever possible.

Full references to Chinese sources, except publishers, appear at first mention within each part. Subsequent references give the author and a short English title *in parenthesis.*

A general bibliography, which appears at the end of Volume Two, contains full references. It is accompanied by a Chinese-Japanese language bibliography and an extensive English-Chinese glossary of international law terms that should prove useful to specialists. The glossary does not in any sense purport to be a dictionary. It merely indicates the English terms that have been found to suit the meanings of the Chinese terms in the particular contexts in which they appear. An index covering both volumes should facilitate access to this work.

Jerome Alan Cohen
Hungdah Chiu

Cambridge, Massachusetts
July 1, 1973

Acknowledgments

We are grateful to Professors Richard R. Baxter, William E. Butler and R. Randle Edwards for valuable comments at various stages of our study. We wish to thank David Finkelstein, Professor C. V. Chen, Lois Tretiak, Rita Howe, Mary Faith Higgins, Alice Stewart, Fred Rockwood, Fuw-daw Chen, and Cassondra Joseph for competent editorial assistance and Bertha Ezell for skillful typing of the manuscript.

We also want to thank the Ford Foundation and the Arms Control and Disarmament Agency of the United States Government for providing funds that supported this research.

Finally, we wish to express our appreciation to the many who have given permission to make use of certain copyrighted materials, and in particular to render acknowledgment in this regard to the following:

American Association for the Advancement of Slavic Studies, for permission to quote from *The Current Digest of the Soviet Press,* Vol. XXI, No. 24, p. 11 (published weekly at The Ohio State University).

The American Society of International Law and Professor Herbert W. Briggs, for permission to quote from Herbert W. Briggs, "American Consular Rights in Communist China," *American Journal of International Law,* Vol. 44 (1950), pp. 243–250.

Association for Asian Studies, Inc., for permission to quote from Arthur Stahnke, "The Place of International Law in Chinese Strategy and Tactics: The Case of the Sino-Indian Boundary Dispute," *The Journal of Asian Studies,* Vol. 30, No. 1 (November 1970), pp. 118–119.

Butterworth & Co. (Publishers) Ltd., for permission to quote from H. Lauterpacht, ed., *International Law Reports,* Vol. 24 (1957), pp. 221–222 (1961).

Carnegie Endowment for International Peace, for permission to quote from Walter Sullivan, "The International Geophysical Year," *International Conciliation,* No. 521 (Jan. 1959), pp. 284–294.

Contemporary China Institute, for permission to quote from Stephen Erasmus, "General de Gaulle's Recognition of Peking," *The China Quarterly,* No. 18, pp. 195–197 (April-June, 1964) and Neville Maxwell, "China and India: The Unnegotiated Dispute," *ibid.,* No. 43, pp. 63–67, 72–76 (July-Sept. 1970).

Cowles Communications, Inc., for permission to quote from Morris R. Wills (as told to J. Robert Moskin), "Why I Chose China," *Look Magazine,* Vol. 30, No. 3, pp. 75–83 (February 8, 1966). Copyright (c) Cowles Communications, Inc. 1966.

Cyrilly Abels, for permission to quote from Allyn and Adele Rickett, *Prisoners of Liberation.* Copyright (c) 1957, 1973 by Allyn and Adele Rickett. Reprinted by permission of Cyrilly Abels, Literary Agent.

The Faculty of Law of the University of British Columbia and the editor of the Canadian Yearbook of International Law, for permission to quote from Edward McWhinney, "Soviet and Western International Law and the Cold War in the Era of Bipolarity," *The Canadian Yearbook of International Law,* Vol. I (1963), pp. 42–45.

Far Eastern Economic Review, Limited, for permission to quote from John Gittings, "A Phoenix Too Frequent," *Far Eastern Economic Review,* Vol. 63, No. 28 (July 10, 1969), p. 118; "Jurisprude," "The Legal Options," *ibid.,* Vol. 61, No. 31 (August 1, 1968), p. 240; Derek Davies, "Twisting the Lions' Tails," *ibid.,* Vol. 61, No. 31 (August 1, 1968), p. 229; and "Traveller's Tales," *ibid.,* Vol. 61, No. 31 (August 1, 1968), p. 22.

The Gazette (Montreal), for permission to quote from Charles Lynch, "Chinese Puzzle," August 19, 1971, p. 6.

Harvard University Press, for permission to quote from Jerome Alan Cohen, ed., *China's Practice of International Law: Some Case Studies* (1972).

Hoover Institution on War, Revolution and Peace, for permission to quote from J. Chester Cheng, *The Politics of the Chinese Red Army: A Translation of the Bulletin of Activities of the PLA* (1966) and Dennis J. Doolin, *Territorial Claims in the Sino-Soviet Conflict: Documents & Analysis* (1965).

Houghton Mifflin Company, for permission to quote from Harold Hinton, *Communist China in World Politics* (1966).

The Johns Hopkins Press, for permission to quote from Bernard Ramundo, *Peaceful Coexistence: International Law in the Building of Communism* (1967).

Professor Luke T. Lee, for permission to quote from his article "Consular Status Under Unrecognized Regime—With Particular Reference to Recent United States Practice," *British Year Book of International Law,* Vol. 32 (1955–56), 1957, pp. 297–298.

Little, Brown and Company, for permission to quote from C. C. Hyde, *International Law, Chiefly as Interpreted and Applied by the United States,* 2nd edition, Vol. I (1947).

Longman Group Limited and David McKay, for permission to quote from L. Oppenheim, *International Law,* Vol. I, 7th ed., by H. Lauterpacht (1948).

Los Angeles Times, for permission to quote from Don Shannon, "Peking Offers to Raise U.N. Contributions—With A Catch," October 10, 1972. Copyright, 1972, Los Angeles Times. Reprinted by permission.

McGraw-Hill Book Company, for permission to quote from *Negotiating with the Chinese Communists: The U.S. Experience, 1953–1967,* by Kenneth T. Young. Copyright (c) 1968 by McGraw-Hill, Inc. Used with permission of McGraw-Hill Book Company.

Nederlands Tijdschrift voor Internationaal Recht, for permission to quote from M.H. Van der Valk, "Documents Concerning the Law of Succession of Foreigners in Communist China," Vol. 7, pp. 191–192, 193–194, 195–198, 204–206 (1960) and "Documents Concerning Conflict of Laws in Matters of Marriage in Communist China," Vol. 8, pp. 323, 325–331 (1961).

The New York Times Company, for permission to quote thirty articles. (c) 1951/52/55/67/, 1968/69/71 by The New York Times Company. Reprinted by permission.

Oxford University Press, for permission to quote from Margaret Carlyle, *Documents on International Affairs 1949–1950* (1953), Denise Folliott, *Documents on International Affairs 1951* (1954) *and 1952* (1955) and Peter Calvocoressi, *Survey of International Affairs 1949–1950* (1953), all published under the auspices of the Royal Institute of International Affairs.

Praeger Publishers, Inc. and Pall Mall Press Ltd., for permission to quote from Theodore H.E. Chen, *The Chinese Communist Regime, Documents and Commentary* (1967), pp. 33–34.

Random House, Inc. and Alfred A. Knopf, Inc., for permission to quote from *The Long Revolution,* by Edgar Snow. Copyright (c)

1971, 1972 by Lois Wheeler Snow. Reprinted by permission of Random House, Inc.

A.W. Sijthoff, for permission to quote from Luke T. Lee, *China and International Agreements* (1969).

Springer-Verlag, for permission to quote from Lennart Petri, "Einige Betrachtungen über Recht und Rechtsprechung in der Volksrepublik China," *Juristische Blätter,* Vol. 93, pp. 26–30 (1971).

The Stamp Magazine, for permission to quote from its "Readers' Forum," April 1968.

Sweet & Maxwell Ltd., for permission to quote from Georg Schwarzenberger, *Manual of International Law.*

Twayne Publishers, Inc., for permission to quote from Robert Ekvall, *The Faithful Echo* (1960), pp. 89–95.

United Press International, for permission to quote from "Chinese Makes Claim in UN to Hong Kong, Macao," *International Herald Tribune,* March 11–12, 1972.

J. A. C.
H. C.

Abbreviations

AJIL	*American Journal of International Law*
BFSP	*British and Foreign State Papers*
CB	*Current Background.* United States Consulate General, Hong Kong
CDSP	*Current Digest of the Soviet Press*
CFYC	*Cheng-fa yen-chiu* (Political-legal research)
CHYYC	*Chiao-hsüeh yü yen-chiu* (Teaching and research)
FBIS	*Foreign Broadcast Information Service*
FEER	*Far Eastern Economic Review*
FH	*Fa-hsüeh* (Legal studies)
FKHP	*Chung-hua jen-min kung-ho-kuo fa-kuei hui-pien* (Collection of laws and regulations of the People's Republic of China)
FLHP	*Chung-yang jen-min cheng-fu fa-ling hui-pien* (Collection of laws and decrees of the Central People's Government)
GAC	*Government Administrative Council*
JMJP	*Jen-min jih-pao* (People's daily)
KCWTYC	*Kuo-chi wen-t'i yen-chiu* (Studies in international problems)
LNTS	*League of Nations Treaty Series*
NCNA	New China News Agency
PC	*People's China*
PR	*Peking Review*
SCMP	*Survey of China Mainland Press.* United States Consulate General, Hong Kong
SGP	*Sovetskoe gosudarstvo i pravo* (Soviet state and law)
TIAS	*Treaties and Other International Acts Series*
TYC	*Chung-hua jen-min kung-ho-kuo t'iao-yüeh-chi* (Collection of treaties of the People's Republic of China)
UNTS	*United Nations Treaty Series*
UST	*United States Treaties and Other International Agreements*
WCC	*Chung-hua jen-min kung-ho-kuo tui-wai kuan-hsi wen-chien-chi* (Collection of documents relating to the foreign relations of the People's Republic of China)

INTRODUCTION

Before undertaking this survey, which shows how the People's Republic of China has assimilated international law, we should briefly discuss the experience of previous Chinese governments, the nature of the PRC's domestic public order, and the evolution of PRC foreign policy. Although each of these factors has had a significant, if indeterminate, impact upon Peking's attitude toward international law, their influence —unlike that of Maoist ideology—may not clearly emerge from the materials that we present.

China's Experience with International Law before 1949

Continuity and change is a principal theme of all studies of contemporary China. Viewing the PRC's attitude toward international law against the background of China's pre-1949 experience will provide some perspective upon our quest and help us appreciate the significance of the PRC's record. This Introduction only briefly recalls the attitude of previous Chinese governments toward international law. Introductory notes to many individual chapters will offer further historical material on specific topics.

Modern international law is, of course, a creation of the West. It emerged in Europe by the middle of the seventeenth century in response to the needs of the new nation-states that had shattered the political and spiritual community which had prevailed on the continent since the Roman Empire. These nation-states developed a "balance of power" system that prevented the domination of any single power and that recognized the sovereign equality of all states. As these dynamic nation-states expanded their activities into East Asia, they discovered a civilization that had not experienced the Renaissance, the Reformation, or the many other forces which in Europe had undermined the concept of a universal state. China had been insulated from the world beyond East Asia by mountains, deserts, and oceans, and by intense suspicion of "barbarians." Thus China, whose name means "the central realm," had continued to preside over relations among the peoples of East Asia according to its own concept of universal state.

THE TRADITIONAL CHINESE WORLD ORDER

Throughout most of two millennia from the founding of the Chinese Empire in 221 B.C. until the onslaught of Western military expeditions in the nineteenth century, the Chinese emperor served as overlord of a rather loose hierarchy of tributary peoples. Status in the hierarchy was proportional to the varying degrees of acceptance of Confucian cultural, ethical, political, and social norms, and of China's writing system and agricultural practices. An elaborate series of rituals governed contacts between the "Son of Heaven" in the Chinese capital and the emissaries periodically sent there by lesser rulers to pay tribute to the emperor and to receive magnanimous gifts from him in return. The hierarchical organization and protocol of the Sinocentric East Asian community were designed to acknowledge not only China's preeminent power, but also its moral superiority as the embodiment of virtues deserving of universal application.[1]

This is not to say that China's vast historical record was devoid of experience in which governments dealt with one another on a basis of equality. During China's preimperial history, from the eighth to the third centuries B.C., there existed in the present north central part of China a number of feudal states which, although nominally vassals of the Chou dynasty, largely functioned as independent entities. The feudal states developed a system of commonly accepted rules, institutions, and processes to deal with each other. Some aspects of that system, like certain aspects of the system that regulated the interaction of the city-states of ancient Greece, bear a striking similarity to the international law that emerged from the multistate system of fifteenth- and sixteenth-century Europe.[2]

Even China's long imperial tradition reveals instances when intergovernmental relations were conducted on an equal basis. The first great unification of China under the Ch'in and Han dynasties came to an end in the third century A.D., and for most of the next three hundred years the country was divided into two or more states—the northern and southern dynasties—which generally treated each other as equals.[3] For over a century during the Northern Sung dynasty (960–1126) Sung rulers had to coexist with the Liao or Chin dynasties in the north and the Hsi-hsia in the west on an essentially equal plane.[4] Moreover, even when unified and powerful, China occasionally dealt with its Central Asian neighbors as equals, as with Tibet during the eighth century [5] and with the monarchs Temür and Shāhrukh during the early fifteenth century.[6]

Yet these instances were exceptions to the dominant Chinese concept of a universal state. They demonstrated that China was capable of accommodating its hierarchical theory and practice to political necessities, but they did not weaken imperial China's continuing insistence upon the tribute system as the proper mode of maintaining "world order." [7]

THE INTRODUCTION OF INTERNATIONAL LAW

China first became acquainted with Western international law during the earliest years of the Ch'ing or Manchu dynasty (1644–1912). In their long series of discussions with Ch'ing officials between 1662 and 1690, representatives of the Dutch East India Company frequently referred to the "law of all nations" and "the custom of all princes" to support their insistence upon such principles as the immunity of envoys from detention or arrest.[8] Ch'ing officials first applied principles of international law during their negotiation with Russia of China's first treaty with a Western power—the Treaty of Nerchinsk of 1689. According to the diary of Father Thomas Pereira, a Portuguese Jesuit missionary who participated in the negotiations on behalf of the Ch'ing court, the Jesuits in Peking had introduced the K'ang-hsi emperor to this new body of learning, and it was utilized in concluding the treaty. Pereira wrote that his own role in the Chinese delegation at Nerchinsk was to make sure that everything was done in accord with the principles of the Law of Nations.[9] In contrast to the situation in 1676, when the mission to Peking of the Russian ambassador, Spathary, had proved abortive because of his failure to comply with court ceremonies required of tribute emissaries,[10] both the Treaty of Nerchinsk and its successor, the Treaty of Kiakhta of 1727, were concluded on the basis of the sovereign equality of China and Russia.

So far as we now know, this initial exposure to international law had no lasting effect upon China. As the Western maritime powers as well as Russia intensified their efforts to persuade China to abandon its isolation and to establish political and commercial intercourse on the basis of sovereign equality, China continued to insist that Western emissaries conform to the protocol of tribute bearers. A number of Western missions to China yielded to these demands and performed the humiliating traditional rites, including the series of abject prostrations before the emperor that have enriched our vocabulary with the word "kowtow" (*k'ou-t'ou*). Beginning with the famous mission of Great Britain's Lord Macartney in 1793, however, the Western states began to balk at complying with the forms of the tribute system, and, as the nineteenth century unfolded, they brought mounting pressure upon China to participate in the Western state system.[11]

Historians tell us that it was not until 1839 that China again applied international law. In a desperate attempt to use the learning of the Western barbarians as an instrument to check their depredations, China sought to invoke international law against Great Britain. In the course of efforts to stop British traders in Canton from importing opium, Imperial Commissioner Lin Tse-hsü learned of the existence of Vattel's *Le Droit des Gens*. He persuaded an American medical missionary, Dr. Peter Parker, and a Chinese who had acquired some Western education while overseas to translate some pages that had a direct bearing on China's plight. These passages acknowledged that it was the right of every state to stop foreign nationals from importing noxious products into its territory; the state could declare those products to be contraband and confiscate the contraband. But Vattel prescribed that, before a state could take such action against the offending foreign nationals, it must first notify their sovereign and request that he restrain his subjects. Accordingly, Commissioner Lin sent off a letter to Queen Victoria, but his letter was never acknowledged. The fateful Opium War of 1839–1842 ensued, resulting in Britain's victory and China's coerced acquiescence in the first substantial Western presence in China.[12]

It is not surprising that Commissioner Lin's unsuccessful invocation of international law failed to inspire Chinese interest in the study of that subject. Nevertheless, the series of treaties that the West imposed upon China between 1842 and 1860 employed the forms of diplomatic equality, even though, because of their substance, they came to be known to twentieth-century Chinese patriots as the first of the "unequal treaties" that introduced China's century of humiliation at the hands of imperialism.[13] Moreover, the process of negotiating those treaties acquainted Chinese officials with some of the institutions and principles of international law, such as the functions, privileges, and immunities of consular officials and diplomats and the requirement that treaty negotiators be endowed with "full powers" to conclude treaties.[14]

It was difficult for the conservative Chinese elite to understand and accept ideas completely alien to the traditional East Asian system of conducting foreign relations. For example, it took decades for China to carry out a reciprocal exchange of permanent diplomatic missions. Although Britain forced China to commit itself to such an exchange in the Treaty of Tientsin in 1858, the British had to shoot their way into Peking before the Ch'ing would actually permit a resident minister to be stationed in the capital in accord with the agreement; China did not send its first resident minister to London until almost two decades later.[15]

By the early 1860's, increasing contacts between China and the West and the efforts of a small group of reform-minded Chinese leaders finally led to the systematic introduction of international law. Chinese officials had become aware of their need to acquire some Western knowledge if they were to be successful in controlling the Western powers. Just as they sought to acquire the secrets of Western military technology, so too did they seek to master international law. Both provided weapons to be used in China's defense.

Soon after the establishment in 1861 of China's first centralized foreign office—the Tsungli Yamen—an Interpreters' College (T'ung-wen Kuan) was founded in Peking to translate Western materials and teach foreign languages to selected students. As part of this effort, an American missionary, W. A. P. Martin, began to translate into Chinese Henry Wheaton's *Elements of International Law,* the then leading text on the subject. Martin believed that knowledge of the legal principles of Christian civilization would not only lead the heathen to Christ but would also help the Chinese cope with overzealous Western diplomats and traders whose demands were often couched in terms of international law. Precisely for the latter reason, some of the foreign diplomats residing in Peking opposed his project. They were convinced that, once the Chinese learned international law, they would appreciate the extent to which the system of extraterritorial privileges recently imposed by the West varied from the treatment accorded the "civilized" sovereign states of Christendom. As a French diplomat correctly predicted, Martin's translation "will make us endless trouble." [16] The Western trading community was also apprehensive about supplying an instrument that might curb newly acquired commercial privileges and prevent the exaction of other concessions. Other diplomats, including Englishmen and Americans, endorsed Martin's effort in the belief that it would show the Chinese that force was not the West's only law and would help them understand and deal with the outside world to the mutual benefit of China and the West.[17]

With the aid of the Tsungli Yamen and several Chinese associates, Martin completed and published his translation of Wheaton in 1864 under the title *Wan-kuo kung-fa* (Laws and regulations of all states). Obtaining imperial approval of publication, however, was not easy. The mandarins at first suspected Martin's translation as the Trojans did "a Greek gift." [18] But Prince Kung, the most enlightened statesman of the era, reminded the throne that, in order to circumscribe the Chinese government's freedom of action, "the craftiest [foreigners] . . . have argued with quotations from Chinese institutional and legal codes to embarrass us. When we want to defeat their statements with [citations of] their practices and precedents, we suffer from not knowing the foreign languages in which all foreign codes and regulations are written." [19]

He pointed out that in the Wheaton book "there are quite a few methods of controlling and bridling the [foreign] consuls, which may be useful [to us]." [20] The Wheaton text immediately demonstrated its utility when China successfully invoked it in a dispute with Prussia. This enabled Prince Kung to report to the emperor that in "the case this year of the Danish ship captured by Prussia outside of Tientsin [in Chinese waters], your ministers used as arguments some sentences from this book without expressly saying so. The Prussian minister immediately acknowledged his mistake and said nothing further." [21]

The new Chinese institutions for Western learning soon offered courses in international law, and China began to send students to Europe and America to study a variety of topics, including international law. Yet for more than a decade Wheaton was the only treatise on the subject available in Chinese. Long after 1877, when missionary Martin and other scholars started to publish translations of other leading texts, Wheaton remained China's bible on the subject, not only for academic purposes but also for the guidance of the government. So far as the Tsungli Yamen was concerned, the book did not merely represent the commentary of a highly qualified publicist constituting a subsidiary source of international law; it *was* international law, although Chinese officials also sought clarifications and advice from Martin, friendly diplomats, foreign-language books and newspapers, and other sources. In 1873, for example, Viceroy Li Hung-chang sought to persuade the emperor to receive foreign diplomats; he cited Wheaton's description of how newly arrived diplomats present their credentials and thereby calmed the emperor's fear that he might personally have to conduct negotiations with the foreigners and that an open dispute might occur at court.[22] And in 1884, during armed conflict between China and France over Vietnam, the Tsungli Yamen used Wheaton to support a recommendation that it would not derogate from China's jurisdiction over French nationals in China if the Russian minister were permitted to protect their interests.[23]

LATE CH'ING APPLICATION OF INTERNATIONAL LAW

The Ch'ing government gradually abandoned its traditional attitude toward foreign relations, recognized many independent countries as sovereign equals, and acknowledged that their relations with China should be ruled by international law. Ch'ing leaders found that, within the narrow limits imposed by their deteriorating power, experience tended to vindicate the original promise of Wheaton's text that international law could be useful as a device for defending China's interests.

When, for example, Peru asked China to conclude a commercial treaty in 1873, the Tsungli Yamen, apparently relying upon the right of a state to protect its nationals abroad, requested that Peru first improve the condition of Chinese laborers in that country.[24] In negotiating the treaty with Peru the following year, China insisted on reciprocal most-favored-nation treatment, instead of the unilateral most-favored-nation treatment that it had extended to Western states in earlier treaties.[25]

China did not confine its application of international law to relations with Western powers; the new learning was also applied within East Asia. In 1874, shortly after the Ryūkyū Islands came under Japanese protection, Japan sent a military expedition to Taiwan to punish the aborigines for having murdered shipwrecked Ryūkyūan sailors. The ensuing dispute between China and Japan was carried on in terms of Western concepts of treaties, customary international law, domestic jurisdiction, territorial claims, and state responsibility for failure to restrain nationals from misbehavior against aliens.[26] Similarly, that very same year Japan protested an incident in which a Japanese warship was fired upon just off the Korean coast. One of the arguments China invoked to justify the Korean action was that it was a legitimate response to infringement of what international law acknowledged to be Korean territorial waters.[27]

In both of these disputes Japan, which had quickly adapted the Chinese publication of Wheaton for its own use,[28] appeared to be more adept at manipulating the applicable legal doctrines than China. Indeed, a number of episodes in the 1870's demonstrated that China had not mastered the new learning. For example, because Prince Kung did not understand that the customary principle of nonextradition of political criminals remained unaffected by the provisions of the Sino-American Treaty of 1844, China in 1874 unsuccessfully persisted in requesting extradition of an alleged political offender who had fled to the United States.[29] More embarrassing, at least to China's first envoy to Britain, was his government's failure to provide him with adequate credentials for presentation upon his arrival in London in 1877.[30] The Chinese government further manifested its unfamiliarity with diplomatic practice by giving the second-ranking member of the mission the title of "Vice-Minister," a position that the British Foreign Office did not know how to classify.[31]

Nevertheless, by the end of the nineteenth century the mandarins of imperial China seem not only to have accepted international law but also to have acquired sufficient experience to feel comfortable in applying it. Their eventual mastery of the Western doctrines and practices, however, made them increasingly aware of the limited value of this legal learning for a China that lacked the military, political, and economic power to defend itself. In certain circumstances, for example, the imperial government might have invoked the principle of *rebus sic stantibus,* which allows a party unilaterally to denounce treaty obligations if there has been a vital change in the circumstances that existed when the treaty was concluded. Or it might justifiably have claimed release from some treaties on the ground of prior violation by the other contracting party. But the political situation precluded such moves, even in relation to relatively friendly countries such as the United States. The enactment by the United States of the so-called Chinese Exclusion Act in 1888 violated the four Sino-American treaties concluded between 1844 and 1880. The Chinese minister to Washington pointed out that this "abrogation . . . of an important treaty stipulation, releases China from the observance of all its treaties with the United States."[32] The United States recognized that China was entitled to denounce the treaties.[33] Yet political considerations prevented China from seizing upon what in theory was a golden opportunity to rid itself of unequal obligations perceived to be contrary to its interests.

As one of China's early diplomats wrote in 1891: "International law is just like Chinese statutory law—reasonable but unreliable. If there is right without might, the right will not prevail."[34] This view is strikingly like that of Fukuzawa Yukichi, Meiji Japan's leading interpreter of the West, who wrote: "A hundred volumes of international law and numerous treaties of amity are weaker than one barrel of cannon."[35] These remarks suggest that Mao Tse-tung is not the first East Asian leader whose experience with the West confirmed the belief that "political power grows out of the barrel of a gun." And scholars in the People's Republic have pointed out how fruitless it would have been for the Ch'ing to demand that foreign powers respect international legal principles such as the integrity of a state's territorial waters.[36]

Perhaps the feeling of powerlessness and futility accounts for the fact that, once having perceived the need to participate in the Western state system, the Ch'ing government appeared to accept all of its rules. Little effort was made to subject them to critical scrutiny with a view to adapting, modifying, or even rejecting those that did not suit China's circumstances. Certainly officials in Peking might justifiably have believed that any effort to change the rules could place China in an even more disadvantageous position and that the best they could hope for would be to restrain the foreigners by persuading them to adhere to the existing system and to admit China to its benefits on the basis of equality.[37]

China's enforced imitation of the West eventually extended to domestic law, for the price of ending the increasingly detested system of extraterritorial jurisdiction that symbolized foreign domination was the adoption of Western internal legal institutions. Japan succeeded in throwing off the yoke of extraterritoriality by modernizing its legal system at the end of the nineteenth century, and this inspired China to seek a similar path to treaty revision. Beginning in 1902, the major Western powers provided China with a substantial incentive to undertake the vast effort "to reform its judicial system and to bring it into accord with that of western nations"; in a series of bilateral treaties they stated that, if China did so, they "will also be prepared to relinquish extra-territorial rights when satisfied that the state of the Chinese laws, the arrangements for their administration and other considerations warrant it. . . ."[38]

Despite efforts to adopt Western international and domestic legal principles in order to end their country's status as a semicolony, late Ch'ing modernizers appear to have been profoundly skeptical that Western nations would apply international law in an even-handed manner in dealing with East Asia. In addition to their previously mentioned observation that the Western powers tended to resort to force rather than law in their foreign relations, imperial Chinese officials also seemed to distrust the manner in which the West resorted to law. For example, apropos of the Vietnam crisis, in 1884 Prince Kung informed the throne that "international law and treaties are not dependable." Although England and Germany were rivals of France, and Germany was especially suspicious of France, he said they would never help China in preference to France, "because they are of the same race [as France] and their countries are close to each other."[39]

This distrust of the West led the Ch'ing to prefer, as modes of conflict resolution, either direct negotiation or mediation, conciliation, or other forms of third-party settlement that did not require China to surrender control over the outcome of the dispute to a third party from a world community in which it lacked confidence. When in 1909 a dispute arose over China's boundary with Portuguese-controlled Macao, China rejected a Portuguese suggestion that the matter be referred to the Permanent Court of Arbitration in the Hague. "European and American countries have a bias against East Asian people," the Chinese negotiator stated. He also pointed out a number of practical reasons why Britain, France, the Netherlands, and other Western countries might favor Portugal's cause. "Having these powers involved," he concluded, "Hague arbitration will definitely defend Portugal's interest. . . . It is better for us to negotiate with Portugal directly so that we may yet have a fifty-fifty chance to succeed."[40]

Despite this distrust of the West, by the time the Ch'ing dynasty collapsed in 1911 China had become a participant in the Western state system and was conversant with its institutions, processes, and norms. Although it had not attained sovereign equality, it had learned to make use of the resources of international law in a modest way to defend against future foreign incursions and to press for the elimination of existing ones. With the exception of the Boxer Rebellion in 1900, when both Chinese and foreign forces committed outrages,[41] late Ch'ing officials gradually brought China's state practice into conformity with international standards, if only to avoid giving the imperialists pretexts for further hostile acts. China was also beginning to play a role in the growth of international law. It participated in the Hague Peace Conferences of 1899 and 1907,[42] adhered to many multilateral conventions dealing with the law of war, the pacific settlement of disputes, and other matters,[43] joined the Universal Postal Union (UPU) and the International Institute of Agriculture (IIA),[44] and sent representatives to the private, but influential, Association for the Reform and Codification of the Law of Nations.[45]

The traditional Sinocentric world order had been virtually destroyed. Its destruction transformed Confucian culturalism into Chinese nationalism and instilled in a proud and once powerful people the determination to have China—no longer "the central realm" but now a nation-state—achieve recognition as the sovereign equal of other states. This was the task that confronted the Republic of China (ROC) upon the overthrow of the last of the imperial dynasties.

THE REPUBLIC OF CHINA AND INTERNATIONAL LAW

In his declaration inaugurating the new Republic on January 1, 1912, Dr. Sun Yat-sen, its founder, stated that its goal was "to obtain the rights of a civilized state" and "to place China in a respectable place in international society."[46] This objective has also guided subsequent leaders of the Republic and even, one may say, the revolutionary leaders of the People's Republic, who have shared with other Chinese patriots the intense desire to attain national self-respect.

In this quest Republican statesmen, like their predecessors during the last half-century of the Ch'ing, regarded international law as a principal asset. They suffered grievous disappointments at the inability of legal arguments to protect enfeebled China against harsh realities of power politics, such as Japan's "Twenty-One Demands" of 1915, refusal of the Paris Peace Conference of 1919 to restore to China former German rights in Shantung Province, and failure of the League of Nations to provide an effective response to Japanese aggression in Manchuria in 1931. Nevertheless, their patient diplomacy, effective mobilization of the resources of international law, and persistent political pressure did gradually succeed in dismantling the elaborate structure of extraterritorial rights, inequitable tariff restrictions, leased territories, concessions, settlements, armed forces, railway, postal, and wireless networks, and other privileges by which the foreign powers had dominated China.[47]

Both before and after World War II the Republic of China contributed to the progressive development of international law, considerably enlarged the number of China's official and academic specialists in the subject, and participated in many international governmental and nongovernmental organizations.[48] It consistently advocated not only that states settle all disputes by pacific means but also that they accept the compulsory jurisdiction of the International Court of Justice (ICJ) in all legal controversies. Although, at the 1945 San Francisco Conference that launched the United Nations, the United States and the Soviet Union successfully opposed an ROC proposal that would have required all states to accept the ICJ's compulsory jurisdiction,[49] the ROC itself accepted the Court's compulsory jurisdiction vis-à-vis those states making a reciprocal acceptance.[50] Thus Republican statesmen proved even more receptive to international law than did their Ch'ing predecessors.

The Republican government's defeat in the Chinese civil war, which required its removal to Taiwan in 1949, has obviously diminished its political influence in the world community. Yet the ROC's attitude toward international law has remained essentially unchanged. Although the sixty-year record of the ROC's theory and practice, like that of the late Ch'ing, deserves far more study than it has received from legal scholars, it seems fair to state that its efforts have contributed to the evolutionary process by which international law is being transformed from an exclusively Western product to one that more truly reflects the composition of the world.

Of course, the extent to which contemporary international law can be said to be universal in character depends in important part on the attitude of the People's Republic. Before presenting the PRC's attitude, for background purposes we should call attention to two other factors, the influence of which does not clearly emerge in the materials: the nature of the Chinese Communist system of public order and the development of Peking's foreign policy.

The PRC's Public Order

Although China is heir to the oldest continuous civilization of any member of the world community, it is poor and backward and shares many of the economic and social problems of the newly developing countries. Upon attaining control of mainland China in 1949, Mao Tse-tung and his associates, like Communist leaders elsewhere, sought to mobilize the nation's resources for development by initiating the abolition of the modified private enterprise system that had existed under previous Chinese regimes. Since the completion of "socialist transformation" of the economy in the mid-1950's, the government has directly controlled virtually all economic activity in the PRC through ownership of the "means of production" by either state organs or collective enterprises under state management. Although private property has not been eliminated, personal possessions—the "means of life"—are generally very modest; even expropriated entrepreneurs, who have been compensated for the loss of their businesses, have found very limited uses for the funds awarded to them. Building upon certain strands of traditional Chinese thought that placed a low value upon commerce and that subordinated the welfare of the individual to that of his social group, Maoism has emphasized the concept of *kung*—contributing to the public good—and has created a negative image of *ssu*—working for private gain.

Rapid "socialist transformation" of the economy was made possible by the Chinese Communists' earlier success in imposing totalitarian rule upon the world's largest population, dispersed over a vast land mass whose physical barriers inhibit easy communication. This unification of mainland China, the goal of all Chinese governments and the greatest achievement since the collapse of the Ch'ing, is more effective than China had ever known. Previous systems of national control had penetrated traditional social groups, such as villages, clans, and guilds, to only a limited extent. In contrast, the reach of the Communist Party, the formal government apparatus, and the elaborate network of semiofficial organizations that replaced traditional groups has extended to virtually every household and work site in the country.[51] Preaching Mao's version of the Marxist-Leninist philosophy of class struggle in lieu of the Confucian precepts of harmony, the party has sought to smash the "feudal" and "bourgeois" institutions of the past in order to improve the lot of the masses, speed economic development, and enhance China's political power.

The role of law in this monumental undertaking has been very limited, far more so than in comparable Soviet efforts, despite the fact that both Communist giants share the Marxist belief that law is the tool of the ruling class. Indeed, much of the PRC's domestic orientation has been explicitly antilegal. To be sure, after an initial period of consolidation from 1949 to 1952, in which a series of party-led "mass movements" ruthlessly suppressed political opposition, from 1953 to 1957 the PRC did begin to adopt a Soviet-style legal system. With the aid of Soviet specialists, a constitution and laws establishing a regular judicial organization were promulgated in 1954; criminal and civil codes were drafted; a few textbooks and law journals were published; law schools were improved; collectives of "people's lawyers" began to operate; and, to the bewilderment of many Communist officials, experiments were conducted with public trials, defense counsel, and other protections of personal liberty.[52]

Yet this attempt to adapt the Soviet legal model to Chinese conditions came to an abrupt end in mid-1957 with the outbreak of the "antirightist" movement, which dramatically reversed a trend toward legal professionalism and judicial erosion of party control. The experimental implementation of constitutional guarantees was not only terminated, but many of those guarantees, such as the independence of the judiciary, were also denounced. The party openly and repeatedly declared that its leadership in legal matters was "absolute." The draft codes that were to be published were pronounced in need of revision. Many scholars and officials were attacked and removed from their posts for having expressed "rightist" views that endowed law with autonomous significance. The intellectual content of legal publications and legal education was heavily diluted by massive doses of ideological indoctrination stressing that law and courts were principal instruments of the people's democratic dictatorship. And the activity of the recently founded lawyers' collectives virtually ended.[53]

After 1957, steps were taken to unify the operations of judges, prosecutors, and public security officials under the control of the public security, which was freed from many of the judicial and administrative restraints provided by the constitutional scheme.[54] Other changes strengthened the control of local party committees over all the law enforcement agencies, so that "the three departments have become one fist, attacking the enemy even more forcefully."[55] At the same time the "mass line" that emerged in 1958, along with the Great Leap Forward and the people's communes, emphasized turning an increasing amount of civil and criminal cases over to the masses for disposition and broadly consulting the masses on the relatively few cases that continued to be handled by official agencies. Because from its inception the Communist government had adapted traditional mediation practices to settle disputes in accord with revolutionary needs, large numbers of interpersonal civil disputes and minor criminal infractions were already being resolved informally by members of people's mediation committees and other persons who were not legal specialists.[56] The advent of the mass line meant that the overwhelming bulk of legal controversies involving individuals would henceforth be processed outside the formal legal system. Moreover, contract disputes between state enterprises have also been resolved either through "persuasion-education" and "criticism and self-criticism" or through administrative decision making; neither courts nor other adjudication institutions, such as the very busy Soviet *gosarbitrazh,* have been found useful for interenterprise disputes in China in most cases.[57]

Yet even this degree of deformalization of the legal system did not meet the radical criteria of the Great Proletarian Cultural Revolution of 1966–1969. During that national paroxysm, not only the courts and the prosecutorial branch but also the public security forces were condemned for having failed to serve as the faithful instruments of the people's democratic dictatorship. The Communist Party itself came under very severe attack. The "handful of top capitalist roaders within the Party headed by Liu Shao-ch'i" was charged with seeking to set up a comprehensive legal system in order to use bourgeois legalism to oppose mass dictatorship and mass revolutionary movements. The Red Guards accused Liu and his chief collaborators of making "every effort to inherit the puppet legal system [of the preceding Chiang Kai-shek regime] and push through the feudal, capitalist, and revisionist legal systems." [58] Repeated Red Guard attacks lumping "revisionism" with feudalism and capitalism made explicit what had usually been left implicit during the anti-rightist movement a decade earlier—that new China had come to scorn the Soviet legal model as indistinguishable from the so-called bourgeois legal dictatorship of Generalissimo Chiang.[59]

The People's Liberation Army assumed a major role in the administration of justice, and in the summer of 1970 the mass line was enshrined in a new draft constitution that pointedly omitted basic guarantees in the Constitution of 1954, including the right of an accused to defend himself in a public trial before an independent tribunal.[60] Moreover, scholarly legal publication and legal education, like all scholarly publication and higher education in China, were suspended during this period, and, in the intensely suspicious, xenophobic atmosphere of the day, contacts with foreigners and their ideas became more difficult than ever for the Chinese people.

As mid-1973 approaches, the Cultural Revolution has subsided, the revolutionary draft constitution has not yet been promulgated, and, in view of the return to moderation in Chinese domestic policy, it is possible that it never will be enacted in its present form. Nevertheless, it seems safe to say that the PRC is unlikely to return to the Soviet model, if only for cosmetic reasons. Rather, it can be expected to continue its search for an autochthonous legal system that will suit its revolutionary political, social, and economic aims and China's circumstances. Whatever that system may turn out to be, the foregoing account should make clear to the reader that there has thus far been little in the PRC's domestic public order to reinforce any other reasons it might have to participate in mankind's halting progress toward a rule of law in world affairs.

The relation between the nature of a state's public order and its attitude toward international law is far from clear, however. Peking's totalitarian order obviously shapes its world outlook and conduct to some extent and restricts the prospects for those modes of international cooperation that would require foreigners to have relatively free access to Chinese society. Yet significant participation in the world community has been achieved by totalitarian or authoritarian governments. In this connection it may provide additional perspective if we say a word about the public order of China's pre-Communist governments.

Although for well over a thousand years imperial China had maintained and developed a sophisticated system of legal codes and of institutions for their application, law did not enjoy the prestige and importance that it gradually attained in Western societies. In China, law was not regarded as a major social achievement and a symbol of rectitude, but rather as a regrettable necessity, principally an instrument to be used by the state to enforce its will upon subjects who had not submitted to other means of social control.[61] The traditional legal system did relatively little to facilitate and regulate the economic activity of private persons, and the only real restraints upon the exercise of imperial power derived from political ethics, rationality and precedent, none of which could always check the caprice of the emperor.[62] The traditional system provided judicial tribunals for the resolution of private disputes as well as the imposition of governmental punishments, but the Confucian philosophy of harmony preferred unofficial conciliation to official adjudication. Traditional social groups disposed of an enormous volume of potential litigation through a variety of techniques that ranged from persuasion to ostracism and coercion. Imperial China never developed a judiciary that was insulated from political authority, or an independent legal profession that strengthened the "law habit," or a legal education that articulated the idea of a rule of law. Yet, as we have seen, the last half-century of imperial rule witnessed an increasing appreciation and application of international law.

Much the same can be said about the Republic of China. Its law reformers carried on the work of the modernizers who, in the final years of the Ch'ing, had sought to transform the imperial legal system in order to strengthen the sagging dynasty and end the incubus of extraterritoriality and other foreign privileges. Following the model of Japan's successful assimilation of Western law, the Republican reformers created a continental-style legal system, including an organized bar, and expanded legal education and scholarly publication. Yet the ROC's record in actually implementing the rule of law at home, both on the mainland before 1949 and in Taiwan, has been less satisfactory than its international performance. The ROC remains an essentially authoritarian, one-party government that has used law as an instrument of state control and that has been reluctant to tolerate the growth of autonomous legal institutions similar to those of advanced Western countries. Martial law, which was proclaimed on Taiwan in 1949, has substantially reduced the protections prescribed by the ROC Constitution of 1947.[63] Nevertheless, the nature of the ROC's domestic public order has not inhibited its adoption of international law and its participation in the world community.

PRC Foreign Policy

In the course of this work, explanatory notes place selected documents in their specific political setting. Here we present a brief and necessarily simplified periodization of the overall development of the PRC's foreign policy in order to provide a broader perspective for those who have not been students of the subject.[64]

Generally speaking, one can divide the evolution of Chinese Communist foreign policy since 1949 into five basic periods. Interestingly, these coincide with the phases that we have noted regarding the development of the PRC's domestic public order, although correlation between Peking's domestic and foreign policies is far from perfect, and within each period there have been both internal and external crosscurrents.

The primary preoccupation of the party leaders during the period 1949–1952 was to consolidate and defend their power against domestic and foreign threats, to reassert Chinese control over Tibet, and to conclude the Chinese civil war by "liberating" Taiwan from the preceding government, which, after mid-1950, was protected by the American Seventh Fleet. The limited foreign policy that the PRC undertook in this era emphasized "Communist internationalism." Even before formal establishment of the People's Republic on October

1, 1949, Chairman Mao, whose earlier efforts to obtain American aid in the Chinese civil war had been rebuffed,[65] announced that new China would "lean to one side"—that of the USSR. In addition to establishing close contacts with existing Communist states, the PRC, like its Soviet big brother, actively encouraged national liberation struggles by Communist-led revolutionary movements in other Asian countries. Peking's propagandists emphasized the Maoist strategy for revolutionary success in China as a model for China's neighbors. The PRC did not neglect diplomatic activity beyond the Communist world and Asia, of course. Yet it enjoyed only modest success in persuading non-Communist states to recognize it as the sole legitimate government of China, and its initial attempts to replace the Nationalist government as the representative of China at the United Nations were frustrated. The entry of Chinese Communist "volunteers" into the Korean conflict, after the United States ignored Peking's repeated warnings not to advance beyond the 38th parallel toward China's border with North Korea, further delayed the PRC's acceptance by the world community, leading to UN condemnation of the PRC as an "aggressor" and the imposition of economic sanctions that sharply curtailed its foreign trade outside the Communist bloc.

By mid-1953 the PRC had demonstrated its ability to defend its borders, and the Korean war had ended in stalemate. It had also become clear to Peking that a policy of encouraging armed struggle against existing governments in Asia would not soon bear fruit. The PRC's domestic situation had become more stable, and the party leaders, who had decided to seek industrialization by applying "the advanced experiences of the Soviet Union," appreciated the need for a relaxation of international tensions to facilitate both China's development at home and its renewed quest for legitimacy abroad. Thus, in this second broad phase of its foreign policy, which lasted until mid-1957, Peking diminished its encouragement of subversion against neighboring governments and began to call for "peaceful coexistence" between Communist and non-Communist states. The PRC particularly sought to win favor with independent African governments as well as neutral Asian governments that it had previously marked for wars of national liberation. The high point of this policy was the Asian-African Conference held at Bandung, Indonesia, in April 1955. The "spirit of Bandung" extended beyond the newly developing countries as the PRC also sought to improve relations with the major Western powers including the United States. Peking had already gained prestige in 1954 through participation in the Geneva Conferences, and it had resumed its campaign to establish diplomatic relations with non-Communist states. At Bandung, Premier Chou En-lai even indicated his willingness to enter into bilateral discussions with the United States. This led to the Sino-American ambassadorial talks in which for several years Peking persistently sought an accommodation with Washington, but only managed to conclude a single agreement concerning the release of each other's nationals.

Just as the period 1958–1965 witnessed renewed militancy, radical innovation, and abandonment of the Soviet model in the PRC's domestic public order, similar changes occurred in its foreign policy. Peaceful coexistence had failed to achieve either détente with the United States or the weakening of the American military position in Asia, which, if anything, seemed to be expanding. Moreover, a decade of economic progress at home and the demonstration of Soviet rocket power offered by *Sputnik* made Chairman Mao confident that "the East wind has prevailed over the West wind" and that the time had come for a direct attack upon the status quo. Peking's more vigorous policy, exemplified by the military and propaganda harassment of the Nationalist-occupied offshore islands of Quemoy and Matsu that provoked a crisis in the late summer of 1958, met with little support from Moscow, which had become increasingly dubious about both the international and domestic wisdom of Mao's radicalism. By 1960 evidence of Sino-Soviet tensions was mounting, and Peking was adopting an increasingly independent foreign policy line from Moscow. The Chinese openly began to compete with the Russians for influence among the other Communist governments and parties of the world and among the non-Communist countries of Asia, Africa, and Latin America. Indeed, on the basis of militant anti-imperialism rather than peaceful coexistence, Peking attempted gradually to forge a "Third World" alliance against both the American and Soviet influence that it saw converging in opposition to revolutionary trends. It even advocated founding an international organization of the "new emerging forces" to rival the United Nations, which had continued to spurn the PRC. In pursuit of its radical, anti-imperialist strategy, Peking resorted to conventional government-to-government relations as well as revolutionary tactics. Between 1958 and 1965 it established diplomatic relations with twenty-two countries, most of them African, and made use of all the accepted forms of influence, such as trade, economic aid, technical assistance, and cultural exchange, while at the same time conducting "people-to-people" diplomacy and encouraging wars of national liberation in selected countries. The PRC also undertook a dramatic reorientation of its foreign trade away from the Soviet bloc and toward Western Europe and Japan.

By 1966 the PRC's policy of militant anti-imperialism was plainly in trouble. Peking had alienated itself from its principal ally and source of aid, the Soviet Union, and had even come to fear a Soviet attack against China. Its handling of the border dispute with India had cost the friendship of another important neighbor, its most prestigious supporter among the nonaligned states. The brutal repression of the attempted Communist coup in Indonesia in September 1965 and the subsequent decline of Sukarno had deprived the PRC of its major partner in the plan to mobilize the "new emerging forces." Peking's unsuccessful effort to reschedule the second Afro-Asian summit conference, after events in Algeria caused a postponement in June 1965, symbolized its inability to persuade most of the developing countries to form a coalition against both their leading benefactors, Washington and Moscow. The burgeoning American military involvement in Vietnam had demonstrated Peking's failure to eliminate Western power from Asia, and Japan's phenomenal economic progress and correspondingly greater political influence had begun to preoccupy Peking. Although domestic issues are commonly thought to have been the focus of the bitter dispute among the Chinese Communist leadership that unleashed the Cultural Revolution, Peking's deteriorating position abroad can hardly have been overlooked.

The Cultural Revolution of 1966–1969 made a shambles of PRC foreign policy. Amid the prevailing turmoil and xenophobia, diplomatic missions in Peking were targets of frequent demonstrations and occasional damage; diplomats, their staff, and their family members were sometimes mistreated by Red Guards and other popular elements, and a number of foreign nationals were jailed on charges ranging from espionage to disrespect for the image of Chairman Mao. Although certain countries considered friendly to the PRC escaped difficulty, many Communist and non-Communist states suffered. It should be noted that the worst abuses occurred in 1967 when extremists seized control of the Foreign Office and even succeeded in subjecting the then Foreign Minister, the late Ch'en Yi, to humiliating "struggle meetings" before large crowds. The Cultural Revolution also led the PRC to hostile actions abroad as well as at home. Peking intensified its public support for wars of national liberation by openly calling for the violent overthrow of specific governments and opposing a negotiated settlement of the Vietnam conflict. It recalled all but one of its ambassadors, and it encouraged those diplomats remaining at their posts, PRC nationals studying or working abroad, and overseas Chinese loyal to the People's Republic to manifest their political activism in ways that many host states deemed objectionable. This often elicited efforts to suppress what was seen to be Peking's interference in internal affairs, and the suppression generally led to a more extreme reaction from the PRC, both in the host country and in Peking. In certain instances, we should point out, it was the host country, rather than the People's Republic, that created the dispute by taking measures that provoked a Chinese response.

By the summer of 1969, after the national paroxysm had passed and stability had been reintroduced at home, the PRC began to indicate an awareness of the incalculable harm that the Cultural Revolution had inflicted upon its stature abroad. While only modestly moderating its revolutionary rhetoric, it again demonstrated serious interest in foreign affairs and set out to convince the world of its rationality and reliability. The security of foreign embassies, diplomats, and nationals was no longer a problem in Peking, and the Foreign Ministry quietly undertook to make amends for previous abuses, even announcing the punishment of the extremist official who was said to have been responsible for ordering them.[66] PRC ambassadors gradually returned to their posts. Peking soon made clear that its interest in representing China at the United Nations had been revived, and it launched another campaign to establish diplomatic relations with non-Communist states.

Peking even proved willing to negotiate with its principal enemies. At the height of the Cultural Revolution it had pushed Moscow to the verge of breaking diplomatic relations, and in the first half of 1969 tensions over the Sino-Soviet border had led to hostilities sufficiently grave to suggest the possibility of a major conflict; yet, shortly afterward, Peking agreed to make another attempt to reach a negotiated solution to the border problem.

By 1971, in addition to extending "people-to-people" diplomacy to American citizens, the PRC showed renewed interest in official contacts with the United States. This culminated in the invitation for President Nixon to visit China and in the moderate Shanghai Communiqué of February 1972, to which the PRC agreed even though the United States did not terminate its commitment to defend Taiwan. At the same time the PRC began to endorse the Vietnamese Communists' proposal for a negotiated settlement of the Vietnam conflict. The exchange of official "liaison offices" between the United States and the PRC in 1973, following the withdrawal of American forces from Vietnam, represented a great leap forward toward a Sino-American détente.

The PRC's entry into the UN and its sudden establishment of diplomatic relations with a great many states virtually achieved its long-sought goal of winning international recognition of its legitimacy. No one can predict how long the current phase of Peking's foreign policy will last, but never since the founding of the People's Republic have prospects been brighter for its full participation in the world community. It is understandable, in these circumstances, that interest in the PRC's views of international law has never been greater.

PART I

The Nature and Basis of International Law

The Introduction to this volume has discussed the nature of the traditional Chinese world order and also the gradual, but virtually total, acceptance of Western international law by late Ch'ing and Republican modernizers. We now seek to present the PRC's views on the nature of international law and the basis upon which it rests. Inevitably, this concerns theory, a matter that has interested Anglo-American students of international law less than our continental European colleagues. Chinese have traditionally attached great significance to correct philosophical orientation, and the importation into China of Marxism-Leninism, a European ideology, has reinforced this trait. It is, of course, difficult to ascertain the extent to which the avowed orthodoxy of Marxism-Leninism actually conditions the world outlook of the contemporary Chinese elite and the extent to which China's international behavior reflects that outlook rather than the influence of other factors. Nevertheless, the reader who becomes too impatient with what may well seem to be sterile academic theorizing should recall Chairman Mao's repeated strictures that theory and practice must be linked and that ideological clarification must precede appropriate action.

Those who are familiar with Soviet writing on international law during the mid-1950's may require an extra ration of patience because of the highly derivative nature of much of the material that follows. They may be compensated, however, by noting the extent to which Chinese scholars have adapted Soviet doctrine to China's experience and situation and the extent to which subsequent Soviet scholarship has moved beyond the views reflected here.

Efforts to Define International Law 1

1-1

Ho Wu-shuang and Ma Chün, "A Criticism of the Reactionary Viewpoint of Ch'en T'i-ch'iang on the Science of International Law," *CFYC*, no. 6:35 (1957).

International law, like all other branches of law, is created in a definite historical stage of mankind's social development. The origin of international law is directly related to the creation of the state. [International law] is created as the political, economic, and other relations among states emerge.

Generally speaking, international law comprises those rules of conduct which states are obligated to observe in their international relations. However, as the definition of international law must reflect and explain many essential problems of international law itself, the above-stated general definition of international law is not a scientific concept because such a general explanation of international law cannot fulfill such a role.

In bourgeois writings on international law, almost every international law scholar has attempted to define international law. According to the Cuban scholar Bustamante's calculation, the number of definitions of international law which have been given exceeds one hundred. However, all such definitions are incorrect and antiscientific. The world view and methodology of the bourgeoisie render it impossible for bourgeois scholars to give a genuine scientific definition. Only when we take a Marxist-Leninist theory of state and law as a basis and start from the practical situation of international law itself can we correctly solve the question of the definition of international law.

The definition of international law which is commonly accepted in Soviet legal circles is: "International Law is the aggregate of various norms adjusting relations among states in the process of their struggle and cooperation, expressing the will of the ruling classes of these states and guaranteed by coercion applied by states individually and collectively." [a]

[a] This is the definition given by Vyshinsky. The editorial department of *SGP*

This definition points out that international law, like all other branches of law, possesses the characteristics of law in general: (1) it expresses the will of the ruling class; (2) it is the aggregate of norms adjusting definite social relations; and (3) it is guaranteed by enforcement measures.

Therefore, international law is a kind of law possessing legal validity; it is not what are called self-executing norms of morality.

On the other hand, the above-stated definition also emphatically points out the characteristics possessed by international law which are different from those of municipal law: for instance, the subjects of international law are states, and the enforcement measures of international law have a special character.

In short, only the definition of international law given by Soviet scholars correctly explains the question of the contents and substance of international law. This definition is adaptable to the international law of various historical periods (the period of the slave system, the period of feudalism, and the period of capitalism). In the meantime, it is also adaptable to modern international law.

Note

By the time the above article appeared in late 1957, the Soviet definition of international law that it recites had been supplemented by the insertion, after the words "struggle and cooperation," of the phrase "designed to safeguard their peaceful coexistence." [1] This change followed the CPSU's promulgation in 1956 of a new policy that required Soviet scholars to recognize that "the purpose of present-day International Law is to promote peaceful coexistence and cooperation between all States regardless of their social systems." [2]

According to an American authority on Soviet law, by the mid-1960's most Soviet text writers defined international law as: "The aggregate of norms which are established by the agreement of states, including those with different social orders; express the wills of these states; regulate their struggle and collaboration on the basis, and in the interest, of the effective maintenance of peace and peaceful coexistence; and enforced when necessary, by collective or individual state action." [3] This reflected "the new emphasis upon negotiated settlement in lieu of force, the existence of special socialist principles of international law, and the emergence of the Soviet state of the entire people to which the concept of a ruling class is alien." [4] Moreover,

---

pointed out in "Recapitulation of Discussion on a Few Problems in Current Theories Concerning International Law" that this definition is a comparatively appropriate definition generally recognized by Soviet international law circles. *SGP*, no. 5(1955).

more recent Soviet writing suggests continuing definitional experimentation that tends to omit reference to class struggle and resort to force.[5]

Although the PRC began to emphasize peaceful coexistence as early as 1954 and although Chinese writers appear to have accepted the post-1956 Soviet modification of the definition of international law to include reference to peaceful coexistence, by the 1960's the Chinese and Soviet views of this slogan and its legal implications differed substantially. For example, on October 8, 1964, Wu Te-feng, then a vice-president of the Supreme People's Court and president of the Chinese Political Science and Law Association, stated: "Imperialism is the basic source of modern war, and American imperialism, moreover, is the most ferocious and ambitious aggressor ever to exist in the history of mankind, and it is the most flagrant violator of the principles of modern international law. Naturally, democratic legal workers in various countries should engage in the thorough exposure of, and determined struggle against it. However, modern revisionists nevertheless make great efforts to propagandize the carrying out of 'peaceful coexistence' with imperialism without being subject to any principles, disseminating the view that contemporary international law is the 'law of peaceful co-existence,' and they propagandize the carrying out of 'full co-operation' with American imperialism."[6] Part II, Chapter 8, traces the evolution of the Chinese view of peaceful coexistence.

The target of attack referred to in the title of item 1–1, Ch'en T'i-ch'iang, until he was dismissed as a "rightist" during the anti-rightist campaign of 1957–1958, served as head of the Division of International Law of the Institute of International Relations of the Chinese Academy of Sciences. Ch'en had been educated at the University of London. His doctoral dissertation, *The International Law of Recognition* (London, 1951), is still regarded as a leading text on the subject. We will see many examples of Ch'en's writing in this study. For criticisms of Ch'en's work, see, for example, items 3–4 and 3–5.

1-2

Ying T'ao, "Recognize the True Face of Bourgeois International Law from a Few Basic Concepts," *KCWTYC*, no. 1:43–44 (1960).

The bourgeoisie carefully conceal the class character of bourgeois international law by using various measures to camouflage this character. This is first reflected by the definition of international law given by bourgeois writers.

Oppenheim, a British bourgeois international law jurist, said that the law of nations is "the name for a body of customary and conventional rules (as distinguished from purely custom, morality and the so-called rules of international comity) which are considered legally binding by civilized states in their intercourse with each other." [a] The German bourgeois international law jurist, Franz von Liszt, defined international law as "an aggregate of rules and regulations about the rights and obligations of civilized countries." [b] There are many other definitions, but they are more or less the same as the two cited above.

These definitions cause us first to realize that bourgeois international law is created for the so-called "civilized states" and does not possess the spirit of democratic legislation in the international big family. Moreover, this creation is synthesized in rules of customs and agreements arising from mutual intercourse among "civilized states" that do not respect other countries on the basis of the concept of equality. Second, these definitions cause us to realize that so-called bourgeois international law is composed of rules governing rights and duties among "civilized states," which implies that so-called "uncivilized states" have a different status.

Here, one would naturally ask: What are the criteria advocated by the bourgeoisie for distinguishing so-called "civilized states" from "uncivilized states"? Among the existing states, which are "civilized states" and which are "uncivilized states"? According to the answer of the bourgeoisie, only "Christian states" are "civilized states," while non-Christian states, mainly oriental states, are "uncivilized states." For instance, Oppenheim said that before the First World War, China, Persia, Burma, Abyssinia, and other oriental states were still "un-

[a] L. Oppenheim, *International Law,* 7th ed., ed. H. Lauterpacht, (London: Longmans, Green and Co., 1948), I, 4. [Note: The words in parentheses appeared only in the Chinese text; they do not appear in Oppenheim's text.]

[b] *Das Völkerrecht,* 11th ed. (1917). [Note: We are unable to locate the book cited in the Chinese article. We found the following book: Franz von Liszt, *Das Völkerrecht, Systematisch Dargestellt, elfte, umgearbeitete Auflage* (Berlin: Verlag von Julius Springer, 1918).]

civilized states," because "their civilization at that time had not yet reached that condition which was necessary to enable their governments and their population in every respect to understand, and to carry out, the rules of international law." [c] Thus, it is evident that the criterion of the bourgeoisie for distinguishing so-called "civilized" and "uncivilized" [states] is neither long history nor culture. Even though China has had 5,000 years of excellent culture, she was not included in the group of "civilized states." The exclusion of oriental states from the exclusive club of "civilized states" reflects exactly the needs of the aggressive interests of the imperialistic monopolistic bourgeoisie.

It should be pointed out here that not all Christian states are rated as equal. In light of the history of the development of bourgeois international law and the practices of the external relations of imperialism, so-called "civilized states" in fact refers only to imperialism itself, or in other words, the big Western capitalist powers. Indeed, bourgeois international law reflects only the will and need of the ruling class of big capitalist powers. Therefore, in the Western capitalist world the suppression of the weak by the strong and the eating of small fish by big fish are not only tacitly condoned by bourgeois international law but are also cloaked with a mantle of "legality." Under bourgeois international law, many oriental states which degenerated into colonies and semicolonies have only the option of accepting butchery, plunder, and slavery and cannot enjoy any right of legal protection. Wherever imperialism extends its devilish arms to socialist states, the latter are branded as lacking "moral" standards or as "uncivilized." Thus, it may be discerned that the bourgeois description of international law as regulations that prescribe rights and duties among "civilized states," and that do not protect "uncivilized states," has profound significance.

Here we wish to emphatically point out that, although bourgeois international law may in certain periods and under certain conditions play a role of mutual restriction among "civilized states," it is mainly a weapon used by "civilized states" to control and oppress what they consider to be "uncivilized states." The "uncivilized states" are their preys. The Chinese people feel very deeply here. In the past, imperialism seized the right of consular jurisdiction in China on the pretext that China was "backward in the rule of law" and "uncivilized." By establishing "spheres of influence," advocating the "open door

[c] Oppenheim, I, 46–47. [Note: The phrase "at that time" does not appear in Oppenheim's text. As a matter of fact, Oppenheim does not say that these states were "uncivilized states"; he only mentions that "the position of [these states] . . . was to some extent doubtful." *Ibid.*, p. 46.]

policy" and "equal opportunity for all," and even trying to partition China, imperialism treated China as a "backward" and "uncivilized" state which could be oppressed. Even now, the deprivation of China's legitimate position in the United Nations is based on the insulting assertion that China has not yet reached the degree of civilization required to carry out international obligations.[7]

1-3

Shih Sung, Yü Ta-hsin, Lu Ying-hui, and Ts'ao K'o, "An Initial Investigation into the Old-Law Viewpoint in the Teaching of International Law," *CHYYC*, no. 4:14 (1958).

Recently, in the "twin-anti" movement [a 1958 campaign against waste and conservatism] we have undertaken an initial investigation of the teaching of public international law. We have uncovered many old-law viewpoints. The old-law viewpoint of one teacher appeared particularly serious.

For example, after the recent antirightist campaign, when our teaching and research office discussed the purpose of offering the course on international law in the department of law, that teacher emphasized that the purpose of such a course is to give students systematic knowledge of international law. His so-called "knowledge" refers to those trifling problems in international law which are of a technical nature. Obsessed by this "pure business" idea, in the course of his lecturing to students he spent substantial time introducing detailed technical problems or explaining terminology and concepts; conversely, he almost never mentioned or only slightly touched upon the vital problem of international struggle and the practices of our foreign policy.

Such a viewpoint is obviously not merely a question of a teaching method; it is a clear illustration of the fact that this comrade failed to recognize that international law is a legal instrument in the service of our foreign policy.

Note

The view that international law is an instrument of foreign policy has been a commonplace among both Chinese and Soviet writers. The following is a typical Chinese formulation: "International law, in addition to being a body of principles and norms which must be observed by every country, is also, just as any law, a political instrument; whether a country is socialist or capitalist, it will to a certain degree utilize international law in implementing its foreign policy."[8]

Occasionally, however, Chinese scholars reflect the fact that the PRC's leaders have maintained a more challenging attitude toward the world community than have their contemporary Soviet counterparts, and they adopt formulations that resemble the more overtly hostile, less sophisticated statements of Soviet writers of an earlier era. During the antirightist campaign, for example, an article published in the authoritative *People's Daily* (*Jen-min jih-pao;* hereafter appears as *JMJP* in headings and notes), the newspaper of the Chinese Communist Party, stated: "International law is one of the instruments for settling international problems. If this instrument is useful to our country, to the socialist cause, or to the cause of peace of the people of the world, we will use it. However, if this instrument is disadvantageous to our country, to the socialist cause, or to the cause of peace of the people of the world, we will not use it and should create a new instrument to replace it. Today we have a majority of the old international law jurists, who still adhere to the purely legalistic viewpoint by restricting themselves to the limited area of international law, and thus they subject themselves to the disposal of imperialism."[9]

Criticism of Bourgeois Theories 2

2-1

Ho Wu-shuang and Ma Chün, "A Criticism of the Reactionary Viewpoint of Ch'en T'i-ch'iang on the Science of International Law," *CFYC*, no. 6:35–38 (1957).

International law and the science of international law are closely related, but the two should not be confused in discussion. The science of international law is the science which takes international law applied among states as its object of study. Everyone knows that international law is not an abstract matter, but possesses class character. However, as the norms of international law are enacted through agreements among states, international law reflects not only the will of the ruling class of a state, *but also the will of the ruling classes of the respective states participating in the agreement.* But, this does not amount to saying that under the current conditions of history (the coexistence of two types of social systems), there exist several types of international law (such as bourgeois international law, socialist international law, and so forth). In fact, the law which is now adjusting the relations between states with different social systems is a type of *general* (generally recognized) *international law.* The possibility of the existence of this type of general international law is determined by the possibility and reality of coexistence and cooperation between states with two different systems in modern times.

As the international law now in existence is general international law, does there also exist a general science of international law?

There now exist two different sciences of international law which are different in character: the bourgeois science of international law and the proletarian science of international law. They are established on two types of economic bases that are opposite in character, and they serve the policy of different classes.

Despite the fact that the characteristics of bourgeois international law as a "science" are expressed differently in one or another capitalist country, or in the writing of one or another scholar (that is, reflecting the interests and demands of the state ruling class of one or another bourgeoisie), its general substance is the same—it is nothing but a theoretical instrument to defend the aggressive or colonial policy of the strong capitalist countries, to do its best to maintain the capitalist "world order" (and to oppose legal principles of socialism). . . .

It should be recognized that, at the end of the nineteenth century and the beginning of the twentieth century, a large number of textbooks on international law were published by capitalist writers. However . . . these books either repeated each other, or engaged in mutual criticism and slander. So far as their contents are concerned, they all started from subjective prejudging by bourgeois scholars and tried to defend the practices of international law (which were actually illegal acts) of the bourgeoisie in their own country. Therefore, despite the fact that the bourgeois science of international law and its writings appear to be full of content and expressed in many forms, they have never really been scientific so far as substance is concerned. Only the proletarian science of international law established on the base of Marxism-Leninism is a genuine science.

Everyone knows that at an early stage Marx and Engels began to study various problems in international law from the proletarian viewpoint. Marx and Engels had made a thorough analysis of the foreign policy and international law of the bourgeoisie before the monopoly stage. The writings of Marx and Engels not only pointed out the economic and political premises of the development of international law, and disclosed the fundamental concept and class essence of the international law at that time, but also proposed applicable principles of international law for the new future society (socialist society). Thus, they established the revolutionary and scientific basis of the proletarian science of international law.

The proletarian science of international law, which is based on Marxism-Leninism, as represented by the Soviet science of international law, is fundamentally opposed to the bourgeois science of international law because it does not defend the interest of the exploiting class or a certain group, but instead defends the interest of the proletariat and all toiling people the world over. The chief mission of the proletarian science of international law is: scientifically to prove and propagandize the system of international law which is serving peace, democracy, and progressive enterprise; and to make such a democratic and progressive system and the principles of international law into an effective weapon for peace-loving countries and all peace-loving people in their struggle to achieve international independence and sovereignty. In contrast to the bourgeois science of international law, the proletarian science of international law has unremittingly engaged in struggle against imperialist acts of breaking international law and has unceasingly exposed the attempts of imperialist countries to conspire to utilize the system of international law . . . to serve their policies of war and aggression.

From the difference in essence between the bourgeois science of international law and the proletarian science of international law, it is not difficult to realize that the science of international law is a science which possesses strong class character; every international law scholar starts from the interests and practical necessity of his own class and attempts to make international law serve the foreign policy of his own class. However, this does not mean that norms of international law can be interpreted at will or distorted. In the course of enacting and at the time of reaching agreement, norms of international law do possess generally recognized and definite content. However, bourgeois scholars cannot always correctly explain the genuine content of norms of international law. The reason is that the limited nature and metaphysical methodology of the bourgeois science of international law have made it impossible for them to reach a correct conclusion. But a more important reason is that the monopoly capitalists demand that their international law scholars interpret international law in accordance with the internationally illegal diplomatic activities of the imperialist countries. In order to fulfill their duty, bourgeois scholars must engage in a distorted interpretation of the various systems of international law. Otherwise, they cannot defend the international law violations of their master. With respect to the proletarian science of international law, since its mission does not contradict the generally recognized fundamental principles of international law, it is unnecessary for the proletarian science of international law to make any distorted interpretation of the norms of international law.

From the foregoing, it seems clear that the proletarian science of international law and the bourgeois science of international law are not comparable because only the former represents the interest of the most progressive class—the interest of the proletariat—and is founded on the basis of Marxism-Leninism. Moreover, their different functions relating to furthering the current peace effort also make genuine comparison impossible. . . .

Since the founding of the People's Republic of China, due to the fundamental change in the character of the state and foreign policy, the science of international law as a science maintaining bourgeois interests and opposing principles of socialism has naturally lost the base for its existence and development.

After the liberation, we must in principle deny the bourgeois "science" of international law, just as we deny other branches of bourgeois social science. Only in that way can we, under the guidance of Marxist-Leninist thought, in accordance with our country's diplomatic practices and upon study of the Soviet science of international law, gradually establish a science of international law consistent with our country's concrete situation and make international law capable of serving our foreign policy.

2-2

Ying T'ao, "Recognize the True Face of Bourgeois International Law from a Few Basic Concepts," *KCWTYC*, no. 1:45–46, 49–51 (1960).

The bourgeoisie formulated many theories concerning the basis of international law, but all of them intentionally avoid discussion of its class character. The most popular theory at present is the theory of "common consent," which says that international law is formulated on the basis of the "common consent" of all members of the international community and its basis is therefore "the common consent of sovereign and equal states." In addition, there is also a theory . . . which considers that the basis of the formulation of international law is a "biological principle." This principle exists "in rules inherited from a natural order which is above the legal order, and the role of the legislators is to transform these rules into legal rules." Historically, international law was once described as reflecting the "will of God," or being born out of "direct or indirect revelation of God."

The advocates of the "common consent" theory expound with great effort on negotiation and conclusion of treaties and other superficial phenomena to show that the theory of "common consent" is real and that such consent is the genuine consent of many countries large and small. However, such are not the facts. Because of the fact that "the weakest goes to the wall" is the essential character of the bourgeoisie, all negotiations and the conclusion of treaties among capitalist countries begin from a position of strength and a battle of wits. It does not permit an equal and free expression of will by countries large and small. The decisive element is the will of the big capitalist powers. Most of the small capitalist countries are on the side of the victims, and the so-called "consent" is reached under circumstances of compulsion, which do not express the genuine wish of these countries. Many facts in history prove this observation. In history it is a well-known fact that various big imperialist powers used the threat of force to compel various weak and small countries to "consent" to the conclusion of a large number of unequal treaties. Today American imperialism uses various means to force various weak and small countries to "consent" to the conclusion of many treaties unilaterally advantageous to the United States. For instance, after the Second World War, in implementing such policies as the "Truman Doctrine," the "Marshall Plan," the "Point Four Program," the "Eisenhower Doctrine," and other aggressive programs, the United States concluded with many countries in Europe (including Britain and France), Asia, and Africa, a series of international agreements in accordance with the definite standards provided in United States law. These agreements include many obligations which obviously encroach upon the sovereignty of other states, invade other states' domestic jurisdiction, and are detrimental to other states' interests. Substantively speaking, can we say that these treaties are the result of genuine "common consent" between the United States and such states?

Furthermore, the matter is not so simple. In view of the unbalanced development of capitalism, the relative strength of imperialist powers varies from time to time. As "each one seeks its own interest" and "the weakest goes to the wall" are the characteristics of capitalist states, "common consent" cannot be easily reached at any time. Thus, "common consent" among members of international society is flexibly interpreted by bourgeois jurists. They say that the so-called "common consent can therefore only mean the express or tacit consent of such an overwhelming majority of the members that those who dissent are of no importance whatever and disappear totally from the view of one who looks for the will of the community as an entity in contradistinction to the wills of its single members." [a] In fact, what they point out as an "overwhelming majority" are the big imperialist powers and those weak and small countries subject to their pressure. Other countries are classified as "those individual elements who dissent" and their dissenting opinion is to be "disregarded totally."

The theory that the basis of international law is a "biological principle" is even more absurd. Speaking of their nature, rules of international law and "biological principles" are two entirely different things. "Biological principles" reflect natural phenomena while international law reflects social phenomena, and natural phenomena and social phenomena are not comparable. [There are four reasons why the bourgeoisie wants to introduce this theory:] First, the bourgeoisie attempts to cover up the fact that bourgeois international law represents its will and to mislead people into regarding bourgeois international law as objective. Second, since natural phenomena have no class character and will not change in a long period of time, by bringing bourgeois international law into the realm of natural phenomena the

[a] L. Oppenheim, *International Law,* 7th ed. by H. Lauterpacht (London: Longmans, Green, 1948), I, 17.

bourgeoisie can claim that legal norms, regulations, and systems are perpetual and unchangeable. Third, since the theory of "the origin of species by means of natural selection and the survival of the fittest" is a part of biological science, the bourgeoisie wishes people to believe that its external aggression is in accord with the principle of natural selection and that its annexation of weak and small countries is in accord with the principle of the survival of the fittest. Fourth, the bourgeoisie attempts to convince people that all its outrageous acts are "just" and consistent with the natural rules of biology. In short, all these theories are introduced in the interest of the bourgeoisie. As for the so-called theory of the "will of God," this is no less than an attempt to sanctify the will of the bourgeoisie and to hoodwink the people of the world. . . .

Bourgeois international law comprises two parts—principles and norms of international law and science of international law. These two parts are different, but have inseparable and close connections. The so-called principles of bourgeois international law are fundamental principles consistent with the external political views of the bourgeoisie, while the so-called norms of bourgeois international law refer to specific rules derived from treaties concluded among bourgeois countries, customs, judicial decisions, and so forth. The science of bourgeois international law must, on the one hand, interpret and defend the external acts of the bourgeoisie and, at the same time, plan for future external acts of the bourgeoisie in order to justify these acts in legal terms. The principles and norms of bourgeois international law are the bases to be studied by the science of bourgeois international law. The latter promotes the development of these principles and norms. Therefore, their relationship is exactly the same as the relationship between theory and practice in the law of the bourgeoisie. The characteristics of principles and norms of bourgeois international law are reflected in the science of bourgeois international law. The situation of the historical development of principles and norms of bourgeois international law and the development of the science of bourgeois international law also consistently follow the interest of the bourgeoisie. The principal schools [of the science of bourgeois international law] are as follows:

Natural Law School—During the period of the bourgeois revolution, the "natural law school" was very popular because it served the need to oppose the feudalistic autocratic system. Natural law jurists considered that natural law was the only source of international law. Anything in accordance with "human nature," "reason" or "justice" was international law. They denied the existence of international law formulated by customs or treaties. What they called "human nature," "reason," or "justice" was actually the natural desires of the bourgeoisie. The object of such desires was to strike down the feudal king's claim that "I am the State" or "the order of the king is law." At that time, natural law jurists denied that customs and treaties were international law because the bourgeoisie had just emerged and seized political power in only a few countries and the bourgeoisie had not yet created their own treaties and customs; the existing treaties and customs were built by the feudal ruling class and did not correspond to the interest of the bourgeoisie.

Positive Law School—After the bourgeoisie seized political power in many countries, consolidated their ruling position, entered the international stage and externally concluded their own treaties and formulated a set of customs through their external practices, the "positive law school" became popular. It recognized only [those rules of] international law formulated by customs and treaties and also considered this kind of international law far more important than the so-called natural international law. Some positivists even completely denied that natural international law was law. If we say that the bourgeoisie at one time used the theory of the natural law school to oppose feudal bondage in order to attain their free development during the period of bourgeois revolution, then we can say that they used the theory of the positive law school to deal with their new opponents in order to keep the latter from breaking the rules prescribed by them.

Middle-of-the-road School—When the free capitalism of some countries entered the stage of imperialism, the positivist theory no longer provided legal justification for the aggressive acts of the bourgeoisie. The "middle-of-the-road school" (also called the Grotian school) began to arise. This school combines the theories of naturalists and positivists . . . by considering "the positive international law of equal importance to the natural international law" and [maintains] "if legal rules based on the practices of various states are inadequate, international law may appropriately supplement itself by borrowing rules of justice or principles of law." [10] This is to say that when one's own treaties and customs are sufficient to serve the purpose of defending aggressive acts, treaties and customs will be invoked. When they are inadequate, then one may borrow such natural law principles as "justice," "reason," or "human nature" to defend aggressive acts. By so doing, imperialism's external aggression may in any case be justified by one theory or the other.

Normativist School—Around the period of the First World War, the aggressive desire of the monopolistic bourgeois interests represented by imperialism increased, and imperialism wished to rule and enslave the whole world. To reflect this desire in legal science, the "normativist school" and the "school of social solidarity" were formed. The normativist school views legal authority as various norms within a hierarchical framework. Within this system of norms, all legal authority and norms constitute a unified entity, and within this unified system of legal authority, international law is above municipal law. International law is the "supreme order of legal authority" and every country must obey this order and be subject to its limitations. Normativists deny state sovereignty and describe sovereignty as the source which causes all disputes in the world. They demand that states abandon sovereignty and advocate the establishment of a supranational "world state," a "world government" and the enactment of a "world constitution." Obviously, the normativist school wishes to clear the road for imperialism's encroachment upon other states' independence and establishment of world domination.

School of Social Solidarity—This school maintains that all parts of the world are interrelated, and the "intercourse" among peoples of the world constitutes a long chain. The "intercourse" among peoples unites respective individuals on the basis of a "relation of solidarity." This "relation of solidarity" is the relation of solidarity created by division of labor. Reasoning from either the nature of "world intercourse" or its constituent elements, intercourse between states is [said to be] in no way different from that between individuals. States are merely the boundaries in international intercourse which can only be implemented by individuals. Therefore, [members of this school] reach the conclusion that only individuals are subjects of international law, while states are not. State sovereignty is a fiction and the "source of international individualism and state anarchy." In order to eliminate this source, a "world government" must be established which will completely eliminate all national states. This conclusion is exactly the same as that of the "normativist school." Today American imperialism is doing its best to sell this theory.

It must be pointed out that it is not at all surprising that there are many schools of the science of bourgeois international law advocating different theories on some questions. The reasons for this situation are: (1) The bourgeoisie all over the world have their own countries with their legislative and judicial organs. (2) The bourgeoisie of various countries all consider only their own interests. Since their situations are different, their interests are also different, and thereby contradictions frequently arise. Since bourgeois international law jurists speak for the interest of the bourgeoisie of their respective countries, the various theories in the science of bourgeois international law are the exact reflections of these contradictions. For instance, the continental school and the maritime school reflect contradictions of interests between capitalist continental countries and maritime countries. For example, the claims of open door and equal opportunity submitted by the United States reflected the contradictions among the United States, Britain, Japan, and other imperialist countries with respect to their plunder and demarcation of spheres of influence in China. Even within the bourgeoisie of a country, several groups are formed because of the difference in interests. This situation accounts for the fact that bourgeois international law jurists of a country may hold different theories and views toward one problem, for they respectively represent the interests of different groups of the bourgeoisie within one country. However, it must be emphatically pointed out that, despite the difference of opinions and views, these differences exist only on questions of secondary importance which do not go beyond or depart from the general interests and demands of the bourgeoisie. The difference of opinions and views among schools of bourgeois international law not only does not confuse the international strategic objective of the bourgeoisie, but, on the contrary, provides them with mobility within which they may use different theories in different situations to achieve their aggressive objectives. To the bourgeoisie, the more theories which exist, the greater is their advantage, not their disadvantage.

* * *

Through the perspective of the above several basic concepts, we can clearly discern that bourgeois international law is the superstructure of a capitalist economic base. Just as the international law in the period of slave society or feudal society, which was the superstructure of the slave economy or the feudal economy, respectively, reflected the respective wills of the slave owner class and feudal lord class, so, too, bourgeois international law reflects exactly the will of the bourgeoisie. Concretely speaking, bourgeois international law is designed in accordance with the needs of the foreign policy of the bourgeoisie at different stages of capitalist economic development, and is formulated through diplomatic means and arbitrary practices. On the other hand, it also serves as an effective weapon to maintain the interest of the bourgeoisie and to promote their external policy. During the early period of capitalism, it once played a progressive role, but, in line with the development of capitalism, it became a tool of oppression used by big capitalist powers against weak and small countries. Today bourgeois international law controlled by the aggressive bloc headed by American imperialism has become extremely reactionary. It is used as a weapon not only to oppose socialist countries, but also to oppose nationalist countries and peoples in colonies and semicolonies. It is even disadvantageous to small capitalist countries. Its ferocious face is more and more clearly exposed before the peoples of the world.

2-3

Chiang Yang, "The Reactionary Thought of 'Universalism' in American Jurisprudence," *JMJP* (Dec. 17, 1963), p. 5.

"Universalism" is a type of reactionary thought which the American monopolistic bourgeoisie have been enthusiastically spreading since the end of the Second World War. The fundamental contents of this type of reactionary thought are: propagandizing about relinquishing national interest, national culture, national tradition and patriotic thought; opposing national independence and the people's struggle for liberation; shouting loudly about eliminating national sovereignty and national boundaries; establishing the so-called "world legal order," "world state," "world government," "world assembly," etc.; and attempting to put all nations and states of the world under the reactionary rule of American imperialism. . . .

In the United States, after the war [World War II], the thought of "universalism" infiltrated into the areas of philosophy, economics, jurisprudence, sociology, literature, arts, etc. In the area of jurisprudence, "universalism" is no longer the characteristic of an individual American bourgeois school of jurisprudence, but rather is the common system of thought of various schools of jurisprudence, including the American sociological school, the realist school, the neo-Thomist school, and so forth, . . . After the Second World War even some reactionary scholars who formerly rarely discussed the question of the relationship between law and international relations, such as the famous representative of the American sociological school, Pound, also joined the chorus of this reactionary thought. . . . "Universalism" has become very fashionable in the United States. . . .

Advocating the establishment of a "world legal order," "world government," or "world state" . . . under the guidance of the United States is central to "universalism" in jurisprudence. Since the ultimate goal of the American reactionaries in promoting "universalism" is the dream of establishing the rule of American imperialism over the world, the American reactionary jurists have done their best to propagandize and to argue in this area.

At the beginning of his "Toward a New *Jus Gentium*," Pound, a jurist in the service of the American monopolistic bourgeoisie, says:

"At the outset I assume the need, and, a very great need, of a world-wide legal order." [a] Why should a "world legal order" be established? The reason given by Pound is that "in view of the economic unification of the world which has been going forward and of the development of transportation and communication which has brought all lands into intimate contact, it seems clear that there is a call for a world order . . . ." [b]

Law is the superstructure of a particular economic base, and it serves a particular economic system. But there is no unified economic system in the modern world. On the contrary, there exist only two fundamental mutually opposed economic systems: the socialist economic system based on the system of public ownership of the means of production and the capitalist economic system based on the system of private ownership of the means of production. Moreover, even in the capitalist economic system, there still exist different hostile and contradictory economic interest groups. "World law," then, is the superstructure of which economic base? What type of economic development does it reflect? Needless to say, the economic development of which Pound speaks is the postwar external economic expansion and economic infiltration of American imperialism, and the neocolonial rule and plunder of vast areas in Asia, Africa, and Latin America by American imperialism. This type of economic unification is the unification of the economies of the various states under the manipulation of American monopolistic capital. Therefore, the "world law" which reflects this type of economic unification can only express the interest and will of the American monopolistic bourgeoisie.

There is a widely fashionable theory in American legal circles of describing the so-called "world law," "world government," and "world state" as a general welfare organization. . . . In fact, the poverty and backwardness of the people of the colonies, semicolonies and various countries in Asia, Africa, and Latin America are the results of a long period of barbarous plunder and oppression by imperialism, especially American imperialism. . . . The only way for them to get rid of such a situation is to rise in revolution and uproot the colonial rule of imperialism. The "universalism" theory of the American reactionary jurists is an ideological weapon preserved for use against the national liberation movement and people's revolutionary struggles in Asia, Africa, and Latin America. Jessup openly confesses this by declaring that, after the establishment of the "world state," the

[a] Filmer Stuart Cuckow Northrop, ed., *Ideological Differences and World Order* (New Haven, Conn.: Yale University Press, 1949), p. 1.

[b] *Ibid.*, p. 2. [Note: The ellipsis represents an omission of words not present in the original Chinese text.]

governments and peoples of various states have no right to oppose it; "the law of a world state would deny the right of revolution. . . ." [c]

In American legal circles, there are also two other relatively fashionable techniques in propagandizing about "universalism." The first is to use the desire of the people of the world for peace to give a false image of "universalism" in order to deceive the people. For instance, Maritain declares: "The lack of a world political organization is the second main obstacle to the establishment of a lasting peace." [11] The other technique is to use atomic blackmail to promote "universalism" and to engage in political speculation. For instance, in a speech entitled "Law and the Idea of Mankind" delivered at the New School for Social Research on November 15, 1961, Jones, professor of law at Columbia University, declared that atomic weapons will destroy all mankind, but such disaster can be avoided if mankind accepts "the law of mankind," "the world rule of law" and "world government." [d] The intention and fraudulent character of the two reactionary fallacies mentioned above are obvious; it is unnecessary to refute them. . . .

With respect to the question of the means of establishing the so-called "world government" or "world state," the American reactionary jurists have made great efforts in formulating a series of concrete projects. In general these projects can be classified into three categories: (1) a majority of the jurists advocate "reforming the United Nations" so as to develop it into a "world government," and remaking the United Nations General Assembly into a "new world legislative organ" or "world parliament"; [others advocate] (2) remaking the North Atlantic Treaty Organization into the so-called "supra-national federation of free states" and afterwards including the whole world in this federation, or (3) establishing "world political organization" by means of the so-called "world constitution" or "world convention." It must be pointed out that in order to make the so-called "world government" into an effective instrument of American imperialism and to enable American imperialism to act effectively as international military police to maintain the so-called "world order," the American reactionary jurists have particularly emphasized that the

[c] Philip Caryl Jessup, *A Modern Law of Nations* (New York: Macmillan, 1948), p. 185. [Note: We are unable to locate the quotation from Jessup's book. He wrote, on p. 185, that: "As is sometimes said, after the establishment of a world state all war would be civil war, and in such a world civil war the power of world government would be directed to the suppression of all resistance against its authority. The right of resistance would not be recognized."]

[d] Harry W. Jones, "Law and the Idea of Mankind," *Columbia Law Review* 62:753 (May 1962). [Note: The speech was delivered November 13, not November 15, according to the *Columbia Law Review*.]

"world government" must maintain a strong "international armed force." They propose to disarm the armies of the various small states and to concentrate all armed forces and nuclear weapons in the hands of the "world government" which would be under the leadership of the United States.[e] Although objectively it is impossible to establish this "world government," "world state," or "world armed force" and although this conspiracy cannot be successful, these proposals of the American reactionary jurists are their response to a series of criminal activities of the American government, such as the intensified manipulation and utilization of the existing international organization—the United Nations—to issue orders and to make the United Nations an instrument of American aggression against and intervention in the affairs of other states. [Another example is] the intensified control of military blocs such as the North Atlantic Treaty Organization to engage in aggression and subversive activities and to conspire on the questions of disarmament and monopoly of nuclear weapons.

On the question of law, the attempt of the American reactionary jurists is to remake international law and the United Nations Charter in accordance with the demands of the American ruling class so as to transform international law and the Charter of the United Nations into "the law of mankind" or "world law"; and then, through the form of this remade "international law," to realize the so-called American-centered "world legal order." Generally, in their program for remaking international law, the American reactionary jurists propose first to change the subject of international law. They say that the subject of international law is no longer the state, but rather the individual—"individuals constitute the foundation of international society." In the meantime, they also propose to enrich the contents of international law in accordance with the contents of the United States Constitution, and the American legislative and judicial system. . . .

In order to realize its ambition for world domination, the head of the United States government has repeatedly advocated the establishment of a "world legal system," "world government," or "world state." The present United States Secretary of State, Rusk, has on a number of occasions declared that the object of United States foreign policy is to establish a "big world family" under the United States' leadership, and to establish the "good world order" desired by the United States. On June 10, 1963, when [President] Kennedy delivered an address at American University to propagandize about American imperialism's so-called "strategy of peace," he also talked a great deal about the function of "world law." He said that in order to prevent

[e] See Grenville Clark and Louis Bruno Sohn, *World Peace through World Law*, 2nd ed. (Cambridge, Mass.: Harvard University Press, 1960).

world revolution and to realize the "world peace" desired by the United States, it "will require a new effort to achieve world law."[12] The thought of "universalism" about which the American reactionary jurists have propagandized is completely consistent with the above-mentioned speeches delivered by the head of American imperialism. The only difference is that American reactionary jurists make more concrete the program of world domination by American imperialism and add some "theoretical basis" to deceive people.

Efforts to Develop a "Socialist" Theory 3

The Chinese criticisms of bourgeois theories of international law that were presented in the previous chapter owe a great debt to Soviet publications. When Chinese writers sought to construct an adequate theory of international law, however, they found Soviet scholarship a less certain, and apparently less persuasive, guide.

Marx and Lenin had written relatively little of a specific nature concerning international law. Yet, almost from its inception, the world's first Communist regime found it expedient to rely on certain principles of international law as a means of self-defense. Thus, Soviet scholars have long confronted the need to explain international law in terms of Marxist theory. A cardinal principle of this theory is that the superstructure of a state, including its legal system, reflects the economic base of the society of that state and serves the interests of the state's ruling class. Therefore, according to Marxism, law necessarily possesses class character. The problem then arises of how to apply this generalization to a legal system that purports to govern relations among states with fundamentally different economic bases and class structures.

During the earliest years of the Soviet regime, when there was very little theoretical writing on international law, some prominent scholars denied the possibility that a legal community could exist between the Soviet Union and the capitalist states. In 1923 the leading jurist in the field, Professor E. A. Korovin, asserted that "an intercourse on the basis of intellectual unity (ideological solidarity) between countries of bourgeois and socialist cultures, cannot exist as a rule, and hence the rules of international law covering this intercourse become pointless." [13] But by the mid-1930's this view had succumbed to the need of Soviet foreign policy to justify and to regulate the Soviet Union's inevitable and increasing contacts with bourgeois states. Since then Soviet legal specialists have striven to develop a theory that, while faithful to Marxist-Leninist dogma, recognizes the universality of international law—the existence of a single, general international law binding upon all states regardless of their economic systems. By 1957, when Chinese writers began to face up to this theoretical problem, a leading Soviet textbook stated: "Although international law, like any other branch of law, has a class character and pertains to the superstructure, it cannot express the will of the ruling class of any particular State. It is the expression of the agreed will of a number of States in the form of an international agreement or custom which has grown up over a long period." [14]

The existence, after World War II, of "people's democracies" further complicated the task of Soviet legal theorists. Not only were they required to reconcile Marxism with a universal theory of a general international law that would provide the Soviet government with legal protection in its relations with bourgeois states, but they were also called upon to adapt this universal theory in a way that would recognize the close collaboration and high standards of behavior that were supposed to mark legal relations among states that had opted for socialism. The need to distinguish the relationships that prevail among socialist states from those that prevail between socialist and capitalist states threatened to fragment the carefully nurtured concept of a general international law. After two decades, Soviet scholars continue to search for a logically consistent, practically satisfying formulation that reconciles the existence of general international law with the existence of what is usually called socialist, or proletarian, internationalism. Although their formulations vary in details and in degrees of precision, at present there appears to be a consensus that contemporary international law consists of general international law and socialist internationalism. [15]

Chinese theorizing on the question has lacked even this degree of consensus. The essays that follow, all of which were written during 1957–1958, a period of intellectual ferment concerning the nature of domestic as well as international law, illustrate the leeway for differences in doctrinal interpretation that is sometimes permitted to exist in China within the confines of Marxist-Leninist-Maoist orthodoxy.

3-1

Chu Ch'i-wu, "Looking at the Class Character and Inheritable Character of Law from the Point of View of International Law," *Kuang-ming jih-pao* (May 13, 1957), p. 3.

Except for primitive communes, we know that slave society, feudal society and capitalist society all created their own international law on the basis of their respective economic bases. Each type of international law expresses the will of the ruling class and serves that class. Its class character is obvious.

Since the great October socialist revolution, there have emerged two types of states with different systems, thereby creating a situation of peaceful coexistence between socialism and capitalism. The law which adjusts relations among these states with different systems is modern international law. But since the latter also adjusts relations among states of the same system, what, then, is the class character of this kind of international law? . . .

In the course of discussing this question in recent years two views which deserve attention have been expressed in the Soviet Union. The first view contends that international law is such a special type of law that the Marxist-Leninist definition of law is inapplicable. It maintains that international law norms themselves possess no class character: if the norms are applied by capitalist states, they become capitalist in character; on the other hand, if the norms are applied by socialist states, they become socialist in character. However, such a view has already been rejected.[a] International law is a type of legal form for the realization of a state's external policy. It is beyond doubt that such a legal form, expressing the will of the ruling class, possesses class character. It is clearly incorrect to deny the class character of international law by regarding it as language—an instrument of mutual communication among human beings.

Another view acknowledges the class character of international law, but contends that it is part of the superstructure not only of socialism but also of capitalism; this resembles the similar norms in Soviet criminal law and capitalist criminal law. For instance, there are provisions against murder and larceny both in socialist codes and capitalist codes, but these crimes possess their respective class essence.[b] Many persons in the Soviet Union support this view, but I do not totally approve of it. International law is a legal system adjusting mutual relations among states; it should not be discussed on the same basis as individual criminal law norms because the two are similar in form but different in substance. Moreover, generally recognized international law norms are commonly observed legal norms created by agreements among states of different systems. These norms constitute yardsticks or standards for evaluating international practices of states with different systems. If we consider that norms of generally recognized international law possess a [special] type of character and content in

[a] Editorial Department, "Present Situation of Soviet Science of Law" [in Russian], *Voprosy Filosofii,* no. 1:8 (1953); *Su-wei-ai fa-hsüeh chung ti chi-ko wen-t'i* (Several problems in Soviet science of law; Peking, 1955), p. 27.

[b] Evgeniia Aleksandrovich Korovin, "A Few Questions of Present Theories of International Law," *SGP,* no. 6 (1954); Chinese translation in *Hsien-tai kuo-chi-fa shang ti chi-pen yüan-tse ho wen-t'i* (Fundamental principles and problems in modern international law; Peking: Fa-lu chu-pan-she, 1956), pp. 317–318.

capitalist states, and possess another type of character and content in socialist states, then we in fact deny the existence of general international law and divide the world into two mutually opposed international law systems—the capitalist international law system and the socialist international law system. This is quite inconsistent with reality. The Soviet Union has been established for almost forty years, but we have never heard it advocating a theory of two types of international law.

The problem of the class character of modern international law is a very complicated one. The solution to the problem depends upon the substance and characteristics of modern international law norms. Speaking simply, such substance and characteristics are: modern international law norms are the commonly observed legal norms created by agreements among states of different systems in the course of their struggle and cooperation in adjusting their mutual relations. They do not express the will of the ruling class of a single state, but rather the will of the ruling classes of states with different systems. Therefore, the formula of the single class character of domestic law cannot be arbitrarily applied to international law. A study of the class character of international law must start from the fact of the peaceful coexistence of states with different systems. Peaceful coexistence produces cooperation among states with different systems. Due to this international cooperation, generally recognized international law norms are formulated among states with different systems. These generally recognized international law norms are common to capitalist and socialist states. . . . In other words, generally recognized international law norms possess the dual class character of capitalism and socialism.

The Charter of the United Nations is an obvious example. . . . It should be noted that to say that generally recognized international law norms possess the dual class character of capitalism and socialism does not mean that such norms are the product of the mixture of the bourgeoisie and the worker class. In forming generally recognized international law norms, states led by the worker class have always insisted on principles of peace, democracy, and socialism. Socialist states can never recognize any international law norms which violate peace and democracy. . . .

Everybody knows that before the October Revolution, only bourgeois international law existed. Since the October Revolution, the law adjusting relations among capitalist states and socialist states is modern international law. The transformation from bourgeois international law to modern international law is not only a historical development, it is also a change of essence. Does modern international law have the characteristic of inheritability?

It must be pointed out that, in the formation of modern international law, the Soviet Union has been a positive and creative element. Since the emergence of the Soviet Union on the international stage, how has it treated bourgeois international law? The Soviet Union neither totally rejects nor totally accepts bourgeois international law. In accordance with the principles of socialism and the interests of the laboring people, it critically recognizes some rules of bourgeois international law. Thus, the Soviet Union denies reactionary principles and systems of international law such as unequal treaties, consular jurisdiction, and the colonial system, and recognizes democratic principles and systems which can be used to safeguard world peace and international cooperation, such as the principle of sovereignty, the principle of equality, and the principle of nonintervention in domestic affairs, and so forth. In the meantime, in the course of its dealing with capitalist states, it has proposed some new principles and systems which have acquired general recognition, such as the principle of peaceful coexistence, the principle of national self-determination, and the system of commercial representatives, and so forth.

On the other hand, since the Second World War a number of people's democracies have been established in Europe and Asia. The socialist states also apply the principle of sovereignty, the principle of equality, the principle of nonintervention in internal affairs, and so forth in their mutual relations. It was pointed out in the October 30, 1956, Declaration of the Soviet Government on the Foundations for the Development and Further Strengthening of Friendship and Cooperation between the Soviet Union and Other Socialist States: "Being united by the common ideals of building a socialist society and by the principles of proletarian internationalism, the countries of the great community of socialist nations can build their mutual relations only on the principles of complete equality, respect for each other's territorial integrity, state independence and sovereignty, and noninterference in each other's internal affairs." [16] Although these principles and systems have acquired new significance by virtue of the essence of socialist states, they are nevertheless international law norms which have already been historically formed.

Therefore, no matter how we look at international law norms as applied among socialist states and capitalist states or among socialist states themselves, modern international law consists of those progressive principles and systems of international law formed in capitalist society, and even of progressive principles and systems, such as the arbitration method, the system of diplomatic envoys, and the principle of *pacta sunt servanda,* which were formed in slave society and feudal society. Despite the change of their essence due to the replacement of one type of social form by another, these progressive principles and systems, as legal norms for adjusting international relations, have continued to exist in the history of the development of international law and thus reveal the inheritable character of law.

However, when we speak of the inheritable character of international law, we do not simply mean the continued existence of those international law norms which have already been historically formed. What we are indicating is that all the progressive international law norms which have already been formed in human society can be criticized, reformed, and absorbed upon a new basis. This is very important.

In short, from the point of view of international law, we maintain that law does possess class character, but such a character does not exclude its inheritability. The inheritable character of law means that law can be critically accepted on a new basis.

From the foregoing, it may be noted that Stalin's theory in his "Marxism and the Problem of Linguistics" that the superstructure is created together with the creation of the base, and is extinguished together with the extinction of the base, must be restricted and supplemented. Stalin said: "The superstructure is the product of the age; its existence and activity depend on the economic base. Therefore, its life will not last long, and it will be extinguished together with the extinction of the base." [c] However, according to the foregoing observations, many international law norms last longer than the base from which they were created; moreover, they continue to develop on a new base. Although the bourgeoisie has never practiced the prinple of sovereignty, the principle of equality, and the principle of nonintervention, they were all originally proposed by the bourgeoisie. The socialist states have not only accepted those principles, but they have also infused new democratic substance into them. Although these international law norms have changed with the change of the socioeconomic base, they have continued to exist as the superstructure. Therefore, we cannot generally hold that all the superstructure is created by the base, and exclude all elements created by historical development.

[c] *Ma-k'o-ssu chu-i yü yü-yen-hsüeh wen-t'i* (Marxism and the problem of linguistics; 2nd ed., Peking, 1953), p. 5.

3-2

Liu Chia-chi, "Some Questions Concerning the Nature and Systems of International Law," *FH*, no. 3:44–45 (1958).

(II) *The so-called question of "the inheritability of international law."* When Comrade Chou Tzu-ya discussed the so-called question of "the inheritability of international law" in his article entitled "The Question of the Nature of Modern International Law [—The Class, Specialty, Compulsion, and Inheritable Character of International Law]" (in *Hsüeh-shu yüeh-k'an* [*Academic Monthly*] no. 7:67, 71–72 [1957]), he stated: "The norms of socialist international law inherit many progressive principles of international law of older periods." The so-called "inheritance" means to "criticize, to absorb, and to reform," and he also cited the principle of nonintervention in explaining his view. Socialist international law is a completely new type of international law which has never existed in a society of exploitation. Therefore, Korovin once pointed out: "It is incorrect to say that socialist international law, which at present is in the course of formulation, is merely a deeper and more thorough realization of those generally recognized norms of international law which have already been formulated in history. . . . In international relations, the transition to socialist democratism is not just an evolutionary stage in the historical development of international law, but a revolutionary change of international law." First, generally recognized or general international law, besides adjusting relations among capitalist countries, is mainly used to adjust relations between countries with two mutually opposed social systems. Socialist international law adjusts relations among countries with the same social and economic structure, and with consistent social and state systems. These two systems of international law are essentially different. Second, various socialist countries, regardless of the legal forms they use, all line up with proletarian internationalism and concretely practice fraternal cooperation. This type of new essence could not exist within the formerly existing bourgeois international law, and it does not exist in generally recognized international law. So even if the "international law of the older periods" has "many progressive principles," it is impossible for it to have proletarian internationalism, which is the soul of socialist international law. Thus, we cannot speak of "inheritance," because proletarian internationalism absolutely cannot be acquired from "criticizing, absorbing, and reforming" the "international law of older periods." Finally, the scope of international cooperation as included in socialist international law is rather wide; it includes political, economic, and cultural cooperation. This type of cooperation not only expresses cooperation among the governments of various countries, but also concretely realizes cooperation among people of various countries because all these governments are governments which represent the will of the people. These characteristics cannot be found in "international law of older periods." Even contemporary, generally recognized international law, regardless of how democratic it is, cannot achieve this type of socialist democracy. It is improper to say that these two systems have relations of "inheritance."

3-3

Yang Chao-lung, "On the Class Character and Inheritable Character of Law," *Hua-tung cheng-fa hsüeh-pao*, no. 3:30 (1956).

International law is the expression of the agreement of wills in the course of international cooperation and struggle among the ruling classes of various states in international society. . . . The agreement of wills may concurrently reflect interests of different types of states, and it thus expresses different [types of] class character. This is because a generally recognized norm or a treaty or convention in which different types of states have participated, though possessing a single form may, with respect to different types of states, satisfy their different needs in different aspects and protect different class interests. The situation is exactly the same in the case of a contract of sale that may benefit both contracting parties. In such circumstances, the class character of public international law is not necessarily expressed in the norms themselves, but is mainly expressed in the practical applications of the norms. . . .[17]

3-4

Chu Li-lu, "Refute Ch'en T'i-ch'iang's Absurd Theory Concerning International Law," *JMJP* (Sept. 18, 1957), p. 3.

Ch'en T'i-ch'iang said that there is one body of international law in capitalist states and another body of international law in socialist states. By so saying, he in fact and in theory denied the existence of a type of general international law in the world which is binding and applicable to all states. I consider that there are a number of norms of international law which are generally recognized, basic, and common; they are equally recognized by and binding on bourgeois states and proletarian states. For instance, respect for state sovereignty, nonintervention in the internal affairs of various states, equality of states large and small, inviolability of each other's territory, various rules of war (Geneva convention on prisoners of war, convention on the prohibition of poisonous gas, and so forth), some systems and customs of diplomacy, and so forth are all generally recognized norms of international law. This is one aspect of the question. Another aspect involves the question of "whether we should use proletarian or monopolistic ideas to interpret the principles of international law." There are fundamental differences between these two approaches. For instance, on the question of respect for state sovereignty, international law scholars of capitalist states maintain that only Caucasian states can possess sovereignty. They even argue that the sovereignty of Caucasian states is absolute and unrestricted, and that they are not bound by any obligation to "respect the legitimate interests of other states" and can, therefore, intervene at will with the sovereignty of other states, especially backward states. Moreover, many bourgeois jurists express the view that colonies in the Orient or trust territories must develop up to certain levels or degrees prescribed by the bourgeoisie before these colonies and territories can be approved as sovereign states. What kind of absurd talk is this? Can we say that only western nations are capable of possessing sovereignty and that Oriental nations should not possess sovereignty? We socialist states take quite a different view. We maintain that the sovereignty of every state should be respected. We respect every state—large or small, Caucasian, Negro, or Mongolian. From this example one can see that there are basic differences between Western international law scholars and socialist international law scholars in ideological standpoint, understanding of the question, etc. In practice, there exist many differences of similar character between the view of Western international law scholars and socialist international law scholars on several questions of international law.

3-5

Lin Hsin, "On the System of International Law after the Second World War," *CHYYC*, no. 1:34, 36, 37–38 (1958).

After the Second World War, the international situation underwent a fundamental change, just as it did after the October socialist revolution. The chief characteristic of this change is the fact that socialism has spread beyond the scope of one country and has thus been transformed into a world system. Therefore, there exist now two world systems on the international stage—the socialist world system and the capitalist world system. Thus, there are now two systems of international law, socialist international law and capitalist international law, corresponding to these two world systems. . . .

Some comrades maintain that if we do not recognize the existence of a general international law, but rather two systems of international law—bourgeois and socialist—then imperialist countries will not observe international law. This view is unscientific since the existence of two systems of international law is an objective fact which will not be changed in accordance with human will. At the same time, I believe that this kind of worry is unnecessary. It is a viewpoint which has unwarranted faith in international law. Although we should pay serious attention to international law, we should not have unwarranted faith in it. It is too innocent to think that simply because of our recognition of a so-called general international law, the imperialists will not dare to do mischief. . . . In fact, those comrades who advocate the view that there exists a general international law concurrently serving both bourgeois and socialist countries have never clearly explained what the so-called general international law is. There are, in the present world, three different kinds of international relations, that is, international relations among socialist countries, international relations among capitalist countries, and international relations between socialist and capitalist countries. They also have not explained why these three different kinds of international relations can be adjusted by the so-called general international law or how the latter adjusts three such different international relations. Their theory is always full of contradictions and lacks logic. On the one hand, they have to recognize the class character of international law, but, on the other hand, they also maintain that so-called general international law is serving both capitalist and socialist countries. How can these two be mixed? We all know that international law serves the external policy of a country and that it is the legal form for realizing a country's external policy. It may be asked how can capitalist and socialist countries, having fundamentally different external policies, apply the same international law? . . .

We know that international law is an instrument for carrying out a country's foreign policy. Socialist international law serves the external policy of socialist countries, and bourgeois international law serves the external policy of capitalism. When socialist and capitalist countries engage in international intercourse, such as negotiating the settlement of an international problem, capitalist countries, by virtue of their class standpoint, naturally would propose a solution to the problem from the viewpoint of bourgeois international law; in other words, they try to apply bourgeois international law. Socialist countries propose a solution from the viewpoint of proletarian internationalism and apply socialist international law. There is then a sharp struggle between bourgeois international law and socialist international law. After a short or long struggle, mutual agreement is reached between capitalist and socialist countries. The agreement is finalized in the form of international law by such means as treaties, agreements, joint statements, joint declarations, and so forth. From the foregoing, it is understandable that the existence of two mutually opposed systems of international law does not exclude the fact that certain agreements can be reached between them. Some people maintain that since there exist two mutually opposed systems of international law, it is impossible for them to reach any agreements. This viewpoint is obviously inconsistent with the facts and is a nondialectical viewpoint. The percentage of elements of bourgeois international law or socialist international law which infiltrates into this mutually agreed upon treaty, agreement, joint statement, or joint declaration, depends mainly upon the strength ratio of the two world systems of socialism and capitalism. Of course, there is a limit to this mutual infiltration, and the limitation is decided by the character of mutual opposition of the two international law systems. In other words, the limitation upon mutual infiltration is the absorbability of the other international law system; otherwise, no agreement can be reached between two sides. Here, whether the capitalist countries dealing with socialist countries are imperialist countries or nationalist countries makes a big difference. Since nationalist countries hope to develop their respective countries' own independent capitalist economy, they do their best to achieve and maintain national independence, they oppose the imperialist policy of war, and they are willing to coexist peacefully with socialist countries. Some of those countries have even joined socialist countries in declaring the five principles of peaceful coexistence. However, imperialist countries are extremely hostile to socialist countries; they have always done their best to subvert socialist countries, and they will not voluntarily coexist peacefully with the socialist countries. . . .

The treaty, agreement, joint statement, joint declaration, and other international law documents mutually agreed upon by capitalist countries, and socialist countries, such as the Charter of the United Nations and the five principles of peaceful coexistence, are not only the composite elements of the bourgeois international law system, but also the composite elements of the socialist international law system. However, capitalist countries accept them from the standpoint of the bourgeois viewpoint and bourgeois interests and socialist countries accept them from the standpoint of the worker-class viewpoint and worker-class interests. At this moment capitalist and socialist countries are sleeping in the same bed, but dreaming different dreams. This kind of mutually agreed upon treaty, agreement, joint statement, joint declaration, and so forth can be absorbed by the respective international law systems. This phenomenon is not surprising, because the international law documents mutually agreed upon by capitalist countries and socialist countries do not themselves reflect the viewpoint of this or that international law. By uniting with the viewpoint of bourgeois nationalism they can be absorbed by the bourgeois international law system and constitute part of bourgeois international law. At the same time, by uniting with the viewpoint of proletarian internationalism, they can also be absorbed by the socialist international law system and constitute part of socialist international law. However, in the course of executing these mutually agreed upon international law documents, there always exists a struggle between the viewpoint of bourgeois international law and socialist international law. This struggle is reflected in the different, even completely contrary, interpretations of a document of international law.

Those comrades who advocate the existence of one general international law, three systems of international law (socialist international law, bourgeois international law, and general international law between socialist countries and capitalist countries), or a general international law and a socialist international law, do not understand that certain agreements can be reached, that is, there can be certain kinds of cooperation between two mutually opposed international law systems. Such mutually agreed upon international law documents themselves do not reflect the viewpoints of this or that international law. Therefore, it is incorrect to say that those international law documents themselves reflect not only the will of the bourgeoisie as the ruling class of capitalist countries, but also the will of the worker class as the ruling class of socialist countries. Only when they unite with the viewpoint of this or that international law theory do they reflect the will of this or that ruling class. When they are absorbed by the bourgeois international law system and constitute part of bourgeois international law by uniting with the viewpoint of bourgeois nationalism, they reflect the will of the bourgeoisie as the ruling class of capitalist countries. When they are absorbed by the socialist international law system and constitute part of socialist international law by uniting with the viewpoint of proletarian internationalism, they reflect the will of the worker class as the ruling class of socialist countries. Those who advocate the existence of one general international law and one socialist international law do not understand this situation. Those who advocate the existence of one general international law in fact unilaterally exaggerate the agreements reached between the socialist international law system and the bourgeois international law system as so-called general international law. They also argue that the class will expressed by this international law is the will of the ruling class of two or more states with different socioeconomic systems (see the article of Professor Chou Tzu-ya of the East China Political Legal Institute entitled "The Question of the Nature of Modern International Law," *Hsüeh-shu yüeh-k'an* [*Academic Monthly*] no. 7 [1957]), and thus abolishes the boundary between bourgeois international law and socialist international law. This is an erroneous rightist viewpoint. Therefore, in our country's legal circles, especially when the rightist elements of bourgeois international law circles were engaged in violent attack against the Communist Party and socialism, they recklessly relied upon this view. Rightist element Wang T'ieh-yai relied on this view to deny the class character of the science of international law and proposed the large-scale translation of writings of bourgeois international law. Rightist element Ch'en T'i-ch'iang even proposed the reactionary view of the necessity of studying Anglo-American international law.

Those comrades who advocate the existence of three systems of international law have recognized the existence of the socialist international law system and its face-to-face stand against the bourgeois international law system. This is correct. But they erroneously describe the agreements reached between these two systems of international law as another independent system of international law—the general international law between socialist international law and bourgeois international law. What is this general international law? What is its character? They do not explain it clearly. Of course, it is impossible to explain it clearly. . . .

It may be asked whether our socialist international law system absorbs those treaties, agreements, and so forth into which some bourgeois international law has infiltrated. If so, is it entirely satisfactory? Certainly so far as those international documents (that is, the mutually agreed upon documents between bourgeois international law and socialist international law) which are adopted under the influence of bourgeois international law are concerned, it is not entirely satisfactory. The Trusteeship System in the Charter of the United Nations is an example. Article 76, paragraph (b), of the Charter provides that one of the basic objectives of the Trusteeship System is to promote the "progressive development toward self-government or independence" of the inhabitants of trust territories. If the Charter did not mention "independence," socialist countries would not agree to the International Trusteeship System. Similarly, since the bourgeois international law system also absorbs treaties, agreements, and so forth, into which socialist international law has infiltrated, from the viewpoint of the imperialist countries, [those documents] are also unsatisfactory. However, such a situation is determined by the law of social development. Because of the unbalanced development of the economy and politics of capitalist countries in the imperialist period, the socialist revolution cannot simultaneously achieve victory in all countries. Therefore, coexistence between capitalist countries and socialist countries is inevitable. When the socialist world system and capitalist world system peacefully coexist in the world, the emergence of the above-mentioned situation is a necessary consequence. Only when all capitalist countries have been transformed into socialist countries will the above-mentioned situation disappear. Such a day will definitely come. The future of the world belongs to socialism.

3-6

Chou Fu-lun, "On the Nature of Modern International Law—A Discussion with Comrade Lin Hsin," *CHYYC*, no. 3:54–56 (1958).

Comrade Lin Hsin's analysis of the struggle in executing the mutually agreed upon documents of international law between states with different systems is likewise incorrect. Although norms of generally recognized international law are recognized by capitalist states, such norms are also frequently violated by them. In the practice of modern imperialist countries, violations of generally recognized norms have become a universal phenomenon because those norms increasingly are obstacles to the realization of the aggressive policy of imperialist countries. However, we should never consider that [as stated in Lin Hsin's article "On the System of International Law after the Second World War"]: "In the course of executing these mutually agreed upon international documents, there always exists a struggle between the viewpoint of bourgeois international law and socialist international law. *This struggle is reflected in the different, even completely contrary, interpretations of a document of international law.*" [Emphasis that of Chou Fu-lun.] When imperialist countries engage in aggression, they often make distorted interpretations of international law to defend their aggressive acts. There are numerous examples in which they describe aggression as "self-defense" or armed intervention as "police action." For instance, when the United Nations discussed the Algerian people's liberation struggle, France even declared that it was an "intervention in internal affairs" of France by the United Nations. Can we say this is a struggle of viewpoint between two mutually opposed theories of international law? No, absolutely not! Such an analysis must reach an extremely erroneous conclusion. Can we say that American imperialism's intervention in the liberation of our territory—Taiwan, an aggressive act which violates international law, is an aggression based on America's viewpoint of bourgeois international law, and the People's Republic of China's opposition to such aggression is based on the viewpoint of socialist international law? If the conclusion follows comrade Lin Hsin's logic—the concurrent existence of two mutually opposed systems of international law—then in the case of executing a common document of international law it is possible to make different interpretations according to mutually opposed viewpoints. This is to say that they have their reasons based on international law and we have our reasons based on international law. Finally, we can only reach the ambiguous conclusion of "you say you are right, and I say I am right." This logic is extremely harmful to our diplomatic struggle, and it is also extremely erroneous. Take a further example: if an aggressive act or illegal act occurs between a capitalist state and another capitalist state, then how should we evaluate it? Should we use the viewpoint of bourgeois international law or socialist international law? If we evaluate the act according to the viewpoint of socialist international law, then what is the legal effect? I think in that case the socialist international law can only have moral force, but not legally binding force, because two mutually opposed systems of international law can only adjust relations among states in their respective world systems. . . .

[Comrade Lin writes:] "We all know that international law serves the external policy of a country and that it is the legal form for realizing a country's external policy. It may be asked how can capitalist countries and socialist countries, having fundamentally different external policies, apply the same international law?" I consider comrade Lin Hsin's doubt about this question to be without foundation. . . . It should also be pointed out that although international law is a tool for carrying out the policy of the ruling class, it has its own special characteristics. Therefore, we cannot conclude that international law is policy. Nor can we merge international law in the concept of policy.

3-7

Keng Fu-ch'eng, "Talks on Current Systems of International Law," *FH*, no. 3:53–54 (1958).

International law is a tool for a state to implement its external policy. When solving a problem, states all use their own viewpoint of international law to carry out their own foreign policy. This is to say that, when solving a problem, socialist countries, based on the standpoint of the worker class, propose a solution from the viewpoint of socialist international law and make efforts to apply norms of socialist international law; capitalist countries, based on the bourgeois standpoint, propose a solution from the viewpoint of capitalist international law and make efforts to apply norms of capitalist international law. At this point a fierce struggle ensues. But, mere struggle is insufficient; they must make appropriate concessions, which naturally should be based on the premise of not impairing the fundamental interests of the respective systems, in accordance with the ratio of strength of the two systems and the situation at that time. Only then can an agreement be reached and the problem be solved. However, one party may still be dissatisfied with some of the contents of the agreement reached. What is the character of the agreement so reached? It depends upon the concrete contents of the agreement and cannot be treated as all the same. Comrade Lin Hsin said: "The percentage of elements of [bourgeois] international law or socialist international law which infiltrates this mutually agreed upon treaty, agreement, joint statement, or joint declaration, depends mainly upon the strength ratio of the two world systems. . . ." I consider such a view inappropriate. Because the treaty, agreement, joint statement, or joint declaration which is mutually agreed upon by countries with different systems (as a matter of fact such a situation also exists among capitalist countries) is not a harmonious and consistent matter, but still is a mixture of various opinions. Its contents are the expression of mutual struggle, and one cannot treat a certain part of the mixture which comes from [the mutual] infiltration [of opinions] [as though it were the same as] the constituent elements. When we analyze an international document, we must (1) understand clearly that the provisions of a document of international law and the norms of international law (substance) are not the same thing, and sometimes they may be contradictory; and (2) in deciding the character of a treaty or agreement we must pay attention to whether a treaty or agreement is in fact implemented.

Those who advocate the existence of general international law have taken the Charter of the United Nations as a representative document of general international law. I consider such a view incorrect. We know that the Charter of the United Nations is based on democratism and peaceful coexistence, but some of its norms are still the expression of the principles of capitalist international law. However, the struggle against capitalist countries launched by a socialist country, the Soviet Union, in accordance with the interests of the Soviet Union and the world worker class and from the viewpoint of socialist international law, has made a substantial part of the Charter also express principles of socialist international law. Therefore, the Charter of the United Nations may be used as a tool in our struggle with capitalist countries. This is the reason why those countries which are victims of aggression, such as Egypt or Tunisia, invoked the Charter of the United Nations to resist Britain and France. However, we must notice that we are not unconditionally to obey everything the United Nations does. We must reserve our independent opinion; otherwise, we cannot resist those resolutions of the United Nations which are adopted under the manipulation of the United States. This is the reason why general international law cannot exist.

Note

Most Chinese writers who took part in the 1957–1958 theoretical dispute argued in favor of the existence of general international law, and all agreed that there is such a thing as socialist international law. But these writers could not agree whether there are two systems of international law (general and socialist) or three systems (general, socialist, and bourgeois). The following extracts are typical:

> In addition, those comrades [who advocate the existence of bourgeois international law] have not pointed out which are today's norms or documents of bourgeois international law. Of course, bourgeois international law does not include the principles of *pacta sunt servanda,* freedom of navigation of the open seas, inviolability of diplomatic envoys, etc., because these principles have today become principles of generally recognized international law and a part of general international law. Some comrades have pointed out that the North Atlantic Treaty, Baghdad Treaty, Southeast Asia Collective Defense Treaty, and so forth are documents of bourgeois international law. They do not know that those documents violate the Charter of the United Nations and general international law. Bourgeois international law has become a relic of history. However, this does not mean that the science of bourgeois international law or the viewpoint of bourgeois international law does not exist.[18]

The existence of capitalist international law is an objective fact. At the same time, it has declined in importance and its scope of application is daily narrowing. The existence and development of the socialist system influences capitalist international relations and, hence, capitalist international law. Therefore, more camouflages have been put on formerly fearless reactionary norms in order skillfully to cover up their reactionary essence. For instance, the notorious North Atlantic Treaty is completely reactionary and violates the Charter of the United Nations, but we must realize that today it still has the function of adjusting capitalist international relations.[19]

Fundamental Principles of International Law

PART II

The designation of certain principles of international law as "fundamental" for purposes of this part necessarily involves a degree of arbitrary choice. Obviously the material presented in Part I could also fall under this rubric, as could some of the material in subsequent parts. Here we address ourselves to a number of general questions.

By what types of argumentation do Chinese officials and publicists support or refute a claim that a given act is or is not in accord with international law? Do they invoke the same categories of prescriptions and exhibit the same reasoning processes as the elites of other states, so that a common mode of discourse can be said to exist? Whom do the Chinese consider to be the relevant actors in the world community? In their view, which entities or persons are entitled to invoke the protection of international law, and which are bound by it? To what extent do the domestic legal processes of the PRC take account of international law?

What is the contemporary Chinese concept of sovereignty? To what extent does it reflect the traditional Chinese world view, nineteenth-century Western concepts, the twentieth-century interdependence of states? According to the leaders of the PRC, what are the principles that guide its relations with imperialist and bourgeois states, with the "third world," and with socialist states? To what extent do China's leaders preach and practice Marxist-Leninist doctrines calling for intervention in the internal affairs of other states, doctrines that have inspired fear and hostility in the non-Communist world since the Bolshevik seizure of power in 1917? Finally, on all such questions, we will want to inquire about the degree to which, despite the Sino-Soviet dispute, Chinese theory and practice reflect Soviet influence.

Before surveying these questions, it may prove useful to offer a few more historical notes for background purposes. As the Introduction suggested, China's tradition offers analogies to certain fundamental principles of modern international law. The multistate system of preimperial China plainly regarded treaties as a source of law, and there were a number of instances in which even imperial China resorted to treaties. Some customary rules, such as those relating to the conduct of warfare or the inviolability of diplomatic envoys, also were recognized. And in both the preimperial and imperial eras prevailing ethical notions, which invoked the sanction of heaven to support concepts such as good faith and the enforceability of promises, played a role somewhat akin to what the West has called natural law and "the will of God."

During the preimperial period the feudal states were the subjects of the law, which purportedly applied equally to all states. Although during the imperial period there were also instances when Chinese emperors dealt with other rulers on the basis of equality, when the tribute system was operating according to theory the states on China's periphery were inferior in status to the Central Realm. Nevertheless, even then both China and the tributary states were expected to conform to their respective, albeit differing, obligations as understood by the hierarchic Sinocentric world.

Sovereignty, of course, is a modern Western concept. Yet the idea that a state generally has exclusive competence to regulate persons, things and events within its territory goes back to the preimperial era in China, and was still being insisted on by the Manchu emperors as the Western powers increasingly intruded into China. The similarity between this Chinese idea and the European concept of territorial sovereignty did not make the Westerners more disposed to accept the exercise of Chinese jurisdiction over them.

As a corollary of the principle that every state had a right to manage its own affairs, preimperial China also recognized that every state had a corresponding duty not to interfere in the affairs of its neighbors. Nevertheless, this general principle was frequently honored in the breach, and there developed a variety of rationalizations of departures from the norm. Strong, self-righteous leaders who were tempted to intervene in other states purported to find justification in doctrines that preached the desirability of the less worthy submitting to the virtuous. Moreover, specific exceptions to the rule of nonintervention came to be recognized. The most obvious of these authorized intervention if necessary to the self-preservation of the intervening state. Another frequently invoked exception permitted intervention against a ruler who oppressed his own people. Also popular was the claim that intervention was a necessary sanction against a state that had failed to carry out its obligations under a treaty. And in many instances one state used military means to install a friendly sovereign on the throne of a neighboring state.[1]

Underlying the imperial tribute system was the theory that China could "intervene whenever and wherever she judged it necessary because the Chinese emperor was responsible for all the peoples under Heaven and because their rulers were viewed as his appointed representatives." [2] This normally latent power of intervention was occasionally exercised.

In 1788, for example, China sent a military expedition to Vietnam to restore to the throne the Lê family, who, until a recent rebellion, had been loyal tributaries of the empire for over a century.[3]

It was, of course, the eventually massive foreign intervention in Chinese affairs that belatedly stimulated the Manchu dynasty and its successor, the Republic of China, to adopt the fundamental principles of Western international law.

Sources of International Law 4

4-1

Ying T'ao, "Recognize the True Face of Bourgeois International Law from a Few Basic Concepts," *KCWTYC*, no. 1:46–47 (1960).

On the question of the sources of international law, although bourgeois jurists also classify the sources into "substantive sources" and "formal sources," their metaphysical interpretation of the "substantive" sources makes the meaning given to this concept categorically different from the meaning given to it by jurists holding the viewpoint of historical materialism. Bourgeois jurists discuss the "substantive" sources in complete isolation from a social material basis, regarding "the psychological elements of judges," "ideal law," "fundamental norms," "moral principles," and so forth as "substantive" sources. In view of the fact that when bourgeois international law jurists discuss sources of international law they generally refer only to formal sources, we shall devote the following to the discussion of these sources. . . .

Bourgeois international law jurists generally classify the sources of international law into the following four categories: (1) treaties, (2) customs, (3) judicial decisions (including arbitral awards), and (4) teachings of publicists. They consider customs and treaties to be the two principal sources of international law, and judicial decisions and teachings of publicists to be subsidiary sources. From their classification, it is clear that their concern is limited to the formality of how international law is expressed. They wish others to study only the formal sources of international law and not the substance of the sources. Although it is necessary to understand clearly the formal sources of international law in order to know how [the rules of international law] are derived and their interrelationship, it is more important academically to study the origin of a matter in order to trace its substantive sources. However, bourgeois international law scholars do not want people to pursue the substantive sources. The reason is very simple. Because international law has a strong class character, the true character of bourgeois international law will be exposed if people pursue the study of the sources of international law to the very end.

We regard the external policy of the bourgeoisie, which is also the will of the ruling class of those big capitalist powers, as the substantive source of bourgeois international law.

Since bourgeois international law scholars state that treaties are the principal source of international law, may we ask where those treaties come from? By referring to the large number of treaties concluded in the period of capitalism, it may be proved that these treaties were all concluded under the guidance of the external policy of capitalist countries, in accordance with the demand of the bourgeoisie and through diplomatic means and arbitrary external practices. For instance, bourgeois international law refers to such documents as "the Covenant of the League of Nations" as an important source of international law. But the "League of Nations" was merely a tool in the hands of imperialism, and the "Covenant" was signed by the victorious powers of the First World War to maintain acquired interests and the kind of international order they needed and to facilitate their further suppression of colonies. Bourgeois international law also considers unequal treaties imposed upon weak and small countries to be sources of international law. The implications of this are only too obvious to everyone.

Bourgeois international law scholars say that custom is also one of the principal sources of international law. The so-called custom refers to those customs formulated by the external practices of big capitalist powers. For instance, the principles concerning the handling of maritime blockade and contraband of war proclaimed by the "Declaration of Paris" in 1856 were later invoked as customs of maritime warfare. However, the "Declaration of Paris" was enacted mainly by the participation of Britain, France, Austria, Prussia, Czarist Russia, and so forth, that is, big powers. The bourgeoisie has never considered and will never consider as customs the resistance of weak and small countries and colonies, the socialist countries' anti-aggression and anti-imperialist wars and opposition to imperialist intervention in internal affairs of other countries, and other just actions, and has never given support to these activities. Again the implication here is obvious.

They say that judicial decisions are a subsidiary source. But who made the so-called judicial decisions? The majority of decisions they invoke are those decisions rendered by the municipal courts or arbitral organs of big capitalist powers and the international judicial or arbitral organs under their manipulation. In accordance with whose will and whose legal standards were these decisions made? Everyone knows that these decisions were made in accordance with the will and demands of big capitalist powers.

They say that teachings of publicists are also one of the subsidiary sources. The so-called "publicists" refers to "publicists" brought up by the bourgeoisie and in the latter's service, and the so-called "teachings" refers to those "teachings" which are formulated solely to carry out the will of the bourgeoisie, to do its legal planning, and to defend it in accordance with the external practices of the bourgeoisie. The teachings of those publicists with a sense of justice and progressive ideas are excluded and are attacked and condemned. Therefore, the substance of this source is easy to understand.

Bourgeois international law is reluctant to trace the genuine substance of its sources. In an attempt to transform into international law all bourgeois acts in obtaining advantages at the expense of others and to treat as the basis of international legislation all greedy and covetous ambitions of the bourgeoisie, [bourgeois international law] limits its sources to surface formalities.

NOTE

Reading Ying T'ao's attack, which draws heavily upon Soviet literature,[4] may lead one to wonder whether there is anything in common between Western conceptions of the sources of international law and those recognized by the People's Republic. Although we do not have information adequate for solid judgment on all aspects of the problem, available evidence suggests that, as in the Soviet case, on a formal level divergences between the PRC and the West are not so great as might be supposed. The remaining items in this chapter illustrate actual Chinese resort to the usual sources of international law.

4-2

"Statement of Chou En-lai, Premier of the Government Administrative Council and Minister for Foreign Affairs of the Central People's Government of the People's Republic of China, on the Question of Korean Armistice Negotiations," in *WCC 1951–1953, II* (1958), 133; UN Doc. A/2378 (March 31, 1953), United Nations General Assembly, *Official Records, Seventh Session,* Annexes, Vol. I, Agenda Item 16 (Headquarters, New York, 1952–1953), p. 56.

As stated above, in the course of the Korean armistice negotiations one question alone—the question of prisoners of war—blocks the realization of an armistice in Korea. And, even with respect to the question of prisoners of war, both sides have reached agreement on all the provisions in the draft armistice agreement on the arrangements relating to prisoners of war except on the question of the repatriation of prisoners of war. Had the Korean armistice negotiations not been interrupted for more than five months, a solution might long since have been found to this issue of the repatriation of prisoners of war.

Now, inasmuch as the United Nations Command has proposed to settle, in accordance with Article 109 of the Geneva Convention, the question of exchanging sick and injured prisoners of war during the period of hostilities, we consider that, subsequent upon the reasonable settlement of the question of sick and injured prisoners of war, it is entirely a matter of course that a smooth solution to the whole question of prisoners of war should be achieved, provided that both sides are prompted by real sincerity to bring about an armistice in Korea in the spirit of mutual compromise.

Regarding the question of prisoners of war, the government of the People's Republic of China and the government of the Democratic People's Republic of Korea have always held and continue to hold that a reasonable solution can only lie in the release and repatriation of war prisoners without delay after the cessation of hostilities, in accordance with the stipulations of the 1949 Geneva Convention, particularly those of Article 118 of the convention.

4-3

"Protests [by Chinese Embassy] to Ghanaian Authorities," *PR* 9.11:7 (Mar. 11, 1966).

The February 28 note reads in part as follows: On February 27, 1966, at about 12 noon, Mr. Chou Chin-wen, leader of the Chinese construction expert team of the Ghana National Integrated Cotton Textile and Knitwear Factory at Juapong, interpreter Chin Chih-tsai, expert Yuan Yun-tsung, and Mr. Kuo Ping-kang, a staff member of the Chinese embassy, were proceeding to the textile factory work site from Accra by car. On their way a group of Ghanaian soldiers stopped the experts and asked them to show their identity cards. While the Chinese experts explained that they came to Ghana on the economic and technical cooperation agreement between the two countries and that no identity card was issued to them by the Ghana government, the soldiers then forced a search on their person and beat them up. Afterward the Chinese experts were taken to the Accra police headquarters [where the "National Liberation Council" of the coup forces was located—*Ed.*]. The soldiers there then stripped the experts naked and carried out brutal assault by using whips, gun stocks, fists, and feet for as long as one hour. Only because of their repeated protests and requests were they sent back to the Chinese embassy. Now the hospital examination proves that there is a fracture of Mr. Chou Chin-wen's hip bone and he is not able to stand. Various wounds are also caused on the bodies and heads of the other three.

The fact that the above-stated atrocities of illegal assault on the Chinese experts and the embassy staff occurred at police headquarters in Accra cannot but be regarded as an act of intentional provocation. It not only seriously impedes the normal work of the Chinese experts, [and] violates the agreement of economic and technical cooperation, but also harms the friendly relations between the peoples of China and Ghana.

The Chinese embassy demands that the authorities concerned should apologize for this incident [and] punish those persons responsible and that effective measures be taken to protect the safety of all members of the Chinese embassy [and] all Chinese experts as well as other Chinese nationals in Ghana and ensure that no such incidents will occur again.

Note

Because the Soviet Union initially stood alone as a revolutionary power in a hostile world, from the outset its legal theorists argued that consent is the sole basis of the validity of international law and that states cannot be bound by norms to which they have not consented. Because a treaty constitutes explicit manifestation of a state's consent, Soviet writers have maintained that treaties are the main source of international law.[5]

Available materials do not permit detailed comparisons, but the Chinese position on the significance of treaties appears generally to resemble the Soviet position. Items 4–2 and 4–3 illustrate the PRC's relatively frequent reference to multilateral and bilateral agreements, respectively, as sources of law. Despite Ying T'ao's attack on bourgeois use of treaties (4–1), Chinese writers acknowledge that treaties are "an important source of international law and an important form of expressing international law."[6]

The Chinese recognize that international conferences can draft multilateral conventions, but maintain that these only acquire binding force upon states that ratify them.[7] Because the PRC was not represented in the United Nations and most other international organizations for over twenty years, it was excluded from participation in their legislative processes. However, although Ying T'ao sought to discredit the Covenant of the League of Nations, he did not criticize the United Nations Charter. As asserted successor to the Republic of China, which ratified the Charter in 1945, the PRC regards itself as bound by the Charter and frequently invokes its support as a source of international law. Moreover, Article 38 of the Statute of the International Court of Justice, which was adopted as "an integral part" of the UN Charter [Article 92 of the Charter] and which directs the ICJ to apply treaties, customs, general principles of law, and, as subsidiary sources, judicial decisions and publicists' teachings, has been listed as a source of law in a book of documents on international law published in 1958 by the Office of Teaching and Research on International Law of the Institute of Diplomacy of Peking.[8]

The Chinese appear to be sensitive to the value of bilateral treaties not only to make law as between the treaty partners but also to serve as indirect sources of general international law. In many bilateral treaties the PRC has incorporated the five principles of peaceful coexistence as a guide for relations between it and the state with which it contracts. As scholar Chou Keng-sheng recognized in 1955 (8–6), these principles are by no means novel and, in somewhat different formulations, have been accepted as principles of international law for some time. Nevertheless, subsequent Chinese scholarship sought to give the impression that it is the incorporation of these principles into a growing number of bilateral treaties, packaged under the label "peaceful coexistence," that has transformed them into general principles of international law.[9] Soviet scholars adopt a similar view.[10]

The materials in later parts of this work provide ample further illustrations of the PRC's reliance on treaties as a source of law, and Part VIII deals with Chinese views concerning the law of treaties.

4-4

"Persecution of Chinese Nationals by Indonesian Right-Wing Forces," note of Nov. 4, 1965, in *PR* 8.48:20–21 (Nov. 26, 1965).

The Embassy of the People's Republic of China in Indonesia presents its compliments to the Ministry of Foreign Affairs of the Republic of Indonesia and has the honour to state the following:

Since the beginning of October 1965, outrageous persecutions of Chinese nationals organized by the Indonesian right-wing forces have incessantly occurred in various parts of Indonesia. According to preliminary information, the principal facts are as follows:

1. Overseas Chinese organizations and schools raided, smashed, and forcibly occupied. . . .

2. Shops and residences of Chinese nationals smashed and ransacked. . . .

3. Chinese nationals illegally subpoenaed, arrested, manhandled, and beaten up. . . .

4. Portraits of the Chinese leaders and Chinese national flags burned and torn up. . . .

5. It must be pointed out in particular that in some places where Chinese nationals were persecuted, the rioters even threatened the civil and military police by announcing that their actions had the support of the army and that their demonstrations must be protected and not stopped. When outrages against Chinese nationals occurred in Semarang, the army personnel on the scene, far from checking the outrages, used their guns to drive passersby to join in damaging and smashing the property of Chinese nationals. In various parts of West Java, many rioters who persecuted Chinese nationals rode in military trucks.

The above-described outrages committed by the Indonesian right-wing forces constitute a brutal encroachment upon the proper rights and interests of the Chinese nationals and their personal safety, and a gross violation of the accepted principles of international law and international practice. The Chinese Embassy hereby lodges a strong protest with the Indonesian government against these outrages.

4-5

"Trial of 28 Japanese in Shenyang," NCNA—English, Shenyang (July 20, 1956) in *SCMP*, no. 1336:23, 26–27 (July 25, 1956).

The trial of 28 Japanese for crimes committed during the war finished today after being in session since July 1. It was conducted before a military court and observed by some 400 representatives of the Chinese People's Political Consultative Conference, local government bodies, factories, schools and the armed forces. Fifty-year-old (Henry) Pu Yi, now in custody, appeared in court to give evidence of what took place while he was puppet "Emperor of Manchukuo" under the Japanese. . . .

The 28 Japanese, who held various important military and administrative positions in the administrative, judicial, and police organizations and in the gendarmes of the puppet Manchukuo regime, were charged with having committed serious crimes during the Japanese war against China, with actively carrying out the aggressive policies of Japanese imperialism, [with] supporting the Japanese war against China, [with] manipulating or participating in the manipulation of the puppet government of "Manchukuo," [and with] violating the sovereignty of China and the principles of international law and humanitarianism.

The special military court sentenced the defendants to varied terms of imprisonment.

NOTE

From the founding of their regime Soviet statesmen and scholars displayed profound distrust of "custom" as a source of international law.[11] Customary norms were inevitably the product of pre-1917 practices which the new revolutionary leaders had never had an opportunity to shape and which they often believed to be adverse to the interests of the Soviet state. Gradually, however, the need to sustain intercourse with the bourgeois world and the recognition that, selectively invoked, custom could be a valuable weapon in dealing with that world, led the Soviet Union to concede the authoritative status of certain customary norms, that is, "rules which have acquired legal significance as a result of their application by states over a prolonged period and their recognition as legal rules."[12] Contemporary Soviet writers maintain that a customary norm is not binding upon a state unless that state has agreed, if only tacitly, to accept it.[13] This emphasis upon agreement, however fictitious, permits the Soviet Union to take a flexible attitude toward customary norms, accepting or rejecting them as Soviet interests appear to warrant.

Chinese scholars have devoted little attention to the many difficult problems relating to resort to custom as a source of international law. From time to time, however, both they and Chinese officialdom have explicitly relied on "international custom" in protesting conduct of other states or in justifying conduct of the PRC.[14] And a 1963 article in the *People's Daily* stated that the primary sources of international law are "international treaties and international customs."[15]

More frequently, the Chinese substitute other formulations for the term "custom." Item 4–5, one of the rare accounts that we have of a Chinese court applying international law, illustrates a favorite variation—"the principles of international law and humanitarianism." When in 1964 Brazil sentenced nine members of an unofficial Chinese trade and cultural exchange delegation to prison for subversive activities, the PRC protested that this "unscrupulously tramples on the standards of international law and dignity and justice and is a serious in-infringement on fundamental human rights."[16] Similarly, when a member of its staff defected to the United States, the Chinese embassy in Burundi claimed that he had been kidnapped "in utmost contempt of the elementary rules of international law and in violation of fundamental human rights." [17] The PRC often charges, as in Item 4–4, that certain hostile acts constitute a flagrant violation of international law and practice. And it sometimes prescribes treaty obligations in terms of "practice," as in the case of the 1961 Sino-Indonesian Friendship Treaty, which provides: "The Contracting Parties agree to continuously consolidate the diplomatic and consular relations between the two countries in accordance with the principle of reciprocity and international practice." [18]

Occasionally, the PRC attempts to demonstrate the unreasonableness of another party to a dispute by accusing it of having departed from an established pattern of conduct that, while not universal or general among states, has nevertheless prevailed in the PRC's relations with the other party and has created expectations of continuation. In protesting the alleged killing of seven Chinese citizens by Burmese border guards in 1967, the Chinese government accused Burma of disrupting the holding of fairs and the visiting of friends and relatives by Chinese and Burmese border residents that "have been the natural result of historical, national and other factors and have been their traditional custom for hundreds of years." [19]

On certain occasions, Peking has relied on patterns of conduct that can in no sense be deemed "historical" but that are of very recent vintage. In 1958, when the Japanese government refused to allow the PRC's trade office in Tokyo to fly the PRC flag, the Chairman of the China Committee for the Promotion of International Trade argued: "The Chinese and Japanese civilian organizations and commodity exhibitions have never in the past had any inconvenience in hoisting their national flags in each other's country caused by the nonrestoration of diplomatic relations between China and Japan." [20] And when in 1963 the Soviet Union demanded the recall of certain Chinese personnel for having "illegally" distributed CCP Central Committee statements in the Soviet Union, the PRC's Ministry of Foreign Affairs replied:

> It is perfectly normal for the official organs and personnel of one socialist country in another socialist country to distribute the published documents of their own government and party. This has always been done by the Soviet organs and personnel in China. In the past six months the Soviet organs and personnel in China have distributed the following documents: [several documents listed] . . .
>
> The principle of reciprocity must be unanimously observed by countries concerned and must in no circumstances be violated at will by any one side.[21]

The extent to which the PRC observes the international customs, principles, standards, rules, law, practice, etc. that it applies to the conduct of others is a question for consideration throughout this study and in subsequent research. Later materials, especially Parts V, VI, and VII, will provide many other illustrations of the PRC's invocation of custom and related concepts.

4-6

Mei Ju-ao, "The Aggressor and the Law," *PC*, no. 5:12 (Mar. 1, 1955). [The author was formerly a judge of the International Military Tribunal for the Far East, the Tokyo equivalent of the Nuremberg tribunal. At the time this article was written, he was a member of the Executive Board of the China Political Science and Law Association.]

With Japan's unconditional surrender in 1945, the Second World War came to an end. China, as a victor nation, naturally has as much right to recover her lost territory from the vanquished foe as France had after the end of World War I to recover Alsace-Lorraine from Germany (Alsace-Lorraine too had been under enemy occupation for nearly fifty years). Any victor is entitled to this fundamental right. This is fair and just. Not only is such right confirmed by the principles of international law and general practice; it is also in conformity with the principles of municipal law in all lands. When a thief is apprehended by his victim or by a constable, his spoils are returned to their rightful owner as a matter of course. No court in the world would decide that they should be handed to a third party, or declared *res nullius*.

The restoration of Taiwan to China after Japan's surrender is an act of restitution, that is, "the restoration of stolen property to its proper owner."

Note

Discussion of Taiwan's status proved to be the occasion for another Chinese scholar to invoke, in the words of Article 38 of the Statute of the ICJ, "the general principles of law recognized by civilized nations." Shortly before his fall from grace for being a "rightist," Ch'en T'i-ch'iang wrote that, since Taiwan had been stolen from China by Japan, "the maxim *ex injuria jus non oritur* (meaning that a person cannot acquire a right through his illegal act) is in point." [22]

Although there is not enough evidence to permit definitive judgment, the above references to widely recognized principles of domestic law suggest that, at least prior to the antirightist movement, Chinese experts may not have shared the view of their Soviet brethren that the "general principles" mentioned as sources of international law in Article 38 of the Statute of the ICJ are limited to general principles of international law and do not include principles of domestic law common to the major legal systems.

Chinese writers rarely invoke judicial decisions as sources or evidence of international law. They more commonly denounce the decisions of both international tribunals and the tribunals of other states as products of capitalist manipulation. Shortly after the PRC's 1958 announcement of the limits of its territorial sea, however, several experts who wrote in justification of the PRC's action made favorable references to the ICJ's decision in the Anglo-Norwegian Fisheries Case. As one article put it:

> The straight baselines method adopted by China to fix the baseline of her territorial sea is suited to the geographical conditions of her coast in many places, and is entirely lawful. Among the other countries which have adopted the straight baselines method to fix the baseline of territorial sea, Norway and Iceland are the most notable examples. Recently Indonesia also announced her intention to adopt this method. Britain had set itself in opposition to the adoption of this method by Norway. But the International Court of Justice in dealing with the fishery disputes between Britain and Norway pointed out in its decision on this case in 1951 that the straight baselines method was not in conflict with international law.[23]

It should also be recalled that in 1958 the Institute of Diplomacy's Office of Teaching and Research on International Law listed among the sources of international law Article 38 of the Statute of the ICJ, which in turn refers to judicial decisions as a subsidiary means for the determination of rules of law.[24] The Chinese position is probably similar to the Soviet position, which views courts as not "making" law but merely "applying" it and which therefore includes judicial decisions among the auxiliary means for determining what the law is. According to a Soviet text, "the International Court's application and interpretation of a legal rule are binding only upon the parties to the given dispute and only concern the particular case in question. . . . Nevertheless, decisions of the Court have a very great importance in stating the existence, or lack, at a given period of rules of International Law." [25]

Also listed among the sources of international law by the Institute of Diplomacy were the Resolution of the United Nations General Assembly on Progressive Development of International Law and Its Codification (December 11, 1946) and the Resolution of the United Nations General Assembly on Affirmation of the Principles of International Law Recognized by the Charter of the Nuremberg Tribunal (December 11, 1946).[26] The significance of the listing of these resolutions is far from clear. In 1963 one Chinese expert wrote:

> The United Nations Organization is one form of international organization of sovereign states. Its resolutions in general have only the character of a recommendation (with the exception of Security Council decisions to maintain peace, taken under Chapter VII of the Charter). Such resolutions cannot *ipso facto* bind member countries. Even the legal drafts prepared by the International Law Commission and adopted by the General Assembly must still go through the procedure of an international conference and the conclusion of a treaty before they acquire binding force.[27]

But General Assembly resolutions have occasionally been cited by Chinese to prove or to disprove the existence of a rule of international law. In 1958 another leading expert argued:

> The recent resolutions of the various organs of the United Nations indicate that the nationalizing state has no legal obligation to grant compensation to foreigners. The United Nations General Assembly resolution of 21 December 1952, states: "the right of peoples freely to use and exploit their natural wealth and resources is inherent in their sovereignty" (Resolution 626) . . . .
>
> Obviously, the above-mentioned 1952 resolution of the United Nations General Assembly recommends that all members, in the exercise of their right freely to use and exploit their natural wealth and resources, have due regard, consistent with their sovereignty, for the need for maintaining the flow of capital in conditions of security, mutual confidence, and economic cooperation among nations. But since the resolution explicitly uses the phrase "to have due regard, consistent with their sovereignty," the nationalizing state still enjoys its sovereign right freely to consider the question of whether it will grant compensation to original owners

> of foreign nationality and, if compensation is to be granted, the amount of such compensation.[28]

The views of these two experts may not necessarily be in conflict The Chinese position may be that the only binding actions of the UN are decisions taken by the Security Council under Chapter VII but that General Assembly resolutions relating to international law, at least in certain circumstances, may constitute evidence of what international law is, just as do decisions of the ICJ, as in the Anglo-Norwegian Fisheries Case. On the other hand, China's experts may disagree on this problem as on some others. Certainly Soviet scholars have not forged a uniform approach to the question of the significance to be attached to the resolutions of international organizations, some even asserting that "resolutions of the General Assembly, adopted unanimously or by a ⅔ majority where that majority includes socialist and capitalist states . . . are binding on the members of the UN and, therefore, have juridical force." [29]

4-7

Chou Keng-sheng, "The Persecution of Chinese Nationals and Infringement of the Right of China to Protect Chinese Nationals by the Indian Government Are Serious International Delinquencies," *JMJP* (Jan. 22, 1963), p. 5.

Measures adopted by India in accordance with its sovereignty cannot be used to extinguish the right of another state to protect its nationals abroad. The protection of nationals abroad is the exercise of the personal supremacy of all sovereign states. No one can deny this minimum standard of international law. It is a standard which must be observed by every state. For instance, the British international law authority Oppenheim points out: "Although aliens fall at once under the territorial supremacy of the state they enter, they remain, nevertheless, under the protection of their home state. By a universally recognized customary rule of international law every state holds a right of protection over its citizens abroad. . . ." [a] Chinese nationals in India naturally should obey Indian laws and as a matter of fact Chinese nationals have been consistently law-abiding; at the same time, the Chinese government has the right and also the duty to protect law-abid-

[a] L. Oppenheim, *International Law,* 8th ed., by H. Lauterpacht (London: Longmans, Green, 1955), I, 686.

ing Chinese nationals. The Constitution of the People's Republic of China (Article 98) provides: "The People's Republic of China protects the proper rights and interests of Chinese residents abroad." The use of discriminatory decrees by the Indian government to persecute law-abiding Chinese nationals is an act that violates international law and impairs the right of China to protect its nationals abroad, which absolutely cannot be justified by what is called an act in accordance with sovereignty or the performance of an act of sovereignty in accordance with domestic law.

NOTE

The PRC frequently attacks the legislative acts as well as the judicial decisions of other states on the ground that they violate international law. Occasionally, as in Item 4–7, Chinese authorities cite the PRC's own constitutional and legislative prescriptions in an effort to demonstrate the legality of the PRC's international acts. We have not found, however, any explicit generalizations relating domestic legislation to the sources of international law, such as Soviet statements that: "National legislation . . . exerts a great influence on the formation of rules of international law. But national legislation acquires the status of a source of international law only when it is recognized as a rule of international law either through international treaty or through international custom. National legislation cannot therefore be considered an independent source of international law." [30] Another Soviet scholar writes that "The democratic laws of individual states (especially the socialist states) promote . . . the process of international legal norm formation and, under certain conditions, serve as possible sources thereof." [31]

Similarly, we have found no general Chinese formulations concerning the weight that should attach to the writings of legal scholars. Yet Chinese publications frequently invoke even the work of bourgeois jurists when the views contained therein coincide with those of the PRC on a given issue; and, of course, they scathingly attack bourgeois scholarship when its views contradict China's needs. Although there is no basis for asserting that the Chinese regard scholarship as a formal, if subsidiary, source of law, it is obvious that they, like Soviet writers, recognize that in practice scholars have an important influence on the interpretation and application of international law.[32]

4-8

Li Hao-p'ei, "Nationalization and International Law," *CFYC*, no. 2:19 (1958).

Recently, the Afro-Asian Jurists' Conference also adopted a resolution on this question [nationalization] at its Damascus meeting held in November of last year. The resolution is given below as the conclusion of this article:

"1. The Conference declares: Nationalization is the legal means to consolidate national economy and, moreover, is the indisputable right of each state in carrying out the principle of state sovereignty and the principle of public use.

"2. The Conference considers: The nationalization of foreign or domestic enterprises within the territory of a state naturally extinguishes the legal personality of the nationalized enterprise by virtue of the act of nationalization, and it should be replaced by the legal personality of the new enterprise.

"3. The Conference further considers: Since it is indisputable that a state has the right to nationalize any enterprise within its territory, the effect of nationalization should extend to all property of the nationalized enterprises, whether it is within the territory of the state carrying out the nationalization or abroad.

"4. The Conference considers: Asia and Africa are the two continents in the world which are most appropriate for carrying out the principle of nationalization.

"The opinion of the Conference adopted after due consideration is: the procedures followed and the measures adopted by Egypt in nationalizing the Suez Canal Company constituted proper application of the above principles.

"Finally, the Conference confirms: the nationalized Suez Canal Company is of Egyptian nationality, and any measure adopted or any law passed in order to change this fact is absolutely void." [33]

NOTE

A Western authority on Soviet views of international law has observed:

> A rather novel feature of Soviet international law thinking in most recent years is a certain pragmatic initiative, accompanied also by a frequent degree of imagination and wit, in bringing to bear the special Soviet concepts of international law in international arenas. In addition to the various traditional "sources" of international law, historically accepted as such and also recognized in Article 38 of the World Court statute, Soviet jurists have

> begun to list a new authoritative source, that is, the opinions and resolutions of public and scientific legal organizations. Since the middle-1950's Soviet Bloc jurists have begun to appear in strength at international professional and technical legal conferences, and to function at those same conferences as co-ordinated and well-prepared and well-researched teams with a concerted programme of action for legal change. Very often the Soviet Bloc delegations to officially private associations like the authoritative International Law Association are headed by the principal legal scientists and advisers in the Foreign Ministries and in the specialized Law Institutes; and the same people very often turn up immediately afterwards in the official national delegations to the United Nations General Assembly meetings and especially in the United Nations' Sixth (Legal) Committee. It is perhaps inevitable, and certainly understandable, that the Soviet Bloc delegates should tend to use the same arguments in each place. Less predictable, from the Western viewpoint, has been the Soviet tactic of leading from arguments or proposals advanced by Soviet jurists in the give-and-take of the International Law Association debates to the assertion of firm propositions of law in the rather different forum of the United Nations: as if by the process of iteration and re-iteration, so to speak, contentions *de lege ferenda* in the International Law Association debates could become converted into binding principles *de lege lata*—a ploy by Soviet jurists which has been partly assisted, it must be admitted, by the frequently rather casual or indifferent record of Western juristic performance in the United Nations' Sixth Committee.[34]

Although the Chinese do not explicitly list the opinions and resolutions of scientific legal organizations as subsidiary sources of norm formation, nevertheless they have also been alert to the possibilities of mobilizing the activities of international professional conferences in support of the PRC's positions on international law, as Item 4–8 indicates. In recent years, however, Chinese jurists have not had as much scope for action as their Soviet counterparts have had. In 1960 the China Political Science and Law Association withdrew from the International Law Association in protest against the admission of lawyers from the Republic of China. Moreover, as a result of the Sino-Soviet dispute, Chinese Communist jurists have often found themselves in a minority position at meetings of the International Association of Democratic Lawyers; these meetings have been held with diminishing frequency and have come to resemble a socialist donnybrook. Of course, the China Political Science and Law Association itself responds with appropriate resolutions whenever requested by the regime.

Subjects of International Law 5

5-1

"Indian Lies about CPR [PRC] 'Intrusions' Refuted," NCNA–English, Peking (Oct. 27, 1966) in *FBIS*, no. 210: BBB 11, 12 (Oct. 28, 1966).

[In its note to the PRC government dated September 30, 1966, the Indian government charged that Chinese herdsmen and patrols had intruded into Bhutanese territory and lodged a protest with the Chinese government on behalf of Bhutan.] In this connection, NCNA is authorized by the [PRC] government to make the following statement: . . .

3. China has consistently respected Bhutan's sovereignty and territorial integrity. China and Bhutan have all along been on friendly terms with each other, without either side committing aggression against the other, and the border between the two countries has always been tranquil. The Bhutan government itself has on many occasions refuted the lies concocted by the Indian side about Chinese "threats" to and "intrusions" into Bhutan. It is true that the China-Bhutan boundary has never been formally delimited, and, if the Bhutanese side's understanding is not quite the same as that of the Chinese side as regards the alignment of the boundary between the two countries at certain specific points, a fair and reasonable solution can very well be found through consultations on an equal footing between the two sides on the basis of mutual understanding and mutual accommodation.

China has successfully settled boundary questions left over by history with such neighboring countries as Burma, Nepal, Pakistan, and Afghanistan through friendly consultations. Nevertheless, it must be explicitly pointed out that the boundary question between China and Bhutan is a matter that concerns China and Bhutan alone and has nothing to do with the Indian government, which has no right whatsoever to intervene in it.

4. The King of Bhutan has long since solemnly declared that "Bhutan is an independent sovereign state and has the right to conduct its own foreign affairs." However, blatantly claiming to be acting on Bhutan's behalf, the Indian government lodged a so-called protest with China. This is a manifestation of downright big-nation chauvinism.

Inheriting the mantle of British imperialism, the Indian government has all along been pursuing an expansionist policy and bullying its neighboring countries. It treats Sikkim as its "protectorate," thus encroaching upon Sikkim's independence and sovereignty. It tries hard to tighten its control over Bhutan, makes every effort to prevent the latter from attaining its due international status, and even intends to send troops directly into Bhutan territory and station them here.

5-2

"China Recognizes Algerian Provisional Government," NCNA–English, Peking (Sept. 22, 1958), in *SCMP*, no. 1861:42 (Sept. 25, 1958).

On September 22, 1958, Foreign Minister Ch'en Yi sent a message to Mohamed Lamine Labaghine, Minister of Foreign Affairs of the Provisional Government of the Republic of Algeria, informing him that the Chinese government has decided to extend recognition to the provisional government of the Republic of Algeria. Full text of the message reads:

> On the happy occasion of the establishment of the provisional government of the Republic of Algeria, I would like, on behalf of the government of the People's Republic of China and the Chinese people, to extend warm congratulations to you and, through you, to the Algerian people. I have the honor to inform you that the government of the People's Republic of China has decided to give recognition to the provisional government of the Republic of Algeria. The Chinese government and people wholeheartedly support the Algerian people's just struggle to win national independence and freedom. I am deeply convinced that the Algerian people will surely achieve complete victory in their struggle. The friendship between the Chinese and Algerian peoples will further develop and be consolidated.

5-3

K'ung Meng, "A Criticism of the Theories of Bourgeois International Law Concerning the Subjects of International Law and Recognition of States," *KCWTYC*, no. 2:44–51 (1960).

One of the fundamental questions of international law is who are the subjects of it. The different attitudes toward this question adopted by the different classes are, as are their attitudes to international law as a whole, determined by their respective class interests. Bourgeois international law serves the bourgeoisie, and its views as to who are the subjects of international law embody the interests of bourgeois countries, especially the interests of strong bourgeois countries. Different views on the question of who are the subjects of international law proposed in different periods are determined by the relative changes of international strength and the concrete needs of the stages in the development of the capitalist system.

The view of the bourgeoisie concerning the subjects of international law is generally as follows: From the early period of capitalism to the October Revolution in Russia, the bourgeoisie generally maintained that only states were subjects of international law; after the First World War, the theory that individuals were subjects of international law began to emerge; and since the Second World War, this theory that "individuals are subjects of international law" has become more popular. Moreover, the bourgeoisie even considers that international organizations are subjects of international law. All such theories are determined by the interests of the bourgeoisie.

The bourgeoisie considered that "states are the only subjects of international law," but in fact it regarded only civilized states as subjects of international law, in order to legalize the practice of national oppression and colonialism by the big capitalist powers.

In the period of the bourgeois revolution and the entire period of capitalism before monopoly, the traditional theory of the bourgeoisie was that only states are subjects of international law.[a]

After overthrowing the despotic dynasties, the Western European bourgeoisie, in order to oppose the intervention of the international feudal force headed by the Pope and the Holy Roman Emperor and to suppress the power of separation and annexation possessed by major and minor feudal lords, from the beginning tightly held the banner of

[a] Franz von Liszt, *Mezhdunarodnoe pravo* (International law, 2nd ed., Moscow, 1912), p. 59. [Note: Chinese reference refers to the 4th edition, which was not available.]

national independence and national sovereignty by raising the status of states so as to oppose the restoration of feudal force and to consolidate its own political power. Similarly, in international law, it particularly emphasized the independence of state sovereignty and the theory that states are the only subjects of international law. This was advantageous to antifeudalism and to the consolidation and development of bourgeois nation-states.

But the bourgeoisie does not recognize the sovereignty and independence of all states and nations. Nor does it recognize all states as subjects of international law. Basically, it recognizes only a handful of Western bourgeois states and their partners in Asia (such as Japan after the First Sino-Japanese War in 1895) as subjects of international law. This is because the ruling class of a capitalist country exploits and oppresses not only the masses of its own country but also of other nations. It engages in colonial expansion and uses every method to encroach upon the sovereignty and independence of weak countries and nations. In order to legitimize all national discrimination and national oppression, these capitalist countries classify themselves as "civilized states," or "full sovereign states" and the respective weak and small nations as "uncivilized nations," "semisovereign states" or "not full sovereign states." According to the theory of the bourgeoisie, international society is a big family of "civilized nations"; international law is the set of rules among "civilized states" and it only protects "civilized nations"; "noncivilized nations" are outside international society; they are either not full subjects of international law or they are not subjects of international law at all. As a matter of fact, this theory of bourgeois international law is an exact reflection of the practices of strong capitalist countries in their international relations. They madly engage in activities of colonial expansion. They have never treated weak or small countries as equal members of the international society; on the contrary, they force those weak or small countries to reduce their status to that of protected states, vassal states, colonies, or mandated territories. Although some of those countries still nominally maintain independence, they are in fact semicolonies (a foreign country has leases and concessions and retains the right of stationing armed forces and of consular jurisdiction, inland navigation, customs administration, and so forth, within their territories). These countries cannot stand on an equal footing with the "civilized countries"; in general they cannot enjoy rights in international law, but can only undertake obligations in "international law" in accordance with the unequal treaties signed by them or agreements concluded between big bourgeois countries.

Some protected states, vassal states, and so forth are permitted, whenever it is advantageous to the suzerain state [that is, the dominant or superior state], to become members of international society and to participate in certain international conferences and international organizations of an administrative character or to sign certain treaties. However, under such circumstances, their representatives are generally instruments used by their respective suzerain states (for instance, they add to the number of those with the right to vote), and they have nothing to do with the interests of the oppressed nations themselves.

From the foregoing, it is clear that the theory of bourgeois international law concerning the subjects (and the scope) of international law serves as a defense of national oppression by strong bourgeois countries and a weapon for those countries in the course of their colonial expansion and plundering aggression. . . .

For more than one hundred years, old China was oppressed and insulted by imperialism and forced to sign a large number of unequal treaties so that it almost lost all sovereignty. Imperialists always considered China an "uncivilized country" or a "semicivilized country" and thus not under the protection of international law. Therefore, when it dealt with imperialism, "China could only comply with the treaties concluded and could not invoke public international law."[b] Some bourgeois scholars consider that before the First World War, Chinese "civilization had not yet reached that condition which was necessary to enable their government and their population in every respect to understand, and to carry out, the rules of International Law."[c] Therefore, China was not a full subject of international law. In fact, the point was not the degree of civilization and understanding of international law. For instance, Japan was recognized as a full subject of international law not because its level of civilization was higher than China's at that time, but because it had joined the imperialist powers by defeating first the Manchu government in China and then Czarist Russia. It became a real accomplice of Western imperialism. . . . As for so-called understanding of "international law," Japan's understanding was not as enlightened as that of the Manchu government. The Japanese version of Wheaton's "Elements of International Law" published in 1865 was only a reprint of the 1864 Chinese edition published by China's T'ung Wen Kuan.[d] At that time, there was not a single Japanese edition of international law.

[b] Hsüeh Fu-ch'eng, *Yung-an wen-pien,* 4 vols. (Collected essays of Hsüeh Fu-ch'eng; Shanghai, 1897). [Note: We are unable to locate the quoted passages from the above work.]

[c] L. Oppenheim, *International Law,* Vol. I, 7th ed., by H. Lauterpacht (London: Longmans, Green, 1948), pp. 46–47.

[d] Kisaburo Yokota, *Kokusai hogaku* (The science of international law; Tokyo: Yuhikaku, 1955), p. 140.

After the First World War, the status of China did not improve. In 1931, after Japan had occupied China's northeastern provinces, its representative openly declared before a meeting of the League of Nations that China was not "an organized country" and did not possess the qualifications of "organized peoples" mentioned in the preamble of the Covenant of the League of Nations. Accordingly, Japan's sending troops to China did not constitute an act of aggression against another member state, but was rather a quite natural thing to do.

Aside from its oppression of nations, international imperialism has also repeatedly used the theory of bourgeois international law concerning the subjects of international law as an instrument against socialist countries.

After the victory of Russia's October Revolution in 1917, the big bourgeois powers felt a deep hatred for this first socialist country from the very beginning. They did not recognize the fact that a government established by the proletariat could be qualified as an equal member in international relations. They started large-scale armed intervention in an attempt to eliminate that government. After such attempts were thwarted, they were compelled to recognize the Soviet Union, but they still imposed various restrictions upon the rights of the Soviet Union as an equal member in international society by restricting its activities on the international stage and by formulating various "theories" to deny its qualifications as a full subject of international law. . . .

Since the establishment of People's China, American imperialism and its followers have used illegal methods to occupy Taiwan and to support the traitorous Chiang Kai-shek clique, which was forsaken by the Chinese people, as the representative of China; and they have excluded China from the United Nations and other international organizations. Thus, they have restricted China's activities in international relations and infringed the rights of China as a subject of international law.

After the October Revolution, the bourgeoisie advocated the theory that individuals are subjects of international law in order to intervene in the internal affairs of other countries on the pretext of protecting "human rights."

After the First World War, with the success of socialist revolution in Russia, two systems came into existence in international relations, putting an end to the situation of bourgeois dominance. At the same time, under the influence of the October Revolution, the imperialist colonial system began to waver. Thus, the theory that only states are subjects of international law was inadequate to meet the new situation. In view of this, the bourgeoisie has shifted to debase [the principle of] state sovereignty and to raise the legal status of individuals in international relations by advocating that individuals as well as states are subjects of international law, thus facilitating the imperialist countries' intervention in the internal affairs of other countries on the pretext of protecting "human rights." After the Second World War, a large number of socialist countries emerged. Particularly, there was the victory of the Chinese revolution. These countries have effected important changes favorable to socialism in the relative strength of classes in the international scene. Moreover, with the rising tide of independence movements in colonies, many new countries have emerged in the vast areas of Asia and Africa. In such circumstances, international imperialism headed by the United States must resort even more to the reactionary theory that "individuals are subjects of international law" in order to achieve its criminal objectives.

After the October Revolution, a large number of Russian counter-revolutionary elements fled to foreign countries and became so-called stateless "refugees." In order to use these persons for anti-Soviet activities, the imperialist countries proposed the so-called question of improving the situation for refugees. For this purpose they concluded three conventions to regulate the "international status of refugees" and issued to refugees in the name of the League of Nations the so-called "Nansen Passport" in order to place them directly under the protection of the League of Nations, to make them tools for anti-Soviet activities, and to intervene in the Soviet Union's affairs on the pretext of the refugee question.

On the other hand, as a result of the redemarcation of state territories after the First World War, the question of national minorities (or religious minorities) arose in certain small European countries. The imperialist countries, especially Nazi Germany, frequently resorted to this question as a pretext for intervention in the internal affairs of those small countries to achieve their own objectives. In order to transform the questions of "refugees" and national minorities into questions of purely international character, imperialism described these individuals as "subjects of international law." Moreover, they also used the theory of "individuals as subjects" to resist the nationalization measures of socialist and nationalist countries.

Before the start of the Second World War, because of the practice of racial discrimination in the Fascist countries, there were a large number of refugees. During the war, many persons fled from the area of Nazi occupation and, moreover, the governments of Fascist countries forcibly transferred large numbers of inhabitants of occupied areas to areas behind the front for hard labor. Thus, the number of refugees greatly increased. Furthermore, as a result of the emergence of a number of new socialist countries in Europe and Asia in the postwar period, some counterrevolutionary elements fled to foreign countries and became so-called "refugees." The imperialist countries headed by the United States, in order to use those persons as tools of opposition to their home countries, have utilized every method to obstruct the repatriation of refugees to their home countries. They carry out reactionary propaganda among the refugees, train those persons who can be used for intelligence service, and forcibly transfer the rest to other countries for cheap labor. On the other hand, they manipulate the International Refugee Organization to intervene in the internal affairs of other countries on the pretext of protecting "human rights." Moreover, the American monopolistic organizations, with their advanced development, have acquired dominant economic and political positions in the capitalist world and have adopted the method of large-scale commodity and capital export to enslave other countries. In order to consolidate their monopolistic positions in foreign countries which allow them to carry out their activities freely in exploiting and plundering the people of backward countries, the monopolistic bourgeoisie demands that such monopolistic organizations be made subjects of international law in order to free them from the jurisdiction of the country in which they are located. The monopolistic organizations in Western European countries on the one hand sell their own national interests and independence in exchange for American dollars, and on the other hand they cooperate with each other in an attempt to recover their own strength. In order to compete they have even established a number of international monopolistic organizations in which states directly participate (such as the European Coal and Steel Community). To facilitate their activities in foreign countries, these monopolistic organizations demand the removal of various restrictions imposed upon their activities by [the principle of] the sovereignty of those foreign countries and claim to enjoy certain privileges (such as tax exemption, diplomatic privileges for their staffs, and even the right to establish their own tribunals) and to enjoy a special status outside the jurisdiction of state sovereignty.

In order to meet the practical needs of the big capitalist powers, certain schools of bourgeois international law in this period advocate the expansion of the scope of the subjects of international law. They depart from the traditional theory of the bourgeoisie by denying that "only states are subjects of international law." For instance, the view of "the school of social solidarity" in France is an obvious example.

The theory of this school (Politis of Greece, Scelle of France, and so forth) is that a state is a fictitious concept and that international society, composed of a number of states, is also a fictitious concept.

International society is the same as a national society, which is an organization constituted of individuals, and the elements of international society are the individuals of the constituent states. Therefore, in international society, regardless of public or private law relations, the subject of law can only be individuals. "International law is merely an aggregate of rules adjusting relations among individuals of different states." States are not [real] subjects of international law. Since the Second World War this theory that individuals are subjects of international law has been more widely accepted, especially in the United States. Although some "jurists" do not deny that states are subjects of international law, they nevertheless emphasize that individuals and legal persons are also subjects of international law. For instance, Jessup proposes that "international law, like national law, must be directly applicable to the individual." He positively advocates including monopolistic organizations as subjects of international law. He maintains that "a state's monopolistic organizations should have the privilege of sovereign immunity before foreign courts." [35] He further says that "in some instances the private corporation may even be factually in a more advantageous position than the government *with which it deals.*"

Other scholars of Western countries also have arbitrarily formulated various "theoretical bases" to prove that individuals are subjects of international law. For instance, Rousseau—a French bourgeois jurist—has used those rules of international law which prohibit genocide, slave trade, the sale of narcotics, the trial of war criminals, and so forth as a "theoretical basis" on which to defend the fallacy that "individuals are subjects of international law."

Since the Second World War, imperialists have done their best to raise the status of international organizations by advocating the view that international organizations are also subjects of international law. Their purpose is to establish world domination through these organizations.

After the First World War, at the contrivance of the principal victorious countries, the United States, England and France, the first permanent international organization of universal character—the League of Nations—was established with the expressed purpose to "achieve international peace." However, the League was in fact merely an instrument of these imperialist countries. (Although the United States nominally did not join the League, through the dispatch of so-called "observers" it exercised important influence behind the scenes.) They used the League to consolidate the "Versailles System," to maintain the "fruits of victory," to prevent the revival of the defeated countries, to isolate and to oppose the Soviet Union, and to oppose the revolutionary movement of proletarians in the various countries and the national liberation movement in colonies and semicolonies. "It is the veil of imperialist artifice" (the words of Stalin). In the later period of the League of Nations (1934), the two Fascist bandits, Germany and Japan, withdrew from the League, and the League once invited the Soviet Union to join (but in 1939 it again expelled the Soviet Union). However, if we look at the entire period of the League's existence, it did not and was unable to undertake the role of maintaining international peace and preventing aggression. On the contrary, it was frequently used by imperialists to carry out their plots against the Soviet Union and to intervene in the internal affairs of other countries.

After the Second World War, on the international scene the United Nations was established. American imperialism has fantastically attempted to establish world domination, and it has done its best to manipulate the United Nations and to transform it into an instrument for realizing American aggression, expansion, and intervention in the internal affairs of other countries. On a number of occasions, the United States government has used the voting machine of the United Nations to pass resolutions opposing socialist countries, to deprive New China of the right of representation and other lawful rights, to usurp the name of the United Nations in sending troops to invade Korea and to insult China by branding it "an aggressor," to intervene in the internal affairs of Hungary, and to conspire to expand the function of certain organs of the United Nations (such as the International Court of Justice) in order to transform the United Nations into a de facto supranational organization above all states. Moreover, in order to guarantee its rule in various areas, it has also established a number of so-called regional organizations, such as the North Atlantic Treaty Organization, the Southeast Asia Treaty Organization, the Baghdad Treaty Organization (and the Organization of American States already in existence), and has concluded large numbers of political and economic international organization "conventions." The United States has done its best to place these international organizations above other states, so that those organizations can encroach upon the territorial sovereignty of the contracting states in order to make them more dependent upon the United States and to serve the policy of war and aggression of the United States.

The view that international organizations are also subjects of international law made its first appearance in the theory of bourgeois international law after the end of the First World War, and it has been even more prevalent since the end of the Second World War. Some bourgeois reactionary schools and scholars have enthusiastically proclaimed universalistic thought by denying or devaluing the significance of state sovereignty and demanding the adoption of "a world constitution" and the establishment of "a world government." For instance, the school of normativists and some English and American reactionary jurists have advocated this view. Many bourgeois jurists in other countries have also argued that international organizations, especially the United Nations, are subjects of international law just as are states. In order to defend their view, they cite the right of the United Nations Organization to conclude international treaties, the diplomatic privileges enjoyed by the personnel of the United Nations Organization and by the Organization itself, and other such facts as proof of their theory. Some jurists even say that the various specialized agencies of the United Nations are also subjects of international law since, according to the Charter, these agencies have the right to "conclude agreements" (Article 63).

In short, from the foregoing we can clearly understand that the different theories as to the question of who are the subjects of bourgeois international law are inseparable from the interests of capitalism in the various stages of its development. In the heyday of capitalism, bourgeois international law emphasized that only bourgeois states were "full subjects" of international law and resorted to the theory of "civilized" and "uncivilized" to deny the sovereignty of weak and small nations. This theory was advantageous to the bourgeoisie. With capitalism in its period of decline, bourgeois international law proposes that individuals and international organizations are also subjects of international law. This theory is also consistent with the interests of capitalism.

The bourgeois theory concerning the subjects of international law is inconsistent with the principles of modern international law.

In the present period, with the coexistence of two systems, the bourgeois theory concerning the subjects of international law, which serves strong imperialistic countries, is not only politically reactionary but it is also inconsistent with the generally recognized principles and norms of modern international law.

First, according to the principles of sovereign equality and national self-determination prescribed in the Charter of the United Nations and the principles of mutual respect for territorial integrity and sovereignty and noninterference in another's internal affairs prescribed in the five principles of peaceful coexistence, all states, regardless of the degree of economic, political, and cultural development are, without exception, subjects of international law. Which type of social system and which form of state a country wishes to adopt is a domestic matter and does not affect the state's qualifications as a subject of international law. Any theory which denies the qualifications of a state as a subject of international law or the sovereignty of a state because of the country's "level of civilization" or social system is illegal.

Besides the existing states, nations which are in the process of forming states and struggling for independence are also subjects of international law. Therefore, an imperialistic war to suppress a colony is absolutely not an "internal conflict" or a "domestic question," but a kind of aggressive war prohibited by international law.

Second, according to the fundamental characteristics of international law (it is the law among states), individuals can only be subjects of municipal law and cannot be subjects of international law. In international relations, individuals are represented by their own countries and if rights and interests (such as entry, residence, employment, and property), are violated in a foreign country, individuals should negotiate with the state concerned through the organs of their home country. Only their home country enjoys the right of diplomatic protection in international law.

Certain individuals (such as heads of state, premiers of governments, diplomatic representatives) do enjoy certain rights (diplomatic privileges) in international relations. This is because they represent their state. In essence, these rights belong to the state, and, after a king abdicates his throne or a president resigns from office, they no longer enjoy such rights. Therefore, invoking the question of diplomatic privileges to prove that individuals are subjects of international law is completely groundless.

Similarly, certain bourgeois scholars (such as Rousseau) attempt to invoke those rules of international law to prohibit genocide, slave trade and the sale of narcotics and to prescribe that war criminals may be punished in accordance with international agreement to prove that individuals are subjects of international crime and thus subjects of international law. This is also groundless because the conventions concluded among the various countries concerning the prohibition and elimination of crimes endangering the life, health, freedom, morality, and property of individuals and the crimes of engaging in aggressive war or violating the law of war are only a means they (subjects of international law) use in their cooperative struggle against the abovementioned crimes. Such conventions merely prescribe certain unified regulations concerning the determination of the existence of crime, procedure for prosecution, jurisdiction, and even criteria for deciding upon punishment, and these become part of the municipal law of the various contracting states to be executed by their judicial organs. Even if certain criminals may be handed over to an international tribunal for trial, such jurisdiction must have prior consent of the various contracting states. In view of this, the fact that individuals who violate international order are held criminally responsible cannot make them subjects of international law.

As to the protection of "fundamental human rights" (Preamble) and respect for "fundamental freedoms" (Article 62) emphasized in the United Nations Charter, the fact that the United Nations General Assembly has adopted the "Declaration of Human Rights" and "Draft Covenant of Human Rights" does not mean, as described by certain bourgeois jurists (such as Lauterpacht and Jessup), that the United Nations Organization, its Economic and Social Council, or its Commission on Human Rights can bypass states to protect the "human rights" of individuals in the various states and thus make individuals subjects of international law. As a matter of fact, the principle concerning fundamental human rights prescribed in the United Nations Charter is that the various member states are obligated to guarantee that individuals under their rule enjoy certain rights. But the fundamental human rights enjoyed by individuals are not conferred on them by an international organization, but rather by the municipal law of the various member states which undertake such obligations. The object of the recommendations adopted by the Economic and Social Council "for the purpose of promoting respect for, and observance of, human rights and fundamental freedoms for all" (Article 62 [paragraph 2]) and of the Declaration of Human Rights adopted by the various member states of the United Nations was recommendatory in nature and was to urge states themselves to guarantee human rights. The object was not to have an international organization bypass states and guarantee the human rights of the citizens of the various states; if it were, it would be intervention in the internal affairs of a state. All individuals, whether citizens within a state or aliens, are under the sovereignty of the state and are not subjects of international law.

Finally, the various international organizations are only a form of cooperation among states; they are neither members of international society nor subjects of international law. Even the functions of an international organization like the United Nations are limited to the scope prescribed by the agreement (the Charter of the United Nations) among member states, and, hence, such an organization is not comparable to a state which possesses sovereignty. The specialized agencies of the United Nations, such as the Universal Postal Union, the International Telecommunication Union, and the International Labor Organization, are merely organs of cooperation among states in various specialized fields; the scope of their activities is restricted by their constitutions (agreements among states). They, also, are not subjects of international law. Aggressive organizations such as the North Atlantic Treaty Organization and the Southeast Asia Treaty Organization, are themselves illegal, so they do not qualify as subjects of international law. . . .

It is true that the right to conclude international treaties and the right to diplomatic immunities are rights enjoyed by subjects of international law and, according to the Charter, the United Nations Organization and its principal organs certainly do have the right to conclude certain treaties. For instance, the Security Council may conclude "special agreements" with member states for the contribution of the latter's "armed forces . . . necessary for the purpose of maintaining international peace and security" (Article 43 [paragraph 1]); the Economic and Social Council has the right to enter into agreements with the various specialized agencies "defining the terms on which the agency concerned shall be brought into relationship with the United Nations" (Article 63 [paragraph 1]). But, the activities of the United Nations and its specialized agencies are strictly regulated by their member states and the scope of the right to conclude treaties is also extremely limited. They do not appear in the capacity of subjects of international law, possessing rights and bearing obligations independently; but rather in the capacity of the representative of all member states (genuine subjects of international law). This is because the treaties only create rights and obligations for member states. Certain immunities enjoyed by delegates of member states of the United Nations, by the United Nations Organization itself and by its officials in accordance with the Charter and other relevant international documents, are merely a guarantee for the successful fulfillment of the functions of the United Nations. Many international conferences among governments are held in various countries and the delegates attending the conferences enjoy immunity privileges, but this fact does not make these international conferences qualified subjects of international law. In view of this, although the United Nations Organization and its specialized agencies do enjoy certain rights belonging to subjects of international law, it does not necessarily follow that they are subjects of international law.

Note

K'ung Meng's views faithfully reflect the views of the majority of Soviet scholars of the 1950's. During the last decade, however, a considerable amount of ferment over the question of subjects of international law has developed among Soviet writers.

A 1964 Soviet textbook concedes that "the UN and certain other international organizations . . . have a special limited form of international personality distinguishable from that enjoyed by states." [36] Another Soviet author notes that, although the question is not yet settled, the legal personality of international organizations is widely recognized.[37] And the leading Soviet authority on international law, Professor G. I. Tunkin, has flatly repudiated the earlier view that international organizations cannot be subjects of international law.[38] This shift in the Soviet position has been attributed by one writer to "Soviet efforts to utilize the United Nations as an instrument of the policy and law of coexistence, and the increased recognition of the need for international organizations to cope with the growing interdependence of states." [39]

Although there has been no comparable change in the traditional Soviet position that neither physical nor juridical persons can be subjects of international law, at least one American scholar has detected signs that this position may also be weakening before the facts of international life and the needs of Soviet foreign policy.[40]

Soviet scholars have also been striving for new ways to develop the thesis, shared by the Chinese, that peoples struggling for national self-determination ought to be accorded international legal status. One recent text suggests that not merely colonial people but also the people of any state in which the organs of state power do not reflect the popular will may create their own organization of state power and attain international legal personality.[41] It should be noted that the PRC was the only state to grant prompt recognition to the Provisional Government of the Republic of Algeria established in 1958 by the National Liberation Front that was struggling to throw off French rule (recall 5–2).

The Relationship between International Law and Municipal Law

6

6-1

Ying T'ao, "Recognize the True Face of Bourgeois International Law from a Few Basic Concepts," *KCWTYC* no. 1:47–49 (1960).

In the writings of the bourgeoisie there are various theories concerning the relation between international law and municipal law. Considering only surface formalities, international law and municipal belong to two different categories. They differ in subjects of law, organs and procedures of legislation, and enforcement of sanctions. However, they both reflect the will of the ruling class and are used by that same ruling class to serve its external and internal policy, respectively. The class characters of the two are identical.

In the early stage of capitalism, the external and internal positions of the bourgeois regimes, particularly the revolutionary regime that followed the French Revolution, collectively and concretely reflected the needs of the bourgeois antifeudalism of that time. In order to destroy the internal and international legal systems of the feudal landlords and to establish its own legal system, the French revolutionary regime not only enacted, through its Assembly, a series of internal legislative acts, but also proclaimed a series of principles of international law. These principles were perfectly in accord with the interests of the newly emerged bourgeoisie. Later, the bourgeoisie gradually built up its own set of norms of international law through its numerous external practices, but the acceptance or rejection of these norms depended upon the self-interest of the bourgeoisie in various countries. For instance, Britain applies, as part of its municipal law, those norms of international law which are consistent with its interest. The United States adopts a flexible means: if the municipal law is in conflict with existing rules of international law, municipal law prevails; if a norm of international law is enacted upon United States sponsorship or with its participation and is in conflict with the existing municipal law, international law prevails and has the effect of amending that municipal law. Although with respect to reconciling municipal law and international law the means used by Britain and the United States are different, they both depend upon the interests of the respective countries. The principle followed by the United States is more consistent with the need of its ruling class in accordance with the development of the existing situation.

At the end of the nineteenth century, bourgeois jurists, represented by Triepel of Germany and Anzilotti of Italy, submitted the theory of dualism. For instance, Anzilotti considered that international law and municipal law deal with two separate, independent, and parallel legal relations. International law can neither in part nor as a whole be ipso facto a part of municipal law. On the other hand, municipal law had no authority to alter or create rules of international law. If municipal law adopts rules of international law, it should not be considered as bound by international law. If municipal law is in conflict with international law, the state concerned should still act in accordance with its municipal law. This theory, which severs any connection between international law and municipal law, serves to cover up the fact of their potential relation in that both laws represent the will of the ruling class. This theory is useful to the bourgeoisie, particularly to capitalist states such as Italy which were not powerful and thereby could not easily play a role in creating international law, by providing a legal basis for resisting international law which reflected the will of large capitalist powers. Thus such a theory aroused the objection of the monists, who represent the interests of large capitalist power. The monists stress that execution by a court of a country of municipal law which is in conflict with international law can only show the weakness of international law and international organization. Despite the fact that the decision of the court of a country is in conformity with its domestic law, that country should still assume the international responsibility arising from international law.

There was once a theory of "external state law" that prevailed in imperialist states such as Germany. According to that theory, municipal law should prevail over international law and, in case of conflict between the two, one should obey the provisions of municipal law. [Moreover, this theory says that] the only guarantee for implementing state sovereignty is force. This theory simply provides an absurd legal basis for imperialist states such as Germany to start wars of aggression. They can thereby encroach upon other states at will on the pretext of municipal law.

After the First World War and particularly after the Second World War, a number of bourgeois international law jurists and politicians made great efforts to propagandize the theory of the supremacy of international law over municipal law. They made a great effort to describe international law as above municipal law and as a special law which plays a decisive role in municipal law. For instance, the bourgeois international law jurist Kelsen wrote: "Since the validity of the respective municipal legal orders is based on the international legal order, and the latter at the same time also determines the scope of the validity of the respective municipal legal orders, international order should be placed above any kind of municipal legal order. . . . There is no question which cannot be solved only by international law, and not by municipal law."[42] Another Austrian bourgeois international law jurist, Verdross, put it more clearly by saying that international law is always, without exception, above those municipal laws which are in conflict with it. He further maintained that only within the scope delimited by international law can municipal law have freedom of development. Although their presentation is different, their central theme is the same, that is, to describe international law as above the municipal law of any country so as to use it or to have it directly regulate any domestic question. In other words, international law is not enacted or used by states, but, on the contrary, it controls states. Here, two questions arise: First, who enacts the international law which controls states and is alleged to be above municipal law? Second, on what basis is this kind of international law enacted? In other words, whose will and interest does this kind of international law reflect? To these questions there can scarcely be more than one answer; that is, the law maker in a capitalist society is the bourgeoisie, which controls the state apparatus, and the law it enacts reflects mainly the will of the bourgeoisie. Of course, the term "bourgeoisie" used here does not refer to the bourgeoisie of all countries, but only to the monopolistic bourgeoisie of big powers because only those members of the bourgeoisie occupy a strong international position and control many international organizations. Regardless of whether they are in the form of treaties and agreements which the bourgeoisie forces weak and small countries to accept, or resolutions and regulations which are adopted by the voting machine operated by the bourgeoisie, they all in practice reflect the will of the bourgeoisie and are in accord with its interest and need. Therefore, [the bourgeoisie] makes great efforts to impose so-called international law upon other countries by using the hypocritical pretext of the supremacy of international law over municipal law in order to achieve its objective of dominating and ruling the world.

In recent years people have often heard American imperialism talking preposterously about such things as a "world state" and a "world constitution" which, as a matter of fact, are only derivations of the theory of "supremacy of international law over municipal law." What they call a "world constitution" is the kind of international law which will reflect the will and interest of the American monopolistic bourgeoisie. After the validity of a "constitution" is conferred upon international law, the "world state" established in accordance with the American model can issue orders to various countries and dominate the whole world according to the "constitution." This is the substance of the so-called supremacy of international law over municipal law. American imperialism is currently engaged in all kinds of activities to promote the sale of this theory and conspiracy. For instance, in 1949, during the discussion of the "Draft Declaration of the Rights and Obligations of States" before the first session of the United Nations' International Law Commission, the United States instructed its servant state Panama to submit a draft which provides, *inter alia,* that "Every State has the duty to conduct its relations with other states in accordance with international law and with the principle that the sovereignty of each state is subject to the supremacy of international law." [43] This is but an attempt to legalize this theory.

In short, regardless of what the bourgeoisie says—supremacy of international law over municipal law, supremacy of municipal law over international law, monist theory or dualist theory—all these theories concretely reflect the will of the bourgeoisie, and their historical changes are solely determined by class interest.

Note

The relation of international law to municipal law is not only of basic theoretical importance, but it is also obviously of the greatest practical importance in the conduct of international activity. Yet Chinese writers rarely discuss this problem, and those who do, like Ying T'ao, almost exclusively confine themselves to criticisms of relevant Western theory and practice. These criticisms follow the arguments set forth in Soviet legal literature. But Soviet authors have, in addition, attempted to construct their own scientific explanations of the relationship between international and municipal law. By 1960, when Ying T'ao published the essay above, the following formulation had evolved in the Soviet Union:

> Such an explanation can be given only on the basis of a recognition of the indivisible link between international law and national (municipal) law and their equal significance. This conclusion is in line with Lenin's postulate regarding the close link between the foreign policy of a state and the domestic policy of the class dominant in it. Lenin also pointed out that the separation of home and foreign policy in order to mislead public opinion was characteristic of bourgeois politicians and theoreticians.

> Proceeding from one and the same supreme authority, both the rules of international law and those of domestic origin should have the same binding force for all organs and nationals of the countries concerned. By concluding an international agreement a governing authority undertakes, if necessary, to bring its domestic legislation into line with the international commitments it has assumed. On the other hand, by promulgating a law clearly contrary to international law, the government concerned commits a violation of international law, for which the state concerned is responsible under international law. . . .
>
> Therefore, international law and national law must not in their very nature either contradict each other or have primacy one over the other.[44]

Whether Chinese writers have consciously shied away from adopting this or other Soviet formulations and what reasons they might have for doing so are legitimate subjects for speculation. Perhaps the Soviet efforts are deemed too cryptic and inadequate to be worthy of acceptance. It is possible that there may be too much risk in venturing any positive view on so important and complex a question.

Accustomed to the unresolved controversies of scholars, international lawyers generally look to state practice on this question as well as others. For example, it is interesting to note that Japanese war criminals, being tried in 1956 before a military tribunal organized by the Supreme People's Court, confessed to having violated "international law and humanitarian principles." [45] The special military tribunal whose decision in another case was summarized in item 4–5 employed a similar formulation. Moreover, certain treaties, such as the 1955 Sino-Indonesian Dual Nationality Treaty, are included in the PRC's official compilation of laws and regulations.[46] And 1964 legislation regulating the travel and residence of aliens in China provides that "cases of violations . . . involving foreign nationals who enjoy diplomatic immunity shall be handled through diplomatic channels." [47] Furthermore, the reader will recall Chou Keng-sheng's assertion in the *People's Daily* [4–7] that "the use of discriminatory decrees by the Indian government to persecute law-abiding Chinese nationals is an act that violates international law. . . ." Other evidence of the PRC's actual position on the relation between international and municipal law will be found scattered throughout this study.

Inviolability of Sovereignty 7

7-1

Ying T'ao, "A Criticism of Bourgeois International Law Concerning the Question of State Sovereignty," *KCWTYC*, no. 3:47–49, 50–52 (1960).

Sovereignty is the supreme power of a state to decide independently its internal and foreign affairs in accordance with its own will. Once a state is deprived of its sovereignty, it loses the status of an independent state. In the course of cooperation and struggle in international relations, sovereignty is a question of paramount importance. Therefore, peoples of the various countries holding high the banner of "inviolability of sovereignty" and the oppressed nations of the world in the past and at present, have launched stubborn struggles against imperialism in defense of their countries' sovereignty. The five principles of peaceful coexistence, which collectively reflect the desire of the great majority of the peoples of the world with respect to principles of modern international law, provide that all countries should respect each other's sovereignty. But bourgeois international law, dictated by the needs of bourgeois interests, vacillates and contradicts itself, and nowadays even openly attempts to bury the principles of inviolability of sovereignty in order to meet the practices of imperialist aggression.

I

In the early stage of capitalism, bourgeois international law jurists introduced some ideas of progressive significance with respect to the question of sovereignty. They generally maintained that sovereignty is the "absolute and perpetual power of a state" and that such power is supreme within a state and is indivisible. They stressed not only "national independence" and "sovereign equality," but also "national sovereignty" and "people's sovereignty." Judging from its background at that time, the introduction of this principle was in perfect accord with the needs of bourgeois interests because at that time the bourgeoisie had only acquired political power in some countries and their rule had not yet been consolidated. They were constantly in danger of foreign attack and intervention in their internal affairs by feudal kingdoms. In international intercourse, these bourgeois countries were constantly being suppressed by feudal countries. Therefore, on the one hand, they described the sovereignty under their control as absolute and indivisible and resorted to "independence" and "equality" to resist the encroachment of feudal kingdoms. On the other hand, they used "national sovereignty" and "people's sovereignty" to mobilize and to rally the masses in their fight with the feudal system of "I am the state" and "sovereignty belongs to the monarch." It must be pointed out that bourgeois international law jurists in that period were by no means unanimous in their views concerning the theory of "indivisibility of sovereignty" and, in fact, debates among them were quite frequent. For instance, some advocated that sovereignty, although it is supreme within a country, is not an absolute power, while others maintained that sovereignty is divisible, saying that "all powers associated with sovereignty need not necessarily be concentrated in one person." According to the view of bourgeois international law jurists, the genesis of the theory of "divisibility of sovereignty" is attributable to facts which international law must recognize, such as the attainment of various degrees of independence by member states of feudal empires, the emergence of a distinction between full sovereign and not-full sovereign states and the transformation of the United States of America from a confederation to a federation and the [accompanying] division of sovereignty between the federation and the member states. Obviously, their view touched only upon the superficial phenomenon without touching upon the substance of the question. (For instance, although the United States is nominally a federation, it is still a state of single sovereignty. The so-called independence of the various member states is fictitious, and there is no question of the division of sovereignty between the federation and the various member states.) However, from this it can be seen that through recognition of these facts the bourgeoisie tried further to liquidate the power of feudal empires. Meanwhile, as a result of the law of the unbalanced development of capitalism, the inherent desire for foreign expansion on the part of the individual, advanced capitalist countries was deliberately reflected in international law by scholars of those countries. This is something that bourgeois international law has tried to conceal. In addition, because of their own interests, those relatively backward capitalist countries naturally could not agree to divide sovereignty. All this, therefore, led to an inevitable controversy in international law. This controversy, however, did not blur the basic character of bourgeois international law which embodies only the will of the bourgeoisie. On the contrary, it exposed the basic character of bourgeois international law even more.

II

The development of capitalism quickly put some countries on the road to expansion. Those countries carried out a policy of foreign aggression and used every method to weaken and destroy the sovereignty of other countries. The most commonly used methods were as follows:

(1) Exterminate countries, put them under colonial rule, and thus destroy their sovereignty nakedly and completely. We can find numerous instances of this in the history of imperialist aggression. Besides those countries which have regained their independence through struggle, many colonies in Asia, Africa, and other areas which are still under the control of Anglo-French imperialism were conquered in this manner.

(2) Coerce weak and small countries to become vassal states or protected states. On the surface, the title of a state is still retained, but all the powers derived from sovereignty are in fact under the control of imperialism. The sovereignty of a vassal or protected state nominally still exists, but in fact it is destroyed. The reason that imperialists resorted to this kind of trick was to reduce resistance so as to facilitate and to consolidate their control over the country. For instance, before the independence of India and Indonesia, there were many native states in India and many feudal dukedoms in Indonesia which were called vassal states and which were put under the colonial rule of England and Holland. During the period between the end of the Sino-Japanese War [1895] and Japan's formal annexation of Korea in 1910, Korea was called Japan's protectorate.

(3) Use armed aggression to separate a part of the existing territory of other countries and place it under the control of a puppet regime so as to conceal the imperialist countries' colonial rule. For instance, "Manchukuo," which was set up by Japan in our country's three northeastern provinces after the September 18 [Mukden] incident in 1931, is an example.

(4) Establish concessions on the territory of other countries and make the imperialist countries themselves the de facto rulers of the concessions, thereby weakening the sovereignty of the countries granting the concessions.

(5) Grab customs privileges and the privilege of consular jurisdiction from weak and small countries. The latter undermines the judicial power of the countries concerned, and the former deprives them of their customs autonomy—an important method with which they resist economic aggression. For instance, in the period from the middle of the eighteenth century to the end of the nineteenth century, England, America, France, and other imperialist countries acquired such privileges in many oriental countries such as Turkey, China, Korea, and Thailand by forcing them to conclude unequal treaties.

There are numerous other instances in which imperialist countries grabbed from weak and small countries the right to navigate on inland waters, open mines, establish factories, and so forth. Because of the aggressive policy of imperialism, the sovereignty of weak and small countries was in fact like meat on the chopping-board of imperialism. In order to meet this situation and the needs of the strong imperialist countries, bourgeois international law further developed the theory of divisibility of sovereignty and reaffirmed the concept of full sovereign states and not-full sovereign states. Vassal states, protected states, and other weak and small states from which imperialism had grabbed many privileges were labeled as not-full sovereign states; "they cannot be full, perfect, and normal subjects of International Law." [a] In the intercourse of the international community, they can only be dominated by full sovereign states, that is to say, large capitalist powers.

Around the period of the First World War, the debate on whether sovereignty is divisible gradually stopped, and the controversy shifted to the question of "how far sovereignty as it presents itself from the point of view of the internal law of the State, namely, as the highest, underived power and as the exclusive competence to determine its jurisdictional limits, is compatible with the normal functioning and development of International Law and organization." [b] That subject of discussion symbolized the following: First, the objective situation had undergone important changes. Capitalism had entered the imperialist stage and imperialism had been resorting more and more to the practice of damaging, restricting, or taking away the sovereignty of the various weak and small countries. Second, bourgeois international law jurists were trying to solve the problem of establishing a "higher legal order" in accordance with imperialism's wish that all countries in their exercise of sovereignty be bound by international law adopted by imperialism and that all countries be at the disposition of the international organizations manipulated by imperialism. From the foregoing, it can be seen that bourgeois international law is nothing but the concrete embodiment of the will of the strong capitalist powers and that bourgeois international law jurists are imperialism's perfect slaves and servants who search and fabricate legal bases for the acts of aggression by those powers. . . .

The history of imperialist aggression against old China is sufficient to illustrate this point. The large imperialist powers not only established spheres of influence in China in an attempt to carve her up, but they also proposed to carry out the "open door," "equal opportunities" and

[a] L. Oppenheim, *International Law,* Vol. 1, 7th ed., by H. Lauterpacht (London: Longmans, Green, 1948), p. 115. [Note: Oppenheim's "they" refers to "all states which are under the suzerainty or under the protectorate of another state, or are member-states of a so-called Federal state."]

[b] Oppenheim, I, 118–119.

"equal privileges" policies in China. They never thought of treating China in accordance with the concepts of "national equality" and "sovereign equality." It is evident that the principles they referred to are insulated and not applied to oppressed nations like China.

7-2

Yang Hsin and Ch'en Chien, "Expose and Criticize the Imperialists' Fallacy Concerning the Question of State Sovereignty," *CFYC*, no. 4:6–11 (1964).

According to the Marxist-Leninist theory of the state, the state is an organ of the ruling class and a tool with which one class oppresses another. There has never been a classless or supraclass state in the world. All states are dictatorships of a particular class. Bourgeois political scientists and jurists describe the state as an aggregate of territory, sovereignty, and population. They attempt to use the concept of sovereignty to replace the concept of class dictatorship. Such a theory completely distorts and conceals the class substance of the state and therefore is basically erroneous. However, this does not mean that in international relations we should deny state sovereignty and the principle of sovereignty or allow a state to infringe the sovereignty of another state. On the contrary, the principle of sovereignty is one of the most important principles in international relations and the whole system of international law. It is the core of all fundamental principles of international law. The principles of nonintervention in internal affairs, mutual nonaggression, equality and mutual benefit, and so forth, are all based on the principle of mutual respect for sovereignty. At the same time, the principle of sovereignty also has important links with other norms of international law. There are many important systems and principles of international law which are, in different degrees, related to the principle of mutual respect for sovereignty. For example, the principle of pacific settlement of disputes, the principle of *pacta sunt servanda*, the system of diplomatic privileges and immunities, and so forth, are all based on the premise of respect for each other's sovereignty and nonimpairment of each other's independence. Therefore, in many problems of international law the principle of sovereignty becomes a legal criterion for judging the legality or illegality of a given act. Because of the foregoing, the struggle revolving around the principle of sovereignty in international law is often very sharp and fierce. . . .

Our government has several times clearly expressed its attitude with respect to the question of sovereignty. On October 1, 1949, Chairman Mao Tse-tung declared in his "Proclamation on the Establishment of the Central People's Government of the People's Republic of China" that "this government is willing to establish diplomatic relations with any foreign government which is willing to observe the principles of equality, mutual benefit, and mutual respect for territorial integrity and sovereignty." [48] On April 19, 1955, Premier Chou En-lai also declared at the general meeting of the Afro-Asian Conference: "Countries, whether big or small, strong or weak, should all enjoy equal rights in international relations. Their territorial integrity and sovereignty should be respected and not violated. The people of all dependent countries should enjoy the right of national self-determination and should not be subjected to persecution and slaughter." [49] From these solemn statements, we discern that our government pays quite serious attention to the principle of sovereignty in international law. We consider that the principle of sovereignty in international law demands mutual respect for sovereignty. It requires that states respect the sovereignty of other states and vice versa. As pointed out by Premier Chou En-lai in his report to the Central People's Government's Council delivered on August 11, 1954, "China has no intention of infringing upon the sovereignty of other nations and will under no circumstances tolerate any infringement upon her own sovereignty by other nations." [50] Our country's interpretation of the principle of mutual respect for sovereignty is the only correct interpretation of the principle of sovereignty in modern international law. . . .

The principle of sovereignty is approved by the great majority of countries of the world. On some occasions, imperialist countries also render lip service to the principle of sovereignty, and, particularly when the concept of "sovereignty" can be used by them to protect their imperialist interests, they appear to be the "positive supporters" of the principle of sovereignty. As a matter of fact, imperialists, to whom plundering is a habit, inevitably carry out a policy of aggression and war and thereby infringe and impair the independence and sovereignty of other countries. We cannot imagine that imperialism would voluntarily observe the principle of mutual respect for sovereignty. In order to meet the needs of the imperialist countries' policies of aggression and war and to conceal the criminal acts of imperialism's destruction of the sovereignty of various countries, imperialist jurists fabricate various "theories" of sovereignty. In general, these theories may be divided into two schools: One school is the theory of absolute sovereignty, and another school is the theory of denial of sovereignty and the theory of restrictive sovereignty.

The advocates of the theory of absolute sovereignty consider that in accordance with its sovereignty a state may, without being subject to any restriction, do anything it wishes to other states. That is to say, a state may impair the sovereignty of another state in order to exercise its own sovereignty. Obviously, this suits the policy of unrestrained aggression and expansion of imperialism. Before the Second World War, although many jurists in imperialist countries gave lip service to "opposition" to absolute sovereignty, they nevertheless considered that it was within a state's "sovereignty" to engage in aggressive war. In their view, insofar as the relations between imperialist countries and weak and small countries are concerned, the "sovereignty" of imperialism to start aggressive war is absolute. That is to say, many jurists in fact advocate that imperialist countries enjoy absolute sovereignty.

The advocates of the theory of denial of sovereignty or the theory of restrictive sovereignty mainly proclaim that states should abandon or restrict sovereignty for the sake of "the general interests of mankind" or "consolidating international legal order." They declare that sovereignty is relative, divisible, and subject to restriction and abandonment, and that as a matter of fact no state has complete sovereignty. The purpose of this theory is to prove that colonial rule and imperialism's infringement on and restriction and elimination of other states' sovereignty are all lawful.

Quite obviously, the theories of absolute sovereignty, restrictive sovereignty and denial of sovereignty advocated by imperialist jurists are completely different from the principle of mutual respect for sovereignty which we advocate. Mutual respect for sovereignty absolutely does not mean that a state (regardless of how strong and large it is) may do whatever it wishes to other states on the pretext of exercising its sovereignty. Respect for sovereignty must be mutual: the principle that other states respect our sovereignty and we respect the sovereignty of other states. The exercise of sovereignty should be based upon the premise of not impairing the sovereignty of other states. . . .

This article will stress a discussion of the more concealed methods of destroying sovereignty adopted by American imperialism in order to deceive the people of the world while it pursues its policy of neocolonialism. We should not only expose those methods adopted by American imperialism to destroy sovereignty, but we must also expose and criticize the "theories" fabricated by its jurists in order to conceal this kind of criminal conduct. One common characteristic of these "theories" is their attempt to distort the concept of sovereignty and to abolish the principle of sovereignty in international law. It may be said that such an attack upon the principle of sovereignty has already become the main current and fashion in American legal circles.

The methods which those jurists in the service of American imperialism use to attack the principle of sovereignty are closely related to the fact that the United States has become the chief representative of neocolonialism.

Unlike colonialism, neocolonialism generally does not directly rule over colonies, but acts through agents set up by the colonialists to rule and exploit. In its pursuit of the policy of neocolonialism, American imperialism often restricts or takes away the sovereignty of other states through various legal forms in order to make them subordinate to the interests of American imperialism. On the one hand, it uses the colonial people's desire for sovereignty and independence and pretends to "approve national independence" and "respect the sovereignty of the various states" in order to facilitate its taking over the position of the former colonialists. At the same time, it adopts various legal camouflages which in fact deny the sovereignty of the various states in order to conceal neocolonial rule over countries which already have achieved independence and over nations which are struggling for independence. . . .

Among various "theories" of denial of sovereignty advocated by American imperialism, the theory most loudly shouted about is: under contemporary conditions, the most important element in state relations is "interdependence" and not independence. We should emphasize the so-called "collective interest," "the interest of international community" and "the common interest of all mankind," and we should not emphasize sovereignty. For example, in 1948 the American jurist, Jessup, wrote: "It may be suggested that it would be more conformable both to the realities and to the desiderata of the international community, if instead of emphasizing that each state is independent of each other, it were frankly asserted that each state is *dependent* on all other states, linked together in the society of nations or in a world government." [a] In 1954 another American jurist, Loewenstein, wrote in an article entitled "Sovereignty and International Cooperation": "The independence and equality of states have disappeared because, in this technological age with its vastly increased density of economic interpenetration and political interdependence, an individual state can exist in isolated sovereignty no more than an isolated individual can in society." [b]

Those persons like Dulles and Kennedy who acted as the chief political representatives of American monopoly capital naturally were not far behind others in proclaiming the theory of abolition of sovereignty. Dulles concluded: "Acceptance of interdependence among states has now replaced the principle of independence." He admonished states that they should not "put what they deem to be their own national rights and interests above the need of the whole society of nations," and he considered that to put national interests above the need of the international community is [to endorse] "concepts of sovereignty which have

[a] Philip C. Jessup, *A Modern Law of Nations* (New York: Macmillan, 1948), p. 37.

[b] Karl Loewenstein, "Sovereignty and International Co-operation," *AJIL* 48.2:223 (April 1954).

become obsolete."[c] Starting from the same standpoint, Kennedy also shouted that "the struggle for independence is coming to an end," and what we should do now is to make an "effort for interdependence." He even considered that the American Declaration of Independence had lost its significance and that we should sign a "Declaration of Interdependence" to replace it![d]

American imperialism's "theory of interdependence" and "theory that sovereignty is obsolete" are not only expressed in words. They are also implemented in its [America's] foreign policy and in its activities. This implementation is manifested particularly in the three areas discussed below.

The first type of manifestation of American imperialism's destruction of the principle of sovereignty is its [America's] control and subversion of, and its intervention in [the affairs of], other states on the pretext of "interdependence." First, it utilizes international organizations to carry out aggression against, and to intervene in [the affairs of], other states in the name of the "collective interest." It once used the United Nations to carry out aggression against the Congo and it uses the Organization of American States to intervene in the internal affairs of Latin American countries. At the 1954 Caracas meeting, the 1959 Santiago meeting, and the 1962 Punta del Este meeting, American imperialism manipulated the Organization of American States to pass a series of "resolutions" which were anti-Communist, and anti-Cuban and which ratified United States intervention in the internal affairs of Latin American countries, all on the pretext of "the common concern" of the so-called "American system."

Next, the military bloc treaties concluded between American imperialism and certain countries generally contain the so-called "mutual defense" provisions. These provisions in fact authorize the United States at any time, on the pretext of "collective self-defense," to send troops to occupy the territory of those countries, to intervene in their internal affairs and foreign relations, and to destroy their sovereignty.[e]

[c] John Foster Dulles, "Challenge and Response in United States Policy," *Foreign Affairs,* 36.1:41, 42 (Oct. 1957). [Note: The original source indicates that the passage "acceptance of interdependence among states has now replaced the principle of independence" is quoted from the above article written by Dulles. However, we are unable to locate the passage in Dulles' article. Dulles did write that "We are . . . unsympathetic to assertions of sovereignty which do not accept the concept of social interdependence" (p. 42).]

[d] [President John F. Kennedy,] "The Goal of an Atlantic Partnership," *Department of State Bulletin,* 47.1203:132 (July 23, 1962).

[e] For example, Article 6 of the 1947 Rio de Janeiro Treaty, Article 25 of the 1948 Charter of the Organization of American States, Article 5 of the 1949 North Atlantic Treaty, Article 1 of the 1951 Japanese-American Security Treaty, and Article 4 of the 1954 Southeast Asia Collective Defense Treaty.

Some of the treaties even openly provide that the application of the United States' privilege of aggression may be extended to noncontracting parties (for instance, Article 4 of the Southeast Asia Collective Defense Treaty). . . .

Another means used by American imperialism to destroy the sovereignty of other states in the name of "interdependence" is "American aid." The so-called "assistance agreements" (for example, the 1948 Convention on European Economic Cooperation) concluded between the United States and certain other countries all generally include provisions for facilitating the entry of American personnel and commodities and for facilitating American supervision and control over the economy and finance of the countries concerned. American laws relating to foreign "assistance" (for instance, the 1949 Mutual Defense Assistance Act, the 1950 International Development Act, the 1951 Mutual Security Act and the Battle Act [the 1951 Mutual Defense Assistance Control Act]), have many restrictions on the sovereignty of "recipient" countries in internal and foreign affairs. For example, the 1951 Battle Act provides that "recipient" countries should not engage in trade with socialist countries. Such treaties obviously violate the principle of sovereignty. Even in an article propagandizing "international cooperation," the American jurist, Loewenstein, had to acknowledge that "one of the effects of international cooperation under the Marshall Plan was that the individual participating states were subjected to controls of their national economic life by both the Economic Cooperation Organization and the United States government to an extent which the traditional concept of national sovereignty would have considered as intervention in domestic and foreign affairs incompatible with the nature of the sovereign state," and this kind of international cooperation "may become instrumental in . . . ultimate self-denial, elimination and destruction [of state sovereignty]." [f]

The second type of manifestation of American imperialism's destruction of the principle of sovereignty is its promoting the idea of the so-called "Transnational Law," in order to use that law to replace international law, which is founded upon the principle of sovereignty and to which sovereign states are subjects. According to the view of the chief propagandist of "Transnational Law," Jessup of the United States, it is no longer possible to distinguish questions of international law and municipal law because the "actions or events that transcend national boundaries" are growing daily and becoming more complex. The concept of the law adjusting relations among states as expressed by the term "international law" can no longer meet the needs of the legal rela-

[f] Loewenstein, p. 238.

tions of the community of mankind. The community of mankind must frequently, through various international and regional organs, directly confer rights on individuals and impose obligations upon them. It must, within the scope of the entire community of mankind, make legal adjustments involving economic, social, technological, and other fields.[g]

The political intention of this theory is very clear. The replacement of international law by "Transnational Law" implies the devaluation of the significance of state sovereignty. The whole world will be directly controlled by a "Transnational Law" which will in fact be subject to any interpretation by imperialism. "Transnational Law" is a tool of imperialism for legal infiltration of other countries, and legal infiltration serves imperialism's economic infiltration of other countries and its political intervention [in their affairs].

We must pay attention to the fact that in recent years jurists of imperialist countries, particularly American jurists, have expressed special interest in the legal problems of foreign investment and commerce. In the United States, many books have been published about laws relating to entry into and exit from various countries, the position of aliens, taxation, investment, trademarks, patents, foreign exchange, and nationalization, as well as other legal books referring to foreign investment of monopolistic capital. The book "International Transactions and Relations: Cases and Materials," edited by Katz and Brewster and published in the United States in 1960, is a typical example. The whole object of the book is to instruct American monopolistic capital in how to use law to engage in economic infiltration of foreign countries, how to avoid taxation and foreign exchange [regulations] of the host countries, how to deal with nationalization by the host countries, and so forth.

These are problems which those jurists in the service of American imperialism believe should be solved by international law and "Transnational Law."

At the same time, we may also note that in imperialist countries the study of comparative law has recently received widespread attention. The jurists in these countries attempt to promote the unification of the laws of various countries through the study of comparative law. The unification of laws has become the main topic of discussion in many imperialist-controlled international conferences of legal science. In the view of the jurists of imperialist countries, the unification of laws is an important step toward "Transnational Law." [h]

With respect to this, we must mention the "Conference on World

[g] See Philip C. Jessup, *Transnational Law* (New Haven: Yale University Press, 1956).

[h] See Eric Stein, "Assimilation of National Laws as a Function of European Integration," *AJIL* 58.1:1–40 (Jan. 1964).

Peace through Law" sponsored by the American Bar Association and held last June and July in Athens, Greece. The study programs adopted by this Conference include "promotion and protection of foreign investments," "development of international trade and economic relations," "international protection of industrial property" and other such items. The declarations and other documents adopted by the Conference advocate that states, individuals, and corporations should be *equally* subject to legal jurisdiction; they must perform all legal obligations and should be subject to compulsory enforcement by the international community. The Conference recommended that organs and procedures for settling international investment disputes be established and that a multilateral convention among states prescribing the rights of foreign investment be concluded. It demanded the abolition of double taxation and "discriminatory" laws relating to investors, and [called for] "prompt, adequate, and effective compensation" for nationalized foreign properties. It recommended that "a model international investment code" and international codes relating to the protection of industrial properties be concluded, and so forth.[1] The contents of the Athens Conference clearly point out the trend of American imperialism's legal circles and the legal means they adopt to protect imperialist interests.

Quite clearly, the theory of "Transnational Law" submitted by jurists of imperialist countries intends to play with legal technicalities to achieve the object of abolishing and restricting state sovereignty. This is an extremely tricky way for imperialism to destroy the principle of sovereignty.

Note

Using Soviet materials, many Chinese scholars have devoted a good deal of attention to analyzing bourgeois manipulation of the murky concept of "sovereignty." Nevertheless, we lack a detailed exegesis of the PRC's own position on the relation of sovereignty to international law. Yet the record amply demonstrates the PRC's understandable sensitivity to past and present incursions upon China's unfettered exercise of those prerogatives that are normally associated with the government of an independent state. Like their Soviet counterparts, the Chinese leaders have frequently invoked sovereignty as a defensive weapon to protect against interference in domestic affairs and to oppose the development of non-Communist international organizations that have supranational authority.[51] Moreover, some Chinese writing, like some Soviet writing, suggests that a state's sovereignty is not subject to the

[1] See Charles S. Rhyne, "The Athens Conference on World Peace through Law," *AJIL* 58.1:138 (Jan. 1964).

supremacy of international law. Recall, for example, Ying T'ao's discussion of the relation of international law to municipal law (6–1). But a number of Soviet and Chinese scholars recognize the untenability of such a position. In the preceding essay (7–2) Yang and Ch'en do not assert that sovereignty signifies the exercise of government power unlimited by any external standard. And it will be recalled that Chou Keng-sheng's article in the *People's Daily* (4–7) argued that India, by characterizing its anti-Chinese legislation as an act of sovereignty, could not justify impairing the PRC's exercise of its sovereign right to protect its nationals abroad; "no one can deny this minimum standard of international law." This illustrates what Yang and Ch'en mean when they write that a state may do whatever it wishes in accord with its sovereignty so long as it respects and does not impair the sovereignty of other states.

The fact that the realities of international life have caused the Chinese to recognize that sovereignty does not license the state to violate the generally accepted principles of international law, although encouraging, is not in itself of great significance. The question remains: in the Chinese view, what is the content of international law to which sovereignty is properly subject? This leads us to renew our quest for further examples of the concrete meaning that the PRC attaches to concepts such as "mutual respect for sovereignty." For examples of Chinese attacks upon Soviet efforts to rationalize the USSR's invasion of Czechoslovakia's sovereignty, see 8–12 and 42–13.[52] For discussion of the relation of sovereignty to suzerainty, see 12–21.

Peaceful Coexistence and Socialist Internationalism

8

The PRC announced that it favored "peaceful coexistence with neighboring countries" as early as 1951 (see 12–20). Indeed, the Chinese government has claimed that "it was China which initiated the Five Principles of Peaceful Coexistence." [53] Yet, as we pointed out in the note following Item 1–1, it was not until 1954, after it had gradually deemphasized its early policy of promoting armed struggle against non-Communist regimes, that Peking began to elaborate that concept. This chapter traces the evolution of Chinese views of peaceful coexistence and its sibling, socialist internationalism.

8-1

"Agreement between the Republic of India and People's Republic of China on Trade and Intercourse between Tibet Region of China and India, April 29, 1954," *TYC 1954*, III (1958), 1; English text in *UNTS* 299:59 (1958).

The government of the Republic of India and the Central People's Government of the People's Republic of China,

Being desirous of promoting trade and cultural intercourse between the Tibet Region of China and India and of facilitating pilgrimage and travel by the peoples of China and India,

Have resolved to enter into the present Agreement based on the following principles:

(1) Mutual respect for each other's territorial integrity and sovereignty,
(2) Mutual nonaggression,
(3) Mutual noninterference in each other's internal affairs,
(4) Equality and mutual benefit, and
(5) Peaceful coexistence.

8-2

"Joint Statement by Chou En-lai and Nehru Issued," NCNA—English, New Delhi (June 28, 1954), in *SCMP*, no. 838:5–6 (June 29, 1954).

Recently India and China have come to an agreement in which they laid down certain principles which should guide relations between the two countries. These principles are: (1) mutual respect for each other's territorial integrity and sovereignty, (2) nonaggression, (3) noninterference in each other's internal affairs, (4) equality and mutual benefit and (5) peaceful coexistence. The Prime Ministers reaffirmed these principles and felt that they should be applied in their relations with other countries in Asia as well as [with] other parts of the world. If these principles [were] applied not only between various countries, but also in international relations generally, they would form a solid foundation for peace and security, and the fears and apprehensions that exist today would give place to a feeling of confidence.

The Prime Ministers recognized that different social and political systems exist in various parts of Asia and the world. If, however, the above-mentioned principles are accepted and acted upon and there is no interference by any one country with another, these differences should not [interfere with] peace or create conflicts. With assurances of the territorial integrity and sovereignty of each country and of nonaggression, there would be peaceful coexistence and friendly relations between the countries concerned. This would lessen the tensions that exist in the world today and help in creating a climate of peace.

8-3

"Text of Premier Chou En-lai's Supplementary Speech at Asian-African Conference," NCNA—English, Bandung (Apr. 19, 1955), in *SCMP*, no. 1031:6–7 (Apr. 21, 1955).

The Chinese delegation has come here to seek unity and not to quarrel. We Communists do not hide the fact that we believe in Communism and that we consider the socialist system a good system. There is no need at this Conference to publicize one's ideology and the political system of one's country, although differences do exist among us.

The Chinese delegation has come here to seek common ground, and not to create divergence. Is there any basis for seeking common ground among us? Yes, there is. The overwhelming majority of the

Asian and African countries and peoples have suffered and are still suffering from the calamities of colonialism. This is acknowledged by all of us. If we seek common ground in doing away with the sufferings and calamities under colonialism, it will be very easy for us to have mutual understanding and respect, mutual sympathy and support, instead of suspicion and fear, mutual exclusion and antagonism. . . .

In our Conference we should seek common ground among us, while keeping our differences. As to our common ground, the Conference should affirm all our common desires and demands. This is our main task here. As to our differences, none of us is asked to give up his own views, because difference in viewpoints is an objective reality. But we should not let our differences hinder us from achieving agreement as far as our main task is concerned. On the basis of our common points, we should try to understand and appreciate the different views that we hold.

Now, first of all, I would like to talk about the question of different ideologies and social systems. We have to admit that, among our Asian and African countries, we do have different ideologies and different social systems. But this does not prevent us from seeking common ground and being united. Many independent countries have appeared since the Second World War. One group of them [is made up of] countries led by the Communist Parties; another group of them are countries led by nationalists. There are not many countries in the first group. But what some people dislike is the fact that the 600 million Chinese people have chosen a political system which is socialist in nature and led by the Chinese Communist Party and that the Chinese people are no longer under the rule of imperialists. The countries in the second group are greater in number, such as India, Burma, Indonesia, and many other countries in Asia and Africa. [Having ended colonial rule, both of these groups of countries have become independent] and are still continuing their struggle for complete independence. Is there any reason why we cannot understand and respect each other and give support and sympathy to each other? There is every reason to make the five principles the basis for establishing friendly cooperation and good neighborly relations among us. We Asian and African countries, with China included, are all backward economically and culturally. [If] our Asian-African Conference does not exclude anybody, why couldn't we understand each other and enter into friendly cooperation?

Secondly, I would like to talk about the question as to whether there is freedom of religious belief. Freedom of religious belief is a principle recognized by all modern nations. We Communists are atheists, but we respect all those who have religious belief. We hope that those [who have] religious belief will also respect those without. China is a country where there is freedom of religious belief. There are in China, not only seven million Communists, but also tens of millions of Islamists and Buddhists and millions of Christians and Catholics. Here in the Chinese delegation there is a pious [Imam] of the Islamic faith. Such a situation is no obstacle to the internal unity of China. Why should it be impossible in the community of Asian and African countries to unite those with religious belief and those without? The days of instigating religious strife should have passed because those who profit from instigating such strife are not those among us.

Thirdly, I would like to talk about the question of the so-called subversive activities. The struggle of the Chinese people against colonialism lasted for more than a hundred years. The national and democratic revolutionary struggles led by the Chinese Communist Party finally achieved success only after a strenuous and difficult course of thirty years. It is impossible to relate all the sufferings of the Chinese people under the rule of imperialism, feudalism, and Chiang Kai-shek. At last, the Chinese people have chosen their state system and the present government. It is by the efforts of the Chinese people that the Chinese revolution has won its victory. It is certainly not imported from without. This point cannot be denied even by those who do not like the victory of the Chinese revolution. As a Chinese proverb says: "Do not do unto others what you yourself do not desire." We are against outside interference; how could we want to interfere in the internal affairs of others? Some people say: There are more than ten million overseas Chinese whose dual nationality might be taken advantage of to carry out subversive activities. But the problem of dual nationality is something left behind by old China. To date, Chiang Kai-shek is still using [a] few overseas Chinese to carry out subversive activities against [those countries] where the overseas Chinese are residing. The People's Government of new China, however, is ready to solve the problem of dual nationality of overseas Chinese with the governments of countries concerned. Some other people say that the autonomous region of Thai people in China is a threat to others. There are in China more than forty million national minorities of scores of nationalities. The Thai people and the Chuang people, who are of the same stock as the Thai people, number more than ten million. Since they do exist, we must grant them the right of autonomy, just as there is an autonomous state for Shan people in Burma [. In China every national minority] has its autonomous region. The national minorities in China exercise their right of autonomy within China; how could that be said to be a threat to our neighbors?

On the basis of strict adherence to the five principles, [we are now] prepared to establish normal relations with all Asian and African countries, with all the countries in the world, and, first of all, with our neighboring countries. The problem at present is not that we are carrying out subversive activities against the governments of other countries, but that there are people who are establishing bases around China in order to carry out subversive activities against the Chinese government. For instance, on the border between China and Burma, there are in fact remnant armed elements of the Chiang Kai-shek clique who are carrying out destructive activities against both China and Burma. Because of the friendly relations between China and Burma, and because we have always respected the sovereignty of Burma, we have confidence in the government of Burma for the solution of this problem.

8-4

"Joint Communique of Bandung Conference," NCNA—English, Bandung (April 24, 1955), in *SCMP*, no. 1033:11, 16–17 (April 24, 1955).

The Asian-African Conference, convened upon the invitation of the Prime Ministers of Burma, Ceylon, India, Indonesia, and Pakistan, met in Bandung from the 18th to the 24th April, 1955. In addition to the sponsoring countries . . . 24 countries participated in the Conference. . . .

The Asian-African Conference considered [problems] of common interest and concern to countries of Asia and Africa and discussed ways and means by which their people could achieve fuller economic, cultural and political cooperation. . . .

The Asian-African Conference gave anxious thought to the question of world peace and cooperation. It viewed with deep concern the present state of international tension with its danger of an atomic world war. The problem of peace is correlative with the problem of international security. In this connection, all states should cooperate, especially through the United Nations, in bringing about the reduction of armaments and the elimination of nuclear weapons under effective international control. In this way, international peace can be promoted and nuclear energy may be used exclusively for peaceful purposes. This would help answer the needs particularly of Asia and Africa, for what they urgently require are social progress and better standards of life in larger freedom.

Freedom and peace are interdependent. The right of self-determination must be enjoyed by all peoples, and freedom and independence must be granted, with the least possible delay, to those who are still dependent peoples. Indeed, all nations should have the right freely to choose their own political and economic systems and their own way of life, in conformity with the purposes and principles of the Charter of the United Nations.

Free from mistrust and fear, and with confidence and goodwill toward each other, nations should practice tolerance and live together in peace with one another as good neighbors and develop friendly cooperation on the basis of the following principles:

1. Respect for fundamental human rights and for the purposes and principles of the Charter of the United Nations.
2. Respect for the sovereignty and territorial integrity of all nations.
3. Recognition of the equality of all races and of the equality of all nations large and small.
4. Abstention from intervention or interference in the internal affairs of another country.
5. Respect for the right of each nation to defend itself singly or collectively, in conformity with the Charter of the United Nations.
6. (a) Abstention from the use of arrangements of collective defense to serve the particular interests of any of the big powers.

   (b) Abstention by any country from exerting pressures on other countries.
7. Refraining from acts or threats of aggression or the use of force against the territorial integrity or political independence of any country.
8. Settlement of all international disputes by peaceful means, such as negotiation, conciliation, arbitration, or judicial settlement, as well as other peaceful means of the parties' own choice, in conformity with the Charter of the United Nations.
9. Promotion of mutual interests and cooperation.
10. Respect for justice and international obligations.

The Asian and African Conference declared its conviction that friendly cooperation in accordance with these principles would effectively contribute to the maintenance and promotion of international peace and security, while cooperation in the economic, social, and cultural fields would help bring about the common prosperity and well-being of all.

The Asian-African Conference recommended that the five sponsoring countries consider the convening of the next meeting of the Conference, in consultation with the participating countries.

8-5

"Treaty of Friendship between the People's Republic of China and the Republic of Ghana, August 18, 1961," *TYC 1961*, X (1962), 17; English text in Chung-hua jen-min kung-ho-kuo wai-chiao-pu pien, *Chung-hua jen-min kung-ho-kuo yu-hao t'iao-yüeh hui-pien* (Collection of friendship treaties concluded by the People's Republic of China; Peking, 1965), 63.

Article II

The Contracting Parties decide to take the Five Principles of mutual respect for sovereignty and territorial integrity, mutual nonaggression, noninterference in each other's internal affairs, equality and mutual benefit, and peaceful coexistence and the Ten Principles laid down at the Asian-African Conference held in Bandung in 1955 as the principles guiding the relations between the two countries.

The Contracting Parties will settle all disputes between them by means of peaceful negotiation.

Article III

The Contracting Parties agree to develop the economic and cultural relations between the two countries in the spirit of equality, mutual benefit, and friendly cooperation.

NOTE

During the period from early 1960 to early 1965 the PRC concluded friendship treaties with Burma, Nepal, Afghanistan, Cambodia, Indonesia, Yemen, Guinea, Ghana, Congo (Brazzaville), Mali, and Tanzania. As in the case of Ghana above, many of these treaties explicitly incorporated the five principles of peaceful coexistence. The texts of all the other treaties referred to at least some of these principles.

During this same period, friendship treaties were also concluded with Mongolia (1960) and North Korea (1961). While these, like earlier friendship treaties with the Soviet Union, East Germany, Czechoslovakia, and Hungary, made reference to one or more of the "five principles," none of the treaties concluded with Communist bloc states included all of the principles or invoked the talismanic phrase "peaceful coexistence."

Four of the eleven friendship treaties concluded with "Third World" states also referred to the ten Bandung principles or their spirit, while none of the Communist bloc treaties contain this reference.

Interestingly, only one of the eleven treaties with Third World states—that with Afghanistan—invoked the UN Charter. Although the four Soviet bloc treaties that were concluded prior to 1960 all invoked the UN Charter, the Mongolian and North Korean treaties did not.

8-6

Chou Keng-sheng, "The Principle of Peaceful Coexistence from the Viewpoint of International Law," *CFYC*, no. 6:38–41 (1955).

As a legal question, the five principles of peaceful coexistence must be considered to be fully consistent with principles of international law and with the development of modern international law. First, the principle of peaceful coexistence should itself be considered as the basic condition of the maintenance and development of modern international relations. This principle is also the premise of the development of modern international law. International law is the set of norms governing relations among states. From the viewpoint of modern international law, the only normal situation in international relations is when peace prevails. Early in 1928, many countries of the world signed the Paris Pact for the Renunciation of War, agreeing not to resort to war as an instrument of national policy or as a method for settling international disputes. The whole spirit of the purpose and principles of the United Nations Charter is to eliminate international war.[a] Therefore, the international relations regulated by modern international law in general are the relations of peace. In modern international law, the law of war has lost the important position and significance it held in traditional international law; the scope of its application has been greatly reduced.[b] On

[a] The Charter of the United Nations first indicates in its preamble the principle of "peaceful coexistence." Then, in Article 1, it also indicates the purpose of "maintain[ing] international peace and security." The article further provides that the United Nations is "to take effective collective measures for the prevention and the removal of threats to the peace, and for the suppression of acts of aggression or other breaches of the peace, and to bring about by peaceful means, and in conformity with the principles of justice and international law, adjustment or settlement of international disputes or situations which might lead to a breach of the peace."

[b] With respect to relations between countries in the democratic socialist camp, Professor Kozhevnikov has stated that all the norms directly belonging to the so-called "law of war" have been completely excluded from the system of socialist international law relations. See his "Looking at Certain Problems of International Law from Stalin's 'Marxism and the Question of the Science of Linguistics,'" translated in *Kuo-chi kung-fa lun-wen chi* (Collected Essays on Public International Law), published by China People's University.

the other hand, together with the development of peaceful relations, including political, economic, and cultural relations, there is a corresponding development in that part of international law which regulates or adjusts this type of international relations. Needless to say, the situation of peaceful coexistence is most favorable to the development of this type of international relations, and thus greatly facilitates the development of modern international law.

It must be pointed out that the principle of peaceful coexistence should be accepted not only in speeches and in literature, but must also be realized in practice. There must be a way for peaceful coexistence to be practiced between countries with different systems. If a type of environment or atmosphere is created in international relations in which some countries are constantly threatened or are treated with hostility by other countries, this obviously is not the way to achieve peaceful coexistence. For instance, the American imperialists' slogans and practices of "preventive war," "cold war," "deterrent policy," "atomic war," policy of "position of strength," "embargo," proclivity for establishing military bases, organizing hostile military groups and other activities for creating tense international situations, and so forth, all contribute to the creation of the above-stated environment and atmosphere and thus completely deny or obstruct the achievement of peaceful coexistence. In order to realize peaceful coexistence, it is necessary to eliminate or change any environment or atmosphere which is unfavorable to peaceful coexistence. The policy of peace, supported by the democratic socialist camp headed by the Soviet Union, constitutes an effort in this direction, especially its advocacy of the solution of international problems through international conferences or the method of pacific negotiations, replacement of hostile military groups by collective security organization, general disarmament and prohibition of atomic weapons, reductions of tense international situations, abolition of foreign military bases, conclusion of peace treaties among big powers, the promulgation by each country of the "law of safeguarding peace" and the prohibition of war propaganda. . . .

To realize peaceful coexistence, it is also necessary to have the spirit and attitude of trying to achieve agreement despite differing opinions, as explained by Premier Chou En-lai at the Bandung Conference. There do exist different ideologies and social systems among the various countries of the world, but this fact does not prevent peaceful coexistence among countries. The most important thing is that everyone must try to establish the foundation of coexistence from the common desire to achieve a peace based upon the spirit of trying to achieve agreement despite differing opinions. The success of the Asian-African Conference proves the important function of this spirit in international relations. On the contrary, the American imperialists' insistence on the spirit of disagreement, their continued emphasis on the exclusive character of different social systems, and President Eisenhower's statement at the Geneva Four-Power Heads of Government Conference that the United States will question the political status of the East European people's democracies, are all calculated to block the path to peaceful coexistence.

The other four principles provided in the Joint Statement of the Premiers of China and India, "mutual respect for territorial sovereignty," "mutual nonaggression," "mutual nonintervention in internal affairs," and "equality and mutual benefit" have always been important principles of international law, and are obligations which states should undertake in international society. They are guiding principles of international relations, and represent the essential conditions for realizing the fundamental principle of peaceful coexistence. Obviously, if these conditions are not observed, genuine peaceful coexistence among states is impossible.[c] Speaking first of the principle of "mutual respect for territorial sovereignty," the term "territorial sovereignty" in fact consists of the two concepts of "sovereignty" and "territorial integrity." These concepts are interrelated, but, by explaining them separately, their meaning will be clearer. Since the birth of modern international law, "state sovereignty," viewed either as the supreme "authority" or as the "situation" of independence, has always been a fundamental concept of international law. The principle of sovereignty is the most important principle of international law, and it is also the legal protection of all countries' survival, independence, and development. . . . The inviolability of territorial integrity is a concrete aspect of respect for state sovereignty, and this principle, according to the express provision of the Charter of the United Nations (Article 2, paragraph 4), has acquired the confirmation of the vast majority of countries of the world. Needless to say, this is also an essential condition for realizing peaceful coexistence. Of course, it frequently happens that through the method of peaceful negotiation, countries for certain reasons do make exchanges of territory or adjustment of frontiers. . . . But such acts do not violate the principle of territorial integrity. Moreover, the independence or liberation of colonies or dependent territories cannot be obstructed or prohibited on the pretext of territorial integrity. But, if any country

[c] The resolution [on the Conditions of a True Peaceful Coexistence among Nations] adopted by the 44th Inter-Parliamentary Conference held in [Helsinki, 25–31] August, 1955, also provides that "the maintenance of peaceful coexistence and the gradual establishment of confident collaboration between the nations require the loyal observance by all governments of the rules of international law and especially of the following principles: (a) mutual respect for the territorial integrity, safety, and equality of each country . . . ; (b) the renunciation of all interference in internal affairs of other countries; (c) nonaggression. . . ." Union Inter-parlementaire, *Compte Rendu de la XLIV Conférence Interparlementaire* (Genève: Le Bureau Interparlementaire, 1956), p. 1130.

openly uses force or the threat of force to invade the territory of another or to obstruct the recovery or unification of another country's territory, or uses other means to promote the division of another country's territory, or refuses to withdraw from territory originally an integral part of another country, this is a violation of the other country's territorial integrity and is inconsistent with the principle of peaceful coexistence. At present [1955], due to obstruction or occupation by a foreign country, China's Taiwan, India's Goa, and Indonesia's West Irian have not yet been liberated. These are obvious examples of violations of territorial integrity. The maintenance of this situation is a factor in the continued tension in the international situation and thus is an obstruction to peaceful coexistence.

Mutual nonaggression is an absolutely essential condition of peaceful coexistence, and it is also an obligation imposed upon states by international law. In order to achieve genuine respect for state sovereignty and territorial integrity, there must be mutual nonaggression. Aggression itself is an act of international banditry and completely destroys the international legal order. In 1928 the Pact of Paris solemnly denounced aggressive war; the purposes and principles of the Charter of the United Nations, especially Article 39, also focus on the suppression of aggression. Before the Second World War, many recommendations and resolutions had already been adopted, such as the 1928 resolution of the Pan-American Conference which declared aggressive war an "international crime." [d] The principle applied by the Nuremberg and Tokyo International Military Tribunals is the same. The principle that a country engaged in aggressive war can no longer exercise its belligerent rights in international law was confirmed by the so-called "Budapest Articles of Interpretation." [e] The United Nations Charter not only affirms the illegality of aggression, but also provides procedures for measures of sanction against aggression (Chapter VII of the United Nations Charter). However, the United Nations Charter does not define aggression; so, in cases of a concrete incident and under special circumstances, a dispute may arise as to the definition of aggression. Thus, an unjust decision may be reached. As a matter of fact, when the Charter was drafted in 1945 at the San Francisco Conference, the

[d] The 1923 Draft Treaty of Mutual Assistance and unratified 1924 Geneva Protocol both declare that aggressive war is an "international crime."

[e] The so-called "Budapest Articles of Interpretation" was an interpretation, consisting of seven articles, relating to the effects of the Pact of Paris. It was adopted in 1934 by the International Law Association during its conference in Budapest. *AJIL* 33:825–826 (1939). The Draft Convention on Rights and Duties in Cases of Aggression, contained in *Harvard Research in International Law*, represents the view of the bourgeois public law jurists and is basically the same as the Budapest Articles. It affirms that an aggressor cannot assert belligerent rights in international law. See *AJIL*, Supp. 33:827–830 (1939).

reason for not defining aggression was due to the consistent opposition of the United States. However, its reasons for opposing the definition of aggression cannot be accepted even by British and American bourgeois international law jurists [f]. . . .

In August, 1953, the Soviet Union proposed that the United Nations make a full consideration of the contents of aggression as further development of the definition of aggression. However, due to the consistent opposition of the United States, the United Nations has not yet made any decision on the question of the definition of aggression. In order to realize the principle of mutual nonaggression and to guarantee that the United Nations exercise impartially and effectively its function of maintaining peace and security, we must continue our effort to carry out the task of defining aggression.

Mutual nonintervention in internal affairs is demanded by the principle of sovereignty. Intervening in the internal affairs of another country represents disrespect for the other country's sovereignty. International law in general prohibits intervention in another country's affairs. The principle of nonintervention is a traditional principle of international law. The principles of the United Nations Charter also prohibit intervention in the internal affairs of other countries (Article 2, paragraph 7, of the Charter). As a matter of fact, if countries intervene in each other's internal affairs, peaceful coexistence becomes impossible. The history of international relations is not lacking in incidents of intervention in the internal affairs of other countries . . . which are inconsistent with the principle or desire for peaceful coexistence. Taking a recent incident for discussion, the liberation of Taiwan is an internal question of China. If a foreign country tries to use any means to intervene in or obstruct the liberation, it is an intervention in China's internal affairs, and thus violates international law and also the principle of peaceful coexistence. However, it must be noted that we cannot take a formal mechanical view of the question of "intervention" or "nonintervention." Sometimes, the imperialists use the good slogan of "nonintervention" to connive at aggression which in fact constitutes indirect intervention. The most notorious example is the Spanish Civil War in 1936. Britain, France, and other countries proposed the so-called "nonintervention agreement" and "nonintervention committee" and so caused the Spanish Republican government finally to be overthrown by the Fascist faction. Moreover, as pointed out by Stalin, there are various forms of imperialist intervention—armed, financial and economic, and even the dispatch of

[f] Oppenheim, *International Law,* 6th ed. (Lauterpacht, 1944), II, 156. Oppenheim, 7th ed., Vol. II (Lauterpacht, 1952), pp. 189–190; L. M. Goodrich and E. Hambro, *Charter of the United Nations,* 2nd ed. (Boston: World Peace Foundation, 1949), pp. 104, 207, 263–264.

spies, terrorists, and subversive persons as well as detective activities through commercial organizations.[g] In recent years, the United States has carried out the so-called "Mutual Security Act" and has appropriated a large amount of money for subversive activities in foreign countries, especially in the people's democracies. Such activities are the most exposed and notorious form of intervention in internal affairs. To realize the principle of peaceful coexistence, we must eliminate all these direct or indirect, open or camouflaged acts of intervention in the internal affairs of other countries. On the other hand, the Western imperialists have, on the pretext [that they constitute] internal questions, failed to submit for discussions at the UN those questions of racial conflict and national self-determination which obviously possess international importance. (Examples are France's attitude toward the question of Algeria and the Union of South Africa's attitude toward the question of the treatment of Indians.) Such acts obviously distort the purposes and principles of the Charter of the United Nations.

Finally, equality and mutual benefit are also important conditions for promoting peaceful coexistence. Equality of states is a traditional principle of international law, and is also a fundamental principle stressed by the United Nations Charter (Article 2, paragraph 1). The principle of equality is inseparable from the principle of sovereignty. The Soviet Union and the respective people's democracies have always advocated, from the viewpoint of the policy of peace, the principle of equality of states, large and small. This is completely consistent with the principles of international law and the principles of the United Nations Charter. Mutual benefit and equality are interrelated. In intercourse between countries, only mutual benefit is genuine equality. Thus, unilateral treaties—particularly those treaties and agreements which in total may be called unequal treaties [and which were] imposed upon China and other Oriental countries by imperialist countries—openly destroy the principle of equality of states. Even those treaties which provide mutual benefit in form but, due to the unequal economic position between two contracting parties, in fact yield unilateral benefits to one side and subject the other side only to exploitation, are neither treaties of mutual benefit nor equal international transactions. The most obvious example is the so-called Sino-American Treaty of Commerce concluded in 1946 between American imperialists and the Kuomintang government. On the contrary, the treaties or agreements concluded between the People's Republic of China and the Soviet Union, the people's democracies, and other countries, such as the 1950 Sino-Soviet Treaty and other agreements and the 1954 Sino-Indian Agreement, are

[g] *Ssu-ta-lin lun hsien-tai kuo-chi-fa ti chi-pen yüan-tse* (Stalin on the fundamental principles of modern international law; Peking, 1950), pp. 41–48.

models for concluding treaties on the basis of equality and mutual benefit. Only thus can the principle of peaceful coexistence between countries be genuinely realized.

International law should serve the peace of mankind. Clarifying democratic principles advantageous to peace and enriching their contents should be the basic role of the modern science of international law. The above-stated five principles of peaceful coexistence belong to this category of democratic principles. In recent years, in diplomatic treaties, declarations, and resolutions the peace-loving governments of many countries have affirmed them as the guiding principles of international relations. They deserve attention and study by international law jurists. Needless to say, to promote the development of modern international law in this direction is to strengthen the legal foundation of international peace.

Note

In the mid-1950's, in an effort to gain greater equality in China's relations with the Soviet Union, the PRC attempted to modify the doctrine of "socialist internationalism," often called "proletarian internationalism," which Stalin had developed as a rationale for maintaining Soviet primacy over and interference in other Communist states. Peking sought to obtain a Soviet admission that the "five principles of peaceful coexistence" were applicable not only to relations between socialist states and non-socialist states but also between socialist states themselves. The high point of this effort came with the following Soviet Declaration (8–7), which was promptly endorsed by the PRC (8–8).

8-7

"Declaration of the USSR on the Foundation for the Development and Further Strengthening of Friendship and Cooperation between the Soviet Union and Other Socialist States, October 30, 1956," *Soviet News*, no. 3502:1–2 (London, Oct. 31, 1956).

The policy of peaceful coexistence, friendship, and cooperation among all states has been and remains the immutable foundation of the foreign relations of the Union of Soviet Socialist Republics.

This policy finds its most profound and consistent expression in the mutual relations between the socialist countries. Being united by the common ideals of building a socialist society and by the principles of proletarian internationalism, the countries of the great community of socialist nations can build their mutual relations only on the principles of complete equality, respect for each other's territorial integrity, state independence and sovereignty, and noninterference in each other's internal affairs. Far from excluding, on the contrary, this presupposes close fraternal cooperation and mutual assistance among the countries of the socialist community in the economic, political and cultural spheres.

It was on this basis that the system of people's democracy in a number of countries of Europe and Asia was formed, gained in strength, and displayed its great viability after the Second World War and the routing of fascism.

The process of building up the new system and the deep-going revolutionary transformations in social relations met with many difficulties, unsolved problems, and direct mistakes, including those in the mutual relations between socialist countries—violations and mistakes which belittled the principle of equal rights in the relations between the socialist states.

The 20th Congress of the Communist Party of the Soviet Union denounced these violations and mistakes with the utmost determination and set the task of consistent application by the Soviet Union in its mutual relations with the other socialist countries of the Leninist principles of equal rights of the peoples. It proclaimed the necessity of taking fully into account the historical past and the distinctive features of each country that has embarked upon the road of building a new life.

The Soviet government is consistently putting into effect these historic decisions of the 20th Congress which create conditions for the further strengthening of friendship and cooperation among the socialist countries on the immutable basis of respecting the full sovereignty of each socialist state.

Recent events have shown that it has become necessary to issue an appropriate statement on the Soviet Union's position with regard to the mutual relations between the USSR and other socialist countries, primarily in the economic and military spheres.

The Soviet government is ready to discuss jointly with the governments of other socialist states measures such as would ensure the further development and strengthening of the economic ties between the socialist countries so as to remove any possibility of violation of the principle of national sovereignty, mutual benefit, and equality in economic relations.

This principle must also be applied to the advisers. It is known that in the first period when the new social system was taking shape, the Soviet Union, at the request of the governments of the people's democracies, sent to those countries a certain number of its specialists—

engineers, agronomists, scientific workers, and military advisers. Recently the Soviet government has more than once raised with the socialist states the question of recalling its advisers.

In view of the fact that skilled national cadres in all spheres of economic and military development have been trained in the people's democracies at the present time, the Soviet government regards it as urgent to examine jointly with the other socialist states the question of the desirability of the further stay of Soviet advisers in those countries.

In military affairs an important foundation for the mutual relations between the Soviet Union and the people's democracies is the Warsaw Treaty, under which the parties to the treaty undertook appropriate political and military commitments, including the commitment to adopt "agreed measures necessary to strengthen their defensive power in order to protect the peaceful labor of their peoples, guarantee the inviolability of their frontiers and territories, and provide defense against possible aggression."

It is common knowledge that Soviet units are stationed in the Hungarian and Rumanian Republics under the Warsaw Treaty and in conformity with government agreements. Soviet military units are stationed in the Polish Republic on the basis of the Potsdam four-power agreement and the Warsaw Treaty. There are no Soviet military units in the other people's democracies.

With the aim of safeguarding the mutual security of the socialist countries, the Soviet government is ready to examine with the other socialist countries that are parties to the Warsaw Treaty the question of the Soviet forces stationed in those countries. In so doing the Soviet government bases itself on the universal principle that the stationing of forces of any state that is party to the Warsaw Treaty on the territory of another state, party to the Warsaw Treaty, is being done on the basis of agreement between all the parties to the treaty and only with the consent of the state on whose territory and at whose request those forces have been so stationed or are to be so stationed.

The Soviet government considers it necessary to make a statement in connection with the events in Hungary. Developments have shown that the working people of Hungary, which has made great progress on the basis of the people's democratic system, are justly raising the question of the need for the elimination of serious shortcomings in the sphere of economic development, for a further improvement in the material well-being of the population, and for a struggle against bureaucratic distortions in the machinery of government. To this just and progressive movement of the working people, however, there soon adhered forces of black reaction and counterrevolution which are trying to exploit the dissatisfaction of a section of the working people in order to undermine the foundations of the people's democratic system in Hungary and to restore there the old regime of landlords and capitalists.

The Soviet government, like the whole Soviet people, deeply deplores the fact that developments in Hungary have led to bloodshed.

At the request of the Hungarian people's government, the Soviet government agreed to the entry into Budapest of Soviet military units in order to help the Hungarian People's Army and the Hungarian authorities to restore order in the city.

Bearing in mind that the further stationing of Soviet military units in Hungary may provide a pretext for making the situation more tense, the Soviet government has instructed its military command to withdraw the Soviet military units from the city of Budapest as soon as the Hungarian government finds it necessary.

At the same time, the Soviet government is ready to enter into appropriate talks with the government of the Hungarian People's Republic and the other parties to the Warsaw Treaty on the question of the stationing of Soviet forces in Hungary.

The defense of the socialist gains of People's Democratic Hungary is today the chief and sacred obligation of the workers, peasants, and intellectuals, of all Hungarian working people.

The Soviet government expresses confidence that the peoples of the socialist countries will not allow external and internal reactionary forces to shake the foundations of the people's democratic system, won and reinforced by the selfless struggle and labor of the workers, peasants, and intellectuals of each country. They will do their utmost, after removing all obstacles standing in the way of the further strengthening of the democratic foundations, independence, and sovereignty of their countries, to develop further the socialist foundations of each country, its economy, and its culture for the sake of the steady advance of the material well-being and cultural standards of all the working people, and they will strengthen the fraternal unity and mutual assistance among the socialist countries for the consolidation of the great cause of peace and socialism.

8-8

"Statement by the Government of the People's Republic of China on the Declaration by the Government of the Soviet Union on October 30, 1956, November 1, 1956," *WCC 1956–1957*, IV (1958), 148–150; *PC*, no. 22, Supp. 1–2 (Nov. 16, 1956).

The government of the Soviet Union on October 30, 1956, issued a declaration on the foundations of the development and further strengthening of friendship and cooperation between the Soviet Union and other socialist countries. The government of the People's Republic of China considers this declaration by the government of the Soviet Union to be correct. This declaration is of great importance in correcting errors in mutual relations between the socialist countries and in strengthening unity among them.

The People's Republic of China maintains that the five principles of mutual respect for sovereignty and territorial integrity, nonaggression, nonintervention in each other's internal affairs, equality and mutual benefit, and peaceful coexistence should be the principles governing the establishment and development of mutual relations among the nations of the world. The socialist countries are all independent, sovereign states. At the same time they are united by the common ideal of socialism and the spirit of proletarian internationalism. Consequently, there is all the more reason why mutual relations between socialist countries should be established on the basis of these five principles. Only in this way can the socialist countries attain a genuine fraternal friendship and solidarity and, through mutual assistance and cooperation, fulfill their desire for a mutual economic upsurge.

As the declaration by the Soviet government pointed out, the mutual relations between the socialist countries are not without mistakes. The mistakes made have resulted in estrangement and misunderstandings between certain socialist countries, and have prevented some of the socialist countries from building socialism more in accordance with their historical circumstances and special characteristics. As a result of these estrangements and misunderstandings, a tense situation has sometimes arisen which would not otherwise have occurred. The handling of the Yugoslav situation in 1948–1949, and the recent happenings in Poland are enough to illustrate this state of affairs. Following the Soviet-Yugoslav joint declaration issued in June 1955, the Soviet government has again taken note of this problem and, in its declaration of October 3, 1956, [has] indicated its willingness to solve various problems in mutual relations by friendly negotiations with other socialist countries on the basis of the principles of full equality, respect for territorial integrity, national independence and sovereignty, and non-intervention in each other's internal affairs. This important step is clearly conducive to removing estrangement and misunderstandings among the socialist countries. It will help increase their friendship and cooperation.

The government of the People's Republic of China notes that the people of Poland and Hungary in recent happenings have voiced demands for a strengthening of democracy, independence and equality and for the raising of the material well-being of the people on the basis of increasing production. These demands are completely proper. Correct satisfaction of these demands not only helps to consolidate the people's democratic system in these countries, but is also favorable to unity among the socialist countries. We note with satisfaction that the people of Poland and their leaders have taken notice of the activities of reactionary elements who attempt to undermine the people's democratic system and unity among socialist countries and the danger therefrom. We consider it absolutely necessary to take note of this and to differentiate between the just demands of the broadest masses of the people and the conspiratorial activities of an extremely small number of reactionary elements. The question of uniting the broadest possible masses of the people in the struggle against an extremely small number of reactionary elements is not only one for an individual socialist country, but one deserving attention by many socialist countries, including our own.

In the socialist countries, because of the unanimity of ideology and aim of struggle, certain personnel are apt to neglect the principle of equality among nations in their mutual relations. Such a mistake is by its nature a bourgeois chauvinistic mistake. Such a mistake, particularly the mistake of chauvinism on the part of a big country, inevitably results in serious damage to the solidarity of the common cause of the socialist countries. For this reason, leading members and personnel of our government and the people of the entire country must at all times take warning and guard against falling into big-nation chauvinistic mistakes in our relations with socialist countries and others. We should at all times carry out education among our personnel and the people of the entire country to resolutely combat such chauvinism. If such an error is committed, it should be promptly corrected. That is a duty to which we should pay the utmost attention in order to strive for peaceful coexistence with all nations and to promote the cause of world peace.

NOTE

The Soviet Declaration of October 30, 1956, and the Chinese statement of November 1, 1956, were followed by the publication, on January 18, 1957, of a joint Soviet-Chinese Declaration, which asserted: "The Socialist countries are united by Communist ideas and the Communist cause. Accordingly, their relations are founded on Marxism-Leninism, on the principles of proletarian internationalism." [54]

The PRC subsequently ceased insisting that the "five principles of peaceful coexistence" be made applicable to relations within the Soviet bloc, but it continued to seek a redefinition of the principles of socialist or proletarian internationalism, which were as vague, abstract, and general as those of peaceful coexistence. Yet socialist internationalism was said to have a distinctive content that described, and called for, the superior standards of conduct that were supposed to prevail in the relations of socialist governments. The standards sought by Peking called not only for the full equality of socialist states but also for the comradely mutual assistance that was said to be the hallmark of the socialist bloc. In 1958, for example, a prominent Chinese writer cited with approval the 1957 statement of G.I. Tunkin, then Legal Adviser to the Soviet Foreign Ministry, that:

> As a principle of international law, socialist internationalism implies that each socialist state has definite rights and obligations. For instance, the right to assistance from other socialist states, and, conversely, the obligation to render such assistance.[55]

An important aspect of this "fraternal mutual aid" was the goal of promoting broad economic cooperation. Although there was no standard formulation of the components of socialist internationalism, some Soviet writers claimed that the norms governing the relations of socialist states genuinely expressed the will of the peoples of those states,[56] and Tunkin's 1957 essay blandly maintained that "violation of international law principles is unknown in relations between the socialist countries." [57]

By the 1960's the PRC obviously realized that the generality of the principles of socialist internationalism permitted the Soviet Union to manipulate them to achieve its own selfish objectives within the bloc and that "mistakes" and "neglect" of the principle of equality among nations were likely to persist unless measures were taken to specify a code of conduct for the socialist countries. The following record of a speech by Ch'en Yi appears to have been a modest effort to give concrete substantive meaning in public to the vague slogans of socialist internationalism.

8-9

"Guiding Principles for Relations between Socialist Countries," *PR* 5.37:11 (Sept. 14, 1962).

[Vice-Premier Ch'en Yi at a reception given by George Kumbiliev, Bulgarian Ambassador to China, on September 8, 1962, in celebration of the eighteenth anniversary of the Bulgarian socialist revolution, said]:

"Socialist countries have the principles of Marxism-Leninism and proletarian internationalism as their common ideological foundation and the building of socialism and communism as their common goal; our fundamental interests are completely identical. In building socialism, therefore, we should and can help and cooperate with each other in the best possible way; and in the struggle against our common enemies, we should and can truly unite as one. In our mutual relations, while we are closely united with and give support to each other, we are each of us fully equal and independent. Every socialist country should abide by the common principles guiding the mutual relations between socialist countries, and safeguard and strengthen the unity of the socialist camp. Anything that runs counter to these common principles and does harm to this unity will not be countenanced by the people of the socialist countries."

"In handling relations between nations," Ch'en Yi added, "the principles adopted by socialist countries are entirely different from those adopted by the imperialist countries."

The following are the major differences noted by the Vice-Premier:

The imperialists engage in subversive activities, whereas socialist countries do not.

The imperialists always try to impose their will upon other countries, whereas socialist countries hold that consultations should be held on an equal footing and no country should impose its will upon another.

The imperialists utilize economic aid as a disguise to realize their true aim of political control over and interference in the internal affairs of other countries; socialist countries stand for equality and mutual support so as to bring about a common upsurge in their economies and culture and are opposed to interference in the internal affairs of other countries.

The imperialists pursue a policy of setting up military bases in other countries, and their troops, once stationed in a foreign country, will hang on there, whereas socialist countries are opposed to the policy of military bases and withdraw on their own initiative the troops which they have sent abroad.

The imperialists enmesh many countries in various military pacts, making them pull the chestnuts out of the fire for them, whereas socialist countries stand for the abolition of all military blocs.

The imperialists do not respect, but undermine the peace and neutrality of other countries; socialist countries, on the contrary, respect and support all countries which follow a policy of peace and neutrality.

The imperialists suppress the national-liberation movement, whereas socialist countries support national independence and the national-liberation movement.

Note

Shortly after Ch'en Yi's speech, relations between China and the Soviet Union deteriorated to the point that each side abandoned veiled reference in favor of more specific indictments. Item 8–10 summarizes the Chinese charges against the CPSU for having violated the norms of socialist internationalism. Item 8–11, which also discusses problems of relations among "fraternal" governments, is primarily a review of the differences that emerged between the Soviet and Chinese views of peaceful coexistence. "The 1957 Declaration" referred to is the "Declaration of Meeting of Representatives of the Communist and Workers' Parties of the Socialist Countries," [58] and "the 1960 Statement" is the "Statement of Meeting of Representatives of the Communist and Workers' Parties of the Socialist Countries." [59]

8-10

Editorial Departments of *People's Daily* and *Red Flag*, "The Leaders of the CPSU Are the Greatest Splitters of Our Times," *JMJP* (Feb. 4, 1964), pp. 1–4; English translation in *PR* 7.6:9–10 (Feb. 7, 1964).

Far from working to consolidate and expand the socialist camp, the leaders of the CPSU have endeavored to split and disintegrate it. They have thus made a mess of the splendid socialist camp.

They have violated the principles guiding relations among fraternal countries as laid down in the Declaration and the Statement, pursued a policy of great-power chauvinism and national egoism toward fraternal socialist countries and thus disrupted the unity of the socialist camp.

They have arbitrarily infringed the sovereignty of fraternal countries, interfered in their internal affairs, carried on subversive activities, and striven in every way to control fraternal countries.

In the name of the "international division of labor," the leaders of the CPSU oppose the adoption by fraternal countries of the policy of building socialism by their own efforts and developing their economies on an independent basis, and attempt to turn them into economic appendages. They have tried to force those fraternal countries which are comparatively backward economically to abandon industrialization and become their sources of raw materials and markets for surplus products.

The leaders of the CPSU are quite unscrupulous in their pursuit of the policy of great-power chauvinism. They have constantly brought political, economic, and even military pressure to bear on fraternal countries.

The leaders of the CPSU have openly called for the overthrow of the party and government leaders of Albania, brashly severed all economic and diplomatic relations with her, and tyrannically deprived her of her legitimate rights as a member of the Warsaw Treaty Organization and the Council of Economic Mutual Assistance.

The leaders of the CPSU have violated the Sino-Soviet Treaty of Friendship, Alliance and Mutual Assistance, made a unilateral decision to withdraw 1,390 Soviet experts working in China, to tear up 343 contracts and supplementary contracts on the employment of experts, and to cancel 257 projects of scientific and technical cooperation, and pursued a restrictive and discriminatory trade policy against China. They have provoked incidents on the Sino-Soviet border and carried on large-scale subversive activities in Sinkiang. On more than one occasion, Khrushchev went so far as to tell leading comrades of the Central Committee of the CPC that certain antiparty elements in the Chinese Communist Party were his "good friends." He has praised Chinese antiparty elements for attacking the Chinese party's general line for socialist construction, the [Great] Leap Forward, and the people's communes, describing their action as a "manly act."

Such measures which gravely worsen state relations are rare even between capitalist countries. But again and again the leaders of the CPSU have adopted shocking and extreme measures of this kind against fraternal socialist countries. Yet they go on prating about being "faithful to proletarian internationalism." We would like to ask, is there a shred of internationalism in all these deeds of yours?

The great-power chauvinism and splittism of the leaders of the CPSU are equally glaring in their conduct vis-à-vis fraternal parties.

Since the 20th Congress of the CPSU, its leaders have tried, on the pretext of "combating the personality cult," to change the leadership of other fraternal parties to conform to their will. Right up to the present they have insisted on "combating the personality cult" as a precondition for the restoration of unity and as a "principle" which is "obligatory on every Communist Party." [a]

Contrary to the principles guiding relations among fraternal parties laid down in the Declaration and the Statement, the leaders of the CPSU ignore the independent and equal status of fraternal parties, insist on establishing a kind of feudal patriarchal domination over the international Communist movement and turn the relations between brother parties into those between a patriarchal father and his sons. Khrushchev has more than once described a fraternal party as a "silly boy" and called himself its "mother." [b] With his feudal psychology of self-exaltation, he has absolutely no sense of shame.

The leaders of the CPSU have completely ignored the principle of achieving unanimity through consultation among fraternal parties and habitually make dictatorial decisions and order others about. They have recklessly torn up joint agreements with fraternal parties, [made] arbitrary decisions on important matters of common concern to fraternal parties and forced *faits accomplis* on them.

The leaders of the CPSU have violated the principle that differences among fraternal parties should be settled through interparty consultation; they first used their own party congress and then the congresses of other fraternal parties as rostrums for large-scale public attacks against those fraternal parties which firmly uphold Marxism-Leninism.

The leaders of the CPSU regard fraternal parties as pawns on their diplomatic chessboard. Khrushchev plays fast and loose, he blows hot and cold, he talks one way one day and another the next, and yet he insists on the fraternal parties dancing to his every tune without knowing whence or whither.

The leaders of the CPSU have stirred up trouble and created splits in many Communist Parties by encouraging the followers of their revisionist line in these parties to attack the leadership, or usurp leading positions, persecute Marxist-Leninists and even expel them from the party. It is this divisive policy of the leaders of the CPSU that has given rise to organizational splits in the fraternal parties of many capitalist countries.

The leaders of the CPSU have turned the magazine *Problems of Peace and Socialism,* originally the common journal of fraternal parties,

[a] "For the Unity and Solidarity of the International Communist Movement," article by the editorial board, *Pravda* (Dec. 6, 1963).

[b] *Cf.* Khrushchev's interview with Gardner Cowles, editor of the US magazine *Look* (Apr. 20, 1962); report by Khrushchev to the Session of the Supreme Soviet of the USSR, Dec. 12, 1962.

into an instrument for spreading revisionism, sectarianism, and splittism and for making unscrupulous attacks on Marxist-Leninist fraternal parties in violation of the agreement reached at the meeting at which the magazine was founded.

8-11

Editorial Departments of *People's Daily* and *Red Flag*, "Peaceful Coexistence—Two Diametrically Opposed Policies," *JMJP* (Dec. 12, 1963), pp. 1–4; English translation in *PR* 6.51:6, 9–14 (Dec. 20, 1963).

Since the 20th Congress of the CPSU, Khrushchev and other comrades have talked more about the question of peaceful coexistence than about anything else.

Again and again the leaders of the CPSU claim that they have been faithful to Lenin's policy of peaceful coexistence and have creatively developed it. They ascribe to their policy of "peaceful coexistence" all the credit for the victories won by the peoples of the world in prolonged revolutionary struggles.

They advertise the notion that imperialism, and US imperialism in particular, supports peaceful coexistence, and they wantonly malign the Chinese Communist Party and all Marxist-Leninist parties as being opponents of peaceful coexistence. The open letter of the Central Committee of the CPSU even slanders China as favoring "competition in unleashing war" with the imperialists.

They describe the words and deeds by which they have betrayed Marxism-Leninism, the proletarian world revolution, and the revolutionary cause of the oppressed peoples and nations as being in conformity with Lenin's policy of peaceful coexistence.

But can the words "peaceful coexistence" really serve as a talisman for the leaders of the CPSU in their betrayal of Marxism-Leninism? No, absolutely not.

We are now confronted with two diametrically opposed policies of peaceful coexistence.

One is Lenin and Stalin's policy of peaceful coexistence, which all Marxist-Leninists, including the Chinese Communists, stand for.

The other is the anti-Leninist policy of peaceful coexistence, the so-called general line of peaceful coexistence advocated by Khrushchev and others.

Let us now examine Lenin and Stalin's policy of peaceful coexistence and the stuff Khrushchev and others call the general line of peaceful coexistence. . . .

In our foreign affairs over the past fourteen years, we have adopted different policies toward different types of countries and varied our policies according to the different conditions in countries of the same type.

1. We differentiate between socialist and capitalist countries. We persevere in the proletarian internationalist principle of mutual assistance with regard to socialist countries. We take the upholding and strengthening of the unity of all the countries in the socialist camp as the fundamental policy in our foreign relations.

2. We differentiate between the nationalist countries which have newly attained political independence and the imperialist countries.

Although fundamentally different from the socialist countries in their social and political systems, the nationalist countries stand in profound contradiction to imperialism. They have common interests with the socialist countries—opposition to imperialism, the safeguarding of national independence and the defense of world peace. Therefore, it is quite possible and feasible for the socialist countries to establish relations of peaceful coexistence and friendly cooperation with these countries. The establishment of such relations is of great significance for the strengthening of the unity of the anti-imperialist forces and for the advancement of the common struggle of the peoples against imperialism.

We have consistently adhered to the policy of consolidating and further developing peaceful coexistence and friendly cooperation with countries in Asia, Africa, and Latin America. At the same time, we have waged appropriate and necessary struggles against countries such as India which have violated or wrecked the Five Principles.

3. We differentiate between the ordinary capitalist countries and the imperialist countries and also between different imperialist countries.

As the international balance of class forces grows increasingly favorable to socialism and as the imperialist forces become daily weaker and the contradictions among them daily sharper, it is possible for the socialist countries to compel one imperialist country or another to establish some sort of peaceful coexistence with them by relying on their own growing strength, the expansion of the revolutionary forces of the peoples, the unity with the nationalist countries, and the struggle of all the peace-loving people, and by utilizing the internal contradictions of imperialism.

While persevering in peaceful coexistence with countries having different social systems, we unswervingly perform our proletarian internationalist duty. We actively support the national liberation movements of Asia, Africa, and Latin America; the working-class movements of Western Europe, North America, and Australasia; the people's revolutionary struggles; and the people's struggles against the imperialist policies of aggression and war and for world peace.

In all this we have but one objective in view, that is, with the socialist camp and the international proletariat as the nucleus, to unite all the forces that can be united in order to form a broad united front against US imperialism and its lackeys.

On the basis of the Five Principles of peaceful coexistence, the Chinese government over the past ten years and more has established friendly relations with many countries having different social systems and promoted economic and cultural exchanges with them. China has concluded treaties of friendship, of peace and friendship, or of friendship, mutual assistance and mutual nonaggression with the Yemen, Burma, Nepal, Afghanistan, Guinea, Cambodia, Indonesia and Ghana. She has successfully settled her boundary questions with Burma, Nepal, Pakistan, Afghanistan, and others, questions which were left over by history. . . .

The General Line of "Peaceful Coexistence" of the CPSU Leaders

It is not we, but the leaders of the CPSU who in fact violate Lenin's policy of peaceful coexistence. The leaders of the CPSU have lauded their concept of peaceful coexistence in superlative terms. What are their main views on the question of peaceful coexistence?

(1) The leaders of the CPSU maintain that peaceful coexistence is the overriding and supreme principle for solving contemporary social problems. They assert that it is "the categorical imperative of modern times" and "the imperious demand of the epoch." [a] They say that "peaceful coexistence alone is the best and the sole acceptable way to solve the vitally important problems confronting society" [b] and that the principle of peaceful coexistence should be made the "basic law of life of the whole of modern society." [c]

(2) They hold that imperialism has become willing to accept peaceful coexistence and is no longer the obstacle to it. They say that "not a few government and state leaders of Western countries are

[a] B. N. Ponomaryov, "Victorious Banner of the Communists of the World," *Pravda* (Nov. 18, 1962), [p. 4.]

[b] Rumyantsev, "Our Common Ideological Weapon," *Problems of Peace and Socialism*, no. 1 (1962), [pp. 8–9.]

[c] N. S. Khrushchev, Speech at the UN General Assembly, Sept. 23, 1960.

now also coming out for peace and peaceful coexistence," [d] and that they "understand more and more clearly the necessity of peaceful coexistence." [e] In particular they have loudly announced a US President's "admission of the reasonableness and practicability of peaceful coexistence between countries with different social systems." [f]

(3) They advocate "all-round cooperation" with imperialist countries, and especially with the United States. They say that the Soviet Union and the United States "will be able to find a basis for concerted actions and efforts for the good of all humanity." [g] and can "march hand in hand for the sake of consolidating peace and establishing real international cooperation between all states." [h]

(4) They assert that peaceful coexistence is "the general line of foreign policy of the Soviet Union and the countries of the socialist camp." [i]

(5) They also assert that "the principle of peaceful coexistence determines the general line of foreign policy of the CPSU and other Marxist-Leninist parties," [j] that it is "the basis of the strategy of Communism" in the world today, and that all Communists "have made the struggle for peaceful coexistence the general principle of their policy." [k]

(6) They regard peaceful coexistence as the prerequisite for victory in the peoples' revolutionary struggles. They hold that the victories won by the people of different countries have been achieved under "conditions of peaceful coexistence between states with different social systems." [l] They assert that "it was precisely in conditions of peaceful coexistence between states with different social systems that the socialist revolution triumphed in Cuba, that the Algerian people gained national independence, that more than forty countries won national independence, that the fraternal parties grew in number

[d] N. S. Khrushchev, Speech at the Gadjah Mada University, Djokjakarta, Indonesia, Feb. 21, 1960.

[e] N. S. Khrushchev, Report to the Session of the Supreme Soviet of the USSR, Jan. 14, 1960.

[f] Editorial article in *Izvestia* (Dec. 4, 1961).

[g] Telegram of greetings from N. S. Khrushchev and L. Brezhnev to John F. Kennedy, Dec. 30, 1961.

[h] See N. S. Khrushchev, Speech at the UN General Assembly, Sept. 23, 1960.

[i] N. S. Khrushchev, Speech at the reception given by the embassy of the Democratic People's Republic of Korea in the Soviet Union, July 5, 1961.

[j] B. N. Ponomaryov, "Some Problems of the Revolutionary Movement," *Problems of Peace and Socialism*, no. 12 (1962).

[k] *Kommunist* (Moscow), no. 2 (1962), p. 89.

[l] B. N. Ponomaryov, "A New Stage in the General Crisis of Capitalism," *Pravda* (Feb. 8, 1961).

and strength, and that the influence of the world Communist movement increased." [m]

(7) They hold that peaceful coexistence is "the best way of helping the international revolutionary labor movement achieve its basic class aims." [n] They declare that under peaceful coexistence the possibility of a peaceful transition to socialism in capitalist countries has grown. They believe, moreover, that the victory of socialism in economic competition "will mean delivering a crushing blow to the entire system of capitalist relationships." [o] They state that "when the Soviet people will enjoy the blessings of Communism, new hundreds of millions of people on earth will say: 'We are for Communism!'" [p] and that by then even capitalists may "go over to the Communist Party."

Just consider. What do these views have in common with Lenin's policy of peaceful coexistence?

Lenin's policy of peaceful coexistence is one followed by a socialist country in its relations with countries having different social systems, whereas Khrushchev describes peaceful coexistence as the supreme principle governing the life of modern society.

Lenin's policy of peaceful coeixstence constitutes one aspect of the international policy of the proletariat in power, whereas Khrushchev stretches peaceful coexistence into the general line of foreign policy for the socialist countries and even further into the general line for all Communist Parties.

Lenin's policy of peaceful coexistence was directed against the imperialist policies of aggression and war, whereas Khrushchev's peaceful coexistence caters to imperialism and abets the imperialist policies of aggression and war.

Lenin's policy of peaceful coexistence is based on the standpoint of international class struggle, whereas Khrushchev's peaceful coexistence strives to replace international class struggle with international class collaboration.

Lenin's policy of peaceful coexistence proceeds from the historical mission of the international proletariat and therefore requires the socialist countries to give firm support to the revolutionary struggles of all the oppressed peoples and nations while pursuing this policy, whereas

[m] Letter of the Central Committee of the Communist Party of the Soviet Union to the Central Committee of the Communist Party of China, March 30, 1963.

[n] Open Letter of the Central Committee of the Communist Party of the Soviet Union to Party Organizations and All Communists in the Soviet Union, July 14, 1963.

[o] B. N. Ponomaryov, "Some Problems of the Revolutionary Movement," *Problems of Peace and Socialism*, no. 12 (1962).

[p] Programme of the CPSU, adopted by the 22nd Congress of the CPSU.

Khrushchev's peaceful coexistence seeks to replace the proletarian world revolution with pacifism and thus renounces proletarian internationalism. . . .

Three Differences of Principle

. . . The first question is: In order to attain peaceful coexistence, is it necessary to wage struggles against imperialism and bourgeois reaction? Is it possible through peaceful coexistence to abolish the antagonism and struggle between socialism and imperialism? . . .

The Five Principles of peaceful coexistence were advanced to combat the imperialist policies of aggression and war. Under these principles, it is impermissible in international relations to encroach upon the territory and sovereignty of other countries, interfere in their internal affairs, impair their interests and equal status or wage aggressive wars against them. But it is in the very nature of imperialism to commit aggression against other countries and nations and to desire to enslave them. As long as imperialism exists, its nature will never change. That is why intrinsically the imperialists are unwilling to accept the Five Principles of peaceful coexistence. Whenever possible, they try to disrupt and destroy the socialist countries, and they commit aggression against other countries and nations and try to enslave them.

History shows that it is only owing to unfavorable objective causes that the imperialists dare not risk starting a war against the socialist countries, or are forced to agree to an armistice and to accept some sort of peaceful coexistence.

History also shows that there have always been sharp and complex struggles between the imperialist and socialist countries, which have sometimes culminated in direct military conflicts or wars. When hot wars are not in progress, the imperialists wage cold wars, which they have been ceaselessly waging ever since the end of World War II. In fact, the imperialist and the socialist countries have been in a state of cold-war coexistence. At the same time as they actively expand their armaments and prepare for war, the imperialist countries use every means to oppose the socialist countries politically, economically, and ideologically, and even make military provocations and war threats against them. The imperialists' cold war against the socialist countries and the latter's resistance to it are manifestations of the international class struggle.

The imperialists push on with their plans of aggression and war not only against the socialist countries but throughout the world. They try to suppress the revolutionary movements of the oppressed peoples and nations.

In these circumstances, the socialist countries, together with the people of all other countries, must resolutely combat imperialist policies of aggression and war and wage a tit-for-tat struggle against imperialism. This class struggle inevitably goes on, now in an acute and now in a relaxed form.

But Khrushchev is impervious to these inexorable facts. He proclaims far and wide that imperialism has already admitted the necessity of peaceful coexistence, and he regards the anti-imperialist struggles of the socialist countries and of the people of the world as incompatible with the policy of peaceful coexistence.

In Khrushchev's opinion, a socialist country has to make one concession after another and keep on yielding to the imperialists and the bourgeois reactionaries even when they subject it to military threats and armed attack or make humiliating demands which violate its sovereignty and dignity.

By this logic, Khrushchev describes his incessant retreats, his bartering away of principles and docile acceptance of the US imperialists' humiliating demands during the Carribean crisis as "a victory of peaceful coexistence."

By the same logic, Khrushchev describes China's adherence to correct principles on the Sino-Indian boundary question and her counter-attack against the military onslaught of the Indian reactionaries, an act of self-defense by China when the situation became intolerable, as "a violation of peaceful coexistence."

At times, Khrushchev also talks about [a] struggle between the two different social systems. But how does he see this struggle?

He has said, "The inevitable struggle between the two systems must be made to take the form exclusively of a struggle of ideas. . . ." [q]

Here the political struggle has disappeared!

He has also said:

> The Leninist principle of peaceful coexistence of states with differing socioeconomic and political systems does not mean just an absence of war, a temporary state of unstable cease-fire. It presupposes the maintenance between these states of friendly economic and political relations; it envisages the establishment and development of various forms of peaceful international co-operation.[r]

Here, struggle has disappeared altogether!

Like a conjurer, Khrushchev plays one trick after another, first

[q] See N. S. Khrushchev, Report to the Session of the Supreme Soviet of the USSR, Jan. 14, 1960.

[r] N. S. Khrushchev, "Answers to the Questions of the Austrian Professor Hans Thirring," *Pravda* (Jan. 3, 1962).

reducing major issues to minor ones, and then minor issues to naught. He denies the basic antagonism between the socialist and capitalist systems, he denies the fundamental contradiction between the socialist and the imperialist camps, and he denies the existence of international class struggle. And so he transforms peaceful coexistence between the two systems and the two camps into "all-round cooperation."

The second question is: Can peaceful coexistence be made the general line of foreign policy for socialist countries?

We hold that the general line of foreign policy for socialist countries must embody the fundamental principle of their foreign policy and comprise the fundamental content of this policy. What is this fundamental principle? It is proletarian internationalism.

Lenin said, "Alliance with the revolutionaries of the advanced countries and with all the oppressed peoples against any and all the imperialists—such is the external policy of the proletariat." ("The External Policy of the Russian Revolution," *Collected Works,* fourth Russian ed., vol. 25, p. 69.) This principle of proletarian internationalism advanced by Lenin should be the guide for the foreign policy of socialist countries.

Since the formation of the socialist camp, every socialist country has had to deal with three kinds of relations in its foreign policy, namely, its relations with other socialist countries, with countries having different social systems, and with the oppressed peoples and nations.

In our view, the following should therefore be the content of the general line of foreign policy for socialist countries: to develop relations of friendship, mutual assistance, and cooperation among the countries of the socialist camp in accordance with the principle of proletarian internationalism; to strive for peaceful coexistence on the basis of the Five Principles with countries having different social systems and oppose the imperialist policies of aggression and war; and to support and assist the revolutionary struggles of all the oppressed peoples and nations. These three aspects are interrelated and not a single one can be omitted.

The leaders of the CPSU have one-sidedly reduced the general line of the foreign policy of the socialist countries to peaceful coexistence. We would like to ask: How should a socialist country handle its relations with other socialist countries? Should it merely maintain relations of peaceful coexistence with them?

Of course, socialist countries, too, must abide by the Five Principles in their mutual relations. It is absolutely impermissible for any one of them to undermine the territorial integrity of another fraternal country, to impair its independence and sovereignty, [to] interfere in its internal affairs, [to] carry on subversive activities inside it, or [to] violate the principle of equality and mutual benefit in its relations with another fraternal country. But merely to carry out these principles is far from enough. The 1957 Declaration states:

> These are vital principles. However they do not exhaust the essence of relations between them. Fraternal mutual aid is part and parcel of these relations. This aid is a striking expression of socialist internationalism.

In making peaceful coexistence the general line of foreign policy, the leaders of the CPSU have in fact liquidated the proletarian internationalist relations of mutual assistance and cooperation among socialist countries and put the fraternal socialist countries on a par with the capitalist countries. This amounts to liquidating the socialist camp.

The leaders of the CPSU have one-sidedly reduced the general line of the foreign policy of the socialist countries to peaceful coexistence. We would like to ask: How should a socialist country handle its relations with the oppressed peoples and nations? Should the relationship between the proletariat in power and its class brothers who have not yet emancipated themselves or between it and all oppressed peoples and nations be one of peaceful coexistence alone and not of mutual help?

After the October Revolution, Lenin repeatedly stressed that the land of socialism, which had established the dictatorship of the proletariat, was a base for promoting the proletarian world revolution. Stalin, too, said, "The revolution which has been victorious in one country must regard itself not as a self-sufficient entity, but as an aid, as a means *for* hastening the victory of the proletariat in all countries." ("The October Revolution and the Tactics of the Russian Communists," *Works,* FLPH [Foreign Languages Publishing House], Moscow, 1953, vol. 6, p. 415.) He added that "it constitutes . . . a mighty base for its further development [*i.e.,* of the world revolution]." (*Ibid.,* p. 419.)

In their foreign policy, therefore, socialist countries can in no circumstances confine themselves to handling relations with countries having different social systems, but must also correctly handle relations among themselves and relations with oppressed peoples and nations. They must make support of the revolutionary struggles of the oppressed peoples and nations their internationalist duty and an important component of their foreign policy.

In contrast with Lenin and Stalin, Khrushchev makes peaceful coexistence the general line of foreign policy for socialist countries and, in so doing, excludes from this policy the proletarian internationalist task of helping the revolutionary struggles of the oppressed peoples and nations. So far from being a "creative development" of the policy of peaceful coexistence, this is a betrayal of proletarian internationalism on the pretext of peaceful coexistence.

The third question is: Can the policy of peaceful coexistence of the socialist countries be the general line for all Communist Parties and for the international Communist movement? Can it be substituted for the people's revolution?

We maintain that peaceful coexistence connotes a relationship between countries with different social systems, between independent sovereign states. Only after victory in the revolution is it possible and necessary for the proletariat to pursue the policy of peaceful coexistence. As for oppressed peoples and nations, their task is to strive for their own liberation and overthrow the rule of imperialism and its lackeys. They should not practice peaceful coexistence with the imperialists and their lackeys; nor is it possible for them to do so.

It is therefore wrong to apply peaceful coexistence to relations between oppressed and oppressor classes and between oppressed and oppressor nations, or to stretch the socialist countries' policy of peaceful coexistence so as to make it the policy of the Communist Parties and the revolutionary people in the capitalist world, or to subordinate the revolutionary struggles of the oppressed peoples and nations to it.

We have always held that the correct application of Lenin's policy of peaceful coexistence by the socialist countries helps to develop their power, to expose the imperialist policies of aggression and war and to unite all the anti-imperialist peoples and countries, and it therefore helps the people's struggles against imperialism and its lackeys. At the same time, by directly hitting and weakening the forces of aggression, war, and reaction, the people's revolutionary struggles against imperialism and its lackeys help the cause of world peace and human progress, and therefore help the socialist countries' struggle for peaceful coexistence with countries having different social systems. Thus, the correct application of Lenin's policy of peaceful coexistence by the socialist countries is in harmony with the interests of the people's revolutionary struggles in all countries.

However, the socialist countries' struggle for peaceful coexistence between countries with different social systems and the people's revolution in various countries are two totally different things. . . .

Acting against this Marxist-Leninist policy, the leaders of the CPSU equate one aspect of the policy to be pursued by the proletariat in power in its state relations with countries having different social systems with the general line of all the Communist Parties, and they try to substitute the former for the latter, demanding that Communist Parties and revolutionary peoples should all follow what they call the general line of peaceful coexistence. Not desiring revolution themselves, they forbid others to make it. Not opposing imperialism themselves, they forbid others to oppose it.

NOTE

It is interesting to observe that in late 1970, after the PRC's long-standing hostile relations with Yugoslavia had begun to improve, Vice-Minister Ch'iao Kuan-hua stated at a reception at the Yugoslav Embassy that the Chinese government has always held that the relations between states should be guided by the Five Principles of Peaceful Coexistence. He said: "These principles should apply to all countries, whether they have the same or different social systems. We note with pleasure that it is precisely on the basis of these principles that the relations between China and Yugoslavia have developed in recent years."[60] Not a word appears to have been said by representatives of either socialist state about the supposedly higher standards of "socialist internationalism" that had previously been deemed to govern relations between socialist states.

The following item, one of many published by the Chinese in their outrage over Soviet intervention in Czechoslovakia in 1968, may provide an explanation. (See also, for example, 42–13.)

8-12

Chi Hsiang-yang, "Smash the New Tsars' Theory of Limited Sovereignty," *PR* 12.21:20–22 (May 23, 1969).

Having long been collaborating and contending with the US imperialists, the Soviet revisionist renegade clique has carried out aggression and expansion everywhere, interfered in other countries' internal affairs, and even embarked on military adventures and thus wildly violated the territory and sovereignty of other countries. Having a guilty conscience, this pack of renegades fabricates all kinds of fascist fallacies to cover up their social-imperialist aggressive nature. The one they trumpet with the most enthusiasm is the so-called theory of "limited sovereignty."

Brezhnev, chieftain of the Soviet revisionist renegade clique, and his gang have raved that the interests of the "socialist community" under their control represent the "highest sovereignty" and that these must be given "first place," while the sovereignty of any one state is "limited." They arrogate to themselves the "right" to "determine" the "destiny" of the members of the "community," including "the destiny of their sovereignty," and allege that "such an act as rendering military aid to a fraternal country to do away with the threat to the socialist system" is in "the common interests of the camp of socialism" and is "upholding" the sovereignty of another country. This is out-and-out gangster logic put out by the new tsars to justify their aggression.

Harping on the "community" right and left, this handful of shameless renegades are maliciously trampling on the sovereignty of other countries and ruthlessly plundering the wealth created by the labouring people there simply on the pretext of the "community." As Vice-Chairman Lin Piao pointed out in his political report to the Ninth National Congress of the Communist Party of China, "the Soviet revisionist renegade clique glibly talks of 'fraternal parties' and 'fraternal countries,' but in fact it regards itself as the patriarchal party, and as the new tsar, who is free to invade and occupy the territory of other countries." The Soviet revisionist renegade clique controls the domestic affairs and foreign policy of those countries in the "community" through the puppets it has installed there, and has become the new tsar in the true sense of the word. The Soviet revisionists use the "Warsaw Treaty" as an instrument to station a large number of armed forces in the member countries of the "community," and freely hand down orders to these countries through their many officers. They also have a firm grip on the economic lifelines of the member nations through the "Council for Mutual Economic Assistance," bilateral agreements, trade, loans, etc. In this way, they have turned these countries into suppliers of raw material, markets for their goods, and auxiliary processing workshops, so as to milk them dry. This has brought enormous disaster to the people of these countries. In a word, Soviet revisionism has put the political, military, and economic power of the "community" completely under its control.

The relationship between Soviet revisionism and the other member countries in this "community" is one between plunderer and the plundered, between master and slave, a relationship between a suzerain state and its colonies and dependencies. "The common interests of the community" preached by the Soviet revisionists are, in fact, the interests of Soviet revisionist social-imperialism. When they advocate putting "the interests of the community" "in first place," they mean giving top priority to their own colonialist interests, that is, they want others to place their sovereignty at the mercy of Soviet revisionism. The armed occupation of Czechoslovakia is a case in point of the "interests of the community." This atrocious act of aggression has met with the Czechoslovak people's vehement resistance, which has been growing in scale recently. In face of this, Soviet revisionism again resorted to sabre-rattling by sending its Defense Minister to direct the Czechoslovak revisionists on the spot in savagely repressing the Czechoslovak people. At the same time, it staged a farce of "swapping horses" by dismissing the puppets who were not sufficiently effective in suppressing the Czechoslovak people and imposed on them other puppets who are even more subservient to Soviet revisionism. In advocating the theory of "limited sovereignty," the Soviet revisionists' sole purpose obviously is to legalize their brutal occupation of Czechoslovakia and the privileges they seized from the member countries of the "community."

What exactly does the theory of "limited sovereignty" mean? It means that the sovereignty exercised by the Soviet revisionist social-imperialists is "unlimited." They can extend at will their own "sovereignty"to other countries and to the whole world, while the sovereignty of other countries is "limited." It means that these countries must be left to the mercies of Soviet revisionism as it carries out aggression and expansion abroad and establishes its social-imperialist hegemony and that these countries must allow Soviet revisionism to intrude into their territory and trample them underfoot as it likes.

This Soviet revisionist fallacy is entirely calculated to serve the purpose of collaborating with US imperialism in a vain effort to redivide the world. US imperialism invented the so-called "free world community," and Soviet revisionism followed suit by concocting the so-called "community of socialist countries." Imperialist and colonialist to the hilt, Soviet revisionism, however, does its utmost to cover up its true imperialist face in the guise of "internationalism." Time and again, it has threatened that whosoever fails to put the interests of the "community" "in first place" "is betraying the principle of proletarian internationalism." This is a gross insult to proletarian internationalism!

In his political report, Vice-Chairman Lin Piao pointed out: "We have always held that the internal affairs of each country should be settled by its own people. The relations between all countries and between all parties, big or small, must be built on the principles of equality and noninterference in each other's internal affairs. To safeguard these Marxist-Leninist principles, the Communist Party of China has waged a long struggle against the sinister great-power chauvinism of the Soviet revisionist renegade clique. This is a fact known to all." The Soviet revisionists have been riding roughshod over other countries in the "community," violating their sovereignty at will, intervening in their internal affairs, and destroying recognized elementary principles of state sovereignty lock, stock, and barrel. Yet they still talk profusely of "proletarian internationalism." What audacity! To put it bluntly, the "internationalism" of the Soviet revisionists is nothing but imperialist cosmopolitanism and big-power chauvinism aimed at conquering and enslaving other nations and establishing world hegemony.

Nonintervention 9

In *Item 8–11*, the *People's Daily* and *Red Flag* state explicitly that, according to their concept of peaceful coexistence, the socialist states "must make support of the revolutionary struggles of the oppressed peoples and nations their internationalist duty and an important component of their foreign policy." The question naturally arises as to how this "duty" can be consistent with the principle of "mutual nonintervention in each other's internal affairs" that the Chinese have consistently espoused as an essential feature of peaceful coexistence (recall 8–1 to 8–4, and 8–6).

Perhaps significantly, although many of the highest-ranking Chinese officials, as well as publicists, have frequently proclaimed the PRC's adherence to the "five principles" and the PRC has bound itself to their observance on numerous occasions, Chairman Mao himself seldom appears to have advocated the principle of "nonintervention." Often, as in his 1949 address to the Preparatory Committee of the Chinese People's Political Consultative Conference, when he has referred to the principles of equality, mutual benefit, and mutual respect for territorial integrity and sovereignty, he has been silent on the subjects of intervention and aggression. At other times, after endorsing other principles of peaceful coexistence, he has actually called for what was tantamount to intervention into the affairs of other states. For example, in his 1956 speech to the CCP's Eighth National Congress, Mao said: "We must endeavor to establish normal diplomatic relations on the basis of mutual respect for territorial integrity and sovereignty and of equality and mutual benefit with all countries willing to live together with us in peace. We must give active support to the national independence and liberation movement in countries in Asia, Africa, and Latin America, as well as to the peace movement and to just struggles in all countries throughout the world."[61] Such statements contrast with those of the highest Soviet officials, such as Khrushchev, who have endorsed nonintervention more often than Mao has.

Although the materials that follow constitute only a sampling of the relevant documentation and literature, they should be sufficient to suggest the concrete meaning that the PRC attaches to "nonintervention" both with respect to its own actions and the actions of other states. Items 9–1 to 9–7 illustrate the extent to which the PRC has invoked this principle as a defensive weapon. Items 9–8 to 9–14 illustrate the extent to which the PRC has ignored this principle "in support of the revolutionary struggles of the oppressed peoples and nations."

9-1
"The Chinese Government Demands Withdrawal of US Forces from Lebanon, Withdrawal of British Forces from Jordan," *PR* 1.21:7 (July 22, 1958).

On July 15, the United States, in flagrant violation of the fundamental principles of the United Nations Charter, landed its armed forces in the Lebanon and launched armed intervention in the Lebanon's internal affairs under the pretext of "protecting American lives" and "defending Lebanese sovereignty." This is an extremely grave [and] warlike adventure on the part of the United States to suppress the national independence movements of the Arab peoples and to create world tension. The government of the People's Republic of China and the Chinese people strongly condemn and protest against the United States act of aggression.

The United States and other Western countries craved for long to carry out armed intervention against the Lebanon, but failed to do so because of the resolute opposition of the Arab peoples and the peace-loving countries and people throughout the world. Now, with colonial rule in the Middle East shaken by the great victory of the national independence movement in Iraq, the United States government, in a sudden rage and panic, has brazenly launched armed intervention against the Lebanon in defiance of universal censure and also attempts to invade Jordan to menace the Republic of Iraq. This act of aggression on the part of the United States is not only an outrageous provocation against the peoples of the Arab states, but also constitutes a grave threat to the peace of Western Asia and the world. The pretexts of "protecting American lives" and "defending Lebanese sovereignty" absolutely cannot cover up this naked act of aggression on the part of the United States. All peace-loving countries and peoples of the world must firmly demand the immediate withdrawal of United States forces from the Lebanon and stop the United States' war provocation.

The people of all countries have the right to choose their own governments, in which no intervention is allowed. The armed intervention against the Arab peoples carried out by the United States imperialists is doomed to failure.

In their struggle for independence and freedom, the peoples of the

Lebanon, Iraq, and other Arab countries by no means stand alone! Together with the peoples of the Asian and African countries and other peace-loving countries and peoples the world over, the 600 million Chinese people will give all-out support to the Arab peoples' just struggle. Should the United States fail to withdraw its forces of aggression from the Lebanon at once, it will have to face the consequences of its action.

9-2

Chou Keng-sheng, "Don't Allow American and British Aggressors to Intervene in the Internal Affairs of Other States" (Summary of Professor Chou's speech delivered at a discussion conference sponsored by the editorial department of the *CFYC* on July 19, 1958), *CFYC*, no. 4:3–4 (1958).

. . . Eisenhower gave three reasons to justify the dispatch of American forces to Lebanon: (1) President Chamoun's appeal; (2) "protection of American nationals abroad"; and (3) the so-called action of "collective defense" taken in accordance with Article 51 of the Charter of the United Nations. These are his so-called legal bases. Let us examine whether these three bases are acceptable. (1) The so-called appeal of President Chamoun's government cannot legalize the dispatch of American forces to Lebanon. The traitorous government of Chamoun, opposed by the people of Lebanon, had to appeal to a foreign state to dispatch forces to maintain its shaky rule and therefore it obviously cannot be considered as a government representing the Lebanese people. As pointed out by Khrushchev, Chairman of the Council of Ministers of the Soviet Union, the "appeal was made by the irresponsible ruler [of Lebanon] without the support of the people and in disregard of the will of the people," [and therefore] "it does not have any constitutional validity." [62] As a matter of fact, the speaker of the Lebanese Parliament had called on the United Nations to request the United States to withdraw its forces; this was, on behalf of the Lebanese people, a repudiation of Chamoun's appeal. Moreover, Chamoun's appeal itself is illegal, because to invite the colonialists to engage in armed intervention in the internal affairs of a state is to betray the independence of that state. American imperialism absolutely cannot conceal the illegal nature of its armed intervention on the pretext of such an illegal appeal. (2) Protection of nationals abroad. One can hardly find such a basis in international law, except in the sixth item of the so-called "intervention by right" in Oppenheim's *International Law* . . . which, however, is merely a theory in defense of the aggressive acts of imperialism. As a matter of fact, the United States frequently intervened in Latin America on the pretext of protecting nationals abroad. . . . In international law, no state can, in the name of protecting nationals abroad, intervene in the internal affairs of other states. The proper way to protect one's nationals abroad is through diplomatic channels, and, in case of necessity, a state can evacuate its nationals living abroad. However, a state absolutely cannot dispatch forces to intervene. . . . [(3)] The so-called "collective self-defense." Self-defense, mentioned in Article 51 of the United Nations Charter, refers to self-defense taken by member states subject to outside armed attack. The Lebanese question is a question of internal affairs, and Lebanon was not subject to outside armed attack. In fact, the United Nations observer corps, which was supposed to find a basis for intervention in Lebanon, could not but recognize the view that Lebanon was not subject to "outside infiltration." Therefore, Article 51 of the United Nations Charter is not applicable to the Lebanese question, and American reliance on Article 51 as its basis for dispatching forces is obviously groundless and cannot be supported.

9-3

"Foreign Ministry Protests to Swiss Government," NCNA–English (Aug. 17, 1967) printed in *FBIS*, no. 160/67: BBB1–2 (Aug. 17, 1967).

(Text) Peking, 17 August—The Chinese Foreign Ministry in a note to the Swiss embassy in China yesterday protested most vehemently against the Swiss government for supporting and encouraging the anti-China activities carried out by the Tibetan bandits in Switzerland. The note severely warns the Swiss government that it must put an immediate end to all the anti-China activities of the Tibetan bandits in Switzerland.

The Chinese embassy in Switzerland delivered a copy of the note to the Swiss government on the same day. The note reads in full as follows:

The CPR [PRC] Ministry of Foreign Affairs requests the Swiss embassy in China to transmit without delay the following note to its government:

A foundation stone-laying ceremony for the so-called "Tibetan Institute" took place at Rikon, Switzerland, on 29 July. It was attended by the mother, the elder brother, and the "personal representative" in Geneva of Dalai, chief of the Tibetan treacherous bandits, and more than 300 other Tibetan bandits. It was also attended by anti-Chinese elements of Britain, France, West Germany, the Netherlands, and Switzerland. The Kuhn brothers, Swiss anti-Chinese elements, went so far as to declare at the ceremony that the said institute is the "spiritual center" of the Tibetan bandits for their activities in Europe. Swiss television, radio, and press took the occasion to play it up and strike up a new anti-Chinese adverse current.

The Chinese government has recently made several representations and protests to the Swiss government against its support and encouragement of the Tibetan bandits' activities, explained its attitude and position concerning this matter, and resolutely demanded that the Swiss government take immediate measures to put an end to such activities. However, in total disregard of this solemn demand of the Chinese government, the Swiss government has persisted in overtly encouraging and supporting the Tibetan bandits in carrying out frantic activities in Switzerland against socialist China. This constitutes a gross intervention in the internal affairs of China, a political provocation which the Chinese people can never tolerate. The Chinese government hereby lodges the strongest protest with the Swiss government.

It must be pointed out that the Tibetan traitorous clique of Dalai, which has fled China, is the enemy of the Tibetan and other nationalities of China. With the support of imperialism, revisionism, and reaction, it is trying to accumulate its forces abroad and look for an opportunity to reestablish the reactionary domination of the serf owners overthrown by the Tibetan people and to subject again the liberated Tibetan people who are leading a happy life to dark and inhuman serfdom. This is a sheer [fantasy] that will never come true.

What rouses indignation is the fact that the Swiss government, which maintains diplomatic relations with China, has, ignoring the repeated advice and protests of the Chinese government, redoubled its efforts in supporting and encouraging the anti-China activities in Europe. This reveals more clearly the reactionary features of the Swiss government which, in collusion with imperialism, revisionism, and reaction, makes itself an enemy of the Chinese people.

The Chinese government severely warns the Swiss government that it must put an immediate end to all the anti-China activities carried out by the Tibetan bandits in Switzerland and refrain from going any farther on the reactionary path against China. The Chinese people who are armed with Mao-Tse-tung's thought are not to be trifled with. If the Swiss government continues to turn a deaf ear to the stern warning of the Chinese government and is bent on being hostile toward the Chinese people and on further aggravating relations between the two countries, it will be lifting a rock only to drop [it on its own] feet.

9-4

I Hsin, "What Does Bourgeois International Law Explain about the Question of Intervention?" *KCWTYC*, no. 4:47–54 (1960).

The principle of nonintervention in the internal affairs of other countries is one of the famous five principles of peaceful coexistence and a fundamental principle of current generally recognized international law. It is enthusiastically supported by all peace-loving countries and peoples throughout the world because it is formulated on the basis of the principle of national equality and is an extension of the principle of inviolability of state sovereignty. It is in accord with the people's desire for freedom and independent existence, and it reflects the will of resistance of peace-loving countries and oppressed nations against the imperialist's coercion in forcing others to follow its will. Bourgeois international law on the question of intervention sometimes superficially recognizes that "intervention . . . concerns the external independence or the territorial or personal supremacy of the State concerned . . . [and, therefore,] intervention is, as a rule, forbidden by the Law of Nations which protects the international personality of the States. . . ." However, it particularly emphasizes that "this rule has exceptions, for there are interventions which take place by right, and there are others which, although they do not take place by right, are nevertheless admitted by the Law of Nations, and are excused in spite of the violation of the personality of the respective States which they involve." It then classifies intervention into "intervention by right," "intervention in default of right," "humanitarian intervention," and so forth. The principle of nonintervention is dismissed in a few words and sentences.[a] This characteristic perfectly reflects the needs of the modern bourgeoisie in international activities.

The principle of nonintervention was proposed in the period of bourgeois revolution, but the historical development of the bourgeois attitude toward this question was the same as its attitude toward other questions. During the period of revolution, the bourgeoisie was frequently subject to the intervention of international feudal reactionary forces. In order to resist foreign intervention and to consolidate its own rule, the bourgeoisie needed the principle of nonintervention. For instance, the French National Convention's 1793 Decree [on Nonintervention] said:

> The National Convention declares, in the name of the French

[a] L. Oppenheim, *International Law,* Vol. 1, 7th ed., by H. Lauterpacht (London: Longmans, Green, 1948), p. 272.

> people, that it will not interfere in any manner in the government of the other powers; but it declares at the same time, that it will sooner be buried under its own ruins than suffer that any power should interfere in the internal regime of the Republic, or should influence the creation of the constitution which it intends to give itself.[63]

This principle of nonintervention was incorporated into an article of the Jacobin Constitution adopted in the same year and was thus confirmed as the supreme law of the state.[64] Both in the American Declaration of Independence of 1776 and in the principles of foreign policy proclaimed later by the United States Secretary of State, Jefferson, the principle of nonintervention was stressed. However, the history of the capitalist countries subsequent to the bourgeois revolution has been different. The development of capitalism reached the stage of imperialism; especially after the Second World War, when capitalism reached the second stage of general crisis, the bourgeois countries found it even more necessary madly to intervene in the internal affairs of other countries. Bourgeois international law is a reflection of this situation, and thus it now talks more of intervention and less of nonintervention.

Let us go one step further by analyzing and criticizing its [bourgeois international law's] various theoretical justifications for intervention.

I

Current bourgeois international law considers that intervention by right in [the internal affairs of] other countries does not constitute infringement. The reason is: "[This] right of intervention is . . . based on a legal restriction upon the independence or territorial or personal supremacy of the State concerned, and . . . the latter is in duty bound to submit to intervention." [b] Oppenheim's *International Law* classifies this kind of intervention into seven categories, but we group them into three major categories: (1) A state intervenes in the affairs of another state for which it has obtained the right of intervention. (2) According to treaties or so-called generally recognized principles of international law, a state has the right to intervene in the affairs of another state which does not observe the treaties or principles. (3) When its nationals are injured abroad or the property of its nationals is damaged abroad, a state has the right to intervene in the affairs of the state where the nationals reside or their property is located. These [cate-

[b] Oppenheim, I, p. 274.

gories of intervention] are all called "intervention by right." Such intervention is alleged to have "legal basis" and therefore seems to be quite righteous and just. We must expose the essence of this bourgeois international law theory and the [related] practices.

The first category of intervention is based upon the right of intervention obtained by one state from another state. First of all, we must point out that such a right of intervention is the result of oppression of weak countries by strong capitalist powers and of small countries by large capitalist powers. A state can be transformed into a protected state, the government of a state can be reduced to a status of dependency and the form of that government can be guaranteed by treaty, or the foreign affairs of one state can be made a part of the foreign affairs of the intervening state. In all these cases, the right of intervention is created on a foundation of imperialist aggression. For instance, the United States once established a type of relationship with some small countries in Central America which provided that the United States had certain rights of intervention. These included important restrictions on the foreign policy of those small countries. In 1903, the United States concluded the Treaty of Havana, which provided that Cuba should never enter into any treaty or engage in any act which would impair or tend to impair its independence. In 1934 the United States agreed to grant independence to the Philippines but prescribed that, for ten years after independence, the United States should directly supervise and control the foreign affairs of the Philippines and also that the United States had the right to intervene in its internal affairs in order to preserve the government and to protect lives and property, as well as for other reasons. After the outbreak of the First World War, Britain also unilaterally declared that Egypt was to be put under its protection. All these cases were in absolute violation of the principle of state sovereignty, but bourgeois international law nevertheless gave them legal status and affirmed that imperialism had the right, which had been grabbed by force, to intervene. The country that was subjected to the intervention was obliged to submit to intervention. The imperialists try to use "law" in this way in order to suppress the resistance of the oppressed nations, to suppress their struggle for liberation, and, thus, to subject them permanently to the status of being oppressed and enslaved.

The second category of intervention is carried out in accordance with treaties or so-called generally recognized principles of international law. It is clear that all these are created in accordance with the will of strong imperialist countries in order to maintain a world order in which the weak are at the mercy of the strong. In 1903 the United States concluded a treaty with Panama which provides that "the same right and authority are granted to the United States for the maintenance of public order in the cities of Panama and Colon, and the territories and harbors adjacent thereto, in case the Republic of Panama should not be, in the judgment of the United States, able to maintain such order." In 1904 the United States intervened in Panama in accordance with this international treaty. This provision was reiterated in Article 10 of the 1936 Treaty between the United States and Panama, which at present is still the "treaty basis" for United States infringement on the territorial sovereignty of Panama. The imperialists have also distorted the Charter of the United Nations and even use it as a basis in international law for their illegal intervention in [the affairs of] other countries. For instance, the struggle of the people of Lebanon against Chamoun's reactionary rule was purely an internal affair of Lebanon, but American imperialists ruthlessly sent troops to intervene on the meaningless pretext of "exercising the right of collective self-defense" under Article 51 of the Charter. . . .

The third category of intervention is carried out in accordance with the protection of the rights of a state's nationals abroad. It must be pointed out that the guiding principle is that a state can only protect the legitimate rights and interests of its nationals abroad. However, in order to carry out its illegal plunder abroad and its other political objectives, imperialism frequently engages in intervention in [the affairs of] other countries on the pretext of protecting its nationals. Around 1926, when the United States intervened in Nicaragua, Coolidge, who was the United States President at the time, even publicly declared that "wherever an American citizen goes, so goes a piece of American territory."[65] This meant that all Americans should enjoy the right of extraterritoriality in any foreign country and that the American government could send troops to those countries to protect the Americans as if they were in their own country. Even as recently as the period after the Cuban revolution, the direct intervention of the United States in [the affairs of] Cuba was still based on the pretext of protecting its nationals. The people of our country have personally experienced the intervention and aggression of imperialist countries on the pretext of protecting their nationals and there are indeed too many cases to enumerate. During the period of the Chinese Revolution, when the Northern Expedition forces captured Nanking in 1927, in order to obstruct the Chinese Revolution through the use of arms, English, American, and other imperialists ordered their warships to shell Nanking on the ground that their nationals and consulates were "encroached upon and harmed by rioters." As a result, more than two thousand Chinese soldiers and civilians were wounded or killed, and the loss of houses and property was considerable. Immediately afterward, the

United States, England, Japan, France, and Italy further discussed plans for sending troops to intervene and lodged an ultimatum with the National Government in Wuhan, demanding the prosecution of criminals, apology, and indemnity and making other unreasonable demands. In 1928, when the Northern Expedition forces entered Tsinan, Japan even declared that in order to "protect Japan's rights and interests" it was sending troops to Shantung. On May 3, Japan massacred more than three thousand Chinese soldiers and civilians and cruelly murdered the Chinese special diplomatic commissioner, Ts'ai Kung-shih . . . . Some bourgeois jurists, such as Hall and others, even directly extended the state's fundamental right of self-defense to the right of "protecting nationals abroad," thus linking and equalizing the protection of a state's nationals with that state's security. They then raise the legal basis for protection of nationals to the level of the legal basis for defending state security in an attempt to "legalize" illegal imperialist intervention. Isn't it clear whose interests they are serving?

II

It is not always possible for imperialism to find a treaty or a legal right as a basis for its intervention in [the affairs of] weak and small countries. Nor does imperialism limit its intervention to "intervention by right." Bourgeois international law, therefore, provides for "intervention in default of right" and other pretexts for imperialism, namely, intervention can be carried out in "self-defense" or in the interests of the "balance of power" and intervention can be based on so-called "humanitarianism." Bourgeois international law makes a great effort to explain that although this type of intervention violates the independence and sovereign integrity of a state and although the state that is subjected to intervention is not legally obliged to submit to it, this type of intervention cannot be considered illegal and is thus permissible and excusable.

On the surface, the grounds for such permissible and excusable intervention are elaborate and high-sounding and make it appear that intervention is a necessary measure for safeguarding peace, justice, national security, and legitimate interests. In fact, so-called "self-defense" is only a pretext used by strong capitalist countries for engaging in foreign expansion. In order to invade other countries it fictitiously cites "self-defense" as the reason for intervention. When its expansion meets obstacles, it may take further intervention on the pretext of "self-defense." When it sees a revolution breaking out in a country and the revolution makes it difficult to preserve the interests it acquired through aggression and makes continuous plunder more difficult, again it may intervene on the pretext of "self-defense." In the history of imperialism we can find a large number of facts relating to this type of intervention. During the three-year period between 1916 and 1919, the United States sent troops to invade Mexico on several occasions in order to "punish infringement on the sovereignty of the United States."[66] In 1958 there was armed intervention by the United States in the revolution of the people of the Arab countries in the Middle East. In recent years, the United States has illegally occupied our territory, Taiwan, by force of arms. All this is done on the pretext of "collective self-defense." Bourgeois international law has unconditionally sanctioned such acts of intervention, and it has done so intentionally in order to enable imperialism unscrupulously to carry out aggression in the name of "self-defense."

So-called intervention in the interests of "the balance of power" is required by the strong imperialists in their struggle and in the consolidation of their already achieved dominant position. They may use it to suppress other newly emerged imperialists; and, similarly, the latter may expand their influence on the same pretext in order to achieve their desire for "balance." In 1895, Russia, Germany, and France forced Japan to return Liaotung Peninsula to our country. In 1899, the United States demanded an "open door" policy with respect to China. These were all in the nature of intervention in the interest of "the balance of power."

So-called "humanitarian intervention" is designed to spread a beautiful carpet over another road of imperalist intervention in the internal affairs of other countries. Its theory is: although "a State can treat its own nationals according to discretion . . . there are limits to that discretion and . . . when a State renders itself guilty of cruelties against and persecution of its nationals, in such a way as to deny their fundamental human rights and to shock the conscience of mankind, intervention in the interest of humanity is legally permissible."[c] It must be pointed out here that the meaning of humanitarianism implies class character. The term "humanity" professed in bourgeois international law means bourgeois humanity. Imperialism considers as "inhumane" those countries in which the proletariat has political power and establishes a dictatorship over the reactionary forces. They consider as "inhumane" the punishment and suppression imposed by the people of a country upon conspiratorial elements who engage in rebellion and subversive activities supported by imperialism. When a revolution breaks out in a country and attacks the reactionary forces,

[c] Oppenheim, I, pp. 279–280.

imperialism considers it "inhumane." When a country adopts certain progressive measures in internal affairs which reflect the demands of the people but which are unfavorable to the minority, the originally privileged class, imperialism also considers it "inhumane." In all these cases, imperialism considers it permissible to intervene. Moreover, in order to achieve its object, which cannot be publicly announced, imperialism can even fabricate the pretext of "humanitarianism" in order to intervene. The Chinese suppression of the rebellion of the upper stratum of the Tibetan reactionary clique supported by reactionaries of foreign countries and the democratic reform of the Tibet Region, which made possible the liberation of a million or more Tibetan compatriots from the dark and cruel serf system, was loudly protested by imperialism, which calumniated the measures as "violations of human rights" and "genocide." Obviously, behind all the shouting is an eagerness to intervene. Some bourgeois jurists follow their master like dogs, barking at sounds and shadows. The calumniating report of the so-called "International Commission of Jurists" relating to the Tibet question is full of rumors and slander for the purpose of fabricating an international legal basis for intervention for reactionaries of foreign countries and imperialism. Moreover, the United States manipulated the General Assembly of the United Nations to pass the so-called resolution on "the Tibet question" in order to cloud the issue and to intervene in the internal affairs of our country. In July 1959, the United States Congress sponsored a "Captive Nations Week" directed at all countries in the socialist camp which have already eliminated exploitation and oppression. It declared that [these submerged nations look to] "the United States, as the citadel of human freedom, for leadership in bringing about their liberation and independence."[67] By thus using a sympathetic pose, imperialism intervenes in the internal affairs of countries in order to achieve its goal of once again enslaving all mankind. This is the "humanitarianism" that imperialism has been promoting. If we look at imperialism itself, how does it carry out "humanitarianism"? The development of capitalism and the means by which capitalists make fortunes and amass wealth are, in the final analysis, achieved by enslaving and plundering the people at home and abroad. Even today, in what capitalist country are the workers, peasants, and other laboring people free from the ruthless exploitation and squeeze of the landlords and the bourgeoisie? And are they not struggling miserably against hunger, cold, and unemployment? With respect to the people in colonies and countries located in economically backward areas, imperialism's rule is even more cruel, its plunder is even more brutal, and its slavery is even more barbarous. The African Negro slave trade was originally the European bourgeoisie's way of making fortunes. The policy used by the American government was that of exterminating the mass of American Indians. Even today, the American government and the white-controlled government of the Union of South Africa continue to discriminate against and persecute Negroes. Despite the fact that the imperialists themselves are completely without humanity, they nevertheless preach "humanity" and "human rights" directly to the socialist countries in an attempt to support the reactionaries in those countries and to find a pretext for imperialist intervention. Bourgeois international law fabricates the legal basis for intervention as follows: "Intervention in the interest of humanity is legally permissible," [68] and "the principle of humanitarian intervention has already become a rule of international law." [69] For this, bourgeois international law distorts the United Nations Charter without hesitation and denies the principle of nonintervention provided in Article 2, paragraph 7 of the Charter by saying that since " 'human rights and fundamental freedoms' have become a persistent feature of the Charter they may have ceased to be a matter which is essentially within the domestic jurisdiction of States." [d] It attempts to fabricate a basis in international law for imperialist intervention. These secrets of bourgeois international law were concisely disclosed by the British international law jurist, Brierly. He wrote: "At present an intervention, which we are forced to stigmatize as illegal, may even deserve moral approval . . . ." [70] Finally, we know that the purpose of the bourgeois international law theory of "humanitarian intervention" is to describe "illegal intervention" as "legal intervention."

In addition to justifying intervention in default of right, bourgeois international law, in order to help imperialism camouflage its intervention, also describes imperialism's intervention in the name of nonintervention as real nonintervention. On the question of nonintervention, bourgeois international law generally describes the Monroe Doctrine of the United States as one of the origins of the principle of nonintervention; but if we study the historical contents of that Doctrine, the story is totally different. Objectively, the so-called Monroe Doctrine did fulfill a definite function in supporting the resistance of the South American countries, which had just won their independence from Spain and Portugal, to the intervention of the Holy Alliance. As far as the United States was concerned, however, the Monroe Doctrine was proposed in order to achieve the object of preventing the intervention of the strong European imperialist countries in the affairs of the various

[d] Oppenheim, I, p. 280, note 2. [Note: Oppenheim does not say *since* " 'human rights . . .' have become a persistent feature of the Charter . . ." but *"possibly, to the extent to which* 'human rights and fundamental freedoms' have become a persistent feature of the Charter they may have ceased to be a matter which is essentially within the domestic jurisdiction of States." (Italics added.)]

American countries, thus establishing its own monopolistic control over those affairs. This is the reason why, when the United States asserted that the Monroe Doctrine was "necessary for the establishment and preservation of the independence of South American countries," those countries all expressed their opposition and considered it an insult to their independence. The facts also prove that just about the time when the Monroe Doctrine was announced, the United States had already begun its expansionist activities in Latin America. In 1806 and 1818, the United States army twice invaded Mexico. In 1822 the United States navy landed in Cuba. In 1836, 1844, and between 1845 and 1848, the United States repeatedly started wars of plunder against Mexico and seized more than one-half of what was originally Mexican territory and now constitutes parts of New Mexico, California, Arizona, Texas, Nevada, Utah, Colorado, and Wyoming in the southwestern part of the United States. Under the banner of the Monroe Doctrine's "nonintervention," the entire nineteenth century became an era of American enslavement of Latin America. For the various countries of Latin America, the nineteenth century was one in which they moved from the colonial rule of Spain and Portugal to enslavement by the United States. The Monroe Doctrine, which was highly praised by bourgeois jurists as the "origin of the principle of nonintervention," subsequently even became the blueprint for the "English Monroe Doctrine," vis-à-vis Europe, which was submitted by English imperialism in 1928 in the course of drafting the General Treaty for the Renunciation of War, and for the "Asian Monroe Doctrine," vis-à-vis China, which was submitted by Japan in 1934. This suffices to show the imperialist essence of the Monroe Doctrine. It can also be seen from this that sometimes imperialism opposes intervention by others in order to facilitate its own intervention. In 1936, Fascist Germany and Italy carried out armed intervention against the Republic of Spain and thus aroused the sympathy and support of the progressive people throughout the world for democratic Spain. Anglo-French imperialism, however, was quite frightened and immediately announced a "nonintervention policy" vis-à-vis Spain. It set up in London a so-called "Non-intervention Committee" to oppose support for the Spanish movement and to give full freedom to intervention by Fascist Germany and Italy. Comrade Stalin once made a shrewd evaluation of this imperialist "nonintervention policy". He said: "The policy of nonintervention indulges aggression, spreads the war, and thus transforms the war into a world war." [c] Today, in a situation where the East wind prevails

[c] Stalin's Report to the 18th Congress of the Communist Party of the Soviet Union [translated from the Chinese].

over the West wind, the United States has been forced to adopt a policy of "genuine preparation for war under the guise of pseudopeace" and has found it all the more necessary to put on the cloak of nonintervention to enable it to engage positively in intervention. In August 1959, at the meeting of Foreign Ministers of the American States, when the United States Secretary of State, Herter, spoke highly of the four principles of the Charter of the Organization of American States, the principle of nonintervention was the one he spoke of first. On February 21, 1960, on the eve of his visit to South America, President Eisenhower again shamelessly and unblushingly said that "in all of Latin America, I repeat, we adhere honorably and persistently to the policy of nonintervention." [71] But the Monroe Doctrine's principle of nonintervention failed to deceive the people of the Americas in the past; today's "principle of nonintervention," as a repetition of the old theme, can only reveal more than it can conceal. In August 1959, Raul Castro, commander in chief of the Cuban armed forces, declared at a news conference held in Caracas: "The Organization of American States is an impotent organ that protects Trujillo and Somoza. The one who leads the organ is a great power which regards itself as the regulator of the people of the various countries and which clearly violates the much-propagated principle of nonintervention." This is a sharp and blunt disclosure by an official of an American state of the hypocritical American imperialist principle of nonintervention; it is a resounding slap on the hypocritical face of American imperialism. Imperialism plays sometimes with the legal basis for intervention and sometimes with the principle of nonintervention. All its manipulations lead to the same goal of carrying out aggression against other countries and of plundering rights and interests. The international law jurists in the service of imperialism naturally echo their master. Whenever intervention is necessary, they justify the legality of intervention; whenever it is necessary to assume the pose of nonintervention, they come out with an affirmation of the reality of their "nonintervention." They also have different justifications for use in defending imperialist aggression and intervention in the internal affairs of other countries.

III

Imperialist intervention in [the affairs of] other countries has been increasing day by day. Particularly since the Second World War, the United States has become the reactionary leader of the whole world. It has not only made full use of old justifications for intervention, but also has gone far beyond the previous scope of intervention by resorting to various [new] forms of intervention in madly carrying out its intervention activities. One method, armed intervention, has been frequently used in the past. Since the war, the United States has used that method in Korea, Taiwan, Indochina and the Middle East. It has concluded many aggressive military treaties, organized many military blocs, and established in foreign countries many military bases which are scattered throughout the world. In addition to being used for armed intervention in [the affairs of] socialist countries, such arrangements also have the goal of obtaining rights of intervention from the allied countries. As a matter of fact, these arrangements have been used to carry out quiet armed intervention and have forced the countries in which the bases are located and the countries which concluded the military treaties to undertake the obligation of submitting to the stationing of American troops and to intervention by military advisory groups.

The second method is intervention through economic "aid." The Truman Doctrine, the Marshall Plan, the Point Four Program, and the Eisenhower Doctrine were all designed to make the countries receiving the aid economically and politically subordinate to the United States. By so doing, the United States achieves its ultimate object of intervening in the internal affairs of those countries. In a letter to Eisenhower, Rockefeller, one of the leading monopolistic capitalists in the United States, admitted this quite frankly by saying: "We must draft a grand economic cooperation program which would insure our political and economic influence in Asia, Africa, and other underdeveloped countries. In order to encourage the investment of private capital in these countries, we must support those people who stand opposed to the present regime. By so doing, we shall have laid the foundation upon which the policy of these countries may turn in a healthier direction. The basic idea of this policy is to bring these countries into our hands for manipulation by developing economic relations with them." [72] In 1952, when the Mossadegh government of Iran adopted the stand of not being dependent upon the United States, the latter [immediately] stopped the aid and conspired to overthrow the Mossadegh government. Then, American aid was used to support the pro-American Zahedi and form a [new] government. It [the United States] not only acquired the petroleum interests in Iran, but also brought Iran into the Baghdad Pact (now renamed the Central Treaty Organization), thus putting Iran under the complete control of the United States. In June 1959 Brazilian President Kubitschek announced that Brazil had decided to discontinue negotiations on obtaining loans from the American-controlled International Monetary Fund "because the conditions for granting loans proposed by this organization constituted an intervention in Brazil's internal affairs." [73] This all shows that American aid is essentially for the purpose of intervening directly in the internal affairs of other countries and of getting the sovereignty of those countries in exchange.

The third method is carrying out internal subversive activities, organizing rebellions, and directing coups d'état to overthrow the governments of other countries. Since the war, imperialism has resorted to this method even more often than before. During the ten-year period between 1948 and 1958, the United States carried out eighteen important subversive incidents on the American continent. In Asia, American imperialism openly supported the rebellious clique in Indonesia. In the Middle East, it succeeded in using subversion to overthrow the Nebulsi cabinet in Jordan. In 1958, the United States Department of State secretly instructed its diplomatic representatives in the various Middle East countries that "they must make an untiring effort to consolidate the internal forces which have Western ideas and such foreign forces as may intervene, at the proper time, with likely developments in the United Arab Republic." [74] There are many similar cases. Another method of intervention is the direct dispatch of special agents, spies, and subversive elements to carry out various activities of sabotage and subversion. In the Mutual Security Act passed by the United States Congress in 1951 and in all similar acts subsequently passed, it is provided that a hundred million dollars be appropriated annually for subsidizing "any selected persons who are residing in or escapees from the Soviet Union, Poland, Czechoslovakia, Hungary, Rumania, Bulgaria . . . or Communist-occupied areas of Germany and Austria . . . either to form such persons into elements of the military forces supporting the North Atlantic Treaty Organization or for other purposes." [75] The expiration date of this act has been extended annually since then by the United States Congress and supplementary appropriations have been made in order to intensify subversive and sabotage activities in socialist countries and to carry out Dulles' "policy of liberation". . . . American imperialism once used its special agents and spy network in West Berlin to precipitate the "Berlin Incident" in the capital of democratic Germany. It used the "Committee of Free Europe" and "Radio Free Europe," spy agencies in West Germany and Austria—countries neighboring Hungary—to plan and direct the counterrevolutionary rebellion in Hungary. Imperialism extensively uses these concealed methods of intervention in an effort to avoid the resistance and condemnation with which open intervention may meet. It thus can stand behind the scenes to achieve the object of intervention. In early July 1959, Eisenhower said: "The United States cannot openly carry out intervention; otherwise we again would be called the dollar imperialists or something else of that kind." [76] This is American imperialism's clearest admission of guilt.

9-5

"Refute the Hue and Cry Over the Hungarian Question by the Western World," editorial, *JMJP* (Nov. 14, 1956), p. 1; English translation under the title "Behind the Hue and Cry over the 'Hungarian Issue,' " in *PC*, no. 23:6–7 (Dec. 1, 1956).

Of course it would be best if the Hungarian government itself could successfully suppress the Fascist armed revolt backed by the West. (Not even the Western countries could deny it was a revolt.) But when the Hungarian government had inadequate strength and asked the Soviet troops for help, it did not alter the essence of the matter one jot. The Soviet Union showed its concern for the freedom of Hungary and defended it.

It is not difficult for any cool-headed person with a political conscience to see that, if Hungary had not requested the assistance of the Soviet troops and if they had not given assistance, Hungary today could only have become a Fascist hell, an imperialist outpost for overthrowing various other East European people's democracies and engineering a new world war. What freedom would this have given to the Hungarian people? And what good could this do to world peace and the progress of mankind? The Soviet government on October 30 issued a declaration repeating its respect for the sovereignty and territorial integrity of the people's democracies, and its readiness to reopen discussions with the Warsaw Treaty nations on the question of Soviet troops in Hungary and other countries. At the same time the Soviet troops had actually withdrawn from Budapest. Certainly the Soviet forces would not have chosen to go through the hardships involved and take action again unless it had been a case of absolute necessity, of being impelled by comradely sympathy, by the duty to share common difficulties with the socialist countries, and by the urgent nature of the situation after the complete exposure of the fascist plot for a comeback. Are not all these things quite obvious?

In helping the Hungarian worker-peasant revolutionary government to suppress the revolt, the Soviet Union did not violate its declaration of October 30, nor the five principles of peaceful coexistence. Soviet forces do not want an inch of Hungarian soil. After the restoration of order in Hungary, the Soviet Union and Hungary will again hold negotiations over the question of stationing troops under the Warsaw Treaty.

Therefore, to mention Soviet assistance to Hungary and the British and French invasion of Egypt in the same breath is either a result of malicious intention or of misunderstanding. The facts are exactly opposite. When the British and French aggressors were engaged in murder and arson in Egypt and Algeria, Western countries were instigating Fascist elements to murder and arson in Hungary with weapons supplied by the West.

While the Soviet government was lending its firm support to Egypt against aggression, it was firmly helping Hungary to combat the restoration of fascism. It is clear that the Soviet Union takes the same stand toward the Hungarian people as it does toward the Egyptian people—it helps them defend freedom and oppose imperialism.

Similarly, many Western countries have the same attitude toward the Hungarian people as they have toward the Egyptian people—they want to slaughter them, to enslave them, to deprive them of their sovereignty and interfere in their internal affairs. . . .

We hold that the actions taken by the Soviet Union in Hungary are entirely just. This is because the Soviet troops are stationed in Hungary not only in conformity with the Warsaw Treaty, and at the request of the Hungarian government to assist in restoring order, but also because that request coincides with the genuine desires of the Hungarian people. It was precisely because of this that the counter-revolutionary forces were quickly smashed and social order throughout Hungary has been steadily and definitely restored. The Hungarian people, though they showed justified dissatisfaction with the work of their former government, never demanded the discarding of socialism and acceptance of fascism. The action to restore fascism by arms was not a "spontaneous" mass action, but one imposed on the Hungarian people by a gang of conspirators instigated by the United States and other Western countries.

9-6

Ho Wu-shuang and Ma Chün, "A Criticism of the Reactionary Viewpoint of Ch'en T'i-ch'iang on the Science of International Law," *CFYC,* no. 6:38 (1957).

Ch'en T'i-ch'iang's antiparty, antisocialist position is also clearly reflected in his articles on questions of international law published after the liberation. For instance, when he mentioned the concept of intervention in his article entitled "The Hungarian Incident and the Principle of Nonintervention,"[a] he wrote:

> . . . Acts of intervention in [the affairs of] a state with the

[a] *Kuang-ming jih-pao* (Apr. 5, 1957), p. 1.

> consent of the government of that state cannot be considered "intervention." Of course if, during a civil war within a state, a foreign state aids the government, which has ruled in a manner contrary to [the interests of] the people, such aid will naturally provoke the people's anger. In particular, if the revolutionary force achieves victory and establishes a new government, the new government may hate that foreign country. *But this is only political ill will* (even to the point of constituting cause of war); *there cannot be legal responsibility.* (Emphasis added by us [Ho and Ma].)

The implications of this viewpoint are quite obvious. Ch'en T'i-ch'iang is supporting the following proposition: American imperialism does not bear legal responsibility for aiding the Chiang Kai-shek clique in fighting the civil war and in suppressing the revolutionary movement of the Chinese people. There is simply ill will on the part of the Chinese people. In other words, from Ch'en T'i-ch'iang's point of view, such acts [by American imperialism] do not violate international law. . . .

American imperialism's act of aiding the Chiang Kai-shek reactionary clique in fighting the civil war is an obvious intervention in the internal affairs of China which violates Chinese sovereignty. Therefore, it directly violates a generally recognized principle of international law—nonintervention in the internal affairs of other countries—and the Charter of the United Nations. As everyone knows, there are many types of intervention, such as direct armed intervention and intervention through using other people. American imperialism's intervention during the Chinese People's Liberation War was intervention of the latter type. This type of intervention also constitutes a breach of international law, and only those rightists who breathe out of imperialism's nostrils would say that it cannot result in legal responsibility and simply results in political ill will.

Note

As the previous items in this section suggest, when foreign troops enter another state at the request of the government of that state in order to assist in restoring order, Peking's opinion of the legality of this action turns upon whether, in its view, "that request coincides with the genuine desires of the [local] people" (9–5). This, of course, permits Peking to decide on the basis of political expediency. To cite a recent example, when the PRC challenged the buildup of US forces in Thailand, "Commentator" wrote in the *People's Daily:*

> [Thai Prime Minister Thanom's] big bug clique even acted as if this clique is the master of Thailand, saying that the US aggressor forces had been invited by it to "help" cope with the revolutionary forces of Thailand. In fact, it is clear to all that Thailand has long been reduced to a colony of US imperialism and that Thanom and his breed are merely a bunch of lackeys fed by US imperialism, lackeys whose sole task is to act as tools of US imperialist aggression against, and enslavement of, the Thai people. It is indeed ridiculous to say that the master is "helping" his slave when it is obviously the slave taking orders from his master![77]

9-7

Ch'en T'i-ch'iang, "We Cannot Allow Hong Kong To Be Used as a Base for Hostile Activities against the Mainland," *JMJP* (Mar. 19, 1956), p. 3.

On January 31, [1956,] an F-86 jet fighter plane of the Chiang Kai-shek clique, after being chased by our air defense forces while undertaking the task of harassing the mainland, fled to Hong Kong and landed on the Kai Tak airfield there. Our Foreign Ministry had drawn the attention of the British government to the incident and requested the British side to detain the plane and its pilot. On [March] 12, the British chargé d'affaires addressed a note to the Foreign Ministry, stating that the pilot had been sent back to Taiwan. According to reports of foreign news agencies, the British authorities are also preparing to despatch the plane back to Taiwan. Our Foreign Ministry has lodged a protest with the British government on the case. This act of the British government is a serious provocation against the Chinese people and cannot but arouse the greatest indignation of the Chinese people.

The principles of international law stipulate that the government of a country has the obligation not to allow the area under its administration to be turned into a base to conduct hostile activities against the government of a foreign country with which it is at peace. Similarly, in the case of civil strife in a country when a state of belligerency has not been recognized, the government of any third country should refrain from taking any action to prevent the legitimate government of that country from making efforts to restore its internal unity and order and should not provide any assistance to the rebels. International law is very clear on this point. The British international law expert, [Professor] Oppenheim, wrote:

> States [referring to the state where the subversive activities are organized] are under a duty to prevent and suppress such subversive activities against foreign Governments as assumes the form of armed hostile expeditions.[a]

[On September 8,] 1900, the Institute of International Law, an association of well-known international law jurists, adopted a draft convention on "Droits et devoirs des puissances étrangères, au cas de mouvement insurrectionnel, envers les gouvernements établis et reconnus, qui sont aux prises avec l'insurrection" at its Neuchatel meeting. Article 2 of the draft convention provides:

> 1. Every third power, at peace with an independent nation, is bound not to interfere with the measures which this nation takes for the reestablishing of internal peace.
> 2. It is bound not to furnish to the insurgents either arms, munitions, military goods, or financial aid.
> 3. It is especially forbidden for any third power to allow an armed hostile expedition against an established and recognized government to be organized within its domains.

In February 1928, a "Convention on Duties and Rights of States in the Event of Civil Strife" was adopted at the Sixth International Conference of American States at Havana. Article 1 of the Convention provides:

> The contracting states bind themselves to observe the following rules with regard to civil strife in another one of them:
>
> 1. To use all means at their disposal to prevent the inhabitants of their territory, nationals or aliens, from participating in, gathering elements, crossing the boundary, or sailing from their territory for the purpose of starting or promoting civil strife.
> 2. To disarm and intern every rebel crossing their boundaries . . . . The arms found in the hands of the rebels may be seized and withdrawn by the government of the country granting asylum, to be returned, once the struggle has ended, to the state in civil strife.

What has been said above are principles universally supported by international law scholars and applied in international relations. The British government is now trampling on these principles.

[a] L. Oppenheim, *International Law,* Vol. I, 7th ed., by H. Lauterpacht (London: Longmans, Green, 1948), p. 260.

As regards the case under discussion, it should first be pointed out that the government of the Chinese People's Republic is the sole legitimate government of China. This government has been formally recognized by, and is at peace with, the British government. Moreover, the British note points out that there is no state of belligerency in existence. This being so, the British government has these obligations only to the legitimate government which it recognizes and has no obligation whatsoever to the Chiang Kai-shek clique, which has no legal status in the sense of international law.

In accordance with the above-stated provisions, the British government at least has the obligation to detain the aircraft and pilot of the Chiang Kai-shek clique so as to prevent the pilot from conducting armed hostile activities against the legitimate Chinese government again. On the contrary, the British government, in defiance of the Chinese government's protest, sent the Chiang Kai-shek pilot back to Taiwan. The British government's note to the Foreign Ministry attempted to defend its action, and said, "It is normal international practice that, if a military aircraft infringes the air space of another country and lands there in the absence of hostile intentions towards the latter or of recognition of a state of belligerency, the aircraft and crew should be allowed to return." Anybody with some knowledge of international law will realize that this statement is completely unreasonable. As everybody knows, a military plane must belong to a state. Since the Chiang Kai-shek clique has no legal status, its plane cannot be considered the lawful plane of any state. If it must be made out to belong to some country, then it must be considered to belong to the People's Republic of China which the British government recognizes. The British note states that such "aircraft and crew should be allowed to return," and this must also mean that they must be allowed to return to the People's Republic of China. This is the natural logical conclusion since the British government recognizes the People's Republic of China and does not admit a state of belligerency to exist. The British government, while recognizing the government of the Chinese People's Republic and stressing nonexistence of a state of belligerency, is putting itself in an untenable position by sending the pilot back to Chiang Kai-shek in Taiwan.

Moreover, the British note said that it had "no intention of permitting Hong Kong to be used as a base for hostile activities against anyone." This is a very good statement. . . . But the fact is that the British authorities have given the Chiang Kai-shek clique the liberty of using Hong Kong as a base for hostile activities to attack the mainland of China and have even encouraged the Chiang Kai-shek clique to so use it. This is a most serious matter.

What is meant by "using an area as a base for hostile activities?" If a country allows individuals to organize armies, enlist troops, store and ship arms within its territory, and to start from this territory an armed attack against another country, there is of course no doubt that the territory is being used for hostile activities. But if an armed expeditionary force does not start from this country, but from another area, and after carrying out hostile activities withdraws to within the territory of this country to evade pursuit, and undertakes within this territory rest, reorganization, and repairs of arms, so that it may leave this territory for another area and then carry out anew hostile activities against the country originally attacked, then on what ground can we say that under these conditions described the said territory is not being used as a base for hostile activities? For one country to allow an armed expeditionary force to start from its territory and for it to allow such a force protection in its territory to preserve and increase its strength, what material difference can be found? The assistance rendered by the British Hong Kong authorities to the aircraft and the pilots of the Chiang Kai-shek clique had actually made Hong Kong such a base. No matter what the British authorities may argue, its deeds are an obvious encouragement to the Chiang Kai-shek clique. Therefore the sophistry contained in the British note does not alter the fact that, in the present case, Hong Kong has been used as base and sanctuary for military activities against the Chinese mainland.

In addition to allowing Hong Kong to be used as a base for hostile activities against the mainland of China, the action of the British authorities is obviously not reconcilable with the various principles of international law referred to above. To allow the Chiang Kai-shek pilot to return to Taiwan is to allow people in British territory facilities for "sailing from their territory for the purpose of starting or promoting civil strife." To send the Chiang Kai-shek plane to Taiwan is to "furnish insurgents with arms." Such acts of the British authorities are obvious violations of the above-mentioned articles. Under general circumstances, when a country neglects to take precautions against individuals engaged in such activities within its territory, it must assume international responsibility. In the present case, the perpetrator of these acts is not any individual, but the British authorities themselves. Such violation of international law must be many times more serious compared with individual acts.

What should Britain do in dealing with this particular case? Article 1, paragraph 2, of the Havana Convention gives a clear answer. That is "to disarm and intern every rebel crossing their boundaries" and to seize or withdraw arms from the rebels and to hand them over to the Chinese government in the future. This is the attitude the British government should adopt.

In short, Britain's handling of the case of the Chiang Kai-shek pilot is in violation of international law and a provocative act against the Chinese people. According to international law, the action of the British authorities in Hong Kong constitutes an international delinquency. As Professor Oppenheim said: "There is no doubt that a foreign state commits an international delinquency by assisting insurgents in spite of being at peace with the legitimate government." [b] A state should assume full responsibility for its international delinquency.

NOTE

When in 1971 the government of Pakistan forcibly sought to suppress East Pakistan's efforts to achieve self-determination and India became progressively embroiled in the struggle to create a separate state of Bangla Desh, PRC sources accused India of subverting Pakistan in the same way India allegedly engineered a rebellion in Tibet in 1959. For example, the *People's Daily* charged:

> [Prime Minister Indira Gandhi, Defense Minister J. Ram and others] said: India "will consider the question of troop withdrawal" after the "return" of East Pakistan's "refugees." In other words, if India fails in its political subversion in Pakistan, then it has the right to resort to military threats against Pakistan and even to occupy Pakistan territory by force. Everybody knows that the so-called "refugee question" is precisely the product of flagrant interference in Pakistan's internal affairs by the Indian government. Now, the Indian government has the impudence to carry out unbridled armed invasion of Pakistan on the pretext of the "refugee question." We are not unfamiliar with such a practice by the Indian government. Didn't the Indian reactionaries also create the "Tibetan refugee question" more than ten years ago? When the rebellion of serf-owners they engineered in the Tibet region of China had failed then, they abducted tens of thousands of Tibetan inhabitants of China to India and made use of this incident to carry out frantic anti-China activities. It is the customary practice of the Indian reactionaries to poison the relations between nationalities in neighbouring countries and create incidents to be used as pretexts for intervention, subversion and aggression against these countries.[78]

The materials thus far presented may lead the reader to believe that the PRC has been almost entirely concerned with forging the principle of nonintervention into a defensive shield for fending off the depredations of all types of imperialism. Actually, of course, this is far from a complete picture of Peking's position, for the PRC has been deeply committed to influencing events abroad through a wide range of actions that raise questions about its view of nonintervention.

[b] *Ibid.*, Vol. II, 7th ed., by H. Lauterpacht, 1952, p. 660.

9-8

Lin Piao, "Long Live the Victory of People's War!" *PR* 8.36:9–10, 22–23, 24–25, 27, 28, 29 (Sept. 3, 1965).

[The author, Vice-Chairman of the Central Committee of the Communist Party of China, Vice-Premier, and Minister of National Defense when this important speech was published, was reported to have died in September 1971 following an abortive attempt to assassinate Mao Tse-tung. Notes omitted.]

Full twenty years have elapsed since our victory in the great War of Resistance against Japan.

After a long period of heroic struggle, the Chinese people, under the leadership of the Communist Party of China and Comrade Mao Tse-tung, won final victory two decades ago in their war against the Japanese imperialists who had attempted to subjugate China and swallow up the whole of Asia.

The Chinese people's War of Resistance was an important part of the world war against German, Japanese, and Italian fascism. The Chinese people received support from the people and the antifascist forces all over the world. And, in their turn, the Chinese people made an important contribution to victory in the antifascist war as a whole.

Of the innumerable anti-imperialist wars waged by the Chinese people in the past hundred years, the War of Resistance against Japan was the first to end in complete victory. It occupies an extremely important place in the annals of war, in the annals of both the revolutionary wars of the Chinese people and the wars of the oppressed nations of the world against imperialist aggression.

It was a war in which a weak, semicolonial and semifeudal country triumphed over a strong imperialist country. For a long period after the invasion of China's northeastern provinces by the Japanese imperialists, the Kuomintang followed a policy of nonresistance. In the early stage of the War of Resistance, the Japanese imperialists exploited their military superiority to drive deep into China and occupy half her territory. In the face of the massive attacks of the aggressors and the anti-Japanese upsurge of the people throughout the country, the Kuomintang was compelled to take part in the War of Resistance, but soon afterward it adopted [a] policy of passive resistance to Japan and active opposition to the Communist Party. The heavy responsibility of combating Japanese imperialism thus fell on the shoulders of the Eighth Route Army, the New Fourth Army, and the people of the liberated areas, all led by the Communist Party. At the outbreak of the war, the Eighth Route and New Fourth Armies had only a few tens of thousands of men and suffered from extreme inferiority in both arms and equipment, and for a long time they were under the cross fire of the Japanese imperialists on the one hand and the Kuomintang troops on the other. But they grew stronger and stronger in the course of the war and became the main force in defeating Japanese imperialism.

How was it possible for a weak country finally to defeat a strong country? How was it possible for a seemingly weak army to become the main force in the war?

The basic reasons were that the War of Resistance against Japan was a genuine people's war led by the Communist Party of China and Comrade Mao Tse-tung, a war in which the correct Marxist-Leninist political and military lines were put into effect, and that the Eighth Route and New Fourth Armies were genuine people's armies which applied the whole range of strategy and tactics of [a] people's war as formulated by Comrade Mao Tse-tung.

Comrade Mao Tse-tung's theory of and policies for [a] people's war have creatively enriched and developed Marxism-Leninism. The Chinese people's victory in the anti-Japanese war was a victory for people's war, for Marxism-Leninism, and [for] the thought of Mao Tse-tung.

Prior to the war against Japan, the Communist Party of China had gone through the First Revolutionary Civil War of 1924–1927 and the Second Revolutionary Civil War of 1927–1936 and summed up the experience and lessons of the successes and failures in those wars, and the leading role of Mao Tse-tung's thought had become established within the party. This was the fundamental guarantee of the party's ability to lead the Chinese people to victory in the War of Resistance.

The Chinese people's victory in the War of Resistance paved the way for their seizure of state power throughout the country. When the Kuomintang reactionaries, backed by US imperialists, launched a nationwide civil war in 1946, the Communist Party of China and Comrade Mao Tse-tung further developed the theory of [a] people's war, led the Chinese people in waging a people's war on a still larger scale, and, in the space of a little over three years the great victory of the People's Liberation War was won, the rule of imperialism, feudalism, and bureaucrat-capitalism in our country ended, and the People's Republic of China founded.

The victory of the Chinese people's revolutionary war breached the imperialist front in the East, wrought a great change in the world balance of forces, and accelerated the revolutionary movement among the people of all countries. From then on, the national-liberation movement in Asia, Africa, and Latin America entered a new historical period.

Today, the US imperialists are repeating on a worldwide scale the past actions of the Japanese imperialists in China and other parts of Asia. It has become an urgent necessity for the people in many countries to master and use people's war as a weapon against US imperialism and its lackeys. In every conceivable way, US imperialism and its lackeys are trying to extinguish the revolutionary flames of people's war[s]. Khrushchev revisionists, fearing people's war like the plague, are heaping abuse on it. The two are colluding to prevent and sabotage people's war. In these circumstances, it is of vital practical importance to review the historical experience of the great victory of the people's war in China and to recapitulate Comrade Mao Tse-tung's theory of people's war. . . .

The International Significance of Comrade Mao Tse-tung's Theory of People's War

The Chinese revolution is a continuation of the Great October Revolution. The road of the October Revolution is the common road for all people's revolutions. The Chinese revolution and the October Revolution have in common the following basic characteristics: (1) Both were led by the working class with a Marxist-Leninist party as its nucleus. (2) Both were based on the worker-peasant alliance. (3) In both cases state power was seized through violent revolution and the dictatorship of the proletariat was established. (4) In both cases the socialist system was built after victory in the revolution. (5) Both were component parts of the proletarian world revolution.

Naturally, the Chinese revolution had its own peculiar characteristics. The October Revolution took place in imperialist Russia, but the Chinese revolution broke out in a semicolonial and semifeudal country. The former was a proletarian socialist revolution, while the latter developed into a socialist revolution after the complete victory of the new democratic revolution. The October Revolution began with armed uprisings in the cities and then spread to the countryside, while the Chinese revolution won nationwide victory through the encirclement of the cities from the rural areas and the final capture of the cities.

Comrade Mao Tse-tung's great merit lies in the fact that he has succeeded in integrating the universal truth of Marxism-Leninism with the concrete practice of the Chinese revolution and has enriched and developed Marxism-Leninism by his masterly generalization and summation of the experience gained during the Chinese people's protracted revolutionary struggle.

Comrade Mao Tse-tung's theory of people's war has been proved by the long practice of the Chinese revolution to be in accord with the objective laws of such wars and to be invincible. It has not only been valid for China, it is a great contribution to the revolutionary struggles of the oppressed nations and peoples throughout the world.

The people's war led by the Chinese Communist Party, comprising the War of Resistance and the Revolutionary Civil Wars, lasted for twenty-two years. It constitutes the most drawn-out and most complex people's war led by the proletariat in modern history, and it has been the richest in experience.

In the last analysis, the Marxist-Leninist theory of proletarian revolution is the theory of the seizure of state power by revolutionary violence, the theory of countering war against the people by people's war. As Marx so aptly put it, "Force is the midwife of every old society pregnant with a new one."

It was on the basis of the lessons derived from the people's wars in China that Comrade Mao Tse-tung, using the simplest and the most vivid language, advanced the famous thesis that "political power grows out of the barrel of a gun."

He clearly pointed out:

> The seizure of power by armed force, the settlement of the issue by war, is the central task and the highest form of revolution. This Marxist-Leninist principle of revolution holds good universally, for China and for all other countries.

War is the product of imperialism and the system of exploitation of man by man. Lenin said that "war is always and everywhere begun by the exploiters themselves, by the ruling and oppressing classes." So long as imperialism and the system of exploitation of man by man exist, the imperialists and reactionaries will invariably rely on armed force to maintain their reactionary rule and impose war on the oppressed nations and peoples. This is an objective law independent of man's will.

In the world today, all the imperialists headed by the United States and their lackeys, without exception, are strengthening their state machinery, and especially their armed forces. US imperialism, in particular, is carrying out armed aggression and suppression everywhere.

What should the oppressed nations and the oppressed people do in the face of wars of aggression and armed suppression by the imperialists and their lackeys? Should they submit and remain slaves in perpetuity? Or should they rise in resistance and fight for their liberation?

Comrade Mao Tse-tung answered this question in vivid terms. He said that after long investigation and study the Chinese people discovered that all the imperialists and their lackeys "have swords in their hands and are out to kill. The people have come to understand this and so act after the same fashion." This is called doing unto them what they do unto us.

In the last analysis, whether one dares to wage a tit-for-tat struggle against armed aggression and suppression by the imperialists and their lackeys, whether one dares to fight a people's war against them, is tantamount to whether one dares to embark on revolution. This is the most effective touchstone for distinguishing genuine from fake revolutionaries and Marxist-Leninists.

In view of the fact that some people were afflicted with the fear of the imperialists and reactionaries, Comrade Mao Tse-tung put forward his famous thesis that "the imperialists and all reactionaries are paper tigers." He said:

> All reactionaries are paper tigers. In appearance, the reactionaries are terrifying, but in reality they are not so powerful. From a long-term point of view, it is not the reactionaries but the people who are really powerful.

The history of people's war in China and other countries provides conclusive evidence that the growth of the people's revolutionary forces from weak and small beginnings into strong and large forces is a universal law of [the] development of class struggle, a universal law of development of people's war. A people's war inevitably meets with many difficulties, with ups and downs and setbacks in the course of its development, but no force can alter its general trend toward inevitable triumphs. . . .

It must be emphasized that Comrade Mao Tse-tung's theory of the establishment of rural revolutionary base areas and the encirclement of the cities from the countryside is of outstanding and universal practical importance for the present revolutionary struggles of all the oppressed nations and peoples, and particularly for the revolutionary struggles of the oppressed nations and peoples in Asia, Africa, and Latin America against imperialism and its lackeys.

Many countries and peoples in Asia, Africa, and Latin America are now being subjected to aggression and enslavement on a serious scale by the imperialists headed by the United States and their lackeys. The basic political and economic conditions in many of these countries have many similarities to those that prevailed in old China. As in China, the peasant question is extremely important in these regions.

The peasants constitute the main force of the national-democratic revolution against the imperialists and their lackeys. In committing aggression against these countries, the imperialists usually begin by seizing the big cities and the main lines of communication, but they are unable to bring the vast countryside completely under their control. The countryside, and the countryside alone, can provide the broad areas in which the revolutionaries can maneuver freely. The countryside, and the countryside alone, can provide the revolutionary bases from which the revolutionaries can go forward to final victory. Precisely for this reason, Comrade Mao Tse-tung's theory of establishing revolutionary base areas in the rural districts and encircling the cities from the countryside is attracting more and more attention among the people in these regions.

Taking the entire globe, if North America and Western Europe can be called "the cities of the world," then Asia, Africa, and Latin America constitute "the rural areas of the world." Since World War II, the proletarian revolutionary movement has for various reasons been temporarily held back in the North American and West European capitalist countries, while the people's revolutionary movement in Asia, Africa, and Latin America has been growing vigorously. In a sense, the contemporary world revolution also presents a picture of the encirclement of cities by the rural areas. In the final analysis, the whole cause of world revolution hinges on the revolutionary struggles of the Asian, African, and Latin American peoples who make up the overwhelming majority of the world's population. The socialist countries should regard it as their internationalist duty to support the people's revolutionary struggles in Asia, Africa, and Latin America.

The October Revolution opened up a new era in the revolution of the oppressed nations. The victory of the October Revolution built a bridge between the socialist revolution of the proletariat of the West and the national-democratic revolution of the colonial and semicolonial countries of the East. The Chinese revolution has successfully solved the problem of how to link the national-democratic with the socialist revolution in the colonial and semicolonial countries. . . .

The new democratic revolution leads to socialism, and not to capitalism.

Comrade Mao Tse-tung's theory of the new democratic revolution is the Marxist-Leninist theory of revolution by stages as well as the Marxist-Leninist theory of uninterrupted revolution.

Comrade Mao Tse-tung made a correct distinction between the two revolutionary stages, that is, the national-democratic and the socialist revolutions; at the same time he correctly and closely linked the two. The national-democratic revolution is the necessary preparation for the socialist revolution, and the socialist revolution is the inevitable sequel to the national-democratic revolution. There is no Great Wall between the two revolutionary stages. But the socialist revolution is only possible after the completion of the national-democratic revolution. The more thorough the national-democratic revolution, the better the conditions for the socialist revolution. . . .

The Chinese revolution provides a successful lesson for making a thoroughgoing national-democratic revolution under the leadership of the proletariat; it likewise provides a successful lesson for the timely transition from the national-democratic revolution to the socialist revolution under the leadership of the proletariat.

Mao Tse-tung's thought has been the guide to the victory of the Chinese revolution. It has integrated the universal truth of Marxism-Leninism with the concrete practice of the Chinese revolution and creatively developed Marxism-Leninism, thus adding new weapons to the arsenal of Marxism-Leninism.

Ours is the epoch in which world capitalism and imperialism are heading for their doom and socialism and Communism are marching to victory. Comrade Mao Tse-tung's theory of people's war is not only a product of the Chinese revolution, but has also the characteristics of our epoch. The new experience gained in the people's revolutionary struggles in various countries since World War II has provided continuous evidence that Mao Tse-tung's thought is a common asset of the revolutionary people of the whole world. This is the great international significance of the thought of Mao Tse-tung.

Defeat US Imperialism and Its Lackeys by People's War

. . . Vietnam is the most convincing current example of a victim of aggression defeating US imperialism by a people's war. The United States has made south Vietman a testing ground for the suppression of people's war. It has carried on this experiment for many years, and everybody can now see that the US aggressors are unable to find a way of coping with people's war. On the other hand, the Vietnamese people have brought the power of people's war into full play in their struggle against the US aggressors. The US aggressors are in danger of being swamped in the people's war in Vietnam. They are deeply worried that their defeat in Vietnam will lead to a chain reaction. They are expanding the war in an attempt to save themselves from defeat. But the more they expand the war, the greater will be the chain reaction. The more they escalate the war, the heavier will be their fall and the more disastrous their defeat. The people in other parts of the world will see still more clearly that US imperialism can be defeated, and that what the Vietnamese people can do, they can do too.

History has proved and will go on proving that people's war is the most effective weapon against US imperialism and its lackeys. All revolutionary people will learn to wage people's war against US imperialism and its lackeys. They will take up arms, learn to fight battles and become skilled in waging people's war, though they have not done so before. US imperialism, like a mad bull dashing from place to place, will finally be burned to ashes in the blazing fires of the people's wars it has provoked by its own actions.

The Khrushchev Revisionists Are Betrayers of People's War

. . . We know that war brings destruction, sacrifice and suffering on the people. But the destruction, sacrifice, and suffering will be much greater if no resistance is offered to imperialist armed aggression and the people become willing slaves. The sacrifice of a small number of people in revolutionary wars is repaid by security for whole nations, whole countries, and even the whole of mankind; temporary suffering is repaid by lasting or even perpetual peace and happiness. War can temper the people and push history forward. In this sense, war is a great school. . . .

In diametrical opposition to the Khrushchev revisionists, the Marxist-Leninists and revolutionary people never take a gloomy view of war. Our attitude toward imperialist wars of aggression has always been clear-cut. First, we are against them, and, secondly, we are not afraid of them. We will destroy whoever attacks us. As for revolutionary wars waged by the oppressed nations and peoples, far from opposing them, we invariably give them firm support and active aid. It has been so in the past, it remains so in the present, and, when we grow in strength as time goes on, we will give them still more support and aid in the future. It is sheer daydreaming for anyone to think that, since our revolution has been victorious, our national construction is forging ahead, our national wealth is increasing, and our living conditions are improving, we too will lose our revolutionary fighting will, abandon the cause of world revolution, and discard Marxism-Leninism and proletarian internationalism. Of course, every revolution in a country stems from the demands of its own people. Only when the people in a country are awakened, mobilized, organized, and armed can they overthrow the reactionary rule of imperialism and its lackeys through struggle; their role cannot be replaced or taken over by any people from outside. In this sense, revolution cannot be imported. But this does not exclude mutual sympathy and support on the part of revolutionary peoples in their struggles against the imperialists and their lackeys. Our support and aid to other revolutionary peoples serves precisely to help their self-reliant struggle. . . .

The struggle of the Vietnamese people against US aggression and for national salvation is now the focus of the struggle of the people of the world against US aggression. The determination of the Chinese people to support and aid the Vietnamese people in their struggle against US aggression and for national salvation is unshakable. No matter what US imperialism may do to expand its war adventure, the Chinese people will do everything in their power to support the Vietnamese people until every single one of the US aggressors is driven out of Vietnam.

NOTE

The PRC has never sought to conceal its ideological and psychological support for Maoist-type revolution abroad, and it has made great efforts to distribute the thought of Chairman Mao widely. This has led a number of countries to take countermeasures. In mid-1967, for example, Kenya accused the PRC of interfering in its domestic affairs and prohibited the importation of a collection of quotations from the works of Mao that had been published in Peking.[79]

Other symbols of the PRC's ideological support for revolutionary upheaval have also been banned by certain countries. The following dispatch is illustrative: "Ceylon said that the recent note by the Chinese embassy constituted unwarranted interference with its sovereignty and internal affairs. The Chinese note followed restrictions placed by the Ceylonese government on the import of Mao badges by Chinese diplomats. Ceylon said that since the embassy staff totaled only 34 persons, it couldn't agree to clear 300 Mao badges—as the bulk of these could be distributed among residents of the island. Ceylon said the only loyalty it requires from its people is toward their country, and it does not admit the truth of Chinese embassy allegations about the presence of either pro-China or anti-China elements in the country."[80]

9.9

"CPC Greets 28th Anniversary of Burmese CP, Firm Support for People's Revolutionary Armed Struggle Led by the Communist Party of Burma," *PR* 10.34:5 (Aug. 18, 1967).

Comrade Thakin Than Tun, Chairman of the Central Committee of the Communist Party of Burma,

The Communist Party of China and the Chinese people warmly greet the 28th anniversary of the founding of the Communist Party of Burma.

The Communist Party of Burma, headed by Comrade Thakin Than Tun, has held high the great red banner of Marxism-Leninism, Mao Tse-tung's thought. It has persevered in taking the revolutionary road of using the countryside to surround the cities and seizing political power by armed force. It has led the people of Burma in carrying out a protracted, heroic struggle against imperialism, feudalism, and bureaucrat-capitalism.

The Communist Party of Burma has withstood all kinds of storms and tests. It has stood up to the pressure of the Soviet revisionist leading clique and China's top party person in authority taking the capitalist road. It has overcome "Left" and "Right" opportunism in the party and has adhered to the revolutionary line of Marxism-Leninism, Mao Tse-tung's thought. It has become the core leading the revolutionary cause of the people of all nationalities in Burma forward.

The Communist Party of Burma has carried out a policy of self-reliance, and has persevered in armed struggle for almost twenty years. It has brought together and developed the revolutionary forces and has dealt heavy blows at the reactionary rule of imperialism and its lackeys in Burma. The armed struggle of the people of Burma has greatly fortified the high resolve of the revolutionary people and deflated the arrogance of imperialism, modern revisionism, and the Burmese reactionaries.

Under the blows of the iron fists of the people's armed force led by the Communist Party of Burma, the reactionary Ne Win government is facing greater and greater difficulties. In order to save itself from its doom, the Ne Win clique has undisguisedly carried out the counter-revolutionary policy of dictatorship, national betrayal, and opposition to Communism, China, and the people. The frantic struggle of the Ne Win clique can only bring it more disastrous defeat.

The Chinese Communist Party and the Chinese people firmly support the people's revolutionary armed struggle led by the Communist Party of Burma. We regard such support as our bounden proletarian internationalist duty.

The Chinese Communist Party extends its heartfelt thanks to the Communist Party of Burma for its warm praise of the great proletarian cultural revolution in China and for upholding and supporting Comrade Mao Tse-tung's proletarian revolutionary line.

Our two parties and the peoples of our two countries have forged a profound friendship in long revolutionary struggle. Let us further consolidate and develop the militant friendship between our two parties and the peoples of our two countries in the joint struggle to liquidate the counterrevolutionary revisionist line of the top person in authority in the Chinese Communist Party who takes the capitalist road.

It is our firm conviction that the Communist Party of Burma headed by Comrade Thakin Than Tun, which persists in the revolutionary line of "to win the war and seize political power," will assuredly further unite the whole party and the people of all nationalities in Burma, overthrow the reactionary Ne Win government, and win complete victory in the revolutionary war in Burma.

Long live the militant friendship between the Communist Parties and peoples of China and Burma!

Long live invincible Marxism-Leninism, Mao Tse-tung's thought!

Central Committee of the
Communist Party of China
August 14, 1967

9-10

"Chinese Foreign Ministry Refutes Indian Government's Slanders," *PR* 9.39:36 (Sept. 23, 1966).

The Chinese Foreign Ministry, in its September 15 note to the Indian embassy in China, categorically rejected the unwarranted charge and protest lodged by the Indian government regarding broadcasts by Chinese frontier guards.

The Chinese note was a refutation of the July 28 note of the Indian Ministry for External Affairs. It said:

> It is entirely within China's sovereign rights for the Chinese frontier guards stationing [*sic*] at Natu La on the China-Sikkim boundary to make broadcasts on Chinese territory advocating the friendship between the Chinese and Indian peoples and setting forth the truth about the Sino-Indian boundary question, and no foreigner has any right to interfere in this. In its note the Indian

> government describes the broadcasts of the Chinese side as an "attempt at subversion" and "interference in the internal affairs of India." This is a slander against China. The note alleges that the Chinese broadcasts call upon the officers and men of the Indian army to "oppose the government of India" and to "support the revolution and establish a true people's republic," and so on and so forth. These are sheer lies and fabrications.

The reply note continued:

> The allegations in the Indian note about subversion and expansionism by China against neighbouring countries are rubbish picked from the anti-China rumor storage of US imperialism and are not worth refuting at all.

The Chinese note pointed out that the Indian government, while unwarrantedly lodging a so-called protest with the Chinese government, has installed broadcasting equipment on Sikkim territory along the China-Sikkim boundary to jam China's broadcasts and hurl venomous calumnies and abuses at the Chinese government. The note said:

> The voice of truth, however, cannot be blocked. Your despicable performances can only expose yourselves and serve to prove once again that you are the disrupter of the friendship between the Chinese and Indian peoples and the creator of tension on the border.

9-11

"Mexico Arrests 13; Links China to Plot," *New York Times* (July 20, 1967), pp. 1, 14.

Mexico City, July 19 (AP)

The government reported in an official statement tonight that it had foiled a plot financed from Communist China that had sought to establish a "popular Socialist" regime in Mexico.

The Attorney General's office said that a Venezuelan and a Salvadorean were among 13 persons arrested in the case.

According to the statement, the group was preparing subversive actions both in Mexico City and the provinces and had already dynamited an army truck in a rural road in the state of Guerrero seeking to procure arms.

The statement said the Mexican branch of Hsinhua [NCNA],

the Chinese Communist press agency, was the channel through which Peking was sending £600, or $1,680, a month to finance armed rebellion.

Javier Fuentes Gutierrez, a civil engineer and former leader of the Mexican Communist Party, the Independent Farmers' Central and the Electoral People's Front, was head of the group, according to the statement.

Mr. Fuentes Gutierrez, a frequent visitor to Cuba, was not among those arrested. The report said he and another Mexican, Federico Emery Valle, also a pro-Chinese leader, flew to Peking June 30. Mr. Fuentes Gutierrez was said to have used for the trip a false passport under the assumed name of Javier Popoca Gutierrez. A bookstore owned by him, called El Primer Paso (The First Step), was said to be the center of activities of the subversives.

Among those arrested, the Attorney General's office identified Silvestre Enrique Marenco Martinez, 36 [years old], a national of El Salvador, who was said to have much experience as a guerrilla leader, especially in Nicaragua. Lately he had been working for Mr. Fuentes Gutierrez in his book store and, according to the statement, preparing to begin intensive training of Mexican guerrillas somewhere in the mountains.

The other foreigner was identified as Daniel Camejo Guanche, a member of the Trotskyite faction, who had promised to help Mexican subversives with medicines, propaganda, and plans.

The arrests were made by the federal security police and the arrested were delivered to the Attorney General's office for investigation.

The list furnished by the Attorney General includes the following names:

Adam Nieto Castillo, one of the intellectual directors of the movement; José Luis Calva Tellez, accused of planning to hold up a bank branch in Mexico City to secure funds to promote the movement; Pablo Alvarado Barrera, a jobless teacher, who was said to be second in command, and Hugo David Uriarte y Bonilla, a civil servant employed by the Ministry of the Treasury, who was accused of acting as general coordinator.

Jungle Camp Reported Planned

Mexico City, July 19 (Reuters)—The Attorney General's document issued tonight said that the alleged conspirators planned to train both rural and urban terrorists at a camp in the jungle of Chiapas, in southern Mexico.

9-12

Tillman Durdin, "Burmese Reds Now Focus on North, With China as Sanctuary," *New York Times* (July 25, 1969), p. 4.

Peking-backed Communist insurgents in Burma have shifted their main sphere of activity from central and lower Burma to areas bordering Communist China in the north.

The shift enables Burmese Communist guerrillas to operate from a haven the way Greek Communists operated from Yugoslavia 20 years ago. Similarly China and North Vietnam provide sanctuary to guerrilla forces in South Vietnam, Laos, and Thailand.

The new strategy has permitted Burmese Communist guerrillas in the north to make considerable though not decisive headway this year, according to informed officials here.

Quiet During Rainy Season

Loosely controlled bands, totaling 8,000 to 9,000 men, are said to dominate an area up to a hundred miles south of the Chinese border stretching from Lashio eastward to the Salween River.

The little northern Shan State of Kokang, east of the Salween, is reported to be ruled by the Communists. Its local sawbwa, or princeling, is an ethnic Chinese who has thrown in his lot with the Communists.

Communist influence also extends up into the Kachin State, in the northernmost section of the country, where factions of an independence movement have accepted weapons and other aid from China.

With the rainy season now on, a lull has settled over northern areas, and it is difficult to determine which areas the Communists control and how effective they are.

4,000 in Motley Army

Both government and Communist forces are reported to be regrouping, resupplying, training, and improving communications, and it may not be until the fall, when the rains stop, that the scope of the new Communist threat in the north will be known.

The strongest Communist contingent in the north is that of Naw

Seng, who is said to command a motley army of some 4,000 in which there are men from the minority peoples of Burma—the Kachins, Shans and Karens—as well as lowland Burmese. The lowlanders make up two-thirds of the 28 million people of Burma.

Naw Seng, a Kachin who went to China in the nineteen-fifties, has risen in the ranks of the Burmese Communist party and was reported to have become a member of the Central Committee last year.

The weakness of the Communist effort in north Burma is similar to its weakness in Thailand. The north of Burma, like the north of Thailand, is an area of minority hill people who are not easily converted to Communism, and, in any case, are not effective in the lowland areas, the most populous and developed areas in the country.

Severe Losses Suffered

The Communist shift of emphasis to the north may be due to a conclusion reached both in the Burmese party leadership and in Peking that the guerrillas have a better chance of success while operating from sanctuary in China. But the change of focus also reflects the severe defeats the Communist insurgents suffered in lower Burma late last year at the hands of government forces.

9-13

"Reports Say Mizo Rebels Asking Chinese Aid," Information Service of India–English, Delhi, Aug. 20, 1967; printed in *FBIS*, no. 162/67: Pl (Aug. 21, 1967).

(Text) Some top-ranking Mizo rebel "army" officers led by self-styled Brigadier General Chhubzawba escaped to China sometime last month to solicit arms and active assistance from the Chinese in their hostile activities in Mizo district, according to an unconfirmed report from usually authentic sources.

Before leaving for China, they contacted the Chinese consulate in Dacca, from which they were reported to have obtained the necessary introduction to military and civil authorities in Peking. Lalnunmawia, president of the Mizo National Front, is credited with the extremists' plan in that he ordered a small group of rebel army officers to proceed to China to negotiate a deal which would facilitate stepping up subversive and other rebel activities in Mizo district and neighboring areas of Manipur.

It is not known which route Mizo hostiles took to China. It is, however, believed in official circles that they might have departed from East Pakistan, itself, or taken some route via northern Burmese territory, as Naga rebels had done toward the end of last year.

Armed hostiles numbering 300 recently returned to Mizo district from East Pakistan after receiving considerable arms and guerrilla training under Chinese military experts there. Five training centers in East Pakistan are giving intensive training to hostiles in military warfare.

Security forces have strengthened border vigilance measures all along the Mizo district-East Pakistan border.

9-14

Ghana Ministry of Information, *Nkrumah's Subversion in Africa* (Accra-Tema, Ghana, n.d.), pp. 7, 8, 18–19.

[This is a report published by the government of Ghana that was formed following the February 24, 1966, coup d'état that deposed Kwame Nkrumah; it details Chinese and Soviet efforts to cooperate with the Nkrumah regime in training nationals of other African states in the arts of revolutionary subversion.]
The record of Chinese activity at this camp follows:

> The written agreement between the governments of Ghana and China, covering the assignment of guerrilla warfare experts to Ghana, was not formalized and signed until August 1965, almost a year after the arrival of the first group of Chinese experts. The agreement was made effective, however, as from 30 September, 1964.
>
> The first group of five Chinese guerrilla warfare experts led by a Chinese colonel arrived at Half-Assini Training Camp in late 1964. Prior to their arrival, conditions at Half-Assini had been steadily deteriorating, and the students had become demoralized over the elementary training in guerrilla warfare they were receiving from inexperienced instructors. It was then that Mr. A. K. Barden decided to have Chinese guerrilla warfare experts assigned to the camp after Nkrumah's approval had been obtained. . . .

The entry of the Chinese guerrilla warfare instructors into Ghana was kept secret at the request of the Chinese embassy. In advance of the instructors' arrival the embassy informed the Bureau of African Affairs that it would not be safe for the men to live in a hotel and that special arrangements should be made for their accommodation in Accra before they proceeded to the camp. The embassy said that this was necessary in view of the delicate nature of their assignment in Ghana and also in view of the various allegations by the imperialists that China was encouraging subversion in certain countries . . . .

At the end of December or in early January the Chinese experts submitted a new program of training for a three-and-a-half-month course which ran from 14 January to 29 April, 1965. The Chinese listed as the objectives and requirements of the course:

> 1. Students are required to have primary understanding of the fundamental thinking in guiding revolutionary armed struggle, basic principles of building a people's revolutionary army, strategic and tactical principles of guerrilla warfare.
> 2. To master simple methods of manufacturing explosive materials, the basic techniques of explosion, uses of mines and how to organize and direct explosion.
> 3. To learn the properties, structure, assembly, and disassembly of weapons; preparation for and conduct of shooting; general knowledge of communication and simple methods of using communication equipment.

The trainees were told: "They, as principal members of guerrilla units, will be able to get a correct direction in their work and general principles of guerrilla warfare. 'Students are required to study with the highest spirit of learning and earnestly and seriously help each other in understanding the techniques and problems and to observe strictly operational rules so as to ensure safety.' "

The Chinese also outlined the "basic guiding" method to be used: "to combine instructors' lectures and demonstrations with students' discussions and actual operations; to combine tactics with techniques; to link their studies with local conditions; and to make use of figurative teachings". . . .

Two hundred and six students completed the course in April 1965. They came from various countries in Africa, including self-governing countries like Niger and Congo (Kinshasa).

According to their final report on the three-and-a-half-months' course, the Chinese found the training results "basically satisfactory." They said:

> After this training, the students have acquired a primary knowledge of the fundamental guiding ideology of armed struggle, the people's war and people's army, the fundamental principles of the strategy and tactics of guerrilla warfare. They have basically mastered the methods of how to organize and direct raid and ambush battles as leaders of a guerrilla unit, how to perform first aid on the battlefield and the simple ways of communication and liaison. They mastered the essential techniques of manufacturing explosives, how to conduct demolition and how to use mines. They have gained a better skill in the use of the three light weapons (semiautomatic rifle, light machine gun, and submachine gun) with a rate of hitting the target up to 88.6 percent in the ball-fire, got a general understanding of some heavy weapons such as mortar, heavy machine gun, etc. As a result, not only have the students gained certain technical proficiencies, but also have raised their ideological level remarkably; thus their fighting will against imperialism and old and new colonialism for national independence has been strengthened.

The Chinese, however, admitted that they fell somewhat short of fitting the Chinese theory and practice into the African situation. They included a certain amount of the "self-criticism" required under Mao's system, since the report was undoubtedly intended for their Chinese superiors as well as for the Bureau:

> Indeed, we have, besides mainly introducing the Chinese revolutionary experiences, made some efforts to connect these experiences with the actual conditions of the African people's revolutionary struggles. However, as we are not very familiar with the African conditions, particularly with the concrete conditions of the above-mentioned countries and regions, the work of [more closely] linking our lectures with the actual conditions of these countries is not sufficient.
>
> Before the next training, the expert team will discuss with the officials of the Bureau of African Affairs the political, economic, and geographic conditions and the situations of armed struggles [in] the countries from which the students come so as to better link the lectures with them.

NOTE

The 1965 agreement to which item 9–14 refers has been reproduced as item 31–17.

The PRC rejected charges of intervention made by the post-Nkrumah government of Ghana:

> In its note, the Ghanaian Ministry of Foreign Affairs hurls at China the absurd slander that she has been "deliberately interfering in the internal affairs of Ghana" and that Chinese personnel "were helping in training saboteurs in Ghana," . . .
>
> As is well known, the military experts as well as the economic and technical experts sent by the Chinese government to work in Ghana were dispatched at the request of the government of the Republic of Ghana and in pursuance of the relevant agreements signed by the two countries. They always worked in accordance with the arrangements made by the Ghanaian government. They are beyond reproach. No one can succeed in distorting all these facts.[81]

In mid-1971 the PRC also rejected Uganda's charges of supporting guerrilla warfare:

> Mou Ping, Chargé d'Affaires ad interim of the Embassy of the People's Republic of China in Uganda, on July 26 called on S. Baingana, Permanent Secretary of the Uganda Foreign Ministry, lodging a protest against the attacks on China made by President Idi Amin at a press conference in London recently. The protest said: "According to the broadcasts over Radio Uganda of July 14 and the Uganda newspaper reports of July 15, President Amin, at a press conference held in London on July 14, went so far as to make the fabrication that Chinese communist instructors along with the guerrillas assailed Uganda from Tanzania and that among the guerrillas there were three Chinese instructors who later escaped. Furthermore, President Amin accused China of interfering in Uganda's internal affairs. These remarks of President Amin are utterly groundless, and constitute a grave incident of undermining the relations between China and Uganda. The Chinese Government hereby lodges a protest with the Uganda Government against this.[82]

It would plainly be impossible here to list all alleged Chinese government interventions.[83] We should, however, note a variety of other forms that such intervention has assertedly taken. For example, in addition to supplying relatively small quantities of weapons to various Arab "liberation" commando organizations and training some of their personnel in China, Peking has also apparently sought to bring about close cooperation with the commandos by at least occasionally sending delegations to participate in planning and maneuvers.[84]

Prince Sihanouk has claimed that, following the military coup that deposed him in Cambodia, the PRC granted him a loan to finance his government-in-exile and free weapons and transport facilities for the fight that his supporters have continued to wage in Cambodia. The Prince quoted Chairman Mao himself as having said: "We are not arms traffickers. We cannot sell you weapons. We can give them to you. As for transport, that's also free."[85] Sihanouk subsequently signed an agreement with the PRC for providing free military aid to his government-in-exile.[86]

At first blush it might appear that Sihanouk's obviously authorized revelations represent an exception to the usual Chinese practice of attempting to keep secret any tangible aid extended to liberation struggles in order to avoid the embarrassment that charges of violating international law might cause. Actually, however, the PRC had continued to recognize Sihanouk as the chief of the Cambodian state, and the Prince made his announcements after the Chinese Government had formally recognized "the Royal Government of National Union Under the Leadership of the National United Front of Kampuchea" as the legal successor to the previous government of Cambodia (see 10–19).[87]

It has been alleged that the PRC has made secret financial payments amounting to bribes to a number of African politicians.[88] And Peking has even been accused of having arranged the assassination of the Prime Minister of Bhutan in 1964, an allegation that it has strongly denied.[89] It is difficult, of course, for academic observers and the public to determine which of the many charges of PRC intervention may be well-grounded.

During the earliest years of the PRC it sought to manipulate overseas Chinese and other groups in certain countries as instruments of its will abroad. By the time of the Bandung conference in 1955, however, Peking had begun to moderate that policy. This led the Prime Minister of Ceylon to suggest that the Chinese Communist Party call upon the Communist parties in Asian and African states to disband. But the *People's Daily* replied that to do so would be an act of interference in the internal affairs of other countries![90] In view of the scope and continuity of the PRC's alleged activities, this expressed solicitude for the principle of nonintervention must have been wryly received by a number of countries. Although Maoist candor sometimes provides a refreshing contrast to the platitudes invoked by other major powers to cloak their own acts of intervention, the reply of the *People's Daily* should remind us that, as earlier materials in this chapter illustrated, the PRC has also not been immune to hypocrisy concerning nonintervention.

For a Chinese scholar's effort to justify PRC support for wars of national liberation in terms of international law, see item 42–11. See also Premier Chou En-lai's interview with James Reston in the Note following item 41–1.

For illustrations of the PRC's attitude toward United Nations resolutions condemning certain domestic policies of certain governments—both before and after the PRC's entry into the UN, see Chapters 38 and 39. For the PRC's views on efforts to influence events in other countries by resort to warfare, see Chapter 42.[91]

Participation in the International Community

PART III

During its first twenty-two years, no problems of international law were more immediate, more enduring, and more important to the PRC than those relating to its identity and to its demands for full participation in the world community. The consequences of the PRC's long-standing failure to achieve general acceptance of its claims to diplomatic recognition and to representation in international organizations were substantial. The refusal of the United States, Japan, West Germany, and over half the countries of the world to recognize its legitimacy did not merely affect the prestige of the regime at home and abroad, but also symbolized the persistence of a hostile environment that threatened its independence, its integrity, and even its very survival.

Until 1971, continuing exclusion from the United Nations, including China's permanent seat on the Security Council, prevented the PRC from acquiring a major power base and the most prominent formal badge of great-power status. Exclusion from the UN and other international organizations also deprived the PRC of many less obvious benefits such as opportunities to participate in many international legislative processes and international economic development programs. Moreover, nonrecognition by individual states precluded the PRC's agents from enjoying diplomatic and consular status in many parts of the world, hampered the establishment of normal trade relations, denied the PRC access to resources that the predecessor regime maintained abroad, narrowed the opportunities for obtaining intergovernmental and multilateral financial assistance, restricted the PRC's access to foreign courts and limited its immunity from foreign process, and circumscribed the foreign areas in which the PRC's laws receive respect.

These consequences of nonacceptance by the world community would be serious enough for any new regime. They were especially grave for one that continued to be locked in a civil war with the prior government, particularly when the prior government, although confined to Taiwan and adjacent islands, continued to enjoy the recognition and representation that its rival had failed to obtain. Thus, the PRC's minimum goal for more than two decades after its founding was to deprive the ROC of the international symbols of legitimacy.

Recognition, Diplomatic Relations, and Their Consequences

10

This chapter deals with the following questions: Do the leaders of the PRC claim to have created a new state or a new government? By what principles do they justify their claim to recognition by other participants in the world community? Do they adopt the "constitutive" theory of recognition? The "declaratory" theory? Do they regard recognition as a "legal" question? As a "political" act that is not subject to legal criteria? Can the PRC's position be adequately described under the traditional doctrinal rubrics? How has the PRC reacted to nonrecognition and its consequences?

Does the PRC assume the burdens as well as the benefits of the principles of recognition that it espouses? When passing upon other regimes' claims to recognition, does it apply the same rules that it invokes in its own case? What distinction does it draw between recognition and establishment of diplomatic relations? Once diplomatic relations have been established, upon what principles does the PRC condition their continuation?

The People's Republic is, of course, not the first Chinese government to deal with problems of recognition. Although the concept of recognition of a state or government in its modern sense was unknown to traditional China, certain modern rules or practices appear to have had ancient counterparts. For example, during the "Spring and Autumn" period (722–481 B.C.) of the preimperial era, "before a territory could be considered a state, it had to have an effective political organization." [1] Moreover, if a ruler of a state seized power by illegal means, such as murder or expulsion of the existing ruler, he was required to legitimize his position by obtaining the approval of the other feudal states. Approval could be expressed, but it also could be implied, as when the other rulers agreed to participate in a conference with the usurper. In the absence of such approval, according to the rules of the multistate system that then prevailed, other rulers would have a legal basis for invading the state in order to restore the ousted ruler or to install his legitimate successor.[2]

After the establishment of the Chinese Empire, a similar rule appears to have been acknowledged, at least on occasion, in relations between the imperial court and tributary rulers. In the seventh century, one of the reasons offered for the T'ang dynasty's invasion of

Korea was that a high Korean official had illegally killed the king.[3] Indeed, as the tribute system evolved, Chinese emperors developed a sense of obligation to protect loyal rulers of tributary states against rebellion. For example, as mentioned in Part II, the Ch'ing dynasty intervened in Vietnam in 1788 in an effort to restore the Lê family to the throne.[4] Significantly, however, when that effort failed, the successful rebel leader immediately paid tribute to China and agreed to journey to Peking to offer his apologies and submission to the Emperor.[5] Under the imperial system, at a formal ceremony envoys of the Son of Heaven gave new rulers of the non-Chinese tribute kingdoms "a patent of appointment and an official seal for use in correspondence. . . ." This ceremony of investiture, which confirmed their ascendancy to the throne, constituted the nearest thing to modern "recognition" that was known to the hierarchical Sinocentric world order.[6]

When the revolution of 1911 overthrew the Ch'ing dynasty, the new government of China was well aware of the fact that its legitimacy would be determined by the rules of Western international law. It sought to comply with those rules by assuming the mantle of a responsible successor government, declaring that the Republic of China would honor the treaty obligations concluded by the imperial government prior to the outbreak of the revolution.[7] Nevertheless, this initial Chinese experience with modern recognition practice was not a happy one, as Japan, Russia, Britain, and other powers sought to impose onerous political and economic conditions upon the feeble and unstable Republic as the price of recognition. Although the Republic was proclaimed early in 1912, it was not until May 1913 that the United States granted recognition, and the other major powers did not follow suit until five months later.[8] This experience, as well as the difficulty encountered by the Bolsheviks in obtaining recognition after the 1917 revolution, was undoubtedly in the minds of the leaders of China's Communist revolution when in 1949 they sought acceptance by the world community [see item 10–17].

10-1

"Concerning the Establishment of Diplomatic Relations and Other Questions," *Shih-shih shou-ts'e* (Current affairs handbook), no. 11:41 (June 10, 1956).

What Is International Recognition? What Is the Significance of International Recognition?

"Recognition" is the affirmation by one state that another state or government exists and that it is willing to recognize it as an object of international intercourse and to establish normal diplomatic relations with it.

There are two types of recognition. The first type is formal recognition, that is, a state unilaterally issues a statement to express its recognition and willingness to establish diplomatic relations with a state or a government. Or, it does not issue a statement, but its recognition is inferred from some conduct involving formal diplomatic relations (such as the conclusion of a treaty or exchange of diplomatic envoys). If both parties participate in an international conference without any reservations, such an act is also considered formal recognition. Another type of recognition is de facto recognition, such as the conclusion of a formal trade agreement or entry into relations of a business nature (concerning certain specific problems), and so forth.

Recognition is the starting point for the establishment of diplomatic relations between two states. Generally, after recognition, two states immediately go on to establish normal diplomatic relations.

What Is the Process of Establishing Diplomatic Relations between States? When Are Formal Diplomatic Relations Considered Established? . . .

Generally, the process of establishing diplomatic relations between states is as follows. The government of a state expresses its intention to recognize the government of another state and its willingness to establish diplomatic relations and exchange envoys. If the government of the other state consents, then both governments will send envoys and establish legations in each other's territory. Thus, diplomatic relations between two states are considered established. [It is also possible that] although two states establish diplomatic relations, for a long time they, possibly due to the lack of any practical need, neither establish legations [in each other's territories] nor send envoys [to each other]. This situation, however, is very rare.

10-2

Mao Tse-tung, "Report to Second Session of Seventh Central Committee" (given March 5, 1949), in *Selected Works,* IV (Peking, 1961), pp. 370–371.

Old China was a semicolonial country under imperialist domination. Thoroughly anti-imperialist in character, the Chinese people's democratic revolution has incurred the bitter hatred of the imperialists who have done their utmost to help the Kuomintang. This has aroused the Chinese people to even deeper indignation against the imperialists and deprived them of their last shred of prestige among the Chinese people. At the same time the whole imperialist system is very much weakened after World War II, while the strength of the world anti-imperialist front headed by the Soviet Union is greater than ever before. In these circumstances, we can and should adopt a policy of systematically and completely destroying imperialist domination in China. This imperialist domination manifests itself in the political, economic, and cultural fields. In each city or place where the Kuomintang troops are wiped out and the Kuomintang government is overthrown, imperialist political domination is overthrown with it, and so is imperialist economic and cultural domination. But the economic and cultural establishments run directly by the imperialists are still there, and so are the diplomatic personnel and the journalists recognized by the Kuomintang. We must deal with all these properly in their order of urgency. Refuse to recognize the legal status of any foreign diplomatic establishments and personnel of the Kuomintang period, refuse to recognize all the treasonable treaties of the Kuomintang period, abolish all imperialist propaganda agencies in China, take immediate control of foreign trade and reform the customs system—these are the first steps we must take upon entering the big cities. When they have acted thus, the Chinese people will have stood up in the face of imperialism. As for the remaining imperialist economic and cultural establishments, they can be allowed to exist for the time being, subject to our supervision and control, to be dealt with by us after countrywide victory. As for ordinary foreign nationals, their legitimate interests will be protected and not encroached upon. As for the question of the recognition of our country by the imperialist countries, we should not be in a hurry to solve it now and need not be in a hurry to solve it even for a fairly long period after countrywide victory. We are willing to establish diplomatic relations with all countries on the principle of equality, but the imperialists, who have always been hostile to the Chinese people, will definitely not be in a hurry to treat us as equals. As long as the imperialist countries do not change their hostile attitude, we shall not grant them legal status in China. As for doing business with foreigners, there is no question; wherever there is business to do, we shall do it and we have already started; the businessmen of several capitalist countries are competing for such business. So far as possible, we must first of all trade with the socialist and people's democratic countries; at the same time we will also trade with capitalist countries.

10-3

"Proclamation of the Central People's Government of the People's Republic of China" (read by Mao Tse-tung at a rally on October 1, 1949), in Theodore H. E. Chen, ed., *The Chinese Communist Regime, Documents and Commentary* (New York: Praeger, 1967), pp. 33–34.

The people throughout China have been plunged into bitter sufferings and tribulations since the Chiang Kai-shek Kuomintang reactionary government betrayed the motherland, conspired with imperialists, and launched the counterrevolutionary war. However, our People's Liberation Army, supported by the people throughout the country, fighting heroically and selflessly to defend the territorial sovereignty of the motherland, to protect the people's lives and property, to relieve the people of their suffering, and to struggle for their rights, has eliminated the reactionary troops and overthrown the reactionary rule of the Nationalist government.

Now the war of the people's liberation has been fundamentally won, and the majority of the people throughout the country have been liberated.

On this foundation, the first session of the Chinese People's Political Consultative Conference, composed of the delegates of all democratic parties and groups, people's various regions, various nationalities, overseas Chinese, and patriotic democratic elements of the whole country has been convened. Representing the will of the people throughout the country, this session of the Chinese People's Political Consultative

Conference has enacted the Organic Law of the Central People's Government of the People's Republic of China, elected Mao Tse-tung as chairman of the Central People's Government . . . form[ed] the Central People's Government Council, proclaimed the founding of the People's Republic of China, and decided that Peking [should] be the capital of the People's Republic of China.

The Central People's Government Council of the People's Republic of China took . . . office today in this capital and unanimously made the following decisions:

Proclamation of the formation of the Central People's Government of the People's Republic of China;

Adoption of the Common Program of the Chinese People's Political Consultative Conference as the policy of the government;

Election of Lin Po-ch'u among the council members as secretary-general of the Central People's Government Council;

Appointment of Chou En-lai as premier of the [Government] Administrative Council and concurrently as minister of the Ministry of Foreign Affairs, Mao Tse-tung as chairman of the People's Revolutionary Military Council of the Central People's Government, Chu Teh as commander-in-chief of the People's Liberation Army, Shen Chün-ju as chief justice of the Supreme People's Court, and Lo Jung-huan as procurator general of the Supreme People's Procuratorate and entrusting them with the task of early formation of the various organs of the government to carry out the work of the government.

At the same time, the Central People's Government Council decided to declare to the governments of all other countries that this government is the sole legal government representing all the people of the People's Republic of China. This government is willing to establish diplomatic relations with any foreign government that is willing to observe the principles of equality, mutual benefit, and mutual respect [for] territorial integrity and sovereignty.

10-4

"The Asian Arena," in Margaret Carlyle, ed., *Documents on International Affairs 1949–1950* (London: Oxford University Press, 1953), pp. 539–541. (Footnotes omitted.)

Telegram From Mr. Gromyko, Russian Deputy Minister Of Foreign Affairs, To [Mr.] Chou En-lai, Foreign Minister Of The People's Republic of China, Announcing the Recognition of the Central People's Government by the Government of the USSR, 2 October 1949

The government of the Union of Soviet Socialist Republics hereby confirms receipt of the declaration of the Central People's Government of China dated October 1 this year with the proposal to establish diplomatic relations between the People's Republic of China and the Soviet Union.

Having examined the proposal of the Central People's Government of China, the Soviet government, moved by the invariable striving to maintain friendly relations with the Chinese people and confident that the Central People's Government of China expresses the will of the overwhelming majority of the Chinese people, informs you that it has adopted a decision to establish diplomatic relations between the Soviet Union and the People's Republic of China and to exchange ambassadors.

The USSR Breaks off Relations with the Nationalist Government: Statement Made by Mr. Gromyko to the Chargé D'Affaires of The Nationalist Government in Moscow, 2 October 1949

Owing to events that have occurred in China which have brought about profound changes in the military, political, and social life of the country, as a result of which the Chinese People's Republic has been formed and a Central People's Government of China has been set up, the government of Mr. Yen Hsi-shan located in Canton has ceased to exercise power in the country, has become a provincial government of Canton and has lost the possibility to maintain diplomatic relations with foreign states on behalf of China.

This circumstance led to the discontinuation of diplomatic relations of China with foreign States.

The Soviet government, taking into account all these circumstances, considers diplomatic relations with Canton as discontinued, and has decided to recall its diplomatic representatives from Canton.

Note from the British Foreign Secretary, Mr. Bevin, to [Mr.] Chou En-lai Announcing the Recognition of the Central People's Government as the DE JURE Government of China by the Government of the United Kingdom, 6 January 1950.

I have the honour to inform Your Excellency that His Majesty's government in the United Kingdom of Great Britain and Northern Ireland, having completed their study of the situation resulting from the formation of the Central People's Government of the People's Republic of China, and observing that it is now in effective control of by far the greater part of the territory of China, have this day recognized that government as the de jure government of China. In these circumstances His Majesty's government, in response to Chairman Mao Tse-tung's proclamation of October 1, 1949, are ready to establish diplomatic relations on the basis of equality, mutual benefit, and mutual respect for territory and sovereignty, and are prepared to exchange diplomatic representatives with the Central People's Government.

Pending the appointment of an ambassador, Mr. J. C. Hutchison has been nominated as His Majesty's chargé d'affaires ad interim. Accordingly I have the honour to request that you will receive him and transact official business with him in that capacity, and further that he may be granted all necessary facilities for the transfer of himself, his staff, and the archives of His Majesty's embassy from Nanking to Peking.

(Signed) Ernest Bevin,
His Britannic Majesty's
Principal Secretary of State for Foreign Affairs

NOTE

Following the Soviet lead, eleven other Communist states promptly recognized the PRC, and all but Yugoslavia immediately thereafter established diplomatic relations with it. Between December 1949 and April 1950, in addition to the United Kingdom, thirteen non-Communist states also recognized the PRC; in many cases, however, substantial periods of time elapsed before diplomatic relations were established, and in one case—that of Israel—they have not yet been established.

The United States and many other countries did not extend recognition to the PRC. The United States claimed to be awaiting satisfactory evidence that the new regime would "recognize its international obligations." [9] On February 1, 1947, thirty-two months before formal founding of the PRC on October 1, 1949, the Central Committee of the Chinese Communist Party had announced that it would not recognize any treaties, agreements, understandings, or loans concluded between the Nationalist government and foreign countries after January 10, 1946, unless such actions had been approved by the Political Consultative Conference, an assembly of representatives of China's major political factions that had first been convened on that date in an effort to work out a settlement of the civil war (see item 30–2). The People's Liberation Army made a similar declaration on October 10, 1947; and termination by the Nationalist government of all agreements that were "detrimental to the Chinese people and their state" had been one of the eight major conditions set forth by the CCP in its 1949 offer to make peace with the Nationalists.[10] On the eve of the PRC's founding, the Common Program, which served as its initial charter of government, proclaimed:

> Article 55: The Central People's Government of the People's Republic of China shall examine the treaties and agreements concluded between the Kuomintang and foreign governments, and shall recognize, abrogate, revise, or renegotiate them according to their respective contents.[11]

Other actions of the Peking government also disturbed the United States. In July 1949 an American vice-consul named Olive was arrested and beaten by Communist police in Shanghai. In October 1949 Angus Ward, the American consul general in Mukden, and four of his staff were imprisoned for a month after having lived under house arrest for almost a year. On January 14, 1950, a day after the United States had defeated a Soviet resolution to expel the Nationalist representative from China's seat on the United Nations Security Council, the Chinese Communists seized American consular compounds in Peking (see 28–1, 28–2).

These events led the United States, which continued to maintain diplomatic relations with, and to provide economic aid to, the Nationalist government, to conclude that in the current circumstances the PRC did not want United States' recognition. As Chairman Mao had said [10–2]: "As long as the imperialist countries do not change their hostile attitude, we shall not grant them legal status in China." And Article 56 of the Common Program had authorized the PRC only to negotiate and establish diplomatic relations "with foreign governments which have severed relations with the Kuomintang reactionary clique. . . ."[12]

Despite the refusal of the United States government to extend recognition to it, the PRC sought through court actions to gain control over assets directly or indirectly owned by the Chinese government in the United States. Item 10–5 reports excerpts of the leading case that emerged from this litigation, and item 10–6 and the subsequent Note reveal the PRC's reaction to its lack of success.

10-5

Bank of China v. Wells Fargo Bank and Union Trust Company, 104 F. Supp. 59 (N.D. Cal., March 17, 1952), at 60–61, 63, 64–66. (Some footnotes omitted.)

GOODMAN, DISTRICT JUDGE. Plaintiff, a Chinese corporation, filed these actions to recover the total sum of $798,584.64 on deposit in the defendant Bank. Defendant Bank filed answers asserting its willingness to pay the sum, but alleging that it was unable to do so because of conflicting claims of corporate authority to receive payment. Thereafter the attorneys for the plaintiff moved for summary judgment in plaintiff's favor. Later, a second group of attorneys, claiming that they were the only attorneys empowered to represent the plaintiff Bank of China, filed a motion to dismiss these actions or in the alternative to substitute themselves as the attorneys for the plaintiff. These motions were argued and submitted to the Court for decision.

On July 17, 1950, the Court filed its opinion[a] wherein it directed the disposition of the cause, in accordance with an order providing as follows:

1. That the trial of this cause will be continued *sine die;*
2. That the said motion for summary judgment is denied without prejudice;
3. That said motion for dismissal or in the alternative for substitution of attorneys is denied without prejudice;
4. That the defendant is hereby permitted to deposit in the Registry of this Court the said sum of $798,584.64, subject to the further order of this Court pending a decision herein on the merits;
5. That the defendant Wells Fargo Bank and Union Trust Co.,

[a] 92 F. Supp. 920. Reference is made to the opinion for a full statement of the legal and factual issues then before the court.

shall be and it is hereby relieved of any and all claims for interest for use of the fund or because of its failure or refusal to pay said fund to plaintiff Bank of China or any other claimant thereto which may now or hereafter be asserted against it by plaintiff or any other claimant to said fund or any part thereof, upon condition that it deposit the sum of $798,584.64 in the Registry of this Court within ten (10) days from the date hereof;

6. That upon the defendant's depositing said sum as provided in paragraph 5 hereof, it shall be and is hereby discharged of and from all liability in the premises either to plaintiff Bank of China or to anyone claiming through or on behalf of plaintiff, and plaintiff and all those persons now before this Court who are assertedly acting in the name of plaintiff are restrained from enforcing or attempting to enforce any claim or claims against said defendant relating to said sum of money or said deposit or from taking any proceedings against defendant in relation thereto;

7. That there is reserved to defendant the right to assert against said fund and to prove its costs and attorneys' fees reasonably incurred in this action.

An appeal was taken from the foregoing order. Subsequently the Court of Appeals dismissed the appeal without prejudice and remanded the cases to this Court, stating: "The District Court may deem it expedient to reexamine the case in the light of changing world conditions and such additional evidence as may be made available to it by the respective parties." 190 F.2d 1010, 1012. Thereafter plaintiff renewed its motion for summary judgment and the intervening attorneys renewed their motion to dismiss or in the alternative for their substitution as attorneys for plaintiff. The motions came on for hearing on November 20, 1951. Additional documentary evidence was presented; the motions were argued and submitted on briefs thereafter filed.

Pursuant to the direction of the Court of Appeals, this Court is now in a position to reexamine the cases in the light of the additional evidence and "changing world conditions."

Not only has additional documentary evidence been submitted, but there is no doubt that "world conditions" *have* materially changed since the Court's decision of July 17, 1950. On the present record, the Court can justly and properly decide these motions without further continuance *sine die*.

The question now presented is essentially one of law. The attorneys who initiated this action contend that the controlling corporate authority of the Bank of China is vested by its Articles of Association in the Nationalist government of China. They note that the Bank of

China was directed by representatives of that government when the deposit in suit was made. The Nationalist government, they point out, not only still exists, but is the only government of China recognized by the United States. The Bank of China, they assert, still functions under the control of the Nationalist government at its present seat on the Island of Formosa and at branch offices in various parts of the world. The Bank of China, so functioning, is the plaintiff in this action, they say, and the rightful claimant to the deposit in suit.

The intervening attorneys contend that the People's government of China, as the successor in fact to the Nationalist government in continental China, has succeeded to the corporate rights of the Chinese state in the Bank of China. They allege that the operations of the Bank of China throughout the Chinese mainland and in certain branch offices abroad are now conducted by new government directors appointed by the People's Government in conjunction with the directors representing private stockholders. It is only through these banking operations, they argue, that the corporate purposes of the Bank of China are now being realized. Only through operations so conducted, they say, can the rights of the Chinese state as majority stockholder and those of the private investors be given any substance. Such corporate operations, the intervening attorneys urge, are the true indicia of rightful ownership of the deposit.

The issue before the Court has therefore been reduced to a comparatively narrow one. It appears from the record, that there are two Banks of China now functioning. The question is: Which Bank of China is legally entitled to the deposit in suit? For convenience, the plaintiff will hereafter be referred to as the "Nationalist" Bank of China, and the Bank of China represented by the intervening attorneys as the "People's" Bank of China. . . .

The issue thus posed focuses attention at the outset on the fact that, of the two governments asserting corporate authority, one is recognized by the United States while the other is not. If this fact, per se, is determinative, the issue is resolved. If whenever this court is called upon to determine whether there is a government justly entitled to act on behalf of a foreign state in respect to a particular matter, the court is bound to say, without regard to the facts before it, that the government recognized by our executive is that government, then nothing more need be said here. To permit this expression of executive policy to usurp entirely the judicial judgment would relieve the court of a burdensome duty, but it is doubtful that the ends of justice would thus be met. It has been argued that such is the accepted practice. But the authorities do not support this view. . . .

This is not to suggest that the courts should regard executive policy in respect to recognition and nonrecognition of foreign governments as meaningless or of little consequence. In any particular situation, executive policy may be crucial, as indeed it appears to be in the present case. But, it is a fact which properly should be considered and weighed along with the other facts before the court.

Turning to the record in this case, it appears that two governments are governments in fact of portions of the territory of the State of China. The "People's" government has supplanted the "Nationalist" government in dominion over the entire Chinese mainland with an area of more than 3,700,000 square miles, and a population of more than 460,000,000. The "Nationalist" government controls one of the 35 provinces of China, the Island of Formosa, which has an area of 13,885 square miles and a population in excess of 6,000,000. It is obvious that the "People's" government is now the government in fact of by far the greater part of the territory of the Chinese state. Nevertheless the "Nationalist" government controls substantial territory, exceeding in area that of either Belgium or the Netherlands, and in population that of Denmark or Switzerland.

Each government, in its respective sphere, functions effectively. Each is recognized by a significant number of the nations of the world. Each maintains normal diplomatic intercourse with those nations which extend recognition. This has been the status quo for more than two years.

Each government is in a position to exercise corporate authority in behalf of the Bank of China. That is, each government is capable of utilizing the corporate structure and certain corporate assets to promote the corporate purposes. The Bank of China was chartered primarily to facilitate Chinese international commercial activities. It was organized as an international exchange bank to deal in domestic and foreign exchange and gold and silver bullion, to discount, purchase, and collect commercial bills and drafts, to issue, service, and redeem government bonds in foreign markets, and to handle public funds deposited abroad. It was also authorized to engage in a general domestic banking business including the acceptance of deposits and valuables for safekeeping, the granting of loans, and the issuance and service of domestic government loans. Each government is in a position to act through the corporate structure of the Bank of China to carry on these international functions in the areas abroad where such government is recognized and these domestic functions within the territory such government controls. Each government is in fact doing so. The Bank of China, as controlled by the Nationalist government, continues to function on the Island of Formosa and through its foreign branches in the United States, Cuba, Australia, Japan, Indochina, and elsewhere where the Nationalist government is recognized.

The People's Government as successor in fact to the Nationalist government on the Chinese mainland is exercising the prerogatives of the government in respect to the Bank of China there. The People's Government has not nationalized the Bank of China, nor confiscated its assets, nor denied the rights of private stockholders. It exercises the authority vested in the government of China as majority stockholder. The Bank of China continues to function in accordance with its Articles of Association under the guidance of the appointees of the People's Government and the majority of the directors previously elected by private stockholders on the Chinese mainland and through branches in London, Hong Kong, Singapore, Penang, Kuala Lumpur, Batavia, Calcutta, Bombay, Karachi, Chittagong, and Rangoon.

This factual situation is without analogous precedent in any reported case. The resulting legal problem, arising as it does out of sweeping historical changes and the claims of rival governments, cannot be met by the application of technical rules of corporation law.

A year and a half ago, this Court felt that the best course was to withhold judgment. At that time the Nationalist forces had only recently retreated to their last stronghold; their ability to consolidate this position was doubtful. The People's Government which had assumed control of the Chinese mainland had not yet demonstrated its stability. Our executive policy had not assumed definite outlines in the wake of these events. The *émigré* directors of the Bank who sought control of the deposit in suit could not demonstrate their authority to do so or their ability to apply the funds to corporate purposes. The Bank of China, under new management on the Chinese mainland, was not yet functioning normally in accordance with its Articles of Association. Whether its assets there would be employed for corporate purposes or diverted to other ends was not known.

Now time has clarified the picture. Both the Nationalist and People's governments have maintained and strengthened their positions. Our national policy toward these governments is now definite. We have taken a stand adverse to the aims and ambitions of the People's Government. The armed forces of that government are now engaged in conflict with our forces in Korea. We recognize only the Nationalist government as the representative of the state of China, and are actively assisting in developing its military forces in Formosa. The Bank of China now operates as two corporate entities, each performing within the area of its operations the functions bestowed upon the Bank of China by its Articles of Association. Each Bank of China is in a position to employ the deposit in suit for corporate purposes.

From a practical standpoint, neither of the rival Banks of China is a true embodiment of the corporate entity which made the deposit in the Wells Fargo Bank. The present Nationalist Bank of China is more nearly equivalent in the sense of continuity of management. The People's Bank is more representative in ability to deal with the greater number of private stockholders and established depositors and creditors. Were the Court to adopt a strictly pragmatic approach, it might attempt a division of the deposit between these two banks in the degree that each now exercises the functions of the Bank of China. Or the Court might award the entire deposit to the bank it deems to be the closest counterpart of the corporation contemplated by the Articles of Association.

But this the Court could not do merely by balancing interests of a private nature. Such a course would ultimately entail determining which bank best serves the corporate interests of the state of China. That determination could not be made while the state, itself, remains divided, except by an excursion into the realm of political philosophy. Were there only one government, in fact, of the Chinese state, or only one government in a position to act effectively for the state in respect to the matter before the Court, the Court might be justified in accepting such a government as the proper representative of the State, even though our executive declined to deal with it. Here, there coexist two governments, in fact, each attempting to further, in its own way, the interests of the State of China, in the Bank of China. It is not a proper function of a domestic court of the United States to attempt to judge which government best represents the interests of the Chinese state in the Bank of China. In this situation, the Court should justly accept, as the representative of the Chinese state, that government which our executive deems best able to further the mutual interests of China and the United States.

Since the Court is of the opinion that it should recognize the Nationalist government of China as legally entitled to exercise the controlling corporate authority of the Bank of China in respect to the deposit in suit, the motion for summary judgment in favor of the Bank of China, as controlled by the Nationalist government, is granted. The motion of the intervening attorneys to dismiss, or, in the alternative, for their substitution as attorneys for the plaintiff, is denied.[13]

10-6

"Kung Ying-ping Protests against US Robbing of Bank of China Deposits," NCNA–English, Peking (July 5, 1952), in *SCMP*, no. 369:12–13 (July 6–8, 1952).

The General Manager of the Bank of China, Kung Ying-ping, issued the following protest against the illegal decision of the American government and its courts which robs the Bank of China of assets that belong to it:

In March this year, the United States District Court for the Northern District of California announced its illegal decision by which this bank's deposits in the Wells Fargo Bank of San Francisco, amounting to 600,000 US dollars [*sic*], were lawlessly seized by the war criminal Kung Hsiang-hsi and a few fugitive directors who have long been removed from office. I hereby lodge a solemn protest at this encroachment on the inviolable rights of the stockholders, depositors of this bank, and all the Chinese people.

All the rights of this bank, at home or abroad, belong to the Chinese people—who include all the private stockholders and depositors of this bank. Our Head Office alone may legally represent these rights; this fact is irrefutable. That our Head Office is the sole legal claimant to the deposits in the Wells Fargo Bank is thus unquestionable. However, the American imperialist government and its courts, applying its reactionary policy, which is traditionally antagonistic to the Chinese people, did not base their decision on the facts, in not returning to this bank (the original owner) its deposits in the Wells Fargo Bank. They have even gone to the absurd lengths of illegally deciding to allow war criminal Kung Hsiang-hsi and a small handful of remnant, fugitive bandits, who have been discarded by the Chinese people, to grab this bank's assets. This again demonstrates the American imperialist government's antagonism to the interests of the Chinese people.

On the basis of the above reasons, I, on behalf of the Bank of China, . . . make the solemn protest that we shall never recognize this sort of utterly absurd, unreasonable, and illegal decision of the American courts. Any action by the American government and its courts concerning this bank's rights in the Wells Fargo Bank or in other banks which is not agreed to by this bank, is invalid. This bank reserves all its rights.

NOTE

In commenting on the *Wells Fargo* case, the *People's Daily* of July 6, 1952, indignantly argued that "even Goodman, American district judge of California," had admitted facts that conclusively established Peking's claim to the assets. It quoted from Judge Goodman's first opinion, of July 17, 1950, in which he stated: "The funds here in controversy belong to a Chinese corporation. . . . It maintains 20 foreign offices for the express purpose of facilitating trade between the Chinese people and the rest of the world. The Bank of China cannot perform its functions while divorced from the Chinese nation. Its depositors, its 5,000 private stockholders, and the Chinese people—who may be characterized as the ultimate owners of the government stockholding—must live under the government which in fact governs throughout the territorial limits of China."

"The émigré directors of the bank are now scattered. . . . The whereabouts of some is unknown. Some of these directors represent a government which is not now, and may never again be, in a position to speak for the Chinese people. . . . The others may or may not be the directors whom the private stockholders now desire to speak for them. It is difficult to perceive how the interests of the corporation, its stockholders, and its depositors will be protected by placing the res in dispute at the disposal of a group of these directors." [14]

The following is Peking's reaction to the failure of another lawsuit to gain control of disputed assets.

10-7

"Chinese General Postal Administration Protests Illegal US Decision," NCNA–English, Peking (June 22, 1953), in *SCMP*, no. 595:9–10 (June 23, 1953).

A statement was issued on June 20 by Su Yu-nung, Director-General of the General Postal Administration of the People's Republic of China, protesting the illegal decision made by the United States Circuit [*sic*] Court for the Southern District of New York, on February 9th. . . .[15]

The following is the full text of Su Yu-nung's statement:

The US Circuit Court for the Southern District of New York, in February, made the illegal decision that the more than 520,000 US dollars deposited with the American Express Company by the Postal Remittances and Savings Bank which has not been taken over by this office should belong to the so-called "Republic of China and the Postal Remittances and Savings Bank." In order to safeguard the inalienable rights of the People's Republic of China and the depositors of this office, I hereby make a serious protest against this illegal "decision."

All the right and interest of the Postal Remittances and Savings Bank in and out of this country belong to the entire people of the People's Republic of China, including all depositors and holders of uncashed money orders of the said bank. It is an undisputed fact that this office, the General Postal Administration of the People's Republic of China, is the sole legitimate representative of this right and interest. Moreover, this office, with a view to protecting their interests from suffering any loss, has cleared at the rate of exchange before liberation all the debts owed by the Postal Remitttances and Savings Bank to its depositors and holders of its uncashed money orders, in accordance with the order of the Government Administrative Council of the Central People's Government. However, the US government and its court, persisting in their reactionary, hostile policy against the Chinese people, have made an illegal decision with regard to the deposit of the Postal Remittances and Savings Bank in the American Express Company, thus enabling the remnant reactionary Kuomintang gang in Taiwan which has long since been spurned by the Chinese people to realize its purpose of open embezzlement. This constitutes a serious infringement upon the legitimate rights of the Chinese people.

On behalf of the General Postal Administration of the People's Republic of China, I hereby solemnly declare that the above-mentioned "decision" of the Circuit Court [*sic*] for the Southern District of New York, USA, is illegal and, therefore, invalid and that any decision taken by the US government and its judiciary regarding . . . the interest of the Postal Remittances and Savings Bank in the American Express Company and other companies or banks without the consent of this office will be invalid too. We reserve all right to demand compensation for the loss.

Note

When, in October 1971, the PRC replaced the ROC as the representative of China in the UN, it was widely anticipated that many states which had until then recognized the ROC as the government of China would transfer their recognition to the PRC. Such a change would have obvious implications within those states regarding property owned by the Chinese government. On December 15, 1971, the ROC reorganized its Bank of China and its Bank of Communications by selling to private interests the stock which the ROC owned in those banks. According to ROC embassy officials in Washington, "the reorganization took place in order to stimulate and expand Taiwan's foreign trade operations." [16] On March 13, 1972, a spokesman for the People's Bank of China, Head Office, in Peking issued the following statement "on the illegal selling of Bank of China and Bank of Communications stocks by the Chiang Kai-shek clique:" [17]

> On December 15, 1971, the Chiang Kai-shek clique formulated a so-called "Bank of China Organization Act" and changed the name of the "Bank of China" into the "International Commercial Bank of China." This is another grave scheme by which the Chiang Kai-shek clique attempts to steal state property through the tactics of putting up a camouflage.
>
> It is well known that the bureaucrat-capital of the Bank of China and the Bank of Communications, which were controlled by the Chiang Kai-shek clique in old China, is sweat and blood of the Chinese people extorted by the Chiang Kai-shek clique over a long period of time. Directly after the founding of the People's Republic of China, it was confiscated by our government by public proclamation, and this bank, the People's Bank of China, was authorized to take it over. All the assets of the branches of those two banks in Taiwan Province and in foreign countries belong to the head offices of the two banks, and only the People's Bank of China and the head offices of the two banks have the right to dispose of them. It is absolutely impermissible for anyone by any means to appropriate or sell them illegally.
>
> At present the Chiang Kai-shek clique is stepping up its scheme of stealing state property. In view of this, this bank hereby declares: Any transferring or selling of the assets of the two banks by the Chiang Kai-shek clique, by whatever means and tactics, is illegal and null and void. This bank and the head offices of the Bank of China and Bank of Communications reserve every right to recover them.[18]

The materials that follow indicate that, to the PRC, a mere offer to establish diplomatic relations did not constitute sufficient proof that an imperialist country had changed its hostile attitude.

10-8

"Foreign Ministry Spokesman on Sino-British Negotiations," *PC*, no. 11:26 (June 1, 1950).

On May 22, a spokesman of the Ministry of Foreign Affairs of the Central People's Government made the following statement:

On January 6, 1950, the British government sent a note to Chou En-lai, Foreign Minister of the Central People's Government of the People's Republic of China, expressing the desire to establish diplomatic relations with the Central People's Government of the People's Republic of China on the basis of equality, mutual benefit and mutual respect for territory and sovereignty. On the same day the British government also announced its withdrawal of recognition from the remnant reactionary clique of the Kuomintang. On January 9, Foreign Minister Chou En-lai of the Central People's Government of the People's Republic of China replied to this note of the British government, expressing willingness to establish diplomatic relations between the People's Republic of China and Great Britain on the basis of equality, mutual benefit and mutual respect for territory and sovereignty. Furthermore, on January 28, he accepted Mr. John C. Hutchison, chargé d'affaires ad interim, as representative of the British government to come to Peking to conduct negotiations on preliminary and procedural questions concerning the establishment of diplomatic relations between the People's Republic of China and Great Britain.

After Mr. Hutchison's arrival in Peking, the negotiations concerning the establishment of diplomatic relations between the People's Republic of China and Great Britain formally began on March 2. In the course of the negotiations, the Central People's Government verbally made it clear to the British representative that, among the preliminary and procedural questions concerning the establishment of diplomatic relations between the People's Republic of China and Great Britain, the most important one, which must first be settled, was the relationship between the British government and the remnant reactionary clique of the Kuomintang. The Central People's Government considered the action of the British delegate in abstaining from voting on the question of Chinese representation in the United Nations, and the question of what actually is the attitude of the British government toward the various organizations of the remnant reactionary clique of the Kuomintang and the national properties and assets of China in Great Britain, Hong Kong, and territories subject to Great Britain, as all pertaining to the question of the relationship between the British government and the remnant reactionary clique of the Kuomintang. The Central People's

Government, therefore, desired the British government to clarify its position with regard to these two questions.

The British government gave some explanations regarding its attitude to the above two questions in a verbal reply delivered by its representative, Hutchison, on March 17. The Central People's Government, however, did not consider these explanations satisfactory.

In fact, the British government has, for five months, consistently abstained from voting on the question of China's right to representation in all the United Nations organs. Furthermore, with regard to the airplanes now at Hong Kong, which are in the possession and directly under the protection of the two airlines—the China National Aviation Corporation and the Central Air Transport Corporation of the Civil Aeronautics Bureau of the Central People's Government of the People's Republic of China—the British authorities in Hong Kong not only have in many ways obstructed their flight to China, but have in fact failed to assume their real responsibility in protecting the airplanes, to the extent that seven of them have been wrecked. All these facts sufficiently indicate that the British government has not been able to demonstrate by its real actions that it has in fact completely severed its relationship with the remnant reactionary clique of the Kuomintang. They also show that it has not paid due respect to the rights of the Central People's Government of the People's Republic of China to its national properties and assets and its right to manage such properties and assets.

In view of this, the Central People's Government addressed, on May 8, a special notification to representative Hutchison for transmission to the British government, asking it to clarify further its position with regard to the following two questions: China's right to representation in the United Nations and China's right to its national properties and assets.

But on the very day following this notification of the Central People's Government, that is, May 9, the British government ordered the Hong Kong court to detain the 70 airplanes of the China National Aviation Corporation and the Central Air Transport Corporation, which were parked on Hong Kong's Kaitak Airfield. This action not only proved that the British government did not respect the rights of the Central People's Government to its national properties and assets and its right to manage such properties and assets, but also represented in fact an extremely unfriendly attitude toward the People's Republic of China. On the one hand, the British government expressed the desire to establish diplomatic relations with the Central People's Government of the People's Republic of China; on the other, after expressing this desire, it again and again demonstrated that it has not in reality completely severed its relationship with the remnant reactionary clique of the Kuomintang. The Central People's Government of the People's Republic of China considers that it is absolutely necessary to ask the British government to clarify further its position with regard to the central questions of this inconsistency between words and deeds.

NOTE

The United Kingdom was faced with a difficult legal problem when the PRC pressed it to recognize that ownership of the Chinese airplanes in Hong Kong lay in two of the PRC's government corporations. On December 12, 1949, more than two months after the formal founding of the PRC and less than a month before the UK recognized the Communist regime in lieu of the Nationalist regime, the Nationalist government had purported to sell the airplanes in question to a private American corporation led by Claire Chennault. Following the UK's recognition of the PRC, the American corporation, seeking a declaration that the airplanes were its property, brought suit in Hong Kong against one of the PRC's corporations. That action was dismissed on the ground that the defendant enjoyed sovereign immunity from the court's jurisdiction.[19] In order to permit a judicial solution of the problem, an Order in Council of May 10, 1950, eliminated the defense of jurisdictional immunity of foreign states in any subsequent proceedings involving the airplanes.[20] New litigation over their ownership was instituted on May 19, 1950, and the Foreign Ministry statement of May 22, reproduced above in item 10–8, reflected the PRC's concern about a possibly unfavorable outcome.

Just one year later, the Hong Kong trial court held that ownership of the airplanes lay with the PRC because the transaction by which the Nationalist government purported to sell them to the American corporation was not valid, as it was a device contrived to deprive the PRC of property that would rightfully belong to it following the UK's impending recognition. This judgment was affirmed by Hong Kong's appellate court, but on further appeal the Judicial Committee of the Privy Council held on July 28, 1952, that the lower courts had erred in declaring the sale invalid; so far as the UK was concerned, the court said, the Nationalist government had been the de jure government of China on the date of the sale and had therefore been entitled to dispose of its property for any reason it saw fit.[21]

Item 10–9 sets forth the PRC's reaction to this decision and its consequences.

10-9

"Chang Han-fu Protests against Seizure of Chinese Planes by British Government in Hong Kong." NCNA–English, Peking (Aug. 2, 1952), in *SCMP*, no. 388:29–30 (Aug. 3–5, 1952).

Chang Han-fu, Vice-Minister for Foreign Affairs of the Central People's Government, made a statement today seriously protesting against the seizure by the British government of aircraft in Hong Kong of the CNAC [China National Aviation Corporation] and the CAC [Central Aviation Corporation] of China and the persecution by the British government of personnel of these two companies. The statement reads:

After the Judicial Committee of the Privy Council of Britain preposterously took up the suit of so-called "property rights of the Central Aviation Corporation," on July 28 of this year, it even "adjudged" the forty planes and other properties in Hong Kong belonging to the Central Aviation Corporation of the People's Republic of China [as belonging] to Chennault's so-called "Civil Aviation Transport Corporation" of the United States.

Immediately afterward, at midnight on July 28, the Hong Kong British government deployed a great number of armed police to make a raid on the Kai Tak Airfield of Hong Kong, and the warehouses of Bailey's Yard and the New Asiatic Chemical Works, where the Chinese aircraft and materials were stored, and beat up, arrested, and imprisoned all of our personnel guarding the aforementioned properties. The Hong Kong British government seized all the properties in Hong Kong, including the 70 planes, belonging to the China National Aviation Corporation and the Central Aviation Corporation of the People's Republic of China.

As early as December 3, 1949, Premier Chou En-lai of the Central People's Government solemnly declared: "The CNAC and the CAC belong to the Central People's Government of the People's Republic of China and are under the direct control of the Civil Aviation Bureau of the Central People's Government. Only the Central People's Government and personnel entrusted by it have the right to deal with the properties of the CNAC and the CAC in Hong Kong, and [no one] is allowed to encroach on, move or damage them by any means." However, for more than two years, the British government, complying with the preposterous demand of the United States government, has worked in collusion with the remnant Kuomintang clique in carrying out a series of conspiratorial activities with [the] intention of seizing the said properties of the People's Republic of China. At first, it tried in every possible way to prevent these airplanes from flying back to China; then it connived with Kuomintang agents and gangsters in blowing up and sabotaging the planes, resulting in destruction of seven of them. Furthermore, it has all along put on acts with legal trimmings by instituting a series of so-called "property rights proceedings." On May 10, 1950, the British government even issued the so-called "order of Privy Council," illegally impounding all the aircraft and other properties in Hong Kong belonging to the CNAC and the CAC. After that, the British government, together with Chennault of the United States, acted with much affectation in several inferior shows of "hearings" and "verdicts" in the British courts of various levels in Hong Kong and London. In addition, the British government has incessantly subjected to unwarranted persecution personnel who have been guarding the aircraft and other properties in Hong Kong of the two aviation corporations. The Central People's Government had reportedly protested to the British government, solemnly condemning the extremely unfriendly attitude of the British government toward the People's Republic of China, and declaring that the British government shall be held entirely responsible for the above-mentioned illegal acts during the last two years.

The Central People's Government considers that the British government, in committing the latest atrocious acts of seizing the properties in Hong Kong of the above-mentioned two aviation corporations and of beating up, arresting, and imprisoning personnel guarding the properties of these two corporations, has gravely demonstrated that it has followed the United States in taking a hostile attitude toward the People's Republic of China. This incident has already aroused tremendous indignation among all people of China. The Central People's Government hereby lodge[s] a serious protest with the British government against the above-mentioned acts of seizure and atrocities. The British government has absolutely no jurisdiction whatsoever over the properties in Hong Kong of the two aviation corporations, [n]or has it any right at all to encroach on, damage, or transfer these properties. The British government should immediately cease its illegal acts of encroaching upon the sovereign rights of the People's Republic of China. It should immediately return the above-mentioned state properties of China, which it seized, to entrusted personnel of the Central People's Government for their disposal. And, furthermore, it should immediately stop persecution of our personnel guarding the said properties and ensure them their freedom and rights. Otherwise, the British government must bear full responsibility and all consequences resulting from these acts.

NOTE

Although the United Kingdom withdrew its recognition of the Nationalist government and recognized the PRC on January 6, 1950, the UK and the PRC did not establish official relations until June 17, 1954. Peking's initial response to British recognition had made it clear that diplomatic relations would have to be "negotiated." We have already seen two questions that had to be settled before an exchange of ambassadors could occur: would the UK support the PRC's representation in the United Nations, and would it respect the PRC's claim to China's property in Hong Kong? There was also a third question, which seemed somewhat less urgent to the Chinese: would the UK continue to maintain a consulate in Taiwan, where the Nationalist government continued to be in control but where the British consul was accredited to the provincial, and not to the Nationalist, government?

The Korean war overtook discussions on these matters, which became more complicated when the UK, following the United States, took the position that the island of Taiwan had not been legally restored to China after World War II (see item 12–9). In 1954, after the Korean armistice and before the PRC obtained satisfaction of any of these issues, the two countries agreed to exchange chargés d'affaires and did so. But they did not establish relations at the ambassadorial level.[22]

Relations between the PRC and the UK became further complicated on April 12, 1955, when the Hong Kong Supreme Court ruled that a warehouse in Hong Kong occupied by CNAC was the property of General Chennault's Zebra Corporation. When CNAC refused to vacate the premises on the ground that they belonged to the PRC, it was ousted by the local police on May 9, 1955. The PRC's Civil Aviation Bureau protested this action.[23]

On May 13, 1966, the Indian government, which maintains diplomatic relations with the PRC, sought to justify to the PRC India's contacts with the Nationalist government by pointing out that the UK had never relinquished its consulate on Taiwan. The Indian note stated that "some countries whose diplomatic missions the Chinese government have received in Peking still maintain consular offices in Taiwan."[24] In a note delivered to the Indian embassy in Peking on July 28, 1966, the PRC rejected this contention:

> As is well known . . . there is indeed an imperialist country which in words recognizes only the People's Republic of China but in practice is willingly serving as the accomplice of the United States in the scheme of creating "two Chinas" and "one China and one Taiwan." For this very reason, China's diplomatic relations

with that country have been prevented from being normalized for the past decade and more. Does the Indian government find such a state of affairs enviable? Is it ready to imitate the past colonial ruler of India on this matter, too? [25]

Subsequently, in the *People's Daily,* "Commentator," a pen name for a high official, wrote that "relations between the two countries to date still remain in a state of semiestablishment of diplomatic relations, although China and Britain have exchanged diplomatic envoys for more than a decade." [26] For the terms upon which the UK eventually managed to exchange ambassadors with the PRC, see the Note following Item 10–16.

10-10

Shao Chin-fu, "The Absurd Theory of 'Two Chinas' and Principles of International Law," *KCWTYC* 2:8–12 (1959); translated in *Oppose the New U.S. Plots to Create "Two Chinas"* (Peking, 1962), pp. 76–85.

In the last few years the US imperialists and their followers have concocted many "theoretical justifications" concerning "two Chinas." Generally they boil down to two sets of logic.

The first set begins with the allegation that the Chiang Kai-shek clique in Taiwan is a "sovereign state" existing side by side with the People's Republic of China. It follows that the relationship between the Chinese people and the Chiang Kai-shek clique is "not a civil war" but an international question. With the United States meddling in as an ally of the Chiang Kai-shek clique, a tripartite relationship between the United States, the Chiang Kai-shek clique, and the People's Republic of China is thereby framed. Then certain principles and concepts of international law are cited, and the efforts of the Chinese people to liberate Taiwan will turn out to be "the use of armed force to seize new territory," "eliminating Free China," "crude violation of the principles upon which world order is based," and consequently they "endanger vital free world positions and the security of the United States." Therefore, China must agree to make "a declaration of renunciation of force" and carry out [a] "cease-fire." On the other hand, by its occupation of China's territory and interference in China's internal affairs the United States is "living up to treaty obligations," helping "a loyal ally" and enjoying the "right of self-defense' 'in the Taiwan area. If China does not accept US demands, then the United States "reserves the right to bring the matter to the United Nations" or to the "International Court of Justice," and so on and so forth.

The second set of logic is for the purpose of refusing to recognize China's sovereignty over Taiwan, alleging that the "legal status of Taiwan is unsettled," that China cannot by a unilateral declaration recover her sovereignty which she had ceded by treaty, that the Cairo Declaration was "merely a declaration of intention" and the question "cannot be solved merely by reference to the Cairo and Potsdam Declarations," and that Taiwan, Penghu, Quemoy, and Matsu "have never been under the authority of the Chinese Communists," and should, therefore, be "placed under UN trusteeship" or "settled by a plebiscite," and so on and so forth.

Obviously these two sets of logic serve two schemes [or] two steps, that is, "isolating Taiwan" and "placing Taiwan under trusteeship." The imperialists use the first set of logic to deny the legality of the right of the Chinese people to liberate Taiwan, claiming that the Chiang Kai-shek clique is another China so as to legalize US intervention in China's internal affairs and its armed occupation of Taiwan. Then they use the second set of logic to deny the Chinese people's sovereignty over Taiwan altogether; that is, to create a legal basis for [evicting] the Chiang Kai-shek regime and placing Taiwan under trusteeship and, as a further step, to seize Taiwan for themselves and use it as a base for extending aggression.

These arguments are gangster logic through and through, which the imperialists have fabricated by distorting historical facts and playing with legal sophistry. Although they have racked their brains in doing so, all the premises of their arguments are fictitious and have nothing to stand on in the face of facts and legal principles.

First of all, the premises of the first set of logic used by the US imperialists that the Chiang Kai-shek clique in Taiwan is a state are extremely absurd.

According to the principles of international law concerning sovereign equality and national self-determination, the adoption of any form of state is the affair of a nation itself. In other words "the establishment of a state organization—a subject of international law—depends upon the free decision of the nation itself."[a] No foreign country has the right to interfere.

China has always been a unified state. Article 3 of the Constitution of the People's Republic of China has made this provision.[b] As

[a] G. I. Tunkin, *Osnovy sovremennogo mezhdunarodnogo prava; uchebnoe posobie* (The basis of modern international law; Moscow: Vysshaia partiinaia shkola pri TsK KPSS), 1956, p. 17.

[b] Article 3: "The People's Republic of China is a unitary multinational state."

national unity is the highest interest of all nationalities in the country and the safeguarding of national unity is their common will, even the reactionary governments of the past could not but recognize this point in their constitutions. In international relations China has always played its part as a unified sovereign state, a single subject of international law. Furthermore, long diplomatic practice has shown that, whether at international conferences or in international treaties, China has always participated or signed in the name of a single state. This basic situation did not change even in the periods of melees between the warlords or revolutionary civil wars. It is still less likely that the question of "two Chinas" will ever arise since the victory of the people's revolution in 1949 when nationwide unification was achieved as never before.

As to the Chiang Kai-shek clique still entrenched in Taiwan, it is the remnant of old China's reactionary ruling clique. It is only a reactionary political clique illegally occupying a corner of land, scheming in vain for a comeback. It is absolutely not a state, and not a subject of international law as between states. This clique depends for its existence entirely on US support and has no mass basis to speak of. It is out of the question that this clique is a "sovereign state." Furthermore, it does not claim to be a new state; on the contrary, it styles itself the "Republic of China," and emphasizes that "Taiwan and the mainland belong to one entity." Notwithstanding its dream for a comeback which will never come true, one point is quite clear, that is, all Chinese recognize Taiwan as a part of China, but not as a state outside of China.

To put the matter in a false light, the US imperialists purposely call the People's Republic of China "Communist China" or "mainland China" to distinguish it from Chiang Kai-shek's so-called "Republic of China," in an attempt to create an impression as though the People's Republic of China is a new member in international relations while the Chiang Kai-shek clique is the continuance of old China. However, people with some common sense all know that the overthrowing of an old government and replacing it with a new one by the people of a country through revolutionary means is an internal question and does not affect the qualification of that country as a member in international relations. In its class nature the People's Republic of China is a new state entirely different from old China, but it is not a new member in the family of nations. In international law she is not a new subject, but continues to exist as a member in international relations in the place of old China. All rights of old China are the rights of new China; all territories of old China are the territories of new China. Taiwan is a part of China. Naturally it is within the sovereignty of new China.

The imperialists' insistent allegations that it is a "state" are nothing but lies with ulterior motives.

The US imperialists' allegation that the local authorities controlled by the Chiang Kai-shek clique in Taiwan are the legitimate government of China is likewise without any foundation.

According to international law, "In such single States there is one central political authority as Government, which represents the State, within its borders as well as without, in its international intercourse with other International Persons."[c] "It [international law] recognizes the government which actually and independently exercises power on the territory of the state as representative of that state in international relations."[d] To quote the Italian jurist Anzilotti, "He who actually holds the power of command has the quality of organ of international personality in international relations; he who in fact loses this power ceases to represent the state internationally."[e] Whether the government of a state is legal or not, only the people of that state can decide; "Nobody has the right to examine into the question of the legality of the government chosen by the people themselves."[f]

The government of the People's Republic of China has been set up after the Chinese people, under the leadership of the Chinese Communist Party, overthrew the Kuomintang reactionary rule through long years of struggle. It exercises state power within the country. Naturally, therefore, it is this government alone that can represent China in foreign relations as the only legitimate government of China.

The reactionary Kuomintang government has already been overthrown by the Chinese people. As to the regime set up in Taiwan by a remnant . . . of old China's reactionary ruling clique, it may at best be regarded as a local authority of China and absolutely has not the qualifications of a central government. Undoubtedly it cannot represent China in foreign relations and has no right to deal with foreign countries. Moreover, since October 1, 1949, "The Republic of China" has ceased to exist. This title, like the titles of the different dynasties in China, has become a historical relic. The using of the signboard of the "Republic of China" up to the present by the Chiang Kai-shek clique is an act of usurpation; it is of course illegal.

The state system and government of the People's Republic of

[c] L. Oppenheim, *International Law,* 7th ed., by H. Lauterpacht (London: Longmans, Green, 1948), I, 161–162.

[d] G. I. Tunkin, *Osnovy sovremennogo mezhdunarodnogo prava; uchebnoe posobie* (The bases of modern international law), 1956, p. 23.

[e] Dionisio Anzilotti, *Cours de Droit International,* tr. Gilbert Gidel (Paris: Librairie du Recueil Sirey, Société Anonyme, 1929), I, 179.

[f] L. A. Modzhoryan, "The Identity, Continuity and Succession of the Subject of International Law," in *SGP,* no. 9:63 (1958).

China have been chosen by the Chinese people themselves and are supported by the whole nation. Even according to the traditional "principle of effective control," this government should be considered the legal representative of China. Other countries have absolutely no right to continue to recognize the remnants of old China's reactionary regime, long ago spurned by the Chinese people, as the legal representative of China.

The relationship between the People's Republic of China and the Chiang Kai-shek clique is the continuation of the internal struggle in the last thirty years between the Chinese people under the leadership of the Chinese Communist Party and the Kuomintang reactionaries. It is China's internal question, a matter between the Chinese themselves. No foreign country, whether it has recognized the People's Republic of China or not, has the right to intervene.

(2)

In order to prove that there exist "two Chinas" the US imperialists try to draw a parallel between the relationship of the Chinese mainland with Taiwan and that of East Germany with West Germany, north Korea with south Korea, and north Vietnam and south Vietnam. This is also preposterous.

Let us first take the case of Germany.

With the defeat and unconditional surrender of Nazi Germany, the situation was: "There is no central government or authority in Germany capable of accepting responsibility for the maintenance of order, the administration of the country and compliance with the requirements of the victorious Powers." [g] On the basis of the relevant provisions of the Crimea statement of February 1945, the declaration of the four powers—the Soviet Union, the United States, Britain, and France—on June 5 regarding the defeat of Germany and the assumption of supreme authority in Germany, and the Potsdam Declaration of August 3 of the same year, the four governments "assumed the supreme authority with respect to Germany" which was exercised by the commanders in chief of the four powers in their respective zones of occupation. Later, on account of the obstructions of the Western powers, a united German government was never set up nor was a peace treaty with Germany concluded. On September 7, 1949, under the manipulation of

[g] Declaration Regarding the Defeat of Germany and the Assumption of Supreme Authority with Respect to Germany by the Governments of the United States of America, the Union of Soviet Socialist Republics, the United Kingdom and the Provisional Government of the French Republic, signed at Berlin, June 5, 1945, *Documents on American Foreign Relations*, 1944–45, VII, 217.

the United States, the "German Federal Republic" was established in the occupation zones of the three Western powers. In October of the same year the people in East Germany set up the German Democratic Republic in the Soviet occupation zone. "At first these two states were subject to certain restrictions by the respective occupying powers in the exercise of their state functions, but gradually these restrictions were removed. Now both are sovereign states though there are essential differences in their conditions." [h]

It can be seen that, first, the Hitler government of Germany was not overthrown by the German people. It was destroyed in its war of aggression, and, according to international agreements, the supreme authority of Germany was assumed by the four victorious powers. Secondly, on account of the obstructions of the Western powers the German people were unable to establish a united government to succeed the old government. Instead they set up two states in the eastern and western occupation zones. From a legal point, "with the appearance of the German Democratic Republic and the German Federal Republic, Germany, formerly a subject of international law, has ceased to exist." [i] Each of the two Germanys becomes at present a subject of international law by itself. Thirdly, the Germany question is one of the important international questions left over by World War II. The existence of two Germanys is a result of this war.

Similarly, the stationing, by agreement, of the Soviet and US armed forces in Korea in 1945 and the Korean Armistice Agreement in July 1953 had a bearing on the division of Korea into northern and southern parts. This was also a question left over from World War II. The division of Vietnam into northern and southern parts was a temporary state of affairs provided by the Geneva Agreements of 1954. Fundamentally speaking, the division of Germany, Korea, and Vietnam was a result of the imperialist policy of aggression, particularly that of the United States. The people of these three countries are striving for the peaceful unification of their motherlands.

What about the Taiwan question?

First, the Chinese people themselves overthrew the old reactionary government by revolutionary means and in its place they set up the People's Government. This does not affect in any degree China's status as a member in the family of nations. Secondly, the question of restoring Taiwan to China was already settled after the Chinese people's victory in the War of Resistance against Japan; it does not belong to

[h] Gerhard Raintantz, "The German Democratic Republic—Subject of International Law," in *SGP,* no. 6:41 (1958).

[i] G. Raintantz, "The German Democratic Republic—Subject of International Law," in *SGP,* no. 6:41 (1958).

the questions left over from World War II. Thirdly, the Chinese people's liberation of Taiwan is a continuation of the Chinese people's revolution after the war. It is purely an internal question which has nothing to do with international agreements and involves no international question. It can be seen, therefore, that the question of China's liberation of Taiwan is different from the cases of the aforementioned countries. The imperialists try to cite the instances of the temporary division of these countries, of which they themselves are authors, to justify their own infamous doings. They will gain nothing except exposing their own helplessness and stupidity.

10-11

Stephen Erasmus, "General de Gaulle's Recognition of Peking," *The China Quarterly*, no. 18:195–197 (April-June 1964).

On January 27 [1964] a communiqué was issued in Paris and Peking which read, somewhat baldly:

> The government of the People's Republic of China and the government of the French Republic have decided in mutual agreement to establish diplomatic relations. For this purpose, the two governments have agreed to appoint their ambassadors within three months. . . .

There is some evidence that General de Gaulle hoped to exchange ambassadors with Peking without breaking off relations with his old wartime comrade Chiang Kai-shek, though precedents indicated that such an arrangement would not be acceptable to the Chinese Communists. M. Faure had said in his interview in *Le Figaro* on January 9 that no conditions were involved in the agreement and described the British arrangement (representation in London and Peking at the level of chargé d'affaires *en titre*) as "bizarre" and in the interests of neither of the parties. As late as January 29 the *Guardian* and other papers reported that a spokesman of the Quai d'Orsay had stated that the agreement to recognize Peking had been made without conditions and that France saw no reason to break with Formosa. There was considerable discussion in the European and American press of the "two Chinas" question and much speculation as to whether the Chinese had, in return for the prize of French recognition, relaxed their hitherto uncompromising attitude.

The fact that the announcement of January 27 somewhat unusually referred to the exchange of ambassadors within three months supports the view that some problems remained to be settled at the time of the announcement. It seems possible that General de Gaulle was not fully briefed on the complexities of the Formosa question when he made his decision and did not realize what was involved in getting an ambassador into Peking—liaison between the General and the ministries which have to carry out his decisions is not always all that it might be. It seems equally possible that the Chinese may have been prepared to leave the issue deliberately vague in the expectation that, once the announcement had been made and the General's prestige engaged, France would be obliged to fall in with China's conditions. Certainly, if there were any doubts about the Chinese attitude [toward] the French remaining in diplomatic contact with the Nationalists, they were resolved by the Chinese Foreign Ministry spokesman's statement on January 28:

> According to international practice, recognition of the new government of a country naturally implies ceasing to recognize the old ruling group overthrown by the people of that country. . . . Consequently, the representatives of the old ruling group can no longer be regarded as representatives of that country to be present side by side with the representatives of the new government in one and the same country or international organization. It was with this understanding that the government of the People's Republic of China reached agreement with the government of the French Republic on the establishment of diplomatic relations and the exchange of ambassadors between China and France.

This statement clearly served warning that no Chinese ambassador would appear in Paris until the Nationalist chargé d'affaires had departed. It was spelled out even more forcefully in the *People's Daily* editorial on January 29, which, in addition, dispelled any illusions that might have remained about China's willingness to accept any kind of "two Chinas" solution:

> Both before and after the establishment of diplomatic relations between China and France, the US press has raised a hullabaloo asserting that China has "mitigated" its opposition to "two Chinas" and that the establishment of diplomatic relations between China and France will "unlock the door" for "two Chinas." This is nothing but a distortion with an ulterior motive and is a daydream.

With the Chinese position thus clearly stated, the French may have been in something of a quandary for, although the Nationalists had lodged a strong protest immediately after the January 27 announcement of the establishment of relations, describing this as "a most unfriendly act," they showed no sign of breaking off relations themselves. The Americans, who made no secret of their displeasure and clearly saw no reason to smooth the General's path, may well have counseled Chiang Kai-shek that it would be to his advantage not to break [off relations]. Meanwhile the Chinese continued to remind the French of their obligations. At a press conference in Mogadishu on February 3, Chou En-lai said:

> The government of the People's Republic of China, as the only legal government of the entire Chinese people, is prepared to send its diplomatic representative to Paris. I emphatically declare that, apart from the diplomatic representative of the People's Republic of China, it is impossible for anyone to act as the diplomatic representative of China in Paris.

It is not clear whether or not the French took any action to precipitate a break with the Nationalists in the face of these uncompromising statements of the Chinese view. In any case Chiang Kai-shek severed relations with France on February 10. The way ahead was then clear and, on February 15, a Chinese Communist chargé d'affaires arrived in Paris; on February 23 a French chargé took up residence in Peking. In April ambassadors were duly appointed.

10-12

Hungdah Chiu, "Chinese Contemporary Practices and Judicial Decisions Relating to International Law (September 1965–April 1966)," *The Annals of the Chinese Society of International Law* 3: 109–110 (1966).

On March 12, 1966, the French police evicted the staff of the Permanent Mission of the Republic of China to UNESCO from the former Chinese embassy building on the ground that "the building belongs to the Chinese state and for France the Chinese state is Peking." In a statement issued by the Ministry of Foreign Affairs of the Republic of China, the Ministry said:

> The French police on March 12 barricaded the premises of the

Permanent Mission of the Government of the Republic of China to the UNESCO in Paris with a view to taking over its premises.

While diplomatic relations still existed between the Republic of China and France, the Chinese embassy formally notified the French government that the embassy premises had been turned over to the permanent mission of the government of the Republic of China to the UNESCO. No objection had been raised at the time by the French government.

The Republic of China is a member state of the UNESCO. Recognition by the French government of the Chinese Communist regime does not in any way affect the status of the Republic of China as a member state of the UNESCO and the diplomatic privileges, immunities, and facilities enjoyed by the permanent mission of the Republic of China.

By attempting to take over the premises of a member state of UNESCO, the French government not only has shown scant regard for international law and practices, but also has violated the existing agreements between France and the UNESCO.

The Chinese government has already requested the UNESCO to take all necessary measures to prevent the French government from taking such outrageous action and to protect the rights and interests of its member nations.[27]

10-13

"French Government Evicts Chiang Kai-shek Gangsters from Two Chinese Buildings in Paris." NCNA–English, Paris (Mar. 12, 1966), printed in mimeographed collection of NCNA telegrams, no. 031322.

On orders of the French government, the French police today expelled the Chiang Kai-shek gangsters from two Chinese buildings here which they had been occupying unlawfully.

A spokesman of the French Foreign Ministry said that the French police had taken over the two buildings located at 11 Avenue Georges V and at 47 Rue Pergolese, in Paris, because the Chiang Kai-shek elements had occupied these two buildings which "belong to the Chinese state, and for France the Chinese state is Peking." The spokesman added that the Chiang Kai-shek gang had been occupying the buildings "illegally and by fraud."

Before France's recognition of China in 1964, 11 Avenue Georges V was used as the "embassy" of the Chiang Kai-shek clique in France, and 47 Rue Pergolese was the location of its "general consulate." After France's recognition of China, the Chiang Kai-shek gangsters continued to occupy these two buildings under a new guise, in the name of the "delegation" to UNESCO. This has gone on until their eviction by the French police today.

Note

A similar problem arose following the establishment of diplomatic relations between the PRC and Japan in late 1972.[28]

By mid-1970, Peking's post-Cultural Revolution return to a policy of moderation again focused public attention on its terms for establishing diplomatic relations with non-Communist states. Not only was there the question of withdrawal of recognition from the Republic of China, but there was also the question of confirmation of Peking's claim to sovereignty over Taiwan. Essentially three formulations were developed for dealing with the status of Taiwan in the various joint communiqués that announced establishment of diplomatic relations. Items 10–14 to 10–16 present examples of these formulas, which enjoyed roughly equal popularity.

10-14

"Joint Communique of Government of People's Republic of China and Government of Canada Concerning Establishment of Diplomatic Relations between China and Canada," *PR* 13.42:12 (Oct. 16, 1970).

The government of the People's Republic of China and the government of Canada, in accordance with the principles of mutual respect for sovereignty and territorial integrity, noninterference in each other's internal affairs, and equality and mutual benefit, have decided upon mutual recognition and the establishment of diplomatic relations, effective October 13, 1970.

The Chinese government reaffirms that Taiwan is an inalienable part of the territory of the People's Republic of China. The Canadian government takes note of this position of the Chinese Government.

The Canadian Government recognizes the government of the People's Republic of China as the sole legal government of China.

The Chinese government and the Canadian government have agreed to exchange ambassadors within six months, and to provide all necessary assistance for the establishment and the performance of the functions of diplomatic missions in their respective capitals on the basis of equality and mutual benefit and in accordance with international practice.

10-15

"Joint Communique Issued by Government of People's Republic of China and Imperial Ethiopian Government on the Occasion of Establishment of Diplomatic Relations between China and Ethiopia," *PR* 13.50:7 (Dec. 11, 1970).

The government of the People's Republic of China and the Imperial Ethiopian government, in conformity with the interests and desire of their respective countries, do hereby agree to establish diplomatic relations at ambassadorial level.

The government of the People's Republic of China and the Imperial Ethiopian government do hereby further agree to develop their diplomatic relations, friendship, and cooperation between their two countries in accordance with the following principles:

— Mutual respect for sovereignty and territorial integrity,
— Mutual nonaggression,
— Mutual noninterference in each other's internal affairs,
— Equality and mutual benefit,
— Peaceful coexistence.

The Imperial Ethiopian government, consistent with the policy they have followed for a long time at the United Nations and other international forums, do hereby affirm that the government of the People's Republic of China is the sole legal government representing the entire Chinese people.

The government of the People's Republic of China do hereby reaffirm that the government and people of the People's Republic of China resolutely support the government and people of the Empire of Ethiopia in their struggle against imperialism, colonialism and neocolonialism.

Addis Ababa—November 24, 1970.

10-16

"Joint Communique on the Establishment of Diplomatic Relations between the People's Republic of China and the Republic of Austria," *PR* 14.23:11 (June 4, 1971).

In accordance with the principles of mutual respect for sovereignty and territorial integrity, noninterference in each other's internal affairs, equality and mutual benefit, the government of the People's Republic of China and the government of the Republic of Austria have decided upon mutual recognition and the establishment of diplomatic relations effective May 28, 1971, and the exchange of ambassadors within six months.

The Chinese government respects the status of neutrality of the Republic of Austria.

The Austrian government recognizes the government of the People's Republic of China as the sole legal government of China.

The Chinese government and the Austrian government have agreed to provide all necessary assistance for the establishment and the performance of the functions of embassies in their respective capitals on the basis of equality and mutual benefit and in accordance with international practice.

Note

The "protocol" signed by the PRC and San Marino was distinctive by virtue of the fact that it did not announce establishment of diplomatic relations but declared that the two governments "have decided, at the present stage, to establish official relations at the consular level as from May 6, 1971." [29]

Although the People's Republic has established diplomatic relations with many countries despite their refusal to acknowledge its sovereignty over Taiwan, it has insisted on at least implicit acceptance of this claim as the price of establishing relations with the United States. Just prior to the secret visit to China of President Nixon's assistant, Henry Kissinger, Premier Chou spelled out the PRC's most flexible position on this question in an interview with three American reporters:

> "How Taiwan will be liberated is our internal affair," he said, adding, "It will not be all that difficult."
>
> "Chiang Kai-shek is opposed to the so-called two Chinas and is also opposed to one China and one independent entity of Taiwan," he continued. "In the past we have been allied with

Chiang Kai-shek, and we became hostile to him, but on this question we have our common point. There can be only one China. So a way can be found."

Premier Chou, remarking that "the world will change," said it would be glorious if United States forces were withdrawn from the Formosa Strait. The United States Seventh Fleet conducts a token patrol of the strait under the 1955 Security treaty with the Chinese Nationalist government, guaranteeing the island against attack.

"Once this problem is solved, then all other problems can be solved," Mr. Chou said. "The Peoples' Republic would then be able to establish diplomatic relations with the United States."

He did not insist on a declaration by the United States recognizing Peking's sovereignty over Taiwan. "If the United States government withdraws all forces from Taiwan and the Taiwan Strait and no longer considers Chiang Kai-shek as the representative of China," he said, "then the logical result would be that Chiang Kai-shek and Taiwan would be matters internal to China. This would be recognition that the People's Republic of China is the only lawful government. There can be no possibility of two Chinas or one China and one Taiwan." [30]

The text of the joint communiqué announcing President Nixon's acceptance of Premier Chou's invitation to visit China stated that "the meeting between the leaders of China and the United States is to seek the normalization of relations between the two countries and also to exchange views on questions of concern to the two sides." [31] In the Sino-American "Shanghai Communiqué" of February 28, 1972, which concluded the President's visit, the US declared:

> The United States acknowledges that all Chinese on either side of the Taiwan Strait maintain there is but one China and that Taiwan is a part of China. The United States government does not challenge that position. It reaffirms its interest in a peaceful settlement of the Taiwan question by the Chinese themselves. With this prospect in mind, it affirms the ultimate objective of the withdrawal of all US forces and military installations from Taiwan. In the meantime, it will progressively reduce its forces and military installations on Taiwan as the tension in the area diminishes.[32]

The meaning and significance of this declaration have been debated by commentators.[33] American officials denied that it represented any change in the position held by the US since 1950 that the status of Taiwan is as yet undetermined (see item 12–9).[34] China, interestingly enough, remained silent for a long period.[34a]

Although the Shanghai Communiqué did not result in the normalization of Sino-American relations, it did stimulate the United Kingdom to cease its long-standing support for the American position that the status of Taiwan is undetermined. Because in 1971 the UK had for the first time supported the PRC's entry into the UN on procedural matters as well as on the merits, this cleared the way for an exchange of ambassadors between the UK and the PRC (recall the Note following item 10–9). The joint communiqué announcing this development stated in part:

> "2. The government of the United Kingdom, acknowledging the position of the Chinese government that Taiwan is a province of the People's Republic of China, have decided to remove their official representation in Taiwan on March 13, 1972." [35]

Foreign Secretary Sir Alec Douglas-Home's accompanying statement to the House of Commons left no doubt that the UK had acceded to the PRC's legal position.[36]

Not long afterward the Netherlands also raised its representation in Peking from the level of chargé d'affaires to that of ambassador, after announcing that it "respects" the view that Taiwan is a province of the PRC.[37] For the experience of Japan in establishing diplomatic relations with the PRC, see 46–3 and Notes preceding and following. For the experience of the United States in exchanging official "liaison offices" with the PRC in 1973, even in the absence of recognition, formal diplomatic relations and clarification of the status of Taiwan, see Note following 29–11.

10-17

K'ung Meng, "A Criticism of the Theories of Bourgeois International Law Concerning the Subjects of International Law and Recognition of States," *KCWTYC*, no. 2:51–53 (1960).

The combination of the theories of bourgeois international law concerning recognition of states and subjects of international law is a deliberate attempt to cope with the independence movement in colonies and the socialist revolution in various countries.

The question of recognition of states (or governments) is closely related to the question of the subjects of international law. The different attitudes toward this question adopted by different classes are determined by their class interests. After the establishment of the capitalist system, the theory of bourgeois international law concerning recognition, combined with its theory concerning subjects of international law, became an instrument for coping with independence movements in colonies and semicolonies and socialist revolution in various countries. The theory of bourgeois international law concerning recognition is consistent with the practices of bourgeois countries. In fact, bourgeois countries themselves monopolize international society and decide whether other countries possess the qualifications for joining this society. For admission of a country into this "big family," it must first have recognition by these bourgeois countries. This means, as for movements in which colonies and semicolonies are struggling for independence, besides de facto suppression by the colonial powers, bourgeois international law also imposes a legal obstruction upon those colonies and semicolonies. To this day imperialist countries still resort to the system of recognition to obstruct the Afro-Asian nations' goal of achieving independence.

Since the bourgeois countries have these rights of determination, a weak or small country has to pay a great price for being recognized. Besides the suzerain state which will normally do its best to retain some privileges, other "civilized" gangsters will also try to extort some interests [in the state seeking recognition]. They conclude insulting treaties with the country at the time of recognition. When a new government is established as a result of a revolution or coup d'état in a weak or small country, strong bourgeois countries frequently demand some interests as a price of their recognition of the new government, openly offer conditions of recognition or conduct intervention. For instance, after the 1911 revolution in China, the big imperialistic powers used the opportunity to make many unreasonable demands as their price for recognizing the Republican government. At that time, Japan made many demands concerning the so-called "Manchurian-Mongolian" question, and Britain made some demands on the question of Tibet as conditions of recognition.

Second, bourgeois countries also use the question of recognition as an instrument for coping with socialist revolution in various countries. During the October Revolution, they used the method of nonrecognition to intervene in the Soviet regime established after the revolution. The American imperialists even withheld recognition until sixteen years later. After the Second World War, they also resorted to this method to cope with some newly established socialist countries. After the victory of the Chinese people's revolution and the establishment of the new government of the people themselves, it received not only the immediate recognition of socialist countries, but also the recognition of many countries in Asia, Africa, and Europe. However, the most evil enemy of the Chinese people, American imperialism, has refused to recognize the legitimate government of the new China, and instead has engaged in an all-out effort to support the remnant antirevolutionary force of the Chiang Kai-shek clique. Moreover, the United States also manipulated the United Nations to pass a resolution branding China as "aggressor" and fabricated absurd theories to insult the Chinese people such as China has not proved that it has reached "the standard of a civilized country." In the past ten years, American imperialism has repeatedly resorted to the measure of threats and oppression to prevent other countries from recognizing the People's Government of China. This is done in order to tarnish the international prestige of the great People's Republic of China and to deprive the new China of its rights in international organizations. As a matter of fact, we do not prize the United States' recognition; the international prestige of new China has not suffered at all, and intercourse between China and the people of the various countries of the world has not been hindered. The conduct of the United States merely reveals more vividly the vicious and ugly face of American imperialism. Similarly, the refusal to restore China's lawful representation in the United Nations simply lowers the prestige of the United Nations more and more each day.

The theories of bourgeois international law concerning the significance of international recognition also reflect the interests of the bourgeoisie. We know that there are two opposing theories concerning the question of the significance of recognition in bourgeois jurisprudence, namely the declaratory theory and the constitutive theory. The declaratory theory considers the establishment of a state as a question of fact; each new state is a subject of international law as soon as it comes into existence. Recognition by other states is merely to declare the existence of this fact. Those scholars who advocate the declaratory theory maintain that, "if a new civilized State comes into existence either by breaking off from an existing recognized State, as Belgium did in 1831, or otherwise, such new State enters of right into the Family of Nations and becomes of right an International Person." [a] The constitutive theory maintains that "through recognition . . . a State becomes an International Person and a subject of International Law," and recognition "is constitutive of the rights and duties pertaining to statehood [and] governmental capacity. . . ." [b] In other words, qualifications of a state are created by recognition. Before it is recognized by other states, a new state is not a subject of international law, and it does not have rights under international law. Although these two theories are mutually contradictory, their existence does no harm to the bourgeoisie. On the contrary, bourgeois countries may apply one or the other theory in accordance with the concrete situation of each case and thus execute their policy without hindrance. However, if we compare the two theories, the constitutive theory is more reactionary. The declaratory theory does have definite progressive significance in the course of the struggle by newly emerging bourgeois countries to achieve equal status and to oppose the intervention of feudal countries. But the constitutive theory is used by big capitalist countries as a "theoretical basis" to oppose any new countries they detest, and it nakedly serves the aggressive force of the imperialists.

In certain writings of bourgeois jurisprudence, there still exists a theory of "conditional recognition" which maintains that "States are free to accord recognition on such terms as they may see fit to impose . . ." and "If the terms on which recognition is conceded be violated by the new State, the group of States according recognition may assert the right to intervene for the purpose of establishing a state of affairs in accordance with the condition specified." [c] This absurd theory attempts to legalize all the harsh conditions and extortion imposed by the bourgeois countries upon newly established countries or governments at the time of recognition.

[a] L. Oppenheim, *International Law*, 7th ed., by H. Lauterpacht (London: Longmans, Green, 1948), I, 121–122.

[b] *Ibid.*, pp. 122, 123.

[c] C. C. Hyde, *International Law, chiefly as interpreted and applied by the United States*, 2nd rev. ed. (Boston: Little, Brown and Company, 1947), I, 151. Franz von Liszt of Germany also maintained the same view; he said that "recognition can be accorded with or without conditions." See the Russian version of his *International Law* (*Mezhdunarodnoe Pravo*, 4th ed. [Yuryev: K. Mattisen, 1917], p. 64).

The theory of bourgeois international law concerning recognition of states violates the generally recognized principles of modern international law.

The reactionary character of the theory of bourgeois international law concerning recognition of states is very obvious. It cannot stand the test of the principles of modern international law.

First, according to the principles of sovereignty and national self-determination, the emergence of a state and its becoming a subject of international law should be decided by the will of the people in that state, that is to say, in accordance with the fact of their establishment as a state. It should not be decided by the will of other states, nor should the new state's qualifications as a subject of international law be conferred upon it by other states. As soon as a new state comes into existence, it is a subject of international law, and it enjoys rights and undertakes duties in international society, regardless of whether or not it is recognized by another state and regardless of how many states recognize it. Recognition in international law merely confirms the fact of the existence of a new state by the existing states. This is because in international society, in order to engage in intercourse, mutual recognition is necessary. Therefore, after an existing state accords recognition to a new state, it is possible for the former to establish diplomatic relations and to engage in normal intercourse with the latter. However, at this moment recognition merely serves as the legal basis for establishing diplomatic relations and intercourse; it cannot create a subject of international law. The bourgeois theory that recognition creates a subject of international law is inconsistent with the principles of sovereign equality and national self-determination.

Second, in accordance with the principle of nonintervention in the internal affairs of other countries, a change of government within a country either as a result of a struggle for power by various political factions through constitutional procedure (no question of recognition in that case) or as a result of a coup d'état, revolution, or other unconstitutional procedure (the question of recognition arises in that case), has nothing to do with international law and is not subject to the review of anyone. From the viewpoint of international law, the government which in fact independently exercises power within a country is the representative of that country in international relations. Even if a country for its own reasons withholds recognition of that government, it should not continue to recognize and to maintain diplomatic relations with the remnant of an old, already overthrown regime (the way that the United States is supporting the Chiang Kai-shek clique). To do so would constitute intervention in the internal affairs of another country.

Third, although recognition of a new state or a new government is a unilateral political act on the part of the recognizing state, on the other hand, recognition is also a system of international law and should not violate the generally recognized principles of international law. That is to say that no state should use recognition as an instrument of its aggressive policy or resort to premature recognition or delayed recognition to acquire illegal interests or to realize its object of aggression.

Fourth, the right to recognize a new state or government is a right belonging to all existing states which cannot be taken away by anyone. Such a right can be exercised individually or collectively and is not subject to anyone's interference. The pressure exercised by strong imperialist countries upon other countries to force them to recognize or not recognize certain new countries or governments (such as the United States' pressure on other countries to withhold recognition of China) is a serious illegal act.

Note

Although the author of item 10–17 undoubtedly would not concede that the PRC has ever violated his strictures against use of recognition for aggressive or otherwise illegal purposes, the PRC has plainly granted and denied recognition for political purposes. By way of illustration, although Yugoslavia recognized it as early as October 5, 1949, the PRC did not reciprocate for more than five years. Although Israel recognized the PRC in 1950, Peking has not yet reciprocated. On the other hand, the PRC was the first state to respond to the Democratic Republic of Vietnam's 1950 request for recognition as the government of all Vietnam, while the Soviet Union hesitated for over two weeks. And the PRC was the only state to grant prompt recognition to the Algerian provisional government proclaimed by the FLN in the autumn of 1958 (recall item 5–2). Items 10–18 and 10–19 illustrate Peking's recent recognition of revolutionary governments, and items 10–20 and 10–21 indicate the criteria to which the PRC purportedly adheres in deciding whether to grant recognition in civil war situations.

10-18

"Premier Chou En-lai Sends Message to President Huynh Tan Phat," *PR* 12.25:5–6 (June 20, 1969).

Chou En-lai, Premier of the State Council of the People's Republic of China, sent a message to Huynh Tan Phat, President of the Provisional Revolutionary Government of the Republic of South Vietnam, warmly congratulating him on the proclamation of the establishment of the Provisional Revolutionary Government of the Republic of South Vietnam. The full text of the message reads as follows:

President Huynh Tan Phat of the Provisional
Revolutionary Government of the
Republic of South Vietnam:

On the occasion of the proclamation of the establishment of the Provisional Revolutionary Government of the Republic of South Vietnam, I extend, on behalf of the Chinese government and people, warm congratulations to you and, through you, to the heroic south Vietnamese people.

The Chinese government has always regarded the South Vietnam National Front for Liberation as the genuine legal representative of the south Vietnamese people, and the Permanent Mission of the South Vietnam National Front for Liberation in China has long enjoyed the status of a diplomatic mission. The south Vietnamese people have waged a long and arduous war under the leadership of the South Vietnam National Front for Liberation, and in so doing their very aim is to defeat the US aggressors, overthrow the South Vietnamese puppet clique and establish their own revolutionary political power. And now, the South Vietnam National Front for Liberation and the Vietnam Alliance of National, Democratic, and Peace Forces, together with the other patriotic forces in southern Vietnam, have held the Congress of People's Representatives and decided to establish the Provisional Revolutionary Government of the Republic of South Vietnam. This is a natural development of the south Vietnamese people's war of resistance against US aggression and for national salvation.

The Chinese government hereby declares that it formally recognizes the Permanent Mission of the South Vietnam National Front for Liberation in China as the Embassy of the Provisional Revolutionary Government of the Republic of South Vietnam in China.

Chou En-lai
Premier of the State Council of
the People's Republic of China
Peking, June 14, 1969

10-19

"Chinese Government Formally Recognizes Royal Government of National Union of Cambodia," *PR* 13.20:14 (May 15, 1970).

Peking, May 5, 1970

Samdech Norodom Sihanouk, Head of State of Cambodia and Chairman of the National United Front of Kampuchea,

Samdech Penn Nouth, Prime Minister of the Royal Government of National Union under the Leadership of the National United Front of Kampuchea.

On the occasion of the formal establishment of the Royal Government of National Union under the Leadership of the National United Front of Kampuchea, I express, on behalf of the Chinese government and people, warmest congratulations and highest respect to you and, through you, to the valiant Cambodian people.

The Royal Government of National Union under the Leadership of the National United Front of Kampuchea is established at a grave juncture when US imperialism has brazenly invaded Cambodia. It is born amidst the raging flames of the armed struggle against US imperialism and its lackey—the Lon Nol-Sirik Matak traitorous clique—waged by the Cambodian people in response to the March 23 solemn call and five-point declaration of Cambodian Head of State Samdech Norodom Sihanouk. Its establishment marks a new historical stage in the Cambodian people's patriotic struggle against US imperialism.

The Chinese government hereby solemnly declares: The Chinese government formally recognizes the Royal Government of National Union under the Leadership of the National United Front of Kampuchea as the sole legal government of the Cambodian people, formally severs all diplomatic relations already long severed with the Lon Nol-Sirik Matak Rightist traitorous clique and will withdraw the Chinese diplomatic mission, personnel, and experts from Phnom Penh.

The Chinese government is deeply convinced that, under the leadership of Head of State Samdech Norodom Sihanouk, the Cambodian people and the Royal Government of National Union, uniting closely with the fraternal Vietnamese and Laotian peoples as well as with all peace-loving countries and people throughout the world and persevering in armed struggle and protracted struggle, will surely win complete victory in their patriotic struggle against US aggression.

U.S. imperialism is bound to be defeated!

The Lon Nol-Sirik Matak traitorous clique is bound to fall!

The heroic Cambodian people are sure to win victory!
Please accept the assurances of my highest consideration.

(signed) Chou En-lai
Premier of the State Council of the People's Republic of China

10-20

"The NFL Is the Sole Representative of South Vietnamese People," editorial, *JMJP* (June 20, 1965), p. 1, translated in *PR* 8.26:10–11 (June 25, 1965).

In its June 1 memorandum on the representation of south Vietnam at the Second Afro-Asian Conference, the Central Committee of the south Vietnam National Front for Liberation [NFL], with good reasons and convincing facts, made it clear that the NFL, not the Saigon puppet authorities, who are the running dogs of US imperialism, is the sole and genuine representative of the south Vietnamese people and that it can only be the NFL, not the puppet regime, which is qualified to represent south Vietnam at the Second Afro-Asian Conference. The Chinese people firmly support the resolute and clear-cut stand of the NFL and its participation in the Second Afro-Asian Conference as the sole and genuine representative of south Vietnam.

Some people ask, why cannot the Saigon regime which took part in the First Afro-Asian Conference ten years ago attend the second conference? The reason is very simple. A tremendous change has taken place in the situation in south Vietnam since 1955. In the past ten years, US imperialism has torn to shreds the Geneva agreements, undermined the peaceful reunification of Vietnam, and followed up its intervention in south Vietnam with a large-scale war of aggression there. The Saigon authorities have long been puppets of US imperialism, its tools of aggression, and its agents to be used against the Asian and African peoples. They were long ago repudiated by the south Vietnamese people. . . .

The facts are crystal clear. Today the genuine representative of the south Vietnamese people can be none other than the NFL which was born out of their just, patriotic struggle against US aggression. Holding aloft the banner of national liberation and uniting the patriotic anti-US forces of all social strata in south Vietnam, the NFL has been leading the 14 million south Vietnamese people to great victories in their unremitting struggle for national independence, democracy, peace, and reunification of their country and against the war of aggression unleashed by US imperialism. Today the liberated areas controlled by the NFL constitute four-fifths of the territory of south Vietnam and contain 10 million people. The NFL has the support of not only the people of the liberated areas but also the people of all strata in the enemy-occupied areas. There is not the slightest doubt that only the NFL can represent the south Vietnamese people.

That the NFL is the sole and legitimate representative of the south Vietnamese people has been universally recognized by the Asian and African peoples and by the people of the world as a whole. . . .

As the representative of the south Vietnamese people, the NFL has established contacts with organizations or governments in 44 countries and set up permanent missions in seven Asian, African, European, and American countries.

Governments of 22 countries, 22 international or regional organizations, and a total of 449 political parties and popular organizations in 92 countries have expressed their sympathy with and support for the statement issued by the NFL on March 22.

The ever higher prestige which the NFL enjoys in south Vietnam and throughout the world shows that it alone has the right to represent south Vietnam at the Second Afro-Asian Conference. This is beyond any dispute.

NOTE

In April 1973, in light of the Paris Agreement on Ending the War in Vietnam (see 46–4), the PRC took the position that both the Provisional Revolutionary Government of the Republic of South Vietnam (formerly the NFL) and the Saigon authorities were entitled to representation at a meeting of the UN Economic Commission for Asia and the Far East (see note 58 on pp. 908–909.).

10-21

Commentator, "Vientiane Authorities Cannot Represent Laotian People," *JMJP* (June 23, 1965), p. 5, translated in *PR* 8.26:11 (June 25, 1965).

Prince Souphanouvong, Chairman of the Neo Lao Haksat and Vice-Premier of the Laotian Tripartite National Union Government, on June 19 sent a cable to the African-Asian Foreign Ministers' meeting reiterating that the Vientiane administration with Prince Souvanna Phouma as "premier" had no right whatsoever to speak on behalf of the Laotian people and stating that only the Tripartite National Union

Government can legally represent the Kingdom of Laos at the Second African-Asian Conference. The Chinese people fully support Prince Souphanouvong's correct stand.

The Laotian Tripartite National Union Government was formed in accordance with the Zurich Agreement and the Agreement of the Plain of Jars signed by the three Laotian Princes. It had won the unanimous support of the three political forces in Laos and the Laotian people. This government was recognized by all the countries taking part in the 1962 Geneva conference and by many other countries as well. It is, therefore, the sole legal government of Laos. But this legal government was subverted by a putsch in Vientiane on April 19, 1964, which was launched by the US imperialists and their lackeys. The administration in Vientiane, illegally recognized, has long changed in essence, although Phouma is still nominally the "premier" and it still hangs out the signboard of a "coalition government."

The Vientiane administration has excluded the Neo Lao Haksat and the patriotic neutralist forces, which are the true upholders of Laotian national interests, and is, therefore, firmly opposed by these two forces. It cannot represent the people of the liberated areas who are half the country's total population and who inhabit three-fifths of the territory. Even in the areas it controls it is opposed by the broad masses of the people.

The Vientiane administration has torn to shreds the various important tripartite agreements and the Geneva agreements. It is an apologist for US imperialist crimes and has colluded with the enemies of the Laotian nation in an attempt to wipe out the Laotian patriotic armed forces and to enable US imperialism to enslave the Laotian people. It permits US imperialism to use Laotian territory to attack south Vietnam and the Democratic Republic of Vietnam.

The Vientiane administration's unilateral decision to represent the National Union Government in the African-Asian Conference is entirely illegal.

Note

In a comprehensive analysis of the first twenty years of the PRC's recognition practice, Professor James C. Hsiung distinguishes essentially two periods: the first decade after 1949, when Peking displayed a "self-oriented" perspective that regarded recognition questions almost exclusively from the point of view of its desire for recognition by other states; and the second decade, when Peking became increasingly preoccupied with developing an "outward-directed" perspective capable of coping with the problems of recognizing a host of newly independent states. Theory and practice forged during the first period had to be adapted to the needs of the second. During the earlier period, the PRC, like many other states, viewed recognition as a factual matter that acknowledged a government's effective control over the territory of a state and that did not imply approval of the way in which the new government came to power, of its sociopolitical system, or of its policies. Beginning in 1958, however, the PRC occasionally departed from these tenets, as in the Algerian and Israeli cases previously mentioned. Professor Hsiung makes a stimulating comparison between the evolution of the PRC's recognition policy and the similar but more gradual shift in American recognition policy from the Jeffersonian "de factoism" of our then still revolutionary government to the gradual adoption of Wilsonian criteria of political acceptability.[38]

A recent, notorious example of Peking's refusal to apply the factual approach occurred in the case of Bangla Desh, which appealed to the PRC to recognize "the heroic success of our national liberation struggle." At his first press conference after being installed as head of the newly-established government, Sheikh Mujibur Rahman said: "I hope that the People's Republic of China will now come forward to recognize the reality of the independent, sovereign People's Republic of Bangla Desh, so that a basis may be established for mutual cooperation." [39] But Peking, which had only recently branded Bangla Desh "a Manchukuo" and a "quisling government," scorned this appeal and subsequently even vetoed the application of Bangla Desh for UN membership (see item 11–8 and preceding Note).

The following materials suggest the principles upon which the PRC appears to condition the continuation of diplomatic relations.

10-22

"Chinese Foreign Ministry Spokesman on Withdrawal of Chinese Embassy in Congo," NCNA–English, Peking (Sept. 18, 1961), in *SCMP*, no. 2584:29 (Sept. 22, 1961).

The spokesman for the Information Department of the Ministry of Foreign Affairs of the People's Republic of China made remarks today on the decision of the government of the People's Republic of China to withdraw the Chinese embassy in the Republic of the Congo (Stanleyville). The remarks follow:

The Chinese government and people consistently supported the lawful government of the Congolese Republic led by Lumumba and Gizenga and the Congolese people in their just and patriotic struggle against US neocolonialism and Belgian old colonialism and in defense of national independence. Basing itself on this stand, the government of the People's Republic of China decided on February 20, 1961, to establish diplomatic relations with the government of the Congolese Republic. This not only reflected the common desires of the Chinese and Congolese peoples, but also strengthened mutual support and assistance between the Chinese people and the Congolese and other African peoples. Of late, the situation in the Congo has changed. The lawful Congolese government led by Acting Premier Gizenga has announced its own termination, while the Leopoldville government in the Congo maintains so-called diplomatic relations with the Chiang Kai-shek clique in Taiwan, which has absolutely no right to represent China. Therefore, the Chinese government has decided to withdraw the embassy of the People's Republic of China in the Congo (Stanleyville) and states most regrettably that the diplomatic relations between the People's Republic of China and the Congo have to be suspended temporarily. As is well known, Taiwan is an inalienable part of China's territory, and the Chinese government and people are resolutely opposed to the US imperialists' forcible occupation of Taiwan and their plot of creating "two Chinas," and to the emergence of a situation of "two Chinas" in any context. We are sure that this solemn and just stand of the Chinese government and people will enjoy the sympathy and support of the Congolese and African peoples.

Note

When Dahomey declared its independence on August 1, 1960, the Republic of China extended its recognition and sent a special envoy to attend the independence celebration. But the People's Republic also extended recognition to Dahomey. On January 19, 1964, Dahomey and the ROC decided to establish diplomatic relations, and an embassy of the ROC was set up in Cotonou.

On November 12, 1964, however, Dahomey and the PRC decided to establish diplomatic relations.[40] Shortly thereafter, the PRC sent a chargé d'affaires ad interim to head its mission in Cotonou, and it appointed an ambassador in February 1965. Two months later, the ROC severed diplomatic relations with Dahomey and closed its embassy. The PRC's ambassador presented his credentials to President Sourou Migau of Dahomey on June 19, 1965.

The third chapter of this tale of two Chinas opened on January 3, 1966, when Dahomey announced that it was severing diplomatic relations with the PRC. In response to this decision the PRC's Foreign Ministry issued the following statement:

> On January 3, 1966, the Minister of Foreign Affairs of the Republic of Dahomey delivered a note to Li Yun-chuan, Ambas-

sador Extraordinary and Plenipotentiary of the People's Republic of China to the Republic of Dahomey, announcing the decision to put an end to the diplomatic relations between China and Dahomey and asking the Chinese embassy to leave Dahomey territory within three days of the notification. This is an extremely serious event in which the government of Dahomey unilaterally and unreasonably tears up the agreement between China and Dahomey on the establishment of diplomatic relations and disrupts the relations between the countries. The government of the People's Republic of China hereby lodges a serious protest against this step.

Since the establishment of diplomatic relations between China and Dahomey, the government of the People's Republic of China has always followed the five principles of peaceful coexistence in working for the development of relations of friendship and cooperation between the two countries in various fields. This consistent stand of the government of China has been generally acknowledged by the people of Dahomey and her numerous patriotic personages. In putting an end to the diplomatic relations between China and Dahomey, the Dahomey authorities have not given any reasons for their action. This unreasonable act on the part of the Dahomey authorities not only damages their own international good faith, but also runs counter to the interests of the patriotic personages and the entire people of Dahomey.

The Chinese government could, with every justification, reject the above-mentioned, unreasonable demand of the Dahomey government. However, the Chinese government, deeming it unnecessary to do so, has decided to recall all the personnel of the Chinese embassy in the Republic of Dahomey. The Chinese government wishes to point out that no one can undermine the friendship between the peoples of China and Dahomey and that the schemes of US imperialism and its followers will eventually be defeated.[41]

On April 21, 1966, the Republic of China and Dahomey announced that they would resume diplomatic relations.

Other countries that broke or suspended relations with the PRC during this period included Burundi, Central African Republic, Ghana, Indonesia, and Tunisia. Although in every case the final decision to sever or suspend relations seems to have come from the other country,[42] this action was generally preceded by Peking's protests against alleged outrages against the PRC committed in the other country.[43] By mid-1973, with the excesses of the Cultural Revolution safely past, Peking had restored relations with Burundi, Ghana and Tunisia as well as with Dahomey (the ROC again severed diplomatic relations). Also, Indonesia had indicated its willingness to resume relations if Peking would promise to stop broadcasting radio propaganda and providing other support to Communist elements in Indonesia.[44]

10-23

"Chinese Embassy Protests Most Strongly against Ceylon Government's Creation of 'Two Chinas,'" NCNA–English, Colombo (Aug. 23, 1967) in *SCMP*, no. 4011:37–38 (Aug. 29, 1967).

The Chinese Embassy here yesterday in a note to the Ceylon Ministry of Defense and External Affairs lodged with utmost indignation the strongest protest with the Ceylon government against its grave steps in barefacedly trailing behind US imperialism in creating "two Chinas," by continuously keeping unseemly connections with the Chiang Kai-shek bandit gang and deliberately undermining the normal relations between China and Ceylon.

The note points out in all seriousness that the Ceylon government must immediately sever all connections with the Chiang bandit gang, and stop the elements of the Chiang bandit gang from coming to Ceylon to carry out underhanded activities, and guarantee that it will not participate in any criminal activities to create "two Chinas."

The note says that the Ceylon Association of Girl Guides invited the Chiang Kai-shek bandit gang in Taiwan to attend the "Asian trainers conference" held in Colombo on August 12, 1967, and that the Chiang Kai-shek bandit gang has also been invited to participate in the "3rd Asian Boxing Championships" to be held in December 1967. The "Trainers Conference" and the "Boxing Championships" are either sponsored or organized by Ceylon and are under the auspices of and financed by official authorities of Ceylon.

It says that in this connection, Hsi Yeh-sheng, chargé d'affaires ad interim of the embassy of the People's Republic of China in Ceylon, made representations to the Ceylon government on August 11, 1967, affirming the Chinese government's stand of resolute opposition to Ceylon's keeping clandestine connections with the Chiang bandit gang to coordinate with the US imperialists in creating "two Chinas," and demanding that the Ceylon government immediately take measures to stop the elements of the Chiang bandit gang from coming to Ceylon to attend the "Asian Trainers Conference of Guides" and guarantee that the elements of the Chiang bandit gang will not be permitted to come to

Ceylon to participate in the "Boxing Championships." Again on August 15, after the Chiang bandit gang element had come to Ceylon to attend the "Trainers Conference," the chargé d'affaires ad interim of the Chinese embassy lodged a stern protest with the Ceylon Ministry of Defense and External Affairs and demanded that the Ceylon government immediately expel the Chiang bandit gang element from the country.

However, the Ceylon government, in disregard of the Chinese embassy's serious representations, protests, and demands, not only has failed to guarantee that the Chiang bandit gang elements will not be permitted to come to Ceylon to participate in the "Boxing Championships," but has openly permitted the Chiang bandit gang element to continue underhand activities in Ceylon. This is a serious incident of hostility toward the Chinese people, a crude interference in the internal affairs of China, and a grave step deliberately taken to undermine the normal relations between China and Ceylon. The Chinese people express their utmost indignation at this.

The note says that it must be pointed out in all seriousness that since it came to power the present Ceylon government headed by the United National Party has all along been very barefacedly following behind the US imperialists in creating "two Chinas" and conniving with the Chiang bandit gang elements' dirty, hostile, anti-China activities toward the Chinese people, and has all along played with the counterrevolutionary dual tactics. The Ceylon government stated that it recognizes only one China, that is, the People's Republic of China. But Ceylon Prime Minister Dudley Senanayake, in his visit to the United States in 1966, made it clear to newsmen that the Ceylon government had not decided how it wanted the United Nations to deal with the question of Taiwan. The official Ceylon broadcasting station, the government newsletter, publications, tender forms, and officially shot newsreels repeatedly described China's territory of Taiwan as "a country." Furthermore, Ceylon has maintained connections with the Chiang bandit gang in many fields. Since 1966 intercourse between Ceylon and the Chiang bandit gang has become even more frequent. The following are some examples:

The Ceylon government has permitted the Chiang bandit gang elements to come to Ceylon to participate in the Conference of the International Commission of Jurists and the world Maha Sangha Conference;

It has permitted a high-ranking official of the Chiang bandit gang's "Foreign Ministry" to come to Ceylon to carry out underhanded activities;

It has permitted the Chiang bandit gang to send to Ceylon a five-man team to survey the tea industry and three so-called rice experts.

NOTE

According to the *Peking Review,* upon receiving the PRC's August 22, 1967, note of protest, "The Ceylon government hurriedly issued a communiqué saying that its position was that 'it recognizes only the People's Republic of China.'" In fact, however, the PRC claimed, Ceylon "has continued to maintain clandestine connections with the Chiang bandit gang," despite repeated protests.[45]

Especially throughout the Cultural Revolution the PRC was similarly alert to protest against other actions that might in any way imply recognition of the Nationalist regime. The following report from the *Peking Review* is typical:

> The Indonesian fascist military regime headed by Suharto and Nasution on September 11 openly "invited" a "trade delegation" which was sent by Chiang Kai-shek, the public enemy of the Chinese people, to visit Djakarta for sinister activities. Lu Tzu-po, chargé d'affaires ad interim of the Chinese embassy in Indonesia, went to the Indonesian Foreign Ministry that day and lodged the strongest protest with the Indonesian fascist military government over this serious political provocation.
>
> Lu Tzu-po said that the Indonesian government, while wildly carrying out anti-China and anti-Chinese activities, had been maintaining open or covert contacts with the Chiang Kai-shek gang in Taiwan and stepping up all-round collaboration with it. Now it has blatantly "invited" the Chiang gang's "trade delegation" to Indonesia. Djakarta newspapers made noisy propaganda about it, saying: "This is the first delegation since relations between Indonesia and Taipei were cut off 20 years ago." Indonesian Foreign Minister Malik also openly declared that Indonesia might establish relations with the Chiang gang "at a level above that of commercial representative." He went so far as to say in an even more flagrant tone: "If Taiwan proclaims the founding of a Taiwan republic, we'll recognize it." Indonesian papers have long described the traitor Chiang Kai-shek, who had been repudiated by the Chinese people, as "the head of state of Taiwan" and referred to the Chiang Kai-shek bandit gang as a "government."[46]

A March 21, 1968, note to the Soviet embassy in China stated:

> The so-called "national emblem" of the Chiang Kai-shek bandit gang has appeared in an inside cover picture publicizing the Olympic Games in *New Books, U.S.S.R.* No. 6, a bulletin published this year by the Soviet revisionists' International Publishers.

> Even more, the Soviet side provocatively sent this bulletin to the Chinese side. This is a new, grave crime committed by the Soviet government in actively collaborating with US imperialism for the creation of "two Chinas," a flagrant political provocation against the 700 million Chinese people, and new ironclad proof of the Soviet government's collusion with the Chiang Kai-shek bandit gang to oppose the great People's Republic of China. The Chinese government hereby lodges a strong protest against this with the Soviet government.[47]

When the British periodical *The Stamp Magazine* recently wrote to the Ministry of Posts in Peking asking for details of new issues of postage stamps, it pointed out that it received "the new issues of Formosa only and wished to record those of the People's Republic of China." The PRC sent the following reply:

> Sirs,
>
> We are in receipt of *The Stamp Magazine* published by you. It is found that in the said journal is printed the information and photo of the stamps issued by the Chiang Kai-shek bandit clique in Taiwan, which was cast off by the Chinese people long ago. The Chiang Kai-shek bandit clique in Taiwan is called "China (Formosa)."
>
> As is well-known, Taiwan is a province of the People's Republic of China and an inalienable part of the sacred territory of China. The so-called "Formosa" is a name imposed on our Taiwan by the imperialists. The Chiang Kai-shek bandit clique, entrenched on Taiwan, is a group of national degenerates, which is utterly hostile to the Chinese people, under the protection of the warships of the US imperialists. The US imperialists have all along been antagonistic to the Chinese people and have attempted in vain to occupy by force our Taiwan for long and have actively pushed ahead the "two-China" plot.
>
> In your stamp journal, you go so far as to act in line with the intrigue of the US imperialists to create "two Chinas." This is a serious case of unfriendliness toward the Chinese people. For this we launch a strong protest against you. We firmly refuse to accept this journal which is returned herewith.
>
> *Secretary of Directorate*
> *General of Posts,*
> *People's Republic of China.*[48]

The Cultural Revolution revealed many other displays of Chinese sensitivity to any conduct that might imply the legitimacy of the rival government on Taiwan. The following excerpt is from the report of one of a number of PRC protests to India:

> A so-called "conference on the application of science and technology to the development of Asia" has been held in New Delhi by the United Nations, a tool of US imperialism and Soviet revisionism. The reactionary Indian government has gone so far as to permit the Chiang gang elements to attend the conference together with delegates of the Soviet revisionist renegade clique.
>
> In his speech at a parliament session on August 9 dealing with the question of participation by Chiang Kai-shek elements in this conference, Indian Minister of State for Education Bhagwat Jha Azad openly used the reactionary, shopworn US imperialist term in calling the People's Republic of China "Communist China," while calling the Chiang Kai-shek gang, the sworn enemy of the Chinese people, the "republic of China." This is a new crime committed by the reactionary Indian government in openly creating "two Chinas."
>
> On August 17, chargé d'affaires ad interim of the Chinese Embassy in India, Chen Chao-yuan, lodged a strong protest with the Indian Foreign Ministry against this outrage. He pointed out that the Indian government had deliberately acted contrary to its repeated assurances to the Chinese government that the Indian government recognized only the People's Republic of China and opposed the creation of "two Chinas." He also noted that at present US imperialism was intensifying its activities of creating "two Chinas" and that the Indian government was also stepping up its anti-China campaign in various fields.
>
> This criminal move by the reactionary Indian government is no accident. In a statement in the United States in September last year Indian Deputy Prime Minister Morarji Desai brazenly described Taiwan, which is China's sacred territory and where the Chiang Kai-shek gang is entrenched, as an "independent country." Later, the reactionary Indian government for the first time allowed 500 anti-Chinese hooligans in India to go to Taiwan to participate in the bogus "national day" celebrations of the Chiang gang. At the same time, a meeting marking the Chiang gang's so-called "national day" was openly held in the Indian capital. Indian M.P.'s and people in diplomatic circles attended this reactionary gathering.
>
> Since the beginning of this year, the reactionary Indian government has on several occasions allowed Chiang Kai-shek elements to attend international conferences in India. Such action on the

part of the reactionary Indian government has greatly pleased the Chiang elements." [49]

Even after the Cultural Revolution had subsided, the protests continued. Peking protested, for example, against the visit of a French Parliamentary Delegation to Taiwan,[50] the repeated reference to Taiwan as a "country" in Soviet propaganda,[51] and an invitation for the Republic of China to send a delegation to the "World Inter-Governmental Conference on Tourism" in Bulgaria.[52] Yet, in its drive to establish diplomatic relations with a majority of the countries of the world, Peking showed a certain flexibility. In the case of some states with which it established relations, it appeared willing to tolerate, at least for a time, the maintenance of a Nationalist Chinese presence as a trade mission or in some similar form.[53]

Although the PRC did not protest at the existence of ROC trade offices in Canada, the question of allowing a news reporter from the ROC to retain a seat in Ottawa's Parliamentary Press Gallery proved more complex, as the following dispatch indicates.

10-24

Charles Lynch, "Chinese Puzzle," *Montreal Gazette* (Aug. 19, 1971), p. 6.

When the Nationalist Chinese removed their embassy from Ottawa, anticipating the arrival of the diplomats from Peking, they left behind Yueh Li, representing the Central News Agency of Taipei.

Li remains in Ottawa as a member of the Parliamentary Press Gallery, and his presence here is an irritant to the People's Republic of China, with which Canada now has formal relations.

As long as Li remains a member of the Press Gallery, Pu Chao-min, the resident correspondent of Peking's New China News Agency, refuses to apply for membership.

The quandary

If Pu were to apply, there is every chance that his membership would be approved. But he will not become a member of any body that includes a representative of Taiwan, and in the eyes of Peking, Li is such a representative since his news agency is an official organ of the Chiang Kai-shek government.

The plot thickens. Several Canadian newspapers and news agencies are seeking to send correspondents to China, but until now they have been unable to obtain the required visas.

The People's Republic likes to handle matters of this kind on a reciprocal basis—a Canadian correspondent in China is matched by a Chinese correspondent in Ottawa. They also have shown a preference for having only one correspondent in Peking from each country with which they have such arrangements, though in the case of Canada there are indications they might be willing to receive more, under certain conditions.

One of those conditions would be that additional Chinese correspondents be admitted to Canada, to augment Pu's Ottawa bureau of the New China News Agency. But this would only be considered by the Chinese if the men they send can become members of the Parliamentary Press Gallery in Ottawa. While Li remains a member, they deem this to be impossible.

What emerges, then, is that as long as Li remains a member of the Parliamentary Press Gallery, there can be no more correspondents from Peking in Canada, and no more correspondents from Canada in Peking.

Apart from such temporary visas as may be granted, this amounts to a freeze on the situation that has obtained since the early '60s, when arrangements were worked out for the Toronto Globe and Mail to have a bureau in Peking, in exchange for the opening of the New China News Agency bureau in Ottawa.

Clearly, Peking feels it is up to the government of Canada, or to the Parliamentary Press Gallery, to do something about Li.

What to do?

The government of Canada would be glad to have something done, but can't figure a way to go about it. The Parliamentary Press Gallery, in its role as housekeeper and monitor of press facilities made available by Parliament, scrupulously avoids involvement in political or diplomatic controversy, limiting itself to the requirement that its members earn the bulk of their income from journalism.

If the government of Canada were to suggest that the Press Gallery expel Li, the Press Gallery almost certainly would tell the government of Canada to go to hell.

One of the many ironies in this situation is that Pu was a member of the Parliamentary Press Gallery when he first arrived here in 1964. Li did not appear on the scene until Pu was recalled to Peking in 1966, at the start of the Cultural Revolution. When Pu returned after the Cultural Revolution, he found Li ensconced in the Chinese seat in the Press Gallery, and refused to go near the place.

This week, Pu softened to the extent of accepting a member's invitation to visit the Press Gallery premises on Parliament Hill, and while he was there, partaking of a friendly beer, Li put in an appearance. The two men pointedly ignored one another, and continued to do so when they both joined the crowd of reporters at a press conference with Acting Prime Minister Mitchell Sharp.

It's all very fascinating and frustrating, especially for those of us who want to get to China and are faced with the fact that until a solution is found to this Chinese puzzle in Ottawa, there is no way.

Representation in International Organizations 11

Part IX will survey the PRC's views of the United Nations, its constitutional problems, its efforts to maintain international peace and security, and its many other activities. It also will suggest Peking's attitude toward the various activities of other international organizations, and will summarize China's pre-1949 experience with international organizations. Here we are interested solely in the PRC's stand on questions relating to its representation in these organizations.

What arguments did the PRC use to support its ultimately successful claim to China's seat in the United Nations? On what terms did it express willingness to participate in the UN? What attitudes has it adopted toward its representation in other public international organizations? According to the PRC, what are the legal consequences of its past nonparticipation in public international organizations? By what criteria does the PRC purport to determine whether other revolutionary governments or states should be represented in such organizations?

Has Peking expressed interest in having nongovernmental groups from China take part in private international organizations? In what circumstances?

11-1

"Exchange of Telegrams between the Minister for Foreign Affairs of the Central People's Government of the People's Republic of China and the Secretary-General," UN Doc. A/1364 (Sept. 14, 1950), in UN General Assembly, *Official Records*, 5th Session, Annexes, Vol. II, Question of the representation of China in the United Nations, pp. 1–2 (New York, 1950).

A. *Telegram dated 26 August 1950 from the Minister for Foreign Affairs of the Central People's Government of the People's Republic of China to the Secretary-General*

Peking, 26 August 1950

The Central People's Government of the People's Republic of China is the sole legal government representing the Chinese people. The so-called "delegates" of the Chinese Kuomintang reactionary remnant clique have no qualification whatsoever for participating in any of the meetings and organs of the United Nations, and must therefore be driven out from all the meetings and organs of the United Nations. Accordingly, on 15 November 1949, I sent on behalf of the Central People's Government of the People's Republic of China a note to you and to Mr. Carlos P. Romulo, President of the fourth session of the United Nations General Assembly, that the so-called "delegation of the Chinese National Government" headed by Tsiang Ting-fu had absolutely no right to represent China. On 8 January, 19 January, 2 February and 30 May 1950, I have repeatedly sent further notes to you and to Mr. Romulo, demanding that the United Nations immediately expel the illegitimate delegates of the Chinese Kuomintang reactionary remnant clique from the United Nations and its Security Council, Economic and Social Council and Trusteeship Council, and notifying that the Central People's Government of the People's Republic of China has appointed Chang Wen-tien chief representative of the People's Republic of China to attend the meetings of the United Nations, including those of the Security Council, Chi Chao-ting representative on the Economic and Social Council, and Meng Yung-chien representative on the Trusteeship Council. Yet until this day the illegitimate delegates of the Chinese Kuomintang reactionary remnant clique are still tolerated by the United Nations in its various organs, but not expelled therefrom immediately. I consider this not only a violation of the United Nations Charter but also a disregard of the rightful claim of the 475 million people of the People's Republic of China. Now that the fifth session of the United Nations General Assembly is due to meet on 19 September, I hereby inform you formally on behalf of the Central People's Government of the People's Republic of China, that the Central People's Government of the People's Republic of China has appointed Chang Wen-tien the chairman of the delegation, and Li Yi-mang, Chou Shih-ti, Chi Chao-ting and Meng Yung-chien the representatives of the People's Republic of China to attend the fifth session of the United Nations General Assembly. Please communicate the same to the parties concerned and make the arrangements necessary for the delegation of the People's Republic of China to attend the fifth session of the United Nations General Assembly. Please reply promptly by cable.

(*Signed*) CHOU En-lai
Minister for Foreign Affairs of the
Central People's Government of the
People's Republic of China

B. *Telegram dated 5 September 1950 from the Secretary-General to the Minister for Foreign Affairs of the Central People's Government of the People's Republic of China*

Lake Success, 5 September 1950

I have the honour to refer to your telegram 26 August designating a delegation of the Central People's Government of the People's Republic of China to attend the fifth session of the General Assembly and requesting me to make the necessary arrangements for the delegation.

Under Headquarters agreement between United Nations and United States approved by the General Assembly on 31 October 1947, transit through the United States to United Nations Headquarters is provided for representatives of Members of United Nations and persons invited to Headquarters by the United Nations. Upon acceptance by the General Assembly of your delegation as representative of the Republic of China or upon the invitation of the General Assembly to your delegation to attend the session, I shall promptly request the entry of your delegation to the United States and shall make arrangements for its reception at Headquarters.

I have circulated your telegram to the Members of the United Nations and shall place it before the General Assembly. I will promptly communicate to you any decisions in this matter made by the General Assembly.

(*Signed*) Trygve LIE

11-2

"Further Exchange of Telegrams between the Minister for Foreign Affairs of the Central People's Government of the People's Republic of China and the Secretary-General," UN Doc. A/1364/Add.1 (Sept. 18, 1950), in UN General Assembly, *Official Records*, 5th Session, Annexes, Vol. II, Question of the representation of China in the United Nations, pp. 2–3 (New York, 1950).

A. *Telegram dated 18 September 1950 from the Minister for Foreign Affairs of the Central People's Government of the People's Republic of China to the Secretary-General*

Peking, 18 September 1950

During the ten months since 15 November 1949, I have stated many times to the various organizations of the United Nations that the Central People's Government of the People's Republic of China is the sole legal government representing the Chinese people, that the Chinese Kuomintang reactionary remnant clique has forfeited all legal and factual basis for representing the Chinese people, and that the United Nations must drive out the illegal "delegates" of the Chinese Kuomintang reactionary remnant clique from all the meetings and organs of the United Nations, and accept the legal delegates of the Central People's Government of the People's Republic of China. Yet at the present time, the illegal "delegates" of the Chinese Kuomintang reactionary remnant clique still remain in all the organs of the United Nations except the Universal Postal Union; this is completely unjustified and constitutes a gross violation of the United Nations Charter.

Now that the fifth session of the United Nations General Assembly is due to meet soon, the so-called "delegation of the Chinese National Government" of the Chinese Kuomintang reactionary remnant clique is going again to New York to participate in the United Nations General Assembly, and to submit to the United Nations General Assembly the item of the so-called "Threats to the political independence and territorial integrity of China and to the peace of the Far East, resulting from Soviet violations of the Sino-Soviet Treaty of Friendship and Alliance of 14 August 1945, and from Soviet violations of the Charter of the United Nations". This is an illegal act of assuming the name of the delegates of the Chinese people, usurping the rights of the Chinese people and insulting the United Nations, an illegal act which the Chinese people firmly oppose and cannot tolerate.

On behalf of the Central People's Government of the People's Republic of China, I hereby solemnly inform you that the so-called "delegation of the Chinese National Government" of the Chinese Kuomintang reactionary remnant clique absolutely cannot represent the Chinese people; they have no qualifications whatsoever for participating in this session of the United Nations General Assembly, let alone any right to make proposals to the United Nations General Assembly. Should the United Nations General Assembly accept the illegal "delegation" of the Chinese Kuomintang reactionary remnant clique, or accept and consider the above-mentioned item or any other items proposed by it, the Chinese People's Government of the People's Republic of China would consider this a most unfriendly action towards the Chinese people on the part of the United Nations, and that, as a result of such action, the United Nations General Assembly would degenerate into an instrument in the service of a handful of fugitive elements, the Chinese Kuomintang reactionary remnant clique, for slandering and provoking the 475 million people of China. Apart from resolutely opposing, on behalf of the Chinese people, such action, the Central People's Government of the People's Republic of China reserves the right to take action on this question.

I hereby inform you once more that the fifth session of the United Nations General Assembly must immediately drive out the illegal "delegates" of the Chinese reactionary remnant clique. At the same time, please make immediately all the arrangements necessary for the delegation of the People's Republic of China to attend this session of the United Nations General Assembly. Should the fifth session of the United Nations General Assembly be held without the participation of the delegation of the People's Republic of China, or, worse still, with the illegal "delegates" of the Chinese Kuomintang reactionary remnant clique tolerated therein, all the resolutions adopted by it concerning China would be illegal and, consequently, null and void.

(*Signed*) Chou En-lai
Minister for Foreign Affairs of
the Central People's Government
of the People's Republic of China

B. *Telegram dated 18 September 1950 from the Secretary-General to the Minister for Foreign Affairs of the Central People's Government of the People's Republic of China*

Lake Success, 18 September 1950

I have the honour to acknowledge receipt of your telegram of the 18th September and to advise you that it will be circulated to the Members of the United Nations and placed before the General Assembly.

(*Signed*) Trygve LIE

11-3

Chou Keng-sheng, "China's Legitimate Rights in the United Nations Must Be Restored," *JMJP* (Dec. 5, 1961), p. 5, translated in *Oppose the New US Plots to Create "Two Chinas"* (Peking, 1962), pp. 55–73.

China is one of the original members of the United Nations and a permanent member of the Security Council. As a subject of international law, the People's Republic of China, established after the victory of the Chinese people's revolution, is the continuation of preliberation China and, therefore, is unequivocally entitled to China's legitimate seat in the United Nations and to all other rights pertaining to it. This is a universally acknowledged principle of international law confirmed in the United Nations Charter and international practice. According to international law, changes in the form of state or political regime of a country which has experienced a revolution do not affect its international personality. In the United Nations Organization, there are member states in which new regimes were established as a result of coups d'état or revolutions. Their seats in the United Nations were not affected. Iraq and Cuba are notable examples.

In his official telegrams addressed respectively to the UN Secretary-General and President of the General Assembly in October 1949 after the proclamation of the founding of the People's Republic of China, Chou En-lai, then Foreign Minister, solemnly declared that the Central People's Government of the People's Republic of China is the sole legal government representing the entire people of the People's Republic of China and demanded that the right of the so-called "delegation of the National Government of China" to represent the Chinese people in the United Nations be nullified. Later he informed them that the government of the People's Republic of China had appointed its representative to attend UN conferences and take part in the activities of the United Nations. But so far, the People's Republic of China has been excluded from the United Nations and is unable to exercise its legitimate rights in that organization, whereas the Chiang Kai-shek clique, which has long been disowned by the Chinese people and which has fled to Taiwan, has for a long time been illegally occupying China's legitimate seat in the United Nations and unlawfully passing itself off as the representative of China. Obviously enough, this is an utterly absurd situation in every sense. It not only encroaches upon China's legitimate rights as a Great Power and a founder of the United Nations, but also violates the UN Charter. Furthermore, the absence in the United Nations of the representatives of the 650 million people of the People's Republic of China has prevented the effective and lawful solution of major questions facing the United Nations and the world. The whole world knows that this situation has been created solely by the United States. Because of its hostility to new China, its interference in China's internal affairs and its attempt to occupy permanently China's territory of Taiwan, US imperialism has from the very beginning opposed the participation of the government of the People's Republic of China in UN activities and has been trying to keep the US-fostered Chiang Kai-shek clique in China's seat. Although the Soviet Union and other socialist countries and all the peace-loving countries have repeatedly demanded that its legitimate seat in the UN be restored to the People's Republic of China, the United States and its followers have been resorting to every trick and device to prevent the People's Republic of China from exercising its legitimate rights in the UN.

In trying to prevent the People's Republic of China from exercising its legitimate rights of representation in the UN, the United States and its followers have been vilifying new China politically with vicious and utterly baseless slanders, alleging, for instance that new China refuses to renounce the use of force and is bellicose and inhuman, and so on. But in addition to these slanders, which have long been bitterly refuted and condemned by the Chinese people and just public opinion the world over, they have also put up certain distorted legal arguments as pretexts for preventing the People's Republic of China from entering the United Nations. They have argued, for instance, that the People's Republic of China has not yet been recognized by the United States and many other UN members; that the People's Republic of China has been branded an "aggressor" in a General Assembly resolution, and even that, according to the name of the state (the Republic of China) listed as a permanent member of the Security Council in Article 23 of the UN Charter, the permanent member referred to should be understood as the "Republic of China" and cannot be replaced by the People's Republic of China. It is crystal clear that these arguments cannot stand in the face of legal principles.

It has been pointed out above that, as a subject of international law, the People's Republic of China is the continuation of preliberation China; the government of the People's Republic of China is therefore the sole legal government representing the entire Chinese people. So far as the United Nations is concerned, the People's Republic of China that has existed ever since October 1949 is the same China that signed the Moscow Declaration of 1943 (proclaiming the decision to establish a general international organization), the Charter of the United Nations in 1945, and other documents. The government of the People's Republic of China, therefore, is undeniably the only government entitled to represent the Chinese people and participate in the activities of the General Assembly, the Security Council, and the other agencies of the United Nations. The exclusion of the People's Republic of China from the UN Organization as a result of the machinations of the United States is by no means a question of refusing to admit a new state as a member; it means depriving one of the founding members and, at that, a permanent member of the Security Council, of its lawful representation. As early as May 22, 1954, at the Geneva Conference, Premier Chou En-lai who was then also Foreign Minister, solemnly pointed out: ". . . the question is not that the People's Republic of China applies for UN membership, but that the People's Republic of China is deprived of its right to participate in the United Nations and hence the rightful place of the People's Republic of China in the United Nations should be restored."

In international relations, the People's Republic of China not only has been recognized by an increasing number of countries, but has established diplomatic relations with them. It took part in the 1954 Geneva Conference and the 1955 Bandung Conference and is now attending the Enlarged Geneva Conference on the Laotian Question. At all these conferences, the representatives of the People's Republic of China have made important contributions toward relaxing international tension, preventing wars of aggression, and promoting and safeguarding world peace—playing the active role of China as a great power. Even the government of the United States which has consistently refused to recognize the People's Republic of China has found it inevitable to hold Sino-American talks at ambassadorial level with the representatives of the government of the People's Republic of China, first in Geneva and later in Warsaw. Anyone who looks squarely at the reality of international politics must admit that no world problems of importance can be effectively settled at all today without the participation of the People's

Republic of China. Though faced with this fact, the UN as an international organization still continues to exclude the People's Republic of China from its organs and allows China's UN seat to be illegally occupied by a handful of the reactionary Kuomintang clique in Taiwan, that is, the so-called "representatives of the Republic of China." This is a violation of the purposes and principles of the UN Charter; it makes a mockery of the United Nations itself and is an insult to the members of that body.

US imperialism has used one pretext after another, such as follows, for opposing the entry of the People's Republic of China into the United Nations: that the People's Republic of China has not yet been recognized by the United States and many other members of the United Nations; that the UN General Assembly passed a resolution in 1951 [labeling] the People's Republic of China an "aggressor." These pretexts are too absurd to require refutation. Juridically, there is no connection between acceptance by the United Nations of the representatives of a state to participate in its activities and recognition of that state and government by UN members. As early as 1950, the UN Secretariat in a memorandum "On Legal Aspects of Problems of Representation of the United Nations," pointed out that from the standpoint of legal theory, the linkage of representation in an international organization and recognition of a government is a confusion of two institutions, and it would appear to be legally inadmissible to [make] acceptance of representation of a government [conditional on] individual recognition prior to it. As a matter of fact, it has never been the case that all UN members are recognized by all other members. A number of newly independent nationalist countries have not been refused admission into the United Nations merely on the ground that for the time being only a few UN members have recognized them. Furthermore, since the People's Republic of China was originally a UN member, how can its legitimate seat in the United Nations be denied merely because the United States and some other countries have not yet recognized it?

As to the UN General Assembly resolution naming China an "aggressor," everybody knows that this was nothing but an utterly vicious slander against new China and was in itself preposterous. In a statement on February 2, 1951, Chou En-lai, then Foreign Minister of China, solemnly pointed out that the US resolution adopted at the United Nations "is an utter perversion of truth and confounds black and white," because "it is obviously the United States government which has engineered the Korean incident, intervened in and invaded Korea, and intervened in and invaded China's Taiwan, yet the United States resolution alleges that the Chinese Communist Party is intervening in Korea. . . ." Moreover, the adoption of that resolution was illegal in procedure and was therefore null and void. As Foreign Minister Chou En-lai pointed out in the same statement, the UN General Assembly and its first committee, "encroaching upon the powers of the Security Council," adopted the resolution, "without the participation of the lawful representatives of the People's Republic of China." It was a disgrace to the United Nations itself that the General Assembly adopted this illegal, invalid, and preposterous resolution as a result of the machinations of the United States. It is against common sense to continue to believe in such a pretext put up by US imperialism to prevent the restoration to China of its legitimate rights in the United Nations.

In an attempt to provide grounds for the so-called "Government of the Republic of China," a puppet gang entrenched in Taiwan under the wing of US imperialism, to continue to grasp at the right of representation in the United Nations, and so deny the People's Republic of China its legitimate rights, the imperialists have even gone so far as to bring up Article 23 of the UN Charter (on the composition of the Security Council) which states that "the Security Council shall consist of eleven members of the United Nations. The Republic of China, France, the Union of the Soviet Socialist Republics, the United Kingdom of Great Britain and Northern Ireland, and the United States of America shall be permanent members of the Security Council." This argument is completely divorced from the essence of the question. The signatory to the Moscow Declaration of 1943 or the UN Charter of 1945 simply represented a state. The representative of China at that time who signed the documents concerning the United Nations Organization represented China in general, a country with a population of 450 million then and 650 million now, not in the sense of a certain government or form of government of China in particular. Any such attempt to draw inferences from the use of the name of the Republic of China as mentioned in Article 23 of the Charter with a view to supporting the remnant Kuomintang reactionary clique in pretending representation in the United Nations is simply a deliberate misinterpretation of the provisions of the Charter. Obviously, the "Republic of China" mentioned in the UN Charter is China; the "Republic of China" was merely the name of China at that time, a name that had begun to be used after the overthrow of the Ch'ing Dynasty in the 1911 Revolution. With the victory of the revolution of the Chinese people in 1949 and the proclamation of the founding of the People's Republic of China, the "Republic of China" was naturally abolished as the name of China. No one had any right to use that abolished name to pass himself off as the representative of China. Since then, the People's Republic of China has been the sole lawful representative of the Chinese people; consequently, the People's Republic of China is naturally entitled to China's legitimate rights in the United

Nations. This is beyond any dispute. The followers of the United States, on the ground that Article 23 of the Charter mentions the "Republic of China" as a permanent member of the Security Council, have asserted that in order to entitle the People's Republic of China to take over the seat in the United Nations, it will require a revision of the Charter. It must be pointed out that such an argument is more preposterous from the standpoint of law. It has been refuted even by Western jurists. For instance, the noted professor Hans Kelsen has pointed out: "Under general international law a state has the right to change its name, and the Charter does not restrict this right of a member state of the United Nations, even if this state is a permanent member of the Security Council mentioned under a definite name in Article 23 of the Charter." He added: "If the Communist government of China should be recognized by the United Nations as the government of China, China will be a member of the United Nations and a permanent member of the Security Council under its new name 'People's Republic of China,' no rewriting of the Charter being necessary." This being so, how can the United Nations refuse to recognize the government of the People's Republic of China as the government of China?

The arguments advanced by U.S. imperialism for preventing the People's Republic of China from recovering its legitimate rights in the United Nations are untenable from the standpoint of both reason and law. In order to realize its scheme to occupy Taiwan permanently by force, it has left nothing undone to keep the so-called "representative of the Republic of China" illegally in China's seat in the United Nations and prevent the People's Republic of China from exercising its legitimate rights in the UN. For many years the United States and its followers have used a moratorium as a means of obstructing the restoration of the legitimate rights of the People's Republic of China. By this means they have illegally deprived the People's Republic of China of those rights in the United Nations for a full 12 years. But the strength of New China is growing, and its international prestige is rising steadily. These arbitrary anti-Chinese tactics employed by the United States have led to its own increasing isolation. Popular resentment has been growing steadily against the US line of trampling the UN Charter underfoot and depriving China of its legitimate rights. This can be convincingly proved particularly by the attitude of the newly-independent Asian and African countries and of certain Latin American countries, such as that expressed in the declaration of the recent Conference of the Heads of State or Government of Non-Aligned Countries.

The majority which the United States managed to scrape together so as to push through the resolution postponing discussion of the "representation of China" in the UN General Assembly has dwindled every year, till last year it was a feeble one of only eight votes (42 vs. 34). It is unlikely that the United States would be able to retain this meagre majority if it sought to get the same resolution passed at the 16th session of the UN General Assembly this year. Confronted with this unfavorable situation, US imperialism has been compelled to switch to a different tactic.

The United States for a time tried to peddle its "two Chinas" plot in the UN in order to extricate itself from its dilemma on the question of China's representation. With the help of some of its satellites in giving publicity to the so-called "two successor states" formula, it planned to retain the seat of the representative of the Chiang Kai-shek clique of Taiwan while accepting participation of the People's Republic of China in the United Nations. This utterly absurd plan instantly met with the resolute opposition of the Chinese people and was bitterly denounced by them. It was even opposed by the Chiang Kai-shek clique in Taiwan. It was also unanimously denounced by just world public opinion. Hasn't Field Marshal Montgomery of Britain, who recently visited China, also openly expressed the opinion that "there should be only one China whom everybody recognizes," and that "Taiwan is part of the People's Republic"? Consequently, the United States must shelve for the time being the so-called "two successor states" formula.

To achieve its purpose of continuing to prevent the People's Republic of China from recovering its legitimate rights in the UN, the US has now resorted to the method of having China's representation discussed at the General Assembly as an "important question" requiring a two-thirds majority vote under Paragraph 2, Article 18 of the UN Charter while at the same time plotting to have the question discussed by an ad hoc committee together with the question of broadening the membership of the Security Council and the Economic and Social Council. This new plot of the United States and its followers must be exposed and opposed. In the first place, there should be a correct understanding of how the question of "China's representation" should be presented. This is the fundamental issue. The Soviet delegate has submitted to the current UN General Assembly session a resolution proposing that the General Assembly discuss the question of restoring to the People's Republic of China its legitimate rights in the United Nations and drive out from all UN organs the representatives of the Chiang Kai-shek clique who are in illegal occupation of China's UN seat. This way of presenting the question is perfectly correct; it gets straight to the gist of the matter. What the peace-loving countries and peoples the world over are interested in and what should be discussed at the 16th UN General Assembly is the question of restoring to the People's Republic of China its legitimate rights in the United Nations. The reason is very simple: the

People's Republic of China's legitimate rights in the UN have long been established and are not a matter for discussion. What is now being submitted for discussion is only the question of the restoration of these legitimate rights, which is also a question of driving out the representatives of the Chiang Kai-shek clique. The resolution proposing to make the question of restoring China's lawful seat in the UN an "important question" as was put forward by Japan, Australia, Colombia, Italy, and the US, with the [last] as the organizer, is utterly preposterous. The United States and its followers want to use the questions of who should represent China and whether representation in the UN should be shared by the so-called "two Chinas" (the so-called two successor states) to spread around their absurd arguments at the UN General Assembly and engage in mud slinging and distortions, so as to drag the dispute on endlessly and continue to postpone a settlement of the question.

By making Japan, Australia, Colombia, and Italy join it in putting forward the resolution to discuss the question of "China's representation," and particularly by seeking to have this question discussed as an "important question," the United States is attempting to turn the question of restoring China's legitimate rights in the United Nations—a question of procedure—into a question of substance requiring a two-thirds majority vote under Paragraph 2 of Article 18 of the UN Charter. In a situation where US imperialism is no longer sure that it can manipulate a simple majority to postpone discussion of this question, it is now attempting, on the pretext of this being an "important question," to rake up a majority for classifying this question as one requiring a two-thirds majority vote so that it can continue to obstruct the restoration of the People's Republic of China's legitimate rights in the United Nations by getting together slightly above one-third of the total number of votes.

It goes without saying that to restore to China lawful representation in the United Nations is a matter of world significance. Nobody can deny this. But this question by no means falls into the category of "important questions" mentioned in Paragraph 2 of Article 18. This paragraph of the UN Charter states that "Decisions of the General Assembly on important questions shall be made by a two-thirds majority of the members present and voting. These questions shall include: recommendations with respect to the maintenance of international peace and security, the election of the nonpermanent members of the Security Council, the election of the members of the Economic and Social Council, the election of the members of the Trusteeship Council in accordance with Paragraph 1 (c) of Article 86, the admission of new members to the United Nations, the suspension of the right and privileges of membership, the expulsion of members, questions relating to the operation of the trusteeship system, and budgetary questions." It should be noted that questions concerning the basic functions of the UN General Assembly with respect to the maintenance of international peace and security, and the composition of its major organs, etc., mentioned under Paragraph 2 of Article 18 are questions of substance. Thus, if a two-thirds majority decision is to be applied to a certain question under this paragraph, that question should also be a substantive one. Questions mentioned under Paragraph 2 are all important questions. But this does not mean that the provisions of this article should be applied to any question that is considered important. The nature of the question should first of all be considered. The question of the restoration of China's legitimate rights in the United Nations is essentially a procedural question. How can provisions for the settlement of substantive questions be applied to procedural ones?

Is it not a fact that for many years the UN General Assembly decided by a majority vote to postpone discussion on the question of China's representation? To postpone discussion itself means not to restore or at least not to restore for the time being China's legitimate rights in the United Nations. This, too, is an extremely important question. Since this could be considered a procedural question and decided by a majority vote, the question of the restoration of the legitimate rights of the People's Republic of China now being discussed is likewise a procedural question. Why then should the latter question be singled out as an important question requiring a two-thirds majority decision? This is self-contradictory and untenable from the standpoint of law.

Paragraph 3 of Article 18 of the UN Charter provides that "Decisions on other questions, including the determination of additional categories of questions to be decided by a two-thirds majority, shall be made by a majority of the members present and voting." To put it briefly, apart from the important questions listed in Paragraph 2, the UN General Assembly may also determine additional categories of questions to be decided by a two-thirds majority. Here only categories of questions, not individual specific questions, are referred to. If it is felt that a specific question should be decided by a two-thirds majority, the General Assembly should first approve a general provision for an additional category and then discuss this specific question as one falling into this category. Western authorities on international law also hold this view. For instance, it is affirmed in Oppenheim's *International Law:* "Unless a question, however important, is comprised within the above enumeration or unless it has been expressly included within a category requiring a two-thirds majority, it can be made the subject of a recommendation by a simple majority." This should be considered a correct interpretation. Otherwise, there will be no limits set. In any case, where they consider it advantageous or convenient for themselves, the imperialists will be in a position to arbitrarily list any question, regardless of its nature, on the pretext of its being an "important question" under Paragraph 2 of Article 18, as one requiring a two-thirds majority vote so that they can oppose or obstruct the solution of such a question. This would lead to repeated misuse of the provisions of Article 18 of the UN Charter and to confusion.

The restoration of the People's Republic of China's seat in the United Nations is simply a specific question which, in accordance with a correct interpretation of Paragraph 3 of Article 18, cannot be classified as one requiring a two-thirds majority decision under Paragraph 2. Therefore, it can be asserted that the resolution tabled by Japan, Australia, Colombia, Italy, and the United States to have the question discussed as an "important question" is obviously designed to misinterpret the scope of application of Paragraphs 2 and 3. The resolution also does not conform to the general practice of the United Nations concerning rules of procedure. Under the UN Charter, provisions relating to procedural matters are made in the Rules of Procedure (the General Assembly's Rules of Procedure under Article 21 and the Security Council's Rules of Procedure under Article 30). According to these rules, procedural questions including the examination of credentials of representatives shall be decided by a simple majority vote, that is to say, they do not require a two-thirds majority decision by the General Assembly and the veto shall not apply to them in the Security Council. Decisions on these rules of procedure themselves are made by a simple majority in the General Assembly and the Security Council, respectively.

The restoration of China's lawful seat in the United Nations is, as remarked above, a procedural question. As far as the Security Council is concerned, this question is one of nullifying the credentials of the representative of the Chiang Kai-shek clique and driving him out of the Council. It is beyond any shadow of doubt that the veto cannot be applied here. The UN Secretariat has already given an explanation on this point. In 1954, the then UN Secretary-General, Dag Hammarskjold, made a public announcement on the question of China's representation, recalling that his predecessor, Trygve Lie, had issued a statement to the effect that the veto could not be used in regard to a decision as to what regime should represent a state on the Security Council and that this was the view of the Legal Department of the UN Secretariat. Western experts in international law have also pointed out that if the examination of credentials of representatives is regarded as a nonprocedural matter and at the same time the veto can be applied in the Security Council on the question of the right of representation, then, after the government of a state has undergone a revolutionary change, the person still acting as representative of the overthrown government of a state having a permanent seat in the Security Council would be able to exclude the representative of the new government by veto while himself forever illegally occupying his seat in the Security Council. Should this be allowed, wouldn't it lead to preposterous results and paralyze the organization of the United Nations?

Thus it is clear and undeniable that, as a procedural question, no veto should be applied in the Security Council to the question of China's lawful seat in the United Nations. Now, if a procedural question can be decided by a simple majority in the Security Council, why then should this selfsame question require a two-thirds majority decision in the General Assembly? What kind of logic is this? By trying to have the question discussed and decided as one of those important questions listed under Article 18, the United States and its followers are deliberately seeking to complicate the issue, in other words, to keep it unsettled.

Moreover, if this question should be discussed as a substantive one, it would necessarily involve the question of whether or not the government of the People's Republic of China represents China. Such a discussion or resolution would constitute a violation of the UN Charter and flagrant interference in the internal affairs of China. The 650 million Chinese people will never tolerate this. The question of who represents China is a matter for the Chinese people themselves to decide, and the 650 million Chinese people have already made their decision. The United Nations has no right whatsoever to meddle in it.

US imperialism is also plotting to have this question, together with the question of broadening the membership of the Security Council and the Economic and Social Council, referred to an ad hoc committee for study. This is to entangle the question of restoring China's seat in the United Nations with the question of broadening these UN bodies and make the question still more complicated. This is another tactic of US imperialism to prevent the People's Republic of China from recovering its legitimate rights.

True, there is some connection between the question of broadening the membership of the Security Council and the Economic and Social Council and that of restoring China's lawful seat. This is because the composition of these two organs is laid down in Articles 23 and 61 of the UN Charter, respectively. A broadening of the membership of these two bodies would necessarily involve a revision of the UN Charter. Under Article 108 of the Charter, a revision of the Charter must be approved by a two-thirds majority of all UN member nations including all the permanent members of the Security Council. In other words, any revision of the Charter must be unanimously approved by the five permanent members of the Security Council. So, if the People's Republic of China as a permanent member of the Council continues to be illegally excluded from the United Nations and does not agree to any revision of the Charter, the revision of any article of the Charter will be considered illegal. But after all, the two questions are of an entirely different nature, one being a substantive question and the other a procedural one. The two cannot be dealt with together. There is no precedent in United Nations practice that a procedural question should be discussed and settled together with a substantive one. In fact, precisely because the two have such a vital relation, as mentioned above, it is all the more necessary for the UN General Assembly to decide first to restore China's lawful seat in the United Nations for a lawful and effective solution of the question of broadening these UN bodies.

To sum up, the question now confronting the 16th session of the UN General Assembly is the restoration of China's original seat and legitimate rights in the United Nations. This is the common demand of the people of the whole world who stand for justice and love peace. The restoration of China's legitimate rights in the UN demonstrates the pressing need to solve important world issues, and particularly Asian problems; it is also the prerequisite for the maintenance of the dignity of the UN Charter, as well as for the fulfillment of the functions of the United Nations Organization. Precisely because this question is of such importance, the United Nations and its members are under all the greater obligation and necessity to give it priority for a speedy solution; it is not a subject entailing "careful study" and "protracted proceedings" as is demanded with deliberate exaggeration by the imperialists.

11-4
"Foreign Minister Ch'en Yi's Press Conference" (Sept. 29, 1965), *PR* 8.41:12 (Oct. 8, 1965).

Concerning the question of restoring to China her legitimate rights in the United Nations, which was raised by the Japanese correspondents, Vice-Premier Ch'en Yi said: The United Nations has long been controlled by the United States and has today become a place where two big powers, the United States and the Soviet Union, conduct political transactions. This state of affairs has not changed although dozens of Afro-Asian and peace-loving countries have [exerted] no small amount of effort in the United Nations. China need not take part in such a United Nations.

During the US war of aggression against Korea, the United Nations adopted a resolution naming China as an aggressor. How can China be expected to take part in an international organization which calls her an aggressor? Calling China an aggressor and then asking the aggressor to join, would not the United Nations be slapping its own face?

The question now is how to reform the United Nations in accordance with the purposes and principles of its Charter and to free it from the control of the United States and other big powers. If the task of reforming the United Nations cannot be accomplished, conditions will no doubt gradually ripen for the establishment of a revolutionary United Nations.

Will the present UN General Assembly adopt a resolution expelling the elements of the Chiang Kai-shek clique and restoring China's legitimate rights? I think this is impossbile as the United Nations is now controlled by the United States: If things really turn out that way, the question would still remain unsolved.

The United Nations must rectify its mistakes and undergo a thorough reorganization and reform. It must admit and correct all its past mistakes. Among other things, it should cancel its resolution condemning China and the Democratic People's Republic of Korea as aggressors and adopt a resolution condemning the United States as the aggressor; the UN Charter must be reviewed and revised jointly by all countries, big and small; all independent states should be included in the United Nations; and all imperialist puppets should be expelled.

NOTE

The conditions that Ch'en Yi set forth for the PRC's participation in the UN represented the stiffest demand Peking had ever made upon the UN. Coming at a time when the People's Republic was searching for a substitute international organization of "newly emerging forces," the Foreign Minister's statement indicated Peking's lack of interest in the UN rather than the necessary conditions for its participation.[54] In 1969, after the Cultural Revolution subsided and Peking began to demonstrate renewed interest in participating in the UN, it reverted to its earlier position of insisting solely upon expulsion of the representatives of the Republic of China, with no independent representation for Taiwan. In the fall of 1971, Peking's return to this position, its foreign policy of moderation and its budding detente with the United States, led to its entry into the UN.

11-5

"Statement of the Government of the People's Republic of China," October 29, 1971, in *PR* 14.45:6 (Nov. 5, 1971).

At its 26th Session, the General Assembly of the United Nations adopted on October 25, 1971 by an overwhelming majority the resolution put forward by Albania, Algeria and 21 other countries demanding the restoration of all the lawful rights of China in the United Nations and the immediate expulsion of the representatives of the Chiang Kai-shek clique from the United Nations and all the organizations related to it. This represents the bankruptcy of the policy of depriving China of her legitimate rights in the United Nations obdurately pursued by US imperialism over the past 20 years and more and of the US imperialist scheme to create "two Chinas" in the United Nations. This is a victory of Chairman Mao Tse-tung's proletarian revolutionary line in foreign affairs and a victory for the people of the whole world and all the countries upholding justice.

However, not reconciled to their defeat, the US and Japanese reactionaries are continuing to spread the fallacy that "the status of Taiwan remains to be determined" and are frenziedly pushing their scheme of creating "an independent Taiwan" in a wild attempt to continue to create "one China, one Taiwan" which is in effect tantamount to "two Chinas." While instigating the representatives of the Chiang Kai-shek clique to hang on in some specialized agencies of the United Nations, they are even vainly attempting to let the Chiang Kai-shek clique worm its way back into the United Nations under the name of a so-called "independent Taiwan." This is a desperate struggle put up by them, and their scheme must never be allowed to succeed. The just resolution adopted by the UN General Assembly must be speedily implemented in its entirety. All the representatives of the Chiang Kai-shek clique must be expelled from the United Nations Organization and all its bodies and related agencies.

Note

Peking Review summarized the historic UN action with evident glee:

> Confronted by this unfavorable situation, the US and Japanese representatives were tearing around, like ants on a hot pan, to put pressure on other countries and to deceive and win them over. Just a few minutes before the formal vote, the United States still

> instigated some countries to ask for a postponement of the vote, "in the hope that it might prevail upon a few still wavering members to support the American resolution" (according to Reuters). But this manoeuvre of the US-Japanese reactionaries was rejected 56 votes to 53, with 19 abstentions, at the General Assembly. Then, the so-called "important question" resolution was voted down 59 votes to 55, with 15 abstentions. Western news agencies reported that "bedlam broke out when the result of the vote appeared on the electronic tabulating board showing that the American proposal had been defeated," that "the announcement of the vote was greeted by prolonged applause from the packed assembly hall" and was "applauded for two minutes," and that representatives of various countries friendly to China were "cheering, singing, shouting," "and some dancing in the aisles."
>
> At this moment, the gloomy-faced US representative George Bush rushed to the rostrum, trying to make a last-ditch struggle. He moved that the provision for the immediate expulsion from the UN of the representatives of the Chiang gang be deleted from the resolution sponsored by Albania, Algeria and 20 other countries before being put to a vote. But his motion was ruled out of order by UN General Assembly President Adam Malik, and this attempt of the US representative was blocked by the opposition of other representatives. Seeing that the situation was hopeless and it was impossible for the Chiang gang to hang on any longer, Chou Shu-kai, the Chiang gang's "foreign minister," had to announce his retreat from the UNO and soon headed his underlings in their dismal departure from the assembly hall.
>
> The resolution sponsored by Albania, Algeria and 20 other countries then was put to a vote and adopted by an overwhelming majority, 76 votes to 35, with 17 abstentions. Resounding loud applause and cheers again burst forth in the assembly hall.[55]

Subsequently, however the PRC appeared to believe that the UN was proving rather slow at liquidating the vestiges of its contacts with the ROC, as the next two items suggest.

11-6
"Huang Hua Sends Note to UN Secretary-General," *PR* 15.3:15 (Jan. 21, 1972).

Huang Hua, Permanent Representative of the People's Republic of China to the United Nations, on January 12 sent a note to Kurt Waldheim, Secretary-General of the United Nations, urging the UN Secretariat immediately to take corresponding measures to cease all contacts with the Chiang Kai-shek clique and immediately stop all the assistance and contacts of the "Development Programme," the "Office of Technical Cooperation" and all other related UN bodies with that clique in accordance with the resolution adopted at the 26th Session of the UN General Assembly on October 25, 1971, restoring to the People's Republic of China all its lawful rights in the United Nations and expelling forthwith the representatives of the Chiang Kai-shek clique from the United Nations and all the organizations related to it.

The note reads:

"The Permanent Representative of the People's Republic of China to the United Nations presents his compliments to the Secretary-General of the United Nations and has the honour to state the following:

"1. At its 26th session, the General Assembly of the United Nations adopted on October 25, 1971, a resolution restoring to the People's Republic of China all its lawful rights in the United Nations and expelling forthwith the representatives of the Chiang Kai-shek clique from the United Nations and all the organizations related to it. Upon the adoption of the above resolution, the United Nations and all its related organizations should immediately cease all their contacts with the Chiang Kai-shek clique and immediately stop all projects of assistance to that clique.

"2. However, it is understood that after the adoption of the above resolution some UN bodies, such as the 'Development Programme' and the 'Office of Technical Cooperation,' are still continuing their on-going programme of assistance to the Chiang Kai-shek clique although they have reportedly decided to stop their projects of assistance to that clique which have not yet begun. The Permanent Mission of the People's Republic of China considers that the continuation of such a state of affairs is in complete violation of the above resolution of the United Nations and is, therefore, impermissible. The Permanent Mission of the People's Republic of China asks the Secretariat of the United Nations immediately to take corresponding measures to cease all contacts with the Chiang Kai-shek clique and to immediately stop all the assistance and contacts of the 'Development Programme' and the 'Office of Technical Co-operation' as well as all the other related UN bodies with the

Chiang Kai-shek clique, including on-going projects and projects which have not yet begun, so that the resolution adopted by the United Nations General Assembly at its 26th session on October 25 last year may be implemented in earnest.

"3. The Permanent Mission of the People's Republic of China hopes that the Secretariat will inform it at an earliest possible date of the results from actions taken in regard to the above question."

11-7

Sam Pope Brewer, "UN, Pressed by Peking, Ousts Two Taipei Newsmen," *New York Times* (Dec. 18, 1971), p. 4.

The United Nations today ousted the two Nationalist Chinese correspondents working at this headquarters, as a result of pressure by the Chinese Communists.

In the unprecedented action, the Secretary-General personally endorsed the order, on the advice of the United Nations general counsel, Constantin A. Stavropoulos of Greece.

Correspondents who questioned the action were told that Mr. Stravropoulos had ruled that the Secretary-General had complete authority to withdraw any accreditation. The action aroused fears among other reporters whose governments are not members.

Both men represented the Central News Agency [at the UN]. They are T. C. Tang, who is 62 years old, was educated in Missouri and has been at the United Nations since it was founded in 1945, and Chen-chi (Frank) Lin, 54, who has been here since 1955.

They had received no warning until they were summoned to the office of the director of press liaison, William Powell, at 10 A.M. today and told that they must hand in their passes by tonight.

Both correspondents seemed dazed by the suddenness of the move. Chinese with Nationalist passports who work for the United Nations have been told that their jobs are safe. The reporters did not have the same protection. . . .

Mr. Powell said in a daily briefing that the action had been taken under pressure from Peking's delegation. He said that the Assistant Secretary-General for the office of public information, Agha Abdul Hamid, had written an order after consulting with Mr. Stravropoulos and that Mr. Thant had approved it.

The spokesman said: "The Central News Agency of China is an official government agency founded on the mainland in 1924. It has since been moved to Formosa where it has been directed by that government."

Peking's representatives, he said, approached the Secretariat and asserted that "the employes are in fact employes of the government in Taiwan, and this is contrary to the principles of the current situation."

The two correspondents are free to remain and work in the United States, though not in the United Nations. The Central News Agency maintains an office in the building of the New York Daily News, at 220 East 42d Street.

Western colleagues were generally indignant at what they considered an infringement of the right to report the news. The newsmen's friends considered the action arbitrary and unjust. United Nations officials took the position that the final decision on the right of a correspondent to work here rested with Mr. Thant.

In a letter to Mr. Powell, Mr. Tang said: "We wish to protest most vigorously Secretary-General Thant's politically motivated decision to withdraw our press accreditations to the United Nations, effective immediately.

"Ever since its inception, our correspondents have been regularly accredited to the United Nations, and our agency has been faithfully covering the activities of the world organization.

"Our agency serves a large number of Chinese and foreign language newspapers throughout the world and now they will be deprived of our United Nations coverage. Whether from the standpoint of universality or a free press, our disaccreditation is unconscionable."

Mr. Powell said that the opinion given by Mr. Stavropoulos was that the General Assembly resolution that admitted the Peking delegation and ousted the Nationalist government on Taiwan applied equally to employes of the official news agency.

The president of the United Nations Correspondents Association, Louis Foy of the Newspaper *Paris-Presse,* said he planned to send a protest to Mr. Thant as soon as he consulted with members of the executive committee. He said that he would tell Mr. Thant that the disaccreditation of the two correspondents was a "dangerous precedent" and ask him to reconsider his decision.

Mr. Foy said that he considered that any correspondent for a legitimate news agency was entitled to accreditation whether or not he was from a country in the United Nations and regardless of political considerations.

NOTE

PRC pressure to eliminate UN contacts with or references to Taiwan proved successful in other respects, also. The Japanese press reported, for example:

> The Japanese government has reached a working decision not to accept new trainees from Taiwan to receive education at the four training institutes set up in Japan with financial assistance from the United Nations, Foreign Ministry sources disclosed over the weekend.
>
> A total of 10 trainees from Taiwan are currently accommodated at three of the four training institutes—the Asia and Far East Crime Prevention Institute, the International Seismological Engineering Institute and the Asia Statistical Institute—all in Tokyo.
>
> The sources said that these trainees will complete their scheduled courses in the first half of this year and return home, and after that, Japan will invite trainees from China, if that country so wishes.
>
> The propriety of giving trainees from Taiwan education at the four training institutes became questionable after the UN Development Program (UNDP) announced Friday that it was terminating technological aid to Nationalist China within three months at a request by Peking, because the institutes were established as part of the UNDP development assistance projects.[56]

Moreover, UN publications eliminated all statistical references to Taiwan or the Republic of China, and even a plaque presented to the UN by the ROC was removed.[57]

It is interesting to note the *Peking Review's* position on the UN decision regarding the representation of Cambodia following the successful coup d'état against Prince Sihanouk in March 1970. The PRC permitted Sihanouk to take up residence in China and recognized the revolutionary government that he purports to head (10–19).

> In disregard of the serious warning by Samdech Norodom Sihanouk, Head of State of Cambodia, UN Secretary-General U Thant openly declared on April 6 the recognition of the Rightist coup d'état clique, US imperialism's running dog, in Cambodia. This proves once again that the United Nations is nothing but a private tool at the beck and call of US imperialism to interfere in and commit aggression against other countries.

> In his cable of April 1 to U Thant, Cambodian Head of State Samdech Norodom Sihanouk pointed out that "the Secretary-General and the United Nations organization should refrain from recognizing the Lon Nol government and consequently from admitting into UNO the 'permanent representatives' or other delegations which would be 'accredited' or 'sent' by men of the March 18, 1970, coup d'état." However, acting on the instruction of US imperialism, U Thant not only refused to distribute among UN member states the copies of Samdech Norodom Sihanouk's cable, but even flagrantly gave official recognition to the Cambodian Rightist coup clique and its "representative" to the United Nations. This act of U Thant's can only indicate that he is an out-and-out faithful cat's paw who, under the cloak of a diplomat, works in the service of US imperialism. Everybody knows that it is US imperialism who [*sic*], after engineering the Cambodian reactionary coup d'état, was the first to recognize the Lon Nol-Sirik Matak regime and tried by all sorts of means to help the reactionary regime to stabilize its rule. Now U Thant has come out in the name of the United Nations to interfere in Cambodia. His aim is to have the United Nations play the role which US imperialism cannot, or fails to, do in this matter.
>
> U Thant alleged in his communiqué that "it is the normal policy of the Secretariat (of UNO) to deal with the authorities which are apparently in control of the government of a member state." This is sheer nonsense. Who are "the authorities which are in control of the government of a member state?" The present Phnom Penh authorities are a hundred per cent conspiratorial coup d'état clique fostered by US imperialism single-handed. It is not only opposed by the people of Cambodia, but also condemned by wide public opinion the world over. The act of the UN Secretariat is proof that it deliberately sets itself against the Cambodian people and defies world opinion.[58]

On August 25, 1972, Peking vetoed the application of Bangla Desh for membership in the UN.[59] This focused world attention upon the PRC's failure to apply the de facto control standard to UN admission, even in behalf of a state that had come into being by virtue of a revolutionary national liberation struggle. In seeking to explain its stand, the PRC made no explicit reference to the possible significance of the establishment of Bangla Desh as a precedent for the formation of an independent state of Taiwan. Yet this concern, as well as political considerations relating to South Asia, undoubtedly affected the PRC's position.

11-8

"Consideration of 'Bangla Desh's' Application for U.N. Membership Opposed," *PR* 15.33:12 (Aug. 18, 1972).

The United Nations Security Council held a meeting on August 10 afternoon to discuss the question of consideration of "Bangla Desh's" application for United Nations membership. In view of the difference of views, the council voted on whether or not the question was to be included in the agenda. The Chinese representative voted against it and the representatives of Guinea, Somalia, and the Sudan did not participate in the voting. The President of the Council declared at the end of the meeting that "Bangla Desh's" application will be referred to the Committee on the Admission of New Members.

Following is the full text of Chinese representative Huang Hua's speech:

The Chinese delegation firmly opposes the Security Council's consideration of "Bangla Desh's" application for membership in the United Nations under the present circumstances. The reason is quite obvious.

1. In the opinion of the Chinese delegation, the application of "Bangla Desh" for membership in the United Nations should in no way be considered in deviation from the relevant resolutions adopted by the United Nations General Assembly and the Security Council last year. As is known to all, on November 21 last year, the Indian government, with the active encouragement and energetic support of the Soviet social-imperialists, brazenly launched a large-scale war of aggression against Pakistan and seriously undermined the peace on the south Asian subcontinent. On December 7 last year, the United Nations General Assembly, breaking through the numerous obstacles raised by the Soviet Union and India, adopted Resolution 2793 (XXVI) with the overwhelming majority of 104 votes, the operative paragraph 1 of which explicitly "calls upon the governments of India and Pakistan to take forthwith all measures for an immediate cease-fire and withdrawal of their armed forces on the territory of the other to their own side of the India-Pakistan borders." Subsequently, on December 21, the Security Council adopted Resolution 307 (1971) with the great majority of 13 votes. Apart from reiterating the demand for troop withdrawal by the two parties, the resolution in its operative paragraph 3 "calls upon all those concerned to take all measures necessary to preserve human life and for the observance of the Geneva Conventions of 1949 and to apply in full their provisions as regards the protection of wounded and

sick, prisoners of war, and civilian population." The Geneva Convention of 1949 referred to in this connection stipulates in article 118 in explicit terms: "Prisoners of war shall be released and repatriated without delay after the cessation of active hostilities."

However, what is the actual state of affairs now? The actual state of affairs is: The Indian government has failed to withdraw all its troops to its own territory in accordance with the UN resolutions concerning troop withdrawal, and has been detaining over 90,000 Pakistan prisoners of war and civilians. "Bangla Desh" is even holding out threats for the trial of Pakistan prisoners of war. This constitutes a gross violation of the relevant resolutions of the UN General Assembly and the Security Council. At the same time, "Bangla Desh" is insisting on its recognition by Pakistan before it can agree to hold negotiations with the latter. This is simply to collude with India in blackmailing Pakistan and in continuing to obstruct the implementation of the relevant resolutions of the United Nations. This is indeed bullying others too much. We would ask: Whether or not Resolution 2793 (XXVI) adopted by the UN General Assembly with 104 votes and the Security Council Resolution 307 (1971) adopted with 13 votes remain valid? Obviously before the true implementation of the relevant UN resolutions and pending a reasonable settlement of the issues between India and Pakistan, and between Pakistan and "Bangla Desh," "Bangla Desh" is not qualified at all to be admitted into the United Nations, and the Security Council's consideration of "Bangla Desh's" application for membership in the United Nations is entirely out of the question. Otherwise, where will the United Nations Charter stand? Where will the relevant resolutions of the UN General Assembly and the Security Council stand? When one refuses to implement the relevant resolutions of the United Nations, how can he possibly speak of "accepting the obligations contained in the present Charter" and of being "able and willing to carry out these obligations?" This is indeed a sheer hoax and a gross mockery of the United Nations.

2. To put it bluntly, in resorting to such [an] unreasonable course of action, the Indian government and its behind-the-scenes supporter the Soviet social-imperialists are [aiming] at encouraging the aggressor through the instrumentality of the United Nations and continuing to maintain the tension on the south Asian subcontinent. A clear evidence is found in the report that after the Simla talks between India and Pakistan, the Indian Prime Minister Mrs. Indira Gandhi claimed that pending the "final settlement" of the Jammu and Kashmir dispute, she would not permit the repatriation of Pakistan prisoners of war. Approval of these acts of theirs would be tantamount to giving aid and abetment to evil-doings. Consequently, in defense of the principles of

the UN Charter and in the interests of the entire people of the south Asian subcontinent, it is essential to insist on the following: Only when the relevant UN resolutions have been truly implemented and only after a reasonable settlement of the issues between Indian and Pakistan and between Pakistan and "Bangla Desh" has been achieved, can the Security Council consider "Bangla Desh's" application for membership in the United Nations.

In view of the above reasons, the Chinese delegation firmly opposes the Security Council's consideration of the application of "Bangla Desh" for membership in the United Nations.

NOTE

In December 1971, while the Indo-Pakistani war over Bangla Desh was raging, the PRC had also opposed efforts to invite representatives of Bangla Desh to relevant UN Security Council meetings. The reasons stated by Ambassador Huang Hua offer broader insight into Peking's view of the problem:

> At our meeting, the Soviet and Indian representatives have repeatedly tried to sell to us their stuff of the so-called "Bangla Desh." They wanted us to join them in inviting to our meeting the representatives of the so-called "Bangla Desh" with red-carpet honours. What kind of thing is the "Bangla Desh" which the Soviet and Indian representatives have lauded so much? I think it will be useful to recall history in this respect, for there is no lack of similar instances in history.
>
> In 1931, the Japanese militarists launched an undeclared war against China and occupied the three provinces of northeast China. Subsequently, they declared the establishment of a puppet government called "Manchukuo." The leader of that government was none other than a traitor who had been reared over a long period by the Japanese militarists. In so doing, the aim of the Japanese militarists was to split China and perpetuate their occupation of the three provinces of northeast China. After its establishment, that puppet government won the recognition of the Japanese militarists, Hitler of Germany and Mussolini of Italy. And what did the League of Nations do about the Japanese aggression against China? Under the manipulation of certain powers, the League of Nations tried to curry favour with Japanese militarism at the expense of China's territory and sovereignty, so as to direct the Japanese militarists' spearhead of aggression to the then Soviet Union. Consequently, the League of Nations did nothing in face of Japanese aggression and let them have their own way. It

was precisely under these circumstances that Japanese militarism further expanded its war of aggression against China, occupying large expanses of China's territory. This greatly inflated the Japanese imperialists' ambitious design for world hegemony, and at the same time abetted the German and Italian facists in their aggression and expansion in Europe. All this finally led to the outbreak of World War II. The events thereafter are well known to everyone present here. World War II brought untold disaster and devastation to the people of various countries.

Japanese militarism created the government of a so-called "Manchukuo" in China; the German Nazis fostered quisling governments in Europe as well. However, the development of history is independent of man's will. Today where has that so-called "Manchukuo" gone? Where are those quisling governments? What has happened to their creators? The "grandiose" plans of the Japanese militarists and Hitlerite and Mussolini fascists for world domination went bankrupt. They were severely punished by the people of various countries. These historical facts are perhaps known even to the schoolboys, but the "erudite" Mr. Malik and the Indian ambassador seem to be ignorant of them.

Now after launching an undeclared war of aggression against Pakistan with the incitement and support of the Soviet Union, the Indian expansionists, with the collaboration of the Soviet government, created a government of the so-called "Bangla Desh" for the purpose of dismembering Pakistan and perpetually occupying East Pakistan. That is a neo-quisling government, a neo-"Manchukuo" government. The Indian government has already openly declared its recognition of that "government." Probably, the Soviet government will also declare its recognition of that "government" tomorrow or the day after tomorrow! Whether recognition or not, what people have now seen is that not only has the Soviet government failed to condemn this neo-quisling government, neo-"Manchukuo" government, but the Soviet representative has shown most solicitous concern and wanted to invite the representatives of that "government" to the Security Council as angels and pay homage to the representatives of the so-called "Bangla Desh" as "heroes" of a national-liberation movement and even wanted others also to take off their hats and salute them.[60]

For further light on the PRC's views concerning admission to UN membership, see items 37–1 and 37–2. For the PRC's views on the 1971 Indo-Pakistan conflict, see item 38–14 and Notes preceding and following.

The PRC has on a number of occasions referred to the legal consequences of its exclusion from the UN. Recall that in his cablegram to the UN Secretary-General dated September 18, 1950 (11–2), Chou En-lai, then Foreign Minister of the PRC, declared that, should the fifth session of the General Assembly be held without the participation of his government's delegation, all the resolutions of the General Assembly concerning China would be illegal, null and void. Similarly, a cablegram from Chou to the UN Secretary-General, dated February 3, 1955, stated that "it must be pointed out that without the representative of the People's Republic of China participating in the name of China in the discussions of the United Nations Security Council, all decisions taken in the Security Council on questions concerning China would be illegal and null and void." [61]

In 1950 Wu Hsiu-ch'üan, the PRC's delegate to the UN for the discussion of the "invasion of Taiwan" case, went even further. Before the Security Council on November 28, 1950, he stated that "so long as the United Nations persists in denying admittance to a permanent member of the Security Council representing 475 million people, it cannot make lawful decisions on any major issues or solve any major problems, particularly those which concern Asia. . . . Without the participation of the lawful representatives of the People's Republic of China, the people of China have no reason to recognize any resolutions or decisions of the United Nations." [62]

Premier Chou En-lai stated, in his 1955 report to the Standing Committee of the National People's Congress on the Asian-African (Bandung) Conference, that: "Many United Nations' resolutions were adopted under the manipulation of the United States, and at the same time the Chinese People's Republic has been deprived of its legitimate place in the United Nations. Therefore, we undertake no obligations towards the resolutions of the United Nations." [63] And in a statement issued on December 12, 1963 a spokesman of the PRC's Foreign Ministry announced that:

> Before China's legitimate rights are restored, the Chinese government considers all activities of the elements of the Chiang Kai-shek clique in the United Nations as illegal, and China cannot be held responsible for any activities of the United Nations. In these circumstances, each action of the United Nations will be judged by China on its intrinsic merits. China will resolutely oppose all evil doing of the United Nations, but will have no objection to the good things, if any, done by the United Nations.[64]

Despite the claim of Chou Keng-sheng (11–3) that any revision of the UN Charter would be illegal without the PRC's consent as a permanent member of the Security Council, the Charter was actually amended on December 17, 1963, to accommodate the widely felt need to enlarge the membership of both the Security Council and the Economic and Social Council.[65] Prior to this action the representative of the Soviet Union, Mr. Fedorenko, stated before the Assembly's Special Political Committee on December 10, 1963, that his government favored increasing the membership of those organs. But he also asserted that an amendment of the Charter would be invalid and unlawful without the approval of all five permanent members of the Security Council, and that such approval could not be obtained until the lawful rights of the PRC in the United Nations were restored. He then explained the PRC's position as follows:

> The Soviet government had consulted the government of the People's Republic of China. . . . The latter government had replied that, since China was still barred from participation in the Organization's work, it would make no commitments on any amendments of the Charter relating to the total number of seats in the principal United Nations organs, and that agreement on its part to revision of the Charter while the Chiang Kai-shek representative was present in the United Nations might lead to the creation of a "two-China situation." The government of the People's Republic of China had thus made it plain that it did not approve of any attempt to settle the question of equitable representation by increasing the membership of the organs in question, and that it favored instead an equitable distribution of the existing seats in those organs.[66]

The Soviet explanation of the Chinese Communist position drew a sharp rebuttal from Peking. In its previously quoted statement of December 12, 1963, the Foreign Ministry claimed that it favored increasing Asian and African membership in the United Nations organs either by expanding these organs or by redistributing the existing seats. Although the statement rejected the idea that this issue should be linked to the Chinese representation question, it somewhat equivocally concluded that, while the People's Republic of China "continues to be excluded from the United Nations, China will undertake no commitment on the question of revision of these articles by the United Nations."[67] It further stated that Foreign Minister Ch'en Yi had already made a statement in this vein on October 2, 1963, and that the Chinese government had repeatedly so notified the Soviet authorities, on October 4, December 5 and 8, 1963.[68]

In spite of this blunt official rebuttal, the representative of the

Soviet Union nevertheless insisted on his own interpretation of the Communist Chinese position and voted against the Charter amendments on the grounds of the Chinese representation question.[69]

An editorial in the *People's Daily* on December 18, 1963, severely criticized the Soviet position as follows:

> We must express our greatest regret at the improper tactics employed by the Soviet delegate over this issue. Using as a pretext his allegation that China opposed an expansion of UN organs, the Soviet delegate refused to support the resolutions for broader Afro-Asian representation in the Security Council and in the Economic and Social Council. Even after the spokesman of the Chinese Foreign Ministry in a statement on December 12 gave a comprehensive and clear-cut explanation of the position of the Chinese government, he still stuck to his misrepresentation of the Chinese position in an attempt to apologize for the action of the Soviet Union. This showed that the Soviet delegate was maneuvering for ulterior motives.[70]

11-9

"Text of Letter to UN Secretary-General Kurt Waldheim from the Permanent Representative of the People's Republic of China, Huang Hua (February 20, 1972)," in *International Legal Materials,* 11.3:652 (May 1972).

Your Excellency:

I have the honour to inform Your Excellency that the Chinese government has received the Secretary-General's letter of January 6, 1972, to the Acting Minister of Foreign Affairs of the People's Republic of China on the contribution due from China to the United Nations budget for the year 1972. I am now instructed by my government to pay to you three million US dollars ($3,000,000), a portion of China's contribution due to the United Nations for the year 1972. Enclosed herewith is a check for the above sum, of which you are kindly requested to acknowledge the receipt. The remainder of China's contribution due for the current year will be paid in a second instalment.

With regard to the question of membership dues, the Chinese government deems it necessary to state as follows: Certain expenditures listed in the UN budget for the year 1972, e.g., the bonds issued for the "UN peace-keeping operations in the Congo" and the "UN Emergency force in the Middle East" as well as the expenditures for the "UN Memorial Cemetery in Korea" and the "UN Commission for the

Unification and Rehabilitation of Korea," etc. are items which constitute a violation of the purposes and principles of the UN Charter or are hostile to the Chinese people. The Chinese government does not recognize the above expenditures and refuses to pay any sum incurred from these operations. As to other items in the UN budget which are in contravention of the purposes and principles of the United Nations Charter, we reserve the right for further statements and actions.

NOTE

Two months later Wang Jun-sheng, PRC representative on a committee of the UN Economic and Social Council, spelled out Peking's position concerning UN resolutions adopted during the 26 years prior to its entry: "Resolutions adopted by the ECOSOC and other UN bodies during this period have no binding force whatsoever on the People's Republic of China," he said. "The Chiang Kai-shek clique's signature or ratification of certain conventions by usurping the name of China are [*sic*] illegal and null and void."[71] See also items 30–5 and 39–1.

Although in 1950 and 1951 the PRC sent a barrage of cablegrams requesting representation in other UN organs, specialized agencies, and intergovernmental organizations, its efforts were generally unsuccessful. In 1952 the PRC began to adopt a more indifferent attitude, at least insofar as direct efforts to obtain representation in most public international organizations were concerned. For example, when the ROC withdrew from the International Civil Aviation Organization (ICAO) in 1953, the PRC made no attempt to join that agency; nor did the PRC register a protest when the ROC rejoined ICAO in 1956. The PRC's brief experience as a participant in the Universal Postal Union (UPU) in 1950–1951 may have been a factor that contributed to this change in attitude.

11-10

"Chinese People's Postal Administration Accepts Universal Postal Convention," NCNA–English, Peking (Dec. 5, 1950), in *SCMP*, no. 24:5 (Dec. 6, 1950).

Su Yu-nung, Director General of the General Post Office of the People's Republic of China, today sent the following telegram to Dr. Fritz Hess, Director of the International Bureau of the Universal Postal Union in Berne. It reads:

On the order of the Central People's Government of the People's Republic of China, I inform you in this telegram that the Chinese People's Postal Administration accepts, as from today, the Universal Postal Convention, the arrangement for postal remittance, the arrangement for letters and boxes with declared value, the arrangement for postal parcels, and the arrangement for consignment against reimbursement as well as their respective annexes, concluded in Paris in 1947. The services of postal parcels, and the consignment against reimbursement are to be temporarily suspended. Requesting you to take note of the aforementioned, and communicate it to the parties concerned.

11-11

"Delegation Headed by Su Yu-nung to UPU Session Recognized as Only Legal Delegation of China," NCNA–English, Peking (Feb. 6, 1951), in *SCMP*, no. 63:16–17 (Feb. 5–8, 1951).

Su Yu-nung, head of the delegation of the Chinese People's Republic to the Joint Commission of the Universal Postal Union and the International Transport Association, addressed the January 25 Session of the Joint Commission denouncing the American delegates for barring the admission of China's delegation, says a Cairo report.

The statement gained the support of the delegates of the USSR and Czechoslovakia. The Commission, after a debate, recognized the delegation headed by Su Yu-nung as the only legal delegation of China for the Session. The so-called "delegation" of the remnant Kuomintang reactionary clique were expelled from the hall. The American design thus failed to materialize.

Denouncing the American intrigue, Su Yu-nung said, "This event is another proof that the representatives of a handful of American monopolists, who insist on being hostile to the 475 million Chinese people, are obstinately trying to prevent the People's Republic of China from taking its legitimate place in international organizations and to hinder the cooperation between the People's Republic of China and the above-mentioned organizations, even in such a purely technical organization like the UPU in which the question of the representation of the People's Republic of China has already been settled."

"Before the Montreux Session, Foreign Minister Chou En-lai of the People's Republic of China had declared that the Central People's Government of the People's Republic of China was the only legal government representing the Chinese people, and that the so-called 'delegates' of the Kuomintang reactionary clique were no longer qualified to participate in any important meeting of the UPU, and should be expelled from the union. This fact and this reasonable demand have been fully recognized by the resolution of the Montreux Session and confirmed by the fact of the invitation of the representatives of the People's Republic of China and by the immediate exclusion of the remnant Kuomintang reactionary clique. After the Montreux Session, the Postal Administration of the People's Republic of China, at the request of the International Bureau of the UPU and with the ratification of the Central People's Government of the People's Republic of China, accepted the invitation of the universal postal convention. This fact further affirmed the relations between the People's Republic of China and the UPU."

Su Yu-nung denounced the UN resolution of December 14, 1950, on which the American delegates based their argument, and declared "As for the resolution concerning the representation of the member nations adopted by the UN on December 14, 1950, it is itself illegal because it violates the arrangement provided for by the UN Charter which was based on the principle of freedom and political independence of all the nations. The said resolution is in fact the outcome of the illegal manipulation of the American delegation. Therefore it is null and void. Moreover, it was illegally adopted without the participation of the representative of the People's Republic of China, and after the official establishment of relations between the People's Republic of China and the UPU. Our Commission has nothing to do with this resolution, and should never be influenced by these political intrigues."

Su Yu-nung concluded by declaring, "The delegation of the People's Republic of China insists that no so-called question of representation of China exists, and that the representative of the People's Republic of China is the only representative qualified to represent China at this Session and all other Sessions of the UPU."

11-12

"Chinese Postal Administration Registers Strong Protest with UPU against Tricks to Oust People's China," NCNA–English, Peking (May 13, 1951), in *SCMP*, no. 104:18–19 (May 11–15, 1951).

A strong protest was lodged with the Universal Postal Union today by Su Yu-nung, director-general of the General Postal Administration of the People's Republic of China, against the attempt to deprive the People's Republic of China of its legal status in the UPU. The protest reads in full as follows:

Dr. Hess, Secretary-General of the Executive and Liaison Commission of the Universal Postal Union, for transmission to all the member nations of the union.

The Central People's Government of the People's Republic of China is the sole legal government representing the Chinese people. The so-called representative of the remnant reactionary Kuomintang clique is not qualified to participate in any international organization or conference including the UPU. As China's only qualified legal delegate, the representative of the General Postal Administration of the People's Republic of China officially participated in the meeting of the Executive and Liaison Commission of the UPU which took place in Montreux in May 1950, and also officially participated in the joint meeting of the Executive and Liaison Commission of the UPU and the International Air Transport Association in Cairo in January and February this year. On the invitation of the UPU, the General Postal Administration of the People's Republic of China accepted on December 5, 1950, the Universal Postal Convention and established regular relations regarding postal business with the Union. These facts of long standing fully prove that the representative of the General Postal Administration of the People's Republic of China is the sole legal representative of China to the UPU. The fact that the so-called representative of the remnant reactionary Kuomintang clique was twice expelled after this was put to the vote and passed by the meetings in Montreux, May 1950, and in Cairo, January 1951, further completely proves that the question of the representation of the remnant reactionary Kuomintang clique no longer exists in the UPU.

However, under the coercion and domination of the United States government, the International Bureau of the UPU ignored the fact of the legal representation of the General Postal Administration of the People's Republic of China by issuing a circular letter on March 8 this year, mentioning the so-called Postal Administration of the remnant reactionary Kuomintang clique on the same footing as the General Postal Administration of the People's Republic of China and consulting the opinions of the Postal Administrations of the member nations on the question of China's representation in the UPU, sternly protesting against this unjustified and absurd action and pointing out that this is a self-contradictory action on the part of the UPU which seriously injures its existent relations with the People's Republic of China and that we can never agree to this.

According to the communication of the UPU on April 21, this year, the result of the consultation was that, among the 86 member nations, 33, including the United States of America and its satellites, supported the remnant reactionary Kuomintang clique, 23 were in favor of my country, while the rest either abstained or gave no answer. The UPU attempts, on the basis of such an absurd, unreasonable, and illegal consultation, to deprive the 475 million Chinese people of their established legitimate right in the UPU. This can never be accepted by the Postal Authority of the People's Republic of China and must be firmly opposed. In fact, even the result of this illegal consultation reveals that the nations following the United States of America are small in number and represent no more than one-fifth of the world population, while 53 nations are not against the legal status of the representative of my country in the UPU.

I am hereby authorized by the Postal Authority of the People's Republic of China to lodge a serious protest with the UPU and to make the following statement: The General Postal Administration of the People's Republic of China is the sole legal postal authority to represent China in the UPU. It is impermissible for the UPU to ignore or deny its established legal status through proceeding with such an illegal consultation. The result of this consultation of the UPU is not only illegal but also invalid. The attempt of the United States of America and its satellites to resort to their usual tricks of manipulation in the UNO to threaten and coerce the UPU into undermining the relations between the UPU and the People's Republic of China is another manifestation of their undermining of international collaboration. We are firmly convinced that this mean action of the government of the United States of America will certainly arouse the opposition of the peoples of the world. Because of its contradictory, perfidious actions in obeying the will of the United States government and illegally attempting to deprive the People's Republic of China of its legal status in the UPU, the UPU will inevitably suffer serious and irreparable loss of international prestige.

Su Yu-nung Director-General of the General Postal Administration of the People's Republic of China. May 13, 1951, Peking.

11-13

"Su Yu-nung Protests against UPU Illegal Action in Not Inviting China to St. Gall Meeting," NCNA–English, Peking (May 20, 1951), in *SCMP*, no. 106:19–20 (May 21–23, 1951).

Su Yu-nung, Director-General of the General Postal Administration, made a statement today strongly protesting against the Universal Postal Union for not inviting the representative of the General Postal Administration of the People's Republic of China to attend the meeting of the UPU Executive and Liaison Commission to be held in St. Gall, Switzerland, on May 21.

His telegram addressed to Dr. Hess, Secretary-General of the UPU Executive and Liaison Commission, states:

> The General Postal Administration of the People's Republic of China is the sole legal postal authority of China. The UPU has the obligatory duty to invite the General Postal Administration of my country to participate in this meeting. All decisions made by all meetings, including the present St. Gall meeting, which do not have the participation and agreement of the representative of the postal authority of the People's Republic of China, or which have the participation of the illegal representative of the remnant reactionary Kuomintang clique, will be illegal and consequently invalid.

NOTE

In the mid-1950's the PRC did demonstrate interest in participating in certain international scientific organizations, as the next two items suggest.

11-14

"Chou En-lai Demands Expulsion of Chiang Clique from Meteorological Organization," NCNA–English, Peking (April 12, 1955), in *SCMP*, no. 1026:17–18 (April 11–13, 1955).

Foreign Minister Chou En-lai today sent a message of protest to G. Swoboda, Acting Secretary-General of the World Meteorological Organization, for transmission to the President of the Second World Meteorological Congress. The message protests against the organization's illegal recognition of the so-called ratification of its convention by the traitorous Chiang Kai-shek clique and its permission for the clique to usurp the position representing China.

The message reads:

> The Government of the People's Republic of China is the sole legal government representing the 600 million Chinese people, and it alone is qualified to participate in the World Meteorological Organization on behalf of China. The traitorous Chiang Kai-shek clique repudiated long ago by the Chinese people has no qualification whatsoever to participate in the World Meteorological Organization. Therefore, as early as May 12, 1950, I on behalf

of the Government of the People's Republic of China informed Mr. G. Swoboda that the delegates of the traitorous Chiang Kai-shek clique must be driven out from all the organs and meetings of the World Meteorological Organization. Moreover, on January 26 and February 6, 1955, Director Tu Chang-wang of the Meteorological Office of the People's Republic of China upon instructions twice cabled Mr. G. Swoboda demanding that the World Meteorological Organization immediately expel the delegates of the traitorous Chiang Kai-shek clique so that the representatives of the People's Republic of China might participate in it. But up to now the World Meteorological organization still illegally recognizes the so-called ratification of the convention of the World Meteorological Organization by the traitorous Chiang Kai-shek clique and allows the traitorous Chiang Kai-shek clique to usurp the position representing China, so that the legitimate position and right of the People's Republic of China in the World Meteorological Organization cannot be restored. Regarding this situation, I hereby raise a protest on behalf of the government of the People's Republic of China.

In order to carry out the purposes of the World Meteorological Organization as specified in its convention and to promote international cooperation in meteorological work, it is imperative that the Second World Meteorological Congress expel the delegates of the traitorous Chiang Kai-shek clique from all the organs and meetings of the World Meteorological Organization so that the representatives of the People's Republic of China may participate in them.

Please circulate the text of this cable to all the delegations to the Second World Meteorological Congress with the exception of the delegates of the traitorous Chiang Kai-shek clique.

11-15

Walter Sullivan, "The International Geophysical Year," *International Conciliation* 521:284–294 (Jan. 1959). (Notes omitted.)

The crisis that marred final preparations for the IGY [International Geophysical Year] concerned the participation of the world's most populous nation—the Chinese People's Republic.

On 12 September 1955, Dr. Chapman, as president of CSAGI [Comité Spécial de l'Année Géophysique Internationale] reported to the CSAGI conference in Brussels on an exchange of telegrams with the Academia Sinica, in Peking, which had built a world-wide reputation for scholarship. The Chinese, he announced, had begun to form an IGY committee headed by Dr. Chu Cho-ching, vice-president of the Academia.

The message from Peking said that participation of the Chinese People's Republic was conditional on nonacceptance of the Chinese Nationalists as participants. This did not appear to be an obstacle since, three years after the initial invitation to participate in the IGY, no response had been received from Taiwan (Formosa).

Following the lead of the Soviet Union, the Chinese People's Republic used the IGY as justification for manifold expansion of its observatories in the fields of weather, geomagnetism, and earthquakes. A list of IGY stations around the world, issued by CSAGI as of 24 March 1957, showed some 27 planned observation posts on the Chinese mainland, ranging from the coastal cities to Lhasa, in Tibet, and Urumchi (Tihwa), in Sinkiang.

A delegation of scientists from Peking took part in the IGY regional conference for Eastern Europe and Asia, held in Moscow from 20 to 25 August 1956. The following month, science closed an eye to politics when delegations from mainland China and the USSR went to Spain, for the CSAGI conference in Barcelona.

About three months later a letter dated 1 November 1956 was received by Dr. Marcel Nicolet, as secretary-general of CSAGI, from Dr. Chu Chia-hua, who identified himself as president of the Academia Sinica. The letter was postmarked Taipei, Taiwan. Thus there were two rival Academia Sinicas, represented by two Dr. Chus—one in Peking and one in Taipei. The latter, in his letter, noted that the Republic of China (on Taiwan) was a member of ICSU [International Council of Scientific Unions] and protested the admittance to the Barcelona conference of "three agents" from the Chinese People's Republic. He said scientists in Taiwan were willing to cooperate in the IGY effort, but demanded deletion of the People's Republic of China from the official list of IGY participants.

Some of the IGY leaders expressed concern at this letter, since they felt that the Chinese Nationalists, having ignored the IGY for more than four years, had been induced to apply only by the news that the Chinese Communists were taking part. Every effort had been made to keep politics out of the IGY and, in the various preparatory conferences, the many political rivals in attendance had assiduously stuck to science. The letter from Taiwan raised an issue which, it was feared, might open a Pandora's box of East-West hostility. The ensuing controversy could wreck the IGY.

Meanwhile, on 18 February, a message reached Brussels from Peking as follows:

> Learned CSAGI intends admit Taiwan to IGY. This directly violates our previous understanding. China will join IGY only on condition Taiwan should not be admitted. Otherwise China will withdraw from IGY.
>
> Chu Choching, Chairman CN IGY.

In a letter to Dr. Nicolet dated 8 April, and one to Dr. Chapman two days later, he rejected their compromise plan.

> We realize [Dr. Chu wrote] that the IGY will accept all bona fide participants to the enterprise it has launched, irrespective of their political creeds; but is it not true that a man of science, as well as a person in any other profession, cannot very well disregard the national consciousness of his own countrymen? We Chinese are very apprehensive of the effort certain powers are making to create two Chinas to the detriment of their fatherland. The Chinese on the continent, and among them the Chinese scientists, therefore will recognize only one Chinese nation, i.e., the People's Republic of China, in existence in any international dealings and enterprises. We do not object [to] scientists from Taiwan coming to the IGY gatherings . . . as long as they agree to this stipulation, implicitly or explicitly.

He described the late adherence of Taiwan as a political move, "for they knew fully well that we would walk out as soon as they were officially admitted."

He argued that the splitting of Germany could not be compared to the Chinese situation, for Germany had been divided on the basis of international agreements growing out of World War II, while "in 1949 the Chinese people overthrew the old corrupt regime and established their own government. It is only owing to foreign intervention that there is the present temporary abnormal situation of Taiwan." Any qualified Chinese geophysicist would be welcomed as a member of the Chinese National Committee, he added, whether or not he resided on the mainland.

He noted that scientists from Peking had already taken part in three IGY conferences and had considerably enlarged their observation network, as requested by various conference resolutions. In a separate letter, on 8 April, Dr. Chu said that Peking would contribute to the CSAGI budget $7,500 in gold for each of the next three years.

No more IGY conferences involving the Chinese were scheduled before the start of the Year, and the Bureau had begun to hope that a showdown could be avoided. However, in his letter to Dr. Nicolet, Dr. Chu said flatly that Peking would take part in the IGY only "on condition . . . that there should not be two National Committees of China."

This proved to be the insurmountable difficulty, for all the Bureau members, with the possible exception of Dr. Beloussov, agreed that acceptance of Taiwan could no longer be deferred.

The CSAGI Bureau, meeting in Uccle from 16 to 19 June 1957, decided to make one final attempt. Taiwan was quietly accepted, but at the same time it was announced to all IGY participants—without any stated reference to the Chinese problem—that henceforth no IGY committees would be listed in CSAGI documents as "national." Letters explaining the situation were sent to Taiwan and Peking. Dr. Chapman, writing on 17 June, thanked the Peking Dr. Chu for his letter of 10 April and explained that a reply had been delayed until the Bureau could meet and discuss the problems that it had raised and that arose from a letter from Taiwan.

> As regards Chinese IGY participation, the Bureau has decided to include, in the list of participating IGY committees, two consecutive entries as follows:
>
> Chinese IGY Committee: Peking
> Chinese IGY Committee: Taipei
>
> The General Secretary will try to avoid the use of the word national in specific references to these two committees. He will also try to ensure that the same practice will be followed by the many others who in some official capacity may have occasion to refer to them. On your own documents the title of your committee is a matter for your own choice. In view of your references, which I was glad to see, to the IGY participation of overseas Chinese geophysicists, I sincerely hope that you will at least tacitly accept this course of action.

On 29 June, eve of the IGY, a cablegram arrived from the Peking Dr. Chu stating that Taiwan was an integral part of China and could not take part as a country separate from the People's Republic of China. He demanded that CSAGI revoke its acceptance of Taiwan; until such action was taken, Peking was withdrawing from CSAGI and all its activities.

Thus when the IGY began, at midnight the following day, the nation whose area ranks third in the world was officially not a participant. Nevertheless, China seems to have carried out all or most of the program originally planned. Satellite-tracking stations were set up across the country from Sinkiang to the coast. The new observatories went to work and, according to Chinese press reports, the number of people working in the geophysical sciences was expanded from 40—most of them weathermen—to 10,000. The roster of weather stations grew more than 20-fold to a total of 1,000. Geomagnetic and seismic networks were established and an oceanographic research vessel fitted out. While the Chinese were obviously feeding their satellite observations into Moscow, it was not clear to what extent their general geophysical data would be made available to the world.

Dr. Pushkov, one of the two Soviet members of CSAGI, wrote Dr. Chapman in February 1958, reporting that data from China was not being received at the Soviet World Data Center. He proposed that the question of Chinese representation be settled by a secret vote in the IGY Advisory Council, which was due to meet in Moscow during the summer of 1958.

Actually, according to some of those who attended the Advisory Council meetings in Moscow, the question of participation of mainland China was never discussed, though why the matter was dropped is not clear. Thus, when the IGY came to an end, the Chinese People's Republic was still not a member, the one nation among 67 to withdraw. It was the only case in which the IGY was significantly affected by political considerations.

NOTE

Following the 1971 resolution of the UN General Assembly to invite the PRC to replace the ROC as the representative of China "at the United Nations and in all the organizations affiliated with it," [72] the UN Secretary-General cabled the text of that resolution to the executive heads of all the organizations of the UN system and requested them to keep him informed of any relevant action taken by their respective organizations. He also drew their attention to General Assembly Resolution 396 (V), of 1950, in which the Assembly had recommended "that the attitude adopted by the General Assembly . . . concerning any such question [of the UN representation of a member state] should be taken into account in other organs of the United Nations and in the Specialized Agencies." [73]

As one of the specialized agencies, in early 1972 the Universal Postal Union (recall items 11–10 to 11–13) asked its member states to vote on whether the General Assembly resolution replacing the ROC with the PRC should be applied to the UPU. Of the members, 66 voted "yes," 11 voted "no," 5 expressly abstained, and 64 were deemed to have abstained because they had not responded by the required date, April 12, 1972. Accordingly, the UPU invited the PRC immediately to replace the ROC.[74] The World Meteorological Organization (recall item 11–14) took similar action, as did ICAO, UNESCO, the International Atomic Energy Agency, the International Labor Organization, the Inter-Governmental Maritime Consultative Organization, and the World Health Organization.

The Food and Agricultural Organization, in which the state of China was not a member because of the ROC's withdrawal in 1951, voted to invite the PRC to take up membership. The General Agreement on Tariffs and Trade, which, although not a UN specialized agency, follows UN decisions on political matters, stripped the ROC of its observer status but has as yet received no application for membership or observer status from the PRC.[75] By July 1973 the withdrawal of the ROC from other specialized agencies except the International Bank for Reconstruction and Development, the International Monetary Fund, the International Development Association and the International Finance Corporation had considerably eased the problem, although the PRC had not yet begun to participate in all of these agencies.

The PRC has, of course, participated in certain Communist international organizations. Some of these have been interstate organizations, while others have been interparty organizations. Activities of both types will be dealt with in Part IX.

Although until recently the PRC was more successful in placing representatives in private (nongovernmental) international organizations than in public ones, its self-imposed political strictures tended to limit the participation of those representatives. Item 11–16 is only one example of numerous instances in which PRC groups have withdrawn from organizations, such as the International Lawn Tennis Federation,[76] which acted on the basis of a "two China" policy. Item 11–17 illustrates what purports to be a PRC delegation's limitation of its participation on political grounds.

11-16

"Firm Opposition to 'Two Chinas' Plot," *PR* 3.32:24–25 (Aug. 9, 1960).

China's Political Science and Law Association has decided to withdraw from the International Law Association and sever all relations with it. This is because the latter, under manipulation of certain of its leaders and ignoring the will of just-minded lawyers of the world, persists in toeing the line of US imperialism and repeatedly engages in conspiratorial activities directed toward the creation of "two Chinas," encroachment on China's sovereignty, and interference in China's internal affairs.

In one of its circulars in May of this year, the International Law Association attempted to put the Chiang Kai-shek clique, long repudiated by the Chinese people, on a par with the People's Republic of China and create a "two Chinas" situation in this organization by listing the "Republic of China" under the heading "visas." Earlier in February, another circular preposterously described the Tibet Region of China as "a country."

In a letter to the International Law Association in June, the Chinese Political Science and Law Association seriously protested against these actions which are contrary to the fundamental principles of international law and constitute a flagrant provocation against the Chinese people. It demanded that these mistakes be corrected and [that] assurance against recurrence of similar incidents be given.

The letter declared:

"There is only one China in the world, that is the People's Republic of China. Taiwan is China's territory. US imperialists have seized Taiwan by armed force, and, in order to legalize their seizure, are now plotting with redoubled effort to create 'two Chinas' and are vainly attempting, in international activities, to counter the People's Republic of China with the Chiang Kai-shek clique which has long been repudiated by the Chinese people."

It further pointed out: "Tibet is an inalienable part of China's territory. The Tibetan people is a member of the large family of the Chinese people. The wild conspiracy of the imperialists and foreign interventionists to create an 'independent Tibet' and interfere in China's internal affairs has already been smashed by the Chinese people, including the Tibetan people. Yet now the International Law Association still vainly attempts to turn Tibet into an independent country. This not only shows that the International Law Association lacks even the most rudimentary knowledge, but fully reveals that it is bent on following the imperialists' scheme of interfering in the internal affairs of China."

However, the International Law Association, on the pretext that it was "a nonpolitical body," refused the just demand of the Chinese association. As the Chinese association pointed out, this refusal proves that far from being "nonpolitical," certain leaders of the International Law Association in fact are merely stubbornly persisting in their political stand of [following] US imperialism. The Chinese association declared that while ready to enter into friendly cooperation with lawyers of other countries, it will absolutely not allow anyone to take advantage of this to encroach upon China's sovereignty and interfere in its internal affairs.

11-17

"Chinese Red Cross Society Decides Not to Attend The Hague Meetings," *PR* 10.38:39–40 (Sept. 15, 1967).

The Red Cross Society of China issued a statement on August 24 announcing its decision not to attend the 29th session of the Board of Governors of the League of Red Cross Societies and the meeting of the Council of Delegates scheduled to be held at The Hague on September 5, and that it would no longer continue as a member of the Executive Committee of the League of Red Cross Societies. The statement strongly condemned some of the leaders of the International Red Cross for consistently following US imperialism, [for] performing services for the latter's hostile plot against the Chinese people and to create "two Chinas," and for aiding aggression against Vietnam.

The statement pointed out that some of the leaders of the International Red Cross, complying with the wishes of US imperialism while disregarding repeated protests from the Chinese Red Cross Society, had smuggled into the 20th International Red Cross Conference elements of the Chiang Kai-shek gang, who had been repudiated by the Chinese people, and staged a "two Chinas" farce. The statement reiterated that "the Government of the People's Republic of China is the only legitimate government representing the Chinese people, and the Red Cross Society of China is the only national Red Cross organization recognized by the government of the People's Republic of China. Only the government of the People's Republic of China and the Red Cross Society of China have the right to attend International Red Cross conferences. Should US imperialism and its followers dare to use the agenda of The Hague meetings to make any scheme aimed at continuing to create 'two Chinas' at the forthcoming International Red Cross conferences, they would be held responsible for all the consequences arising therefrom."

The statement cited facts denouncing some of the leaders of the International Red Cross for having become tools serving US imperialist aggression against Vietnam and accomplices in suppressing the just struggle of the Vietnamese people. The Red Cross of Soviet revisionism had also taken an active part in the plots of the leaders of the International Red Cross and had worked hand in glove with US imperialism, betraying the interests of the Vietnamese people.

The statement declared that, in the absence of its delegation, the Chinese Red Cross Society would in no way be committed to, or undertake any responsibility for, any resolution adopted at the 29th session of the Board of Governors or at the meeting of the Council of Delegates.

NOTE

The PRC did not, however, withdraw from the International Committee of the Red Cross (ICRC) or from the International League of Red Cross Societies.[77] Nevertheless, it rejected participation in the 21st International Conference of the Red Cross, held in Istanbul in September 1969, because the list of conference members included "the Chiang Kai-shek bandit gang . . . and its so-called 'Red Cross organization.' "[78] This did not prevent the Chinese Red Cross from cooperating with the League of Red Cross Societies in 1970, when the PRC proved to be the second largest contributor of aid to Peruvian earthquake victims.[79] On the other hand, even though the ICRC was careful not to invite the Republic of China to participate in a conference of thirty-nine governments that was held in Geneva in the spring of 1971 to consider revisions of the 1949 Geneva Conventions relating to protection of prisoners of war and civilians, Peking refused to attend.[80] In 1972 it refused to attend a similar ICRC meeting, but it did attend the following meeting in January 1973. In 1971 the PRC Red Cross Society also protested against the League of Red Cross Societies' invitation to "the 'red cross societies' of the Saigon Nguyen Van Thieu puppet clique and the Phnom Penh Lon Nol-Sirik Matak puppet clique" to attend the 31st session of the Board of Governors of the League.[81]

Claims to Territory

PART IV

Part III illustrated the PRC's invocation of legal principles to foster acceptance of its identity as the legitimate government of China. Part IV deals with the PRC's invocation of legal principles to foster acceptance of its definition of China's identity.

Because a government's political power is based upon its ability to order activity within a given area and because international society is organized along territorial principles that generally recognize a state's claim to exclusive formal authority within its territory, the governments of all states regard the definition of state territory as a matter of great importance. This was true of China even long before it became acquainted with Western principles of international law.

As early as the eighth century B.C. the feudal states of the pre-imperial Chou dynasty had developed certain rules regarding modes of acquiring territory. Conquest was the usual way, and the stronger states gradually swallowed up the weaker, facilitating the eventual unification of China. Often military victory led to the formal cession of territory by the loser. The Chou rulers sometimes distributed land to reward persons of merit. There were also instances in which territories were exchanged or purchased.[1]

During the more than two thousand years of its existence, the territorial identity of imperial China altered considerably and almost cyclically. By the end of the first century A.D. the Han emperors "had not only consolidated control over all the chiefs of the Turkestan oases but had advanced, for the first and only time, to the edge of Europe on the Caspian Sea."[2] Although the Chinese tide receded, during other periods of China's strength it flowed strongly again, as under the T'ang Emperors of the seventh and eighth centuries and the Ming Emperors of the fifteenth century. The Mongols and Manchus, who conquered China in the thirteenth and seventeenth centuries, respectively, and who each then reigned as Chinese dynasties, ruled territory of even vaster dimensions. The Manchu or Ch'ing dynasty, as it came to be known, stood at its zenith at the beginning of the nineteenth century when the Chinese Empire began to feel the increasing pressures of Western maritime power as well as Russian land power.

Although conquest was the principal means of acquiring territory during the imperial era, other means also supplemented it or substituted for it. Treaties of cession, for example, were occasionally employed, as in 1142 when the Sung dynasty ceded all of its territory north of the Huai River and Ta-sun Kuan to the state of Chin.[3] Treaties were also sometimes used to regulate the establishment of defense installations along existing boundaries. In 1004, for example, the Sung concluded an agreement with the state of Liao providing that neither side would erect new walls in its cities along their boundary.[4] Given the presuppositions of the traditional East Asian world order, over which China presided as a civilization rather than as a nation-state, the boundaries separating the Central Realm from its tributary states were often imprecise. Some natural boundaries, such as those imposed by oceans and rivers, were clear, but, however difficult they may have been to surmount, the barriers presented by mountains and deserts provided less certainty. The prime example of Chinese resort to an artificial boundary is, of course, the Great Wall that was constructed over two thousand years ago to separate the agricultural Chinese in the south from the nomadic "barbarians" in the north, but it came to be regarded more as a line of defense than a delimitation of the exercise of Chinese authority, which extended north of the Wall into Inner Mongolia.

More important for our background purposes than the details of China's premodern experience with territorial problems is the traditional Chinese psychology regarding territory, which Professor C. P. Fitzgerald has sought to encapsulate:

> China was the civilized world; for centuries this was perfectly true as far as Chinese experience reached, and the idea remained firm in Chinese minds long after it had ceased to be true in fact. Territory once won for civilization must not be given back to barbarism; therefore, territory which was once Chinese must forever remain so, and if lost, must be recovered at the first opportunity. Such loss cannot be legal or valid; it is at best a recognition of passing weakness. The whole growth of the Chinese empire, throughout more than 3,000 years, had been built on this principle; the barbarians were conquered, then absorbed and turned into Chinese by slow assimilation and cultural influence. To deny this process, to claim that it had, or should, come to an end, was to Chinese thought a denial of the right, a recognition of failure.[5]

When in the 1860's Ch'ing officials finally accepted the necessity of learning Western international law, they promptly applied those principles that pertained to territory. Even before publication of the translation of Wheaton's textbook by W. A. P. Martin and his Chinese associates in 1864, resort to their manuscript had helped China's newly established foreign office to prevail upon the Prussian minister to release three Danish ships he had ordered seized in the Gulf of Pohai. The seizure, it was successfully argued, had been illegal because it had occurred in waters that constituted part of China's "inner ocean." [6]

In 1874, Japan, having recently taken control of the Ryūkyū Islands, which for centuries had paid tribute to both the emperor of China and the daimyo of Satsuma, sent a punitive expedition to the island of Taiwan. The Japanese action was ostensibly in retaliation for the slaughter by Taiwanese aborigines of fifty-four shipwrecked Ryūkyūans. Japan justified its action in part by arguing that Taiwan was not Chinese territory. China, it maintained, had failed to display the function of a state on the island by establishing effective control over it. China replied that the manner in which the territory was to be governed was exclusively a matter of Chinese concern and that, even though China did not maintain effective control over the area of Taiwan in which the aborigines resided, it was a common phenomenon for a government not to have penetrated all areas over which it had sovereignty. The dispute ended when China compensated Japan for the harm to the Ryūkyūans and acknowledged that Japan's action was justifiable. In the course of the diplomatic exchanges, the leading Chinese statesman of the day, Prince Kung, both admitted and demonstrated his lack of mastery of customary international law. Moreover, although the basis for terminating the dispute implicitly recognized China's sovereignty over Taiwan, it also implicitly conceded Japan's right to protect residents of the Ryūkyūs, and eventually Peking gave up all claim to those islands.[7]

Also in 1874, when Japan protested against Korea's firing upon a Japanese warship off the coast of Korea, China defended the Korean action by claiming that the Japanese ship had violated Korean coastal waters.[8] And in 1895, when it was announced that the Treaty of Shimonoseki concluding the Sino-Japanese War provided for the cession of Taiwan to Japan, the governor and people of the island vainly sought to persuade the Ch'ing government to annul that provision on the ground that international law precluded ceding territory without consulting its inhabitants. One of the governor's telegrams to Peking expressly referred to the 1880 Chinese translation of Bluntschli's text on international law.[9]

As the introduction to this study suggests, the mastery of the principles of international law that Ch'ing officials finally achieved before the end of the dynasty in 1912 did not enable them to terminate the restrictions upon China's territorial sovereignty that had been imposed by the imperialist powers. The task of putting an end to extraterritorial jurisdiction, leased territories, demilitarized zones, and foreign concessions, settlements, spheres of influence, and armed forces, fell to the Republic of China.

In seeking to persuade the members of the world community to give up their special privileges in China, the Republic made clear that it had adopted the generally accepted principles of international law regarding territory. The ROC signed the 1919 Convention relating to the Regulation of Aerial Navigation, which recognized "that every Power has complete and exclusive sovereignty over the air space above its territory." [10] At the 1930 Hague Conference on Codification of International Law, the ROC endorsed the view that the breadth of territorial waters should be three miles (see introduction to Chapter 13). It subsequently indicated that it considered airplanes and ships as floating portions of its territory.[11] And there were no essential differences between the Republican and commonly accepted conceptions of either the modes of acquiring and losing state territory or of delimiting boundaries.[12] In view of the preoccupation of the People's Republic with territorial unification and delimitation of its borders on the basis of equality and reciprocity, it is worth noting that, beginning with the inauguration of the Nationalist regime in 1928, the Republic attached extreme importance to the same goals.[13]

As the PRC's first decade wore on, the great powers and China's neighbors became increasingly concerned with the territorial views of the Communist elite. Diplomatic furor over Tibet and Taiwan focused attention on certain territorial issues in the regime's early years. Moreover, it gradually came to light that maps printed in China often showed large portions of territory in neighboring states as parts of China, and some Chinese books provided a rationalization for these cartographic manipulations by claiming that vast areas now in other countries had been illegally taken from China by the imperialists.[14] The Chinese government, however, did not rush to spell out its views on most territorial questions, and the positions that it did take were more moderate than those reflected in the semiofficial maps and books that may have been designed primarily for domestic Chinese consumption, including the teaching of history. Nevertheless, official statements such as those relating to the Sino-Indian and Sino-Soviet borders and to the breadth of China's territorial sea stimulated anxiety, protest, and occasionally even military clashes. Thus, there has been a high degree of interest in the PRC's perception of the many legal issues involved in ascertaining the scope of China's territory.

After asserting that the criminal law of the PRC is applicable to the entire territory of the country, a 1957 textbook prepared by the Central Political-Legal Cadres School in Peking went on to provide:

> According to internationally recognized principles, a state's territory includes:
> (1) The land within the borders of the state;
> (2) The territorial waters within the borders of the state (inland seas, inland rivers, inland lakes) and part of the waterways bordering other states (middle lines of the waterways are the border lines, but if the waterways are navigable, the border lines are the middle of the navigable channels);
> (3) [The territorial seas] the border lines of which are to be drawn at a given distance from the low water marks of the sea coast (in some states twelve nautical miles, in other states three nautical miles);
> (4) The territorial air space within the borders of the state (including the air space over the land, the waters, and the coasts).
>
> In addition, all the Chinese warships and military aircraft navigated on or over the open sea (oceans) or moored at the ports of any foreign state, or the nonmilitary vessels and aircraft with the flag of the People's Republic of China navigated on or over the high seas, are also considered as part of Chinese territory[15]

Although a useful starting point, this definition raises more questions than it answers. It tells us virtually nothing about how the borders of the state are to be determined. For example, according to the Chinese Communists, what are the permissible modes by which a state may acquire territory? In demarcating an international boundary, what weights does the PRC attach to factors such as historic occupation, topographic configurations, contemporary political administration, and the language and culture of the region's residents? What is the breadth of the territorial sea claimed by the PRC, and what principles does it invoke to support this claim? How does the PRC define airspace? What institutions and procedures does the PRC endorse for the resolution of territorial disputes, and what time perspectives does it envisage as appropriate?

The materials in this part do not exhaust available information relating to these and other legal aspects of territorial problems, but they do provide a basis for evaluating Chinese theory on the subject. Materials in other chapters supplement this body of data (recall, for example, items 5–1 and 8–6).

Land 12

1. *General Principles Governing Acquisition*

12–1

Hsin Wu, "A Criticism of Bourgeois International Law on the Question of State Territory," *KCWTYC*, no. 7:44–51 (1960).

II

Bourgeois international law sums up the various methods by which imperialist countries have historically seized territory by classifying them. Methods of acquiring territory are divided into "original acquisition" and "derivative acquisition" according to the different owners of the annexed territory. Methods of acquiring territory are divided into "acquisition by means of treaty" or "acquisition not by means of treaty" according to the different methods adopted at the time of annexation. All these methods of acquiring territories are given legal status, and beautiful legal terms are used to conceal the reactionary essence of these actions. Let us now strip off the legal covers to see what is meant by "original acquisition," "derivative acquisition," "acquisition by means of treaty" and "acquisition not by means of treaty."

"Original Acquisition:" According to the explanation of bourgeois international law, acquisition of land "without an owner" [terra nullius] is "original acquisition." What is land "without an owner"? Colonialists do not conceal the fact that this is not land which is entirely uninhabited, but merely land inhabited by what they do not regard as a "civilized people." They regard the vast lands in Asia, Africa, and Latin America as lands "without an owner," despite the fact that millions of owners live there and various nations exist there. They regard those people and nations as "barbarous" and "backward" and believe that they cannot be the owners of those lands. Thus, the lands should be occupied by "civilized" people and the acquisition of this territory by "civilized" countries is proper; it is a legitimate method of "original acquisition." In the words of the American scholar Hyde: "If the inhabitants of the territory concerned are an uncivilized or extremely backward people, deemed to be incapable of possessing a right of sovereignty, the conqueror may, in fact, choose to ignore their title, and proceed to occupy the land as though it were vacant."[a] This statement shows how this authoritative American bourgeois scholar unabashedly defends aggressors. His reactionary theory is extremely absurd.

The inhabitants of so-called lands "without an owner" are by no means the kind of people whom colonialists and bourgeois scholars have described as barbarous, ignorant, willing to be slaves, and unable to exercise sovereignty. These descriptions are a great insult and defamation to these inhabitants. The true situation is that, whether it was in Asia, Africa, or Latin America, the indigenous inhabitants all had their own excellent cultures. Bourgeois scholars may consider Africa, for example, as the most barbarous land. But, everyone knows that the African people once had excellent civilizations in the Nile River region, the Congo River region and in Carthage. Long before their contact with Europeans, the Africans were experts in various handicraft skills and technology and were able to refine iron and other mineral ores. They could make various instruments of production, weapons, and furniture. In certain areas of Africa, national art already had reached a comparatively high standard. African folk literature was rich, colorful, and full of attraction. The allegation that they were willing to become slaves and were unable to exercise sovereignty is a lie inconsistent with history. The indigenous nations which were conquered by colonial powers have always firmly resisted foreign conquerors. People may still remember that since 1521 the Filipinos have had numerous uprisings against invading colonialists . . . . History proves that they were not willing to be slaves but were forced to be slaves by the colonialists. It was not that they were unable to exercise sovereignty but rather that they were prevented from exercising their sovereignty by colonialists' use of massacre and suppression.

It should be pointed out that there has been a change in the view of bourgeois international law concerning the methods of "original acquisition." At first, bourgeois scholars argued that "occupation" was one method of "original acquisition," that is, a state which "first discovered a land 'without an owner' " should be the owner of that piece of land. It was through this method of acquisition that Portugal and Spain, two of the earliest colonial powers, occupied a large number of colonies. Later, bourgeois scholars proposed the view of "effec-

[a] Charles C. Hyde, *International Law, Chiefly as Interpreted and Applied by the United States,* 2nd ed., Vol. I. (Boston: Little, Brown, 1947), p. 357.

tive occupation." So-called "effective occupation" was meant to oppose symbolic occupation. If a state wanted to make a land "without an owner" its own territory, it must solidly occupy and actually establish its own power over that land and also have the strength to exercise such power. For instance, "Oppenheim's International Law" maintains that "possession and administration are the two essential [conditions] that constitute an effective occupation."[b] Here we discern that bourgeois international law serves powerful strong imperialist countries. The theory of "occupation" did not meet the desire of the powerful imperialist countries that subsequently emerged, while "effective occupation" provides them with a legal basis for redistribution of the spoils.

"Derivative Acquisition:" Bourgeois international law holds that the difference between "derivative acquisition" and "original acquisition" is that the former does not refer to the method of acquiring territory without an owner but refers to the method of acquiring territory originally belonging to another state. The imperialist powers' plundering of foreign territory naturally would not be limited to lands "without an owner." After lands "without an owner" were carved up, they naturally would plunder lands "with an owner." Lenin said: "When the whole world had been divided up, there was inevitably ushered in an era of monopoly ownership of colonies, and, consequently, of particularly intense struggle for the division and redivision of the world."[c] There is no limitation on imperialism's ambition with respect to plundering territory. This ambition will continue until it dominates the whole world. Imperialist countries also have territorial ambitions toward each other, and they frequently engage in annexation of each other's territory. In the course of their activities they adopt a number of specific methods of plundering territory. Some are covert, and others overt. Sometimes, imperialism nakedly uses the method of aggressive war forcibly to seize another state's territory; sometimes it uses camouflaged measures or various pretexts to force another state in fact to place its territory under imperialism's occupation. In order to prove the legality of the above-stated methods of seizing territory, bourgeois international law further classifies "derivative acquisition" into acquisition by means of treaty and acquisition not by means of treaty.

What are the methods of "derivative acquisition" by means of treaty? Bourgeois international law considers cession one of these

[b] L. Oppenheim, *International Law,* 8th ed., by H. Lauterpacht (London: Longmans, Green, 1948), I, 509.

[c] *Lieh-ning ch'üan-chi* (Collected works of Lenin; Chinese version), XXII, 293.

methods. Every country has the right to cede its territory, and it has the right to acquire ceded territory. "Oppenheim's International Law" says: "Cession of State territory is the transfer of sovereignty over State territory by the owner-State to another State . . . . As far as the Law of Nations is concerned, every State as a rule can cede a part of its territory to another State . . . . The only form in which a cession can be effected is an agreement embodied in a treaty between the ceding and the acquiring State. Such a treaty may be the outcome of peaceable negotiations or war, and the cession may be made with or without compensation." [d] What is the meaning of these passages? It can be summed up like this: Territory acquired through the method of cession is legal, regardless of the circumstances under which the cession was made. But "Oppenheim's International Law" does not clearly say which states usually ceded territory, which were the states that acquired territory through cession, and what the relations between them were. Of course, "Oppenheim's International Law," like all other writings of bourgeois international law, cannot make a statement on this point; if it did, it would expose the truth about the imperialist countries' seizure of territory. Despite their efforts to conceal and to evade this point, it cannot be covered up completely. In a discussion on the form of cession, "Oppenheim's International Law" described the annexation of Korea in 1910 by Japanese imperialism and the annexation of the Congo in 1908 by Belgian colonialists as a method of acquiring ceded territory through peaceable negotiation. But everyone knows that Korea was forcibly occupied by Japanese bandits and the Congo was a victim of the colonial system. From these instances, we may clearly discern that countries which ceded their territories were all under compulsion and that they were either weak, small, or defeated countries. Countries which acquired ceded territories were all imperialist countries engaging in territorial expansion. Bourgeois international law writings have never been able to cite a single case in which an imperialist power ceded its territory to a weak or small country. Therefore, it can be said that cession of territory is a method of plundering the territories of weak and small or defeated countries used by imperialist countries through the use of war and threat of force. The special characteristic of cession is that the "transfer" of territorial sovereignty is fixed through the use of the formality of the unequal treaty. Sometimes bourgeois scholars do not deny that territorial cession does not come of the free will of the small and weak countries but results, instead, from pressure exerted by imperialist countries. However, they nevertheless shamelessly declare that

[d] Oppenheim, 7th ed., I, 499–500.

territorial cession, no matter what its motive, is legal when there has been a treaty of cession. Most outspoken on this point is the American scholar Hyde, who writes in his book "International Law, Chiefly as Interpreted and Applied by the United States": "The validity of a transfer of rights of sovereignty as set forth in a treaty of cession does not appear to be affected by the motives which have impelled the grantor to surrender them."[e] Obviously, according to such an interpretation, it was legitimate for Japan to force the Manchu government of China to cede Taiwan and Penghu through the unequal Treaty of Shimononseki of 1895, after the Sino-Japanese War. This is tantamount to saying that if a robber steals property by brandishing a dagger before an owner and by threatening his life forces him to put his fingerprint on a document indicating his consent, then the act of robbery becomes legal. Is that not absurd? No wonder bourgeois international law has sometimes been described as the law of bandits. There is no exaggeration in such a description.

Besides cession, bourgeois international law also considers lease as a method of "derivative acquisition" of territory by means of treaty. This is to say that a state leases a part of its territory to another state for a definite period, and the latter administers that territory in accordance with the treaty or lease. Like cession, it is a method by which imperialist countries seize territory from weak and small countries. In 1898 Germany leased Kiaochow Bay, Britain leased Wei-hai-wei, and France leased Kuang-chou Wan from China. These leases were acquired by concluding unequal treaties. These unequal treaties absolutely were not concluded through "peaceable negotiations" as described by bourgeois international law. As a matter of fact, lease of the above-mentioned Kiaochow Bay and other places was executed under threat of force. In November 1897 Germany sent four men-of-war to Kiaochow Bay to occupy Tsingtao on the ground that its missionaries had been killed. It was under these circumstances of armed occupation that the "Treaty of the Lease of Kiaochow" was concluded. The leases of Wei-hai-wei and Kowloon were also obtained under similar conditions. Although formally a lease is different from cession because the former generally prescribes a definite period, there is substantively no difference between the two. Generally, the period of a lease is very long, and the lessee can do whatever he likes on the leased land; as if it were the lessee's own territory.

Bourgeois international law considers "conquest" a method of acquiring territory where no treaty exists. So-called conquest means that a state uses its armed forces for long-term occupation of the territory or a part of the territory of another state. Undoubtedly, this

[e] Hyde, I, 363.

is a savage and aggressive act. Bourgeois international law, however, considers such a method of acquiring territory lawful, even though it does not go through the process of concluding a treaty. In analyzing the causes of war, "Oppenheim's International Law" states: "If . . . territory . . . cannot be acquired by peaceable means, acquisition by conquest alone remains if International Law fails to provide means of peaceful change in accordance with justice." [f] Charles Rousseau, Professor of International Law at the University of Paris, in his book "Principes Généraux du Droit International Public" held that conquest is a means of acquiring sovereignty over a certain territory. The British jurist Schwarzenberger held: "In the international society law is subordinate to the rule of force . . . . If the whole State machinery [of the defeated State] has collapsed, conquest would permit acquisition of title to the territory of this State." [g] According to these theories, colonial wars or other aggressive wars started by imperialist countries in order to annex territories of other countries are lawful. Thus, the Japanese seizure of China's three northeastern provinces, Italy's annexation of Ethiopia, and Fascist Germany's occupation of Poland, Czechoslovakia, and so forth were all lawful.

"Prescription" is also considered a method of "derivative acquisition" of territory not by means of treaty. According to the explanation of bourgeois international law, "prescription" means the acquisition by a state of title to a territory through prolonged occupation. Obviously, this recognizes imperialism's acquisition of legal title to a territory through prolonged occupation by force. "Oppenheim's International Law" held that "a State is considered to be the lawful owner even of those parts of its territory of which originally it took possession wrongfully and unlawfully, provided that the possessor has been in undisturbed possession for such a length of time as is necessary to create the general conviction that the present condition of things is in conformity with international order." [h] This means that any country, regardless of its motive or the means it used—whether by

[f] L. Oppenheim, *International Law,* 7th ed., II, 222. [Note: The relevant passages of Oppenheim's statement are: "A constant increase of population must, if unchecked or deliberately encouraged, in the end force upon a State the necessity of acquiring more territory; and if it cannot be acquired by peaceable means, acquisition by conquest alone remains if International Law fails to provide means of peaceful change in accordance with justice."]

[g] Georg Schwarzenberger, *A Manual of International Law,* 2nd ed. (London: Stevens, 1950), p. 50. [Note: Translated from the Chinese, the relevant passages of Schwarzenberger's statement are: "In the international society law is subordinate to the rule of force, and, at least under international customary law, States are free to resort to war against each other. . . . Only in the case of debellatio (when the whole State machinery of the defeated enemy has collapsed) is conquest the title—and, in this case, the original title—to territory. This is the position under international law."]

[h] Oppenheim, 7th ed., I, 526.

way of annexation or aggression—as long as it has the power to be in prolonged occupation by force of the territory of another state, may consider its aggressive act as "lawful." History shows that colonialists in fact frequently used the concept of "prescription" to plunder the territory of other countries. Even recently, in certain countries, certain persons in power and bourgeois scholars have attempted to resort to the concept of "prescription" as a legal basis for putting certain territory of China's Tibet under the jurisdiction of another country.

In view of the foregoing, the "derivative acquisition" either by means of treaty or not by means of treaty mentioned by bourgeois international law is a general term which describes the various methods used by imperialist countries to plunder the territory of colonized countries and weak and small countries.

IV

With the emergence of new imperialist means of plundering territories, bourgeois international law has also changed its tone. The emergence of the first socialist country—the Soviet Union—after the First World War was a great encouragement to the independence movement in colonies and semicolonies. After the Second World War, the formation and strength of the socialist camp and its strong support of the national independence movement resulted in a steady momentum of anticolonialism throughout the world. Such a situation should not only force imperialism to disgorge the territories it had plundered, but should also prevent it from plundering new territories. However, imperialism is still imperialism, and it will not terminate its ambitions to plunder territories before it goes into the grave. For this reason it has endeavored, without making any real change, to adopt a new set of measures [to cope with the new situation].

The first of these measures is to plunder the territories of other countries in the name of an international organization. The mandate system prescribed in the Covenant of the League of Nations following the conclusion of the First World War was a means whereby imperialist countries recarved former colonies in the name of an international organization. As everybody knows, when Germany and its allies were defeated, the colonies which they had were transformed into colonies of Britain, France, Japan, and others in the form of mandates. According to Article 22 of the Covenant of the League of Nations, the victorious countries would, in the name of the League of Nations, entrust to certain countries the administration of those colonies which had been separated from the defeated countries. The mandatories were to administer the territories in accordance with the mandates concluded between them and the League of Nations. The article also specifically classified mandated territories into three types: Type A was those areas where "their existence as independent nations can provisionally be recognized," such as Iraq, Syria and others, which were under the mandate of Britain and France, respectively. Type B was those areas where "the Mandatory must be responsible for the administration of the territory," such as Cameroons, Togoland, and so forth, which were under the mandate of Britain, France, and Belgium. Type C was those areas that were completely to be "administered under the laws of the Mandatory as an integral portion of its territory," such as South West Africa, Nauru, and so forth, which were under the mandate of Britain, Australia, and others.

After the Second World War, the mandate system was nominally abrogated, but imperialism again attempted to maintain its colonial system through the United Nations Organization. In the course of drafting the Charter of the United Nations, on May 5, 1945, the United States submitted a draft on the international trusteeship system which consisted of eleven articles. The basic spirit of this draft was that the colonies of the defeated countries were to be recarved in the name of trusteeship. As everyone knows, the Soviet Union opposes any form of colonial system and therefore waged a determined struggle in the course of discussing the United States' proposal. Finally, although the trusteeship system was incorporated in the Charter of the United Nations, the Charter nevertheless could not disregard the view of the Soviet Union and expressly pointed out that the object of trusteeship is to promote the "progressive development towards self-government or independence" [1] [of the inhabitants of the trust territories].

According to the decisions of the United Nations, the former Japanese-mandated colonies, such as the Marshall, Caroline, and Mariana Islands in the Pacific were to be placed under the trusteeship of the United States; the Cameroons and Togo, under Britain and France; Tanganyika, under Britain; Nauru, under Britain, Australia, and New Zealand; New Guinea, under Australia; West Samoa, under New Zealand; and Somaliland, under Italy for ten years.

But, in the past ten or more years, the administering countries have not acted in accordance with the spirit of the provisions of the United Nations Charter. On the contrary, they have carried out colonial policy in the trust territories in an attempt to realize their hope of prolonged occupation. Therefore, they have in fact maintained the

[1] Article 76(b), UN Charter.

old colonial system in the form of trusteeship. This is tantamount to plundering the territories under their trusteeship. In fact, it is no longer a secret that imperialist countries used the trusteeship system prescribed by the United Nations Organization to plunder territories. . . . In order to achieve its prolonged occupation of Japan's Ryūkyū Islands and Bonin Islands, American imperialism demanded that Japan agree to have these islands put under the United States' "trusteeship" and allow the United States to act as the "only administering authority" of these islands. Such a demand was openly made in the San Francisco Peace Treaty, which was drafted solely by the United States. These islands coveted by the United States have not only failed to proceed to "progressive development towards self-government or independence" under the United States' "trusteeship," but, as part of a United States plot, are also being gradually absorbed into the territory of the United States. According to an article which appeared in the Japanese "Red Flag" on July 21, 1959, the United States Congress "was considering" a bill for the purchase of the Bonin Islands for six million US dollars. This was the objective that American imperialism attempted to achieve through the trusteeship system.

Second . . . [when imperialism] is forced to recognize the independence of colonies because of their intense resistance and imperialism's inability to suppress such resistance, it still attempts to reserve part of its power and jurisdiction through the method of maintaining old treaties or by means of concluding agreements. . . . When in 1952 the United States granted "self-government" to its colony Puerto Rico and also promulgated a Constitution for it, [that Constitution] provided that the United States Congress, the President, and the Supreme Court have, respectively, veto powers over the corresponding organs of Puerto Rico. The United States established eleven military bases in Puerto Rico. Four-fifths of the land of Puerto Rico's Vieques Island was appropriated for the use of American armed forces. Hundreds of thousands of the island's inhabitants lost their land and were driven to other places. Therefore, the colonial status of Puerto Rico has not yet changed. Moreover, the United States has repeatedly planned to incorporate Puerto Rico into the territory of the United States. According to a report of United Press International on March 7, 1960, American President Eisenhower forced Puerto Rico to "consent" to become a state of the United States. According to the London Agreement on the Cyprus question, signed not very long ago by Britain, Turkey, and Greece, Britain may continue to occupy its military bases in Cyprus and may enjoy absolute sovereignty over those bases. It has gone to the extent of asking Cyprus to prescribe such matters in its future constitution. . . . This year, Belgian colonialists were forced to give the

Congo independence, but they still attempted to retain their political privileges and to continue to control the Congo economically.

Third, imperialist countries are madly building military bases on the territory of other countries. This is in preparation for the realization of their frantic attempt to annex the territories of socialist countries and is a practical means for plundering the territory of those countries which permit the establishment of military bases. At present, the United States has established a network of military bases throughout the world, treating Greece, Turkey, and others as its strategic points and the American continent as a "unified military base." In the Far East, the area from South Korea, Japan, Taiwan, the Philippines, and South Vietnam to Thailand and Pakistan is dotted with American military bases. In Japan alone, there are over 800 American military bases, and, in the eyes of the United States, South Korea is its most important army and air force base.

The United States has comprehensive rights over its military bases. It uses its domestic law to govern not only its own armed forces but also all the inhabitants of the bases. According to the Agreement for the Lease of Defense Sites in the Republic of Panama concluded in 1942, the United States government "shall have . . . exclusive jurisdiction in all respects over the civil and military personnel of the United States situated therein, and their families . . . and [the right] to arrest, try, and punish all persons who, in such areas, maliciously commit any crime against the safety of the military installations therein. . . ." The United States controls the political life and economic resources of these countries and also undermines their sovereignty and territorial integrity.

There is no essential difference between the method which the United States has used in establishing military bases in various parts of the world and that which Britain, France, and others employed in exacting leased territories from China. Both bases and territory were obtained by means of concluding unequal treaties. But the means which the United States has adopted are more diversified. Directly or indirectly connected with this question are the establishment of military blocs, mutual defense or security agreements, economic "aid," "filling of the vacuum," and so on. Countries participating in the military blocs of American imperialism must provide it with certain land for use as American military bases; even Britain and France are no exceptions. The "Japanese-American Security Treaty" has become the legal basis for prolonged occupation of Japan by American imperialism. The "Defense Agreement between the United States and the Republic of Iceland" even provides that "the people of Iceland cannot themselves adequately secure their own defenses and the United States must make . . . use of facilities in Iceland in order to defend Iceland."[16] To put it in a straightforward way, the territory of Iceland must be turned over to the United States for use. By providing Turkey and Greece with "aid" of 400 million dollars, the United States has established military bases in these two countries. In 1952, the United States publicly announced that countries which refused to accept the American "Mutual Security Act" would not be given American economic and technical "aid." This is really the concurrent use of threat and enticement. If the United States considers a certain area a "vacuum," it will fill it with American power.

Four, imperialist countries fabricate many absurd reasons for occupying the territory of other countries. . . . At present, West Germany's ruling clique is inheriting, with the support of the United States, the ambitions of Hitler and Fascism and is making a great effort to propagandize the theory of "lebensraum." On March 8 of this year [1960], the West German Minister of Defense, Strauss, stated in his talk at Athens that, because of West Germany's "limited territorial space," West Germany could have only part of its military training facilities installed on its territory and that inasmuch as the West German troops "must have appropriate training facilities," it would be necessary for West Germany to establish military bases abroad. American imperialism also fabricates many excuses to occupy our Taiwan, claiming that Taiwan is needed for American national defense and is the hope of the United States in obtaining the "moral leadership" of the United States in Asia. Later, it claims that "the status of Taiwan is undetermined," and so forth, in order to attempt to engage in prolonged occupation by force of our territory. The United States and other imperialist countries also fabricate many excuses in order to attempt to occupy West Germany and West Berlin permanently. They use all means to delay the signing of a peace treaty with Germany and to use sophistry to justify their prolonged occupation. In the ranks of imperialism, American imperialism has used the greatest number of such means. American imperialism is fantastically attempting to establish world hegemony. It attempts not only to occupy the territory of the whole world, including the North Pole and South Pole, but also to control the whole universe. In its practice of occupying the territories of other countries, it has always resorted to such pretenses as joint resistance to Communism and defending the "free world." But eventually the countries whose territories are occupied will realize that they have been used and that they have sacrificed their territorial sovereignty.

How are the varied means which imperialism has adopted in plundering the territory of other countries reflected in bourgeois international law? At present, when imperialism engages in plundering territories or in aggression, it always confronts a great obstacle, that is, the principle of sovereignty in the current generally recognized international law. Therefore, bourgeois international law has undertaken the mission of removing this obstacle. It exerts great effort to advocate the abandonment of the principle of sovereignty and the establishment of world government, and it claims that the principle of sovereignty is the "principle of the state of international anarchy" and the source of all disasters. It argues that only by abolishing state sovereignty and eliminating national states "can world peace be maintained and can mankind be guaranteed enough food and clothing." Naturally, this spirit of bourgeois international law is needed by imperialism, particularly American imperialism, in order to realize its rule over the whole world and to enslave all mankind. . . .

In order to realize the intention of imperialism in its legal aspect, bourgeois international law scholars specifically propose the theories of "provisional sovereignty," "suspended sovereignty," "shared sovereignty," "potential sovereignty," and so forth. They consider that a state may, in accordance with a treaty, let another state exercise its sovereignty for a definite period. The right enjoyed by imperialism in this state is "provisional sovereignty." A state may turn over its territorial sovereignty to another state, and in that case the former is in a position of "suspended sovereignty." The sovereignty of a state over its territory may be "shared" with another state. [Bourgeois international law scholars] also hold that, while a state has sovereignty over its territory, it nevertheless may let another state exercise its practical sovereignty and control its territory. In that case, the [first] state's sovereignty becomes "potential sovereignty." They also hold that sovereignty may be separated from jurisdiction. If a state lets another state exercise its territorial jurisdiction, the sovereignty of the [weaker] state is not violated. . . . These absurd theories try to conceal the imperialist criminal act of plundering territory with roundabout legal concepts, and they enable the territory of other countries to fall into the grasp of imperialist devils.

12-2

Shih Sung, Yü Ta-hsin, Lu Ying-hui, and Ts'ao K'o, "An Initial Investigation into the Old Law Viewpoint in the Teaching of International Law," *CHYYC*, no. 4:15–16 (1958).

III

When this comrade [the authors did not say who he is] lectured on the chapter on "territory," he specifically presented the section entitled "modes of acquiring territory." This caption amounts to telling students that, according to international law, states can "acquire" territory, and there are various "modes" of acquisition.

It should be pointed out that modern international law does not have such norms; nor can one find such international law documents. Conversely, some important documents of modern international law explicitly prescribe the principle of the inviolability of territory. For example, Article 2, paragraph 4, of the United Nations Charter provides: "All members shall refrain in their international relations from the threat or use of force against the territorial integrity or political independence of any state, or in any other manner inconsistent with the purpose of the United Nations." Article 1 of the famous five principles of peaceful coexistence is "mutual respect for each other's territorial integrity and sovereignty." The 1955 Asian-African Conference Communiqué also explicitly prescribes "respect for the sovereignty and territorial integrity of all nations."

There are a number of provisions on the question of territory in documents of modern international law. The provisions of the Charter of the United Nations on the trusteeship of territory are an example. But the trusteeship system absolutely does not mean that the trust state can "acquire" the territory under the trusteeship; the basic objective of the trusteeship system is to impel the trust areas toward "independence." . . .

In short, [we] cannot find provisions on the so-called "modes of acquiring territory" in modern international law documents.

Then where does the mention of so-called "modes of acquiring territory" come from? Originally, this was taken without the slightest change from the writings of bourgeois international law. In "Oppenheim's International Law," the discussion of the so-called question of "modes of acquiring [state] territory" occupies about one-fifth of the chapter on "territory." [We] all know that there are many questions in international law on "territory"; but bourgeois scholars nevertheless use one-fifth of the chapter on territory to discuss this question, and this shows that the question is seriously considered by bourgeois scholars of international law. Why? Because the so-called "theory" of "modes of acquiring territory" described in the bourgeois science of international law justifies acts of robbery committed by the so-called Western "civilized" countries—external expansion, plundering of colonies, carving and recarving the world—and fabricates "legal" bases for this kind of robbery and aggression. . . .

We all know that the principle of inviolability of territory is one of the fundamental principles of generally accepted modern international law and that it is also prescribed in a series of international law documents. According to the viewpoint of modern international law, state territory is the material expression of state independence and state sovereignty. An encroachment of the territorial integrity of a state is an infringement of its sovereignty and is [therefore] an aggressive act in violation of international law.

The principle of inviolability of territory does not imply that the present situation of territory is "absolutely stabilized." Such an interpretation of the principle of inviolability of territory violates the fundamental concept of history. Practical situations illustrate that territory can undergo a change in status. According to the practice of modern international law, these changes may occur: (1) According to the international law principle of national self-determination, colonial people have the right of political self-determination, including the right to determine the destiny of the territory they inhabit. In order to continue its colonial rule, imperialism frivolously alleges that colonies are its "metropolitan" territory and that its relationship with colonies is an "internal" question. Quite clearly, this theory is inconsistent with the international law principles of national self-determination and national sovereignty. Colonial people have the perfect right to decide to form an independent state and to be independent of the control of imperialism. . . . (2) In order to rectify the unjust situation created by history, a state must recover sovereignty over its own territory. This is confirmed by the practice of modern international law. (3) It is also possible that neighboring states may exchange a part of their frontier area in accordance with generally accepted principles of international law. Of course, this type of exchange will contribute to the friendship and peace of the states concerned.

But all these changes have nothing to do with the so-called "modes of acquiring territory." We all know that state territory is a portion of the earth under a state's sovereignty. May we ask: except for the changes in territorial status in accordance with the above-mentioned principles (national self-determination and so forth), from whom can one "acquire" territory today?

12-3

"Statement of the Chinese Government [in Support of India's Recovery of Goa, December 19, 1961]," *PR* 4:51:10–11 (Dec. 22, 1961).

On December 18, 1961, the Indian government announced the dispatch of its troops into Goa to terminate Portuguese colonial rule over Goa. Goa is an inalienable part of India's territory. To oppose colonialism and safeguard national independence and the unity of their country, the Indian people have for a long time been demanding the recovery of Goa and have waged an unremitting struggle for this purpose. The action of the Indian government in recovering Goa reflects the just demand of the Indian people. The Chinese government and people express their resolute support for it.

The colonial rule of the Portuguese colonialists over India's Goa has already lasted over 400 years. After India attained independence, the Indian government has repeatedly proposed to settle the Goa question by peaceful means, but has each time met with the unreasonable refusal of the Portuguese authorities. Even now the Portuguese authorities are still attempting to use force to prevent the return of Goa to India. All this proves that imperialism and colonialism will never of their own accord abandon their colonial rule and interests. Only by waging resolute struggles can the people in various countries drive out imperialism and colonialism from their own soil and win genuine independence and freedom.

What calls for serious attention is that the imperialist powers headed by the United States of America openly oppose and unjustifiably censure the Indian people's just demand for recovering Goa and support continued Portuguese occupation of Goa. Apart from taking separate diplomatic moves, the imperialist powers have lined up to use the United Nations Security Council to pressurize [*sic*] India in a strenuous attempt to obstruct India's effort to recover Goa. This shows that at the present time, when the United Nations is controlled by the imperialist powers headed by the United States, it is sheer illusion to wish that the United Nations would make the old and new colonialists abandon their colonial rule in various parts of the world.

The Chinese people and government have consistently given active support to the Asian, African and Latin American peoples in their just struggles to oppose imperialism and colonialism and to win and safeguard national independence and state sovereignty. Such struggles are not only an important factor in defense of world peace, they are also a very powerful support to the Chinese who resolutely oppose the occupation of China's territory Taiwan by US imperialism.

12-4

Chang Su-p'ing, "Facts on the West Irian Question," *JMJP* (Feb. 26, 1957), p. 5.

The Origin of the Question

We know that after Indonesia became independent on August 17, 1945, the Dutch colonialists, supported by British and American imperialism, launched several armed attacks against Indonesia in an attempt to overthrow this young republic. But all attacks shamefully failed. Indonesia and the Netherlands signed the Linggadjati Agreement (March 1947) and the Renville Agreement (January 1948). No question of West Irian was raised in these agreements. For instance, Article 3 of the Linggadjati Agreement provides: "The United States of Indonesia shall comprise the entire territory of the Netherlands Indies. . . ." [Article 1 of the six additional principles for the negotiations towards a political settlement of] the Renville Agreement also provides: "Sovereignty throughout the Netherlands Indies is and shall remain with the Kingdom of the Netherlands until, after a stated interval, the Kingdom of the Netherlands transfers its sovereignty to the United States of Indonesia." Even the 1949 Charter of the Transfer of Sovereignty signed by the Netherlands and Indonesia also quite explicitly provides: "The Kingdom of the Netherlands unconditionally and irrevocably transfers complete sovereignty over Indonesia to the [independent and sovereign state of] the Republic of the United States of Indonesia. . . ." However, when transferring her sovereignty to Indonesia, the Netherlands suddenly tore up all previous agreements and insisted upon the maintenance of her colonial rule in West Irian. This was the origin of the question of West Irian.

In order to obtain a just and reasonable solution of the West Irian question and the early return of the West Irian people to the breast of Indonesia, the Indonesian government conducted several negotiations with the Netherlands in April 1950, December 1950, December 1951, and between January and March of 1952. The Indonesian government also made important concessions in negotiations such as the recognition of the present interests and privileges of the Netherlands in West Irian, the employment of Dutch in various organs in West Irian, and the guarantee of Dutch immigration to West Irian, and so forth. But the Dutch colonialists, with the support of imperialism, still refused to return West Irian to Indonesia in an arbitrary manner. The strange thing was that in 1952, when negotiation was still progressing, the Dutch colonialists, in disregard of the strong opposition of the people of Indonesia and the Netherlands, hastily passed a bill to amend Chapter I of "the Constitution of the Kingdom of the Netherlands." According to that amendment, West Irian was listed as within the territorial scope of the Kingdom of the Netherlands. Since 1954, the Netherlands has refused to negotiate the West Irian question with Indonesia. This explains the ambition of the Dutch colonialists' attempt to arbitrarily occupy West Irian by force for a long period.

Irrefutable Proof in Race and History

The pretext used for the Dutch colonialists' arbitrary occupation of West Irian by force is that the people of West Irian have no racial affinity with Indonesia. But this is an absurd theory, contrary to science and facts.

The Indonesian Republic is a multinational state. National groups in Indonesia are primarily divided into Papuans . . . and Malayo, and these groups are again subdivided into several minor racial groups. From ancient times, these national groups have lived together. They have close connections in philology, culture, habits, and customs, and such connections existed as early as prehistory. Through the research conducted by several scientists of world reputation . . . it has been proved that the West Irian language and languages in other parts of Indonesia all belong to the same language family, that is to say, the Austronesian language family. In addition to other common characteristics, they have the same prefixes and suffixes, and the similarity in numerical names is especially obvious. From the human relics excavated from these areas, these scientists further proved that in the prehistoric period, some immigrant groups from Southeast Asia settled in various parts of Indonesia, and some of them settled in West Irian. Their obvious similarities in habits, customs, ways of life, and languages confirm these facts.

Even the Dutch colonialists themselves could not deny these facts. In a 1949 report to the United Nations submitted by the Netherlands, it is written: "Indonesia consists of a series of island groups in the region of the equator. . . . Racially, the indigenous peoples may be broadly divided into Malayo in the West and Papuans in the East. As these races have intermixed to a considerable extent, they are not separated by clearly defined boundaries."

Another pretext for the Dutch colonialists' arbitrary occupation of West Irian by force is that there was no historical connection between West Irian and other parts of the Republic of Indonesia. This claim is also absurd in the extreme and cannot stand on its own footing. From ancient times, West Irian and other parts of Indonesia have had close connections. Even Western colonialists could not but recognize this fact. . . .

As early as Western colonialists began to penetrate into the East Indies, they recognized that West Irian is a part of Indonesia. Before the Dutch came to Indonesia, Portuguese traders called Irian a Papuan island. In 1494, because of the dispute between Portugal and Spain over Indonesia's spices and their contest for sea power, Pope Alexander VI of Rome mediated their dispute, and the Treaty of Tordesillas was concluded. According to this agreement, Indonesia was divided into two parts at 180 degrees east longitude. Only Portuguese traders could enter the western part; while the eastern part, including West Irian, was the sphere of Spanish traders. Soon after that, Spanish traders called Irian New Guinea.

In 1648, the Netherlands totally acquired monopolistic privileges over various islands in eastern and western Indonesia, and in several subsequent international agreements concluded by the Netherlands, such as the 1648 Münster Treaty, the 1713 Utrecht [Treaty] . . ., the 1814 London Agreement, and others, the Netherlands also recognized West Irian as a part of Indonesia. In 1884, when Britain declared southeastern Irian its protectorate, Britain and the Netherlands used the line of 141 degrees east longitude as their boundary; the western area, that is, the present West Irian, belonged to the Dutch East Indies. Before the Second World War, the Dutch colonialist government included West Irian in the [administrative] scope of the provincial government of the Molucca Islands, one of its administrative units. It is worth noting that in all Dutch constitutions, West Irian was also included in the territorial scope of Indonesia as its integral part. In a 1949 report submitted to the United Nations by the Netherlands, it is written: "The principal groups [of Indonesia] are the Greater Sunda Islands, the Lesser Sunda Islands, the Moluccas, and New Guinea west of 141 degrees E."

Note

Items 12–3 and 12–4 illustrated the PRC's resort to "the international law principle of national self-determination" to justify territorial changes. The materials relating to the PRC's specific territorial disputes will provide examples of the other two types of circumstances in which, according to the authors of item 12–2, modern international law sanctions territorial change: when, "in order to rectify the unjust situation created by history, a state must recover sovereignty over its own territory;" and when neighboring states freely agree to exchange parts of their frontier area.

That these formulations lend themselves to flexible application was demonstrated by Mao Tse-tung long before the Chinese Communists attained nationwide power. When in September 1939 the Soviet Union responded to the German invasion of Poland by occupying eastern Poland, Mao obviously felt called upon to reconcile this action with Marxist-Leninist principles. He stated:

> Many people in China are bewildered by the fact that Soviet troops have entered Poland. . . . As for the Soviet Union, its actions have been perfectly just. It was confronted by two problems. The first problem was whether to let the whole of Poland fall under the rule of German imperialism or to help the minority nationalities of eastern Poland win their liberation. It chose the second course. A vast stretch of territory inhabited by Byelorussians and Ukrainians had been snatched from the newborn Soviet state by the German imperialists as far back as 1918 when the Treaty of Brest-Litovsk was signed, and it was later arbitrarily put under the rule of the reactionary Polish government by the Treaty of Versailles. What the Soviet Union has now done is merely to recover its lost territory, liberate the oppressed Byelorussians and Ukrainians and save them from German oppression.[17]

More recent Chinese Communist policy vis-à-vis Poland's borders has reflected less sympathy for the plight of minority nationalities. Seeking to assuage Polish fears of having to surrender former German territory which had been incorporated into Poland after World War II, Foreign Minister and Vice-Premier Ch'en Yi marked the sixteenth anniversary of the founding of the Polish People's Republic in 1960 by declaring: "The Chinese government and people firmly support the Polish government's just stand on the question of Poland's western frontier. We have always held that the Oder-Neisse [Odra-Nysa] frontier is a final frontier which is absolutely not subject to change."[18]

2. *Specific Territorial Disputes*

(a) ISLANDS IN THE SOUTH AND EAST CHINA SEAS

12-5

Shao Hsun-cheng, "Chinese Islands in the South China Sea," *PC*, no. 13:25–27 (July 1, 1956).

The Philippine Foreign Minister, Mr. Carlos Garcia, told a press conference on May 19, according to foreign news agency dispatches, that a group of islands in the South China Sea, including Taiping (Itu Aba) Island and Nanwei (Spratly) Island "should rightly" belong to the Philippines—because it is so close to them. This was a preposterous claim. The islands have always belonged to China. Therefore the Chinese Foreign Ministry issued a statement on May 29 which read in part:

> . . . Taiping Island and Nanwei Island in the South China Sea, together with the small islands in their vicinity, are known in aggregate as the Nansha Islands. These islands have always been a part of Chinese territory. The People's Republic of China has indisputable, legitimate sovereignty over these islands.

The statement described the pretext of proximity—advanced by the Philippine government—as utterly untenable, a mere cover-up for its attempt to invade and occupy a part of China's territory. And indeed, common sense itself shows how absurd it is to assume that a claim to possession can arise purely out of nearness. If this were the case, each country could claim the adjacent lands of its neighbour, and vice versa.

Now for the actual situation. There are over 150 islets in the South China Sea, and they can be divided into four groups. The Nansha Islands, which were mentioned in the statement, lie 115°E. and 10°N. Taiping is the biggest; and Nanwei one of the more important of them. The other three groups are the Sisha Islands (also known as the Paracels, 112°E., 16°N.); the Chungsha Islands (115°E. and between 15° and 16°N.) and the Tungsha Islands (117°E., 21°N.).

Historical Records

China's indisputable sovereign rights over all four groups are old and for centuries were never challenged. This can be seen from her historical records, and from previous diplomatic contacts with other countries on the matter.

Let us first look at the Tungshas. In an illustration attached to the book *Lands Across the Sea* written by Chen Lun-chiung around the year 1730, the Tungshas were already listed among China's coastal islands. They were repeatedly mentioned in the book *Records of the Sea,* dictated by Hsieh Ching-kao and written by Yang Ping-nan in 1820. They were also clearly marked as one of the archipelagos along China's seacoast, and part of her territory in the *China Sea Pilot* compiled for the British Admiralty and published in 1894.

Chinese Islands

For centuries, Chinese people living along the coast of Kwangtung Province have made frequent visits to the Tungsha Islands. Yet in 1907, vainly hoping to seize them, a Japanese merchant named Kitchiji Nishizawa falsely claimed to be their "discoverer." He built some houses there and began to exploit rich local resources of guano and marine products. When the Chinese authorities became aware of this Japanese trespassing on the Tungshas, Li Chun, naval commander of Kwangtung Province, sent men to keep Nishizawa under surveillance. At the same time, Chinese officials in Kwangtung lodged a protest with the Japanese consul in Canton. The Japanese government knew it had no case, and the Tungsha Islands were handed back to China.

As to the Sishas, they were frequently mentioned in the old Chinese historical work as "Ocean of Seven Islands." The book *Journeys by Junk* by Fei Hsin, a famous traveller of the fifteenth century who sailed on one of the ships of the great Ming dynasty navigator Cheng Ho, and *Geographical Notes* by Ku Tsu-yu, a geographer of the seventeenth century, mention that, from early times, Chinese seamen have made use of these islands. An illustration in *Lands Across the Sea,* already mentioned earlier, shows clearly that the Sishas were included among China's offshore territories. That the Chinese people have frequented or settled on them since the remote past is beyond all doubt.

After Li Chun had made an inspection tour of the Tungsha Islands in 1907, he took his fleet to the Sishas for the same purpose. There he met Chinese fishermen collecting tortoise-shells, sea slugs, and kelp, a thing they did each year.

In and after 1921, a number of Japanese intruded on the Sisha Islands where they surreptitiously exploited the guano deposits and built docks, railways, and factories. This aroused strong opposition among the Chinese people. In 1926, after the Canton-Hongkong General Strike which marked a high tide of antiimperialist feeling, the Japanese deemed it more prudent to withdraw. Chinese fishermen then resumed and expanded their operations.

The Chungsha Islands are shoals submerged by the sea. China's sovereign rights over them have always been taken as a matter of course.

The Nanshas

The Nansha Islands, which some elements in the Philippines covet, are as undeniably Chinese as the fact that the Tungsha, Sisha, and Chungsha groups are. The biggest cluster of shoals in the Nansha archipelago has always been known, in Chinese history, as "The Sandbank and the Rock." Chinese fishermen have always gone to the Nanshas, at fixed periods, to fish and collect various marine products, and some Chinese have been domiciled there permanently.

China's sovereignty over the Nansha Islands was repeatedly recognized by other countries. In 1883, the Germans undertook a survey there, but stopped when China protested. Art. III of the special treaty defining the boundary line between China and the then French possessions in Indochina signed in 1887 also confirms that these islands belong to China. In 1917, Japan sent a party to investigate and exploit the natural resources of the Nanshas. But, having no right to be there, they too were forced to withdraw.

In 1933, France forcibly occupied nine of the archipelago's islets, including the Taiping and Nanwei, alleging that they "were mere uninhabited shoals and sandbanks which were often submerged in the sea." These allegations were ridiculous and could not be sustained either from history or from contemporary facts.

The *China Sea Pilot* (Vol. III, 2nd edition, 1923) published for the Hydrographic Department of the Admiralty by His Majesty's Stationery Office, London, records:

> Hainan fishermen, who subsist by collecting trepang and tortoise-shell, were found upon most of these islands; some of them remain for years amongst the reefs. Junks from Hainan annually visit the islands and reefs with supplies of rice and other necessaries, for which the fishermen give trepang and other articles in exchange. . . .

The same book also mentions the Shuangtze Shoal where "the cays are frequented by Chinese fishermen from Hainan, who collect bêche-de-mer, turtle shell, &c. . . ."

On August 21, 1933, France had to admit that Chinese fishermen were living on two of the islets she had seized. Nonetheless, she still tried to occupy them on the pretext of building lighthouses to facilitate navigation. The then Chinese government reacted with a strong protest, calling the attention of the French government to the fact that Chinese people had been living on the islands, and Chinese fishermen frequenting them, for many years. It added that there were Chinese temples and cemeteries on the Nanshas and China's sovereignty over them was undoubted. The French government failed to make any answer.

During the War of Resistance to Japanese Aggression, the Nansha group and other Chinese islands in the South China Sea fell into Japanese hands. When Japan surrendered in 1945, all of them were returned to China, which sent a fleet, in 1946, to take them over officially. Stone monuments were reerected on Yunghsing (Woody) Island, in the Sishas, and Taiping Island, in the Nanshas. Surveys and mapping were undertaken and weather and radio stations set up. That all the islands in the South China Sea were returned to China after Japan's defeat is known to the whole world.

But despite these irrefutable historical facts, certain forces abroad continued to cherish ambitions with regard to the islands. In July 1946, when the Chinese people were waging their war of Liberation, the Philippine Foreign Ministry made a completely unfounded statement claiming an interest in the Nanshas. In May 1950 when the whole Chinese mainland had been liberated, the Philippine authorities again made a provocative statement of this kind.

No Encroachment Allowed

Article II, Chapter II, of the so-called "peace treaty with Japan" dictated by the United States government in 1951 provided that Japan must renounce all rights to the Sisha and Nanwei Islands, but deliberately avoided any mentioning of the fact that these islands had in fact already been returned to China. This was an evident attempt by the US imperialists to cancel the facts of the case. It led to a statement by Chou En-lai, the Chinese Foreign Minister, on August 15, 1951, in which he solemnly declared:

> Just like the entire Nansha Islands, Chungsha Islands and Tungsha Islands, the Sisha Islands (the Paracel Islands) and Nanwei Island (Spratly Island) have always been China's territory. Although they had been occupied by Japan for some time during the war of aggression waged by Japanese imperialism, they

> were all taken over by the then Chinese government following Japan's surrender. The Central People's Government of the People's Republic of China hereby declares: whether or not the US-British Draft Treaty contains provisions on this subject and no matter how these provisions are worded, the inviolable sovereignty of the People's Republic of China over Nanwei Island (the Spratly Island) and Sisha Islands (the Paracel Islands) will not be in any way affected.

The facts of history cannot be denied or twisted. The Nansha, Sisha, Chungsha, and Tungsha Islands have always been part of China's territory. The attitude of the Chinese people on the matter has been voiced in a Foreign Ministry statement:

> Encroachment on China's legitimate sovereignty over the Nansha Islands by any country under whatever pretext and by whatever means will absolutely not be tolerated.

12-6
"Chinese Warning on South Vietnam Intrusions,"
PR 2.9:9 (Mar. 3, 1959).

On the night of February 20, a South Vietnam gunboat was prowling about Peh Island in the Hsisha [Sisha] Archipelago. The next day it intercepted several Chinese fishing vessels and at gunpoint seized an old Chinese fisherman to get information on the Hsisha Islands out of him. In the morning of the 22nd, the gunboat's crew landed on Shenhang (Tenghing) Island. They tore down Chinese national flags and finally made off with 82 captured Chinese fishermen, five fishing vessels, and other property.

A South Vietnam aircraft flew over the islands on reconnaissance.

In connection with this outrage, the Chinese Foreign Ministry, on February 27, issued the following statement:

> According to reports from our national coast guard, South Vietnam naval men made an illegal intrusion on Shenhang Island of the Hsisha Islands of our country on February 22, 1959, kidnapped 82 Chinese fishermen and took away five Chinese fishing vessels and other property. In regard to this, the Ministry of Foreign Affairs of the People's Republic of China is authorized to state:

The Hsisha Islands are part of China's territory. The government of the People's Republic of China made solemn statements concerning this fact on August 15, 1951, and May 29, 1956. Now the South Vietnam navy has openly violated China's territorial integrity and sovereignty and kidnapped Chinese fishermen and fishing vessels. This has aroused the great indignation of the Chinese people.

The Ministry of Foreign Affairs of the People's Republic of China gives solemn warning that the South Vietnam authorities must immediately release all the Chinese fishermen kidnapped, return all the fishing vessels and other property carried away, compensate for the losses of these fishermen and guarantee that similar unlawful incidents will not recur in the future; otherwise, the South Vietnam authorities must accept responsibility for all consequences.

Note

The status of the islands in the South China Sea has continued to be in dispute. When in May 1960 the PRC accused the United States of violating Chinese air space over the Sishas, the US denied that the islands were Chinese territory. This led the *People's Daily* to renew the PRC's claim.[19] In the summer of 1971 it was reported that Chinese Nationalist soldiers were manning gun emplacements on Itu Aba (Taiping) island of the Spratly (Nansha) group and had fired on a Filipino party that sought to land there. The Philippine government sent a note to Taipei asking that the Nationalist garrison be withdrawn. The ROC stated that it had stationed troops on the Nansha group but that no shooting had taken place. At the same time a report from Washington suggested that the PRC had undertaken construction of what appeared to be a naval base on the Sishas;[20] and NCNA protested against a renewed Philippine claim to the Nanshas and a renewed South Vietnamese claim to both the Sishas and the Nanshas.[21]

By the end of 1970 a more serious dispute over five uninhabited islets in the East China Sea north of Taiwan had come to public attention. The islands, known as Senkaku in Japanese and as Tiaoyü or Tiao Yü T'ai in Chinese, have little value in themselves, but in 1968 a study by the United Nations Economic Commission for Asia and the Far East revealed that the seabed of the East China Sea could be one of the richest oil producing areas in the world. Thus ownership of the islands became important because of the rights the country that owned them would have to the adjacent territorial sea and continental shelf. When it was announced that the United States planned to return the

US-administered Ryūkyū Islands to Japan in 1972 and that the Senkaku, which had been administered as part of the Ryūkyū, would also revert to Japan, the dispute became apparent.

In July 1970 the Republic of China granted the Japanese subsidiary of an American oil company drilling rights over the seabed of a vast area of the East China Sea including the islands.[22] ROC officials also claimed Chinese sovereignty over the islands, and ROC acting Foreign Minister James C. H. Shen informed the Japanese ambassador to Taipei on October 23, 1970, that these islands are part of Taiwan.[23] The ROC also asked the United States to stop Ryūkyū local patrol boats from chasing Chinese fishermen from the area.[24] Ryūkyū officials had also removed a ROC flag from one of the islands and had placed "no trespassing" markers on each of them.[25]

Although neither Japan nor the ROC was willing to enter into formal negotiations over the question of sovereignty over the islands, they did begin an informal exchange of views over the question of the exploitation of the resources of the continental shelf. The Japanese also suggested that Japan, the ROC, and South Korea cooperate in developing the undersea resources of the East China Sea without prejudice to their respective legal claims.[26] At this point the PRC entered the dispute, unofficially at first with item 12–7 and similar claims, and then, a year later, with the official statement reproduced in item 12–8.

12-7

"US and Japanese Reactionaries Out to Plunder Chinese and Korean Seabed Resources," *PR* 13.50:15 (Dec. 11, 1970).

A group of Japanese reactionary politicians and pro-US monopolist bigwigs led by arch war criminal Nobusuke Kishi rigged up on November 12 a "liaison committee" in Seoul, in collusion with the Chiang Kai-shek gang and the Pak Jung Hi puppet clique. They noisily declared that, beginning in 1971, they would "jointly exploit" the undersea oil in the water areas around China's Taiwan Province and its appendant islands and in the shallow water areas close to China and Korea. This is a new crime by Japanese militarism in plotting aggression against China and Korea with US imperialist support, a serious provocation by the US and Japanese reactionaries against the Chinese and Korean people.

The formation of the Japan-Chiang-Pak "liaison committee" shows that the Japanese militarist forces are embarking more recklessly on the criminal path of aggression against China and Korea. At the instigation of the Japanese militarist forces, the first undertaking of this committee is its decision to set up under it two "special committees" for "ocean development" and "economic co-operation" and its declaration that "joint development" of the undersea oil in the water areas around China's Taiwan Province and its appendant islands and in the shallow water areas close to China and Korea will begin next year. To this end, they have planned to set up a so-called joint-stock company for ocean development and decided that the "special committee for ocean development" will meet in Tokyo in December to determine the proportion of members' investment in the company and the nomination of its staff.

What they call "joint development" is merely the established practice of the Japanese militarist pirates in viciously plundering others. The "joint development" to be undertaken by Japanese militarism together with Chiang Kai-shek and Pak Jung Hi, dregs of history long spurned by the Chinese and Korean people, is an outright dirty deal between aggressor and traitors.

The Japanese militarists have adopted a series of new and more vicious tricks for the purpose of plundering the undersea oil of China and Korea. They will temporarily "shelve" or "freeze" the title of China and Korea to the islands and the undersea resources and begin "joint development" first. What do "shelving" and "freezing" mean? By "shelving" and "freezing," they want the people of China and Korea to surrender their sovereignty and let Japanese militarism ravage and occupy the islands and resources at will. Such wild piratical behaviour by the Japanese reactionaries has shocked even the Japanese bourgeois press which declared that "this is something that has seldom been seen in the world."

There are indeed rich oil, natural gas, and other mineral resources on the sea floor in the water areas around China's Taiwan Province and its appendant islands and in the shallow water areas close to China and Korea. While feverishly plundering the rich resources of China's Taiwan Province, US imperialism, aggressive by nature, long ago stretched its claws of aggression on to the sea floor of China's vast shallow water areas. In recent years, US imperialism and the Japanese reactionaries have conducted large-scale surveys of the undersea resources in China's shallow water areas. Their aircraft and ships equipped with various kinds of instruments have made prolonged and repeated surveys above and on the surface of China's shallow water areas. The scope of their surveys included the vast water areas of the Yellow Sea, the East China Sea, and the South China Sea, which are close to China and the Taiwan Straits. These activities are still going on.

Japanese militarism is feverishly carrying out arms expansion and war preparations and stepping up the militarization of the national economy. Thus, it is particularly in need of all kinds of strategic materials, especially petroleum. Apart from viciously plundering oil in the Middle East, Southeast Asia, and other places, the Japanese reactionaries have been casting covetous eyes on China's undersea resources in particular. Together with the US armed forces in Okinawa and the US imperialist-controlled UN Economic Commission for Asia and the Far East, the reactionary Sato government has jointly surveyed the sea floor in the shallow water areas close to China and around China's Taiwan Province. Cheek by jowl, it is now scheming with the Chiang Kai-shek gang to prospect for undersea oil in China's Taiwan Straits area. Supported by US imperialism, the reactionary Sato government is also seeking various pretexts for incorporating the Tiaoyu, Huangwei, Chihwei, Nanhsiao, Peihsiao, and other islands and water areas which belong to China into Japan's territory.

This new act of aggression by the US and Japanese reactionaries in league with the Chiang Kai-shek gang and the Pak Jung Hi clique has aroused great indignation among the 700 million Chinese people and the 40 million Korean people. The US and Japanese reactionaries will reap their own bitter fruits if they do not pull in their claws of aggression.

12-8

"Statement of the Ministry of Foreign Affairs of the People's Republic of China" (Dec. 30, 1971), in *PR* 15.1:12 (Jan. 7, 1972).

In the past few years, the Japanese Sato government, ignoring the historical facts and the strong opposition of the Chinese people, has repeatedly claimed that Japan has the so-called "title" to China's territory of the Tiaoyu and other islands and, in collusion with US imperialism, has engaged in all kinds of activities to invade and annex the above-mentioned islands. Not long ago, the US Congress and the Japanese Diet one after the other approved the agreement on the "reversion" of Okinawa. In this agreement, the governments of the United States and Japan flagrantly included the Tiaoyu and other islands in the "area of reversion." This is a gross encroachment upon China's territorial integrity and sovereignty. The Chinese people absolutely will not tolerate this!

The Tiaoyu and other islands have been China's territory since ancient times. Back in the Ming dynasty, these islands were already within China's sea defence areas; they were islands appertaining to China's Taiwan but not to Ryukyu, which is now known as Okinawa. The boundary between China and Ryukyu in this area lies between Chihwei Island and Kume Island and fishermen from China's Taiwan have all along carried out productive activities on the Tiaoyu and other islands. During the 1894 Sino-Japanese War, the Japanese government stole these islands and in April 1895 it forced the government of the Ching dynasty to conclude the unequal "Treaty of Shimonoseki" by which "Taiwan, together with all islands appertaining to Taiwan" and the Penghu Islands were ceded. Now the Sato government has gone to the length of making the Japanese invaders' act of aggression of seizing China's territory in the past a ground for claiming that Japan has the so-called "title" to the Tiaoyu and other islands. This is sheer and outright gangster logic.

After World War II, the Japanese government illicitly handed over to the United States the Tiaoyu and other islands appertaining to Taiwan, and the United States government unilaterally declared that it enjoyed the so-called "administrative rights" over these islands. This in itself was illegal. On June 28, 1950, shortly after the founding of the People's Republic of China, Foreign Minister Chou En-lai, on behalf of the Chinese government, strongly condemned US imperialism for sending its Seventh Fleet to commit aggression against Taiwan and the Taiwan Straits, and solemnly declared that the Chinese people were determined to "recover Taiwan and all territories belonging to China." Now the US and Japanese governments have once again made an illicit transfer between themselves of China's Tiaoyu and other islands. This encroachment upon China's territorial integrity and sovereignty cannot but arouse the utmost indignation of the Chinese people.

The Ministry of Foreign Affairs of the People's Republic of China hereby solemnly declares: Tiaoyu Island, Huangwei Island, Chihwei Island, Nanhsiao Island, Peihsiao Island, etc. are islands appertaining to Taiwan. Like Taiwan, they have been an inalienable part of Chinese territory since ancient times. It is utterly illegal for the US and Japanese governments to include China's Tiaoyu and other islands in the so-called "area of reversion" in the Okinawa "reversion" agreement. Their act cannot in the least alter the sovereignty of the People's Republic of China over her territory of the Tiaoyu and other islands. The Chinese people are determined to liberate Taiwan! The Chinese people are determined to recover the Tiaoyu and other islands appertaining to Taiwan!

NOTE

Peking Review embellished the PRC's official claim that the Tiaoyu have been China's since ancient times:

> To resist harassment by Japanese invaders, China's Ming dynasty in 1556 appointed Hu Tsung-hsien commander of the punitive force in charge of military action against the Japanese invaders in the coastal provinces. Tiaoyu Island, Huangwei Island, Chihwei Island, and other islands were then within the scope of China's coastal defence. It was more specifically stated in the records of missions sent to the Ryukyu Islands by China's Ming and Ching dynasties and in geography and history books that these islands belong to China and that the demarcation line between China and the Ryukyu Islands lies between Chihwei Island and Kome Island, namely, present-day Kume Island.
>
> In 1879, when Li Hung-chang, Minister Superintendent of Trade for the Northern Ports of China of the Ching dynasty, held negotiations with Japan on the title to the Ryukyus, both the Chinese and Japanese sides held that the Ryukyus comprised 36 islands. Tiaoyu and the other islands were not among those 36 islands at all.
>
> The Tiaoyu and other islands were under China's jurisdiction for several centuries, and it was only in 1884 that the Japanese "discovered" them. The Japanese government immediately plotted to annex them, but dared not lay hands on them then. It was in 1895 when the defeat of the government of the Ching dynasty in the Sino-Japanese War had become inevitable that these islands were grabbed by Japan. The Japanese government then compelled the Ching dynasty government to sign the "Treaty of Shimonoseki" which ceded "Taiwan, together with all islands appertaining to Taiwan" and the Penghu Islands to Japan.[27]

On March 8, 1972, the government of Japan, through its Foreign Ministry, issued a statement of its position regarding the islands in dispute:

> After 1885 the Japanese government carried out a series of careful on-the-spot surveys of the Senkaku Islands through the assistance of the Okinawa prefectural authorities and by other means. Having thus ascertained carefully that the islands were not only uninhabited but without any trace of control by China (Ching dynasty), the Japanese government [made a] cabinet decision on January 14, 1895, to set up posts on the Senkaku

Islands to manifest Japan's territorial sovereignty and thereby formally incorporated these islands into the territory of Japan.

Since then the Senkaku Islands have been consistently a part of Japan's territory of Nansei Shoto. Naturally, these islands are not included in the islands of Formosa and the Pescadores, which were ceded to Japan under Article 2 of the Sino-Japanese Peace Treaty which entered into force in May, 1895. At the time of the San Francisco Peace Treaty, therefore, the Senkaku Islands were not renounced by Japan under Article 2 of the Treaty but were placed under the administration of the United States together with other islands of Nansei Shoto in accordance with the provisions of Article 3. Now the administration over the Senkaku Islands and over the other islands of Nansei Shoto is to be returned to Japan under the Agreement between Japan and the United States of America concerning the Ryukyu Islands and the Daito Islands signed on June 17, 1971. All these facts testify in the clearest possible manner to the status of the Senkaku Islands as a territory of Japan.

For a long time, since the entry into force of the San Francisco Peace Treaty, China [has] raised no objection to the fact that the Senkaku Islands are included in the area placed under United States administration in accordance with the provisions of Article 3 of the Treaty. In fact, neither the government of the Republic of China nor the government of the People's Republic of China had taken up the question of sovereignty over the islands until the latter half of 1970 when movements relating to exploitation of oil resources deposited in the East China Sea continental shelf surfaced. All [of] this clearly indicates that China had not until recently regarded the Senkaku Islands as a part of Formosa.

None of the alleged historical, geographical, and geological arguments set forth by the governments of the Republic of China and the People's Republic of China are acceptable as valid under international law to substantiate China's territorial claim over the Senkaku Islands.[28]

Peking Review responded by pointing out that "the Chinese government and people" had never recognized Japan's transfer to the United States of "administrative rights" over the Tiaoyu and by challenging Japan's version of relevant nineteenth-century history:

The "official statement" brought forth by Foreign Minister Fukuda and the Japanese Foreign Ministry alleged that "the islands were never ruled by the Ching dynasty of China. This was confirmed by a survey made in the 18th year of the reign of Meiji (1885)." The Japanese government attempts to describe China's territory Tiaoyu and other islands as "belonging to nobody" so as to create "grounds" for its occupation of them. This is a complete distortion of historical facts to confuse the issue. When the Japanese government clandestinely made a so-called "survey" there in 1885, these islands had been under China's jurisdiction for several centuries. Historical facts cannot be changed. The "grounds" fabricated by the Sato government in distorting the historical facts can deceive nobody.

Another "reason" dreamt up by Foreign Minister Fukuda and the Japanese Foreign Ministry is that in the 28th year of the reign of Meiji (1895) the Japanese cabinet decided to incorporate the islands into Japanese territory. This is precisely a confession of the criminal act of the old Japanese militarists in annexing China's territory Tiaoyu and other islands. Historical facts show that Japanese militarism had cast a covetous eye on China's Tiaoyu and other islands for ten years since 1885, but never dared to lay a hand on them until 1895, when, taking advantage of the defeat of the Ching dynasty government in the Sino-Japanese War, it forcibly "incorporated" the Tiaoyu and other islands into Japanese territory. In April the same year, the government of the Ching dynasty was compelled to sign the unequal "Treaty of Shimonoseki," by which Taiwan together with all the islands appertaining to it and the Penghu Islands were ceded to Japan. Now the Sato government has gone so far as to take the aggressive act of grabbing China's territory by the Japanese aggressors in the past as "grounds" to support its standpoint that it should have title to the islands. This is absolute gangster logic.[29]

In the interim the dispute had also been brought before the UN Committee on the Peaceful Uses of the Sea-Bed and the Ocean Floor Beyond the Limits of National Jurisdiction, where both the Japanese and PRC representatives made strong statements.[30] And, five days after the May 15 reversion to Japan of the "administrative rights" over the Tiaoyu Islands, Huang Hua, the PRC's Permanent Representative to the UN, sent a letter to UN Secretary-General Waldheim and to the President of the Security Council for the month, asserting that "The Chinese Government and people will never accept it." [31] Subsequently, however, what had been developing into a tense situation gradually subsided as the advent of the new Tanaka government in Japan led to an improvement of relations between Tokyo and Peking. By that stage the dispute had begun to spawn a body of legal literature.[32]

(b) TAIWAN

The islands in the South and East China Seas have obvious strategic and economic significance for the PRC. Yet, given Peking's overall objectives and policies, the status of those islands has proved to be a very minor matter. The same can hardly be said about the status of the island of Taiwan. As indicated in Part III, their failure to "liberate" Taiwan has left the Communist leaders with a profound sense of deprivation; of all the major territories that they claim outside the bounds of mainland China's traditional eighteen provinces, only Taiwan has remained beyond their control. Manchuria, Inner Mongolia, and Sinkiang were all subdued by the time that the Communists achieved nationwide power in 1949, and, as we shall see in Section d, below, Tibet yielded in 1950.

The frustration felt over their inability to achieve what is perceived to be China's territorial unification is intensified, of course, by the fact that Taiwan is the refuge of the predecessor Nationalist regime that continues to claim jurisdiction over all of China and to carry on the civil war. In light of modern China's "century of humiliation" at the hands of imperialism, perhaps the most galling aspect to the Communists is that this situation has been made possible because the leading non-Communist power of the era, the United States, interposed its fleet in the Taiwan strait beginning June 27, 1950, subsequently built up a substantial military establishment on the island in support of the Nationalist forces, and committed itself by treaty to defend the island against attack. If history makes the wound more grievous to a historical-minded elite, it also holds out the hope that Peking's ambition might eventually be fulfilled. The difficulty that the new regime on the mainland has had in subjugating the old regime that is now based on Taiwan bears certain resemblances to the difficulty in the seventeenth century that China's new Manchu dynasty had in subduing partisans of its predecessor, the Ming dynasty, after they had retreated to Taiwan in 1662. In 1683, however, the Manchus finally succeeded.

Although Chinese contacts with Taiwan date back at least as far as 605 and although Chinese had begun emigrating to the island centuries before the advent of the Manchus, the Manchu regime was the first Chinese government to maintain reasonably effective control over Taiwan. It treated the island as a part of the mainland's Fukien province until 1885, when it made Taiwan a separate province. In 1895, however, Taiwan had to be ceded to Japan under the terms of the Treaty of Shimonoseki, which ended the Sino-Japanese War.

Despite this history and despite the fact that as early as 1938 the Nationalist government claimed Taiwan,[33] Mao Tse-tung apparently did not regard Taiwan as rightfully belonging to China prior to the Second World War. The following excerpt is from his famous 1936 interview with Edgar Snow:

> Question: "Is it the immediate task of the Chinese people to regain all the territories lost to Japanese imperialism, or only to drive Japan from North China, and all Chinese territory above the Great Wall?"
>
> Answer: "It is the immediate task of China to regain all our lost territories, not merely to defend our sovereignty south of the Great Wall. This means that Manchuria must be regained. We do not, however, include Korea, formerly a Chinese colony, but when we have reestablished the independence of the lost territories of China, and if the Koreans wish to break away from the chains of Japanese imperialism, we will extend them our enthusiastic help in their struggle for independence. The same thing applies for Taiwan [Formosa]. . . ." [34]

The Chinese Communists adopted a markedly different position about Taiwan as a result of wartime diplomatic and military developments described in the following materials. As indicated by the materials in this part and those in Part VIII (see Note following item 31–11 and see items 31–21 and 34–1) the Communists have consistently adhered to this position for over two decades.

Item 12–9 presents relevant portions of the statement made in 1950 by the representative of the PRC who had been invited by the United Nations Security Council to attend its discussion of the PRC's charge that the United States had committed "direct armed aggression against the territory of China" by placing its fleet in the Taiwan strait.

12-9

"Extracts from a Speech by Mr. Wu Hsiu-ch'üan, Representative of the PRC at the Security Council's Discussions on the Question of 'Invasion of Taiwan,' November 28, 1950," United Nations Security Council, *Official Records*, 5th Year, 527th Meeting, No. 69, at 5–7, 9–10 (S/PV.527)

People with any common sense know that Taiwan is an inseparable part of the territory of China. Long before Christopher Columbus discovered America, the Chinese people were already in Taiwan. Long before the United States achieved its own independence, Taiwan had already become an inseparable part of the territory of China. Precisely because of this irrevocable historical fact that Taiwan is part of China, civilized nations of the whole world have never conceded that the occupation of Taiwan by imperialist Japan during the fifty-year period from 1895 to 1945 was justifiable. Moreover, the people of Taiwan have always opposed the rule of Japanese imperialism. During the fifty years under Japanese imperialist rule, the people of Taiwan lived like beasts of burden and underwent all the sufferings of a subject people. But during these fifty years the people in Taiwan never ceased conducting a dauntless struggle against the alien rule of Japanese imperialism and for their return to the motherland. In their heroic struggle against Japanese imperialism, the people in Taiwan have written with blood and fire into the pages of history that they are a member, an integral part, of the great family of the Chinese nation. Even the White Paper, *United States Relations with China,* compiled by the United States Department of State, has to admit that: "The native population for 50 years had been under the rule of a foreign invader and therefore welcomed the Chinese forces as liberators. During the Japanese occupation the principal hope of the people had been reunion with the mainland." [35]

Precisely because Taiwan is an inseparable part of China, the Cairo Declaration jointly signed on 1 December 1943 by the governments of China, the United States of America, and the United Kingdom explicitly stipulated that "it is their"—the three great Powers'—"purpose . . . that all territories Japan has stolen from the Chinese, such as Manchuria, Formosa, and the Pescadores, shall be restored to the Republic of China."

Taiwan is an integral part of China. This is not only an unshakable historical fact, but also one of the main aims for which the Chinese people fought unitedly against imperialist Japan. The Cairo Declaration signed on 1 December 1943 by the United States, the United Kingdom, and China clearly reflected this aim of the people of China. Moreover, the Cairo Declaration is a solemn international commitment which the United States government has pledged itself to observe. As one of the principal provisions concerning the unconditional surrender of Japan, this solemn international commitment was again laid down in the Potsdam Declaration which was signed jointly on 26 July 1945 by China, the United States, and the United Kingdom, and was subsequently adhered to by the Soviet Union. Section 8 of the Potsdam Declaration, which provides the terms of the unconditional surrender of Japan, states: "The terms of the Cairo Declaration shall be carried out and Japanese sovereignty shall be limited to the islands of Honshu, Hokkaido, Kyushu, Shikoku, and such minor islands as we determine."

On 2 September 1945, Japan signed the Instrument of Surrender, the first article of which explicitly provided that Japan "accepts"—I am quoting from the original wording—"the provisions set forth in the Declaration issued by the heads of the Governments of the United States, China and Great Britain on July 26, 1945, at Potsdam, and subsequently adhered to by the Union of Soviet Socialist Republics." When the Chinese government accepted the surrender of the Japanese armed forces in Taiwan and exercised sovereignty over the island, Taiwan became, not only de jure, but also de facto, an inalienable part of Chinese territory, and this has been the situation as regards Taiwan since 1945. For this reason, during the five postwar years from 1945 to 27 June 1950, no one has ever questioned the fact that Taiwan is an inseparable part of Chinese territory, de jure or de facto.

This state of affairs was so clear that on 5 January 1950, even President Truman of the United States could not but admit the following:

> In the joint Declaration at Cairo on December 1, 1943, the President of the United States, the British Prime Minister, and the President of China stated that it was their purpose that territories that Japan had stolen from China, such as Formosa, should be restored to the Republic of China.
>
> The United States was a signatory to the Potsdam Declaration of July 26, 1945, which declared that the terms of the Cairo Declaration should be carried out. The provisions of this Declaration were accepted by Japan at the time of its surrender. . . .
>
> For the past four years the United States and the [other] Allied Powers have accepted the exercise of Chinese authority over the island.
>
> The United States has no predatory designs on Formosa or on any other Chinese territory. . . . Nor does it have any intention of

> utilizing its armed forces to interfere in the present situation. The United States government will not pursue a course which will lead to involvement in the civil conflict in China.

Thus, even President Truman admitted that Taiwan is Chinese territory. . . .

There is not the slightest justification for the United States government's invasion and occupation of Taiwan. Yet, to carry out that aggression, the United States government had somehow to find a justification. Thus, we have the story that "the status of Taiwan is not yet determined" and that, therefore, the armed occupation of Taiwan by the United States cannot be regarded as invasion and occupation of Chinese territory by the United States. Can you call this a "justification"? Did not President Truman declare, at the time the order for armed aggression against Taiwan was issued, that: "The determination of the future status of Formosa must await the restoration of security in the Pacific, a peace settlement with Japan, or consideration by the United Nations"?

Let us first of all deal with the question of the status of Taiwan and its relationship to the peace treaty with Japan. Does it hold water to say that, since the status of Taiwan is not yet determined, the invasion of Taiwan by United States armed forces constitutes no aggression against China? No, it does not. Here we have in the first place the Truman of 5 January 1950 contradicting the Truman of 27 June 1950. On 5 January, this year, Mr. Truman stated: "The United States and the other Allied Powers have accepted the exercise of Chinese authority over the island."

Surely, at that time, Mr. Truman did not consider that the peace treaty with Japan had already been signed. Then, we have President Roosevelt contradicting President Truman. On 1 December 1943, President Roosevelt solemnly declared, in the Cairo Declaration, that: "All the territories Japan has stolen from the Chinese, such as Manchuria, Formosa, and the Pescadores, shall be restored to the Republic of China."

Surely, neither President Roosevelt nor anyone else considered at that time that, in the absence of a peace treaty with Japan, the Cairo Declaration would be invalid and that Manchuria, Taiwan, and the Penghu Islands would remain in the possession of Japan.

The facts of history in the course of the past several centuries and the situation during the last five years, since the surrender of Japan, also contradict Mr. Truman, because the facts of history and the situation following the Japanese surrender have long determined the status of Taiwan to be an integral part of China. The status of Taiwan was determined long ago; there is no such question as that of Taiwan's status.

Article 107 of the Charter of the United Nations clearly provides that: "Nothing in the present Charter shall invalidate or preclude action, in relation to any state which during the Second World War has been an enemy of any signatory to the present Charter, taken or authorized as a result of that war by the governments having responsibility for such action." Therefore, the United Nations has no right whatsoever to alter the status of Taiwan, all the less as the question of the status of Taiwan does not exist.

President Truman declared that the so-called question of the status of Taiwan must await consideration by the United Nations. However, after the People's Republic of China had charged the United States before the United Nations with armed aggression against Taiwan, the United States government indicated that it would welcome consideration by the United Nations of the question of Taiwan and investigation by the United Nations. The United States representative at the fifth session of the United Nations General Assembly introduced the so-called "Question of Formosa," and made use of its voting machine in the General Assembly to put this matter on the agenda. All these moves of the United States government aim at stealing the name of the United Nations to legalize its illegal acts of armed aggression against Taiwan and to consolidate its actual occupation of Taiwan.

My government has protested in strong terms to the United Nations General Assembly, resolutely opposing the inclusion of the so-called "Question of Formosa"—concerning the status of Taiwan—on the agenda of the fifth session of the General Assembly. Whatever decision the United Nations General Assembly may take on the so-called question of the status of Taiwan, whether it be to hand over the island to the United States so that it might administer it openly under the disguise of "trusteeship," or "neutralization," or whether it be to procrastinate by way of "investigation," thereby maintaining the present state of actual United States occupation, it will, in substance, be stealing China's legitimate territory and supporting United States aggression against Taiwan in opposition to the Chinese people. Any such decision would be unjustifiable and unlawful. Any such decision would in no way shake the resolve of the Chinese people to liberate Taiwan; nor would it prevent action by the Chinese people to liberate Taiwan.

12-10

Mei Ju-ao, "The Aggressor and the Law," *PC*, no. 5:10–14 (Mar. 1, 1955).

Taiwan is an inseparable part of Chinese territory. This is an irrevocable historical fact confirmed by international agreements. It is just as true as the fact that Long Island is a part of the territory of the United States and the Isle of Man of the United Kingdom. Just as any invasion of Long Island, or the Isle of Man, by any foreign power would be a violation of the sovereignty of the United States or Britain, respectively, equally the invasion of Taiwan by any foreign power is and always will be a violation of the sovereignty of China. . . .

In its eight years of war against Japan, China suffered heavily. Over ten million Chinese citizens lost their lives, and property losses were immeasurable. At such a cost, China defended her national independence, sovereign rights, and territorial integrity.

As victor, China is entitled to recover Taiwan; no third party is permitted to deny or strip China of this right.

China's determination to recover Taiwan was in fact made known to the world early in 1941. Declaring war on Japan on December 8, 1941, China announced that all treaties between China and Japan were abrogated. It was under the Treaty of Shimonoseki that Japan claimed its right to occupy Taiwan. Once this treaty was abrogated, Japan immediately lost the ground for its rule in Taiwan.

Victory over Japan made it actually possible for China to carry out her declaration of December 8, 1941. On October 25, 1945, Japan surrendered Taiwan to China. China then declared that, "From today on, Taiwan and the Penghu Islands are once again officially incorporated into the map of China." Thus China acted on its own declaration. From that day on, the sovereignty of China over Taiwan and the Penghu Islands was in fact restored. . . .

The fact is that the Cairo Declaration was further incorporated into the Potsdam Declaration made by China, the United States, and Great Britain on July 26, 1945, later joined by the Soviet Union, and the Instrument of Surrender signed between Japan, on the one hand, and China, the Soviet Union, Britain, the United States, Australia, Canada, France, the Netherlands, and New Zealand, on the other, on September 2 of the same year. It has become an integral part of both those documents. The Potsdam Declaration says that "the terms of the Cairo Declaration will be carried out." Article 1 of the Instrument of Surrender provides that Japan is to accept "all the terms laid down in the Potsdam Declaration." These three documents are so closely interrelated that to deny one of them means to deny the other two. We say to those who deny the binding force of the Cairo Declaration: If you do this, you must at the same time deny the binding force of the Potsdam Declaration and the Instrument of Surrender. If that is the case, the surrender of Japan must be considered as having been invalid and the over six year postwar occupation of Japan by the United States as illegal. In other words, if [this] view is taken, all international relations in the Far East since the Second World War must be considered as having absolutely no legal grounds. Can such a thing enter anyone's mind?

Some people have vainly tried to distort the truth by trying to prove that the so-called "Peace Treaty" with Japan did not say anything about which country Taiwan belongs to. But this is an equally trashy piece of sophistry. First of all, China was not a party to the 1951 San Francisco "Peace Treaty" with Japan. It is therefore obvious that this US-made treaty is not legally binding on China. Moreover it is a matter of course that any country has the right to recover its own territory from an enemy when the latter is subjugated, before a peace treaty is concluded. Many European countries invaded by the Nazis recovered their territory immediately after Germany's defeat—even though no peace treaty with Germany has yet been signed. Similarly Alsace-Lorraine was formally restored to France on November 11, 1918, the actual day of the cessation of hostilities in the First World War, long before the signing of the Versailles Peace Treaty, and this fact is clearly stated in the Treaty itself (Article 51). In the same way, China was entitled to take back Taiwan and the Penghu Islands after the defeat of Japan, and in fact did so. . . .

In the light of all this, the utterances prodigally repeated by some British officials in recent weeks are manifestly absurd. . . .

In his statement made at the House of Commons on January 26 Anthony Eden, the British Foreign Secretary, said: "Formosa has never in this century been a part of China." Again on February 4 this year in a written reply to a Labor question he said: "Formosa and the Pescadores are, in the view of Her Majesty's Government, territory the de jure sovereignty over which is uncertain or undetermined." On February 1, Sir Winston Churchill, the British Prime Minister, also said that the Cairo Declaration "contains merely a statement of common purpose," and he added that since it was made "a lot of things have happened."

One test we can apply to such statements is to compare them with earlier ones, also made by officials and recorded in Hansard. Such a comparison will show them to be completely self-contradictory. . . .

On August 25, 1954, a spokesman of the British Foreign Office said: "The Cairo Declaration said that Formosa should be handed back to the Chinese government, which was done."

It was not only the British who once saw the real status of Taiwan much more clearly than it suits them to do now. The same inconsistency may be seen by comparing the frequent contentions of the United States government with its own earlier official statements. . . .

On January 5, 1950, Dean Acheson, the then US Secretary of State, stated that "the Chinese have administered Formosa for four years. Neither the United States nor any other ally ever questioned that authority and that occupation. When Formosa was made a province of China nobody raised any lawyer's doubts about it. It was regarded as being in accordance with the commitments."

On February 9, 1950, the United States Department of State made another statement which reads: "Formosa has been administered by China since 1945. . . . It was incorporated into China as a province. . . . The Allied Powers associated in the war against Japan have not questioned these steps. The United States government has not questioned these steps because they were clearly in line with its commitments made at Cairo and reaffirmed at Potsdam. In other words, the Allied Powers including the United States have for the past four years treated Formosa as a part of China. . . . For the United States government . . . to seek to establish a non-Chinese administration on Formosa . . . would be almost universally interpreted in mainland China and widely interpreted throughout Asia as an attempt by this government to separate Formosa from China in violation of its pledges and contrary to its long-standing policy of respecting the territorial integrity of China."

12-11

Shao Chin-fu, "The Absurd Theory of 'Two Chinas' and Principles of International Law," *KCWTYC*, no. 2:12–17 (1959); translated in *Oppose the New U.S. Plots to Create "Two Chinas"* (Peking, 1962), pp. 85–97.

While discussing the Taiwan question, former US Secretary of State Dulles advocated that "no country should use armed force to seize new territory," and that it was a principle "upon which world order is based." He demanded that China agree to "make a declaration of mutual and reciprocal renunciation of force, except in self-defense" and to carry out "cease-fire" and "peaceful solution," and so on.

True, "to refrain from the use of armed force to seize new territory" is a generally recognized "principle upon which world order is based." But this is a principle of international law. International law consists of principles for the settlement of questions concerning the relations between states, but not principles for settling internal questions of a state. An internal question is different in nature from an international question. Municipal law and international law have different scopes of application; the two should never be confused. The well-known German bourgeois jurist Liszt said, "International law is the body of legal norms which define reciprocal rights and obligations between states" [a] and "International law concerns only states as states." [b] The Soviet jurist Tunkin said, "International law does not apply to the internal relations of a country. As is laid down by the United Nations Charter, international law cannot be invoked in internal disputes and conflicts." [c] Even the American scholar Wilson also admitted: "Its scope should not be extended so as to interfere with domestic affairs or to limit domestic jurisdiction." [d] Since the Chinese people's liberation of their own territory, Taiwan, is China's internal question; naturally it has nothing to do with international law. It should be settled by the Chinese government according to its municipal law. Here Dulles purposely evaded the nature of the Taiwan question and applied, without the least justification, a principle of international law to China's internal question. What was he after if he was not deliberately calling black white and confusing truth with falsehood?

It is the business of the Chinese people themselves as to how the Chinese government is to deal with the Chiang Kai-shek clique and what form is to be adopted to liberate Taiwan. The Chinese government has the absolute right "to recover these areas by all suitable means at a suitable time." [e] To use or not to use force, "cease-fire" or no "cease-fire," "peaceful solution" or otherwise—these questions are not within the scope of application of international law. The United States can in no way meddle in.

Since there is no firing between China and the United States in the Taiwan area, there is no "fire" to "cease." When the United States brings up this question, it is raising a hue and cry for no reason.

US imperialists' assertion of the "right of self-defence" in this connection is also out of place. It is true that both international law and

[a] Franz von Liszt, *Mezhdunarodnoe pravo,* 4th ed. (International law) (1923), p. 1. [Note: We are unable to locate the place and publisher of this source.]

[b] *Ibid.,* p. 3.

[c] G. I. Tunkin, "Time to Restore China's Representation in the United Nations," *International Affairs: A Monthly Journal of Political Analysis* (Moscow), No. 10:27 (Oct. 1956).

[d] George Grafton Wilson, *International Law* (New York: Silver, Burdett and Company, 1935), p. 5.

[e] "Declaration on China's Territorial Sea, September 4, 1958," *PR* 1.28:21 (Sept. 9, 1958).

the United Nations Charter recognize that each country enjoys the "inherent right of individual or collective self-defence" (Article 51 of the UN Charter). But such a right can only apply to the relations between states and only a "state" can enjoy it, because "the purpose of the nonaggression principle is to maintain international peace; it only applies to relations between states," [f] but not to internal conflicts within a country. Therefore, as far as the Chiang Kai-shek clique is concerned, there is no right of self-defence to speak of.

As to the United States, it is the side which first used force towards the Chinese territory (Taiwan), grossly violating the obligation "not to be the first to use force towards another country." Still less is it entitled to the right of self-defence.

Sometime ago US imperialists declared that they would bring the question of the situation in the Taiwan Straits before the United Nations for settlement. Dulles openly announced at the 12th session of the UN Assembly that "The United States reserves the right to bring the matter to the United Nations." He also said he would submit it to the International Court of Justice for settlement, and so on.

But we would like to ask: What question did he want the United Nations to settle? If he meant settling the question between the Chinese government and the Chiang Kai-shek clique, obviously it is sheer nonsense. It is expressly stipulated in Article 2, Paragraph 7, of the UN Charter that "Nothing contained in the present Charter shall authorize the United Nations to intervene in matters which are essentially within the domestic jurisdiction of any state. . . ." The United Nations, therefore, has no right to discuss this question. Likewise, the International Court of Justice, as the principal judicial organ of the United Nations, has no jurisdiction over China's internal question. If Dulles meant the settlement of disputes between China and the United States over the Taiwan area, then as China's right of representation in the UN has been illegally deprived of and has not hitherto been restored, the United Nations is morally or legally not qualified to deal with such a question. As to the International Court of Justice, since China has never agreed to accept its jurisdiction, it has no right to handle cases concerning China.

(4)

The US ruling circles have time and again displayed the so-called "Mutual Security Treaty" signed between the United States and the Chiang Kai-shek clique in 1954 as a legal basis for their dispatching

[f] G. I. Tunkin, *Osnovy sovremennogo mezhdunarodnogo prava; uchebnoe posobie* (The bases of modern international law; Moscow: Vyssha partinaia shkola pri TsK KPSS, 1956), p. 29.

armed forces to the Taiwan Straits area and interfering in China's internal affairs, and they term the movements of the US forces in the Taiwan area as "living up to treaty obligations." But this so-called "treaty" is illegal and invalid with regard either to its subjects or to its contents.

First, according to international law, "The subjects of a treaty are states." [g] American jurist Wilson also said, "The parties to the treaty must have the international capacity to contract, i.e., ordinarily they must be states." [h] Since Taiwan is not a state, and the Chiang Kai-shek clique is not the legal representative of China, it has absolutely no right to conclude a treaty and cannot be a subject of a treaty. A treaty concluded by an unqualified subject should of course be regarded as null and void.

Secondly, as to the contents of the treaty, "The treaties must be in conformity to law, as embodied in the generally recognized principles of international law and the established usages of states," [i] and "obligations which are at variance with universally recognized principles of International Law cannot be the object of a treaty." [j] Article 103 of the UN Charter states: "In the event of a conflict between the obligations of the Members of the United Nations under the present Charter and their obligations under any other international agreement, their obligations under the present Charter shall prevail." In other words ". . . to the extent of their [treaties'] inconsistency with the Charter all these agreements are, for all practical purposes, void and unenforceable." [k] The aim of the US-Chiang "treaty" is "to resist armed attack and Communist subversive activities directed from without against their territorial integrity and political stability" (Article II). Here, "to resist armed attack" means to resist the Chinese people's liberation of Taiwan, on the pretext of which the United States can provoke war at any time. To resist "Communist subversive activities" means that the United States can send troops to suppress the Taiwan people because the United States and the Chiang Kai-shek clique are always in the habit of [designating] any revolutionary activity as "directed from without." The contents of the US-Chiang "treaty" are to empower the United States to split China, provoke war, and interfere in China's internal affairs. This, of course, contravenes the principles of international law and the UN Charter, and what contravenes these principles has, of course, no validity at all.

[g] Kozhevnikov, ed., *Mezhdunarodnoe pravo* (Moscow, 1957), p. 242.
[h] Wilson, *International Law*, p. 219.
[i] *Ibid.*
[j] Oppenheim, 7th ed., I, 808.
[k] Oppenheim, 7th ed., I, 807.

(5)

The imperialists' second set of logic is also baseless.

Since ancient times Taiwan has been a part of China. More than 1,000 years ago China set up government offices in Taiwan and Penghu to administer these places. After the Sino-Japanese War of 1894 the government of the Ch'ing Dynasty by signing the Treaty of Shimonoseki ceded Taiwan and Penghu to Japan. With the outbreak of China's War of Resistance against Japan in 1937, in accordance with international law, the treaties between the two countries became null and void. The Treaty of Shimonoseki was no exception. In 1945, after China's victory in the Anti-Japanese War, China recovered these two places from Japan. No question has ever been raised about the legal status of Taiwan. Since Taiwan has always been Chinese territory, it is a matter of course for China to take it back like a thing restored to its original owner. It is not a case of China taking a new territory from Japan which must be affirmed by a peace treaty. Particularly since the United States and Britain signed the Cairo Declaration which clearly recognizes that Taiwan and the Penghu Islands are "territories Japan has stolen from the Chinese," and "shall be restored" to China, they are still less in a position to raise the so-called "question of legal status of Taiwan." Despite the US and British imperialists' clamours that the Cairo Declaration was "merely a declaration of intention" and was not in the nature of a treaty, anyone with some legal knowledge realizes that the Cairo Declaration, like the Yalta Agreement and the Potsdam Declaration, was neither a unilateral expression of the policy of one allied country nor merely a statement of general principles between allies. It was an agreement reached between the heads of governments of Allied Powers on a specific question in the interest of joint military operations during the war, having definitely a legal binding force. Regarding the nature and contents of such documents, even the bourgeois authorities on international law admit their validity. For example, Oppenheim's *International Law* says: "Official statements in the form of Reports of Conferences signed by the Heads of States or Governments and embodying agreements reached therein may, in proportion as these agreements incorporate definite rules of conduct, be regarded as legally binding upon the States in question." [1]

In fact, in October 1945 the Chinese government at that time had already recovered Taiwan from the Japanese aggressors, exercised sovereignty there, and made it one of the provinces of China. Such hard facts were known to the whole world and were publicly recognized

[1] Oppenheim, 7th ed., I, 788.

even by the Truman administration. The Chinese people overthrew the reactionary rule and set up the People's Republic of China; the sovereignty of this Republic naturally extends to Taiwan. The Chinese people's liberation of Taiwan, like their liberation of other places in the whole country, is a legal act of exercising their sovereign rights. It can never be called "extending new territories."

Dulles said, "Neither Taiwan (Formosa) nor the islands of Quemoy and Matsu has ever been under the authority of the Chinese Communists." This is true, but who does not know that it is precisely owing to US aggression that Taiwan has up till today been unable to come under the authority of the People's Republic of China? This point brought up by Dulles can on no account deny the Chinese people's sovereign rights over Taiwan. On the contrary, it is a confession on the part of the United States of its occupation of Chinese territory and intervention in China's internal affairs.

As to "plebiscite" and "UN trusteeship," which the United States and some of its accomplices clamour for, they are even less grounded.

Of the total population in Taiwan, 98 percent are Hans who are exactly the same as the Hans on the mainland. Only a very small section are Koshans who have become a member of China's big family for a long time, and China is their motherland. Here the question of national self-determination does not exist; nor is there any controversy over the territory. On what grounds do the imperialists want them to vote in a plebiscite? Since they do not want to establish a new state or belong to any foreign country, what is the objective of imposing a plebiscite on them?

The United Nations trusteeship system is the result of mutual compromise between the Allied Powers after World War II on questions dealing with the colonies of the defeated nations and the former League of Nations mandates. The "basic objectives" of the system are to promote the local inhabitants' "progressive development towards self-government or independence" (Article 76 of the UN Charter), and, according to Article 77, the "Trust Territories" are confined to: (1) territories now held under mandate; (2) territories which may be detached from enemy states as a result of the Second World War, and (3) territories voluntarily placed under the system by states responsible for their administration. China was a victorious Power in World War II, and Taiwan, being always China's territory, is entirely different from the three categories of territories mentioned above. Obviously the "trusteeship system" is not applicable.

It can be seen therefore that both sets of the imperialists' gangster logic are full of loopholes and untenable. There are no two Chinas in this world whether in law or in fact, and Taiwan is Chinese territory de facto and de jure. Foreign aggressors fancy they can use their preposterous theory of "two Chinas" to apologize for their acts of aggression, but they will never achieve their end.

(6)

The "two Chinas" scheme is a temporary tactic rather than the aim of the US policy towards China. For, as far as its original intention goes, the United States does not even wish to see a truly independent China. It only wants a China of "open door and equal opportunity," a colonial or semicolonial China. It helped the Chiang Kai-shek clique fight civil war with the object of maintaining the continued existence of such a China. At present it adopts the policy of creating "two Chinas," its purpose being precisely to occupy by force a part of Chinese territory, [to] foster a counterrevolutionary clique on it so as to detach it from China and make it a base for extending aggression, and to look for an opportunity to overthrow the people's state power and further its aggression on the whole of China.

Today the US imperialists are just treading the old path of the Japanese bandits in their aggression against China. The aims and even many concrete measures of the two are identical.

In 1931 when Japan launched aggression against China's Northeast, it claimed that it had "vital interests" in "Manchuria," and that its purpose was for "maintaining peace in the Orient." Today, in occupying Taiwan, the United States claims that Taiwan concerns the "US defence interests" and its purpose is for "the security of the free world." In order to detach the Northeast from China, Japan used the feudal remnants of the Ch'ing Dynasty such as Puyi and Cheng Hsiao-hsu, who had been long ago repudiated by the Chinese people, as figureheads to set up the so-called "Manchukuo." In order to sever Taiwan from China, the United States supports the so-called "Republic of China"—the remnants of the reactionary Kuomintang ruling clique. In order to deny China's sovereign rights over the four northeastern provinces, the Japanese militarists said that these were the "old imperial domain" of the Ch'ing Dynasty and should be "detached from the China proper," [m] in other words, to be turned over to Japan. In order to deny China's sovereign rights over Taiwan, the United States and its accomplices say that "the legal status of Taiwan is not decided" and it should be placed

[m] From the Opinion of the Japanese Government on the Lytton Report, November 18, 1932. Reported in Kuzuu Yoshihisa, *The Unofficial History of Japan-China Negotiations* (in Japanese) [Note: The author of the original source does not give publication information.]

under "United Nations trusteeship," in other words, be turned over to the United States. In order to create a "legal basis" for occupying the Northeast, the Japanese government signed a "Japan-Manchukuo Protocol" with its collaborator Cheng Hsiao-hsu. For a similar purpose the United States has concluded a "Mutual Security Treaty" with the Chiang Kai-shek clique. The "Japan-Manchukuo Protocol" states: "Manchukuo and Japan, recognizing that any threat to the territory or to the peace and order of either of the High Contracting Parties constitutes at the same time a threat to the safety and existence of the other, agree to cooperate in the maintenance of their national security; it being understood that such Japanese forces as may be necessary for this purpose shall be stationed in Manchukuo." (Article 2).[n] The US-Chiang "Security Treaty" states: "Each party recognizes that an armed attack in the West Pacific area directed against the territories of either of the parties would be dangerous to its own peace and safety and declares that it would act to meet the common danger in accordance with its constitutional processes" (Article V), and the United States has "the right to dispose such United States land, air, and sea forces in and about Taiwan and the Pescadores as may be required for their defence, as determined by mutual agreement" (Article VII). Is there any difference in phraseology between the Japanese and US imperialists? When Japan attacked China's northeast, it said that it was exercising the "right of self-defence," and that the action of the Japanese army "conforms with Webster's definition of right of self-defence."[o] Now the United States claims that it enjoys the right of self-defence in the Taiwan area which is Chinese territory and that this is based on the "United Nations Charter." Again, how similar are their claims!

The matter is crystal clear. The so-called "Manchukuo" was only a signboard; Puyi, Cheng Hsiao-hsu and others were only a group of puppets in the hands of the Japanese invaders who regarded them as negligible elements. The real motive of the Japanese was to turn "Manchuria" into an "imperial domain," in other words, a Japanese colony. Today the so-called "Republic of China" is also a signboard. The Americans, too, regard the Chiang Kai-shek clique as negligible elements. As the US Vice-President Nixon said that the Americans never intended "to keep the symbol of Chiang Kai-shek on the Taiwan island" but [to] "look beyond Chiang." [*sic*] In other words, if the

[n] East-Asiatic Economic Investigation Bureau, *The Manchukuo Yearbook, 1934* (Tokyo, 1934), p. 152.

[o] From the Opinion of the Japanese Government on the Lytton Report, November 18, 1932. Webster, the American Secretary of State, defined the necessity of self-defence as being "instant, overwhelming, and leaving no choice of means and no moment for deliberation." Oppenheim, 7th ed., I, 266, n. 1.

Chiang Kai-shek clique refuses to act obediently as puppets, the Americans will kick them out and turn round to "keep the symbol of a free government." In the last analysis, US imperialists only want to turn Taiwan into an "island of freedom," in other words, [to] seize it as their own and turn it into a colony of the United States.

12-12

"Statement by the Spokesman of the Chinese Government—A Comment on the Soviet Government's Statement of August 21, 1963," September 1, 1963, in *People of the World, United, For the Complete, Thorough, Total, and Resolute Prohibition and Destruction of Nuclear Weapons* (Peking, 1963), pp. 52–53.

We have not forgotten and will not forget the support the Soviet people have long given China on the question of Taiwan.

Likewise, however, we have not forgotten and will not forget what the Soviet leader, Khrushchev, said about the question of Taiwan after his visit to the United States in October 1959.

He said that the question of Taiwan was an incendiary factor in the international situation and that, because the United States supported Chiang Kai-shek and the Soviet Union supported China, the atmosphere was like that on the eve of a great war; but the Soviet Union stood for the creation of all conditions to ease international tension and eliminate war.

He said, further, that there was more than one way to solve every complicated question, depending on what basis you took. For example, after the October Revolution, the Far Eastern Republic was established in the Soviet Far East, and Lenin recognized it at the time; this was a temporary concession and sacrifice since later on it was united with Russia.

The meaning of this statement by the Soviet leader was quite clear. To put it bluntly, it was asking China to agree to the US scheme of creating "two Chinas."

This absurd view was of course rebutted and rejected by China, whereupon the Soviet leader made several speeches hinting that China [had a] "craving for war like a cock for a fight," and, like Trotsky, wanted "neither peace nor war," etc.

In accordance with the procedure mutually agreed upon by the Soviet Union and the United States, the Chiang Kai-shek clique, swaggering like a sovereign state, has now signed the tripartite [nuclear test ban] treaty. Not only has the Soviet leader asked the Chinese government to sign the same tripartite treaty along with the Chiang Kai-shek clique spurned by the Chinese people, [thus creating] a two-Chinas situation, [but] he has also threatened that, if the Chinese government opposed this treaty and refused to be bound by it, the United States would help the Chiang Kai-shek clique to manufacture nuclear weapons. It turns out that in order to "save millions of Chinese from nuclear death," one China has to become two Chinas! It is evident that the Soviet leaders will stop at nothing in order to curry favour with the US imperialists. The international position of the German Democratic Republic is beneath their notice and so is China's sovereignty and territorial integrity.

Although the truth has been so fully exposed, they still assert that the nuclear strength of the Soviet Union guarantees China's independence and sovereignty. What effrontery!

12-13

"US-Chiang Kai-shek Illegal 'Status Agreement,' A New Step To Make Taiwan [A] US War Base," NCNA–English, Peking (Feb. 13, 1966), in *SCMP*, no. 3640:26–27 (Feb. 17, 1966).

The so-called "agreement" on the status of the US aggressive force in Taiwan, which was illegally signed by the US and the Chiang Kai-shek gang and was "passed" recently by the "Legislative Yuan" of the Chiang gang is part of US imperialism's criminal efforts to perpetuate its occupation of the Chinese territory Taiwan and to turn it into a base for the expansion of its aggressive war in Asia.[36]

Following, as it does, the illegal signing of the so-called "mutual defense treaty" with the United States of 1954, this is a further serious crime by the Chiang Kai-shek gang, a further step in the selling out of the national interests.

The "status agreement" stipulates that the US forces of aggression in Taiwan (including military and civil service personnel and their dependents) have the right to use land and existing equipment in Taiwan for the purposes of their aggressive war making activities and that the US military authorities in Taiwan have the right to designate certain areas, entry to which is limited to those authorized by the local US commanders.

This means the legalizing of the US privilege of stationing troops in Taiwan and of delimiting its own occupation areas. The aggressive forces of the US can thereby march into Taiwan and delimit their occupation areas at will, turning Taiwan into a military base for the US, for the expansion of its aggressive war in Asia.

According to the "agreement," the aggressive forces of the US stationed in the occupation areas in Taiwan have the right "to adopt every measure necessary" to maintain the "order and security" of the occupation areas, and [they] are thus empowered to commit whatever crimes they please.

The "agreement" also stipulates that when US military personnel on "official duty" commit offenses outside the occupation areas, the Chiang Kai-shek gang cannot interfere. Furthermore, the question of whether the US offender is on "official duty" is to be defined in accordance with American laws. Although the "agreement" allows the Chiang Kai-shek gang to pass "judgment" on the US offender if he is not on "official duty," the offender must be put in the custody of the US military authorities in Taiwan. This recognizes de facto the military jurisdiction by the US forces in Taiwan.

The "agreement" also stipulates that the aggressive US forces in Taiwan enjoy privileged exemption from the Chiang Kai-shek gang's regulations governing the issue of visas and the registration of foreigners. This amounts to allowing them full freedom to move into or out of Taiwan or to stay in Taiwan for good.

The US forces of aggression in Taiwan, according to the "agreement," also enjoy immunity from taxation, the right to set up post offices and to demand compensation for "damage." These privileges give US troops the right to [rob] the people of Taiwan and to [practice] large-scale smuggling.

[The] "agreement" is declared [to be "still in force while"] the illegal "mutual defense treaty" signed by the US and the Chiang Kai-shek gang ["remains in force"], and the "treaty" is supposed to remain effective indefinitely. This warrants special attention because it means the legalizing of permanent occupation of Taiwan by US imperialism.

This "agreement" was signed at a time when US imperialism is shifting the focus of its counterrevolutionary global strategy from Europe to Asia. Its obvious purpose is to meet its needs in relation to the expansion of its aggression in Vietnam and the war in Indochina and to turn Taiwan still more into a US colony and base for aggression.

On January 12, the day after the "Legislative Yüan" of the Chiang Kai-shek gang "passed" the "agreement," an AP dispatch from Taipei frankly declared: "The last obstacle to stationing substantial American forces in Formosa (Taiwan) was cleared Tuesday when the Legislative Yuan (of the Chiang gang) approved the agreement governing the status of American forces."

It was [at] about [this] time that the US started large-scale extension of its military bases in Taiwan and sent aggressor troops and aircraft there.

As early as December 8, 1954, the Chinese government solemnly declared: "The Chiang Kai-shek clique of national betrayal has no authority whatsoever to conclude any treaty with any country."

The so-called "agreement" governing the status of the US aggressor forces in Taiwan signed between the US and the Chiang gang, is no more than a piece of wastepaper. The Chinese people absolutely will not tolerate US imperialism using this "agreement" to turn Taiwan into a base for the expansion of its aggressive war in Vietnam.

Note

For recent developments regarding the views of the United States and the United Kingdom regarding the legal status of Taiwan, recall the Note following item 10–16.[37] For recent changes in Japan's position, see 46–3 and the Notes preceding and following.

(c) HONG KONG AND MACAO

Although both Hong Kong and Macao are overwhelmingly Chinese in population, although both areas constituted part of the Chinese Empire, and although the Nationalist regime had sought to end imperialist control of these areas, the PRC has never made their immediate "liberation" one of its major goals.

Great Britain had annexed the island of Hong Kong under the Treaty of Nanking, which terminated the Opium War in 1842. Further hostilities culminating in the 1860 Treaty of Peking had forced China to cede Britain the Kowloon Peninsula facing the island, and in 1898 the badly weakened Ch'ing dynasty had been required to "lease" Britain, for a period of ninety-nine years, a much larger area including the remainder of Kowloon and the so-called "New Territories." The "lease" convention, which made no provision for payment of rent, contained the following stipulation:

> It is at the same time agreed that within the city of Kowloon the Chinese officials now stationed there shall continue to exercise jurisdiction except so far as may be inconsistent with the military requirements for the defence of Hong Kong. Within the remainder of the newly leased territory, Great Britain shall have sole jurisdiction. Chinese officials and people shall be allowed as heretofore to use the road from Kowloon to Hsinan.[38]

It should be noted that no Chinese government since the Ch'ing has sent officials to administer the City of Kowloon, which is actually only a small enclave in Kowloon.

Portuguese control over the tiny peninsula of Macao and its adjacent islands has a much longer and more complex history. After half a century of efforts to establish a trading depot somewhere on the Chinese coast near Canton, in 1557 Portugal received the local authorities' permission to locate at Macao; thus Macao is the oldest outpost of Western colonialism in East Asia. The nature of the rights conferred upon the Portuguese has been a subject of dispute ever since that time. By building a wall across the isthmus leading to the mainland, the Chinese soon made it clear that the Portuguese were to confine themselves to Macao, but China did not surrender all powers over the peninsula. For most of the next three centuries it continued to receive rent for Portugal's use of Macao, to collect land taxes and customs revenues, to station an official in Macao, and, at least occasionally, to exercise some of the other functions associated with the Western concept of "sovereignty." Nevertheless, Portugal, which enjoyed considerable autonomy within this system, has continued to claim sovereignty over Macao.

That Portugal recognized the unsatisfactory basis for its legal claim was implicit in the efforts that it made from time to time to impose an agreement upon China that would clear up the question of its title to Macao. Finally, in 1887, China yielded to Portuguese demands in the hope of obtaining Portugal's cooperation in stopping the smuggling of opium into China; the "Protocol of Lisbon" provided, in somewhat ambiguous language, that: "China confirms perpetual occupation and government of Macao and its dependencies by Portugal, as any other Portuguese possession."

In 1945, after the end of extraterritoriality had been achieved in China proper and before the British reentry into Hong Kong at the close of the war, the Nationalist regime called for the liquidation of foreign control over Hong Kong and Macao. But the Nationalists became too preoccupied by the civil war with the Communists to fulfill these long-held goals of their "rights recovery" campaign.

Given this background, it was surprising to many observers that from 1949 until the outbreak of the Great Proletarian Cultural Revolution in 1966 the Chinese Communists did little to disturb the status quo in Hong Kong and Macao. The case of Macao is especially interesting in view of the facts that Portugal continued to maintain diplomatic relations with the Nationalists rather than the Communists, allowed the ROC to maintain an official representative in Macao until 1965, tolerated anti-Communist intelligence and espionage activities there, and permitted Macao to serve as a haven for fugitives and refugees from the mainland. In 1952 some border clashes shattered the tranquility and stimulated a newspaper campaign in neighboring Kwangtung province for the "liberation" of Macao, but settlement of this dispute led to fourteen more years of relatively quiet acquiescence in the status quo. To be sure, Macao elected representatives to the National People's Congress in Peking (as well as to the Portuguese legislature) and from time to time Peking asserted its title to Macao and branded Portuguese possession "illegal." But even after the Soviet Union and its allies began to accuse Peking of being hypocritical and cowardly in tolerating the "stench of colonialism" with regard to China's own territories while exhorting others to militant anticolonial warfare, the Chinese Communists, for both political and economic reasons, preferred not to focus attention on the legal status of Macao.

Indeed, the events of late 1966 and early 1967, when the frenzy of the Cultural Revolution spilled over into Macao and caused rioting that shattered the myth of Portuguese control, suggest that Peking does not yet want to reincorporate Macao. At that time, the power exerted by leftist groups among Macao's Chinese residents was so great that, according to widely credited reports, in December 1966 Portugal offered to surrender Macao upon Peking's request, if allowed to make a dignified departure. Peking, however, contented itself with humiliating Portugal, which was required to comply with the demands of the local Chinese community, to suppress all signs of Nationalist activities, to refuse to admit refugees, and to accept without protest the entry of Communist gunboats into Macao's harbor. The policy, as defined by the New China News Agency, was simply to "pull tighter and tighter the noose Portuguese imperialism has put around its neck." [39]

Much the same can be said of the PRC's attitude toward Hong Kong. Peking has not been above inspiring local violence there during various Asian political crises, thereby reminding Britain of its vulnerability. Yet from 1949 to 1967, although it occasionally reiterated that "Hong Kong is Chinese territory" and asserted special interest in the welfare of residents of the City of Kowloon, it did not offer any serious challenge to Britain's present possession of the territory. And while the furor over the strikes and violence that paralyzed Hong Kong in the spring of 1967, and over the border incidents that followed in the summer, led Peking to reemphasize China's previous claim to Hong Kong, it produced no evidence of Peking's intention to vindicate that claim in the near future.

Items 12–14 through 12–18 illustrate Peking's vigilance in maintaining its claims to Hong Kong and Macao while awaiting the opportunity for a final settlement.

12-14

Observer, "A Warning to the Portuguese Authorities in Macao," *JMJP* (Oct. 26, 1955) p. 1; NCNA–English, Peking (Oct. 26, 1955), in *SCMP*, no. 1158:36 (Oct. 27, 1955).

The Portuguese authorities in Macao originally announced plans for large-scale "celebrations" this November of the 400th anniversary of their seizure of Macao. This news has evoked the utmost indignation of the Chinese people.

Macao is Chinese territory. The Chinese people have never forgotten Macao, nor have they forgotten that they have the right to demand the recovery of this territory from the hands of Portugal. Indian Prime Minister Nehru also pointed out in the House of People of the Indian Parliament on September 17th that Macao should be returned to China as a matter of course and that there was no doubt about this point at all. The fact that Macao has not yet been returned to China does not mean that the Chinese people can tolerate long continuation of occupation of Macao.

Apparently the Portuguese authorities in Macao mistake the Chinese people's peace policy as a sign of weakness. They made [an] outrageous attempt to show off, by "celebrations" of the 400th anniversary of their seizure of Macao, their colonialist position to the Chinese people who have already freed themselves from the yoke of colonialism. The Chinese people will never tolerate this.

The provocative action of the Portuguese authorities in Macao is a challenge not only to the Chinese people but to the people throughout Asia. . . .

We warn the Portuguese authorities in Macao that China today is not the China of six years ago, let alone the China of 400 years ago. If the Portuguese authorities in Macao think that they can provoke this great Chinese people by taking advantage of China's peace policy, they are mistaken. The Chinese people have never allowed and never will allow the provocateurs to reap what they sow.[40]

12-15

"China Protests against British Attempt to Demolish Premises in Kowloon City," NCNA–English, Peking (Jan. 17, 1963), in *SCMP*, no. 2903:26–27 (Jan. 22, 1963).

The British authorities in Hong Kong have recently attempted to use compulsory means to demolish premises in the City of Kowloon which . . . [belong] to China, and to resettle the residents by force.

This act by the British authorities in Hong Kong is a serious encroachment upon China's sovereignty. The Chinese Foreign Ministry has lodged a serious protest on this matter with the British government.

The City of Kowloon is situated on the northeast part of Kowloon and [is] inhabited by more than 20,000 people. Traditionally it has been part of China's territory and under China's jurisdiction.

In the past few years, repeated attempts have been made by the British authorities in Hong Kong to demolish premises in the City of Kowloon and resettle the residents by force. But all attempts failed because of strong opposition by the residents. Of late, the British authorities in Hong Kong [have,] in the most arrogant way, fixed a deadline for the demolition and resettlement. This could not but arouse the serious attention of the Chinese government.

In May 1960 the British authorities in Hong Kong published the "Kowloon Planning Areas 8 or 11 Outline Development Plan," drawing the City of Kowloon into its scope. It was opposed by local residents and a protest was lodged with the "Hong Kong Town Planning Board."

On March 19, 1962, some 30 persons were dispatched by the Hong Kong British Resettlement Department to post resettlement notices on premises along Tung Tau Village Road, Lung Shing Street, Lung Tzun Street, Kwong Ming Street, and other streets in that area and to carry out a survey and registration. It was also announced that, according to the provisions in "stage two of Tung Tau Resettlement Estate Scheme," the premises on these streets were to be demolished and the residents resettled.

In November and December of last year, staff members of the Hong Kong British Resettlement Department repeatedly entered the City of Kowloon and forcibly issued resettlement notifications to residents in these streets. Scores of armed police from the Hong Kong Police Force were deployed as if they were facing a strong enemy when the resettlement notifications were issued on December 28. Local residents expressed great indignation at this truculent act by the British authorities in Hong Kong.

On January 1, 1963, Sung Chih-kuang, Deputy Director of the West European Affairs Department of the Chinese Foreign Ministry, summonded T. W. Garvey, British chargé d'affaires in China, and expressed deep concern about the action taken by the British authorities in Hong Kong to demolish the premises and resettle the residents in the City of Kowloon. He asked the British chargé d'affaires to tell the British authorities in Hong Kong to give serious consideration to the matter. The British government has not, however, changed its attitude. Furthermore, on January 7, the British Resettlement Department in Hong Kong issued "demolition and resettlement notifications" to residents in these streets, declaring truculently that the premises of the residents were to be demolished separately before the 8th, 12th, 14th, 19th and 20th of February. Some two hundred premises and more than 2,000 residents are involved.

The flagrant announcement by the British authorities in Hong Kong of a time limit for the demolition and resettlement, in spite of the warning issued by the Chinese government, is a grave violation of China's sovereignty and is intolerable. The truculent action of the British authorities in Hong Kong in bringing increasing pressure to bear upon the residents in the City of Kowloon has aroused their strong opposition and protests. Local landlords and other residents with estate interests in the area refused to accept "resettlement notifications" and "demolition and resettlement notifications." Many residents in the City of Kowloon pointed out that if the forced demolition and resettlement were carried out, their homes would be destroyed and their means of making a living lost. Residents with estate interests in the area would sustain heavy losses and thousands of residents would be thrown into desperate straits. The newspapers *Wen-wei Pao* and *Ta-kung Pao* in Hong Kong on January 14 carried statements by the leaders of the Anti-Demolition and Anti-Resettlement Committee of the Residents of the City of Kowloon and many other representatives of local residents. They expressed the most resolute protest against the measures taken by the British authorities in Hong Kong, which violated China's sovereignty and damaged the vital interests of local residents.

The forced demolition and resettlement of residents of the City of Kowloon has long been plotted by the British government. The utterly truculent and vicious attitude taken by the British authorities in Hong Kong upon instruction from the British government in pressing forward further and further has aroused the grave concern of the Chinese government. On January 17, the Chinese Foreign Ministry lodged a strong protest with the British government, seriously pointing out that the City of Kowloon is China's territory, and within China's jurisdiction and that this has all along been so in history. The Chinese

Foreign Ministry demanded that the British government instruct the British authorities in Hong Kong to withdraw immediately the decision on the demolition of premises in the City of Kowloon and stop all actions relating to such demolition and resettlement.[41]

12-16

"A Comment on the Statement of the Communist Party of the USA," editorial, *JMJP* (Mar. 8, 1963), p. 1; in *PR* 6.10, 11: 61–62 (Mar. 15, 1963).

With an ulterior purpose, the statement of the CPUSA referred to Taiwan, Hong Kong, and Macao. It said that the Chinese comrades were "correctly not following the adventurous policy in Taiwan, Hong Kong, and Macao that they advocate for others. Why this double standard approach?"

We know from what quarter they have learned this ridiculous charge. And we know, too, the purpose of the person who manufactured it.

Here we should like to answer all those who have raised this matter.

For us there never has been a question of a "double standard." We have only one standard, whether dealing with the question of Taiwan, whether dealing with the questions of Hong Kong and Macao, or whether dealing with all international questions, and that standard is Marxism-Leninism, proletarian internationalism, the interests of the Chinese people and of the people of the world, the interests of world peace, and the revolutionary cause of the people of all countries. In international struggles we are opposed both to adventurism and to capitulationism. These two hats can never fit our heads.

Inasmuch as some persons have mentioned Taiwan, Hong Kong, and Macao, we are obliged to discuss a little of the history of imperialist aggression against China.

In the hundred years or so prior to the victory of the Chinese revolution, the imperialist and colonial powers—the United States, Britain, France, Tsarist Russia, Germany, Japan, Italy, Austria, Belgium, the Netherlands, Spain, and Portugal—carried out unbridled aggression against China. They compelled the governments of old China to sign a large number of unequal treaties: the Treaty of Nanking of 1842, the Treaty of Aigun of 1858, the Treaty of Tientsin of 1858, the Treaty of Peking of 1860, the Treaty of Ili of 1881, the Protocol of Lisbon of 1887, the Treaty of Shimonoseki of 1895, the Convention for the Extension of Hong Kong of 1898, the International Protocol of 1901, and others. By virtue of these unequal treaties, they annexed Chinese territory in the north, south, east, and west and held leased territories on the seaboard and in the hinterland of China. Some seized Taiwan and the Penghu Islands, others occupied Hong Kong and forcibly leased Kowloon, still others put Macao under perpetual occupation, and so forth.

At the time the People's Republic of China was inaugurated, our government declared that it would examine the treaties concluded by previous Chinese governments with foreign governments, treaties that had been left over by history, and would recognize, abrogate, revise, or renegotiate them according to their respective contents. In this respect, our policy towards the socialist countries is fundamentally different from our policy towards the imperialist countries. When we deal with various imperialist countries, we take differing circumstances into consideration and make distinctions in our policy. As a matter of fact, many of these treaties concluded in the past either have lost their validity, or have been abrogated or have been replaced by new ones. With regard to the outstanding issues, which are a legacy from the past, we have always held that, when conditions are ripe, they should be settled peacefully through negotiations and that, pending a settlement, the status quo should be maintained. Within this category are the questions of Hong Kong, Kowloon, and Macao and the questions of all those boundaries which have not been formally delimited by the parties concerned in each case. . . .

Why is it that after the Caribbean [Cuban missile] crisis this correct policy of ours suddenly became a topic of discussion among certain persons and a theme for their anti-China campaign?

These heroes are apparently very pleased with themselves for having picked up a stone from a cesspool, with which they believe they can instantly fell the Chinese. But whom has this filthy stone really hit?

You are not unaware that such questions as those of Hong Kong and Macao relate to the category of unequal treaties left over by history, treaties which the imperialists imposed on China. It may be asked: In raising questions of this kind, do you intend to raise all the questions of the unequal treaties and have a general settlement? Has it ever entered your heads what the consequences would be? Can you seriously believe that this will do you any good?

Superficially, you seem to agree with China's policy on Hong Kong and Macao. Yet, you compare it with India's liberation of Goa. Anyone with a discerning eye can see at once that your sole intention is to prove that the Chinese are cowards. To be frank, there is no need for the Chinese people to prove their courage and staunchness in combating imperialism by making a show of force on the questions of Hong Kong and Macao. The imperialists, and the US imperialists in particular, have had occasion to sample our courage and staunchness. Shoulder to shoulder with the Korean people, the finest sons and daughters of the Chinese people fought for three years and shed their blood on the battlefields of Korea to repulse the US aggressors. Don't you feel it "stupid" and "deplorable" on your part to taunt us on the questions of Hong Kong and Macao?

We know very well, and you know, too, that you are, to put it plainly, bringing up the questions of Hong Kong and Macao merely as a fig leaf to hide your disgraceful performance in the Caribbean crisis. But all this is futile. There is an objective criterion for truth, just as there is for error. What is right cannot be made to look wrong; nor can wrong be made to look right. To glory in your disgraceful performance will not add to your prestige. How can the correct policy of the Chinese people on the questions of Hong Kong and Macao be mentioned in the same breath with your erroneous policy in the Caribbean crisis? How can such a comparison help you to whitewash yourselves?

12-17

"Khrushchev Group Turns World Youth Forum into Anti-China Forum," NCNA–English, Moscow (Sept. 25, 1964) in *SCMP*, no. 3309:39–40 (Oct. 1, 1964).

The World Youth Forum manipulated by the leaders of the Soviet youth organization adopted at its evening session on September 23 two anti-China resolutions on Hong Kong and Macao and the Sino-Indian boundary question.

The adoption of these two resolutions interfering in the internal affairs of China and encroaching on its sovereignty in the teeth of the opposition and protest of the youth delegates of China and many other countries has thoroughly revealed the despicable scheme of the revisionist Khrushchev group to turn "the World Forum of Solidarity of Youth and Students in the Fight for National Independence and Liberation, and for Peace" into a forum against China.

The entire proceedings of this Forum which wound up its sessions amid wild anti-China ravings have furnished proof that the leaders of the Soviet youth organization are the most rabid splitters in the international democratic youth movement.

After the Forum went into group discussions on September 20, the leaders of the Soviet youth organization continued their dirty anti-China intrigues. A draft resolution put forth by the Soviet delegation at the first group committee demanded the granting of "independence" to Macao which is part of China's territory.

However, in the face of denunciation and opposition by many delegates who saw through the sinister motives behind this draft resolution, the Soviet delegates [retreated] and withdrew it. But they made the Ceylonese youth delegate table another draft resolution at the group meeting calling for the elimination of colonies in Asia. The resolution put Hong Kong and Macao, which are China's territory, on a par with Timor Island, Papua, Oman, Aden, and South Arabia and demanded "independence" for the two places in accordance with the UN declaration.

The Chinese delegate at the group meeting sternly condemned the erroneous approach of identifying Hong Kong and Macao in the two draft resolutions. He pointed out that Hong Kong and Macao are Chinese territory occupied by British and Portuguese imperialism on the strength of unequal treaties. The Chinese people will recover them without fail at an appropriate time. To demand "independence" for the two places, as done in the draft resolution, means in fact to demand their detachment from China. The Chinese delegate lodged a serious protest against this.

However, the manipulators of the meeting brushed aside this just protest, set the voting machine in motion and rammed through the draft resolution put forward by the Ceylonese delegate.

12-18

Commentator, "Hong Kong Is Chinese Territory," *JMJP* (Aug. 20, 1967), p. 2; NCNA–English, Peking (Aug. 20, 1967) in *SCMP*, no. 4007:23 (Aug. 23, 1967).

The British imperialist radio stations and newspapers in Hong Kong have recently been frenziedly babbling that Hong Kong is "British territory," that members of people's communes in Kwangtung Province [have been] "encroaching upon" [what is] "British territory" when they went to farm their land in the "New Territories," and that the Chinese people were "interfering with the domestic affairs of Hong Kong" when they support their fellow countrymen there in their struggle against British atrocities. This is nothing but gangsters' language; it is a grave provocation against the Chinese people.

Hong Kong has been Chinese territory since ancient times. This is a fact known to all, old and young, in the world. More than a century ago, British imperialism came to China by pirate ships, provoked the criminal "opium war," massacred numerous Chinese people, and occupied the Chinese territory of Hong Kong. Later it snapped [up] the Chinese territory of Kowloon and the Chinese territory of the "New Territories." This is an enormous blood debt British imperialism owes to the Chinese people. Sooner or later, the Chinese people will make a thorough-going liquidation of this debt with British imperialism.

Because Hong Kong has always been Chinese territory and was occupied by the British imperialists, the peasants of Kwangtung Province living near the "New Territories" have for generations tilled the land there. Now the British imperialists have gone so far as to call this an "encroachment upon British territory." This is absolutely preposterous! Have members of our people's communes gone to till the land on the British Isles? They have not taken a step out of their own country. On the contrary, it is the British imperialists who have come from thousands of miles away to seize our land by force and kill our compatriots. We must tell the British imperialists that not only have the Chinese peasants the right to till the land in the "New Territories," but the whole of Hong Kong must return to the domain of the motherland.

This is not the old era when the British colonialists seized Hong Kong by force. Our compatriots in Hong Kong have the powerful backing of their strong socialist motherland. How can it be imagined that Hong Kong will always be under the rule of British imperialism? Of course it can't; it is absolutely unthinkable. It is idiotic wishful thinking for the British imperialists to imagine that they can prevent the great Chinese people from assisting their Hong Kong compatriots' fight against British violence. Hong Kong is an inalienable part of Chinese territory, and our compatriots in Hong Kong are blood brothers and sisters of the Chinese people. The Chinese people cannot possibly turn a deaf ear to the British imperialists' fascist atrocities of barbarously suppressing our countrymen in Hong Kong.

Today the fate of Hong Kong is in the hands of the Chinese people and our countrymen in Hong Kong. Hong Kong's affairs must be decided by the Chinese people and our countrymen in Hong Kong. It is absolutely impermissible for British imperialism to ride roughshod over Hong Kong!

NOTE

The PRC's entry into the UN provided it with a major forum for recording its claim to Hong Kong and Macao as well as other territories. When the UN General Assembly's Special Committee on Colonialism included Hong Kong and Macao in its list of colonial territories,

Chinese Ambassador Huang Hua, in a letter to the chairman of the committee dated March 10, 1972, stated:

> As is known to all, the questions of Hong Kong and Macao belong to the category of questions resulting from the series of unequal treaties left over by history, treaties which the imperialists imposed on China.
>
> Hong Kong and Macao are part of Chinese territory occupied by the British and Portuguese authorities. The settlement of the questions of Hong Kong and Macao is entirely within China's sovereign right and does not at all fall under the ordinary category of colonial territories.
>
> Consequently, they should not be included in the list of colonial territories covered by the declaration on the granting of independence to colonial countries and people.
>
> With regard to the questions of Hong Kong and Macao, the Chinese government has consistently held that they should be settled in an appropriate way when conditions are ripe. The United Nations has no right to discuss these questions.
>
> For the above reasons, the Chinese delegation is opposed to including Hong Kong and Macao in the list of colonial territories covered by the declaration and requests that the erroneous wording that Hong Kong and Macao fall under the category of so-called colonial territories be immediately removed from the documents of the special committee and all other United Nations documents.[42]

(d) TIBET

The character of Tibet's relations with China has changed with time. Tibet had to some extent become dependent upon China as early as the thirteenth century, and the Ch'ing dynasty had managed to dominate that remote region fairly effectively from the middle of the eighteenth century to the middle of the nineteenth. From that point on, however, the Ch'ing government progressively deteriorated, thereby providing foreign powers and the Tibetans themselves with an incentive to attempt to detach Tibet from the Chinese Empire. As the nineteenth century wore on, British and Russian imperialism increasingly challenged the Chinese position in Central Asia, and the question of Tibet's legal status became correspondingly more complex and controversial. Belated Ch'ing efforts to make a vigorous response to this challenge in the early years of the twentieth century came to an end with the Revolution of 1911.

The political and legal maneuvering that took place both before and after the overthrow of the Ch'ing dynasty and its replacement in

1912 by the Republic of China will be alluded to not only in this section but also in the following section on the Sino-Indian border dispute. What should be emphasized here for background purposes is that every government that has come to power in China since the fall of the Ch'ing has announced its intention to reassert Chinese control over Tibet. That control had ended soon after founding of the Republic and was not reestablished until Communist troops "liberated" Tibet in October 1950. A scholarly commentator has aptly summarized the reaction that "liberation" evoked:

> Tibet appealed to the United Nations for help. It won no support, however, from the Great Powers which upon occasion had stood for self-determination and the independence of peoples. The resolution asking for UN intercession on behalf of Tibet was put forward by little El Salvador. Naturally, Moscow supported Peking's assertion of right to rule Tibet. The Chinese Nationalists voiced as firmly as the Communists the claim to an unqualified Chinese sovereignty over Tibet. The United States was governed by a past acceptance of the Chinese claim and bound besides by its liaison with the Nationalists. Britain also was committed to past legal positions. Under the circumstances, the Western delegations seemed happy to defer to the country then having primary interest in the fate of Tibet—India. And India asserted that it had reason to hope that a satisfactory political settlement could be worked out.[43]

Item 12–19 indicates the arguments exchanged in the course of India's attempt to persuade the PRC to negotiate the status of Tibet, which India, and colonial Britain before her, had regarded as a valuable buffer against Chinese power. Item 12–20 reproduces the "agreement" reached between the PRC and Tibet as a result of the PRC's application of force.

12-19

"Exchange of Notes between the Government of India and of the People's Republic of China Concerning the Advance of Chinese Army Units into Tibet," October-November, 1950 in "Central People's Government's Reply to Indian Note on Tibet," NCNA–English, Peking (Nov. 16, 1950) in NCNA, *Daily News Release*, no. 549:135–140 (Nov. 17, 1950).

(1) *Indian Note to China, October 28, 1950.*

We have seen with great regret reports in newspapers of official statement made in Peking to the effect that "People's Army units have been ordered to advance into Tibet." We have received no, repeat no, intimation of it from your ambassador here or from our ambassador in Peking. We have been repeatedly assured of the desire of the Chinese government to settle Tibetan problem by peaceful means and negotiations. In interview which India's Ambassador had recently with the Vice-Foreign Minister, the latter, while reiterating resolve of Chinese government to "liberate" Tibet, had expressed continued desire to do so by peaceful means. We informed Chinese government through our ambassador of decision of Tibetan delegation to proceed to Peking immediately to start negotiations. This delegation actually left Delhi yesterday (25th). In view of these facts the decision to order advance of China's troops into Tibet appears to us most surprising and regrettable. . . .

2. Now that the invasion of Tibet has been ordered by Chinese government, peaceful negotiations can hardly be synchronised with it, and there will naturally be fear on part of Tibetans that negotiations will be under duress. In the present context of world events, the invasion by Chinese troops of Tibet cannot but be regarded as deplorable and, in the considered judgement of the government of India, not in the interests of China or of peace. The government of India can only express their deep regret that in spite of the friendly and disinterested advice repeatedly tendered by them, the Chinese government should have decided to seek a solution of the problems of their relations with Tibet by force instead [of] by the slower and more enduring methods of peaceful approach. . . .

(2) *Chinese Reply to India, October 30, 1950.*

The Central People's Government of the People's Republic of China would like to make it clear: Tibet is an integral part of Chinese territory, the problem of Tibet is entirely a domestic problem of China. The Chinese People's Liberation Army must enter Tibet, liberate the Tibetan people, and defend the frontiers of China. This is the resolved policy of the Central People's Government. The Central People's Government has repeatedly expressed the hope that the problem of Tibet may be solved by peaceful negotiations, and it welcomes, therefore, the delegation of the local authorities of Tibet to come to Peking at an early date to proceed with peaceful negotiations. Yet the Tibetan delegation, under outside instigation, has intentionally delayed the date of its departure for Peking. The Central People's Government, however, has not abandoned its desire to proceed with peaceful negotiations. But regardless of whether the local authorities of Tibet wish to proceed with peaceful negotiations, and whatever results may be achieved by negotiations, the problem of Tibet is a domestic problem of the People's Republic of China, and no foreign interference shall be tolerated.

In particular, the problem of Tibet and the problem of the participation of the People's Republic of China in the United Nations are two entirely unrelated problems. If those countries hostile to China attempt to utilize as an excuse the fact that the Central People's Government of the People's Republic of China is exercising its sovereign rights in its territory Tibet, and threaten to obstruct the participation of the People's Republic of China in the United Nations organisation, it is then but another demonstration of the unfriendly and hostile attitude of such countries toward China.

Therefore, with regard to the viewpoint of the government of India on what it regards as deplorable, the Central People's Government of the People's Republic of China cannot but consider it as having been affected by foreign influences hostile to China in Tibet and hence expresses its deep regret.

(3) Indian Note to China, November 1, 1950.

Indian ambassador in Peking has transmitted to the government of India the note handed to him by the Vice-Foreign Minister of the People's Republic of China on 30 October. The government of India have read with amazement the statement in the last paragraph of the Chinese government's reply that the government of India's representation to them was affected by foreign influences hostile to China and categorically repudiate it. At no time has any foreign influence been brought to bear upon India in regard to Tibet. In this, as in other matters, the government of India's policy has been entirely independent and directed solely towards a peaceful settlement of international disputes and avoidance of anything calculated to increase the present deplorable tensions in the world.

2. The government of China are equally mistaken in thinking that the Tibetan delegation's departure to Peking was delayed by outside instigation. In their previous communications the government of India have explained at some length the reasons why the Tibetan delegation could not proceed to Peking earlier. They are convinced that there has been no possibility of foreign instigation.

3. It is with no desire to interfere or to gain any advantage that the government of India have sought earnestly that a settlement of the Tibetan problem should be effected by peaceful negotiations, adjusting legitimate Tibetan claim to autonomy within the framework of Chinese suzerainty. Tibetan autonomy is a fact, which, judging from reports that they have received from the Indian ambassador in China and also from other sources, the Chinese government were themselves willing to recognise and foster. The government of India's repeated suggestions that Chinese suzerainty over Tibet and Tibetan autonomy should be reconciled by peaceful negotiations were not, as the Chinese government seem to suggest, unwarranted interference in China's internal affairs, but well-meant advice by a friendly government which has a natural interest in the solution of problems concerning its neighbours by peaceful methods.

4. Wedded as they are to ways of peace, the government of India had been gratified to learn that the Chinese government was also desirous to effect a settlement in Tibet through peaceful negotiations. Because of this the government of India advised the Tibetan government to send their delegation to Peking, and were glad that this advice was accepted. In the interchange of the communications which had been taking place between the government of India and the government of China, the former had received repeated assurances that a peaceful settlement was aimed at. In the circumstances the surprise of the government of India was all the greater when they learned that military operations had been undertaken by the Chinese government against a peaceful people. There has been no allegation that there has been any provocation or any resort to non-peaceful methods on the part of the Tibetans. Hence there is no justification whatever for such military operations against them. Such a step involving an attempt to impose a decision by force could not possibly be reconciled with a peaceful settlement. In view of these developments, the government of India are no longer in a position to advise the Tibetan delegation to proceed to Peking, unless the Chinese government think it fit to order their troops to halt their advance into Tibet and thus give a chance for peaceful negotiations. . . .

6. The government of India have repeatedly made it clear that they have no political or territorial ambitions in Tibet and they do not seek any novel privileged position for themselves or for their nationals in Tibet. At the same time they have pointed out that certain rights have

grown out of usage and agreements which are natural between neighbours with close cultural and commercial relations. These relations have found expression in the presence of an agent of the government of India in Lhasa, the existence of trade agencies at Gyantse and Yatung and the maintenance of post and telegraph office at the trade route up to Gyantse. For protection of this trade route a small military escort has been stationed at Gyantse for over 40 years. The government of India are anxious that these establishments, which are to the mutual interests of India and Tibet, and do not detract in any way from Chinese suzerainty over Tibet, should continue. The personnel at the Lhasa Mission and the agencies at Gyantse and Yatung have accordingly been instructed to stay at their posts.

(4) *Chinese Reply to India, November 16, 1950.*

On November 1, 1950, the Ministry of Foreign Affairs of the People's Republic of China received from H.E. Ambassador Panikkar a communication from the government of the Republic of India on the problem of Tibet.

The Central People's Government of the People's Republic of China, in its past communications with the government of the Republic of India on the problem of Tibet, has repeatedly made it clear that Tibet is an integral part of Chinese territory, the problem of Tibet is entirely a domestic problem of China. The Chinese People's Liberation Army must enter Tibet, liberate the Tibetan people, and defend the frontiers of China. This is the firm policy of the Chinese government. According to the provisions of the Common Programme adopted by the Chinese People's Political Consultative Conference, the regional autonomy granted by the Chinese Government to the national minorities inside the country is an autonomy within the confines of Chinese sovereignty.[44] This point has been recognised by the Indian government in its aide memoire to the Chinese government dated August 26 this year. However, when the Chinese government actually exercised its sovereign rights, and began to liberate the Tibetan people and drive out foreign forces and influences to ensure that the Tibetan people will be free from aggression and will realise regional autonomy and religious freedom, the Indian government attempted to influence and obstruct the exercise of its sovereign rights in Tibet by the Chinese government. This cannot but leave the Chinese government greatly surprised.

The Central People's Government of the People's Republic of China sincerely hopes that the Chinese People's Liberation Army may enter Tibet peacefully to perform the sacred task of liberating the Tibetan people and defending the frontiers of China. It has therefore long since welcomed the delegation of the local authorities of Tibet which has remained in India to come to Peking at an early date to proceed with peace negotiations. Yet the said delegation, obviously as a result of continued outside obstruction, has delayed its departure for Peking. Further, taking advantage of the delay of the negotiations, the local authorities of Tibet have deployed strong armed forces at Changtu of Sikang Province in the interior of China, in an attempt to prevent the Chinese People's Liberation Army to liberate Tibet. On August 31, 1950, the Chinese Ministry of Foreign Affairs informed the Indian government through Ambassador Panikkar that the Chinese People's Liberation Army was going to take action soon in West Sikang according to set plans, and expressed the hope that the Indian government would assist the delegation of the local authorities of Tibet so that it might arrive in Peking in mid-September to begin peace negotiations. In early and middle September, the Chinese Chargé d'Affaires Shen Chien and later Ambassador Yuan Chung-hsien both in person told the said delegation that it was imperative that it should hasten to Peking within September, otherwise the said delegation should bear the responsibilities and be held responsible for all the consequences resulting from the delay. In mid-October, the Chinese Ambassador Yuan again informed the Indian government of this. Yet still owing to outside instigation, the delegation of the local authorities of Tibet fabricated various pretexts and remained in India. Although the Chinese Government has not given up its desire of settling the problem of Tibet peacefully, it can no longer continue to put off the set plan of the Chinese People's Liberation Army to proceed to Tibet. And the liberation of Changtu further proved that through the instrument of Tibetan troops, foreign forces and influences were obstructing the peaceful settlement of the problem of Tibet. But regardless of whether the local authorities of Tibet wish to proceed with peace negotiations, and regardless of whatever results may be achieved by negotiations, no foreign intervention will be permitted. The entry into Tibet of the Chinese People's Liberation Army and the liberation of the Tibetan people are also decided.

In showing its friendship with the government of the Republic of India, and in an understanding of the desire of the Indian government to see the problem of Tibet settled peacefully, the Central People's Government of the People's Republic of China has kept the Indian government informed of its efforts in this direction. What the Chinese government cannot but deeply regret is that the Indian government, in disregard of the facts, has regarded a domestic problem of the Chinese government—the exercise of its sovereign rights in Tibet—as an international dispute calculated to increase the present deplorable tensions in the world.

The government of the Republic of India has repeatedly expressed its desire of developing Sino-Indian friendship on the basis of mutual respect for territory, sovereignty, equality, and mutual benefit, and of preventing the world from going to war. The entry into Tibet of the Chinese People's Liberation Army is exactly aimed at the protection of the integrity of the territory and the sovereignty of China. And it is on this question that all those countries who desire to respect the territory and the sovereignty of China should first of all indicate their real attitude toward China. In the meantime, we consider that what is now threatening the independence of nations and world peace is precisely the forces of those imperialist aggressors. For the sake of maintenance of national independence and defence of world peace, it is necessary to resist the forces of these imperialist aggressors. The entry into Tibet of the Chinese People's Liberation Army is thus an important measure to maintain Chinese independence, to prevent the imperialist aggressors from dragging the world toward war, and to defend world peace.

The Central People's Government of the People's Republic of China welcomes the renewed declaration of the Indian government that it has no political or territorial ambitions in China's Tibet and that it does not seek any new privileged position. As long as our two sides adhere strictly to the principle of mutual respect for territory, sovereignty, equality, and mutual benefit, we are convinced that the friendship between China and India should be developed in a normal way, and that problems relating to Sino-Indian diplomatic, commercial, and cultural relations with respect to Tibet may be solved properly and to our mutual benefit through normal diplomatic channels.

12-20

"Agreement between the Chinese Central People's Government and the Tibetan Government on the Administration of Tibet," Peking, May 23, 1951; English translation in "Agreement on Peaceful Liberation of Tibet," Peking, May 27, 1951, NCNA, *Daily News Release* [English], no. 708: 112 (May 28, 1951).

1. The Tibetan people shall unite and drive out imperialist aggressive forces from Tibet so that the Tibetan people shall return to the big family of the motherland—the People's Republic of China.

2. The local government of Tibet shall actively assist the People's Liberation Army to enter Tibet and consolidate the national defenses.

3. In accordance with the policy toward nationalities laid down in the Common Programme of the Chinese People's Political Consultative Conference, the Tibetan people have the right of exercising national regional autonomy under the unified leadership of the Central People's Government.

4. The central authorities will not alter the existing political system in Tibet. The central authorities also will not alter the established status, functions, and powers of the Dalai Lama. Officials of various ranks shall hold office as usual.

5. The established status, functions, and powers of the Panchen Ngoerhtehni shall be maintained.

6. By the established status, functions, and powers of the Dalai Lama and of the Panchen Ngoerhtehni are meant the status, functions, and powers of the Thirteenth Dalai Lama and of the Ninth Panchen Ngoerhtehni when they were in friendly and amicable relations with each other.

7. The policy of freedom of religious belief laid down in the Common Programme of the Chinese People's Political Consultative Conference shall be carried out.

The religious beliefs, customs and habits of the Tibetan people shall be respected, and lama monasteries shall be protected. The central authorities will not effect a change in the income of the monasteries.

8. Tibetan troops shall be reorganized step by step into the People's Liberation Army and become a part of the national defense forces of the People's Republic of China.

9. The spoken and written language and school education etc. of the Tibetan nationality shall be developed step by step in accordance with the actual conditions in Tibet.

10. Tibetan agriculture, livestock raising, industry, and commerce shall be developed step by step, and the people's livelihood shall be improved step by step in accordance with the actual conditions in Tibet.

11. In matters related to various reforms in Tibet, there will be no compulsion on the part of the central authorities. The local government of Tibet should carry out reforms of its own accord, and, when the people raise demands for reform, they shall be settled by means of consultation with the leading personnel of Tibet.

12. Insofar as former pro-imperialist and pro-Kuomintang officials resolutely sever relations with imperialism and the Kuomintang and do not engage in sabotage or resistance, they may continue to hold office irrespective of their past.

13. The People's Liberation Army entering Tibet shall abide by all the above-mentioned policies and shall also be fair in all buying and selling and shall not arbitrarily take a needle or thread from the people.

14. The Central People's Government shall have the centralized handling of all external affairs of the area of Tibet, and there will be peaceful coexistence with neighboring countries and the establishment and development of fair commercial and trading relations with them on the basis of equality, mutual benefit, and mutual respect for territory and sovereignty.

15. In order to ensure the implementation of this agreement, the Central People's Government shall set up a military and administrative committee and a military area headquarters in Tibet, and, apart from the personnel sent there by the Central People's Government, shall absorb as many local Tibetan personnel as possible to take part in the work.

Local Tibetan personnel taking part in the military and administrative committee may include patriotic elements from the local government of Tibet, various districts and various principal monasteries; the name list shall be set forth after consultation between the representatives designated by the Central People's Government and various quarters concerned and shall be submitted to the Central People's Government for appointment.

16. Funds needed by the military and administrative committee, the military area headquarters, and the People's Liberation Army entering Tibet shall be provided by the Central People's Government. The local government of Tibet should assist the People's Liberation Army in the purchase and transport of food, fodder and other daily necessities.

17. This agreement shall come into force immediately after the signatures and seals are affixed to it.

Signed and sealed by delegates of the Central People's Government with full powers . . . [and] delegates with full powers of the local government of Tibet . . . .

Note

Despite growing concern over the manner in which Peking was implementing the agreement on Tibet's "regional autonomy," in the fall of 1952 India, at the PRC's request, changed the status of its mission in the Tibetan capital of Lhasa, so that it was no longer accredited to the Tibetan government but was accredited as a consulate general to the central government in Peking. Moreover, the April 1954 Sino-Indian agreement regulating trade and travel between India and "the Tibet region of China" [8–1], in addition to initiating the era of "peaceful coexistence," provided further tacit recognition of Chinese sovereignty over Tibet. India agreed to withdraw military units stationed at the trading points of Yatung and Gyantse and to turn over to the PRC India's telegraph, telephone, and postal systems and trade route rest houses in Tibet. The agreement also provided that India and China could each maintain three trading agencies in the other's territory, and it prescribed six routes to which trade and pilgrim traffic would be limited.

As Chinese party, military, and government cadres descended upon Tibet in increasing numbers, their impact upon the politics, economy, religious life, and educational system of that region became correspondingly more pronounced. When they were followed by masses of Chinese immigrants, violence began to break out in sections of Tibet. By April 1958 the rebellion of one fierce Tibetan tribe, the Khambas, who had sought to evade the wave of Chinese immigration by resettling near the Nepalese border, had attained serious dimensions, and the PRC charged that arms were reaching the Khambas via Nepal. In July 1958 the Khambas demanded that the Chinese leave Tibet, a demand that was widely suspected to have been instigated by foreign powers. At that time the PRC sent India a protest alleging "subversive and disruptive activities against China's Tibetan region carried out in Kalimpong [, India] by American and Chiang Kai-shek clique special agents, Tibetan reactionaries and local special agents." [45]

When the PRC sought to have the Tibetan government suppress the Khambas, this triggered a full-fledged revolt. In March 1959 Tibet denounced the 1951 agreement with the PRC and declared its independence. But the PLA quickly put down the revolt, and, no longer restrained by the 1951 agreement, the PRC followed up this military action with a thorough and reportedly bloody purge of Tibetan leaders. It dissolved the Tibetan government and turned its duties over to the Preparatory Committee for the Tibetan Autonomous Region, which had originally been set up under Tibet's principal leader, the Dalai Lama, but which, upon his flight to India after failure of the revolt, fell under the control of Peking's puppet, the Panchen Lama. All obstacles had thus been removed for what the Communists called "the democratization of Tibet."

Despite the efficiency of the PLA and despite India's earlier recognition of China's claim to sovereignty over Tibet, the rebellion stimulated Peking's fears that a new chapter in the history of foreign attempts to detach Tibet might be taking place. And Peking could not have been comforted by the fact that, after the rebellion had failed, thousands of Tibetans crossed into India and Nepal, mysteriously obtained arms there, and returned to Tibet. Thus, in May 1959 the PRC's ambassador to New Delhi reasserted that Tibet was "an inalienable part of China's territory" and that no one had a right to "make Tibet semi-independent or even to turn it into a sphere of influence of a foreign country or buffer zone." The following article, published several weeks later in the authoritative *People's Daily*, was designed to provide the legal basis for this position.

12-21

Yü Fan, "Speaking about the Relationship between China and the Tibetan Region from the Viewpoint of Sovereignty and Suzerainty," *JMJP* (June 5, 1959), p. 7.

What Is Sovereignty: What Is Suzerainty?. . . .

Speaking simply, state sovereignty is the supreme power of a state, within its own territorial sphere and in accordance with its own will, independently to decide its internal and external affairs.

According to the principle of sovereignty, a state has the power, in accordance with its own will, to decide its own form of state, political system, and social-economic system, and intervention by other states in those matters is absolutely not permissible. What particularly should be carried out and what should be reformed in internal affairs are matters concerning a state's own affairs. Intervention by other states in those matters is absolutely not permissible. Consequently, one can deduce the important principle of nonintervention in the internal affairs of other states from the principle of sovereignty.

The principle of sovereignty is one of the fundamental principles of generally recognized modern international law and the principle of nonintervention in the internal affairs of another state, deduced from the principle of sovereignty, is another fundamental principle of generally recognized modern international law. A sovereign independent state must maintain its own sovereignty and, at the same time, should demand respect for its sovereignty from other states. Since this is a most fundamental principle, no further explanation is necessary.

What is suzerainty? Suzerainty was a special form of rule used by a big state to control a small state during the feudalistic period. The state with the suzerainty was called a suzerain state and the state subject to the control of the suzerain state was called a vassal state. The vassal state's dependent relationship toward the suzerain state was called vassalage. Under this relationship the external affairs of the vassal state were generally administered by the suzerain state. Internally, the vassal state enjoyed a certain degree of self-governing authority or self-government, but it had to fulfill a definite obligation to the suzerain state, particularly the obligation to pay tribute. The unequal relationship between the suzerain state and the vassal state fully expressed the characteristic of international relations in the feudal period, and thus suzerainty can also be called feudal ruling authority.

Before the independence of India and Pakistan, there were about 500 vassal states of different sizes in India. In order to facilitate [its policy of] divide and rule, Britain retained all these vassal states and the British King dispatched the Governor-General (Viceroy) of India to rule over them. The British King was not only "the King of Great Britain, Ireland and of the British Dominions beyond the Seas," but was also the "Emperor of India," and a self-installed suzerain. Thus, it is clear that British imperialism employed the form of feudal suzerainty to conceal its colonial policy of expansion, and its cruel colonial rule. Such a ruling relationship used by a big state to control a small state was used by colonialists as one of the forms of colonial rule, and suzerainty thus became an imperialist tool for concealing its aggression and expansion.

Historically, the suzerain relationship established between the Ottoman Empire and Egypt had another meaning.

Egypt was originally a province of the Ottoman Empire. In the nineteenth century a tense struggle between Britain and France over the leadership of Egypt ensued, and a civil war broke out between the Turkish Sultan and the Egyptian Pasha, Mehemet Ali. France supported Egypt and Britain supported Turkey. Turkey was defeated by Egypt and requested British help. Britain then united with Austria, Prussia, Czarist Russia, and Turkey to conclude the so-called "Convention for the Pacification of the Levant" on July 15, 1840, in London. A separate act annexed to that Convention prescribed the arrangement between the Turkish Sultan and Mehemet Ali as follows:

(1) The Sultan granted to Mehemet Ali Egypt as his hereditary land and the administration of the southern part of Syria for life.

(2) Mehemet Ali was to pay annually some tribute to the Sultan.

(3) All the treaties and laws of the Ottoman Empire were still applicable to Egypt. Mehemet Ali could collect taxes in the name of the Sultan.

(4) The military and naval forces commanded by Mehemet Ali were to become part of the forces of the Ottoman Empire.

Thus, in order to facilitate further aggression against Egypt, Britain guaranteed the Turkish position as a suzerain state over Egypt through the form of a treaty which, in fact, denied the sovereignty of Turkey over Egypt. [This situation] continued until December 18, 1914, when Britain unilaterally announced the termination of Turkish suzerainty over Egypt and established a protectorate relationship over Egypt. This was done on the ground that Turkey had joined the side of Germany in the European war. As a matter of fact, Britain had controlled Egypt since

1840, and Turkey merely maintained the empty title of suzerain state over Egypt. This is a device used by imperialism when it plots to seize a certain part of the territory of another state by recognizing the latter's suzerainty over the part of its territory.

The Form of Chinese Rule over Tibet is in the Form of Complete Sovereignty

What is the relationship between China and Tibet? History tells us that, as early as the middle of the thirteenth century, the Yüan dynasty [1280–1368] unified the Tibet Region and incorporated it into Chinese territory. During the Ch'ing dynasty, Tibet's relationship with the Central Government became closer. The Ch'ing dynasty's rule over Tibet was not in the form of suzerainty, but was in the form of complete sovereignty. The Shun-chih Emperor [1644–1662] of the Ch'ing dynasty prescribed not only the title of "Dalai Lama," but also the political system, laws, and regulations of Tibetan local government. In 1728, the Ch'ing government began to dispatch one Resident [Amban] and one deputy Resident to Tibet to administer governmental affairs together with the Dalai [Lama] and Panchen [Lama]. The "Royal Regulations of 29 Articles" promulgated in 1793 (the 58th year of the Ch'ien-lung Emperor [1736–1796]) provided for various aspects of Tibetan local administration: for example, the question of the reincarnation of the children of the Dalai, Panchen, and other Hu T'u Kalons, the question of mutual relationships and powers between the Dalai and Panchen and Residents, the rules of organization and personnel regulations of Tibetan local government (Ko-hsia or Kashag); regulations of Tibetan taxation, finance and currency, judicial organization and litigation procedure; administration of religious temples; administration of aliens; foreign trade; the frontier inspection system and so forth. The power of Residents was very great; even the official documents from the Dalai and Panchen to the Residents were called Kung Ying (a document submitted by a subordinate to his superior). [Ch'ing] rule over Tibet was absolutely not in the form of suzerainty; it was in the form of sovereignty.

When British imperialism started its aggression against Tibet, even the elements of British imperialism had to recognize the above-stated facts. Colonel Younghusband, who led British forces in invading Tibet (he was later called Sir Francis Younghusband and, on September 7, 1904, he represented Britain at Lhasa when Britain compelled the Tibetan local government to sign the illegal "Anglo-Tibetan Treaty"), pointed out in his book "India and Tibet" (1910) that three days after he signed the "Anglo-Tibetan Treaty," he still saw with his own eyes the announcement of the Resident. The concluding language of the announcement said: "The Dalai Lama will be responsible for the Yellow-cap faith and monks, and will only be concerned slightly in the official matters while the Amban will conduct all Tibetan affairs with the Tibetan officials and important matters will be referred to the Emperor." [46]

Since the Resident's power was so impressive, in the fall of 1908, the 13th Dalai in Peking petitioned the Empress Dowager Tz'u-hsi [1875–1908] that he be allowed to bypass the Resident and appeal directly to the Emperor. But the Empress Dowager Tz'u-hsi refused. Until the end of the Ch'ing dynasty, the institution of Residents remained. This shows that the Chinese relationship with Tibet has always been one of sovereignty, not suzerainty. Tibet has always been an inalienable part of Chinese territory.

The Hsin-hai Revolution [1911] overthrew the Ch'ing dynasty. China was renamed "the Republic of China," and the national flag was changed into a five-color flag. The five colors—red, yellow, blue, white, and black—symbolized the "five-nation republic"—Han, Manchu, Mongolian, Moslem and Tibetan. This shows that, after the Hsin-hai Revolution, Tibet remained part of Chinese territory and was not what is called a dependent [vassal] state.

British Conspiracy to Fabricate "Chinese Suzerainty over Tibet" Has Never Been Realized

In fact, imperialists also know very clearly that Tibet is an inalienable part of Chinese territory. When Britain premeditated its aggression against Tibet, the British government seriously considered this point. How to undermine Chinese sovereignty over Tibet in order to achieve its objective of aggression against Tibet was the main question carefully considered by British imperialism.

Lord Curzon of Britain advocated positive aggression against Tibet, and he was called the "vanguard" of the "forward policy" of aggression against Tibet. In January 1903, as Governor-General (Viceroy) of India, he submitted a report to the British Secretary of State for India in London. He wrote:

> We regard the so-called suzerainty of China over Tibet as a constitutional fiction—a political affectation which has only been maintained because of its convenience to both parties.[47] (The term "parties" refers to Tibet and India—author's [Yü Fan] note.)

The instruction of Hamilton, Secretary of State for India, nevertheless expressed caution. It said:

> His Majesty's government cannot regard the question as one concerning India and Tibet alone. The position of China, in its relations to the powers of Europe, has been so modified in recent years that it is necessary to take into account those altered conditions in deciding on action affecting what *must still be regarded as a province of China.* [Emphasis added.] [48]

On January 14, 1904, the British Secretary of State for Foreign Affairs also pointed out in his instruction to the British ambassador to Russia "the utility and necessity of maintaining the political status quo in that *province* [that is, Tibet] *of the Chinese Empire.*" [49]

So the British imperialists clearly knew that the relationship between China and the Tibet Region was one between the Central Government and the local government, and recognized that Tibet is "a province of the Chinese Empire" and an inalienable part of Chinese territory and that the relationship between China and Tibet is clearly one of sovereignty. . . .

Throughout the history of British aggression against Tibet, in order to negate the real sovereignty of China over Tibet, Britain tried several times between 1904 and 1914 to make a fiction of "Chinese suzerainty over Tibet" through treaties. However, China agreed to none of those treaties.

The first attempt was made on April 27, 1906, when T'ang Shao-i (Tong Shao-yi), Vice-Minister of the Ministry of Foreign Affairs of the Ch'ing government, negotiated . . . the signing of the "Six Article Convention between Great Britain and China respecting Tibet." We have stated before that Colonel Younghusband of Britain once led British forces in invading Tibet and on November 7, 1904, concluded the illegal "Anglo-Tibetan Treaty" with the Tibetan local government which, [in the absence] of the Resident in Lhasa, had absolutely no power over its foreign relations. Britain thereby acquired a position of special privilege in Tibet. The Ch'ing government then protested to the British government and thereafter negotiations were reopened between China and Britain on another Tibetan treaty. Britain demanded that the new treaty should have one article providing that "Great Britain agrees to recognize China as Tibet's superior state." [50] The Chinese representative opposed the term "superior state". . . .

The term "superior state" in the foregoing provision . . . refers to a suzerain state. It is clear that Britain certainly proposed the provision . . . in the draft of the treaty in an attempt to impose fictitious suzerainty on the relationship between China and the Tibet Region. Even though it was stupid and incompetent, the Ch'ing government did not dare to fall into that trap. Therefore, although Britain extracted many privileges from the 1906 Convention between China and Great Britain respecting Tibet, there was no so-called provision on "Chinese suzerainty over Tibet."

The second attempt was expressed in the Convention between Great Britain and Russia relating to Persia, Afghanistan, and Tibet, signed at St. Petersburg on August 31, 1907, which clearly expressed "the suzerainty of China over Tibet. . . ." The third part of the Convention, that is, the part relating to Tibet, provides in Article 2: "In conformity with the admitted principle of the suzerainty of China over Tibet, Great Britain and Russia engage not to enter into negotiations with Tibet except through the intermediary of the Chinese government. . . ."

This Convention, however, was concluded between Britain and Russia and can only be effective between Britain and Russia. Since China is not a contracting party, according to the principle of *"pacta tertiis nec nocent nec prosunt"* of the law of treaties, this Convention naturally cannot bind China. How can a convention of which China was ignorant impose fictitious "suzerainty" on the relationship between China and Tibet?

The third attempt was expressed in the notorious (draft) "Simla Convention between China, Britain, and Tibet." After the Hsin-hai Revolution, the pro-British elements of the Tibetan upper class used the opportunity to start a rebellion. When the Yüan Shih-k'ai government sent troops to Tibet, the British Minister, Jordan, arbitrarily intervened, and then the so-called "Tripartite Conference of China, Britain, and Tibet" was convened in Simla, India. The meeting started on October 13, 1913.

The so-called "Simla Convention" is an extremely absurd document. The so-called Tibetan representative, Lonchen Shatra, ruthlessly made the absurd demand of "independence for Tibet," and the British representative, McMahon, superficially appeared in the posture of [mediator] between the Chinese government and Tibet. He submitted a so-called mediating draft of eleven articles, Article 2 of which provides:

> The governments of Great Britain and China, recognizing that Tibet is under the suzerainty of China, and recognizing also the autonomy of Outer Tibet, engage to respect the territorial integrity of the country, and to abstain from interference in the administration of Outer Tibet (including the selection and installation of the Dalai Lama), which shall remain in the hands of the Tibetan government at Lhasa. The government of China engages not to convert Tibet into a Chinese province. The government of Great Britain engages not to annex Tibet or any portion of it.

It is worthwhile to note that this article not only describes China as a suzerain state over Tibet, but also describes Tibet as a state in such phrases as "the country," etc. . . .

After the conclusion of the discussion of the draft, the Chinese representative, Ivan Chen, upon the instruction of the then Ministry of Foreign Affairs, refused to sign the convention. . . .

On April 29, 1954, the Central People's Government of the People's Republic of China and the government of the Republic of India concluded at Peking the Agreement on Trade and Intercourse between India and the Tibetan Region of China. The preamble of the Agreement provides as follows:

> The Government of the Republic of India and the Central People's Government of the People's Republic of China,
>
> Being desirous of promoting trade and cultural intercourse between Tibet Region of China and India and of facilitating pilgrimage and travel by the peoples of China and India,
>
> Have resolved to enter into the present Agreement based on the following principles:
>
> (1) mutual respect for each other's territorial integrity and sovereignty,
>
> (2) mutual nonaggression,
>
> (3) mutual noninterference in each other's internal affairs,
>
> (4) equality and mutual benefit, and
>
> (5) peaceful coexistence.

The term "Tibet Region of China" referred to in the preamble shows clearly that Tibet is an inalienable part of Chinese territory and the term "the peoples of China and India" also clearly points out that the Tibetan people are part of the Chinese people. China is a multinational country and the people of Tibet are an element of the big family of various nationality groups of Great China. This is a very important point. The fact that the Indian government solemnly signed and ratified this agreement indicates that India also already confirms that Tibet is part of Chinese territory and that China has complete sovereignty over the Tibet Region.[51]

(e) SINO-INDIAN BORDER

If the PRC suspected India's intentions in Tibet, India also suspected the PRC's intentions. Shortly after the Chinese reestablished control over Tibet in 1950, India, concerned over the need to bolster its northern frontier, moved to occupy most of the Northeast Frontier

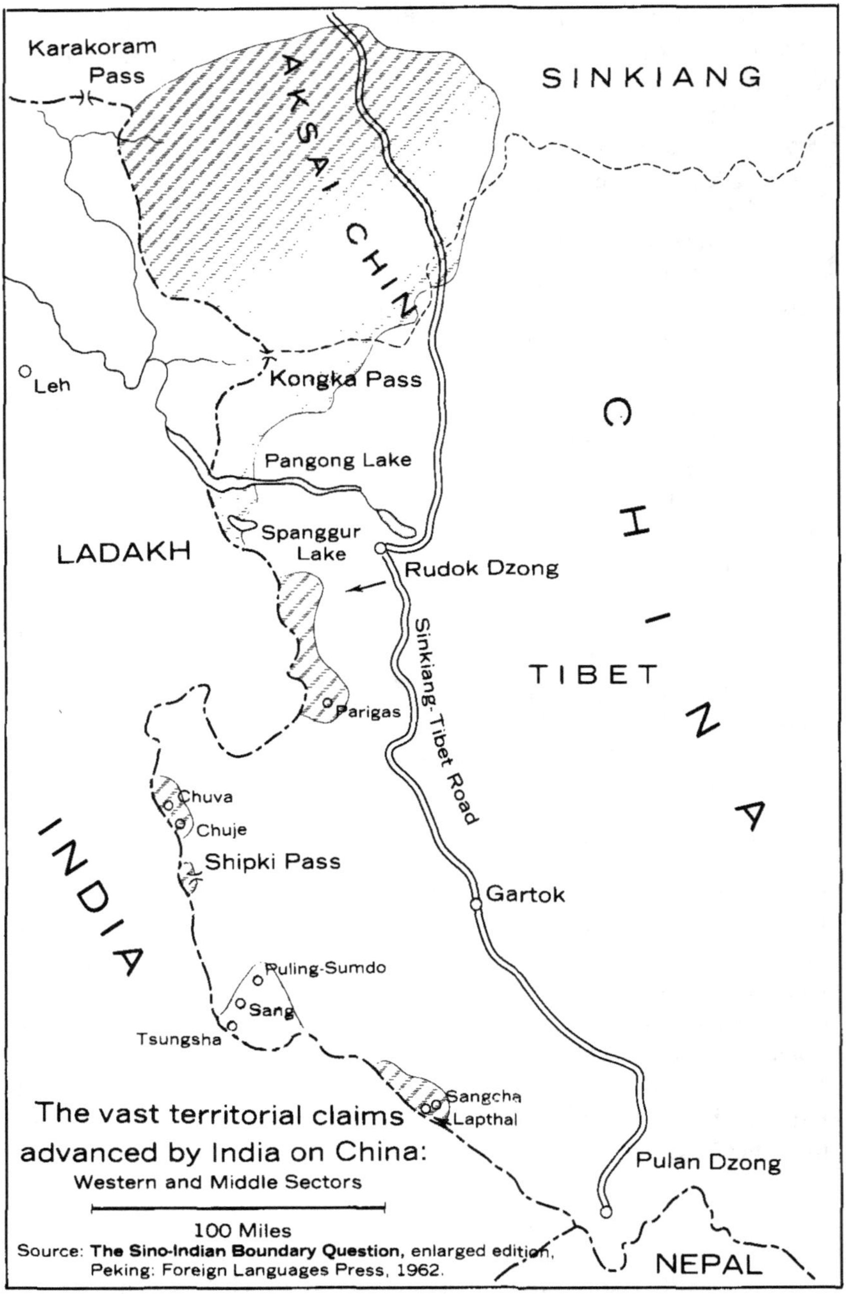

The vast territorial claims advanced by India on China: Western and Middle Sectors

Source: **The Sino-Indian Boundary Question**, enlarged edition, Peking: Foreign Languages Press, 1962.

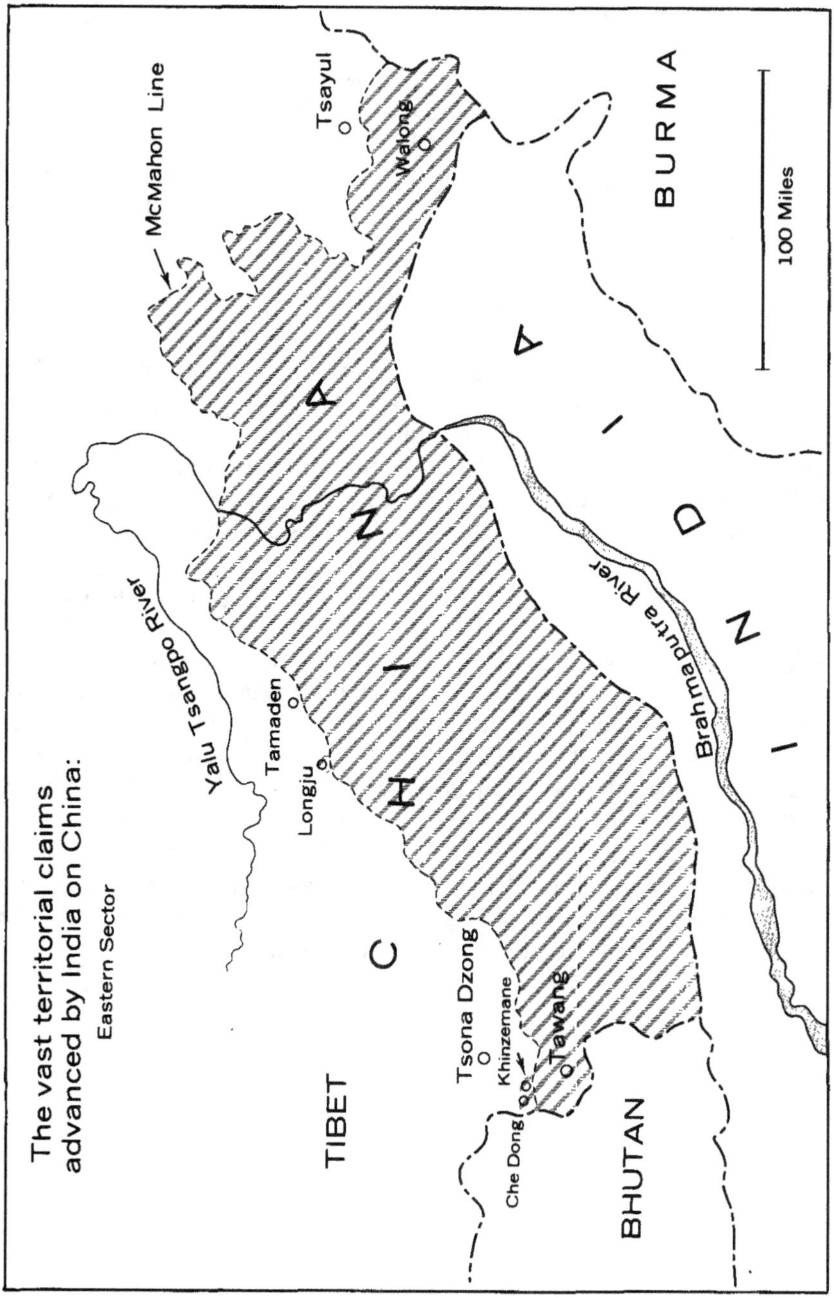

The vast territorial claims advanced by India on China:
Eastern Sector

Agency, which item 12–22 refers to as the "eastern sector" of the Sino-Indian border. Although the Indians did not learn until 1958 that in the "western sector" the PRC had constructed a road from China's Sinkiang province to Tibet via the Aksai Chin plateau claimed by both states, tensions gradually mounted in the early 1950's as the Chinese sought to consolidate their hold on Tibet. Moreover, growing unrest among India's Naga tribes situated near the Chinese border created a potentially ripe situation for Chinese interference, and Indian nervousness increased in 1952 when a leader of an unsuccessful revolt in Nepal escaped to China. When the PRC began to publish maps claiming large portions of territory that were also claimed by India, it became obvious that a border dispute of considerable political significance was brewing. Nevertheless, neither side wished to press the issue at the time that they negotiated the April 1954 agreement on trade and travel between India and "the Tibet Region of China." From that point on, however, each side increased its military patrols and exploratory missions in the border areas, and India began to publish maps that expanded upon previous Indian claims in the areas involved.

India's Prime Minister Nehru and the PRC's Premier, Chou En-lai, held the first of a series of discussions on border problems in the fall of 1954. In late 1958, after India protested the newly discovered Chinese road on the Aksai Chin plateau, Nehru initiated more formal exchanges in the form of diplomatic correspondence. In 1959 this correspondence continued amid sharply heightened tension created by the Tibetan revolt, the PRC's efforts to seal what it claimed to be the Sino-Indian border, and the ensuing clashes between Chinese and Indian troops. At the end of 1959, in response to India's request that it spell out the historical foundation for its border claims, the PRC delivered the following note, which states the Chinese position as clearly as any document in the voluminous exchanges on the merits of the question.

12-22

"Note of the Ministry of Foreign Affairs of the People's Republic of China to the Indian Embassy in China," December 26, 1959, *WCC 1959*, VI (1961), 125–148; translated in *The Sino-Indian Boundary Question* (Peking: Foreign Languages Press, 1962), pp. 51–92.

The Ministry of Foreign Affairs of the People's Republic of China presents its compliments to the Embassy of the Republic of India in China and has the honour to make the following observations on the Sino-Indian boundary question, which the Embassy is requested to transmit to the Indian government:

On September 8, 1959, Premier Chou En-lai wrote to Prime Minister Jawaharlal Nehru, giving an overall account of the historical background and the present actual situation of the Sino-Indian boundary question and the stand and policy of the Chinese government. Afterwards, Premier Chou En-lai and the Chinese Government received Prime Minister Nehru's letter of September 26 and the Indian Ministry of External Affairs' note of November 4. In the said letter and note, the Indian government indicated that it could not agree to Premier Chou En-lai's account of the facts regarding the boundary.

The Chinese government is desirous at all times of maintaining friendship with the Indian government and people, and, on the boundary question, of holding discussions with the Indian government calmly and amicably and with an attitude which is fair both to itself and to others so as to seek a rapprochement of the views of the two sides. In view of the fact that the Sino-Indian boundary question is rather complex and that it would be extremely difficult to bring about a settlement through the exchange of letters, the Chinese government has always maintained that face-to-face talks should be held speedily between the representatives of the governments, first of all between the Prime Ministers of the two countries, so as more effectively to exchange views and reach agreement. But since the talks between the two Prime Ministers are yet to be decided on through consultations between the two sides, and the Indian government has moreover complained that the Chinese government has given no reply to the parts of the abovementioned letter and note concerning facts about the boundary, the Ministry of Foreign Affairs of China is instructed to make further observations on the major questions concerning the facts about the boundary, with reference to Premier Chou En-lai's letter of September 8, Prime Minister Nehru's letter of September 26 and the note of the Indian Ministry of External Affairs of November 4.

China and India are two peace-loving, big countries with a long history of mutual friendship and with many great common tasks both at present and in the future. Friendship between China and India is in the interests not only of the two peoples, but also of world peace, particularly of peace in Asia. The Chinese government is therefore very reluctant to engage in arguments with the Indian government over the boundary question. Unfortunately, the Sino-Indian boundary has never been delimited, Britain left behind in this respect a heritage of certain disputes, and moreover the Indian government has made a series of unacceptable charges against China, thereby rendering these arguments unavoidable. Because the Indian government has put forth a mass of detailed data on the boundary question, the Chinese government feels sorry that, though trying its best to be brief, it cannot but refer in this reply to various details so as to clarify the true picture of the historical situation and the views of the two sides.

For convenience's sake, in the following paragraphs the section of the boundary between China's Sinkiang and Tibet on the one hand and Ladakh on the other will be termed the western sector; the section of the boundary from the southeastern end of the western sector to the converging point of China, India, and Nepal, the middle sector; and the section of the boundary east of Bhutan the eastern sector.

Question One:
Has the Sino-Indian Boundary Been Formally Delimited?

The reason for the present existence of certain disputes over the Sino-Indian boundary is that the two countries have never formally delimited this boundary and that there is a divergence of views between the two countries regarding the boundary. According to the Indian maps, the boundary line in the western sector cuts deep into Chinese territory, including an area of over 33,000 square kilometres in India; the boundary line in the middle sector is relatively close to the delineation on the Chinese maps, but still a number of areas which have always belonged to China are included in India; and in the eastern sector, the whole boundary line is pushed northward, including in India an area of 90,000 square kilometres which originally belonged to China. The Chinese government, therefore, considers it necessary to conduct friendly negotiations to bring about a reasonable settlement. The Indian government, however, holds that the greater part of the Sino-Indian boundary line as shown on current Indian maps is defined by international agreements and therefore sees no reason to hold overall boundary negotiations. Thus, the negotiations themselves have run up against difficulties and there is the danger of the boundary disputes remaining deadlocked for a long time. The Chinese government considers that to say that the greater part of the Sino-Indian boundary has been formally delimited by international agreements is totally inconsistent with the facts. The Chinese government wishes to make the following explanations:

(1) Concerning the western sector. The Indian government holds that the boundary line it claims was fixed by a treaty concluded between the authorities of the Tibet Region of China and the Kashmir authorities in 1842.

But firstly, this treaty merely mentioned that the boundary between Ladakh and Tibet would be maintained as it had been and that both sides would hold to their confines and refrain from encroaching on each other. The treaty contained no provision or hint whatsoever about the concrete location of the boundary. None of the arguments advanced by Prime Minister Nehru in his letter of September 26, 1959, to Premier Chou En-lai to the effect that the location of the boundary has been long established can prove that the boundary line now claimed by the Indian government is well founded.

Secondly, the 1842 treaty was concluded between the authorities of the Tibet Region of China and the Kashmir authorities, but the greatest part (about 80 per cent) of the area now disputed by the Indian government is part of China's Sinkiang which was no party to the treaty. It is obviously inconceivable to hold that, judging by this treaty, vast areas of Sinkiang have ceased to belong to China but have become part of Ladakh. The British government proposed in 1899 to delimit the boundary between Ladakh and Kashmir on the one hand and Sinkiang on the other, but nothing came of it. It is also inconceivable to hold that the territory of another country can be annexed by a unilateral proposal.

Thirdly, there are many indisputable positive evidences to show that the western sector of the Sino-Indian boundary is not delimited. For instance, (a) Between 1921 and 1927, the British Indian government made many representations to the authorities of China's Tibet Region, asking to delimit the boundary between Ladakh and Tibet, but without any result. This is testified by many documents exchanged between the two sides at the time, and is also confirmed by Sir Arthur Lothian, the Briton who acted as the representative of India, in his letter to the London *Times* published on December 11, 1959. (b) According to data now available to the Chinese government, no boundary line was drawn at all in the western sector of the Sino-Indian border on the official map published by the Survey of India as late as 1943. On the official Indian map of the 1950 edition, the present version of the boundary line was shown in a most equivocal way, but was still marked by the words "Boundary Undefined." It is only since 1954 that this undelimited sector of the boundary has suddenly become a delimited boundary. (c) Referring to this sector of the boundary in the Lok Sabha of India on August 28, 1959, Prime Minister Nehru declared that: "This was the boundary of the old Kashmir state with Tibet and Chinese Turkestan. Nobody had marked it." All the above-mentioned facts are absolutely incompatible with the allegation that this sector of the boundary was delimited long ago. It is unthinkable that the Indian government which held that this sector of the boundary had explicitly been delimited in 1842 or 1899 would, between 1921 and 1927, still ask continually for negotiations to delimit it; that it would in 1943 still admit the absence of any determined boundary; that it would in 1950 still declare the mere existence of a boundary undefined; and that it would in 1959 still proclaim that nobody had marked the boundary.

(2) Concerning the middle sector. The Indian government considers that the specification in Article IV of the 1954 Sino-Indian Agreement of six passes in this area as passages for traders and pilgrims of both countries indicates that the Chinese government has already concurred in the Indian government's opinion about this sector of the boundary. The Chinese government holds that this allegation is untenable both factually and logically.

The question of the boundary between the two countries was not touched on at all in the 1954 Sino-Indian Agreement or during its negotiations. The Chinese side's draft wording for Article IV of the Agreement was that "The Chinese Government agrees to open the following mountain passes in the Ari district of the Tibet Region of China for entry and exit by traders and pilgrims of both parties." The Indian side disagreed with the Chinese draft; its own draft wording was that "Traders and pilgrims from India and western Tibet may travel by the routes traversing the following localities and passes." Later on the two sides agreed to change the wording into: "Traders and pilgrims of both countries may travel by the following passes and route." The concession made by the Chinese government was only to adopt a wording which does not involve the ownership of these passes. Nobody can draw from this the conclusion that this sector of the boundary between the two countries has thus been fixed. On the contrary, the Chinese representative, Vice-Foreign Minister Chang Han-fu, in his talk with the Indian representative, Ambassador Mr. N. Raghavan, on April 23, 1954, clearly stated that the Chinese side did not wish, in those negotiations, to touch on the boundary question. And Ambassador N. Raghavan agreed forthwith. The Chinese government therefore maintains that there is no ground to say that this sector of the boundary has been delimited and that there is no need to conduct negotiations for its delimitation.

(3) Concerning the eastern sector. The Indian government holds that the so-called McMahon Line is the product of the 1914 Simla Conference jointly attended by Britain, China, and the Tibet Region of China, and is therefore valid. The Chinese government holds that the so-called McMahon Line is wholly illegal, and the Indian government's assertion is utterly unacceptable to the Chinese government.

Firstly, it is known to the world that the Simla Convention itself is void of legal validity. The Chinese representative Ivan Chen attending the Simla Conference not only refused to sign the Simla Convention, but acting under instructions from the Chinese government formally declared at the conference on July 3, 1914, that the Chinese government would not recognize any treaty or similar document that might then or thereafter be signed between Britain and Tibet. Similar declarations were made in formal notes delivered to the British government on July 3 and 7 the same year by Minister of the Chinese government in Britain, Lew Yuk Lin. All Chinese governments since then persisted in this stand. Many dirty unequal treaties signed by the past Chinese governments under imperialist oppression have already been proclaimed null and void. The Chinese government feels perplexed why the government of India, which has likewise won independence from under imperialist oppression, should insist that the government of its friend China recognize an unequal treaty which the Chinese government has not even signed.

Secondly, the Indian government asserts that the boundary between India and Tibet was discussed at the Simla Conference, that the Chinese government never objected at the time or afterwards to the discussion of the boundary between India and Tibet at the conference, and that therefore the agreement which resulted from the conference in regard to the McMahon Line boundary between India and Tibet must be regarded as binding on China. But this line of argument, from beginning to end, is inconsistent with the facts. As a matter of fact, the Simla Conference only discussed the boundary between the Tibet Region and the rest of China and the boundary between so-called Outer and Inner Tibet; it never discussed the boundary between China and India. The so-called McMahon Line boundary between China and India was the result of the exchange of secret letters at Delhi on March 24, 1914, between the British representative and the representative of the then Tibet local authorities. It was in no way made known to China. It also means that it was never placed on the agenda of the Simla Conference. A section of the red line shown on the map attached to the Simla Convention corresponds with the so-called McMahon Line, but that red line was presented as the boundary between Tibet and the rest of China, and it was never stated that part of the red line was the boundary between China and India. Since the so-called question of Sino-Indian boundary never existed at the Simla Conference and in the Simla Convention, the Chinese government naturally would not refer to this question or the question of the so-called McMahon Line in its memorandum and its suggestions for the revision of the Simla Convention. The Indian government has pointed to the fact that the Chinese government at the time did not raise any objection to the so-called McMahon Line. But this fact only shows that the Chinese government was completely unaware of the existence of the question of the so-called McMahon Line, and can in no way prove that the Line was legal or was accepted by the Chinese government. It can thus be seen that the so-called McMahon Line is more unsavoury and more unpresentable than the Simla Convention, and it is indeed all the more strange to assert that it is binding on the Chinese government. The Chinese government would like to ask the Indian government whether, among all the proceedings of the Simla Conference, it can point to any particular date of the conference or any particular article of the Convention when and where the Sino-Indian boundary question, and particularly the question of the so-called McMahon Line, was referred to.

In addition, it must also be pointed out that it is beyond doubt that Britain had no right to conduct separate negotiations with Tibet. Indeed, the Chinese government made repeated statements to this effect; as to the British government, it too was strictly bound by the 1907 agreement on Tibet concluded between it and the old Russian government not to enter into negotiations with Tibet except through the intermediary of the Chinese government. Therefore, judging by this treaty obligation alone which was undertaken by the British government, the secret exchange of letters in 1914 between the British representative and the representative of the Tibet local authorities behind the back of the Chinese government is void of any legal validity.

Thirdly, the assertion that China did not raise any objection to the so-called McMahon Line boundary between China and India is also inconsistent with the fact. It was during the most difficult period of China's War of Resistance to Japanese Aggression that the so-called McMahon Line gradually and unofficially appeared on Indian maps, and after 1943 the Tibet local authorities were under the firm control of British imperialism and their relations with the Chinese Central Government steadily deteriorated. Nevertheless, on learning that Britain had gradually encroached on Chinese territory south of the so-called McMahon Line, the Kuomintang government four times protested by addressing notes to the British embassy in China after the conclusion of the Anti-Japanese

War, in July, September, and November of 1946 and January of 1947. Since Britain shifted its responsibility onto India, the Kuomintang government protested by note with the Indian embassy in China in February 1947. Even up to November 18, 1949, Lo Chia-lun, ambassador to India of the Chiang Kai-shek clique which then still maintained diplomatic relations with the Indian government, delivered a note to the Indian Ministry of External Affairs, repudiating the Simla Convention which the Indian government held to be valid. The government of the People's Republic of China, since establishing diplomatic relations with the government of India, has repeatedly stated the fact that the Sino-Indian boundary has not been delimited. During Prime Minister Nehru's visit in China in 1954, Premier Chou En-lai made it clear that the Sino-Indian boundary was yet to be delimited. Premier Chou also said that the reason why the delineation of old maps was followed in Chinese maps was that the Chinese government had not yet undertaken a survey of China's boundary, nor consulted with the countries concerned, and that it would not make changes in the delineation of the boundary on its own. This was reiterated in the memorandum delivered to the Indian embassy in China by the Chinese Ministry of Foreign Affairs on November 3, 1958. Besides, even the local authorities of Tibet did not regard as reasonable the so-called McMahon Line, which was the product of underhand schemes; they repeatedly objected to this line and asked for the return of occupied Chinese territory south of the Line. This fact is not denied even by the Indian government.

Fourthly, not only the so-called McMahon Line boundary between China and India has never been recognized by the Chinese government; its validity was for a long time questioned by the Indian and the British governments. The so-called McMahon Line was not adopted on the official map, *Tibet and Adjacent Countries,* published by the Survey of India in 1938, nor on the map "India" in the sixth edition of the *Oxford Advanced Atlas,* 1940, compiled by John Bartholomew, cartographer to the King of Britain. Neither was the so-called McMahon Line followed in drawing the eastern sector of the Sino-Indian boundary on the map "India 1945" attached to the 1951 3rd edition in English of *The Discovery of India,* written by Prime Minister Nehru himself and first published in 1946. Although the so-called McMahon Line was drawn on the official maps of India published by the Survey of India in 1950, 1951, and 1952, it was still marked as undemarcated. Up to 1958, on the map "China West and Tibet" in the *Times Atlas of the World,* edited by John Bartholomew, cartographer to the King of Britain, the traditional Sino-Indian boundary line and the so-called McMahon Line were both drawn with the words "Disputed Area" marked between the lines. All these authoritative facts squarely refute the Indian government's argument that this sector of the boundary has been delimited. The Indian government contends that Britain withheld the publication of the Simla Convention for years in the hope that there would be an agreement about the status and boundary of Inner Tibet. That this assertion cannot help the Indian government out of its difficulties is already explained as [*sic*] above; the assertion moreover adds to its difficulties. What meaning can the Simla Convention have, when the British government also admitted that no agreement was reached on it? And since the Convention itself has not acquired validity, what can be said for the so-called Sino-Indian boundary line which was never proposed to the Chinese government and which the British unilaterally meant to smuggle into this Convention? In fact, British officials who once held posts in India, though by no means pro-Chinese, also admit that the McMahon Line is legally untenable and actually ineffective. For instance, Henry Twynam, who was Acting Governor of Assam, India, in 1939, testified in his letter to the London *Times* published on September 2, 1959, that this line "does not exist, and never has existed."

From what has been said in the above, the following incontestable conclusion can be drawn: The entire Sino-Indian boundary, whether in its western, middle, or eastern sector, has not been delimited. The 1842 Treaty, on which the Indian government bases itself, did not define any boundary line for the western sector of the Sino-Indian border; and, moreover, China's Sinkiang Region, which is most concerned with this sector of the boundary, was no party to this treaty. The 1954 Agreement, on which the Indian government bases itself, did not involve the middle or any other sector of the Sino-Indian boundary. The 1914 Convention, on which the Indian government bases itself, is itself void of legal validity, and the Sino-Indian boundary was never discussed at the 1914 Conference. That the Sino-Indian boundary is yet to be delimited has been recognized by the Indian and British governments over a long period of time, and is borne out by indisputable evidences. In order to achieve a reasonable settlement of the Sino-Indian boundary dispute satisfactory to both sides, there is no other way except the holding of friendly negotiations.

Question Two:
Where Is the Traditional Customary Sino-Indian Boundary Line?

Although the Sino-Indian boundary has not been formally delimited, both sides acknowledge the existence of a traditional customary line, that is, the line formed by the extent of jurisdiction exercised historically by each side. The present question is that the two sides hold very different conceptions of the position of the traditional customary line. In drawing the boundary (mainly the eastern and western sectors) on its maps, the Indian government has gone far beyond the extent of its original actual jurisdiction; it asserts that this is not only based on international treaties, but is the traditional customary line itself. The Chinese government holds that the delineations of the Sino-Indian boundary on current Indian maps, which differ greatly from those on Chinese maps, are not based on any international treaty, as stated above, and, what is more, are not based on tradition and custom.

(1) Concerning the western sector. The area of over 33,000 square kilometres now disputed by India has always belonged to China. This is conclusively borne out by Chinese official documents and records. Except for the very small area of Parigas which has been occupied by India in recent years, the remaining broad area has always been under the effective control of the Chinese government. The major part of this area is under the jurisdiction of Hotien County of the Sinkiang Uighur Autonomous Region of China, while the minor part [is] under that of Rudok Dzong of the Tibetan Autonomous Region of China. Though sparsely populated, this area has all along been a place for pasturage and salt mining for the Uighur and Kirghiz people living in the southwestern border of Sinkiang and a part of the Tibetan people living in the northwestern border of Tibet. Many places of this area are named in the Uighur language. For instance, Aksai Chin, which is part of Hotien County of Sinkiang, means "the desert of white stones" in the Uighur language; while the Karakash River which flows through this area means "the river of the black jade" in the Uighur language.

This area is the only traffic artery linking Sinkiang and western Tibet, because to its northeast lies the great Gobi of Sinkiang through which direct traffic with Tibet is practically impossible. Therefore, since the middle of the 18th century, the government of the Ching Dynasty of China had established Karens (checkposts) to exercise jurisdiction over and patrol this area. In the decades from the founding of the Republic of China till the liberation of China, there were troops constantly guarding this area. After the liberation of Sinkiang in 1949, the Chinese People's Liberation Army took over the guarding of the frontier in this area from Kuomintang troops. In the latter half of 1950, it was through this area that the Chinese government dispatched the first units of the Chinese People's Liberation Army to enter Tibet. In the nine years since then, the Chinese troops stationed in the Ari district have regularly and frequently brought up indispensable supplies from Sinkiang through this area. From March 1956 to October 1957, the Chinese government built along the customary route a motor road from Yehcheng of Sinkiang to Gartok of Tibet of a total length of 1,200 kilometres, of which a section of 180 kilometres runs through this area, and over 3,000 civilian workers took part in its construction.

These unshakable facts should have been sufficient to prove beyond dispute that this area is Chinese territory.

The Indian Government asserts that this area "has been associated with India's culture and tradition for the last two thousand years or so, and has been an intimate part of India's life and thought." But firstly, the Indian government fails to give any concrete facts to support its contention. On the contrary, Prime Minister Nehru said in the Rajya Sabha of India on September 10, 1959, that this area "has not been under any kind of administration." On November 23, 1959, he said again in the Rajya Sabha of India: "During British rule, as far as I know, this area was neither inhabited by any people nor were there any outposts." Though Prime Minister Nehru is in no position to judge correctly the conditions prevailing on the Chinese side, his words do prove authoritatively that India has never exercised control over this area.

Secondly, the Indian government says that it has been sending regular patrols to this area, and that this is one way India exercises its jurisdiction. According to data available to the Chinese government, however, armed Indian personnel intruded only three times into this area to carry out reconnaissance, namely, in September 1958, July 1959, and October 1959, and on each occasion they were promptly detained and then sent out of China by Chinese frontier guards. Apart from these three intrusions, they have never been to this area. It is precisely for this reason that the Indian government has been so unaware of the long-term activities of the Chinese personnel in this area that it declares that it was in 1957 that Chinese personnel first entered this area.

Thirdly, the Indian government has referred to a number of maps to corroborate what it has claimed to be the traditional customary line. But the situation in this respect is not favourable to India's arguments either. Despite slight discrepancies at some places, the delineations of the western sector of the boundary on the maps published in China in the past one to two hundred years have in the main been consistent. The Indian government says that the delineation of the western sector of the boundary on an official Chinese map published in 1893 approximates to [*sic*] that of the Indian maps. The Chinese government does not know what map is referred to here and, consequently, is unable to comment on it. As to the atlas published in 1917 by the British-owned paper, the *North China Daily News and Herald,* it can only represent the British view but not the Chinese, and there is no need to discuss it here.

By contrast, there have been considerable contradictions and confusion in the delineations of the boundary on maps published in Britain and India in the past century and more. This is because, after occupying Kashmir, Britain actively tried to use it as a base for aggression against China's southern Sinkiang and northwestern Tibet, and, therefore, it continually made arbitrary changes in the traditional customary boundary line in the western sector and sent surveying parties to intrude into China for this purpose. Prime Minister Nehru says that "accurate" maps, that is, maps in agreement with the current Indian maps, became possible only from 1865 after surveys. But, even so, some reputed surveyors did not wish to misrepresent the facts at will. For instance, the delineations of the boundary on the *Sketch Map of Eastern Turkestan* of 1870, by G. W. Hayward and on the *Sketch Map of the Country North of India* of 1871, by Robert Shaw—both surveyors being referred to by Prime Minister Nehru in his letter of September 26—are close to the traditional customary line as shown on Chinese maps. In his article in the *Journal of the British Royal Geographical Society,* Vol. XL, 1870, Hayward stated explicitly that the boundary ran along the main chain of the Karakoram Mountain[s] to the passes in Changchenmo, that is to say, it is the Chinese maps, rather than the current Indian maps, that have correctly delineated this sector of the boundary. What is of special significance is the fact that no boundary line, let alone an "accurate" boundary line, was drawn at all for this sector on the official map compiled by the Survey of India as late as the 1943 edition. On its 1950 map, though the same colour for Kashmir was painted in the area disputed by India, still no boundary line was drawn, and there were marked the words "Boundary Undefined." This fact has already been pointed out above.

Fourthly, the Indian government says that the traditional customary line claimed by it possesses, in addition, distinct geographical features, that is, it runs along the watershed. However, to begin with, the principle of watershed is not the sole or main international principle for the delimitation of boundaries. It is particularly impermissible to use the watershed as a pretext for seeking a boundary line within the territory of another country. Next, the traditional customary line claimed by the Indian government, instead of separating the Hotien River system from the Indus River system, actually cuts across the Hotien River system. On the contrary, the traditional customary line as shown on Chinese maps truly reflects the geographical features of this area, that is, having no steep slopes in the north-south direction, the area is easily passable and, therefore, naturally forms the only route linking Sinkiang and western Tibet. To the west, however, there lies between this region and Ladakh the towering Karakoram Mountain range which is extremely difficult to pass through. The Indian government also admits that this area is extremely difficult of access from Ladakh.

It can thus be seen that judging by the actual administrative jurisdiction at all times or by the maps and geographical features referred to by India, the line claimed by India to be the traditional customary boundary line in the western sector is without any foundation; while the traditional customary line for which China stands is truly well founded.

(2) Concerning the middle sector. The disputed areas involved here owing to difference of conception between the two sides regarding the traditional customary line—Chuva, Chuje, Shipki Pass, Sang, Tsungsha, Puling-Sumdo, Wuje, Sangcha, and Lapthal—are all traditional Chinese territory. Except Sang and Tsungsha which were invaded and occupied by Britain earlier, they were all occupied or intruded into by India only after the signing of the 1954 Sino-Indian Agreement.

The local authorities of the Tibet Region have kept up to now the land-conferring documents or land deeds concerning these places issued in the past few centuries. For example, the mandate issued in the name of the 7th Dalai Lama in the 18th century stated specifically that Wuje was within the territorial limits of Daba Dzong of Tibet. Furthermore, the local authorities of the Tibet Region have all along been collecting taxes in these places, and the census record and taxation papers of some of these places have been preserved down to the present time.

Nearly all those who have lived long in these places are of the Tibetan nationality of China. Despite foreign occupation of their places of residence, they still did not wish to be separated from their motherland. For instance, after Sang and Tsungsha were occupied by Britain, the local population still considered themselves Chinese nationals, and on more than one occasion pledged their allegiance to the local government of the Tibet Region of China in statements made to the local authorities of the Tibet Region.

It must be pointed out in particular that among the above-mentioned places, Puling-Sumdo is one of the ten places which the Chinese government agreed to open as markets for trade in the Ari district of Tibet as specified in Article II, Section 2 of the Sino-Indian Agreement of 1954. It was opened together with the nine other markets in compliance with request made by Mr. N. Raghavan, representative of the Indian government and Indian ambassador, at the first meeting of the negotiations. Puling-Sumdo, however, was occupied by India soon after the signing of the 1954 Agreement.

The Indian government claims that it has all along been exercising jurisdiction over the above-mentioned places. However, in the note annexed to Prime Minister Nehru's letter of September 26, 1959, apart from some extremely strained arguments in connection with Sang and Tsungsha, there are no concrete facts whatever to show that jurisdiction has always been exercised over the seven other places.

The principle of watershed put forward by the Indian government cannot be applied here either, as it does not conform with the jurisdiction actually exercised by each side.

The maps published by the two sides also show that it is China, not India, which has abided by the traditional customary line. The delineations of this sector of the boundary on past Chinese maps, though leaving a few very small pieces of Chinese territory outside of the Chinese boundary, on the whole reflected the correct traditional customary line. On the other hand, no boundary line was drawn for this sector on official Indian maps even as late as 1950, and only the words "Boundary Undefined" were marked.

(3) Concerning the eastern sector. The area between the so-called McMahon Line and the boundary line at the southern foot of the Himalayas as shown on Chinese maps has always belonged to China, and was until recently still under Chinese jurisdiction. This is proved by a mass of facts.

As early as the middle of the 17th century, the local government of the Tibet Region of China had begun to exercise jurisdiction over this area comprising Monyul, Loyul, and Lower Tsayul. Take the Monyul area for example. In the middle of the 17th century, when the 5th Dalai Lama unified Tibet, he sent his disciple Mera Lama and tribal chief Namka Drukdra, Dinpon of Tsona, to the Monyul area to establish their rule there. By the beginning of the 18th century, the local government of the Tibet Region had unified the whole of Monyul and divided the area gradually into thirty-two "tso" (a few named "din"). At Tawang, the capital of Monyul, an administrative committee known as "Tawang Shidrel" and a nonpermanent administrative conference of a higher level known as "Tawang Drudrel" were set up to direct the affairs of the whole area. The local government of the Tibet Region used always to appoint the officials of the administrative organs at various levels in Monyul, collect taxes (mainly grain tax, twice a year) and exercise judicial authority in all parts of the area. Monyul was included in every census conducted in Tibet in the past and was not treated as an exceptional case. The religious, economic, and cultural life of the local people, the Monbas, has been deeply influenced by the Tibetan nationality; they believe in Lamaism, can speak the Tibetan language, and used Tibetan currency. It is from the Monyul area that the 6th Dalai Lama, Tsanyun Gyaltso, hailed, and his house there received for all generations the mandates conferred by successive regimes of the Tibet Region.

In addition, it must be pointed out that even after the so-called McMahon Line was defined and made public, the local government of the Tibet Region continued to exercise extensively and for a long period of time its jurisdiction over this area. For instance, the Tibetan administrative institutions in Monyul had been almost kept intact until 1951. In Loyul and Lower Tsayul, up to 1946, the administrative organs of "tso" and "din" were maintained quite extensively, and the people continued to pay taxes and render corvée to the Lhasa authorities.

Therefore, the allegations of the Indian government that "the Tibetan authorities have not exercised jurisdiction at any time in this area," that the local "tribes have not been affected in the slightest degree by any Tibetan influence, cultural, political, or other," and so on are incredible.

The Indian government claims that it has always exercised jurisdiction over this area. However, in Prime Minister Nehru's own words, Indian administration had "gradually moved up" to this area; the tribes had generally been left "more or less to look after themselves" until around 1914; and British political officers only "visited these areas." And what did the British officers who had visited this area say? The Captain Bailey referred to by Prime Minister Nehru in his letter on September 26, 1959, who was specially sent by the British Indian government in 1913 to southeastern Tibet to conduct illegal exploration and survey for the purpose of defining the so-called McMahon Line, described the jurisdiction of the Tibet local government over the Monyul area at the time in his book, *No Passport to Tibet,* published in 1957; he further stated in his letter to the London *Times* published on September 7 this year that, "When we reached Tawang (i.e., capital of Monyul), we found a purely Tibetan administration in force." Even Christoph von Fürer-Haimendorf, then Special Officer of the Indian External Affairs Department in Subansiri, who was sent by the Indian Assam authorities in 1944, that is, thirty years after the so-called McMahon Line was defined, to explore this area, also testified in his book, *Himalayan Barbary,* published in 1955, that the frontier in this area was undefined and unsurveyed, and remained unadministered by the Indian authorities. It can thus be seen how untenable are the assertions that the area has belonged to India for tens and hundreds of years, that the current boundary has always been the historical boundary, etc., etc.

The Indian government says that the British concluded a number of agreements with some of the local tribes between 1844 and 1888 and that these agreements are evidence of Indian jurisdiction. However, the 1853 agreement with the Monbas cited by Prime Minister Nehru begins with the statement by the Monbas: "We . . . being deputed by the Daba Rajas to carry letters of friendship to the Agent, Governor-General, North-East Frontier, desiring that the former friendly relations which existed between the government of India and our Lhasa government . . . should be again resumed. . . ." This passage proves exactly and indisputably that the Monbas belong to Tibet, not India, and that it was under the premise of recognizing them as belonging to Tibet that the Indian government concluded the agreement with them. The Daba Rajas referred to here was the Regent of the local government of the Tibet Region. As to the agreements with the Abors and the Akas cited, it can also be seen clearly from their texts that the areas of those tribes were not British territory. Some of the agreements even stated explicitly that British territory "extends to the foot of the hills (i.e., southern foot of the Himalayas)." And these peoples were not British subjects.

It can be seen from the above historical data provided by the Chinese and Indian sides, respectively, that this area always belonged to China, not to Britain or India.

This conclusion is further confirmed forcefully by the authoritative maps published in the two countries. The maps published in China as a rule include this area in Chinese territory, that is, marking the boundary line along the true traditional boundary at the southern foot of the Himalayas. According to material now available to the Chinese government, the same delineation was followed on the official maps published by the Survey of India up to and including the 1938 edition. After 1938 and up to 1952, the Survey of India changed its delineation by marking the boundary in accordance with the so-called McMahon Line, but still using the marking for undemarcated boundary. Since 1954, it has again changed the undemarcated boundary into demarcated boundary. By these successive changes it shifted from its original position of recognizing this area as Chinese territory to that of claiming this area as India's lawful territory at all times. Nevertheless, the delineation on current Indian maps has not been accepted internationally. As stated above, the atlas edited by John Bartholomew, cartographer to the King of Britain, and published in 1958, still considered it a disputed area, while the delineation on the map "India 1945," attached to Prime

Minister Nehru's book, *The Discovery of India,* was still the same as that on Chinese maps.

In the face of these authoritative facts, the *Atlas of the Chinese Empire,* published in London in 1906 by the China Inland Mission, a British church organization, to which the Indian government referred, is obviously without significance.

It can be seen from what has been said in the above that the Chinese government's view of the traditional customary line is based on objective facts and confirmed by a mass of factual data in all its sectors, western, middle, and eastern. On the other hand, the boundary line marked on Indian maps, with the exception of the middle sector which for the most part conforms to reality, does not represent at all the traditional customary line. The eastern and western sectors of this boundary line, it can in particular be seen beyond any shadow of doubt, are the product of the British policy of aggression and expansion in modern history.

It should not have been necessary to discuss the British policy of aggression and expansion in modern history, as the history of India itself, the history of India's adjacent countries which had once been a part of British India or its dependency, the history of China, and, in particular, the history of China's Tibet Region adjoining India, all bear witness to this policy. While embarking on armed aggression against Tibet and conspiring to cause Tibet to break away from China, Britain also nibbled at the frontiers of Tibet both on the maps and in deed, which resulted in this boundary line that was later inherited by India and is marked on current Indian maps. Of course, the great Indian people, who treasure peace, can in no way be held responsible for all the acts of aggression committed by Britain with India as its base. It is, however, surprising that the Indian government should claim the boundary line which Britain unlawfully created through aggression against Tibet and which even includes areas to which British authority had not extended as the traditional customary boundary line, while perversely describing the true traditional customary boundary line pointed out by the Chinese government on the basis of objective facts as laying claim to large tracts of Indian territory. How would the Indian government feel, if it were in the position of the Chinese government? If this assertion is maintained, the inevitable conclusion to be derived would be that the British colonialists were most fair-minded while oppressed China was full of undisguised ambitions; that the powerful British imperialism was, for the past one hundred years and more, invariably upholding the traditional Sino-Indian boundary, while the weak China was ceaselessly encroaching upon British territory! The Chinese government believes that no one would accept this conclusion.

NOTE

There have been a number of studies of the legal aspects of the Sino-Indian border dispute that reach a variety of conclusions.[52] A recent analysis of China's use of international law in this dispute concludes:

> In reviewing the entire sequence of events . . . perhaps the most striking feature of the Chinese part in them was the extent to which her behavior was consistent with the practice of international relations by nonrevolutionary regimes. While one could expect, perhaps, that a government committed to principles sharply at odds with those supported by Western states would behave in a similarly conflicting manner, the record does not bear out such an expectation. Peking's strategy and tactics showed a willingness to operate within customary boundaries and her performance showed an ability to do so in an effective manner as well.
>
> More specifically, the Chinese government demonstrated a keen perception of the utility and limitations of international law as a guide and constraint in international behavior. Peking's leaders skillfully manipulated legal principles and quasi-legal arguments as they sought to legitimize their claims. There is no indication in any of the relevant official correspondence that Peking viewed accepted principles of international law with alarm or distrust; repeatedly, she voiced the intention of behaving according to their precepts.
>
> A better case, perhaps, can be made to the effect that the Chinese Communist elite had learned its lessons on international relations too well, and that it had mastered the art of manipulating the law to its own purposes, while it did not allow legal factors such a dominant place in its considerations as to be a straitjacket. Its intention clearly was to move in discourse from legal to political or moral considerations frequently and freely, and its style was to tie these several types of arguments together in one neat package.
>
> It should also be noted that Peking understood the need to correlate argument with action, explaining the latter with frequent references to legal as well as political considerations and supporting legal claims (or threats) with evidence of serious intentions. In spite of the ultimate failure to obtain Indian concurrence with its own view on boundary claims, the evidence above indicates that the Chinese government must be credited with having a sophisticated understanding of the workings of international politics

and the important place international law holds in that larger process.[53]

For an elaboration of Peking's view of the appropriate procedures for settling this dispute, see items 41–2 and 41–3.[54]

As the following excerpts suggest, the PRC and India have also bickered over the boundaries between China, on the one hand, and, on the other, the Himalayan states of Bhutan and Sikkim over which India claims a protectorate.

> In its September 30 [1966] note to the Chinese government, the Indian government concocted stories about "intrusions" into Bhutanese territory by Chinese herdsmen and patrols and, claiming to be acting on behalf of Bhutan, lodged a so-called protest with the Chinese government. Following that, the Indian government set its propaganda machine in motion with much fanfare, raising a hue and cry about "Chinese intrusions into Bhutan." Indian Prime Minister Indira Gandhi personally stepped forth to carry out anti-China propaganda. The Hsinhua News Agency has been authorized to issue a statement sternly refuting the Indian government's slanders.
>
> The statement says that the Indian government's outcries about Chinese "intrusions" into Bhutanese territory are an out-and-out lie. The Donghan grassland (referred to as "Doklan pasture" by the Indian side) where the Indian government alleged that Chinese "intrusions" had taken place is located near the place where the boundaries of China, Bhutan, and Sikkim meet. It has always been under Chinese jurisdiction, and Chinese herdsmen have grazed cattle there for generations. When Bhutanese herdsmen cross the border to graze cattle on this grassland, they pay for the pasturage to the Chinese side, according to practice. During the second half of 1965, Indian troops crossed the China-Sikkim boundary five times and intruded into this grassland to carry out reconnaissance and harassing activities, against which the Chinese government protested to the Indian government on August 27, 1965 and again on January 31, 1966. The Indian government did not at that time deny the fact that this grassland belongs to China. That the Indian government should now assert that the Chinese side has "intruded" into China's own territory is positively ludicrous and not worth refutation.[55]
>
> The Chinese Foreign Ministry on April 11 [1967] sent a note to the Indian embassy in China, strongly protesting against the fresh aggression and provocation against China committed recently

by Indian troops who crossed the China-Sikkim boundary and surreptitiously put up false border markers on the Chinese side of the boundary.

Indian troops recently constructed seven stone piles, each over a metre high, on the Chinese side of Kailu La on the China-Sikkim boundary and demolished a Mani pile at Kailu La, which was regarded as a traditional boundary mark by the border inhabitants of both countries. These seven stone piles, clandestinely erected by the Indian troops, go well beyond the original Mani pile into Chinese territory. It is perfectly clear that this action by the Indian troops is a vain attempt to unilaterally alter the China-Sikkim boundary and thereby create new tension along the border and sabotage the friendship between China and Sikkim.

The note said: "The boundary between China and Sikkim has long been formally delimited, and there is neither any discrepancy between the maps nor any dispute in practice. This has been recognized by the Indian government as well. However, acting contrary to what it has said, the Indian government has continually made use of Sikkim territory to commit acts of aggression against China." [56]

(f) SINO-BURMESE BORDER

Like the Sino-Indian border, the Sino-Burmese border presents complex legal problems that trace back to British imperialism's nineteenth-century intrusion into the sinocentric world. The Kingdom of Burma had for centuries paid periodic tribute to the emperors of China. In 1886, however, more than half a century of British effort culminated in the absorption of Burma into British India. Britain, taking advantage of the Ch'ing dynasty's declining strength, induced it to renounce all rights over Burma in exchange for Britain's promise to permit Burma to continue to send a tribute mission to China every ten years, a promise that was soon repudiated. This 1886 agreement also called for joint boundary settlement and was followed in 1894 and 1897 by other agreements that led to the demarcation of much, but not all, of the Sino-Burmese frontier.

Little was heard of the remaining border problems with Burma during the early years of the Republic of China. But the dispute over one of the border regions, referred to in item 12–23 as "the Kawa area," flared up in the 1930's when silver was discovered there. A League of Nations commission surveyed the area and by 1937 demarcated a boundary that purported to compromise the British and Chinese claims. This boundary, known as the Iselin line, or, as in 12–23, "the 1941 line," was accepted by Britain, and, in 1941, by China's then embattled Nationalist government. Nevertheless, the Nationalists never accepted Britain's claims to two other portions of the frontier, referred to in 12–23 as "the section to the north of the High Conical Peak" and "the Namwan triangular area." After the end of World War II, as Burma's independence from Britain approached, the Nationalists began to reassert their claims to those two areas.

A series of atlases published shortly after they attained nationwide power made it clear that the Chinese Communists intended not only to maintain the claims inherited from the Nationalists but also to challenge the Nationalists' acceptance of the 1941 line. Apparently the Communists did not anticipate a prompt settlement, for a 1953 map noted that "these problems . . . await the establishment of a people's Burma and the final victory of the Asian people's revolution; then they can receive a complete and reasonable solution."[57] Indeed, during the PRC's early years a prompt settlement was not desired, for this was an era when China's Communist leaders were emphasizing the path of violent revolution, and, apart from Vietnam, Burma was the only country on China's borders where local Communists were actively engaged in armed struggle. The PRC was providing asylum, training, and arms to some Burmese Communist units. It was making efforts to lure certain of Burma's minority nationalities—the Kachins and Shans—to cross into China to join their brothers there. Also, Chinese Communist troops were frequently reported to have entered Burmese territory, probably in an effort to suppress the thousands of Nationalist troops who had entered Burma in 1950 following the Communist victory in China. And many Chinese refugees, some of whom had left China with Peking's permission, continued to move into Burma, thereby extending Chinese influence. A border settlement would have impeded all these activities to some degree, and Burma's attempts to open negotiations met with little enthusiasm.

This situation changed in the mid-1950's. The "Bandung spirit" called for nonintervention in the affairs of one's neighbors and harmonious resolution of disputes. Moreover, as the revolt of the Khamba tribesmen in eastern Tibet became more serious, the PRC became increasingly preoccupied with cutting them off from possible sources of aid in Burma. Thus, in 1956 the PRC began to show interest in negotiations to stabilize the frontier, and Sino-Burmese talks got underway. Item 12–23 was the first public statement of the official Chinese position on questions relating to the Burmese border.

12-23

"Report on the Question of the Boundary Line between China and Burma Delivered by Chou En-lai, Premier and Foreign Minister, at the Fourth Session of the First National People's Congress," July 9, 1957, in *WCC 1956–1957*, IV (1958), 341–347; translated in *A Victory for the Five Principles of Peaceful Coexistence; Important Documents on the Settlement of the Sino-Burmese Boundary Question* (Peking: Foreign Languages Press, 1960), pp. 16–27.

Fellow Deputies,

The question of the boundary line between China and Burma is an important question in the foreign relations of our country, a question in which our people are greatly interested. The government therefore deems it necessary to make a special report on this matter to the National People's Congress.

We have inherited from the past questions of undefined boundary lines between our country and many neighbouring countries, and the one between China and Burma has attracted public attention particularly. This is because of the prolonged disputes created by Britain over the boundary line between China and Burma when Burma was under British rule, and because in recent years the forces of imperialism have constantly used the boundary question between China and Burma to sow discord between the two countries in an attempt to create a tense situation.

Our government has consistently held that a fair and reasonable settlement of all outstanding questions between China and other countries should be sought through peaceful negotiation. The boundary question between China and Burma is of long standing as well as complicated; so from the moment our government began to tackle it, it has taken a careful attitude to seek, step by step and through suitable preparatory work, a settlement of the question.

During the years immediately after the founding of our state, our government was engrossed in a series of urgent, major tasks at home and in its relations with foreign countries, and was therefore unable at that time to make comprehensive and systematic preparations for the settlement of the Sino-Burmese boundary question. However, since the Premiers of China and Burma proposed in the communiqué on their talks issued on December 12, 1954 that the question of the undefined boundary line between the two countries should be settled "at an appropriate time through normal diplomatic channels," our government has proceeded to make the necessary preparations for the settlement of the question. The various government departments concerned have, jointly with the provincial authorities of Yunnan, undertaken a systematic and detailed examination and study of relevant historical data and actual conditions.

In November 1955, just as the Chinese and the Burmese sides were respectively making active preparations for the settlement of the boundary question, an armed clash unfortunately occurred owing to misunderstanding between the outpost units of the two countries in the border region. This incident was properly dealt with through the joint efforts of both sides, but at the same time it made the governments of both countries realize the need for an early settlement of the boundary question between the two countries.

Since the beginning of 1956 the Chinese and the Burmese governments have entered into frequent contacts on the boundary question. In November of the same year, Chairman U Nu of the Burmese Anti-Fascist People's Freedom League came to Peking at our invitation to hold consultations with our government. In line with our foreign policy of peace and on the basis of the results of our examination and study of the boundary question, our government made, through Chairman U Nu, to the Burmese government a proposal on the principles for the settling of the boundary question. The proposal received the approval of the Standing Committee of the National People's Congress at its 50th meeting on November 5, 1956.

The greater part of the boundary line between China and Burma is fixed, but there are three sections regarding which outstanding issues remain to be settled. Our government made a proposal on the principles concerning these three sections and held that the various points mentioned in the proposal should be considered as an integrated whole. Let me now explain the contents of the proposal made by the government.

The first point concerns the section in the Kawa area. This section was explicitly provided for in the two treaties on the Sino-Burmese boundary line signed between China and Britain in 1894 and 1897, respectively. But as the related provisions are self-contradictory, this section was for long not demarcated. To create a *fait accompli,* Britain sent troops in the earlier part of 1934 to attack the areas under the jurisdiction of the Panhung and Panlao tribes and met with heroic resistance from the Kawa people of these areas. This was the well-known "Panhung Incident." In 1941, taking advantage of the critical situation in which China was placed during the War of Resistance to Japanese

Aggression and using the closing of the Yunnan-Burma Road as a pressure measure, Britain effected, in an exchange of notes with the Kuomintang government on June 18, a demarcation in the Kawa area to her advantage. This was the so-called "1941 line." But since the Pacific War broke out soon afterwards, no markers were erected along the line. In the course of the discussion between the Chinese and Burmese governments in 1956 on the boundary question, Burmese leaders indicated that they could understand the Chinese people's dissatisfaction with the 1941 line but, in view of the fact that this section of the boundary had been demarcated by an exchange of notes between the Chinese and the British governments responsible at that time, they asked our government to recognize the line and to withdraw the Chinese troops from the area to the west of the 1941 line which they had entered in 1952 when chasing after remnant Kuomintang troops. It was the opinion of our government that on the question of boundary lines, demands made on the basis of formal treaties should be respected according to general international practice, but this by no means excluded the seeking by two friendly countries of a settlement fair and reasonable for both sides through peaceful negotiation between their governments. In order to promote such a fair and reasonable settlement and to create a favourable atmosphere for it, our government in its proposal about principles to the Burmese government expressed its preparedness to withdraw its troops from the area to the west of the 1941 line. At the same time, our government asked that, pending a final agreement between the Chinese and Burmese governments on the question of the 1941 line and the setting up of boundary markers, Burmese troops should refrain from entering the area to the west of the 1941 line evacuated by the Chinese troops; however, the working personnel of the Burmese government may enter this area.

The second point concerns the Meng-Mao triangular area, otherwise called the Namwan triangular area, situated at the junction of the Namwan River and the Shweli River and measuring about 250 square kilometres. This is Chinese territory, a fact which Britain also recognized in explicit terms in the treaty. But before the signing of the Sino-British treaty on [the] Sino-Burmese boundary line in 1894, Britain, without obtaining China's consent, built by compulsion a highway through this area to join Bhamo with Namhkan. By the time China and Britain signed another treaty on the Sino-Burmese boundary line in 1897, Britain under the name of "perpetual lease" further secured jurisdiction over this piece of Chinese territory. Following her independence, Burma succeeded to the "perpetual lease" of the area. In its proposal about principles to the Burmese government, our government pointed out that it would be inconsistent with the relations of equality and friendship now existing between China and Burma for Burma to continue the "perpetual lease" of a piece of Chinese territory. Our government expressed its readiness to negotiate with the Burmese government so as to decide upon the concrete steps to abrogate the "perpetual lease" of the Meng-Mao triangular area.

The third point concerns the section to the north of the High Conical Peak. This section of the boundary line has never been delimited in the past. Britain continually created disputes in this area and took the opportunity to expand its colonial territory. The most serious of such disputes was the armed occupation of the Hpimaw area by Britain in the early part of 1911. The "Hpimaw Incident" aroused the righteous indignation of the whole Chinese people and protest movements spread with gathering force through all parts of China. Under such circumstances, the British government could not but acknowledge formally in its note dated April 10, 1911, to the then Chinese government that the villages of the Hpimaw, Kangfang, and Gawlum area belong to China, but it continued unreasonably to occupy this area. On the basis of the results obtained from an examination and study of the historical facts and actual conditions, our government made to the Burmese government the following proposal concerning the demarcation of this section of the boundary line: The section from Isurazi Pass northward to Diphu Pass can be demarcated along the customary boundary line. The section from Isurazi Pass to the High Conical Peak can in principle be determined along the watershed between the Nu River, the Shweli River (otherwise called the Lungchuan River) and the Taiping River on the one side and the Nmai Hka River on the other, with the exception of the Hpimaw, Kangfang, and Gawlum area which should be returned to China. Our government asked at the same time that, during the same period as the Chinese troops would be withdrawing from the area to the west of the 1941 line, the Burmese government should withdraw its troops from Hpimaw, Kangfang, and Gawlum. Pending the final demarcation of this section, the Burmese government might retain its administration over Hpimaw, Kangfang, and Gawlum, and the Chinese government would undertake to refrain from sending Chinese troops into these places before this section had been finally demarcated.

After the above proposal was made by our government, Chairman U Nu expressed the view that it was a fair and reasonable proposal taking account of the interests of both sides. In the joint press communiqué issued after the talks held between Chairman U Nu and the leading personnel of our government, it was declared that the governments of China and Burma had arrived at an understanding that from the end of November 1956, Chinese troops would withdraw from the area to the west of the 1941 line and Burmese troops would withdraw from Hpimaw, Kangfang, and Gawlum, the withdrawal to be completed before the end of the year. By the end of 1956, the two governments had completed the withdrawal of troops respectively. Thus a good start was made for the settlement of the Sino-Burmese boundary question. The leading personnel of the two governments again had opportunities to continue their friendly talks on the boundary question in Rangoon in December 1956 and in Kunming in March 1957. During these talks the standpoints of the two sides were further clarified, and a general agreement of views was obtained.

People of all walks of life in our country take a great interest in the settlement of the Sino-Burmese boundary question. In order to obtain views from a wider circle of our people, on behalf of the government I made a report on this question in the middle of March this year to the third plenary session of the Second National Committee of the Chinese People's Political Consultative Conference. Present at the meeting also were deputies to the National People's Congress who were in Peking at the time, members of the government, and specially invited experts. At the end of March this year I made in Kunming another report on the question to a meeting called by the Yunnan Provincial Committee of the People's Political Consultative Conference and attended by representatives of people of all walks of life of Yunnan Province and representatives of various fraternal nationalities. Earnest discussions took place at these two widely representative meetings which gave the government an opportunity to listen to the opinions from different quarters and reply to relevant questions raised, thus bringing into closer agreement the views of the people of different quarters in the country on the Sino-Burmese boundary question.

Such, in brief, is what has taken place in the handling of the Sino-Burmese boundary question by our government up till the present. I should like now to say a few words on the basic policy followed by the government in dealing with this boundary question between China and Burma.

Ever since the founding of the People's Republic the policy persistently followed by our country in international affairs has been to strive for the easing of the world situation and for peaceful coexistence with all countries in the world, and particularly with our neighbours. This policy is beneficial to our country's socialist construction; it also conforms to the interests of the peoples of all countries in the world. It is precisely this basic foreign policy of peace that our government has followed in handling the Sino-Burmese boundary question.

Like so many outstanding questions existing among Asian and African countries, the question of the boundary line between China and

Burma is the result of the policy of aggression carried on over the years by the imperialists. Both China and Burma have now achieved independence and are making efforts to secure a peaceful international environment so that they can engage in peaceful construction in their own countries. Together with India, China and Burma were the first to initiate the Five Principles of Peaceful Co-existence. We all treasure our national independence and national interests and know full well that our national independence and national interests can best be safeguarded only through peaceful coexistence and friendly cooperation. However, the imperialists have never ceased exploiting the differences existing among Asian and African countries to create tension and discord among them and are trying hard to carry out again their aggressive policy of "divide and rule" against these countries. In view of all this, our government, in discussing the boundary question with the Burmese government, has always stressed that both sides should act in a spirit of sincerity and carry out friendly negotiation in accordance with the Five Principles of Peaceful Co-existence so that a fair and reasonable settlement may be arrived at. The settlement of the Sino-Burmese boundary question in this manner will not only further consolidate and develop the friendly relations between China and Burma, but also benefit the solidarity among Asian and African countries. The stand which our government takes in solving the boundary question between China and Burma is based on a desire to protect our national interests as well as promote Sino-Burmese friendship and the solidarity among Asian and African countries.

The boundary question between China and Burma has behind it a complicated historical background. Therefore, in dealing with this question, the treatment of historical data has become an important problem. In the days when China was under feudal rulers, its boundaries, like the boundaries of many other countries in the feudal era, were not too well defined. Throughout the ages the feudal dynasties in China maintained different relations, varying in nature and degree, with the nationalities living in the border areas. Therefore it is almost impossible to define the boundaries such as existed under Chinese feudal empires. Furthermore, during the past sixty years or so there have been many vastly different ways of drawing the undefined boundary between China and Burma in the maps published at home and abroad. All this cannot but cause confusion in wide circles as regards the undefined boundary between China and Burma. Our government holds that in dealing with the Sino-Burmese boundary question we must adopt a serious attitude towards historical data, we must take a correct stand and viewpoint so as to make a scientific analysis and appraisal of such data and to distinguish between the data which can be used as a legal and reasonable basis and those which have only reference value as a result of changed conditions. At the same time we must bear in mind the fundamental changes of historic importance that have taken place in China and Burma, respectively, i.e., China has cast away its semicolonial status and Burma its colonial status and both have become independent and mutually friendly countries. The Burmese government has suceeded to the territory formerly controlled by Britain, and the Union of Burma has been established by combining the various national autonomous states and Burma proper, while our government has taken over the territory under the jurisdiction of the Kuomintang government. In dealing with this boundary question, attention must be paid to these historical changes, and the treaties signed in the past which concern the boundary between China and Burma must be treated in accordance with general international practice. Only when we take all the above-mentioned points into account can we use historical data correctly and secure a fair and reasonable settlement of the Sino-Burmese boundary question.

The Sino-Burmese boundary question has a direct bearing on the interests of the nationalities living in compact communities on the Sino-Burmese borders. Therefore, in tackling this question we must specially take into account the interests of these nationalities. We know that the boundary line between two countries is often found dividing into two parts a nationality living in compact communities on the borders. This is the result of historical development. On the various sections of the defined boundary between China and Burma and on the borders between China and many other neighbouring countries we find people of the same nationality living on both sides of the boundary line. So when we solve the question of the undefined boundary line between China and Burma, we must realize beforehand that it will be hard to avoid separating the nationalities concerned by the boundary line. In view of this, it is all the more necessary for us to take measures, in consultation with the Burmese government, to make the future defined boundary a boundary of peace and friendship, and further cement the close ties of the peoples of the two countries living on the borders.

Fellow Deputies! After repeated contacts and consultations in a spirit of friendship and in accordance with the Five Principles of Peaceful Co-existence, the Chinese and Burmese governments have arrived at a general agreement of views on the boundary question. We believe that when the views of both sides on concrete problems are brought into accord through continued negotiations, the boundary question between China and Burma will receive a comprehensive, fair, and reasonable settlement.

NOTE

Despite the fact that the parties had reached "a general agreement of views on the boundary question," they were slow to come to an understanding on "the concrete problems" involved until the outbreak of violence on the Sino-Indian border in 1959 stimulated both sides to cooperate. Burma then sought to avoid India's predicament, and the PRC was eager to oblige in order to demonstrate India's unreasonableness and to isolate India from her neighbors. Item 12–24 is the preliminary agreement that was concluded in early 1960 as a result of these pressures. Its provisions were promptly carried out, and a final boundary treaty was signed on October 1, 1960,[58] the National Day of the PRC.

12-24

"Agreement between the Government of the People's Republic of China and the Government of the Union of Burma on the Question of the Boundary between the Two Countries," January 28, 1960, in *TYC 1960*, IX (1961), 65–68; English text in *A Victory for the Five Principles of Peaceful Coexistence; Important Documents on the Settlement of the Sino-Burmese Boundary Question* (Peking: Foreign Languages Press, 1960), pp. 33–37.

The government of the People's Republic of China and the government of the Union of Burma,

With a view to promoting an over-all settlement of the Sino-Burmese boundary question and to consolidating and further developing friendly relations between China and Burma,

Have agreed to conclude the present Agreement under the guidance of the Five Principles of Peaceful Co-existence and have agreed as follows:

Article I

The Contracting Parties agree to set up immediately a joint committee composed of an equal number of delegates from each side and charge it, in accordance with the provisions of the present Agreement, to discuss and work out solutions on the concrete questions regarding the Sino-Burmese boundary enumerated in Article II of the present Agreement, conduct surveys of the boundary and set up boundary markers, and draft a Sino-Burmese boundary treaty. The joint committee shall hold regular meetings in the capitals of the two countries or at any other places in the two countries.

Article II

The Contracting Parties agree that the existing issues concerning the Sino-Burmese boundary shall be settled in accordance with the following provisions:

(1) With the exception of the area of Hpimaw, Gawlum, and Kangfang, the entire undelimited boundary from the High Conical Peak to the western extremity of the Sino-Burmese boundary shall be delimited along the traditional customary line, that is to say, from the High Conical Peak northward along the watershed between the Taiping, the Shweli, the Nu (Salween) and the Tulung (Taron) Rivers on the one hand and the Nmai Hka River on the other, up to the place where it crosses the Tulung (Taron) River between Chingdam and Nhkumkang, and then along the watershed between the Tulung (Taron) and the Tsayul (Zayul) Rivers on the one hand and all the upper tributaries of the Irrawaddy River, except for the Tulung (Taron) River, on the other, up to the western extremity of the Sino-Burmese boundary. The joint committee shall send out joint survey teams composed of an equal number of persons from each side to conduct surveys along the above-mentioned watersheds so as to determine the specific alignment of this section of the boundary line and to set up boundary markers.

(2) The Burmese government has agreed to return to China the area of Hpimaw, Gawlum, and Kangfang which belongs to China. As to the extent of this area to be returned to China, it is to be discussed and determined by the joint committee in accordance with the proposals put forward and marked on maps by the governments of Burma and China on February 4, 1957, and July 26, 1957, respectively. After determining the extent of this area to be returned to China, the joint committee shall send out joint survey teams composed of an equal number of persons from each side to conduct [an] on-the-spot survey of the specific alignment of this section of the boundary line and to set up boundary markers.

(3) In order to abrogate the "perpetual lease" by Burma of the Meng-Mao triangular area (Namwan Assigned Tract) at the junction of the Namwan and the Shweli Rivers, which belongs to China, the Chinese government has agreed to turn over this area to Burma to become part

of the territory of the Union of Burma. In exchange, the Burmese government has agreed to turn over to China to become part of Chinese territory the areas under the jurisdiction of the Panhung and Panlao tribes, which are west of the boundary line from the junction of the Nam Ting and the Nampa Rivers to the No. 1 marker on the southern delimited section of the boundary as defined in the notes exchanged between the Chinese and the British governments on June 18, 1941. As to the extent of these areas to be turned over to China, the Chinese and the Burmese governments put forward proposals marked on maps on July 26, 1957, and June 4, 1959, respectively. The area where the proposals of the two governments coincide will definitely be turned over to China. Where the proposals of the two governments differ as to the area under the jurisdiction of the Panhung tribe, the joint committee will send out a team composed of an equal number of persons from each side to ascertain on the spot as to whether it is under the jurisdiction of the Panhung tribe, so as to determine whether it is to be turned over to China. After the extent of the areas under the jurisdiction of the Panhung and Panlao tribes to be turned over to China has been thus determined, the joint committee will send out joint survey teams composed of an equal number of persons from each side to conduct [an] on-the-spot survey of the specific alignment of this section of the boundary line and to set up boundary markers.

(4) Except for the adjustment provided for in paragraph (3) of this Article, the section of the boundary from the junction of the Nam Ting and the Nampa Rivers to the No. 1 marker on the southern delimited section of the boundary shall be delimited as defined in the notes exchanged between the Chinese and the British governments on June 18, 1941. The joint committee shall send out joint survey teams composed of an equal number of persons from each side to carry out delimitation and demarcation along this section of the boundary line and set up boundary markers.

Article III

The Contracting Parties agree that the joint committee, after working out solutions for the existing issues concerning the Sino-Burmese boundary as enumerated in Article II of the present Agreement, shall be responsible for drafting a Sino-Burmese boundary treaty, which shall cover not only all the sections of the boundary as mentioned in Article II of the present Agreement, but also the sections of the boundary which were already delimited in the past and need no adjustment. After being signed by the governments of the two countries and coming into effect, the new boundary treaty shall replace all old treaties and notes exchanged concerning the boundary between the two countries. The Chinese government, in line with its policy of being consistently opposed to foreign prerogatives and respecting the sovereignty of other countries, renounces China's right of participation in mining enterprises at Lufang of Burma as provided in the notes exchanged between the Chinese and the British governments on June 18, 1941.

Article IV

(1) The present Agreement is subject to ratification and the instruments of ratification will be exchanged in Rangoon as soon as possible.

(2) The present Agreement will come into force immediately on the exchange of the instruments of ratification and shall automatically cease to be in force when the Sino-Burmese boundary treaty to be signed by the two governments comes into force.

Done in duplicate in Peking on the twenty-eighth day of January 1960, in the Chinese and English languages, both texts being equally authentic.

For the Government of the People's Republic of China:	*For the Government of the Union of Burma:*
(Signed) Chou En-lai	*(Signed) Ne Win*

NOTE

Shortly after putting an end to its frontier dispute with Burma, the PRC moved to resolve similar problems with a number of other neighbors. Professor Hinton has aptly described the course of negotiations with Nepal:

> In March, 1960, shortly before he was to visit India to discuss the Sino-Indian border dispute, Chou En-lai received a visit from Prime Minister B. P. Koirala of Nepal. They signed a boundary agreement that provided in effect, since the differences were not large or very controversial, that they should be settled on the ground by teams of both sides. It also provided that each side should demilitarize a zone twenty kilometers deep on its side of the boundary. It later developed that by the time the agreement was signed the PRC had already agreed in principle that the boundary should run through the summit of Mt. Everest, rather than to the south of it as on earlier Chinese maps. The Nepalese, however, continued to hold out for the entire mountain, on the

theory that it had never been climbed to the summit except from the Nepalese side. Thereupon the PRC claimed that on May 25, 1960, two Chinese and one Tibetan mountaineer had reached the summit from the northern side for the first time in history. This claim is regarded with the greatest skepticism by non-Chinese mountaineers, and it had little effect. The final boundary treaty, which was signed during a visit by King Mahendra of Nepal to the PRC in October 1961 and published on October 13, merely described the boundary as "passing through" Mt. Everest, without specifying the location of the boundary with respect to the summit. The problem was left unresolved in the public mind by the announcement in January 1963 that a protocol had been signed specifying the location of the boundary markers, which had already been erected. Any one anxious to settle the question in his mind would presumably have to go to the mountain himself.[59]

On March 2, 1963, the PRC and Pakistan published an agreement providing for delimitation of the border between China's Sinkiang Province and that part of Kashmir occupied by Pakistani forces; the two parties recognized that, if future settlement of the Kashmir dispute between Pakistan and India left the latter in control of the territory involved, negotiations on the boundary question would have to be reopened.[60] Several weeks later Peking announced that the PRC and the People's Republic of Mongolia had exchanged ratifications of a treaty that fixed the location of their lengthy mutual frontier.[61] And in November 1963 the PRC and Afghanistan concluded a treaty that disposed of problems related to their short boundary.[62]

The Chinese made no secret of at least one of their major motives for this flurry of boundary settlement activity. Peking's May 31, 1962, note to India stated:

> Since the Burmese and Nepalese governments can settle their boundary questions with China in a friendly way through negotiations and since the government of Pakistan has also agreed with the Chinese government to negotiate a boundary settlement, why is it that the Indian government cannot negotiate and settle its boundary question with the Chinese government? [63]

(g) SINO-SOVIET BORDER

By the time that the Sino-Mongolian boundary treaty was announced on March 26, 1963, there was evidence that Peking's strategy in making a concentrated effort to settle certain territorial disputes was designed to put pressure on the Soviet Union as well as on India. Less than three weeks earlier the *People's Daily* had pointedly mentioned Tsarist Russia as one of the imperialist powers that had carried out aggression against China during the century that began with the Opium War, and it had included three Sino-Russian treaties in a list of "unequal treaties": the 1858 Treaty of Aigun, which ceded Russia a vast area in Manchuria north of the Amur River; the 1860 Treaty of Peking, which ceded Russia the Maritime Province bounded on the west by the Amur and Ussuri Rivers and on the east by the Sea of Japan; and the 1881 Treaty of Ili, actually concluded at St. Petersburg, which capped two decades of Russian expansion into Central Asia by ceding Russia part of the strategic Ili River valley in Chinese Turkestan (12–16).

In early 1963, however, the time had not yet come when the Chinese Communists thought it appropriate to make public mention of the Soviet Union's own record of territorial aggrandizement at the expense of China. Although in a series of statements made between 1918 and 1920 the Bolshevik leadership had proclaimed its intention to repudiate the treaties under which the Tsars had acquired vast areas of China and a variety of privileges on Chinese territory,[64] it had soon become apparent to a succession of pre-Communist Chinese governments that by one device or another Soviet Russia intended to retain most of the Tsarist holdings in Asia. In Central Asia, Siberia, and the Far East, the Bolsheviks organized "autonomous" republics and regions whose people, it was claimed, had chosen incorporation into the Bolshevik polity, and a tremendous effort was made to industrialize and populate these areas. In 1921 Soviet Russia guided the new Mongolian People's Revolutionary Party in setting up a government in Outer Mongolia, which declared itself the Mongolian People's Republic in 1924. Nevertheless, in the Sino-Soviet agreement concluded on March 14, 1924, Soviet Russia recognized "that Outer Mongolia is an integral part of the Republic of China" and promised to respect Chinese sovereignty there and to withdraw Soviet troops from the area.[65] But Soviet influence continued to grow in Outer Mongolia, and the situation came to bear a suspicious resemblance to that which the Tsar had created there on the eve of World War I: Chinese suzerainty but Outer Mongolian autonomy under actual Russian control.[66]

Stalin's diplomacy at the close of World War II could have left no Chinese patriot in doubt about the extent to which the "anti-imperialist" Soviet regime had inherited the territorial ambitions of the Tsars. Indeed, in the Yalta Agreement of February 11, 1945, as part of the price for Soviet participation in the war against Japan, Stalin exacted from the United States and Great Britain a pledge that "the former rights of Russia violated by the treacherous attack of Japan in 1904 shall be restored."[67] With respect to Manchuria the Agreement specifically provided that:

> (b) the commercial port of Dairen shall be internationalized, the preeminent interests of the Soviet Union in this port being safeguarded and the lease of Port Arthur as a naval base of the USSR restored,
>
> (c) The Chinese-Eastern Railroad and the South-Manchurian Railroad which provide an outlet to Dairen shall be jointly operated by the establishment of a joint Soviet-Chinese Company, it being understood that the preeminent interests of the Soviet Union shall be safeguarded and that China shall retain full sovereignty in Manchuria; . . .[68]

In the Sino-Soviet Treaty of Friendship and Alliance and related agreements concluded with the Republic of China on August 14, 1945, Stalin acquired even broader control over the Manchurian ports and railroads than the Yalta Agreement had called for. Moreover, the ROC agreed to recognize the formal independence of the Mongolian People's Republic if a plebiscite determined that independence was the wish of its inhabitants.[69] The ROC made these concessions in return for Soviet promises to respect the sovereignty and territorial and administrative integrity of China and to provide aid only to the Nationalist government of the ROC and not to the Chinese Communists; Soviet failure to fulfill these promises led the Nationalists in 1953 to repudiate their recognition of Outer Mongolian independence.[70]

In February 1950, shortly after attaining nationwide power, the Chinese Communists moved to abrogate the 1945 Sino-Soviet arrangements and to conclude a Sino-Soviet Treaty of Friendship, Alliance, and Mutual Assistance and other agreements. One of the latter, item 12–25, scheduled the liquidation of Soviet territorial privileges in Manchuria. But, as item 12–26 indicates, part of the price that the Soviet Union exacted for this concession and for various pledges to aid China was that the PRC accede to the independence of Outer Mongolia. Soon after, the PRC also agreed to the establishment of several Sino-Soviet joint-stock companies.[71]

Because of the Korean war, agreement on a date for completion of the Soviet withdrawal from Manchuria was delayed until October 1954, when Item 12–27 fixed the date for the actual Soviet departure from Port Arthur. At that time the Chinese also persuaded the Soviet Union to sell China its interest in the joint-stock companies that had been set up in 1950.[72]

12-25

"Agreement between the Union of Soviet Socialist Republics and the People's Republic of China Concerning the Chinese Changchun Railway, Port Arthur and Dairen," signed at Moscow, on February 14, 1950, *UNTS* 226:38–42 (1956).

The Presidium of the Supreme Soviet of the Union of Soviet Socialist Republics and the Central People's Government of the People's Republic of China note that since 1945 the following radical changes have taken place in the situation in the Far East: Imperialist Japan has suffered defeat; the reactionary Kuomintang government has been overthrown; China has become a People's Democratic Republic; and there has been established in China a new People's Government which has united all China, applied a policy of friendship and cooperation with the Soviet Union, and proved its ability to uphold the state independence and territorial integrity of China and the national honour and dignity of the Chinese people.

The Presidium of the Supreme Soviet of the Union of Soviet Socialist Republics and the Central People's Government of the People's Republic of China consider that, because of this new situation, a new approach to the question of the Chinese Changchun Railway, Port Arthur, and Dairen is possible.

In accordance with these new circumstances, the Presidium of the Supreme Soviet of the Union of Soviet Socialist Republics and the Central People's Government of the People's Republic of China have decided to conclude this Agreement concerning the Chinese Changchun Railway, Port Arthur, and Dairen.

Article 1

The two Contracting Parties have agreed that the Soviet government shall transfer to the government of the People's Republic of China, without charge, all its rights to joint administration of the Chinese Changchun Railway together with all property belonging to the railway. The transfer shall be effected immediately after the conclusion of a peace treaty with Japan, but in any case not later than the end of 1952.

Until the transfer is effected, the present status of the joint Soviet-Chinese administration of the Chinese Changchun Railway shall remain unchanged; however, after this Agreement has come into force, the procedure whereby posts are occupied by representatives of the Soviet and

Chinese Parties shall be altered and a system of rotation of posts (Manager of the Railway, President of the Board of Directors, etc.) at fixed intervals shall be established.

The specific means of effecting the transfer shall be agreed and determined by the governments of the two Contracting Parties.

Article 2

The two Contracting Parties have agreed that Soviet troops shall be withdrawn from the jointly used naval base of Port Arthur and that the installations in this area shall be transferred to the government of the People's Republic of China immediately after the conclusion of a peace treaty with Japan, but in any case not later than the end of 1952; the Government of the People's Republic of China shall compensate the Soviet Union for the expenditure incurred by the Soviet Union since 1945 in respect of the reconstruction and erection of the said installations.

Pending the withdrawal of Soviet troops and the transfer of the aforesaid installations, the governments of the Soviet Union and China shall appoint an equal number of military representatives to constitute a Joint Sino-Soviet Military Commission, over which the two Parties shall preside in rotation and which shall administer military affairs in the Port Arthur area; specific measures for this purpose shall be determined by the Joint Sino-Soviet Military Commission within three months after the entry into force of this Agreement and shall be applied after they have been approved by the governments of both Parties.

The civil administration in the aforesaid area shall be under the direct control of the government of the People's Republic of China. Until the Soviet troops are withdrawn, the zone in which Soviet troops are quartered in the Port Arthur area shall remain unchanged in accordance with the existing boundaries.

Should either of the Contracting Parties become the object of aggression by Japan or any state which might join with Japan, and as a result be involved in hostilities, China and the Soviet Union may, on the proposal of the government of the People's Republic of China and with the consent of the Soviet government, jointly use the naval base of Port Arthur for the conduct of joint military operations against the aggressor.

Article 3

The two Contracting Parties have agreed that the question of the port of Dairen shall be examined after the conclusion of a peace treaty with Japan.

The administration of Dairen shall be wholly in the hands of the government of the People's Republic of China.

All property at present in Dairen which is temporarily administered by or leased to the Soviet Party shall be taken over by the government of the People's Republic of China. For the purpose of effecting the transfer of the said property, the governments of the Soviet Union and China shall appoint three representatives from each Party to constitute a joint commission, which shall within three months after the entry into force of this Agreement determine specific measures for effecting the transfer of the property and shall, after the joint commission's proposals have been approved by the governments of both Parties, complete their application in the course of 1950.

Article 4

This Agreement shall come into force on the date of its ratification. The exchange of the instruments of ratification shall take place at Peking.

DONE at Moscow, on 14 February 1950, in two copies, each in the Russian and Chinese languages, both texts being equally authentic.

By authorization of the Presidium of the Supreme Soviet of the Union of Soviet Socialist Republics:

(Signed) A. Y. Vyshinsky

By authorization of the Central People's Government of the People's Republic of China:

(Signed) Chou En-lai

12-26

"Exchange of Notes Concerning the Abrogation of the Treaty of Friendship and Alliance and of the Agreements of the Chinese Changchun Railway, Dairen, and Port Arthur, Signed on 14 August 1945, and Concerning the Recognition of the Independence of the Mongolian People's Republic," *UNTS* 226:16–18 (1956).

I

Moscow, 14 February 1950

Sir,

In connexion with the signature this day of the Treaty of Friendship, Alliance, and Mutual Assistance between China and the Soviet Union and the Agreement concerning the Chinese Changchun Railway, Port Arthur, and Dairen, I hereby state that an understanding was reached between the two Contracting Parties on the following points:

1. In view of the signature of the aforesaid Treaty and Agreement and in accordance with the said Treaty and Agreement, the two Contracting Parties agree to declare that the Chinese-Soviet Treaty of Friendship and Alliance and the Agreements on the Chinese Changchun Railway, Dairen, and Port Arthur, concluded on 14 August 1945 between China and the Soviet Union, and all annexes thereto, have ceased to have effect.

2. The two Contracting Parties recognize that the independent status of the Mongolian People's Republic has already been fully secured as a result of the referendum held in Outer Mongolia in 1945, which confirmed its desire for independence, and of the establishment by the People's Republic of China of diplomatic relations with that Republic.

If you confirm this understanding of the two points referred to above, this note and your reply thereto will constitute part of the Treaty of Friendship, Alliance, and Mutual Assistance between China and the Soviet Union.

I have the honour to be, etc.

Chou En-lai

A. Vyshinsky
Minister of Foreign Affairs of the USSR

II

Moscow, 14 February 1950

Sir.

I confirm the receipt of your note of 14 February 1950, which reads as follows:

[*See note I*]

I have the honour to state hereby that I fully concur in this understanding of the two paragraphs referred to above, and agree that your note and this reply thereto shall constitute part of the Treaty of Friendship, Alliance, and Mutual Assistance between the Soviet Union and China.

I have the honour to be, etc.

A. Vyshinsky

Mr. Chou En-lai
Chairman of the State Administrative Council
and Minister of Foreign Affairs
of the Central People's Government
of the People's Republic of China

12-27

"Communiqué by the Union of Soviet Socialist Republics and the People's Republic of China Concerning the Withdrawal of Soviet Military Units from the Jointly Used Chinese Naval Base of Port Arthur and the Transfer of the Said Base to the Full Control of the People's Republic of China," signed at Peking, on October 12, 1954, *UNTS* 226:54 (1956).

Having regard to the change which has taken place in the international situation in the Far East with the cessation of the war in Korea and the restoration of peace in Indochina, and taking into account the enhanced defensive power of the People's Republic of China, the government of the Soviet Union and the government of the People's Republic of China, acting in accordance with the relations of friendship and cooperation which have been established between the two states and are constantly being strengthened, have agreed that Soviet military units shall be withdrawn from the jointly used naval base of Port Arthur and that the installations in that area shall be transferred, without compensation, to the government of the People's Republic of China.

The two Parties have agreed that the application of measures connected with the withdrawal of Soviet military units and the transfer of the installations in the area of the naval base of Port Arthur to the government of the People's Republic of China shall be entrusted to the Joint Soviet-Chinese Military Commission in Port Arthur which was constituted under the Agreement of 14 February 1950.

The withdrawal of the Soviet forces and the transfer of the installations in the area of the naval base of Port Arthur to the government of the People's Republic of China shall be completed by 31 May 1955.

12 October 1954
(*Signed*) *A. I. Mikoyan*
Chou En-lai

Note

During the PRC's first decade there were no indications of any serious territorial dispute with the Soviet Union. To be sure, until 1953 Chinese maps had claimed for China a large portion of what the Soviet Union calls Tadzhikistan, but subsequent maps were adjusted to reflect the Soviet version of the boundary. And the fact that there was uncertainty over the ownership of some islands near the confluence of the Amur and Ussuri Rivers in Manchuria did not seem to be troublesome.

By September 1963, however, charges and countercharges from Moscow and Peking alleged border violations dating back to 1960. The Soviet government claimed:

> Beginning in 1960, Chinese servicemen and civilians have been systematically violating the Soviet border. In the single year of 1962, more than 5,000 violations of the Soviet border from the Chinese side were registered. Attempts are also being made to "develop" some parts of Soviet territory without permission. . . . [It was then indicated that this charge related mainly to the disputed islands in the Amur and Ussuri Rivers.]
>
> The Soviet government has a number of times offered to the CPR [PRC] government that consultations be held on the question of ascertaining separate sections of the border so as to exclude any possibility of misunderstanding. However, the Chinese side evades such consultations, at the same time continuing to violate the border. This cannot but make us wary, especially in view of the fact that Chinese propaganda is making definite hints at the unjust demarcation of some of the sections of the Soviet-Chinese border allegedly made in the past.

> However, the artificial creation today of any territorial problems, especially between socialist countries, would be tantamount to embarking on a very dangerous path. . . .[73]

The Chinese accused the Soviets of inciting dissident elements in Sinkiang Province to flee across the border into the Soviet Union. When negotiations on boundary questions took place in early 1964, the Russians were reported to have limited the agenda to the clarification of minor frontier disputes, while the Chinese were said to have argued for a comprehensive discussion of the entire border problem.[74] That these negotiations had failed to resolve the difficulties became clear when Chairman Mao conducted his celebrated interview with some Japanese visitors in the summer of 1964. Item 12–28 excerpts the relevant remarks by Mao, and item 12–29 contains *Pravda*'s interesting rebuttal.

12-28

"Chairman Mao Tse-tung Tells the Delegation of the Japanese Socialist Party that the Kuriles Must Be Returned to Japan," *Sekai Shuko,* Tokyo, August 11, 1964; translated in Dennis J. Doolin, *Territorial Claims in the Sino-Soviet Conflict* (Stanford, Calif: Hoover Institution on War, Revolution, and Peace, 1965), pp. 42–44.

On July 10, a five-man group of parliamentary deputies, headed by Kozo Sasaki, from . . . the Japanese Socialist Party had a lengthy talk in Peking with Mao Tse-tung, Chairman of the Chinese Communist Party. In the course of this talk, Mao Tse-tung declared that he "supported the position of Japan on the question of the return of the Kuriles." After arriving in Hong Kong on July 12, the group told this to a group of Japanese correspondents accredited there. The contents of the talk deserve special attention. . . .

Chairman Mao Tse-tung bitterly criticized the Soviet Union for its territorial ambitions. . . .

The territorial question: The head of the delegation of the staff of the Socialist Party on the island of Hokkaido, Tetsuo Ara, asked, "At a time when we were kept in ignorance, the Kuriles were taken away from us in accordance with the Yalta Agreement and the Potsdam Declaration. We demand their return [by the Soviet Union] and, in this connection, would like to hear Chairman Mao's opinion."

The following was said in reply: "There are too many places

occupied by the Soviet Union. In accordance with the Yalta Agreement, the Soviet Union, under the pretext of assuring the independence of Mongolia, actually placed the country under its domination. Mongolia takes up an area which is considerably greater than the Kuriles. In 1954, when Khrushchev and Bulganin came to China, we took up this question, but they refused to talk to us. They [*i.e.,* the Soviet Union] also appropriated part of Rumania. Having cut off a portion of East Germany, they chased the local inhabitants into West Germany. They detached a part of Poland, annexed it to the Soviet Union, and gave a part of East Germany to Poland as compensation. The same thing took place in Finland. The Russians took everything they could. Some people have declared that the Sinkiang area and the territories north of the Amur River must be included in the Soviet Union. The Soviet Union is concentrating troops along its border.

"The Soviet Union has an area of 22 million square kilometers and its population is only 220 million. It is about time to put an end to this allotment. Japan occupies an area of 370,000 square kilometers and its population is 100 million. About a hundred years ago, the area to the east of [Lake] Baikal became Russian territory, and since then Vladivostok, Khabarovsk, Kamchatka, and other areas have been Soviet territory. We have not yet presented our account for this list. In regard to the Kurile Islands, the question is clear as far as we are concerned—they must be returned to Japan."

12-29

"On Mao Tse-tung's Talk with a Group of Japanese Socialists," editorial, *Pravda* (Sept. 2, 1964), p. 2, translated in *International Affairs,* no. 10:80–85 (Oct. 1964).

An interview which Mao Tse-tung gave a group of Japanese Socialists visiting Peking was recently published in Japan. Bourgeois newspapermen played up his statements—they liked what the Chairman of the Communist Party of China had to say. The content of the talk was such that at first it was hard to believe its authenticity. For bourgeois newspapers write all sorts of things in their effort to poison the international situation and sow strife among the Socialist countries.

One expected Peking to deny the report, but there was no denial. On the contrary, Chinese leaders intimated that the Mao Tse-tung interview published in the Japanese press had indeed taken place. When a Soviet representative in Peking asked Chinese Deputy Foreign Minister

Wang Ping-nan for an explanation, the latter replied: "If Mao-Tse-tung has said so, I agree with him." On August 1, the Japanese newspaper, *Asahi,* published a statement by Chou En-lai which contained, in effect, the same thoughts as those voiced by Mao Tse-tung.

This left no doubt that the statement printed in the Japanese press had really been made by the Chairman of the Communist Party of China. . . .

Mao Tse-tung's reference to the territorial question shows clearly how far the Chinese leaders have gone in their cold war against the Soviet Union. He is not just claiming Soviet territory but presenting his claims as part of a "general territorial question."

We are faced with an openly expansionist programme with far-reaching pretensions. This programme did not emerge today or yesterday. A history textbook published in China in 1954 contained a map showing China as she was, in the opinion of the authors, before the first Opium War. The map showed Burma, Vietnam, Korea, Thailand, Malaya, Nepal, Bhutan, and Sikkim, all as part of China. In the north the border ran along the Stanovoi Mountain range, cutting all the Far Eastern territory from the USSR. In the west a part of Kirghizia, Tajikistan, and Kazakhstan (up to Lake Balkhash) was also included in China. Sakhalin was also marked as Chinese territory. If we are to believe the textbook, all these areas and countries were "Chinese national territory" and had been seized from China.

In those days it was thought that the publication of such a textbook was the result of an oversight or a piece of provocation by nationalistic elements. Subsequent events, however, proved this assumption to be wrong. Maps showing various parts of the Soviet Union and other countries neighbouring on China as Chinese territory continued to be published in the CPR [PRC].

Chinese spokesmen have lately been referring more and more frequently to hundreds of thousands of square kilometres of Soviet territory as allegedly belonging "by right" to China.

A recent issue of the Peking magazine Lishih Yenchiu (No. 4 for 1964) affirms that "Russia seized large expanses north of the Heilungchiang [Chinese name for the Amur River.—ed.] and east of the Ussuri River . . ." and that "various times Russia annexed extensive areas in Sinkiang, and the North-East Region."

Now, in his talk, Mao Tse-tung declares: "About 100 years ago the area to the east of Baikal became the territory of Russia, and since then Vladivostok, Khabarovsk, Kamchatka, and other points have been the territory of the Soviet Union. We have not yet presented a bill on this account."

By what right do the Chinese leaders lay claim to areas which did not belong to China? They argue that hundreds of years ago Chinese troops appeared in those areas and that the Chinese emperor collected tribute from their population. Really, if the question were not such a serious one, these "historical arguments" could only be described as childish.

Human history is replete with examples of the rise and fall of states and [the] migration of whole peoples in the course of which national borders were repeatedly altered. By resorting to the method of "historical references" in the question of borders, one can prove anything. One can prove, for instance, that England is a French territory because she was once the possession of a Duke of Normandy. It may be proved, on the other hand, that France is a British possession because she was almost entirely conquered by the English during the Hundred Years' War. With the aid of such arguments, it may be proved that the CPR [PRC] borders run along the Great Wall, which is less than 100 kilometres from Peking. For, at one time, in fact, it was there that China's border ran, and the Wall itself testifies to this.

But even if these references to "historical rights" are taken seriously, it turns out that in this case they are wholly at odds with the facts. For in the middle of the 17th century China's possessions are known to have extended only to the Khingan Mountain range, that is, very much further south of the Amur. The territories to the north of the Khingans were populated by indigenous tribes (the Evenks, Daurs, etc.) which from time to time were subjected to raids by the Manchus and paid them tribute. There was no indigenous Manchu or Chinese population in the Amur area. With Russia developing the northern half of the Amur basin and China the southern, there began the process of delineating the factual border. It was formalised more than 100 years ago in the Aigun and Peking Treaties.

No one argues the point that the tsarist government pursued a policy of aggrandisement just as, to the extent of their abilities, did the Chinese emperors.

At various times, now one, now the other proved stronger and gained the upper hand. This led to certain changes in settlement of peoples. But the working people did not think of any territorial conquests. They worked on the land on which they had to live and watered it with their sweat. It is amazing that there are people who challenge the right of the workers and peasants to the land on which they have lived and worked for ages for the sole reason that in antiquity one emperor defeated another and was then defeated himself.

Have those who question the Soviet Union's possession of a territory covering more than 1,500,000 square kilometres given any thought to how their claims will be regarded by the Soviet people, who have lived and worked on this land for several generations and consider it their homeland, the land of their ancestors.

That is why we say that the present border has been formed historically and consolidated by life itself, and the border treaties are a basis that cannot be disregarded.

The CPSU led the Russian working class and toiling masses in battle against tsarism and routed it. The Soviet government is known to have abrogated all the unequal treaties with China in its very first years. Continuing its Leninist policy, it gave up the Port Arthur naval base and turned over to the CPR, without any compensation, all its rights to the joint administration of the Chinese-Changchun Railway, together with all its assets. Lenin wrathfully condemned the tsarist government's seizure of Port Arthur and infiltration of Manchuria. But it was also Lenin who said: "Vladivostok is far away, but it is ours."

The Soviet Union is an absolutely new state entity, the result of the voluntary union of the Soviet republics built on the ruins of the tsarist empire. And whereas the frontiers of tsarist Russia were determined by a policy of imperialist rapine, the Soviet Union's borders are the result of the voluntary expression of the will of the peoples based on the principle of free self-determination of nations. The peoples that constitute the Soviet Union will never allow anyone to encroach upon their right to shape their own destiny.

In his interview Mao Tse-tung bemoans the fate of Mongolia, on whom, he says, the Soviet Union has "imposed its rule." This can arouse nothing but indignation. The Mongolian People's Republic has been a sovereign Socialist state for more than forty years and enjoys all the rights of an independent country. Why did Mao Tse-tung want to make such a patently absurd statement? The fact is that the existence of an independent Mongolian state, which maintains friendly relations with the USSR and other Socialist countries, does not suit the Chinese leaders. They would like to deprive the MPR of independence and make it a Chinese province. It was this that the CPR leaders offered N. S. Khrushchev and other Soviet leaders to "settle" during their visit to Peking in 1954.

N. S. Khrushchev, naturally, refused to discuss the question and told the Chinese leaders that the Mongolian people's destiny was not determined in Peking or Moscow but in Ulan Bator and that the question of Mongolia's statehood could be decided only by the working people of that country themselves, and by no one else.

As has been said, the Chinese leaders are trying to elevate territorial claims to a kind of general principle. And that is something that involves the fundamentals of international relations. What would happen if all states were to follow the Peking recipe and started presenting each other with claims for the revision of historically evolved frontiers? It is not difficult to answer this question. It would mean an inevitable increase of international tension and would be fraught with military conflicts and all that this involves.

The question of territorial disputes and borders is exceptionally complex. One must distinguish the nature of territorial issues. It is one thing when peoples justly seek to eliminate the remnants of the disgraceful colonial system and recover the imperialist-held territories traditionally inhabited by people of their own nationality. The Indian people, for instance, had an incontestable right to reunite Goa with the homeland. Equally incontestable was Indonesia's right to reunite West Irian with the Republic. We have always said that People's China has every right to accomplish the liberation and reunion of Taiwan and Hong Kong, which are part of the country and the majority of whose population is Chinese. The list of such cases could be continued.

It is an altogether different thing when territorial claims stem from attempts to revise historically evolved borders between states, to impose, in one form or another, a revision of treaties and agreements concluded after the Second World War as a result of the defeat of Hitler's Fascism and Japanese militarism. The peoples who won victory at the cost of millions and millions of lives will never countenance such ambitions. . . .

If we proceed from Mao Tse-tung's so-called historical principle, we shall see that all rights to this territory belong to the Soviet Union. But Chairman Mao treats the principles he himself propounds with an utter lack of principle. He invokes them when it suits him and forgets them when it does not suit his political designs. . . .

Mao Tse-tung canot help realising that the Chinese leaders' stand on the territorial question is a far cry from internationalism. To smooth this over, he appeals not only to history but to "justice." In effect, his argument amounts to this: the population of the globe is unevenly distributed and hence justice requires a redistribution of territory.

The demagogy of this is quite plain. The distribution of the human race over the globe is the result of a long and complex process of development, as a result of which different peoples live in different conditions. What the Communists are fighting for is a better life for everybody. When Socialism triumphs throughout the world and the productive forces everywhere reach a high level, the integration of nations will result in the differences in the living conditions in various countries gradually disappearing and national boundaries losing their importance. In these circumstances it will become possible to solve the problem of a more even distribution of people over the globe.

But this is a thing of the future. And it is extremely harmful to raise such a question today, when there are opposing social systems and when an objective process of the strengthening of statehood and sovereignty is going on.

It should not be forgotten, incidentally, that history knows of many cases when the most reactionary wars were started to expand "living space." So that Mao Tse-tung's talk about the "unjust distribution of territories" is not so new. He has predecessors of whom he can hardly be proud.

NOTE

A detailed study of the evolution of the Sino-Soviet boundary dispute until mid-1964 has concluded:

> In sum, a careful analysis of the public record dispels the notion that the territorial element contributed a significant dimension to the Sino-Soviet controversy, at least at the incubating stage. Rather, the foregoing debate over frontiers bears every earmark of an intricate game played for intrinsic political stakes in accordance with a series of well-defined rules. Style is crucial: the parties show keen awareness of what can properly be said, how it should be worded, and that they must observe throughout the exchange the principle of proportionality, lest the fixed limits of the colloquy be transcended and the contest unwittingly take on a riskier character than intended by the opponents. The territorial issue undoubtedly helps inflame the tempers on both sides, nasty enough already, and so aggravates the circumjacent politico-ideological struggle waged by Moscow and Peking, without, however, achieving a raison d'être of its own or gaining a stature sufficiently dominant to steer the overarching conflict into new and uncharted channels.
>
> The role assigned to international law in the process fits the picture just outlined. The weapon of law is used sparingly, and for good cause. Law is rigid, and everybody concerned seeks to maintain maximum flexibility of action. Law deals with right and wrong and ascribes guilt and innocence. Amicable compromise holds out a better promise of attaining success. Law means a collision at a state level, and the present *malentendu* is, by unanimous vote, pictured as a quarrel between rival teams of dedicated Marxist-Leninists. Law has other defects as well. Arguments drawn from the fund of general international law are ideologically impure and, in any case, probably are out of place in a conversation between "fellow-socialists." And "socialist international law" sheds no light on the matter, for the very phenomenon which now

> requires a solution is a priori barred as an impossibility under the terms of membership in the "socialist Commonwealth"—hence, the dilemma and the wispy quality of the legal accompaniment to the political solos. Note that even on those rare occasions where, as we have recently learned, genuine international legal formulas were invoked—the thalweg rule, for instance, during the 1964 negotiations—the fact was not made public until many years later. Granted, the rationale for citing the principle—the dispute over the status of the river islands—was itself at the time a relatively well-kept secret, but then one wonders if fear of precipitating a legal quarrel or of being caught breaking a doctrinal taboo or introducing alien standards into a family "debate" was not perhaps a prime motive for maintaining the silence to begin with, since the topic could hardly be discussed intelligently without venturing into the legal sphere.[75]

The situation on the Sino-Soviet border deteriorated rapidly after the 1964 negotiations broke off without a settlement of the dispute. Thousands of border incidents subsequently occurred, culminating in some serious armed clashes in the late winter of 1969 on the Ussuri River border between Manchuria and the Soviet Union's Maritime Provinces. This led each side to articulate its legal claims in some detail. Item 12–30 states the Chinese position. For the PRC's views on the appropriate mode of settling this dispute, see 41–4. It should be noted that in Chinese statements the Ussuri River is referred to as the Wusuli, the Amur River as the Heilung, and Damansky Island as Chenpao. Moreover, the Treaty of Nerchinsk is called the Treaty of Nipchu and the Treaty of Kiakhta the Burinsky Treaty.

12-30

"Statement of the Government of the People's Republic of China, May 24, 1969," in *PR* 12.22:3–7 (May 30, 1969).

On March 29, 1969, the Soviet government issued a statement on the Sino-Soviet boundary question. On April 1, 1969, Vice-Chairman Lin Piao of the Central Committee of the Communist Party of China pointed out in his report to the Ninth National Congress of the Communist Party of China: In its statement, the Soviet government was "still clinging to its obstinate aggressor stand, while expressing willingness to resume 'consultations.' Our government is considering its reply to this."

The Communist Party of China and the Chinese government have always held that boundary questions should be settled by negotiations through diplomatic channels and that, pending a settlement, the status quo of the boundary should be maintained and conflicts averted. This was our stand in the past and remains our stand at present. The development of the Sino-Soviet boundary question to its present state is wholly the responsibility of the Soviet side. The Chinese government hereby states the truth about the Sino-Soviet boundary question and its consistent position as follows:

I. Chenpao Island Is China's Territory and the Chenpao Island Incident Was Deliberately Provoked by the Soviet Government

Chenpao Island has always been China's territory. Before 1860, the Wusuli River where Chenpao Island is situated was still an inland river of China. It was only after the Opium War in the 19th century when the capitalist powers, one after another, imposed unequal treaties on China that the Wusuli River was stipulated as forming part of the boundary between China and Russia in the "Sino-Russian Treaty of Peking" of 1860. According to established principles of international law, in the case of navigable boundary rivers, the central line of the main channel shall form the boundary line and determine the ownership of islands. Situated on the Chinese side of the central line of the main channel of the Wusuli River, Chenpao Island indisputably belongs to China and has always been under China's jurisdiction.

The Soviet government invoked the map attached to the "Sino-Russian Treaty of Peking," asserting that in the area of Chenpao Island the demarcation line shown on this map "passes directly along the Chinese bank of the Ussuri River" and vainly attempting to prove thereby that Chenpao Island belongs to the Soviet Union. But this attached map can in no way help it out of its present predicament.

The map attached to the "Sino-Russian Treaty of Peking" was drawn unilaterally by tsarist Russia before the boundary was surveyed in 1861. And in 1861, China and Russia surveyed and marked only the land boundary south of the Hsingkai Lake but not the river boundary on the Wusuli and Heilung Rivers, and a red line was drawn on the attached map on a scale smaller than 1:1,000,000 only to indicate that the two rivers form the boundary between the two countries. The red line on this attached map does not, and cannot possibly, show the precise location of the boundary line in the rivers, still less is it intended

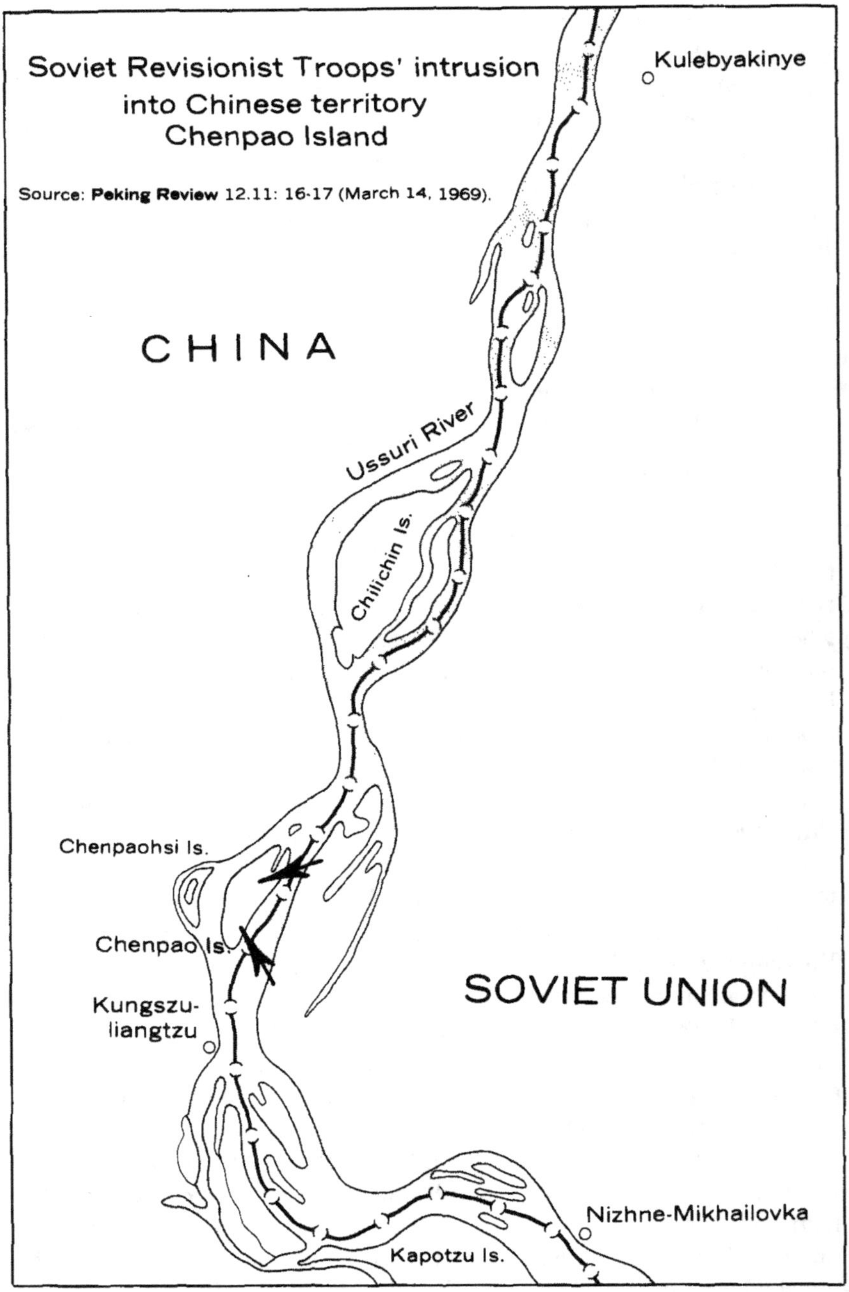
Soviet Revisionist Troops' intrusion
into Chinese territory
Chenpao Island
Source: Peking Review 12.11: 16-17 (March 14, 1969).
Kulebyakinye
CHINA
Ussuri River
Chilichin Is.
Chenpaohsi Is.
Chenpao Is.
Kungszu-
liangtzu
SOVIET UNION
Nizhne-Mikhailovka
Kapotzu Is.

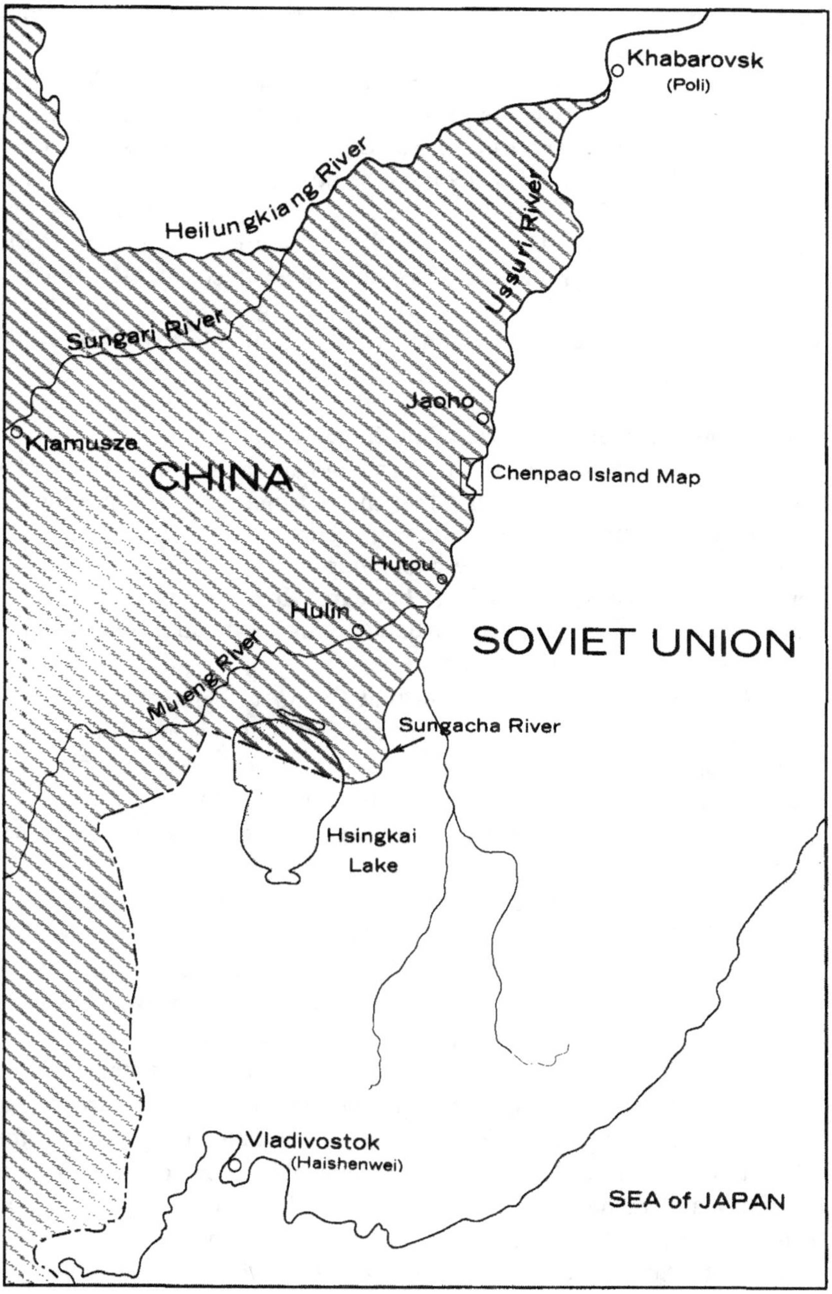
Khabarovsk
(Poli)
Heilungkiang River
Ussuri River
Sungari River
Jaoho
Kiamusze
CHINA
Chenpao Island Map
Hutou
Hulin
SOVIET UNION
Muleng River
Sungacha River
Hsingkai
Lake
Vladivostok
(Haishenwei)
SEA of JAPAN

to determine the ownership of islands. Hence, it can in no way prove that Chenpao Island belongs to the Soviet Union.

In fact, after the conclusion of the "Sino-Russian Treaty of Peking," the two sides always took the central line of the main channel for determining the ownership of islands and exercised jurisdiction accordingly. This was also repeatedly borne out by letters from the frontier officials of tsarist Russia to the Chinese side. For instance, in his letter of May 8, 1908, to a Chinese official, the frontier commissar of the Amur Region of tsarist Russia, Kuzmin, made it clear: "If countries are divided by a river, then the line running along the middle of the river should be taken as the boundary line between them. On navigable rivers, this line should be drawn along the channel." Again, in his letter of September 6 of the same year to the Chinese official, Kuzmin stated: "Islands in the rivers are divided by the river channel."

During the Sino-Soviet boundary negotiations in 1964, the Soviet representative also had to admit that the red line on the map attached to the "Sino-Russian Treaty of Peking" cannot show the precise alignment of the boundary line in the rivers, nor can it possibly determine the ownership of islands; he could not but agree that the central line of the main channel should be taken for determining the boundary line on the rivers and the ownership of islands.

It should also be pointed out that Chenpao Island was originally not an island, but a part of the bank on the Chinese side of the Wusuli River, which later became an island as a result of erosion by the river water. To this day, Chenpao Island still connects with the Chinese bank at low water, and the river arm to the west of the Island has never become a waterway.

The Chenpao Island incident was deliberately provoked by the Soviet side. In recent years, Soviet troops have repeatedly been sent in helicopters, armoured cars, and vehicles to intrude into China's territory, Chenpao Island, for provocations. During the first two months of this year alone, they intruded into the Island as many as eight times. They kidnapped Chinese inhabitants, assaulted and wounded Chinese frontier guards, and seized arms and ammunition. With regard to the provocations by the Soviet side, the Chinese side all along exercised the utmost forbearance, persisting in reasoning things out on the basis of the facts and demanding that the Soviet side stop its intrusions and provocations. However, thinking that China was weak and could be bullied, the Soviet side became ever more unbridled. When they intruded into China's Chenpao Island on February 16, the Soviet troops flagrantly clamoured that they would use force of arms should the Chinese frontier guards go there for patrols again. Following that, the

Soviet Far Eastern frontier troops entered into No. 1 combat readiness. On March 2, large numbers of Soviet troops in armoured cars and vehicles intruded into China's territory, the Chenpao Island area, simultaneously from Nizhne-Mikhailovka and Kulebyakinye, launched a sudden attack on the Chinese frontier guards on normal patrol duty and were the first to open fire with guns and cannons, killing and wounding many Chinese frontier guards on the spot. Driven beyond the limits of forbearance, the Chinese frontier guards were compelled to fight back in self-defence. On March 15, Soviet troops again intruded into Chenpao Island and shelled areas deep within Chinese territory on the Chinese side of the river, thus creating a new incident of bloodshed. Such is the truth about the Chenpao Island incident. No amount of lies will help the Soviet government escape the responsibility for its crimes.

II. The Treaties Relating to the Present Sino-Soviet Boundary Are All Unequal Treaties Imposed on China by Tsarist Russian Imperialism

Tsarist Russia. a European country, was originally not contiguous to China. Tsarist Russia began to expand eastwards in the 16th century, and it was not until the latter half of the 17th century that there arose the question of a boundary with China. In 1689, China and Russia concluded their first boundary treaty, the "Treaty of Nipchu," which defined the eastern sector of the Sino-Russian boundary. In 1727, China and Russia concluded the "Burinsky Treaty," which defined the middle sector of the Sino-Russian boundary (the larger part of this sector of the boundary has now become Mongolian-Soviet boundary). As for the western frontier of China, it was then at the Balkhash Lake, a great distance from the boundary of tsarist Russia.

After the Opium War of 1840, China was gradually reduced to a semicolony, while Russia was gradually becoming a military-feudal imperialist country. Beginning from the fifties of the 19th century, tsarist Russia colluded with the Western imperialist countries in pursuing the aggressive policy of carving up China. Within the short space of half a century, it forced China to sign a series of unequal treaties, by which it annexed more than 1.5 million square kilometres of Chinese territory, an area three times that of France or twelve times that of Czechoslovakia.

While the allied Anglo-French imperialist forces were attacking Tientsin and threatening Peking in their aggression against China, tsarist Russian imperialism seized the opportunity to compel the authorities of the Ching Dynasty by force of arms to sign the "Sino-Russian Treaty of Aigun" on May 28, 1858, by which it annexed more than 600,000 square kilometres of Chinese territory north of the Heilung River and south of the Outer Khingan Mountains and placed the Chinese territory east of the Wusuli River under the joint possession of China and Russia.

Taking advantage of the military pressure brought about by the occupation of Peking by the allied Anglo-French forces invading China, alleging that it had made contribution in mediation and threatening that "it is not difficult to renew the war," tsarist Russia forced the Ching dynasty government to sign the "Sino-Russian Treaty of Peking" on November 14, 1860, by which it forcibly incorporated some 400,000 square kilometres of Chinese territory east of the Wusuli River into Russia.

By the "Sino-Russian Treaty of Peking" and by the "Tahcheng Protocol on the Delimitation of Sino-Russian Boundary" which tsarist Russia forced the Ching dynasty government to sign on October 7, 1864, tsarist Russia further annexed more than 440,000 square kilometres of territory in the western part of China.

In 1871 tsarist Russia sent troops to forcibly occupy China's Ili area, who entrenched themselves there for as long as ten years; on February 24, 1881, it forced the Ching dynasty government to sign the "Sino-Russian Ili Treaty." By the "Sino-Russian Ili Treaty" and the subsequent protocols on boundary delimitation, tsarist Russia further incorporated more than 70,000 square kilometres of Chinese territory into the territory of tsarist Russia.

The great teachers of the world proletariat, Marx, Engels, and Lenin, had long made brilliant conclusions on the unequal nature of these treaties. Commenting on the "Sino-Russian Treaty of Aigun" in 1858, Marx said that ". . . by his second opium war he [John Bull] has helped her [Russia] to the invaluable tract lying between the Gulf of Tartary and Lake Baikal, a region so much coveted by Russia that from Czar Alexey Michaelowitch down to Nicolaus, she has always attempted to get it." [a] Engels also pointed out in the same year that Russia despoiled "China of a country as large as France and Germany put together, and of a river as large as the Danube" and that "Not satisfied with this, she has obtained the establishment of a Russo-Chinese Commission to fix the boundaries. Now, we all know what such a commission is in the hands of Russia. We have seen them at work on the Asiatic frontiers of Turkey, where they kept slicing away piece after piece from that country, for more than twenty years." [b] Things turned out to be exactly as Engels had wisely foreseen. After 1858, tsarist Russia was "slicing away piece

[a] Marx, "The British and Chinese Treaty," *Collected Works of Karl Marx and Frederick Engels,* Chinese ed., Vol. 12, pp. 625–626.

[b] Engels, "The Progress of Russia in Far-East," *Collected Works of Karl Marx and Frederick Engels,* Chinese ed., Vol. 12, pp. 662, 664.

after piece" of Chinese territory with the signing of each treaty and with every survey of the boundary. Lenin also bitterly denounced tsarist Russia more than once for its crimes of aggression against China. Lenin pointed out that ". . . the European governments (the Russian government among the very first) have already started to partition China. However, they have not begun this partitioning openly, but stealthily, like thieves" and that "The policy of the tsarist government in China is a criminal policy." [c]

While glibly talking about being "true to Lenin's behests" in its statement of March 29, the Soviet government in the very same statement directly opposed the brilliant conclusions made by Marx, Engels and Lenin and thoroughly betrayed their teachings.

In order to suit the needs of its social-imperialist policy, the Soviet government even described tsarist Russian imperialist aggression against semi-colonial China after the mid-19th century as "disputes" between "Chinese emperors and tsars," in which there was no question of who was the aggressor and who the victim of aggression, nor was there any question of whether the treaties concluded between them are equal or not. This is a gangster logic in defense of tsarist Russian imperialist aggression.

In his time the great Lenin warmly supported China and all other oppressed countries in opposing aggression by tsarist Russian imperialism and all other imperialists. He said that ". . . if tomorrow, Morocco were to declare war on France, or India on Britain, or Persia or China on Russia, and so on, these would be 'just,' and 'defensive' wars, *irrespective* of who would be the first to attack; any socialist would wish the oppressed, dependent and unequal states victory over the oppressor, slave holding and predatory 'Great' Powers." [d] Today when people review these teachings of Lenin's, they can only come to one conclusion: Such energetic propagation of the imperialist gangster logic by the Soviet government is not only "alien to the Leninist policy," but is also a most shameless betrayal of Leninism.

III. The Fact That There Exists a Boundary Question between China and the Soviet Union Cannot Be Obliterated

There exists a boundary question between China and the Soviet Union not only because tsarist Russia annexed more than 1.5 million

[c] Lenin, "The War in China," *Collected Works,* Chinese ed., Vol. 4, pp. 335–336, 338.

[d] Lenin, "Socialism and War," *Collected Works,* Chinese ed., Vol. 21, pp. 280–281.

square kilometres of Chinese territory by the unequal treaties it imposed on China, but also because it crossed in many places the boundary line stipulated by the unequal treaties and further occupied vast expanses of Chinese territory. Even tracts of Chinese territory which have always been under the Chinese government's jurisdiction have been drawn as Soviet territory. For instance, in the Pamir area, tsarist Russia occupied more than 20,000 square kilometres of Chinese territory in violation of the stipulations of the "Protocol on Sino-Russian Boundary in the Kashgar Region" of 1884. Again, for instance, in the sector of the Wusuli and Heilung Rivers, the Soviet government, in violation of the "Sino-Russian Treaty of Aigun," the "Sino-Russian Treaty of Peking" and the established principles of international law, has gone so far as to draw the boundary line almost entirely along the Chinese bank and in some places even on China's inland rivers and islands, marking as Soviet territory over 600 of the 700 and more Chinese islands on the Chinese side of the central line of the main channel, which cover an area of more than 1,000 square kilometres.

With regard to the unequal treaties imposed on China by tsarist Russia, the great Lenin always stood for their annulment.

On September 27, 1920, the Government of Soviets led by Lenin solemnly proclaimed: It "declares null and void all the treaties concluded with China by the former Governments of Russia, renounces all seizure of Chinese territory and all Russian concessions in China and restores to China, without any compensation and forever, all that had been predatorily seized from her by the Tsar's government and the Russian bourgeoisie."

Furthermore, the "Agreement on General Principles for the Settlement of the Questions between China and the Soviet Union" signed on May 31, 1924, stipulates that at the conference agreed upon by both sides, they are to "annul all Conventions, Treaties, Agreements, Protocols, Contracts, etcetera, concluded between the government of China and the tsarist government and to replace them with new treaties, agreements, etcetera, on the basis of equality, reciprocity, and justice, as well as the spirit of the Declarations of the Soviet government of the years of 1919 and 1920" and "to redemarcate their national boundaries . . . , and pending such redemarcation, to maintain the present boundaries."

In pursuance of the 1924 Agreement, China and the Soviet Union held talks in 1926 to discuss the redemarcation of the boundary and the conclusion of a new treaty. Owing to the historical conditions at the time, no agreement was reached by the two sides on the boundary question, no redemarcation of the boundary between the two countries was made, and no new equal treaty was concluded by the two countries, and thus this proletarian policy of Lenin's failed to come true.

The above facts fully show that the treaties relating to the present Sino-Soviet boundary are all unequal treaties, that they should all be annulled, and that the Sino-Soviet boundary question remains an outstanding issue. In its statement, the Soviet government did not even say a single word about the fact that under the above-mentioned Declarations and Agreement, it is "all" the treaties concluded with China that are to be annulled and it is "all" the seized Chinese territory that is to be renounced, but uttered the nonsense that the 1924 Agreement did not "consider" the boundary treaties "as being among the unequal treaties" and that "there was no talk of their being annulled." This is indeed a "juggling with history, adapting it to its territorial claims."

Chairman Mao spoke highly of the declaration of the annulment of the unequal treaties between China and Russia made by the Government of Soviets led by Lenin. However, from Chairman Mao's words no conclusion whatsoever can be drawn that there does not exist a boundary question between China and the Soviet Union. The same is true of Dr. Sun Yat-sen's remarks. As for the "Sino-Soviet Treaty of Friendship, Alliance, and Mutual Assistance" and the "Sino-Soviet Agreement on Navigation on Boundary Rivers," they are in no sense a treaty or agreement for the settlement of the boundary question, still less can they prove that there does not exist a boundary question between China and the Soviet Union.

IV. The Soviet Government Has Violated the Status Quo of the Boundary and Provoked Border Conflicts

It is understandable that the boundary question existing between China and the Soviet Union was not settled when China was under reactionary rule. The founding of the People's Republic of China created all the necessary conditions for a reasonable settlement of the Sino-Soviet boundary question. Owing to various reasons, no start was made to settle the question at the time, yet the Sino-Soviet border was all along tranquil.

Since 1960 the Soviet government has gone farther and farther down the road of betraying Marxism-Leninism. It restores capitalism at home and pursues a social-imperialist policy abroad, it allies with US imperialism and opposes socialist China and it has incessantly violated the status quo of the boundary and tried to occupy Chinese territory which has always been under the Chinese government's jurisdiction, thus aggravating the Sino-Soviet boundary question. The Soviet government directed Soviet frontier troops to push their patrol routes into Chinese territory, build military installations within Chinese territory, assault and kidnap Chinese border inhabitants, sabotage their production, and carry out all sorts of provocative and subversive activities. In 1962 the Soviet government incited and coerced more than 60,000 Chinese citizens in the Ili and Tahcheng areas of Sinkiang, China, into going to the Soviet Union, and it has up to now refused to send them back.

Since 1964, the Soviet government has sent large reinforcements to the Sino-Soviet border, stepped up its violation of the status quo of the boundary, carried out armed provocations and created incidents of bloodshed. From October 15, 1964 to March 15 this year, the Soviet side provoked as many as 4,189 border incidents, two and a half times the number of those it provoked from 1960 to 1964 with its tactics getting even more vicious and its behaviour even more unbridled. Soviet troops intruded into Chinese territory, indulging in murder and arson; killing barehanded Chinese fishermen and peasants by beating and running armoured cars over them or even throwing them alive into the river. Lenin indignantly condemned the Russian government for its atrocities of slaughtering peaceable Chinese inhabitants in these words: ". . . they flung themselves upon it [China] like savage beasts, burning down whole villages, shooting, bayonetting, and drowning in the Amur River unarmed inhabitants, their wives, and their children."[e] What difference is there between the present-day atrocities committed by the Soviet government against Chinese inhabitants on the Wusuli and Heilung Rivers and the atrocities by the tsarist Russian government which were bitterly denounced by Lenin in those days!?

The Chenpao Island incident is the inevitable result of the Soviet government's violation of the status quo of the Sino-Soviet boundary and pursuance of its social-imperialist policy over a long period of time. The sanguinary conflicts on Chenpao Island were deliberately engineered by the Soviet government in order to cover up its capitulation on the Berlin question and curry favour with US imperialism, so that it can further ally with US imperialism against China. By this action, the Soviet government tells the United States that China is the common enemy of the United States and the Soviet Union.

NOTE

In early June 1969 another serious armed clash occurred between the PRC and the USSR, this time in Central Asia on the border between the northwest portion of China's Sinkiang Uighur Autonomous Region and Soviet Kazakhstan. Shortly afterward, the USSR responded to the PRC's May 24, 1969, statement, declaring:

[e] Lenin, "The War in China," *Collected Works,* Chinese ed., Vol. 4, p. 336.

The Ussuri River was defined as the boundary line between Russia and China by the 1860 Treaty of Peking, and in accordance with the protocol appended to it in 1861 the "border line" in the sections where it runs along the river was indicated by a red line on the map. In the vicinity of Damansky Island it runs directly along the Chinese bank of the river; consequently, this island, since it is located on the Soviet side of the "border line," belongs to the Soviet Union and not to China.

It is common knowledge that in international law there is no norm that automatically establishes the border line on frontier rivers as running along the middle of the river's main channel. In concluding treaties involving such situations, states mark the border in the way that they believe most suitable and in accordance with the circumstances. There are examples in interstate relations in which a border has been established along the bank of a river, not along its channel. The 1858 treaty between Costa Rica and Nicaragua stipulates that the border line runs along the right bank of the San Juan River and that "the Republic of Nicaragua has the exclusive right of possession and sovereign jurisdiction with respect to the waters of this river." Similar determinations of river borders are to be found in agreements between other countries

The 1860 Russo-Chinese Treaty of Peking is another such example. Recognition of the fact that the border line does not necessarily coincide with the channel was also reflected in the Soviet-Chinese agreement on the procedure for navigation on border rivers concluded in 1951. Art. I of this agreement states that the ships of both parties may navigate the main channels of border rivers, "regardless of where the state border line runs."

During the Peking consultations in 1964 the Soviet side expressed its willingness to meet halfway the wishes of the Chinese side with reference to the interests of the Chinese population living near the river and to come to an agreement regarding the location of the USSR-CPR border line along the Amur and Ussuri Rivers on the basis of mutual concessions, given the condition that the Chinese side in turn displayed a willingness to recognize the corresponding interests of the Soviet population in certain sections of the border. This would have been a reasonable arrangement, based on the desire of both sides to eliminate tension and maintain tranquility of the border.

No agreement was reached at that time, since the Chinese representatives complicated the consultations by advancing unfounded territorial and other demands that called into question both the location of the existing border line and all the treaties defining the Soviet-Chinese border.

The CPR government statement of May 24, 1969, alleges that in circumvention of the 1884 "Description of the State Border between China and Russia in the Kashgar Region" the latter country occupied over 20,000 sq. km. of Chinese territory. However, the May 22, 1884, Protocol, which the Chinese side is talking about, bears no relation whatever to the Pamir region, as anyone who takes the trouble to look at this protocol can see for himself. The Russian and Chinese commissioners dealt with the location of the border in the region of the Tien Shan Mountains between what was then Russia's Fergana Province and China's Kashgar Province, in the section from Bedel Pass to Uz-Bel Pass, and upon completion of their work they signed the above-mentioned May 22, 1884, Protocol. The demarcation in the Pamirs was accomplished by means of an exchange of notes in 1894; at this time, the two sides agreed "not to go beyond the limits of the positions they now occupy" in the Pamirs along the Sarikol Range. This line and no other exists up to the present.

In the light of known facts, arguments alleging that the western border of China "runs along Lake Balkhash" seem ridiculous at best.[76]

The Soviet interpretation of the Treaty of Peking was categorically rejected by the PRC's Foreign Ministry. On October 8, 1969, it stated:

> The attached map [attached to the Treaty] is on a scale smaller than 1:1,000,000. The red line on it only indicates that the rivers form the boundary; it does not, and cannot possibly, show the precise location of the boundary line in the rivers. . . .
>
> In order to deny the principle of international law that the central line of the main channel shall form the boundary line in the case of navigable boundary rivers, the Soviet government cited as an example the treaty concluded between Costa Rica and Nicaragua in 1858 . . . [and] it impudently alleged that the "Sino-Russian Treaty of Peking" was likewise a case in point. Of course, there are exceptions to any established principle of international law, and the same is true of the principle that the central line of the main channel shall form the boundary in the case of navigable boundary rivers. But explicit stipulations must be made in treaties for any exceptional case. . . . Now we want to ask the Soviet government: Where is it stipulated in the "Sino-

> Russian Treaty of Peking" that the boundary line between China and Russia runs along the Chinese bank of the [Amur] and [Ussuri] Rivers? [77]

The PRC also pointed out that the Soviet border regulations of 1960 unambiguously asserted that "the state boundary of the USSR on navigable boundary rivers runs along the center of the main channel or the thalweg of the river." [78] According to this view China would not only be entitled to Chenpao Island and other minor islands but also to a much larger and more important one occupied by the USSR that is within easy shooting distance of the important Soviet city of Khabarovsk.

The Chinese note of October 8, 1969, also answered the Soviet position regarding the bearing of nineteenth-century agreements upon the dispute over the Pamir region:

> The 1884 "Protocol on Sino-Russian Boundary in the Kashgar Region" clearly stipulates that in the Pamir area, from the Uz-Bel Mountain Pass "the boundary of Russia turns southwestwards, the boundary of China runs due south." This is the only treaty stipulation relating to the Sino-Russian boundary in the Pamir area. Yet the Soviet government alleged that this Boundary Protocol "has nothing at all to do with" the ownership of the Pamir area and that it was the notes exchanged in 1894 which were the documents of "demarcation."
>
> What are the facts? The facts are: In 1892, tsarist Russian imperialism, in violation of the stipulation of the 1884 Boundary Protocol, dispatched its troops to the Pamir area again and further occupied by force of arms more than 20,000 square kilometres of Chinese territory west of the Sarykol range. At the time, the troops of the two sides faced each other along the range. In April 1894, China and Russia exchanged notes, and the Chinese government was forced to agree to the tsarist government's proposal to maintain temporarily the respective positions of the troops of the two sides pending a final settlement of the Pamir question. However, the Chinese government made explicit reservations at the time, declaring that "in adopting the above-mentioned measure, the Chinese government does not at all mean to abandon the rights China possesses over the territories of the Pamirs which are situated beyond the positions occupied by the Chinese troops at present. It considers that it should maintain the rights based on the 1884 Protocol until a satisfactory understanding is reached." Find-

> ing itself devoid of justification, tsarist Russian imperialism dared not insist that the Sarykol range should form the boundary.
>
> The present Soviet government has gone farther than the old tsars. It wants to force on China as the Sino-Soviet boundary line the line of military occupation of the old tsars and itself. How can this be regarded as taking the relevant treaty as the basis for determining the alignment of this sector of the boundary? [79]

October 20, 1969, the Chinese and Russians undertook another effort to resolve their boundary dispute through negotiations in Peking at the level of Vice-Minister of Foreign Affairs. As of mid-1973, however, no settlement was yet in sight. In April 1960, at the end of the first decade of the PRC's relations with the USSR, Premier Chou En-lai had dismissed a suggestion of border troubles between the two Communist giants by stating that "There are insignificant discrepancies in the maps, easy to solve peacefully." [80] Subsequent events have failed to vindicate his optimism.

Late in 1970 the London *Sunday Times* claimed that, according to reliable intelligence reports, the PRC had quietly dropped a claim against North Korea for cession of a hundred-square-mile strip of territory in the Mount Paektu area along the border between China and Korea. The Chinese had reportedly sought this area as "fraternal compensation" for PRC aid in the Korean conflict. The claim was initially made in 1965 when North Korea appeared to be shifting to Moscow's position in the Sino-Soviet rift. The claim was abandoned on the twentieth anniversary of the entry of Chinese forces into the Korean conflict.[81]

Water 13

As the introductions to this study and this part mention and as item 13–1 recalls, the law of the sea was among the first principles of Western international law invoked by China's Ch'ing dynasty. Resort to international law had helped China's foreign office to prevail upon the Prussian minister to release three Danish ships seized in the Gulf of Pohai in 1864. The seizure, it was successfully argued, had been illegal because it had occurred in waters that constituted part of China's "inner ocean." [82] Thus, for over a century China has been aware of the service that the law of the sea can render national security by obliging other states to refrain from unwanted military action in whatever coastal waters can legitimately be claimed as Chinese.

At the current stage of our research into late Ch'ing application of international law, the scope of territorial waters claimed by the Ch'ing remains unclear. In 1874, when Chinese Viceroy Li Hung-chang sought to justify Korea's action in firing upon a Japanese warship that appeared near the Korean coast, he stated that, according to international law, the width of the territorial sea was ten *li* (approximately 3 nautical miles).[83] An 1899 treaty with Mexico provided: "The two Contracting Parties agree upon considering a distance of 3 marine leagues [approximately 9 nautical miles], measured from the line of low tide, as the limit of their territorial waters for everything relating to the vigilance and enforcement of the Custom-house Regulations and the necessary measures for the prevention of smuggling." [84] What the imperial government officially claimed to be its territorial waters in the absence of treaty is uncertain. The following is a Chinese Communist scholar's explanation of this phenomenon:

> From the time our country opened five of our ports to foreign trade after the Opium War of 1842, we lost, one after the other, our rights of navigation and trade along the coast and inland rivers. Vessels belonging to imperialist countries not only plied between our coastal ports to engage in trade, but even sailed freely to Chungking—a port 1,350 nautical miles from the seashore—and did business all along the way. Moreover, warships also cruised up and down at will, invading and encroaching upon our rights under the excuse of protecting their merchant

vessels. As our country was then in a semicolonial state, how absurd it would have been for us to bring up the question of the extent of our territorial sea! [85]

Soon after assuming command of the Republic of China, the Nationalist government clarified China's position on this question. At the 1930 Hague Conference on Codification of International Law it took the position that the breadth of the territorial sea should be three nautical miles, measured from the low-water marks along the coast, and that within that area it enjoyed full sovereignty, subject to the right of foreign vessels to innocent passage.[86] A 1934 Chinese statute added that for purposes of enforcing China's customs laws a limit of twelve nautical miles would be enforced.[87] The ROC has maintained this position, despite the fact that an increasing number of states have come to claim territorial seas of greater breadth than three nautical miles in an effort both to enhance national security and to obtain title to a larger portion of the riches of the sea. In 1958, however, at the first Geneva Conference on the Law of the Sea, the ROC supported efforts to reach a compromise between those states that advocated a twelve-mile limit and those that argued for a narrower coastal belt; it voted for an unsuccessful United States proposal that the territorial sea be six miles in breadth, with coastal states having a right to regulate fishing for another six miles subject to certain historical fishing rights.[88]

Before 1958 relatively little was known about the Chinese Communist regime's position on the scope of the territorial sea, for it had published no statutes, regulations, or official pronouncements on the subject. On the basis of the imprecise formulation contained in the 1957 criminal law textbook, quoted in the introductory note to this part, it might have appeared that the PRC would adopt the Soviet view. But an article by a scholar named Wei Wen-han, published in June 1957 and specifically devoted to the breadth of the territorial sea, indicated that Peking was discussing the wisdom of taking an independent view, one that would take account of the circumstances which distinguished China's situation from that of the Soviet Union. For example, the criminal law textbook stated that the border lines of the territorial sea are to be drawn at a given distance from the low-water marks of the seacoast; this is the so-called "normal baseline" method which is used by most countries. But Wei argued that at least the southern section of China's 11,000 kilometer coastline was sufficiently indented and dotted with islands to justify application of the "straight baseline" method of measurement which had been applied by Norway and upheld by the International Court of Justice in the Anglo-Norwegian Fisheries Case.[89]

The advent of the Geneva Conference on the Law of the Sea

in the spring of 1958 led the PRC, as well as other governments, to evince increasing interest in legal aspects of territorial waters. The PRC leaped to the defense of Indonesia when, shortly before the conference, that country claimed a twelve-mile limit as applied by the straight baseline method, thereby evoking strong protests from some of the major maritime countries.[90] But, even though it had not been invited to attend the Law of the Sea Conference, which had been held under UN auspices, the PRC waited to spell out its own position until well after the conference had concluded its labors and another country, Iceland, had chosen to follow the precedents set by Norway and Indonesia.[91]

The Taiwan Strait crisis of late summer 1958 finally spurred Peking to state its claims to the territorial sea. On September 4, as the United States was preparing to convoy Nationalist ships from Taiwan to points only three miles from the mainland's offshore island of Quemoy, which is held by the Nationalists, the PRC announced that its territorial sea was twelve miles in breadth as measured by the straight baseline method.[92] This immediately elicited protests from both the United States and Great Britain, although Communist states, including the Soviet Union, North Korea, and North Vietnam, as well as certain "neutralist" states, rallied to Peking's support. Moreover, the United States actually challenged the PRC's claim by carrying out its plan to escort Nationalist ships up to points three miles from Quemoy. Peking responded with "a serious warning." [93]

After the crisis had passed, the United States articulated the legal grounds for its protest:

> In addition, the United States considers that international law recognizes only a 3-mile limit, that it is not possible for a country by unilateral action to take unto itself that which is the common property of all nations, and that this is, moreover, in violation of the universally accepted principle of the freedom of the high seas. The United States position finds support in the report of the United Nations International Law Commission wherein it is stated that "international law does not require states to recognize a breadth [of territorial sea] beyond 3 miles."
>
> Further, a country is not free to choose whether its territorial sea will be measured from the low-water mark on the coast, which is the normal baseline, or whether it will use straight baselines connecting salient points or offshore islands. While article 4 of the Geneva Convention on the Territorial Sea and the Contiguous Zone adopted by the recent Geneva Conference on Law of the Sea permits the establishment of straight baselines in localities

> where the coastline is deeply indented and cut into or if there is a fringe of islands along the coast in its immediate vicinity, it is clear that the Chinese coast along which the straight lines described in the statement of September 4 are drawn does not conform to the geographic conditions which are set forth in article 4. There is even less legal basis for drawing straight baselines from outermost points on a group of islands and claiming waters thereby included as internal waters. Similar attempts by other countries to claim, as internal waters, large areas of high seas within groups of islands or archipelagoes have been protested by many countries. The straight baselines described in the statement of September 4, 1958, are accordingly regarded by the United States as completely arbitrary and without any basis in recognized international law.[94]

Item 13–1 states the Chinese case as persuasively as any of the official or scholarly rebuttals of these arguments that has appeared.

13-1

Fu Chu, *Kuan-yü wo-kuo ti ling-hai wen-t'i* (Concerning the Question of our Country's Territorial Sea; Peking, 1959), pp. 1–21, 26.

I. Important Significance of Our Government's Declaration on Territorial Sea

On September 4, 1958, our government issued the Declaration on the Territorial Sea. The Declaration solemnly announced: (1) The breadth of the territorial sea of the People's Republic of China shall be twelve nautical miles (1 nautical mile = 1.852 kilometers), (2) The straight baseline method shall be adopted to delimit the breadth of the territorial sea, (3) No foreign vessels for military use and no foreign aircraft may enter our country's territorial sea or the territorial air space above it without the permission of our government, and any foreign vessels navigating in our territorial sea must observe the relevant laws and regulations of our government, (4) The Taiwan and Penghu area are still occupied by the United States armed forces. This is an unlawful encroachment on our territorial integrity and sovereignty. Our government has the right to recover these areas by all suitable means at a suitable time. This is China's internal affair, in which no foreign interference can be tolerated. This Declaration is an important measure for protecting our country's sovereignty and territorial integrity and has rather important significance for consolidating our country's national defense and security and protecting our economic interest.

Territorial sea is an important composite part of a state's territory which is completely under the sovereign jurisdiction of the state. State sovereignty extends to its territorial sea and the territorial air space above and the subsoil beneath. The encroachment upon a state's territorial sea or the territorial air space above the territorial sea by any foreign power by any means is an encroachment upon that state's territorial sovereignty. This is considered to be an aggressive act in violation of international law. The victim state has the right to adopt all means of self-defense until the injurious act is eliminated.

The territorial sea of a coastal state is important mainly to its economy and national defense. As for the economic significance, the territorial sea is the place where a coastal state and its inhabitants can acquire sea resources. The inhabitants of a coastal state have exclusive rights to engage in fishing and exploration of natural resources within their own country's territorial sea. As for the significance in terms of national defense, the territorial sea separates the mainland from the open sea and is very important in preventing aggression by the enemy and in safeguarding national defense and security.

Every independent state which is adjacent to the sea has its own territorial sea. Mutual respect of sovereignty over territorial sea has already become a generally accepted principle of international law. Socialist countries have consistently and strictly observed this principle and engaged in uncompromising struggle with imperialist countries which have used various means to encroach upon the territorial sea of other countries. Socialist countries not only cannot tolerate the encroachment on their own territorial sea by foreign powers, but also oppose the encroachment on the territorial sea of other countries. Many bourgeois scholars of international law also recognize the principle of respecting other countries' sovereignty over territorial sea. However, in practice, imperialist countries ruthlessly trample on and undermine this principle. The most obvious example is the dispatch of warships by the United States, Britain, and other imperialist countries to the territorial sea of other countries for demonstration and provocation.

Our country has a very long coastal line of 11,000 kilometers, and, therefore, the protection of our country's sovereignty over the territorial sea has a further important significance in the consolidation of the national defense and security of our country. However, before the liberation, since old China was for a long period in a semicolonial position, the reactionary ruling class of old China concluded a series of unequal treaties with the United States, Britain, Japan, and other imperialist countries, permitting foreign warships not only to enter and leave our territorial sea freely, but also to penetrate without obstacles into our inland rivers. Our sea coast and cities and villages along the banks of inland rivers were constantly under the threat of imperialist warships, and therefore we completely lost our sovereignty. Thus, at that time [old China] could not in fact speak of any territorial sea. . . . In 1949, the People's Republic of China was established; it terminated at last the rule of imperialist forces and their lackeys in China, abolished all unequal treaties and cancelled all privileges of imperialism in China. From then on, imperialists could no longer do what they wished in Chinese territory. The period in which imperialist warships could freely enter and leave China's territorial sea without being subject to any punishment has been declared ended forever. . . . Internationally, our Declaration on the Territorial Sea has received the unanimous and unreserved support of the governments and public opinion of [the following] socialist countries: the Soviet Union, Bulgaria, Hungary, Rumania, Czechoslovakia, the German Democratic Republic, Poland, Albania, Korea, Vietnam, and Mongolia. . . . In addition to fraternal countries, we also have the support of the governments and peoples of other friendly countries. . . .

II. The Question of the Breadth of the Territorial Sea

(i) The Breadth of the Territorial Sea of the Various Countries Should Be Respectively Decided by Each of These Countries.

The breadth of the territorial sea of the various countries should be decided, within reasonable scope, in accordance with the respective needs of those countries. This is a principle accepted in theory and in practice. Theoretically speaking, since international law recognizes that territorial sea should be under the sovereignty of the coastal country, the right to enact a reasonably broad territorial sea and the method of measuring it should naturally belong to this country. Practically speaking, the breadth of territorial sea of the various countries of the world has always been decided by the respective countries. When the various countries determine the breadth of their own territorial sea, they generally consider the various aspects of their interests (which naturally cannot prejudice the interests of other countries), including economic interest, interest in national defense and security, interest in sea transportation and other relevant historical and geographical circumstances. Once the breadth of the territorial sea has been determined, it should be announced in a proper form. Generally, the various countries use the form of enacting a municipal decree or governmental declaration to announce [the breadth of the territorial sea]. For instance, in its 1923 and 1927 Statutes on the Protection of the State Boundaries, the Soviet Union prescribed the breadth of its territorial sea as 12 nautical miles; the United States Congress enacted the 3 nautical mile breadth of the territorial sea in 1794; the Customs Consolidation Act promulgated by Great Britain in 1876 provided the 3 nautical mile breadth of the territorial sea; the statement of the Indonesian government in 1957 declared the 12 nautical mile breadth of the territorial sea; and recent statements of the governments of Iraq and Panama also declare the 12 nautical mile breadth of the territorial sea.

Since the act of determining the breadth of the territorial sea is a sovereign act of a state, such act becomes effective immediately after promulgation. It does not require the recognition of other states, nor do other states have the right to oppose.

(ii) It Is Necessary for Our Country To Declare the 12-Nautical Mile Breadth of the Territorial Sea.

In the Declaration on the Territorial Sea, our government declared that the breadth of our territorial sea shall be 12 nautical miles. This was decided completely in accordance with the concrete needs of our country. First, it was considered from the point of view of the national defense and security of our country. Our country's coastline is very long, and the southeastern coast is the door of our national defense. Imperialism always uses its fleets to engage in aggression and sabotage activities. Consequently, we must have sufficient breadth of territorial sea so as to enable us effectively to suppress the imperialist military provocations and war threats, to make it impossible for imperialist airplanes and warships to show their strength in places near our coasts or to threaten the construction of our coastal cities and villages and the security of people's life and property. Particularly in the present situation, when American imperialism occupies our territory of Taiwan by force and puts its Seventh Fleet in the Taiwan Strait to engage in military threats and provocations against our country, our regulation of a 12 nautical mile breadth of territorial sea is even more advantageous to our present struggle opposing American aggression.

Second, it was considered from the point of view of the economic interest of our country. Our country is a country with abundant aquatic resources. Aquatic products occupy a comparatively important position in the income of our national economy. There are more than 12 million fishermen on our coasts who for a long period have made their living on fishing, and the number of fish caught annually is very large and constitutes one of the important sources of food to satisfy the needs of the people. . . . Following the Great Leap Forward in our industrial and agricultural production, the exploration and use of sea resources shall be broader and broader; therefore, the resources must be more carefully protected. Now that our country has decided that our territorial sea shall be 12 nautical miles in breadth, all sea resources within the area of our territorial sea are owned by our people and only our people have the right to exploit them; any plundering acts of imperialism shall be severely suppressed. This has important significance with respect to the security and production of our fishermen, the protection of our industrial and agricultural construction and the need for preserving sea resources.

(iii) The 12-Nautical Mile Breadth of the Territorial Sea Declared by Our Country is Consistent with the Principles of International Law.

Our country's declaration of the breadth of our own territorial sea is the exercise of our sacred sovereignty and an act which is completely justifiable and consistent with the principles of international law. Moreover, the 12 nautical mile breadth of territorial sea also has a perfect basis in international law. First, it is within the scope of a state's sovereignty to declare the breadth of its territorial sea; and, second, there is no uniform breadth of territorial sea either in international law or in international practice. The United States, Great Britain, France, and other big sea powers make a great effort to claim that the breadth of territorial sea of the various countries is restricted to 3 nautical miles and cannot be exceeded by other countries. They describe the 3 nautical mile theory as the "legal breadth of territorial sea." However, their claim has encountered the opposition of a large majority of countries and has not been adopted as an accepted principle of international law. Conversely, the breadth of territorial sea for the majority of the countries of the world exceeds 3 nautical miles. Fourteen countries (excluding our country), including the Soviet Union, Indonesia, the United Arab Republic, and others, have adopted the 12 nautical mile breadth of territorial sea. Article 3 of the "Articles Concerning the Law of the Sea," adopted by the United Nations International Law Commission in its Eighth Session in 1956, provides: "The Commission recognizes that international practice is not uniform as regards the delimitation of the territorial sea." The Commission holds that international law does not permit an extension of the territorial sea beyond twelve nautical miles. In other words, the Commission holds that if the breadth of the territorial sea does not exceed 12 nautical miles it is legal. The imperialist bloc headed by the United States decried our declaration of the 12 nautical mile breadth of territorial sea, fabricating some so-called "reasons" to defame and to oppose our country. For instance, in disregard of the facts, they arbitrarily said that "the legal sphere of territorial sea is 3 nautical miles," opposed "the unilateral expansion of territorial sea," and made the senseless claim that "the United States has never recognized any claim of 12 nautical miles," [95] and so forth. Particularly, United States Secretary of State Dulles further shamelessly said: "[The breadth of the territorial sea] cannot be effected unilaterally by any nation any more than it [that is, a state] can grab territory. . . ." [96]

The so-called 3 nautical mile "rule" has never been a "legal" principle of international law. Historical facts can explain this point. Early in the seventeenth century, the Dutch jurist Grotius recognized that the control of a coastal state over the sea extends to that part of the sea which it can control from the coast. This principle was further expanded and illustrated by another Dutch jurist, Bynkershoek, in the eighteenth century. He held that the [coastal] country's authority is limited to the range of its batteries and at that time the range of batteries was approximately 3 nautical miles. This rule was therefore called the cannon shot rule. In 1872, the Italian, Galiani, also submitted a similar claim. At that time, there were some countries which actually had adopted the 3 nautical mile breadth of territorial sea in accordance with the then technical conditions. However, this rule was not considered a universal principle of international law, because, while some countries had adopted the 3 nautical mile breadth of territorial sea, many had not. For example, the Kingdom of Denmark in 1745 had decided its breadth of territorial sea was to be 4 nautical miles. Later, Sweden also adopted this limit. Since 1760 Spain has always considered its breadth of territorial sea as 6 nautical miles. This is also the breadth of territorial sea of Portugal. As a result of scientific developments the range of batteries had already exceeded 3 nautical miles, and thereby the 3-nautical-mile breadth had lost its original basis. Many bourgeois jurists also do not recognize 3 nautical miles as an accepted principle of international law. For instance, the Italian jurist Anzilotti acknowledged that "since the abolition of the cannon shot rule, an accepted rule of international law has not been formulated." [97] Even Oppenheim acknowledged that "there is still no unanimity on the breadth of the territorial sea on account of the fact that such range is day by day increasing," [98] and "technical developments in sea transport and communications, in the range of guns, and other changes have not been altogether without effect upon the three mile rule." [99] The textbook on International Law by the joint authorship of Soviet scholars (1957) also affirmatively says: "But there is no rule in International Law laying down a definite limit for territorial waters."[100] Therefore, the so-called "legal" and "traditional" 3 nautical miles is completely without any basis.

In practice, . . . in accordance with the data collected by the Secretariat of the Conference on the Law of the Sea convoked by the United Nations between February and April 1958, among the 68 states which reported their current breadth of territorial sea, only 21 states have 3 nautical miles (the United States, Japan, Britain and its Dominions, France, and the Netherlands); 3 states have 4 nautical miles (Sweden, Norway, and Finland); 1 state has 5 nautical miles (Cambodia); 12 states have 6 nautical miles (Italy, Spain, and others); 1 state has 9 nautical miles (Mexico); 1 state has 10 nautical miles (Albania); 11 states have 12 nautical miles (the Soviet Union, Bulgaria, Rumania, United Arab Republic, Indonesia, Saudi Arabia, Ecuador, Ethiopia, Guatemala, Venezuela, and Libya); 1 state has 50 kilometers (Chile); 1 state has 200 nautical miles (El Salvador). Besides, there are some states which do not indicate the breadth of their territorial sea. Therefore, only a small part of the 60-odd states have the 3 nautical mile breadth of territorial sea and the majority of states have a breadth exceeding 3 nautical miles.

When the question concerning the breadth of territorial sea was discussed at the Conference on the Law of the Sea at Geneva in 1958, there was a fierce controversy. The United States at first insisted upon the 3 nautical mile limit to territorial sea, but after encountering the opposition of a great majority of states, it was compelled to abandon its proposal and to put forward a compromise proposal of allowing a maximum breadth of 6 nautical miles. This, the Conference again failed to adopt. At the conference, the Soviet delegation put forward a reasonable proposal providing that every state has the right to determine its own breadth of territorial sea by taking into account the related historical and geographical conditions, economic interests, the interests of security and international navigation. According to existing practice, in principle a state should determine its breadth of territorial sea within the range of 3 to 12 nautical miles. The proposal submitted by India and Mexico also provided that every state has the right to determine the breadth of its territorial sea within the range of 12 nautical miles. Both proposals won the approval of many states, but were not adopted since they failed to obtain a two-thirds majority. . . . The circumstances of the discussion at the conference clearly prove that the so-called doctrine of a traditional and legal 3 nautical mile breadth of territorial sea is completely without any basis.

As a matter of fact, the United States itself has not, as it is so alleged, consistently supported the "range of 3 nautical miles." For instance, on October 16, 1864, United States Secretary of State Seward proposed to Great Britain an expansion of the breadth of its territorial sea to 5 nautical miles. In 1952, the United States member, Hudson, acknowledged before the Fourth Session of the United Nations International Law Commission that "in the present state of international law and practice, it is possible to say that the minimum width of the territorial sea of each coastal state is three marine miles, but it is not possible to say that any maximum width has been established." At the Geneva Conference on the Law of the Sea, the United States representative also put forward an opinion in favor of a 6 nautical mile breadth of territorial sea. The above-mentioned series of opinions and proposals of the United States all loudly slap the face of the United States. They clearly show that the United States has had every intention of utilizing the so-called traditional and legal "3 nautical mile breadth" to oppose the breadth of the territorial sea prescribed by our country. It is an attempt to undermine the proper right of our country to exercise its sovereignty.

As for the so-called "unilateral expansion of the territorial sea" alleged by imperialist countries headed by the United States, this is not even worthwhile refuting. As we have already stated, the determination of the breadth of the territorial sea is a sovereign act of a state, so it naturally follows that such an act does not require any negotiation or the conclusion of any treaties. For instance, the United States' declaration of its range of territorial sea in 1793 [*sic*] and Great Britain's declaration of its range of territorial sea in 1878 [*sic*] were unilateral determinations. Moreover, in 1866 Italy also unilaterally declared that the breadth of its territorial sea was 10 nautical miles (it is now 6 nautical miles); Spain and Portugal also unilaterally determined the breadth of their respective territorial seas. There are also many recent examples; for instance, India in 1953 declared the extension of its territorial sea to 6 nautical miles; Indonesia at the end of 1957 declared a 12 nautical mile limit to its territorial sea, and recently both Iraq and Panama declared a 12 nautical mile limit to the territorial sea. [All these determinations of the breadth of territorial sea] were unilateral determinations and were not "ratified" by the United States. Since the great majority of the countries of the world consider their acts to be justified, prior consultation with foreign powers is not necessary for our country to make a declaration as to its own reasonable breadth of territorial sea. It is completely groundless for the United States and other imperialist countries arbitrarily to oppose the so-called "unilateral expansion of the territorial sea."

Why does the imperialist bloc headed by the United States so enthusiastically focus on 3 nautical miles and so fiercely oppose our country's determination of our own 12 nautical mile breadth of territorial sea? The reason is very simple: Imperialism is imperialism; they have evil intentions which cannot be openly told. They desire a narrower territorial sea for other countries or no territorial sea at all so that they can freely engage in military aggression and economic plundering. The United States, Great Britain, and other imperialist countries are called "strong sea powers" and possess enormous fleets which are used as their capital to engage in aggression against other countries. If a country's territorial sea is expanded, then the aggressive activities of imperialist countries are subject to definite restrictions. . . .

III. The Question of the Methods of Delimiting Territorial Sea

(i) The Methods of Delimiting Territorial Sea.

We have stated before that territorial sea is a sea area within a definite breadth from the coast (or island or islands). Where should this breadth be measured from?

There are two methods of measuring in international law and international practice:

The first method is called the "normal baseline method," which takes the low-water mark as baseline (that is, the outermost line where the ocean tide retreats from the coast) and then measures a definite breadth of sea area as territorial sea. This is illustrated in sketch map No. 1. The AB line in the map is the low-water mark, which is also the baseline of the breadth of territorial sea. The CD line parallel to the AB line is the outer limit of territorial sea. The sea area between AB and CD is the area of territorial sea.

Another method is called the "straight baseline method," which first determines several points as base points on the mainland or coastal islands, then joins all the base points by straight lines, thus forming a broken line as the baseline of the territorial sea, and then measures outward to decide the territorial sea. This is illustrated in sketch map No. 2. A, B, C, D, E, F, G, H, and so forth, on the map are base points, and a baseline of the territorial sea is formed by the connecting straight lines between base points. The MN line parallel to the baseline of the territorial sea is the outer limit of territorial sea and the water area between the baseline and the outer limit is the territorial sea area. This method of delimiting the breadth of territorial sea is usually used by a state with a very indented or cut into coast and complicated coastal

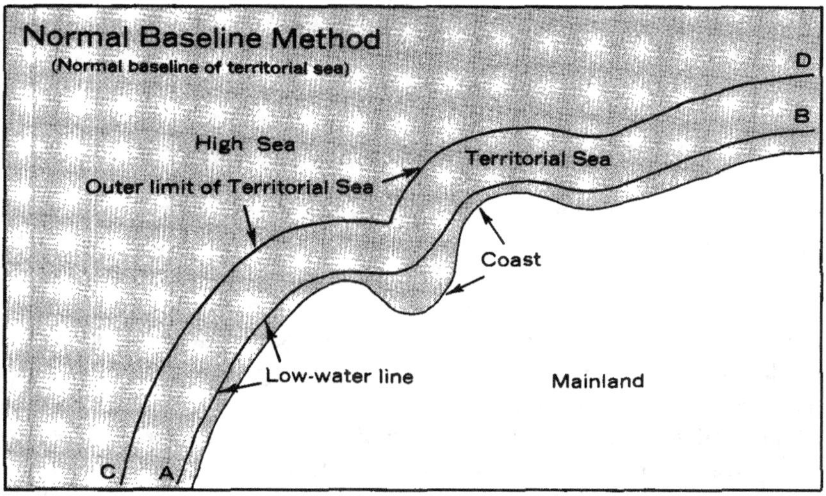
Normal Baseline Method
(Normal baseline of territorial sea)
D
B
High Sea
Territorial Sea
Outer limit of Territorial Sea
Coast
Low-water line
Mainland
C
A

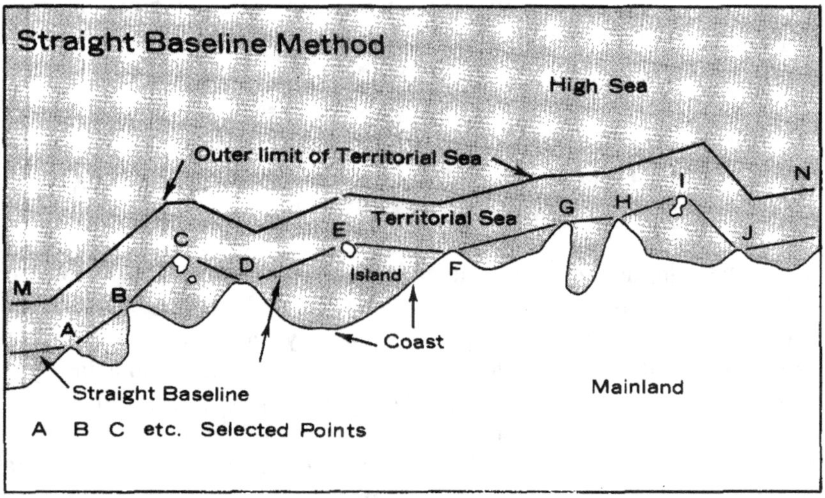
Straight Baseline Method
High Sea
Outer limit of Territorial Sea
N
I
G
H
Territorial Sea
J
C
E
D
Island
F
M
B
A
Coast
Straight Baseline
Mainland
A B C etc. Selected Points

islands. In this case the use of the normal baseline method can hardly draw an accurate boundary line of the territorial sea.

(ii) The Method Delimiting the Territorial Sea of Our Country.

In the Declaration on the Territorial Sea issued by our government, the "straight baseline method" to delimit the territorial sea is used. The Declaration states: "China's territorial sea along the mainland and its coastal islands takes as its baseline the line composed of the straight lines connecting base points on the mainland coast and on the outermost of the coastal islands; the water area extending twelve nautical miles outward from this baseline is China's territorial sea." The adoption of the straight baseline method to delimit the territorial sea declared by our government is completely based on the concrete situation of our country, because it is very difficult to adopt the normal baseline method as our coast is indented or cut into and there are many islands and sand stretches along the seacoast. The adoption of the straight baseline method will facilitate the accurate delimitation of the outer limit of the territorial sea and, at the same time, will facilitate more accurate identification of the limits of the territorial sea by navigators on the ocean and in the air.

(iii) The Adoption of the "Straight Baseline Method" to Delimit the Breadth of the Territorial Sea Declared by Our Country Is Legitimate.

The adoption of the straight baseline method as the method to delimit the baseline of territorial sea is not only consistent with the needs of the practical situation of our country, but also with principles of international law and international practice. International law provides that any sovereign state has the right, in accordance with its own concrete situation, to adopt the "normal baseline method" or the "straight baseline method" or both methods to delimit its own territorial sea. For example, the above-mentioned "Articles Concerning the Law of the Sea" provides in Article [5] that: "Where circumstances necessitate a special regime because the coast is deeply indented or cut into or because there are islands in its immediate vicinity, the baseline may be independent of the low-water mark. In these cases, the method of straight baselines joining appropriate points may be employed." The Convention on the Territorial Sea and Contiguous Zone adopted by the Geneva Conference on the Law of the Sea also provides in Article 4 that: "In localities where the coastline is deeply indented and cut into or if there is a fringe of islands along the coast in its immediate vicinity, the method of straight baselines joining appropriate points may be employed in drawing the baselines from which the breadth of the territorial sea is measured." In practice, there are some states which have adopted the straight baseline method. For example, on July 12, 1935, the King of Norway promulgated a royal decree declaring the adoption of the straight baseline method, that is, a straight line would be drawn from point to point on the outer part of coastal islands and rocks along Varangerfjord in the Arctic Ocean to Traena in the County of Nordland. In 1952 Iceland also declared the adoption of the straight baseline method. Recently Indonesia also adopted this method. Thus, the adoption of the straight baseline method by our government is reasonable and legitimate.

However, imperialist countries arbitrarily and groundlessly expressed their opposition to the adoption of the straight baseline method by our country, as they did to the 12 nautical mile breadth of territorial sea declared by our country. For example, the note sent by the British government to our government on September 13, 1958, not only refused to recognize the breadth of territorial sea declared by our country, but also opposed the method to delimit territorial sea adopted by our government. This clearly reflects the aggressive essence of imperialism. The large amount of materials in international law and international practice stated above strongly refutes the unreasonable attitude of Britain. It is particularly worthwhile to mention that Britain itself once lost a case because of its unreasonable opposition to the Norwegian adoption of the straight baseline method. The facts of the case are: As a result of the adoption by the Norwegian government in 1935 of the straight baseline method to delimit territorial sea, a substantial number of British fishing boats were subject to substantial restrictions on the right to fish in Norwegian territorial sea. On September 28, 1949, the British government instituted proceedings before the International Court of Justice against Norway on the ground that Norway had violated international law. In its application, the British government asked the Court "to declare the principles of international law to be applied in defining the baselines, by reference to which the Norwegian government is entitled to delimit a fisheries zone, extending to seaward 4 sea miles from those lines and exclusively reserved for its own nationals." However, the result of the judgment of the International Court of Justice denied the application of Britain and found "that the method employed for the delimitation of the fisheries zone by the Royal Norwegian Decree of July 12, 1935, was not contrary to international law"; and "that the baselines fixed by the said Decree in application of this method are not contrary to international law." [101]

It is clear that the International Court of Justice considers that the method adopted by Norway to delimit Norwegian territorial water and the baselines used in applying this method are all legitimate. Britain met with shameful failure in this incident of opposing the Norwegian adoption of the "straight baseline method." Now, Britain again is opposing our country's adoption of the straight baseline method; the British government will gain nothing, but it will arouse the grave indignation and severe condemnation of our people. In its reply note, our government has categorically rejected this act of naked intervention in the internal affairs of our country.

The opposition of imperialist countries to the adoption by our country of the straight baseline method in delimiting territorial sea, similar to their opposition to the 12-nautical-mile breadth of territorial sea prescribed by our country, is motivated by their imperialist aggressive ambition. They fear that this measure adopted by our country will be disadvantageous to imperialist military aggression and economic plundering. . . .

IV. Internal Sea and Internal Sea Islands

The water area within the baseline is called internal sea. . . .

Islands situated in the internal sea are called internal sea islands. Internal sea islands are also the territory of a coastal state. . . .

V. Bays and Gulfs
The Gulf of Pohai (Chihli) is China's Internal Sea Gulf

Simply speaking, sea water indented into the land is called a bay or gulf. The situation of bays or gulfs is a comparatively complicated one. The coast of a bay or gulf may belong to one state or separately belong to several states. The Persian Gulf, for example, belongs to several states; its coast separately belongs to Iraq, Iran, and Saudi Arabia, and other countries. Each state has its own territorial sea in the bay or gulf. The sea area outside the territorial sea is open sea.

With respect to the gulf or bay whose coast belongs to one state, it may be an internal gulf or bay of the state or it may be that that state has its territorial sea in the gulf or bay, but the sea area outside the gulf or bay remains open sea. In accordance with international law and international practice, a bay or gulf must possess one of the following conditions in order to constitute an internal bay or gulf:

First, in a state which adopts the straight baseline method to delimit the breadth of its territorial sea, if a bay or gulf is situated inside the baseline, then the bay or gulf is an internal bay or gulf of the state.

Second, if the distance between the low-water marks of the natural entrance points of a bay or gulf does not exceed 24 nautical miles, a line called the closing line between the two low-water mark points may be drawn. The sea area inside the closing line is internal sea and the bay or gulf thereby becomes the internal bay or gulf of the coastal state. If the mouth of a bay or gulf has many islands and thus has several entrances, each of the entrances shall be measured, respectively, in accordance with the above method.

The second method is internationally recognized. For instance, the "Convention on the Territorial Sea and Contiguous Zone," adopted by the International [Geneva] Conference on the Law of the Sea on April 29, 1958, provides: "If the distance between the low-water marks of the natural entrance points of a bay does not exceed twenty-four miles, a closing line may be drawn between these two low-water marks, and the waters enclosed thereby shall be considered as internal waters" (Article 7, paragraph 4).

Third, although the natural entrance of some bays or gulfs exceeds 24 nautical miles, if the bays or gulfs are important to the national defense and economy of the coastal states and for a long period the coastal states have repeatedly exercised jurisdiction over the bays or gulfs, they may be regarded as historical bays or gulfs. Regardless of whether or not the mouths of these bays or gulfs exceed 24 nautical miles, they may also be considered as the internal bays or gulfs of the coastal state.

International law and international practice all recognize historical bays or gulfs. For example, Article 7, paragraph 4, of the "Articles Concerning the Law of the Sea" drafted by the Eighth Session of the United Nations International Law Commission and Article 7, paragraph 6, of the "Convention on the Territorial Sea and Contiguous Zone" both expressly recognize the existence of historical bays or gulfs. There are many such instances in international practice. For instance, France [holds] the Bay of Cancale with a breadth of 17 nautical miles at the entrance as its internal bay; Norway [holds] the Varangerfjord with a breadth of 32 nautical miles at the entrance as its internal bay; Canada [holds] Hudson Bay with a breadth of 50 nautical miles at the entrance as its internal bay. These bays are all treated as the internal bays of the respective states on the ground that they are historical bays. On July 21, 1957, the government of the Soviet Union also reasserted that Peter the Great Bay was the internal sea of the Soviet Union (the width of the mouth of the bay is 120-odd nautical miles) on the ground that it is a historical bay.

Our seacoast is indented and cut into, and there are many bays and gulfs. The famous Gulf of Pohai, Hangchow Bay, Gulf of Ch'u [Pearl] River Mouth, and so forth, are important internal bays of our country. The reason for only mentioning the Gulf of Pohai in the Declaration on the Territorial Sea is that it is the largest bay among the bays of our country. Viewed from any one of the three above-stated situations, the Gulf of Pohai in every case absolutely should be an internal gulf of our country.

First, in its Declaration our government has declared the adoption of the straight baseline method to delimit our own territorial sea, and the Gulf of Pohai is completely situated inside the baseline of our territorial sea; therefore, it can only constitute an internal sea and nothing else.

Second, the mouth of the Gulf of Pohai connects the Liaotung Peninsula and the Shantung Peninsula, a distance of 45 nautical miles. However, a series of islands along the mouth constitutes eight entrances, and the largest entrance is the entrance between Liaotung Peninsula and Pei Huang Chen Island (Lao T'ieh Shan waterway), which has a breadth of 22.50 nautical miles, but is less than 24 nautical miles. Therefore, even if we use this method of measuring, the Gulf of Pohai should be considered as our internal sea.

The Gulf of Pohai is also a historical bay of our country. In several thousand years of history it has been constantly under the actual jurisdiction of our country, and not only has our country always considered it as an internal sea, but also [the fact] is internationally recognized. For instance, in 1864 when Prussia and Denmark were at war with each other, the Prussian gunboat *Gazelle* captured a Danish ship in the Gulf of Pohai; the then Chinese government protested to the Prussian government on the ground that Pohai is China's internal sea and compelled the Prussian government to free the Danish ship.[102] This is the most obvious example of international recognition, a hundred years ago, that the Gulf of Pohai is our internal sea.

The extremely important relationship of the Gulf of Pohai to the economy and national defense of our country is quite obvious. For instance, from the point of view of national defense, the Gulf of Pohai is our northern door and is quite important to the protection of our capital, Peking. . . .

VI. Straits

Chiungchow Strait is Our Internal Strait

A strait is a narrow waterway which passes through land and links two separate oceans, such as the Bosphorus Strait and the Dardanelles Strait linking the Black Sea and the Mediterranean Sea, the Strait of

Gibraltar linking the Mediterranean Sea and the Atlantic Ocean, and the Straits of Magellan linking the Atlantic Ocean and the Pacific Ocean.

There are many straits in the world, and their nature is rather complicated. Where a strait passes through land, in some cases the two shores do not belong to the same state and in other cases they do. Consequently, international law provides various regulations governing these [two] kinds of straits.

(i) In the Case Where the Land a Strait Divides Belongs To Two Separate States:

(a) If the distance between the coasts of two states is shorter than the total breadth of the territorial seas of the two states, the boundary of the territorial sea should be delimited by agreement of the two states; if there is no such agreement, the midchannel line should be the boundary unless a special situation demands that the boundary should be otherwise delimited. For example, the two shores of the Corfu Channel are respectively subject to the jurisdiction of Albania and Greece. The widest distance between the two shores of the channel is approximately 8.80 nautical miles, the narrowest distance is approximately 4.40 nautical miles, and the total breadth of the territorial seas of Albania and Greece is 16 nautical miles (the breadth of the territorial sea of Albania is 10 nautical miles, and the breadth of the territorial sea of Greece is 6 nautical miles); therefore, the boundary of the territorial sea in the channel should be decided through negotiation between Albania and Greece.

(b) If the distance between the shores of two states is wider than the total breadth of the territorial seas of the two states . . . the sea area between the territorial seas of the two states is open sea. For example, the two shores of the Strait of Malacca belong to Malaya and Indonesia, respectively; the widest distance of the strait is 110 nautical miles, the narrowest distance is approximately between 22 to 28 nautical miles, both being more than the total breadth of the territorial seas of the two states (the breadth of the territorial sea of Indonesia is 12 nautical miles and the breadth of the territorial sea of Malaya is 3 nautical miles); therefore, the sea area outside the territorial seas of the two states should be open sea.

(ii) In the Case Where Both Shores of a Strait Belong To a Single State:

(a) If the breadth of a strait does not exceed twice the breadth of the territorial sea declared by the coastal state, this kind of strait should generally be the territorial sea of the coastal state (because there is territorial sea adjacent to both shores of the strait). For example, both shores of the Solent Strait and the Menai Strait are British territory and the breadth [of these straits] does not exceed twice the breadth of the British territorial sea (the breadth of the British territorial sea is 3 nautical miles); therefore, they are both territorial straits of Britain.

(b) If the breadth of the strait is wider than twice the breadth of the territorial sea declared by the coastal state, then the sea area outside the territorial sea should be open sea. There are many straits belonging to this category, and the Taiwan Strait also conforms to this situation. Both shores of the Taiwan Strait are our territory, but the breadth of the strait is from 83 to 140 nautical miles, which is wider than twice the breadth of the territorial sea declared by our government. Therefore, the Declaration on the Territorial Sea issued by our government expressly points out that there is open sea [in the Taiwan Strait].

(c) When a coastal state adopts the straight baseline method to delimit the breadth of its territorial sea, if a strait is inside the baseline, then this strait should be the internal strait of the coastal state. Our Chiungchow Strait is this kind of strait because it is situated inside the baseline of our territorial sea. Therefore, our Declaration on the Territorial Sea declares it to be our internal sea.

Our country has many internal straits and Chiungchow Strait is only the largest among them. Since it is situated between the mainland and Hainan Island, it is an important sea route linking the mainland with Hainan Island and a convenient navigation route between our country and southeast Asian countries. It has an extremely important meaning for our economy and national defense. Historically, it has always been subject to our sovereign jurisdiction and has constituted an inalienable, composite part of our territory. Since liberation our country has always administered it as an internal strait. The present Declaration on the Territorial Sea issued by our government is merely to reaffirm once more a historical fact.

X. Our Government's Regulation Concerning the Territorial Sea Applies to All Territories of Our Country

Our government provides clearly in the Declaration on the Territorial Sea that: "The principles provided in paragraphs (2) and (3) likewise apply to Taiwan and its surrounding islands, the Penghu Islands, the Tungsha Islands, the Hsisha Islands, the Chungsha Islands, the Nansha Islands, and all other islands belonging to China." . . . The above regulation of our government is in perfect accord with the principles of international law. In accordance with international law and international practice, the islands of a state should have the same breadth of territorial sea as its mainland; the relevant laws and regulations concerning the territorial sea promulgated by that state are also perfectly applicable to the territorial sea surrounding the islands. The respect paid by other states to sovereignty over the territorial sea also includes the respect paid to sovereignty over the territorial sea surrounding islands. . . .

NOTE

In 1970 the New China News Agency began to voice strong support for the intensifying efforts of Latin American countries to win acceptance of a 200 nautical mile limit for their territorial waters. The following excerpt is typical:

> The Latin American countries have formed a united front to defend the 200 nautical mile territorial limit and to oppose firmly the schemes of US imperialism and social-imperialism to divide up and dominate the oceans, thus setting an example for small and medium-sized countries of struggling through joint efforts against the power politics of the two superpowers. In view of the intensified collusion between the two superpowers and their schemes to encroach on the sovereign rights of small- and medium-sized countries over their territorial waters and to plunder their ocean resources, more and more Latin American countries have risen in joint actions in the past year. Last year, many Latin American countries held meetings on the law of the sea—3 countries in January, 9 in May, and 21 in August. At the Lima meeting in August, 14 countries—Chile, Peru, Salvador, Ecuador, Nicaragua, Argentina, Panama, Uruguay, Brazil, Mexico, Guatemala, Honduras, Costa Rica, and Colombia—approved the "Declaration of Latin America on the Law of the Sea," reaffirming the right of various countries to establish the limits of sea sovereignty and jurisdiction in accordance with their respective geographical, biological, and geological characteristics and the need to make rational use of their resources.
>
> This year, the Latin American countries have, on the one hand, further co-ordinated their actions in the struggle in defence of the 200-nautical-mile territorial waters and, on the other hand, strived to win support from countries in Asia, Africa and other regions, so as to form a wider united front to confront the two superpowers at the so-called international conference on the law of the

> sea to be held in Geneva in 1973. In mid-January, 9 Latin American countries held another conference on defending ocean rights in Lima which stressed the necessity to unite with the Asian and African countries, and put forward the resounding slogan of "eliminating maritime colonialism." In the first half of February, 23 Latin American countries held a consultative conference and reached further agreement on questions related to the law of the sea.
>
> What is noteworthy is that in the first quarter of this year, the Latin American countries struck hard at the premeditated provocations by the United States in sending a big fleet of piratic fishing vessels to intrude into their territorial waters for plunder. They successively detained US piratical vessels which intruded into their territorial waters for illegal fishing, and had a big trial of strength with the power politics of US imperialism.[103]

Peking's support became increasingly official. For example, when, in mid-1971 some Peruvian cabinet officers visited the PRC, Premier Chou En-lai "reiterated the firm support of the government of the People's Republic of China for Peru and other Latin American countries in their struggle to persist in defending their rights over 200 nautical mile territorial waters and their maritime jurisdiction." [104]

Not long afterward, in the joint communiqué announcing its establishment of diplomatic relations with Peru, the PRC "recognize[d] the sovereignty of Peru over the maritime zone adjacent to its coasts within the limit of 200 nautical miles." [105] And the joint communiqué announcing establishment of diplomatic relations with Argentina contained a similar declaration.[106]

In the PRC's maiden speech before the UN Committee on the Peaceful Uses of the Sea-Bed and the Ocean Floor Beyond the Limits of National Jurisdiction, An Chih-yüan, its representative, stated:

> The superpowers have tried hard to find pretexts in international law for their own defence. First they asserted that "the breadth of the territorial seas of states has been defined by international law to be three nautical miles." Then, under the pressure of circumstances, they changed their tune and said that it should be "12 nautical miles." By this they attempt to attack the Latin American countries' proclamation of 200 nautical miles territorial seas as "violation of international law." But this is of no avail. As everyone with some knowledge of international law is aware, there has never been in history a unified and internationally recognized breadth of territorial seas. The breadth of the territorial sea of

> each country in the world is determined by the country itself, and this is within its state sovereignty. With regard to the breadth of territorial seas of various countries in the world, there are at present more than ten different stipulations, ranging from 3 to 200 nautical miles. What is most ridiculous, when a superpower says 3 nautical miles today, others must not say no; when tomorrow it, in collusion with the other superpower, says the breadth must not exceed 12 nautical miles, others have again to follow suit. By this logic, only the superpowers have the final say, while the other one hundred and scores of countries in the world can only submissively obey and let themselves be trampled upon at will. Can this be "international law"! It is crude violation of the principle of state sovereignty. It is imperialist logic, pure and simple. . . .
>
> We hold that it is within each country's sovereignty to decide the scope of its rights over territorial seas. All coastal countries are entitled to determine reasonably the limits of their territorial seas and jurisdiction according to their geographical conditions, taking into account the needs of their security and national economic interests and having regard for the requirement that countries situated on the same seas shall define the boundary between their territorial seas on the basis of equality and reciprocity.
>
> We maintain that all coastal countries have the right of disposal of their natural resources in their coastal seas, sea-bed, and the subsoil thereof so as to promote the well-being of their people and the development of their national economic interests.[107]

And a few weeks later Shen Wei-liang, the PRC's deputy representative, delivered the following thinly veiled attack on the Soviet Union's view of the breadth of the territorial sea before subcommittee two of the UN committee.

13-2

"Refuting Superpowers' Sophistry at the Sea-Bed and Ocean Floor Committee's Meeting," March 24, 1972, *PR* 15.13:17–18 (Mar. 31, 1972).

Some people have recently echoed the other superpower with hypocritical arguments, flagrantly attacking the just stand of the developing countries for the protection of their maritime resources and in defence of their national sovereignty and security, and openly defending the policies of aggression, plunder and hegemony. In this connection, the Chinese delegation deems it necessary to state its position.

At the recent meetings, some people tried to find a theoretical basis for the superpowers' wilful plunder of the fishery resources of other countries. They asserted that fish can live only a limited period of time, that leaving it uncaught will cause unnecessary losses, and that with the catch of fish protein which man needs will increase for the benefit of mankind. Under the cover of these fine words, they stubbornly oppose the exercise of any jurisdiction by the developing countries over the seas beyond 12 nautical miles. They even asserted that if this practice is carried out, "the interest of most of the states will suffer," and demanded that "the interests of the states the fishermen of which carry out distant water fishing be taken into account." This means that the superpowers' fishing vessels should be allowed to continue to run amuck on the seas and oceans and plunder the fishery resources of other countries. They claimed that such plunder is meritorious rather than criminal, because it can make a so-called "valuable contribution" to the solution of the question of starvation on the globe. On the other hand, they maintained that it was improper and guilty for the developing countries to take the acts of widening their territorial seas and fishery areas to defend their state sovereignty, develop their national economy and protect their maritime resources, because such acts harm the "interests of most states." It is sheer deceptive sophistry for them to claim as representing "most states" by reversing the right and wrong. The people of the world will never accept such fallacy spread by the superpowers that "it is meritorious to plunder and criminal to defend one's sovereignty."

In order to justify the superpowers' theory for plundering the fishery resources of other countries, those people have further put forth the argument that "fish does not recognize the borders imposed by man." This seems to be very plausible. However, it should be pointed out that fish recognizes neither the 200 nautical mile limit nor the 12 nautical mile limit. Therefore, this argument can in no way help the superpowers prove their claim for a 12 nautical mile limit to be more justifiable than that of 200 nautical miles, but can only make themselves an object of ridicule.

In trying to restrict the territorial seas and fishery areas of various countries within the limit of 12 nautical miles, the purpose of the superpowers is not only to facilitate their wilful plunder of maritime resources, but, what is more important, to push their hegemony over the world. In their opinion, a country which first gains control of the sea-bed will control the whole world. Consequently, apart from large numbers of ocean-going fishing vessels, they have sent out what they call "research vessels" to carry out activities everywhere and are stepping up the development of nuclear submarines and the establishment of various military installations, using the sea-bed for arms expansion and war preparation. Facts are more eloquent than words. No amount of high-sounding words about the "peaceful uses of the sea-bed and ocean floor" at the meeting can cover up their wild ambition for big-power hegemony and world domination.

Posing themselves as the protector of the landlocked countries, those people are saying profusely that they cannot ignore the deprivation of the right of dozens of landlocked countries to use the maritime resources. This is aimed at sowing discord in the relations between the landlocked and coastal countries and sabotaging the unity among the developing countries so as to extricate the superpowers from their political isolation. However, this is utterly futile. Despite the difference of geographical conditions between the landlocked and coastal countries, the countries of the third world are bound together by their common goal of opposing imperialism and colonialism and safeguarding national independence; they share the same basic interests. We believe that all the developing countries will co-operate with and support each other and arrive at a reasonable settlement of the questions between them on the basis of mutual understanding and mutual accommodation. This is borne out by the fact that during the present session, the developing countries of Asia, Africa and Latin America, through full consultation, have reached agreement on a common list of questions concerning the law of the sea. This demonstrates the developing countries' desire and determination for unity.

NOTE

The PRC's arrival in the UN and the increasing worldwide concern about the law of the sea stimulated domestic Chinese news media to devote renewed attention to international legal questions relating to the sea, as the following item illustrates.

13-3

"Answers to Readers," *Kuo-chi chih-shih* (International knowledge), No. 44, in *JMJP* (April 12, 1972), p. 6.

Recently some readers inquired about the meaning of the terms territorial sea, strait, continental shelf, high sea, ocean floor, and other terms related to the sea mentioned in the United Nations Sea-Bed Committee. Now [we] explain these terms as follows:

Territorial Sea. The territorial sea is a part of the sea area extended to a designated width from the low-water line or the selected baseline (called baseline of the territorial sea) along the entire coast of a coastal state and is under the sovereign jurisdiction of that state. At present, the width of the territorial sea of coastal states (also called littoral states) of the world is extremely inconsistent. Their width starts from 3 nautical miles and may be extended to 4, 6, 10, 12, 18, 25, 30, 130 and up to 200 nautical miles.

Strait. A narrow waterway connecting with oceans at both ends is called a strait. For instance, the Strait of Malacca connects the Pacific Ocean and the Indian Ocean, while the Strait of Gibraltar connects the Mediterranean Sea and the Atlantic Ocean.

The coast of both sides of a strait may either belong to one state or to several states. If a strait is entirely located within the baseline of the territorial sea of a state, it is an internal sea of that state. For instance, our country's Chiungchow Strait is our internal sea.

Continental Shelf. The sea-bed extends gradually downward and outward from the coast, usually with increasing declivity, to a depth at which there is a marked increase of declivity. This sea-bed area of comparatively great declivity is usually called the continental slope. The shallow sea area from the sea coast to the continental slope is called the continental shelf. Because the continental shelf is close to the continent and is not very deep, it is unusually rich in biological resources. The three largest fishing zones of the world are all located on the continental shelf. The continental shelf also contains plentiful petroleum, natural gas, and other mineral resources. Its economic value grows more important every day.

High Sea. Except for those internal seas and territorial seas which belong to the various coastal states, all oceans on the earth are regarded as high seas. The high seas are not subject to the sovereign jurisdiction of any state.

Ocean Floor. The ocean is like a basin and the deepest part of the bottom of the basin is called the ocean floor. It is a broad and flat [area] and constitutes the major portion of an ocean. Although the declivity of the deep water plain [abyssal plain] in the ocean floor is moderate, there are still some medium-sized hills which emerge toward the outer edge of the [ocean floor]. The surface of the ocean floor is covered by a not very thick layer of soft soil and below that is a hard rock layer.

Note

In addition to other attacks upon Soviet views of the law of the sea, Peking also condemned the Soviet Union for its efforts to muster support for the view that the Strait of Malacca is an international strait.

Although the following report from *Peking Review* is "unofficial" and only states the PRC's view by implication, it offers a presumably reliable indication of Peking's position.

13-4

"Malaysia and Indonesia Oppose Soviet Government's Conspiracy," *PR* 15.11:20–21 (March 17, 1972).

In collusion with the reactionary Sato government of Japan, the Soviet government recently raised the absurd idea that the Strait of Malacca should be "internationalized." The aim is to have a hand in the affairs of the strait and encroach upon the sovereignty of the states on both sides of it. This conspiracy is opposed by the governments of Malaysia and Indonesia.

A March 3 Kyodo report said that when Soviet Ambassador to Japan Troyanovsky called on Japanese Vice-Foreign Minister Haruki Mori that day he conveyed to the Sato government the Soviet government's position regarding the Strait of Malacca as an "international strait."

The Kyodo report said the Soviet ambassador told Haruki Mori that "the Soviet Union regards it as an international strait linking the high seas, through which free navigation should be allowed." He asked, "What is the opinion of the Japanese government?"

A spokesman of the Foreign Ministry of Malaysia reiterated to the press on March 6 that the Strait of Malacca is not an international strait and that Malaysia will oppose any attempt to "internationalize" it. Indonesian Foreign Minister Malik said in Djakarta on March 5 that Indonesia cannot agree with the Soviet view. He said: "The Russians can say whatever they wish but we have our own view about the Strait of Malacca."

Malaysia, Singapore, and Indonesia issued a joint statement on November 16, 1971, declaring tripartite joint responsibility for the affairs of the Strait of Malacca and the Strait of Singapore. The statement clearly stated that the two straits are not international and in order to protect the interests and rights of the states on both sides of the Strait of Malacca, it expressed opposition to any plot to "internationalize" it.

It is no accident that Soviet revisionist social-imperialism is casting a covetous eye on the Strait of Malacca, the main passage between the Indian Ocean and the South China Sea. In recent years, it has carried out frantic expansionist activities on the seas in doing all it can to build up naval hegemony in the vast area from the Black Sea, the Mediterranean, the Red Sea, the Indian Ocean, and the West Pacific to the Sea of Japan. Of late, quite a number of Soviet warships have entered the Indian Ocean through the Strait of Malacca and carried out activities which have seriously threatened the security of all countries in that area.

Peddling the "internationalization" of the strait in league with the Japanese reactionaries who claim "the Strait of Malacca is the lifeline of Japan," Soviet revisionist social-imperialism has now further exposed its ambition of expansion and aggression.

NOTE

Item 13–5 offers the PRC's most recent official formulation of its views concerning the issues that confront the third UN Conference on the Law of the Sea.

13-5

"Chinese Representative Speaks at Sub-committee of UN Sea-Bed Committee," *Hsinhua Weekly*, no. 15: 17–18 (Apr. 9, 1973).

Chinese representative Shen Wei-liang stated at the March 29th Meeting of the Sub-committee II of the UN Sea-Bed Committee that the outmoded four Geneva conventions on the law of the sea are in the interests of the superpowers in pursuing maritime hegemony. He said that the Chinese delegation resolutely supports the opinion of many small and medium-sized countries that at the third Conference on the Law of the Sea, a new and comprehensive convention should be worked out to replace the four Geneva conventions.

Shen Wei-liang pointed out that "in 1958 when the first conference on the law of the sea was held, many Asian and African countries had not yet won independence. Asian, African and Latin American countries made up only about half of the eighty-odd countries then participating in the conference. And owing to manipulation by the imperialist powers, their many reasonable propositions were not adopted. Thus, the four Geneva conventions have completely failed to reflect truly the reasonable demands of the numerous developing countries. In the decade and more since then, profound changes have taken place in the world situation. All countries, big or small, should be equal. International affairs should be settled by all countries through consultations on an equal footing. Opinions of the third world should be fully respected. The representatives of many countries have now pointed out that the four conventions do not meet the needs of our epoch and should be rewritten. This is well-founded. This just demand was reflected in the list of subjects and issues relating to the law of the sea approved last year by the sea-bed committee, which covered various topics relating to the maritime law to be discussed at the third Conference on the Law of the Sea. However, the superpowers are doing their utmost to maintain the four Geneva conventions. As everyone is aware, one of the superpowers demanded the inclusion in the list of an item entitled: 'Measures Which Must Be Taken to Ensure the Universal Participation of States in . . . The Geneva Conventions of 1958'. This attempt failed only because of the strong opposition of many countries.

"What is the real purpose of the superpowers in defending so obstinately the outmoded four Geneva conventions? The answer can be found by a mere glance at the main provisions of the four conventions."

Speaking on the convention on the territorial sea and the contiguous zone Shen Wei-liang pointed out: "The superpowers with their unbridled ambition to carve up and dominate the seas and oceans, are trying hard to narrow down the territorial seas of other coastal states. At the 1958 Conference on the Law of the Sea, the head of the delegation of a superpower attempted to impose upon other countries the three-nautical-mile breadth of the territorial sea as a so-called principle of international law. But after the conference he publicly admitted that he was opposed to a broader territorial sea not 'simply' from consideration of international law, but 'for compelling military and commercial reasons'. Because, if a broader territorial sea was agreed on, the operations of the air and naval forces of his country would be 'seriously impeded'. The other superpower opposed the three nautical mile rule, being at the time nominally for 'safeguarding the sovereignty of all states'. But as its own territorial sea was twelve nautical miles, it tried to confine those of all other countries to the same breadth. Though they held two propositions, the purpose was the same, that is, to contend for the domination of the seas and oceans."

"Another important question concerning the territorial sea is the right of passage through the territorial sea. Article 14 of the aforementioned convention provides in general terms that ships of all states shall enjoy the right of innocent passage through territorial seas. That is to say, it may be interpreted that foreign military ships enjoy the same right. This is obviously unacceptable to many countries. As is well known, legislations of many countries expressly provide that prior approval or notice is imperative for foreign military ships to pass through their territorial seas. This is a matter within the sovereignty of a coastal state—a point even admitted by the draft convention originally put forward by the international law commission. However, the above-mentioned article in the convention has actually written off at one stroke this lawful right of the coastal states. Besides, article 16 of the convention stipulates that there shall be no suspension of the innocent passage of foreign ships through straits which are used for international navigation. This blatantly deprives coastal states with such straits of the right to exercise sovereignty over their own territorial seas. Consequently, foreign warships and submarines can intrude unimpedely into the straits within the territorial sea limits of coastal states in disregard of their security. Is it not crystal clear whose interests these unjustifiable provisions serve?"

Speaking on the convention on the high seas, Shen Wei-liang said, "A small number of maritime powers have long dominated and run amuck on the seas and oceans by utilizing the so-called 'freedom of the high seas'. The convention on the high seas further stipulates explicitly the so-called 'four freedoms' of the high seas (that is, so-called freedom of passage, freedom of fishing, freedom of laying and maintenance of submarine cables or pipelines at seabed and freedom of flying over high seas—Ed.)." He said: "The 'four freedoms' of the high seas are, in essence, freedoms of superpower aggression, threat and plunder against other countries, particularly the developing countries, and freedoms of superpower hegemony and power politics. Should such 'freedoms' be permitted to continue today in the 1970's?"

Shen Wei-liang then spoke of the convention on fishing and conservation of the living resources of the high seas. He said, "Article 7 of the convention requires that measures taken by coastal states for the conservation of fishery resources 'do not discriminate in form or in fact against foreign fishermen'. This, in reality, serves to provide legal justification for the superpowers to plunder the fishery resources of other countries. At present, the one or two superpowers, relying on their maritime superiority, are dispatching large numbers of fishing fleets to wantonly intrude into the off-shore areas of other countries and plunder their fishery resources on a large scale. The above-mentioned provision serves no other purpose than to leave the door wide open to such acts of their piracy. This has been fully proved by the fact that in the last decade the annual catch of the Soviet Union from distant water fishing constitutes over three fourths of its total output."

Speaking on the convention on the continental shelf, Shen Wei-liang said, "Three out of the only seven articles forming the operative part of the convention are designed to uphold 'the freedom of the high seas'. For instance, article 3 stipulates that the rights of a coastal state over the continental shelf do not affect the legal status of the superjacent waters as high seas, or that of the air space above those waters. Article 4 includes a specific clause against impediment to the laying and maintenance of submarine cables or pipelines on the continental shelf. Under article 5, there are many more specific provisions: paragraph I stipulates that exploitation of the continental shelf must not interfere with navigation, fishing, the conservation of resources and scientific research. Paragraph 6 says that installations or devices for exploitation must not interfere with international navigation. Paragraph 8 stipulates that a coastal state shall not normally withhold its consent to the request of 'purely scientific research' into the continental shelf, etc. In a word, no one is allowed to prejudice or affect the so-called 'four freedoms' of the superpowers."

He continued, "It is worth noting that the Soviet representative stated at the conference that "if no kind of scientific research into the continental shelf could be undertaken without the consent of the coastal state, much valuable purely scientific work would be stopped.' But later the Soviet government promulgated its own legislation which prohibits surveying or any other activities on its continental shelf unless there is agreement or special permission. This double standard fully reveals the true features of a maritime overlord."

The Chinese representative said in conclusion: "The outmoded four Geneva conventions on the law of the sea are fundamentally in the interests of the superpowers in pursuing maritime hegemony and not to the advantage of the large numbers of developing countries in their just struggle to defend their sovereignty and national economic interests. If the four Geneva conventions should be taken as the basis in the forthcoming new Conference on the Law of the Sea, it would in effect mean forcing all other countries to accept the maritime overlord position of the superpowers and submit to their orders and manipulation. This is absolutely unacceptable to us. Therefore, the Chinese delegation firmly supports the opinion of the delegations of many small and medium-sized countries that at the third Conference on the Law of the Sea a new and comprehensive convention should be worked out to replace the four Geneva conventions. We are deeply convinced that this will be in the interests of the people of all countries."

Air Space and Outer Space 14

Peking's 1957 textbook on criminal law stated that, "according to internationally recognized principles, a state's territory includes . . . the territorial air space within the borders of the state (including the air space over the land, the waters, and the coasts)." [108] The PRC's practice has left no doubt that it claims territorial sovereignty over air space above both land and water belonging to China. The Chinese government has repeatedly protested intrusions by foreign military aircraft, including high altitude reconnaissance planes and weather balloons,[109] and the air force of the Chinese People's Liberation Army has frequently shot down foreign military aircraft over territorial waters and the mainland itself.[110] On the other hand, despite occasional pre-*Sputnik* statements by scholars that "there is no upper limit to the territorial air of a state," [111] practice indicates that the PRC does not claim sovereignty over superjacent space to an unlimited height. Its failure to protest against artificial earth satellites orbiting through that part of outer space that may be thought to be above its territory suggests that the PRC does not regard outer space as subject to state sovereignty. It is far from clear, however, what the PRC may regard as the dividing line between territorial air space and higher reaches.

Even though more than fifteen years have passed since *Sputnik* introduced the space age and even though Peking itself began to launch artificial earth satellites in 1970,[112] the PRC has issued no pronouncement on this subject similar to its 1958 declaration on the territorial sea. Moreover, although the difficult problems presented by the spectacular new technological achievements in space have elicited a great deal of scholarly attention in other countries, Peking's publicists have almost been silent. To our knowledge only four articles concerning space law have been published in the PRC between the advent of *Sputnik* and 1973. Two of these were tendentious political commentaries by the *People's Daily* that shed no light on the delimitation of territorial air space.[113] The third article was a translation from a Soviet legal journal.[114] Excerpts from the fourth article are reproduced here as item 14–1.[115]

14-1

Liu Tse-yung, "The Question of the Legal Status of Cosmic Space," *KCWTYC*, no. 8:45–47 (1959).

II. Does State Sovereignty Extend to Cosmic Space?

The problems which closely relate to state sovereignty, security and international peace, that is, whether state sovereignty extends to cosmic space and the related problems of the scope of a state's territorial air space and how to use cosmic space, are among the most important legal problems of cosmic space. . . .

In order to explain the problem [of whether state sovereignty extends to cosmic space], it is necessary to begin with state sovereignty over territorial air space.

State territory in a broad sense includes land, territorial sea, and territorial air space. Territorial air space refers to the space over the land territory and territorial sea. How far upward in territorial air space does state sovereignty extend? . . . The existing international law on sovereignty over air space provides: Every state has complete and exclusive sovereignty over the air space above its territory (see the Paris Convention of 1919 and the Chicago Convention of 1944). This is a universally recognized principle of international law. However, neither international treaties nor the municipal law of the various states has ever mentioned how far upward in air space above territory this sovereignty can be exercised.

In recent years, in the opinion of many international law jurists, a state's territorial air space should be limited; in other words, state sovereignty cannot be exercised in cosmic space. They have submitted the following reasons:

(1) Some consider that since no state has opposed or has regarded as a violation of its territorial air space the orbiting of artificial satellites launched by the Soviet Union and the United States at an altitude between 600 or 700 kilometers and 1,000 or more kilometers, it may be considered that such an altitude has been tacitly recognized by states as beyond the scope of air space. However, other jurists believe that the launching of artificial satellites by the Soviet Union and the United States is conducted in accordance with the scientific research project of the International Geophysical Year agreed upon among states, and, therefore, that the lack of objection by states to the orbiting in the space above them of satellites launched for peaceful purposes cannot demon-

strate that they have already recognized that such an altitude is beyond the scope of their sovereignty. We do not regard the first theory as sufficiently convincing. Nor is the second theory perfectly correct. Since not all states participated in the agreement, the lack of objection by nonparticipating states is not due to the existence of the agreement.

(2) Some base their theory upon an interpretation of existing conventions. They point to the nature of the aerial navigating apparatus (flying machines) referred to in various technical provisions of the Paris Convention of 1919 and the Chicago Convention of 1944 and say that the air space [above state territory] referred to in those conventions is not unlimited because flying machines, whether lighter than air (balloons, aerostats, and so forth) or heavier than air (the various aircraft), all depend upon air for ascent and navigation and cannot fly if there is no air or if the air is too thin. Therefore, they reach the conclusion that the sovereignty over territorial air space referred to in the existing conventions does not extend to the altitude in space in which ordinary flying machines cannot fly. We consider that this view . . . is not very persuasive, particularly since not all states are participants in these two conventions.

(3) [Some consider that] territorial air space is limited because of practical circumstances or scientific facts. For instance, a German scientist, Meier, considers that the great distance between cosmic space and land practically makes states unable effectively to exercise sovereignty over cosmic space and that such a great distance also makes the accurate demarcation of territorial air space between states impossible. If a certain incident occurs in space at such great altitude, it cannot be confidently determined in which state's space the incident actually took place. The British jurist, C. W. Jenks, holds the same view. He says that as a result of the revolution of the earth [on its own axis], a particular area of space may at one moment be above one state and at another moment above another state.[a] Therefore, in view of these circumstances, one can hardly imagine that state sovereignty can extend to the space of unlimited altitude above a state; or at least one may say that state sovereignty must lose its practical meaning at a certain altitude. From the foregoing, one may naturally reach the conclusion that the territorial air space of a state is limited and that state sovereignty cannot in fact be exercised in the space of unlimited altitude above a state. At present, the great majority of international law jurists, including jurists of socialist countries such as Korovin, Kovalev, and Galina of the Soviet Union, Machowski of Poland and Reintanz of the German Democratic Republic, all consider that

[a] C. W. Jenks, "International Law and Activities in Space," *International and Comparative Law Quarterly* (1956), pp. 99–114; A. Galina, "On the Question of Interplanetary Law," *Sovetskoe Gosudarstvo i Pravo*, no. 7:52–58 (1958).

cosmic space is beyond the scope of state sovereignty and cannot be appropriated by any state.[b]

III. How Far Upward Does the Territorial Air Space of a State Extend?

Since cosmic space is beyond the scope of a state's territorial air space, the question of the altitude of territorial air space naturally arises. However, this question has so far not yet been settled. . . .

(3) Some advocate the use of the scope of the earth's atmosphere as the criterion [for determining the altitude of territorial air space].[c] The reason is: the atmosphere of the earth is an integral part of the whole earth structure, and therefore the atmosphere above a certain state's territory is an integral component part of the state's territory and constitutes the territorial air space of that state. This seems natural; however, the upper limit of the atmosphere cannot be accurately delimited. Therefore, one cannot directly determine the specific altitude of territorial air space on the basis of [this criterion]. However, the concept of taking the atmosphere as the scope of territorial air space is basically natural and reasonable, and it is an old concept reflected in the meaning of the term "territorial air space" in various European languages. The terms "vozdushnoe prostranstvo" in Russian, "l'espace aerien" in French, "air space" in English, and "luftraum" in German, all imply "space of air." Moreover, recently many jurists, such as Korovin of the Soviet Union, and Jenks of Britain, have been frequently using the term "space beyond atmosphere" to replace the term "outer space" or "cosmic space." In view of this, the idea of using the earth's atmosphere as [a criterion for determining] the territorial air space of a state is comparatively popular among international law jurists. However, this is only a general concept and cannot be used to determine the specific altitude of territorial air space. Until the specific altitude is determined, [we] may provisionally keep this general concept and wait for future legal, reasonable, and specific provisions on altitude reached on the basis of scientific research and international negotiations.

Note

For the position adopted by the PRC on space problems following its entry into the United Nations, see item 30–5.

[b] E. Korovin, "International Status of Cosmic Space," *International Affairs* (Moscow), no. 1:53–59 (1959).

[c] For example, in 1949 Polish scholar Berezowski proposed this view. See Marek Zylicz, "Sur quelques problèmes de droit astronautique," *Revue Générale de Droit International Public*, 62.4:657, n. 10 (1958).

The Exercise of Territorial Jurisdiction

PART V

Part IV surveyed the PRC's views concerning the scope of China's territory. Part V illustrates various ways in which the regime has exercised authority within that territory. Here we confront questions such as the extent to which: the PRC seeks to control entry into and departure from Chinese territory, claims comprehensive, continuous, and exclusive control over China's resources, including its waters, air space and land masses, recognizes international restrictions upon its competence to deal with the persons and property of resident Chinese nationals, treats resident aliens differently from resident nationals, and acknowledges responsibility for injuries suffered by aliens.

Although modern international law did not make an impact upon China until the latter part of the nineteenth century, the concept of territorial jurisdiction was not unknown to traditional China. The feudal states of preimperial China recognized the exclusive competence of each state to exercise authority in its territory. For example, it was customary for envoys to obtain permission to pass through third states that lay en route to the state of their destination. Those who attempted to pass without permission were seized, and some were executed. And practices of granting asylum and ordering extradition were based on the premise of territorial jurisdiction.[1]

By the time of the T'ang dynasty (618-906) the Chinese Empire had to contend with a large number of foreign merchants, travelers, religious figures, students, and other "barbarians," and it developed a relatively comprehensive legal framework to regulate them. Foreigners who crossed into China without permission and Chinese who left China without permission were both subject to punishment. Once foreigners arrived in China, they were generally subject to the laws and customs of the empire. Foreign merchants bringing goods to China were usually required to pay a "tribute gift," and aliens had to obtain official credentials permitting them to travel and trade in China. T'ang law eventually prohibited foreigners from marrying Chinese and from owning real property in China, and, upon a foreigner's death, it subjected his other property to rather sophisticated inheritance rules. Both foreigners and Chinese who engaged in espionage in China were put to death. The T'ang exempted from Chinese law foreigners who committed crimes or brought lawsuits against persons of their own nationality; they were tried according to their own customs, laws, and modes of administering justice, under the jurisdiction of their own resident chieftain. In all other cases involving foreigners Chinese law and institutions applied, in principle if not always in practice.[2]

During the first two centuries of the Ch'ing dynasty, which was founded in 1644, the advent of European missionaries, merchants, sailors, officials, and warships in ever increasing numbers posed a far more direct challenge than foreigners had ever before presented to the traditional Chinese political and social order. The Ch'ing code prohibited the unauthorized entry of foreigners into China and provided that Chinese law should be applied to all foreigners committing offenses on Chinese territory. According to an authority on the period,[3] the emperor and his officials claimed to have an exact idea of the territorial bounds of Chinese law. Yet, in order to control the foreigners, Ch'ing rulers adopted a policy of treating them with generosity and leniency, while taking care not to allow them to disturb public order or frontier security. Although Ch'ing laws prescribed often highly detailed measures for restricting the entry, travel, contacts, and information of aliens, it also sought to establish the conditions for mutually profitable trade and peaceful foreign relations. In practice the laws, which were carefully communicated to the foreign community, were frequently not enforced with rigor. Building upon the tradition of earlier dynasties, the Ch'ing largely delegated to the leaders of the foreign community responsibility for maintaining control over their own people, and Chinese officials devised flexible procedures for facilitating the resolution of local disputes between foreigners and Chinese. Only in the most serious cases did the government impose sanctions upon alien offenders. Merchants and seamen, whose activities were confined to China's ports, usually received more lenient treatment than did missionaries, who were greatly feared because they sought to subvert the millennial traditions of the interior.

Despite Chinese self-restraint in the exercise of criminal jurisdiction over aliens, there were bitter disputes over the relatively rare cases in which jurisdiction was exercised. Finally, after the Opium War of 1839-1842, the Western powers forced China to accept the extraterritorial system. Under that system, in both theory and practice, most Westerners, and later Japanese, were exempted from responsibility to the Chinese government for a broad variety of acts committed in Chinese territory and were subject only to the jurisdiction of foreign consular officials. As the Chinese gradually familiarized themselves with international law, they became increasingly aware of the extent to which extraterritoriality was in derogation of the sovereignty that nation-states normally enjoyed. The concept of the territorial state's competence to regulate events and resources within its boundaries was, it will be recalled, one of the first principles of international law that China invoked. As the Introduction to this study pointed out, when in 1839 Commissioner Lin Tse-hsü sought to stop the British from importing opium into China, his determination to take a firm stand was strengthened by knowledge that international law gave every state a right to prohibit the entrance of foreign merchandise.[4] In 1864, even before the Chinese translation of Wheaton's textbook had been published, China successfully utilized the new learning in its protest against Prussia's seizure of a Danish vessel in China's "inner ocean."[5] In 1874 China also invoked the concept of territorial jurisdiction both in justifying Korea's firing upon a Japanese warship that had entered Korean waters without permission[6] and in arguing that Japan had no business launching a punitive expedition against the Chinese territory of Taiwan. In the latter case the Chinese government paid a large indemnity to Japan because Taiwanese aborigines had slaughtered shipwrecked Ryūkyūan sailors who had recently come under Japanese protection; China thus recognized the principle of state responsibility for injuries suffered by foreign nationals within its territory in circumstances that imply the state's negligent failure to prevent the injuries.[7]

As we have seen in the Introduction, late Ch'ing modernizers became increasingly determined to throw off the yoke of extraterritorial jurisdiction and the elaborate structure of inequitable tariff restrictions, leased territories, concessions, settlements, armed forces, communications networks, and other privileges by which the foreign powers deprived China of the ability to be master within its own borders. Ch'ing officials also vainly sought to put an end to the discriminatory application of the doctrine of state responsibility for international delinquencies, according to which the great powers made China the virtual guarantor of the security of their nationals' persons and property while at the same time refusing to comply with even the ordinary understanding of the doctrine in cases of China's claims for wrongs done to its nationals.[8] These became the principal goals of Republican statesmen, whose perseverance gradually succeeded in placing China on a plane of formal equality with other states.[9] The materials in this part reveal the PRC's evaluation of Republican accomplishments and the extent to which China's "century of humiliation" has made the revolutionary leaders in Peking determined to brook no interference with the exercise of their territorial jurisdiction.

Entry and Exit 15

Every country strives to maintain close supervision over its borders. As "the Bamboo Curtain" implies, the People's Republic, like traditional Chinese governments, has been preoccupied with insulating its people against undesired foreign influences and has been especially careful about who enters and leaves its territory.

The only constitutional prescriptions relating to entry or exit concern the right of asylum. Article 60 of the PRC's preliminary charter of government, the 1949 Common Program of the Chinese People's Political Consultative Conference, provided: "The People's Republic of China shall accord the right of asylum to foreign nationals who seek refuge in China because they have been oppressed by their own governments for supporting the people's interests and taking part in the struggle for peace and democracy." [10] The Constitution of the PRC that replaced the Common Program in 1954 contains, in Article 99, a somewhat broader formulation, one that is similar to that contained in the constitutions of the Soviet Union and the East European "people's democracies": "The People's Republic of China grants the right of asylum to any foreign national persecuted for supporting a just cause, for taking part in the peace movement, or for engaging in scientific activity." [11]

Although some foreigners sympathetic to Communist aims have been permitted to live in China, it is not possible to state the extent to which their residence there can be regarded as a formal exercise of the right of asylum. Part VI will present Peking's reaction to other states' grant of asylum to Chinese citizens who have sought refuge from the mainland government, but the following excerpt from a Chinese scholar's analysis of bourgeois theory and practice relating to aliens should be of interest:

> The bourgeois international law jurists do their best to defend the mistreatment of and discrimination against aliens by imperialism. In an attempt to dispose of just condemnation and opposition on the international scene they argue that "a state can freely decide upon the treatment of aliens." Obviously, there are other intentions behind such a theory. It is true that international law recognizes that a state has the right, in accordance

with its sovereignty, to refuse the entry of a particular alien and to adopt laws granting particular treatment to aliens. But it totally violates the principles of modern international law and the principles of equality and friendly intercourse among peoples of various countries to discriminate against aliens on the basis of race, color, nationality, religion, language and so forth in matters of entry, exit, and treatment.

Regarding such questions as expulsion, asylum, and extradition, bourgeois international law also does its best to provide bases and defenses for bourgeois discrimination against and hostility toward laboring people and progressive elements. For instance, on the question of expulsion of aliens, [bourgeois international law] never mentions the fact that most aliens expelled from capitalist countries were working people and progressive elements; rather, it intentionally invokes the right of a state to expel aliens in order to conceal the truth. In order to provide a legal basis for extradition by various capitalist countries of Communists and progressive elements engaging in peace movements, it gives a distorted interpretation of the principle of non-extradition of political criminals by saying that "whoever undermines the foundation of social order" is no political criminal. Particularly with respect to the question of the right of asylum, capitalist countries on the one hand refuse to grant asylum to political criminals subject to persecution because of their having engaged in progressive activities and on the other hand they abuse the right of asylum by sheltering reactionary elements, criminal offenders, and even war criminals who have fled from various countries, mainly from socialist countries, in order to use them to engage in subversive and destructive activities. Bourgeois international law jurists do not consider this conduct to be a violation of the principles of international law.[12]

Item 15–1 is the basic legislation currently in force that regulates the movement of foreigners into, out of, and within China. It is supplemented by other national legislation, by provincial and municipal regulations, and by agreements with other countries. For example, in addition to rules found in this chapter, detailed provisions governing entry and departure at ports and airports may be found in Chapters 17 and 18, respectively.

As item 15–1 indicates, in principle the PRC recognizes that foreign diplomats enjoy immunity from its jurisdiction. Part VII will devote extensive consideration to problems of diplomatic and consular immunity, including the vexing problem posed by Peking's refusal to grant the applications of certain foreign diplomats to leave China during the Cultural Revolution.

15-1

"Act Regulating the Entry, Exit, Transit, Residence, and Travel of Foreign Nationals" (passed at the 114th meeting of the Standing Committee of the NPC, March 13, 1964; promulgated by the Premier of the State Council, April 13, 1964), *JMJP* (Apr. 20, 1964), p. 2.

Chapter I
General Principles

Article 1: The entry into, exit from, and transit through the national boundaries of the People's Republic of China by foreign nationals as well as the residence and travel within China of such persons shall be dealt with in accordance with the provisions contained in this act.

This act is also applicable to stateless persons.

Article 2: Foreign nationals in China shall observe the laws and decrees of China.

Article 3: The entry, exit, transit, residence, and travel of foreign nationals shall be approved by the competent organs of the Chinese government.

Article 4: Chinese government organs abroad which handle applications of foreign nationals for entry, exit, and transit shall be Chinese diplomatic and consular organs.

Chinese government organs within China which handle applications for entry, exit, transit, residence, and travel of foreign nationals shall be the public security bureaus in the areas concerned. Applications by diplomatic envoys, consular officers, and the staff of diplomatic and consular organs of foreign countries in China shall be handled by the Ministry of Foreign Affairs and by alien affairs offices in the areas concerned; applications by other foreign nationals holding diplomatic or official passports shall be handled by the Ministry of Foreign Affairs, the alien affairs offices, or the public security bureaus in the areas concerned.

Article 5: Organs handling applications for entry, exit, transit, residence, and travel of foreign nationals have the authority to refuse to issue visas and certifying documents, and also the authority to cancel or declare null and void the visas or certifying documents already issued.

Article 6: Residence and travel of foreign nationals in important national defense and military localities and restricted areas shall be prohibited.

Chapter II
Entry, Exit, and Transit

Article 7: Foreign nationals who wish to enter into, exit from, or transit through [the territory of the People's Republic of China] shall apply for a visa.

Article 8: With regard to entry, exit, or transit, foreign nationals shall abide by ports of entry and exit, means of communications, and routes prescribed in the visas within the valid period as indicated. Foreign nationals entering the country may proceed only to the place of destination noted in the visas. In the course of entry, exit, or transit, no stays on the way shall be permitted without authorization.

Article 9: Foreign nationals who come under the scope of an agreement signed between the Chinese government and a foreign government concerned, which mutually exempts visa arrangements, shall proceed through open ports which the Chinese government has designated to the foreign governments. Upon entering the country, such foreign nationals should explain at national border checkpoints their places of destination, and proceed via the route and by means of communications designated at the national border checkpoints. In the course of entry, exit, or transit no stays on the way shall be permitted without authorization.

Chapter III
Residence

Article 10: Foreign nationals residing in China shall apply for residence registration within the stipulated period of time.

Article 11: Foreign nationals residing in China shall observe the household control system and register the inhabitants in the household as prescribed.

Organs, schools, enterprises, organizations, hotels, and private residents accommodating foreign nationals shall register the inhabitants as prescribed.

Article 12: Foreign nationals residing in China shall proceed to public security organs within a specified period of time designated by the public security organs to present documents for examination.

Article 13: Foreign nationals residing in China who change places of residence shall apply for certified documents of moving.

Chapter IV
Travel

Article 14: Foreign nationals who are to travel in areas out of the travel bounds set forth by city or county people's councils shall apply for documents authorizing travel within the specified period of time.

Article 15: Foreign nationals who travel shall proceed within the valid period noted in the travel documents, and in accordance with the points of travel, means of communications, and routes of travel as authorized, which shall not be altered on their own initiative. In the course of travel, no stays shall be permitted on the way without authorization.

Article 16: Public security organs shall set up checkpoints in necessary localities of passage to check on foreign nationals, or dispatch people's police to check on foreign nationals with regard to their observance of the provisions in this act. Foreign nationals shall accept such checks.

Chapter V
Punishment

Article 17: Local public security organs shall, according to the gravity of the matters involved, give foreign nationals who violate the provisions of this act punishment in the form of warning, fine, detention, orders to leave the country within a time limit, expulsion, and so forth or they shall pursue these violators for criminal responsibility according to law.

Cases of violation of the provisions of this act involving foreign nationals who enjoy diplomatic immunity shall be handled through diplomatic channels.

Chapter VI
Supplementary Rules

Article 18: Concrete measures regulating the entry, exit, transit, residence, and travel of foreign nationals shall be formulated by the Ministry of Public Security and the Ministry of Foreign Affairs.

Article 19: This act shall be in effect from the day of promulgation. The "Provisional Rules Governing the Entry, Exit, and Residence of Foreigners" promulgated by the Government Administrative Council of the Central People's Government on November 18, 1951, and the "Provisional Rules Governing Residence Registration and Issuance of Residence Certificates for Foreigners," "Provisional Rules Governing Travel of Foreigners," and "Provisional Rules Governing Exit of Foreigners" ratified by the Government Administrative Council of the Central People's Government and promulgated by the Ministry of Public Security on August 10, 1954, shall be abrogated simultaneously.

NOTE

Item 15–2 arose when American lawyer A. L. Wirin sought to visit China to gather evidence for the defense in *United States v. Powell,* a case in which three Americans were prosecuted for "sedition" for having published, in a magazine in China, material that accused the United States of waging aggression and germ warfare during the Korean war.[13]

15-2

"Americans Arrive at Shumchun," NCNA–English, Canton (Jan. 7, 1958) in *SCMP,* no. 1688:1 (Jan. 10, 1958).

Defense lawyer A. L. Wirin in the Powell case presented his American passport for entry at Shumchun yesterday afternoon. On examining the passport in which the US State Department described the Chinese People's Republic as "those portions of China . . . under Communist control," the Chinese frontier inspector pointed out to the holder that such words showed the US government's hostility toward China and said that the passport could not be accepted.

However, he told Mr. Wirin, in the light of the fact that it was not the fault of the holder and since Mr. Wirin had come from far away; "we give special consideration and grant you a visa on a separate paper and allow you to enter."

A similar statement was made by Chinese officials at the Shumchun frontier inspection post to the family members of three convicted US special agents on their arrival yesterday, as their American passports carried similar hostile words to China.

15-3
"Abolition of Visas," NCNA–English, Peking (Feb. 10, 1967), in *FBIS*, no. 30:BBB 9 (Feb. 13, 1967).

A representative of the Foreign Ministry of the People's Republic of China, in a verbal statement to the Soviet embassy here [February 10, 1967], lodged the strongest protest with the Soviet government against its unilateral scrapping of the agreements of the two countries on the abolition of visas.

The statement said that on 9 February, the deputy director of the consular bureau of the Soviet Foreign Ministry, Konzhukov, in a verbal communication to An Chih-yüan, chargé d'affaires ad interim of the Chinese embassy in the Soviet Union, said that, beginning 12 February, all Chinese citizens destined for the USSR or traveling across the territory of the USSR must obtain corresponding visas on a common basis from the embassies or consulates abroad of the USSR. Citizens of the People's Republic of China leaving the USSR must possess exit visas of the USSR.

In connection with this, the Chinese Foreign Ministry makes the following statement:

> Proposals for agreements between China and the USSR on the abolition of visas were put forward by the Soviet side at different times since 1956. Proceeding from the desire of promoting the friendship between the two peoples, the Chinese side agreed to the proposals of the Soviet side, and agreements were reached on different occasions on the abolition of visas.
>
> Now the Soviet government has unilaterally scrapped the agreements of the two countries on the abolition of visas. This is yet another serious step taken by the Soviet revisionist leading group to intensify the opposition to China, undermine the friendship between the Chinese and Soviet peoples, and worsen still further the relations between the two countries. Against this, the Chinese government lodges the strongest protest with the Soviet government. As the Soviet government has unilaterally taken this unjustifiable decision, the Chinese government decides that beginning 12 February, all Soviet citizens must obtain Chinese visas on entering, leaving, or passing through Chinese territory.

15-4

"Statement of the [PRC] Ministry of Public Health," NCNA–English, Peking (June 29, 1967) in *FBIS*, no. 127:BBB11–12 (June 30, 1967).

In connection with the unilateral scrapping of the Sino-Soviet agreement on the mutual abolition of certificates of vaccination against smallpox by the Ministry of Public Health of the USSR and its slandering of China as a smallpox and cholera infested area, the Ministry of Public Health of the People's Republic of China states the following:

According to a report by the frontier quarantine station of the People's Republic of China, the Soviet Union has unjustifiably decided that from 1 July 1967, Chinese citizens entering the Soviet Union must produce their international certificates showing vaccination against smallpox and cholera. The Soviet Ministry of Public Health is also going to make this known to the countries of the world through the World Health Organization (WHO)—an agency of the United Nations which is a tool of US imperialism. This is another grave step taken by the Soviet revisionist ruling clique in uniting with the United States to oppose China, in sabotaging still more the friendship between the Chinese and Soviet peoples and aggravating the relations between the two countries. On this score, the Ministry of Public Health of the People's Republic of China lodges the strongest protest with the Public Health Ministry of the Soviet Union.

On 28 May 1960, the Soviet Public Health Ministry proposed to the Ministry of Public Health of the People's Republic of China that the two countries sign an agreement on the mutual abolition of certificates of vaccination against smallpox. Proceeding from the desire to promote friendship between the two peoples, the Chinese side at that time agreed to the Soviet proposal. Agreement on the mutual abolition of certificates of vaccination against smallpox was then reached. Now the Soviet side has unilaterally decided that, as of 1 July 1967, Chinese citizens entering the Soviet Union must produce their smallpox vaccination certificates; this is a unilateral scrapping of the agreement between the two countries. The Soviet side must bear full responsibility for all the consequences of this action.

The Soviet revisionist ruling clique not only unilaterally scrapped the Sino-Soviet agreement on mutual abolition of certificates of vaccination against smallpox, but announced this unreasonable decision through the World Health Organization of the United Nations.

15-5

"Act on the Frontier Defense Inspection" (passed at the 155th plenary meeting of the State Council, April 30, 1965; promulgated by the Premier of the State Council, April 30, 1965), *JMJP* (May 7, 1965), p. 2.

Article 1. In order to defend the sovereignty and national security of the PRC and to facilitate the passage of persons and the means of communication and transportation for entering or leaving the country, frontier defense inspection stations are established at the harbors, airports, and national boundary [transportation] stations and small passageways which are open to the outside, and at the specially permitted arrival and departure ports.

Article 2. The frontier defense inspection stations are responsible for carrying out the frontier defense inspection of persons entering or leaving the country, their passports or other certificates for entering or leaving the country, their accompanying baggage and goods,. the means of communication and transportation for entering or leaving the country, and [the goods] they are carrying.

Article 3. The persons and the means of communication and transportation for entering or leaving the country shall pass through the harbors, airports, and national boundary [transportation] stations and small passageways which are open to the outside and at the specially permitted arrival and departure ports.

Persons entering or leaving the country shall observe the laws and decrees and the frontier defense inspection system of the PRC.

Article 4. Persons entering or leaving the country shall surrender for inspection to the frontier defense inspection stations their passports or other certificates for entering or leaving the country.

The frontier defense inspection stations shall prohibit the entrance into or departure from the country of those persons who refuse to surrender for inspection their passports or other certificates for entering or leaving the country; and persons who surrender for inspection passports or other certificates for entering or leaving the country that are not in accord with the Chinese system governing the entrance into and departure from the country shall be prohibited from entering into or departing from the country or shall be ordered to complete [their] certificates of entrance into or departure from the country.

Article 5. Persons entering or leaving the country should accept the inspection of their baggage and goods by the frontier defense inspection stations.

The frontier defense inspection stations should handle the baggage and goods of diplomatic envoys and consular officers of various countries and of other people enjoying preferential treatment in accordance with the relevant rules of the PRC.

Article 6. Captains of entering or departing vessels shall report the manifests of their crew members and passengers to the frontier defense inspection stations and accept inspection by the frontier defense inspection stations.

Crew members and other personnel wishing to embark or disembark shall surrender their valid certificates for embarkation and disembarkation to the frontier defense inspection stations for inspection and shall secure the permission of the frontier defense stations.

Entering or departing vessels, while sailing within territorial waters, harbors and bays, or rivers of the PRC, are prohibited from embarking or disembarking persons or loading or unloading cargo on the way.

In case of distress, entering or departing vessels and other foreign vessels authorized to enter harbors of the PRC which are not open to the outside shall accept the inspection of local frontier defense forces or public security organs. The above-mentioned vessels shall leave immediately upon the disappearance of the reason for entry.

Article 7. Pilots-in-command of airplanes entering or departing the country shall report the manifests of their crew members and passengers to the frontier defense inspection stations and accept the inspection of the frontier defense inspection stations.

Prior to landing at designated airports and prior to leaving the country after taking off from designated airports, entering and departing airplanes are prohibited from landing, parachuting persons, or dropping goods on the way. In case of danger or accident when airplanes are forced to make a landing, parachute persons, or drop articles on the way, the pilots-in-command shall immediately submit a detailed report of the situation and the cause to the frontier defense inspection stations or the local public security organs through the civil aviation stations.

Article 8. Upon entering or departing the country, chief train masters [chief conductors] or train masters [conductors] of railway trains shall report to the frontier defense inspection stations the number of crew members and passengers and the composition of the trains, and accept inspection by the frontier defense inspection stations.

While running between the line of national demarcation and the railway station within the national boundary of the PRC, entering and departing trains are prohibited from embarking or disembarking persons or loading or unloading cargo or from stopping on the way without a reason.

Article 9. Upon entering or departing the country, persons in charge of automobiles or other motor vehicles shall report to the frontier defense inspection stations the number of crew members and passengers and the details of the vehicles' cargo, and accept inspection by the frontier defense inspection stations.

Nonmotorized vehicles and horse transportation groups entering or departing the country shall accept the inspection of the frontier defense inspection stations.

Article 10. In the event that the vessels, airplanes, trains, automobiles, and other means of communication entering or departing the country carry persons seeking to cross the national boundary secretly or goods endangering the security of China, those in charge of the means of communication shall report immediately to the frontier defense inspection stations and wait for disposition.

Article 11. Frontier defense inspection stations shall, according to the actual circumstances of the matters involved, handle persons who violate the stipulations of this act according to law.

Article 12. This Act shall be in force from the date of promulgation.

Note

The following account describes one of the more ambitious, if unsuccessful, attempts by foreigners to enter China at a time when Americans were not yet welcome:

> The last of the six Americans who had crewed the yacht Phoenix to Shanghai and back, in a vain attempt to enter China on a goodwill mission, was released from detention at Nagasaki last week. Spurned by the Chinese, and then harassed by the Japanese immigration authorities, they had learnt the hard way that good intentions are not enough.
>
> For five days they had hovered off the Chinese coast, some 17 miles from the nearest land, pleading with Chinese coastal patrols for permission to proceed to Shanghai. But the Chinese Foreign Ministry had already decided to refuse them entry. The grounds for this decision, as relayed by the patrol boat, were that "no Americans may enter China" so long as Taiwan, China's province, remains under US occupation. The officers in charge of the two boats with which the Phoenix came into contact were prepared to debate the case—"go back and struggle at home," they

suggested—and to provide fuel and supplies for the return trip. But they were adamant that the yacht was "violating territorial waters" and that it could not proceed further. Finally one patrol boat employed threatening manoeuvres to drive the Phoenix out of Chinese waters (similar to the tactics used by Soviet gunboats against Chinese fishermen on the Ussuri River. Perhaps they train by the same manuals).

The crew of the Phoenix had excellent credentials. They included Quakers, pacifists, and one Buddhist monk, all strongly opposed to US policy in Asia. The skipper is 59-year-old Earle Reynolds, who had previously sailed his boat into US nuclear testing grounds in the Pacific, and who last year sailed to North Vietnam (where he was welcomed with open arms) with medical supplies and aid. Also on board was Professor Jonathan Mirsky of Dartmouth College, who acted as interpreter, exchanging arguments and Mao-quotations by voice-hailer with the Chinese naval patrol.[14]

From time to time foreigners enter China inadvertently. They have generally been released and returned to the border after being held for questioning for a period that has extended from days to years. In 1967, for example, two Hong Kong policemen of Chinese descent claimed to have ridden a motorcycle across the border by mistake. They were held for two months during which they were subjected to political indoctrination and were given Communist publications to read. They signed statements in which they admitted crossing the border without proper authority and attacked the Hong Kong authorities for oppressing the Chinese people under their jurisdiction. They were released according to a secret agreement in which the Hong Kong government deported five persons who had entered the British colony from China in exchange for the two policemen.[15] The People's Republic has always welcomed the return to the mainland of persons serving or living under the jurisdiction of the Republic of China on Taiwan, who are, of course, regarded not as foreigners but as Chinese nationals.[16]

The problem of exit control has proved troublesome to both the PRC and to aliens resident in China, as the following excerpts from the Sino-Indian diplomatic correspondence and the personal interview recorded in item 15–6 suggest:

In its notes of April 13 and June 30, the Indian government referred time and again to the questions of the nationality and exit of Ladakhi lamas on pilgrimage to China's Tibet Region. The

Ministry of Foreign Affairs in its note, dated December 31, 1959, reiterated that the Chinese government had never had the intention of regarding the Ladakhi lamas as Chinese. At the end of 1959 alone, more than one hundred and twenty Ladakhi lamas were given permission to leave China. According to recent reports, by the end of May this year, the great majority of Ladakhi lamas who remained in Lhasa and Shigatse on pilgrimage were also given permission one after another to leave China. Proceeding from the desire of upholding the traditional friendship between China and India, the authorities in China's Tibet Region, at the time of their departure, took the initiative in supplying them with means of transportation, and also helped those lamas in difficult economic straits by supplementing them with travelling expenses and food rations on the way. Such warm attentions of goodwill have won the praise of all Ladakhi lamas who left China, who before leaving China more than once expressed their heartfelt gratitude for the friendly solicitude shown by the authorities in China's Tibet Region. In its note, dated April 13, the Indian government also stated that it was "gratified at the arrival of some Ladakhi lamas" in India. At present, the remaining small number of Ladakhi lamas are all those who stayed behind of their own accord to continue their pilgrimage. In deference to their religious desire, the Chinese government has given them facilities to continue with their stay. The Chinese government would like to reiterate that if anyone among them wishes to apply for exit, he will likewise be given permission and friendly attentions by the Chinese government. Disregarding the incontrovertible facts mentioned above, the Indian government in its note of June 30, 1960, to the Chinese government, nonetheless raised in a self-contradictory manner the nonexistent question of the nationality of Ladakhi lamas and the question of their exit which has been smoothly settled long ago so as to pester the Chinese government unjustifiably. The Chinese government cannot but express its deep regret at this.[17]

3. Reference [to] Indian national Dawa Thondup's request for permission for his family of Chinese nationality to leave China[.] [A]ccording to the regulations of the Chinese government, a Chinese national should go through necessary exit formalities before he goes abroad. On this question Dawa Thondup not only failed to cooperate with the local authorities, [but] India unreasonably prevented his family from fulfilling the formalities for going abroad, refused to observe decrees and regulations of the Chinese government, and brazenly filled the name of his family who are of Chinese nationality in his Indian traders' cer-

tificate in an attempt to change their nationality surreptitiously and sneak them out of China. This was an offence against the law for which the Chinese authorities gave Dawa Thondup a severe reprimand. As to exit of Basang Chulma [deemed by the PRC to be a Chinese] the local authorities in regard for the union of the whole family expressed consent once again on 10 November 1959 for them to leave China and gave them facilities by allowing them to go through the exit formalities locally.[18]

See also item 25–27.

15-6
Interview

Li was an overseas Chinese from Indonesia who had gone to China in 1960 to obtain a university education. By 1962 he became disillusioned with conditions at the university to which he was assigned in the city of Tientsin, and applied to the neighborhood police station for permission to return to Indonesia. When permission was not forthcoming, he and a fellow student decided to try to leave the country by covertly crossing the China-Burma border. They traveled by rail on an ostensible sightseeing trip to Yunnan Province at the Burmese border. Soon after they left the train, in a town that was approximately a five-hour hike from the border, they were questioned by two local policemen who noted them in a restaurant. Not long afterward, as they started to walk out of town, two plainclothes officials stopped them to ask where they were going and who they were. From their appearance and accent, it was obvious that they were not natives of the region. Unimpressed by their claim to be tourists, the officials took them to the town police station, where the station chief subjected them to further interrogation and searched them. The station chief found their story implausible, especially after a search revealed possession of canned goods, knives, and other articles that suggested an intent to pass through rough countryside en route to the border. He issued warrants for their arrest and confined them in a cell for the night to think about his admonitions to confess. When the next morning the prisoners persisted in their story, the station chief transferred them to the jail maintained by the local court.

At the jail Li and his companion were put in separate cells, each of which was occupied by approximately twenty inmates. Conditions were very primitive in the cells, where the prisoners were required to work from dawn to dusk while their cases were being processed. In each cell evenings were devoted to four hours of "small group discussion" in which the inmates would criticize the mistakes in thinking and behavior that each had made in the course of the day. Nonconformists would be "struggled against" before larger groups, and hard-core recalcitrants would be subjected to handcuffs and leg irons.

On the day after his arrival at the jail, Li was summoned for interrogation by a plainclothes public security officer, who spent 45 minutes probing Li's motives in seeking to cross the border. Li denied the accusation that he had hoped to join the irregular units of the Nationalist Chinese Army that continue to inhabit remote areas of Burma near the Chinese border, and he confessed to nothing. The interrogator, whose attitude was very harsh, gave Li three days "to think it over." A second interrogation focused on Li's behavior back in Tientsin. After a week's interlude a third interrogation sought to determine whether Li's attempt to sneak across the border had been aided by others and whether an anti-Communist conspiracy existed. It also explored the political views of Li and his companion in order to ascertain whether they harbored counterrevolutionary thoughts. Although Li admitted having complained about difficult living conditions, he denied any anti-Communist sentiments and still refused to confess to attempted border crossing.

He subsequently decided that further resistance was futile, however. Four days later, when summoned for another interrogation, he admitted attempting to leave the country illegally and said that the training and thought reform he had received while in jail had led him to see the error of his ways. Li promised to study hard and lead a better life if given an opportunity to redeem himself. The interrogator expressed satisfaction at Li's change of heart and told him to spend the next three evenings writing a detailed report about his crime, his thought reform, and his plans for the future. About a week after he submitted this report, he was summoned for yet another interrogation, this one by the Secretary of the Communist Youth League unit at his university and by two public security officers from Tientsin, who wanted to know how he had acquired funds to reach Yunnan and ration books that were honored all over China. They asked him to submit a written report on these questions.

A few days after he prepared this report, at a meeting of all the inmates of the jail, Li's case was one of four discussed. It was announced that he had committed the crime of "betrayal of the motherland" (*pei-p'an tsu-kuo*) by attempting to reject China and to cross the border illegally and that he could be sentenced to twenty years in prison or to death. [Article 11 of the "Act of the PRC for Punishment of Counterrevolution" (see Note following item 19–7) provides that "Those who, with a counterrevolutionary purpose, secretly cross the borders of the state shall be punished by not less than five years of imprisonment, life imprisonment, or death."] However, because he had confessed, recognized his wrongdoing, and promised to reform, he was going to be released to continue his study. After returning to the university in Tientsin, Li again applied for permission to return to Indonesia, and three months later it was granted.

NOTE

Li was interviewed in October 1963 in Macao, where he was awaiting the Indonesian government's permission to return. Part VI will deal with the status of overseas Chinese, especially those in Indonesia.

Foreign residents of China who do not enjoy diplomatic immunity have often had difficulty in obtaining permission to leave the country. Some have been forcibly detained on charges of violating the criminal law, as Chapter 19 will demonstrate. Others have been detained by virtue of "noncriminal" administrative measures, as illustrated in Chapter 21. Some of these foreigners have been held under informal "house arrest" (21–14 and Note following 21–10). More often, they have simply been denied exit visas for extended periods (21–9 and Note following 21–10).

Of course, when the regime has deemed it politically propitious, it has not hesitated to deport or expel foreigners, including those whom it has previously been detaining. This frequently follows criminal conviction (see 19–8, 19–11, 19–16, and 19–21), but those who have not run afoul of the criminal process may also be promptly ousted (21–13).

As in item 15–6, overseas Chinese who have served a criminal sentence are often permitted to choose whether to stay in China or to return to the country of their previous residence (19–4).

Covert departure from the country by small numbers of persons, such as those in item 15–6, who were simply intent upon trying their luck elsewhere, is, of course, less of a concern to the PRC than illegal border crossings by armed groups. Item 15–8, from a secret Chinese military journal obtained by American intelligence services, illustrates the PRC's abiding concern to suppress groups of armed rebels that operate in remote border regions, sometimes receiving aid from abroad and sometimes themselves crossing into neighboring countries for shelter, supplies, and training before covertly returning to China.

The following item was the PRC's response to Japan's efforts to secure the repatriation of Japanese nationals detained in or otherwise residing in China.

15-7

"Foreign Ministry Communiqué on Sino-Japanese Talks," NCNA–English, Peking (Feb. 11, 1956), in *SCMP*, no. 1230:27 (Feb. 17, 1956). (The following is a statement of the spokesman of the PRC Foreign Ministry issued on August 16, 1955. This statement was attached to the PRC Foreign Ministry's Communiqué issued on February 11, 1956.)

Japanese civilians residing in China who desire to return to Japan have always been provided facilities by the government of the People's Republic of China. By the end of March 1955, out of the original total of about 35,000 Japanese civilians, about 29,000 who desired to return to Japan had done so through the joint efforts of the Red Cross Society of China and the Red Cross Society of Japan, the Japan-China Friendship Association and the Japan Peace Liaison Council. There are [over] 6,000 Japanese civilians who are still residing in China. They have expressed their desire to reside in China permanently or for the time being. Should any of them change their mind and apply for returning to Japan, the Chinese government will still provide them facilities; and the Red Cross Society of China will also give them assistance as it best can. This was agreed upon between the delegation of the Red Cross Society of China and the Red Cross Society of Japan and other Japanese organizations when the former visited Japan. Nevertheless, the Japanese government now made the complaint that allegedly "there was no more progress on the question of evacuating civilians." This complaint is completely groundless. On the other hand, there are tens of thousands of Chinese civilians residing in Japan whose legitimate rights and interests have not been properly cared for, whose contacts with their fatherland and families are still being obstructed and who have no facilities to return to China. In can thus be seen that, so far as matters of Chinese and Japanese civilians are concerned, what awaits negotiation and settlement is not the question of Japanese civilians residing in China, but the question of Chinese civilians residing in Japan.

Next, regarding the question of Japanese war criminals. We have already stated that we are prepared to deal with them in accordance with a policy of clemency. In August 1954, 417 former Japanese military men who committed various crimes during the Japanese war of aggression against China and the Chinese people's liberation war were exempted from punishment and returned to Japan. Thereafter, the Red Cross Society of China further provided the Red Cross Society of Japan with a namelist of 1,069 war criminals and information concerning their conditions. These war criminals will be dealt with by the government of the People's Republic of China in accordance with Chinese juridical procedures. This is a matter of Chinese sovereign rights, in which the Japanese government has no right to interfere.

Apart from the above-mentioned Japanese civilians and war criminals, there are here in China no such Japanese whose situation is unknown. However, the Japanese government raised the so-called question of 40,000 Japanese of unknown situation; this cannot but be surprising. The Japanese militarists pressed a great number of Japanese to take part in the war of aggression against China, during which many Japanese died in China. The certain death of some of the Japanese has perhaps not been [made known to] their relatives by the Japanese government up to now. The concern of the relatives for their cases is quite natural, and calls for sympathy. The Red Cross Society of China, upon humanitarian principles . . . reached an agreement with the Red Cross Society of Japan and other Japanese organizations on the question of investigating the fate of individual Japanese, that is, if the Red Cross Society of Japan submitted concrete data, the Red Cross Society of China was ready to carry out investigations as far as possible. But it should be pointed out that this was an expression of the Chinese people's friendship towards the Japanese people and has nothing to do with the so-called question of 40,000 Japanese of unknown situation remaining on the Chinese mainland as alleged by the Japanese government.

15-8

"An Outline of the 1961 Plan for the Work of Building Up National Defense," *Kung-tso t'ung-hsün* (Bulletin of Activities), No. 7 (Feb. 1, 1961) [secret; dispatched to regimental level], published by the General Political Department of the Chinese People's Liberation Army; English translation by J. Chester Cheng *et al.*, eds., *The Politics of the Chinese Red Army: A Translation of the Bulletin of Activities of the PLA* (Stanford, Calif.: The Hoover Institution on War, Revolution, and Peace, 1966), pp. 190–191.

E. Continue To Fight the Rebels and Aim to Destroy Them

In Kansu, Chinghai, Szechwan, Tibet, and Yunnan, and in some other places armed rebels, after we spent the whole of last year to destroy them, have already been reduced to submission. There are still, however, about 3,000 scattered and roaming about. This is a great victory in our drive against them. This year, although there are not many bandits left, most of them are leaders of the most rabid of the rebels, familiar with the terrain, equipped with combat experience against us; we at the same time have even calculated that, because superior fighting skill had not yet developed far enough in some places owing to insufficient training and [because] the counterrevolutionaries inside had not been purged, the counterrevolutionaries outside were still in communication with those inside, and there is in some places the danger of repeated uprisings and new uprisings. In addition, rebels who had escaped abroad may return for further action. Therefore there must be no lightening of our hold upon them.

The suppression of the rebellion in 1961 ought to carry through thoroughly the direction already set, especially to arouse the people and absorb the experience of last year. We should organize a few more expeditions to surround the rebels or search them out and try to destroy all the rebels and bandits. All the military units which joined the suppression should energetically spread the usefulness of the working teams, and, under the unified leadership of the local party committee, develop the work among the people with great energy.

In places near the border of neighboring countries, as the Sino-Indian border, the Sino-Nepalese border, and the Sino-Sikkim border, while proceeding with military action against the bandits, we must strictly respect the ruling not to exceed the limit of entry into the neighboring country beyond 20 kilometers. Regarding bandits returning from abroad to fight, we must also strictly observe the principles contained in the Southwest Region Border Defense Regulations promulgated by the Military Affairs Commission, together with the rulings of the eight documents.

F. We Must Continue To Preserve Our Southwest and Northwest Border, and Gradually Strengthen Various Kinds of Work for the Building Up of a National Defense System

1. We must work hard to make our Southwest and Northwest regional borders peaceful and secure. This is the best way to settle the problem of our border regions. Therefore, all those army units which are responsible for the peace and security of the border must continue to see through deeply and clearly the Southwest Region Border Defense Regulations promulgated by the Military Affairs Commission, together with the rulings of the eight documents, and according to these regulations strictly respect and put them into operation.

2. In the neighboring countries (including fraternal nations and nationalistic countries) if and when in these border regions there occurs any international incident, it is required to report quickly to superiors and await the decision and orders, if any. Under no circumstances should an officer upon his own personal responsibility take steps to carry out an unauthorized decision.

3. In the border regions involving friendly foreign countries, our military units may carry on recreational activities with them, but ought to invite each other properly before the event and go through thorough and proper preparations in order to get better results.

4. If there are questions concerning building up border defense which need solution, it should be ascertained whether they be serious or light, slow or urgent, and [they] should be quickly settled according to a plan.

Internal and Territorial Waters 16

One of the many symbols of China's "century of humiliation" was gunboat diplomacy in which the warships of various countries plied China's territorial and internal waters to back up the political and economic demands of their respective governments. Item 16–1 suggests the extent to which the Chinese Communists feel themselves the heirs to this bitter national heritage and are bent upon obliterating it.

16-1

Mao Tse-tung, "On the Outrages by British Warships[a]—Statement by the Spokesman of the General Headquarters of the Chinese People's Liberation Army"[b] (April 30, 1949), in *Selected Works*, IV (Peking: Foreign Languages Press, 1961), pp. 401–403.

We denounce the preposterous statement of the warmonger Churchill.[c] In the British House of Commons on April 26, Churchill

[a] On April 20–21, 1949, while the People's Liberation Army was fighting its way across the Yangtse, the *Amethyst* and three other British warships intruded into the river, an inland waterway of China, and, together with Kuomintang warships, fired on our army, causing 252 casualties. The People's Liberation Army returned the fire; the *Amethyst* was disabled and forced to anchor near Chinkiang; the other three British warships escaped. The British authorities requested that the *Amethyst* should be allowed to leave, and its captain, acting on the orders of Brind, Commander-in-Chief of the British Far Eastern Fleet, conducted negotiations with the representative of our army. During these negotiations, the British side consistently prevaricated and refused to admit its criminal acts of aggression. While the negotiations were continuing, on the night of July 30, the *Amethyst* forced her way alongside a passenger ship, the *Liberated Chiangling,* which was going downstream off Chinkiang, and escaped by using that ship as a shield. When our army signalled a warning to the *Amethyst* to stop, she opened fire, collided with and sank a number of junks, and escaped from the Yangtse River.

[b] This statement was drafted by Comrade Mao Tse-Tung for the spokesman of the General Headquarters of the Chinese People's Liberation Army. It expressed the solemn stand of the Chinese people who fear no threats and resolutely oppose imperialist aggression; it also set forth the foreign policy of the new China which was soon to be established.

[c] On April 26, 1949, speaking in the British House of Commons, Churchill, the chieftain of the British Conservative Party, slandered as an "atrocious outrage" the action taken by the Chinese People's Liberation Army in counterattacking the

demanded that the British government should send two aircraft carriers to the Far East for "effective power of retaliation." What are you "retaliating" for, Mr. Churchill? British warships, together with Kuomintang warships, intruded into the defense area of the Chinese People's Liberation Army and fired on the People's Liberation Army, causing no less than 252 casualties among our loyal and gallant fighters. Since the British have trespassed on Chinese territory and committed so great a crime, the People's Liberation Army has good reason to demand that the British government admit its wrongdoing, apologize, and make compensation. Isn't this what you should do, instead of dispatching forces to China to "retaliate" against the Chinese People's Liberation Army? Prime Minister Attlee's statement is also wrong.[d] Britain, he said, has the right to send her warships into China's Yangtse River. The Yangtse is an inland waterway of China. What right have you British to send in your warships? You have no such right. The Chinese people will defend their territory and sovereignty and absolutely will not permit encroachment by foreign governments. . . . The People's Liberation Army demands that Britain, the United States, and France quickly withdraw their armed forces—their warships, military aircraft, and marines stationed in the Yangtse and Whangpoo Rivers and other parts of China —from China's territorial inland waters, seas, land, and air and that they refrain from helping the enemy of the Chinese people to wage civil war.

16-2

Fu Chu, *Kuan-yü wo-kuo ti ling-hai wen-t'i* (Concerning the question of our country's territorial sea) (Peking, 1959), pp. 15–16, 21–26.

In international law there are similarities and differences between internal sea and territorial sea. For instance, they are both composite parts of the territory of the coastal state and are subject to the sovereign jurisdiction of the coastal state. These are the similarities. The main differences are: Foreign merchant vessels can innocently pass through

---

British warships which had fired on our army, and demanded that the British government "get in Chinese waters one aircraft carrier, if not two, capable of . . . effective power of retaliation."

[d] On April 26, 1949, British Prime Minister Attlee declared in the House of Commons that British naval vessels had been within their rights in going up the Yangtse on their "peaceful missions," because they had the permission of the Kuomintang government of China. At the same time, when speaking about the negotiations which the British representative was holding with the representative of the Chinese People's Liberation Army, Attlee lied, saying that the Chinese People's Liberation Army "would be prepared to allow the ship [the *Amethyst*] to proceed to Nanking, but only on condition that she should assist the People's Liberation Army to cross the Yangtse."

the territorial sea of another state under the condition of observing the laws and regulations of the coastal state. However, the entry of foreign merchant vessels into the internal sea of another state must have the prior permission of that state. The different regulations are due to the fact that the territorial sea immediately connects with the open sea and thereby is related in an important way with sea communication. In order to facilitate navigation and economic intercourse among various states, international law recognizes that foreign merchant vessels can innocently pass through the territorial sea of another state. This is not the situation in the case of the internal sea, which is separated [from the open sea] by the territorial sea. . . .

VII. The Coastal State Has the Right to Enact Laws, Orders and Regulations Concerning Its Territorial Sea

The laws, orders, and regulations which should be observed by ships passing through the territorial sea are to be enacted by the coastal state. The coastal state generally enacts them in the form of municipal law.

As the territorial sea is territory under the sovereign jurisdiction of the coastal state, the enactment of laws, orders, and regulations effective within its own territory should be the necessary consequence of the exercise of sovereignty by the coastal state. Any ship, whether it is a national or foreign ship, passing through the territorial sea should observe all the relevant laws, orders, and regulations promulgated by the coastal state. All violations and undermining acts are acts infringing on the sovereignty of the coastal state, and [the latter] has the right to adopt all necessary measures to rectify them.

At present the various states of the world have already enacted many laws and orders of this category, including navigation, trade, customs, and sanitary, security, and other laws. If necessary, the coastal state can at any time enact new laws and orders or amend or repeal old laws and orders. . . .

In order to protect our sovereignty over the territorial sea more effectively, our government has enacted some laws and orders such as a Customs Law, Provisional Regulations Governing Harbors, Regulations Governing Foreign Vessels Leaving and Entering Ports, and Regulations on Frontier Sanitation and Inspection. On September 4, 1958, our government, in the Declaration on the Territorial Sea, made clear regulations on the system which should be observed by foreign vessels and aircraft entering our territorial sea and the territorial air space above the territorial sea. All foreign vessels and aircraft entering our territorial sea and the territorial air space above the territorial sea must observe these regulations without the slightest violation. . . .

VIII. The Entry of Foreign Aircraft or Warships into Our Territorial Sea and the Territorial Air Space above Our Territorial Sea Must Be with Prior Permission

Our government provides in its Declaration on the Territorial Sea that: "No foreign vessels for military use and no foreign aircraft may enter China's territorial sea and the air space above it without the permission of the Government of the People's Republic of China." This provision has very great significance for the protection of the national defense and security of our country. . . .

This provision has an excellent basis in international law and international practice.

First, since international law recognizes that state sovereignty extends to the territorial sea and the territorial air space above the territorial sea, it is a quite natural and indisputable right of the coastal state, for the sake of its own security, to require all foreign aircraft and vessels for military use to have prior permission before entering its territorial sea. Any state which really respects the sovereignty and territorial integrity of other states should respect the exercise of this right by the coastal state.

Second, in international practice, a number of states have provisions in their municipal law which are similar to those provided in our Declaration on the Territorial Sea. For instance, on March 28, 1931, the Soviet Union promulgated the Provisional Regulations Governing the Entry of Foreign Warships into Soviet Waters (including territorial sea and internal sea), which provides that prior consent is required for the entry of foreign warships into the Soviet territorial sea. . . . In addition to the Soviet Union, other socialist states such as Bulgaria and Albania, and also states such as Indonesia, the United Arab Republic, and Turkey all have the same regulations.

Of course, some states permit the unconditional passage of foreign warships [through their territorial sea]; others provide that prior notification, but not permission, is necessary. These provisions are enactments of municipal law in accordance with the interests of the respective states and are an expression of the exercise of their sovereignty. Whenever it is considered necessary, a state also has the right to cancel or amend the original provisions.

Imperialism raises the so-called "right of innocent passage" of warships in an attempt to deny our exercise of sovereignty and to get certain advantages for themselves. An example of this is the [recent] note of British imperialism to our government. This is, of course, an intemperate illusion, which can never be realized.

First, it must be pointed out that our government's regulation is a proper exercise of state sovereignty, which does not require the consent and permission of any imperialists. Whether you agree or disagree, the above regulation must be strictly executed. If imperialist bandits attempt to undermine [our regulation], they themselves will be in trouble.

In practice, the so-called "right of innocent passage" of foreign warships advocated by the imperialists has never been an accepted principle of international law. For instance, Article 24 of the "Articles Concerning the Law of the Sea" expressly provides: "The coastal state may make the passage of warships through the territorial sea subject to previous authorization or notification." Many bourgeois scholars of international law also hold the same opinion. For instance, the British scholar Hall long ago denied that foreign warships enjoy the "right of innocent passage." Another famous British international law scholar, Oppenheim, also writes . . . : "A right for the men-of-war of foreign states to pass unhindered through the maritime belt is not generally recognized."[19] In view of this, the "right of innocent passage" of warships claimed by imperialists is absolutely without basis and cannot stand on its own feet in international law; it only further exposes the imperialists' aggressive aims.

With respect to foreign aircraft, all international air conventions uniformly confirm that no foreign aircraft has a right of innocent passage through the air space above the territorial waters. This is [due to the fact] that, if aircraft are used as tools of aggression, they present greater danger than warships to the national defense and security of the coastal state.

IX. Any Foreign Vessel Must Observe the Laws and Regulations of Our Country While Navigating Our Territorial Sea

The Declaration on the Territorial Sea promulgated by our government further provides: "While navigating Chinese territorial sea, every foreign vessel must observe the relevant laws and regulations laid down by the government of the People's Republic of China." The term "every foreign vessel" also includes, except for foreign warships and aircraft which have acquired prior permission to pass through our territorial sea, foreign merchant ships. We will discuss below the question of the passage of foreign merchant ships through territorial sea.

We have stated before that international law recognizes that foreign merchant ships enjoy the right of innocent passage through territorial sea. However, this right is not unconditional and unrestricted. For example, the passage must be innocent. Simply speaking, so-called innocent passage requires that the ship refrain from doing any act which will impair the economic interest and national defense and security of the coastal state; otherwise, it is not innocent but injurious. For instance, imperialists often use the opportunity of their merchant ships passing through the territorial sea of the coastal state to smuggle, avoid taxes, dispatch special agents, collect intelligence and so forth. Such acts obviously cannot be considered innocent passage. In these circumstances, the coastal state, in order to protect its own interest, has a perfect right to adopt all necessary measures to suppress or refuse to permit the passage of foreign merchant vessels.

Second, in the course of passing through the territorial sea of another state, foreign merchant vessels should observe the relevant laws and decrees enacted by the coastal state. . . . With respect to this, the Declaration on the Territorial Sea issued by our government has a clear provision providing that the passage of foreign merchant vessels through our territorial sea must be under the condition of "observ[ing] the relevant laws and regulations laid down by the government of the People's Republic of China"; otherwise, no passage is allowed. . . . This regulation by our country is perfectly in accord with Article 17 of the [1958 Geneva] "Convention on the Territorial Sea and Contiguous Zone." It provides: "Foreign ships exercising the right of innocent passage shall comply with the laws and regulations enacted by the coastal state . . . and, in particular, with such laws and regulations relating to transport and navigation."

All civil and criminal cases occurring in the course of passage through the territorial sea of a state by foreign merchant ships should be in principle subject to the jurisdiction of the coastal state. The courts or other relevant organs of the coastal state have the right to deal with these cases according to its own law. . . .

In order to meet the needs of national defense and security, the coastal state can delimit a particular area within its own territorial sea as a prohibited zone, refusing passage through it to all vessels. Once a prohibited zone is delimited, [the coastal state] should notify all relevant parties by appropriate means. While navigating through the territorial sea, foreign merchant vessels cannot enter the prohibited zone, but must make a detour. The coast guard or relevant authorities can fire at a violator without previous warning; the violating ship should bear all the consequences of violating the regime of the prohibited zone.

Establishment of a prohibited zone within a state's territorial sea is an act within the scope of the sovereignty of the coastal state; it does not require the consent of other states, nor do other states have the right to express opposition.

Note

Fu Chu does not refer to the fact that the PRC had already proclaimed certain areas within its territorial sea as military zones in which all foreign merchant vessels were either prohibited from navigation or permitted to enter only upon prior authorization. (See item 16–7 and the Note that follows it.)

The PRC was not invited to participate in either the International Law Commission's preparation of Draft Articles on the Law of the Sea or the 1958 Geneva Conference that considered the Draft Articles. Moreover, the PRC has never attempted to accede to the Convention on the Territorial Sea and Contiguous Zone that was signed at Geneva. Nevertheless, the PRC's Declaration on the Territorial Sea and the gloss that Chinese scholars have put upon it have obviously taken careful account of these international efforts. On many questions Peking's position follows that adopted in the Convention. In certain respects, however, Peking has departed from the rules set forth in the Convention.

Fu Chu, the author of item 16–2, tells us that Article 24 of the ILC's Draft Articles expressly provided that, "The coastal state may make the passage of warships through the territorial sea subject to previous authorization or notification." But he does not tell us that at Geneva this article was deleted from the Convention over the vigorous objections of the Soviet Union, which acceded to the Convention with a reservation on this important principle.[20] Another Chinese scholar, Liu Tse-yung, faced the problem more candidly. He wrote:

> At the Conference on the Law of the Sea held this year, this article was deleted. Nevertheless, all vessels of foreign states, including men-of-war, in passing the territorial sea, must observe the relevant laws and regulations of the coastal state; this is a principle generally accepted by all nations, and it is also stipulated in the convention adopted by the Conference on the Law of the Sea. Therefore, if the coastal state provides that the passage of foreign military vessels through its territorial sea must have its approval beforehand, they must not enter its territorial sea before they are permitted. . . . The provisions on this question embodied in the recent declaration of the Chinese government are most necessary and in full conformity with the law.[21]

Fu Chu pointed out that the PRC was not alone in supporting the Soviet position on this question. At Geneva a number of states filed reservations similar to the USSR's. And an authoritative study has concluded that "the support of the Soviet view by many nations at the Geneva Conference which did not enter reservations . . . suggests that no international consensus has been reached on the passage of warships, notwithstanding a strict reading of the Convention." [22]

Article 19 of the Convention precludes the coastal state from exercising jurisdiction over any crimes committed on board foreign ships during their passage through territorial waters except in specified cases such as those where the consequences of the crime extend to the coastal state or to the good order of its territorial sea. Fu Chu, on the other hand, asserts for the PRC full jurisdiction, at least in principle, over both criminal and civil cases arising on foreign merchant ships in the course of passage through the territorial sea.

Item 16–3 suggests that another important difference between the PRC's position and that of the Convention on the Territorial Sea and Contiguous Zone concerns jurisdiction over straits. A knowledgeable commentator has described the Chiungchow strait as being

> near the southern end of the Chinese coast, separating the Leichow Peninsula and Hainan Island and linking the South China Sea with the Gulf of Tonkin. It is about 50 miles long and from 9.8 to 19 miles wide. The Strait has been the main shipping route between Hong Kong and Haiphong, and will probably become part of a major highway for international traffic for a much broader area, since Communist China has been building a major port at Chankiang on the Leichow Peninsula to serve Southeast Asia and the route to Europe.[23]

16-3

"Rules Regulating Passage of Foreign Nonmilitary Vessels Through the Chiungchow Strait" (passed at the 145th plenary meeting of the State Council, June 5, 1964; promulgated and put into effect by the Premier of the State Council, June 28, 1964), *JMJP* (June 28, 1964), p. 2.

Article 1. According to the "Declaration on the Territorial Sea of the government of the People's Republic of China," Chiungchow Strait is China's internal sea. No foreign military vessels are allowed to pass through it, and all foreign nonmilitary vessels, if they need to pass through, must apply for approval in accordance with these Rules.

Article 2. For the convenience of exercising control over the

Chiungchow Strait, the "Chiungchow Strait Administration of the People's Republic of China" is established. (Hereafter referred to simply as Chiungchow Strait Administration.)

The execution of these rules shall be supervised by the Chiungchow Strait Administration.

Article 3. The area under the control of the Chiungchow Strait Administration (hereafter simply referred to as the administrative area) is provisionally decided as follows: Water areas west of the line (referred to simply as east line) drawn between the Mu-lan-tao light post (about 20 degrees, 9 minutes, 37 seconds north latitude and 110 degrees, 41 minutes east longitude) and Sheng-kou-hou-sha light post (about 20 degrees, 26 minutes north latitude and 110 degrees, 30 minutes, 22 seconds east longitude), and east of the line (referred to simply as west line) drawn between the Chiao-wei-chiao light post (about 20 degrees, 13 minutes, 30 seconds north latitude and 109 degrees, 55 minutes, 30 seconds east longitude) and the Lin-kao-chiao light post (about 20 degrees, zero minutes, 22 seconds north latitude and 109 degrees, 42 minutes, 6 seconds east longitude).

Article 4. If foreign nonmilitary vessels need to pass through the Chiungchow Strait, the following procedures must be followed:

(1) Forty-eight hours prior to the vessel's entry into the administrative area or prior to the vessel's departure from a port, it must cable the Chiungchow Strait Administration the details about its name, nationality, tonnage, speed, color of the body of the ship, and smokestack marks, as well as the date and time and the name of the place of embarkation and disembarkation, and request [approval] to pass through the strait.

(2) After receiving notification of approval to pass through the strait, the vessel should definitely report to the Chiungchow Strait Administration, 24 hours before it enters the administrative area or two hours after it sails from a port, the time of entry into the administrative area.

All cables requesting passage through the strait and approval for passage through the strait, and so forth will be relayed by the Haikou Branch of the China Foreign Shipping Agency Company.

Article 5. With respect to foreign nonmilitary vessels which have been approved for passage through the strait, the Chiungchow Strait Administration may, whenever it deems necessary, notify [such vessels] that the passage is prohibited.

Article 6. The time for foreign nonmilitary vessels to pass through the administrative area is limited to daytime. They shall enter the administrative area after sunrise and leave the district completely before sunset. The Chiungchow Strait Administration will [make] the concrete time allotments for vessels' entry into and departure from the strait in accordance with the speed of the vessels applying for [approval] to pass through the strait.

Article 7. Foreign nonmilitary vessels must use midchannel while entering and leaving the Chiungchow Strait, but [those] specially permitted by the Chiungchow Strait Administration shall not be subject to this restriction.

Article 8. When passing through the administrative area, all foreign nonmilitary vessels can only navigate within the scope of the following navigation area: Water areas north of the line drawn from a point four nautical miles from the Mu-lan-tao light post on the east line to a point four nautical miles from the Lin-kao-chiao light post on the west line, and south of the line drawn from a point six nautical miles from the Mu-lan-tao light post on the east line through a point four nautical miles due south of the Chiao-wei-chiao light post to a point 14 nautical miles from the Lin-kao-chiao light post on the west line.

Article 9. Foreign nonmilitary vessels passing through the Chiungchow Strait shall strictly follow the time reported and the navigation area provided for their passage. Whenever signals dispatched from the shore or warships or boats are noticed, the vessels that are entering or passing through the strait should answer immediately and also unconditionally execute the directions given by the signals. The vessels will bear all the consequences incurred if they do not observe the above regulations.

Article 10. When passing through the Chiungchow Strait, foreign nonmilitary vessels may not use radar. If in the course of navigation [they] encounter circumstances of poor visibility, such as heavy fog or storm, which necessitate the use of radar, they should at that time report to the Chiungchow Strait Administration, stating their reasons as well as their position, their speed, and so forth. Radar can only be used when approval is granted. In case of emergency situations which endanger the safety of the navigation of the vessels, the vessels may on the one hand apply [for permission] and report [the situation] and at the same time use radar, subsequently submitting to the Chiungchow Strait Administration for the record a detailed report on the situation and the total time during which radar was used.

Article 11. When passing through the Chiungchow Strait, foreign nonmilitary vessels are not allowed to take pictures, to make surveys, or to engage in conduct that violates the laws and decrees of the People's Republic of China.

Article 12. Foreign nonmilitary vessels which violate these rules will be handled in accordance with the following provisions:

(1) If the vessels have not yet entered the administrative area,

they may be ordered not to enter the area, to return to their original route and to make a detour around Hainan Island; or they may simply wait until all procedures for passing through the strait are followed and approval is granted to pass through the strait.

(2) If they have already entered the administrative area, they may be ordered to stop navigation and may be sent under surveillance to Haikou Port for inspection. Sanctions will be given in accordance with the [finding] of the inspection. After handling the matter, [the Administration] may, considering the situation, permit the vessels to pass through the administrative area, or order them to withdraw from the administrative area until they are withdrawn from the strait under custody.

NOTE

On the eve of the 1958 Geneva Conference, a Western authority on international law summarized the rules pertaining to jurisdiction over straits as follows:

> In relation to portions of the territorial seas which form international straits and, for purposes of free communication, are assimilated to the high seas, the [International Court of Justice] has affirmed clearly the right of innocent passage of both men-of-war and merchant ships in time of peace. In the *Corfu Channel* (*Merits*) case (1949), the Court held: "It is, in the opinion of the court, generally recognized and in accordance with international custom that states in time of peace have a right to send their warships through straits used for international navigation between two parts of the high seas without the previous authorization of a coastal state, provided that the passage is *innocent*. Unless otherwise prescribed in an international convention, there is no right for a coastal state to prohibit such passage through straits in time of peace." In situations pertaining to a *status mixtus* between peace and war, the Court conceded to the coastal state the right of regulating the passage of warships, but short of prohibiting such passage or making it dependent on special authorization.[24]

A leading Soviet text of that period went even further to curb the authority of coastal states, stating that straits that link open seas and that are important as international waterways "are free both in time of war and peace for the passage of merchant vessels and men-of-war. This rule also applies when the waters of such straits do not exceed the width of the territorial waters of their littoral states." [25]

Article 16, paragraph 4 of the Convention on the Territorial Sea and the Contiguous Zone also recognized a right of innocent passage for all ships through straits which are "used for international navigation between one part of the high seas and another part of the high seas or the territorial sea of a foreign state." [26]

Had the PRC employed the normal baseline method of delimiting its territorial sea, the Chiungchow Strait would have been part of China's territorial sea and therefore clearly subject to innocent passage by nonmilitary vessels, and, if one accepts the PRC's view on military vessels, to innocent passage by military vessels that had obtained prior authorization. By choosing to employ the straight baseline method, however, the PRC transformed this strait into China's internal waters. This was apparently deemed a satisfactory basis for absolutely prohibiting military vessels and for allowing nonmilitary vessels to pass only upon prior authorization under closely circumscribed conditions. Because a state generally has the right to prohibit all ships from passing through its internal waters, one might have viewed the PRC's adoption of a somewhat less inhospitable standard for the Chiungchow Strait as a concession to the need to maintain international commercial communication through the strait regardless of the label imposed upon it. But, although the PRC and its scholars are reluctant to acknowledge the point, Article 5, paragraph 2, of the Convention on the Territorial Sea and Contiguous Zone provides that where a coastal state's resort to straight baselines transforms into internal waters areas formerly considered as part of the territorial sea, foreign vessels are to have the same rights of innocent passage through these newly created internal waters as through the territorial sea. Whether prior to the PRC's 1958 Declaration Chiungchow Strait was regarded as entirely territorial waters (assuming a twelve-mile maritime belt) or as high seas in part (assuming a three-mile maritime belt, as under the ROC), the PRC's regulation of the strait obviously fails to preserve the pre-1958 rights of foreign vessels.

Although no protests have been made against the extent of jurisdiction which the PRC has claimed over the Chiungchow Strait, it is difficult to know whether this should be attributed to recognition of its reasonableness or to the fact that, as indicated in Chapter 13, some of the major maritime powers have protested generally against PRC use of the straight baseline method upon which the legal regime of the strait rests and therefore have not seen a need to protest against this specific consequence of resort to that method.

The PRC's entry into the UN and participation in the work of the UN Committee on the Peaceful Uses of the Sea-Bed and the Ocean Floor Beyond the Limits of National Jurisdiction provided an occasion for Peking to restate its views on the regulation of straits and to spell out its evolving disagreement with Soviet views of the law of the sea. In reading item 16–4, which consists of excerpts from a speech delivered on July 24, 1972, by Shen Wei-liang, Chinese Representative to Subcommittee Two of the Sea-Bed Committee, note how the PRC gives the impression that the Soviet Union has changed its position with respect to both straits and innocent passage generally.

16-4

"No Superpowers' Control of the Seas Is Allowed," *PR* 15.33:13–15 (Aug. 18, 1972).

On the right of passage through straits within the territorial seas of coastal states, Representative Shen Wei-liang pointed out, "Everybody understands that territorial seas are different from the high seas. Every state in the world has the right to define the extent of its territorial seas, and that is its sovereign right. Even if straits within the territorial seas of coastal states are often used for international navigation, this fact does not change their status of territorial seas into that of the high seas. Permitting innocent passage is of course not closing the straits. It merely requires that foreign ships, while passing through the straits, should not impair the peace, good order, and security of the coastal states and should observe their laws and regulations. Prior consent should be obtained before foreign warships and military aircraft may pass. We hold that these requirements are entirely justified and reasonable. In advocating 'freedom of transit' and 'freedom of overflight' for foreign ships and planes, whether civilian or military, through straits within the territorial seas of coastal states, the superpowers are seeking to treat territorial seas as the high seas in order to serve their purpose of maritime hegemony."

US Attitude Changes

He said, "Before World War II, the United States acknowledged that foreign warships had no right of free transit through the territorial seas of other countries. In 1910, the former US Secretary of State Elihu Root stated that foreign warships might not pass without consent into the zone (the territorial waters) because they threatened." But "after World War II, the United States intensified its expansion to the seas and oceans. It sent out great numbers of warships, nuclear-powered submarines and military planes, and established numerous naval bases all over the world in an attempt to control the seas and oceans. To meet the needs of its policy of expansion and aggression, the United States changed its attitude on the question of the right of passage through territorial seas. At the 1958 Geneva Conference on the Law of the Sea the US delegate spoke strongly in favour of the 'innocent passage' of warships through the territorial seas of other countries without the latter's prior consent."

"On January 20, 1960, while testifying before the US Senate Committee on Foreign Relations," the Chinese representative noted, "the president of the US delegation to the 1958 law of the sea conference said 'Our navy would like to see as narrow a territorial sea as possible in order to preserve the maximum possibility of deployment, transit, and manoeuvrability on and over the high seas, free from the jurisdictional control of individual states.' In a foreign policy report issued in February 1972, the US government asserted in an even more blatant way that 'the United States relies on the seas to meet its global responsibilities. Our security, and that of our friends, depends upon freedom of navigation and overflight of the high seas, and on free movement through and over international straits.' In short, the United States wants to treat the territorial seas of other countries as the high seas and demands the right of free transit through straits within the territorial seas of coastal states. It was guided by this thought that the United States drafted the articles on straits it submitted to the Sea-Bed Committee in July 1971."

The Soviet Union Follows in US Footsteps

Referring to the attitude of the Soviet Union on this question in the past, the Chinese representative said, "For a long time in the past the Soviet Union adhered to the principles of innocent passage and prior consent as regards the question of the right of passage through straits within territorial seas. Take for instance the Corfu Channel case dealt with by the International Court of Justice in 1949. The then Soviet judge Krylov explicitly pointed out that foreign warships were different from commercial ships for they had no right of passage through the territorial seas of other states. He also held that, in the absence of rules prescribed in a special convention, the right to regulate passage through straits belonged to the coastal states.

"During the discussions on the Convention on Territorial Sea and Contiguous Zone at the 1958 Geneva Conference on the Law of the Sea, the Soviet delegate Nikolaev stated: 'In the exercise of its sovereignty each coastal state has the right to subject the passage of foreign warships in its territorial waters to an application for prior authorization.'

"What is more noteworthy, the Soviet government made the following reservation with respect to article 23 (rules applicable to warships) of the 1958 Convention on Territorial Sea and Contiguous Zone: 'The government of the USSR considers that a coastal state has the right to establish procedures for the authorization of the passage of foreign warships through its territorial waters.' Up to this day that reservation is still printed in a United Nations document of 1972.

"The 1960 regulations for the defence of the state frontier of the Soviet Union provides: foreign nonmilitary vessels shall enjoy the right of innocent passage through the territorial waters of the USSR; foreign warships shall pass through the territorial waters subject to the prior authorization of the government of the USSR. The 1967 USSR rules for the visits by foreign warships in territorial waters and ports of the USSR stipulates that visits by foreign warships in territorial waters of the USSR shall be subject to the authorization of the government of the USSR, and that authorization shall be requested not later than 30 days before the date of the proposed visit. It was on the grounds of these rules and regulations that in August 1967 two US coast guard ships were refused passage through the Vilkitsky Straits that are within the Soviet territorial waters."

Representative Shen Wei-liang pointed out, "However, in his statement on March 24, 1972, the Soviet delegate made a 180-degree about-face from the original position of his government by trumpeting with all his might for 'freedom of transit' through straits. He said that freedom of transit through international straits is 'the principle generally recognized in international law and international practice,' and that, without freedom of transit through the straits that were not regulated by an international convention, 'the realization of freedom of the high seas is practically impossible.' In line with these assertions, one may ask whether the Soviet government is ready to open straits within Soviet territorial waters to all other countries and allow warships of all countries freedom of transit. The answer is 'no,' for the Soviet delegate added that 'the extension of territorial waters to 12 nautical miles should not of itself lead to the change of the legal status of a considerable number of international straits.' It transpires that the Soviet delegation stands for the maintenance of the status quo. In other words, straits of the Soviet Union, which were declared closed to free transit by the Soviet government on the basis of its 12-mile territorial waters limit, will remain closed to free transit. But if other states claim jurisdiction over straits on the strength of the 12-mile territorial waters limit, that [is] impermissible, for it would be regarded as changing the status quo, violating the 'principle generally recognized in international law and international practice,' and undermining 'freedom of the high seas.' This is acting just like the magistrates in an ancient fable, who allow themselves to burn down houses while forbidding the common folk to light lamps. This is in effect to say that you have no freedom of transit through my straits, but I must have freedom of transit through your straits. This is utterly absurd, and nothing but hegemonic behaviour."

What This Change Means

Shen Wei-liang went on to say, "It is ironical that at the 1958 Geneva Conference on the Law of the Sea the Soviet Union opposed the US stand for 'the passage of warships in territorial waters as a matter of right.' Quoting the US delegate as having recognized at the 1930 Hague International Law Codification Conference that the passage of warships in territorial waters was only a 'gesture of international courtesy' and not a right, the Soviet delegate Tunkin pointed out then the change of attitude on the part of the United States. But in 1972, it is the turn of the Soviet Union to make a similar change by following in the footsteps of the United States. The Soviet Union, which in 1958 was opposed to such a US stand, now asserts, through its delegation, that the US proposal of July 1971 for the freedom of transit of ships and planes through international straits 'can serve as the basis of articles on straits.' This only shows that the Soviet Union is following the example of the United States and attempting to become another hegemonic sea power."

He pointed out: "The 56 countries, which constitute a majority in the Sea-Bed Committee, have set forth their position on the question of straits in the list of subjects and issues concerning the law of the sea, which they have jointly put forward. The demand of the two superpowers for freedom of transit through straits within the territorial waters of coastal states is unacceptable because it denies the sovereignty of the coastal states."

China's Stand

The Chinese representative emphasized, "We hold that straits within territorial waters, whether or not they are often used for international navigation, should be subjected to regulation by the coastal states concerned. Foreign commercial ships may have innocent passage through them but must observe the relevant laws and regulations of the coastal states. Foreign warships must obtain prior authorization before they can pass through straits within the territorial waters of coastal states."

In conclusion, he said, "We hold that a fair and reasonable solution to this question should be sought by all countries in accordance with the principles of mutual respect for sovereignty and territorial integrity, mutual nonaggression and noninterference in each other's internal affairs, and that the hegemony of the superpowers trying to partition and control the seas must be firmly opposed."

16-5

"China's 338th Warning Against US Military Provocations," NCNA–English, Peking (Oct. 29, 1964), in *SCMP*, no. 3330:37 (Nov. 3, 1964).

A US warship twice intruded into China's territorial waters east of Pingtan and Meichow Island of Fukien Province between 01:02 hours and 03:00 hours and between 06:09 hours and 10:21 hours on October 29.

A spokesman of the Chinese Foreign Ministry has been authorized, in relation to these military provocations by the US warship, to issue the 338th serious warning.

Note

Perfunctory warnings such as that illustrated by item 16–5 have become commonplace to readers of the Chinese press. As the statement indicates, the PRC claims to be meticulous in recording and protesting alleged violations of its territorial waters. From time to time it issues cumulative figures. It claimed, for example, that between September 7, 1958, and April 27, 1962, 261 American warships intruded into its territorial sea on 144 occasions.[27]

Item 16–6 illustrates the PRC's response to a more unusual instance of lack of respect for its jurisdiction in territorial waters.

16-6

"China Protests against British Government's Action over *Pak Tang* Incident," NCNA–English, Peking (July 1, 1957), in *SCMP*, no. 1563:27 (July 5, 1957).

The Ministry of Foreign Affairs lodged a serious protest today with the British government over the *Pak Tang* incident. The protest was contained in a second note to the British chargé d'affaires' office here today.

The full text of the note reads:

The Ministry of Foreign Affairs of the People's Republic of China presents its compliments to the Office of the Chargé d'Affaires of Britain and hereby makes the following statement and request with regard to the note dated June 21, 1957, of the Foreign Ministry to the Office of the Chargé d'Affaires and the return note dated June 24, 1957, of the Office of the Chargé d'Affaires concerning the seizure and sailing to Hong Kong of the motorized sailing vessel *Pak Tang* of the Kwangtung Sea Products Company. It is requested that the following be transmitted immediately to the British government.

The motorized sailing vessel *Pak Tang* of the Kwangtung Sea Products Company, in sailing from Tam Kung Island to Tong Ka Wan, while passing by Chih Chou Island in Chinese territorial waters at about eight a.m. on June 12, 1957, was suddenly seized forcibly by ruffians mingled among the passengers. After killing one of the working personnel on board ship, these ruffians forced the vessel to sail for Hong Kong. The above facts have been confirmed by the communiqués issued by the Hong Kong British authorities on June 12 and 23, respectively.

In view of the fact that this criminal offense of murder was committed on board a Chinese vessel in Chinese territorial waters, the British government and the Hong Kong British authorities should, in conformity with international practice, assist in handing back all the working personnel and passengers on board to Chinese authorities concerned according to the request of the note of the Foreign Ministry dated June 21, 1957, so that the case may be dealt with according to law. However, on June 23, 1957, the Hong Kong British authorities only returned the vessel and 11 of the passengers and working personnel, and, under the name of deportation, sent 25 passengers to Taiwan, including the murderer and suspects [in] the case.

It should be pointed out that such an act of the Hong Kong British authorities of sending to Taiwan the murderer and suspects involved in this case who should be handed over, according to international practice, to be dealt with by the Chinese authorities concerned, is in fact to connive at the murderer's escaping from law and thus obstructing the Chinese government from dealing with such a grave criminal offense. The Chinese government hereby lodges a serious protest with the British government and the Hong Kong British authorities for this extremely unfriendly act in flagrant violation of international practice and resolutely demands that the British government be responsible for handing back to the Chinese authorities concerned all those persons who have been sent to Taiwan, including the murderer and suspects involved in this case. The Chinese government declares at the same time that it reserves the right to make further demands in this matter.

NOTE

Peking's views on preserving exclusive sovereignty over the territorial sea have been expounded in connection with tensions in both Vietnam and Korea.

When in 1965 the United States proclaimed a "combat zone" off the Vietnamese coast, the "Observer," an influential spokesman in the *People's Daily,* stated:

> US President Lyndon Johnson issued an executive order on April 24, arbitrarily designating Vietnam and the waters adjacent to it as "an area in which armed forces of the United States are and have been engaged in combat." This "combat zone," defined in the form of law with its limits given in exact terms of latitude and longitude, actually covers the whole of Vietnam, a large expanse of the high seas, and even some of China's territorial waters. This is a serious move by US imperialism to continue expanding the war of aggression in Vietnam and to heighten the tension in Indochina and Asia. It is an act of piracy in flagrant violation of international law. . . .
>
> Johnson's order also constitutes a menace to China's security and an encroachment on China's sovereignty. This "combat zone" flagrantly defined by US imperialism extends to the very door of China and even includes part of Chinese territorial waters in the vicinity of China's Hsisha Islands. We solemnly declare: China will brook no infringement by anyone on its territorial waters or air space. Anyone who disregards this will have to shoulder the responsibility for all the grave consequences arising therefrom.[28]

When in 1968 the North Korean regime seized the USS *Pueblo,* the government of the PRC issued a statement which said in part:

> On January 23, naval units of the Korean People's Army captured on the seas off Wonsan an armed US spy ship *Pueblo,* which had intruded into Korea's territorial waters for espionage activities. On January 27, the government of the Democratic People's Republic of Korea issued a statement pointing out that this provocation by US imperialism "is another flagrant violation of the Korean armistice agreement, and an open aggression against the Democratic People's Republic of Korea. . . . It is entirely right that the Korean people have taken the decisive measure of self-defense. . . . The US imperialists, no matter how they act, can never conceal their ugly nature of aggression nor surprise the Korean people." The Chinese government and people firmly support the just stand of the Korean government and people in countering US imperialism's flagrant provocation.
>
> It is by no means accidental that the US warship intruded into Korea's territorial waters for espionage activities. To save themselves from doomed defeat on the Vietnam battlefield, the US aggressors are plotting to expand the war of aggression against Vietnam and stepping up their activities of aggression and war throughout Asia. This incident of provocation against the Korean people by US imperialism is part and parcel of these criminal US activities.[29]

The outrage voiced by "Observer" over the American-proclaimed "combat zone" off the Vietnamese coast was directed not only against its infringement of Chinese territorial waters but also against its interference with "a large expanse of the high seas." The Johnson administration was indicted for believing that "the high seas can be regarded as its own to meet its needs of aggression and expansion. . . ."[30] Peking's official and semiofficial spokesmen have issued ringing testimonials to the vitality of the international law principle of freedom of the high seas. According to the *People's Daily:*

> The high seas are that part of the ocean or sea the use of which is shared by all nations. On the high seas ships and nationals of all states are free to navigate, to fish, to hunt, and to engage in other maritime enterprises as well as to lay submarine cables. The principle of the freedom of the high seas has been recognized by international law and all nations.[31]

States that have purported to exclude other states from access to portions of the high seas have frequently been condemned by the Chinese Communist press. For example, when in 1958 the United

States undertook nuclear tests in specified areas of the Pacific Ocean, *Ta-kung pao,* a major newspaper, stated that "no country has the right to occupy part of the high seas and exclude flight and navigation there by the planes and ships of other countries." [32]

Yet there have been other occasions when the PRC has foregone the opportunity to invoke freedom of the high seas. In 1957, for example, when protesting against the United Kingdom's scheduled hydrogen bomb tests in the Pacific, the *People's Daily* relied on other grounds. And the Chinese Communist press did not protest at all against the subsequent temporary suspension of navigation in Pacific target areas.[33] This occasional reluctance to invoke freedom of the seas as a barrier to nuclear testing probably reflected the PRC's growing interest in becoming a nuclear power. It may also have reflected awareness of the fact that the PRC itself had already claimed to exercise jurisdiction for certain purposes over areas of the high seas near its territorial sea.

Shortly after its founding, the PRC issued regulations that prohibited all fishing by trawlers, whether Chinese or foreign, in a zone that extended from China's Korean border to Chekiang Province and that appeared to be broader than even the twelve-mile maritime belt Peking later claimed.[34] This conservation zone was expanded by a 1957 regulation.[35] It was the "unofficial" agreement concluded in 1955 between the Chinese Fisheries Association (CFA) and its Japanese counterpart, the Japan-China Fishing Council (JCFC), that focused public attention on the scope of the PRC's claims to control events in adjacent high seas. This agreement was renewed until 1958, and, after a lapse of five years, was followed by a similar agreement concluded in 1963 (31–24). What interests us here are the claims that the CFA referred to, and that the JCFC acknowledged, in the exchange of letters that accompanied the agreements. Item 16–7 reproduces the 1963 exchange.

16-7

"Letters between the Delegation of China Fishery Association and the Delegation of Japan-China Fishery Council," *TYC 1963*, XII (1964), 267–270; translated in *CB*, no. 724:4–6 (Dec. 6, 1963).

A. "Letter from the Delegation of China Fishery Association to the Delegation of Japan-China Fishery Council."

To: Jisaku Ekuchi, Head of the Delegation of Japan-China Fishery Council of Japan,

Acting on instructions from the government of the People's Republic of China, the delegation of the Fishery Association of the PRC hereby notifies the delegation of the Japan-China Fishery Council of Japan of the following:

I. The government of the People's Republic of China has, in the interests of defense security and military needs, made the following provisions for the sea areas along the Chinese coast:

(1) The sea area west of the line running from a point at 39 degrees 45 minutes N and 124 degrees 9 minutes 12 seconds E to a point at 37 degrees 20 minutes N and 123 degrees 03 minutes E is a military security area. Japanese fishing boats are not allowed to sail into this area without permission of the competent department of the Chinese government.

(2) The sea area within the line formed by a point at 31 degrees N and 122 degrees E, a point at 30 degrees 55 minutes N and 123 degrees E, a point at 30 degrees N and 123 degrees E, a point at 29 degrees 30 minutes N and 122 degrees 30 minutes E, and a point at 29 degrees 30 minutes N and 122 degrees E, [is] a military area in which navigation is forbidden. Japanese fishing boats are forbidden to sail into this area.

II. The sea area south of 27 degrees N and east of the coast of mainland China, including the periphery of Taiwan is now in a state of military operation. On account of this, Japanese fishing boats are advised not to enter into this area for fish catching; otherwise, all the consequences resulting therefrom shall be the responsibility of the fishing vessels concerned.

III. With a view to protecting the fishery resources along the coast of China, the government of the People's Republic of China has ruled that the sea area west of the line formed by a point at 37 degrees 20 minutes N and 123 degrees 03 minutes E, a point at 36 degrees 48 minutes 10 seconds N and 122 degrees 44 minutes 30 seconds E, a point at 35 degrees 11 minutes N and 120 degrees 38 minutes E, a point at 30 degrees 44 minutes N and 123 degrees 25 minutes E, a point at 29 degrees N and 122 degrees 45 minutes E, a point at 27 degrees 30 minutes N and 121 degrees 30 minutes E, and a point at 27 degrees N and 121 degrees 10 minutes E, is an area in which motorboat trawler fishing is forbidden. Chinese motorboat trawlers are forbidden to catch fish in this area. At the same time, Japanese motorboat trawlers may not enter into this sea area for fish catching.

On these grounds, the China Fishery Association requests the Delegation of the Japan-China Fishery Council of Japan to give the above notification its fullest attention and to urge the Japan-China Fishery Council of Japan to take effective measures to insure that all the fishing boats of Japan observe the above provisions.

Yang Yü, Head of the Delegation of the China Fishery Association

Hsiao P'eng, Deputy Head of the Delegation of the China Fishery Association

November 9, 1963

B. "Letter from the Delegation of Japan-China Fishery Council to the Delegation of China Fishery Association."

To: Mr. Yang Yü, Head, and
Mr. Hsiao P'eng, Deputy Head, of the Delegation of China Fishery Association of the PRC

In reply to your letter dated November 9, 1963, delivered to us by you at the time of signing the "Fishery Agreement for the Yellow Sea and the East Sea between the Japan-China Fishery Council of Japan and the China Fishery Association of the People's Republic of China" in Peking on November 9, 1963, the Delegation of Japan-China Fishery Council of Japan wishes to state the following:

I. Concerning the following three military areas, we consider that the measures taken by your government are applicable to all boats irrespective of their nationality and are not merely intended for Japanese fishing boats. With this understanding:

(1) Without permission of the competent department of your government, Japanese fishing boats will not enter into the military security area west of the line formed by a point at 39 degrees 45 minutes N and 124 degrees 09 minutes 12 seconds E, and a point at 37 degrees 20 minutes N and 123 degrees 03 minutes E.

(2) Japanese fishing boats will not enter into the military forbidden navigation area formed by a line drawn through a point at 31 degrees N and 122 degrees E, a point at 30 degrees 55 minutes N and 123 degrees E, a point at 30 degrees N and 123 degrees E, a point at 29 degrees 30 minutes N and 122 degrees 30 minutes E, and a point at 29 degrees 30 minutes N and 122 degrees E.

(3) Concerning the military operation area south of 27 degrees N, our side, understanding the spirit of your advice, will notify all Japanese fishing boats to observe it.

II. With reference to the fishing area in which motorboat trawlers are forbidden, defined by your government with a view to protecting fishery resources along the Chinese coast, west of a line drawn through a point at 37 degrees 20 minutes N and 123 degrees 03 minutes E, a point at 36 degrees 48 minutes 10 seconds N and 122 degrees 44 minutes 30 seconds [E], a point at 35 degrees 11 minutes N and 120 degrees 38 minutes E, a point at 30 degrees 44 minutes N and 123 degrees 25 minutes E, a point at 29 degrees N and 122 degrees 45 minutes E, a point at 27 degrees 30 minutes N and 121 degrees 30 minutes E, and a point at 27 degrees N and 121 degrees 10 minutes E, while holding that the internal law of a country cannot be directly binding on the people of another country on the open sea, we, noting the spirit in which your government establishes the fishery area forbidden to motorboat trawlers, pledge ourselves to stop of our own accord the operation of Japanese motorboat trawlers in the forbidden area.

Our purpose in making the above measures clear according to your advice is to insure peaceful coexistence of Japanese and Chinese fishing boats on the Yellow Sea and the East Sea fishing grounds and to promote friendly relations between Japan and China.

Jisaku Ekuchi, Head of the Delegation of the Japan-China Fishery Council

Peking, November 9, 1963

NOTE

The military security areas designated by parts I (1) and (2) of the CFA letter are apparently entirely within the PRC's territorial sea and constitute examples of the exercise of what Fu Chu termed the coastal state's right to establish prohibited zones within its waters (16–2). The sea area between the mainland of China and Taiwan includes a broad portion of high sea, but since part II of the CFA letter merely "advised" Japanese fishing boats not to fish there because of "a state of military operation," the JCFC did not choose to regard this advice as the exercise of jurisdiction by the PRC over the high sea.

It is only part III of the CFA letter that purported to assert binding authority over the high sea, and, while reserving its right not to be bound by this Chinese claim, the JCFC nevertheless agreed, "of [its] own accord," to conform to it.

The PRC has enforced observance of these prohibitions by Japanese fishing boats. In May 1958, after Sino-Japanese relations sharply deteriorated as a result of the Nagasaki Flag Incident (see Note after 29–6), the CFA protested to the JCFC against alleged violations of the fisheries arrangements, and in a single week sixteen Japanese fishing boats and 194 crew members were seized for allegedly intruding into a prohibited fishing area and the sea between Taiwan and the mainland. All but four boats and two men were subsequently released by the Shanghai Public Security Bureau as a result of representations made by the JCFC and the Japan-China Friendship Association. The two men who continued to be detained were convicted of military espionage, as item 16–8 reveals. Through the good offices of the Chinese Red Cross and the Japan-China Friendship Association, both were released after serving one year of their sentences.[36]

16-8

"Japanese Criminals Sentenced to Jail," NCNA–English, Shanghai (Oct. 31, 1958) in *SCMP*, no. 1889:39–40 (Nov. 5, 1958).

Two Japanese criminals who penetrated into China's coastal waters and gathered military information have been sentenced to three and four years' imprisonment respectively, the Shanghai Municipal Intermediate People's Court announced today.

They are chief trawler Yoshio Kinoshita and radio operator Sachio Kinoshita of the Japanese fishing ships *Himejima Maru* and *Mijima Maru*. Yoshio Kinoshita was sentenced to four years and Sachio Kinoshita to three years. The two ships were confiscated by decision of the court.

These sentences, the court announcement said, were passed in accordance with the regulations governing the punishment of counter-revolutionaries.

The Japanese fishing ships, *Himejima Maru* and *Mijima Maru,* were detained by Chinese naval vessels after they intruded into an area of China forbidden to motor trawler fishing on May 6 this year.

According to the depositions of Yoshio Kinoshita and Sachio Kinoshita, the two ships invaded China's military patrolled areas and areas forbidden to motor trawler fishing on 21 occasions in the period between 1955 and May this year. On the instruction of the Japanese Coastal Safety Board, they gathered information about the movements of Chinese naval vessels and aircraft, the military facilities on Chinese coastal islands and the depth of water, the structure of the sea floor, and water currents along Chinese coastal areas.

As early as in 1954, Yoshio Kinoshita and Sachio Kinoshita gathered information about the movements of Chinese naval vessels and aircraft on the waters off northern Kiangsu Province and outside the Yangtze River estuary and tried to find out the radio call signals of Chinese naval vessels and aircraft.

In the winter of 1956, the two criminals sent information to the Japanese Coastal Safety Board about Chinese naval vessels sailing in the southern part of the Yellow Sea.

Moreover, when they intruded into Chinese waters in the Wenchow Bay, Tachen Island, and the Taishan Islands, Yoshio Kinoshita and Sachio Kinoshita destroyed the fishing gear of Chinese fishermen on six occasions. After being arrested, they destroyed part of the evidence in an attempt to evade the consequences of their crimes.

In February this year, under the instruction of US intelligence in Japan and for the purpose of intensifying its reconnoitering activities into Chinese military information, the Coastal Safety Board of the Japanese Kishi government called a meeting of the leading members of a number of Japanese fishing companies and forced part of the crew members of Japanese fishing ships to carry out such activities as collecting Chinese military information.

The Japanese Coastal Safety Board has also directed part of Japanese fishing ships to get close at any cost to the waters in the vicinity of Tungfu Shan Island, Huaniao Shan Island, [the] Chiushan Islands, [and the] Yushan and Taishan Islands of China and collect information about the types, movements, and equipment of Chinese naval vessels and aircraft and, particularly, to reconnoiter the fortresses, artillery positions, airfields, barracks, radar and radio facilities on China's coastal islands.

The Japanese Coastal Safety Board has also issued to the Japanese fishing ships engaged in collecting military information equipment for military reconnaissance and communications, including special secret codes and liaison call letters, cameras with telephoto lenses and precision telescopes. It instructed the crew members of Japanese ships who were carrying out intelligence activities that they must destroy all evidence of crimes if they were discovered and arrested by the Chinese side when carrying out military intelligence activities.

It has been proved by the data concerned that in March and April this year, crew members of Japanese ships who had been assigned to intelligence missions photographed military facilities on the Chinese islands of Yushan, Chiushan, Tungfu Shan and Tung, and sent the pictures to the Japanese Coastal Safety Board. The Japanese Coastal Safety Board has sent the military information thus collected to the intelligence organizations of the US forces stationed in Japan.

The Shanghai Municipal Intermediate People's Court decided to make out light sentences on Yoshio Kinoshita and Sachio Kinoshita in view of the fact that they committed their crimes of spying under the compulsion of the Coastal Safety Board of the Japanese Kishi government.

Note

On February 16, 1969, Chinese armed vessels were reported to have intercepted and detained three yachts bound from Hong Kong to Macao as they passed through waters claimed by the PRC as part of its twelve-mile territorial sea.[37] On April 3, 1969, two of the yachts and thirteen of the fifteen persons who had been detained were released, after two of the yachtsmen signed statements declaring that they had intruded into Chinese territorial waters. All of this group had been interrogated on a number of occasions by PRC authorities but had been "treated very well." [38] The two persons who were not then released were American residents of Hong Kong, one of whom owned the yacht that continued in detention. Their released companions reported that the two Americans had thrown their passports over the side of their yacht as it was being boarded. Interviews with British officials in Hong Kong revealed that the Americans' boat was unusually well equipped with electronic equipment due to the fact that its owner was in the electronics business, that at the time the yacht was being boarded the owner sent out an electronic signal contrary to Chinese regulations, and that the two Americans lied about their citizenship for their first few days in detention. On December 7, 1969, after almost ten months' captivity, the two were finally released, together with the yacht, after having signed numerous statements of confession and repentance. In announcing their release the New China News Agency noted that the two had "destroyed their papers" and "at first adopted a very dishonest attitude" but that, after the Chinese authorities had looked into the facts, the Americans "admitted their mistakes of trying to conceal their identity and intruding into China's territorial sea." [39]

The PRC has occasionally taken ad hoc action against fishermen from neighboring states, even in their own territorial waters adjacent to Chinese waters. In mid-1968, for example, "Chinese Communist junks accompanied by a naval gunboat swept into a fleet of sampans about a mile and a half from Hong Kong, took 14 in tow, and sailed four miles back into Chinese waters."[40] Apparently all of the sixty Hong Kong residents who were seized were released within a few days, but the fate of the sampans is unknown.

The following two items indicate how, after its entry into the UN, the PRC spelled out its views on the right of coastal states to exercise jurisdiction over areas adjacent to the territorial seas. These items contain excerpts from speeches made on July 21, and August 2, 1972, respectively, by Chinese Representative Chen Chih-fan before Sub-Committee Three of the UN Committee on the Peaceful Uses of the Sea-Bed and the Ocean Floor Beyond the Limits of National Jurisdiction.

16-9

"Superpowers' Plunder of Fishing Resources Opposed," *PR* 15.32:14 (Aug. 11, 1972).

Representative Chen Chih-fang said: "The Chinese delegation has studied the statements made by the representatives of various countries at sessions of the Sea-Bed Committee. The representatives of many developing and other small- and medium-sized countries have stated the determination to safeguard their state sovereignty and national interests, expressed dissatisfaction with the superpowers and another distant-water fishing power for their current practice of plundering fishery resources everywhere and expressed resolute opposition to the maritime hegemony of the superpowers. The Chinese delegation fully supports these just propositions and would like to explain its own position on some of the questions concerning the development of sea fishery."

In the past few years, he recalled, "70–80 percent of the total annual catch of these powers was that made in distant oceans, while the annual catch of some developing countries has been on the decrease year by year. Owing to the fact that these distant fishing powers disregard the interests of coastal states and sometimes concentrate their fishing fleets in one area for intensive catches, serious damage has been caused to the fishery resources. For instance, the resources of herring, cod, and haddock in the northern Atlantic and the northern Pacific have drastically decreased, and those of some fishes are almost exhausted.

"Sea fish resources are an important component of the natural resources of coastal states. And the shallow sea waters along the coasts are important places for the main sea fishes to spawn, feed, and hibernate. At present, more than 80 percent of the world's total catch is made in the shallow sea waters, which comprise only 7.8 percent of the total sea area on the globe. The domination of the few distant fishing powers over the seas and their reckless plunder of fishery resources in the shallow sea waters of other coastal states have already caused tremendous damage and posed a serious threat to the economic interests and state sovereignty of many coastal states, particularly those in Asia, Africa, and Latin America."

"In the face of this grave situation, it is only natural and right for the coastal states to adopt necessary and pertinent measures to protect their fishery resources. The Chinese delegation supports the coastal states, and particularly the developing states, in their just struggle to develop their national economy, safeguard state sovereignty, and oppose the superpowers' plunder of sea fishery resources. We hold that the coastal states have every right to delimit, according to their geographical conditions and in the light of the needs of their national economic interests, certain economic zones beyond their territorial seas, so as to protect their fishery resources," the Chinese representative stressed.

On the question of other countries coming to the sea area adjacent to a coastal state for fishing, he said: "We hold that a reasonable solution should be sought through negotiations between the coastal state and the country or countries concerned on the precondition of non-encroachment on the sovereignty of the coastal state. We are deeply convinced that the coastal states are fully capable of protecting and rationally exploiting the fishery resources in their own economic zones."

16-10
"On Prevention and Control of Marine Pollution,"
PR 15.34:12 (Aug. 25, 1972).

Chen Chih-fang noted the differences of opinion on the prevention and control of marine pollution. He supported the statements made by many representatives who maintained that coastal states have the right to exercise direct jurisdiction and control over areas within given limits, which are adjacent to their territorial seas, for the purpose of preventing, reducing, or eliminating the serious harms of pollution. He condemned the superpowers for their opposition, under various pretexts, to this right of the coastal states.

The Chinese representative stated: "We think that coastal states, being the direct victims of marine pollution, have the full right as well as necessity to exercise direct jurisdiction and control over areas within given limits, which are adjacent to their territorial seas, in order to protect the health and security of their people and meet the needs of their economic development. The proposals submitted by representatives of many countries at the Sea-Bed Committee with a view to safeguarding the rights of the coastal states are of positive significance to the prevention of marine pollution. Any argument aimed at opposing or weakening such jurisdiction of coastal states is detrimental to the prevention of marine pollution and runs counter to the desire of the peoples of the world to preserve the marine environment and is therefore unacceptable."

Note

In addition to other Chinese actions to close off portions of the territorial sea and adjacent areas of the high sea, we should also mention the "Regulations Concerning Japanese Vessels Destined for China" which the Japan-China Trade Promotion Association received from its Chinese counterpart in 1952. They provided:

> 2. The ports of entry for a Japanese vessel navigating in Chinese waters are Shanghai and Taku. Within the sea area 15 nautical miles from the Chinese coast, no hovering is permitted. Moreover, it may not enter any port other than the one it has been scheduled to enter.
>
> 3. A Japanese vessel destined for China shall observe all Chinese maritime regulations upon entering the sea area 15 nautical miles from the Chinese coast. It shall not hoist any signs. But it must inform by telegram, through its agent at the port of destination, the port authorities of its present location at sea in degrees of latitude and longitude. The contact shall be made with international signals for maritime use. In case there is any suspicion on the part of a Chinese patrol boat against a Japanese vessel, the latter must obey an order and submit to visit and search by the former.[11]

Whether these regulations continued to be in effect after the PRC's 1958 claim to a twelve-mile maritime belt and after promulgation in 1957 of item 17–1 is unclear.

Finally, we should take note of the "Rules For Investigation and Handling of Incidents Involving Maritime Losses," promulgated in 1959, Article 13 of which asserts jurisdiction over foreign-flag ships not only for incidents occurring in the PRC's territorial waters but also for other incidents that cause damage to property of Chinese people. In addition, it authorizies port authorities to order foreign-flag ships to put up a guarantee and to prohibit the departure of such ships before a required guarantee is presented.[42]

For further examples of the PRC's views regarding the justifiability of exercising jurisdiction beyond the scope of a state's territory, see Part VI, especially Chapter 26.

Ports and Boundary Rivers 17

Although ports are recognized as part of a state's internal waters by the PRC as well as by other countries, they have proved sufficiently important in the PRC's international relations to warrant special treatment in this chapter, together with the related problem of boundary rivers. Imperial China's attempt to assert jurisdiction over foreign merchants and sailors who visited Chinese ports constituted one of the principal frictions in Sino-Western relations from the latter part of the eighteenth century until the "unequal treaties" formally initiated the extraterritorial system in China in the middle of the nineteenth century. Extraterritoriality gradually nourished the spirit of Chinese nationalism that has stimulated both the Nationalists and the Communists to strive to end the humiliations that began with lack of jurisdiction over the treaty ports. A recent Chinese treatise on jurisdiction in international law proudly stated: "In the days of old China, as a result of treaty provisions imposed by foreign powers, foreign ships entering Chinese ports were not subject to Chinese jurisdiction. . . . Since the Chinese people have won their liberation, the days when foreigners were within Chinese territory but not under Chinese law have gone forever." [43]

Recall items 12–25 and 12–27 regarding Soviet efforts to retain certain privileges in the ports of Dairen and Port Arthur for at least a temporary period in the early 1950's.

17-1

"Measures Governing Foreign Vessels Entering and Leaving Port" (ratified by the State Council, February 21, 1957; promulgated by the Ministry of Communications, March 14, 1957), *FKHP 1957*, V, 208–210.

Article 1. Foreign vessels entering and leaving ports of the PRC shall observe these measures, in addition to observing the Provisional Customs Law of the PRC and other relevant laws and regulations.

Ports mentioned in these measures shall mean those Chinese ports which the Ministry of Communications of the PRC has authorized foreign vessels to enter and leave.

Article 2. In order to arrange necessary entrance procedure, the captain of a foreign vessel shall, through its agent in port, submit to the local port affairs administration a week before its scheduled arrival in the destined port (or prior to its sailing at the port of departure) the scheduled time for arrival in port of the vessel, its draft before and after entering port, its quantity of cargoes, and the number of passengers. Twenty-four hours before its arrival in the destined port, he shall also report to the port affairs administration, through the vessel's agent in port, the exact time of the vessel's arrival.

Article 3. A foreign vessel entering or leaving port shall hoist all specified signal flags and in the daytime shall hoist the national flag of the country to which the vessel belongs.

Article 4. A foreign vessel entering or leaving port shall follow the national frontier sanitary epidemic inspection rules and the epidemic inspection organ shall conduct such inspections.

Article 5. A foreign vessel shall not leave or enter port or navigate in port or transfer its mooring unless the port affairs administration has designated a pilot to direct it.

Article 6. A foreign vessel entering or leaving port shall be subject to inspections by the port affairs administration and other relevant inspection organs in accordance with the provisions of Provisional General Rules for Inspection of the Crew, Passengers, and Baggage of Inbound and Outbound Vessels.

Article 7. The captain of a foreign vessel, upon its entering port, shall report to the port affairs administration the descriptions and quantities of the weapons and ammunition and the items listed in paragraph (2) of this article which the vessel carries and shall observe the following provisions:

(1) Weapons and ammunition shall be sealed and kept in store;

(2) Use of wireless transmitters, radio-telephones, radar, radio sounding machines, sextants, rocket signals, flame signals and signal guns is forbidden in port.

Vessels facing disaster or sending out emergency notices may unseal and use the articles listed in paragraph (2). After these are used, a report shall be immediately submitted to the local port affairs administration.

Article 8. The captain of a foreign vessel, upon entering port and being moored, shall fill out a foreign vessel inbound report, and lists of its crew, its passengers, and its import cargoes for examination by the port affairs administration. At the same time he shall submit for inspection the certificate relating to the nationality of the vessel, the sea and machine room log book, and other relevant certificates.

Before leaving port, the captain of a foreign vessel shall fill out a foreign vessel outbound report, a report on changes in its crew (this shall not be necessary if there are no changes), a passenger list and a list of the cargoes of the vessel. These shall be submitted to the port affairs administration for inspection and for the arrangement of clearance procedures.

Article 9. Following the completion of inspections by the relevant organs, a crew of a foreign vessel, if they desire, may apply to the frontier defense inspection organ for crew landing certificates.

Article 10. Passengers and crew of a foreign vessel shall not be allowed to engage in photographing or sketching in port.

Article 11. A foreign vessel entering or leaving port or transferring its mooring in port shall not conduct sounding unless this is undertaken with the consent and under the supervision of the pilots.

Article 12. The captain of a foreign vessel that experiences maritime problems along the Chinese coast shall make a maritime problems report to the port affairs administration within 48 hours of arrival. If maritime problems are met in port, he shall immediately submit a maritime problems report.

Article 13. The local port affairs administration may forbid the departure of any foreign vessel in any of the following cases:

(1) Violation of the regulations on vessel certificates, conditions of seaworthiness, freight loading, and provisions and installations relating to the vessel's technical safety conditions or of any other regulations.

(2) Failure to make the following payments: (a) various port charges; (b) fines for violation of the measures; (c) indemnity for damage to construction, navigation signals and other items of property.

The foreign vessel may be released if it has provided an appropriate guaranty sufficient to satisfy all the payments outstanding against her.

Article 14. These measures have been ratified by the State Council for promulgation and enforcement by the Ministry of Communications. The "Provisional Measures Governing Foreign Vessels Leaving and Entering Port" promulgated by the Ministry of Communications on May 20, 1952, shall meanwhile become null and void.

Note

The 1957 port measures expressly annulled the provisional measures of 1952. Nothing was said, however, about their impact upon the "Regulations Concerning Japanese Vessels Destined for China," some provisions of which were reproduced in the Note following item 16–10. It is unclear whether Japanese vessels continued to be subject to special regulations in Chinese ports.

Certain states have come to enjoy special privileges in Chinese ports as a result of treaties concluded with the PRC. For example, Article 8 of the Sino-Soviet Treaty of Commerce and Navigation of April 23, 1958, provided:

> Article 8. The vessels and the cargoes on vessels of either of the Contracting Parties shall be accorded in the ports of the other Party most-favoured-nation treatment in all that concerns entering, clearing, and stationing. Such treatment is in particular applicable in respect of the following: all kinds of dues and charges collected in the name of and for the state, the local authorities and other organs; mooring, loading and discharging in port and at anchorages; the use of pilots, navigation routes, lock gates, bridges, signals and lights for navigation; the use of cranes, weighbridges, warehouses, shipyards, dry-docks, and repair yards; supplies of fuel, lubricants, water, and food.
>
> The provisions of this Article shall not apply to the performance of port services, including pilotage and towage or to coastal shipping. Nevertheless, the vessels of either of the Contracting Parties proceeding from one port of the other Party to another for the purpose of landing cargo brought from abroad, or of taking on board cargo for a foreign destination, shall not be considered as engaged in coastal shipping.[44]

And, a few months earlier, the PRC and the USSR concluded item 17-2, an agreement governing ports, navigation, and commerce in the waters touching their joint frontier.

17-2

"Agreement between the Government of the People's Republic of China and the Government of the Union of Soviet Socialist Republics Concerning the Navigation by Merchant Vessels on Boundary Rivers and Lakes and Those Adjoining Them," signed at Moscow on December 21, 1957, *TYC 1957*, VI (1958), 278–282.

The government of the People's Republic of China and the government of the Union of Soviet Socialist Republics, being desirous of further developing exchange of materials between their two countries and of reciprocally providing convenient conditions for navigation by merchant vessels on the Amur, Sungari, Ussuri, Argun, Cherny Irtysh, Ili, and Sungacha Rivers and on Lake Khanka, have agreed as follows:

Article 1: The Contracting Parties shall, on the principle of reciprocity and equality, takes measures, including port and navigational fees, to ensure that during the period of navigational seasons merchant vessels of both Parties find navigation to be free and practicable at any time of the day and night along the entire navigable length of the Amur River (including the lower course of that river in the territory of the Union of Soviet Socialist Republics up to and including its mouth), the Sungari, Ussuri, Argun, Cherny Irtysh, Ili, and Sungacha Rivers, and Lake Khanka, and in all ports concerned.

The navigation authorities of the two Contracting Parties shall jointly draw up lists of ports and other places for navigation by merchant vessels on the rivers and lake specified above, in the light of the requirements of Soviet-Chinese exchange of materials. Such lists shall be drawn up well in advance of the start of navigation so as to enable the navigation enterprises to begin operations as soon as the rivers and lake are open for navigation.

Article 2. Each Contracting Party shall extend to the other favorable conditions in all matters pertaining to navigation by merchant vessels on the rivers and lake specified in Article 1, above, including the stay of vessels of either Contracting Party in ports of the other, the carrying out of port operations (including the work of loading and unloading), the use of port facilities and warehouses, the supply of fuel and food to vessels, the payment of fees and charges, and, when necessary, the rendering of medical assistance, and so forth.

Article 3. Sino-Soviet transport of goods and transit transport along the rivers and lake specified in Article 1, above, shall be reasonably shared among the navigation enterprises of the two Contracting Parties with due regard for the interests of the said enterprises, so that each shall satisfactorily participate in such transport.

The navigation enterprises of the two Contracting Parties may enter into agreements regarding technical and other questions resulting from the implementation of this Agreement.

Article 4. A vessel of either Contracting Party shall, while in the waters of the other Contracting Party, comply with the laws and orders in force in those waters. Matters concerning internal order on board the vessel shall be governed by the laws and orders of the Contracting Party whose flag the vessel is flying.

Each Contracting Party shall recognize the regulations of the other Contracting Party applying to its vessels concerning the construction and equipment of vessels, the composition of the crews and ship's papers.

Vessels of either Contracting Party navigating the waters of the other Contracting Party shall not be required to use the services of pilots of the other Contracting Party. However, all necessary measures shall be taken to ensure that any request by a ship's captain for pilots shall where possible be granted immediately.

Article 5. Each Contracting Party shall take the measures within the scope of its laws and regulations to expedite and simplify as far as possible the application of customs, health, and other regulations concerning navigation at its ports and along the national boundary.

Article 6. In accordance with the law in force of a Contracting Party, the customs authorities shall be entitled to take customs supervision over goods in transit through the territory of that Contracting Party.

Article 7. A vessel of either Contracting Party calling at a port of the other Contracting Party not for the purpose of loading or unloading goods but to take on supplies shall not be subject to customs formalities and shall be exempt from customs duties and other dues. However, it shall be subject to the supervision of the customs authorities until it leaves port.

Article 8. A vessel of either Contracting Party, on calling at a port of the other Contracting Party for loading or unloading goods and on leaving port, shall be exempt from customs duties and other dues, and from the requirement of import or export permits for articles of equipment, installation, or spare parts carried aboard the vessel.

The supplies on board the vessel destined for the crew and passengers, or for the operation and maintenance of the vessel, shall be exempt from customs duties and other dues both on entering and on leaving the port, and shall also be exempt from the requirement of import or export permits, provided that the regulations concerning custom supervision of the Contracting Party in whose waters the vessel has docked are observed.

The supplies which are destined for the crew and passengers, or for the operation and maintenance of the vessel, and which have been placed under the customs supervision in a port of the other Contracting Party shall be exempt from customs duties and other dues and from the requirement of import or export permits.

Goods not mentioned in this article shall be subject to the applicable customs regulations of the Contracting Party in whose waters the vessel has docked.

Article 9. Each of the Contracting Parties shall recognize the crew member's identity paper, with attached photograph, issued by a competent agency or local political authority of the other Contracting Party. This identity paper, in the case of a member of the crew of a

Chinese vessel, shall be the crew member's identity paper issued by the Ministry of Communications of the People's Republic of China and in the case of a member of the crew of a Soviet vessel, shall be the USSR seaman's pass.

Article 10. The identity papers specified in Article 9, above, shall entitle the persons who are described therein and who are aboard a vessel of either of the Contracting Parties to cross the state frontier of the other Contracting Party in either direction without a passport or business travel papers, provided that the name of the person concerned appears on the vessel's register.

A person in possession of an identity paper issued by one of the Contracting Parties shall, during the stay of his vessel in a port of the other Contracting Party, enjoy the right to go ashore and to move freely in the town in which the port is situated. Proper process should be executed for movement beyond the limits of the town. All persons going ashore shall be required to pass through the health, passport, and customs inspections of the locality concerned and to comply with local laws and decrees in force.

Article 11. A person in possession of an identity paper issued by one of the Contracting Parties, as specified in Article 9, above, and of a business travel paper issued by a navigation enterprise indicating his itinerary and destination, if required to do so in the course of his official duties, may cross to his destination at specified points of the state frontier of the other Contracting Party. However, in that case he shall not linger unnecessarily in the territory of the other Contracting Party.

Article 12. An employee of a navigation authority or enterprise of either Contracting Party who desires to cross the state frontier of the other Contracting Party in pursuance of his official duties must be in possession of a properly processed official identity paper, with attached photograph, or of the identity paper specified in Article 9, above, and of a business travel paper which has been issued by the navigation enterprise which indicates his itinerary and destination.

Article 13. No vessel of a Contracting Party shall dock in, or ride at anchor off, a port of the other Contracting Party without the special permission of the appropriate political authorities of the other Contracting Party, except in cases of force majeure or of inability to continue navigation. In such cases the persons aboard the vessel must remain on board and may not leave the vessel without the permission of the appropriate shore political authorities.

If necessary, the captain may send two or three members of the crew to go ashore to notify the nearest shore political authorities.

If the lives of the persons aboard the vessel are in jeopardy, they may go ashore. However, they may not leave the place at which they land until the arrival of the personnel of the political authorities summoned by members of the crew. Persons who have gone ashore must implement the lawful instructions of such authorities.

Article 14. Navigation enterprises of the two Contracting Parties may act as each other's agents in connection with passenger and freight transport at places along the rivers and lake specified in Article 1 of this Agreement.

Navigation enterprises of one Contracting Party may, if necessary and by agreement between the navigation authorities of both Contracting Parties, establish agencies in the territory of the other Contracting Party.

Such agencies shall be established and operated in accordance with the laws and regulations of the Contracting Party in whose territory they are situated.

Agencies of navigation enterprises of one of the Contracting Parties, set up in the territory of the other Contracting Party, shall be exempt from all taxes and dues imposed in that territory.

Article 15. Navigation enterprises of the Contracting Parties shall be subject to taxes directly connected with their passenger and freight transport business and shall pay them only to the state in which their supervising authority (administrative bureau) is situated.

Article 16. This Agreement is subject to ratification by the Contracting Parties and shall enter into force on the date of exchange of the instruments of ratification. The exchange of the instruments of ratification shall take place at Peking. The Agreement shall remain in force until it is denounced by one of the Contracting Parties, which shall give notice to the other Contracting Party three months before the end of the calendar year.

Done at Moscow on 21 December 1957 in duplicate, in the Chinese and Russian languages, both texts being equally authentic.

For the Government of the People's Republic of China:
Chu Li-chieh

For the Government of the Union of Soviet Socialist Republics:
S. Shashkov

NOTE

Agreements concerning ports did not preclude the PRC from unilaterally promulgating new measures relating to matters not covered in the agreements. As the 1960's wore on, steadily increasing tensions along the Sino-Soviet border led Peking to perceive a need for stricter control over border ports and rivers than the bilateral agreement with the USSR provided. Item 17–3 was promulgated just as the Great Proletarian Cultural Revolution that had been gathering force burst into view. It placed Chinese ports on the Soviet border under controls that are similar to, and in certain respects even stricter than, the controls that have prevailed in the PRC's ocean ports.

17-3

"Measures Governing Foreign Vessels on Bordering Rivers" (ratified by the State Council; promulgated by the Ministry of Communications on April 19, 1966), *JMJP* (Apr. 20, 1966), p. 2.

Article 1. These measures are enacted specially to safeguard the sovereignty of the PRC, to facilitate foreign vessels entering or leaving Chinese ports on rivers forming borders between China and other countries (hereinafter named briefly as ports on bordering rivers) or Chinese rivers reaching neighboring countries (hereinafter named briefly as rivers reaching neighboring countries), and to insure safe passage for foreign vessels.

Article 2. All foreign vessels entering or leaving ports on bordering rivers or rivers reaching neighboring countries shall observe these measures.

Article 3. Port Affairs Supervision Offices of the PRC are set up at ports on bordering rivers and ports on rivers reaching neighboring countries.

The Port Affairs Supervision Offices undertake to insure the thorough implementation of these measures and other decrees, laws, and regulations concerning navigation. They have the authority to review and approve the applications of foreign vessels entering or leaving port, to enforce compulsory pilotage on these vessels and organize joint inspection, to supervise the technical condition of foreign vessels and maintain order and safety of navigation, and to investigate and handle cases of average or accidents sustained by foreign vessels.

Article 4. No foreign vessel should enter or leave a port on a bordering river or a river reaching a neighboring country, except in accordance with the agreement on navigation by merchant vessels signed between the governments of China and the country to which the vessel belongs, or with the approval of the Chinese government. Each time a vessel enters or leaves port or river, it must apply for approval from the Port Affairs Supervision Office concerned, in accordance with the provisions of Article 5 and paragraph 2 of Article 9 of these measures.

Article 5. When applying for permission to enter or leave a port on a bordering river or a river reaching a neighboring country, the captain of a foreign vessel should, before the vessel departs from the last port of call, report, through its agent in the destined port, to the Port Affairs Supervision Office for review and approval in the destined port on a bordering river or the first port on the river reaching a foreign country, the name of the vessel, the number of vessels in the fleet, the deepest draft, the names and quantities of cargoes, and the number of passengers the vessel carries, and the scheduled time for arrival in port on a bordering river and for reaching the anchorage for joint inspection (pilotage) on a river reaching a foreign country. If the last port of call is situated on the opposite bank of the bordering river on which lies the port for which a foreign vessel is destined, a simplified procedure may be adopted, that is, the vessel may apply for entry by means of signals specified by the Port Affairs Supervision Office concerned.

Article 6. A foreign vessel entering or leaving a port on a bordering river or sailing on a river reaching a foreign country should hoist all specified signal flags. In daytime, it should also hoist the national flag of the country to which it belongs. When sailing on a river reaching a foreign country, it should also hoist atop its foremast the national flag of the PRC.

Article 7. A foreign vessel entering or leaving a port on a bordering river or a river reaching a foreign country must apply to the Port Affairs Supervision Office concerned for pilotage. During its anchorage in a port, a foreign vessel may not transfer its mooring without the direction of a pilot. If the pilot-anchorage has not been demarcated in a port on a bordering river owing to special circumstances, the Port Affairs Supervision Office concerned may exempt a foreign ship entering or leaving port from application for pilotage.

Article 8. When a foreign vessel enters a pilot-anchorage, its captain should report to the Port Affairs Supervision Office concerned the names and quantities of all the weapons, ammunition, wireless transmitters, radiotelephones, radar, rocket signals, signal guns, and so forth on board, and observe the following provisions:

(1) Weapons and ammunition should be delivered to the Port Affairs Supervision Office for custody;

(2) Use of wireless transmitters, radiotelephones, radar, rocket signals, signal guns and so forth is forbidden.

A vessel facing disaster or having an accident may unseal and use articles listed in paragraph (2) of this article, but [the captain] should immediately report to the Port Affairs Supervision Office concerned after such use.

Article 9. The captain of a foreign vessel entering pilot-anchorage should fill in the forms specified by the Port Affairs Supervision Office and submit them, together with the documents related to his vessel, for inspection by this Office. He should also accept joint inspection by the Port Affairs Supervision Office and the departments concerned.

When a foreign vessel leaves port, its captain should, through its agent in port, send in an application [for clearance] to the Port Affairs Supervision Office for review and approval and then fill in the specified forms and accept joint inspection. It may not leave port before receiving a certificate of [clearance] issued by the Port Affairs Supervision Office.

Article 10. When a foreign vessel sails on a river reaching a foreign country, the Port Affairs Supervision Office or other inspection departments concerned may send their personnel to work on board and the captain of the vessel should give them assistance where necessary.

Article 11. A foreign vessel entering port on a bordering river or a river reaching a foreign country, together with its crew and passengers on board, is forbidden to do the following:

(1) Photographing and sketching;

(2) Swimming, fishing, and hunting;

(3) Sounding;

(4) Jettisoning or discarding of ballast, cinders, refuse, exhaust fuel oil, greasy water from the ship, and so forth when in port.

Article 12. A foreign vessel is forbidden to moor, anchor, embark, and disembark its crew, load and unload cargo at any unspecified spot on the Chinese bank of a bordering river or on a river reaching a foreign country. There may be an exception when the ship is encountering maritime accidents or meets with accidents beyond its control. But its captain should immediately report the matter to the Port Affairs Supervision Office concerned or the local People's Council.

Article 13. When a foreign vessel has a maritime accident in a port on a bordering river or a river reaching a foreign country, its captain should expeditiously report the maritime accident to the Port Affairs Supervision Office concerned and wait for inspection and handling by the Port Affairs Supervision Office.

Article 14. The Port Affairs Supervision Office may forbid the departure of any vessel in any of the following cases:

(1) The vessel has lost its seaworthiness;

(2) The vessel violates the regulations governing safe navigation;

(3) The vessel has not paid its port charges;

(4) The vessel has not paid the indemnity payable and has not offered any suitable guaranty.

Article 15. The Port Affairs Supervision Office should deal with any foreign vessel and any of its crew and passengers that violate these measures and other decrees, laws, and regulations concerning navigation as the situation may be.

Article 16. These measures are applicable to all vessels except as otherwise stated in an agreement on navigation by merchant vessels signed between the governments of China and the country to which the vessels belong.

Article 17. All related People's Councils of provinces, autonomous regions, and municipalities under the direct jurisdiction of the Central People's Government may draw up and enforce bylaws according to these measures and in the light of local concrete conditions.

Article 18. These measures are promulgated for enforcement by the Ministry of Communications with the ratification of the State Council.

Note

The PRC has apparently been vigorous in enforcing its various measures and agreements relating to ports. Yet, until the Cultural Revolution, the subject attracted little attention, and information concerning actual practice is fragmentary. An enterprising scholar has discovered that the crimes of the two Japanese fishing boat officers who were convicted of military espionage in 1958 (16–8) included misbehavior in port; according to an interview with a former crew member, after the two vessels had been detained in port their logbooks were thrown into the harbor, but subsequently retrieved by the authorities.[45]

The following statement by a leading Chinese authority on jurisdiction, written "merely as a matter of reference" for the Communist government, summarizes what, at least until 1966 and in the absence of special agreement, was probably the PRC's view on jurisdiction over crimes committed on board foreign ships in port:

> According to the principle of territorial sovereignty, any crime committed on board a foreign ship in a Chinese port must, as a matter of course, be submitted to the Chinese authorities concerned. If, however, it merely involves the internal order and discipline of the ship, the said authorities may decide, in accordance with the relevant laws and regulations and the actual situation, whether they will accept jurisdiction over the case. For example, in the case of a drinking bout, quarreling, or other similar conduct among the ship's crew that does not affect the security and interests of the Chinese people, we ourselves would decide whether to claim jurisdiction. But if the case is so

> serious as to disturb the tranquillity of the port, or the victim is a Chinese citizen, the port authorities should proceed to deal with it immediately. . . . If homicide or other serious crimes should be committed on board a foreign ship, whether the murderer or the victim is a Chinese, a member of the crew, or a stranger, or whether the captain has reported it or requested assistance, it should be dealt with by the port authorities.[46]

With the advent of the Cultural Revolution, Peking's jurisdiction over ports became a matter of worldwide interest through a series of incidents, involving Soviet ships and personnel, that were reminiscent of the disputes between the Western maritime powers and the Ch'ing government during the decades preceding the Opium War.

17-4
"Soviet Ship Violating Chinese Harbor Regulations Ordered to Leave China," NCNA–English, Dairen (Dec. 28, 1966), in *SCMP*, no. 3851:39–40 (Jan. 3, 1967).

The Soviet SS *Zagorsk,* which violated China's harbor regulations and acted contemptuously toward China's sovereignty, was today ordered to leave China by the superintendent of the Dairen Harbor of the People's Republic of China.

The superintendent issued an order to the Soviet SS *Zagorsk* berthing at the Dairen Harbor on the decision to punish it for violating China's harbor regulations and acting contemptuously toward China's sovereignty.

The decision states: "In order to safeguard the sovereignty and the dignity of the harbor regulations of the People's Republic of China, it is hereby proclaimed:

"1. Nawmov, Captain of the Soviet SS *Zagorsk* is persona non grata and must immediately leave the domain of China; hereafter he is not allowed to enter any Chinese harbor;

"2. Impose the punishment of a serious warning on Kolbaenkov, Chief Officer of the Soviet SS *Zagorsk;* and

"3. Send the Soviet SS *Zagorsk,* under custody, out of the harbor."

The decision points out that while the Soviet SS *Zagorsk* was leaving the Dairen Harbor on December 8, 1966, its Captain Nawmov, in defiance of China's harbor regulations, repeatedly refused the pilot-orders of the Chinese pilot, and on his own accord, lifted anchor and mooring rope, started the engine and steered out. This made it impossible for the Chinese pilot to pilot the ship and seriously threatened the safety in the Chinese harbor. The Chinese pilot promptly issued orders to the captain: stand by anchor, hard port, and stop engine! so as to ask for instructions from the harbor master as to how to handle the question. However, the captain ignored the orders and insisted on moving the ship out of the basin. The Chinese pilot again ordered the captain to stop the engine. He refused to stop the engine and, moreover, asked the Chinese pilot to leave the ship in an attempt to move it out and evade responsibility. It was only after the Chinese pilot persistently refused to leave the ship that the captain had to stop the engine. The ship's chief officer, Kolbaenkov, even cursed the Chinese pilot twice and shook his fist at him in a provocative and threatening manner in the presence of the captain.

The decision stresses that "Captain Nawmov of the Soviet ship seriously violated China's harbor regulations and acted contemptuously toward China's sovereignty, and that the chief officer of the ship, Kolbaenkov, insulted a worker of the Chinese state in an utterly vile manner. However, proceeding from the desire for friendship between the Chinese and Soviet peoples, we decided to treat the matter leniently, only calling on the Soviet captain to recognize his mistakes, apologize for them, insure that no similar events recur in the future; then the whole matter would be finished. However, the Soviet captain not only refused to recognize his error and apologize, but, on the contrary, reversed right and wrong, falsely slandered the Chinese pilot as having given the wrong orders, and even lodged an unwarranted protest with the Chinese harbor authorities and asked for compensation."

"Deliberately making the incident even bigger, the representative of the Soviet Embassy in China openly supported this arrogant and unreasonable big-nation chauvinist attitude of the Soviet captain, thus repeatedly delaying settlement of the question."

After the announcement of the decision, the Dairen Harbor superintendent immediately dispatched ships to send the Soviet *SS Zagorsk* out of the harbor under custody.

Note

The Soviet version of the *Zagorsk* incident was indeed markedly different from the PRC account, as the following statement by the competent USSR ministry illustrates:

> On 8 December 1966, Chinese authorities of Port Dalny [Dairen] unlawfully detained the Soviet motor ship *Zagorsk* and held her until 28 December.

In this or in other ways to justify their actions, grossly violating the generally accepted norms and practices laid down by the legislation of shipping nations, including the regulations in force in the port of Dalny, the authorities of this port made the absolutely groundless charges that the Soviet ship had "violated regulations."

What really happened in Port Dalny regarding the Soviet motorship *Zagorsk?* Moored to quay 28 of Port Dalny, the motor ship *Zagorsk* finished loading cargo on 8 December, and, having completed all the necessary formalities, prepared to leave for the sea. Two Chinese pilots boarded the motor ship at 16:10. They gave the order to cast off and steered the *Zagorsk* toward the harbor mouth. Neither the skipper of the Soviet ship, nor the other members of the crew interfered with the actions of the Chinese pilots until, in the immediate vicinity of the port entrance, the pilots suddenly ordered the motor ship to change course. Compliance with this command would have inevitably resulted in the collision of the *Zagorsk* with the pier, presenting the danger of a serious accident or even the sinking of the vessel.

In this situation, the skipper of the *Zagorsk* could not, and, of course, should not have carried out the pilot's command. Precisely this enabled the ship safely to pass through the gates of the port, after which the skipper immediately stopped the ship and anchored it at the request of the Chinese pilots. When the ship had been anchored, armed Chinese guards and representatives of the port authorities came aboard, prohibited further movement of the ship, and tried to force their way into the navigator's room of the motor ship to seize maps and the ship's papers.

Soviet seamen, cherishing the interest of friendship between the peoples of the USSR and China, displayed self-control and patience, striving from the very beginning to settle this incident.

Despite repeated requests of the *Zagorsk* skipper to the port administration to investigate the case with the participation of members of the Soviet ship's crew and the Chinese pilots who were aboard the motor ship, representatives of the port authorities categorically refused to carry out any investigation and continued to detain the Soviet ship. These absolutely groundless and challenging actions of the Chinese authorities are unprecedented, the more so in relations among socialist nations.

On 10 December the Soviet Embassy in Peking asked the PRC Foreign Ministry to facilitate the sailing of the *Zagorsk* from the port of Dalny. However, the PRC Foreign Ministry spokesman, deliberately exaggerating the concocted charges against Soviet seamen, alleged that the motor ship *Zagorsk* had "violated the sovereignty of China." The Chinese authorities continued to insist on their demands and the motor ship and its crew were guarded at the outer roadsteads of Port Dalny.

On 17 December the Soviet side lodged a protest with the PRC embassy in Moscow, in view of the illegal arrest of the motor ship *Zagorsk,* and demanded its immediate release. The statement fully exposed the charges against the motor ship's skipper and other Soviet sailors invented by the Chinese authorities. It pointed out, specifically, that according to generally accepted international standards and practices laid down by the legislation of shipping nations, the pilot is an adviser (consultant) to a ship's skipper. Regardless of the presence of a pilot aboard, the ship's skipper is not stripped of responsibility for steering the ship during the maneuvering, and he bears full responsibility for the safety of the ship entrusted to him. According to Chinese official data, this practice exists also in PRC ports. Neither the sailing directions nor local regulations of Port Dalny contain any restriction on these rights of the skipper during piloting.

The Chinese pilot, who was aboard the motor ship *Zagorsk,* issued such instructions as might create the threat of an accident or even the loss of the ship. The actions of the skipper, in conformity with existing rules, insured the safety of the ship and were lawful. The charges by the Chinese side that the skipper of the motor ship *Zagorsk* allegedly "violated the sovereignty of China" were farfetched and groundless from beginning to end.

However, the Chinese side, far from taking any steps to release the ship, did not even reply to the statement of 17 December, made to the PRC embassy in Moscow. In this connection, the Soviet side again lodged a resolute protest on 24 December against the detention of the Soviet motor ship.

Only after that were Chinese authorities compelled, on 28 December, to let the Soviet motor ship *Zagorsk* leave the port. In order to conceal from world public opinion the true nature of their actions, they are trying now, by distorting facts, to find, in retrospect, justification for the unlawful 20-day detention of the Soviet ship and its crew. This is precisely the purpose of the 28 December NCNA report which was broadly circulated in the press and broadcast by the PRC radio. The unseemly goals of this report are perfectly obvious.

The USSR Ministry of the Merchant Marine cannot fail to

draw attention to the fact that the actions of the Chinese authorities are incompatible with generally accepted principles of relations in international trade navigation; they seriously prejudice cooperation between Soviet and Chinese seamen, and jeopardize normal shipping between the ports of the USSR and China.

The USSR Ministry of the Merchant Marine reserves the right to demand from the appropriate PRC authorities compensation for the losses caused by the unlawful, long detention of the motor ship *Zagorsk*.[47]

17-5

"Chinese Foreign Ministry Most Strongly Protests against Soviet Provocation of Insulting Chairman Mao," NCNA–English, Peking (Aug. 13, 1967) in *SCMP*, no. 4002:41–42 (Aug. 16, 1967).

The Chinese Foreign Ministry in a note to the Soviet Embassy in China today lodged the strongest protest with the government of the USSR against the serious provocative incident in which the Soviet revisionist ruling clique recently gave instructions to the crew of the Soviet diesel ship *Svirsk* to wilfully insult the great leader of the Chinese people, Chairman Mao.

The note was delivered to A. A. Brezhnev, chargé d'affaires ad interim of the Soviet Embassy in China, by a responsible member of the Department of the Soviet Union and the Eastern European Countries of the Chinese Foreign Ministry, who summoned the Soviet chargé d'affaires to an interview this afternoon.

The note says: On August 6, second mate Stanislav Ivanov and another crew member of the Soviet diesel ship *Svirsk* which lay at anchor in Port Dairen, China, asked on their initiative for a badge with the profile of Chairman Mao, the great leader of the Chinese people, from the Chinese frontier guard inspector, and then willfully insulted it and threw one badge into the sea in the face of the inspector. This was an intolerable act of sacrilege toward Chairman Mao, the great leader of the Chinese people and the revolutionary people of the whole world, an open insult to the socialist Chinese People's Republic and the 700 million great Chinese people, and an extremely serious provocative incident against China.

After the occurrence of the incident, all the Chinese port personnel and the broad revolutionary masses in Dairen, filled with indignation, put in many demands that the Chinese authorities concerned severely punish the culprits and handle this matter in a serious manner. The

Chinese department concerned twice ordered the captain of the Soviet ship to transfer the offenders to the Chinese department concerned for summons and trial.

But Soviet Captain Victor Korzhov adopted an arrogant attitude and stubbornly resisted, repeatedly refusing to produce the offenders. He even said that he was following orders from the Soviet embassy in China. This fully proved that the serious political provocation was made entirely on the instructions of the Soviet embassy in China. Its purpose was to further worsen the relations between China and the Soviet Union and to step up the perverse anti-China campaign throughout the world started by the Soviet revisionist ruling clique in collaboration with US imperialism. The Chinese government lodges the strongest protest with the Soviet government against the serious incident deliberately created by the Soviet revisionist ruling clique in insulting Chairman Mao, the great leader of the Chinese people.

The note says: It is no wonder that the Soviet revisionist ruling clique attacks and slanders Chairman Mao, the great leader of the Chinese [people, in] such a hysterical manner at a time when the world has entered the era of Mao Tse-tung's thought and when China's proletarian cultural revolution is gaining momentum. In the irresistible torrent of China's great proletarian cultural revolution and in the gigantic movement in which the invincible thought of Mao Tse-tung takes command of the hundreds of millions of people, the Soviet revisionist clique feels the approaching doom. These revisionists fear that once the Soviet people under their domination grasp the weapon of Mao Tse-tung's thought, they will rise in rebellion against them and unhorse them. Therefore the revisionists are adopting the most despicable means and using abusive terms to curse Chairman Mao. Yet how can mayflies topple a giant tree? The abuses of the Soviet revisionists against our great leader are no more than the buzzing of a few dying flies. They can by no means obscure the radiance of Mao Tse-tung's thought, but will only multiply the agony of their own doom. Their evil behavior all the more proves the greatness and correctness of Chairman Mao, the Lenin of our time. It will further elevate the boundless love for Chairman Mao among the broad masses of the Soviet people and accelerate the process of the grasping of Mao Tse-tung's thought by the Soviet people and the revolutionary people all over the world.

The note points out: Second mate S. Ivanov and another crew member of the Soviet diesel ship *Svirsk* brazenly insulted our great leader Chairman Mao in Port Dairen, and Captain V. Korzhov refused to carry out the order from China's department concerned and has so far refused to hand over the culprits. The Chinese authorities concerned therefore have decided to drive both V. Korzhov and S. Ivanov out of China and never allow them to come back again, meanwhile forcing the Soviet diesel ship *Svirsk* to leave Chinese territory under armed escort.

The Chinese government solemnly warns the Soviet government: Should you continue to instigate your men to stir up similar incidents, the Chinese authorities concerned will mete out severe punishment to them, the note concludes.

Note

Again the Soviet version of the events in question was dramatically different from the PRC's account. The following is a report of the incident made by the captain of the *Svirsk,* V. A. Korzhov, to staff correspondent P. Demidov, upon receiving a hero's welcome after arrival at Vladivostok:

> At about 8 p.m. on Aug. 7 ten armed border guards summoned the ship's captain. This in itself was unusual since a captain is never summoned with the assistance of members of the armed forces. The border guards demanded the surrender of Second Mate Stanislav Vladimirovich Ivanov, who had refused to pin on his chest a button with a picture of Mao Tse-tung, which a border guard standing at the ramp had offered to him as a "present." This rather insignificant episode sufficed for the unleashing of a vile uproar around the Soviet ship's crew.
>
> On the morning of Aug. 8 Captain V. Korzhov lodged a categorical protest and said he would not surrender the second mate to the Chinese authorities until he knew the true nature of his guilt.
>
> Aug. 9 came. Together with the first mate, Captain V. A. Korzhov went to the entry control station to learn the gist of the border guards' demands. It was discovered there that Second Mate Ivanov was charged with violating the sovereignty of the country. The conversation, accompanied by curses, insults, and shouting from the Chinese side, lasted a good seven hours. In this way still another day passed.
>
> At 5 a.m. on Aug. 10 the loading of the ship was completed, but the shipping papers, which were supposed to be filed immediately after completion of the loading, were not filled out until 2 p.m. The port authorities did not board the ship to register its departure. The captain concluded from this that the ship was under arrest.

The day of Aug. 11 began with a conversation between the captain and representatives of the entry control station. He was told to wait for a telephone call that would convey their decision. Forty minutes later the telephone did actually ring; the captain was asked to come to the entry control station for foreign seamen, which had never been the case before with respect to Soviet people.

There armed guards shoved the Soviet seamen into a room. The captain reiterated his protest against the arrest and the illegal detention of the ship. The border guards reconfirmed their terms—they would release the ship if the second mate were surrendered. The captain categorically refused to comply with their demand. Then a sheet of paper, clearly prepared in advance, appeared on the table. It said that from that moment the ship's captain was under arrest. Two border guards immediately tied Korzhov's hands behind his back and, with the help of several armed people, tossed him into a car. The captain of the *Svirsk* was put in prison. There he was subjected to a humiliating search, his watch was torn off, his pockets were cleaned out and his papers taken, and he was pushed into a dirty, small, isolated cell.

An hour and a half later Korzhov was transferred to another cell, to [the] ceiling [of which] a loudspeaker was attached. From 3 p.m. until 11 p.m. some sort of speeches, cries, slogans, and so on, were broadcast in Chinese. It was subsequently learned that scenes of the *hung weiping* [Red Guard] attack on the *Svirsk* were being described.

At about 3 p.m. on Aug. 12 the captain was led to the exit under escort. In the corridor he came face to face with 200 armed *hung weiping*. The wild mob rushed at him, Viktor Antonovich recalled. He was knocked off his feet, sworn at, and kicked while the border guards silently stood aside and watched this brutal violence. Korzhov was then dragged across the prison yard to the street. There he was met by a huge mob. He was put in a truck with his hands tied behind his back, was forced to bow his head, and in this position was driven around the city for three hours.

Afterwards Korzhov was brought to the port. When Viktor Antonovich looked at the ship, his self-control abandoned him, probably for the first time. The entire ship, from keel to truck, was packed with armed hooligans. They hung on the masts, on the shrouds, on the superstructures. The entire hull of the vessel was covered with slogans and obscenities.

Another truck arrived, and through an amplifier the demand was again made that the second mate be surrendered or else the *hung weiping* would take him by force. Five minutes were given to think it over.

A kind of trial was organized aboard the ship at the pier. Everything had been rehearsed in advance. In the raging mob there was always someone vested with power, at whose command the mob would begin to chant, storm the ship, yell, and so forth.

The *hung weiping* forced their way onto the ship, broke the radio shack window and tried to enter the cabins. They seized Piskunov, a sailor, mistaking him for Second Mate Ivanov, dragged him onto the bridge alongside the captain and smeared him with paint. They released him only when they found out they had made a mistake.

In the roads, meanwhile, two Chinese warships were anchored with their artillery pointed at the peaceful Soviet vessel.

The trial on the pier lasted several hours. The *hung weiping* dragged out Soviet sailors by force, one by one, and, failing to find Ivanov, drove them onto the roof of one of the holds.

Finally a border guard identified Ivanov and turned him over to the *hung weiping.* The navigator was placed alongside the captain. For two and a half hours Captain Korzhov and Second Mate Ivanov, the navigator, were driven around the city. Then they were taken to the *hung weiping* headquarters.

They were separated. Korzhov was taken from the office, and Ivanov was subjected to a "trial by ordeal"—with his hands tied behind his back, [he was] curse[d] and insult[ed].

The interrogation lasted all night. On the morning of Aug. 13 Ivanov was sent to prison and three hours later was brought to the headquarters; after a long and humiliating interrogation, he and Captain Korzhov were driven around the city on an open truck. They were brought to a stadium. A huge mob of people had gathered there. It was felt that the entire shameful spectacle had been well prepared.

From the stadium the captain and the second mate were taken back to the ship. They walked past columns of armed *hung weiping* and boarded the vessel. Under the escort of eight tugboats and a military launch the *Svirsk* finally put out to sea.

This is the story the captain of the *Svirsk* related to me as the ship entered its home port.[48]

Captain Korzhov had obviously been subjected by the Red Guards to what the Chinese call a "struggle meeting" or, as another Soviet press release condescendingly put it, "a trial patterned on Chinese culture." [49] The fact that many of the alleged outrages were committed by unofficial persons did not, in the Soviet view, lessen the PRC's responsibility. In the words of a Soviet commentator: "All these scandalous acts of lawlessness and arbitrariness are being carried out under the eyes of the official Chinese authorities and with their direct connivance. This in itself indicated that these provocations were planned in advance and are directed toward further complicating Soviet-Chinese relations." [50]

The Red Guards ended all hostile acts against the *Svirsk* and its crew less than twenty-four hours after dispatch of "the message of Comrade Kosygin," an extraordinary public telegram sent to Premier Chou En-lai just one day after a normal diplomatic protest had been filed. Kosygin protested the PRC's "violation of elementary norms of international law," demanded an immediate end to it, and pointedly noted that the Chinese action "is making doubtful the fulfillment of existing trade agreements between the Soviet Union and the [PRC]." [51]

17-6

Commentator, "A Clumsy Anti-China Performance," *JMJP* (Apr. 29, 1968), p. 6, translated in *PR* 11.20:29 (May 17, 1968).

The Soviet revisionist ruling clique has made a big noise and whipped up another anti-China campaign lately over the expulsion of the captain and second mate of the Soviet ship *Komsomolets Ukrainy* and over the ship's expulsion from a Chinese port under armed escort. From Vladivostok to Moscow it held "mass" rallies, gave press conferences and issued "statements" and "appeals." It has turned on its propaganda machine, keeping up the din in its press and on television and radio.

The Soviet revisionist clique's foul farce is an extremely clumsy one. It tried hard to appear as if it had been wronged, that the second mate of the *Komsomolets Ukrainy* had never surreptitiously taken photographs of Chinese naval vessels at a Chinese port and the topography of the Humen Fortress, nor had he carried out espionage activities. Similarly, it pretended that the ship's captain had never openly violated Chinese law, nor had he directed his crew to stage provocations against the Chinese side. However, all the evidence is there. The captain of your ship has confessed all and has made a written confession. How can you possibly deny this? When your men violated Chinese law and port regulations on Chinese territory, we certainly were obliged to take necessary measures to safeguard our state sovereignty and the dignity of our law. We can tell you frankly: If you dare to carry out espionage activities in China, you are surely going to be severely punished.

NOTE

Although it fails to present information concerning the PRC's allegations against the crew of the *Komsomolets Ukrainy,* the following account by an *Izvestia* correspondent is nevertheless of interest:

> It was a difficult voyage. Usually these words are spoken about the stormy Antarctic latitudes, the silent Arctic ice, or the fiery skies of Vietnam. Now, unfortunately, voyages to China have also become difficult. . . .
>
> Today the tanker *Komsomolets Ukrainy* is being welcomed in Vladivostok. As is known, it was illegally detained by the Chinese authorities in the Port of Whampoa.
>
> At 10:10 p.m. on March 26 the Chinese authorities signed the cargo documents. This meant that the *Komsomolets Ukrainy* had fulfilled its assignment and was ready to leave port. However, the Chinese authorities, under farfetched pretexts, did not give the vessel permission to leave port and committed high-handed acts against its crew.
>
> At 11:00 a.m. on March 30 representatives of the port administration came aboard the tanker and read an order for the arrest of the second mate, A. P. Panomarchuk. Naturally, the captain, Ivan Gavrilovich Kosyakov, protested, since such an action runs counter to international norms. Soviet ships enjoy immunity; no person can be detained, much less arrested, without the knowledge of our embassy and our government. This was followed by the insolent statement that the captain has no rights here and must only answer questions. When a border guards officer came on board, he was followed by 24 armed men with submachine guns, who blockaded the living quarters.
>
> At night there was another visit. This continued during the next three days.
>
> At 5:00 a.m. on April 3, 11 armed soldiers came on board, and a representative of the state security agency demanded that the ship's log and radio log be produced. Since this was at variance with international regulations, the captain refused. Then followed another demand to turn over the second mate. The captain read a collective protest from the crew, but the officer Li

Chang-cho read an order of the Kwang[tung] (Canton) Province border control service concerning the violation of Chinese laws by the Soviet vessel. The state security representative whispered several orders and a few minutes later a naval landing vessel approached carrying no less than 200 regular troops with submachine guns.

Several soldiers forced their way into the wardroom and began to unfurl a canvas; from all indications, their aim was to cover the captain with it and carry him away since there was an order for his arrest. Our seamen surrounded their commander and formed a living wall in front of the soldiers. Then the soldiers literally began to attack. They were unable to overcome the seamen's resistance by sheer force, and therefore they began to seize them one by one, beating them, striking them in the face, head, and legs and dragging them about by the ears. How much resistance can 12 men put up? But one soldier would constantly be replaced by another. One seaman was torn from the ranks. Then a second. A third. A blow to the head, and he is thrown like a sack onto the wardroom floor. Anatoly Zhansky tried to get up—his chest met the muzzle of a submachine gun. Vladimir Malinovsky and Aleksei Kovpak faced submachine gun barrels. After two hours only 3 out of the 12 remained on their feet.

With his hands tied behind his back, the captain was lowered down the ship's ladder. As the seamen withstood the last siege, when the pressure from the Chinese soldiers was especially strong, from the wardroom of the Soviet tanker resounded the words of the "Internationale." Our seamen were singing the party hymn. The captain was led down the ladder. He was thrown into a car. Then a cell with bars on the windows. A cot. The interrogation, at a table covered with a black cloth. Threats, insults, blackmail.

The seamen were compelled to declare a collective hunger strike as long as the captain did not return to the ship.

By this time the homeland knew about the outrages committed by the Chinese authorities. Our government lodged a resolute protest.

At 4:48 a.m., Peking time, April 5, the homeland received a radiogram from the Soviet tanker *Komsomolets Ukrainy* saying that the ship was in international waters.[52]

The Soviet Union was not the only country to run afoul of the impact of the Cultural Revolution on China's ports, as the following dispatch suggests:

G. Eckford and D. I. Twitchen, crew members of the British merchant ship *SS Lord Gladstone* anchored in the Chinese port of Talien, on May 7 and 15 insulted portraits of Chairman Mao, the great leader of the Chinese people. They also wrote a reactionary slogan "Long live the US" on board the ship. These extremely grave acts of political provocation and hostility towards China have aroused tremendous indignation among the Chinese people.

The Chinese authorities concerned have detained the culprits in accordance with law, and announced that the British captain of the ship, E. C. Marsden, who connived in these incidents, was forbidden to call at any Chinese port in the future.

These political provocations by British crew members are inseparable from the British government's hostile attitude all along towards the Chinese people. The Chinese Ministry of Foreign Affairs addressed a note of strong protest to the Office of the British chargé d'affaires to China on May 19.[53]

The PRC subsequently protested against a total of seven alleged incidents of British sailors insulting Chairman Mao. "A responsible member" of the Department of Consular Affairs of the Foreign Ministry handed the British chargé d'affaires a detailed memorandum that concluded:

> "We must sternly warn you that the days when the imperialists could ride roughshod in China are long since gone for ever. If the British government is wise enough, it must immediately take effective measures to prevent the recurrence of similar acts of political provocation. Otherwise, the Chinese authorities concerned will mete out severe punishment. Don't say that you have not been warned in advance.[54]

Seamen from other countries also had problems coping with the Red Guards during 1967.[55]

Even after the activities of the Red Guards had been curbed, foreigners' difficulties with port regulations continued. For example, in April 1968 Peter Crouch, a British ship's officer, was taken off a freighter in Shanghai for allegedly violating harbor regulations. He was held without trial for two and one-half years before being released.[56] In March 1970 Shanghai authorities arrested an officer from each of two British cargo ships on charges of infringing harbor regulations that prohibit marking the position of buoys on charts, an international navigational practice disapproved of by the PRC. One of the ships was released after the crew had suffered five days of intimidation and propaganda. The other ship and the two officers were detained another fortnight.[57]

Although consideration of the PRC's claims to exercise jurisdiction over Chinese ships and personnel in foreign ports should properly be deferred until Part VI, the following statement is presented here because it provides a nice contrast with the PRC's claims to control events within its own ports. Moreover, item 17–7 suggests that, contrary to the view expressed by a 1957 Chinese textbook (recall the introduction to Part IV), the PRC claims the equivalent of territorial jurisdiction over its nonmilitary vessels even while they are situated within foreign ports.

17-7

"Political Provocation," NCNA–English, Peking (July 31, 1967), in *FBIS*, no. 147/67:BBB4–6 (July 31, 1967).

Peking, 31 July—Chinese seamen and the commercial representative of the China Council for Promotion of International Trade are waging a tit-for-tat struggle in Venice against a grave political provocation by the Italian authorities. A report from Venice indicates that the Italian authorities have obstructed Sino-Italian trade and carried out acts of provocation against the Chinese people.

Quotations from Chairman Mao Tse-tung displayed aboard two Chinese ships—the SS *Sungkiang* and SS *Yuhao* (Friendship)—were made the excuse for this provocation. The two freighters belonging to the China Ocean Shipping Company arrived in Venice on 22 and 26 July, respectively, laden with cargo of Chinese goods scheduled for discharge in Italy.

On the ships were hung these quotations from Chairman Mao: "People of the world, unite and defeat the US aggressors and all their running dogs! People of the world, be courageous, dare to fight, defy difficulties, and advance wave upon wave. Then the whole world will belong to the people. Monsters of all kinds shall be destroyed." Also hung on the ships were the slogans: "Salute to the Italian working people!" and "Long live the friendship between the Chinese and Italian people!"

The Italian authorities unjustifiably intervened and demanded that all the quotations and slogans be removed. The Chinese crew refused to comply with this unreasonable demand, pointing out that Chinese seamen consider they have a duty and a right to study and publicize

Mao Tse-tung's thought [aboard] their own ships and to display slogans expressing their friendship for the Italian people. This right, they claim, is not to be interfered with by anyone under any pretext.

After this sharp and justified rebuke, the Italian authorities sent a large police force [aboard] threatening and attempting to intimidate the Chinese crew. The ships were cordoned off, and unloading was stopped. The Italian authorities forbade Chinese seamen to go ashore and refused to allow the shipping agent [aboard] to make the necessary business contacts.

More serious still is the Italian authorities' obstruction of the normal functions in Venice of personnel of the commercial representative bureau in Italy of the China Council for Promotion of International Trade. The vice representative of the bureau, Liu Jo-ming, and two of its staff were kept on board and were not allowed to carry out their normal duties.

The Chinese captains strongly protested a number of times against the Italian authorities' crude violation of the elementary principles of international law. The Italian authorities, however, paid no attention to their protests and cut off all supplies of food, drinking water, and fuel to the ships. They even threatened to dispatch the Chinese ships out of Italian territorial waters under "armed escort."

Informed of what had happened in Venice, the Chinese commercial representative bureau in Italy on the afternoon of 27 July lodged a most serious protest with general manager Scala of the Italian Foreign Trade Institute. This protest pointed out that the incidents in Venice constituted a grave political provocation on the part of the Italian authorities, were hostile to the Chinese people, and were in accordance with the anti-China line of US imperialism. It demanded that all these provocative measures be called off immediately, that unloading of the ships be resumed, and that the Chinese foreign trade personnel and seamen be guaranteed the right to go about their legitimate activities. The bureau again lodged similar protests on the evening of 27 July and the next morning.

The more than 80 Chinese seamen involved, armed with the thought of Mao Tse-tung, waged an heroic struggle against the outrageous provocation by the Italian authorities. Defying the threat of violence made by the Italian armed policemen, they sternly and justly repudiated the provocations of the Italian authorities. With heads erect, they read aloud together quotations from Chairman Mao and sang those passages set to music. This left the Italian policemen speechless and caused great confusion in their ranks.

The Italian people's warm reception of the visiting Chinese ships was in strong contrast to the action of the authorities. When the two ships carrying cargo of Chinese materials and the Chinese people's profound friendship for the Italian people arrived in Venice, they were warmly welcomed by the Italian working people. The SS *Sungchiang,* the first to arrive, was greeted by many Italian workers and the waving of the five-star red flag of China. Their friendship was also demonstrated by various gestures. When the ship was alongside the wharf, dockers and other working people exchanged very friendly greetings with the Chinese seamen, besieging them with requests for badges with the profile of Chairman Mao. Some copied quotations from Chairman Mao displayed in Italian in the ship's mess room and others shouted "Long live Mao Tse-tung!" All their actions expressed sincere admiration for Chairman Mao and their deep friendship with new China.

Following the political provocation of the Italian authorities, the Chinese quarters concerned are closely watching all developments.

NOTE

The tensions of the Sino-Soviet conflict that manifested themselves in Chinese ports also affected the operations of the Sino-Soviet Joint Commission for Navigation on the Boundary Rivers, as indicated by the following message sent by the chairman of the Chinese side to the chairman of the Soviet side on June 6, 1969.

17-8

"Chairman of Chinese Side of Sino-Soviet Joint Commission for Navigation on Boundary Rivers Replies to Chairman of Soviet Side," *PR* 12.24:3,39 (June 13, 1969).

Your telegram of May 23 has been received.

On May 11 this year, the Chinese side proposed to your side that the 15th regular meeting of the Sino-Soviet commission for boundary river navigation be held in Poli [Khabarovsk] in the middle of June.

In its telegram of May 23, the Soviet side, while proposing that the meeting be convened on June 18, again stood facts on their head and falsely alleged that the Chinese side "did not show the desire to hold the 15th meeting last year" and that the "14th meeting" held in Harbin the year before last "ended up without any result because the Chinese side attempted to bring up for discussion problems that were not within the competence of the commission." These slanders and attacks made by the Soviet side on the Chinese side are utterly groundless.

The Chinese side made it perfectly clear in its telegram to the Soviet side dated May 11 this year that the responsibility for the failure to hold the regular meeting last year rests entirely on the Soviet side. As for the fruitless outcome of the 14th regular meeting held the year before last, that, too, was solely the making of the Soviet side. At the 14th regular meeting, basing itself on the relevant agreement between the two countries and proceeding from its stand of respecting each other's sovereignty and safeguarding normal navigation on the Sino-Soviet boundary rivers, the Chinese side discussed with the Soviet side all the questions raised by the latter and reasonable solutions were indeed found for some of them. The Soviet side, however, adopted a truculent attitude of big-power chauvinism and refused to discuss and solve the questions advanced by the Chinese side, asserting that they "were not within the competence of the commission." Furthermore, in violation of the established practice, the Soviet side refused to enter into the notes of the meeting the different views of both sides, and thus broke up that regular meeting.

Now, in deliberately distorting the truth about the 14th regular meeting and attacking the Chinese side, the Soviet side is attempting to place in advance obstacles to the coming 15th regular meeting. If the Soviet side still has any sincerity for making the coming regular meeting a success, it must change its wrong attitude and earnestly discuss all the questions put forward by the two sides concerning navigation on the Sino-Soviet boundary rivers.

I now inform you that the Chinese side agrees to the date of June 18 for holding the coming regular meeting and that it will send to the meeting at the scheduled time a delegation of ten headed by Chang Chan-teh, the new chairman of the Chinese side of the Sino-Soviet Joint Commission for Navigation on the Boundary Rivers. You will be notified later of the specific time of the Chinese delegation's arrival at Poli.

Note

The meeting of the Joint Commission was held from June 18 until August 11, 1969. The Chinese press subsequently reported: "Proceeding in the spirit of making a success of the meeting and settling issues, the Chinese delegation patiently conducted negotiations with the Soviet side, reached agreement with the Soviet side on certain specific issues relating to navigation on the boundary rivers between the two countries and signed the minutes of the meeting."[58] Late in December 1970 it was announced that the Joint Commission had met again and concluded another annual agreement relating to technical navigation matters.[59]

18 Territorial Air Space

In the course of his discussion of the legal status of outer space (14–1), Liu Tse-yung set forth the PRC's position on the extent to which a state may exercise jurisdiction over its territorial air space. "Every state," he wrote, "has complete and exclusive sovereignty over the air space above its territory (see the Paris Convention of 1919 [for the Regulation of Aerial Navigation] and the Chicago Convention of 1944 [for International Civil Aviation]). This is a universally recognized principle of international law." Although Liu relied on the Paris and Chicago conventions as evidence of customary international law supporting this broad general principle, the Chinese Communist regime has not acceded to either convention, and its position on certain basic problems of air law appears to rest upon customary international law that differs from principles adopted in those conventions. The most obvious example concerns the extent to which international law permits foreign aircraft to enter a state's air space without prior permission.

It will be recalled from Fu Chu's discussion (16–2) that the PRC's 1958 Declaration on the Territorial Sea provided that: "No foreign vessels for military use and no foreign aircraft may enter China's territorial sea and the air space above it without the permission of the Government of the People's Republic of China." In supporting the legal position of his government, Fu Chu asserted that "all international air conventions uniformly confirm that no foreign aircraft has a right of innocent passage through the air space above the territorial sea." He attributed this to recognition of the increased security problems that a state would encounter were it unable to restrict the entry of all foreign planes.

While the PRC's refusal to admit foreign aircraft into its air space without prior authorization expresses the customary rule of international law, it is not quite accurate to state, as Fu Chu does, that no international conventions recognize a "right of innocent passage" for any aircraft. Fu Chu should have pointed out that with respect to civil aircraft the Paris Convention established a distinction between scheduled international airlines and unscheduled ones. The latter, if they belonged to parties to the Convention, were given "freedom of innocent passage" through the air space of other parties, subject to certain conditions set forth in the Convention. Scheduled airlines, on the other hand, were to have no right of passage without prior authorization.[60] The Chicago Convention maintained this distinction in somewhat more precise terms. It gave nonscheduled airlines the right, without prior authorization, to "make flights into or in transit *nonstop*" through the air space of a party and to "make stops for nontraffic purposes," subject to a number of qualifications and restrictions laid down by the Convention. State aircraft, including military aircraft, were required to have prior authorization.[61]

Within the limits of its military power, the PRC has vigorously enforced its claim to exclusive control over its air space. It has repeatedly protested alleged intrusions and from time to time has issued cumulative statistics on these violations. In 1954, for example, it was reported that in previous years American planes had illegally entered the PRC's air space on a total of 32,995 occasions for bombing, strafing, and reconnaissance missions.[62] It was subsequently alleged that between September 7, 1958, and April 27, 1962, 334 American military planes had violated the PRC's air space on 161 occasions.[63] The PRC's air force has frequently shot down intruding aircraft. The following three items and the intervening Note reveal the PRC's responses to challenges to its sovereignty over air space. Chapter 19 contains further examples.

18-1

"Chinese Air Force Downs Three US Imperialist Warplanes," *PR* 10.19:30 (May 5, 1967).

An air force unit of the Chinese People's Liberation Army shot down a pilotless military reconnaissance plane of US imperialism on April 29 somewhere over Kwangsi. The plane had intruded into China's air space for reconnaissance and provocation. On May 1, two intruding A–4B attack planes of US imperialism were also shot down over Kwangsi. The heroic Chinese air force units had, within the short space of eight days, brought down five intruding US imperialist warplanes. This is a tremendous victory for the great proletarian cultural revolution, for the proletarian revolutionary line represented by Chairman Mao and for the immensely brilliant, great, and invincible thought of Mao Tse-tung.

The Military Commission of the Central Committee of the Chinese Communist Party has issued orders commending the air force units concerned. The Commission's May 1 order pointed out that the successive victories scored by Chinese air force units had greatly raised the morale of the revolutionary people and punctured the arrogance of

US imperialism. The order extended the warmest congratulations to all the commanders and fighters who took part in the engagements. It added: "Recently, while steadily escalating its bombing of north Vietnam, US imperialism has repeatedly sent military planes to intrude into China's air space in deliberate war provocations. We must raise our vigilance and deal seriously with them. We hope you will hold still higher the great red banner of Mao Tse-tung's thought, vigorously give prominence to proletarian politics and energetically revolutionize your thinking, earnestly sum up your experience, keep up your militancy, guard against arrogance and rashness, give full play to our style of fighting—courage in battle, no fear of sacrifice, no fear of fatigue, and continuous fighting—and win new and greater victories."

[A] *Renmin Ribao* [People's Daily] commentator published an article on May 2 in congratulation of the victories. [The] commentator stressed: "We want to tell US imperialism again in all seriousness: The 700 million Chinese people and the Chinese People's Liberation Army are invincible. The US air bandits will certainly come to no good end if they should dare to continue to intrude into our air space. The Chinese people and the PLA are waiting at all times with their iron fists for the US aggressor bandits. We will strike hard at them whenever they come. If they should dare to come, we will see to it that they will never get away!"

18-2

"China Protests against Spy Flight of an American U-2 Plane," *PR* 5.38:7 (Sept. 21, 1962).

Following is the text of the statement issued on September 14, by the Government of the People's Republic of China protesting against the provocative spy flight of an American U–2 plane over China.

On September 9, 1962, a US-made U–2 plane of the Chiang Kai-shek gang intruded into the air space over eastern China on an espionage mission and was shot down in the act by the air force of the Chinese People's Liberation Army. This intrusion constitutes a crime of flagrant aggression by US imperialism against China. It is a serious challenge by US imperialism to peace in the Far East and the world. While warmly celebrating this great victory of the defenders of the territorial air of their country, the 650 million Chinese people cannot but express their strong indignation against the US imperialist aggressor who has all along been hostile to the new China.

After the incident took place, the United States government, on the one hand, declared that the U–2 plane was purchased by the Chiang Kai-shek clique from the American Lockheed Aircraft Corporation, attempting to show thereby that the whole affair had nothing to do with the United States, but on the other hand it admitted that the United States obtained information collected through the activities of such espionage aircraft. This is indeed a futile attempt; it is also a self-contradictory statement. The United States has U–2 planes stationed in many parts of the world. Wherever the U–2 planes go, the danger of war follows. The people in all countries where American U–2 planes are stationed strongly demand that the United States withdraw them. It is well known that all these U–2 planes are under the direct control of the United States itself. How can Taiwan be an exceptional case? The servicing, maintenance, use, and command of these planes are all in the hands of the United States. The present U–2 intrusion into China was solely directed by the United States. The US government is the chief culprit in this aggressive crime. The Chinese government hereby lodges the strongest protest with the US government.

The intrusion of this American U–2 aircraft into China is by no means an accidental or isolated incident. For a long time, US aeroplanes and warships have continually intruded into China's air space and territorial waters. Not long ago, the United States even incited and encouraged the Chiang Kai-shek gang to prepare for an adventurist invasion of the southeastern coastal areas of China. After this scheme was exposed, the US government still made flat denials; it indicated again and again that it had no intention of attacking China with armed force, and declared that it would not allow the Chiang Kai-shek clique to invade the Chinese mainland. The present U–2 incident sufficiently shows, however, that all these statements are just a hoax. And this incident itself represents an important step taken by the US government in inciting and encouraging the Chiang Kai-shek gang to invade the mainland of China.

Note

Peking's scholars have also been alert to answer arguments that might relieve the United States from legal responsibility for having launched balloons that violated Chinese air space. Ch'en T'i-ch'iang responded to certain contentions:

> The United States recently launched large numbers of military reconnaissance balloons over the territorial air of China, the Soviet Union, Czechoslovakia, the Democratic Republic of Germany, Bulgaria, Albania, and Sweden. The spokesman of the

> Chinese Ministry of Foreign Affairs protested against this provocation in a statement released on February 7. Similar protests were made by the Soviet Union and other countries. The Soviet protest of February 4 pointed out that the US action constituted a rude infringement of the Soviet territorial air and a violation of the principles of international law.
>
> In face of the protests from various parts of the world, the US authorities tried every means and used different excuses to whitewash its crime. These excuses, however, contradicted each other and were of little help to lessen US crimes in violating international law. For instance, the US Navy declared on February 6 that the balloons were not equipped with cameras. On the same day, a spokesman of the US State Department admitted that the balloons were fitted with cameras and radio sets but that they were intended to collect meteorological data. US Secretary of State Dulles explained at a press conference on February 7 that the cameras attached to the balloons were to take pictures of cloud conditions and, quite accidentally, they took some pictures of the ground. In trying to defend the illegal US action and write off the sovereignty of a country over its territorial air, Dulles said: "The question of the ownership of the upper air is a disputable question, and also of the ether above the air."
>
> Dulles' allegation is nothing but a flight of fancy in the field of international law. . . .
>
> Other US excuses are equally pointless. The American allegation that the balloons did not interfere with traffic [was] smashed by the tragic air crash in Czechoslovakia.[64]

Hsu Tun-chang met the argument that a state is free to launch balloons in its own air space even if they subsequently float elsewhere. His view was summarized in an NCNA dispatch:

> Professor Hsu Tun-chang went on to point out that according to universally acknowledged principles of international law, a country must bear legal responsibility for any damages to another country arising from its violation of international obligations or abuse of its rights. "According to this principle, a country must exercise restraint regarding any act that may harm the interests of other countries and prevent the occurrence of any such incidents. This is why a country should not do anything to a river that may damage the interests of other countries along it, or adopt any measure within its own territory that may pollute the air of its neighboring countries."

The American international law expert C. C. Hyde was quoted as having declared in his *International Law, Chiefly as Interpreted and Applied by the US:* "A state is obliged to make reasonable and constant endeavor to prevent uses of the domestic areas in such a way as to pollute the air or water within adjacent foreign territory."

Professor Hsu continued: "In view of the present highly developed air traffic, it is impermissible for any country to carry out within its territory or in areas under its effective jurisdiction any activities that encroach on the territorial air of other countries or are detrimental to their aviation or international security.

"The launching of balloons by the US military authorities from many military bases is an abuse by the US of its rights, and an encroachment on the rights of other countries. The US must bear legal responsibility for this." [65]

The reaction of another Chinese scholar, Ch'en Wei, to the American meteorological balloons suggested that the PRC was willing to permit use of its air space for properly authenticated international scientific observation, as indeed was demonstrated by its cooperation in preparation for the International Geophysical Year that was to begin July 1, 1958 (recall 11–15):

The aerial boundaries of a country are as inviolable as its boundaries on land and sea. Since the military reconnaissance balloon is a flight instrument of a military nature, its intrusion over another country is clearly a violation of the latter's territorial air. The nonsense uttered by Dulles, therefore, cannot change the universally accepted principle of international law or free the United States from responsibility for its criminal action.

Another pretext deserving our attention is the US attempt to misconstrue the launching of balloons as a kind of scientific research activity, and even to link it with the plans of the forthcoming International Geophysical Year. This way of putting it can hardly deceive people with a little common sense. The International Geophysical Year, as is generally known, is an activity of a purely scientific research nature universally planned by the scientists of the world. Although this comprehensive scheme envisages the gathering of meteorological data in different parts of the world, it has nothing in common with the launching of US balloons of a military reconnaissance nature. Furthermore, the preparatory committee of the International Geophysical Year has already assigned relevant scientific organizations of

> various countries to proceed with the work of gathering meteorological data. It has not entrusted the US military authorities with any task of contributing scientific materials. The US claim of launching balloons for the sake of scientific research is only intended to undertake, under similar pretext, the type of reconnaissance activities they [*sic*] previously failed by means of aircraft over peaceful and democratic countries.[66]

Together with other scholars, Ch'en Wei also criticized the United States' effort to avoid responsibility for the launching of propaganda balloons by private organizations:

> It should be pointed out here that in its reply to the Soviet government and other official statements, the US government tried to evade its responsibility for the practice by certain US organisations of sending propaganda balloons over the people's democracies in Eastern Europe. It tried to argue that the criminal activities of the US-backed Radio Free Europe and the Crusade for Freedom had no connection whatever with the United States.
>
> Dulles said that since these activities undertaken outside the US territory were of a private nature, it was not their concern to think of controlling them. [The] facts before us, however, indicate that it is very difficult for the United States to deny its close relations with these reactionary organs.
>
> It is common knowledge that Radio Free Europe in Munich, West Germany, is a special agency founded by General Lucius D. Clay, former commander of US occupational forces in West Germany, to conduct espionage against the Soviet Union and the people's democracies. The American magazine, *Newsweek,* reported several years ago that Americans decided on the policy and offered technical assistance in operating this radio station. It added that the broadcasting station of Radio Free Europe would not duplicate the effort of the Voice of America but would broadcast what the Voice of America, an agency of the US State Department, could not do.
>
> The point to be emphasized here is that Radio Free Europe is a private organisation and therefore it can broadcast whatever it pleases without having to bother about diplomatic reactions or [any] mess it might bring about. Clay himself also predicted at the time when this organization was inaugurated in 1950 that there would be no limit to what they could and would do. Over the years, whenever the US ruling clique found it necessary to intensify the cold war or international tension, it would,

like the masters letting loose their hounds, direct this reactionary organ to launch frantic subversive and sabotage activities against peaceful democracies in Europe. The launching of balloons is one of its criminal activities in recent years. Obviously, only the United States can stop activities undertaken by this organ. Therefore, in denying its connection with Radio Free Europe, the United States was only showing that it would try to continue its provocations against the people's democracies in Europe and to interfere with their internal affairs.[67]

18-3

"Foreign Ministry Note to Britain on [F-86]," NCNA–English, Peking (June 22, 1957), in *SCMP*, no. 1558:36–37 (June 26, 1957).

The Ministry of Foreign Affairs of the People's Republic of China today lodged a strong protest with the office of the British chargé d'affaires in Peking against the permission granted on March 22 by the Hong Kong British authorities for the Chiang Kai-shek clique to ship back to Taiwan an F-86 jet fighter plane which escaped to and took refuge in Hong Kong last year.

This plane intruded over Fukien and Kwangtung provinces on January 1, 1956. It was pursued by Chinese People's Liberation Army aircraft and landed in the Kai Tak airfield in Hong Kong.

The protest stressed that the British authorities in Hong Kong must take responsibility for all consequences of their connivance in the use of Hong Kong by the Chiang Kai-shek clique to threaten China's security.

As regards this incident, the Ministry of Foreign Affairs on the afternoon of the same day, orally and, on February 4, in a note to the British chargé d'affaires in Peking, demanded that the British government detain the Chiang Kai-shek military plane and its crew. In defiance of international precedents and the just demand of the Chinese government, the British government on March 12, 1956, permitted the return to Taiwan of Li Sheng-lin, the plane's pilot. In its note of reply dated March 16, 1956, to the office of the British chargé d'affaires, the Chinese Ministry of Foreign Affairs made a strong protest and reiterated its firm demand that the Hong Kong British authorities detain this plane and that the plane shall not be handed over to Taiwan by any means. The Foreign Ministry also stated that the Chinese government would never tolerate connivance at Chiang Kai-shek's use of Hong Kong to threaten China's security. The British government has up to now failed to reply to the note of the Chinese Ministry of Foreign Affairs dated March 16, 1956. The British government has now once again disregarded the solemn statement and just demand of the Chinese government by permitting the Chiang Kai-shek clique to take the plane to Taiwan. This is another very unfriendly act by the British government and the Hong Kong British authorities toward the Chinese government and people. It cannot but arouse protest and condemnation by the Chinese people.

NOTE

The PRC has also accused the USSR of a great many intentional intrusions into China's air space, charges that have been vigorously denied by the USSR.[68]

The only multilateral air agreement to which the PRC has acceded is the Warsaw Convention of 1929 (Convention for the Unification of Certain Rules Relating to International Transportation by Air).[69] Of course, Peking's participation in multilateral air regulation efforts might be more substantial if it had succeeded in its 1950 attempt to oust the delegates of the Republic of China from the International Civil Aviation Organization (ICAO) and to replace them with Chinese Communist representatives.[70] In the present circumstances, however, details relating to the PRC's exercise of jurisdiction over foreign civil aviation in its air space must be found in its unilateral prescriptions and in its bilateral agreements.

Articles 7 and 10 of the Act on the Frontier Defense Inspection (15–5) illustrate relevant provisions that are scattered in various internal promulgations. Item 18–4 announces the publication of flight regulations, the text of which is not yet available. Item 18–5 is an example of the bilateral air agreements that the PRC has concluded with a number of countries. It is considerably more detailed than air agreements that the PRC has concluded with Communist neighbors such as North Vietnam.[71]

18-4

"China Publishes Flight Rules Governing Foreign Civil Aircraft," NCNA–English, Peking (Jan. 28, 1964) in *SCMP*, no. 3151:18 (Jan. 31, 1964).

The flight regulations to be observed by all foreign civil aircraft entering or leaving the People's Republic of China or flying within China have been made public here by the Civil Aviation Administration of China. The "Flight Rules Governing Foreign Civil Aircraft" were approved by the State Council at a recent plenary meeting.

The regulations provide that foreign civil aircraft can enter or leave China or fly within China only in accordance with agreements on air communication concluded between the Chinese government and the government of the foreign countries concerned, or with the permission of the Chinese government obtained through diplomatic channels. Foreign civil aircraft must obey the orders of the air traffic control departments designated by the Civil Aviation Administration of China and abide by the flight regulations.

Foreign civil aircraft and the crew members and the passengers on such flights, while in China, must abide by the laws of the People's Republic of China and the decrees and regulations for entrance and departure and transit through China.

Foreign civil aircraft granted permission to fly within China must bear identifying markings. The aircraft and their documents, members of the crew, passengers, freight, and luggage, are subject to inspection by the relevant departments of China.

Chinese People's Liberation Army air defense planes on duty may order foreign civil aircraft to land at designated airfields if they violate the rules governing flight within China. Such aircraft may continue their flight only with permission from the Civil Aviation Administration of China.

18-5

"Air Transport Agreement between the Government of the People's Republic of China and the Government of the Union of Burma," (signed and entered into force on Nov. 8, 1955), in *Air Laws and Treaties of the World,* I (Washington, D.C.: Government Printing Office, 1965), pp. 438–443.

The government of the People's Republic of China and the government of the Union of Burma, desiring to establish scheduled civil aviation services between their countries in order to promote their economic and cultural relations, have agreed upon the following:

Article I. (A) Each Contracting Party, pursuant to the provisions of this Agreement, agrees to grant the right to the designated air transport enterprise of the other Contracting Party to carry on flights, by its aircraft for civil transport purposes, on the following air route:

Course for aircraft of the People's Republic of China: Kunming-Mandalay-Rangoon

Course for aircraft of the Union of Burma: Rangoon-Mandalay-Kunming-Canton.

For civil aircraft of the People's Republic of China, the above-mentioned right to conduct transport flights shall mean the transporting of passengers, baggage, goods, and mail (1) from Kunming to Mandalay and Rangoon, (2) from Rangoon and Mandalay to Kunming; for civil aircraft of the Union of Burma, the above-mentioned right to conduct civil transport flights shall mean the transporting of passengers, baggage, goods, and mail (1) from Rangoon and Mandalay to Kunming and Canton, (2) from Canton and Kunming to Mandalay and Rangoon.

(B) In accordance with the principle of mutual respect for sovereignty over territorial air, each Contracting Party shall designate independently that part of the air route, which Section (A) of this Article prescribes, that passes through its own territory. Entrance and exit points on the common border of the Contracting Party shall be designated jointly through consultation.

Article II. (A) The government of the People's Republic of China shall designate the "China Civil Aviation Administration" as the air transport enterprise to manage the air route prescribed in Article I of this Agreement. The government of the Union of Burma shall designate the "Union of Burma Airways Board" as the air transport enterprise to manage the air route prescribed in Article I of this Agreement. The frequency of scheduled flights of the air transport enterprise of each Contracting Party shall not exceed two a week in each direction. Each Contracting Party shall decide for itself as to the date of inauguration of such scheduled flights, provided the other Contracting Party has been notified sixty days prior to such inauguration. Either Contracting Party may request consultation, which shall be conducted on a fair and equal basis, with the other Contracting Party with a view to initiate any change in the schedule of flights.

(B) The right of principal ownership and the right to make final decisions in the management of the designated air transport enterprise shall belong to the government of each Contracting Party.

Article III. The designated air transport enterprises of the Contracting Parties, in accordance with the Protocol, which is based on joint needs and mutual benefit, of this Agreement, shall receive fair and equal opportunity and consideration regarding the distribution of business and utilization of service facilities including communication services, navigational aid, meteorological information, accommodations of airports, schedule of flights, rates charged for the carriage of passengers and goods, business agency, transshipment and fiscal matters.

Article IV. (A) Rates to be charged for the carriage of passengers, baggage and goods on the designated air route prescribed in Article I of this Agreement, shall be fixed at a reasonable level, with due consideration for all factors including presupposition of economy in operation and expectation of a reasonable amount of profit. The designated air transport enterprises of the Contracting Parties shall establish a uniform minimum standard for rates to be charged on either the whole common air route or on different but equal sections of it.

(B) Minimum rates to be charged on the air route prescribed in Article I of this Agreement or any section of it shall be resolved by the air transport enterprises of the Contracting Parties and ratified by the Contracting Parties. In the event an agreement cannot be reached by the air transport enterprises or in the event the minimum rates agreed upon fail to acquire the required ratification, the Contracting Parties shall devise ways and means through which mutual agreement may be secured. Unless a new decision on minimum rates is reached, the rates in force at the time shall continue to be effective.

Article V. Matters concerning the carriage of mail on the designated air route prescribed in Article I of this Agreement shall be dealt with by the postal authorities of the Contracting Parties through negotiation.

Article VI. (A) Every civil aircraft of the designated air transport enterprise of each Contracting Party, while in flight on the designated air route prescribed in Article I of this Agreement, shall carry domestically designed markings for international flight, registration certificate, certificate of airworthiness, flight logbook, permit for radio equipment, passenger list, and manifest of goods and mail; flight personnel shall possess valid licenses and certificates of fitness.

(B) Each Contracting Party shall recognize as valid the above-mentioned documents issued or validated by the other Contracting Party. But the standard of minimum requirement set by one Contracting Party for the issuance or approval of such certificates and licenses shall equal or exceed that which is or may, at some future time, be set by the civil aviation authorities of the other Contracting Party.

Article VII. Pilots and other members of flight service who operate aircraft of the designated air transport enterprises of the Contracting Parties on the designated air route prescribed in Article I of this Agreement shall be citizens of the People's Republic of China and the Union of Burma, respectively.

Article VIII. Each Contracting Party shall permit the use by the other Contracting Party of its airports necessary for the operation of the designated air route prescribed in Article I of this Agreement and shall be responsible for providing the kind of radio service essential to aircraft in flight under normal conditions, meteorological service and other flight facilities, and shall adopt the approved standards as set forth in the Protocol of this Agreement.

Article IX. Neither Contracting Party shall, under any circumstances, charge civil aircraft of the other Contracting Party for using its airports and other facilities rates higher than those paid by its own aircraft. Each Contracting Party shall publish these rates and notify the civil aviation authorities of the other Contracting Party.

Article X. (A) Aircraft of the designated air transport enterprise of each Contracting Party shall comply with laws and regulations of the other Contracting Party governing the entry into and departure from its territory in international flight, business transactions, flight within its borders and prohibited and restricted areas.

(B) Pertinent laws and regulations in force [for] each Contracting Party governing entering the country, leaving the country, release permit, customs, immigration, quarantine, and so forth shall apply to flight personnel, passengers, baggage, goods, and mail carried by civil aircraft of the other Contracting Party. The Contracting Parties shall avoid any unnecessary delay while applying the provisions of these laws and regulations.

(C) In order to ensure observance of the provisions of this Agreement, the proper authorities of each Contracting Party shall have the right to inspect, within its territory, grounded civil aviation aircraft of the other Contracting Party. In doing so, unreasonable delay shall be avoided.

Article XI. (A) Supplies of fuel, lubricating oils, spare parts, regular equipment, and other aviation stores retained on board aircraft of the designated air transport enterprise of one Contracting Party shall be exempt in the territory of the other Contracting Party from customs duties, inspection fees, or similar duties or charges, even though such supplies be used by such aircraft within that territory. When permitted by the customs authorities of the other Contracting Party, such tax-exempt supplies may be unloaded and kept under the custody of the customs authorities until reloading is desired.

(B) Supplies of fuel, lubricating oils, spare parts, regular equipment, and other aviation stores introduced into the territory of the other Contracting Party, to be used exclusively for aircraft of the air transport enterprise designated by, or on behalf of, one Contracting Party, shall, in accordance with the principle of equality and mutual benefit, be exempt from customs duties, inspection fees or similar duties or charges, provided pertinent regulations of the other Contracting Party, whose customs authorities may supervise such supplies, have been observed.

Article XII. (A) Each Contracting Party shall render every possible assistance and convenience, within its territory, to the other Contracting Party in its technical maintenance and repair activities necessary for the operation of the designated air route prescribed in Article I of this Agreement.

(B) The designated air transport enterprise of each Contracting Party shall make arrangements, and shall, when requested, make every effort to provide, within its territory, the designated air transport enterprise of the other Contracting Party with fuel and lubricating oils necessary for the operation of the designated air route prescribed in Article I of this Agreement. If one Contracting Party, for the purpose of operating that part of the designated air route that lies within the territory of the other Contracting Party, imports its own fuel and lubricating oils, the other Contracting Party shall permit such practice and render every possible assistance and convenience.

(C) Each Contracting Party shall adopt security measures in its airports for safeguarding aircraft, fuel, lubricating oils, and equipment of the other Contracting Party.

Article XIII. The Contracting Parties, considering the needs in the operation of the designated air route prescribed in Article I of this Agreement, shall, respectively, accord to the designated air transport enterprise of the other Contracting Party the following: To the designated air transport enterprise of the People's Republic of China, the right to establish its own offices at Rangoon and Mandalay. To the designated air transport enterprise of the Union of Burma, the right to establish its own offices at Canton and Kunming.

With the exception of persons who are hired locally, each Contracting Party shall employ its own citizens to staff such offices. Each Contracting Party shall render such offices of the designated air transport enterprise of the other Contracting Party every assistance and convenience.

Article XIV. Each Contracting Party agrees to accord to the designated air transport enterprise of the other Contracting Party necessary convenience in matters concerning foreign exchange, in order that profit resulting from operating the designated air route prescribed in Article I of this Agreement may be converted into the desired currencies.

Article XV. Each Contracting Party shall direct its civil aviation authorities to conduct regular and routine consultations and to maintain close cooperation with the civil aviation authorities of the other Contracting Party, in order to uphold the principles of this Agreement and to ensure the application of its provisions.

Article XVI. The civil aviation authorities of each Contracting Party shall undertake, or direct its designated air transport enterprise to undertake, to make prompt exchange of current data on traffic between the Contracting Parties. These data include regulations concerning transportation, timetables, price lists, and papers pledging that the provisions of this Agreement will be fully adhered to. Each Contracting Party shall also direct its designated air transport enterprise to furnish the civil aviation authorities of the other Contracting Party with monthly statistics on traffic, including places of embarkation and destination, between the Contracting Parties.

Article XVII. Either Contracting Party may request consultation with the other Contracting Party with a view to initiate any amendments to this Agreement. Consultation shall take place within sixty days after the initial request. Resulting new or amended provisions shall immediately enter into force.

Article XVIII. In the event one Contracting Party or its designated air transport enterprise fails to act according to the provisions of this agreement, the other Contracting Party reserves the right to detain or terminate the operating license granted. This action, however, shall not be taken until negotiation has taken place.

Article XIX. (A) Each Contracting Party shall deem it its responsibility to furnish suitable equipment and take practical steps to aid aircraft in distress of the other Contracting Party, and to permit, subject to control by local authorities, the other Contracting Party to provide measures of aid as may be necessitated by circumstances. The Contracting Parties, when searching for missing aircraft or aiding distressed aircraft, shall cooperate in concerted measures.

(B) In the event of an accident within the boundaries of the other Contracting Party to an aircraft of the designated air transport enterprise of one Contracting Party, involving death or serious injury, or indicating serious damage of the aircraft, the Contracting Party in whose territory the accident has occurred shall, according to its pertinent regulations, undertake to investigate the circumstances of the accident. The Contracting Party which owns the aircraft shall have the right to appoint observers to be present at the investigation, and the Contracting Party conducting the investigation shall communicate the report and findings to that Contracting Party.

Article XX. The protocol and notes exchanged between the Contracting Parties in connection with this Agreement shall be regarded as component parts of this Agreement and shall be included in its application.

Article XXI. In the spirit of friendship and mutual understanding, the Contracting Parties shall settle any dispute arising from the interpretation or application of this Agreement and the protocol through consultation and negotiation.

Article XXII. This Agreement shall enter into force on the day it is signed. After this Agreement has been in force for one year, either Contracting Party may at any time give written notice to the other Contracting Party expressing its desire to terminate this Agreement. If such notice is given, this Agreement shall terminate one year after the date of receipt of the notice by the other Contracting Party, unless the notice is withdrawn by mutual agreement three months before the expiration date.

Done in duplicate at Rangoon on the eighth day of November, 1955, in the Chinese and Burmese languages. Both texts shall have equal authority.

NOTE

Although prior to entering the UN the PRC had not articulated its legal position with respect to the increasingly troublesome problem of hijackings of international air flights, it appeared to be opposed to hijacking. For example, the PRC exuberantly supported some other activities of Palestinian terrorists, but it remained silent when they hijacked a number of planes in 1970.[72] And, when in the spring of 1971 some Philippine radicals hijacked a Philippine Air Lines jetliner and forced it to fly to China, the PRC released the passengers, crew, and plane, without the hijackers, within twenty-four hours. The Chinese authorities, who said this was their first case of hijacking, treated the passengers and crew courteously, made the hijackers apologize to them, and stated that they disapproved of air piracy.[73]

Entry into the UN required Peking to face up to the problem in a general way. The PRC participated in a decision of the Security Council, adopted by consensus on June 20, 1972, which stated:

> Members of the Security Council are gravely concerned at the threat to the lives of passengers and crews arising from the hijacking of aircraft and other unlawful interference with international civil aviation. In these circumstances, they wish to reaffirm Security Council resolution 286 (1970) of 9 September 1970 and to recall that the General Assembly has expressed its deep concern about the situation.
>
> Members of the Security Council condemn and consider it necessary to put an end to acts that are directed against the safety of civil aviation and that are being perpetrated in various parts of the world presenting serious obstacles to the normal use of air transportation, an important means of international intercourse.
>
> The Security Council calls upon States to take all appropriate measures within their jurisdiction to deter and prevent such acts and to take effective measures to deal with those who commit such acts.
>
> The Security Council invites all States to expand and intensify cooperative international efforts and measures in this field, in

> conformity with Charter obligations, with a view to ensuring the maximum possible safety and reliability of international civil aviation.[73a]

Security Council resolution 286, adopted prior to the change in China's representation at the UN, appealed to all parties concerned immediately to release all passengers and crews held as a result of hijacking or other interference with international travel, and called on states to take all possible steps to prevent further hijacking or other interference with international civil air travel.[73b]

Crimes Committed in Chinese Territory 19

We have already seen many examples of the PRC's claim to exercise criminal jurisdiction over aliens as well as Chinese nationals within its territory. The vaguely worded enforcement provisions of the legislative and administrative prescriptions reproduced in items 15–1, 15–5, and 17–3 all authorized, explicitly or implicitly, resort to the criminal process. In item 16–2 Fu Chu stated that in principle the coastal state has jurisdiction over all cases occurring on board foreign merchant ships in the course of their passage through its territorial sea. And the Note following item 17–3 presented another Chinese scholar's assertion that the PRC has jurisdiction over all crimes committed on board foreign ships in Chinese ports, even though it may choose to forego the exercise of jurisdiction in appropriate circumstances. We have also seen in item 17–2 an agreement between the PRC and the USSR prescribing that, when the vessel of one party is in the waters of the other, "matters on board the vessel shall be governed by the laws and regulations of the Contracting Party under whose flag the vessel is sailing."

Part V has already presented a number of cases of the actual exercise of criminal jurisdiction by the PRC over both nationals and aliens: the conviction of an overseas Chinese who was an Indonesian national for illegally attempting to leave China (15–6); the PRC's effort to pressure the UK to return Chinese who fled to Hong Kong after allegedly committing crimes on board a PRC ship in Chinese territorial waters (16–6); the conviction of two Japanese fishing boat officers for military espionage (16–8) and the detention of foreign maritime personnel and yachtsmen (17–5, 17–6, Note following 16–8, and Note preceding 17–7).

Frictions with many countries have arisen out of the PRC's exercise of territorial criminal jurisdiction. This was especially true in the regime's earliest years, when a variety of foreign nationals who had chosen to remain in China after the Communist takeover were convicted of espionage and other counterrevolutionary crimes. Missionaries, academic administrators, professors, students, and businessmen—many, but not all, from the United States—ran afoul of the law in this period. In addition, the PRC's relations with Japan were clouded by the exercise of criminal jurisdiction over two distinct categories of persons:

fishermen and prisoners of war. It has been reported that between 1950 and 1954 "the PRC detained 158 Japanese fishing vessels and 1,909 crewmen under the charges of espionage and other illegal activities. Fifty-four vessels and all the crewmen (except 17 who died during captivity) were later returned to Japan."[74] And item 4–5 illustrated the PRC's conviction of Japanese prisoners of war as war criminals.

Here we present material on the general scope of the PRC's territorial jurisdiction over crime, the extent to which the international law of human rights is perceived to be a limitation upon the exercise of that jurisdiction over citizens of the PRC, and the experiences of diverse types of foreigners with the criminal process.

19-1

Chung-yang cheng-fa kan-pu hsüeh-hsiao hsing-fa chiao-yen-shih pien, *Chung-hua jen-min kung-ho-kuo hsing-fa tsung-tse chiang-i* (Lectures on the general principles of criminal law of the PRC; Peking, 1957), pp. 36–37.

The criminal law of the People's Republic of China is universally applicable to the entire territory of the country.[a] Following the establishment of the People's Republic of China, the Chinese people have completely abolished the concessions, leased territories, and consular jurisdiction [b] which the United States, Britain, and other imperialist countries acquired in old China, thereby ending the humiliating position of China as a semicolony and restoring the state's sovereignty and independence. Therefore, all the offenses committed within the territory of our country will be subject to the punishment of our criminal law. This is a natural conclusion based on the principle of state sovereignty. . . .

Here it should be pointed out that in ordinary circumstances the problem of determining the commission of an offense within the territory of the People's Republic of China can be easily solved. But it is also possible to have the following circumstances: A criminal act takes

[a] [Omitted.]

[b] Consular jurisdiction is a privilege provided for in the unequal treaties imposed upon the old Chinese government by imperialist countries. It started with the Sino-British Hu-men [the Bogue] Treaty of 1843 and the Sino-American Wanghsia Treaty of 1844. This privilege is: when nationals of those countries which enjoyed the right of consular jurisdiction in China were defendants in civil or criminal cases, Chinese courts had no right to adjudicate those cases, and they could only be adjudicated by consuls of the respective foreign countries.

place outside Chinese territory, but its consequences take place inside Chinese territory; or a criminal act takes place inside Chinese territory, but its consequences take place outside Chinese territory. For example, a criminal element blows up an international train with a time bomb. He places the bomb in the train when it is in foreign territory; then the train enters our territory and blows up. Or the opposite situation might occur. In either case we should consider the offense committed within our territory, and therefore, our criminal law shall apply.

19-2

Ch'ien Szu, "A Criticism of the Views of Bourgeois International Law on the Question of Population," *KCWTYC*, no. 5:41–43 (1960).

In international relations, imperialism frequently uses the pretext of "protecting human rights" to intervene in the internal affairs of socialist countries. The tunes of bourgeois international law scholars also serve this imperialist goal. Under the socialist system, the elimination of the system of private ownership of the means of production has led to the elimination of the economic basis which gives rise to political and legal inequality, and thereby guarantees the genuine realization of the human rights of the vast laboring people. The rights of landlords and bourgeoisie arbitrarily to oppress and enslave laboring people are eliminated; the privilege of imperialism and its agents to do mischief, kidnap, rob, rape, and massacre is also eliminated. To the vast masses of people, this is a wonderfully good thing; this is genuine protection of the human rights of the people. The bourgeoisie and the bourgeois international law scholars, however, consider this to be a bad thing, since it encroaches upon the "human rights" of the oppressors and exploiters. The socialist countries' suppression of counterrevolutionary criminals and rebellious elements supported and dispatched by imperialism in an attempt to sabotage the people's regime is a necessary measure adopted to protect the interests of the people. However, the bourgeoisie and the bourgeois international law scholars decry such measures as encroachments upon "human rights." In fact, they try to use the pretense of protecting "human rights" to slander socialist countries, and thus pave a legal way for their intervention. For instance, after our country pacified the rebellion of the upper class reactionary clique of Tibet, in 1959 the imperialist-supported "International Commission of Jurists" slandered our country on the pretext of "human rights" and "freedom." In their so-called "Summary of the Report on the Question of Tibet" and "The Question of Tibet and the Rule of

Law" and other reactionary documents, they increasingly cried that the Chinese government "deprived the Tibetan people of their fundamental human rights and freedoms" and that the Tibetan people have been subjected to "massacre, imprisonment, banishment, and forced labor." They demanded that the United Nations and other international organizations concerned "assist the struggle of the people of Tibet to achieve justice and freedom" and "punish" the "crimes" committed by the Chinese government. They put on a false face of kindness and justice and dressed themselves up as the defenders of the human rights of the Tibetan people. This is indeed hypocrisy and shamelessness to the extreme. All people can see that when the vast masses of Tibetan people were serfs and were subject to oppression, being whipped, having their eyes gouged and their limbs cut off, and being killed at will by feudal serf owners, it [the International Commission of Jurists] did not consider these acts to be violations of human rights and did not come out with an appeal for the oppressed and the injured. Only when the Central People's Government with the support of the Tibetan people pacified the rebellion of the upper-class reactionary clique of Tibet and began to reform the Tibetan serf system so that the vast masses of Tibetan people might genuinely obtain freedom and liberation did it feel sorry and lose no time in accusing us of disrespect for "human rights," "humanity," and so forth. This is indeed a strange sense of "kindness." To put it bluntly, they do not want to protect human rights; they want to protect Tibetan serf owners' privileges of oppressing and massacring the vast masses of Tibetan people and to find an excuse to intervene in the internal affairs of China.

Imperialism often uses the pretext of respecting and protecting human rights to launch aggression and carry out intervention in the internal affairs of nationalist countries. For instance, when the revolutionary [courts] of Iraq and Cuba sentenced counterrevolutionaries and spies of imperialism to imprisonment, American imperialism and its agents all invoked the "abuse of human rights" and other arguments in their threats and provocations against Iraq and Cuba. During his visit to Brazil, Argentina, Chile, and Uruguay in early 1960, President Eisenhower further proposed to organize an "Inter-American Commission on Human Rights" to protect the "democratic freedoms" of the Latin American people.[a] As a matter of fact, this was an attempt by the United States to use the "Inter-American Commission for Human Rights" for further control over Latin American countries, since it may, at any time, intervene in the internal affairs of various American countries on the pretext of "protecting human rights."

[a] Ch'ing-li-pao, Argentina, Feb. 3, 1960. [Note: We are unable to locate this source.]

In short, the "human rights" referred to by bourgeois international law and the "human rights" it intends to protect are the rights of the bourgeoisie to enslave and to oppress the laboring people, that is to say, the human rights of the bourgeoisie. Internally, they are used to conceal the real encroachment upon the rights and freedoms of the laboring people by the bourgeoisie; externally, they provide pretexts for imperialist opposition to socialist and nationalist countries. They are reactionary from head to toe.

Bourgeois international law's views of genocide are the same as those on the question of human rights, and are mainly used to malign and to oppose socialist countries.

The bourgeoisie have committed the crime of genocide many times in history. The American treatment of Indians is an example. According to statistics, there were as many as 14 million to 40 million Indians in Columbus' time. However, as a result of the policy of extermination carried out by the American bourgeoisie, there were only 400,000 Indians according to the 1957 statistics of the United States Bureau of the Census. Essentially, all Indians in the United States have been exterminated. During the period of the Second World War, German Fascist bandits carried out the policy of exterminating all Poles, Czechs, Jews, and other nationalities, and killed millions of good people. This is another example of genocide which shocked the world. Under pressure from the people of the whole world who were angered by Fascist atrocities, the United States, the United Kingdom, and France were obliged to assume a hypocritical pose, and at the United Nations General Assembly in 1948 they reluctantly agreed to adopt the Genocide Convention. However, they smuggled something of their own into the Convention. They not only concealed the class origin of genocide, but also intentionally did not prescribe criminal responsibility for propagandizing about genocide, thereby providing an exit for future criminals to avoid responsibility. In fact, even though the Convention has been signed for more than ten years, the crime of genocide has never been stopped either in the United States or in the Union of South Africa. Bourgeois international law scholars have never forcefully accused or condemned those criminals. On the contrary, in order to meet the needs of imperialist opposition to socialist countries, they have fabricated some false accusations of genocide to slander and malign socialist countries. For instance, at the eleventh session of the General Assembly of the United Nations in 1956, the United States and the United Kingdom and other imperialist countries manipulated to submit an agenda item on the so-called "Question of Deportation of Hungarian Citizens" which fabricated the story that the Soviet Union engaged in genocide activities by large-scale massacre and exile of Hungarians. United Nations intervention was demanded. In 1959, after our country pacified the rebellion of the upper-class Tibetan reactionary clique, the so-called "International Commission of Jurists" mentioned above also groundlessly fabricated the story that "the Chinese even attempted to resort to massacring Tibetans, by means of serious physical and mental persecution, in order to exterminate the nation and religion of Tibet." It also stated that "such actions constitute the crime of genocide" and therefore the United Nations should intervene. Obviously, all this slander is designed to serve the ultimate object of an attempt by American imperialism and international reactionaries to use the question of Tibet to intervene in the internal affairs of our country. The foregoing further exposes the real face of bourgeois international law which serves only the aggressive interests of imperialism.

Note

Ch'ien Szu's arguments were an elaboration of some of those advanced by the PRC in protesting against a resolution on the question of Tibet adopted by the UN General Assembly in 1959 (see 38–3 and Note preceding it).

Despite their professed scorn for bourgeois manipulation of symbols such as "human rights" to interfere in China's domestic affairs, PRC scholars have not been reluctant to play the game themselves. In 1959, for example, when the United Arab Republic moved to detain a resident Lebanese Communist, the China Political Science and Law Association condemned this as "persecution." Shen Chün-ju, then President of the Supreme People's Court, termed the UAR's action an outrage "against human rights and humanitarianism, international law and the minimum code of international relations." Another Supreme Court judge, Chang Chih-jang, stated that it "violated the fundamental principles of modern international law safeguarding basic human rights."[75]

19-3

The following account summarizes a series of articles published in the *Hong Kong Tiger Standard* (Oct. 10, 13, 14, and 15, 1960) by Yim Yuen-lo, a Chinese resident of Hong Kong, who had left mainland China as a child when his parents became refugees.

In 1959 Yim was a reporter on the staff of United Press International in Hong Kong. Through the Hong Kong branch of the China Travel Service, the tourist agency of the PRC, he arranged for permission to go to Canton for the purpose of interviewing William Downey, an American who was in China at that time to visit his brother, detained in prison. En route to Canton, Yim took photographs of soldiers, peasants, workers, and flood conditions. In Canton he took "tourist photos" of streets, houses, people, and construction. After several days of fruitless efforts to arrange the interview he sought, Yim decided to return to Hong Kong. As he was preparing to leave his hotel, he was notified that the city Public Security Bureau wanted to see him. Upon arrival at the Bureau, he was questioned by two officials, who accused him of being an "American reporter" and of having entered the country illegally. They said that he should have reported to the Public Security Bureau upon entering the city, and he had not. The officer confiscated his papers, told him not to communicate with anyone or to try to leave Canton, and ordered him to return the next day for further questioning.

For seven days in succession, usually at night, Yim was interrogated at the Bureau and allowed to return to his hotel to sleep. At that point he decided to send a telegram asking his Hong Kong office for help. The next day, having received no response, he attempted to place a telephone call to Hong Kong. Within minutes, a public security official entered his room and said: "Haven't you forgotten our discipline?" Yim was taken back to the Bureau, where he was told to "think over" his mistakes. At that time, in addition to illegal entry, he was accused of working for an American imperialist propaganda organ and collecting military, political and economic information. Afraid that his life was in danger, Yim confessed to "violating the sovereignty" of the PRC.

The next day he was shown arrest and search warrants, which he was asked to sign. Since these documents contained no formal charges, when signing his name he added "I do not know the reason for my arrest." He was then transferred to a prison, where he was kept in a small, solitary cell where the light remained on all night. From time to time he was interrogated by a "sweet-talker" and a "shouter," who tried to extract information about spying and other illegal activities. The rest of the time, although subject to no physical mistreatment and no "violent form of brainwashing," he was exposed to thought reform through talks with the warden and guards and through newspapers, books, and radio broadcasts.

One day, after about six months, he was taken to a room in the prison, where he was confronted by two men from the prosecutor's office. They gave him a paper with charges written on it: "collecting military, political, and economic information" and "lobbying against the people with money and material under the direction of the US imperialist Merick [the Hong Kong UPI Bureau Manager]." The prosecutors asked whether Yim wanted a lawyer to defend him. He declined: "What is the use of a lawyer? I had already confessed the charges earlier, knowing that was the only way I would ever gain freedom."

The following afternoon he was taken to court for a show trial, replete with newsreel cameras and floodlights. Yim was told to speak in Mandarin rather than the local Cantonese because a film and a tape recording of the trial were being made for national distribution in the cinema and over the radio. There were approximately three hundred spectators in the courtroom. At the front of the room, behind a table, sat a judge and two "people's assessors," all dressed in Chairman Mao's favorite style high-necked tunics. At a table to the right sat the two prosecutors who had interviewed Yim. At a table to the left sat a defense attorney, despite the fact Yim had requested none and had not known that counsel had been assigned. Microphones were in front of all the participants.

After reading the charges, the judge questioned Yim with the "same old questions." When Yim finished his testimony, a series of witnesses appeared including a cab driver who testified about driving Yim to the telegraph office; a travel service representative who told of Yim's effort to discuss politics; and a hotel waitress who described Yim's attempt to leave her a tip. With one exception (a man who claimed that Yim had sought to be smuggled out of Canton), the witnesses, although rehearsed, "basically told the truth." But the court, Yim felt, put a distorted interpretation upon all the facts. For example, his attempt to discuss politics was said to be "collecting political information," and tipping the waitress became an "attempt to 'corrupt' her." After the prosecution rested its case, and Yim declined a proffered opportunity to call his own witnesses, he was asked to identify his camera, unused film, typewriter, and notebooks.

A prosecutor then rose to review the case against Yim, accusing him of being a "stooge" of American imperialists. When the judge asked defense counsel whether he had anything to say, the lawyer uttered his only words at the trial: "According to the accused's confession, he has realized that he violated the sovereignty of the PRC. That means he has taken the first step toward reforming himself. I suggest you give him a light sentence." The trial, which had thus far lasted one hour, then recessed. Fifteen minutes later, Yim was summoned back to the courtroom to hear that he was guilty as charged and was sentenced to one year in prison, with credit being granted for the six months already served while awaiting trial.

19-4
Interview

Liu was an overseas Chinese from South Vietnam who had returned to China for higher education and had been admitted to Nanking University. In December 1962 public security officers came to the university and arrested Liu and three overseas Chinese companions, two of whom were from Indonesia and one from Malaya. The arrest warrants simply charged them with "political crimes." The four suspects were taken to the Nanking Public Security Bureau's main detention quarters, "booked," fingerprinted, searched, and placed in separate cells. Liu's small cell had 19 other inmates, all of whom worked from dawn to dusk making matches amid squalid conditions and under close supervision.

On the fourth day of detention Liu was summoned by an armed guard to his first interrogation. The public security officer who questioned him did not specify the nature of Liu's alleged political crimes but urged him to avoid heavy punishment by freely confessing his guilt. Nothing could be gained by resistance, the interrogator said, because the government already had proof of Liu's guilt. When Liu refused to talk, he was sent back to his cell to "think it over."

Six days later Liu was taken back to the interrogation room. By this time he was miserable—hungry, tired, dirty, and ragged. When the interrogator began to increase the pressure to confess, Liu decided that he had little to lose by confessing to a few minor infractions. He admitted selling on the black market a small number of matches that had been sent to him from Hong Kong, having an affair with a girl, and listening once to the Voice of America. The interrogator angrily told him that he was not being honest and had better return to his cell to reflect more profoundly about his wrongdoing.

At their next meeting, four days later, the interrogator told Liu that his friends had confessed, implicating him, and read Liu a few excerpts from their statements to prove it. The interrogator said that Liu appeared to be the least guilty of the four and that, if he honestly confessed, his case would not be sent to court but would be disposed of administratively. Liu then decided to tell all. He spent the entire session describing his many black market transactions, including the names and addresses of his sources of supply and his customers. The next day was devoted to a detailed account of the times, places, partners, and expenses involved in his illicit sexual activities. On the third day, he discussed his bourgeois political background and thinking and admitted listening to the Voice of America regularly and going to the Indonesian embassy in Peking in an effort to obtain its help in getting out of China.

The interrogator told Liu that, before the case could be disposed of, his story would have to be verified by investigators. Some two months later the interrogator reported that the investigation had shown his confession to be "relatively honest." The file, he said, would now have to be checked by higher law enforcement personnel, including lawyers, who would recommend an appropriate punishment for the approval of the Provincial Communist Party committee. Two weeks later the interrogator called Liu in and told him that because he came from abroad, had not been the leader of his group, had confessed thoroughly and had behaved well in prison, he would be given the light punishment of serving six months in "rehabilitation through labor" under the supervision of the party committee of his university. Although this was understood to be an administrative rather than a criminal sanction, he was said to have committed a crime that consisted of a combination of economic speculation, moral violations, and bourgeois political thinking.

A week later Liu was sent back to Nanking and transferred to a university farm outside the city. There, under virtually no supervision, he was assigned to work eight hours a day hoeing fields and to spend the evenings in political "study." At the end of six months he was informed that he could not return to university study but that he either could find a job or, if his parents agreed, he could leave the country. Liu chose the latter course. His parents, who were in South Vietnam, wrote their consent, and in the fall of 1963 he left the PRC for Macao, where he was interviewed.

19-5

Ch'ien Szu, "A Criticism of the Views of Bourgeois International Law on the Question of Population," *KCWTYC*, no. 5:46–47 (1960).

III

With respect to the question of the legal status of aliens, especially the question of the status and treatment of aliens after entry, the demands of imperialism concerning the status and treatment of its own nationals abroad and the status and treatment granted to citizens of foreign countries within its territory are totally different.

The status and treatment of citizens of capitalist countries in foreign countries have undergone the following historical development and change. During the period of feudalism, aliens were without any rights. Their rights were not accorded the legal protection they deserved. After the bourgeois revolution, however, the development of the capitalist economy had burst the fence of self-sufficiency that characterized the period of feudalism. Foreign trade developed and expanded, and intercourse between people of the various countries increased. It was, therefore, necessary to change some of the restrictions imposed on the rights and status of aliens during the period of feudalism. Moreover, under the added influence of ideas such as "equality" and "human rights" which were put forth in the early period of the bourgeois revolution, a fundamental change in the status and treatment of aliens occurred. The principle that aliens and nationals alike enjoy equal rights in civil affairs gradually became generally recognized in bourgeois international law. It was also known as the principle of granting "national treatment" to aliens. This and the subsequently proposed principle of "most favored nation treatment" (that is, that a state shall accord to nationals of another state rights and privileges no less favorable than those which are or may in the future be accorded to the nationals of any third state) became principles of bourgeois international law on the treatment of aliens in the formative period of capitalism. These principles played a definite function in promoting capitalist economy and trade.

After capitalism advanced to the imperialistic stage, the desire of the monopolistic bourgeoisie to acquire excessive profits became greater and greater. In order to facilitate plunder and exploitation, it was no longer satisfied with having "equal rights" with the nationals of the victim state; instead, it demanded better or privileged treatment. An extraordinary example of this kind of privileged treatment is the fact that the nationals of imperialist countries enjoyed extraterritoriality in host countries and thus were not subject to the latter's judicial jurisdiction. In order to exclude the jurisdiction of local laws and courts over their nationals so as to facilitate their doing mischief at will, imperialism forced victim states to accept the system of consular jurisdiction on the fabricated grounds of "cultural backwardness," "imperfect judicial facilities," and "nonapplicability of the laws of non-Christian countries to peoples of Christian countries," and so forth. There were many instances of this in old China. For instance, Article 13 of the "General Regulations for British Trade at the Five Ports" concluded in July 1843 between Britain and China in accordance with the Treaty of Nanking, provided that British criminals should be punished by the British government in accordance with British law. Similar provisions existed in the unequal treaties between China and France, the United States, Czarist Russia, Japan, Germany, Italy, Holland, and other imperialist countries. While residing within the territory of China, all nationals of those countries were outside the judicial power of China and enjoyed the right of not being subject to the jurisdiction of Chinese laws and courts. Indeed, they fully exploited this privilege to do mischief at will, to rob and plunder, to regard Chinese laws as useless paper, and to regard the lives of Chinese as being valueless. During the Ch'ing dynasty and the Kuomintang government period, the Chinese government could not do anything about this. Sometimes, it even helped imperialism oppress the Chinese people and thus brought extreme suffering to the Chinese people.

The right of consular jurisdiction within Chinese territory existed for more than one hundred years. It also existed for a very long period in many other oriental countries besides China. Later, particularly after the October Revolution, the people of the oppressed countries awakened. They were deeply impressed by the fact that the socialist Soviet Union abolished all unequal treaties concluded by Czarist Russia and advocated a policy of national equality. The courage of the people of oppressed countries to struggle for the abolition of privileges for foreigners was heightened. Under such circumstances, imperialism realized that the system of privileges in its naked form could no longer be maintained, and it was obliged to announce the abolition of this system, at least on the surface. As a matter of fact, however, citizens of imperialist countries have continued, even to this day, to enjoy special privileges [in foreign countries]. For instance, members or dependents of members of American forces stationed at foreign military bases who have committed such crimes as robbery, rape, and murder against the residents of the host countries are not subject to the legal sanctions of the host countries and remain outside the law. This is the most obvious example.

NOTE

PRC spokesmen have always been quick to seize upon any evidence that the Republic of China on Taiwan has failed to put an end to foreign jurisdictional privilege. The 1957 Reynolds case, in which an American soldier stationed in Taiwan who had killed a Chinese national was acquitted of homicide charges by a United States military tribunal, was a cause célèbre in Taiwan and gave Peking a welcome opportunity. Reynolds was immune from trial by Chinese courts because a February 9, 1951, exchange of notes between the United States and the ROC provided that members of the American Military Assistance Group "will, in their relations with the Chinese government, operate as a part of the United States embassy, under the direction and control of the Chief of the United States Diplomatic Mission." [76]

Item 19–6 gives Peking's reaction to the Reynolds case, and 19–7, its explanation of the meaning of extraterritoriality. For its view of the 1965 status of forces agreement concluded between the US and the ROC, see 12–13.

19-6

"International Law Experts Condemn US Army," NCNA–English, Peking (May 29, 1957), in *SCMP*, no. 1543:38–39 (June 4, 1957).

Statements by Chinese international law experts condemning the US army in Taiwan as lawless were carried in today's *Kuang Ming Jih Pao*.

The acquittal of Robert Reynolds was a violation of international law viewed from any angle, declared Chou Keng-sheng, Vice-President of the Institute of Foreign Affairs. He said that the extraterritoriality enjoyed by a foreign army applied to the army as a whole. It did not mean that each individual soldier could enjoy this prerogative even off duty. The killing of Liu Tzu-jan was Reynolds' personal misconduct, he continued. According to international law, the local court had full authority to handle this murder case and the US army had no right to interfere, he stressed.

Chou Keng-sheng said that by stationing troops in China's territory of Taiwan in peacetime, the United States had infringed the sovereignty of China. Its lawlessness had become all the more intolerable by taking advantage of extraterritoriality to shield its serviceman who was guilty of murder, he added.

Mei Ju-ao, a judge of the former Far East International Military

Tribunal, reviewed the Chinese people's struggle in the past century to rid themselves of the extraterritoriality provision imposed on them by imperialism. But the United States, while conspiring militarily with the Chiang Kai-shek clique, forced anew this provision on the compatriots in Taiwan. . . . "This is a grave insult to the Chinese people. The Chinese people will not tolerate it," he stated.

Ch'en T'i-ch'iang, international law expert and member of the Council of the Political Science and Law Association of China, pointed out that under international law criminal offenses by foreign soldiers must be tried by local courts. Agreements on exemption were generally limited to offenses committed within the garrison area, against the offender's own countrymen, or when the offender was on duty. He noted that the Reynolds case did not come under these stipulations.

19-7

"Answer to readers: What is 'extraterritoriality?' " *Kuang-ming jih-pao* (Enlightenment Daily; May 30, 1957), p. 4.

Question: According to a recent report, American aggressors abused their extraterritoriality in Taiwan by illegally releasing a murderer named Reynolds, and thereby provoked extensive anti-American and patriotic demonstrations in Taipei. What is this so-called "extraterritoriality?"

Answer: Extraterritoriality has two meanings in general usage: one is what international law refers to as "diplomatic privilege," and the other refers to the "right of consular jurisdiction" created by treaties.

Under international law, diplomatic envoys are immune from the judicial and administrative jurisdiction of the receiving state. This is generally referred to as "diplomatic privilege." The reasons for granting this privilege to a diplomat envoy, who represents his state and its head of state abroad, are to maintain his honor and dignity and to enable him to effectively carry out his functions. Under customary law it is recognized that a diplomatic envoy in the receiving state may enjoy certain privileges such as special protection over his person, life, freedom, honor, residence, and correspondence (that is, inviolability); nor is he subject to the judicial, police, or taxation jurisdiction of the receiving state.

This type of diplomatic privilege granted to diplomatic envoys is the origin of extraterritoriality under international law. Later, extraterritoriality was extended to the head of a state, military forces stationed in foreign territory, or warships in foreign territorial waters.

The extraterritoriality accorded to a head of state consists basically of the same privileges accorded to a diplomatic envoy.

When military forces and warships enter the territory or territorial waters of a foreign state in accordance with the [explicit or] implied consent of that state, in principle they are immune from the judicial and administrative jurisdiction of that state. This kind of extraterritoriality also exists under international customary law. However, when a member of the military forces or a warship leaves his camp or warship and acts in his capacity as a private person (not carrying out official business), he does not possess extraterritoriality. That is to say, in such a situation he would be subject to the administrative or judicial jurisdiction of the host state. The extraterritoriality of military forces or warships concerning the immunity from the judicial or administrative jurisdiction of a foreign state, is usually explicitly provided in a military treaty between the two states.

The other meaning of extraterritoriality is the right of consular jurisdiction. This means that a national of a state residing in another state is not subject to the juridical jurisdiction of the latter state. Moreover, the national's home state, in accordance with its own judicial power at home, may try or handle [the national's case] in the state where the national resides. This is a unilateral privilege which imperialism compelled the weak and small states to grant them. Its nature is totally different from the extraterritoriality generally referred to in international customary law. It is prescribed in an unequal treaty. In the past, our country has received such unequal treatment from imperialism. Now, after a hundred years or so of struggle, we have abolished it.

It is said that the "diplomatic privilege" enjoyed by the American forces of aggression in Taiwan is based upon a 1951 agreement on the stationing of an American military advisory group in Taiwan between the United States and the Chiang Kai-shek clique. The stationing of American forces in Taiwan is itself an illegal act of aggression against our country, and naturally such an agreement between the United States and the Chiang [clique] is illegal. Moreover, even in accordance with the provisions of this illegal agreement, the American right to try its own armed forces is limited to acts of official duty. The American forces' unilateral trial and release of the murderer Reynolds is obviously a serious violation of general international law principles.

Note

Article 59 of the 1949 Common Program provided: "The People's Government of the People's Republic of China protects law-abiding foreign nationals in China."[77] Curiously, the 1954 Constitution contained no similar sentence, although the draftsmen were careful to include in the Constitution provisions similar to those of the Common Program that granted asylum to persecuted foreigners and that guaranteed the PRC's protection of "the proper rights and interests of Chinese resident abroad." [78]

The PRC has not yet enacted a criminal code, many of its criminal proscriptions are unpublished, and those that are published are often extremely vague and permit the authorities to exercise the broadest discretion. Thus, it is difficult for foreigners to know the law by which they are required to abide. Some of the published proscriptions, such as the "Act of the PRC for Punishment of Counterrevolution" [79] and the "Act of the PRC for Punishment of Corruption" [80] do not state that they apply to foreigners, but they plainly do. Other laws, such as the "Security Administration Punishment Act of the PRC," [81] are explicit that foreigners as well as citizens fall within their ambit.

19-8

Chung-yang cheng-fa kan-pu hsüeh-hsiao hsing-fa chiao-yen-shih pien, *Chung-hua jen-min kung-ho-kuo hsing-fa tsung-tse chiang-i* (Lectures on the general principles of criminal law of the PRC; Peking, 1957), pp. 40, 41–42, 213–214.

Chinese criminal law is applicable to all criminal acts taking place within Chinese territory, regardless of the nationalities of the offenders, whether they are Chinese, foreigners, or stateless persons. Our criminal law is effective against foreigners and stateless persons. Article 4 of the "Provisional Rules Governing the Entry, Exit and Residence of Foreigners" issued on November 28, 1951, by the Government Administrative Council [superseded by item 15–1] provides: "Foreign residents within Chinese territory shall observe the laws and decrees of the Chinese People's Government"; Article 11 provides: "Stateless persons shall be handled according to these rules." From this it can be seen that both foreigners and stateless persons within Chinese boundaries are required to observe Chinese law; and those who violate Chinese laws and whose violations constitute offenses are all subject to the punishment of Chinese criminal law, whether their offenses are counterrevolutionary or general criminal offenses. This principle has been fully implemented in our judicial practice. . . .

Under certain conditions, if a foreigner or a stateless person commits an offense outside Chinese territory, he is also subject to

Chinese criminal law. These conditions are: (1) the offender is responsible for his act according to our criminal law; and (2) his act injures the People's Republic of China or its citizens. In our opinion, the scope of his criminal responsibility should be in principle the same as that of a Chinese offender in a foreign country.

With respect to a foreigner or stateless person who commits a given offense endangering the state or citizens of the People's Republic of China if he has been tried or his punishment has been executed by a foreign country, the principle of solving such a question is the same as that which applies in the case of a Chinese who commits a given offense abroad in the above-stated circumstances [that is, Chinese authorities can still prosecute the offender, but his punishment may be mitigated or dispensed with if he has served the sentence in the foreign country concerned]. . . .

This punishment [expulsion from the country] is only applicable to foreigners or stateless persons who have committed crimes within the territory of our country. All foreigners and stateless persons who commit offenses within the territory of our country are subject to the jurisdiction of our law. They are not only subject to expulsion from the country but also to other punishments. Expulsion from the country should be applied to those foreigners or stateless persons whose offenses are not very serious. This will eliminate the possibility that they might commit crime again in our country. At the same time, it must be made clear that, when applying punishment to a foreigner or a stateless person who commits a crime in our country, we should not only take the degree of his offense into account but should also consider the situation of the international struggle. Aside from other punishments, we have the punishment of expulsion from the country. This enables us better to serve the interests of this struggle.

Expulsion from the country may be applied independently or accessorily. When applied as an accessory punishment, it should be executed after execution of the principal punishment has been completed.

19-9
"Judgment of Military Tribunal on US Spies in the Arnold-Baumer Espionage Case," translated in *PC*, no. 24 (supp.): 3–5 (Dec. 16, 1954).

Judgment of the Military Tribunal of the Supreme People's Court of the People's Republic of China.

(54) M.T. No. 1.

Prosecutor: Yao Lun, Military Procurator of the Supreme People's Procuratorate of the People's Republic of China.

Defendants: John Knox Arnold, Jr., male, 41, of Washington, D.C., USA, commanding officer (colonel) of the US 581st Air Re-supply and Communications Wing, now under detention;

William Hurl Baumer, male, 32, of Pennsylvania, USA, operations officer (major) of the 91st Strategic Reconnaissance Squadron of the US Far East Air Force, now under detention.

(Wang Hou-li, instructor in law of the China People's University, acting as defending counsel for the aforementioned two defendants.)

[The judgment goes on to list the nine other defendants, all of whom were Americans, and their counsel.]

The aforementioned eleven defendants were indicted by Yao Lun, Military Procurator of the Supreme People's Procuratorate of the People's Republic of China, for having clandestinely crossed the Chinese border by plane to conduct espionage activity with the aim of jeopardizing the security of the People's Republic of China. The present tribunal, after examining the evidence, has established the following facts:

In attempting to extend armed aggression, jeopardize world peace, and intensify espionage and subversive activity against the Soviet Union and the people's democracies, the United States aggressors have formed, through air force channels, special air wings for the purpose of dropping special agents. These air wings serve the ends of the United States Central Intelligence Agency. The 581st Air Re-supply and Communications Wing is one of these wings, and its task is to drop special agents into the territories of the Soviet Union and the people's democracies, to provide these agents with supplies, to evacuate them, and to maintain contact with special agents on the ground. The 581st Air Re-supply and Communications Wing was formed in July 1951 at the Mountain Home Air Base, Idaho, USA. After a year's special training in recruiting special agents, in air-dropping and resupplying, as well as in maintaining liaison with agents on the ground, the 581st Air Re-supply and Communications Wing was transferred in July 1952 to the Clark Air Base in the Philippines, to conduct hostile activities against the coastal areas of China and against the maritime provinces of the Soviet Union in the Far East. The Vaadi and Chappelle crews of this Wing were later assigned to the 91st Strategic Reconnaissance Squadron of the US Far East Air Force Bomber Command, which has China and the Soviet Union as its main field of reconnaissance. The Vaadi crew was attached to the Air Re-supply Squadron of the 581st Air Re-supply and Communications Wing. The plane in which they flew was a remodelled B-29, No. 44–62217. This plane could fly long distances, and was specially remodelled for the dropping of special agents. Defendant Eugene John Vaadi of that crew was the aircraft commander (captain) of the US 581st Air Re-supply and Communications Wing; Elmer Fred Llewellyn was the navigator (captain); John Woodrow Buck was the bombardier (lieutenant); Wallace Lamer Brown was copilot (second lieutenant); Howard William Brown was technical sergeant; Steve Edward Kiba was radio operator (sergeant); Harry Martin Benjamin, Jr. was left scanner and jump master (corporal); Daniel Chris Schmidt was central scanner (corporal); and John Walker Thompson was right scanner (corporal)—all of the US 581st Air Re-supply and Communications Wing.

John Knox Arnold, Jr., was the commanding officer (colonel) of the U.S. 581st Air Re-supply and Communications Wing. William Hurl Baumer was the operations officer (major) of the 91st Strategic Reconnaissance Squadron of the US Far East Air Force. Baumer had many times flown planes to invade China's territorial air and carry out reconnaissance of China's national defense works. On January 12, 1953, John Knox Arnold, Jr., with the aid of William Hurl Baumer, led the Vaadi crew and violated China's territorial air over Liaoning Province in Northeast China. The plane in which they flew was shot down by an antiaircraft unit; it fell to the west of Hwangwan Village, west of Wulungpei in Antung. John Knox Arnold, Jr., and the others were captured at Hsinkang and Laokukou Villages, Wulungpei District. Van Voorlis, Alvin D. Hart, Jr., and Henry D. Weese, who were in the same plane as the defendants were killed when the plane was shot down. The portable radio transmitting and receiving set, arms, documents, and other equipment which the defendants carried to enable themselves to live in the woods, as well as other evidence of criminal intent, were captured.

That the 581st Air Re-supply and Communications Wing served the US Central Intelligence Agency in carrying out criminal activity against China and the Soviet Union, such as the dropping of special agents, resupplying, and maintaining liaison with and evacuating special agents on the ground, has been admitted by the defendant, John Knox Arnold, Jr. The Vaadi crew was attached to the 91st Strategic Reconnaissance Squadron of the US Far East Air Force Bomber Command; its field of strategic reconnaissance was China and the Soviet Union. William Hurl Baumer, who was in the same plane with John Knox Arnold, Jr., was the operations officer of the 91st Strategic Reconnaissance Squadron, and had many times violated China's territorial air by plane to conduct reconnaissance of China's national defense works. All this has been admitted by William Hurl Baumer himself. The plane in which the defendants flew was shot down in China's territorial air. Besides the remains of the damaged plane, other evidence, such as the portable radio transmitting and receiving set, arms, documents, and other equipment which the defendants carried to enable themselves to live in the woods, fully prove the crimes committed by the defendants. On the basis of this evidence, it is established that the defendants, in carrying out the policy of the United States aggressors to extend armed aggression against China and undermine the cause of people's democracy, clandestinely crossed the Chinese border by plane to conduct espionage and reconnaissance activity; they also attempted to resupply and maintain liaison with other US special agents. All these crimes seriously jeopardize China's national security, and the evidence is conclusive.

Defendant John Knox Arnold, Jr., is the ringleader in this criminal case; as he played the leading role, he should therefore bear the main responsibility. Defendant William Hurl Baumer had many times conducted reconnaissance against China aimed at jeopardizing China's national security. He, too, should be severely punished, but since he has, during the investigations and trial, shown repentance, his punishment will be appropriately lightened. Defendant Eugene John Vaadi was aircraft commander; as his responsibilities in this criminal case are heavy, he should be severely punished according to law [along with] defendants Wallace Lamer Brown, Elmer Fred Llewellyn, John Woodrow Buck.

Howard William Brown, Steve Edward Kiba, Harry Martin Benjamin, Jr., Daniel Chris Schmidt, and John Walker Thompson do not bear the main responsibility; they will therefore be given mitigated sentences.

In accordance with the provisions of Articles 6, 11, and 16 of the Law of the People's Republic of China on the Punishment of Counterrevolutionaries, judgment is hereby passed:

1. Defendant John Knox Arnold, Jr., sentenced to 10 years' imprisonment.

2. Defendant William Hurl Baumer, sentenced to eight years' imprisonment.

3. Defendant Eugene John Vaadi, sentenced to six years' imprisonment.

4. Defendants Elmer Fred Llewellyn and Wallace Lamer Brown, each sentenced to five years' imprisonment.

5. Defendants John Woodrow Buck, Howard William Brown, Steve Edward Kiba, Harry Martin Benjamin, Jr., John Walker Thompson, and Daniel Chris Schmidt, each sentenced to four years' imprisonment.

6. The remains of the plane shot down, the portable radio transmitting and receiving set, arms, and other material evidence captured are to be confiscated.

Chia Chien, Chief Judge
Chu Yao-tang, Judge
Chang Hsiang-chien, Judge

Military Tribunal of the Supreme People's Court of the People's Republic of China.

November 23, 1954

19-10

"Judgment of Military Tribunal on US Spies in the Downey-Fecteau Espionage Case," translated in *PC*, no. 24 (supp.): 6–8 (Dec. 16, 1954).

Judgment of the Military Tribunal of the Supreme People's Court of the People's Republic of China.

(54) M.T. No. 2.

Prosecutor: Yao Lun, Military Procurator of the Supreme People's Procuratorate of the People's Republic of China.

Defendants: John Thomas Downey, alias Jack Donovan, male, 24, of Connecticut, USA, United States special agent, now under detention;

Richard George Fecteau, male, 27, of Massachusetts, USA, United States special agent, now under detention.

(Chao Hsi-lun, defending counsel appointed by the state for the aforementioned two defendants).

[The judgment goes on to list the nine other defendants, all of whom were Chinese, and their counsel.]

The aforementioned eleven defendants were indicted by Yao Lun, Military Procurator of the Supreme People's Procuratorate of the People's Republic of China, for having stealthily crossed the Chinese border by plane to conduct espionage activity in order to jeopardize China's national security, and some of them for having committed high treason against their mother country. The present tribunal, after examining the material evidence, has established the following facts:

John Thomas Downey, the defendant, joined the US Central Intelligence Agency, a United States espionage organization, in June 1951, and was transferred in December of the same year to the espionage organization of the US Central Intelligence Agency stationed at Atsuki (Japan). Richard George Fecteau, the defendant, joined the US Central Intelligence Agency in June 1952, and was transferred in October of the same year to the espionage organization of the US Central Intelligence Agency stationed at Atsuki (Japan). Both defendants have undergone special training for terrorist subversive activity and armed riots against the Soviet Union and the people's democracies. In the spring of 1952, John Thomas Downey, together with another US agent, on orders of the chief of the Atsuki espionage organization, selected special agents from the training center for agents of the US Central Intelligence Agency on Saipan Island—Li Chun-ying, Chang Tsai-wen, Hsu Kwang-chih, Yu Kwan-chou, Luan Heng-shan, Wang Chin-sheng—and brought these agents to a secret training camp in Chigasaki, Japan, belonging to the Atsuki espionage organization. John Thomas Downey also transferred there Wang Wei-fan and radio operators, Niu Sung-lin and Chung Tien-hsing from another training center for agents of the US Central Intelligence Agency. John Thomas Downey organized Chang Tsai-wen, Hsu Kwang-chih, Yu Kwan-chou, [and] Niu Sung-lin into a team called "Team Wen," and secretly dropped them from a US C-47 plane into Kirin Province in northeast China in July 1952. John Thomas Downey also organized Luan Heng-shan, Wang Wei-fan, Wang Chin-sheng, Chung Tien-hsing, and others into another team called "Team Shen" and secretly dropped them from a US B-17 plane into Kirin Province in northeast China in September 1952. Besides this, he had Li Chun-ying dropped from a US plane into Kirin Province in October 1952, to keep in contact with the other agents and to conduct subversive activity. In August 1952 John Thomas Downey himself secretly entered Kirin Province in northeast China in a US plane to drop food and supplies for the agents of "Team Wen," who had been dropped into Kirin Province. Finally, on the night of November 29, 1952, John Thomas Downey and Richard George Fecteau secretly violated the territorial air over northeast China in a US C-47 plane and again made contact with and provided supplies for the agents who had been dropped into our country. They also attempted to pick up the agent Li Chun-ying to give them a report on work, so as to continue the dropping of large numbers of special agents into our country. The plane in which they came, however, was shot down, and John Thomas Downey and Richard George Fecteau were captured.

The nine defendants, Chang Tsai-wen, Hsu Kwang-chih, Yu Kwan-chou, Niu Sung-lin, Luan Heng-shan, Wang Wei-fan, Wang Chin-sheng, Chung Tien-hsing, [and] Li Chun-ying were all former military officers of the Chiang Kai-shek gang. They took part in the civil war against the people and fled to Hong Kong after the collapse of the Chiang Kai-shek regime. They were taken up in 1951 by the "Free China Movement," a US espionage organization in Hong Kong. Under the guise of being employed by the "Far East Development Company" for work on Guam, they were flown in groups to espionage training centers of the US Central Intelligence Agency in Chigasaki, Kanagawa Prefecture, Japan, and on Saipan Island, for secret training. The training courses were mainly how to carry out assassination, demolition, armed riots, the collection of intelligence, secret communications, and other espionage activity in China. After training, they were selected by John Thomas Downey and another US special agent to receive training under the personal direction of Downey. They were later organized into groups and dropped in succession from US planes into Kirin Province in northeast China to set up "bases" there for armed agents and "safety points" for sheltering agents, to build "parachuting grounds" to receive air-dropped supplies and agents, to establish secret communication lines connecting the "bases" with Shenyang (Mukden), to collect information about the national defenses of China, location of industrial areas and meteorological conditions, to rescue such intruding American airmen as were shot down and to gather lurking elements of the traitorous Chiang Kai-shek gang in order to foment armed riots. The mission of defendant Li Chun-ying after being dropped was to report on the activities of "Team Wen" and engage in liaison work and subversive activity. These defendants were all captured on different occasions.

All the defendants in this case have after capture admitted the crimes committed by them. Their crimes are also borne out by a vast amount of captured material evidence such as weapons, ammunition, radio sets, maps, parachutes, equipment for dropping special agents, forged safe-conducts of the Chinese People's Liberation Army, certificates for wounded soldiers, passes, as well as gold, paper currency, and other equipment for conducting espionage activity. In view of such conclusive evidence of their crimes, it is beyond doubt that the defendants were dropped into Chinese territory in order to conduct espionage activity, thereby seriously jeopardizing the security of China, in an attempt to carry out the plan of the American aggressors to extend their aggression against China and undermine the cause of people's democracy in China.

The defendant John Thomas Downey actively assembled and

trained special agents and had them secretly dropped into Chinese territory to conduct subversive activity. He also personally violated China's territorial air to carry out criminal activity. He is the chief criminal in this case and should be punished with the full rigor of the law. The defendant Richard George Fecteau, who assisted John Thomas Downey in entering China to conduct espionage activity, should also be severely punished. The defendants Hsu Kwang-chih, Wang Wei-fan, Wang-Chin-sheng, and Yu Kwan-chou committed high treason against their native land by joining the US espionage organization. They were dropped into China to carry out subversive activity at the instigation of the US espionage organization. They have committed the heinous crime of endangering the security of the state and should all be severely punished according to the law. The defendants Chang Tsai-wen, Luan Heng-shan, Chung Tien-hsing, Li Chun-ying, and Niu Sung-lin have committed crimes of equal gravity, but as the defendants Chang Tsai-wen, Luan Heng-shan, Chung Tien-hsing, and Li Chun-ying have shown repentance during the trial, they are therefore given lighter sentences. The defendant Niu Sung-lin has shown true repentance during the trial and will be given a mitigated sentence.

In accordance with Articles 6, 3, 7, 11, 14, and 16 of the Law of the People's Republic of China for the Punishment of Counterrevolutionaries, judgment is hereby passed:

(1) The defendant John Thomas Downey, sentenced to life imprisonment.

(2) The defendant Richard George Fecteau, sentenced to 20 years' imprisonment.

(3) The defendants Hsu Kwang-chih, Yu Kwan-chou, Wang Wei-fan, and Wang Chin-sheng, all sentenced to death, deprived of political rights for all time.

(4) The defendants Chang Tsai-wen, Luan Heng-shan, Chung Tien-hsing, and Li Chun-ying, all sentenced to life imprisonment, deprived of political rights for all time.

(5) The defendant Niu Sung-lin, sentenced to 15 years' imprisonment, deprived of political rights for 10 years.

(6) The captured weapons, ammunition, radio sets, maps, parachutes, and equipment for air-dropping are to be confiscated.

Chia Chien, Chief Judge
Chu Yao-tang, Judge
Chang Hsiang-chien, Judge

The Military Tribunal of the Supreme People's Court of the People's Republic of China.

November 23, 1954

19-11

"The Case of the United States Airmen," Denise Folliot, ed., *Documents on International Affairs 1954* (London: Oxford University Press, 1957), pp. 335–340.

(a) *Note from the United States government to the Chinese government regarding the imprisonment of United States airmen on charges of espionage, November 26, 1954* [a]

The United States government vigorously protests the wrongful action of the Chinese Communist authorities in sentencing on November 23rd eleven members of the United States Armed Forces and two American civilians employed by the Department of the Army to terms of imprisonment on political charges which are without foundation. These Americans were in planes which were attacked over the recognized combat zone in Korea, or over international waters, in the course of the Chinese Communist aggression against Korea. Their detention is in patent violation of the Korean Armistice Agreement.

The sentencing of the members of the United States Armed Forces to penitentiary terms in these circumstances is grossly contrary to the substance and spirit of all recognized international standards as to the protection of prisoners of war. The maltreatment of the two civilian American citizens, whose names were wilfully and deceitfully withheld by the Chinese Communist representatives at Geneva last June from the list of American civilians held in Chinese Communist jails, is equally reprehensible.

The United States government calls upon the Chinese Communist authorities to release these unjustly detained American nationals forthwith, in accordance with the provisions of the Korean Armistice Agreement and in conformity with the elementary precepts of justice and humanity.

The Chinese Communist authorities are under an obligation to redress insofar as possible the wrong they have inflicted on these American nationals and their families. The United States government reserves the right to claim compensation as may be determined appropriate, and to demand the punishment of the Chinese Communist officials responsible for the denial of the rights of these persons.

The Chinese Communist authorities should bear in mind that the long list of Chinese Communist outrages against American nationals, which the American people have borne with restraint thus far, is sig-

[a] "US Protests Sentencing of Americans by Chinese Communists," *Department of State Bulletin* 31.806:856–857 (Dec. 6, 1954).

nificantly extended by the Chinese Communist announcement of November 23rd.

(b) *Explanatory memorandum accompanying the United States request for the inclusion in the General Assembly's agenda of a complaint of a violation of the Korean Armistice Agreement, December 4, 1954* [b]

Complaint of Detention and Imprisonment of United Nations Military Personnel in Violation of the Korean Armistice Agreement

A United States Air Force B-29-type aircraft, on a mission of the United Nations Command in Korea, was attacked fifteen miles south of the Yalu River near the North Korean town of Sonchon and shot down on 12 January 1953. The officers and men of the United States Air Force on the plane were captured. More than a year and a half later, and long after the conclusion of the Korean Armistice Agreement providing for the release of all captured personnel desiring repatriation, eleven officers and men from the above-mentioned aircraft were brought before the Chinese Communist military tribunal and sentenced to long terms of imprisonment.

This is a clear-cut violation of the Armistice Agreement.

The United States government first learned of this action by the Chinese Communist authorities through a broadcast of the Peking radio on 24 November 1954. Immediately thereafter, the United States government sought to communicate with the Chinese Communist authorities, both directly in Geneva and through the United Kingdom government, to protest this serious violation of the Korean Armistice Agreement. The Chinese Communist authorities rejected these representations.

The government and people of the United States are shocked and outraged by the treatment thus accorded to its airmen who were serving the cause of peace under the Charter, and hold these same feelings for the men of other nations who are held prisoner. The governments of other nations having troops in Korea share this feeling of indignation at this violation of the Armistice Agreement.

The United States believes this conduct of the Chinese Communist authorities has created a serious situation for the United Nations, which called for the action in Korea to repel Communist aggression and which requested the United States to provide a Unified Command of United Nations forces in Korea. The United States believes the United Nations must now act promptly and decisively to bring about the release of these eleven officers and men and all other captured personnel of the United Nations Command still detained.

[b] UN Doc. A/2830 (Dec. 4, 1954), p. 2.

(c) *Resolution adopted by the General Assembly on December 10, 1954* [c]

The General Assembly,

Having considered the item proposed by the United States of America as the Unified Command regarding eleven members of the United States armed forces under the United Nations Command captured by Chinese forces when undertaking a mission on 12 January 1953, at the direction of the United Nations Command,

Recalling the provisions of article III of the Korean Armistice Agreement regarding the repatriation of prisoners of war,

1. *Declares* that the detention and imprisonment of the eleven American airmen, members of the United Nations Command, referred to in document A/2830, and the detention of all other captured personnel of the United Nations Command desiring repatriation is a violation of the Korean Armistice Agreement;

2. *Condemns,* as contrary to the Korean Armistice Agreement, the trial and conviction of prisoners of war illegally detained after 25 September 1953;

3. *Requests* the Secretary-General, in the name of the United Nations, to seek the release, in accordance with the Korean Armistice Agreement, of these eleven United Nations Command personnel, and all other captured personnel of the United Nations Command still detained;

4. *Requests* the Secretary-General to make, by the means most appropriate in his judgment, continuing and unremitting efforts to this end and to report progress to all Members on or before 31 December 1954.

(d) *Cable from Mr. Chou En-lai to the Secretary-General of the United Nations, Mr. Dag Hammarskjöld, regarding the General Assembly's resolution, 17 December 1954* [d]

The ninth session of the United Nations General Assembly, under the domination of the United States and its followers, adopted on 10 December 1954 an absurd resolution under the title of "Complaint of detention and imprisonment of United Nations military personnel in violation of the Korean Armistice Agreement," which slanders China's conviction of eleven United States spies as contrary to the Korean Armistice Agreement. To this the government of the People's Republic

[c] *General Assembly, Official Records, Ninth Session, Supplement No. 21, Resolutions* (A/2890), 906 (IX), p. 56. This resolution was sponsored by Australia, Belgium, Canada, Colombia, Ethiopia, France, Great Britain, Greece, Luxembourg, the Netherlands, New Zealand, the Philippines, Siam, South Africa, Turkey, and the USA. It was adopted by 47–5–7.

[d] UN Doc. A/2889 (Dec. 17, 1954).

of China is resolutely opposed. The said eleven United States spies and two others intruded into Chinese territory and were caught in China. After examining evidences which conclusively proved that they had conducted espionage activities in China, the Chinese Court on 23 November 1954 passed judgments on them according to law. To convict foreign spies caught in China is China's internal affair. There is no justification at all for the United Nations to try to interfere in China's conviction of full-proved United States spies, while failing to condemn the United States' dispatching, in violation of the United Nations Charter, of spies to intrude into China to carry out subversive activities. The case of these United States spies has nothing to do with the question of the prisoners of war in Korea. If one speaks of the question of the prisoners of war in Korea, it is the United States and the United Nations Command side which has violated the Korean Armistice Agreement. . . . The Chinese people are opposed to war, but they will never be frightened into submission by threats of war. The Chinese people desire peace, but they will never beg for peace at the expense of their territory and sovereignty. No amount of clamour on the part of the United States can shake China's just stand of exercising its own sovereign right in convicting the United States spies. Mr. Secretary-General, I request that you circulate the text of this cable to the delegations attending the United Nations General Assembly with the exception of Chiang Kai-shek's Kuomintang representatives.

(e) *Cable from Mr. Hammarskjöld to Mr. Chou En-lai, 10 December 1954* [e]

The General Assembly of the United Nations has requested me to seek the release of eleven United Nations Command personnel captured by Chinese forces on 12 January 1953 as well as of all other captured personnel of the United Nations Command still detained. Taking into consideration all facts and circumstances the Secretary-General must, in this case, take on himself a special responsibility. In the light of the concern I feel about the issue, I would appreciate an opportunity to take this matter up with you personally. For that reason I would ask you whether you could receive me in Peking. I would suggest a visit soon after 26 December and would, if you accept my proposal, ask you what date at about that time would be suitable to you.

(f) *Mr. Chou's reply, 17 December 1954* [f]

I acknowledge the receipt of your cable of 10 December 1954 in which you indicated your wish to visit China. Regarding the case of the United States spies mentioned in your cable, our position has been

[e] UN Doc. A/2888 (Dec. 17, 1954), p. 1.
[f] *Ibid.*, p. 2.

set forth in my other cable addressed to you. In the interest of peace and relaxation of international tension, I am prepared to receive you in our capital, Peking, to discuss with you pertinent questions. We welcome you to China. Please decide for yourself the date of your visit and inform us of your decision.

(g) *Report to the United Nations by the Secretary-General on the release of the United States airmen, 9 September 1955* [g]

1. The General Assembly, by resolution 906 (IX) of 10 December 1954, requested the Secretary-General to seek the release, in accordance with the Korean Armistice Agreement, of eleven United Nations Command personnel and all other captured personnel of the United Nations Command still detained. It further requested the Secretary-General to make, by the means most appropriate in his judgment, continuing and unremitting efforts to this end and to report progress to all Members on or before 31 December 1954.

2. On 31 December 1954, I submitted a report [h] informing Members that, following an exchange of communications with the Prime Minister of the State Council and Minister for Foreign Affairs of the People's Republic of China and a meeting in Stockholm with General Keng Piao, ambassador of the People's Republic of China, arrangements were made for the Secretary-General to visit Peking.

3. As stated in my annual report to the General Assembly on the work of the Organization, my visit to Peking was made necessary because of the need to establish a direct contact with the Central People's Government of the People's Republic of China, since this government was not represented in any organs of the United Nations. The visit, aimed primarily at clarifying the substantive and legal aspects of the matter, established this direct contact on a personal basis. It thus provided possibilities to pursue the discussion concerning the problem raised by the detention of the United Nations personnel referred to in the General Assembly resolution.

4. After my return from Peking I continued, within the framework of the contact thus established, an exchange of views with Mr. Chou En-lai, Prime Minister and Minister for Foreign Affairs of the People's Republic of China. The contact was maintained mainly through a series of communications transmitted by the Swedish embassy in Peking. I received valuable assistance also from representatives of the governments of other Member states.

5. A renewed personal contact with a representative of the Central People's Government of the People's Republic of China, Ambassador Keng Piao, was made by me in Stockholm on 23 April 1955.

[g] UN Doc. A/2954 (Sept. 9, 1955).
[h] UN Doc. A/2891 (Dec. 30, 1954).

6. By a letter to me, given to the Swedish ambassador in Peking in the early afternoon of 29 May 1955 (New York time), Mr. Chou En-lai announced that an investigation of the cases of four detained fliers had been completed and that it had been decided that they should be deported immediately from the territory of the People's Republic of China. The four men arrived in Hong Kong on 31 May 1955.

7. By an oral message to me, given to the Swedish ambassador in Peking at 1 o'clock in the morning, 1 August 1955 (New York time), and transmitted by him, Mr. Chou En-lai announced that the Central People's Government of the People's Republic of China had decided to release as soon as feasible the eleven American fliers who had been detained and imprisoned, and that an announcement to that effect would be made in Peking at 10 a.m. on 1 August 1955 (New York time). The eleven men arrived in Hong Kong on 4 August 1955.

8. Mr. Chou En-lai has expressed his hope that the contact established will be continued. In reply I have stated that this hope is shared by me.

NOTE

The PRC released the eleven American airmen but did not release the two Americans who the United States claimed were "civilians employed by the Department of the Army." Indeed, as item 19–11 indicates, the American protest against the PRC's conviction of these men was not couched in the same terms as the protest concerning the airmen, since the former were not said to be part of the United Nations Command. For this reason the US did not include them in its complaint to the UN, and the Resolution of the UN General Assembly did not authorize the Secretary-General to seek their freedom.

Although the Chinese press also rejected American claims that the airmen had not been spying, it enjoyed a field day answering factual allegations made by the US in behalf of the two civilians. If Downey and Fecteau were civilian employees of the Army, it was said, was it not unusual that no records to this effect could be found in Tokyo, where they were supposed to have been based? Moreover, why had the US Defense Department claimed that the two men "were authorized passengers on a routine flight from Seoul to Japan in a plane which was under military contract to the Far East Air Force," while a US Far East Air Force spokesman claimed that the two had hitched a ride on a civil air transport and that "for some still unexplained reason" it was not disclosed that the two men were on board when the plane vanished? And why, it was asked, had the Christian Science Monitor reported that Fecteau's family understood that he had been engaged in intelligence work? [82]

In order to secure the release of Downey and Fecteau, as well as other Americans in and out of Chinese prison, the US subsequently relied on direct negotiations with the PRC at the ambassadorial level in Geneva. These talks began on August 1, 1955, the date on which Peking announced the release of the eleven airmen, a gesture that launched the negotiations on an auspicious note. Part VIII will deal with the Sino-American agreement that emerged from the Geneva negotiations. For subsequent developments regarding Downey and Fecteau, see item 19–15.

The PRC's release of the eleven airmen in no way signified recognition of the validity of the American challenge to the legality of their conviction. According to the PRC, since their detention the airmen had observed proper discipline and had behaved well, thereby warranting the exercise of leniency that commuted their sentences and deported them to the US.[83] The following items are typical of the Chinese scholars' spirited defense of the legality of the PRC's conviction of the airmen.[84]

19-12

"Uniformed Spy is a Spy, Says Legal Expert Ch'en T'i-ch'iang," NCNA–English, Peking (Dec. 25, 1954), in *SCMP*, no. 955:31–32 (Dec. 24–28, 1954).

American efforts to deny spy charges by claiming that military uniforms were worn are refuted by international law, states Ch'en T'i-ch'iang, a member of the Executive Council of the Political Science and Law Association of China in today's *Peking Jih Pao*.

The Americans, the Chinese legal expert writes, hinge their argument around the point that these spies, being in military uniform, could not have engaged in clandestine activities and could not be considered as spies as defined in the Hague Regulation [the Hague Regulations on Land Warfare of 1907].

He recalls that Henry Cabot Lodge in the United Nations General Assembly admitted that John Knox Arnold and the other US spies flew in a plane painted black and that the plane's flame outlets were covered. "Is this not proof that their action was clandestine?" the writer asks. He refers to the Hague Regulation which states that clandestine activities constitute one of the elements of spying.

"As for Arnold and ten other spies, they flew in a plane painted black which sneaked into China at night. The plane carried radio sets for use on the ground and other equipment for espionage purposes."

There are two ways to use aircraft for espionage, the legal expert points out. One is for the aircraft to land for espionage purposes. The other is to bring spies or pick them up, or give them supplies or make contact with them.

J. M. Spaight, a British expert on the laws of warfare, demonstrated that the spies [who] landed during the First World War all wore uniforms. Spaight devoted a whole chapter of his book "Air Power and War Rights" to the use of aircraft for espionage by European countries.

Quoting Spaight, Ch'en T'i-ch'iang writes, "They do this so that in the event of being caught they can pose as members of the armed forces and request that they be treated as prisoners of war. If they land safely and are not discovered, they change into civilian dress."

"Wearing uniforms," the legal expert continues, "has been used by imperialist states to violate the Hague Regulation. They hope that by virtue of wearing military uniforms a spy may not be proved a spy. But it is precisely this that may at times characterize a spy, namely, that he is functioning in such disguise.

"It is for this reason that Spaight declared: 'If he were in uniform but accompanied by clear evidence of his intended mission, his position would be more doubtful, and would depend upon the exact circumstances of the case.' "

In view of all these facts and the provisions of international law, Ch'en T'i-ch'iang says that the US claim that Arnold and the ten other US spies should be considered Korean war prisoners is untenable.

As to the case of the US spies John Thomas Downey and Richard George Fecteau who were caught in China, Ch'en T'i-ch'iang points out that the United States government has admitted that Downey and Fecteau were not members of the armed forces. They flew in a plane which carried no markings. The plane carried a special device for picking up agents. On their persons they had a detailed map of Antu County in Kirin Province of China and a Chinese-English conversation sheet. Downey admitted that earlier he had trained agents who were air-dropped into China and had contacted them.

"Any one with the slightest familiarity with international law knows that only captured members of the armed forces of a belligerent can be considered prisoners of war by the captor side. No state of war exists between China and the United States. US spies who have intruded into China for espionage are not prisoners of war."

From this it then follows, the legal expert declares, that the sentencing of criminals within China's territory by a Chinese court of law is "simply the exercise of China's domestic judicial authority, irrespective of the nationality of the criminals."

He points to the international provisions governing this exercise of justice within a country. "The exercise of the judicial right is stipulated in Article 2, paragraph 7, of the United Nations Charter as 'essentially within the domestic jurisdiction of any state,'" he notes. "The United Nations has no right to intervene. Submission of the spy cases to the United Nations and discussion of this matter by the United Nations General Assembly are illegal. It follows, therefore, that adoption by the General Assembly of the US-sponsored resolution is completely illegal and a violation of the UN Charter."

19-13

"Law Expert Refutes US Allegation on Spies," NCNA–English, Peking (Dec. 20, 1954), in *SCMP*, no. 952:5 (Dec. 21, 1954).

US efforts to distort international law in the United Nations can never alter the fact that its spies are real spies, says Wang Tieh-yai, Professor of International Law of Peking University, in an article in today's *Kuang Ming Jih Pao*.

Refuting the allegation that men in uniform cannot be spies, he refers to the "Rules of Land Warfare" issued by the United States itself in 1917. The rules state, "The fact that a person charged with being a spy is in the uniform of his state does not render it impossible for him to be a spy in fact, since he may have gained admission into the enemy's line under the privilege of the Red Cross and have taken advantage of the opportunity afforded him for obtaining information." Professor Wang Tieh-yai writes that the decisive factor in judging a spy is his espionage activities, not his clothes.

The professor advises Henry Cabot Lodge to refer to international law documents before arguing a case. Professor Wang cites a case included in the writings of the prominent American international lawyer, Charles C. Hyde, that during the American War of Independence a British major was sentenced to death by the United States for spying although he wore a uniform. "Commenting on this case," Professor Wang Tieh-yai continues, "an American Major-General, H. W. Halleck, wrote in an article in the American Journal of International Law (Volume 5): 'Superficial writers are sometimes disposed to attach undue importance to a change of dress, forgetting that disguise does not consist in dress alone, and that any false pretense, coupled with other circumstances, may make a man a spy.'"

The Peking University international law expert declares: "If Lodge wants to prove his denial by the literature on international law by Americans, this literature shows that his denial is quite untenable according to international law."

The two groups of American spies in question made their way into China by air, which was very rarely practiced in the days at the beginning of this century, Professor Wang Tieh-yai says. "But," he continues, "L. Oppenheim, the famous international law expert . . . said long ago that 'spying can well be carried out by dispatch-bearers, or by persons in an air-vessel. The mere fact that a balloon or air-vessel is visible does not protect the persons using it from being treated as spies since spying can be carried out under false pretenses quite as well as clandestinely.' This is a clear explanation of espionage activities being conducted from an airplane. Even this bourgeois scholar admitted that it is chiefly the espionage activities and not clothes that determine whether a person is a spy."

NOTE

A previous NCNA release had summarized an earlier article by Wang T'ieh-yai, who was later declared a "rightist" in 1957, but not apparently on grounds related either to the foregoing or the following views:

> An expert in international law today tears to shreds the US attempt to shield US spies in China by reference to the terms of the Korean Armistice Agreement. Writing in the *Kuang Ming Jih Pao,* Wang T'ieh-yai, Professor of International Law at Peking University, points out that "spies are entirely different from POWs." Spies cannot be included as prisoners of war who should be released or repatriated under the Provisions of the Korean Armistice Agreement. And this applies with particular force to the US spies who intruded by air into Chinese territory to carry out espionage.
>
> He goes on, "The Geneva Convention [Relative to the Treatment of Prisoners of War, 1949] contains nothing concerning spies. No article in it accords any protection to spies." It is empty and meaningless to attack the judgments rendered in the two spy cases as violating the Geneva Convention for there is not a single article in it to justify such a contention, he points out.
>
> In international law, he asserts, every state has the right to punish spies. All international law experts, including bourgeois international law experts, acknowledge this.[85]

Item 19–14 reveals the PRC's response to an American protest over the 1960 conviction of Bishop James Walsh.

19-14

"Chinese Ambassador's Statement on Sentencing of US Espionage Criminal Walsh," NCNA–English, Warsaw (Mar. 24, 1960), in *SCMP*, no. 2227:46 (Mar. 30, 1960).

Chinese Ambassador Wang Ping-nan, representative to the Sino-US ambassadorial talks, issued a statement here at 1900 hours (local time) today on the sentencing of James Edward Walsh, US espionage criminal, by the Chinese judicial authorities. The statement reads:

The American James Edward Walsh was sentenced to imprisonment according to law by the Chinese judicial authorities on March 18, 1960, for his espionage activities in China and [his] attempt to subvert the Chinese government. Ambassador Wang Ping-nan informed American Ambassador Beam of this at their Warsaw meeting on March 22. Ambassador Beam went so far as to lodge a protest against the sentencing. Ambassador Wang Ping-nan categorically rejected Beam's protest, and pointed out that Walsh was guilty of serious crimes which were conclusively proved by evidences and beyond denial, and that it is China, not the United States, which has reason to lodge a protest. The so-called protest of the United States further proves that Walsh's criminal activities in China constitute a link in the persistent scheming activities of the US government aimed at subverting the Chinese government.

Ambassador Wang Ping-nan pointed out that the Chinese government consistently protects law-abiding foreign nationals and respects freedom of religious belief. However, it absolutely will not allow imperialist spies to carry on activities aimed at subverting the Chinese government under the cloak of religious activities. Speaking of humanitarianism and the standards of international law and behavior among civilized nations, it is precisely the United States, which persists in encroaching on Chinese territory, being hostile to the Chinese people and plotting to subvert the Chinese government, that has violated these principles. The Chinese court has every right to punish any foreign spy who offends the Chinese law. The dignity of the Chinese law and China's judicial sovereign rights are absolutely not to be interfered with by the United States.

Note

On July 10, 1970, the 79-year-old Bishop Walsh, who had been in prison since 1958 and was in ill health, was released and permitted to leave China. Simultaneously the PRC announced that Hugh Redmond, 50, an American businessman who had been serving a life sentence in China after having been convicted of espionage in 1951, had committed suicide three months earlier.[86]

In late 1971, shortly before President Nixon was scheduled to visit China, the PRC announced the release of Richard Fecteau and another American who had been held over three years without trial and also the commutation of John Downey's life sentence to five more years in prison (recall items 19–10 and 19–11).

19-15

"China's Organs of Dictatorship Dispose of Cases of US Culprits," *PR* 14.51:23 (Dec. 17, 1971).

China's organs of dictatorship recently granted leniency to two imprisoned spies of the US Central Intelligence Agency, John Thomas Downey and Richard George Fecteau, in accordance with the proletarian policy of leniency towards those who confess their crimes and severe punishment of those who refuse to do so. The life sentence originally passed on J. T. Downey was commuted into five years' imprisonment. R. G. Fecteau was released before the expiry of his term. . . .

In view of the fact that the two criminals, Downey and Fecteau, admitted their crimes during the trial and their behaviour was not bad while serving their terms, China's organs of dictatorship decided to grant them leniency by commuting Downey's sentence into five years' imprisonment (starting from the date of the commutation) and releasing Fecteau before the expiry of his term. Fecteau was set free and left China via Shumchun on December 13.

It was also learnt that Mary Ann Harbert, an American woman, illegally intruded into China's territorial waters near Tamkon Island off the Pearl River estuary in Kwangtung Province aboard a yacht on April 21, 1968, and was promptly detained by China's people's police. Investigations by the Chinese auhorities concerned verified the abovementioned fact. The culprit, M. A. Harbert, admitted her mistakes in intruding into China's territorial waters. She was set free and left China on December 13.

Another American, Gerald Ross McLaughlin, male, who illegally intruded into China's territorial waters on the same yacht with M. A. Harbert, was also detained. During detention, the culprit behaved badly, resisted investigation and, taking the warders unawares, committed suicide on March 7, 1969. McLaughlin's yacht was confiscated according to law.

NOTE

At a news conference on January 31, 1973, President Nixon conceded that John T. Downey had been an agent of the Central Intelligence Agency. On March 9, 1973, after the President informed Premier Chou En-lai that Downey's mother had become critically ill, the PRC fully commuted Downey's sentence, permitting him to leave China shortly thereafter.[86a]

The following account, written by Allyn Rickett, a Fulbright Scholar whose release from Chinese prison was secured in 1955 as a result of the Sino-American ambassadorial talks, is from a fascinating book that vividly and objectively describes the exercise of the PRC's criminal jurisdiction over an American husband and wife who were both convicted of counterrevolutionary espionage. Earlier portions of the book describe their 1951 arrest and confinement and interrogation processes that closely resemble those reported in items 15–6 and 19–4.

19-16

Allyn and Adele Rickett, *Prisoners of Liberation* (New York: Cameron Associates, 1957), pp. 149–151, 272–275.

Finally, driven to a point of angry desperation, I exploded, "Well, I don't see why I couldn't have had a lawyer."

Immediately shouts came flying from all sides. What did I want a lawyer for? What had I to defend? Was I or was I not a spy?

"The only reason you want a lawyer," broke in Liao, "is so you can avoid having to pay for your crimes. That's the way it is in a capitalist society. If a man has money he can hire a lawyer to get him out of almost anything, while the poor man goes to jail. And what's more, if this were the old China you wouldn't even have had to hire a lawyer. All you'd have had to do was call your Consulate friends and they'd have had you out in no time."

I was silent. How could I answer such an attack? What they said might be true, but to my mind it was irrelevant. According to our traditions, whether a man was guilty or not he had a right to a lawyer.

As if to answer this unexpressed thought, Liao went on, "If you had committed an ordinary crime and this were a civil court, you would have a right to a lawyer and organized defense. But you're forgetting that we're not only living through a revolution here at home. There is also a war going on in Korea. You have been guilty of counterrevolutionary espionage. That puts your case under martial law and before a military tribunal a person has little in the way of normal legal rights.

Academically speaking, I could see his point. A revolution by its very nature is the antithesis of formal legality. It is a social explosion which takes place when one part of society rises up and forcibly asserts its will over its former ruler. To disagree with such a situation is like disagreeing with the universe. However, when it was a matter of my own life being involved, academic logic seemed cold and barren, and I could find little satisfaction in it.

"Incidentally," spoke up Ma suddenly, "since you seem to have so much resentment about not having a lawyer, what about it? Was your confession true or not?"

I vehemently denied that there was any question about the veracity of my confession. Heaven knows the government had been painstaking enough in searching for the truth during those endless hours of intensive questioning. Every point had been gone over and over, yet the investigating judge [interrogator] had never tried to put words in my mouth. In fact, once when I had tried to accept the blame for an affair in which I had been involved but for which I had not actually been responsible, he had reprimanded me for not taking my confession seriously enough and had crossed that part out of my statement.

My quick response to Ma's questions seemed to satisfy him, for the moment at least, but he had no way of knowing what was seething in my mind. Actually what I objected to but did not dare put into words was the very idea of having to make a confession. To me this was a violation of basic civil rights, without which there could be no safeguard for justice. Supposing I had not been guilty but had been arrested on the basis of false evidence? If I had refused to confess, what would have happened? I would have run the risk of being shot. Under the pressure of knowing this a person might very well decide to play safe and confess to something he had not done, in the hopes of pleasing the authorities.

This same point has often been raised by people we have met since our return home. Actually, as I came to realize later on, the court did not determine a person's guilt on the basis of his confession alone. It had to be substantiated by extensive outside evidence. Furthermore, his case was reviewed once a year until final sentence was passed, and even then every prisoner had the right to appeal.

Especially from the latter part of 1952, the government seemed to become increasingly aware of the danger of false confessions. Not only was every confession checked and rechecked for corroboration of the facts, but, in order to avoid undue pressure, prisoners were no longer allowed to "help" each other with their confessions or even discuss the details of their cases in the cell. The use of handcuffs and leg irons as punishment for those people who refused to confess to what the government felt it had substantial proof of was also greatly reduced. Prisoners were frequently encouraged to think over their cases and make any rectifications which would bring their statements more in line with the facts, and it was stressed that any deviation from the facts, whether by way of exaggeration or concealment, was equally dishonest.

It became clear to me that the confession itself served not so much to verify a prisoner's guilt as to give him a chance to make his first step toward reform. That is one of the reasons why the authorities were so careful to see that it adhered strictly to the facts, for only if the prisoner made a really accurate confession could he begin to appreciate what he had done. If he admitted to something he had not done, then, to excuse his reluctance to reform, he would certainly use the rationalization that he was being treated unjustly.

My four years' experience in prison led me to the conclusion that, in spite of the tense internal situation which led to counterrevolutionary and espionage cases being handled by military courts—with the resulting restrictions on normal legal rights—the Chinese government sincerely attempted to see that justice was done. Injustices certainly occurred, as has been admitted by the government itself, but as the internal situation has improved many of the more severe restrictions have been done away with, and at the recent meeting of the National Congress in the summer of 1956 the Chief Justice of the Chinese Supreme Court asserted that the treatment of counterrevolutionary cases was being further liberalized. . . .

Rick: By late spring of 1955 it had become clear that my long-awaited release was near at hand. In April I was informed that Dell [Mrs. Rickett] had left and that my own case would soon be settled. Then one evening in late August, 1955, I was called out of the cell and directed toward a big room near the interrogation offices. I entered, the guard remained on the outside and I found a man and woman waiting for me there.

The man stood up, bowed politely, and asked if I were Li Ko. When I replied in the affirmative, he motioned to a comfortable chair and said pleasantly, "We are from the Procurator-General's office. The Public Security Bureau has turned your case over to us and we would like you to tell us about your crime. You should speak freely and you may disregard any statements you have made before."

I told him that my last statement written in the summer of 1954 was correct to the best of my knowledge. I then proceeded to give him a rough outline of my relations with the Consulate and the British Negotiation Mission.

When I had finished he leaned back for a moment and asked, "Have you any complaints or requests which you would like to make?"

I faltered, "What do you mean? Requests or complaints about what?"

"About the way you were treated and the handling of your case."

I told him that I considered my treatment fair and my punishment just, but that I hoped that some day I would be able to return to the United States.

"Well," he said, standing up by way of dismissal, "we think your wish will probably come true."

September 11 [1955], was a Sunday. Han and I had a big project afoot. My Chinese-English dictionary had become so battered it was falling apart. Han, who had once lived next door to a bookbindery, had suggested that we try to rebind it ourselves. Saturday evening we had spent dismantling the volume and twisting cotton threads to sew the pages together again. We had just started arranging the guide strings Sunday morning when Supervisor Shen appeared at the door.

"Li Ko, put on some presentable clothes and come along," he said.

He stood waiting while I scrambled into a pair of clean slacks and shirt and then led me over to his office, where a blue-uniformed cadre presented me with a typewritten sheet bearing the stamp of the Superior Municipal Court of Peking.

"These are the charges against you," he said. "Read them over and see if they are correct."

I read them carefully. I had been charged with supplying information to the American Consulate and the British Negotiation Party, as well as carrying on activities intended to sabotage the revolution.

After assuring him that they were correct and signing the statement, I was led out to the courtyard where a jeep was waiting. We rode through the streets of Peking to the Municipal Court Building, where I was ordered into a small waiting room. In a few minutes the little interpreter who had accompanied us ushered in a man whom she introduced in English as Professor Wang of the Peking University Law School.

"He is to act as your lawyer," she said.

"I don't need a lawyer," I replied in Chinese. "I'm guilty of the charges against me."

"That's not the point," broke in the professor. "Let me explain. In the first place, since this is not a military court, the law entitles you to legal advice. If you are not satisfied with me, you can choose anyone you want to represent you. Expenses will be taken care of by the government. Secondly, you may plead guilty or not guilty. But even if you plead guilty you still want to have your sentence reduced as much as possible. There are a number of points which can be argued in your favor."

"What?" I asked.

"The fact that you made a full confession and that your attitude since arrest has shown that you regret your past actions. And then, too, perhaps there were extenuating circumstances which forced you to commit your crime. All of these factors should be considered by the court."

We discussed my case for about half an hour and he then left with the interpreter, whose services had not been needed.

About twenty minutes later an attendant appeared to summon me to the courtroom. I walked down a broad corridor to a side door of a long, narrow room. To my left across the back of the room was a gallery of about twenty-odd people some of whom I seemed to recognize. They were probably witnesses called to testify against me if I should plead not guilty. Toward the front of the room on either side were long tables. I was motioned to take a chair at the foot of the table nearest me, where I noticed my lawyer sitting. The young woman on the other side of him turned out to be the court stenographer.

At the table opposite us sat the man from the Procurator-General's office who had interviewed me a few weeks before in prison. Next to him sat a clerk from his office and the interpreter.

I had hardly sat down when the court was called to order and three men filed in to take their places at the bench on the dais which filled the front of the room. The man in the middle, a heavy-set person of forty or so with a fierce-looking mustache, announced in a clear Peking accent that the court was about to consider my case and told me to stand up. He first asked me if I wished an interpreter, and when I declined, he introduced himself as the judge and the men on his right and left as people's asseyors [assessors]. From their appearance they might very well have been college professors. After he had ascertained that I was represented by counsel, the trial got under way.

The man from the Procurator-General's office read off the charges.

I was asked whether I pleaded guilty or not guilty.

"I wish to plead guilty," I stated.

The judge then told me that I was free to make any statement in my defense.

I declined, but my lawyer stood up and made a plea for clemency. He cited the points which he had mentioned to me before. I was again asked if there were anything I wished to say and after I had declined for the second time the court record was read back to us and I was asked to sign it. The judges filed out and I was led back to the waiting room. The whole trial could not have taken more than half an hour.

I sat watching the clock as it ticked off the minutes. When twenty-five of them had gone by, the attendant appeared again to lead me back to the courtroom. This time I was ordered to stand in the center of the room.

The judge and two jurors [assessors] returned to take their places again on the dais. After clearing his throat the judge began to read off the decision, a lengthy document. I was guilty on two counts but in view of my record since arrest, the plea for clemency was granted in part and my sentence was six years, dating from the time of arrest.

"Six years!" I thought, a little stunned. Perhaps I had not heard right. I had been so sure that I was already on my way home. But when I was asked to sign the decision and given a copy, I could see it clearly in black and white—six years.

Court was adjourned and I was led out. By the time I had reached the waiting room the initial shock had worn off.

"Six years is not so bad. I could have been given much more," I thought. "With only two more to go, I'll be home in no time."

While waiting for someone to take me back to prison, I began making plans as to how I would spend those next two years. The list of books I would ask Dell to send me was already taking shape in my mind. Much to my surprise, however, the court attendant reappeared to direct me to a small room opposite the courtroom. It seemed filled with people.

As I stood at attention, a man informed me that I was now before the Peking Lao-gai Wei-yüan Hwey (Labor Reform Committee, which acts as a sort of parole board). My case had been referred to the committee and in view of my record it was decided that my six years' sentence should be commuted to immediate release.

Mumbling some sort of thanks, I left the committee room in a state of joyous confusion and as I almost flew back to the waiting room my lawyer had a hard time catching up with me to explain that I had three years or three days (I was too excited to hear him clearly) to appeal my sentence. In any case I assured him that no appeal would be necessary.

NOTE

In a 1971 article on the administration of justice in the PRC, Lennart Petri, former Swedish ambassador to Peking, wrote:

> In meting out punishment for a crime committed in China by a foreigner, the nationality of the defendant can be of importance. The matter is regarded in the light of the political relations existing at the time in question between China and the concerned country. For maltreatment of a Chinese, a Pole or an Indian has to expect, at the present time, a more severe punishment than a Swede or a Rumanian, for instance. In 1964, when a Swedish sailor was held responsible for having injured two Chinese stevedores by thrusting a knife at them on board a Swedish ship in a Chinese seaport, it was said that the court, in examining the crime, had considered, among other things, the good relations between China and Sweden, the good behavior of the Swedish commander and of the crew, as well as the sympathy of the Swedish embassy for the victims of the maltreatment. This, together with the repentance shown by the defendant, resulted in his not being sentenced to a punishment. On the other hand, in conjunction with "the ship," he was required to compensate the victims for expenses of their hospital care and the "losses caused because of the injury," which had been fixed at a sum that was rather high for Chinese conditions. It was said that the "ship" had neglected to maintain the necessary discipline among its men and to provide sufficient protection for the Chinese stevedores. Neither the shipping company nor the commanding official of the ship nor "the ship" had been accused.[87]

Ambassador Petri also noted that in recent years foreigners have repeatedly been apprehended without their embassies being able either to discover the reasons for the apprehension or to make contact with the persons apprehended.[88] The case described in items 19–17 through 19–20 illustrates the difficulty that many states had, even during the period between the turmoil of the PRC's earliest years and the turmoil of the Cultural Revolution that erupted in 1966.

19-17

"Note Given by the Ministry of External Affairs, New Delhi, to the Embassy of China in India, 2 March, 1964," *White Paper,* no. 11:50–52 Jan. 1964—Jan. 1965).

2. On the 29th October, 1963, Shri Makham Lal Das, an Indian national resident in Shanghai, was arrested by the local authorities on alleged criminal charges. On 1st November, 1963, a consular official of the embassy of India, Peking, met an official of the Consular Department of the Chinese Foreign Office and requested him that information on the circumstances leading to the arrest of Shri Das be furnished to the embassy, urgently. As no information was made available for some time, the embassy sent a note dated 6th December, 1963, to the Chinese Foreign Office, requesting an early reply and also seeking facilities for an embassy representative to meet Shri Das in prison, in accordance with international law and practice. On 7th December, 1963, Mr. Feng Hsien-pi, the Assistant Director and Section Chief of the Consular Department of the Chinese Foreign Office, received the Indian chargé d'affaires and informed him that the matter was still under investigation. The chargé d'affaires was also told that, according to the report of the local authorities, it was a case of criminal assault. However, no further information was given as to when the alleged offence was said to have taken place or even in regard to the name of the alleged victim. Regarding facilities for an embassy representative to meet Shri Das, Mr. Feng Hsien-pi stated that the Foreign Office would contact the local authorities, but that, as far as they knew, it would be impossible to meet him before Shri Das had been sentenced! No further details were given to the chargé d'affaires, beyond stating that "the local authorities have made very detailed and serious investigations."

3. Following a reminder from the embassy dated January 4, 1964, for the details earlier requested in its note of 6th December, 1963, the Assistant Director of the Consular Department of the Chinese Foreign Office again received the Indian chargé d'affaires. He however, made no concrete reply to the points raised by the chargé d'affaires who was seeking facilities under international law, but merely repeated, over and over again, the meaningless statement that "the Chinese government have always given reasonable treatment to the nationals of other countries living in China" and that "there is no discrimination against Indians in this regard." Mr. Feng Hsien-pi informed the chargé d'affaires again that they would be getting in touch

with the local authorities. During this interview Mr. Feng Hsien-pi, however, provided the extraordinary piece of information that the alleged victim of the "assault" had already given birth to a child and stated that "this child very much resembles an Indian." Shri Das was arrested on October 29, 1963, on alleged criminal charges, and Mr. Feng Hsien-pi gave this piece of information in January, 1964. All this cannot but arouse serious doubt about the bona fide nature of the charges levelled against Shri Das.

4. In a note dated 11th January, 1964, the embassy of India in Peking had reiterated their request, in conformity with normal consular privilege, recognised in international law and practice, for the following facilities:—

(i) To meet Shri Das in prison;
(ii) to be present at his trial; and
(iii) to arrange for his defence.

5. It is indeed surprising that the Chinese government in their note under reference should have adamantly refused to grant any of the legitimate facilities requested by the embassy. The Chinese government have perversely tried to justify their stand on various excuses, stating that: "according to stipulation of the authorities concerned, during the period of trial, the request from any person to see the defendant is unacceptable; at the same time, the case is concerned with social morals, so no public hearing can be held. Therefore, visitors are unacceptable. As regards the question of arranging a defender, the local authorities concerned will accord the facilities in accordance with the regulations of the Chinese side."

6. The government of India feel compelled to ask whether the "regulations of the Chinese side" conform to normally accepted international law and practice or not in these matters relating to the arrest, detention, and trial of foreign nationals. One of the main functions of any embassy is to protect the interests of its nationals living in the country of its accredi[ta]tion, within the limits of international law. As the Chinese government are fully aware, it is well recognised international law and practice that a consular officer has the right to be informed of the arrest of nationals of his country, to visit them if they are in prison, custody, or detention, and to converse and correspond with them and also to arrange for their full and proper legal representation, whenever and wherever found necessary. The embassy in its notes dated 6th December, 1963, 4th January, 1964, and 11th January, 1964, has accordingly repeatedly requested the Ministry of Foreign Affairs of the [People's] Republic of China to have the matter in-

vestigated, and the facts of the case and the reason for the arrest ascertained and communicated. The embassy, at the same time, had requested that facilities referred to in paragraph 4 above to be extended to it by the Chinese government. However, the Chinese Ministry of Foreign Affairs has flatly denied these facilities on the flimsiest pretexts, completely ignoring international law and practice recognised all the world over.

7. The laws and regulations of all governments are required to give full effect to the purpose for which specific rights have been accorded to consular officers under international law. The laws and regulations of the receiving state must give full effect to the purposes for which consular rights have been accorded to a consular officer under international law, and the laws and regulations of a receiving state cannot nullify the rights which accrue from international law. That these rights have always been recognised in the law and practice of all states will be evident from the fact that they are embodied in Article 36 of the Vienna Convention on Consular Relations, 1953 [1963]. The Indian embassy in Peking has the right, under international law, to visit Shri Das in prison and also to arrange for his legal representation before the court which is supposed to try him for the alleged criminal offence, and the Chinese government would be flouting international law and convention if it continues its present stand.

8. The Chinese government have stated that no public hearing is to be held and arrangements for Shri Das's defence can be made only in accordance with "the regulations of the Chinese side." This attitude of the Chinese authorities clearly indicates that they have no intention of administering proper justice to Shri Das. This is not only a denial of justice to the accused, but is also a clear violation of international law.

9. In view of the above facts, the government of India earnestly urge the Chinese authorities to reconsider their stand and to provide immediately facilities to the Indian embassy in Peking to visit Shri Das in prison, arrange for his defence, and also for the embassy officials to be present at his trial, when the trial takes place.

19-18

"Note Given by the Ministry of External Affairs, New Delhi, to the Embassy of China in India, 14 April, 1965," *White Paper*, no. 12:116–117 (Jan. 1965—Feb. 1966).

2. The Chinese government has stated in the above note that "the way the Chinese side dealt with the case is unimpeachable and in full accord with international practice. However, regardless of the facts described above, the Indian government in its note deliberately distorted the content of the aforesaid conversations, made unwarranted charges against the Chinese government, and deliberately attempted to interfere in a matter within sovereign jurisdiction of the Chinese government. This is entirely impermissible."

3. Contrary to the Chinese government's claim, full facts about the case were never given to the government of India in spite of repeated requests.

4. To give another instance of Chinese reluctance to give information, Shri Das's case was decreed on the 25th July, 1964, by the People's Court of Shanghai and both the Chinese Foreign Ministry and the Foreign Affairs Bureau in Shanghai were fully aware of this. During his visit to Shanghai on the 4th August, 1964, the Indian chargé d'affaires repeatedly urged Mr. Lwo, an official of the Foreign Affairs Bureau, Shanghai, to expedite the disposal of the case. At that time the chargé d'affaires was not informed that Shri Das had already been found guilty and sentenced to imprisonment.

5. The embassy of India in Peking repeatedly asked for certain facilities in conformity with normal consular privileges recognised in international law and practice. Instead the government of India is being asked to be satisfied with the unsubstantiated assertion of the Chinese government that "the evidence of his (Shri Das's) guilt was incontrovertibly established." The government of India cannot but point out that the accused was denied elementary justice in blatant violation of international practice.

6. Furthermore, when officers of the Indian embassy in Peking asked for permission to see Shri Das in jail, restrictions were placed on the subjects they could discuss with him, and no conversation was allowed regarding the case itself. The result was that Shri Das was not allowed to communicate with the embassy either during or after the trial; nor was he allowed to engage a lawyer to defend himself. Moreover, Shri Das's interview in jail with one of the officers of the embassy was abruptly terminated by the jail authorities before it had

lasted even five minutes. Though the jail regulations allow prisoners to receive visitors twice a month, on the first and third Tuesday, his parents were not allowed to see him except on those specific occasions when the embassy made a request on their behalf to the Chinese Foreign Ministry. It is not known what kind of treatment and food Shri Das is receiving in jail, but when he was seen in jail by an officer of the embassy and later by his parents, he was looking ill and emaciated. The letters which he wrote to the embassy were not forwarded to the destination by the jail authorities. All this cannot but raise serious suspicion that Shri Das is being subjected to grave ill-treatment. It is clearly the responsibility of the Chinese government to issue instructions to jail authorities not to ill-treat him in jail and to provide him adequate diet and medical attendance.

7. The government of India emphatically lodges a protest to the Chinese government on the denial of justice to one of their nationals Shri M. L. Das, and urges the Chinese authorities to provide immediately facilities to the accused for appealing to a higher court as it has been established beyond doubt that justice has not been meted out to him by the People's Court of Shanghai.

19-19

"Note Given by the Ministry of Foreign Affairs, Peking to the Embassy of India in China, 15 September, 1965," *White Paper*, no. 12:118–120 (Jan. 1965—Feb. 1966).

The Ministry of Foreign Affairs of the People's Republic of China categorically rejects the so-called "strong protest" of the Indian Ministry for External Affairs, which is utterly unwarranted, in connection with the rape of a Chinese girl by Makham Lall Das.

1. Indian national in China M. L. Das forcibly raped a Chinese girl, seriously violating the right of person and damaging the physical and mental health of the victim, disrupting public order and breaking Chinese law. It is proper and unimpeachable that the Chinese local judicial authorities sentenced him to imprisonment according to law.

2. The Ministry of Foreign Affairs of the People's Republic of China had repeatedly acquainted the Indian embassy in China with the case long ago, and the Indian Ministry for External Affairs had acknowledged the fact in its reply notes. Yet in its latest note the Indian Ministry for External Affairs haggled unreasonably, asserting that it had not been told the "full facts" and the "circumstances." We would like to state clearly once again that Indian national M. L. Das

had committed in China a very serious offence of raping a juvenile girl. Even the official of the Indian embassy in China, Mr. Damodaran, admitted in his conversation with Assistant Director Mr. Feng Hsien-pi of the Chinese Ministry of Foreign Affairs on December 7, 1963, that he considered the offence a "shame." Yet now the Indian Ministry for External Affairs has appealed to so-called international law and practice and asked the Chinese government to furnish it again with the "full facts" and "circumstances." This is entirely impermissible.

M. L. Das is guilty of the raping of a Chinese girl. Out of regard for the future and the name of the injured girl, the judicial authorities of the Chinese government decided on a private trial. Hence it was entirely reasonable to deny attendance at the trial to officials from the Indian embassy in China. This had been made clear by the Chinese Ministry of Foreign Affairs in its note to the Indian embassy in China on January 31, 1964. However, in its note under reference, the Indian Ministry for External Affairs still talked drivel, alleging that the Chinese government had "dealt with the case in complete secrecy." This is not only a vicious slander against the Chinese government, but also an illegal interference with China's exercise of its sovereign rights.

In order to cast such slanders on China, the Indian Ministry for External Affairs groundlessly stated in its note that "M. L. Das was not allowed to engage a lawyer to defend himself." The fact was that the Chinese authorities concerned offered him a lawyer to defend him, but he refused and decided on defending himself.

The Indian Ministry for External Affairs also said in its note that M. L. Das was not allowed to communicate with the embassy either during or after the trial. According to the regulations of the Chinese authorities concerned, visits to prisoners are allowed after they have been sentenced. From September 1964 to April 1965, a total of six requests were made by officials of the Indian embassy in China and relatives of the criminal to meet the latter in prison; each request was met by the Chinese authorities concerned, and not one was rejected. Even when the official of the Indian embassy in China, Mr. Damodaran, failed to go to the prison at the specified time, the Chinese authorities concerned gave him special consideration and let him visit the criminal against the rule. These facts clearly show that the slanders made by the Indian Ministry for External Affairs against the Chinese government cannot stand refutation.

The assertion in the note of the Indian Ministry of External Affairs that the interview of an official of the embassy with the criminal "was abruptly terminated by the jail authorities before it had lasted even five minutes" is also a sheer distortion of the fact. The fact was that the visit to M. L. Das had to be stopped because the press attaché of the Indian embassy in China, Mr. P. V. Srinivasan, violated the regulations concerning visits although he had been informed of the regulations in detail beforehand by the jail authorities.

As is well known, the Chinese jail authorities always treat criminals humanely. The assertion of the Indian Ministry for External Affairs about M. L. Das being "ill-treated" is an absurd fabrication pure and simple. Instead of taking shame at the scandal caused by such a bad element as M. L. Das, the Indian government has kept on haggling about it. Does it really think that this will bring it any honour?

It must be further pointed out that although the Middle People's Court of Shanghai Municipality on January 27, 1964, passed a fair sentence on the offence committed by M. L. Das, at his request the authorities concerned permitted him to appeal to the Higher People's Court of Shanghai Municipality. After going through another careful examination and full debate in court, the Higher People's Court of Shanghai Municipality confirmed that the evidence of M. L. Das's offence was conclusive, decided to uphold the original sentence and reject his appeal, and concluded that this was the sentence of the final trial and that no further appeal might be made.

3. The Chinese government has dealt with the offence committed by M. L. Das in accordance with Chinese law. This is in full conformity with international practice, and also reasonable and unimpeachable as a judicial measure which any sovereign state is bound to take in order to safeguard public order and protect personal safety. The Chinese authorities concerned have rendered facilities to meet all the reasonable requests made by the Indian embassy in China concerning the case of M. L. Das, but the Indian government has repeatedly made baseless and malicious slanders against the Chinese government and openly interfered in matters which are within China's sovereign rights. This course of action is obviously pursued by the Indian government with ulterior purposes, and the Chinese government expresses its deepest regret at it.

19-20

"Note Given by the Ministry of External Affairs, New Delhi to the Embassy of China in India, 2 November, 1965," *White Paper*, no. 12:120, 121 (Jan. 1965–Feb. 1966).

It was only on the 11th September, 1964, that the Chinese government informed the Indian embassy, that Shri M. L. Das had been sentenced to five years imprisonment. Right from the time of the arrest of Shri Das it was repeatedly pointed out by us to the Chinese government that the 70-year-old parents of Shri M. L. Das were in a state of nervous shock on account of their anxiety for their son. The Chinese government, in callous disregard of all accepted canons of humanity and international law, gave evasive replies for more than ten months and withheld permission for Shri M. L. Das's parents to meet their son in prison.

In its note under reply, the Chinese government has boasted of its magnanimity towards Shri M. L. Das in permitting officials from the Indian embassy to visit him after September, 1964. Yet on the 21st September, 1965, barely a week after handing over the note under reply, when an official of the Indian embassy in Peking visited Shanghai for the purpose of meeting Shri M. L. Das in prison, the Chinese government, notwithstanding the fact that they had been given prior intimation of this visit, refused to let this official meet Shri M. L. Das. In defence of this they advanced the flimsy excuse that the prisoner had "violated prison regulations."

In its frantic attempt to find justification for the ill-treatment of Shri M. L. Das, the Chinese government has deliberately misquoted an official of the Indian embassy in Peking and claimed, in its note dated 15th September, 1965, that this official had expressed "shame" at the offence allegedly committed by Shri Das. If they have the slightest regard for the truth, the Chinese government will recall that on being informed of Shri M. L. Das's arrest on 7th December, 1963, the First Secretary of the Indian Embassy in Peking had merely stated that such an incident, *if it had taken place,* was [a] shameful event. It is regrettable that the Chinese government should have distorted the context and the meaning of words in this manner.

The allegation of the Chinese government that Indian officials visiting Shri M. L. Das at the Shanghai jail have "violated regulations concerning the visits" is absurd. As a matter of fact, during each visit Indian embassy officials counselled Shri M. L. Das to observe the jail "regulations" however distasteful they may be. The truth is that on more than one occasion the Chinese government have forcibly prevented Shri M. L. Das from communicating with Indian embassy officials. On one occasion while he was narrating facts regarding his treatment in prison to a visiting Indian official, Shri Das was physically dragged by the prison authorities back into his cell in the middle of the interview. The government of India condemn these actions to the Chinese authorities and the denial to Shri M. L. Das of the right, under international law, to communicate with the representatives of his country. The government of India urge that the Chinese government stop the persecution of Shri M. L. Das and review his case on the basis of universally accepted canons of justice and law, and provide facilities to the Indian embassy in Peking to extend to Shri M. L. Das full consular protection.

NOTE

Although always alert to the danger of espionage, during the xenophobic Cultural Revolution of 1966 to 1969 the Chinese Communists again became as preoccupied with the problem as they were in the earliest years of their regime. Items 19–21 and 19–22 illustrate the application of the criminal process against foreigners during that era. Both of these cases, it should be noted, arose in Lanchow, which is the site of China's gaseous diffusion plant and is a major support base for the country's nuclear test facilities.

19-21

"British Spy Case Broken in Lanchow," *PR* 11.12:14–15 (Mar. 22, 1968).

Acting in accordance with the information supplied by the revolutionary masses, the Public Security Bureau in Lanchow, Kansu Province, recently broke a case in which British spy George Watt (British) carried out espionage activities in the People's Republic of China.

George Watt came to China on December 14, 1966, as an engineer for British Vickers Zimmer, Ltd. Watt was assigned the job of gathering intelligence by the British imperialist spy P. F. W. Jay, a responsible member of Vickers Zimmer, Ltd., before he got to China. Since his arrival Watt, in the guise of an engineer, had engaged in espionage activities directed against the People's Republic of China and rendered active service to the British imperialist policy of aggression. During his stay in China, he spied out and stole important intelligence about China's military, political, and economic affairs and the great proletarian cultural revolution, and had furtively taken many photographs of prohibited areas in China. Thus, he had committed grave crimes, thereby seriously endangering the security and undermining the socialist construction of China.

At the time the Lanchow Public Security Bureau broke this case, it discovered that Peter Deckart (West German), an engineer for Vickers Zimmer, Ltd., had also engaged in espionage activities in China.

"Make trouble, fail, make trouble again, fail again . . . till their doom; that is the logic of the imperialists and all reactionaries the world over in dealing with the people's cause, and they will never go against this logic." Using the cover of trade, British imperialist intelligence organizations had sent spies through Vickers Zimmer, Ltd., and this company had undermined China's socialist construction through blackmail and deception in the economic and technical fields, but their criminal activities were eventually brought to light. Though they had been extremely crafty in their espionage activities, they were eventually caught by the mighty arm of the Chinese people who are armed with Mao Tse-tung's thought and maintain high revolutionary vigilance at all times.

The crimes of George Watt and Peter Deckart in carrying out espionage activities aroused immense indignation among the revolutionary masses who unanimously demanded that the British spies be severely punished.

Rally for Announcing Sentence

At a rally on March 15, the intermediate people's court in Lanchow announced that Watt had been sentenced to three years in prison. At the same time, the Lanchow Public Security Bureau announced that Peter Deckart would be immediately deported from the People's Republic of China. . . .

Held in Lanchow's Hall of Anti-Revisionism, the rally was attended by proletarian revolutionaries, the revolutionary masses, and representatives of the Chinese People's Liberation Army units stationed in Lanchow. All the participants angrily denounced British imperialism for sending spies into China and strongly condemned the British imperialist spies for their monstrous crimes of stealing intelligence and undermining the socialist construction of our country. Filled with indignation, everyone shouted: "Down with British imperialism!" "Down with US imperialism!" "Down with Soviet modern revisionism!" "Severe punishment for the British spies!" and "We'll resolutely smash all the plots and sabotage activities of the special agents of the US-Chiang Kai-shek gang, British imperialism, Soviet revisionism and Japan!". . . .

British imperialist spy Watt was taken to the rally amid angry shouts of "Down with British imperialism!" and "Severe punishment for the British spy!" Trembling with fear, this spy who had committed grave crimes looked pale and bowed his head as he stood on the accused stand.

A representative of the Lanchow intermediate people's court read out the verdict which listed the crimes of the spy. It pointed out that he should be severely punished for his crimes as a spy, of which there was irrefutable evidence and to which he had admitted, but considering the fact that he had shown repentance, he was therefore given a light sentence of three years' imprisonment in accordance with our country's policy of leniency toward those who acknowledge their crimes but severe punishment for those who stubbornly refuse to do so.

After the verdict was read, the rally burst into thunderous applause. Everyone raised his arm and shouted: "We resolutely support the just sentence passed by the Lanchow intermediate people's court on the British spy Watt!" "Long live the great, glorious, and correct Chinese Communist Party!" "Long live the all-round victory in the great proletarian cultural revolution!" "Long live the victory of Chairman Mao's proletarian revolutionary line!" "Long live the invincible thought of Mao Tse-tung!" "Long live the great leader Chairman Mao! A long, long life to him!"

NOTE

Not only did the PRC impose criminal sanctions against Vickers-Zimmer employees, but it also imposed civil sanctions upon the company itself (see 21–11). On July 30, 1970, almost three years after his detention, George Watt was released and deported.[89]

By the summer of 1968 more than thirty foreigners were reported to have been imprisoned by Chinese authorities, including ship's officers and passengers, bankers, trade representatives, engineering personnel, journalists, and even Communists who had lived in Peking and worked for the PRC for many years.[90] Many of these persons were released by the fall of 1969, as the Cultural Revolution subsided. Some were ordered deported following conviction for espionage, but in most instances the case appears simply to have been dropped. The following announcement served notice that the PRC would not relax its vigilance against espionage. At the same time that Peking announced the conviction of Trutz von Xylander, it also released four other West German employees of the Lurgi Company and the family of one of them, who had not been imprisoned but who had been confined to a Peking hotel and immediate environs for fourteen months while the investigation proceeded (see Note following 21–11).

19-22

"US Imperialist Spy Case Broken by Lanchow's Organs of Dictatorship," *PR* 12.44:4–5 (Oct. 31, 1969).

The organs of dictatorship in Lanchow, Kansu Province, have broken a case in which the US imperialist spy Trutz von Xylander (of West Germany) carried out espionage activities in the People's Republic of China. The spy case was broken with the cooperation of the revolutionary masses armed with Mao Tse-tung Thought at a time when China's Great Proletarian Cultural Revolution has won tremendous victories. The sentence passed on the spy has been openly pronounced.

US imperialist spy Trutz von Xylander came to China in October 1965 as an "equipment inspector for unpacking" for the "Lurgi Gesellschaft für Mineraloetechnik M.B.H." of West Germany. Before leaving for China, he accepted from a US imperialist intelligence organization in West Germany the job of secretly collecting intelligence about China. After his arrival, Trutz von Xylander, first in the guise of an "equipment inspector for unpacking" and then of a "plant site clerk," conducted espionage activities aimed at subverting the People's Republic of China. He furtively took photographs of prohibited areas and gathered important intelligence about China's military, political, and economic affairs and the Great Proletarian Cultural Revolution, rendering active service to the US imperialist policies of aggression and war and seriously endangering China's security. His crimes were grave, of which there were [*sic*] irrefutable evidence.

The revolutionary masses were deeply indignant at the espionage crimes committed by US imperialist spy Trutz von Xylander and unanimously demanded that severe punishment be meted out to him. In accordance with the law of the People's Republic of China, the organs of dictatorship in Lanchow, Kansu Province, sentenced US imperialist spy Trutz von Xylander to ten years' imprisonment.

Note

Von Xylander was released in 1973 as part of a systematic PRC effort to clear its jails of Western prisoners as relations with the West improved. After Japan established diplomatic relations with the PRC, Peking also released all but one of a number of Japanese businessmen who had been detained on espionage charges for approximately six years; the businessman who remained was convicted of espionage and sentenced to twenty years in prison.[90a]

According to an agreement reached at Geneva in 1954, the

Chinese Red Cross received from the American Red Cross monthly deliveries of parcels and mail for Americans detained in Chinese prisons. These deliveries were made at China's border with Hong Kong. The PRC also permitted relatives of imprisoned Americans to visit them on a few occasions.[91]

Aliens' Personal Affairs 20

We have already seen in item 15–1 the strict regulations to which aliens who wish to enter, leave, and travel in China are subject. Previous materials have also suggested the extent to which the PRC scrutinizes other activities of foreign nationals. Chapter 21 will deal with the PRC's regulation of aliens' economic opportunities. In this chapter we introduce some of the fragmentary documentation that is available concerning limitations placed upon two major aspects of aliens' personal lives: their freedom to marry and divorce in China, and their freedom to transfer property at death and to inherit it. These documents date from the PRC's first decade; since that time material relating to the domestic legal system has become increasingly scarce. In some respects, the documents probably no longer reflect current practice in the PRC.

Before presenting materials concerning marriage and inheritance problems, we ought to note that even less is known about the PRC's regulation of other aspects of aliens' lives. For example, although Article 11 of the 1954 Constitution provided that "The state protects the right of citizens to own lawfully earned incomes, savings, houses, and other means of life" (as distinguished from "means of production," discussed in Chapter 21),[92] nothing was said about any such right for aliens. Detailed study of the PRC's regulation of these aspects, including treatment of overseas Chinese who have returned to China as dual nationals, should prove rewarding.

The most interesting aspect of item 20–1 is the extent to which, at least at that early stage, the revolutionary Chinese Communist regime was prepared to give effect to the family law policies of other states. If it has not subsequently adopted less lenient laws regulating the marriage of foreigners to Chinese, it has nevertheless done a great deal by administrative and informal methods to discourage its citizens from marrying foreigners or even coming into contact with them. Therefore some of the problems discussed in this item, which is a Dutch scholar's English translation of the Chinese texts, are undoubtedly less pressing than they were during the earlier period.

20-1

M. H. van der Valk, translator, "Documents Concerning Conflict of Laws in Matters of Marriage in Communist China," in *Nederlands Tijdschrift voor Internationaal Recht* (Netherlands international law review) 8:323, 325–331 (1961).

III

VIEWS OF THE COMMISSION OF LEGISLATIVE AFFAIRS OF THE CENTRAL PEOPLE'S GOVERNMENT CONCERNING THE PROBLEM OF MARRIAGES OF CHINESE WITH FOREIGN RESIDENTS AND THAT OF FOREIGN RESIDENTS WITH FOREIGN RESIDENTS

ANSWER TO THE OFFICE OF AFFAIRS OF FOREIGN RESIDENTS OF THE MILITARY AND POLITICAL COMMITTEE OF THE SOUTH CENTRAL GREATER ADMINISTRATIVE AREA. NOVEMBER 8, 1950.

The method of dealing with marriages and divorces in China between Chinese and foreign residents, and between foreign residents and foreign residents, as devised by the Ministry of Foreign Affairs is fundamentally satisfactory. We now supplement it with our views in the following way:

1. When in China a Chinese has married a foreign resident, or has been divorced from a foreign resident; or when in China a foreign resident has married a foreign resident, or been divorced from him; and thereupon he makes a request to have it registered by the Chinese organs for the registration of marriages, it seems that these organs, when dealing with these matters, must not only apply the Chinese Marriage Law, but also pay heed within proper limits—to put it differently: to apply to considering the circumstances—to the (foreign) party's national marriage law, in order to avoid [a situation where] the marriage or divorce of that party is recognized as void by his own country.

For example, as regards marriage, as from February 15, 1947, Soviet Russia forbids its citizens to conclude marriages with foreigners; suppose a person from the Soviet Union intends to conclude a marriage in China with a Chinese or a Korean, then Soviet Russia will recognize this marriage as absolutely void if the Chinese organs for the registration of marriages merely apply the Chinese Marriage Law and register it. (See private international law by Professor [Lunts.]) Thus the marrying parties will be put into a most unfortunate position; therefore it seems that under these circumstances the Chinese organs for the registration of marriages must also pay heed to the laws and ordinances of Soviet Russia, and it is suitable that they do not allow registration of these marriages. As regards divorce, as from July 8, 1944, in Soviet Russia it is required that in cases of divorce a court of first instance mediates, and thereupon a court of second instance gives judgment allowing it; finally it is registered by the organ for the registration of divorces, which issues a certificate of divorce; only then is it lawful. Suppose that two persons from Soviet Russia both want to divorce, and the Chinese organs for the registration of marriages, merely applying the provision of article 17 of the Marriage Law, register the divorce and issue a certificate of divorce, then such a divorce shall also be recognized as void in Soviet Russia. (See p. 306 of the work quoted above.) Thus, if the parties to the divorce conclude marriage with another person, the Russian courts shall recognize this as bigamy; on account hereof the parties will be put into a most unfortunate position. Therefore under these circumstances it seems that the Chinese organs for the registration of divorces must also pay heed to the Russian marriage law; they may not immediately proceed to the registration of the divorce, but perhaps propose to the parties that they make a request for divorce to their national law court, or propose that a Chinese law court first give judgment after which (the divorce) is registered by the organ for the registration of divorces.

Under circumstances that parties to the marriage or to the divorce do not intend to reside in China, but whose permanent domicile is in their own country, it is even more important to take into consideration the national marriage law of the parties.

2. Within which limitations shall the Chinese organs for registration apply the national marriage law of the parties? The reply is: within the limitation that the national marriage law of the parties is not detrimental to public order in China—to put it differently: if it is not detrimental of Chinese public interests, nor in contravention of Chinese present fundamental policies—the Chinese organs for the registration of marriages shall apply the national marriage law of the parties; but where the national marriage law of the parties is going to be detrimental to public order in China—to put it differently: if it is detrimental to Chinese public interests, or in contravention of Chinese present fundamental policies—it shall therefore not be applied, but merely the Chinese Marriage Law, in order to settle the problem whether or not to allow the registration of marriage or divorce.

A *As Regards Marriage:*

1. As related above, the Russian law forbids its citizens to marry foreigners. Suppose a Russian citizen concludes a marriage with a Chinese in China, (then) the Chinese organs for the registration of marriages shall apply the (rule of) the Russian law of not allowing the registration of marriages; because the point of departure of this Russian law is not racial discrimination, China shall apply it, and it is not detrimental to Chinese public order.

2. Several American states forbid marriage between persons of the white and of the black race. Suppose a white American wishes to conclude marriage in China with a black American, then the Chinese organs for the registration of marriages shall not apply these American laws, but merely apply the Chinese Marriage Law and allow the registration, for these laws of American imperialism are in contravention of the Chinese policy of racial equality and, if China applies them, it will be detrimental to Chinese public order.

3. As regards the lowest marriageable age, the main thing is that there is a difference in the rate of physical development of the citizens of several countries (and therefore) the legal provisions in the several countries are also different. For example, the German code considers that the lowest marriageable age for the man is 21, for the woman 16; the French code considers that the lowest marriageable age for the man is 18, for the woman 15; the English law considers that the lowest marriageable age for men and women is 16; the Japanese code considers that the lowest marriageable age for the man is 17, for the woman 15. The lowest marriageable age as provided for in the parties' national law commonly can pay heed to the rate of physical development of the parties and is not detrimental to the public order of China; therefore commonly it must be applied. On account of this, if a German man has already reached the age of 20 but not yet that of 21, China must not allow the registration[.] [A]lthough according to the Chinese Marriage Law he has reached the marriageable age, [he has] not yet [done so] according to his national law. If a French woman has already reached the age of 15 but not yet that of 18, then China must allow the registration because according to her national law she has reached the marriageable age, although according to the Chinese Marriage Law she has not.

4. As regards the prohibitions to marriage between near relatives: owing to the fact that the nations hold divergent views on eugenics and have different opinions on ethical principles, the provisions in the laws of the nations are consequently also mutually different. For example, German law does not prohibit marriage between uncle and

niece. If a German wishes to marry his niece in China—she also being of German nationality—and requests registration by the Chinese organs for the registration of marriage, it would seem not to be greatly detrimental to Chinese public order if our organs for the registration of marriages apply the German law, allowing marriage between uncle and niece, although these marriages are contrary to Chinese custom and prohibited by the Chinese Marriage Law. Hence it would seem (the German law) can be applied and the registration of marriage allowed. But if one of the parties intending marriage, uncle and niece, is a German and the other a Chinese, the Chinese organs for the registration of marriages must apply the Chinese Marriage Law, and the registration of the marriage is not allowed.

5. Several Mohammedan countries allow one man to have four wives. Suppose a man from such a country, who already has one wife, wants to marry another woman in China. As monogamy is an important policy of China with regard to marriage, it would be detrimental to public order in China if, applying the national law of that party, the registration of marriage were allowed. Therefore under these circumstances the national marriage law of parties shall not be applied, but merely the Chinese Marriage Law, and the registration of the marriage shall not be allowed.

B *As Regards Divorce:*

1. The laws of several countries stipulate that, for a divorce, judgment by a law court is required—for example, Russia, Germany, France are all like this; under these circumstances China can pay heed to the national law of the parties and suggest that parties first institute proceedings with a Chinese law court; after judgment of divorce has been given by that court, it can thereupon be registered by our organs for the registration of divorces. When trying these divorce cases, the courts shall naturally grant the divorce if both the Chinese Marriage Law and the national marriage law of the parties recognize that a divorce shall be granted; if both recognize [that] it shall not be granted, then it shall naturally not be granted. But when the Chinese Marriage Law recognizes [that] it shall be granted, [but] the parties' national marriage law however [recognizes] that it shall not be granted; or the reverse: that the Chinese Marriage Law recognizes that it shall not be granted, but the parties national law recognizes [that] it shall be granted, then the question if judgment shall be given by application of the Chinese law or by application of the national marriage law shall be settled by considering if [the] parties intend to reside in China or in their own country, as well as if application of the national marriage law

of the parties is detrimental to Chinese public order. If [the] parties intend to reside in China, or if the application of the parties' national marriage law is to be detrimental to Chinese public order, it is not possible to apply the parties' national marriage law, but judgment shall be given [by] merely applying the Chinese Marriage Law. On the other hand, if the application of the parties' national marriage law is not detrimental to Chinese public order, judgment shall be given merely [by] applying the parties' national marriage law. If parties have their permanent domicile in their own country but [only a temporary abode in China], the law courts shall even pay more heed to the national marriage law of the parties, upon condition that it is not detrimental to public order in China.

3. Our organs for the registration of marriages when dealing with the marriages or the divorces of foreigners, as well as the Chinese law courts when trying divorce cases of foreigners, may order the foreign party to give evidence concerning his national marriage law for reference. That foreign party's consulate in China or legal specialists may guarantee this, [but,] if the party can produce an original text of the marriage law, sealed by his national government, so much better.

IV

INTERPRETATIVE ANSWER OF THE COMMISSION OF LEGISLATIVE AFFAIRS OF THE CENTRAL PEOPLE'S GOVERNMENT CONCERNING THE PROBLEM IF THE FOREIGN WIFE OF A CHINESE ACQUIRES CHINESE NATIONALITY. MARCH 9, 1951.

As regards the problem how the foreign wife of a Chinese acquires Chinese nationality: as long as no Chinese nationality law has been promulgated, in special cases one may deal with it in accordance with the following principle:

1. Where the foreign wife of a Chinese desires to acquire Chinese nationality, she shall make a request to the local government to be naturalized; after investigating the circumstances the local government shall give its opinion, and it shall report the case to the Ministry of the Interior for investigation and decision.

2. A Chinese man cannot donate immoveable property to a wife who was originally a foreigner.

VI

LETTER IN REPLY OF THE MINISTRY OF JUSTICE OF THE CENTRAL (PEOPLE'S GOVERNMENT) CONCERNING THE PROBLEM OF MARRIAGES BETWEEN CHINESE AND JAPANESE CADRES

ANSWER TO THE SOCIAL SERVICE DEPARTMENT OF THE *Manchurian Daily* (TUNG PEI JIH PAO). APRIL 25, 1951.

We have received the letter you transferred on February 10 for Yang Shu-heng of the local medical college; we have exchanged views with the Ministry of the Interior about the problem of marriage between Chinese and Japanese cadres, about which you made enquiries, and the solution is as follows:

The principle when dealing with the problem of marriages between Chinese and foreign cadres is: army cadres and foreign office cadres are absolutely not allowed to marry foreign cadres; in general, marriages between cadres and foreign cadres must not be in contravention of the provisions of the Chinese Marriage Law. If the foreign cadres' country has already established diplomatic relations with China, attention must also be paid to the law of the foreign cadres' own country.

In the letter on the part of Yang Shu-heng is mentioned that a Chinese lecturer requests to marry a Japanese nurse; in accordance with the principle related above we recognize: if their marriage is not in contravention of the Marriage Law of the Chinese People's Republic it can be allowed.

20-2

"What Are the Procedures for Sending a Certificate of Authorization Abroad?" *Kung-jen jih-pao* (Workers' daily; Dec. 22, 1956), p. 3.

Comrade Editor:

I came back [to China] from Indonesia two years ago, and I am now studying at a college in Peking. My father died in Indonesia in January this year. When he was alive he owned houses and coconut plantations in Indonesia. Now my mother and I are to inherit his property. She sent a certificate of authorization for me to sign so as to authorize her to act for me in the procedures of succession. I signed and affixed my seal on the document and sent it back to her. A few days later she returned it to me saying that my signature should be verified by someone. I then asked my college to verify my signature and affix its seal on the document as a sign of the verification. But shortly after I sent it to Indonesia, my mother returned it to me again saying that it was still no good. Thus we tried again and again for over half a year without any success. This poses a difficulty to me and adversely affects my studies. What shall I do? Please help me resolve the problem.

Ch'en I-mei

Comrade Ch'en I-mei:

Concerning the question of verifying your certificate of authorization, you may apply to the notarizing organ for verification. According to international practice, any document sent abroad by an individual which would have legal effects there must be notarized in the country where the sender resides. Only after being notarized will the document be recognized as valid by the foreign government. If the document is not notarized by a notarizing organ according to the proper procedure but only verified by a private individual, a district or village government or any other organ, a foreign government will not be able to tell whether it is authentic or not, and thus will not recognize it as a valid document. Thus in the case of your certificate of authorization, although your college verified your signature and affixed its official seal on the document as a sign of the verification, yet it will not have any legal effect abroad.

When you apply to a notarizing organ for notarization of a document you should write the document yourself and send it to the notarial office of the place where you live. If you live in Peking, send the document to the Notarial Office of the City of Peking. Since the certificate of authorization sent to you by your mother is in the Indonesian language, you must translate it into Chinese and then have the original and the Chinese version notarized by the Notarial Office of the City of Peking. Thereafter you should bring it to the Ministry of Justice of the People's Republic of China for certification and finally bring it to the Foreign Ministry of the People's Republic of China and the Indonesian embassy in our country for verification. Then you can send it to Indonesia. This certificate of authorization will then have a legal effect and will enable you to obtain your father's property in Indonesia.

The Editors

20-3

"Public Notice of the Office of the Notary, Harbin, Public Notice ('59) No. 1," *Ha-erh-pin jih-pao* (Harbin Daily; Jan. 9, 1959).

Foreigner [indecipherable Russian name] died December 28, 1958. He left immovable property which is situated at No. 47 Manchuria Street, Nan Kan District, and some movable property (furniture and clothing). Within six months of the date of the published notice, anyone who is a legal heir shall bring legal documents to our office to complete the procedure of succession. When the period expires, the case will be handled by escheat [chüeh-ch'an].

20-4

"Public Notice of the High Court of Shanghai," *Chieh-fang jih-pao* (Liberation Daily; July 8, 1960).

This Court handles the succession case, Shanghai High Court No. 41, 1960, of P.L. Coviot [?], male, a foreigner of French nationality, who was born in 1895 and lived at No. 87 Wu Hsin Road. He died because of illness on April 5, 1960, in Shanghai. He left cash, clothing, and other items. We, therefore, give notice to those who are favored to succeed to the above property that they must bring the documents concerned to this court to make application within six months of the date of this published notice. When this period expires, the case will be handled according to law. We herewith publish this notice.

20-5

The following documents are translations of (a) a judicial decision that determined the right of a Soviet resident of China to inherit property from another Soviet resident; and (b) the will that the deceased had made shortly before her death.

(*a*) *Uncontested Decision of the People's Court of Harbin File No. Fei-662, 1950. September 5, 1951*

The Applicant: Ivar Spessa, a citizen of the Soviet Union, residing at 32, San-t'ang Street, Ching-wei, Tao-li District, Harbin.

In the case of the above-mentioned applicant for a determination of his right to inherit, the Court decides as follows:

Decree: It is decided that the attached will is valid.

Facts and Reasons: Julia G. Orlovskaya, a citizen of the Soviet Union, died on September 10, 1950, and left an amount of movables listed in the paper attached to the will. Before her death, she had made a notarial will at this court (File No. I-26, 1950). Since the decedent did not have any statutory heirs, she bequeathed her property to the applicant, Ivar Spessa, with whom she had lived for thirty-two years. After the death of the testator, the applicant requested this Court to determine the validity of her will.

According to the death certificate [of the decedent] issued by the Northeast Red Cross Hospital and her notarial will, File No. I-26, 1950, made at this Court, the aforesaid facts can be held true. The case is therefore decided as the decree indicates.

Judge T'ien Chia-ho

(*b*) *The Notarial Will* *File No. I-26, 1950. The People's Court of Harbin, May 25, 1950*

The Testator: Julia G. Orlovskaya, a citizen of the Soviet Union, sixty-five years of age, doing household affairs, residing at 32, San-t'ang Street, Tao-li District, Harbin, now temporarily receiving treatment at the Jewish Hospital, 44 Chung-kuo Wu-tao Street, Tao-li District, Harbin, presents an Alien Resident Certificate, No. 09800, issued to her on November 29, 1946, by the Public Security Bureau of Harbin City and a [Membership] Certificate, No. 2693, issued to her on May 25, 1950, by the Resident Soviet Citizens' Association in Harbin, to show that he [she] has no statutory heirs.

The Heir: Ivar Spessa, a citizen of the Soviet Union, fifty-nine years of age, holding a teaching job, residing at the same place as listed above, is the paramour of the testator.

The Contents of the Will: I, Julia G. Orlovskaya, make the following disposition [of my property] in this will. Since I do not have any statutory heirs, I bequeath to my unregistered husband, Ivar Spessa, a citizen of the Soviet Union, all my clothes, underwear, shoes, a manual sewing machine branded "*Sheng-chia,*" an old dentist's chair, and all other items, including all other movables. I bequeath everything to him after my death, including all I have left and all those things which will belong to me in the future and all those things to which I will have a claim in the future.

Those who witness the making of this will are all citizens of the Soviet Union. They are:

1. ————, sixty-seven years of age, merchant, at 26 Szu-t'ang Street, Tao-li District, Harbin, holding an Alien Resident Certificate, No. 14668, issued on December 18, 1946, by the Public Security Bureau of Harbin;

2. ————, sixty-four years of age, engineer, residing at 12 Szu-t'ang Street, Tao-li District, Harbin, holding an Alien Resident Certificate, No. 07162, issued on November 29, 1946, by the Public Security Bureau of Harbin.

They attest that the testator was in good health and good memory when she made this will.

Signature of the testator
Signature of the witness
Signature of the witness

This is to certify that the above-named testator understands the contents of this will. She declared to this court that she made the will of her own volition. She signed her name above to show that no mistake has been committed.

Judge Li Hou-sheng (*Seal*)

Clerk Wa-hsi Lien-kuo (*Seal*)

The People's Court of Harbin City
May 30, 1950
This is a copy differing nothing from the original.
Clerk Wa-hsi Lien-kuo (*Seal*)

NOTE

Article 12 of the PRC's 1954 Constitution provided that "the state protects the right of citizens to inherit private property according to law."[93] The Constitution said nothing, however, about the right of aliens. The following item illustrates the early groping of Chinese Communist authorities for appropriate rules to govern inheritance problems relating to foreigners. Note, for example, the seemingly inconsistent position that the various documents take with respect to the right of foreigners to inherit land. These documents also suggest the slow process by which law has developed in the PRC. Especially interesting is their confirmation of the existence of secret instructions and of executive interference in judicial decision making, and the explicit recognition that other countries would deem these practices improper.

20-6

M. H. van der Valk, translator, "Documents Concerning the Law of Succession of Foreigners in Communist China," in *Nederlands Tijdschrift voor Internationaal Recht* 7:191–192, 193–194, 195–198, 204–206 (1960).

I

HOW TO DEAL WITH THE PROBLEM OF THE SUCCESSION TO AND THE LEGACIES OF IMMOVEABLE PROPERTY BELONGING TO A FOREIGN RESIDENT

Upon the death of a foreign resident the problem of succession to and the legacies of his immoveable property, the two parts, houses and land, shall be separately dealt with; if what is left is land, it shall be recovered by our government and no person whosoever can inherit or be legatee. If it is a house, it can only be inherited by his spouse as well as his lineal relatives, or be legated to his relatives and friends of Chinese nationality. If the heirs as mentioned are not in our country, then by our organs concerned a measure can be devised to notify or publicly summon them to petition for the inheritance within a specified period of time; on the other hand, the inheritance of the deceased shall for them be managed by our organs concerned. If after the set period of time no one appears to petition the succession, the inheritance shall be nationalized by our government. If the deceased is a foreign resident, a citizen of a state with which our country has already established foreign relations, then, besides a public summons (to petition the succession) within a certain period of time by our organ concerned, a notification shall be made again to his embassy and consulate in China, requesting it to devise a means to notify (the heirs).

If there is no spouse nor a lineal relative to inherit, [nor] a will making a legacy to his relatives and friends of Chinese nationality, then it shall be nationalized by our government. These houses in general cannot be legated to nonlineal relatives or friends of foreign nationality; neither can they be legated to foreign government organs or associations of foreign residents.

[Part II omitted]

III

PRINCIPLES OF DEALING WITH THE PROBLEM OF THE SUCCESSION TO PROPERTY OF FOREIGN RESIDENTS (ISSUED BY) THE MINISTRY OF FOREIGN AFFAIRS OF THE CENTRAL (GOVERNMENT), 6TH JANUARY 1953

I. The scope of moveables and immoveables: immoveables comprise land, houses as well as parts that are inseparably attached to the land and the houses—such as dikes, bankments, fences, walls that are built on land, trees that have been planted on the land, water, electricity, central heating, airconditioning, hygiene, fire prevention, and similar additional installations; all the others are moveables.

II. Principles of dealing with the succession to moveables and immoveables of foreign residents: (they shall be) dealt with according to the general customs and rules, being: immoveables shall be dealt with according to the law of the country of residence—the principles of dealing with the succession to immoveables have already been (set forth in) a reply of our Ministry of 19th February 1952, character fa pan su, number 52/159, notifying the Offices of Foreign Affairs everywhere to put them into execution. Moveables shall be dealt with according to the law of the country of the owner, but it shall be (on condition of) the principle of reciprocity, being that the government of the state of the opposite party also recognizes this principle.

The share certificates and the industrial installations owned by a foreign resident: if according to the laws and ordinances of the Chinese People's Republic, or its policies, foreigners cannot enjoy the right of ownership of certain business enterprises or of share certificates in real estate companies, or if they may not establish certain factories, then the share certificates of companies as enumerated above, in the past kept by foreigners, as well as factories and establishments as enumerated owned by them, cannot be inherited by or assigned to foreigners or foreign governments.

III. The method of dealing with the succession to moveable and immoveable property of foreign residents: Cases of succession to property of foreign residents shall be jointly dealt with by the organ of foreign affairs and the law court, but towards the outer world it shall always be presented in the name of the law court. It is not proper that the organs for foreign affairs present it.

IV. The points as mentioned above are all principles of management of the Ministry of the Interior. If hereafter analogous cases come up, it is as yet necessary individually to apply for instruction to the Ministry of Foreign Affairs to give a decision.

IV

INSTRUCTION OF THE MINISTRY OF FOREIGN AFFAIRS AND THE SUPREME COURT OF THE CENTRAL PEOPLE'S GOVERNMENT CONCERNING THE ISSUING OF THE "PRINCIPLES OF DEALING WITH THE PROBLEMS OF SUCCESSION TO PROPERTY IN CHINA OF FOREIGNERS," CHARACTER FA PU OU (54), NUMBER 1689/787, . . . SEPTEMBER 1954.

Character fa hsing mi, number 5.

After the Ministry of Foreign Affairs, together with the Supreme Court, the Central Bureau for the Management of Industry and Trade, the Central Commission of Legislative Affairs, the Central Commission of Overseas Chinese Affairs, as well as the Ministry of the Interior have examined the proposed "Principles of dealing with the problems of the succession to property in China of foreigners," they have already been amended by the Government Administrative Council and on the 7th June 1954 been approved to be practiced for trial—copy added as an appendix to the reply, number (54) hsing cheng mi hsi of the 7th June 1954, of the Administrative Council. At present we issue one copy to your Ministry—Court—and request that you will immediately begin to practice it for trial; if in doing so you have any views, we hope that as yet you will report them to our Ministry—Court—for examination.

PRINCIPLES OF DEALING WITH THE PROBLEMS OF SUCCESSION TO PROPERTY IN CHINA OF FOREIGNERS

1. The law of our country as yet has no explicit provisions concerning the law of succession; therefore, in dealing with the problems of succession to property in China of foreigners, we must base ourselves on the Common Program as well as on the policy, the laws and the ordinances of the government of our country.

2. Land of foreigners on Chinese territory shall be dealt with on the basis of the principles set forth in our Administrative Council's (document entitled) "No rights of foreigners to property of land in China shall be recognized"; they shall not be within the scope of foreign inheritances.

3. The circle of heirs to inheritances in China of foreigners is the

same as the circle of heirs to inheritances of Chinese, as dealt with by our law courts.

Where a foreigner by will legates his property in China to a person who is not a legitimate heir, it shall in general be allowed that his property is received as a legacy by a Chinese. Cases where by will houses and a large amount of property are legated must be reported to the Ministry of Foreign Affairs for approval.

4. The succession to property [of foreigners in China] may be executed in accordance with the will if the object of the legacy is not in conflict with the third item, but the testator may not deprive his minor children of the successional portion.

If the legacy by will is in conflict with the third item the will is void, the property shall as yet be inherited by the lawful heirs. Where the will is void, or if there is no will, the order between the lawful heirs to the succession of the property and the successional portion can be the same as the order to the succession and the successional portion of Chinese, as dealt with by our law courts.

5. A will made in China by a foreigner must before the opening of the succession be certified by (one of) our law courts. The will made abroad by a foreigner, if made by the subject of a country with which China has established relations, must before the opening of the succession be certified by our embassy (or) consulate abroad, or in China by an organ in charge of foreign affairs; if made by the subject of a country with which China has not established relations, it must before the opening of the succession be transferred to and certified by our embassy (or) consulate in a country with which China has established relations, or, in China, by an organ in charge of foreign affairs.

6. If the inheritance in China of a foreigner is refused acceptance by all the lawful heirs and the legatees, or if it is not clear whether or not there is an heir, and upon the expiry of the period of calling upon the heirs—the limit of the period of the public notification is six months—no person petitions the succession, it shall therefore be considered as being without an heir, and it shall be nationalized. The dealing with inheritance as mentioned before shall be reported to the Ministry of Foreign Affairs for approval.

7. Moveable property belonging to the inheritance in China of a foreigner may, based on the principle of reciprocity, be dealt with according to the national law of the testator.

Moveable property left behind by a person without an heir, subject of a country with which China has established relations, may, based on the principle of reciprocity, be delivered to be received by the embassy (or) a consulate of his own country in China.

8. As from the day of giving out of these principles, the prob-

lems of succession to property in China of foreigners shall all be executed according to the provisions of these principles. Problems of the succession to property in China of foreigners that have already been dealt with (either) before (or) after the establishment of the Chinese People's Republic shall in general not again be searched to the bottom; where there has already been [an inheritance] but the procedure of transferring the property has not yet been effected, the land shall be recovered; about the rest, a public notice calling upon the heirs shall be made. When according to the provision of item 6 there are no lawful heirs, it shall be nationalized. But if there are special problems (the case) shall as yet be reported to the Ministry of Foreign Affairs to be dealt with.

9. Cases of succession to property in China of foreigners shall be jointly dealt with by the Office of Foreign Affairs, and the law court; the more important ones shall be reported to the Ministry of Foreign Affairs to be dealt with; but towards the outside world they shall all be presented in the name of the law court—such as succession to property, a declaration that the inheritance shall be nationalized when there are no legitimate heirs, and so forth. The Office of Foreign Affairs shall not directly present (the matters concerned).

10. The provisions embodied in the items of these principles are all principles set for internal (use) and are not promulgated to the outer world. In the text of court decisions they may [not] be mentioned. But in a suitable form they may be [communicated] to the foreigners in China concerned.

11. After these principles have been issued, they shall be the standard if previously drafted items of regulations by the Ministry of Foreign Affairs are in conflict with them.

V

REPLY OF THE SECRETARIAT OF THE MINISTRY OF FOREIGN AFFAIRS CONCERNING THE VIEWS ON THE PRINCIPLES OF DEALING WITH THE PROBLEMS OF SUCCESSION TO PROPERTY IN CHINA OF FOREIGNERS, 14TH FEBRUARY 1955

The report of your office of 29th November 1954 has been received. As regards your views concerning the "Principles of dealing with the problems of succession to property in China of foreigners," we have consulted the Supreme People's Court, and at present we answer you as below:

1. Where a foreigner by will legates his inheritance in China to a foreigner who is not a lawful heir, a distinction shall be made as according to the nationality of the deceased and the opposite party, legatees, and the relations between them, and it shall be dealt with distinguishing as according to concrete circumstances, such as the nature of the inheritance and the value and such like; in general, however, it shall not be allowed.

2. When regarding the inheritance of a foreigner in China one of the circumstances as mentioned below exists, a public notice calling up the heirs shall be given:

a. When the place of abode of the heir is not clear;

b. When it is not clear whether there is an heir;

c. Where all the lawful heirs and legatees reject the inheritance.

Unless there are these circumstances, no public notice can be given.

VI

REPLIES OF THE MINISTRY OF FOREIGN AFFAIRS OF THE CHINESE PEOPLE'S REPUBLIC CONCERNING SOME CONCRETE PROBLEMS BROUGHT UP WHEN DEALING WITH THE PROBLEM OF SUCCESSION TO PROPERTY IN CHINA OF FOREIGNERS. 1ST MARCH 1955, CHARACTER FA PAN OU (55), NUMBER 16/181; GIVEN TO THE OFFICES—SECTIONS—OF FOREIGN AFFAIRS EVERYWHERE

A. Concrete Problems

[omitted]

B. Answers to Problems

I. Inheritances

1. Business enterprises with foreign capital, as well as houses and land of foreign merchants that are among the inheritance in China of a foreigner, share certificates in companies, can all be inherited; but as regards share certificates that (according to) the provisions of our Ministry of the Interior cannot be transferred, they shall be limited by the Bureau of Industry and Trade at the time when the procedure of transfer is put into effect.

2. It can be allowed that objects of art and antiques among the inheritance in China of a foreigner are inherited.

3. During the period of the public notice of calling up the heirs, the moveable property in China left by a foreigner shall for him be kept in custody by the law court; objects that cannot easily be kept in custody shall be converted into money and the price kept in custody. If upon the expiry of the period of public notice no person files a petition, it shall therefore be considered as without an heir and be dealt with according to the seventh item of the "Principles of dealing with the problems of succession to property in China of foreigners."

4. If upon the death of a foreigner there is no relative (or) friend to manage the affairs, we can be repaid with part or the whole of the inheritance in China for the funeral expenses we have made for them, but the receipt of the costs must be kept. If the inheritance in China is insufficient to repay the funeral expenses, it can be supplemented by our organs of aid.

5. Where Soviet Russia has already delivered to (one of) our consulates the moveable property of a Chinese resident in Soviet (Russia), who is without an heir, to deal with, then on this account we can deal with the moveable property left by a Soviet resident in China in accordance with item 7 of the "Principles of dealing with the problems of succession to property in China of foreigners."

II. Heirs

1. Where the lawful heir is of a different nationality than the deceased it can be allowed that he succeeds to the property in China.

2. If a foreigner has a wife and children both in China and abroad, his inheritance in China shall by both sides be jointly enjoyed; where there is no will the wife and children in China can inherit by preference if there is not much to inherit; where the inheritance is of a large size and the circumstances are confused it shall be reported to the Ministry to deal with.

III. Representatives of the Inheritance

1. Where the heirs of an inheritance in China of a foreigner are abroad, it is allowed that a petition for the succession is filed by the consulate in China of the testator's or heirs' own country, or by the relatives and friends in China, representing the heir. But it is necessary that the official formalities for commissioning a representative have been performed; the proxy must have been certified by our consulate in that country—in the case of a subject of a country with which China has not established relations, by our embassy or [the] consulate in a country with which we have established relations, or in China by an Office of Foreign Affairs.

2. If a foreigner has commissioned a representative for his possessions in China, (then) after his death we do not recognize the power of representation of his representative. The trustee of the inheritance in China of a foreigner, the manager of an inheritance, and the long-term executor of a will shall not be recognized.

IV. Obligatory Rights and Duties

Obligatory rights in China of a foreigner can be inherited by his heirs. Among the obligatory duties in China: what is due to public funds, such as voluntary contributions, costs of electricity and water, wages for workmen, and so forth, can by preference be deducted by our law courts from the inheritance in China; in general the obligatory duties towards private persons shall be settled by the heirs themselves. But the heir is only responsible up to the actual value of the inheritance that has been left for the obligatory duties of the testator.

V. The Relations with the Embassy and Consulate in China when Dealing with the Problems of the Death and Inheritance of Foreigners in China

1. Where (the citizen of) a country with which relations have been established dies in China, in general such need not be notified to his embassy (or) consulate in China; if under special circumstances it is necessary to notify his embassy (or) consulate it can be done, having acquired the consent of offices of foreign affairs everywhere.

2. A petition for the succession shall be filed by the embassy (or) consulate in China for the inheritance in China of a subject of a country with which relations have been established; or, (in virtue of) the principle of reciprocity, his moveable property, when there is no heir, shall be received by his embassy (or) consulate in China; when necessary an inventory shall be made and the embassy (or) consulate shall be notified to send an official to take part in it. He shall be requested to sign the inventory, and a duplicate copy shall be delivered to it [the embassy or consulate] to be kept. In all other cases of dealing with the inheritances of foreigners in China it is not necessary to notify the embassy (or) consulate in China to partake in it; if it [the embassy or consulate] makes a move and requires it, it [the embassy or consulate] can be allowed to partake in it.

3. It is in general not necessary that by us means are devised to notify the heirs abroad to the inheritance in China of a foreigner; to give a public notice calling up heirs is possible. When needed, in case of the subject of a country with which we have established relations, the embassy (or) consulate in China of the testator can be notified by

us to pass on the notice. The form of notifying the embassy and the consulate—orally or in writing, both are possible—and the notification to the embassy (or) consulate shall be effected by the Ministry of Foreign Affairs; the notification to the consulate, by the Office of Foreign Affairs.

VI. Notification on the Execution of the Inheritance

After the right of the heirs to the inheritance in China of a foreigner has been established, a notification allowing the succession may be issued. This notification need not list the concrete contents of the inheritance; it is only allowed to state clearly the heir and the part of what is to be inherited consisting of land, of which it shall be noted that it is property of the Chinese People's Republic. A person who is not a lawful heir cannot succeed to the property; a certificate shall not be issued when he claims it.

VII. Public Notice Calling the Heirs to an Inheritance

In general a public notice shall be published in the newspapers, the cost of the publication in the newspapers can be paid by the heir to the inheritance if there is one. If there is none, it shall be made good with part of or the whole of that inheritance. If the value of the inheritance is very small, the notification can be made separately at the gate of the deceased's residence as well as at the gate of the law court.

VIII. Dealing With Cases of Inheritance

1. We must all make a move to deal with cases of inheritance in China of foreigners.

2. In general cases of inheritances can be dealt with on the basis of the principles of dealing with the problems of succession to property of foreigners in China; it is not necessary to report cases to the Ministry as they come up, but periodically a summary shall be reported to the Ministry.

Aliens' Economic Activities

21

The triumph of Communism in 1949 obviously boded ill for foreign industrial and commercial interests in China; it was far from clear how long and in what circumstances foreign business would be tolerated. The 1949 Common Program[94] offered few clues about what to expect. Article 3 pledged the PRC to "abolish all the prerogatives of imperialist countries in China." On the other hand, Article 47 provided, equally vaguely, that the PRC "may restore and develop commercial relations with foreign governments and peoples on a basis of equality and mutual benefit."

Since the PRC was unlikely to grant foreign businessmen better treatment than Chinese businessmen, Communist policy toward the latter was obviously of interest to the former. Yet, to the extent that its general terms indicated a policy orientation, the Common Program offered little consolation to either group. The state, Article 26 proclaimed, would "coordinate and regulate" all sectors of the economy, including all phases of the operations of "the private capitalist economy," and take into account both public and private interests. Article 28 provided that "All enterprises relating to the economic life of the country and exercising a dominant influence over the people's livelihood shall be under the unified operation of the state." These enterprises included, of course, the holdings of major industrialists who had opposed the Communists and whose resources constituted "bureaucratic capital," which, according to Article 3, was to be confiscated. Although "socialist," state-owned resources were to be the leading force of the entire economy, Article 29 stated that the People's Government would foster the development of the "semisocialist," cooperative economy and "accord it preferential treatment." But Article 30 claimed that the government would also "encourage the active operation of all private economic enterprises beneficial to the national welfare and to the people's livelihood and . . . assist in their development." Whatever hopes this provision might have raised were immediately dampened by Article 31, which ominously stated that "whenever necessary and possible, private capital shall be encouraged to develop in the direction of state capitalism," the term used to describe the "public-private joint enterprise," a business unit in which the state and private capital ostensibly share ownership, control, and profit but which is actually under state control.

In practice, what happened to Chinese business was that the regime confiscated most of the major industrial and commercial firms and gradually increased its control over the remaining private firms to the point where their incentives "voluntarily" to become "public-private joint enterprises" became overwhelming. By the time the PRC had adopted a formal Constitution in September 1954,[95] this process of "socialist transformation of capitalist industry and commerce" was well under way, as a result of harassing techniques which included extremely high taxes, fines, and penalties assessed against the great many firms that were found to have engaged in corrupt dealings with the previous government, generous loans that increased a firm's debt obligations, manipulation of government monopolies over essential raw materials and markets, artificially inspired labor troubles, selective applications of terror, and propaganda and social pressures from organizations that were supposed to represent business interests.

The Constitution, promulgated in 1954, must have put an end to any doubts about the future of private enterprise in China, for it proclaimed its goal to be the "transition to socialism," which would be achieved, in the words of Article 4, by "the gradual abolition of systems of exploitation." Article 10 solemnly stated that "the state protects the right of capitalists to own means of production and other capital according to law," but it went on to make clear the fragility of this protection by announcing that "the policy of the state towards capitalist industry and commerce is to use, restrict, and transform them." Although the Constitution emphasized that the process of replacing capitalist ownership with "ownership by the whole people" was to be a gradual one, the task was basically completed by 1956.

It was in this environment that foreign business had struggled to continue functioning. Moreover, the prospects for foreign firms had never looked bright since the autumn of 1950, when the PRC became involved in hostilities with the United Nations in Korea. It is difficult to say what the speed of "socialist transformation" of foreign business might have been had this not occurred, but the Korean conflict undoubtedly accelerated the process, as the PRC took economic measures against some of the major Western powers in retaliation for measures which the latter had previously adopted against the PRC. Some foreign interests in China were confiscated or requisitioned, others were placed under control or "frozen," and many foreign firms were harassed so severely that continuing operations appeared intolerable. The materials in this section illustrate the PRC's attitudes and actions taken toward various types of foreign economic activity. Chapter 22 will present the PRC's view on the question of state responsibility for the nationalization of foreign property within its territory.

21-1

Ch'ien Szu, "A Criticism of the Views of Bourgeois International Law on the Question of Population," *KCWTYC*, no. 5:47–48 (1960).

It should be pointed out that extraterritoriality is only one of the privileges which imperialism has secured for its citizens. There are many other privileges; for example, American citizens unilaterally enjoy the right of free entry into and exit from the territory of other countries, and preferential rights in investment and trade. Even in an imperialist country such as France, the United States likewise secured these rights for its citizens. For instance, according to the Economic Cooperation Agreement between the United States and France concluded in 1948, France permits Americans freely to enter France without a visa, but the United States does not permit the French to enjoy the same right.[96]

But today the most frequently employed and the most shrewd method by which American imperialism tries to secure practical privileges for its citizens remains the use of beautiful terms such as "equality" and "mutual benefit." For instance, many treaties concluded between the United States and other countries on economic cooperation and commerce and navigation provide what appear in form to be equal rights of the citizens of the contracting parties freely to engage in commerce, trade, enterprises, and so forth, in the territory of the other party. Article 2 of the "Sino-American Treaty of Friendship, Commerce and Navigation" concluded in November 1946, provides that "the nationals of either High Contracting Party shall, through the whole extent of the territories of the other High Contracting Party, be permitted, without interference, to engage in and to carry on commercial, manufacturing, processing, scientific, educational, religious, and philanthropic activities not forbidden by the laws and regulations enforced by the duly constituted authorities," and in order to realize the above-stated objectives, they enjoy the rights "to acquire, hold, erect or lease, and occupy appropriate buildings, and to lease appropriate lands." It further provides that both parties "shall [not] prevent the nationals of either High Contracting Party from entering, traveling and residing in the territories of the other High Contracting Party." This means that the citizens of both parties shall be permitted to enjoy, in the territory of the other contracting party, the rights of entry, movement, and residence. On the surface, these provisions seem to be equal and the rights provided can be equally enjoyed by citizens of both parties. However, the so-called "Sino-American Treaty of Friendship, Commerce, and Navigation" is a perfectly unequal treaty. This is because there was a drastic difference in the economic strength of old China and American imperialism; old China was a poor backward country dependent upon the United States, and the Chinese bourgeoisie was extremely weak. How could the Chinese bourgeoisie have had the ability to establish factories in the United States, to carry on commerce, and to engage in scientific and cultural enterprises in order to realize the rights given to them by the "Sino-American Treaty of Friendship, Commerce, and Navigation?" Only the American monopolistic bourgeoisie and its representatives were in a position really to enjoy these rights. The facts that American capital and commodities flooded everywhere and that the United States controlled the economic lifeline of China show this very clearly. From the foregoing, it is clear that so-called "equality" and "mutual benefit" exist on paper only. The United States' tricky use of the form of equality shows the shrewd plot of imperialism; at the same time, it proves that, in front of the awakened people throughout the world, the United States cannot resort to previously used naked methods, but has to resort to further concealed and camouflaged methods [of aggression].

Bourgeois international law does not consider the acts of imperialism to secure privileges for its nationals abroad to be illegal. On the contrary, it fabricates various reasons in order to provide bases and defenses for such acts. Besides . . . slanderous theories directed against weak and small countries, such as that they are "uncivilized" or "imperfect in the rule of law," another important theory is that aliens should be treated in accordance with the so-called "international standard." According to their [bourgeois international law jurists'] view, there is an international standard for the treatment of aliens and no country may accord treatment to aliens that falls below that standard. Oppenheim wrote: "[Every State enjoys] the right of protection over its subjects abroad. . . . The home State of the alien has, by its right of protection, a claim upon such State as allows him to enter its territory that such protection shall be afforded, and it is no excuse that such State does not provide any protection whatever for its own subjects." [a] Another bourgeois international law jurist, Brierly, also wrote that "if a state has a low standard of justice towards its own nationals, an alien's position is in a sense a privileged one, for the standard of treatment to which international law entitles him is an objective one, and he need not, even though nationals must, submit to unjust treatment." [b] Another bourgeois jurist, Hall, even declared: "The rule . . . that

[a] Oppenheim, 7th ed., I, 627.

[b] J. L. Brierly, *The Law of Nations,* 5th ed. (London: Oxford at the Clarendon Press, 1954), p. 220.

an alien must accept the institutions of a foreign state is [correct, but is] qualified by the requirement that those institutions must conform to the standard set by international law."[c] In their statements they do not conceal the fact that the treatment consistent with the international standard demanded by them is higher than that which the host countries accord to their own nationals. In fact, they use such terms as "international standard" to cover the privileged treatment enjoyed by citizens of imperialist countries. This also proves that the "international standard" is not an objective and fair standard, but a subjective standard used by imperialism to plunder colonies and weak and small countries. It completely violates the generally recognized modern international law principles of equality, mutual benefit, and respect for sovereignty.

21-2

"Control of Economic Relations with Communist China," *Department of State Bulletin* 23.599:1004 (Dec. 25, 1950).

The United States government is taking measures today [December 16, 1950] to place under control all Chinese Communist assets within United States jurisdiction and is issuing regulations to prohibit ships of United States registry from calling at Chinese Communist ports until further notice as steps necessary to accomplish the effective control of the economic relationships between the United States and Communist China envisaged by the institution, on December 3, 1950, of the requirement that no exports would be permitted to Communist China from the United States without validated export licenses.

This action has been forced upon us by the intervention of Chinese Communist military forces in Korea. In view of the commitment of Chinese resources in this unprovoked aggressive activity, this government cannot permit the Chinese Communists to have access to United States supplies or assets in the United States, the use of which under present circumstances clearly runs counter to the interests and objectives of the United Nations in the Far Eastern crisis.

It is not our desire that this be a permanent restriction. As long as a willful group of Chinese Communist leaders are willing to subvert their national interests and the welfare of the Chinese people to the designs of international Communist imperialism, it is impossible for this government to act otherwise. If the Chinese Communists choose

[c] Quoted from *ibid.*, p. 221.

to withdraw their forces of aggression and act in conformity with United Nations principles, this government will be prepared promptly to consider removing restrictions and restoring normal trade relations.

The same controls also are being applied to North Korean assets at this time. This is purely an administrative measure since North Korean assets are [negligible].

The Departments of Commerce and Treasury are issuing the necessary regulations.

21-3

"Government Administrative Council Issues Order for the Control of American Government and Private Property in China," NCNA–English, Peking (Dec. 28, 1950), in *SCMP*, no. 38:1–2 (Dec. 28, 1950).

Order No. "Tsun Tsai" 412 of the Government Administrative Council of the Central People's Government follows:

The US government announced on December 16, 1950, the control of the public and private property of the People's Republic of China within United States jurisdiction, and a ban on the sailing of American registered ships to Chinese ports, in an attempt to further rob the property of the Chinese people economically, following its armed aggression on our Taiwan, bombing of our northeast, and shelling of our merchantmen.

The Central People's Government of the People's Republic of China, in view of such daily aggravated aggressive and hostile action of the United States government toward our nation, and in order to prevent it from carrying out economic sabotage on our territory and endangering the interest of our nation and our people, takes herewith the following measures:

1. The local people's government shall control and inventory all property of the American government and American enterprises. They may not be transferred or disposed of unless authorized by the regional People's Government or the Military Control Committee. In the case of provinces and municipalities which are under the direct jurisdiction of the Central People's Government, such transfers and disposals should only be authorized by the Financial and Economic Committee of the Government Administrative Council. The owners and those in charge of the property shall be responsible for the protection of the property and shall in no way cause damage to them.

2. All American public and private deposits within the territory of the People's Republic of China shall be frozen. Necessary expenses to maintain lawful business and the living of individuals may only be withdrawn upon approval by the local people's government. The amounts are to be regulated by the Financial and Economic Committee of the Government Administrative Council in a separate order.

The above order takes effect immediately on the date of proclamation.

Premier Chou En-lai

December 28, 1950

21-4

"Six US Real Estate Companies in Shanghai under Military Control," *Shanghai News* (Jan. 4, 1951), in *SCMP*, no. 55:6 (Jan. 24, 1951).

The Public Housing Department of the Shanghai People's Government has, following the instruction of the Shanghai Military Control Committee [SMCC], taken over the control of six American-owned real estate companies.

The six enterprises now subject to military control are: the Asia Realty Co., Fed. Inc. USA; the China Realty Co., Ltd.; the Kiangsu Realty Co.; the Pacific Products Corp.; the Hubertus Properties, Fed. Inc. USA; and the Blackstone Apartments.

The employees and workers of these companies accorded a warm welcome to Pi Hsiu-shan, the Military Control Commission, and the liaison officers when they [arrived].

Military Commissioner Pi read the instruction of the SMCC and immediately ordered the companies to submit their inventories to the authorities concerned. He told the employees and workers to stay at their posts and continue work as usual. However, he said, the properties of the companies must not be transferred or disposed of in any way without prior approval obtained from the authorities.

21-5

"GAC Committee on Financial and Economic Affairs Announced Measures Governing Drawing on Deposits by American Firms and Individuals," NCNA, Peking (Jan. 15, 1951), in *SCMP*, no. 48:3–4 (Jan. 14–15, 1951).

The GAC Committee on Financial and Economic Affairs of the Central People's Government announced on Jan. 14 stipulations concerning application for drawing on deposits by American firms and individuals. The full text follows:

Stipulations by the GAC Committee on Financial and Economic Affairs concerning application for drawing on deposits by American firms and individuals:

1. Drawings will not be restricted in case individual deposits by an American national do not exceed JMP \$30,000,000.[97] In case deposits exceed JMP \$30,000,000, a monthly drawing of JMP \$10,000,000, shall be permitted.
2. Drawings will not be restricted in case deposits by an American firm do not exceed JMP \$500,000,000. In case deposits exceed JMP \$500,000,000, payments shall be approved by the local control and examination organ according to its needs.
3. Drawings on deposits in foreign currency shall be converted at the official rate of exchange in accordance with the aforementioned provisions.

Chen Yun, Chairman

21-6

"Properties of British-Owned Shell Co. of China Requisitioned," NCNA–English, Peking (Apr. 30, 1951), in *SCMP*, no. 101:13 (May 1–3, 1951).

The full text of the order signed by Premier Chou En-lai, requisitioning the properties of the British-owned Shell Company of China, Limited, issued today by the Government Administrative Council, follows:

In order to safeguard China's security and the public interest, it is hereby decided to requisition all the properties of the British-owned Shell Company of China, Limited, other than the offices of its head office and branches and sales agencies within the territory of China, and to requisition by purchase all its existing stocks of petroleum.

The responsible personnel of the Shell Company of China, Limited, in various places must immediately draw up inventories of all the properties (including all movable and immovable properties) other than the offices of its head office and branches and sales agencies pending disposal by the local military control committee and (or) the local people's government. These responsible personnel must be responsible for protecting and handing over these properties. Pilfering, destruction, transfer, concealment and other unlawful acts will be severely punished.

This order will come into force on the day of issue.

21-7

"GAC Promulgates Measures for Disposal of American-subsidized Christian Bodies," NCNA, Peking (July 26, 1951), in *SCMP*, no. 144:8–10 (July 27–28, 1951).

Measures for Disposal of American-Subsidized Christian Bodies (Promulgated by GAC, July 24, 1951)

In accordance with the "Decision on Policies of Disposal of American-subsidized Cultural-Educational and Relief Agencies and Religious Bodies" passed at the 65th meeting of GAC on December 29, 1950, and with the principle laid down in Vice Premier Kuo's report approved at the same meeting that American-subsidized religious bodies in China should be changed into bodies operated by Chinese Christians themselves and that the government should encourage their campaign for independence, self-support and independent propagation of faith, the following measures are hereby enacted for the disposal of American-subsidized Christian bodies:

1. All Chinese Christian churches and bodies should immediately sever their ties with American missions and other non-American missions principally supported by American funds. The above-mentioned missions in China should cease their activities at once.

2. American personnel working in Christian churches and bodies in China should be dealt with according to the following principles:

i. Those who speak and act against the People's Government should be dismissed, and those committing crimes should be reported to the government for punishment according to law.

ii. Those who wish to leave China shall be permitted to return to their home country.

iii. Those who do not speak or act in a reactionary way and whom the churches and bodies consider it necessary to keep and are willing to support may be retained in service provided they will assume no administrative functions in churches and bodies.

3. In the case of social service enterprises such as medical and welfare agencies originally operated by self-supporting Christian churches and bodies, operations may continue where they can support [themselves, but] a board of directors must be organized to ensure the carrying out of government laws and ordinances. [A list of those serving on the board of directors should be submitted to the government for approval]. Where they [social service enterprises] cannot support [themselves, they] may request [that] the government [subsidize them or] take over. But all universities, middle and primary schools (except theological schools) operated by churches and missionary bodies should be separated from churches. Buildings used for the schools should, in principle, be transferred to the schools; if the school buildings are for common use with churches and missionary bodies, the local people's government should separately draw up measures for their disposal in accordance with concrete conditions.

4. In case a foreign mission voluntarily wishes to donate its properties in China (excluding landholdings) to Chinese Christian churches and bodies, the Chinese Christian churches and bodies, following government review and approval, may accept all or part of these properties provided no condition is attached to this gift.

5. In the case of Chinese Christian churches and [the] YMCA and YWCA, which have carried out self-support measures, the buildings used directly for churches and offices may be exempted by the government from real estate tax.

6. In regard to house properties offered for rent by Chinese churches and bodies, tenancy rights should be protected and tax paid to the government according to government laws and ordinances. In the case of church buildings borrowed by the government, settlement may be made by consultation in light of the local situation and Church needs, and contracts will be signed if necessary.

7. Christian churches and bodies which have carried out self-government, self-propagation, and self-support, and which deposited their funds outside the country prior to Dec. 29, 1950, and require their withdrawal, should furnish exact and detailed evidence with an explanation of their source and use and submit them to the government

for consideration and approval. Any concealment, false reporting, and forgery of evidence should be the legal responsibility of the [responsible and relevant] persons.

8. All churches subsidized by foreign countries as well as their subordinate agencies should register in accordance with the GAC "Regulations Governing Registration of Cultural-Educational and Relief Agencies and Religious Bodies Subsidized by Foreign Countries or Operated with Foreign Funds" without delay or refusal under any pretext. In respect to such agencies and bodies which have actually carried out self-support, this registration will be allowed to be cancelled.

NOTE

During the Cultural Revolution, one of the Red Guards' first antiforeign acts to gain international attention was the takeover of a missionary school.

> The Peking Municipal People's Council announced on August 26 the banning of the Franciscaines Missionnaires de Marie and took over the school, Sacre-Coeur, run by the mission. The action was taken in response to the demand of Peking's Red Guards and revolutionary masses and to safeguard China's security and the interests of the people. The Public Security Bureau of Peking announced a deportation order on August 28 and deported Olga Fedorowicz and seven other foreign nuns who had engaged in counterrevolutionary activities. In the custody of public security personnel and the Red Guards, they were deported from China on August 31.
>
> The Franciscaines Missionnaires de Marie was founded in 1915 on the instructions of its headquarters in Rome, at a time when imperialism was carrying out aggression against the Chinese people. Before liberation, the mission worked in collusion with the reactionary ruling classes abroad and at home, consistently took an antagonistic attitude towards the Chinese people, and tried to undermine the cause of the liberation of the Chinese people. After liberation, under the direction of its Rome headquarters and under the cloak of religion, the mission used the school as a cover and secretly collaborated with a number of counterrevolutionaries in the Catholic churches in Peking, Hopei, Shansi, Inner Mongolia, and Harbin, spied for information about China, printed reactionary documents, fabricated and spread rumours, instigated counterrevolutionaries to engage in plots to create riots, and committed a series of acts of sabotage seriously detrimental to China's sovereignty.

> During the present vigorous and great proletarian cultural revolution, which is unprecedented in history, the young Red Guards, armed with Mao Tse-tung's thought and holding aloft the great red banner of Mao Tse-tung's thought, are sweeping away the reactionary forces of imperialism and revisionism with the momentum of an avalanche and the force of a thunderbolt. They no longer would permit the counterrevolutionary mission which served imperialism to commit evil on Chinese territory. On August 24, Red Guards from more than a dozen schools in Peking rose against the counterrevolutionary mission. Their revolutionary action immediately won the most resolute and warmest support from the workers, peasants, soldiers, revolutionary cadres, and revolutionary intellectuals.
>
> When the Peking Public Security Bureau announced the deportation of Olga Fedorowicz and seven other foreign nuns engaged in counterrevolutionary activities at a mass rally on the evening of August 28, the people gathered inside and outside the compound where the mission was located expressed warm support for the deportation order.[98]

Western religious institutions were not the only ones confiscated during the Cultural Revolution. The Indian government accused the PRC of permitting Red Guards to desecrate Indian temples and then confiscating three Indian Sikh temples and a Parsi temple and cemetery in Shanghai. Peking's response stated:

> 1. The persons in charge of the Indian Sikh temples in Shanghai have long kept in secret Japanese military swords, military sabres, a rifle bayonet, pistol cartridges and a portrait of the bandit Chiang Kai-shek, thus seriously violating China's laws and decrees and jeopardizing public order. The Indian in charge of the Parsi temple and cemetery, under cover of religion, collected military and economic intelligence and supported and provided shelter for a reactionary clique to carry out counterrevolutionary activities in the temple. The evidence for these criminal activities is well established and allows of no denial. It is therefore a matter of course for the Chinese local authorities to ban these unlawful religious institutions, and the judicial sanctions taken against those in charge of these institutions are due punishment meted out to them for their crimes. This is entirely the Chinese people's internal affairs. But in its note the Indian embassy still repeated its hypocritical arguments refuted long ago on many occasions,

tried hard to distort the facts and viciously slandered the Chinese government's policies on religion. What is more, the note flaunted such words as "desecration" and "religious sentiments" in a vain attempt to deceive people and achieve the criminal aims of covering up the Indian nationals' criminal acts against the law and of opposing China by inciting the religious sentiments of those believers who were ignorant of the actual facts. This is utterly futile. The protest raised by the embassy on this matter cannot but be regarded as deliberate trouble-making. The Ministry of Foreign Affairs categorically rejects this protest.

2. As everybody knows, it has been the consistent policy of the Chinese government to protect religion. The great numbers of Buddhists, Christians and Moslems all enjoy their freedom of religious belief in China, and their temples, churches, or mosques have been duly protected. The Indian nationals' Sikh temples in China have similarly been protected by the Chinese government and have all along enjoyed the privilege of exemption from real estate taxation. In order to show consideration for the Sikhs' religious life, the Shanghai local authorities have provided extra supplies to the Sikh temples each month. Over a long period of time, the local authorities gave preferential treatment to the dairies run by the Sikhs, such as the purchase of their milk and cow dung at a price higher than the market price and [providing] a higher supply quota of cattle fodder to the Sikhs than to the Chinese breeders, etc.

However, the Chinese government absolutely will not allow anyone to carry out under cover of religion unlawful and criminal activities harmful to the Chinese people. In June, 1949, the Shanghai local authorities issued the decree of confiscating all illegal weapons. But the Sikh temples secretly kept Japanese military swords, military sabres, a rifle bayonet, and pistol cartridges over a long period without reporting and handing them over to the authorities concerned. Hidden behind the glass frame holding a religious image was a portrait of Chiang Kai-shek, the public enemy of the Chinese people. The military swords and sabres found there all bear the mark of the Japanese army. Yet, you describe these weapons used by the Japanese militarists to slaughter the Chinese people during their aggression against China as "holy swords." This precisely reveals your ugly feature of acting as a cat's paw. The persons in charge of the Parsi temple and cemetery, in league with the social scum of China, carried on activities harmful to the Chinese people. All these are what the Chinese people absolutely will not tolerate.[99]

21-8

"Public Apology Published in Shanghai Paper by Two Foreign Firms," *Shanghai News* (Jan. 18, 1952), in *SCMP*, no. 259:14–15 (Jan. 20–21, 1952).

Public Apology

Owing to the lack of understanding of government regulations on the part of former members of the Company's Board of Directors, certain transactions were effected after liberation in contravention of the Temporary Regulations Governing Exchange Transactions in the East China Region.

As the above has been pointed out by the Finance Bureau, the present Board of Directors realizes the mistake made and hereby expresses its deepest regrets.

The Culty Dairy Co., Ltd.

Shanghai, Jan. 15, 1952.

Public Apology

The undermentioned firm having accepted an order from the Cathay Engineering Co., Shanghai, for one lot of calculators and microscopes during June of 1951 permitted part of the foreign exchange from their profit to remain abroad, therefore violating the order of foreign exchange control. Besides making efforts to remit the foreign exchange involved within the time limit into the country, we hereby guarantee that there will be no repetition of such violation in the future.

Holdo Stromwall

Shanghai, Jan. 15, 1952

21-9

"[China's] Relations with the West," Denise Folliot, ed., *Documents on International Affairs 1952* (London: Oxford University Press, 1955), pp. 460–462, 464–466.

(*I*) *Note from the British Chargé d'Affaires in Peking to the Chinese People's Government Regarding the Difficulties of British Firms in China, 12 April 1952.*[a]

Peking, 12th April, 1952.

British firms have been facing increasing difficulties in China which have been handicapping them in carrying out their legitimate trading activities. Among these difficulties are the following:

(i) The making of each individual manager *personally* responsible for the policy and acts of his company, in some cases for acts before he became manager.

(ii) The increasing restrictions on the entry and exit of foreign staff.

(iii) The cancellation by the Chinese government's trading organisations of former contracts, even though raw materials have been paid for and processed.

(iv) Taxation and legal judgments which both appear to be discriminatory against foreigners.

(v) Uncertainty caused to British subjects by the fear of arrest and detention *incommunicado* and without charges being preferred.

(vi) Pressure by the labour unions and reluctance by the local authorities to give any protection to firms who are being accused by the unions of malpractice.

If this situation continues it can only result, sooner or later, in the elimination of British business interests in China to the detriment of friendly relations between China and the United Kingdom. I am therefore instructed by Her Majesty's government, at the request of the

[a] Great Britain, Foreign Office, *Correspondence between the Government of the United Kingdom of Great Britain and Northern Ireland and the Central People's Government of China on British Trade in China, Peking, 12th April-5th July 1952, with Statement by the Secretary of State for Foreign Affairs in the House of Commons on 20th May 1952* (Cmd. 8639) (London: HMSO, 1952), pp. 2-3.

British firms principally concerned, to bring this unsatisfactory state of affairs to the notice of the Chinese government.

I have, & c.

L. H. Lamb.

(*II*) [omitted]

(*III*) *Note from the British Chargé d'Affaires in Peking to the Chinese People's Government Regarding the Closing of British Firms in China, 19 May 1952.*[b]

Peking, 19th May, 1952.

As stated in my note of 12th April, 1952, British firms in China have for a long time and for reasons beyond their control been facing increasing difficulties. The increasing extent to which many of the functions formerly handled in China by private merchants and industrialists are being taken over by organisations operating on a state basis is correspondingly reducing need for maintenance in their existing form of many British-owned and established enterprises.

2. Nearly all, if not all, of the British companies in China have come to the conclusion that this change in conditions necessitates a corresponding change in the nature of their organisations and in the scope of their activities. Many feel they can no longer operate satisfactorily in China and can serve no useful purpose in the future. Consequently they feel that the proper course is for them to arrange for the transfer as going concerns, custody or closure, of their businesses. The needs of individual companies will vary with their particular circumstances, and applications appropriate thereto will be made by them in due course.

3. A number of important British companies, whilst recognising that in existing conditions their present organisations are or may become redundant, believe that they can still perform a useful service in the interests of Sino-British trade. They therefore contemplate setting up a new form of organisation which is better suited to current conditions. This would take the form of an association of representatives of manufacturers and overseas buyers who would maintain direct contact with the appropriate Chinese authorities. This body could, in fact, act as a permanent Trade Mission.

4. Her Majesty's government trust that the Central People's Government will issue appropriate instructions to the departments con-

[b] Cmd. 8639, pp. 3–4.

cerned to facilitate the measures for which individual British companies will make application in pursuance of the above decisions. The particular points in respect of which the good offices of the Central People's Government are requested are:

(a) approval of the termination of the services of redundant staff;
(b) the issue of exit permits for non-Chinese staff;
(c) the setting up of machinery to deal with custody or transfer as going concerns of any business to which this treatment is appropriate;
(d) taking of the necessary steps to deal with the suggestion in paragraph 3, above.

5. In view of the prolonged period during which many companies have been operating under economically adverse circumstances, Her Majesty's government request that early and favourable consideration will be given to the representations made herein.

I have, &c.

L. H. Lamb.

(*IV*) [omitted.]

(*V*) *Statement by the Chinese Vice-Minister for Foreign Affairs, Mr. Chang Han-fu, on British Trade with China, 5 July 1952.*[c]

The Ministry of Foreign Affairs of the Central People's Government of the People's Republic of China has already received from Mr. Lamb, the representative for negotiations of the British government, Note No. 53 of 18th April, 1952,[100] on Sino-British trade, and Note No. 69 of 19th May, 1952, on the suggestions of the British industrial and commercial firms in China to wind up their business and to set up a new form of organisation, and has further taken notice of the related statement made by Mr. Eden, the Secretary of State for Foreign Affairs of the British government, on 20th May, in the House of Commons of Britain.

Mr. Chang Han-fu, Vice-Minister for Foreign Affairs of the Cen-

[c] Cmd. 8639, pp. 5–6.

tral People's Government, considers it necessary to issue the following statement:

(1) The Central People's Government has repeatedly declared: China is willing to restore and develop international trade relations with governments and peoples of other countries, on a basis of equality and mutual benefit; all foreign residents and firms in China, who abide by the laws of the Chinese government, will receive protection from the people's governments of all levels. In accordance with this policy of the Central People's Government, all the private and state trade organisations of China have been and still are striving to establish normal trade connections with foreign industrial and commercial firms.

Since October 1949 the trade between China and Britain has had a considerable revival and development. Consequently, the activities of the British firms in China have gradually become brisk. For more than two years, the private and state trade organisations of China have further signed trade contracts of various forms and contracts for processing and orders with foreign industrial and commercial firms in China, among which chiefly are the British.

Recently, at the International Economic Conference, convened in April of this year in Moscow, the Chinese and British delegations reached an agreement for trade exchange to the amount of £10,000,000 on either side in 1952. On the basis of this agreement, the Chinese and British representatives for trade negotiations signed on 9th June, in Berlin, a *pro forma* contract to the amount of £6,500,000 for the first installment of goods. All these facts amply prove that the Chinese government and people are willing to develop, between China and Britain, a normal trade relationship on an equal and mutually beneficial basis.

(2) However, the British government has persistently carried out a discriminatory trade policy against China, thus hindering the establishment of a normal economic relationship between the British people and the People's Republic of China. It can be recalled that since 1950, under the incessant pressure of the United States, the British government has adopted a series of unfriendly measures of control in respect of trade against the People's Republic of China. On 18th May, 1951, in the United Nations Assembly, under the domination and coercion of the United States government, the delegate of the British government voted for the preposterous proposal of the United States for an embargo against the People's Republic of China. Immediately afterwards, on 19th June, 1951, the British government further declared all the export items to China and Hong Kong to be under the control of special permits. The British government has thus followed the United States government in carrying out the policy of trade control and em-

bargo, hostile to the People's Republic of China, and calculated to obstruct the trade exchange between China and Britain. Since then, the trade between China and Britain has abruptly declined in volume.

Under such a trade policy of the British government, the British industry and commerce have met serious but unnecessary difficulties. This is especially so in the case of the British companies and manufacturing firms in China, many of which have been reduced to the straits of retrenchment or closure of their business by the depressed state of the trade between the two countries, in addition to their bad management. For some time in the past, they have taken a wait-and-see attitude with anxiety. The government authorities of all levels of the People's Republic of China have taken such measures as the advancing of loans and supplying of raw materials in order to aid them. However, the measures of trade control and embargo taken by the British government have not shown the least sign of relenting, and the resulting difficulties, before which the British firms in China are powerless, have shown the tendency to become increasingly greater, instead of the slightest sign of abating.

The predicament of the British firms in China is the bitter fruit of the policy of trade control and embargo of the British government. This alone suffices to prove that by following the United States in carrying out the trade control and embargo, the British government not only contravenes but also jeopardises the interests of the British people.

(3) Due protection shall be afforded to the British companies and manufacturing firms in the territories of the People's Republic of China by the authorities of the people's governments of all levels, provided that they abide by the laws of the Chinese government. In case they wish to wind up their business voluntarily, no matter what form of windup they may take, they may apply at the people's government at their respective localities, and the competent authorities will deal with each case according to its own merits and the regulations. In the course of winding up, any question that may arise relating to the termination of services of employees and workers, the application for exit permit, and the disposal of the enterprises may be expeditiously and reasonably settled on the merits of each case and in accordance with the regulations.

(4) The Central People's Government considers that the active promotion of the trade relations between China and Britain on a basis of equality and mutual benefit is conducive to the recovery and development of industrial and agricultural production in both countries, as well as to the improvement of the living conditions of the peoples of both countries. Therefore, any British companies and manufacturing firms,

or any such in the territory of China, as well as any organisation jointly formed by the British companies and manufacturing firms, provided that they do not harbour monopoly designs and are willing to trade with China on a basis of equality and mutual benefit, may all approach at any time the private and state trade organisations of China, establish contacts with them, and conduct specific business negotiations with them.

21-10

"Canton Military Control Committee Requisitions Property of Butterfield and Swire," *Nan-fang jih-pao* (Feb. 25, 1953), in *SCMP*, no. 519:15 (Feb. 25–26, 1953).

In the interests of the Chinese public, the Canton Military Control Committee of the Chinese People's Liberation Army on the afternoon of February 24 issued an order requisitioning the wharves and godowns (excluding the business offices) in Canton of the British firm, Butterfield and Swire, as well as all the assets of its building, No. 16, West Bund. Tsao Yo-ming, Director of the Foreign Affairs Office of the Canton Military Control Committee, on the morning of February 24, at 10 a.m., called in the representatives responsible for the control of the said property [and] read before them the order. The text of the order is as follows:

Canton Military Control Committee,
Chinese People's Liberation Army.

Order No. Chun Chu Chen Series, 102.
Dated: February 24, 1953

In the interests of the Chinese public, it has been decided to requisition the whole of the assets in Canton of the British firm Butterfield & Swire, including all wharves and godowns (but excluding the business offices) and the building, No. 16 West Bund.

Responsible members of the said firm shall prepare an inventory of all the assets and await attention by the military representative of the Committee. Such responsible members shall seriously undertake the protection and transfer of all property requisitioned, and there shall be no stealing, damaging, transfer, concealment, and other illegal acts, failing which severe punishment shall be inflicted.

This order takes effect on the day of its issuance.

Canton Military Control Committee.

Following the reading, Director Tsao Yo-ming announced the appointment of Comrade Sha Fu as the military representative of the Military Control Committee.

When Military Representative Sha Fu arrived at the wharves and godowns of Butterfield and Swire to carry out the order, he was enthusiastically welcomed by the whole body of employees and workers thereat and other transport workers. Representatives of the employees and workers expressed their readiness to take concrete action to assist the government's act of requisition and control. All of them celebrated the occasion.

NOTE

A 1963 report by the Committee on Foreign Affairs of the US House of Representatives estimated that in 1949 the value of American investments in mainland China was $56 million. This estimate excluded the value of various American-owned schools and universities, such as Peking Union Medical College, St. John's University in Shanghai, and Yale-in-China and also US embassy and consular property.[101] At a 1966 hearing of the Foreign Affairs Committee, however, the representative of an American company whose assets were taken over by the PRC claimed that those assets alone were worth more than $56 million. Mr. Kenneth Sprague, Vice-President of American & Foreign Power, Inc., stated:

> American & Foreign Power owned a majority interest in Shanghai Power Co., the leading electric power company in Shanghai, China, until December 1950 when the Chinese Communist regime confiscated its properties, as well as the properties of its subsidiary, Western District Power Co., in Shanghai. Over 80 percent of the common stock of Shanghai Power Co. is owned, directly or indirectly by nationals of the United States, including American & Foreign Power. . . .
>
> In 1950, when the Chinese Communist regime confiscated the company's properties, books, and records, the investment of the company in plant and equipment was approximately $60 million exclusive of some $2 million representing the properties of its subsidiary, Western District Power Co. No compensation for any of the properties seized has been offered to or received by the company. It proved impossible for the company to secure any legal relief in the courts of China against the seizure and, in fact, the company was never even accorded a hearing by the Communist Chinese authorities.
>
> Over 15 years have now passed since the seizure of the com-

> pany's properties in Shanghai. The Chinese Communist regime has totally disregarded proper international standards and has shown no interest whatever in providing the victims of its property confiscations with any opportunity for the submission of proof of their claims.[102]

The 1966 hearing was on a bill that, in the words of one of its proponents, "would empower the [US] Foreign Claims Settlement Commission to determine the amount and validity of claims against the 'Chinese Communist regime,' arising since October 1, 1949, for losses resulting from the nationalization or other taking of property of nationals of the United States in violation of international law. . . ."[103] The bill received support from the Deputy Legal Adviser of the Department of State, on the ground that "we are confident that at some stage in the future there will be a Chinese government with which we will be able to deal and with which we will be able to negotiate a claims settlement for all this property which was taken."[104] And American & Foreign Power Co., Inc., urged the bill's passage "to emphasize the importance which the United States attaches to the view that nations must observe in their relations with each others' nationals at least a basic standard of morality and fair dealing."[105]

The bill was enacted, and, as of March 31, 1971, the Foreign Claims Settlement Commission had processed and validated 375 awards to American business, religious and educational institutions and individuals who suffered losses as a result of PRC action against their property. These awards, which represent unpaid claims against the PRC, total almost $200 million exclusive of interest. By May 1973, Sino-American negotiators reported that they were close to a settlement of this question as well as the question of almost $80 million in PRC assets that had been "frozen" by the United States during the Korean war.[106]

The following colloquy concerning British assets located in China took place in the House of Lords on October 20, 1954:

> Lord VANSITTART: My Lords, I beg to ask the Question which stands in my name on the Order Paper.
>
> [The Question was as follows:
>
> To ask Her Majesty's government whether, as widely stated in the Press, the Communist government of China have already reduced the assets of British firms in Shanghai from £300 million to less than £40 million, and whether the British government have protested against this form of peaceful coexistence.]
>
> The MINISTER of STATE, FOREIGN OFFICE (The

MARQUESS OF READING): My Lords, it is impossible to make an exact estimate in money terms, but the general scale of the loss may well be of the order indicated by the noble Lord. There has certainly been a very serious reduction in the assets of British firms in China, which are concentrated mainly in Shanghai. Command Paper No. 8639, published in August, 1952, dealt with the representations made by Her Majesty's government to the Chinese government about the position of British firms. Other representations have frequently been made to the Chinese government about the difficulties which British enterprises have met with in China. It is clear that it is the deliberate policy of the Chinese government to render it impossible for most British and foreign firms to remain in China and to force them to surrender their assets. The reduction in assets is mainly due to the Chinese authorities forcing British firms into debt by restrictions, regulations, and taxes *et cetera,* so that they have been unable to carry on, and in order to be able to liquidate and leave China they have had to surrender all their assets to the Chinese authorities. Only a comparatively small part of the reduction in assets is due to direct expropriation and confiscation by the Chinese.

Lately, and in particular since the Geneva Conference, the Chinese have been more accommodating in such matters as the issue of entry and exit permits, but their fundamental attitude towards British and other foreign firms has remained unchanged.[107]

Article 3 of the 1954 Provisional Regulations Governing the Departure of Foreign Residents from China provided: "A foreign resident applying for departure from the country shall conform with the following formalities: . . . (3) The possession of valid evidence to prove that he had no debt disputes in China, no arrears in the payment of taxes due, and no involvement in civil or criminal cases not yet settled in court. . . ." [108] The Regulations were promulgated on August 10, 1954, and were replaced in 1964 by item 15–1, which does not contain an article similar to Article 3 of the 1954 Regulations.

Harassment of foreign businessmen, although muted from the mid-1950's until the Cultural Revolution, nevertheless continued. Refusal to grant them exit visas remained a principal sanction. An extreme case was that of a Belgian bank manager in Shanghai, Frank von Roesebrook. Claiming that his bank owed it $30 million, which had been transferred out of China in behalf of the Nationalist Chinese just before the Communist takeover, the PRC refused to permit him to leave China even after it approved liquidation of the bank's Shanghai branch in 1952. In 1968, he was arrested by security police and lost contact with his wife and children, who had been permitted to leave China in 1966. In late 1971, as part of the agreement between the PRC and Belgium to establish diplomatic relations, arrangements were finally made for von Roesebrook's release a few months later.[109]

The recurrence of xenophobia and spy scares inspired by the Cultural Revolution led not only to reemphasis upon the use of criminal sanctions against aliens, but also to other renewed restrictions upon the few remaining foreign efforts to conduct private business activities in the PRC. British banking personnel in Shanghai, for example, had by mid-summer of 1968 been waiting a year to leave China, even though their replacements had long since arrived.[110] And the 1967–68 experiences of three British technicians make further unattractive reading for those who hope to profit from a vast China market:

> In June of this year three engineers who had been working for the firm of *Farmer Norton,* installing machinery in a steel plant on the outskirts of Peking, arrived back in Hong Kong. The story of that firm's travails in China has not been reported in the world's press, but they well illustrate the dangers faced by any foreign firm undertaking a contract in China today.
>
> Three men, Messrs. Ward, Magee, and Krnic (a British citizen of Yugoslav descent), had been working under the most trying circumstances since last October. Their job should have been over in a few weeks, but absenteeism and a lack of cooperation by the Chinese authorities kept them in Peking for many months. They were subjected to a great deal of propaganda, and the nerves of Mr. Krnic in particular began to suffer. Just before the installation they were working on was about to go into production, Krnic apparently suffered most acutely and reduced the furniture of his hotel to ruins. When he attempted to force open the window of the room with his bare hands he cut an artery, drenching the room with blood. He was taken to hospital where he needed at least a dozen stitches. At one stage the Chinese authorities attempted to accuse Mr. Krnic's colleagues of having beaten him up. By mid-June, their machinery was functioning satisfactorily, and the men asked for permission to leave China. But they were told that the financial terms of the contract (which the Chinese authorities themselves had signed) were now deemed to be unsatisfactory and a reduction in payment of approximately HK$300,000 was demanded. Although the three men were only technical employees of *Farmer Norton* and were certainly not able to negotiate on the firm's behalf, the Chinese threatened to keep them prisoners or hostages in China until the matter of payment had been settled

to their satisfaction. Finally, the men were grudgingly allowed to leave—one suspects because the Chinese did not wish to risk a further incident.[111]

Item 21–11 is the sequel to item 19–21. Knowledgeable sources have claimed that "the *Vickers-Zimmer* contract with China quite plainly provides for arbitration in Stockholm—a provision which the Chinese have ignored." [112] Furthermore, the damage verdict assessed against the company was equal to the sum that the company claimed was due to it for goods that it had delivered to the Chinese enterprise under their contract.[113]

21-11

"Verdict in British Vickers-Zimmer, Ltd., Fraud Case Pronounced in Peking," *PR* 11.28:4, 29 (July 12, 1968).

On July 3, the Peking Municipal Intermediate People's Court held a mass meeting at which the great red banner of Mao Tse-tung's thought was held high and the verdict in the fraud case of the British Vickers-Zimmer, Ltd., was announced. The verdict was read out in the absence of the defendant, the Vickers-Zimmer, Ltd., which dared not appear at the meeting.

To safeguard the security and socialist construction of our country and the fruits of victory of the great proletarian cultural revolution, the Peking Municipal Intermediate People's Court [declared]: The contract concerning a plant signed on November 25, 1964, between the defendant, the Vickers-Zimmer, Ltd., and the China National Technical Import Corporation is to be annulled immediately as of the date of the present judgment; personnel of the Vickers-Zimmer, Ltd., still in China must leave the country within ten days as of the date of the present judgment; and the Vickers-Zimmer, Ltd., shall pay an indemnity of 650,000 British pounds to the China National Technical Import Corporation for economic losses suffered by the latter. This just verdict fully demonstrated the great might of the dictatorship of the proletariat of our country.

When the meeting opened, the revolutionary masses present read in unison the great leader Chairman Mao's teaching: "The imperialists and domestic reactionaries will certainly not take their defeat lying down, and they will struggle to the last ditch. After there is peace and order throughout the country, they will still engage in sabotage and create disturbances in various ways and will try every day and every minute to stage a comeback. This is inevitable and beyond all doubt, and under no circumstances must we relax our vigilance."

A representative of the Peking Municipal Intermediate People's Court read the verdict.

The verdict pointed out: "The defendant, the British Vickers-Zimmer, Ltd., signed a contract with the China National Technical Import Corporation on November 25, 1964, relative to the supply of a plant. In the course of more than three years, while the contract was under execution, abundant facts showed that the defendant had no intention to fulfill the contract and had been deliberately perpetrating a fraud. Among the so-called technical personnel it had sent to China, some are incompetent while others were spies disguised as technical personnel. Before the spy George Watt came to China, he had been assigned the task of collecting intelligence by P. F. W. Jay, a responsible member of the defendant company. During his stay in China, George Watt stole a large quantity of important intelligence about China's military, political, and economic affairs and the great proletarian cultural revolution, thus rendering active service to the British imperialist policy of aggression and opposing the People's Republic of China. The above offender had already been sentenced by the intermediate people's court of Lanchow in Kansu Province. Another so-called engineer Peter Deckart, who also carried out espionage activities in China, had been expelled from the country by our public security authorities."

The verdict added: "It was stipulated in the contract that the defendant Vickers-Zimmer, Ltd., undertook to supply the China National Technical Import Corporation with the most up-to-date design and techniques, the best equipment and materials, and ensure the realization of the guaranteed values as stated in the contract. But facts have proved that the defendant had not grasped the main techniques concerning the contracted plant, and had repeatedly resorted to chicanery. In addition, with regard to delivery of technical documents, the supply of equipment and materials, and arrangements for trainees and other matters, the defendant had always defrauded by resorting to such tricks as procrastination, shirking responsibility, and flat denials."

The verdict declared: "The criminal activities of the defendant Vickers-Zimmer, Ltd., were deliberate political and economic sabotage and fraud, under the camouflage of trade, against the People's Republic of China, in an attempt to endanger China's security and undermine its socialist construction."

All those present at the meeting enthusiastically applauded in support of the solemn judgment of the Peking Municipal Intermediate People's Court. The revolutionary masses pointed out: China is a great socialist country exercising the dictatorship of the proletariat. The

Chinese people wish to have friendly cooperation with the people of all countries in the world and develop international trade on the basis of equality and mutual benefit, but they will never allow any enemy to take advantage of this to sabotage and make trouble in China. The revolutionary masses also shouted: "Down with US imperialism!" "Down with British imperialism!" "Long live the dictatorship of the proletariat!" "Long live all-round victory in the great proletarian cultural revolution!" and "Long live the great leader Chairman Mao! A long, long life to him!"

At the end of the meeting, everyone sang *Sailing the Seas Depends on the Helmsman.*

Note

On October 31, 1969, four engineers of a West German firm, the Lurgi Construction Company, and the wife and two children of one of them were released after fourteen months of confinement to a Peking hotel and immediate environs. The group had been detained as it was about to leave China after work on a construction project in Lanchow. They were told that customs and departure formalities would take a while. According to one of the group, they were frequently accused of breaking Chinese laws, but were never told which laws had been broken. No accusations of spying were made against them.[114] However, another Lurgi engineer was sentenced to ten years in prison for espionage as a result of the investigation that had obviously been conducted into the Lurgi case (recall 19–22 and Note following).

The three items that follow relate to Peking's regulation of the activities of news media. Item 21–12 summarizes an "unofficial" agreement between Chinese and Japanese organizations that established an exchange of correspondents. (For "unofficial" Sino-Japanese efforts to exchange resident trade missions, see items 29–5 and 29–6 and related Notes.) Items 21–13 and 21–14 indicate the impact of the Cultural Revolution upon various agreements authorizing the operation of newspaper reporters in China.

21-12

"China and Japan to Exchange Correspondents," NCNA–English, Peking (Apr. 19, 1964), in *SCMP*, no. 3205:27–28 (Apr. 24, 1964).

An agreement on the exchange of correspondents between China and Japan was reached here today by the Liao Cheng-chih office and Tatsanosuke Takasaki office, after the talks between their representatives held in Peking from April 14 to 18.

Taking part in the talks were Sun Ping-hua and Wang Hsiao-yun of China, and Yutaro Takeyama, Kaheita Okazaki, Yoshimi Furui, and Tomoharu Okubo of Japan.

According to the agreement, the decision to exchange correspondents between the two countries was taken as a result of the talks between Mr. Liao Cheng-chih and Mr. Kenzo Matsumura.

Arrangements for the exchange of correspondents, including entry formalities, are to be made by the Liao Cheng-chih office and the Takasaki office.

The number of the correspondents to be exchanged from each side is not to exceed eight. In principle each newspaper (or news agency, broadcasting station, television station) will send a correspondent. Either side may make readjustment within the number if necessary.

The first group of correspondents will be dispatched in June 1964. The exchange will take place simultaneously.

Each term of residence for the correspondents of both sides is within a year.

Each side should be responsible for the security of the correspondents of the other side.

Each side should provide facilities for reporting for the correspondents of the other side.

The correspondents of both sides should abide by the rules governing foreign correspondents and enjoy the same privileges as given to other foreign correspondents.

Each side should insure freedom of correspondence for the correspondents of the other side.

21-13

"French Reporter Ousted by Peking; Accused of 'Lying,'" *New York Times* (May 8, 1968), p. 6.

PEKING, May 7 (Agence France-Presse)—Jean Vincent, head of the Agence France-Presse bureau in Peking, was ordered to leave China today. He was declared persona non grata and instructed to leave within three days.

Mr. Vincent, who had been at the Peking post since Feb. 11, 1966, was called to the Chinese Foreign Ministry today. The head of the ministry's press service read him a long statement declaring that his services were no longer "acceptable." The statement said that despite several warnings, Mr. Vincent had recently sent certain dispatches that were considered "slanderous and lying."

Two Agence France-Presse correspondents were accredited in Peking, Mr. Vincent and Rene Flipo.

The expulsion of Mr. Vincent follows a series of ousters over the last twelve months, including those of three Soviet correspondents, a correspondent of the Tanjug, the Yugoslav news agency, a Czechoslovak correspondent, Jaroslav Struhal, and three Japanese correspondents. The departure of Mr. Vincent will leave only four Western correspondents in Peking: Mr. Flipo, correspondents of the Toronto *Globe and Mail* and the West German news agency, and Anthony Grey, a Reuters correspondent, who has been confined to his apartment by the Chinese authorities since last August. Other foreign journalists here are two Soviet reporters, two Poles, one Hungarian and four Japanese correspondents. There were eleven Japanese here two years ago.

21-14

Derek Davies, "Twisting the Lions' Tails," *FEER* 61.31:228 (Aug. 1, 1968).

Anthony Grey, the Reuters correspondent in Peking, has now spent more than a year imprisoned in a room in his house which overlooks the roofs of the Forbidden City in Peking. Six PLA soldiers are on guard inside the house, while three are on duty outside, preventing anyone from attempting to glimpse his tragic figure. When he attempts to speak to his military warders, they do not reply, and his repeated requests for permission at least to study the Chinese language have elicited no response. His only form of "relaxation" is the opportunity to read the turgid prose of the *Peking Review* for one hour every week.

He stands accused of no crime, nor have the Chinese authorities suggested that he has behaved improperly in any way. He is purely and simply a hostage for the action taken by the Hong Kong government against the two members of the New China News Agency and twelve other Communist journalists who were convicted of crimes connected with the Maoist revolution in Hong Kong last year.

Grey's detention began on July 21 last year. For about one month there were some contacts with him, and he played chess over the telephone with a diplomat friend until the Chinese cut the telephone off. In August there were reports that his three-story house, No. 15 Nanchitze, had been invaded by a band of Red Guards. Formal approaches by Reuters News Agency to the Chinese government and personal messages to Chou En-lai ("in the name of common humanity") were unanswered. Except for a cable sent last Christmas by Grey saying that he was in sound health "in spite of difficulties," there was no news of him until last April 23, when Sir Donald Hopson, the British chargé d'affaires, and one member of his staff were allowed "consular access" to Grey for 20 minutes. The conversation, in the presence of three uniformed policemen, was held entirely in "standard English" at the Chinese insistence. Although Grey said he was in good physical condition, the diplomats had the impression that, not surprisingly, he had been "affected by his long months of solitude." Since then nothing more has been heard of him.

The treatment of Grey is obviously unjustified and uncivilised. Reuters maintain a correspondent in Peking because the New China News Agency maintains a bureau in London; its presence in the Chinese capital has no connection whatever with Hong Kong or with the presence of NCNA men in the British colony. However, Grey's imprisonment inspired only faint public remonstrance from Reuters, while the British press—usually so vocal in attacking any encroachments on its liberties—has also been relatively restrained in its comments on the Chinese behaviour. This muted approach was adopted after consultations with the British Foreign Office, who advised that a wave of public protest might "do more harm than good." The Foreign Office advice was doubtless influenced by the consideration that such a campaign would probably spark off embarrassing demands in Britain for reprisals against the NCNA men in London.

Evidently, Reuters accepted the advice, partly because that news agency is proud of its independent status (it is now owned by a trust of British newspapers) and official protests in its behalf might tend to identify it in the public mind with the British government. Further, of course, Reuters is anxious to maintain its right to a correspondent in Peking, being the first non-Communist news agency allowed to operate there. The British press cooperated, and the illegal detention of a British journalist for over a year has been systematically "played down."

Now, a year later, it has become all too obvious that appeals to sweet reason (based on the hopes that the Chinese would return to their civilised norm) have so far failed.

Note

On October 4, 1969, twenty-six months after his confinement began, Mr. Grey was released, following the release in Hong Kong of the last of the thirteen Chinese journalists who had been imprisoned during the 1967 disturbances there. Chinese authorities made it clear that this was the reason for Grey's release.[115] For the PRC's official justification of its treatment of Grey, see item 29–8. During his long confinement British diplomats were allowed to visit Grey on only three occasions.[116] Upon his return to London, Grey described how, about a month after his house arrest had begun, two hundred Red Guards beat him and painted him, vandalized his house, and killed his cat.[117]

A week after the PRC lifted the house arrest on Grey, it released a 69-year-old free-lance journalist, Norman Barrymaine, who had been charged with spying during a two-day stopover in Shanghai as a passenger on a Polish freighter. He had been detained for nineteen months after Communist authorities found in his possession a photograph of gunboats that he had taken at the entrance to the port of Shanghai.[118]

At the height of the Cultural Revolution the Peking central telegraph office at one point refused to transmit press cables reporting the existence of wall posters attacking Premier Chou En-lai. It was believed to be the first time that a foreign correspondent's cables had been refused in Peking since the establishment of the PRC. The Reuters correspondent involved was permitted to telephone the news to Tokyo, however.[119]

Although, as we have seen, the Soviet Union and other East European Communist states became involved in many disputes with the PRC in the 1960's, during the 1950's they enjoyed good relations with Peking. Because their socialist economic systems precluded their nationals from privately owning property in China or operating businesses there, these states avoided many of the frictions that arose from the PRC's efforts to regulate the economic activities of nationals of capitalist states. Of course, until 1954, when the Soviet Union sold the PRC its interest in the four Sino-Soviet joint-stock companies that had been organized in 1950, and by which time the USSR had transferred to China its rights to joint administration and ownership of the

Chinese Changchun Railway, there must have been a certain amount of friction over the fetters these arrangements imposed on China's exercise of territorial jurisdiction (recall 12–25 and Note preceding it). Item 21–15 illustrates Peking's willingness to cooperate with the Soviet Union in economic activity on equal terms in the late 1950's.

21-15

"Treaty of Commerce and Navigation between the People's Republic of China and the Union of Soviet Socialist Republics, signed in Peking, April 23, 1958," *PR* 1.9:21–23 (Apr. 29, 1958).

The chairman of the People's Republic of China and the Presidium of the Supreme Soviet of the Union of Soviet Socialist Republics, desirous of promoting further development and consolidation of the economic relations between the two countries, have resolved to conclude the present Treaty of Commerce and Navigation, and have appointed as their plenipotentiaries for this purpose:

The Chairman of the People's Republic of China:

Yeh Chi-chuang, Minister of Foreign Trade of the People's Republic of China;

The Presidium of the Supreme Soviet of the Union of Soviet Socialist Republics:

Ivan Grigoriyevich Kabanov, Minister of Foreign Trade of the Union of Soviet Socialist Republics;

who, having communicated their full powers, found in good and due form, have agreed upon the following articles:

Article 1. The Contracting Parties shall, in accordance with the spirit of friendly cooperation and mutual assistance, adopt all necessary measures to develop and consolidate the commercial relations between the two countries on the basis of equality and mutual benefit.

For this purpose, the governments of the Contracting Parties will, in accordance with the requirements of the national economy of the respective countries, conclude various agreements, including long-term agreements, to ensure the development of the flow of goods between the two countries.

Article 2. The Contracting Parties shall grant each other most-favoured-nation treatment in respect of all questions relating to commerce, navigation, and all other economic relations between the two countries.

Article 3. In accordance with the provision of Article Two of this Treaty, the Contracting Parties shall grant each other most-favoured-nation treatment in respect [to] all questions relating to customs, particularly the following: customs duties and other duties; storage of goods in the custody of the customs office; regulations and formalities applicable while the goods are in the custody of the customs office.

Accordingly, natural or manufactured products of either Contracting Party shall not be liable, on importation to the territory of the other Party, to any customs or duties, other or higher, or to regulations or formalities, other or more burdensome, than those imposed on similar natural or manufactured products imported from any third country.

Similarly, natural or manufactured products of either Contracting Party intended for export to the territory of the other Party shall not be liable to any customs or duties, other or higher, or to regulations or formalities, other or more burdensome, than those imposed on similar natural or manufactured products intended for export to any third country.

Article 4. Natural or manufactured products of either Contracting Party, on importation to the territory of the other Party through the territory of one or more third countries, shall not be liable to any customs or duties, other or higher, or to regulations or formalities, other or more burdensome, than those imposed on similar products shipped direct from the producer country.

The provisions of this Article also apply to goods which, passing through the territory of one or more third countries, have had their packing or wrappings changed or were stored for a period of time.

Article 5. Within the time limit prescribed by the customs authorities, the following certified articles being reexported or reimported shall be exempted from customs or other duties:

a. articles for fairs, exhibitions, or competitions;
b. articles for testing or experimentation;
c. articles imported for repairs and shipped back after being repaired;
d. tools and implements carried by or mailed to installation technicians;
e. natural or manufactured products imported for processing or remodelling and shipped back after such processing or remodelling;
f. empty wrappers bearing trade marks imported for wrapping purposes and the wrappers of the imported goods themselves.

Samples of goods sent purely as samples and within amounts customary in trade practice shall be exempted unconditionally from customs and other duties.

Article 6. Natural or manufactured products of either Contracting Party shall under no circumstances be liable, after importation into the territory of the other Party, to higher internal taxes on their production, processing, circulation, or consumption than those imposed on similar products of any third country.

Article 7. Neither of the Contracting Parties shall impose on importations from or exportations to the territory of the other Party any restrictions or prohibitions which are not applicable to all other countries.

However, in the interests of national security, public order, protection of public health, protection of animal and plant life, preservation of works of art and historical relics, the Contracting Parties may reserve the right to stipulate restrictions or prohibitions on the import and export of related articles, provided that, in like circumstances, these restrictions and prohibitions are also applicable to all third countries.

Article 8. The vessels and the cargoes on vessels of either of the Contracting Parties shall be accorded in the ports of the other Party most-favoured-nation treatment in all that concerns entering, clearing, and stationing. Such treatment is in particular applicable in respect of the following: all kinds of dues and charges collected in the name of and for the state, the local authorities and other organs; mooring, loading, and discharging in port and at anchorages; the use of pilots, navigation routes, lock gates, bridges, signals, and lights for navigation; the use of cranes, weighbridges, warehouses, shipyards, dry-docks, and repair yards; supplies of fuel, lubricants, water, and food.

The provisions of this Article shall not apply to the performance of port services, including pilotage and towage, or to coastal shipping. Nevertheless, the vessels of either of the Contracting Parties proceeding from one port of the other Party to another for the purpose of landing cargo brought from abroad, or of taking on board cargo for a foreign destination, shall not be considered as engaged in coastal shipping.

Article 9. If any vessel of either of the Contracting Parties should run aground or be wrecked on the coast of the other Party, such vessel and its cargo shall enjoy the same treatment as the other Party would give to its own vessels and cargoes in similar circumstances.

The other Contracting Party shall give the same necessary help and assistance to the master, crew, and passengers, both as regards their persons and as regards the vessel and cargo as it would give to its own vessels in similar circumstances.

Rescue shall be carried out in accordance with special agreements if related agreements have been concluded.

Article 10. The nationality of vessels shall be reciprocally recognized on the basis of the documents and certificates on board the vessel issued according to law by the proper authorities of the Contracting Party whose flag the vessel flies.

Any tonnage certificates and other shipping documents issued by the proper authorities of either of the Contracting Parties shall be recognized by the proper authorities of the other Party.

In accordance with this provision, vessels of either of the Contracting Parties which are provided with a valid tonnage certificate shall be exempted from remeasurement in the ports of the other Party, and the net capacity of the vessel entered in the certificate shall be accepted as the basis for calculating tonnage tax and harbor dues.

Article 11. The Contracting Parties shall undertake, in respect of the conveyance of goods, passengers, and luggage by rail, road, or waterways in the same direction and over the same distance, to extend to each other most-favoured-nation treatment in respect [to] all that concerns acceptance for conveyance, methods, and costs of conveyance and other changes connected with such conveyance.

Article 12. Natural or manufactured products of either of the Contracting Parties, being conveyed through the territory of the other Party to the territory of a third country, shall be exempted from customs and other duties.

The transit of the above products shall enjoy, in respect [to] regulations and formalities, no less favourable treatment than that granted to the transit of goods of any third country.

Article 13. Either of the Contracting Parties may set up an office of its commercial representative in the capital of the other Party, the legal position of which shall be determined by the provisions of the Annex to the present Treaty, which shall constitute an integral part thereof.

Article 14. The juridical or natural persons of either of the Contracting Parties shall enjoy in the territory of the other Party in all respects no less favourable treatment than that granted to the juridical or natural persons of any third country.

Article 15. The provisions of this Treaty shall not apply to advantages or favoured treatment which are or may hereafter be granted by either of the Contracting Parties for the purpose of facilitating trade between its border regions and a neighbouring country.

Article 16. The Contracting Parties undertake to implement the awards of arbitration of any dispute relating to commercial or other contracts concluded between the juridical persons or organs of the Contracting Parties, if both parties to the dispute have through proper means agreed to its arbitration by a special tribunal set up for this purpose or [by] a standing tribunal.

The decrees of implementation as well as the implementation itself of the arbitration awards shall be carried out in accordance with the laws and regulations of the Contracting Party implementing the arbitration awards.

Article 17. The present Treaty shall be ratified as soon as possible and shall enter into force on the day of the exchange of ratifications, which shall take place at Moscow.

The present Treaty shall remain in force for six months after the day either of the Contracting Parties gives notice of its desire to terminate the Treaty.

Done in duplicate, at Peking, on April 23, 1958, in the Chinese and Russian languages, both texts being equally authentic.

(signed) Yeh Chi-chuang. (signed) Ivan Grigoriyevich Kabanov

Responsibility for Causing Injury to Aliens in China

22

We have seen cases in which the PRC has demanded that other states assume responsibility for alleged violations of international law committed in Chinese territory. When British warships entered the Yangtse River without the PRC's permission, Chairman Mao himself called on the British government to "admit its wrongdoing, apologize, and make compensation" (16–1). And the PRC has vigorously opposed efforts of the United States to avoid responsibility for sending U–2 planes and reconnaissance balloons into China's air space (18–2 and Note following it).

We have also seen that the PRC has insisted on the responsibility of other states to protect Chinese nationals within their territory. After a 1961 incident in Ghana, it will be recalled (4–3), the Chinese embassy there demanded: "that the authorities concerned should apologize for this incident [and] punish those persons responsible, and that effective measures be taken to protect the safety of all members of the Chinese embassy, all Chinese experts as well as other Chinese nationals in Ghana and ensure that no such incidents will occur again." Parts VI and VII present numerous other examples.

Peking's complaint against the alleged unilateral scrapping by the Soviet Union of the Sino-Soviet agreement on mutual abolition of certificates of vaccination against smallpox (15–4) has already indicated the PRC's recognition of the principle that a state must be responsible for breach of a treaty obligation. We will return to that question in Part VIII.

Here we present a discussion of the circumstances in which the PRC recognizes its own international responsibility for acts committed within its territory. The preceding chapter set forth the range of methods by which the PRC has succeeded in liquidating most foreign economic interests in China. It also indicated that the United States considers Peking's "nationalization or other taking of property of nationals of the United States [to be] in violation of international law" and that, according to the Minister of State in the British Foreign Office, "it is the deliberate policy of the Chinese government to render it impossible for most British and foreign firms to remain in China and to force them to surrender their assets" (Note following 21–10). As the Foreign Office pointed out, only a comparatively small part of the dramatic reduction in British assets in China is due to "direct expropriation and confiscation." Neither officials nor scholars in Peking have addressed themselves to all the thorny legal questions implicit in claims arising out of the PRC's acts against foreign economic interests in China. But scholarly writing suggests what Peking's position is likely to be on some of the principal questions, including the problem of the standard by which the international validity of the nationalization of foreign assets should be determined.

We have already read the scorn that one Chinese writer has heaped upon the attempts of bourgeois scholars to assert the existence of an international standard for the treatment of aliens that all states must observe regardless of how they treat their own citizens (21–1). That position does not necessarily contradict the view of another Chinese scholar who has argued that there is a minimum standard of international law that protects aliens from discriminatory decrees such as those by which India has persecuted allegedly law-abiding Chinese nationals (4–7). Yet one can hardly be confident of understanding the PRC's position on the basis of these brief discussions. The first two items in this chapter provide more reliable insights into Peking's view. They are typical of a number of scholarly articles that appeared after the PRC announced its support of Egypt's nationalization of the Suez Canal.[120]

22-1

Li Hao-p'ei, "Nationalization and International Law," *CFYC,* no. 2:10–15 (1958).

I

Although nationalization is not [a phenomenon] new to this century, it has nevertheless occurred more frequently in this century because socialist, nationalist, and imperialist countries have in this period all adopted measures of nationalization. Soviet nationalization after the October Revolution and nationalization by the various people's democracies after the Second World War basically changed the economic structure of those countries by transforming the system of private ownership into a system of socialist ownership. In 1951 Syria nationalized water, electricity, and public transportation enterprises and in 1956 Egypt nationalized the Suez Canal Company. Both incidents struck blows at imperialist economic aggression and made possible the development of national capital in those two countries. Finally, the imperialist country of Great Britain nationalized the Bank of England, coal mines, the transportation enterprises, and others in 1945. In 1936-37 France nationalized its military supply industry and railways and in 1946–48 its electricity, gas and banking enterprises, and others. However, this nationalization by the two countries did not really change their economic structures.

The objects of this nationalization were not individual properties of individuals, but were certain categories of properties or enterprises. Although the purposes of this nationalization were not uniform, the questions of public and private international law raised by this and other similar nationalization are by and large the same. These questions are: (1) Whether the state has the right to adopt nationalization measures; (2) Whether the nationalizing state is obligated to compensate the original owners of foreign nationality; and (3) What is the extraterritorial effect of nationalization laws? This paper studies these problems.

II

The question of whether a state has the right to adopt nationalization measures is a public international law question. Public international law regards nationalization as lawful exercise of state power. This is because each state, being possessed of sovereignty, naturally has the right within its own territory to prescribe whatever economic and social system it chooses to establish. Speaking more concretely, each state has the exclusive right to regulate ownership relations within its own territory—the subject, object, kinds, and contents of ownership as well as the conditions of acquisition, loss, and transfer of ownership. Consequently, when one approaches this question from the standpoint of the principle of state sovereignty, one must recognize that states enjoy the right to adopt nationalization measures. Nationalization belongs to matters of domestic jurisdiction and therefore, according to Article 2, paragraphs 4 and 7, of the Charter of the United Nations, neither the United Nations nor other states have a right to intervene.

The principle that a state has the right to nationalize properties or enterprises within its territory was confirmed by the Permanent Court of International Justice in the Chorzow Factory Case.[a] Since states of all types have adopted nationalization measures, this principle has been generally accepted by all states. Even Great Britain and France did not deny this principle in regard to the question of the

[a] Judgment No. 13, Case Concerning the Factory at Chorzów (Claim for Indemnity) (The Merits), September 13, 1928, in *PCIJ* [Permanent Court of International Justice], Ser. A, No. 17, pp. 46–47 (Leyden: A. W. Sijthoff's, 1928).

Egyptian nationalization of the Suez Canal Company. They instead founded their legally and factually groundless opposition to the nationalization on the ground of the so-called special status of the Suez Canal Company.[b] It can thus be seen that this principle has become unquestionably established in public international law.

III

Whether or not the nationalizing state must compensate original owners of foreign nationality is also a public international law question. Opinions with respect to this question are not unanimous; they can be classified into three types. The first theory maintains that the nationalizing state must make compensation to owners of foreign nationality and that the compensation must be adequate, effective, and prompt. The second theory maintains that the nationalizing state should make partial compensation to owners of foreign nationality. The third maintains that no compensation is required.

1. The first theory is obviously based upon the sanctity and inviolability of private property advocated by the bourgeoisie. This theory can be further classified into two views. The first maintains that the validity of nationalization is conditioned on the making of adequate, effective, and prompt compensation to owners of foreign nationality. The second maintains that, although the validity of nationalization is not conditioned upon such compensation, the nationalizing state still has an obligation to make compensation.

The first view is the one officially adopted by the United States. It is stated in a note dated April 3, 1940, from United States Secretary of State Hull to Mexico with respect to Mexican nationalization of certain land and petroleum enterprises which involved the interests of certain American capitalists. He stated: ". . . the right to expropriate property is coupled with and conditioned on the obligation to make adequate, effective, and prompt compensation. The legality of an expropriation is in fact dependent upon the observance of this requirement."[c] The Supreme Court of British Aden Island also adopted this attitude in its judgment on the Rose-Mary case decided in 1953.[d]

[b] "Nationalization of the Suez Canal Company," [Note] *Harvard Law Review,* 70.3:480–490 (Jan. 1957); Robert Delson, "Nationalization of the Suez Canal Company: Issues of Public and Private International Law," *Columbia Law Review,* 57.6:755–786 (June 1957).

[c] Green Haywood Hackworth, *Digest of International Law* (Washington, D.C.: Government Printing Office, 1942), III, 662.

[d] *Anglo-Iranian Oil Co.* v. *Jaffrate et. al.,* Supreme Court of the Colony of Aden, January 9, 1953, reported in William W. Bishop, Jr., "Judicial Decisions," *AJIL,* 47.2:325–328 (Apr. 1953).

Reactionary international law jurists such as Hyde and Shawcross [?] also advocate this view.[e] However, the great majority of bourgeois jurists have adopted the second view of this theory.[f]

2. Although the second theory also starts out from the principle of protecting private property, it takes into consideration the nationalizing state's ability to make compensation. It thus leans towards compromise. Among bourgeois international law scholars, Lauterpacht and La Pradelle have adopted this view.[g] The alien compensation agreements concluded between various countries from the end of World War I to the present generally provide only partial compensation and are thus frequently cited as support for this theory.

3. The rationale of the third theory is: since the end of World War I, many states have nationalized property in order to carry out large-scale economic and social reform. To require the nationalizing state to make compensation to owners of foreign nationality may frustrate the exercise of the sovereign right of a state to carry out economic and social reform, because it may be unable or difficult for such state to assume an obligation to make compensation. Therefore, this theory maintains that the nationalizing state only has an obligation not to discriminate against foreigners; if it does not compensate nationals who are owners, then it has no obligation to compensate owners of foreign nationality. Among international law jurists in the People's democracies, Bystricky of Czechoslovakia strongly supports this theory; and among international law jurists in bourgeois countries, Williams of Great Britain strongly advocates it.[h] Other international

[e] C. C. Hyde, *International Law, Chiefly as Interpreted and Applied by the United States*, 2nd ed., (Boston: Little, Brown, 1945), II, 710–720; Shawcross, "Several Problems of Nationalization in International Law," in *Fifth International Conference of Lawyers* (Fa-lu chia ti-wu-tz'u kuo-chi hui-i; 1954), p. 14. [Note: The reference to Shawcross is translated from the Chinese; we are unable to locate this source.]

[f] Joseph, "International Aspects of Nationalization," in *Fifth International Conference of Lawyers,* 1954, p. 3 [Note: The reference to Joseph is translated from the Chinese; we are unable to locate this source.]; Nicholas R. Doman, "Postwar Nationalization of Foreign Property in Europe," *Columbia Law Review,* 48.8: 1127–1161 (Dec. 1948).

[g] L. Oppenheim, *International Law,* 8th ed., by H. Lauterpacht, (London: Longmans, Green, 1955), I, 352; M. A. de La Pradelle, "Les effects internationaux des nationalisations," *Annuaire de L'Institut de Droit International,* Vol. 43, tome 1 (1950), pp. 42–46.

[h] Bystricky, "On Several Problems of Socialist Nationalization in International Law," in *Proceedings of the Committee on Private International Law of the Sixth Congress of the International Association of Democratic Lawyers* (Kuo-chi min-chu fa-hsieh ti-lu-tz'u ta-hui kuo-chi ssu-fa wei-yüan-hui), pp. 15ff. [Note: The reference to Bystricky is translated from the Chinese; we are unable to locate this source.]; John Fisher Williams, "International Law and the Property of Aliens," *British Year Book of International Law,* 9:1–30 (1928).

law jurists, such as Décencière-Ferrandière[?] . . . Friedman of France and Ross of Denmark, adopt this theory.[i]

IV

We believe that the third theory is correct. With respect to the question of compensation, public international law has only established the rule of equal treatment between nationals and foreigners; it has not established the rule that foreigners must be compensated. Therefore, if a state does not compensate its own nationals, it need not compensate foreigners. In practice, the nationalizing state sometimes pays more or less [*sic*] compensation to foreigners, but this is not because public international law has already established the rule that a state must compensate owners of foreign nationality. [A state may compensate foreign nationals] because it also pays some compensation to its own nationals who were owners; or because of certain practical considerations (such as a desire to resume normal international economic relations, to obtain the release of frozen properties, or to conclude credit agreements); or even because of the illegal exercise of compulsion by imperialist countries. We will try to prove the correctness of this view.

(A) We can reach this conclusion from studying several famous nationalization cases of the past hundred or more years.

1. The Case of the Sicilian Sulphur Monopoly. In 1836, the Kingdom of the Two Sicilies granted to a French company the monopoly right to purchase and export sulphur from its country. Great Britain protested about this action to the Two Sicilies on the ground that the monopoly violated the 1816 Treaty of Commerce between the Two Sicilies and Great Britain—which, in addition to the most-favored-nation clause, provided that British nationals in the Two Sicilies should be entitled to dispose of property of any kind without the slightest loss and without any limitation being placed on exercise of such rights—and on the ground that the monopoly impaired the rights of British nationals. The government of the Two Sicilies replied to the British government that foreigners could not enjoy more rights than nationals,

[i] *Proceedings of the Committee on Private International Law of the Sixth Congress of the International Association of Democratic Lawyers: A Study of Nationalization* (Kuan-yü kuo-yu-hua ti yen-chiu; publication of the International Association of Democratic Lawyers, 1957); Samy Friedman, *Expropriation in International Law* (London: Stevens, 1953); Alf Ross, *Larebog i Folheret* (*A Textbook of International Law*, Kuo-chi-fa chiao-pen, 1947) Copenhagen, 1949. [Note: The references, except those by Samy Friedman and Ross, are all translated from the Chinese; we are unable to locate these sources.]

and it still granted the monopoly right to the French Company in disregard of the [British] protest. The British government, disagreeing with the view of the government of the Two Sicilies, made a show of naval force against the Two Sicilies. The result was that the Two Sicilies submitted, cancelled the monopoly agreement and set up a commission to decide upon the demand for compensation made by British nationals. The amount of compensation decided upon by the commission was duly paid by the Two Sicilies. In this case, three points are worthy of notice: first, the government of the Two Sicilies expressly advocated the principle of equality of treatment between foreigners and nationals; second, the British demand was based upon a treaty and not upon any principles of public international law; and third, the Two Sicilies' submission [to the British demand] was due to the British show of naval force, and not to the persuasiveness of the British claim. Therefore, this case cannot be cited as a basis for claiming that any state adopting nationalization measures assumes an obligation to compensate foreigners.[j]

2. Italian Life Insurance State Monopoly Case. In 1911, the Italian government submitted to its Parliament a proposal for the establishment of a state life insurance monopoly with no provision for compensating existing insurance companies doing business in Italy, many of which were foreign. Therefore, the British, United States, German, and Austro-Hungarian governments all protested to the Italian government. At that time, the famous French international law jurist Clunet, in his capacity as an expert, delivered an opinion to the effect that the foreign companies were entitled to compensation. Other famous international law jurists, such as Anzilotti, Asser, von Bar, Holland, Grabba, Lammasch, Lyon-Caen, Roguin, and Rolin, expressed agreement with this opinion. However, the Italian Parliament nevertheless persisted in adopting the original government proposal. The only concession made was that the existing life insurance companies were allowed ten years in which to conclude their business. This case clearly illustrates that a state adopting nationalization measures does not have an obligation to compensate owners of foreign nationality. (See Williams, "International Law and the Property of Aliens.")

3. Uruguayan Life Insurance State Monopoly Case. In 1911,

[j] "Correspondence between Great Britain and Sicily, relative to the Sulphur Monopoly in Sicily—1837–1839," *British and Foreign State Papers,* Vol. 28, 1839–1840 (London: Harrison and Sons, 1857), pp. 1163–1242; *ibid.,* 1840, Vol. 29, 1840–1841 (London: Harrison and Sons, 1857), pp. 175–204; "Correspondence between Great Britain and Sicily, relative to the Claims of British Subjects, for Losses Consequent upon the Sulphur Monopoly, in Sicily—1840–1842," *ibid.,* Vol. 30, 1841–1842 (London: James Ridgway and Sons, 1858), pp. 111–120.

the Uruguayan Parliament adopted an act providing for a state monopoly over life insurance enterprises. The British government immediately protested to the Uruguayan government on the ground that the proposed law involved the expropriation of the British companies established in Uruguay; that all the assets inherent in the companies' "good will" were to be eradicated without compensation; and that the law was consequently of a confiscatory character. The result was that this law was not promulgated or put into effect by the Uruguayan government (see Williams, "International Law and the Property of Aliens"). The facts of this case are basically the same as those of the Italian Life Insurance State Monopoly Case, but the result is entirely different: Italy put the monopoly into effect in disregard of the protest; Uruguay cancelled the monopoly immediately after the protest. The different results are due to the difference in strength of the two countries at that time. Therefore, the cancellation of the monopoly by Uruguay cannot prove that there is a principle that the nationalizing state must grant compensation to foreigners.

4. The Case of Land Reform by Rumania and Other Countries. After the First World War, Rumania, Czechoslovakia, and Yugoslavia carried out land reform on some lands acquired from the Austro-Hungarian Empire. The land reform encountered the opposition of those landlords who had chosen Hungarian nationality. The Hungarian government negotiated with Rumania on behalf of those landlords. Hungary claimed that the landlords who had chosen Hungarian nationality should receive full compensation in accordance with international law and Article 250 of the Treaty of Trianon. Rumania and the other countries strongly maintained that compensation to foreign landlords could not exceed the amount prescribed by the laws of Rumania and the other countries; nor could it exceed the amount to which their own landlords were entitled. For instance, the compensation Rumania was willing to grant was equivalent only to 1 percent of the Hungarian demand. After a long period of controversy the respective disputant states agreed that Rumania and the other countries jointly [were to] set up a land reform compensation fund, but that each of these states should pay only the amount of compensation its own laws required.[k] Therefore, this case can merely support the principle that foreigners and nationals are entitled to equal treatment and compensation.

5. The Case of Mexico's Nationalization of Land and Petroleum Enterprises. In the dispute between Mexico and the United States

[k] See Friedman [*Expropriation*], pp. 82–86.

arising out of Mexican nationalization of land and petroleum enterprises, the legal points held by both parties have been described above. The result of the dispute was that the parties could not agree with each other's legal points. Although Mexico, under strong pressure from American imperialism, in practice had to yield to the United States' demand to a relatively large degree, it did not make one concession in principle. Article [18] of the November 19, 1941, exchange of notes between the United States and Mexico relating to the compensation of nationals of the United States expressly provides: "Nothing contained in this note shall be regarded as a precedent or be invoked by either of the two governments in the settlement between them of any future difficulty, conflict, controversy, or arbitration. The action herein provided for is considered as singular and exceptional, appropriate solely to this case. . . ."[1] Consequently, this case only specifically exposes two opposing views; it does not have the value of a precedent.

6. The Case of Soviet Nationalization of Land and Enterprises. After the October Revolution, the Soviet nationalization of land and enterprises also struck a blow to imperialists, and thereby caused the latter to protest. Imperialist countries convened two conferences—the 1922 Genoa Conference and the Hague Conference—in an attempt to compel the Soviet Union to grant compensation to the imperialists. But the Soviet Union invoked the French bourgeois revolution's precedent of no compensation and, moreover, submitted a counterclaim against imperialist countries for damage done to the Soviet Union by their 1919–1920 armed intervention. Their attempt was thus fruitless. Finally, those countries had to conclude separate bilateral treaties with the Soviet Union in which they expressed or implied renunciation of their claims against the Soviet Union. On April 16, 1922, Germany concluded with the Soviet Union the Treaty of Rapallo in which the two countries renounced their claims against each other. On August 8, 1924, Great Britain concluded with the Soviet Union a treaty in which Great Britain in principle agreed with the counterclaim submitted by the Soviet Union with respect to British armed intervention. Moreover, it also recognized the mutual cancellation of this counterclaim and the claims of British nationals against the Soviet Union arising out of Soviet measures of nationalization. Although this treaty did not go into effect because the British Conservative government,

[1] Exchange of notes constituting an agreement relating to the compensation of nationals of the United States of America whose properties, rights, or interests in the petroleum industry in Mexico were affected by acts of the government of Mexico subsequent to 17 March 1938, Washington, 19 November 1941 (Filed and recorded at the request of the United States of America on October 30, 1952). *UNTS*, 148:367–373 (New York, 1952).

which replaced the Labor government shortly after the conclusion of the treaty, refused to ratify it, Great Britain afterwards did not seriously submit claims against the Soviet Union regarding the question of Soviet nationalization. On October 26, 1924, France recognized the Soviet Union. The Soviet Union agreed that France could reserve its claims, and, moreover, it permitted the French government temporarily to take possession of Soviet property in France. As a practical matter, this solved the nationalization dispute between France and the Soviet Union because France afterwards did not seriously submit its claims. The claims of the United States against the Soviet Union were similarly solved. The November 16, 1933, Litvinov-Roosevelt Agreement provided that "preparatory to a final settlement of the claims and counterclaims between the governments of the Union of Soviet Socialist Republics and the United States of America and the claims of their nationals," the Soviet Union agrees to assign to the United States government all sums that American nationals might owe the Soviet government as the successor to former Russian governments. Subsequently, the United States did not continue to press its claims. Therefore, it may be considered that in practice the United States also tacitly renounced its claims. Thus, this case was ended by the expressed or implied renunciation by the various countries of their claims for compensation against the Soviet Union. It thereby proves that the view that foreigners have the right to compensation is without foundation. Soviet permission to have the French government temporarily take possession of its limited amount of property in France and its assignment to the United States government of a small amount of money owed by United States nationals to the Soviet Union were merely measures to achieve the normalization of economic relations with those two countries (see Friedman, *Expropriation in International Law.*)

7. The Case of Nationalization of Land and Enterprises by the Various Eastern European People's Democracies. After the Second World War, nationalization by various Eastern European people's democracies caused the United States, Britain, and other imperialist countries to attempt to protect the so-called "vested interests" of their nationals. A British jurist summarized these endeavors as:

> [British] success in these endeavors was about as disappointing as that of the United States. Neither the United Kingdom nor the United States succeeded in protecting in these countries the individual rights of their citizens by means of diplomatic intervention. The disintegration of the concept of property rights in Europe has gone so far that no individual claimant seems to

> have been able to obtain full satisfaction. Only where timely economic countermeasures were taken against the confiscating states could compensation agreements be concluded which provide for some measure of compensation.[m]

Take Britain as an example. As a result of the conclusion of a compensation agreement with Yugoslavia on December 23, 1948, Britain received compensation in the amount of £4,500,000; as a result of the conclusion of a compensation agreement with Czechoslovakia on September 28, 1949, Britain received compensation in the amount of £8,000,000. However, there are [two points] worthy of note: first, the amount of compensation paid by Yugoslavia and Czechoslovakia merely constitutes a small portion of the amount of compensation claimed by British nationals.[n] Second, the conclusion of these agreements was due to the concurrent conclusion of financial and trade agreements with Yugoslavia and Czechoslovakia. Moreover, Great Britain also granted a substantial credit that enabled Yugoslavia to purchase commodities scheduled in the trade agreement. Therefore, the granting of a small amount of compensation to Great Britain by Yugoslavia and Czechoslovakia was due to considerations of finance and trade, and not to the legal obligation to make compensation. The circumstances of Yugoslavia's granting partial compensation to the United States were similar. Since the United States agreed to release $47,000,000 of blocked Yugoslavian gold, Yugoslavia consented to sell $17,000,000 of the gold, and the proceeds were given to the United States as compensation.[o]

(B) The recent resolutions of the various organs of the United Nations indicate that the nationalizing state has no legal obligation to grant compensation to foreigners. The United Nations General Assembly resolution of 21 December 1952 states: "the right of peoples freely to use and exploit their natural wealth and resources is inherent in their sovereignty. . . ." (Resolution 626). Article 1, paragraphs 1 and 2, of the Draft Human Rights Covenants adopted by the Third Committee of the United Nations General Assembly after twenty-nine sessions, states:

[m] Alfred Drucker, "Compensation for Nationalized Property: The British Practice," *AJIL* 49.4:477–486 (Oct. 1955).

[n] According to the calculation in the report of the London "Foreign Compensation Commission," the amount of compensation paid by Yugoslavia to Britain did not reach 18 percent of the amount claimed by British nationals and the amount of compensation paid by Czechoslavakia to Britain did not reach 8 percent of the amount claimed; see Drucker, ["Compensation"], p. 485.

[o] J. E. S. Fawcett, "Some Foreign Effects of Nationalization of Property," *British Year Book of International Law* 27:355, 375 (1950).

> [1] All peoples have the right of self-determination. By virtue of this right they freely determine their political status and freely pursue their economic, social, and cultural development.
>
> [2] The people may, for their own ends, freely dispose of their natural wealth and resources without prejudice to any obligations arising out of international economic cooperation, based upon the principle of mutual benefit and international law." [p]

As peoples have the right, in accordance with sovereignty and the principle of self-determination, freely to pursue their economic development and freely to dispose of their wealth and resources, nationalization is naturally a proper measure. Since Article 1 does not state that the exercise of the right "freely to dispose of their natural wealth and resources" by adopting nationalization measures is contingent upon granting compensation to foreigners, the obligation to compensate aliens is obviously not an existing principle. Obviously, the above-mentioned 1952 resolution of the United Nations General Assembly recommends that all members, in the exercise of their right freely to use and exploit their natural wealth and resources, have due regard, consistent with their sovereignty, to the need for maintaining the flow of capital in conditions of security, mutual confidence, and economic cooperation among nations. But, since the resolution explicitly uses the phrase "to have due regard, consistent with their sovereignty," the nationalizing state still enjoys its sovereign right freely to consider the question whether it will grant compensation to original owners of foreign nationality or, if compensation were to be granted, the amount of compensation.

(C) In public international law, the best treatment foreigners may claim is merely equal treatment with nationals. Their treatment cannot surpass that of nationals; otherwise foreigners would be in a privileged position similar to their position under the consular jurisdiction system and the sovereignty of the state concerned would of necessity be impaired. This principle was confirmed by the report submitted in 1926 by the Committee of Jurists on the codification of international rules concerning the question of state responsibility, which was under the auspices of the League of Nations.[q] In 1928 the Economic Committee of the League of Nations also adopted the principle of equality of treatment of nationals and foreigners in the provisions of Article 11 of the Draft Convention on the Treatment of

[p] See James N. Hyde, "Permanent Sovereignty over Natural Wealth and Resources," *AJIL* 50.4:854–867 (Oct. 1956).

[q] League of Nations Documents, C.46, M.23 (1926); [reprinted in *AJIL*, Supp. 20:177, 182 (1926).]

Foreigners concerning compensation by a state which carries out expropriation or requisition. The Committee states: ". . . foreigners established in a country and enjoying the protection of its laws and the advantages of its administration must share in its burdens on the same footing as nationals, even if those burdens are of an exceptional character and involve sacrifices amounting in certain cases to total or partial deprivation of property." [r] These provisions were approved by the great majority of states at the International Conference on the Treatment of Foreigners held at Paris in 1929.[s] The Committee also expressed the same opinion in its commentary to Article 11 concerning treatment with respect to taxation. . . .

(D) Even in bourgeois countries, deprivation of private property without compensation has occurred repeatedly. For instance, first of all, the abolition of feudal property after the French bourgeois revolution was carried out without any compensation.[t] Second, in 1926 the United States prohibited the manufacture and sale of alcoholic liquor, which resulted in considerable injury to private property rights, but no compensation was granted.[u] Third, in almost all bourgeois states there is very little difference between the result of currency inflation and depreciation and the result caused by nationalization without compensation; yet bourgeois states believe that no claim for compensation can be presented on the ground of the injury done [by inflation] to foreigners.[v] Finally, all bourgeois states recognize that if the tax collected by a state from foreigners is entirely the same as that collected from the state's own nationals and if there is no discrimination, then even if the tax rate is so high that it can hardly be distinguished from nationalization without compensation, there is no room for the foreign state to present a diplomatic claim.[w] Since compensation is not required in these situations, on what ground can it be claimed that compensation must be granted in cases of nationalization?

[r] League of Nations Documents, C.[1] 74, M.53 (1928), II, Commentary p. 29; [Publications of the League of Nations, II. Economic and Financial, 1928, II, 14.]

[s] "Comptes Rendus de la Conférence Internationale sur le Traitement des Étrangers," in League of Nations Documents, C. 97, M. 23, 1930, II, 274.

[t] The Decree of the French National Assembly of 3 November 1789.

[u] See Friedman [*Expropriation*], p. 51.

[v] See Williams, "International Law and the Property of Aliens," pp. 15ff.

[w] Fauchille, *Traité de droit international public,* I, 933.

22-2

Chou Keng-sheng, Ling Ch'i-han, and Ni Cheng-ao, "The Legal Basis for the Nationalization of the Suez Canal Company," *JMJP* (Aug. 13, 1956), p. 5.

The "nationalization" of the Suez Canal Company and the "international character" of the Suez Canal itself are legal questions of categorically different natures. The nationalization of the Canal Company refers to the transformation of the privately operated Canal Company into a state-owned Canal Company by the Egyptian government. The international character of the canal refers to the guarantee of freedom of navigation in the canal subject to the principle of not impairing the sovereignty of the state through whose territory the Canal passes. The former—the nationalization of the Canal Company—is a question of domestic law, while the latter—the international character of the canal—is a question of international law. These two questions must be strictly differentiated. Currently the Western countries have been intentionally confusing these two questions in order to create an internationally tense situation. This is absolutely erroneous.

It should first be pointed out that *nationalization is a question of domestic law and not a question of international law.* Nationalization is absolutely not a new thing. Capitalist countries like Britain, France, the United States, and other countries each have taken nationalization measures. To declare state ownership over an item of private property or to transform a private enterprise into a state enterprise is called "nationalization." This is a sovereign act of a state within its territory and therefore is a question of domestic law and not a question of international law.

Whether nationalization is accompanied by compensation is also a question of domestic law and not a question of international law. But Western countries usually consider that nationalization without compensation or without adequate compensation is not permissible under international law. Therefore, they arbitrarily lump together nationalization, which is within the sphere of domestic law, with international law. In reality, the reason nationalization—essentially an internal affair—may become an international dispute or an international problem is that the object of nationalization includes the interests of foreigners. At present, the announcement by the Egyptian government of the nationalization of the Universal Suez Canal Company is the most obvious example.

We will analyze several questions involving the nationalization of the Suez Canal Company, such as the legal status of the canal, the legal status of the company, and whether the nationalization of the Canal Company will seriously injure shareholders of foreign nationality, and so forth. Then we can reach a clear conclusion as to whether this nationalization measure is legal.

(I) *The Suez Canal is [part of] Egyptian territory.* Scholars of international law in all countries unanimously agree that a canal is a part of the territory of the state of the [canal's] river bed. . . .

(II) *The Suez Canal Company is an Egyptian company and is subject to the jurisdiction of Egyptian law.* A company is a kind of legal person and a legal person must have nationality. The judicial precedents of the European continental countries maintain that the "siège social" indicates the nationality of a company; Anglo-American judicial precedents consider the place of incorporation as indicating the nationality of a company. However, as monopolistic capital in capitalist countries engages in economic expansion, it frequently occurs that "the center of administration or board of directors of a shareholder company, which is established or incorporated in one country is located in another country, and the industrial activities or business is in still a third country. Moreover, the shareholders and leaders of this enterprise are persons of various citizenships or nationalities." (Lunts, *Mezhdunarodonoe chastnoe pravo,* 1949; Chinese version, 1951, p. 175). The Universal Suez Canal Company is a most vivid example of this situation. . . .

(III) *The Egyptian Nationalization Law provides generous arrangements for compensation.* Article 1 of Egyptian Law No. 285 regarding nationalization of the Universal Company of the Suez Maritime Canal [promulgated] on July 26, 1956, provides: "Shareholders and holders of foundation bonds will be compensated for the shares and bonds they possess, at their value estimated at the closing rate on the Paris Bourse prior to the date on which this Law entered into effect. Payment of this compensation shall take place after completion of the handover to the state of all the funds and property of the nationalized company." The par value of the shares are, in accordance with the 1856 Statute, 500 francs per share which in total amount to 400,000 shares at a value of 200,000,000 francs. In 1924, the number of shares was increased to 800,000 shares and the par value of a share proportionately reduced to 250 francs per share. But in accordance with investigation, the exchange price of the shares in the fall of 1951 had increased to 100,000 francs per share. Now the Nationalization Law provides that compensation to shareholders "will be . . . at their [the shares'] value estimated at the closing rate on the

Paris Bourse prior to the date on which this Law entered into effect." It must be pointed out that this closing rate was recorded before the promulgation of the Nationalization Law and was definitely not affected by the nationalization measure. This generous arrangement of compensation should be considered as consistent with the condition, consistently advocated by Britain and France, that nationalization must provide "timely, just, and effective" compensation. If shareholders still disagree, they can appeal to the Egyptian court.

On the basis of the various above-mentioned reasons, this conclusion should be reached: The nationalization of the Universal Suez Canal Company by the Egyptian government is lawful, and the measures promulgated for carrying out nationalization are reasonable.

NOTE

The nationalization of alien property, of course, is only one of many actions that a state may take within its territory that may lead another state to demand satisfaction for alleged violation of international law. Other states have frequently sought to hold the PRC responsible for acts that the Peking regime has viewed as legitimate exercises of its territorial sovereignty and therefore not appropriate instances for state responsibility to be engaged. One example is the PRC's refusal to acknowledge any basis for the United States' protest against the conviction of eleven American fliers and two civilian employees (19–11). Item 22–3 offers another example, and more will be seen in subsequent chapters.

In some instances, however, the PRC has been responsive to the claims of other states. Items 22–4 to 22–8 are illustrative.

22-3

"Vice-Foreign Minister Chang Han-fu Sends Reply to British Representative Trevelyan on Naval Incident," NCNA–English, Peking (Sept. 29, 1953), in *SCMP*, no. 660:11–12 (Sept. 30, 1953).

Chang Han-fu, Vice-Foreign Minister of the Central People's Government of China, today sent a letter to H. Trevelyan, representative for negotiations of the British government, in reply to the latter's letter of September 12 regarding the provocations and attacks against a Chinese naval vessel by British gunboat and aircraft.

On September 9, a gunboat and two "Mosquito" fighter-bombers of Britain sought to provoke and made surprise attacks on a patrol vessel of the Chinese navy sailing on waters within the mouth of the Pearl River southwest of Inner Lin Tin Island and between that island and Houng Chow. They fled only after the Chinese vessel and air defense units on the island fired back in self-defense.

Three days later, however, the British representative for negotiations, H. Trevelyan, sent a letter of protest to Vice-Foreign Minister Chang Han-fu in an attempt to cover up the provocations and attacks by the British gunboat and aircraft on September 9.

The full text of the reply of Vice-Foreign Minister Chang Han-fu to H. Trevelyan reads as follows:

Mr. H. Trevelyan,

Representative for negotiations of the British government.

I have the honor to acknowledge the receipt of your letter Number 213 dated the 12th of September 1953. I am instructed to make the following reply and request that Your Excellency convey it to the British government.

According to confirmed reports received by the Central People's Government of the People's Republic of China, at 14:04 hours (local time) on September 9, a patrol vessel of the navy of the People's Republic of China, while sailing on waters within the mouth of the Pearl River southwest of Inner Lin Tin Island, and between Inner Lin Tin Island and Houng Chow, discovered an armed gunboat, displaying no national flag whatever, sailing towards it. Our patrol vessel then made inquiries through international signals. The gunboat, whose actions were questionable and whose purposes [were] unclear, made no reply and increased its speed of approach. In view of the fact that pirate vessels have long harassed the waters in that locality, the patrol vessel of the navy of the Chinese People's Republic fired three shots into the air, warning the said gunboat to come to a halt. The gunboat not only disregarded the warnings, but, on the contrary, rushed provocatively at the patrol vessel; the patrol vessel of the People's Republic of China again fired two shots into the air to give warning. At that moment, the said questionable gunboat launched a surprise attack upon the patrol vessel of the People's Republic of China, firing more than ten shots at it. Accordingly, the patrol vessel of the People's Republic of China fired back in self-defense. As a result, the intruding gunboat fled southward to the open seas.

It can now be judged from the above-mentioned facts and from the contents of your letter that the said gunboat, which did not display any national flag, which ignored inquiries made through international signals, which disregarded repeated warnings, and which sought to provoke and made a surprise attack upon the patrol vessel of the People's Republic of China, was a gunboat of the British navy.

Again according to reliable reports, at between 14:18 and 15:05 hours on September 9, the two "Mosquito" fighter-bombers, definitely identifiable as belonging to the British government, first dived and strafed at the patrol vessel of the People's Republic of China, which was situated within the mouth of the Pearl River, and then intruded above Inner Lin Tin Island in an attempt to seek provocation. It was only after resisting shots fired by air-defense units on the island that the two airplanes then flew in the direction of Hong Kong.

The facts being as stated above, the Central People's Government is of the opinion that the protest lodged by the British government is unacceptable. The Central People's Government hereby lodges a strong protest with the British government regarding the above-mentioned provocations and surprise attacks by the British navy and the two British "Mosquito" fighter-bombers, and wishes that the British government immediately take necessary measures to prevent the recurrence of such incidents.

I avail myself of this opportunity to express to Your Excellency the assurance of my highest consideration.

Chang Han-fu, Vice-Minister of the Ministry of Foreign Affairs of the Central People's Government of the People's Republic of China.

22-4

"Unexpected Incident at Sino-Nepalese Border Explained," *PR* 3.27:24–25 (July 5, 1960).

When the unexpected incident at the Sino-Nepalese border was reported, the spokesman for the Department of Information of the Chinese Foreign Ministry issued a statement on June 30 saying that the Chinese government was extremely concerned over the news and had immediately instructed the authorities concerned to find out what had actually happened. Upon receiving a report on the incident from the frontier guards in the Ari district of China's Tibet Region, Premier Chou En-lai sent a letter to the Prime Minister of Nepal, B. P. Koirala, on July 2. In his letter, Premier Chou En-lai explained the course of the incident as follows: At 16:45 hours on June 28, a unit of the Chinese People's Liberation Army suppressing Tibetan rebel bandits within our territory near the Sino-Nepalese boundary discovered, at about one kilometre north of the Kore Pass, a group of men with horses advancing towards it. Mistaking them for Tibetan rebel bandits, the Chinese troops opened fire, killing one man, and [capturing] ten (one of whom was wounded). It was then found that they were not Tibetan rebel bandits but were Nepalese. Premier Chou En-lai said that it can be seen from the course of the incident that this was an unfortunate incident resulting entirely from misunderstanding. The incident occurred at a point north of the Kore Pass, and not in the Mustang area in Nepal. And according to the maps exchanged between the Chinese and Nepalese sides in March this year, the Kore Pass lies to the north of the Sino-Nepalese traditional boundary line. Therefore, the place of the incident is clearly within Chinese territory and Chinese troops have not entered the territory of the Kingdom of Nepal.

Nevertheless, Premier Chou En-lai said, this unexpected and unfortunate incident was due to carelessness on the part of certain low-ranking personnel of Chinese troops. The Chinese government expresses deep regret at this, apologizes to His Majesty's Government of Nepal and condoles on the unfortunate dead. The Chinese government has already instructed the troops in the locality to look at once into the responsibility for the incident, and to return the ten Nepalese personnel detained and the dead body, together with the horses of these Nepalese personnel and all articles carried by them, to the Nepalese side on July 4. Premier Chou En-lai also said that the Chinese government is willing to accept the Nepalese side's demand for compensation. He said in his letter that he was convinced that the profound friendship between China and Nepal will by no means be affected by this unexpected incident. He reaffirmed that China will continue to make unceasing efforts, as heretofore, to maintain and develop the traditional friendly relations between China and Nepal.

June 30 Statement

The June 30 statement of the spokesman of the Information Department of the Chinese Foreign Ministry reads as follows [*WCC 1960*, VII (1962), 180–182]:

According to foreign news agency reports of June 29, an incident took place on the Sino-Nepalese border on June 28, in which Chinese troops killed and captured personnel of the Nepalese side. The Chinese government is extremely surprised at the news and greatly concerned over it. It immediately instructed the authorities concerned to find out what actually happened.

Earlier, on June 26, the Chinese government, through Chinese ambassador to India and Nepal, P'an Tzu-li, and the Tibet Bureau of Foreign Affairs, had notified the Nepalese ambassador to India and China, Lieutenant General Daman Shamsher Jung Bahadur Rana, and

Nepalese Consul General in Lhasa, U. B. Basnyat, respectively, the following: "A batch of rebel bandits are carrying out harassments within our territory close to the Sino-Nepalese border. This not only affects local public security, but also hampers the implementation of the Sino-Nepalese agreement on the boundary question. We have decided to send troops to suppress them so as to ensure tranquility on the border between the two countries and so that Sino-Nepalese friendly relations will not be affected thereby. In the course of the suppression, our troops will strictly confine their operations within our territory and will in no case go beyond our own territory. Our side would not cross the border to pursue the rebel bandits if they should flee into Nepalese territory. When the suppression comes to an end, our troops sent for the purpose will at once withdraw from the areas within 20 kilometres on the Chinese side of the boundary. Strictly observing the stipulations of the Sino-Nepalese boundary agreement, our side will neither station troops nor send armed personnel for patrol in these areas." The Nepalese government announced on June 28 that it had received the above notification from the Chinese government.

On learning of reports of the occurrence of an unexpected incident at the Sino-Nepalese border, instructions were at once cabled by the Chinese government at four o'clock in the morning of June 30 to our ambassador to India and Nepal, P'an Tzu-li, and the Tibet Bureau of Foreign Affairs that they respectively convey to Nepalese ambassador to India and China, Lieutenant General Rana, and Nepalese Consul General in Lhasa, U. B. Basnyat, the following: The Chinese government was greatly concerned over this report and had immediately inquired of local authorities as to what had actually happened and would inform the Nepalese government as soon as a report was received.

At ten o'clock on June 30, Premier Chou En-lai received a message from Nepalese Prime Minister, B. P. Koirala, which was forwarded to him through Ambassador P'an Tzu-li by Nara Pratap Thapa, Foreign Secretary of the Nepalese government. In the message, Prime Minister Koirala lodged a protest against the reported killing and capturing of Nepalese personnel by Chinese armed forces at the Chinese-Nepalese border, and demanded immediate release of the captured Nepalese personnel and so on.

Premier Chou En-lai at 21 hours on the same day sent a reply to Prime Minister Koirala saying that the Chinese government was greatly concerned over this news and was inquiring of local authorities as to what had actually happened. He also indicated that if an unfortunate case of Nepalese being killed as mentioned in the Nepalese Prime Minister's message had actually occurred, the Chinese government would express extreme regret and that, if any Nepalese were indeed detained, they would of course be speedily released.

There is traditional friendship between China and Nepal. This year, through the mutual visits between the Prime Ministers of the two countries and the signing of the Sino-Nepalese treaty of peace and friendship and the Sino-Nepalese agreement on the boundary question, friendly relations between the two countries have entered a new stage. The Chinese government is confident that when the truth is revealed after investigation of this unexpected incident on the Sino-Nepalese border, it will certainly be settled appropriately on the basis of the facts and in the spirit of friendship between the two countries. The scheme of the imperialists and foreign reactionaries to make use of this incident to spread slanders, sow discord between China and Nepal, and once more whip up an anti-Chinese campaign will never succeed.

22-5

"Detained Nepalese Handed Over," *PR* 3.28:26 (July 12, 1960).

In accordance with the proposal made by Premier Chou En-lai in his letter to Nepalese Prime Minister B. P. Koirala on July 2, Chinese frontier guards on July 4 at Manitui, 250 metres southeast of the Kore Pass, handed over to the representative sent by the Nepalese side all the ten Nepalese personnel, their horses, and all of their articles, as well as the dead body of a Nepalese, detained in the recent unexpected incident resulting from a misunderstanding which occurred inside Chinese territory at the Sino-Nepalese border.

At 16:40 hours on the 4th, a representative of the Chinese frontier guards met in the locality a representative sent by the Nepalese side and at once handed over one by one to the Nepalese representative the ten Nepalese personnel, a dead body, together with the horses of these Nepalese personnel and all articles carried by them. A receipt in Nepalese was instantly signed by the Nepalese representative. The work of handing over and receiving was completed smoothly at 17:50 hours. In the process of handing over and receiving, both sides more than once expressed wishes for the promotion of friendship between the two countries and harmony along the border.

22-6

"Premier Chou's Letter to Nepalese Prime Minister," *PR* 3.30:26 (July 26, 1960).

On July 12, Premier Chou En-lai again wrote to Nepalese Prime Minister, B. P. Koirala [on the unexpected incident that had occurred on the Sino-Nepalese border on June 28]. In the letter, Premier Chou expressed pleasure in noting that, because both sides had assumed an attitude of friendship and understanding, this unfortunate incident had been dealt with promptly and satisfactorily, and those who sought by every means a chance to undermine the friendship between China and Nepal had failed in their sinister objective. Premier Chou said that, as regards the entry of Chinese troops into Chinese areas close to the Sino-Nepalese boundary to suppress Tibetan rebel bandits, the Chinese government had notified the Nepalese government [of it] beforehand, on June 26. In the notification, the Chinese government especially emphasized that the Chinese troops would under no circumstances cross the boundary to pursue the rebel bandits and that as soon as the task of suppressing them was completed, the Chinese troops would withdraw from the areas within 20 kilometres on the Chinese side of the boundary. This fully shows that the Chinese government respects the agreement on the boundary question and attaches great importance to Sino-Nepalese friendship. After the occurrence of the unexpected incident on the Sino-Nepalese border on June 28, the Chinese government, in order to avoid any recurrence of misunderstanding, ordered Chinese troops, in suppressing Tibetan rebel bandits, not to enter areas within 10 kilometres of the Chinese side of the boundary. It is now estimated that the work of suppressing the bandits would be concluded at the end of July, at which time all Chinese troops would be withdrawn from the areas within 20 kilometres on the Chinese side of the boundary. Premier Chou En-lai said that he noted with pleasure that Prime Minister Koirala in his letter of July 7 had given assurance that armed Tibetan rebel bandits entering Nepalese territory had been and would always be dealt with according to international law. Premier Chou En-lai expressed the conviction that, with the elimination of the Tibetan rebel bandits along the Sino-Nepalese border, tranquility along the two countries' borders would be ensured and [that] the agreement between the two countries on the boundary question [would be] smoothly implemented. Premier Chou En-lai accepted the demand of the Nepalese side for compensation to the value of 50,000 rupees for losses incurred in the incident and indicated that the sum would be remitted to the Nepalese government in the immediate future.

On July 18, Chinese ambassador to India and, concurrently, to Nepal, P'an Tzu-li, wrote to Nara Pratap Thapa, Foreign Secretary of the Nepalese government concerning the compensation and enclosed 50,000 Indian rupees.

22-7

"Note from British Chargé d'Affaires in Peking to PRC," July 24, 1954, *Parliamentary Debates* (Commons) 531:37–38 (1953–1954).

I have been instructed by Her Majesty's Principal Secretary of State for Foreign Affairs to bring the following matter to your attention.

On the morning of 23rd July, a DC4 passenger aircraft of the British company Cathay Pacific Airways, registration No. VRHEU, crashed into the sea near Hainan while on a regular scheduled flight from Bangkok to Hong Kong. The last signal received from the aircraft was an emergency call at 7:45 a.m., Peking time, and it stated that the port engine was on fire. The aircraft was carrying 17 persons, including the crew. Subsequently 10 survivors, including the pilot, were rescued by amphibious aircraft and brought to Hong Kong.

The pilot, who is injured, has now stated that, while flying at 9,000 feet, about 30 miles from Hainan, in position 18 degrees north, 110 degrees east, his copilot drew attention to two cream-coloured, low-wing piston engined fighter aircraft, rather like Japanese-type Zeros with red filled-in markings. These aircraft were on the tail of the passenger aircraft and opened fire, apparently with incendiary bullets, setting two engines on fire. The instrument panel was marked by bullets. The pilot of the passenger aircraft took evasive action as the fighter aircraft followed him and continued firing. He landed in the sea at 160 miles per hour. It seems clear the fighter aircraft which attacked the aircraft VRHEU could only have come from Chinese territory. I have been instructed to protest most strongly against this wanton attack on a British civil aircraft flying on a normal scheduled flight. Her Majesty's Government in the United Kingdom must hold the People's Government of the People's Republic of China responsible for the tragic loss of life and the injuries sustained. Her Majesty's Government reserve the right to claim full compensation.

22-8

"Chang Han-fu Answers Trevelyan on Case of British Aircraft," NCNA–English, Peking (July 26, 1954), in *SCMP*, no. 856:1 (July 27, 1954).

Your note No. 122, dated July 24, 1954, has been received. In respect of the case of a British transport aircraft, I am instructed by the Central People's Government to give an account of the circumstances obtained through investigation as follows, which you are requested to transmit to the British government.

The Chinese people as well as the peoples of the world rejoice at the easing of the international situation through the recent holding of the Geneva Conference and the agreement reached on the restoration of peace in Indochina. Meanwhile, however, aircraft of the remnant Chiang Kai-shek gang in Taiwan have enlarged further their sphere of harassment, covering the coastal areas and islands of China, including Hainan Island, dropped secret agents over China, and practiced piratical interception and robbery of merchant vessels of various nations sailing to China for trade in a desperate attempt to create tension in Asia. Therefore, fighting has frequently taken place over the coastal areas and islands of China.

According to the report received by our military authorities from Hainan Island, on the morning of July 23rd, patrol aircraft of the People's Republic of China, while carrying out patrol duty over Port Yulin of Hainan Island, encountered an aircraft of the Chiang Kai-shek gang in that area, and fighting took place. Upon receiving this report, the government of the People's Republic of China undertook an investigation through various channels, which revealed that the aircraft involved was actually a British-owned transport aircraft, mistaken by our patrol aircraft as an aircraft of the Kuomintang gang on a mission to raid our military base at Port Yulin. The occurrence of this unfortunate incident was indeed entirely accidental.

The Central People's Government of the People's Republic of China expresses its regret at this accidental and unfortunate incident of the British transport aircraft and is taking appropriate measures in dealing with it; it extends its sympathy, concern, and condolences to the dead and injured in this incident and to their relatives; it is willing to give consideration to the payment of appropriate benefit and compensation for the loss of life and property damage involved.

I avail myself of this opportunity to renew to you the assurance of my highest consideration.

NOTE

On July 27, 1954, the British government sent another note to the PRC, which pointed out that the lost airliner had been unarmed and clearly marked as a British aircraft. It asked that the PRC airmen responsible for its loss be punished and that immediate measures be taken against any recurrence of such an action. It also delivered a further protest on July 28 against a PRC warning that any rescue aircraft in the area, other than one already there, would be fired upon. On September 15 the British government presented a claim to Peking for £367,000, which the PRC government accepted as its total liability for all losses sustained through the destruction of the British airliner.

Subsequent parts of this work will offer many examples of PRC efforts to engage the responsibility of other states for alleged wrongs against the PRC and its nationals.

The Exercise of Extraterritorial Jurisdiction

PART VI

Part V dealt with the PRC's exercise of jurisdiction within its territory. Part VI describes the PRC's efforts to assert jurisdiction over and to protect persons and assets outside Chinese territory and to influence events abroad. Part VII will discuss the extent to which the PRC claims immunity from the local jurisdiction for its agents abroad and grants such immunity at home. Treatment of diplomats, consuls, trade representatives, and other agents of international relations will be deferred until then. As a transition to Part VII, at the end of this part we will briefly present PRC views relating to the sovereign immunity from the local jurisdiction of foreign state property.

In view of the fact that most of the claims with which this part is concerned reflect Peking's desire to regulate or protect the activities of Chinese nationals abroad, at the outset we should ascertain its views about the nature of nationality and the proper means for determining Chinese nationality and resolving problems of dual nationality. We will then examine the variety of claims that the PRC has made to regulate and especially to protect its nationals abroad. A final chapter will illustrate the PRC's attempts to influence events and to safeguard interests abroad that do not directly involve the protection of nationals.

Determination of Chinese Nationality

23

"Nationality" as a legal concept was introduced into China in the mid-nineteenth century, together with other aspects of the nation-state system that had crystallized in Europe during preceding centuries.[1] For millennia prior to that time, there had been commercial and diplomatic contacts between China and neighboring lands, and Chinese traders had settled not only in areas contiguous to China but also in areas accessible only by sea. Nevertheless, after the cessation of China's voyages of exploration in the 1430's, Chinese governments showed little interest in protecting Chinese abroad and therefore had less reason than the more dynamic, expansionist Western governments to clarify the criteria for determining the persons over whom authority could be exercised on a nonterritorial basis.

According to the traditional view, Chinese who were so unwise and disloyal as to prefer living among barbarians to remaining in China to tend the ancestral tombs and share the benefits of civilization were unworthy of the protection of the imperial government. Indeed, at various times during the Ch'ing (Manchu) dynasty, the law sought to prevent or discourage Chinese from residing permanently abroad.[2] Confucian disdain for trade reinforced the regime's antipathy toward an emigration that was initially inspired by the lure of commercial gain. When toward the end of the nineteenth century Chinese began to leave their homeland because of political as well as economic discontent, the imperial attitude increasingly reflected distrust as well as disdain. And the fact that some overseas Chinese engaged in piracy, brigandage, and more conventional criminal activity, frequently through secret societies, did nothing to endear them to the Chinese government, not to mention the local authorities.

The official Chinese policy toward emigration and overseas Chinese underwent a significant change in the latter half of the nineteenth century. Shortly after the Opium War (1839–1842), the economic development of Southeast Asia created a need for cheap labor that stimulated a massive influx of peasants from China's populous coastal provinces of Kwangtung and Fukien. A similar situation prevailed in the United States and elsewhere in the western hemisphere. To facilitate Chinese emigration, several foreign powers exerted pressure on the Ch'ing dynasty to lower its barriers. In 1859 the authorities of Kwangtung Province proclaimed that Chinese had a right to leave the country, settle abroad, and return without fear of prosecution.[3] The following year saw the ratification of treaties between the West and China which committed the emperor to command the authorities of every province to proclaim that Chinese "choosing to take service" in British or French colonies or elsewhere were free to make contracts to do so with subjects of those countries.[4] The Burlingame Treaty of 1868 between China and the United States went even further, recognizing "the inherent and inalienable right of man to change his home and allegiance." [5]

As the swelling overseas Chinese communities began to prosper, they gradually attracted the interest of progressive Chinese officials, who recognized not only their economic importance but also the contribution that the more educated overseas Chinese might make to the modernization of China by communicating the principles of Western power that they had learned through experience abroad. Mindful of the Western practice of protecting nationals overseas, beginning in 1868 China undertook to negotiate treaty provisions that authorized her to send consuls abroad to protect overseas subjects, and within a decade she became reconciled to the need actually to station both diplomats and consuls abroad.[6] The establishment of permanent representation in other countries, a historic departure from Chinese tradition, in turn intensified China's awareness of the achievements and the problems of the overseas Chinese.

This awareness was heightened by the spirit of nationalism that began to affect both the Chinese on the mainland and those overseas at the end of the nineteenth century. This spirit of nationalism was fostered by a host of reformers and revolutionaries from the mainland who traveled among the overseas Chinese to organize political support for their programs, the former to modernize the Ch'ing regime and the latter to overthrow it. Although destined to become the first victim of this political awakening, the Ch'ing government sought to control it by sending a series of ad hoc missions to Southeast Asia to win the loyalty of the overseas Chinese. In the Netherlands East Indies, for example, these missions encouraged the local Chinese to set up commercial associations and a cultural association that sought to reconcile Chinese nationalist education with Confucian precepts. The change in the imperial attitude was illustrated by an 1899 edict that spoke of the emigrants' unswerving loyalty to their native country and that instructed ambassadors and consuls to assist and to protect overseas Chinese as much as possible.[7]

As a result of these developments, despite China's evident weakness, overseas Chinese increasingly came to view China as their national protector as well as the native place of their ancestors and the source of their cultural heritage. If we again take the Netherlands East Indies as an example, we find that, by the turn of the century, the large numbers of Chinese there, although better treated than the indigenous people, looked to China to intervene in their behalf with the Netherlands in order to eliminate the humiliating discriminations and restrictions that Chinese suffered in comparison with Europeans and, after 1899, with Japanese. As a means of facilitating their protection, they urgently sought the establishment of Chinese consulates in the Indies, especially after the Netherlands attempted in late 1907 to force the Chinese residing in Java to become Dutch subjects and after it made a consular agreement with Japan in 1908.

One of the arguments put forward by the Dutch in the course of resisting the repeated efforts of the Manchu government to obtain permission to establish consulates in the colony was that China lacked a proper nationality law that could justify her claim to the allegiance of the overseas Chinese.[8] To meet this objection, in 1909 the imperial government promulgated China's first nationality law.[9] According to its draftsmen, it was designed to achieve two purposes: to "set up high qualifications for naturalization so that only desirable aliens should be admitted to Chinese nationality, and . . . to keep natural-born Chinese from falling under foreign dominion." [10] The law not only made it difficult for foreigners to become Chinese subjects but so profound was imperial fear of foreign subversion that it also restricted the right of naturalized persons to serve China in the military or in high public office.[11] The law sought to attain its second purpose by adopting the principle of jus sanguinis as the major basis for obtaining Chinese nationality, providing that a child born of a Chinese father was Chinese, regardless of the country in which the child was born.[12] Moreover, the law provided that no Chinese could divest himself of his nationality without first obtaining government consent, which was to be granted if the petitioner was not involved in litigation and if certain other conditions were fulfilled.[13]

After the fall of the Ch'ing, although details varied, the successive nationality laws that were enacted by Republican governments in 1912, 1914, and 1929 all adopted the principles of the 1909 law summarized above. The 1929 law, which was promulgated by the Nationalist government shortly after its rise to power, was still in effect at the time of the Communist take-over in 1949 and has continued to be enforced by the Nationalist government since its removal to Taiwan.[14]

China's invocation of the principles of jus sanguinis and no denationalization without government consent guaranteed the occurrence of dual nationality problems between China and states that granted nationality to children born within their territory and to persons who met naturalization requirements. With no state were these problems resolved during the four decades from 1909 to the establishment of the People's

Republic. Thus, it was with some trepidation that the states of Southeast Asia awaited the unfolding of the nationality policy of a new, powerful, and revolutionary Chinese government.

The Common Program of the Chinese People's Political Consultative Conference (CPPCC), which on September 29, 1949, proclaimed the establishment of the People's Republic and which served until 1954 as an interim charter of government, declared in its preamble that it had been adopted by representatives of the overseas Chinese as well as representatives of a variety of groups within China.[15] Article 13 provided that overseas Chinese and these other groups would continue to be represented in the CPPCC, "the organizational form of the people's democratic united front," which would serve as an interim national legislature and would establish the organs of state power. Article 58 stated that "The Central People's Government of the People's Republic of China shall do its utmost to protect the proper rights and interests of Chinese residing abroad." But duties were also imposed on Chinese nationals. Article 8 provided: "It is the duty of every national of the People's Republic of China to defend the fatherland, to abide by the law, to observe labour discipline, to protect public property, to perform public and military service, and to pay taxes."

The Constitution of the PRC that was adopted in 1954 by the First National People's Congress contained similar provisions to those of Articles 8 and 58 of the Common Program.[16] Moreover, Article 23 of the Constitution stated that the National People's Congress (NPC) would contain deputies elected by "Chinese resident abroad." Indeed, the electoral law that had been promulgated in 1953 had actually allocated thirty seats in the NPC to deputies who were to be elected by overseas Chinese.[17]

None of these measures should have surprised other states, for they closely resembled provisions enacted by the preceding regime, the Republic of China. It too had pledged to protect the rights and interests of Chinese residing abroad,[18] and had granted them representation in the National Assembly, the Legislative Yüan and the Control Yüan[19] of government. But, unlike the preceding regime, the PRC failed to enact any legislation to define who would be deemed Chinese nationals. The ambiguous wording of Article 17 of the Common Program—that "all of the reactionary Kuomintang government's laws, decrees, and judicial systems that oppress the people shall be abolished"—suggested the possibility that the new regime might recognize the nationality law of 1929 as continuing in effect. But Article 17 was authoritatively interpreted as abolishing the entire body of laws enacted by the Republic of China.[20] Other states were thus quite uncertain about China's attitude toward the overseas Chinese, a group that in 1954, according to the PRC's only official census, comprised 11,743,320 persons.[21] In the absence of Chinese legislation, the only recourse of other states was to scrutinize the PRC's state practice, its policy statements, and any attempts it might make to deal with the situation on an international basis.

How would Peking define Chinese nationality? Would it seek to resolve or to mitigate the long-standing problems of dual nationality? Would it follow the predecessor regime's policy of vigorously urging overseas Chinese to retain their Chinese nationality and to resist integration into the local society?

For the first few years after attaining nationwide power—during the period when they were hopeful of inspiring successful revolutions in a number of neighboring countries—the Communists followed the previous policy of encouraging Chinese nationalism among the overseas Chinese. As the Introduction to this study makes clear, however, by 1954 the PRC had decided to cease overt attempts to undermine the neutralist, anticolonial governments of the new Afro-Asian states and sought instead to gain their support. In accordance with this major change in its foreign policy, the PRC began to alter its views on the overseas Chinese so as to allay the anxieties of China's neighbors.

In his September 23, 1954, report to the First National People's Congress on the work of the government, Premier Chou En-lai, who at the time was also serving concurrently as Foreign Minister, stated:

> For our part, we are willing to urge overseas Chinese to respect the laws of the governments and the social customs of the countries in which they live. It is worth pointing out that the question of the nationality of overseas Chinese is one which the reactionary governments of China in the past never tried to solve. This placed overseas Chinese in a difficult situation and often led to discord between China and the countries concerned. To improve this situation, we are prepared to settle this question, and are ready to settle it first with the Southeast Asian countries which have established diplomatic relations with us.[22]

Shortly thereafter negotiations began between the PRC and the Indonesian government, which was eager to ameliorate a difficult situation in which it found itself torn between the desire to improve relations with Peking and the need to placate a surging tide of nationalist sentiment demanding that discriminatory measures be taken against the economically dominant Chinese minority of approximately 2.5 million persons. These negotiations culminated in the signing of a Sino-Indonesian dual nationality treaty on April 22, 1955, during the Asian-African Conference at Bandung.

Item 23–1 presents the PRC's perception of this background information and its characterization of the significance of the treaty. Item 23–2 is the treaty itself.

23-1

Wang Chi-yuan, "Nationality of Overseas Chinese," *PC*, no. 12:7–9 (June 16, 1955). (Mr. Wang was identified as a member of the Standing Committee of the Peking Returned Overseas Chinese Association.)

There are some 12 million Chinese residing abroad, most of whom live in the countries of Southeast Asia, notably in Malaya, Thailand, Indonesia, Vietnam, and Burma.

As far as we know, Chinese travellers were going to India and the East Indies as long ago as the Later Han dynasty (in the first century A.D.). By the time of the Tang dynasty (618–907), many Chinese had emigrated to other lands.

In the past hundred years the migration has been particularly great. During this century, China's economy all but collapsed under the dual exploitation of imperialism and feudalism, culminating in the reactionary rule of the Kuomintang. Because life was so hard, the people of China's seacoast, especially of Kwangtung and Fukien Provinces, were forced by poverty to seek their living abroad.

Chinese Abroad

China, unlike the capitalist powers, has never used her citizens abroad to turn the countries in which they have settled into colonies. Overseas Chinese and the people among whom they have settled have lived and worked together in peace and friendship. Side by side with the original inhabitants, they have played an important part in the economic development of the countries in which they reside, and a large number of Chinese emigrants have intermarried with people in their new homes and brought up their children there.

Among the Chinese living abroad those who come from China are known as "newcomers" and those born in the countries of their domicile as "overseas-born." Most of the "overseas-born" still lead a Chinese way of life and have relatives in the motherland. But some, whose families have lived abroad for generations, no longer speak Chinese and have few or no ties with China.

In view of these circumstances, the question of the nationality of the overseas Chinese should have been reasonably settled long ago. But the Western colonial powers did not do this. Ignoring the fact most foreign-born Chinese still retain their own customs and way of life, speak Chinese and are closely connected with their motherland, they made arbitrary provisions with regard to their nationality. These provisions were not made in the interests of the overseas Chinese but for greater convenience in exploiting and suppressing them.

The Question of Dual Nationality

By British law, for instance, all overseas Chinese born in Great Britain, its colonies, and ships under British flags, and all, whatever their place of birth, whose grandfathers and fathers were born on British territory, are considered "British subjects" or "citizens of the British Commonwealth of Nations." The Netherlands, during their rule over Indonesia, issued a decree in 1910 on the position of Dutch subjects which provided that all natives of Dutch colonies and nonnatives born there were "Dutch subjects." Similar arbitrary determination of the nationality of foreign-born Chinese was made by governments of some countries in Southeast Asia.

The traditional practice of the Nationality Law of China was based on jus sanguinis, that is, every descendant of Chinese nationals, irrespective of place of birth and of residence, was considered to be of Chinese nationality. Hence the problem of nationality of Chinese born abroad has become an outstanding issue.

A reasonable solution of the question could be found only by diplomatic negotiations between the governments concerned. Any attempt to settle it by one-sided decisions would naturally tend to injure diplomatic relations between that country and China. The Chinese people and the majority of the overseas Chinese would never consent to it. When the decree on the position of Dutch subjects was issued, the overseas Chinese affected declared that they would never accept it.

Under the reactionary rule of the Manchu dynasty and the Kuomintang [government] China was a semicolony, and its governments cared very little about the interests and aspirations of overseas Chinese. This is why the question of their double nationality remained unsettled for so long.

The Sino-Indonesian Treaty

After the Chinese people took power into their own hands, the government of the People's Republic of China gave its attention to this question. Only then was it possible to reach a just and reasonable settlement. On April 22, 1955, after six months of friendly negotiations, a treaty on the question of dual nationality was signed between the People's Republic of China and the Republic of Indonesia. . . .

Since the founding of our People's Republic, Chinese residing abroad have been urged to respect the laws and customs of the countries where they live and not to take part in the political activities of these countries. This is in line with the firm Chinese policy of opposing outside intervention and forbidding interference in the internal affairs of other countries. The embodiment of this principle in the Treaty is another blow at the slander that China might conduct "subversive activities" abroad through the dual nationality of overseas Chinese.

A Contribution to Peace

The significance of this treaty between China and the Republic of Indonesia extends much further.

The signing of the Treaty is a victory of the will to seek common ground in international relations, of the spirit that prevailed at the Asian-African Conference held at Bandung last April. It represents the putting into practice of the five principles of peaceful coexistence and is a model for the settlement of international disputes by peaceful negotiations. It goes to prove that any difference between nations can be reasonably settled by peaceful negotiation if the will to friendly cooperation exists. Such reasonable settlement of the question of dual nationality is in the interests of the overseas Chinese, and at the same time helps to promote friendship between the peoples of China and Indonesia and the development of good-neighbourly relations between them. Above all, it is an important contribution to the cause of peace in Asia and the world.

The signing of this treaty has set a precedent for the settlement of the dual nationality question between China and other countries in Southeast Asia. The Chinese government is ready to settle it with other governments concerned, first of all with those which have diplomatic relations with the Chinese government.

China's position in this matter is clear. It should serve to remove all apprehensions inherited from history or arising from exterior influences. It is to be hoped that it will lead to the settlement of this question between China and other countries concerned.

23-2

"Sino-Indonesian Treaty on Dual Nationality, April 22, 1955," *TYC 1959*, VIII (1960), 12–17; English translation in NCNA–English, Peking (Apr. 25, 1955), in *CB*, no. 326:1–4 (Apr. 27, 1955).

The Government of the People's Republic of China and the Government of the Republic of Indonesia,

In order to achieve a reasonable solution [to] the [problem] of the nationality of persons who hold simultaneously the nationality of the People's Republic of China and the nationality of the Republic of Indonesia,

Have agreed to conclude the present treaty in accordance with the principles of equality and mutual benefit and noninterference in each other's internal affairs and on the basis of friendly cooperation, and

Have appointed as their respective plenipotentiaries: the Government of the People's Republic of China, Minister for Foreign Affairs of the People's Republic of China, Chou En-lai; the Government of the Republic of Indonesia, Minister for Foreign Affairs of the Republic of Indonesia, Sunarjo.

The plenipotentiaries of both parties, after having examined each other's credentials and found them in good and due order, have agreed upon the following provisions:

Article I

The high Contracting Parties agree that all persons who hold simultaneously the nationality of the People's Republic of China and the nationality of the Republic of Indonesia shall choose, in accordance with their own will, between the nationality of the People's Republic of China and the nationality of the Republic of Indonesia. All married women who hold the above-mentioned two nationalities shall also choose, in accordance with their own will, between the two nationalities.

Article II

All persons who hold the two nationalities mentioned in Article I and who have come of age when the present treaty comes into effect, shall choose their nationality within two years of the coming into effect of the present treaty. For the purpose of this treaty, persons who have come of age are understood to be persons who have attained the age of 18 years and married persons under the age of 18 years.

Article III

Any person holding the two nationalities mentioned in Article I [and] desiring to retain the nationality of the People's Republic of China must declare before the appropriate authorities of the People's Republic of China that he or she renounces the nationality of the Republic of Indonesia, and shall after such declaration, be considered as having chosen voluntarily the nationality of the People's Republic of China. Any person holding the two nationalities mentioned in Article I desiring to retain the nationality of the Republic of Indonesia [must declare] before the appropriate authorities of the Republic of Indonesia that he or she renounces the nationality of the People's Republic of China, and shall, after such declaration, be considered as having chosen voluntarily the nationality of the Republic of Indonesia. The above-mentioned appropriate authorities of the People's Republic of China are as follows: in the People's Republic of China, government organs designated by the government of the People's Republic of China; in the Republic of Indonesia, the embassy of the People's Republic of China in the Republic of Indonesia, the consulates of the People's Republic of China in the Republic of Indonesia, and such temporary offices established by the above-mentioned embassy or consulates as necessary and with the consent of the government of the Republic of Indonesia. The above-mentioned appropriate authorities of the Republic of Indonesia are as follows: in the Republic of Indonesia, government organs designated by the government of the Republic of Indonesia; in the People's Republic of China, the embassy of the Republic of Indonesia in the People's Republic of China, the consulates of the Republic of Indonesia in the People's Republic of China, if there be any, and such temporary offices established by the above-mentioned embassy or consulates as necessary and with the consent of the government of the People's Republic of China.

In order to facilitate the choosing of their nationality by persons holding the two nationalities mentioned in Article I, the high Contracting Parties agree to adopt a convenient method for the said declaration. The method of choosing nationalities as stipulated in this article also applies in principle to those persons who reside in places outside the territories of the People's Republic of China and the Republic of Indonesia and who hold the two nationalities mentioned in Article I.

Article IV

The high Contracting Parties agree that any person holding the two nationalities mentioned in Article I shall automatically lose the nationality of the Republic of Indonesia upon choosing, in accordance with the provisions of this treaty, the nationality of the People's Republic of China; and that any person holding the two nationalities mentioned in Article I shall automatically lose the nationality of the People's Republic of China upon choosing, in accordance with the provisions of this treaty, the nationality of the Republic of Indonesia.

Article V

The high Contracting Parties agree that the nationality of those persons who hold the two nationalities mentioned in Article I and who fail to choose their nationality within the period of two years prescribed in Article II shall be determined in the following manner: if their fathers are of Chinese origin, they shall be considered as having chosen the nationality of the People's Republic of China; if their fathers are of Indonesian origin, they shall be considered as having chosen the nationality of the Republic of Indonesia. The nationality of those of the above-mentioned persons who fail to choose their nationality within the prescribed period and who have no legal relationship with their fathers or whose father's nationality is unascertainable, shall be determined in the following manner: if their mothers are of Chinese origin, they shall be considered as having chosen the nationality of the People's Republic of China; if their mothers are of Indonesian origin, they shall be considered as having chosen the nationality of the Republic of Indonesia.

Article VI

All those persons who hold the two nationalities mentioned in Article I and who have not come of age when the present treaty comes into effect shall choose their nationality within a year of their coming of age. Pending their coming of age, they shall be considered as only holding the nationality chosen by their parents or their fathers in accordance with the provisions of the present treaty. In case they have no legal relationship with their fathers or their fathers have died without choosing a nationality or their father's nationality is unascertainable, those persons shall, pending their coming of age, be considered as only holding the nationality chosen by their mothers in accordance with the provisions of the present treaty. If they fail to choose their nationality within the period prescribed in this article after their coming of age, they shall be considered as having chosen voluntarily the nationality held by them before they come of age.

Article VII

All those persons holding the two nationalities mentioned in Article I who, after having chosen the nationality of the Republic of Indonesia and lost the nationality of the People's Republic of China, leave the Republic of Indonesia and take up permanent residence outside its territory shall automatically lose the nationality of the Republic of Indonesia if they regain, in accordance with their own will, the nationality of the People's Republic of China. All those persons holding the two nationalities mentioned in Article I who, after having chosen the nationality of the People's Republic of China and lost the nationality of the Republic of Indonesia, leave the People's Republic of China and take up permanent residence outside its territory shall automatically lose the nationality of the People's Republic of China if they regain, in accordance with their own will, the nationality of the Republic of Indonesia.

Article VIII

All children born in the Republic of Indonesia acquire, upon their birth, the nationality of the People's Republic of China if both their parents or only their fathers hold the nationality of the People's Republic of China; all children born in the People's Republic of China, acquire, upon their birth, the nationality of the Republic of Indonesia if both their parents or only their fathers hold the nationality of the Republic of Indonesia.

Article IX

Any child holding the nationality of the People's Republic of China, if legally adopted by a citizen of the Republic of Indonesia before attaining five years of age, acquires the nationality of the Republic of Indonesia and automatically loses the nationality of the People's Republic of China; any child holding the nationality of the Republic of Indonesia, if legally adopted by a citizen of the People's Republic of China before attaining five years of age, acquires the nationality of the People's Republic of China and automatically loses the nationality of the Republic of Indonesia.

Article X

In the case of a citizen of the People's Republic of China marrying a citizen of the Republic of Indonesia, each party retains after their marriage his or her original nationality. However, if one party applies for and acquires the nationality of the other party in accordance with his or her own will, he or she shall automatically lose his or her original nationality upon acquiring the nationality of the other party. The said applications shall be made to the appropriate authorities of the country concerned.

Article XI

With a view to improving the conditions under which citizens of one country reside in the other, each high Contracting Party agrees to encourage its own citizens residing in the other country, that is citizens of the Republic of Indonesia residing in the People's Republic of China and citizens of the People's Republic of China residing in the Republic of Indonesia, to respect the laws and social customs of the country in which they reside and not to take part in political activities of that country. Each high Contracting Party affirms its willingness to protect according to its laws the proper rights and interests of the citizens of the other party residing in its territory.

Article XII

The high Contracting Parties agree that matters relating to the implementation of the present treaty which are not provided for in this treaty may be decided upon through negotiations between the two parties.

Article XIII

Should disputes arise between the high Contracting Parties over the interpretation or implementation of the present treaty, the two parties will settle such disputes through negotiations.

Article XIV

The present treaty shall be ratified by the high Contracting Parties in accordance with their respective constitutional procedures and shall come into effect upon the date of the exchange of ratifications, which shall take place in Peking. The present treaty shall be valid for 20 years and shall remain in force thereafter. If, after the expiration of the period of 20 years, one party requests its termination, it must so notify the other party one year in advance and in written form; and the present treaty shall be terminated one year after the tendering of such notification.

In faith whereof, the plenipotentiaries of the high Contracting Parties put seals and signatures thereon. Done in Bandung on the 22nd day of April, 1955, in duplicate in the Chinese and Indonesian languages, both texts being equally authentic.

NOTE

In commenting on the substance of the treaty, Wang Chi-yuan, the author of item 23–1, went on to state:

> Many notable features can be found in the Treaty. Among them is the principle of choice of nationality at one's own free will for men and women alike. Moreover, both men and women have the right and freedom to retain their original nationality after marriage. . . .
>
> [Article VIII] reflects the new equality between two sovereign and independent countries. It is in sharp contrast with the one-sided provisions of the Western colonial powers and of the governments of some countries in Southeast Asia regarding the nationality of foreign-born Chinese.[23]

Another article in a Chinese journal sought to explain the meaning of dual nationality:

> Simply speaking, a person's nationality is the qualification of becoming a member of the people of a certain state, that is to say, the qualification for becoming a citizen of this state. Who can become a citizen of a state is prescribed by the municipal law of that state. Because of the different prescriptions in the municipal law of various states, a person from one state who resides in another state may easily acquire two or more nationalities. For instance, the British-born son and daughter of German parents are regarded as British in accordance with British municipal law. They are regarded as German in accordance with German municipal law. A person with two nationalities is called a dual national, and a person with more than two nationalities is called a multiple national.[24]

Reactions to the treaty were much less bland in Indonesia, where it provoked a major controversy. Especially offensive to many persons of Chinese descent who had long since come to regard themselves as Indonesians was the provision requiring them once again to undergo the painful process of opting for Indonesian citizenship, with the consequent uncertainties to which their status would be subjected during the two-year option period.[25] Moreover, the treaty appeared to be vague about the implications of its termination provisions. Item 23–3 constituted an effort to meet these objections.

23-3

"Note from Mr. Chou En-lai to Dr. Sastroamidjojo on the Dual Nationality Treaty," June 3, 1955, NCNA–English, Peking (June 15, 1955) in *SCMP*, no. 1070:20–21 (June 16, 1955).

On April 22, 1955, the People's Republic of China and the Republic of Indonesia signed the Treaty on the Question of Dual Nationality. During Your Excellency's visit to the People's Republic of China, our two governments further exchanged views fully in Peking on the purpose and the method of implementation of this treaty and have come to an understanding which I now confirm as follows:

ONE. The purpose of the above-mentioned treaty on dual nationality is to solve the question of dual nationality between the People's Republic of China and the Republic of Indonesia, a question which we inherited from the past and the settling of which is in conformity with the interests of the peoples of both countries. To achieve the above-mentioned purpose, the two governments agree to take all necessary measures and provide all facilities while implementing the above-mentioned treaty so that all persons holding dual nationality can choose their nationality according to their own will.

TWO. The government of the People's Republic of China and the government of the Republic of Indonesia agree that, among those persons who hold simultaneously the nationality of the Republic of Indonesia and that of the People's Republic of China, there is a category of persons who can be considered as holding only one nationality and not holding dual nationality because, according to the opinion of the government of the Republic of Indonesia, their social and political status testifies that they have already implicitly renounced the nationality of the People's Republic of China.

Persons belonging to the category mentioned above, since they hold only one nationality, are not required to make their choice of nationality in accordance with the provisions of the treaty on dual nationality.

If so desired, a certificate to that effect can be issued to such persons.

THREE. To eliminate any misunderstanding with regard to the provision of the 20-year period of validity in Article 14 of the above-mentioned treaty on dual nationality, the two governments agree to the following interpretation: those persons who have once chosen their nationality in accordance with the above-mentioned treaty are not required to choose it again after the expiration of the period of 20 years.

FOUR. In order that the above-mentioned treaty shall be implemented satisfactorily, the two governments agree to set up in Djakarta a joint committee composed of representatives of the Republic of Indonesia and of the People's Republic of China. The function of the joint committee is to discuss and work out the methods of implementation of the above-mentioned treaty on dual nationality.

FIVE. Prior to the expiration period of two years provided for the choosing of nationality, the present status of persons holding dual nationality should remain unchanged until they have made their choice of nationality in accordance with the provisions of the above-mentioned treaty.

If the above points receive Your Excellency's confirmation, the present note and your reply shall form an understanding arrived at between the government of the Republic of Indonesia and the government of the People's Republic of China on the implementation of the question of dual nationality and should come into effect at the same time as the above-mentioned treaty.

NOTE

The exchange of notes mollified the Indonesian Chinese only to a modest extent, and considerable doubt remained about its actual implementation. Furthermore, important segments of the indigenous Indonesian population were becoming increasingly concerned that the exchange of notes made it easier for Chinese of questionable loyalty to become Indonesian nationals. Because of the continuing controversy over the treaty and because of the vicissitudes of Indonesian internal politics, some of which related to a new Indonesian nationality bill that was being considered in tandem with the treaty, the treaty was not ratified by Indonesia until December 17, 1957. When the Standing Committee of the PRC's National People's Congress granted its ratification shortly thereafter, it was expected that exchange of ratifications would soon take place and that the treaty would then go into effect. But ratifications were not exchanged until January 20, 1960, more than two years later. In part the delay was caused by the PRC's dissatisfaction at the manner in which Indonesia unilaterally undertook to implement the provisions for identifying those persons of Chinese descent who were to be exempted from the option provision.[26] The fact that in 1958 and 1959 the Indonesian government greatly intensified its discriminatory measures against persons of Chinese ancestry also undoubtedly contributed to the delay.[27]

After Foreign Minister Ch'en Yi's vigorous protests in late 1959 against new Indonesian regulations providing for an all-Indonesian committee to determine the scope of the exemption,[28] Indonesia agreed to establishment of a Sino-Indonesian Joint Committee to negotiate the difficult questions of detail relating to the definition of dual nationality and the procedures for option. Item 23–4 was the product of negotiations that lasted from January 25 to October 19, 1960.[29] And item 23–5 represented the PRC's response to inquiries from its public security officials about the procedures to be followed by dual nationals residing in China who wished to opt for Chinese nationality under the treaty.

23-4

"Arrangement for the Implementation of the Treaty Concerning the Question of Dual Nationality," signed in Djakarta, December 15, 1960, *PR* 3.52: 9–12 (Dec. 27, 1960).

Preamble

The government of the People's Republic of China and the government of the Republic of Indonesia, in the spirit of friendly consultation and in accordance with the principles of equality and mutual benefit and noninterference in each other's internal affairs, hereby implement the Treaty Concerning the Question of Dual Nationality and consider this to be in the interests of the peoples of the two countries.

Both Parties agree to take all necessary measures and provide all facilities to make it possible for all persons holding dual nationality to choose their nationality according to their own will.

For this purpose, the two Parties have, on the basis of the provisions of the Treaty Between the People's Republic of China and the Republic of Indonesia Concerning the Question of Dual Nationality signed on April 22, 1955, and of the notes exchanged between the Prime Ministers of the two countries on June 3, 1955, made the following Arrangement for the Implementation of the Treaty Concerning the Question of Dual Nationality:

Chapter One
Scope of Persons to Choose Nationality

ARTICLE I

1. According to the provisions of the Treaty Concerning the Question of Dual Nationality, those entitled to declare their choice of the nationality of the People's Republic of China and their renunciation of that of the Republic of Indonesia or their choice of the nationality of the Republic of Indonesia and their renunciation of that of the People's Republic of China are persons who, at the time when the Treaty comes into force, hold simultaneously the nationality of the People's Republic of China according to the laws of the People's Republic of China and the nationality of the Republic of Indonesia according to the laws of the Republic of Indonesia.

2. The two Parties agree that, in accordance with the principle of respect for one's own will, those who had not come of age between December 27, 1949, and December 27, 1951, and had renounced their nationality of the Republic of Indonesia along with their parents or had it renounced by their parents on their behalf are considered as still holding dual nationality and consequently enjoying the right to choose their nationality.

ARTICLE II

1. Among those who hold simultaneously the nationality of the People's Republic of China and the nationality of the Republic of Indonesia, one category of persons are considered as having already implicitly renounced the nationality of the People's Republic of China and holding only the nationality of the Republic of Indonesia.

2. The scope of the category of persons referred to above in Paragraph 1 shall be determined by the government of the Republic of Indonesia which will provide a list of names of such persons to the government of the People's Republic of China for its information.

3. [Those citizens of the Republic of Indonesia of Chinese origin, who are proved by certificates issued by the Indonesian Election Committees or other evidence to have taken part in elections of the All-Indonesia People's Congress or local people's congresses, shall be added to the categories of those who are considered as unquestionably possessing only the nationality of the Republic of Indonesia according to the laws of the Republic of Indonesia.]

Chapter Two
Organs Receiving Declarations on the Choice of Nationality

ARTICLE III

Any of the persons referred to in Article I of the present Arrangement desiring to retain the nationality of the People's Republic of China must declare his renunciation of the nationality of the Republic of Indonesia before the following organs:

1. In the People's Republic of China: the Public Security Bureaus of the counties (or cities) where the declarants reside;

2. In the Republic of Indonesia: the embassy, consulate-general, and consulates of the People's Republic of China in the Republic of Indonesia and the temporary offices established by them;

3. In places outside the territories of the People's Republic of China and the Republic of Indonesia: the diplomatic or consular missions of the People's Republic of China stationed there or nearby.

ARTICLE IV

Any of the persons referred to in Article I of the present Arrangement desiring to retain the nationality of the Republic of Indonesia must declare his renunciation of the nationality of the People's Republic of China before the following organs:

1. In the Republic of Indonesia: judges of the local courts of the administrative districts where the declarants reside;

2. In the People's Republic of China: the embassy and consulate of the Republic of Indonesia in the People's Republic of China and the temporary offices established by them;

3. In places outside the territories of the Republic of Indonesia and the People's Republic of China: the diplomatic or consular missions of the Republic of Indonesia stationed there or nearby.

ARTICLE V

The temporary offices of the People's Republic of China and the Republic of Indonesia shall, on the basis of equality and reciprocity, enjoy proper protection and all facilities in carrying out their tasks; the personnel of the temporary offices shall, according to their status, enjoy the immunities and privileges due to similar personnel of the embassy or consulate.

ARTICLE VI

The number and location of the temporary offices to be established by the People's Republic of China and the Republic of Indonesia shall be specifically discussed by the Joint Committee and approved by the governments of both Parties before their establishment, in the light of the number and distribution of persons simultaneously holding the nationality of the People's Republic of China and that of the Republic of Indonesia and in accordance with the principle of facilitating their fulfillment of the procedure of declaration on the choice of nationality.

Chapter Three Procedure for the Choice of Nationality

ARTICLE VII

Declarations on the choice of nationality made by persons referred to in Article I of the present Arrangement within two years after the coming into force of the Treaty Concerning the Question of Dual Nationality shall be valid. Declarations may be made orally or in writing. The procedure of declaration may be fulfilled by the declarant personally at an organ receiving such declarations or by mail. In fulfilling the procedure of declaration on the choice of nationality, the declarant may also receive the assistance of local public organizations concerned.

ARTICLE VIII

In fulfilling the procedure of declaration, persons referred to in Article I of the present Arrangement shall fill in a simple form of declaration. The organs receiving declarations shall provide the declarants with every assistance and facilities. No taxes or fees shall be imposed on the procedure of declaration.

ARTICLE IX

1. After receipt of the form of declaration, the organ receiving declarations shall, as quickly as possible (not exceeding three months at the most), sign and stamp it and return a copy of the form to the declarant as his certificate of nationality. The organ receiving declarations may, if it deems it necessary, ask the declarant to furnish evidence of his holding two nationalities; if the evidence furnished by the de-

clarant is accepted, the date on which he first submits his form of declaration shall be counted as the date of declaration.

2. Detailed administrative and technical regulations concerning declaration on retaining the nationality of the People's Republic of China and renouncing that of the Republic of Indonesia, or on retaining the nationality of the Republic of Indonesia and renouncing that of the People's Republic of China may be laid down, made public, and implemented by the governments of the two countries respectively, so far as those regulations are not in conflict with the relevant provisions of the Treaty Concerning the Question of Dual Nationality, the notes exchanged between the Prime Ministers of the two countries, and the present Arrangement.

ARTICLE X

1. If the organ receiving declarations considers that a declarant is not within the scope of persons referred to in Article I of the present Arrangement, it shall reply in writing to the declarant explaining the reasons and reject his declaration.

2. The declarant, however, is entitled to apply to the Joint Committee for an examination of his case. If the Joint Committee considers the case well grounded, it shall forward the same to the government concerned and suggest that the rejection be reexamined and the case be dealt with anew.

ARTICLE XI

Declaration on the choice of nationality by persons referred to in Article I of the present Arrangement shall be free from any interference or obstruction which will affect his choice of nationality according to his own will. Should such a situation occur, the Joint Committee shall recommend that the government of the country concerned adopt effective measures to stop it.

Final Provisions

ARTICLE XII

Questions requiring specific discussion, that is, other matters concerning dual nationality not provided for in the present Arrangement, shall be settled by the Joint Committee through consultation, and supplementary arrangement made public by it.

ARTICLE XIII

The present Arrangement shall come into force the date of its publication.

Done in Djakarta on the fifteenth day of December 1960, in duplicate in the Chinese and Indonesian languages, both texts being equally authentic.

23-5

"Ministry of Public Security Rules for the Declaration of Choice of the Nationality of the PRC by Persons Possessing the Nationality of Both the PRC and the Republic of Indonesia," promulgated April 25, 1961, *FKHP 1960–1961*, XII, 35–36.

1. In accordance with the relevant provisions made in the Arrangement between the government of the People's Republic of China and the government of the Republic of Indonesia for the implementation of the Treaty Concerning the Question of Dual Nationality (hereinafter referred to as "the Arrangement," for short), all those who hold simultaneously the nationality of the People's Republic of China and the nationality of the Republic of Indonesia shall choose between the two said nationalities as they wish.

Persons declaring their choice of the nationality of the People's Republic of China should go through declaration formalities with such offices as may have been designated by the government of the People's Republic of China for this purpose, within the period specified in the Treaty. In the People's Republic of China, such offices are the bureau of public security of the counties (or municipalities) where the declarants reside.

2. Declarants must complete in triplicate and return a "Form of Declaration on the Choice of the Nationality of the People's Republic of China by Holders of the Nationality of Both the People's Republic of China and the Republic of Indonesia," and submit three two-inch photographs showing their faces. When proceeding with declaration formalities, they may do so either by contacting the offices concerned in person or through correspondence. Oral declarants, if they have difficulty in completing declaration forms, may ask the offices concerned for assistance in doing so.

3. When deemed necessary by the offices receiving their declarations, declarants should provide proof of their status as holders of dual nationality.

4. Minors holding dual nationality are not required to go through formalities of declaration on the choice of nationality separately. They may be included in the declaration forms of their fathers, or, in the event of there being no legal relations between them and their fathers, or where their fathers die before choosing either nationality, or where the nationality of their fathers is obscure, in the declaration forms of their mothers.

5. Declarants are not required to pay any fee in going through formalities of declaration on the choice of nationality.

6. If, after receiving and considering their declaration forms, offices designated for this purpose are satisfied that the declarants are among those specified in the first article of the Arrangement, they should, as soon as possible (in any case not later than three months), sign and stamp the said forms and return a copy thereof to the declarants as proof of their nationality.

Note

The exchange of ratifications of the dual nationality treaty at the beginning of 1960 and the successful negotiation of the implementation Arrangement by the end of that year marked a gradual improvement in Sino-Indonesian relations. Although the Arrangement formula made it possible for many more Chinese to opt for Indonesian nationality than could have done so under the unilateral Indonesian formula and although the Chinese embassy and local Chinese organizations sought to facilitate the choice of Indonesian nationality, fewer dual nationals opted for that choice than had been anticipated.[30] As of 1968, official Indonesian estimates reported that only half of the approximately 3 million persons of Chinese origin were regarded as Indonesian nationals; one estimate claimed, however, that only 100,000 of the 1.5 million Chinese nationals had passports of the PRC.[31]

The dramatic deterioration in Sino-Indonesian relations that followed the abortive Communist coup of September 30, 1965, and the widespread suspicion of Peking's alleged involvement in it lent renewed momentum to anti-Communist and anti-Chinese feelings in Indonesia. This led to increasing popular pressure to abrogate the treaty.[32] Renewed animosity against the Chinese minority stimulated an increasing demand for Indonesian citizenship among persons of Chinese descent who feared that further sanctions would be imposed upon Chinese aliens. Many claimed recently to have come of age and therefore to be eligible to exercise the right of option provided by Article VI of the treaty. This sudden rush for citizenship, combined with charges of bribery and of fraud regarding birth dates, added grist to the mill of those favoring abrogation.[33] After a considerable period of hesitation, Indonesia did unilaterally abrogate the treaty on April 10, 1969.[34] For the PRC's view of Indonesia's abrogation, see item 35–8.

Because the Sino-Indonesian Dual Nationality Treaty of 1955 did not actually go into effect until 1960, it was not the PRC's first international commitment relating to dual nationality. An exchange of notes between Nepal and China, dated September 20, 1956, provided:

> The two Parties agree that any person residing in the Tibet Region of China born of parents holding respectively the nationality of the People's Republic of China and the nationality of the Kingdom of Nepal and of eighteen years of age or above, may, according to their own will, choose the nationality of the People's Republic of China for themselves and their children who are under the age of eighteen, by completing relevant procedures at the Chinese government. After the completion [of] the above-mentioned procedures, they and their children under the age of eighteen shall be considered to have lost automatically the nationality of Nepal.[35]

A commentator has pointed out that "this agreement purports only to solve the problem of persons with dual nationality residing in Chinese territory." [36]

A few weeks later Premier Chou En-lai was reported to have laid down the following principles concerning the Chinese in Singapore:

> (1) The Chinese government wishes to see the Chinese in Singapore acquire Singapore citizenship as they themselves so wish, and give exclusive loyalty to the land where they live. The Chinese government believes that this is conducive to the welfare of those Chinese themselves, to the stability and peace of Singapore, and to the development of friendly relations between China and Singapore.
>
> (2) Any Chinese residing in Singapore who voluntarily adopts Singapore citizenship immediately ceases to have Chinese citizenship though, of course, his inherent racial and cultural affinity remains.
>
> (3) Any Chinese who has acquired Singapore citizenship may, if he wishes, adopt Chinese citizenship after relinquishing Singapore citizenship in accordance with the laws of Singapore.
>
> (4) People with Chinese citizenship should respect the laws and decrees of the local government and refrain from taking part in local political activities. But their proper rights and interests should be respected and not subjected to discrimination.

> The Premier said that, after Singapore has attained full independence, the Chinese government will be ready to affirm the above principles in legal form with the Singapore government through negotiation.[37]

Chou En-lai made similar statements shortly thereafter in both Burma and Cambodia.[38] In 1957 a Chinese writer offered a scholarly elaboration of his government's evolving position. Item 23–6 presents useful excerpts.

23-6

Liu Chia-chi, "On the Question of Dual Nationality," *FH*, no. 3:20, 22–24 (1957).

How should the question of dual nationality be solved? . . . The solution adopted by bourgeois countries disregards the principle of national self-determination and is unilaterally compulsory in nature. For example, in 1930 the Conference on Codification of International Law held under the auspices of the League of Nations adopted the "Convention on Certain Questions Relating to Conflict of Nationality." The essentials of the Convention are as follows: (1) A state "may not afford diplomatic protection to one of its nationals against a state whose nationality such person also possesses" (Article 4). (2) A person with dual nationality ["]who habitually resides in one of the countries whose nationality he possesses, and who is in fact most closely connected with that country, shall be exempt from all military obligations in the other country.["] This exemption may involve his loss of the nationality of the other country ("Protocol on Military Obligations in Certain Cases of Double Nationality" annexed to the Convention).

The Soviet Union does not adhere to the above-quoted 1930 Nationality Convention. The Convention was not even accepted by the great majority of capitalist countries. The fact that Article 4 of the Convention unilaterally provided that a country shall not protect a person with dual nationality and nevertheless failed to grant him the right to choose one of the two nationalities amounts to depriving the person with dual nationality of his free will. The consequence is that, until the question of dual nationality is solved, the person with dual nationality is placed in a situation in which no country can protect him.

Socialist countries, on the one hand, do not allow the continuation of dual nationality, and, on the other hand, take into consideration the free will of the person possessing dual nationality. . . .

The principle of option [choice of nationality] is the fundamental principle of our country for solving the question of dual nationality. . . .

Does the principle of option have any basis in international law? The principle of option is similar to the system of "plebiscite" in international law; both represent the way to implement national sovereignty by the people. Article 1, paragraph 2, of the United Nations Charter provides that [the purposes of the United Nations are] "to develop friendly relations among nations based on respect for the principle of equal rights and self-determination of peoples." The principle of option, on the one hand, enables the person with dual nationality to decide for himself to which country he wishes to belong and, on the other hand, removes the pretext of imperialist countries to undermine friendly international relations. This principle is also consistent with the Preamble and Article 1 of the Draft Covenant on Human Rights adopted by the tenth session of the General Assembly in 1955. [Article 1] provides: "[1.] All people have the right of self-determination. By virtue of this right they freely determine their political status and freely pursue their economic, social, and cultural development."

NOTE

The above excerpt should not be understood to imply that the USSR disapproves of the principle enunciated in Article 4 of the 1930 Convention on Certain Questions Relating to Conflict of Nationality. A recent study by George Ginsburgs has concluded: "Within the frontiers of the USSR, the Soviet regime simply refuses to recognize the legal consequences of dual (or multiple) nationality in cases involving persons also in possession of a valid Soviet citizenship." [39] Nor should one accept at face value Liu Chia-chi's statement that "socialist countries . . . do not allow the continuation of dual nationality." Ginsburgs' view is that "in its fifty-year history, the USSR has but rarely evinced willingness to initiate positive steps to deal with that 'endemic ailment.' " [40] Liu's statement was undoubtedly influenced by the fact that, at the time he wrote, the USSR was in the process of concluding bilateral dual nationality conventions with nine other "socialist" countries including North Korea and Mongolia but, interestingly, not China.[41]

The Soviet conventions differed from the Sino-Indonesian treaty in a number of respects. They provided that application for choice of citizenship had to be filed within one year from their effective date.[42] If a dual national failed to declare his choice of nationality, he would be treated as a national of his country of residence rather than as a national of his father's country.[43] The Soviet conventions failed to provide a solution for dual nationals residing in third countries, they did not deal with the situation where marriage between nationals of different states leads one of the partners to acquire the nationality of the spouse, and they provided no continuing option for children reaching their majority, instead stipulating that parents were to choose the nationality of minor children. On the other hand, Soviet treaties permitted states to reject persons as their nationals in certain circumstances, and on occasion they provided that the nationality of a child should follow that of the mother in preference to that of the father.[44]

23-7

"Ngo Dinh Diem's Persecution of Overseas Chinese," *PC*, no. 12:40 (June 16, 1957).

On May 20 the Overseas Chinese Affairs Commission issued a statement couched in strong terms on the action of the government of South Vietnam in forcing half a million Chinese born there to give up their own nationality and accept South Vietnamese citizenship. "The South Vietnamese government," it said, "must accept the full responsibility for any consequences which arise from such unreasonable measures," and demanded their immediate withdrawal.

In the past twelve months the South Vietnamese government has taken a series of measures to restrict the legitimate rights and interests of overseas Chinese there and force them to give up their own nationality. The first blow fell in March 1956, when the South Vietnamese government deprived Chinese of their right to correspond with their homeland by refusing to accept mail for the People's Republic of China. Later, on August 21, 1956, it issued a decree that all Chinese born in South Vietnam should be considered as South Vietnamese citizens. To carry this scheme into effect the South Vietnamese government has applied all sorts of pressure and restrictions, both economic and cultural, on the overseas Chinese there. On August 30 last it announced that the principals of middle schools for overseas Chinese in South Vietnam must be South Vietnamese citizens. On September 6 it issued an order forbidding foreign residents (mainly overseas Chinese) to run eleven categories of industry and commerce. In March 1957 it started making a general investigation of all overseas Chinese other than native-born Chinese. In April it declared the aliens' identity cards of all native-born Chinese invalid, and ordered them to surrender such cards to the government not later than May 9, 1957, or "be considered as persons of illegal status." And now the South Vietnamese government is tightening its grip on overseas Chinese still more by forcing them to change their nationality.

"The government of the People's Republic of China," says the statement, "has many times shown its readiness to settle the question of the nationality of overseas Chinese together with the countries concerned in a spirit of friendly negotiation and in accordance with the principles of international law. It is apparent that the question of the nationality of the overseas Chinese in South Vietnam can only be reasonably solved through negotiations between the countries concerned and taking account of the wishes of the overseas Chinese themselves. The steps now taken by the South Vietnamese government to force overseas Chinese to change their nationality is not only a wanton violation of the proper rights and interests of the overseas Chinese in South Vietnam but also a serious transgression of the principles of international law."

In condemning this act of the Ngo Dinh Diem government, Chinese public opinion has laid bare the real reasons behind it. First, that that government hoped, by trampling on the legitimate rights and interests of the overseas Chinese industrialists and businessmen, to ease the economic crisis in South Vietnam, divert the attention of its people, and allay their discontent with the Ngo Dinh Diem clique. Secondly, that Ngo, falling in with the US policy of military expansion, has recently announced the introduction of compulsory military service and hoped to enlist young overseas Chinese as cannon fodder. The South Vietnamese vice-minister of defence, as early as September 24, 1956, told the press that when such overseas Chinese were recognized as "Vietnamese citizens" the government would make them liable for military service.

The Chinese press has also had some strong words to say about the United States, for, as Western news agencies have made clear, the persecution of overseas Chinese by the South Vietnamese authorities has Washington's tacit approval and support.

NOTE

Item 23–7 illustrates the PRC's attitude toward an attempt by another state unilaterally to impose a solution upon the dual nationality problem. It is interesting to note that Peking did not argue, as it might have in light of China's pre-Communist position,[45] that overseas Chinese could not divest themselves of Chinese nationality without the permission of the Chinese government. Rather, it maintained that South Vietnam was illegally forcing its Chinese residents to give up Chinese nationality. This suggests the possibility that, so long as overseas Chinese are permitted to make a truly voluntary choice, the PRC might permit those who choose to be nationals of their state of residence thereby to divest themselves of Chinese nationality even in the absence of any affirmation of these principles "in legal form," as Chou En-lai had contemplated in the case of Singapore.[46]

It has been reported that South Vietnam's measures prompted a change in Nationalist China's traditional position that the overseas Chinese should remain Chinese. After vigorously protesting against South Vietnam's actions, the Republic of China gradually came around to a reluctant acceptance of a policy of "free choice." This was clearly established in 1963 when, soon after the Chinese ambassador to the United States, the noted scholar Dr. T. F. Tsiang, had made a statement that seemed to encourage overseas Chinese to adopt the citizenship of their countries of residence, Mr. Kao Hsin, then chairman of the ROC's Overseas Chinese Affairs Commission, issued the following clarification:

> The government has never encouraged the overseas Chinese to become the nationals of foreign countries. However, if the overseas Chinese, in order to adapt themselves to the circumstances, voluntarily acquire the nationality of the countries they reside in, the government will let them have their free choice, and has never interfered with their option.[47]

All of the material thus far presented in this chapter concerns dual nationality and Peking's views of how to cope with it. Contrary to the usual treatment of nationality problems, we have postponed focussing explicitly on the Chinese Communist view of how Chinese nationality may be acquired. Nevertheless, the foregoing material has suggested Peking's endorsement of the jus sanguinis principle. Also, the Sino-Indonesian Dual Nationality Treaty (23–2) provided that a dual national who rejects Chinese nationality may in certain circumstances subsequently reacquire it (Article VII), that an Indonesian child acquires Chinese nationality if legally adopted by a Chinese national before attaining the age of five (Article IX), and that the Indonesian spouse of a Chinese national may be granted Chinese nationality upon application (Article X). In the absence of nationality legislation or policy statements dealing in detail with the acquisition of nationality, one has to look to practice, and published evidence of practice has been fragmentary and rather slow to appear.

To be sure, the reader will recall that item 20–1, published in a 1954 judicial manual, makes it clear that even in the absence of a treaty a foreign wife of a Chinese national can become a naturalized Chinese national if her application is approved by the Ministry of Interior. No criteria were set forth to guide the Ministry's decision. A naturalized wife, it should be noted, was subjected to the discriminatory treatment of being disqualified from acquiring immovable property by gift from her husband.

On the basis of "information from a foreign diplomatic source," a German scholar of nationality law reported in 1959 that "a child from the marriage of a Chinese national and a foreigner acquires Chinese nationality regardless of whether the father or the mother is Chinese." [48] The latter rule, it should be noted, differs from the version of the jus sanguinis principle adopted by pre-1949 Chinese governments and by the Sino-Indonesian Dual Nationality Treaty of 1955, both of which made nationality ordinarily follow the nationality of one's father.[49]

The same German source also reported that an official document of the PRC's Ministry of Foreign Affairs, transmitted on November 3, 1958, to the mission of a foreign government in Peking stated:

> 1. A Chinese woman marrying a foreigner does not lose her nationality, nor does she lose her nationality if her husband acquires a foreign nationality. If she wants to acquire [a foreign] nationality, she must first follow the necessary procedure to renounce her Chinese nationality. . . .
>
> 3. If a Chinese woman who has renounced her Chinese nationality because of her marriage with a foreigner wants to reacquire her Chinese nationality, she has to follow the necessary procedure for the reacquisition of her original nationality.[50]

As the Sino-Indian dispute intensified beginning in 1959, more became known about the acquisition of Chinese nationality by persons who were not ethnically Chinese. Before taking up this question, a background word about the ethnic composition of China might be useful. Although it is usually said that people of Han Chinese origin constitute roughly 94 percent of China's population,[51] the Han Chinese are themselves a mixed people whose ethnic composition has been importantly influenced by the races that invaded China from the north and by those that the Chinese conquered in the course of their southward expansion. If the influence of the Hsiung-nu, the Ch'iang, and the Mongols has only been a minor one, "the Hsien-pei, the Khitan, and the Ju-chen, later reinforced by the Manchus, certainly had an enormous if not easily ascertainable effect on the Chinese as a people." [52] The 6 percent of China's population that are considered ethnically distinct from the Han Chinese include Tibetans, Mongols scattered over the north and northwest areas, and a variety of Turkish peoples in Sinkiang. There are also other peoples such as the Lo-lo and Tai peoples of the extreme southwest and the Miao-yao group in parts of southern China who are ethnically rather close to the Han people living in their areas.[53]

The Chinese Constitution of 1954 took account of this heterogeneous ethnic situation. Article 3 provided:

> The People's Republic of China is a single multinational state. All the nationalities are equal. Discrimination against, or oppression of, any nationality, and acts which undermine the unity of the nationalities are prohibited.
>
> All the nationalities have freedom to use and foster the growth of their spoken and written languages, and to preserve or reform their own customs or ways.
>
> Regional autonomy applies in areas where people of national minorities live in compact communities. National autonomous areas are inalienable parts of the People's Republic of China.[54]

The translation of the Chinese term *min-tsu* as "nationality" is misleading for purposes of international affairs, and might better be rendered as "race" or "people." The important point to note is that under the Constitution the minority peoples living in China were plainly regarded as Chinese citizens, *kung-min,* and Chinese nationals, *kuo-min.*[55] Neither the Constitution nor other documents came to grips with the problem of how to distinguish the minority peoples who are Chinese nationals from persons of minority extraction who are regarded as foreigners either by other states, by themselves, or by the PRC. Tensions with India, however, caused the PRC to begin to spell out its position on this difficult question.

On November 6, 1959 India's Ministry of External Affairs sent the following note to the Chinese embassy:

> The government of India wish to draw attention to the following incidents, which have recently been reported by the Indian representatives in Tibet:
>
> (i) Kesong Tsering, who is the gardener attached to the dispensary of the Indian Trade Agency in Yatung, was arrested by the Chinese authorities on the 22nd October, 1959. Kesong Tsering is an Indian protected person, and his arrest without any reason is open to serious objection. The Indian Trade Agency in Yatung took up the matter with the local Foreign Bureau and sought permission under the terms of the 1954 Agreement to meet him. In reply the Trade Agency was informed that Kesong Tsering is a Chinese national. This is completely contradictory to the facts.
>
> Kesong hails from Sikkim and even though he has been in the employment of the Indian Trade Agency, he continues to own property in Lachan. His father and his relations are similarly residing in Sikkim. There are no grounds on which Kesong Tsering can be regarded as a Chinese national. In fact the name of Kesong Tsering was included in the list of the Indian nationals furnished

to the Foreign Bureau in May this year, and no objection was raised that Kesong Tsering was a Chinese national. The government of India strongly protest against the arbitrary detention of an Indian protected person and the denial of the rights of access to him by the Trade Agent in accordance with international usage. The 1954 Agreement [between India and China] provides for Indian representatives meeting Indian nationals even if they may have been taken into custody for justifiable reason. In this case no justification has yet been provided. The government of India urge that instructions should be issued for Kesong Tsering's release immediately.

(ii) Dawa Thondup, retired head clerk of the Indian Trade Agency, Gyantse, who had been residing in Yatung as a small trader, requested permission some time ago to send his family to India. Dawa Thondup is an Indian national holding an Indian trader's certificate. It is true that his wife was born in Tibet, but, by virtue of her marriage, she is fully entitled to Indian nationality. Indeed, one of his sons has been in India for some time, and Dawa Thondup now desires to send his eldest son for study, [along with] the rest of the family, back to India. It may also be pointed out that the mother of Dawa Thondup's wife was also an Indian national and thus, according to the Tibetan custom by which the nationality of the daughters is derived from their mothers, the claim of Dawa Thondup's wife to Indian nationality is well grounded.

The general question of nationality of Indian nationals in Tibet has already been explained in the government of India's note of the 24th September, 1959. The Chinese government have recognized in principle in the Sino-Nepalese Agreement [56] that persons resident in the Tibet region born of mixed parentage are entitled to exercise the option to choose one of the two nationalities. In the circumstances, the government of India see no justification for placing restrictions on the return of Dawa Thondup's family to India.

The government of India request that immediate instructions be issued for release of Kesong Tsering and for necessary permission to Dawa Thondup's family to leave for India.[57]

On December 31, 1959 the Ministry of Foreign Affairs in Peking sent the following reply (also recall note preceding 15–6):

According to the principle of the government of the People's Republic of China in dealing with the question of a nationality, a person born of a Chinese parent, father or mother, is a Chinese (except [as] otherwise provided by treaty or agreement). Kesong Tsering's mother and Basang Chulma's [58] father are Chinese. Therefore, according to the above said principle, Kesong Tsering and Basang Chulma are Chinese. Kesong Tsering was arrested on account of offense against the law and was meted due punishment corresponding with his guilt by the local authorities. This is entirely a matter of China's internal affairs.

[In] reference [to] Indian national Dawa Thondup's request for permission for his family of Chinese nationality to leave China according to the regulations of the Chinese government, a Chinese national should go through necessary exit formalities before he goes abroad. On this question Dawa Thondup not only failed to cooperate with the local authorities; on the contrary India unreasonably prevented his family from fulfilling the formalities for going abroad, refused to observe decrees and regulations of the Chinese government, and brazenly filled the name of his family who are of Chinese nationality in his Indian trader's certificate in an attempt to change their nationality surreptitiously and sneak them out of China. This was an offense against the law for which the Chinese authorities gave Dawa Thondup a severe reprimand. As to [the] exit of Basang Chulma, the local authorities, in regard for the union of the whole family, expressed consent once again on 10th November, 1959, for them to leave China and gave them facilities by allowing them to go through the exit formalities locally.[59]

On the same day the PRC also sent item 23–8.

23-8

"Note Given by the Ministry of Foreign Affairs of China to the Embassy of India in China," December 31, 1959, *White Paper*, no. 3:120–121.

Regarding [the] question of [the] nationality of the Indians and Ladakhi Lamas residing in the Tibet Region of China and the Kajis [Kashmiri Muslims] in the Tibet Region of China which has been raised by the government of India on several occasions the ministry would like to set forth the Chinese government's views as follows:

1. Concerning the nationality of the Indians and Ladakhi Lamas residing in the Tibet Region of China:

The Chinese government would like to reiterate that it has never had the intention of regarding Indian residents who are of Indian origin and the Ladakhi Lamas as Chinese. The local authorities have all along regarded them as having Indian nationality provided that they hold valid certificates of their Indian nationality. It should be pointed out that up till now many among the above-mentioned persons still hold no legal certificates of nationality and so their nationality cannot be identified. Five years have passed since conclusion of the 1954 Sino-Indian Agreement on Trade and Intercourse between the Tibet Region of China and India yet the government of India have still failed to deal with the matter of the certificates which its nationals must hold in accordance with the provisions of the Agreement. This is an abnormal situation which it is hoped will be rectified speedily.

2. Concerning the nationality of the Kajis in the Tibet Region of China:

As pointed out by the Ministry of Foreign Affairs of China in its note to the government of India, dated 18 September 1959 the ancestors of these persons moved to and settled in Tibet as early as several centuries back, and they have become long since part of the Tibetans of China. There are adequate proofs to show that they have always been treated as the Tibetans of China by the local government of the Tibet Region of China. Since 1951 most of them have been abroad with either Chinese passports or certificates for Chinese citizens going abroad, and transit or exit visas were issued by the Indian consul general in Lhasa on all the Chinese passports. Neither the government of India nor the persons concerned ever complained about their status and treatment as Chinese nationals or asked that they renounce Chinese nationality. As Chinese they are naturally entitled to the rights and bear the obligations due to Chinese citizens. It is therefore entirely proper that they now continue taking part in various social activities and enjoy the right to education. The Chinese government cannot agree to the fact that [the] government of India should lodge a so-called "strong protest" against this matter which is purely within the scope of China's internal affairs.

Even though, according to the Indian laws, people can apply for and acquire Indian nationality the government of India cannot ignore China's principle governing the handling of the question of nationality. It is universally acknowledged that, according to international law and practice, if, in dealing with a question of nationality there should arise any clash between the laws of two countries it must be dealt with in accordance with the law of the country in which the person concerned resided, before the two countries have come to an agreement through consultations. The Chinese government absolutely cannot agree to the view expressed in government of India's note and the practice of Mr.

S. C. Chibber formerly Indian consul general in Lhasa which would force persons of Chinese nationality living in China to unilaterally accept the Indian law.

Nevertheless, the Chinese government, in line with its stand to settle the question of nationality through friendly consultations and respecting the desires of the persons concerned themselves in regard to their nationality, is willing to settle the question of nationality of the Kajis in the Tibet Region in a sympathetic and reasonable manner. The Chinese government therefore hold that those of them who desire of their own will to acquire Indian nationality must go through the legal procedure of renouncing Chinese nationality in accordance with the regulations of the authorities of the Tibet Region of China before they can choose Indian nationality. As to those who do not go through the procedure of renouncing Chinese nationality, they no doubt remain Chinese and will continue to enjoy the treatment due to Chinese.

NOTE

India's response is worth quoting at length:

> 2. The government of India have stated clearly that, in terms of the relevant clauses of the Indian Constitution and the Citizenship Act of 1955, persons of Indian origin, who have been residing in the Tibet Region of China, are entitled to the privileges of Indian citizenship and that, under the Indian law, registration with the diplomatic and consular missions for Indian nationalities is a matter of option without any time limit. No general grounds can, therefore, be advanced by which Indian nationals can be deemed to have lost their claim to Indian citizenship. It is an accepted canon of international law, which was specifically upheld in a declaration by the Permanent Court of International Justice in 1923, that the question of nationality law lies solely within [the] domestic jurisdiction of a state. The government of India are therefore under no obligation to accept any law of nationality or executive decree promulgated in the People's Republic of China, which, in effect, would amount to depriving the persons so entitled of their rights to Indian citizenship. Further, the Convention on Certain Questions Relating to the Conflict on Nationality, concluded at the Hague Conference in 1930, stated that the law of each state on nationality shall be recognized by the other states in so far as it is consistent with international conventions, international custom and the principles of law generally recognized with regard to nationality. The government of India and the then

government of China subscribed to this convention. The Indian laws on the subject are fully consistent with well-accepted international principles of nationality. On the other hand, the government of India were not aware of any law on nationality promulgated by the government of the People's Republic of China. The traditional practice of the government of China in regard to nationality was apparently based on the principles of jus sanguinis, that is, every descendant of Chinese nationals, irrespective of residence, was considered to be of Chinese nationality. The Chinese note under reference admits that the Kashmiri Muslims and the Ladakhi Lamas resident in Tibet are of Indian origin. The government of India are, therefore, all the more surprised that the Chinese government should endeavor to challenge the right to Indian citizenship of the persons of Indian origin. This right is based on a principle to which the Chinese central authorities have traditionally and specifically subscribed, and even now continue to subscribe.

3. It may be added that the considerations which the Chinese government have adduced are totally irrelevant to the legal right to Indian nationality of this group of persons who came from India. For example, the fact that these persons did not hold Indian nationality certificates has no relevance since, as pointed out earlier, there is no time limit prescribed under Indian laws, within which they must register with Indian missions abroad. Such registration abroad is a matter of option. Actually, as far as these persons residing in the Tibet Region are concerned, they did endeavor to approach the Indian consulate general for the necessary papers and it was the Chinese authorities which obstructed them from doing so. The government of India immediately drew the attention of the Chinese authorities to this in the letter sent by the consul general on 13th May, 1959, to the Chinese Foreign Bureau in Lhasa. Indeed, the local authorities went [so] far as to forcibly confiscate the registration forms and papers of Indian nationals who had succeeded in obtaining them from the consulate general.

4. It is also equally irrelevant that the Tibetan local authorities treated these persons as Chinese Tibetans. Under international practice the treatment meted [out] by any local government cannot unilaterally be deemed to confer or determine the question of nationality of foreign citizens.

5. The Chinese government in their note have also contended that many of the Indian nationals had been abroad with Chinese travel papers. Although some Indian nationals might have, for

the sake of convenience and out of ignorance, taken Chinese papers, the government of India believe that such assertion does not apply to the bulk of Kashmiri Muslims. In this connection it would not be inappropriate to recall, as was pointed out in the Indian note of 24th September, that as soon as these persons reached India, they claimed the benefits which were reserved for Indian citizenship even though they might be holding Chinese papers. They proceeded to the Haj as Indian nationals in pilgrim ships which were intended for Indian citizens only. In any case, the possession of Chinese passports and certificates does not necessarily result in their loss of Indian nationality.

6. From such information and representations as have been received by the government of India, they must categorically reject the Chinese government's assertion that the Indian nationals were satisfied at being treated as Chinese nationals. Apart from the fact that Chinese nationality as such was [never] conferred on them, from all evidence these people appear to be waiting impatiently to return to the places in India from where they originated, whatever their economic losses.

7. The basic facts remain that these persons are of Indian origin and, by tradition, common to both China and India, and, under Indian laws, they are fully entitled to be treated as foreign nationals in Tibet with the right to return to the country of their origin. The Ladakhi Lamas went to the Tibet Region for the theological studies during their lifetime. The Kashmiri Muslims even though they may have been in Tibet for more than a generation, have retained their separate identity and their traditional connection with their homeland. There is no evidence that these persons have expressly renounced their right to Indian citizenship and, as such, any unilateral attempt to treat them as Chinese nationals is contrary to international law and practice, apart from being at variance with the spirit of friendship between the two countries.

8. It is therefore unfair and illegal to insist that these persons should renounce their Chinese nationality when in fact there is nothing to suggest that they had acquired Chinese nationality much less that they had surrendered their Indian nationality.

9. Even if these Indians, by virtue of their residence, are deemed to have fulfilled the conditions which would qualify them for Chinese citizenship, they would be entitled to the benefit of dual nationality. According to the international conventions and the application of China's own practice *mutatis mutandis,* in another context, Indian nationals retain the right title to Indian citizenship.

The government of the People's Republic of China have the sovereign right to confer its own citizenship on foreigners, but they cannot claim the right to deprive foreigners of their nationality.

10. In this connection, it may be expedient to recall the treaty between the People's Republic of China and the Republic of Indonesia on the question of dual nationality. Article I of the treaty upholds the principle that all persons who simultaneously hold the nationality of the two signatory countries have the right to choose according to their own will which nationality they would wish to adopt. Further, an authoritative comment on this treaty made by Mr. Wang Chi Yuan, member of the Standing Committee of Peking—[R]eturned Overseas Chinese Association, published in "People's China" of June 16, 1955, may be recalled in this connection.[60] It referred to the notable features which can be found in the treaty. Among them, he stated, is ["]the principle of the choice of nationality of one's own free will for men and women alike. . . .["] He went on to say that "The signing of this Treaty has set a precedent for the settlement of the dual nationality question between China and other countries in Southeast Asia. The Chinese government is ready to settle it with [the] other government concerned." The government of India seek nothing more than the application of these same principles to persons of Indian origin.

11. Moreover the same principle of choice was in the agreement concluded between the People's Republic of China and the Royal Nepal Government in 1956 in respect of the persons of mixed parentage residing in the Tibet Region of China. In fact, only recently, a decree issued in Lhasa has reiterated the terms of the agreement.

12. The government of India finds it patently illogical that the Chinese government should affirm the right of persons of Chinese origin living for generations in foreign countries to Chinese nationality, regardless of their residence and birth, [to] pledge themselves to the principle of option implicit in dual nationality, and at the same time persistently refuse to give the freedom to exercise the same option to the persons of Indian origin residing in the People's Republic of China. Such an attitude is as inconsistent as it is unfair from the humanitarian point of view.[61]

Peking in turn rejoined:

The Chinese government has always considered the Kajis to be Chinese and is fully entitled to deal with such questions as their

> nationality . . . as China's internal affairs. The Chinese government would naturally respect the wishes of the Kajis concerned, who do not want to remain Chinese, and settle the question of their nationality in accordance with the regulations of the Chinese government. The Chinese government would also give facilities, in accordance with the regulations concerned, to those among them who request to leave the country. Therefore, the question has never arisen of any obstruction on the part of the Chinese government in settling the question of the nationality and exit of the Kajis. Hereafter, should they, of their own will, apply to the Chinese government for exit or ask to settle their nationality, the Ministry of Foreign Affairs believes that the Chinese government, in view of the friendship between the Chinese and Indian peoples, will as before effect a sensible and rational settlement of their questions, and will be prepared to give whatever possible consideration to those who apply for exit.[62]

The PRC's denial of any obstruction flatly contradicted India's earlier assertions that local Chinese authorities had crudely placed various kinds of obstacles in the path of Kajis who sought to register as Indian nationals. It is interesting to note, however, that one of India's protests had claimed that three Kashmiri Muslims had recently been brought before "a mass gathering" in an athletic stadium in Lhasa and sentenced to prison terms of from 11 to 15 years for "incitement of Ladakhi Muslims to claim a foreign nationality"; one of the defendants was also charged with "continuing the movement for foreign nationality among his people." [63] The PRC defended these convictions as "a matter entirely within the scope of China's sovereign rights in which the Indian government has no right to meddle." [64] This led an Indian scholar to comment: "It should be noted that the factual allegations about the barbarous method of trial, and of the nature of the crime for which the prisoners were tried, were not denied by the Chinese authorities. China has indeed the unique distinction of being probably the only country in the world where inducing a dual national to opt for one of his two nationalities is made a crime punishable with 15 years' imprisonment." [65]

As a consequence of the border treaty concluded between China and Nepal in 1961, the PRC had to make known its views about another aspect of acquiring and losing Chinese nationality.

23.9

"Sino-Nepalese Exchange of Notes Concerning the Questions of Choice of Nationality, Transfrontier Cultivation of Lands and Transfrontier Pasturing by the Inhabitants of Certain Border Areas," August 14, 1962, *TYC 1962*, XI (1963), 16.

I. The inhabitants of the areas to be transferred by one party to the other in pursuance of the provisions of Article 1 of the Nepalese-Chinese Boundary Treaty shall, after the transference of the areas to the other party, be definitely considered citizens of the country to which the areas belong. Any inhabitants of these areas who do not wish to become citizens of the country to which the areas belong may retain their previous nationality by making declaration to that effect within one year of the coming into force of the agreement contained in the exchanged notes. Persons who make such declarations may either stay where they are as foreign residents or at any time move into the territory of their country of nationality. In order to implement the above provisions, the following arrangements are adopted:

1. Specific provisions concerning the choice of nationality shall be jointly carried out by the appropriate local authorities in both countries. The declaration on choice of nationality shall be filed by the inhabitants in person with the appropriate local authorities. For those who are minors according to the law of the country where they reside, the declaration shall be made by their parents or, in case the parents are deceased or cannot exercise their right, by their [legal] guardians.

2. If the inhabitants of the area concerned choose to retain their original nationality and continue to reside in the area, the government of the country governing the area shall, in accordance with its municipal law, protect their proper rights and interests and shall allow them to keep their movable and immovable property during the period of their stay.

3. If an inhabitant of the area concerned chooses to retain his original nationality and to move to the country of his original nationality, he is entitled to carry all movable property with him. Unless permission is granted to retain his immovable property in the area concerned, he shall, within one year after moving out of the area, sell his immovable property in accordance with the relevant rules of government for the area; otherwise, the government shall take over the property, and he shall be granted compensation to be decided jointly by the local officials of both countries under Article 4 of this Note. The money collected from sale or compensation may be transferred to the country of the

nationality of the inhabitant. If the money the inhabitant possesses (including money collected from the above-mentioned sale or compensation) at the time of moving is legal tender in the area in which he then stays but is not legal tender in the country of his nationality, the local authority shall provide him the facility to exchange it for currency of the country of his nationality in accordance with a reasonable exchange rate.

Note

Before concluding our presentation of materials relating to the acquisition and loss of nationality, we should expose the reader to the Chinese view of how bourgeois states manipulate the relevant doctrines to achieve preferred results. The following excerpt, like so many other academic efforts of the PRC's first decade, largely derives from Soviet scholarship.

23-10

Ch'ien Szu, "A Criticism of the Views of Bourgeois International Law on the Question of Population," *KCWTYC*, no. 5:43–45 (May 1960).

On the question of nationality, bourgeois international law likewise reflects the needs of the bourgeoisie at different periods. In the early period of capitalism, since the strength of bourgeoisie was still weak and it was necessary to rally the people around the bourgeoisie in order to cope with foreign intervention, bourgeois international law stressed that birth, naturalization, and reintegration or resumption were the ways of acquiring nationality, and that a state has personal supremacy and territorial supremacy over its citizens. After capitalism developed to the stage of imperialism, it was necessary to invade and occupy the territory of other states and to enslave and exploit peoples in colonies. Bourgeois international law then asserted that subjugation and cession are also lawful ways of acquiring nationality. It further maintained that, regardless of the wishes of the people in the subjugated or ceded territories, their nationality will automatically be changed. For instance, after discussing birth, naturalization, and reintegration as three ways of acquiring nationality, Oppenheim wrote that "the fourth and fifth modes of acquiring nationality are by subjugation after conquest and by cession of territory, the inhabitants of the subjugated and the ceded territory acquiring *ipso facto* by the subjugation or cession the nationality of the State which acquires the territory. These modes of acquisition of nationality are modes settled by the customary International Law of Nations. . . ." [a] He further wrote that "in all cases of cession the inhabitants of the territory who remain lose their old citizenship and are handed over to a new sovereign whether they like it or not," [b] and "enemy subjects as are domiciled on the annexed territory and remain there after annexation become *ipso facto* by the subjugation subjects of the subjugating State." [c]

Subjugation is a way in which imperialism plunders colonies. So-called cession in bourgeois international law refers to the forcible division of the territory of weak and small countries through war or pressure. In substance, it is another way in which imperialism plunders colonies. The fundamental reason for imperialism's violent insistence on transforming the nationality of the people who remain on the subjugated or ceded territories into the nationality of the "subjugating state" or the "new sovereign" is to facilitate imperialism's plunder and exploitation.

Everyone knows that unceasingly to plunder people in colonies and to force them to engage in slave labor is one of the main methods of ensuring the maximum profit for the imperialist monopolistic clique. From the point of view of the monopolistic bourgeoisie, the colonial people are not only the ideal supply of cheap labor, but they are also the bearers of all taxes and military service obligations. They are the ideal objects of cruel exploitation and enslavement. In order to facilitate their plunder of colonial people and to avoid the condemnation of the people of the world, the imperialist monopolistic clique fabricates a set of legal excuses by arbitrarily prescribing as principles of international law that the inhabitants who remain on subjugated territory lose their original nationality and acquire the nationality of the subjugating state, and that the relations between those inhabitants and the ruler of the subjugating state are the same as the relations between citizens of a state and their government. By so doing, they try to bring the question of the treatment of people in colonies into the sphere of internal affairs, and thus they seem to be able to do whatever they like and to reject the condemnation of the people of the world on the ground of "nonintervention in internal affairs." This is the real object and intention of bourgeois international law. This is also frankly admitted by Oppenheim: "Different from the fact that enemy subjects become through annexation subjects of the subjugating State is the question what position they acquire within it. This question is one of Municipal and not of International Law. The subjugating State['s] . . . Municipal Law can put them in any position it likes, and can in particular grant or refuse them the same rights as

[a] L. Oppenheim, *International Law*, 7th ed., by H. Lauterpacht (London: Longmans, Green, 1948), I, 598.

[b] *Ibid.*, p. 503.

[c] *Ibid.*, p. 522.

those which its citizens by birth enjoy." He also wrote: "Being now their sovereign, it may indeed impose any burdens it pleases on its new subjects—it may even confiscate their private property, since a sovereign State can do what it likes with its subjects. . . ." [d] Moreover, they further maintain that since the inhabitants who remain on the ceded or subjugated territory acquire new nationality, they *ipso facto* lose their original nationality. They call this way of losing nationality "substitution"; that is to say, their original nationality is extinguished by the substitution of a new nationality. This is necessary in the words of Oppenheim, "since otherwise the whole population of the ceded territory might actually consist of aliens and endanger the safety of the acquiring State." [e] Bourgeois international law jurists have considered both sides of the quest for imperialism.

After the Second World War, some bourgeois international law scholars further proposed the theory of "world citizenship" in response to American imperialist aggression and expansion against the entire world. They maintain that an individual should not be the citizen of a certain state, but should be the citizen of a world state and thereby have world citizenship. In order to propagandize about this view, there have been established in the United States monopolistic capitalist-subsidized organizations such as the "League for World Citizenship" and "World Citizens [Association]." The fundamental object of the advocates of world citizenship are the abolition of the sovereignty of a state in the field of determining the rights and duties of its own inhabitants and the transfer of the exercise of that part of sovereignty to a "world state" or "world government." Obviously, this view is a direct reflection of the wish of American imperialism to establish world domination, and it is an attempt to provide the legal basis for American imperialist intervention in the internal affairs of other countries.

Bourgeois international law's treatment of dual nationality, especially the question of statelessness, is the same. The majority of stateless persons in capitalist countries are laborers. The bourgeoisie have oppressed and mistreated them economically and politically, and they have been completely reduced to the status of persons without any rights. Bourgeois international law explains this as follows: "Since stateless individuals do not own a nationality, the principal link by which they could derive benefits from international law is missing, and thus they lack protection as far as this law is concerned. Their position may be compared to vessels on the open sea not sailing under the flag of a state, which likewise do not enjoy any protection. . . . However much

[d] *Ibid.*, pp. 524, 522.
[e] *Ibid.*, pp. 504–505.

they are maltreated, international law as at present practiced cannot aid them. . . ." [f]

Since the October Revolution and particularly since the Second World War, imperialism has arbitrarily treated as stateless persons those citizens of the Soviet Union and other socialist countries who were reduced to the status of refugees by Fascist persecution, and it has thereby frustrated the repatriation of these refugees to their home countries.

NOTE

In a similar vein another publicist has written:

> Imperialist countries certainly allow the situation of dual nationality to continue in order to facilitate their organizing centers for spy and destructive activities abroad. For example, both the German [nationality] law of 1913 and 1935 and the Japanese [nationality] law of 1899 as amended in 1924, openly legitimized dual nationality. Recently, the United States even tried to use dual nationality to annex another country. For instance, the princess of a small European country—Monaco—was an American movie star and her child will eventually succeed to the throne. On January 23, 1957, when she bore a girl, the United States Department of State informed its consul in Nice that according to the United States Immigration and Naturalization Act, this princess of Monaco may acquire United States nationality. Although this wishful "recommendation" was rejected by the Prince of Monaco, and thus was not realized, it fully exposed the United States' ambition to expand its territory through dual nationality.[66]

[f] *Ibid.*, pp. 610–611.

Regulation of Chinese Nationals Abroad 24

24-1

Chung-yang cheng-fa kan-pu hsüeh-hsiao hsing-fa chiao-yen-shih pien, *Chung-hua jen-min kung-ho-kuo hsing-fa tsung-tse chiang-i* (Lectures on the general principles of criminal law of the People's Republic of China; Peking, 1957), pp. 38–40.

Section 2.
Validity of the Criminal Law in Terms of Persons

A. *Validity to Our Fellow Countrymen*—Chinese criminal law is applicable to the Chinese people who commit offenses within Chinese territory. This is beyond doubt. However, whether Chinese criminal law is applicable to all those Chinese who commit offenses outside Chinese territory is a matter worth our study.

Our law protects the interests of the state as well as the proper rights and interests of our citizens abroad. Our country has jurisdiction over Chinese citizens abroad. Therefore, our criminal law is applicable to those of our citizens who commit offenses abroad. But when a Chinese citizen commits an offense abroad, the implications are somehow different. Because the offense is committed in the territory of another country, it inevitably involves a question between one country and another. We may carry out our sovereignty, but the country in which the offense is committed also has its own sovereignty. Thus in solving the question of a Chinese citizen who commits an offense abroad, we should follow the principle of maintaining our own sovereignty, on the one hand, and respecting the sovereignty of the other country, on the other. The scope of the validity of Chinese criminal law in this context may be considered from several aspects stated below.

In solving the question of criminal responsibility of a Chinese citizen who commits an offense abroad, we should first make sure that the offense committed is a criminal act under our criminal law. The diversity of social systems in the various countries makes it possible that an act may be an offense in a foreign country (mainly in a capitalist country), but not an offense in our country. In the case where an act is held to be an offense by a foreign country but not an offense by our country, the problem of the offender's criminal responsibility does not exist.

When a Chinese citizen commits an offense abroad, our criminal law should apply. However, because the overseas Chinese citizens generally do not quite understand the situation in their motherland and do not have the opportunity to receive legal, disciplinary, and social education in their motherland, we cannot treat them in the same way as we treat our citizens at home. At the same time, the criminal act takes place abroad. Therefore, we consider that with respect to an offense committed by a Chinese citizen abroad, he is responsible to our criminal law only to the extent that the nature of his offense is serious or the degree of his offense is relatively serious, such as in the case of a counterrevolutionary offense, piracy, or forgery of national currency or valuable securities. Other offenses that are relatively serious should also be subject to criminal responsibility in accordance with our criminal law. With respect to the question whether a given offense is serious, our future criminal legislation should consider making provisions on the basis of the minimum statutory punishment prescribed for a given offense. For instance, we can provide that only offenses with a minimum statutory punishment of three or five years of imprisonment should be subject to criminal responsibility in accordance with our criminal law; other offenses with a minimum statutory punishment of less than three or five years of imprisonment or a punishment short of imprisonment for a definite period (such as detention, control, fine, or reprimand), should not be subject to criminal responsibility in accordance with our criminal law. At the same time, if the minimum statutory punishment for a given offense is three or five years of imprisonment, but, according to the law of the foreign country where the offense was committed the offender should not be punished, our criminal law shall not apply. For in such circumstances to punish the offender is not necessary. By acting in such a manner, the people's courts will be able to concentrate their strength upon struggling with criminal elements at home and with those Chinese citizens who commit serious crimes abroad.

Finally, in order to solve the question of criminal responsibility of those Chinese citizens who commit offenses abroad, we may have to face the following situation: what should we do when a Chinese offender has been tried or his punishment has been carried out by a foreign country? The People's Republic of China is a sovereign state. For this reason, when in a foreign country, a Chinese citizen commits an offense that is subject to trial under our criminal law, the fact that he has been tried or his punishment has been carried out by another country does not bar our country's right to prosecute him; we can still prosecute and try him in accordance with our criminal law. However, if the offender's punishment has been carried out abroad, we might take this fact into account when making our decision to punish him. On the basis of the concrete situation, we may reduce or remit his punishment. As regards those Chinese citizens who commit offenses abroad but refuse to return to their own country, we can extradite them to this country through diplomatic channels.

Note

A footnote to the last sentence of item 24–1 states:

Extradition means the transfer of a criminal from the country where he is staying to another country for purposes of trial or punishment.

The following countries may ask for the extradition of a criminal from the country where he is staying: (1) the country of which the criminal is a national; (2) the country in which the offense was committed; (3) the country that is injured by the offense.

When asking for the extradition of a criminal, countries in the last two categories should inform the country of which he [the criminal] is a national of the facts on which the extradition is based. When several countries request the extradition of a criminal, the criminal is generally extradited to the country in which the offense was committed.

The extradition of a criminal is based on the treaties concluded between the countries concerned and on the laws promulgated in those countries.[67]

24-2

"Hsiao Wei-ch'ang Case" *Hua-ch'iao wan-pao* (Overseas Chinese evening news, Hong Kong; July 30, 1966).

On March 15, 1966, a girl named Hsü Yen-yü was murdered in Macao (Portuguese colony). The suspected murderer, Hsiao Wei-ch'ang escaped to mainland China. The victim's relatives reported the case to the Public Security Bureau in Canton. A few days later, the Bureau informed the victim's father in Macao of the suspect's arrest and asked him to go to Canton to confront the suspect. When the father arrived in Canton and confronted the suspect, the latter confessed the commission of the crime. The Public Security Bureau informed the victim's father that the suspect would be tried in Canton and after the trial he would serve his punishment in mainland China.

NOTE

It is unclear whether the action taken in the above case was perceived by Chinese authorities as a claim to punish a Chinese national for conduct committed abroad. The action may have been based on the assumption that Macao, despite its long-standing occupation by Portugal, is Chinese territory. Recall item 12–14.

Although there is no evidence that the PRC was directly responsible for the punishment described in the following report, it may nevertheless be worth noting:

> In Hong Kong today, Lam Bun, a leading radio personality, died from serious burns he received when terrorists threw a gasoline bomb into his car. A cousin, Lam Kong-hoi, who was with him and was initially identified as his brother, was still on the critical list.
>
> Lam Bun had been producing a radio program ridiculing Communist agitation against the Hong Kong government. . . .
>
> In Hong Kong, Communist newspapers supported the attack on Mr. Lam and his cousin. They said it was the work of the "anti-traitors assault corps," which they said had the task of severely punishing anyone who opposed the Communists.
>
> *Ta-kung pao,* a major Communist paper, said all who supported the Hong Kong government should take warning from the "punishment" imposed on Mr. Lam.[68]

Even before the Cultural Revolution, pro-Peking Chinese occasionally inflicted punishment upon anti-Communist Chinese living abroad. In India, for example, when "subsidies" or "loans" from the Chinese embassy or the Bank of China failed to elicit the loyalty of overseas Chinese businessmen, newspaper editors, or cultural leaders, there were sometimes violent reprisals against them and their organizations.[69]

The Cultural Revolution stimulated the PRC to assert other claims to regulate Chinese in Macao. These were made in the course of a bitter dispute with Portugal during the winter of 1966–67 that at least nominally had its origins in the allegedly brutal suppression by the Portuguese authorities in Macao of Chinese residents of Taipa Island who sought to renovate a building for school purposes.[70]

The Foreign Affairs Bureau of the Kwangtung Provincial People's Council demanded, among other things, that the Portuguese authorities "effectively guarantee that no agents of the Chiang Kai-shek gang will ever be permitted to operate in Macao in any manner," and that they "immediately return for disposition by the Chinese government the seven agents of the Chiang Kai-shek gang" who had been detained ever since 1963.[71] These agents, who had been on a military maneuver, had been arrested and held on charges of illegal entry into Portuguese waters and illegal hoarding of weapons, but the Portuguese government had on several occasions given assurances to the Republic of China that it would not turn them over either to the PRC or to the ROC. Nevertheless, on December 20, 1966, as the Communist campaign to mobilize internal and external pressure against the Portuguese authorities reached its peak, they turned the seven men over to the PRC. Moreover, during this period they also forced ROC-sponsored refugee relief agencies, schools, and other organizations to cease functioning and banned the display of the ROC flag. These concessions were formalized on January 29, 1967, when Portugal, which maintains diplomatic relations with the ROC and not the PRC, signed a protocol that was delivered in China to a representative of the Foreign Affairs Bureau of the Kwangtung Provincial People's Council. The *Peking Review* summarized its contents:

> In their protocol to the Foreign Affairs Bureau of the Kwangtung Provincial People's Council, the Portuguese authorities gave assurances that they would banish all Chiang Kai-shek bandit organizations and personnel in Macao, prohibit the use of the sign and the name of the Chiang Kai-shek gang, such as the hanging or the use of its flag and emblem in Macao, prohibit Chiang Kai-shek gang organizations and personnel from carrying out any activity against the People's Republic of China, and drive them all out of Macao. Should any agents of the Chiang Kai-shek gang turn up in Macao and carry out activities in the future, the Portuguese authorities would arrest them immediately and turn them over to the department concerned in the Kwangtung Provincial People's Council.[72]

Undoubtedly to avoid embarrassment to the PRC, the *Peking Review* failed to report another concession embodied in the protocol: Portugal's agreement to surrender to the PRC all future Chinese refugees who seek to enter Macao from mainland China. Portuguese authorities immediately began turning over incoming refugees to Chinese authorities at the border gate.[73] The Republic of China, which repeatedly protested in vain against Portugal's concessions, also sent a note to the Secretary-General of the United Nations for circulation to all UN members. It stated:

> These acts of the Portuguese authorities are clearly contrary to international practice and in total disregard of human rights, and constitute specifically a flagrant violation of the principle of

> nonrefoulement of the 1951 Convention Relating to the Status of Refugees, of which Portugal is a contracting state. Under Article 33 of that Convention, no contracting state shall expel or return a refugee in any manner whatsoever to the frontiers of territories where his life or freedom would be threatened.[74]

Item 25–13 will provide additional information on the PRC's dispute with Macao.

There have been numerous other instances when the PRC has sought to exert pressure upon other governments to regulate hostile Chinese nationals. Recall item 9–3, where Peking remonstrated with Switzerland for tolerating the activities of a refugee Tibetan organization. During the 1950's, when Sino-Indian relations were friendly, the PRC prodded New Delhi to curb the political activities of pro-Nationalist Chinese residents. They were prohibited from displaying the Nationalist flag in celebrating the anniversary of the founding of the Republic of China; their leading newspaper was ordered to use the term "Chinese Communists" rather than "Communist bandits" in describing the elite in Peking; and some prominent Nationalists were expelled from India.[75] Even as late as 1959, India issued instructions to prevent all future pro-Nationalist meetings and demonstrations, threatened to expel foreigners who indulge in such "objectionable activities" and promised not to permit "any activities designed to promote the idea of two Chinas."[76]

For the PRC's demand that the UN cease assistance to Chinese refugees in India, Macao, and Hong Kong, see item 39–9.

The following 1971 newspaper dispatches report one of the most bizarre instances of the PRC's efforts to control its nationals abroad:

> The Chinese traveler who was seized by Orly Airport policemen yesterday from a group trying to take him aboard a Shanghai-bound plane remained under heavy guard today.
>
> Officials said that the man, who was identified as Dr. Chung Shi-jung, a 31-year-old physician from Peking, was still unable to answer questions.
>
> However, it began to appear that he had done considerable talking even yesterday, while he was being pried with difficulty from the hands of 10 protesting comrades, although he had been described as being apparently in a drugged state.
>
> Sources in Algiers—where the press has not yet mentioned the affair—said that Dr. Chung had been assigned to a Chinese medical aid mission of about 30 people at Medea, about 60 miles south of Algiers.
>
> There were reports that he had appealed for asylum to the

French embassy in Algiers. A spokesman said that the embassy was "not officially aware" of any such appeal and was under strict orders not to get involved in matters of asylum. But the spokesman declined to deny that a man might have come and banged on the gate.

The first story of a chance discovery by customs officers did not stand up. The version offered in semiofficial circles today is that an anonymous telephone caller told an Air France hostess that a Chinese was being kidnapped. But other circles add that the call came as no surprise to the French counterintelligence services.

Dr. Chung, bundled in sweaters, was hustled by the police to an office at the airport, accompanied by 10 shoving and shouting companions. Contrary to yesterday's police reports that the man was unconscious or dazed, it is now acknowledged that, at least at times, he talked animatedly with a Chinese embassy official. At those times, it is reported, he refused treatment by a French physician.

When he was finally taken away from the others and placed in an ambulance, however, he apparently talked animatedly and amicably with a Secret Service agent who spoke Chinese.

Chinese diplomats called at the Foreign Ministry this morning and again this afternoon; . . . Apart from noting that the Chinese had lodged a protest, officials declined to shed any light on the case.

Speculation arose that the intelligence services had arranged the rescue of Dr. Chung without consulting the Foreign Ministry. The two agencies are not always friendly.

Press comment suggested that relations between France and China might not be gravely damaged by the affair. *France-Soir,* which is progovernment, observed that such incidents "have only the importance that the governments concerned choose to give them."[77]

The Foreign Ministry denied and described as slanderous today a newspaper report that said France had refused to give asylum to a Chinese Communist official. The paper was apparently *The International Herald Tribune.*

The official, Chung Shi-jung, 31 years old, left for home yesterday. At Orly airport nine days ago the police clashed with Chinese diplomats who tried to bundle him semiconscious onto a plane for Peking.

Today's *Herald Tribune* said Mr. Chung had been sent home after being told he was not welcome in France. The paper said France did not want to jeopardize relations with Peking.[78]

Protection of Chinese Nationals Abroad 25

As indicated at the outset of this part, treatment of the PRC's efforts to protect its official and semiofficial agents abroad will be deferred until Part VII. Thus, PRC instrumentalities that function abroad such as banks, transportation companies, trade agencies, and political, scientific, and technical assistance delegations will not be discussed here. Given Chinese theory and practice, there is, of course, no sharp dividing line between the activities of Chinese abroad that should be denominated "semiofficial" and those that should be regarded as essentially private. For example, students assigned to study at foreign universities, members of a fishing collective sent to fish outside of territorial waters, and laborers permitted to cross into a neighboring country every day for purposes of employment might be deemed, at least by Peking, to be semiofficial agents of the Chinese government. Even more clearly, the officers of overseas organizations of Chinese nationals can be viewed as serving the motherland in a type of representative capacity. Nevertheless, we have chosen to deal with the latter categories of activity in this chapter, together with the activities of ordinary overseas Chinese. It will be helpful, however, for the reader to note the relation of these materials to those presented in Part VII.

At its inception the PRC was verbally vigorous in adhering to its formally proclaimed commitment to "do its utmost to protect the proper rights and interests of Chinese residing abroad."[79] The past two decades have provided many occasions for testing the sincerity with which this promise was made. Some observers have detected a reluctance or an ambivalence on the part of Peking with respect to the protection of overseas Chinese during the period from 1955 to 1965, but surely there was little trace of such an attitude during the Cultural Revolution of 1966 to 1969.

Literally, volumes could be devoted to this subject, and should be, for dozens of thorough case studies are needed before useful generalizations can be constructed with confidence about Chinese practice in protecting nationals. All that we can do here is to introduce the reader to the range of claims that the PRC has made against various countries over a twenty-year period.

We have already seen a few examples of such claims (recall items 4–3, 4–4, and 15–7) and of the efforts of Chinese publicists to cope with the problems of state responsibility for the treatment of aliens (compare items 4–7, 21–1, 22–1, and 22–2). We have also been introduced to the views of Chinese publicists about the proper means of enforcing claims to protect nationals (recall 9–2 and 9–4). In Part V we surveyed the PRC's own practice toward aliens. This chapter will fill out the picture of Peking's conception of the right of states to protect citizens abroad and the corresponding responsibility of states to prevent international delinquencies. Later parts will provide further examples (for example, 31–24).

When considering the following materials together with earlier ones, the reader will want to bear in mind three of the basic questions that motivate our entire inquiry. To what extent do the PRC's theory and practice diverge from the theory and practice of other states? To what extent does the PRC apply the double standard of expediency, depending on whose ox is being gored? To what extent does its own behavior appear to be similar to its perception of the behavior of bourgeois states? In addition to the extent and nature of the PRC's invocation of international law, we should also note the variety of authorities that issue statements in its behalf, ranging from the chairman of the PRC to the spokesmen of "mass organizations."

We begin with one Chinese writer's view of how some bourgeois states have acted toward Chinese and other minorities within their boundaries.

25-1

Ch'ien Szu, "A Criticism of the Views of Bourgeois International Law on the Question of Population," *KCWTYC*, no. 5:48–49 (1960).

With respect to the status and treatment of citizens of weak and small countries within the territory of imperialist countries, the situation is exactly the reverse. They cannot enjoy any privileges, not even the minimum privilege of equal rights. Imperialism publicly discriminates against and mistreats them.

It is a well-known fact that the United States and some Western European countries discriminate against and mistreat Negroes and other colored races. For instance, the United States discrimination against and mistreatment of the "yellow race," mainly the Chinese, with respect to entry and fundamental human rights, date back many years. The methods and means of such discrimination and mistreatment are extremely violent and unconcealed. As a matter of fact, the Chinese working people made notable contributions to the economic development of American capitalism. Everyone knows that when gold mines were discovered in San Francisco in 1848, in order to use China's cheap labor force for mining, the United States resorted to various deceitful propaganda and even kidnapping and other shameless methods in recruiting Chinese laboring people to work as gold miners and to do other labor in the United States. By 1868, the number of Chinese workers in the United States had sharply increased to tens of thousands, thus enabling American capitalists to pocket billions of dollars in profits. However, as a result of the further development of American capitalism, economic crises frequently occurred; there was a surplus of labor and mass unemployment. In such circumstances, Chinese laborers were no longer needed. Thus, the United States not only refused to admit more Chinese, but it also openly excluded those Chinese who had settled in the United States and who had made notable contributions to the development of the United States. The United States enacted the "Chinese Exclusion Act," thereby openly legalizing the American atrocities in excluding Chinese. According to statistics, between 1882 and 1913 alone there were no fewer than fifteen Chinese exclusion acts that overlapped with each other to a certain extent. The position of the Chinese in the United States was extremely miserable, and the persecution to which they were subject can hardly be described. The Chinese exclusion acts were nominally abolished in 1943, but discrimination still exists in practice.

The Union of South Africa's acts "rival" those of the United States. The discrimination against Indians by the government of the Union of South Africa is well known. According to incomplete statistics, there have been promulgated as many as 65 statutes discriminating against Indians alone. These include statutes for racial segregation, deprivation of the right of Indians to earn a living, prohibition of mixed marriage between whites and Indians, and so forth.

In addition to racial reasons, there are also political reasons for imperialism's mistreatment of and discrimination against citizens of foreign countries. For instance, the United States has adopted extremely strict quotas on immigrants from Eastern European countries. It has also persecuted progressive-minded aliens in the United States without any just reason. On the other hand, it greatly facilitates the entry into the United States of those reactionary elements or traitors from the various socialist or nationalist countries in order to use them to carry out sabotage against these countries and to intervene [in their affairs].

The bourgeois international law scholars do their best to defend the imperialists' mistreatment of and discrimination against aliens. In an attempt to dispose of just condemnation and opposition on the international scene they argue that "a state can freely decide upon the treatment of aliens." They obviously had other intentions. It is true that international law recognizes that a state has the right, in accordance with its sovereignty, to refuse the entry of a particular alien and to adopt laws granting particular treatment to aliens. But it totally violates the principles of modern international law and the principles of equality and friendly intercourse among peoples of various countries to discriminate against aliens on the basis of race, color, nationality, religion, language, and so forth in matters of entry, exit, and treatment.

Regarding such questions as expulsion, asylum, and extradition, bourgeois international law also does its best to provide bases and defenses for bourgeois discrimination against and hostility toward laboring people and progressive elements. For instance, on the question of expulsion of aliens, it never mentions the fact that most aliens expelled from capitalist countries are laboring people and progressive elements; rather, it intentionally invokes the right of a state to expel aliens in order to conceal the truth.

25-2

Li Ta, ed.,[so] *Chung-hua jen-min kung-ho-kuo hsien-fa chiang-hua* (Lectures on the Constitution of the People's Republic of China; Peking, 1956), pp. 233–234.

[Article 98 of] the Constitution of our country provides: "The People's Republic of China protects the proper rights and interests of Chinese residing abroad."

Overseas Chinese are Chinese citizens residing abroad. The number of our country's overseas Chinese is approximately 12 million. As old China was a semifeudal and semicolonial state with an extremely low international status, Chinese people residing abroad not only were the object of imperialists' plunder and oppression, but also were subject to various kinds of discrimination and insults. Kuomintang reactionaries not only did not actively protect Chinese residing abroad, but, on the contrary, blackmailed them and imposed exactions on them. Therefore, the proper rights and interests of overseas Chinese did not receive any protection. Since the establishment of the People's Republic of China, the situation of the overseas Chinese has undergone a fundamental change. Now foreign imperialists do not dare openly to oppress, to discriminate against, and to insult overseas Chinese. Furthermore, our country has taken a series of measures to protect overseas Chinese, and the constitutional provision concerning the protection of the proper rights and interests of overseas Chinese is the summing up of our country's work to protect overseas Chinese. The era of abandonment of overseas Chinese has been declared at an end. Thus, people formerly called "overseas orphans" are now receiving the care and the concern of the mother country, and they have also strengthened their patriotism toward the mother country. Now, the broad overseas Chinese have linked their destiny to the destiny of the mother country, and they are constantly giving fond devotion and consideration to the mother country. They hope that the mother country will become increasingly prosperous, wealthy, and strong, and in various aspects they support and sustain the socialist construction of the mother country.

25-3

Ni Cheng-ao, *Kuo-chi-fa chung ti ssu-fa kuan-hsia wen-t'i* (The question of judicial jurisdiction in international law; Peking, 1964), pp. 55, 91–92.

A state's jurisdiction over a foreigner who has committed a crime in a foreign state is a question which has become increasingly complicated. The exercise of this type of jurisdiction cannot be explained on the basis of any method of simplified classification. First, we must affirm that criminal acts committed abroad which endanger the security and interest of the prosecuting state are punishable. But, at the same time, we should also make it clear that this jurisdiction should not be used at will as an instrument for conducting persecution. Any state which, for the purpose of persecuting progressive persons or promoting racial discrimination or other criminal policies, conducts criminal prosecution against foreigners for acts done before entry into its territory is adopting a barbarous and arbitrary measure in violation of rules of international law and is not properly exercising its jurisdiction. Second, since the judgment of the "Lotus" case, the right of the state to which the victim belongs to prosecute foreigners for acts done [before entry] has gradually received broad recognition. At present legislation that provides for such jurisdiction is not subject to strong criticism as it was in the past. Finally, the principle that every state can exercise jurisdiction over piracy and war crimes cases has been generally recognized. The above examples constitute exceptions to the principle of territorial jurisdiction over crimes committed by foreigners. . . .

It sometimes happens that Chinese coastal fishing boats are sunk or destroyed as a result of a collision with a ship of foreign nationality. If the foreign ship concerned carries out rescue and salvage after occurrence of the accident and agrees to wait for investigation or applies for its release by furnishing a guarantee, the case may reach a negotiated settlement and litigation may not arise. Even if litigation should arise, in these circumstances the case is still comparatively easy to settle. However, if the foreign ship escapes after the accident and then is captured by a Chinese naval vessel which brings her to a Chinese port, or if after entering a Chinese port the foreign ship, with the intent to conceal or to shift the responsibility for the accident, does not take the initiative to submit a maritime accident report, then the Chinese port authorities concerned naturally have the right to handle the matter in accordance with law. Even when this type of maritime accident does not take place in China's territorial seas or ports, in view of the fact that the foreign ship has caused damage to the property of Chinese people and has entered or has been brought into a Chinese port, the Chinese courts can adjudicate the case if the parties concerned cannot reach a negotiated settlement. But if the parties concerned agree, they may submit the case to the arbitration of an arbitral organ or to the decision of the port administrative organ. If a foreign ship sinks a Chinese fishing boat in the high seas and then enters a port of a third state, China may request the assistance of the third state to seize the ship in accordance with the relevant situation. The port authorities of the third state have the right to exercise jurisdiction over the foreign ship, as it is the first port which the foreign ship enters after the accident and it is also the port where the foreign ship is seized or exempted from seizure by virtue of having furnished a guarantee.

Note

Ni Cheng-ao's description of China's exercise of the passive nationality principle reflects Article 13 of the PRC's "Rules for Investigation and Handling of Incidents Involving Maritime Losses," which asserts jurisdiction over foreign-flag ships not only for incidents occurring in Chinese territorial waters but also for other incidents that cause damage to property of Chinese people.[81] Some years earlier the PRC's leading textbook on criminal law had stated:

> Under certain conditions, if a foreigner or a stateless person commits an offense outside Chinese territory, he is also subject to Chinese criminal law. These conditions are: (1) the offender is responsible for his act according to our criminal law; and (2) his act injures the state or citizens of the People's Republic of China. In our opinion, the scope of his criminal responsibility should be in principle the same as that of a Chinese who committed an offense abroad.
>
> With respect to a foreigner or stateless person who commits a given offense endangering the state or citizens of the People's

> Republic of China, if he has been tried or his punishment has been executed by a foreign country, the principle of solving such a question is the same as that which applies in the case of a Chinese who commits a given offense abroad under the above-stated circumstances [that is, Chinese authorities can still prosecute the offender, but his punishment may be mitigated or dispensed with if he has served the sentence in the foreign country concerned].[82]

Most PRC claims to protect the interests of nationals abroad are manifested not in the exercise of jurisdiction by a competent tribunal but rather in the form of protests against the conduct of other states. The following item is illustrative of a series of PRC protests against American bombing of Chinese fishing vessels on the high seas.

25-4

"Strongest Protest against US Piratical Act," *PR* 9.23:11 (June 3, 1966).

US imperialist military aircraft again bombed and strafed Chinese fishing boats bearing the national flag of the People's Republic of China on the high seas on May 28. A Chinese fisherman, a fisherwoman, and her daughter were killed, and 18 others were wounded. A Chinese fishing boat was sunk, and three were damaged.

A spokesman of the Chinese Ministry of National Defense has expressed the strongest protest against these flagrant, serious provocations by the US military aircraft.

On the 28th, while two fishing boats, No. 6503 and No. 6505, of the Wanwei Brigade of the Chiangping People's Commune of Tunghsing Multi-National Autonomous County in the Kwangsi Chuang Autonomous Region were fishing on the high seas in northern Bac Bo Gulf, two US military aircraft, flying separately from the directions of the southwest and northwest, circled over them at 15:30 hours. Then the US aircraft savagely dropped seven bombs aimed at the two boats and strafed successively with machine guns, killing Chinese fisherman Chen Cheng-wei, wounding six other fishermen, and sinking one Chinese fishing boat and damaging another.

At 15:50 hours on the same day, two US imperialist military aircraft bombed and strafed Chinese fishing boats, No. 2241, No. 2242, No. 2325, and No. 2326, of the Hoping Fishing Brigade and Chiying Brigade of the Chisha People's Commune of Tunghsing Multi-National Autonomous County, while they were fishing on the high seas in northern Bac Bo Gulf. Chinese fisherwoman Huang Feng-ying and her three-year-old daughter were killed, and twelve others were wounded. Two Chinese fishing boats were damaged.

The spokesman of the Chinese Ministry of National Defense points out that the sending of military aircraft by the US government to sabotage fishery production on the high seas and wantonly bomb and strafe Chinese fishing boats engaged in peaceful labor and [the] murdering or wounding [of] Chinese fishermen prove that the Johnson administration is the most barbarous and most ferocious aggressive gangster of present times. "We resolutely protest against the piratical act of US imperialism. We sternly warn the US government that it must immediately stop such acts of piracy. The great Chinese people armed with Mao Tse-tung's thought are not to be trifled with. We shall definitely settle the blood debts incurred by US imperialism," he said.

25-5

"US Imperialist Persecution of Chinese Fishermen Condemned," *PR* 10.7:29 (Feb. 10, 1967).

Forty-eight Chinese fishermen, abducted by the US imperialists and sent to South Vietnam, recently returned to their motherland after more than a month of heroic struggle and after repeated negotiations by the Red Cross Society of China. After their return, the fishermen accused US imperialism, in collusion with the Chiang Kai-shek gang and the South Vietnamese puppet clique, of brutally persecuting them and of resorting to various means to extort military, political, and economic intelligence from them. In an article published on February 2, *Renmin Ribao* [People's Daily] Commentator said: "This is a major political intrigue jointly engineered by US imperialism and its flunkeys, the Chiang Kai-shek gang and the South Vietnamese puppet clique; it is another serious provocation by US imperialism against the great Chinese people. The Chinese people hereby express their strong indignation and their serious protest against the US government!"

Early last December when the 48 Chinese were fishing on the high seas in the Gulf of Bac Bo, they were caught in a huge gale which blew their vessels southwards. They were later intercepted and taken to Nha Trang, South Vietnam, by US warships and all the fishermen were locked up in a 12-square-metre room in a jail of the puppet police bureau. Working together, the US imperialists, members of the Chiang gang on Taiwan and the South Vietnamese puppet authorities resorted to threats and bribery in a vain attempt to extort intelligence about China from them, induce them to betray their country and force them to join organizations of the US-Chiang agents. US military officers taking part in questioning them mentioned on many occasions the repeated spying activities by US aircraft in reconnaissance flights over China's territory, and asked them again and again about the possibility of US warships entering ports on Hainan Island. This fully reveals the criminal intention of US imperialism to launch aggression against China.

Having abducted the Chinese fishermen, the US imperialists made a lot of propaganda about "saving Chinese fishermen from danger." This was pure fiction aimed at deceiving people and covering up their vile abduction in a vain attempt to hide their heinous crime of repeatedly sending planes and warships to invade China's air space and territorial waters and bombing and strafing Chinese fishing vessels and fishermen, and to evade the just condemnation of the people of the world.

Note

The American press gave a somewhat less sinister account of the above incident. For example:

> [48 Chinese] fishermen were rescued from a large junk and two small sampans. The sampans were breaking up, and the junk had suffered severe damage when the United States ships came to their assistance. The fishermen and the junk were taken to Nhatrang, South Vietnam, and kept there while arrangements were made for their repatriation.
>
> A United States military transport plane flew the Chinese to Hong Kong today. They were described as being "in a cheerful mood" on their arrival. They were dressed in clothing given them by the navy when they landed at Hong Kong, but changed into blue trousers and jackets, the standard wear in China, before leaving for the border. . . .
>
> The 48 Chinese fishermen who were repatriated today after having been rescued by the United States navy after a storm at sea were accompanied by two American Red Cross representatives, Melville G. Jewel of Monmouth, Ill., and John P. Schag of Albuquerque, N.M. They were met inside the border by Chinese Red Cross representatives. The transfer, the Americans said, involved only a brief, friendly ceremony that went "very smoothly and without any incident."
>
> The fishermen spent more than an hour in a restricted airport lounge in Hong Kong. Officials of the China Travel Service then handed them small red books containing quotations of Chairman Mao.
>
> Mr. Jewell described the fishermen as "obviously hardworking,

simple and honest people who did not even know where Hong Kong was."[83]

25-6

"Red Cross Society Refutes New Japanese Fabrication," NCNA–English, Peking (Apr. 8, 1958), in *SCMP*, no. 1749:45 (Apr. 11, 1958).

The trumped up story by the Japanese government that Liu Lien-jen was not abducted to Japan but went there by "agreement" was refuted by a spokesman of the Red Cross Society here today.

Interviewed by a NCNA correspondent, the spokesman said that investigations that had been made had verified that Liu was abducted in October 1944 at his home village of Chao Po, in Ching Ko Hsiang, Kaomi County, previously Chucheng County, in Shantung Province. Members of Liu Lien-jen's family and his neighbor Chiu Hsien-chieh were eyewitnesses of this outrage.

Thanking the friendly Japanese people and organizations that had shown sympathy to Liu and had helped him, the spokesman said "a letter was received from the Japanese Red Cross Society, the Japan-China Friendship Association, and the Japanese Peace Liaison Committee dated February 27 saying that they would assist Liu Lien-jen to return by the next ship leaving Japan to take back Japanese nationals from China." He added that this was not only happy news for Liu's family but a matter in which all Chinese people are interested. In contrast to the friendly attitude of the Japanese people, said the spokesman, "not only was there no sign of apology from the Japanese government for the outrage committed by the Japanese militarists in violation of international law and humanitarian principles, but they were trying out a new provocation in the form of the fabrication about Liu's 'illegal entry' into Japan."

The spokesman expressed indignation when he referred to the remark by Osamu Itagaki, Director of the Asian Affairs Bureau of the Japanese Foreign Ministry, who in answering questions in the House of Councillors on March 25 said that "Liu Lien-jen was not abducted, but went to Hokkaido by 'agreement.' "

The spokesman commented: "Liu Lien-jen is a Chinese civilian who was abducted to Japan by the Japanese aggressive forces after the so-called 'immigration of Chinese laborers' directive was adopted on November 27, 1942, at the Japanese Diet meeting, with the aim of using the Chinese people as slaves. The files of the Japanese Foreign Ministry bear this out.

"At that time when the Japanese militarists were treating China as a colony and the Chinese people as their slaves, was there any likelihood of an 'agreement'?" He asked: "Can the thrusting of a bayonet at the chest of Liu Lien-jen and, after binding him, dragging him off be regarded as the implementation of an 'agreement'?"

"We hold that the Japanese government must take full responsibility for the case, give a responsible account for it, compensate all his losses, and send him back to the People's Republic of China," he expressed.

"Liu Lien-jen is only one of tens of thousands of Chinese civilians seized by the Japanese forces during the Japanese aggression. Forced hard labor, torture, and maltreatment caused the loss of many Chinese lives and many others were never heard of again," he said. "The Japanese government now should take full responsibility for these press-ganged Chinese citizens who had not responded at all. Liu Lien-jen's case gives us ground for suspecting that there may be two, three, or more similar cases of people who are suffering the same trouble in Japan. We demand of the Japanese government that it undertake a thorough investigation into the situation regarding Chinese citizens who were forcibly removed to Japan by the Japanese forces during their aggression on China and report concretely the findings of this investigation."

25-7

"Clash Is Averted at Hong Kong Line," *New York Times* (Aug. 6, 1967), p. 12.

A tense border incident was ended as an amicable tea party today after the restrained intervention of a British army officer.

The incident occurred this morning at Nankamto, a crossing point for produce from Communist China to Hong Kong, when Chinese workers grabbed a Hong Kong policeman's submachine gun and a Gurkha soldier's rifle.

About 30 people who live on the Chinese side but work on the Hong Kong side handling produce from China had just crossed the border. As they walked by two police officers outside the police post, two men suddenly seized the weapons held by the policeman and the Gurkha nearby.

A Hong Kong government spokesman said that six more armed policemen were in the post but that their officer instructed them "not to fire." The spokesman said there was a platoon of 40 soldiers just up the road from the police post and "they also held their fire."

Gurkhas Sent to Area

Senior army and police officers went to the scene, two miles east of the official crossing point at Lowu, and a second platoon of Gurkhas took up positions opposite the group of Chinese workers. Brig. Peter Martin, commander of the 48th Gurkha Brigade, talked to the workers an hour and a half.

A spokesman for the workers complained that posters that they had put up the day before had been taken down and also said they had been instructed to support their "compatriots" in Hong Kong. This was a reference to local Communists, who have been engaged in a trial of strength with the British colonial authorities for three months.

Brigadier Martin said that inflammatory posters were prohibited by law in Hong Kong but that the authorities did not object to posters quoting sayings of Mao Tse-tung, the Communist party Chairman in China.

Tea Brought on Trolley

The government spokesman said the conversation was "amicably conducted" and at one time tea was brought from the Chinese side on a trolley and served to all present.

The workers were assured that they would be free to display posters quoting Chairman Mao and to sing Chinese Communist songs. This assurance, and a promise that no reprisals would be taken against the workers, was made in writing by Brigadier Martin and Trevor Bedford, the district officer for the area.

During the discussion, Chinese troops arrived on the scene. However, they did not interfere in the proceedings. Three hours after the weapons were seized, they were handed back and the workers returned to the Chinese side.

It was the second serious border incident in three days. On Thursday, demonstrators crossed into British territory at Lowu and threw stones at a police post. British troops drove them back with tear gas, and Chinese soldiers brought the situation under control by preventing further demonstrators from crossing into Hong Kong.

25-8

"Strongest Protest against British Imperialist Armed Provocation along the Border," *PR* 10.29: 35 (July 14, 1967).

Vice-Minister of Foreign Affairs Lo Kuei-po on the morning of July 9 summoned D. C. Hopson, British chargé d'affaires to China and handed him a note from the Chinese Foreign Ministry. It lodges the most urgent and strongest protest with the British government against the serious armed provocation committed against the Chinese people by the British authorities in Hong Kong on July 8. The note says:

> On July 8, people on our side of Sha Tau Kok and Chinese inhabitants of the "New Territories," Kowloon, held a rally on our side to voice support for our patriotic countrymen in Hong Kong and Kowloon in their just struggle against brutal persecution by the British authorities in Hong Kong. After the rally, they demonstrated along different routes. When the Chinese inhabitants were returning to the "New Territories," Kowloon, from the demonstration, fully armed policemen and "riot police" of the British authorities in Hong Kong flagrantly carried out a premeditated sanguinary suppression of them, throwing tear gas bombs and opening fire at them, and at the same time fired at our side. The Chinese frontier guards at once fired warning shots against such atrocities and provocations by the British side. But, in total disregard of the warnings from our side, the policemen and "riot police" of the British authorities in Hong Kong continued to fire at the demonstrators, killing one and wounding eight of them. Our frontier guards also fired back at the policemen and "riot police" of the British authorities in Hong Kong.

The Chinese government in the note raised the following demands to the British government:

> 1. Make public apologies for the July 8 armed provocation in Sha Tau Kok;
> 2. Immediately punish the culprits, compensate for all the losses suffered by the inhabitants of Sha Tau Kok and by the dead and wounded, and release all the inhabitants arrested since June 24 in the Sha Tau Kok region;
> 3. Guarantee that no similar incidents will occur in the future.

The British government and the British authorities in Hong Kong, the note points out, have gone further to create tension along the border. This is increasingly aggravating the Hong Kong situation. The Chinese government hereby sternly and solemnly warns the British government: If you persist in being hostile to the Chinese people to the end, then you must bear all the grave consequences arising therefrom.

25-9

"*Jen Min Jih Pao* Denounces Songgram's Outrage against Overseas Chinese," NCNA–English, Peking (July 23, 1952), in *SCMP*, no. 381:13–14 (July 24, 1952).

The Thai government's insistence on raising the annual fee for foreign nationals' identification cards from 20 to 400 Baht per head is denounced as "an outrage" in today's Peking *Jen Min Jih Pao.* It is obviously aimed at the masses of overseas Chinese in Thailand, the paper notes. The commentary continues as follows:

In recent years, the Luang Pibul Songgram government of Thailand has been following the American aggressors' policy of armament expansion and war preparation. Its embargo against China has caused the price of tin, rice, and rubber in Thailand to drop, resulting in a general business depression and a declining revenue. Now, by pushing up the annual fee for foreign nationals' identification cards to a level beyond what the Chinese residents can bear, the Thai government intends to exact large sums of money from them to make up the deficit in its finances for war preparation.

The Thailand *Chuan Min Pao* of February 1952 reported a high official of the Thai police department as saying that the present hike in this annual tax "will net them a total revenue of 480 million Baht. If the number of foreign residents taking out identification cards increases, the revenue will be even greater."

What monstrous exploitation! At the same time, the Thai government is attempting, by means of this outrageous measure, to force Chinese residents who cannot pay this annual tax to serve [terms at] hard labor, or even [to] compel them to become soldiers for the Chiang Kai-shek gang in Taiwan, thus providing cannon fodder for the American imperialists to pursue their aggressive policy of extending war, using Thailand as a war base. We must keep a close watch on this disgraceful scheme.

This increased fee places the overwhelming majority of Chinese residents in Thailand in a desperate position. China has more than three and a half million overseas Chinese in Thailand. Most of them are shop assistants, workers, small traders, and peasants who live a very difficult life. An ordinary wage earner only gets three or four hundred Baht a month, which is insufficient for the minimum requirements for a family of five. In 1950, when the Thai government raised the annual fee for foreign nationals' identification cards from four to twenty Baht, many Chinese residents there found this tax too difficult to bear. Now by the sudden twenty-fold increase, a family of five will have to pay two thousand Baht a year. This will make it utterly impossible for the overwhelming majority of Chinese residents to keep going; it will beggar them.

Since this decree was passed by the Thai government on February 4, 1952, it has drawn widespread opposition from the masses of Chinese residents in Thailand. In many cities and villages, Chinese residents have developed a petition movement to state their case. They are firmly demanding of the Thai government that it reduce this burden which is beyond their means. This activity of the Chinese residents to protect their right to existence is perfectly justified and lawful. It is winning widespread sympathy among the Thai people of all strata and has the firm support of the people in the motherland.

As early as March 11, 1952, Chairman Ho Hsiang-ning of the Overseas Chinese Affairs Commission made a statement denouncing the vicious increase in the annual fee for foreign nationals' identification cards as a means used by the Thai government to attack the Chinese residents in that country. Now, once again, we warn the Thai government that its vicious, unreasonable action is a serious encroachment on the right to existence of several million Chinese residents in Thailand and will certainly not be tolerated by the Chinese people. The Thai government must end this ruthless persecution and extortion or it must hold itself responsible for the grave consequences resulting from this act of persecution of Chinese residents in Thailand.

NOTE

Compare the following item with the PRC's 1963 protest against the British attempt to undertake urban redevelopment in the City of Kowloon, an area that the PRC claimed has traditionally been "part of China's territory and under China's jurisdiction" in a way that the rest of Hong Kong has not (Item 12–15).

25-10

"Official Protest to British Government over Hong Kong Evictions," NCNA–English, Peking (Sept. 10, 1957), in *SCMP*, no. 1609:41–42 (Sept. 13, 1957).

A strong protest was lodged today with the British government against the action of the British authorities in Hong Kong. It was from the Foreign Ministry in a note to the British Chargé d'Affaires' Office here concerning the continued eviction of Chinese residents in the Kowloon area, the tearing down of their houses and [the] levelling of their farms in disregard of the previous protest of the Chinese government and the vehement opposition of the Chinese residents in Hong Kong and Kowloon.

The note also refuted the arguments made by the British government in defense of the unjustifiable actions of the British authorities in Hong Kong in its reply of August 5. This was in answer to the Chinese Foreign Ministry note of July 24.

Today's Foreign Ministry note stated that in its reply of August 5, the British government had rejected the solemn protest and reasonable demand of the Chinese government. Distorting facts, it had also maliciously slandered the Chinese government in an attempt to deny the responsibility of the British authorities in Hong Kong for seriously jeopardizing the legitimate interests of the Chinese residents in Kowloon.

Since July 29 the British authorities in Hong Kong had resumed their campaign of forcible eviction and had made more Chinese residents homeless and destitute, disregarding their protests and opposition.

The Chinese government, therefore, lodged this second serious protest at the same time expressing its extreme wrath.

The Foreign Ministry's note then refuted the vicious calumny against the Chinese government in the British government's reply of August 5.

The plans of the Hong Kong British authorities to evict the people in the district north of the Kaitak airport had from the outset met with vehement opposition and protest from the local Chinese inhabitants, the Foreign Ministry's note pointed out. It was only under the armed threat of a large number of policemen that they finally left their homes under compulsion. Since then, many had not been properly accommodated. Although the authorities had given some compensation to some of the inhabitants, this was done very unreasonably. The compensation was far from sufficient to cover the heavy losses of the inhabitants, and a large number of the inhabitants received no compensation at all.

Yet in its reply the British government alleged that the unreasonable action of the Hong Kong British authorities in forcibly turning Chinese inhabitants of the Kowloon area into homeless, bankrupt vagrants, was a "purely humanitarian action" which the local inhabitants regarded as "fair and reasonable" and met with their "cooperation." This is sheer distortion of facts, a reversal of the truth, the note said.

According to the British reply the initial stage of the eviction plan affected only "7,000 people," the note continued, and it was not planned to carry out extensive eviction in areas to the north and east of Kaitak airport. But according to the statement issued to the Hong Kong press by representatives of ten villages of Kowloon, the number of inhabitants affected by the initial stage of the eviction plan far exceeded 7,000. Statements issued by the Hong Kong authorities on April 6 and May 30 openly admitted that the areas to the north and east of Kaitak airport would in the future also come under the long-term development plan.

Thus the British government deliberately understated the eviction area and the number of inhabitants who would be affected in an attempt to minimize the gravity of the case and so reduce its responsibility, the note stated.

It said that most inhabitants of Hong Kong and Kowloon were Chinese and the Chinese government had the duty and right to demand that the Hong Kong authorities respect and protect their traditional rights and peaceful life. The British government in its reply described the solemn protest and reasonable demands put by the Chinese government to the Hong Kong authorities as "intervening in the internal affairs of another government." This was entirely groundless and could not but be regarded as an attempt to deny the Chinese government its legitimate rights to protect from infringement the legitimate interests of the Chinese residents in Hong Kong and Kowloon. This was, therefore, against the general principles of international law.

The note finally reiterated that the British government and the British authorities in Hong Kong must stop carrying out the unreasonable and forcible eviction of Chinese residents and give them just and reasonable compensation for their loss of property. The traditional rights and normal life of the Chinese residents in Hong Kong and Kowloon had to be honored, it said, otherwise the British government and the British authorities in Hong Kong would have to bear responsibility for all consequences.

25-11

"Foreign Ministry Protests at Hong Kong Flag Incident," NCNA–English, Peking (June 10, 1958), in *SCMP*, no. 1791:34 (June 13, 1958).

The Chinese Foreign Ministry sent a note to the office of the British chargé d'affaires here today strongly protesting against the action of the Hong Kong British authorities in interfering with and prohibiting Chinese residents in Hong Kong from hanging up the Chinese national flag and singing the Chinese national anthem.

The note pointed out that on May 1, 1958, a number of Chinese schools in Hong Kong and Kowloon hoisted the Chinese national flag to celebrate International Labor Day, but the Hong Kong British authorities unreasonably interfered in this matter both before and after the event to force the Chinese schools not to hang up the Chinese national flag.

The Hsinchiao Middle School in Hong Kong had planned to hold school anniversary celebrations on May 10, 1958, but the Hong Kong British authorities prohibited the school from hoisting the Chinese national flag and singing the Chinese national anthem. These actions of the Hong Kong British authorities had aroused great indignation among the Chinese residents in Hong Kong and the entire Chinese people.

The note added that, as Chinese, the Chinese residents in Hong Kong had a sacred and inviolable right to hang up the Chinese national flag and to sing the Chinese national anthem. Instead of respecting this right, the Hong Kong British authorities had crudely violated it. This was an extremely unfriendly action toward the Chinese government and the Chinese people. The Chinese government therefore lodged a strong protest with the British government and demanded that the Hong Kong British authorities immediately stop such infringements on the sacred rights of the Chinese residents in Hong Kong.

25-12

"Hong Kong British Authorities' Unreasonable Action in Cancelling Registration of Chung Wah Middle School Protested," *PR* 11.35:29–30 (Aug. 30, 1968).

A responsible member of the West European Affairs Department of the Chinese Foreign Ministry on the afternoon of August 26 summoned P. Cradock, chargé d'affaires ad interim of the Office of the Chargé d'Affaires of Britain, and lodged a serious protest with the British government against the Hong Kong British authorities' unreasonable action in cancelling the registration of the Chung Wah Middle School.

The responsible member said: On August 3, I clearly expressed to Mr. Hopson the serious concern of the Chinese government over the question of the British authorities in Hong Kong contemplating to cancel the registration of the Chung Wah Middle School in Hong Kong, and I sternly warned the British government that it must enjoin the British authorities in Hong Kong immediately to adopt effective measures to meet the just demands of the teachers and students of that school. However, in disregard of this stern warning of the Chinese government and the strong opposition voiced by the teachers and students of the Chung Wah Middle School and our patriotic countrymen of all circles in Hong Kong and Kowloon, the British authorities in Hong Kong flagrantly announced on August 14 the decision to cancel the registration of that school. This is a grave incident in which the British government and the British authorities in Hong Kong wilfully persecute patriotic Chinese educational undertakings and renew tension in Hong Kong.

The responsible member pointed out: the Chinese government has long ago solemnly stated that Chinese inhabitants in Hong Kong have every right to study and propagate Mao Tse-tung's thought and to carry out relevant activities there, and that they have every right to engage in patriotic educational undertakings in Hong Kong. These sacred rights of theirs brook no encroachment by anybody. On the pretext of an accidental explosion in that school's laboratory, the British authorities in Hong Kong forcibly closed the Chung Wah Middle School last November and unwarrantedly arrested Huang Tsu-fen, the headmaster of the school, thereby seriously depriving several hundred teachers and students of the school of their right to work and study. Now the British authorities in Hong Kong have even resorted to further political persecution against that school by cancelling its registration on the same specious pretext. This move by the British authorities in Hong Kong can only be regarded as a grave political provocation against the Chinese people and their patriotic countrymen in Hong Kong. The Chinese government expresses its indignation over this unreasonable action of the British authorities in Hong Kong. I am instructed to lodge a serious protest with the British government against this.

In conclusion, the responsible member emphasized: the British government has talked glibly about its "desire to ease Sino-British relations" and its "desire to see the settlement of outstanding differences," but in fact it has been committing one brazen provocation after another against the Chinese people and our patriotic countrymen in Hong Kong. The British government and the British authorities in Hong Kong must be held fully responsible for the consequences arising therefrom.

NOTE

For information relating to events that preceded and followed those described in the next item, recall the Note on Macao following item 24–2.

25-13

"Chinese People Armed with Mao Tse-tung's Thought Are Not to Be Trifled with," *PR* 9.51:16, 17–18 (Dec. 16, 1966).

On December 3, the patriotic teachers and students in Macao sent their delegates to lodge a serious protest with the Portuguese authorities against their brutal massacre of Chinese residents on November 15, and to reaffirm that the five demands made by the Taipa residents on November 18 must be accepted: 1. the culprits who engineered the sanguinary incident must be severely punished; 2. the Portuguese authorities on Taipa Island must not obstruct the repair of school buildings and must not violate the proper rights and interests of the residents; 3. the Portuguese authorities on Taipa Island and the Portuguese police in Macao must compensate the injured for all their medical expenses as well as for all their losses resulting from this incident; 4. the unreasonable sentence given to their delegates by the Portuguese office of the judicial police in Macao should be annulled; 5. the Portuguese authorities in Macao must guarantee against any recurrence of similar incidents of residents being beaten. Employing the most despicable means, the Portuguese authorities in Macao induced the delegates to enter the "Governor's Office" where they were shut in and savagely beaten. At the same time, large numbers of troops and policemen, armored vehicles and tanks were sent to open fire on Chinese shops, homes, and residents, thus precipitating an unprecedented tragic incident in which Chinese residents were massacred. Shooting at Chinese residents was still taking place on December 5. According to incomplete statistics, there was a total of more than one hundred casualties on December 3 and 4, including eight killed. White terror reigned over all Macao. The lives and property of Chinese compatriots there were under grave threat. . . .

A statement by the Director of the Foreign Affairs Bureau of the Kwangtung Provincial People's Council on December 9 protested in the strongest terms against the fascist atrocities of the Portuguese authorities in Macao.

"Taking up the minor issue to avoid the major one," the statement said, "the Portuguese authorities in Macao have now feigned acceptance of the demands of the Chinese residents on Taipa Island in an attempt to evade their grave responsibility for the criminal massacre of Chinese residents on a big scale since December 3. This is a fraud which will never succeed. The Foreign Affairs Bureau of the Kwangtung Provincial People's Council is instructed to lodge the strongest protest against the fascist atrocities of the Portuguese authorities in Macao. The Chinese people firmly support the just actions of the patriotic compatriots in Macao. The Portuguese authorities in Macao must

1. Immediately and unconditionally accept the five demands put forward on November 18 by the Chinese residents on Taipa Island, Macao;

2. Immediately and unconditionally accept the five demands put forward on December 5 by the Chinese Students' Union in Macao; [1. Fully accept and comply with the five demands put forward by the Taipa residents; 2. punish Octavio Figueiredo, the chief culprit who directed the suppression of the patriotic teachers and students; 3. immediately stop the criminal shooting of Chinese compatriots in Macao; 4. undertake to compensate the victimized persons for all their losses; 5. guarantee against any recurrence of the atrocities in suppressing Chinese compatriots in Macao.—*Peking Review* Ed.]

3. Immediately apologize to the Chinese residents and severely punish the chief culprits: army commander Carlos Armando da Mota Cerveira, police commandant Octavio Figueiredo, deputy police commandant Antonio Vaz Antunes, and acting island administrator Rui de Andrade;

4. Effectively guarantee that no agents of the Chiang Kai-shek gang will ever be permitted to operate in Macao in any manner; immediately return for disposition by the Chinese government the seven agents of the Chiang Kai-shek gang whom the Portuguese authorities in Macao took off [*sic*] in June 1963 by intruding into Chinese waters.

> We must solemnly warn the Portuguese authorities in Macao that the Chinese people, armed with the great thought of Mao Tse-tung, are not to be trifled with and that the Chinese residents in Macao must in no way be bullied. The Portuguese authorities in Macao must immediately accept and fully comply with all the just demands put forward by the Chinese side. Should you try to seek the intervention of the Chiang Kai-shek gang and US and British imperialism in Macao's affairs, the Chinese people absolutely will not tolerate it.

On December 11, *Renmin Ribao* carried an article by its commentator which sternly warned the Portuguese authorities in Macao. The article said that the four-point proposition in the above statement expressed the firm stand of the 700 million Chinese people. "The Portuguese authorities in Macao must immediately accept and fully comply with the just demands of the Chinese side. Otherwise, you will eat the fruits of your action," the article concluded.

Note

According to the *Peking Review*, in addition to signing the protocol in which they guaranteed the PRC that they would prohibit ROC activities, personnel, and symbols in Macao and would return future refugees to the PRC, the Portuguese authorities also "signed a document admitting their bloody crimes of last November 15 and December 3." They "accepted in full the four-point demand put forward in the statement by the director of the Foreign Affairs Bureau of the Kwangtung Provincial People's Council and the six-point [*sic*] demand raised by Chinese compatriots in Macao. . . . They said that they would bear full responsibility for these crimes, punish the chief culprits and pay indemnity for all losses incurred in the incidents, admit their crimes and apologize to all the Chinese in Macao, and truly guarantee the safety of Chinese lives and property and the protection of their legitimate interests."[84]

The activism that the Cultural Revolution inspired in Chinese students abroad led to diplomatic frictions between the PRC and a number of states. The events described in the following excerpt of a statement of the Chinese Foreign Ministry brought Sino-Soviet relations to a new low and set in motion a chain of hostile actions.

25-14

"Strongest and Most Vehement Protest against Fanatic Suppression by Soviet Revisionists of Chinese Students Returning from Europe," *PR* 12.6: 21–22 (Feb. 3, 1967).

On January 25, 1967, with feelings of boundless respect for the great revolutionary teacher of the proletariat Lenin and the great Marxist-Leninist Stalin, 69 Chinese students returning from Europe via Moscow proceeded in an orderly and neat column to Lenin's Mausoleum and Stalin's tomb to lay wreaths. They read out quotations from Chairman Mao Tse-tung, the reddest, reddest red sun in the hearts of the revolutionary people of the world, to express their boundless faith in and boundless love for Marxism-Leninism [and] Mao Tse-tung's thought.

This action of the Chinese students is an entirely revolutionary one. It is fine! All revolutionary students, youths, and people of China and the world, including those of the Soviet Union, will warmly support and praise them.

However, these Chinese students were subjected to barbarous suppression by the Soviet revisionist ruling clique. When they were reading out quotations from Chairman Mao Tse-tung, the Soviet government called out the two or three hundred soldiers, policemen, and plainclothesmen planted there in advance to encircle and savagely assault them, injuring over 30 of them with four seriously wounded, of whom one is in a critical state with broken ribs.

The Chinese government and people express the utmost indignation at this fascist atrocity by the Soviet revisionist ruling clique and lodge the most, most vehement protest against it.

In wildly suppressing the Chinese students before Lenin's Mausoleum and Stalin's tomb, the Soviet revisionist ruling clique has once again revealed their features as renegades from Marxism-Leninism. Listen, you chieftains of Soviet revisionism Brezhnev, Kosygin, and the like: All those who suppress student movements, all those who enforce fascist rule over the people, and all those who betray the revolution will come to no good end! The German, Italian, and Japanese fascists came to no good end. Chiang Kai-shek came to no good end. The Czar of Russia came to no good end. Kautsky came to no good end. Khrushchev came to no good end. And you will definitely come to no good end either! This is not the first time that Chinese students have shed their blood on the streets of Moscow. A new debt has been incurred before the old ones are cleared. All these debts must be repaid in full!

NOTE

At the same time as the Foreign Ministry in Peking issued the above protest, the Chinese Embassy in Moscow lodged a protest with the Soviet Foreign Ministry "in the strongest and most serious terms." According to the *Peking Review*:

> The protest note pointed out that the bloody suppression of the Chinese students by the military, police, and plainclothesmen of Soviet revisionism was a grave incident planned and engineered beforehand by the Soviet government. It demanded that the Soviet government apologize publicly, punish the culprits, and assume responsibility for all consequences arising therefrom. Because justice was not on its side and it was short of arguments, the Soviet Foreign Ministry at first refused to receive the Chinese chargé d'affaires ad interim and took refuge in stalling tactics. The Chinese chargé d'affaires insisted and Soviet Vice-Foreign Minister Firyubin finally had to agree to an interview. Firyubin did not have a leg to stand on in face of ironclad facts and lamely threatened that the Soviet side would "prohibit Chinese citizens from travelling via the Soviet Union." The Chinese chargé d'affaires threw this back in his teeth.[85]

The Soviet version of the events in question, related by *Pravda*, was markedly different from China's:

> On January 25, in Moscow's Red Square, a group of Chinese citizens passing through the USSR and CPR embassy staff members accompanying them, in crude violation of the established and commonly known rules for visiting the V. I. Lenin Mausoleum, created disturbances, annoyed other visitors, forced their way ahead of them and prevented them from entering the Mausoleum, which actions they accompanied with anti-Soviet shouts, jeering, and other unseemly outbursts. The provocative behavior of the Chinese citizens at this site, sacred to every Soviet man, aroused the just indignation of Soviet people in Red Square.
>
> In view of the outrageous hooligan actions of the Chinese citizens in Red Square, the USSR Ministry of Foreign Affairs has lodged a resolute protest to the CPR embassy in Moscow. The USSR Ministry of Foreign Affairs has demanded that the embassy take all the necessary measures to ensure that Chinese citizens in the USSR behave in a proper manner. It is emphasized that any violations by Chinese citizens of laws and of public order in the Soviet Union will be halted in the most decisive manner and that

the Chinese side will bear full responsibility for possible consequences.[86]

Demonstrations against the Soviet action by Chinese students in other countries immediately led to fresh incidents that in turn elicited further Chinese protests. For example:

> Ten Chinese students studying in Iraq went to the Soviet embassy in Baghdad on January 28 to deliver a letter protesting the fascist atrocity perpetrated in Moscow three days earlier by the Soviet revisionist ruling clique in sanguinarily suppressing Chinese students returning from Europe. The Soviet embassy, with Counsellor A. S. Novikov in the lead, mustered over 30 of its thugs to savagely beat up the Chinese students and the correspondent of the Hsinhua News Agency. Five of the Chinese students were injured and the correspondent was seriously injured and his camera smashed.
>
> On January 30, the Chinese Foreign Ministry sent a note to the Soviet embassy in China lodging the strongest and most vehement protest against the incident. This, said the note, was a "continuation and development of . . . bloodshed created by the Soviet revisionists on the Red Square of Moscow," and was "one more proof of the crimes of the Soviet revisionist ruling clique in uniting with the United States against China and in being hostile to and opposing China's great proletarian Cultural Revolution." "Your embassy has already become a lair for a mob of fascist hooligans in perpetrating counterrevolutionary atrocities. This constitutes not only another grave provocation against the Chinese people but also a serious provocation against the people of Asia and the world," the note added.[87]

25-15

"Chinese Students' Valiant Struggle in Paris," *PR* 12.6:30 (Feb. 3, 1967).

Forty-nine Chinese students who had studied in Rennes, France, made their way to the Soviet embassy in Paris on the evening of January 27 to lodge a protest against Soviet revisionism's January 25 bloody suppression in Moscow of Chinese students. Before they reached the embassy, the French police authorities called in about 200 policemen to launch a surprise raid on the students who were surrounded on the sidewalk from three sides and arrested by force. The French policemen brutally dragged the men students by their necks or ears and the women students by their hair or plaits into a police van. The students defended themselves heroically. All 49 of them, 19 of them were women, were beaten up by the police. Some received head wounds and bled, while others suffered internal injuries.

Violating the Chinese students' deep feelings for Chairman Mao-Tse-tung, the most respected and beloved leader of the Chinese people, the police tore up his portraits and trampled on copies of *Quotations From Chairman Mao Tse-tung.*

Yi Su-chih, First Secretary of the Chinese embassy in France, lodged a protest with Etienne Manach, Director of the Asian Department of the French Foreign Ministry. Because justice was not on his side, Manach had nothing to say and did not dare reject the verbal protest of the Chinese side. All the arrested Chinese students were released at three o'clock on the afternoon of January 28. . . .

On the same day, Peking's revolutionary masses, including workers and young Red Guards, angrily demonstrated in front of the French embassy to voice their protest. Holding portraits of Chairman Mao and red-covered copies of *Quotations From Chairman Mao Tse-tung,* the demonstrators warned the Paris authorities that the Chinese people armed with Mao Tse-tung's thought were not to be trifled with and that those who worked with the Soviet revisionists against China would come to no good end. They also lodged the strongest protest against the criminal French police action of tearing up Chairman Mao's portraits and trampling on the *Quotations.* The walls of the embassy building and the grounds outside were posted with the slogans: "Down with imperialism!" "Rebel against whoever is hostile to the Chinese people!" and "Bash in the French thugs' heads!"

NOTE

The Cultural Revolution was not the first occasion on which the French government was thought by Peking to have interfered with Chinese students. In 1952, during the Korean war and over a decade before France established relations with the PRC, France decided to dissolve the Chinese Students' Association in Paris. The All-China Students' Federation, in addition to sending a message of support to the Association, sent a protest to French Premier Pinay that stated: "This hostile act of the French government was obviously pressed for by the remnant Chiang Kai-shek brigands as part of the attack on our students in France and violation of the proper rights and interests of our overseas Chinese abroad. On behalf of the students throughout China, we lodge a solemn protest with you and demand that you immediately require the French government to withdraw its unreasonable decision."[88]

Because a rising tide of economic nationalism has led many newly independent Southeast Asian countries to impose discriminatory business regulations upon the economically powerful Chinese minority within their midst, the PRC has had many opportunities to seek to protect its nationals against such discrimination. As in the case of other claims to protection, whether the PRC has actually gone to the aid of the overseas Chinese community in question has depended on Peking's perception of the political expediency of doing so; the two periods of particular activism to date have been the regime's earliest years and the Cultural Revolution.

Nevertheless, even at times when Peking has preferred "to treat the Chinese abroad as an embarrassing nuisance complicating the implementation of [its] grand strategy" of winning the cooperation of neighboring Southeast Asian governments,[89] economic discrimination has occasionally been so blatant that Peking could not ignore it. Such a case occurred when Indonesia promulgated the infamous Presidential Regulation No. 10 of November 16, 1959, which prohibited alien, that is, Chinese, retailers, distributors, and middlemen from doing business in the rural areas of Indonesia. The following indicates the PRC's response.

25-16

"Foreign Minister Ch'en Yi's Letter on December 24 to Indonesian Foreign Minister," NCNA–English, Peking (Dec. 25, 1959), in *SCMP*, no. 2167:47–49 (Dec. 31, 1959).

Foreign Minister of the People's Republic of China, Ch'en Yi, on December 24 sent a letter to the Foreign Minister of the Indonesian Republic, Subandrio, in reply to his letter of December 11. The reply reads:

His Excellency Dr. Subandrio,
Minister of Foreign Affairs of the
Republic of Indonesia,
Djakarta.

Your Excellency,

I thank Your Excellency for your letter dated December 11, 1959.

I note with pleasure that Your Excellency has indicated in your letter that the Indonesian government wishes to strengthen the friendly relations between our two countries, that it agrees to exchange the instruments of ratification of the Treaty on the Question of Dual Nationality and institute a joint committee, and that it will not undertake to obstruct those overseas Chinese who wish to return to China but is prepared to consider rendering assistance to them. However, I note at the same time that the Indonesian government has failed to show a definite attitude toward the Chinese government's proposal that the two sides immediately appoint representatives to hold negotiations for an overall settlement of the overseas Chinese question. Considering the present grave situation in connection with the overseas Chinese question, and for the sake of safeguarding the friendly relations between our two countries, the Chinese government eagerly hopes that the Indonesian government will adopt a positive and cooperative attitude and agree to undertake negotiations at once.

The contentions made by Your Excellency in your letter concerning the role of the overseas Chinese in Indonesia and the root cause of the present activities of antagonism and discrimination against the Chinese, and the charges levelled against the Chinese representative organs in Indonesia are all unacceptable to the Chinese government. The Chinese government, however, considers that endless arguments about these matters will only hamper the joint efforts of the governments of our two countries for the settlement of the urgent question of overseas Chinese. Here I would only give necessary presentation of some of the most important facts.

The overwhelming majority of the overseas Chinese in Indonesia are working people. For generations, they have lived amicably with the Indonesian people and have played their part in the economic development and the cause of national independence of Indonesia. They are fundamentally different from the colonialists backed up by gunboats and harboring the aim of oppressing and plundering another country. It is true that a very small number among the overseas Chinese do not behave well. But it would be unfair, merely on account of this, to describe the entire overseas Chinese community as a monopoly group which hinders Indonesia's economic development and to make them the main target of discrimination and attack.

How to adjust the economic position of the overseas Chinese in the course of the development of Indonesia's national economy is a complicated question. That is why the foreign ministers of our two countries in their joint communiqué issued on October 11 this year expressed the common view that "an appropriate way should be sought for the solution of this question so that it will be in the interest of the economic development of Indonesia and that the proper rights and interests of the Chinese nationals will be respected"; they also mutually agreed that "the economic resources of those Chinese nationals will still play a useful role in the economic development of Indonesia." As a matter of fact, the Chinese government has always advised and encouraged the overseas Chinese in Indonesia to take an active part in local economic construction, and has suggested on more than one occasion that the Indonesian government take suitable steps to lead and turn overseas Chinese capital step by step from trade to industry. Unfortunately, the regulation on the prohibition of alien small or retail trade in rural areas has been utilized to make concentrated attack on overseas Chinese, and even to enforce the forcible evacuation of overseas Chinese on a large scale, so that tens of thousands of overseas Chinese have lost their homes and properties, become displaced, and landed in a desperate situation. This state of affairs is not only inconsistent with the principles set forth by the two foreign ministers in their joint communiqué, but also inconsistent with His Excellency President Sukarno's call for maintaining a cooperative atmosphere as made by him in the political manifesto of August 17, 1959. Under these circumstances, overseas Chinese are not to be blamed for making complaints about their difficulties and asking for fair and reasonable treatment of their own accord.

The Chinese government has always encouraged the overseas Chinese to abide by the laws and decrees of the Indonesian government, and has never interfered in Indonesia's internal affairs. As Your Excellency has also agreed in your letter, however, it is the obligation of the government of the People's Republic of China to protect the rights of the overseas Chinese. The execution by the Chinese representative organs in Indonesia of their duty to protect their own nationals, while the latter's proper rights and interests are seriously impaired, can in no way be interpreted as agitation to incite overseas Chinese to defy the orders of the local government, even less can it be used justifiably as an excuse for placing discriminative restrictions on the Chinese diplomatic representative organs. The Chinese government cannot accept the protest contained in Your Excellency's letter, and asks once again that the Indonesian government lift at once the discriminative restrictions imposed on the Chinese representative organs.

I presume Your Excellency will share my view about the gravity of the present issue concerning the overseas Chinese. At present, the imperialists are taking advantage of the situation to sabotage the relations between our two countries and divert the people of the Asian countries from the goals of their struggle. Therefore, whether a proper overall settlement of the overseas Chinese question can be achieved quickly not only concerns the destiny of millions of overseas Chinese and the friendship between our two countries, but also has a bearing on our common cause of opposing colonialism and safeguarding peace. It is precisely on the basis of this understanding that I, on behalf of the Chinese government, put forward in my previous letter the three-point proposal for an overall settlement of the overseas Chinese question. Your Excellency has in your reply set forth the opinions of the Indonesian government on the Chinese government's three-point proposal. In order to bring the opinions of the two sides closer to each other, I would like to give further explanations on behalf of the Chinese government. . . .

The exchange of instruments of ratification and the establishment of a joint committee by the two sides, which will provide the legal basis and the necessary institution for the implementation of the dual nationality treaty, will indeed be a happy progress. However, in the present conditions in which activities of antagonism and discrimination against the Chinese continue to spread in Indonesia, those who originally inclined to choose Indonesian nationality are beset with great misgivings and, what is even more important, those who are capable of making contributions to Indonesia's economic development also feel unsure about their future in staying on in Indonesia. The Chinese government has never had, nor will have, any intention of interfering in Indonesia's internal affairs. However, I believe Your Excellency will also agree that matters involving the proper rights and interests of overseas Chinese should be negotiated and settled reasonably by the two sides in accordance with the principles agreed upon long ago.

It is also necessary to point out that now already a fairly large number of overseas Chinese have lost their means of livelihood or do not wish to stay on in Indonesia. To send these overseas Chinese back to China as quickly as possible is a pressing question to be tended to right now. The sending of overseas Chinese back to China not only involves a series of detailed organizational work, but also contains the question of protecting the interests and safety of the overseas Chinese. For this reason, too, the two governments should immediately hold consultations and make proper arrangements so that the work of sending back these overseas Chinese can start at an early date.

The Chinese government has always held that a reasonable overall settlement of the overseas Chinese question is possible only if those overseas Chinese who wish to remain in Indonesia can do so in a friendly atmosphere and under secure conditions, while others who wish to leave Indonesia are enabled to do so with their interests and safety fully taken care of.

Out of the above-mentioned considerations, the Chinese government once again suggests that the two governments immediately appoint representatives to hold negotiations on the Chinese government's three-point proposal for an overall settlement of the overseas Chinese question and any corresponding proposals the Indonesian government may put forward. Following the Indonesian government's agreement to this suggestion of the Chinese government, Ambassador Huang Chen as the representative of the Chinese government will enter into negotiations with the representative to be appointed by the Indonesian government.

I avail myself of this opportunity to renew to Your Excellency the assurance of my highest consideration.

(signed) Ch'en Yi,
Minister of Foreign Affairs
of the People's Republic of China

NOTE

At the time that Ch'en Yi wrote the above letter, well over a million overseas Chinese nationals also held or claimed Indonesian nationality.[90] Yet the PRC did not limit its protection to overseas Chinese who did not claim to be Indonesian nationals. Recall publicist Liu Chia-chi's criticism of Article 4 of the 1930 Convention on Certain Questions Relating to Conflict of Nationality, which prohibited a state from affording diplomatic protection to one of its nationals against a state whose nationality such person also possesses (23–6). But also recall Peking's position regarding India's asserted right to protect persons of Indian origin residing in China who were claimed as nationals by both countries (23–8).

Relations between China and Indonesia gradually improved after 1959, and enforcement of Regulation No. 10 was correspondingly relaxed until "the measure had to all intents and purposes been forgotten." [91] The PRC's alleged involvement in the unsuccessful September 30, 1965, coup d'état, however, caused Sino-Indonesian friendship to deteriorate to such an extent that diplomatic relations were "suspended" in October 1967. During the postcoup era, persons of Chinese descent in Indonesia suffered terribly from a variety of abuses, and the PRC issued a stream of protests of which we have already seen one (4–4). The following Note of November 27, 1965 is typical of the series.

25-17

"China Lodges Strongest Protest with Indonesia," *PR* 8.49:8, 9–10 (Dec. 3, 1965).

The embassy of the People's Republic of China in Indonesia presents its compliments to the Ministry of Foreign Affairs of the Republic of Indonesia and has the honor to state the following:

(1) Since October 1965, serious outrages of persecution of overseas Chinese have occurred one after another in Semarang, Solo, Magelang, Pekalongan, and many other countries and districts in Central Java.

(2) The properties of overseas Chinese have been severely damaged. After its arrival in Solo on October 22, the Regiment of Paratroop Commando of the Indonesian Army (RPKAD) paraded in armored cars and trucks in the main streets of the city. Shielded by these military cars, the organized right-wing hooligans wantonly smashed up and burnt down shops and residences of Chinese nationals along the streets. Of many of the houses of Chinese nationals on Djalan Warung Pelem only broken walls are left, and all properties have been reduced to ashes. It is a horrible sight. On the night of October 25, hooligans also burnt down Chung Hua Chung Hui and the Chung Hua School in Kebumen. On the morning of October 26, hooligans in the city and its vicinity again assembled and went in groups to smash up shops and residences of Chinese nationals. None of the houses and factories of Chinese nationals on Djalan Kolopaking was spared. More than 90 per cent of the Chinese nationals in the city suffered extremely serious losses, and there are quite a number of people who have been thus rendered propertyless and homeless. Eight of the overseas Chinese organizations and schools were burnt down or completely wrecked.

(3) The personal safety of Chinese nationals is seriously threatened. Between the end of October and the middle of November, over 40 Chinese nationals were unwarrantedly arrested by troops or police in Semarang, Pekalongan, Purwodadi, Salatiga, Sragen, Tjepu, Jogdjakarta, and Solo of Central Java, and over 20 of them are still in custody, including many responsible officials of the overseas Chinese organizations in various places. Frame-up charges were brought against them, and they have time and again been unwarrantedly interrogated. Many have even been beaten up or cruelly tortured. In the dead of the night of October 29, the Regiment of Paratroop Commando of the Army forcibly broke into and searched the Hua Ing Middle School in Semarang and brazenly insulted the teachers and students, abusing them as "China dogs" and savagely threatening them with the remarks, "If we fail, we'll kill you

first" and "when [the] time comes, we'll kill you all, women as well as men."

On November 10, the residence of the Chinese national Oei Tjong Kwi in Djepara County was searched by the Regiment of Paratroop Commando of the Army, and Oei Tjong Kwi himself was taken away. After "interrogation" a document was issued him proving him to be innocent. But when he was going home from Bangsri under the escort of the police, a gang of hooligans, with weapons in their hands, blocked his way, knocked him down, and then poured kerosene on him and burnt him to death. On November 15 the Chinese national Liem Dioen Kwang and his son Liem Djin Ho were kidnapped in Solo by a gang of hooligans during the curfew and then brutally killed in a pasture nearby.

It is clear from all [of] the above that the outrageous persecution of the Chinese nationals stage-managed by the Indonesian-right-wing forces in Central Java has reached serious proportions in its cruelty. It must be stressed that the embassy has repeatedly sent notes to the Indonesian government urging it to put a speedy and effective stop to the persecution of Chinese nationals in various parts of Indonesia. However, up to now we have not received any effectual reply; what is more, the persecution of Chinese nationals by the right-wing forces is daily widening in scope, and their outrageous actions are becoming still more rampant. In Semarang, Solo, and Magelang, Central Java, the Regiment of Paratroop Commando of the Army of Indonesia has gone to the length of supporting the hooligans openly and with armed force, so that the latter are emboldened to do whatever they like. This fully testifies to the role played by the troops of the Indonesian army in the outrageous persecution of Chinese nationals. For this the Indonesian government has the unshirkable responsibility.

The Chinese embassy hereby lodges the strongest protest with the Indonesian government and demands that it take immediate and effective measures to put an end to the outrageous persecution of Chinese nationals in all parts of Indonesia, punish the instigators and those who murdered Chinese nationals, give relief to the dependents of the innocent victims, speedily release the Chinese nationals who have been unwarrantedly arrested, compensate the Chinese nationals concerned for all their losses, and effectively safeguard the personal safety and property of the Chinese nationals.

Because of communications difficulties in various parts of Indonesia, the Chinese embassy is now still in no position to have full information about the serious persecution of Chinese nationals and their losses, and it reserves the right to raise further demands.

The embassy avails itself of this opportunity to renew to the Ministry of Foreign Affairs the assurance of its highest consideration.

NOTE

That in this case the PRC's perception of the harm suffered by overseas Chinese was not unduly distorted has been carefully documented by a leading scholar of Indonesian affairs, who has characterized the events of 1965–1967 as a "continuing anti-Chinese pogrom [in which] the restraining gestures and pacifying efforts of the Indonesian authorities frequently seemed to have a rather perfunctory character." [92]

Item 25–18 illustrates Peking's efforts to protect overseas Chinese workers against the hostile actions of foreign governments. It presents the PRC's perception of the labor dispute, and the chain of events that it precipitated, leading to the major Sino-British difficulties over Hong Kong during 1967–1969 (see 25–23 and 29–8). This document is especially interesting because it explicitly recognizes the connection between the extraterritorial spread of the Cultural Revolution, on the one hand, and the reaction of the local government and ensuing PRC protest, on the other.

25-18

"Hong Kong Incident Note from CPR [PRC] Foreign Ministry to British Chargé d'Affaires to China, May 15, 1967." NCNA–English, Peking (May 15, 1967), printed in *FBIS*, no. 94:BBB3–5 (May 15, 1967).

On the afternoon of 6 May 1967, Chinese workers of the Hong Kong Sanpokong artificial plastic flower works launched a struggle against intensified capitalist exploitation. To shield capital and suppress labor, the British authorities in Hong Kong brazenly turned out on the same day more than 200 armed policemen and "riot police," sanguinarily suppressing the workers of the factory and other Chinese residents, beating and wounding many of them, and arresting 21 persons. Afterwards they also arrested the president of the federation of the rubber and plastic trade unions and workers' representatives who went to [the] Hong Kong police station to protest.

On the afternoon of 11 May the British authorities in Hong Kong carried out another sanguinary suppression on an even bigger scale by turning loose on the bare-handed workers, representatives of various circles, young students, large numbers of armed troops, policemen, and "riot police" totaling more than 1,000, who repeatedly attacked them with clubs, riot guns, and tear gas bombs, and even turning out military vehicles and helicopters. Many persons (including newsreel cameramen and journalists) were arrested. After 12 May the British authorities in Hong Kong still continued large-scale arrests of the demonstrating masses. By the morning of 14 May more than 400 had been arrested. At present the situation is still being aggravated.

It must be pointed out that these large-scale sanguinary atrocities perpetrated by the British authorities in Hong Kong are the result of long premeditation and are a component part of the British government's scheme of collusion with US imperialism against China. On the one hand, in coordination with the US imperialist war escalation in Vietnam, the British government is continuing to provide the United States with Hong Kong as a base for aggression against Vietnam in disregard of the repeated solemn warnings of the Chinese government, and, on the other, it is steadily stepping up various hostile measures against China in Hong Kong. Particularly since the unfolding of the great proletarian cultural revolution in China, the British authorities in Hong Kong have carried out repeated military and police maneuvers hostile to China and aimed at the sanguinary suppression of Chinese residents in Hong Kong, vainly attempting to exclude the great influence of China's great proletarian cultural revolution by high-handed tactics. The persecution of Chinese residents and workers by the British authorities in Hong Kong by making use of the labor-capital dispute of the artificial plastic flower works is a big exposure of this criminal plan of sanguinary suppression. Their fascist atrocities have aroused boundless indignation among the Chinese residents in Hong Kong and the entire Chinese people. The Chinese government hereby lodges the most urgent and the strongest protest with the British government against these atrocities.

The sanguinary atrocities wholly perpetrated by the British authorities in Hong Kong show that they mortally fear and bitterly hate China's great proletarian cultural revolution. This great revolutionary movement, which is without parallel in history, has dealt a telling blow to imperialism, modern revisionism, and world reaction, completely shattered their dream of counterrevolutionary capitalist restoration in China, and greatly encouraged and impelled the liberation struggles of the oppressed people and oppressed nations of the whole world. In particular, this great revolutionary movement has caused our Chinese compatriots in Hong Kong to love still more ardently the thought of Mao Tse-tung, and they are vigorously unfolding the movement of creative study and application of Chairman Mao's works. Armed with the ever victorious thought of Mao Tse-tung, the masses of our patriotic compatriots are more militant than ever in fighting imperialism. Frightened out of their wits by this, the British authorities in Hong Kong vainly attempted by violent suppression to restrict the influence of Mao

Tse-tung's thought and to maintain their control, and thus committed the barbarous fascist atrocities.

The Chinese government must sternly warn the British government that in so doing you have completely miscalculated and misjudged your opponent. Succeeding to the glorious tradition of anti-imperialist struggle of over a century, the Chinese workers and residents in Hong Kong armed with Mao Tse-tung's thought are neither to be cowed nor crushed. Holding high the great red banner of Mao Tse-tung's thoughts, they are resolute, fear no sacrifice, and are surmounting every difficulty to win victory in this struggle against the atrocities committed by the British authorities in Hong Kong.

Heroic, stanch, and unyielding, they have greatly developed the glorious anti-imperialist and patriotic tradition and are indeed fine sons and daughters of the Chinese nation. The British authorities in Hong Kong are blustering and baring their fangs, but as Chairman Mao, the great leader of the Chinese people, has pointed out: "In the final analysis, their persecution of the revolutionary people only serves to accelerate the people's revolutions on a broader and more intense scale." In sanguinarily suppressing Chinese residents, the British authorities in Hong Kong can only end up like one "lifting a rock only to drop it on one's own feet."

The Chinese government hereby solemnly declares: The Chinese government and the 700 million Chinese people firmly support their compatriots in Hong Kong in their heroic and just struggle and resolutely stand behind them as their powerful backing. The Chinese government demands in all seriousness that the British government instruct the British authorities in Hong Kong as follows:

Immediately accept all the just demands put forward by Chinese workers and residents in Hong Kong;

Immediately stop all fascist measures;

Immediately set free all the arrested persons (including workers, journalists, and cameramen);

Punish the culprits responsible for these sanguinary atrocities, offer apologies to the victims, and compensate for all their losses;

Guarantee against the occurrence of similar incidents.

The British government and the British authorities in Hong Kong must immediately and unconditionally accept the above-mentioned solemn and just demands of the Chinese government. The Chinese government and people are determined to carry the struggle through to the end. Should the British government and the British authorities in Hong Kong cling to their perverse course, they must be held responsible for all the grave consequences arising therefrom.

NOTE

The language used in the Chinese press to describe Britain's determined effort to control the unrest in Hong Kong was more colorful than that of the Foreign Ministry. The very high official whose articles in the *People's Daily* are signed "Commentator" published a number of broadside attacks of which the following reminders of the Chinese Communists' historic sense of grievance are samples:

a. The sanguinary persecution of Chinese residents by Hong Kong British authorities is an out-and-out fascist outrage. However, the British imperialists have stubbornly refused to admit their crimes. As soon as he heard the words "fascist outrage," British Foreign Secretary Brown, touched to the quick, gave vent to a hysterical outburst. We ask Brown: What are you making such a fuss about? You turned out thousands of police and "riot police" and used helicopters and tear gas bombs to suppress completely unarmed Chinese residents. What is this if not a fascist outrage? On the main thoroughfares and in the sidestreets, you severely beat up and arrested Chinese workers, students, journalists, and even ten-year-olds. What is this if not a fascist outrage? You sent a large number of plainclothesmen and special agents, illegally kidnapped patriotic Chinese compatriots, tried them secretly and savagely beat them up. What is all this if not an out-and-out fascist outrage?

Furthermore, Brown had the cheek to lodge a "protest" with the Chinese people against their just action of condemning the fascist atrocities of the British authorities in Hong Kong. Shut up! Instead of hanging your head and admitting your guilt after killing, arresting, illegally trying, and cruelly persecuting Chinese compatriots in Hong Kong, you British imperialists made countercharges. You have really overreached yourselves! Today, in the 1960's are you still dreaming of your good old days of the Opium War?

It must be pointed out in all seriousness that the British government is now playing with fire in Hong Kong.[93]

b. Just as our patriotic compatriots in Hong Kong and Kowloon were valiantly unfolding their struggle against persecution, the British imperialist aircraft carrier *Bulwark* suddenly appeared in the seas off Hong Kong on May 26. In these last few days, six British warships have sailed to Hong Kong. These are shameless threats and intimidations made by British imperialism against our patriotic compatriots in Hong Kong and Kowloon in a vain attempt to repeat the old nineteenth-century imperialist trick of "gunboat-policy."

On the same day, British governor of Hong Kong, David Trench, who is the chief culprit in the sanguinary suppression of our patriotic compatriots, clamored that the British authorities in Hong Kong had "the fullest support of the British government in maintaining peace and order." That is to say, backed by the British government's "gunboat policy," the British authorities in Hong Kong are in a position to do even greater evil and suppress our compatriots there in a still more unrestrained way. Look, this decayed British imperialism is trying a bluff before the great Chinese people—how extremely silly and ridiculous it is! [94]

25-19

"Note from CPR [PRC] Foreign Ministry to Burmese Embassy in China, July 4, 1967," NCNA–English, Peking (July 4, 1967), printed in *FBIS*, no. 129:BBB7–9 (July 5, 1967).

Of late, the Burmese government has been frantically conducting anti-Chinese activities, subjecting overseas Chinese to inhuman and heinous persecution and massacre, and the situation continues to deteriorate.

At the instigation and with the connivance of the Burmese government, thousands of ruffians have been brutally massacring overseas Chinese since 22 June, and according to preliminary information, more than 100 overseas Chinese have been murdered in Rangoon alone. On 27 June ruffians broke into the office of the Overseas Chinese Teachers Federation in Burma and committed the most shocking fascist atrocity of beating 27 persons to death. The number of wounded overseas Chinese over the last few days is far greater.

What is still more intolerable is that after instigating ruffians to slaughter overseas Chinese on a large scale, the Burmese government has even refused to let the families of the deceased identify and examine the bodies. This is indeed arbitrary and insolent to the extreme!

While ruthlessly massacring overseas Chinese, the Burmese government has arrested and imprisoned a large number of them. On 27 June over 600 students of the former Overseas Chinese Middle School and the former Nan Yan[g] Middle School and their parents as well as overseas Chinese in several suburban areas of Rangoon were arrested and held en masse in army barracks. The Burmese radio admitted on 1 July that more than 1,300 overseas Chinese were held in the Mingaladone army barracks in Rangoon. Meanwhile, the Burmese government has imposed military control over those districts of Rangoon where the homes of the overseas Chinese are concentrated and dispatched troops and policemen to surround these districts, so that the broad masses of overseas Chinese are deprived of freedom and are unable to maintain their subsistence.

During the last few days, the Burmese government has instigated ruffians to engage in large-scale looting and destruction of the shops of overseas Chinese and burned their houses and property, inflicting heavy losses on them.

Far from abating, the anti-Chinese atrocities engineered by the Burmese government have spread to some medium and small cities in Burma despite the repeated strong protests of the Chinese government. Thousands of ruffians have persecuted the overseas Chinese in Mandalay, Magwe, Bassein, Yenangchaung, and other places.

These incidents of large-scale persecution of overseas Chinese are entirely engineered by the Burmese government in an organized, planned, and systematic way. Against this the Chinese government once again lodges the most urgent and strongest protest with the Burmese government. The Chinese government solemnly points out: The broad masses of overseas Chinese who have lived in Burma for generations have forged a profound militant friendship with the Burmese people. They have contributed greatly to the friendship between the Chinese and Burmese peoples, to the anti-imperialist revolutionary struggles of the Burmese people, and to the development of Burma's national economy. No one will ever succeed in the attempt to write off this contribution made by the broad masses of overseas Chinese. Out of the needs of its reactionary domestic and foreign policies, the Burmese government has now acted against the interests and wishes of the Burmese people and perpetrated in a planned way the above barbarous fascist anti-Chinese atrocities regardless of all consequences. This is what the people of China as well as those of Burma absolutely cannot tolerate.

The Chinese government must tell the Burmese government in all seriousness that in so frantically opposing China and so brutally persecuting and massacring overseas Chinese, you are playing with fire only to get yourselves burnt and hasten your own doom.

In view of the fact that the fascist outrages of opposing China and persecuting overseas Chinese perpetrated entirely by the Burmese government are continuing to spread and expand, the Chinese government demands that the Burmese government must speedily adopt effective measures:

1. To immediately stop the persecution of overseas Chinese, effectively guarantee the security of their lives and property, immediately release the arrested overseas Chinese, lift the armed siege of the overseas Chinese quarters, and allow them to resume their normal activities.

2. To immediately provide the Chinese government with the numbers and others detailed information concerning those overseas Chinese who were killed, wounded, or arrested. The Chinese embassy in Burma will immediately dispatch personnel to go together with the families of the dead and missing overseas Chinese and the representatives of the overseas Chinese organizations to examine the bodies of the murdered overseas Chinese, console their families, and visit and comfort the arrested and the wounded overseas Chinese. The Burmese government must send officials to go together with them.

3. To severely punish the instigators and culprits of the murder of overseas Chinese, assume responsibilities for the funerals of the murdered overseas Chinese, pay relief to the families of the victims, and undertake to give medical treatment to the wounded.

4. To compensate for all the losses suffered by the overseas Chinese and relieve and provide for those overseas Chinese who are now deprived of means of livelihood.

5. To publicly apologize to the Chinese government and people and the broad masses of overseas Chinese in Burma and guarantee against the recurrence of incidents of persecuting overseas Chinese in the future.

At present the Chinese embassy in Burma is still unwarrantedly surrounded by Burmese troops and police and its normal functions are seriously hampered. The Burmese government must promptly lift its unwarranted siege of the Chinese embassy and guarantee the normal performance of all the embassy's functions. In the circumstances in which the Chinese embassy is unable to obtain overall information of the grave persecution and losses suffered by the overseas Chinese, the Chinese government reserves the right to raise further demands and adopt other necessary measures.

25-20.

"Protest against Murder of Overseas Chinese Leader by Burmese Government," *PR* 10.36:38 (Sept. 1, 1967).

The Chinese embassy in Burma, in a note to the Foreign Ministry of Burma on August 22, lodged the strongest protest with the reactionary Ne Win government against its fascist atrocity in cruelly murdering Liu Ying-chao, a leader of the patriotic Chinese nationals in Burma and chairman of the Federation of Overseas Chinese Workers in Burma, in prison.

Liu Ying-chao was illegally arrested on June 26 at the height of the anti-China and anti-Chinese outrages engineered by the Ne Win regime. The arrest took place when he went to the former Overseas Chinese Middle School to visit patriotic students in their courageous struggle against the reactionary Ne Win government's unreasonable ban on wearing badges with a profile of Chairman Mao. Thereafter, the Chinese embassy, in its two notes to the Burmese Foreign Ministry, sternly warned the reactionary Ne Win government that it must not victimize Liu Ying-chao and other detained patriotic Chinese and demanded that it immediately set them free. The reactionary government, however, completely ignored the warning and demand and continued to persecute and savagely torture the detained Chinese. Liu Ying-chao died as a result of continuous persecution and torture. . . .

Having murdered Liu Ying-chao, the reactionary Burmese government spread the lie that he died of illness in prison. Furthermore, in disregard of repeated warnings by the Chinese embassy, it staged behind the back of the embassy a fraudulent postmortem examination in an attempt to get rid of incriminating evidence and evade the responsibility for the crime.

The Chinese embassy in its August 22 note solemnly declared that the Chinese people will take revenge for Liu Ying-chao's death and settle accounts with the reactionary Burmese government for this blood debt.

The Chinese embassy firmly demanded that the reactionary Burmese government: 1. immediately arrange for the embassy's personnel to go to Insein prison near Rangoon to meet the arrested Chinese and other people concerned for an on-the-spot investigation of the murder of Liu Ying-chao; 2. severely punish the culprits and their instigators and make compensation to the family of the victim; 3. hold a large memorial service and funeral in honor of Liu Ying-chao; 4. release immediately and unconditionally all innocent patriotic Chinese nationals under arrest; 5. put an immediate end to the illegal interrogation and persecution of the unwarrantedly arrested Chinese nationals.

NOTE

The Cultural Revolution, of course, was not the first period in which the PRC had sought to protect overseas Chinese against physical harm. The earliest years of the regime also witnessed vigorous efforts, especially in behalf of militant Communists who were attempting to undermine existing governments such as those that then ruled in Thailand and in colonial Vietnam and Malaya.[95]

The following report, again from the Cultural Revolution period, illustrates the PRC's attitude toward the criminal trial of "patriotic Chinese nationals" on various charges of disrupting public order.[96]

25-21

"Burmese Government Must Cease Anti-China Activities and Release Patriotic Chinese Nationals," *PR* 11.9:29–30 (Mar. 1, 1968).

The Chinese embassy in Burma sent a note to the Burmese Foreign Ministry on February 22, strongly protesting against the reactionary Ne Win government for manipulating a Burmese court in sentencing Chen Po-fu and ten other patriotic Chinese nationals, who were illegally arrested, to prison terms on framed-up charges on February 20. This serious political persecution is a vile scheme of the reactionary Burmese government to continue to stir up anti-China provocations, and an attempt to evade responsibility for its monstrous crimes committed during last year's frantic anti-China and anti-Chinese campaign.

The Chinese embassy's note pointed out that the eleven patriotic Chinese were not guilty and that their court trial, which was manipulated by the Burmese government, and [whatever sentence was] passed on them were illegal. The note strongly demanded that the Burmese government act in accordance with the five just demands raised by the Chinese government, put an immediate end to its anti-China and anti-Chinese criminal acts, call an immediate halt to the illegal "trials" of innocent patriotic overseas Chinese, and unconditionally release Chen Po-fu and the ten others, as well as all other patriotic overseas Chinese unwarrantedly arrested. Otherwise, the note declared, the Burmese government would have to bear responsibility for all the serious consequences arising therefrom.

Chen Po-fu and the ten others were arrested and detained last

June when the reactionary Burmese government stirred up a massive anti-China and anti-Chinese adverse current. At that time, the reactionary Burmese government organized large numbers of thugs to launch savage attacks on the Chinese embassy, killed a Chinese aid worker, savagely slaughtered hundreds of innocent overseas Chinese, and committed monstrous crimes rarely heard of in the history of international relations. The masses of the patriotic overseas Chinese rose in self-defense. Chen Po-fu and the ten others were indomitable, feared no sacrifice, and resolutely defended the dignity of their motherland. After their unwarranted arrest by the reactionary Burmese troops and police, the reactionary Burmese government directed fascist thugs to torture them ruthlessly. Sixty-eight-year-old Chen Po-fu was so severely beaten that he twice coughed blood, while Yuan Yung-tang was injured all over his body. Despite all this, the eleven studied Chairman Mao's works every day in prison and put up a valiant and resolute fight. The enemy's attempt to use force to bring them to their knees ended in ignominious failure.

The reactionary Burmese government had the eleven on "trial" since last October on the trumped-up charge of "creating fear among the people." Resorting to every vile means, it even hired a large number of "witnesses" to give "testimony" against the innocent victimized Chinese. But lies can never cover up the truth. The eleven turned the enemy's court into a forum to scathingly denounce the reactionary Burmese government and expose its anti-China farce.

On February 20, they demonstrated in the enemy's court their firmness in upholding justice and their staunch and unyielding spirit. They fully displayed the heroism of patriotic Chinese nationals in Burma in showing their boundless loyalty to Chairman Mao, Mao Tse-tung's thought, and their socialist motherland.

In face of their valiant struggle, the reactionary Burmese government showed great fear and dismay. Fully armed troops and police were posted inside and outside the court and [plainclothesmen] prowled all over the place. Only a few of the family members of the persecuted Chinese were admitted into the courtroom. Immediately after the judge finished reading the rigged-up "sentences," a patriotic Chinese national, Chen Tien-huang, voiced a strong protest. Almost instantly, the eleven and their family members present recited in unison the following quotations from Chairman Mao: "Be resolute, fear no sacrifice, and surmount every difficulty to win victory." "All reactionaries are paper tigers. In appearance, the reactionaries are terrifying, but in reality they are not so powerful. From a long-term point of view, it is not the reactionaries but the people who are really powerful." The undaunted eleven who had received harsh sentences walked out of the court with their heads up. Raising their handcuffed hands, they waved their greetings to about 300 patriotic overseas Chinese and Burmese friends outside the court. Despite threats from the reactionary troops, police, and special agents, the angry crowd raised their fists and shouted: "Long live Chairman Mao!" and "Down with the Burmese reactionaries!" In the police van, the eleven patriotic Chinese kept singing Chairman Mao's quotations set to music.

NOTE

The PRC has often sought to protect overseas Chinese journalists and newspapers. Its protests have necessarily been most frequent during periods, such as the earliest years of the regime and the Cultural Revolution, when Peking has emphasized revolutionary action against foreign governments and its sympathizers abroad have followed suit and thereby provoked countermeasures. In 1951, for example, the PRC protested against Cuba's search and closing of a Chinese newspaper and its arrest of thirteen members of the staff.[97] Item 25-22 provides another example.

25-22

"Peking Spokesman Protests against Songgram Government's Arrest of Chinese Journalists," NCNA-English, Peking (Feb. 18, 1951) in *SCMP*, no. 69:1–2 (Feb. 18–19, 1951).

The spokesman of the Commission of Overseas Chinese Affairs of the Central People's Government has made a statement concerning the Thailand government's arrest of the editor in chief and publisher of the *Chuan Min Pao* daily of the overseas Chinese in Bangkok and the scheme for large-scale persecution of the overseas Chinese. The statement reads as follows:

> Since American imperialism began its aggressive war in Korea, and the signing of the economic and military agreement of an aggressive nature between the Thailand government and the United States, the Thailand government has more openly carried out the bidding of American imperialism, further persecuted the overseas Chinese in Thailand, and made an enemy of the Chinese people.
>
> Recently, the Thailand government illegally arrested the editor in chief Tsai Chih-hung and publisher Wu Chien-chung of the *Chuan Min Pao* on the pretext that this paper published by the

patriotic overseas Chinese in Bangkok carried news about the patriotic anti-American movement of the local overseas Chinese. It proclaimed that they would be deported. The *Chuan Min Pao* has always stood for peace in Asia and the world, promoted the friendship of the people of China and Thailand, and strongly defended the interests of the overseas Chinese, and it is deeply loved by the local overseas Chinese. But the Thailand government has ceaselessly subjected it to threats and persecution. In January this year, the Thailand government also unreasonably confiscated the calendars with the flag of the People's Republic of China which were published by the *Chuan Min Pao*. Such acts of the Thailand government fully demonstrate its hostility to the Chinese people.

Earlier, the Thailand government had unreasonably closed down several hundred overseas Chinese schools, crushed the industry and commerce of overseas Chinese, and deported overseas Chinese. Recently, it plotted to carry out again on a larger scale the venomous 1941 anti-Chinese "Forbidden Areas" system. According to the "Forbidden Areas" regulation, which has already been brought up in the National Assembly of Thailand, 18 regions in Thailand thickly populated by overseas Chinese will be marked off as "Forbidden Areas," and large numbers of Chinese nationals living there will be forced to move away. Once this regulation is implemented, masses of overseas Chinese will be deprived of homes and means of livelihood.

The overseas Chinese in Thailand are now reasonably demanding that the Thailand government release the illegally arrested responsible members of the *Chuan Min Pao* and safeguard the freedom of speech and other legitimate rights of the overseas Chinese. The Chinese people and all just people support this just and reasonable demand.

We strongly protest against the outrageous acts of the Thailand government in intensifying the crushing of the legitimate rights and interests of the overseas Chinese. We firmly demand that the Thailand government immediately release the responsible members of *Chuan Min Pao,* put an end to all illegal measures of persecuting the overseas Chinese, and safeguard all legitimate rights and interests of the overseas Chinese.

Note

Item 25–23 summarizes perhaps the most important Chinese protest against the suppression of journalists and their newspapers. This was the culmination of a series of Chinese notes responding to Britain's efforts to maintain order in Hong Kong in the face of large-scale disruptions that began with the labor disturbances described in item 25–18.

25-23

"Most Vehement Protest against Persecution of Patriotic Press by Hong Kong British Authorities," *PR* 10.35:22 (Aug. 25, 1967).

In the past two months or more, the British authorities in Hong Kong have illegally kidnapped and unwarrantedly arrested 14 reporters of the Hong Kong office of the Hsinhua News Agency and news publications run by patriots, and illegally arrested five directors or publishers of three newspapers. On August 17, the British authorities went so far as to order the *Hong Kong Evening News,* the *Tin Fung Daily News,* and the *Afternoon News* to cease publication and brought illegal lawsuits against the *Ta Kung Pao,* the *Ching Pao,* and the Nam Cheung Printing Company and the Hong Kong Press Enterprise which print the patriotic newspapers. On August 19, they again sent armed police and special agents to assault the offices of the three banned newspapers and illegally arrested 34 of their staff members.

On the evening of August 20, D. C. Hopson, British chargé d'affaires in China, was summoned to the Chinese Foreign Ministry where he was handed a note by a leading member of the Ministry's West European Affairs Department. The note lodged the most urgent and strongest protest with the British government.

The note says: It is entirely just for the patriotic Chinese press and journalists in Hong Kong and Kowloon to report truthfully and expose the Hong Kong British authorities' fascist atrocities of suppressing our fellow countrymen there in blood. It is their sacred duty to do so. The Hong Kong British authorities are carrying out all kinds of brutal political persecution against them under various trumped-up charges. This can only serve to thoroughly reveal the British government's utterly hideous and ferocious features of fascist imperialism to the people of the world.

The note solemnly states that the British government and the British authorities in Hong Kong must, within 48 hours, cancel the ban on the three newspapers, declare the 19 patriotic Chinese journalists and 34 staff members of these three newspapers innocent and set them free, call off the illegal lawsuits against the two newspapers and two printing firms, and make it possible for them to resume normal operations. Otherwise, the British government must be held responsible for all the consequences arising therefrom.

The Foreign Ministry's protest note received the firm support of the revolutionary journalists in the capital. Two thousand of them and a number of foreign revolutionary journalists in Peking held a demonstration on August 21. They read a letter of protest to British diplomatic officials outside the Office of British Chargés d'Affaires.

The All-China Journalists' Association also issued a statement supporting the Foreign Ministry protest note.

NOTE

It should be pointed out that, before taking the relatively extreme step of issuing an ultimatum to protect Chinese nationals, the PRC resorted to a number of other instruments of pressure in addition to strong diplomatic protests. When, for example, Britain failed to respond to the demands made in the PRC's note of May 15, 1967, concerning the labor disturbances (25–18), Vice-Foreign Minister Lo Kuei-po summoned Donald Hopson, British chargé d'affaires in Peking, and declared:

> Because the British government has taken a hostile attitude toward the Chinese people, and especially because the British authorities in Hong Kong have perpetrated sanguinary atrocities against Chinese inhabitants in Hong Kong, the arrangement made in 1954, in which the Chinese government, out of consideration for the request of the British government, agreed to the British Chargé d'Affaires's Office posting personnel in Shanghai in charge of the affairs of British nationals there, has now entirely lost its original meaning. Therefore, the Chinese government decides to annul this arrangement and demands that Mr. P. M. Hewitt leave Shanghai within 48 hours.[98]

And the next day Lo walked out when Hopson tried to deliver a protest against the closing of the Shanghai office.[99]

When "correspondents of the NCNA Hong Kong branch and other patriotic reporters" were subsequently convicted of crimes and sentenced by the British courts in Hong Kong, on July 21, 1967, the PRC announced that in retaliation for this "illegal persecution" it was restricting the freedom of Reuters correspondent Anthony Grey (recall 21–14). Shortly before this announcement, it was reported that China had failed to respond to a Hong Kong request for more water in addition to the annual quota from China upon which the colony was dependent and which had already been exhausted.[100]

Popular pressures were also mobilized against Britain both in China and in Hong Kong. For example, "more than 15,000 Peking journalists, film workers, and [members of the] Red Guard assembled on August 4 to angrily denounce the fascist atrocities of the British authorities in Hong Kong." [101] And the Communists in Hong Kong experimented with a general strike and with a long-term suspension of trade.[102]

For "the consequences" arising from Britain's refusal to comply with the PRC's ultimatum, see item 27–18.

The first decade of the PRC's relations with India was blissfully free of serious disputes over the treatment of the approximately 20,000 persons of Chinese descent residing in India. In 1959, however, the outbreak of the Tibetan revolt and the flare-up of the Sino-Indian border dispute stimulated a reversal of India's policy of toleration toward persons of Chinese descent who sympathized with Peking and of restriction of those who sympathized with Taipei. Between 1959 and the occurrence of large-scale Sino-Indian hostilities in October 1962, India's "ill-treatment" of Chinese nationals as well as official and semiofficial Chinese representatives became a constant subject of dispute between Peking and New Delhi.[103] But it was the Indian response to the escalation of the border conflict in the fall of 1962 that presented some distinctive questions of international law relating to the protection of nationals.

Following his proclamation of national emergency on October 26, 1962, President Radhakrishnan of India issued the Defense of India Ordinance, which suspended the exercise of certain individual rights during the emergency. Promulgated under this ordinance and its successor, the Defense of India Act, were the Defense of India Rules, which provided for the restriction of movement and detention of suspected persons, both citizens and aliens.[104]

Besides these special emergency powers, the Indian government invoked the Foreigners Act of 1946 [105] to issue a number of far-reaching orders that regulated the Chinese community during the crisis. These orders authorized restrictions on movement, deprivation of certain basic rights, and arrest and internment or detention.

There were two major orders restricting the movement of Chinese nationals. The Foreigners (Restriction on Chinese Nationals) Order, October 25, 1962, prohibited a Chinese national from leaving the limits of his city or village or absenting himself from his registered address for longer than 24 hours without prior written permission from his registration officer, who was authorized to impose whatever conditions he deemed appropriate to the granting of permission.[106] The Foreigners (Restricted Areas) Order, January 14, 1963, prohibited all Chinese nationals and all persons of Chinese origin from entering or remaining in designated restricted areas (the state of Assam and some districts of West Bengal, Uttar Pradesh, and Punjab) without a permit, even if they were Indian citizens and residents of those areas.[107]

President Radhakrishnan promulgated on October 30, 1962, the Foreigners Law (Application and Amendment) Ordinance, which made the Registration of Foreigners Act of 1939,[108] the Foreigners Act of 1946, and all rules and orders issued thereunder, applicable to "any person not of Indian origin who was at birth a citizen or subject of any country at war with, or committing external aggression against, India. . . ." [109] Another order issued on the same day suspended for the duration of the emergency the right of such persons, as well as foreigners, to move any court for the enforcement of basic constitutional protections against the arbitrary deprivation of life or liberty.[110] In order to effectuate the Indian government's intention to subject all Indian citizens of Chinese origin to both of the October 30 measures, the scope of these measures was soon broadened to include "any person who, or either of whose parents, or any of whose grandparents was at any time a citizen or subject of any country at war with, or committing external aggression against, India. . . ." [111] This became the definition of "person of Chinese origin" as that term was used in subsequent measures, such as the Foreigners (Restricted Areas) Order, 1963, mentioned above. The effect of these measures was to deny the almost 900 Indian citizens of Chinese origin the benefits of citizenship and to subject them to the same restrictions and controls as Chinese aliens.

A similar formula—"any foreigner who is, and any person not of Indian origin who was at birth (a citizen of a country at war with India)"—was used to designate those persons who without cause were subject to arrest and "internment" in camps under the Foreigners (Internment) Order of November 3, 1962. The order also authorized the arrest without warrant and the "detention" of any foreigner who is reasonably suspected of "having acted, of acting, or of being about to act, with intent to assist a country at war with or committing external aggression against India, or in a manner prejudicial to the public safety or to the safety of any building or machinery." [112]

In accordance with the foregoing measures, by early 1963 the Indian government reported that 2,165 persons of Chinese descent, both aliens and citizens, had been arrested for alleged "anti-Indian activities" and taken to a permanent internment camp and that an additional 143 had been detained in various local jails.[113] The large number of persons of Chinese descent who were not interned or detained suffered a variety of other disabilities. Some were forced to move their homes from the "restricted" areas. Many had to give up their businesses. Chinese employees and workers were dismissed from their positions in Indian firms and factories. Chinese seamen and ship repairers were barred from harbors, docks, and shipyards. The fact that Chinese were forbidden to leave their residential area for longer than 24 hours without a permit handicapped them in their work and in their children's schooling. Chinese restaurants in some Indian cities even found it prudent to adopt Japanese names.[114]

The measures taken and the actions permitted by India against the overseas Chinese resulted in a substantial addition to the already bulky Sino-Indian diplomatic correspondence. The following commentary by one of the PRC's leading scholars of international law summarizes the major claims made by Peking in behalf of its nationals. In addition, it does what the PRC seemed reluctant to do in its official communications: provide a detailed rejoinder to India's attempt to justify its conduct by reference to the 1949 Geneva Convention Relative to the Protection of Civilian Persons in Time of War.

25-24

Chou Keng-sheng, "The Persecution of Chinese Nationals and Infringement of the Right of China to Protect Chinese Nationals by the Indian Government Are Serious International Delinquencies," *JMJP* (Jan. 22, 1963), p. 5.

The Indian government . . . maligns China by saying that China invaded India; it resorts to this pretext to stir up large-scale anti-Chinese movements in India, forcibly take over the main and branch offices of the Bank of China, restrict the freedom of movement of personnel of the Chinese embassy and consulates, and discriminate against and mistreat Chinese nationals. Immediately following the announcement of a "state of emergency" by the President of India on October 26, the Indian government promulgated, on October 31, the so-called 1962 "Foreigners' Law (Application and Amendment) Ordinance" which in fact is directed against Chinese nationals. Even after the Chinese government took the initiative for cease-fire and withdrawal measures and the armed conflict in fact ceased, the Indian government, resorting to the pretext of border conflict, nevertheless unilaterally tore to pieces the Sino-Indian Agreement on Establishing Consulates and closed the Chinese consulates in India. This was obviously done intentionally so that Chinese nationals would lose the protection of their consulates and

Indian authorities could engage in unscrupulous persecution of Chinese nationals.

Recently, the Indian government's acts of persecution of Chinese nationals have become more and more cruel and violent; a large number of Chinese nationals have been deprived of their personal freedom or their life and property have been infringed. . . . Undoubtedly, the various measures adopted by India to persecute Chinese nationals are acts which unabashedly undermine the minimum standards of international relations. . . . The Chinese embassy has the duty to protect its nationals and has requested the Indian government on several occasions to permit it to visit those Chinese nationals under arrest and to apprise itself of the circumstances involved. But, even these perfectly proper requests, which can be easily satisfied, were flatly rejected. Instead, the Indian government described its acts of persecution of Chinese nationals as a security measure taken because of Chinese "aggression." It says that its acts are within the sovereignty of India's domestic law and that the treatment of the internees is "consistent" with the "provisions" of "the Geneva Convention." The Indian story is obviously an artificial argument which distorts the facts, and it cannot stand on its own. . . .

What is aggression? From the legal point of view, one of the basic characteristics of aggression is the initiation of an armed attack. This concept was already reflected in several well-known conventions defining aggression, known as the London Convention, concluded in 1933 between the Soviet Union and a number of states such as Afghanistan and Persia. Article 2 of the London Convention provides that in an international dispute, "the aggressor . . . shall be considered to be that State which is the first to commit . . . invasion by its armed forces . . . of the territory of another State." This definition confirms the fact that India is an aggressor by virtue of its having first invaded Chinese territory. . . .

The Indian government states that its acts are necessary for internal security. This is purely an unreasonable pretext which cannot conceal the criminal acts of cruel and violent persecution of Chinese nationals by the Indian authorities. As everyone knows, the border conflict between China and India was unilaterally created by India. This cannot be said to constitute a threat to India's national security. Moreover, Chinese nationals are all self-contented, law-abiding, and peaceful residents. In no circumstances can this border conflict constitute a ground for the large-scale arrest and detention of law-abiding Chinese nationals. During the Sino-Indian border conflict, did not the Indian nationals in the territory of China, including those residing in the Tibet Region, which was directly affected by the border conflict, continue to have a peaceful and happy life without being arrested or interned?

In contrast to the Indian way of handling the matter, it can be seen that the treatment of Chinese nationals by India is not necessary for security, but is for other reasons. Since China initiated the cease-fire and withdrawal and the Chinese border forces will withdraw behind the line of actual control of November 7, 1959, the border conflict has already ceased. But India nevertheless [increases its] internment of Chinese nationals. It certainly cannot be said that this is necessary for national security. It is merely a pretext to continue and to expand the anti-Chinese movement stirred up long ago.

The Indian government argued that its treatment of Chinese nationals is a measure adopted in accordance with the sovereignty of its domestic law. Who would deny that the adoption and execution of domestic law by India are acts of sovereignty, but who can think that India may use its domestic law to deny the human rights and fundamental freedoms of peaceful and law-abiding alien residents or freely to infringe their life, property, and security? An act of sovereignty by India cannot be used to extinguish the right of another state to protect its nationals abroad. The protection of nationals abroad is the exercise of the personal supremacy of all sovereign states. No one can deny this minimum standard of international law. It is a standard which must be observed by every state. For instance, the British international law authority Oppenheim points out that "although aliens fall at once under the territorial supremacy of the State they enter, they remain, nevertheless, under protection of their home State. By a universally recognized customary rule of international law every State holds a right of protection over its citizens abroad. . . ."[a] Chinese nationals in India naturally should obey Indian laws and as a matter of fact Chinese nationals have been consistently law-abiding; at the same time, the Chinese government has the right and also the duty to protect law-abiding Chinese nationals. The Constitution of the People's Republic of China (Article 98) provides: "The People's Republic of China protects the proper rights and interests of Chinese residing abroad." The use of discriminatory laws and decrees by the Indian government to persecute law-abiding Chinese nationals is an act that violates international law and impairs the right of China to protect its nationals abroad, which absolutely cannot be justified by what is called an act in accordance with sovereignty or the performance of an act of sovereignty in accordance with domestic law. The so-called "Foreigners' Law Ordinance" promulgated by India seems on its face to deal with all foreigners generally, but it is particularly intended to deal with Chinese nationals and it is applicable even to those persons of Chinese origin who have already acquired Indian

[a] L. Oppenheim, *International Law*, 8th ed., by H. Lauterpacht (London: Longmans, Green, 1955), I, 686.

nationality and have become Indian citizens. Regardless of India's play with words, this is naked racial discrimination. . . .

Chinese nationals in India are generally deprived of personal freedom. Their residence and freedom of movement are subject to control, and they are even deprived of the freedom to exit and to return to their home country. In international practice, this is a rare instance of unreasonableness and nonobservance of rules of international relations.

Foreign nationals generally have the freedom of exit. This is a rule generally accepted by international law and international custom. As one western international law jurist points out: "Since a State holds only territorial and not personal supremacy over an alien within its boundaries, it can never, in any circumstances, prevent him from leaving its territory, provided he has fulfilled his local obligations, such as payment of rates and taxes, of fines, of private debts, and the like. An alien leaving a State can take his property away with him on the same conditions as a national, and a tax for leaving the country, or tax upon the property he takes away with him, cannot be levied." [b] The Indian government's prevention of Chinese nationals from leaving India and returning to their home country and its various other unreasonable measures in the treatment of Chinese nationals, are obviously in violation of international law and can under no circumstances be justified by invoking domestic law.

The Indian government superficially mentioned the Geneva Convention and the visit of the International Committee of the Red Cross to the interned Chinese nationals. The Geneva Convention it mentioned naturally is the Fourth Geneva Convention, that is, the Geneva Convention Relative to the Protection of Civilian Persons in Time of War. We do not deny that the Geneva Convention has positive meaning in protecting civilians in time of war, but in a situation in which normal diplomatic relations between China and India still exist, what right does India have to deny the legitimate right of the Chinese embassy to protect Chinese nationals? Despite the fact that the Chinese consulates in India were compelled to close, China still has an embassy in India and one of the functions of diplomatic envoys generally accepted by international law is to protect their nationals in the accredited state. "Oppenheim's International Law" explains this clearly: "A third task of diplomatic envoys is the protection of the persons, property, and interests of such subjects of their home States as are within the boundaries of the State to which they are accredited," and the envoys "must be allowed [by the accredited States] to afford them protection." [c] The

[b] *Ibid.*, p. 690.
[c] *Ibid.*, p. 786.

"Convention on Diplomatic Relations" adopted by the 1961 Vienna Conference also confirms the above-mentioned rule of international law. The Convention provides (Article 3) that one of the functions of diplomatic envoys is to protect the interest of nationals of the home state in the accepting state. In order to carry out its function of protecting Chinese nationals, the Chinese embassy accredited to India naturally has the right to visit Chinese nationals illegally interned by India in concentration camps and request that it be apprised of the circumstances by the Indian government, and be given a list of the internees. India's domestic law absolutely cannot deprive the Chinese embassy of this right, and the Geneva Convention does not have any provisions which negate this right. Article 13 of the Geneva Convention states that "the provisions . . . are intended to alleviate the sufferings caused (to populations of the conflicting states) by war." The fundamental spirit of the Convention is in time of war to protect peaceful residents from mistreatment. The relevant provisions of the Convention are intended to restrict the measures which can be taken against peaceful residents by the parties to a conflict and to make those measures consistent with humanitarianism. They do not authorize a party to a conflict freely to persecute nationals of another party. Moreover, in general only when a state of war exists between two states and diplomatic relations are severed is it necessary to entrust the nationals of one state residing in the other state to the protection of a third state. Although this time a border armed conflict did arise between China and India, diplomatic relations between China and India were not severed. In these circumstances, India has no reason, nor can it find any basis in the Geneva Convention, to prevent the Chinese embassy from exercising its right to protect Chinese nationals. On what ground can the Indian government refuse to allow the Chinese embassy to visit Chinese nationals under detention? On what legal basis can the Indian government substitute the visit by the International Committee of the Red Cross to detained Chinese nationals for a visit by the Chinese embassy? The Indian government (note of December 31, 1962) states: "The officially accredited representative of the International Committee of the Red Cross in India has also visited the camp and was fully satisfied with the arrangement made." Does the Indian government consider that the International Committee of the Red Cross has already performed its function of protection? According to Article 10 of the Geneva Convention, the protective activities undertaken by the International Committee of the Red Cross must be "subject to the consent of the Parties to the conflict concerned." May one ask if the Indian authorities acquired the consent of China with respect to the visit by the representatives of the International Committee of the Red Cross to detained Chinese nationals?

Even more absurd is the fact that India proposed to exchange information concerning the internees "on a reciprocal basis" through the International Committee of the Red Cross. We want to ask why information concerning detained Chinese nationals cannot be given directly to the Chinese embassy, which has the right to protect its nationals, but must be given through a group like the International Committee of the Red Cross? What is the meaning of the so-called reciprocal basis? Obviously, it cannot refer to Indian nationals in China since, as we have pointed out before, there are no detained Indian nationals within China's boundaries. Therefore, the question of exchange of information about internees just does not exist. Then what is the meaning of the so-called reciprocity on the Indian side? Does it mean reciprocity between peaceful and law-abiding Chinese nationals unreasonably detained in concentration camps by the Indian authorities and the Indian soldiers taken prisoners by Chinese border forces during the armed conflict? Everyone with common sense should know that the legal status of peaceful foreigners detained in the territory of one side and personnel taken prisoner in an armed conflict is different. They absolutely cannot be regarded as the same. . . . India has detained Chinese nationals on a large scale and refuses to allow the Chinese embassy to visit them; it does not permit Chinese nationals freely to leave the country, and it does not reply to the Chinese government's proposal to dispatch ships to India to pick up detained Chinese nationals and those who have no way of making a living in India as a result of other kinds of persecution and who are willing to return to their home country. (Note given by the Ministry of Foreign Affairs of the People's Republic of China to Indian embassy of December 18, 1962.) It even states that it will carry out so-called "differentiation" among the several thousands of Chinese nationals innocently interned in concentration camps. In fact, all these are pretexts for the unlimited detention of Chinese nationals. In view of the above-mentioned facts, one cannot but express the suspicion that the Indian government has other objectives which it dares not reveal. It plans to hold large numbers of Chinese nationals as hostages to blackmail the Chinese government. It must be pointed out that Article 34 of the Geneva Convention explicitly provides that "the taking of hostages is prohibited." Therefore, the Indian government's attempt to hold Chinese nationals as hostages is an extreme violation of humanitarianism, an absolute violation of the Geneva Convention, and also a violent undermining of generally accepted rules of international relations.

A spokesman for the Indian Ministry of External Affairs said on December 19 of last year that India's treatment of the internees is consistent with the provisions of the Geneva Convention. We want to ask: In what respect is the Indian treatment of Chinese nationals consistent with the Geneva Convention? First, is it consistent with the provisions of the Geneva Convention to obstruct nationals who wish to leave India and return to their home country? Does not Article 35 of the Geneva Convention provide that "all protected persons who may desire to leave the territory at the outset of, or during a conflict, shall be entitled to do so, unless their departure is contrary to the national interests of the State"? Therefore, the various obstacles faced by Chinese nationals who wish to leave India and return to their home country violate the provisions of the Geneva Convention. Second, the Indian authorities have unreasonably deprived several thousand Chinese nationals of their personal freedom by arresting or detaining them. Is this also consistent with the provisions of the Geneva Convention? According to the provisions of Article 5 of the Convention, only an individual protected person who is really suspected of, or engaged in, activities endangering the security of the state [in which he resides], loses the rights and privileges granted by the Convention. According to the provisions of Article 42, the internment or placing in assigned residence of protected persons may be ordered only if the security of the detaining power makes it "absolutely necessary." India has placed a large number of innocent, peaceful, and law-abiding Chinese nationals in concentrated internment, and such an extreme measure has been taken during a period of limited border conflict. Where is the "absolute necessity"? Moreover, after the Chinese government has taken the initiative of declaring a cease-fire and withdrawal of Chinese border forces, the Indian government continues to intern and persecute Chinese nationals. Where are the similarities between these measures and the provisions of the Geneva Convention? Article 43 of the Geneva Convention provides that "the Detaining Power shall, as rapidly as possible, give the Protecting Power the names of any protected persons who have been interned or subjected to assigned residence. . . ." At present, China and India still maintain normal diplomatic relations, and the one who has the duty of protecting Chinese nationals can only be the Chinese embassy, but the Indian government has so far refused to submit the list of interned Chinese to the Chinese embassy. Is this consistent with the provisions of the Geneva Convention? . . .

The Geneva Convention prescribes rules for the treatment of interned persons. For example, "parties to the conflict who intern protected persons shall be bound to provide free of charge for their maintenance, and to grant them also the medical attention required by their state of health;" "the Detaining Power shall provide for the support of those dependent on the internees, if such dependents are without adequate means of support or are unable to earn a living" (Article 81); "the Detaining Power is bound to take all necessary and possible measures to ensure that protected persons shall, from the outset of their internment, be accommodated in buildings or quarters which afford every possible safeguard as regards hygiene and health. . . . The premises shall be fully protected from dampness. . . ." The Geneva Convention also protects the personal property of the internees. Article 33 of the Convention states that "pillage is prohibited" and "reprisals against protected persons and their property are prohibited." Article 97 of the Convention further provides that "internees shall be permitted to retain articles of personal use." However, the properties and monies of Chinese nationals arrested in India have been pillaged; the Chinese nationals are not even permitted to take their clothes and belongings with them; the conditions of their quarters are bad; and there is no medical care for sickness. Is this consistent with the provisions of the Geneva Convention?

In short, the Indian government's use of the existence of an armed border conflict, which India nevertheless provoked, to justify the large-scale persecution of Chinese nationals has fundamentally violated the Geneva Convention Relative to the Protection of Civilian Persons in Time of War. The living conditions and the treatment of interned Chinese nationals in the concentration camps are also completely inconsistent with the provisions of the Geneva Convention.

The Indian government's idea of "differentiating" several thousand Chinese nationals interned in concentration camps is even more incredible. One can hardly find any basis in the Geneva Convention for carrying out the so-called "differentiation" among peaceful and law-abiding interned civilians. Originally, the Indian government intended to rely on the pretext that its interning of a large number of Chinese nationals was necessary for security. Now it fabricates the so-called "espionage" or "subversive" activities and similar fairy tales to carry out "differentiation" in an attempt wantonly to make criminal charges against Chinese nationals. It looks like a fabrication of pretexts with an intention to intern Chinese nationals for a long period. This is a measure of extremely violent persecution of Chinese nationals, and it violates the Geneva Convention's fundamental spirit of protecting civilians. The use of this Sino-Indian armed conflict to justify the intensified large-scale persecution of Chinese nationals by the Indian government and even involving all persons of Chinese origin is clearly a part of a plot by the Indian government to carry out an anti-Chinese movement for a long period. The Indian government absolutely cannot use the lie of so-called "safeguard[ing] the security of the country endangered by massive Chinese invasion" and the pretext of a decree promulgated in accordance with Indian sovereignty in order to cover up a serious crime which is inhumane, which undermines international custom and international law, and which also violates the object and spirit of the Geneva Convention and its specific provisions. The Indian government's unreasonable persecution of Chinese nationals has violently infringed the legitimate right of China to protect its nationals abroad. From the point of view of international law, any infringement by one state of the person or property of a foreigner impairs the right of the state of which that foreigner is a national to protect its nationals abroad; and such an infringement constitutes an international delinquency.[d] India's persecution of Chinese nationals and impairment of China's right to protect its nationals abroad are definitely international delinquencies for which the Indian government should bear major responsibility.

With respect to India's unreasonable and illegal large-scale persecution of Chinese nationals, the Chinese government has on several occasions (November 8, 24, and December 18, 1962) sent notes of strong protest to the Indian government. In particular, the December 18 note presented three demands to the Indian government: (1) Immediately stop persecuting Chinese nationals; release all arrested and interned Chinese nationals; return to them their property and compensate them for their losses; immediately supply the number, name list, and places of detention of the arrested Chinese nationals; and facilitate requests for visits and other reasonable requests made by the Chinese embassy. (2) Ensure the freedom of departure of Chinese nationals wishing to return to their mother country and allow them to take with them their money and property; ensure the personal freedom of Chinese nationals wishing to stay on in India and the safety of their person and property, without discriminating against them in any way. (3) Give due cooperation and necessary facilities to the Chinese government in [implementing] measures for sending home its victimized nationals. The report of the Indian government's persecution of Chinese nationals made by the Chinese government in these notes is perfectly accurate. The three demands presented to the Indian government are based on the legitimate right of China to protect its nationals abroad and are reasonable and justifiable. However, the Indian government has so far insisted upon its unreasonable stand and in its recent (December 31) reply to the Chinese government's note of December 18, it still repeats the old set of lies and empty phrases, such as the so-called Chinese "invasion," "in the . . . interests of national security," "within . . . sovereign competence," and "conformity with . . . the Geneva Convention of 1949," and it fails to make an explicit reply to the demand of the Chinese government for cooperation in sending home Chinese nationals. On

[d] *Ibid.*, pp. 343–344.

the contrary, attempting to continue its detention of Chinese nationals, it puts forth the unreasonable measure that is described as "conducting review" of interned Chinese.

NOTE

Another leading Chinese commentator, after mustering essentially similar arguments against India's actions, stated:

> In addition, according to the above-mentioned Foreigners' Law (Application and Amendment) Ordinance, all Indian citizens of Chinese origin are regarded as foreigners and are to be treated as foreigners; this in reality deprives a group of people of nationality by virtue of discrimination toward a certain race. This measure of the Indian government can rarely be seen in international relations and also violates fundamental human rights. . . .
>
> It is worthwhile to notice that the current violent acts and measures toward Chinese nationals adopted by the Indian government are not permissible even when belligerents treat enemy nationals. . . .
>
> The Indian Government's atrocity of discrimination and persecution against Chinese nationals is a serious international delinquency. According to international law, a state should undertake state responsibility for a delinquency committed through its organs. Now, the government of India, on the one hand, madly persecutes Chinese nationals and, at the same time, connives with ruffians to assault Chinese nationals and to destroy and rob Chinese shops, causing the life and property of Chinese nationals to suffer serious threat and damage. For this the Indian government must be held responsible.[115]

As item 25–20 illustrated, the PRC has frequently demanded that its diplomats and consuls be granted access to Chinese nationals who have been confined or imprisoned by other governments. Other examples will be referred to in Part VII. Yet, as the Shri Das case (19–17 to 19–20) and the case of Anthony Grey (21–14) indicated, the PRC has often prevented or hindered foreign governments from making contact with their nationals who have been detained by Chinese authorities. It is interesting that, although Article 14 of the 1959 consular treaty between the USSR and the PRC (28–5) authorizes consuls to "protect the rights and interests of their state and of citizens and juridical persons of the sending state" and to "address themselves to the authorities of their consular district and . . . make representations to them concerning [violations]," the agreement, like similar agreements that the USSR has concluded with other socialist states, failed to provide specifically for consular access to detained nationals.[116]

As chapter 44 shows, the PRC has also rigidly resisted the efforts of other states to persuade it to comply with the provisions for access to prisoners of war set forth in the 1949 Geneva Convention Relative to the Treatment of Prisoners of War, to which the PRC has bound itself. This undoubtedly accounts for the attempt of the PRC and scholar Chou Keng-sheng to separate the question of Indians held as POW's from that of Chinese civilians detained in India. This may also explain why the PRC appeared reluctant to invoke the 1949 Geneva Convention Relative to the Protection of Civilian Persons in Time of War in its official communications concerning its nationals. Despite the fact that this Convention offered Peking some excellent possibilities for embarrassing India, the similarities between the Civilian Convention and the companion POW Convention are so significant that the PRC's leaders may have decided that any detailed reliance upon the former would only call further attention to its failure to observe the latter (see item 44–13).

25-25

"Chinese Government to Send Relief Material to Chinese Nationals in Burma," NCNA–English, Peking (July 26, 1967), in *SCMP*, no. 3991:27–28 (July 31, 1967).

Disregarding the advance warning of the Chinese government, the reactionary Ne Win government has gone so far as to unjustifiably place obstructions in the way of the Chinese government's decision on the shipment of relief material to Rangoon for the Chinese nationals in Burma.

A responsible official of the First Department of Asian Affairs of the Chinese Foreign Ministry yesterday received U Maung Maung Gyee, counsellor of the Burmese embassy in China, and lodged the strongest protest with him against the unreasonable obstructions put up by the Burmese government. The responsible official of the Foreign Ministry stressed that the Chinese government will send relief material according to plan.

When U Maung Maung Gyee yesterday met by appointment the responsible official of the First Asian Department of the Chinese Foreign Ministry, he delivered a reply note in connection with the Chinese government's decision. The note says that the Burmese government "in principle forbids foreign governments and their organizations to send in any material for use of their nationals" and consequently cannot agree to China's shipment of relief material to the Chinese nationals.

The Chinese official immediately lodged the strongest protest against the unreasonable obstructions placed by the Burmese government. He also sternly pointed out that the Burmese government had perpetrated the fascist outrages in frantically massacring and persecuting the Chinese nationals. This blood debt has yet to be paid. And now without any justification, it places obstructions in the way of the Chinese government's shipment of material to Rangoon for the relief of the Chinese nationals, the victims of persecution. This once again lays bare the fascist and reactionary features of the Burmese government.

He pointed out that the Chinese government has every right to protect and relieve the victimized Chinese nationals in Burma. In its note the Burmese government has failed to give any reason for its refusal of China's shipment of relief material. This is because the obstructions placed by the Burmese government are entirely without any justification. The Chinese nationals in Burma are victims of ruthless persecution by the Burmese government and are in deep suffering. It is entirely just and reasonable for the Chinese government to send relief material to them. No government has any justification whatsoever to refuse such arrangements if it respects the right of a foreign government to protect its nationals and recognizes the most elementary norm of international relations.

He noted that after its ruthless slaughter and persecution of the Chinese nationals in Burma, the Burmese government had behaved hypocritically, setting in motion its propaganda machine and tried in a thousand and one ways to absolve itself from its crimes. But to be frank, the Ne Win government cannot evade the responsibility for its monstrous crimes against the Chinese people. Now you have groundlessly obstructed the sending of relief material by the Chinese government. This shows that you are redoubling your efforts in persecuting the broad masses of Chinese nationals and exposes your diabolic scheme of putting them to death. This is what the government and people absolutely cannot tolerate.

The Chinese official stressed that the Chinese government's decision to send relief material to Rangoon for the Chinese nationals shows the warm concern of the 700 million Chinese people for their fellow countrymen. The Chinese government will send relief material to Burma as scheduled. If the Burmese government continues to put up obstructions, it can only be committing a new crime on top of old ones and will be strongly condemned by the Chinese and other people the world over.

NOTE

Two weeks after the above protest, the Foreign Ministry in Peking made another, stating that:

> The reactionary government of Burma went so far as to disregard even the minimum standards governing international relations and forcibly held back the first batch of relief goods when they were flown to Rangoon airport on 31 July. The situation has been like this for more than 10 days now. This absolutely cannot be tolerated. . . . Sending supplies to relieve their own compatriots is one of the sacred rights of the Chinese government and people of which nobody can deprive them.[117]

For a few weeks the PRC persisted in its demand that these relief supplies be released, maintaining that emergency shipment differed from ordinary goods brought in by governments for use of their nationals.[118] Finally the question was dropped. Shortly thereafter, however, Peking announced that it would send to Burma an investigation and relief mission organized by its Overseas Chinese Affairs Commission. Predictably, Burma refused permission.[119]

25-26

"Chinese Embassy in Burma Protests against Obstructions to Overseas Chinese," NCNA–English, Peking (July 25, 1967), in *SCMP*, no. 3990:23–24 (July 28, 1967).

The Chinese embassy in Burma, in a note to the Burmese Foreign Ministry on July 20, strongly protested against the obstructions the reactionary Ne Win government has placed in the way of the persecuted patriotic overseas Chinese who went to the Chinese embassy to apply for passports and visas to return to their motherland, according to a Rangoon report.

The note said: "It is the legitimate and inviolable right of overseas Chinese to apply to the Chinese embassy for passports and visas, and the consular section of the embassy is fully entitled to make and maintain contact with overseas Chinese. The reactionary Burmese government absolutely has no right to interfere with all this. By violating our diplomatic rights and breaking the elementary norms governing international regulations, you are merely further discrediting yourself and proving that you are a group of monsters mortally afraid of the sunshine. You are sure to receive severe punishment from the Chinese people and the people of the whole world."

The note pointed out that as a result of the anti-China and anti-Chinese fascist outrages perpetrated by the reactionary Burmese government, tens of thousands of patriotic overseas Chinese families have been ruined and rendered destitute and homeless. Large numbers of patriotic overseas Chinese, desirous of returning to their motherland, resolutely demand to come to the Chinese embassy and apply for passports and visas. Yet they have been hindered in every conceivable way by your soldiers, policemen, and plainclothesmen from coming to the Chinese embassy. Some overseas Chinese were three times forcibly turned back by your special agents on their way to the embassy for passports and visas, while others were summoned by your army men and police for "interrogation" or what you call "scrutiny." What is more, some were even unwarrantedly arrested and imprisoned by you, and these patriotic overseas Chinese have thus been subjected once again to your fascist torture and ill-treatment. Their very survival is endangered.

The note pointed out: While the remains of the patriotic overseas Chinese slain by you have hardly turned cold, you bloodthirsty fascists are plotting an even more massive massacre. Your persecution has rendered the masses of overseas Chinese destitute and made their life precarious. Now when they desire to go back to their motherland, you come out with a host of obstacles to obstruct them in a thousand and one ways. We want to ask: What on earth are you after? Have you decided to exterminate all the patriotic overseas Chinese to your satisfaction? If so and if you have the audacity, you may well announce this gangster decision of yours to the Burmese people and the people of the whole world! You don't dare. You are out-and-out fascists, but you are taking great pains to present yourselves as philanthropists in order to fool the world's people. If this can be tolerated, what else cannot? Having massacred countless patriotic overseas Chinese, you come out with crocodile tears and sanctimoniously publish photos in your press to show your "solicitude" for overseas Chinese, in an effort to hoodwink the people of the world. This is indeed despicable!

The Chinese embassy has repeatedly made representations and protests with you in this connection, but you have turned a deaf ear to our just demand. Should your reactionary Burmese government dare to persist in your own way and continue your criminal acts in disregard of our just demand and serious warnings, you must bear the full responsibility for all the grave consequences arising therefrom, the note warned.

25-27

"Huang Hua Accuses US of Detaining 5,000 Chinese Students," NCNA–English, Geneva (May 26, 1954), in *SCMP*, no. 818:20–21 (May 28, 1954).

The spokesman of the Chinese delegation to the Geneva Conference Huang Hua told foreign correspondents here this afternoon that American nationals were always granted exit permits to leave China provided they apply for them and so long as the applicants were not involved in unsettled civil or criminal cases. Huang Hua accused the US government of unwarrantedly detaining Chinese nationals residing in the US including over 5,000 Chinese students.

His press statement reads: Since the establishment of the Central People's Government of People's Republic of China, that government has consistently accorded protection to foreign nationals residing in China, including American nationals, as long as they abide by laws and decrees of the Chinese government. They can lead a peaceful life and carry on their business operations smoothly. If they want to leave China, for whatever reasons, they can apply to the People's Government at various levels in accordance with legal procedure. As long as he or she is not involved in any unsettled civil or criminal cases, an exit permit is always granted.

As a matter of fact, as a result of the hostile attitude of the US government toward the People's Republic of China and the blockade and embargo it launched against China, many foreign nationals including American nationals, have lost their business in which they have engaged all along and have to leave China. We are sympathetic with these foreign nationals, including American nationals who have been ruined by various policies of the US government which are antagonistic to the Chinese people. The People's Government of China has not deterred them [from] leaving China. So far as I know, from 1950 to the end of 1953, about 1,500 American nationals had left China and only over 80 American nationals are now still in China.

This very fact suffices to prove that assertions made by certain quarters of the United States to the effect that the Chinese government prevented American nationals from leaving China are nothing but malicious fabrications. As to the fact that the Chinese government has arrested and prosecuted in accordance with law a few Americans who had breached the law, China is merely carrying out the functions and duties common to any sovereign state. For every one who has been arrested as a result of his lawbreaking acts, we have in our possession sufficient evidence. Among those American nationals who have been arrested because of their lawbreaking acts, there are those who have been resident in China, and also those who had been brought down from air over China or had sneaked in by sea. In spite of this, we are still willing to render assistance to these few persons who have been arrested because of their lawbreaking acts, if their relatives have messages to be forwarded to them.

On the other hand, however, since 1950 the US government has outrageously oppressed and forcibly retained Chinese nationals resident in the United States, particularly more than 5,000 Chinese students. Many Chinese nationals and students, when they asked to leave the United States for China, received notifications from the US Immigration Office stating: "You are hereby ordered not to depart or to attempt to depart from the United States, whether or not you have a permit to depart, until you have been notified that this order has [been] revoked." The United States Immigration Office further threatened that, if they should violate this order, they would "be fined not more than 5,000 dollars or imprisoned for not more than five years or both." Not a few of them have even been subjected to maltreatment, arrest, and imprisonment because they applied for return to their country. Since 1951, the United States government has gone to such lengths as to take away all passports from Chinese students, thus making it impossible for them to leave the United States.

The Central People's Government of the People's Republic of China has received messages from many Chinese students in the United States recounting how the United States government has forcibly retained them with no justification whatsoever. Families of many students who are now in the United States have also applied to the Central People's Government for helping the return of their sons and daughters who have been forcibly retained by the United States government.

Chinese students in the United States have not committed any crime, yet the United States government has deprived them of their freedom to leave the United States and return to their motherland and has deprived them of their right to go back to their homeland to rejoin their families. This not only contravenes principles of international law, but it is entirely incompatible with humanitarianism.

If the United States government respects the principles of international law and humanitarianism, it should immediately put an end to the forcible retention and maltreatment of Chinese students and Chinese nationals and restore to them their inalienable right to leave the United States for their mother country to rejoin their families.

Note

Ambassador Huang Hua's justification of China's prolonged detention of certain American nationals was made in response to the United States' claim that a relatively large number were being illegally confined by the PRC. Some of the better-known cases have been presented in the previous part (recall 19–9 to 19–16). The PRC repeatedly emphasized the distinction between forbidding the exit of foreign nationals held under criminal charges and forbidding the exit of foreign nationals who are law abiding but whose departure is deemed contrary to the security of the host state.

During the course of the 1954–55 Sino-American negotiations on the exchange of each other's nationals, a Chinese publicist stated:

> As a matter of fact the problem is very simple. The students and the spies are entirely different classes of people. The Chinese people absolutely have the right to punish the American spies who secretly entered our country for sabotage activities, while the United States Department of State has no reason whatsoever to detain the Chinese students. There is no room for discussion of the problem. This illegal action on the part of the United States government in detaining our Chinese students to serve as hostages, an irresponsible act, does not have support even within the United States. The *Washington Star* in its editorial on December 15 stated that up to that time, the Chinese students did not obtain the permission to leave the United States on the ground that they all possess special skill which might prove useful to the Communists. It must be admitted (said the paper) that the explanation is not satisfactory, for, should the students desire to return home, the State Department must let them go, the sooner the better. When even the *Washington Star* considers the detention of the Chinese students to be unreasonable and contrary to conscience, what more has the Department of State to say? . . .
>
> The Chinese delegation had taken up the matter with the United States delegation in the hope that both parties would respect the right to leave for their homes of nationals of the other party in their respective countries who are law abiding. But the American delegation rejected the proposal. The Chinese delegation followed up with another proposal for third-nation diplomatic representatives assigned by the two parties themselves to look after the interests of the nationals of the respective countries. But this was also rejected by the American delegation. On what grounds does the United States government detain our students?
>
> On this matter the United States Department of State actually stated that the United States government had detained these students because they are skilled in various sciences and are useful for war. It added that, once they are allowed to leave the United States, they may take with them [a] very valuable scientific tech-

nique that will be contrary to the best interests of the United States. Then the reason for detaining our students is to utilize them to serve the war policy of the United States ruling clique.

International law stipulates that any country under whatever circumstances cannot prevent a foreign national [from leaving] its territory, as long as he abides by the law of the country of his residence. Since the United States government cannot name the crimes committed by the Chinese students, what right has it to prevent them from leaving the United States to return to their fatherland? [120]

25-28

"US Hinders Return of Chinese Students," *PC*, no. 18:40–41 (Sept. 16, 1955).

During the past few years, the US government has resorted to various measures, including intimidation and persecution, to prevent Chinese students from returning home. While the Sino-American talks at ambassadorial level on the question of the return of civilians of both sides to their respective countries have continued, the US State Department has frequently stated that since early April all restrictions had been lifted from those Chinese students who had applied to leave the United States. But the fact of the matter is that these students are still not free to leave.

A commentary by Observer in the *People's Daily* of August 24 says that, while China certainly welcomes the US statement that the students are free to come back, the facts are at variance with this statement. To this day, Chinese students are, in practice, detained in the United States by various obstacles put in their way. The only change compared with the past is that the US authorities have shifted from open to camouflaged obstruction.

Observer cites the case of the scientist, Dr. Chien Hsueh-shen, who has been trying to return to China ever since August 1950. For this, he was illegally arrested by the American authorities and held for 15 days. He was ordered not to leave America, or even to travel outside the bounds of the county in which he lives. This continued even after last April when restrictions on the departure of Chinese students held in the US had allegedly been lifted. Even as late as on June 15, Dr. Chien had to write to Chen Shu-tung, Vice-Chairman of the Standing Committee of the Chinese National People's Congress, asking for help. He wrote, "I have been detained by the US government for five years. Not a day, not an hour, not a minute passes without my thinking of returning home and taking part in the great work of national construction."

Observer points out that deliberate obstacles were also placed in the way of the small number of Chinese students who had been allowed to leave the US. The American Immigration Service knows very well that the students have to find travelling expenses and need time to complete arrangements for their departure. But they are ordered to leave within two weeks after permission is given. If they are unable to leave within the time specified, they are subjected to "deportation procedure," which includes detention, interrogation, and demands for bail. In this predicament, the students are then told that, if they want to avoid such trouble, they must apply for permanent residence permits or political asylum in accordance with the so-called Refugee Act of 1953.

The American government also persecutes in other ways Chinese students who want to return home. After notifying them that they must leave within a short period, the Immigration Service constantly summons them and, in an attempt to compel them to reveal their political convictions, impertinently puts questions to them such as "Why do you want to go back?" and "What are your views on the Communist Party?" They are then ordered to sign records of what they say under oath. Immigration and FBI agents can then charge them with "perjury" any time they like on the pretext that the answers are not always identical. Chinese students have been subjected to intimidation and obstruction even when already on their way home.

The Chinese press has published a number of interviews with Chinese students who have, after many difficulties, recently returned from the United States. They show that the American government persecuted them in the past and continued to the last to try to prevent them from returning home.

Huang Pao-tung, a chemistry student who received a doctor's degree at the Brooklyn Polytechnic Institute, said he was arrested and imprisoned for 116 days on Ellis Island by the US Immigration and Naturalization Service in May 1951, on the second day after he had made arrangements to return home. Finally released on bail, he was confined to the district covered by the New York Immigration Service. He had to report in person every Monday and was not allowed to attend meetings of any sort.

Shih Li-chi, who studied biochemistry at Columbia University said: "This April the Immigration Service notified me that I was free to leave America and go home, but demanded that I leave in two weeks' time. However, it was very difficult to get a steamship ticket at such short notice, let alone a visa. When I approached the Immigration

Service on the question, an official of that service threatened that, if I did not leave before the time limit, I should have to apply to be a political refugee. When I refused, he detained me half a day on a charge of 'illegal stay.' I was only released on a bail of 1,000 US dollars. The immigration authorities confined my activities to a radius of 25 miles, and I had to report to them regularly."

Hsieh Chia-lin, who holds a doctor's degree in physics from Stanford University, said that when he was on his way home via Honolulu in September 1951 he and eight other Chinese students were suddenly put under detention at Honolulu and the US authorities declared that they would not be allowed to return home. Hsieh was forced to go back to America. From then on, he was constantly subjected to interrogation by the FBI and had to report to the Immigration Service every three months. While on his way home this time, further obstacles were put in his way to prevent him [from] getting to China. US officials in Yokohama, Manila, and Hong Kong all used various threats and tricks to try and force him to go back to America.

These returned students pointed out that if the US government stops its intimidation, obstruction, and persecution, many Chinese students now in the United States will certainly apply for permission to leave and return to their homes in China.

NOTE

On September 10, 1955, the US and the PRC announced an agreement for the exchange of each other's nationals. For discussion of the agreement and its implementation, see items 31–3 to 31–6.

The case of Dr. Chien Hsueh-shen received a good deal of publicity again in the late 1960's when Peking revealed that, since his return home in 1955, he had directed the development of the PRC's nuclear missile program.[121]

At the same time that the PRC was having difficulty obtaining the release of certain nationals from the United States, it was having similar problems with Japan. On October 17, 1955, Peng Chen, then Secretary-General of the Standing Committee of the National People's Congress, and Eikichi Kanbayashiyama, leader of a Japanese Diet mission to China, announced an agreement that had been reached between the PRC's highest officials and the Diet mission. This provided, among other things, that:

> Five. Both China and Japan should actively look after their nationals residing in each other's country, enabling them to travel freely to and from their home country.

> Six. China and Japan have in the past sent back to each other the remains of the dead. Hereafter the two sides should continue to send back the remains of the dead to their home country as speedily as possible.[122]

Soon after, however, Japan infuriated PRC leaders by allegedly forcing 132 Chinese nationals to go to Taiwan, and it also "illegally detained" five of 161 Chinese who decided to return to mainland China.[123] Item 25–29 illustrates the PRC's response to the latter situation.

25-29

"Chinese Red Cross Protest at Japanese Government Action," NCNA–English, Peking (Nov. 22, 1955), in *SCMP*, no. 1176:29 (Nov. 23, 1955).

The Chinese Red Cross Society yesterday expressed deep regret over the series of obstructions recently imposed by the Japanese government against Chinese nationals in Japan desiring to return home.

The society pointed out that these obstructions "are against the desire of the Chinese and Japanese people for the free movement of nationals between the two countries and are unfriendly acts of discrimination against the Chinese nationals in Japan."

In a telegram to the Liaison Office of the Japanese Red Cross Society, the Japanese Peace Liaison Committee and the Japan-China Friendship Association, the Chinese Red Cross Society cited as examples the recent arrest in Nagoya of Hung Chin-shan and the detention of four other Chinese—Pan Kuang-kun, Huo Chuan-tsao, Ku Min-sheng and Tsai Chin-hsiu—at Hamamatsu center.

All these Chinese have expressed their desire to return home.

[The telegram protesting the Hung Chin-shan case] said, "The Chinese people are closely watching this problem. The liaison office of your three organizations is requested to make representation to the Japanese government quickly so that the above-mentioned five Chinese nationals can board the Koan Maru to return to China as they desire."

The Chinese Red Cross Society notified the three Japanese organizations that the number of Japanese nationals desiring to return home and now assembled at Tientsin had increased to about 190. "This shows that we have been consistently providing all facilities and all possible assistance to Japanese nationals desiring to return to Japan."

The Chinese Red Cross Society thanked the Japanese Executive Committee for commemorating Chinese martyrs for its decision to send back to China the remains of the 131 Chinese martyrs at Hokkaido,

Osaka, Shimonoseki, Moji, and other places. It also sent its welcome to Katsuo Takenaka and 17 other representatives who are coming to China on the Koan Maru with the remains of the Chinese martyrs.

NOTE

The PRC has not only protested against the refusal of other states to permit the departure of its nationals, but it has also protested when other states have expelled or otherwise compelled the departure of its nationals. The following materials suggest the range of hostile actions and PRC responses.

25-30

"Spokesman of Ministry of Foreign Affairs Protests US and French Abduction of Chinese in Vietnam," NCNA–English, Peking (Jan. 19, 1955), in *SCMP*, no. 972:14 (Jan. 20, 1955).

A spokesman of the Ministry of Foreign Affairs of the People's Republic of China today issued the following statement on the abduction of Chinese residents in the northern part of Vietnam by the Chiang Kai-shek clique with the assistance of the French authorities at the instigation of the United States:

"Since the Geneva Agreement was reached on the restoration of peace in Indochina, the United States, the traitor Chiang Kai-shek's clique, and the French authorities have abducted and persecuted Chinese residents in Hanoi, Moncay, and other places in a planned way. They openly sent planes and vessels to carry Chinese residents away to Haiphong, Saigon, and Taiwan. Chinese residents abducted to Haiphong and Saigon have suffered all the distress of displacement, hunger, and illness. Some have been tortured or murdered. Overseas Chinese youth and students abducted to Taiwan have been forcibly impressed by the traitor Chiang Kai-shek's clique into its armed forces for use as cannon fodder.

"This atrocity perpetrated by the United States has evoked great indignation among the mass of the Chinese people and Chinese residents abroad. It was denounced by a spokesman of the Overseas Chinese Affairs Commission of China on August 16th, 1954. Nevertheless, the United States, the traitor Chiang Kai-shek's clique, and the French authorities did not end their criminal actions of abducting overseas Chinese, but have recently intensified these actions. US, French, and Chiang Kai-shek's special agents are now resorting to every imaginable vicious measure to coerce Chinese residents in Haiphong, Quangyen, Bayinh, Hoangbi, and other places to move south and are intensifying their criminal activities of abducting overseas Chinese.

"By instigating the French authorities to help the traitor Chiang Kai-shek's clique to persecute, plunder, and abduct overseas Chinese, the United States has completely violated the terms of paragraph 8 of the Final Declaration of the Geneva Conference dated July 21st, 1954, which reads: 'The provisions of the agreements on the cessation of hostilities intended to ensure the protection of individuals and of property must be strictly applied and must, in particular, allow everyone in Vietnam to decide freely in which zone he wishes to live.'

"The Chinese people cannot tolerate this action by the United States and the French authorities in deliberate violation of the Geneva Agreement on the restoration of peace in Indochina, and [they] declare that the United States and the French authorities must immediately end the criminal action. Otherwise, the United States and the French authorities must bear full responsibility for all consequences."

25-31

"Songgram's Attempt to Deport Overseas Chinese to Taiwan Denounced by Returned Overseas Chinese in Peking," NCNA–English, Peking (Feb. 5, 1952), in *SCMP*, no. 269:3–4 (Feb. 6, 1952).

The Chinese who have returned from abroad warned the government of Thailand against its sinister scheme to deport the patriotic overseas Chinese in Thailand to the Chiang Kai-shek remnant clique in Taiwan.

In a statement issued here yesterday, the spokesman of the Returned Overseas Chinese Society in Peking stated that the government of Thailand in last December unreasonably arrested Wu Tien-yung, editor-in-chief of the *Chuan Min Pao,* and an employee of the paper, Shih Po-hsing, and also secretary of the Chinese Chamber of Commerce, Chen Hwai-tien. He said that the Thai government had planned to deport the patriotic overseas Chinese secretly to Taiwan and place them in the hands of Chiang Kai-shek butchers. When this plot was exposed, Banyat Phehastin, Thailand's Minister of the Interior, while verbally refusing to admit that he had given such an order, openly stated that the destination of deported overseas Chinese would depend on where ships were going; in other words, if American ships headed directly for Taiwan, they would be sent to Taiwan. This shows that the authorities of Thailand have still not given up their vicious intentions of massacring the patriotic overseas Chinese through Chiang Kai-shek. All they have done is to make a shameless denial and try to transfer responsibility to so-called destination of the ships.

The Foreign Minister of Thailand, Nai Varakarn Bancha, made an even more scandalous statement. He could not but admit in words that, according to international convention, deported foreign residents should be sent back to their native land, but, on the pretext that Thailand has not established relations with China, he arbitrarily claimed that he had the "right" to deport the patriotic overseas Chinese to Taiwan.

"We solemnly denounce this plot of the Thailand government to massacre the patriotic overseas Chinese," the statement continues. "It must be pointed out that such arbitrary and shameless behaviour of the Thai government constitutes open and direct acts of hostility toward the Chinese people, which can never be tolerated. The Thai government must immediately put an end to this vicious scheme to deport the patriotic overseas Chinese to Taiwan for Chiang Kai-shek brigands to slaughter; otherwise, the Chinese people will have every reason to settle accounts with the Thai government for any bloodshed caused by such outrages."

Note

The fact that a state might deport Chinese nationals to mainland China rather than to Taiwan has not significantly assuaged the PRC's displeasure. During the British struggle to repress Communist guerrilla warfare in Malaya, an NCNA dispatch stated:

> In all, 9,052 overseas Chinese have been deported from Malaya by the British imperialists, without reason, since November 24, 1950.
>
> These overseas Chinese, who have arrived in 14 separate groups, were first thrown into concentration camps and then deported under the so-called "emergency regulations" which the British colonial government has put into force since June 1948. Available statistics alone estimate that overseas Chinese have sustained losses amounting to 4.9 million Straits Dollars (equivalent to over 36 billion yuan) as a result of destruction by burning and plundering of their houses, plantations, and other properties. Many Chinese have been wounded or crippled through sadistic torture and maltreatment.
>
> Disregarding serious protests lodged by the Chinese people, the British colonial government in Malaya has continued its persecu-

> tion of Chinese residents there during the past year. It has deported [almost] 10,000, at the same time, constantly throwing further numbers into concentration camps. A report from Singapore places [the] number of overseas Chinese now in concentration camps at over 20,000. In addition, the British colonial government compelled over 400,000 Chinese to move into so-called "migration camps" and burned and looted their homes and property. The British imperialists must be held responsible for consequences of this persistent persecution of the Chinese residents in Malaya and for encroaching upon their legitimate rights and interests.[124]

The following is a more recent example.

25-32

"Strong Protest against Burmese Government's Unwarranted Expulsion of Patriotic Chinese Nationals," *PR* 11.25:29 (June 21, 1968).

The Chinese embassy in Burma, in a note to the Ministry of Foreign Affairs of the Union of Burma on June 13, strongly protested against the Burmese government's order for the unwarranted expulsion from Burma of illegally arrested patriotic Chinese nationals.

The note said: Recently, the Burmese government has notified the Chinese embassy, in a series of notes, of its outrageous decision to expel from Burma Chen Fu-shun and scores of other patriotic overseas Chinese who have been illegally arrested. This is another serious step taken by the Burmese government which is persisting in its policy of hostility toward China and stepping up its persecution of Chinese nationals.

The note added: The Burmese government has committed a series of atrocities, brutally massacring and ruthlessly persecuting Chinese nationals in the anti-China and anti-Chinese incidents which it instigated in June last year. Soon afterwards, using various absurd excuses and fabricating evidence, it arrested a large number of patriotic Chinese, tortured them while they were on trial, passed heavy sentences on them, and threw them into prison. The Chinese embassy has repeatedly asked the Burmese government to release at once all patriotic overseas Chinese who have been unwarrantably arrested and convicted. However, the Burmese government has not only refused to accept this just demand, but has continued to arrest more in various parts of Burma. Now it has gone further and notified the Chinese embassy of its decision to expel a large number of these illegally arrested Chinese. It is quite obvious that the Burmese government is obdurately pursuing its set plans and schedules in persecuting the masses of patriotic Chinese in Burma and completely depriving them of their proper and legitimate right of subsistence.

In persecuting the overseas Chinese who love their motherland and who have always lived amicably with the Burmese people, the note went on, the Burmese government is motivated by its sinister political objectives, which are to cater to the needs of US imperialism and Soviet revisionism and further worsen relations between China and Burma. It must be pointed out that the Burmese government should not think that it can persecute the overseas Chinese unscrupulously and at will. The debt it owes the Chinese people will be settled sooner or later.

The note said in conclusion: The Chinese government will resolutely protect the proper rights and interests of the overseas Chinese and their personal safety. The Chinese embassy once again sternly demands that the Burmese government immediately release all the patriotic overseas Chinese unjustifiably arrested and convicted in Rangoon and other parts of Burma, put an end to all anti-China and anti-Chinese activities immediately, and give practical guarantees for the freedom and safety of Chinese nationals. Failing this, the Burmese government will be held fully responsible for all the consequences.

25-33

"Strongest Protest against Soviet Government's Unjustifiable Expulsion of All Chinese Students," *PR* 9.44:10–11 (Oct. 28, 1966).

Yu Chan, director of the Soviet Union and East European Department of the Chinese Foreign Ministry, on October 22 summoned Razdukhov, chargé d'affaires ad interim of the Soviet embassy in China, and handed him a note lodging the strongest protest with the Soviet government against the intensification of its anti-China activities and the deterioration of Sino-Soviet relations by its unjustifiable decision to suspend the studies of all Chinese students in the Soviet Union. Finding himself devoid of all argument, the Soviet chargé d'affaires ad interim refused to accept the note. Comrade Yu Chan declared that this unreasonable attitude of Razdukhov is most regrettable.

The note of the Chinese Foreign Ministry says that, by a notification of the Ministry of Higher and Secondary Special Education of the USSR dated October 7, 1966, the Soviet government has unilaterally decided to suspend the studies of all Chinese students in the Soviet Union and ordered them to leave the Soviet Union in October this year. This is a grave incident in which the Soviet government has flagrantly violated the Agreement on Cultural Co-operation Between China and the Soviet Union and further worsened the relations between the two countries.

This incident has been deliberately engineered by the Soviet government. On September 20, 1966, the Ministry of Higher Education of the People's Republic of China notified the Soviet embassy in China that as the great proletarian cultural revolution is going on in all institutions of higher education in China, where classes have been completely suspended, all foreign students in China are to suspend their studies for one year, and those who are to graduate next summer or by the end of this year may graduate ahead of time. The Soviet students in China are originally scheduled to graduate by the end of this year, and as they have already completed their major courses, they may graduate ahead of schedule. After an agreement in principle has been reached through consultation with the Soviet side, the time of their graduation will be decided concretely by the school authorities in consultation with the Soviet students in the light of the progress each student has made in his studies. Although the Chinese side has repeatedly asked for a reply in this connection, the Soviet side has thus far failed to give any answer, but has instead recalled on its own the Soviet students in China. On the very next day following the departure of the Soviet students, the Soviet government went so far as to falsely accuse the Chinese government of having unilaterally decided to suspend the studies of the Soviet students and, on the pretext of what is called the principle of reciprocity, suddenly announced ordering all Chinese students to leave the Soviet Union within a set time limit.

The note says, the pretext of the Soviet authorities is utterly untenable. The whole world knows that a great cultural revolution is in progress in China and the suspension of studies for one year does not apply to the Soviet students alone but to all foreign students in China. Since in the Soviet Union the case does not exist in which all foreign students are required to suspend their studies for one year, the unilateral decision to suspend the studies of the Chinese students there is clearly a discrimination against the Chinese students exclusively.

The Soviet leadership has long plotted to sabotage the exchange of students between China and the Soviet Union. For a long time, the Soviet side has obstructed in every possible way China's dispatch of students to the Soviet Union and has tried hard to cut down their number; it has created all kinds of difficulties for their studies, unilaterally altered their specialties, placed restrictions on their reading materials and training programs, driven them back to China on fabricated excuses, and even tried to incite them to betray their own country, and now it has finally ordered all of them to leave the Soviet Union. It is futile for you to turn things upside down and try to shift on to us the responsibility for sabotaging the exchange of students.

NOTE

For the agreement referred to in item 25–33, see item 31–16, and for further discussion of its alleged violation, see Note following 35–4.

As the Cultural Revolution reached its peak, the PRC encountered similar difficulties with other "sister socialist states" and responded in similar fashion. Five Chinese students studying in Hungary "were unwarrantedly ordered to leave the country. . . ." [125] "The Mongolian revisionist leading clique unwarrantedly deported . . . three Chinese teachers . . . because they had enthusiastically propagated the infinitely brilliant thought of Mao Tse-tung among Chinese children and the broad masses of the patriotic Chinese nationals in Mongolia." [126] The Bulgarian government was accused of "unwarrantedly declaring three Chinese students in Bulgaria '*persona non grata.*' " [127] And the Czechoslovak government's "flagrant provocation" in refusing to readmit ten Chinese students who had temporarily returned home to take part in the Cultural Revolution "received a stern rebuff from the Chinese side. . . ." [128] (See 35–9.)

Indonesia thus far holds the record for informally having driven out the largest number of overseas Chinese. Approximately 100,000 left for China after Indonesia substantially intensified its discriminatory regulations in late 1959.[129] Over four thousand more left after the attempted coup of September 30, 1965, revived the harshest aspects of Indonesian xenophobia. The following report indicates the PRC's reaction to the latter series of measures:

> The Chinese Foreign Ministry sent a note to the Indonesian embassy in China on October 21, lodging a strong protest with the Indonesian government against its inhuman persecution and expulsion of Chinese nationals.
>
> The note pointed out that the Indonesian government was becoming increasingly rampant in its persecution of Chinese nationals and that this persecution had reached the serious stage of expelling Chinese nationals en masse. Taking advantage of the dispatch of ships by the Chinese government for bringing back its persecuted nationals, the Indonesian government had now gone so far as to wantonly rob the Chinese nationals of their property, deprive them of their means of livelihood, and try to drive them out of Indonesia in groups. This was something which the Chinese government absolutely could not tolerate; nor could this ever succeed.[130]

The massive Indonesian campaigns of 1959–1960 and 1965–1968 against persons of Chinese origin presented the PRC with its gravest challenge to protect nationals and made it obvious that Peking's efforts to ameliorate the overseas Chinese problem by urging its nationals to take on Indonesian citizenship and characteristics had failed. Despite frequently bitter protests and veiled threats, especially during the latter period, there is no evidence that the PRC seriously contemplated resort to military sanctions to prevent the expulsion of its nationals; nor did it take the initiative in breaking off trade or diplomatic relations.[131] Rather, in both periods the PRC adopted the pragmatic position of making a new effort to settle the problem by facilitating the repatriation of all those Chinese who no longer found life tolerable in Indonesia. Foreign Minister Ch'en Yi articulated this position in his letter of March 15, 1960 to Indonesian Foreign Minister Subandrio:

> Seeing that the Indonesian government stresses the overseas Chinese can no longer adapt themselves to the economic development of Indonesia, and that in fact a considerable part of the overseas Chinese have already been deprived of their means of livelihood and reduced to great distress, the Chinese government has deemed it necessary, in its proposal for the overall settlement of the overseas Chinese question, to raise the question of sending back to China those overseas Chinese who are unable to make a living and do not wish to continue to reside in Indonesia. This is a major effort made by the Chinese government to open a way out of the difficult situation on the overseas Chinese question. The Chinese government has repeatedly asked the Indonesian government to take up the responsibility of sending overseas Chinese back to China in accordance with their own will, and has made preparations for the reception and settlement of the returned overseas Chinese. Since the Indonesian government has indicated that for the present it has difficulties in providing ships, the Chinese government has taken the initiative in sending ships to transport overseas Chinese back to China. These facts fully show the sincere desire of the Chinese government to settle the overseas Chinese question.[132]

The PRC's position led one American student of Southeast Asian affairs to write: "The sheltering of the refugees may have been a humane act, but it also constituted admission that China was not prepared to prevent their expulsion. . . . China thus not only retreated from the defense of her overseas citizens, she agreed to be an accomplice in their persecution." [133]

Both in 1959–1960 and in 1965–1968 Indonesian authorities actually appeared ambivalent or divided about the wisdom of driving out large numbers of Chinese and about the conditions for permitting them to leave. Many obstacles were placed in the way of their departure. For an example of the protests such conduct evoked from the PRC in 1959, see item 25–16.[134] The following item derives from the more recent period.

25-34

"Chinese Foreign Ministry Note to Indonesian Embassy," *PR* 9.28:41 (July 8, 1966).

The Ministry of Foreign Affairs of the People's Republic of China presents its compliments to the embassy of the Republic of Indonesia in China and has the honor to state the following:

On May 18, the Chinese government sent the Indonesian government a note in which the Chinese government stated its decision to send ships to Indonesia in the near future to transport back the persecuted Chinese nationals who desire to return to China of their own will and demanded that the Indonesian government give a speedy reply and make the necessary arrangements. However, despite the constant inquiries by the Chinese government over the past month and more, the Indonesian government has deliberately delayed the reply on the repeated pretext that the Indonesian side had to make a study. On June 15 the Indonesian Ministry of Foreign Affairs asserted that "no Chinese nationals have made any request for returning to China" and asked the Chinese embassy to supply a list of the Chinese nationals who desire to return to China of their own will. This fully shows that the Indonesian government is deliberately placing obstacles and unreasonably creating difficulties and raising obstructions with regard to the urgent problem of the Chinese government sending ships to transport back the persecuted Chinese nationals.

As everyone knows, the fact that large numbers of Chinese nationals under persecution desire to return to China is caused entirely by the Indonesian government which is frantically opposing China and persecuting Chinese nationals. It should be the Indonesian government's unshirkable responsibility to arrange ships to assist in the return of the persecuted Chinese nationals. The Chinese government has raised the proper and reasonable demand to the Indonesian government which, however, peremptorily rejected it. In these circumstances, out of concern for the safety of the persecuted Chinese nationals the Chinese government decided to send its own ships to transport them back to China. But again you are trying hard to raise obstructions. We would like to ask: what are you up to? Is it that you will not feel satisfied until you have driven to complete destruction those Chinese nationals who have lost their means of livelihood because of persecution? Such a truculent and unreasonable attitude of the Indonesian government has aroused the great indignation of the Chinese people.

Your assertion that "no Chinese nationals have made any request for returning to China" is a downright lie. Tens of thousands of the persecuted Chinese nationals, rendered homeless and deprived of all their property or means of subsistence, are in dire distress. It is only natural that in order to survive they should ask to return to China. As a matter of fact, they raised long ago to the Indonesian government the demand for departure for China, and the Chinese embassy and consulates have constantly received applications of the persecuted Chinese nationals. In asking the Chinese embassy to supply a list of the persecuted Chinese nationals who desire to return to China of their own will, you actually want to carry out further persecution of the Chinese nationals on the list and force them to give up their demand for returning to China. The Chinese government firmly opposes the vicious scheme of yours.

It must be pointed out in all seriousness that it is the inalienable right of the Chinese government to protect its nationals by sending ships to transport them back to China in the circumstances in which the Chinese nationals are savagely persecuted and there is no guarantee at all for the safety of their lives and property. Arrangements have already been made for the Chinese ships which are ready to sail at any time. The Chinese government firmly demands that the Indonesian government immediately make an unequivocal and positive reply with regard to the question of the dispatch of ships by China to transport back the persecuted Chinese nationals who desire to return to China of their free will. The Chinese government once again protests that the governments of the two countries should immediately hold negotiations on the question of concrete arrangements for the dispatch of ships by the Chinese government to transport back its nationals and that the negotiations should start in the second week of July. The Chinese government has appointed Mr. Yao Teng-shan, chargé d'affaires a.i. of the Chinese embassy in Indonesia, as the chief delegate of the Chinese side and Mr. Hsu Jen, the Chinese consul general in Djakarta, as the delegate. The Chinese government demands that the Indonesian government speedily appoint corresponding delegates.

Note

After dragging their feet on the question of allowing Chinese ships to enter for repatriation purposes, the Indonesian authorities finally permitted three to come. When a fourth arrived, however, they presented it with even greater difficulties, eliciting this comment in a protest from "a responsible member of the [PRC] Commission for Overseas Chinese Affairs"[:] "On each of the three previous occasions when China sent a ship to Medan for victimized Chinese . . . the Indonesian reactionaries had made trouble but had failed ignominiously. This time, the Indonesian reactionaries deliberately obstructed proceedings by unreasonably putting restrictions on the number of visas they would issue for members of the group in charge of bringing back the victimized Chinese." [135] As one student of Indonesian politics has written, "there was more than a kernel of truth in Peking's charge." [136] The fourth ship was finally permitted to take home its passengers, bringing to 4,251 the number of repatriated Chinese.[137] But by mid-1967 it had become clear that Indonesia would not permit the departure of the much larger number of Chinese who were living in intolerable conditions in evacuation camps while awaiting the opportunity to emigrate.

Indonesia is not the only country to which the PRC has had to send ships to repatriate nationals. At the end of his long article on India's persecution of Chinese nationals (25–24), Chou Keng-sheng reported the demands contained in the PRC's note to India of December 18, 1962. These included ensuring the freedom of departure of Chinese nationals who wished to return to China and granting due compensation and the necessary facilities to the PRC for carrying out the return of its victimized nationals. After some prolonged negotiations the two sides concluded an agreement on repatriation arrangements, reproduced as item 25–35. Before long, a controversy developed over implementation of this agreement, as item 25–36 makes clear.

25-35

"Letter Given by the Ministry of External Affairs, New Delhi, to the Embassy of China in India," April 9, 1963, in *White Paper*, no. 9:117–118. [The source fails to identify either the author of the letter of the Ministry of External Affairs or the author of the Chinese embassy's letter.]

I write to acknowledge the receipt of your letter dated the 9th April, 1963, which reads as follows:

> In the course of the discussions recently held between the embassy of the People's Republic of China and the Ministry of External Affairs of the government of India on matters concerning some concrete arrangements for the Chinese government to send

ships to bring back those Chinese nationals and members of their families interned by the Indian government as well as other members of their families elsewhere in India, who desire to come back to China, the following points have been agreed upon by the two sides:

(1) The Chinese government will send ships to bring back the above-mentioned interned Chinese nationals and members of their families by stages and by groups, with each group numbering from 800 to 1,000 persons. All members of the family of an internee mentioned above shall come back to China together with the [internee] in the same ship.
(2) The Indian government will issue exit permits to the above-mentioned interned Chinese nationals and members of their families and give them necessary facilities while they are leaving India.
(3) The Indian government will make arrangements for all the above-mentioned interned Chinese nationals and the members of their families to undergo necessary health formalities and issue them valid health certificates, as agreed upon between the two sides.
(4) The Indian government will be responsible for transporting each group of the above-mentioned interned Chinese nationals and members of their families to the port, namely Madras. Before their arrival at Madras and embarkation on board the ships, the Indian government will be responsible for providing and making proper arrangements for all their transportation, boarding, and lodging as well as health facilities etc. The safety of their person and property shall be ensured.
(6) The Chinese and the Indian governments will designate officials respectively to maintain contact with each other at the port in regard to the work of shipping back the above-mentioned interned Chinese nationals and members of their families, and to settle, at any time and through consultations, problems which may arise, so that the work may proceed smoothly in time.

I shall be glad if you will please confirm that the foregoing correctly sets out the points of agreement reached between the two sides.

I confirm that the foregoing correctly sets out the points of agreement reached between the two sides.

25-36

"Memorandum Given by the Embassy of China in India, to the Ministry of External Affairs, New Delhi, April 27, 1963," in *White Paper*, no. 9: 125–127.

The Chinese embassy has to point out with regret that, during the time when the Chinese government sent ships at the middle of April 1963 to bring back to China a group of Chinese nationals interned by the Indian government and members of their families, the Indian side should have violated the six-point agreement reached between China and India concerning concrete arrangements of bringing back the Chinese nationals, created various difficulties, and unjustifiably placed obstacles and made harassment, thus causing numerous inconveniences and obstructions to the said work:

(1) The so-called name list supplied by the Indian government to the Chinese side of the first group of the interned Chinese nationals and their families who desire to return to China consisted of 995 persons. But, at the time of the handing over at the port of Madras, the Indian side withheld more than eighty of them in the list and deprived them of the right to go back to their motherland. Besides, contrary to the agreement, some of the internees and members of their families were not transported to the port to sail for China.

(2) According to the agreement, members of the family of an internee shall come back to China together with the internee in the same ship. Some of the internees, however, were not accompanied by members of their families while returning to China.

(3) Under the agreement, the Indian side should be responsible for making proper arrangements for the transportation, boarding, and lodging as well as health facilities for the victimized Chinese nationals on their way to the port, and it should also ensure the safety of their property. But, the embassy has learnt that during the long journey of 3 to 4 days in the hot weather from the concentration camps to the port, the victimized Chinese nationals were under armed escort like prisoners, and even subjected to restrictions and harassment when they got down [from] the train for drinking water. The aged, the young, and the sick were not given necessary care. A pregnant woman had begun to feel birth pangs on the

way, but received no due attendance. While the victimized Chinese nationals were going on board the ship, there were three old men, extremely weak and unable to walk, who had to be carried to the deck on stretchers. But this had not been intimated by the Indian side to the Chinese side in advance to enable the latter to make arrangements for special care. From the concentration camps to the port and before embarkation, the victimized Chinese nationals and their luggage were subjected to several searches. Even [their few] valuables were forcibly taken away from a number of them. Money was also taken away from many of them, and their request for a receipt was rejected. All these are in violation of the agreement reached between the two sides.

(4) It had been verbally agreed between the two sides that the two Chinese ships for bringing back the Chinese nationals should berth at the wharf at the same time near to each other. But, at the port, the Indian side persisted that only one ship was permitted to berth at one time. This has caused unnecessary difficulties and delay in the work of shipping back the Chinese nationals. Moreover, after the victimized Chinese nationals embarked on board the ships, the Indian side asked the ships to leave the wharf immediately, thus making it impossible for the officials of the embassy to undertake necessary registration and other formalities among the Chinese nationals returning to China. Before the chargé d'affaires and other officials of the Chinese embassy got down from the ship, the ladder placed to the ship was being removed in an attempt to render it difficult for them to come back to the wharf. On the evening of April 13, when a diplomatic official of the embassy was leaving the harbour, Indian policemen even wanted to search his briefcase and prevented him from leaving the place for as long as over ten minutes. Such practice as mentioned above not only goes against the agreement that the Indian government would give the Chinese officials facilities in their work, but also contravenes international practice and lacks minimum diplomatic courtesy.

(5) It should also be pointed out that the Indian authorities have taken away from many Chinese nationals passports and other papers issued to them by Chinese government organs, and did not return them to the Chinese nationals even when they embarked on board the ships for their motherland. Such an outrageous act of forcible seizure of passports issued by China is in grave violation of [the] code of conduct in international relations.

The various facts listed above show that the Indian side lacks cooperation and sincerity in regard to the work of shipping back the Chinese nationals. The Indian side not only violated the agreement reached between China and India concerning concrete arrangements of bringing back the Chinese nationals, but even broke the various promises it had made during the discussions as well as in the Annex to its note dated March 26, 1963. This has brought many difficulties and [much] delay to the work of bringing back the Chinese nationals, and consequently it could not proceed smoothly and in time. To this, the Chinese embassy hereby draws the serious attention of the Indian Ministry of External Affairs.

The Chinese embassy now informs the Indian Ministry of External Affairs that Chinese ships for bringing back the second group of the victimized Chinese nationals will arrive in India by the middle of May 1963. The embassy hopes that, in the forthcoming work of bringing back the Chinese nationals, the Indian government will strictly abide by the agreement reached for the purpose, and the promises it has made, [and] fully cooperate with the Chinese officials and ensure due facilities to them. In order to ensure the smooth proceeding of the work of shipping back the second group of the victimized Chinese nationals, the Chinese embassy requests that the Indian government:

(1) supply within a week the name list of the returning victimized Chinese nationals and members of their families, which includes, besides the original items, names in Chinese, age, and health conditions, requiring special care;
(2) immediately release the returning victimized Chinese nationals to go back to their original places of residence to dispose of their property;
(3) immediately make known the contents of the six-point agreement between China and India and the eight-point promises contained in the Annex to the Indian note dated March 26, 1963, to the returning victimized Chinese nationals and members of their families.

NOTE

During 1963 the PRC repatriated 2,395 nationals from India in three shiploads. When it offered to repatriate another batch of nationals, India refused on the ground that none of the remaining overseas Chinese wished to return to China.[138]

Early in China's bitter 1967 dispute with Burma, the Chinese embassy in Rangoon transmitted a note that stated: "Out of solicitude and loving concern for the overseas Chinese, the government of the People's Republic of China has decided to send civil aircraft immediately to Burma to bring back home for medical care and treatment those patriotic overseas Chinese who have been beaten up and wounded by ruffians organized and directed by the Burmese government."[139] Burma refused to comply with this request on the ground that the wounded could not be permitted to leave the country until the crisis had been resolved.[140]

The Republic of China's attitude toward repatriation, necessarily conditioned by overpopulation in Taiwan, has been summarized by one authority on Asian politics:

> The repatriation of overseas Chinese to Taiwan is by no means favored by the Nationalist government. Some persons have come from abroad to seek haven on the island, but ordinarily Taipei argues that there is no room for repatriates. Even possession of a Nationalist passport is no guarantee of admission. The government on Taiwan must come close to being unique in claiming the right to deny entry onto its territory to its own citizens. A rather embarrassing diplomatic dialogue between Manila and Taipei went on for some years over this issue. The Philippine government planned to deport Nationalist Chinese who overstayed their Philippine visas, but Taiwan refused to admit them.[141]

Protection of Other Interests Abroad 26

We have seen that the PRC's leading criminal law textbook asserted the power to punish foreigners for criminal acts committed abroad that "injure the People's Republic of China or its citizens." [142] Item 25–3 indicated that criminal acts committed abroad that injure the PRC are those "which endanger the security and interest of the prosecuting state. . . ." We do not know whether the PRC has actually exercised criminal jurisdiction over foreigners for acts committed abroad that did not harm Chinese nationals, their property, or property of the PRC but that were otherwise deemed to have harmed the PRC's "security and interest." As in the case of the protection of nationals, the PRC's efforts to protect other interests are usually known not through the exercise of judicial jurisdiction but rather through the protests that it has lodged with other states.

Recall also the PRC's regulations, policy statements, and enforcement actions regarding its claims and those of other coastal states to control events in international waters adjacent to territorial seas (16–7, 16–9, and 16–10 and related Notes). And see Part IX for examples of PRC efforts to achieve effects abroad through participation in the UN.

As the materials in the preceding chapters have indicated, the PRC's efforts to protect overseas Chinese have frequently been perceived by host states as interference in their internal affairs. If this has been the case with respect to the protection of nationals, it has been much more so with respect to the protection of other Chinese interests abroad. The reader may recall that, when the PRC protested against Ceylon's refusal to permit the importation of 300 Chairman Mao badges, Ceylon claimed that the Chinese embassy's note constituted unwarranted interference with its sovereignty (Note following 9–8). Part VII will provide similar examples relating to the privileges and immunities of diplomats and other agents of international relations. Here we will merely illustrate some other attempts by Peking to influence events and to safeguard interests abroad, including the assertion of immunity from local jurisdiction of Chinese government property abroad.

26-1

"Protest against Anti-China Provocation in Britain," *PR* 10.29:40 (July 14, 1967).

While millions upon millions of people throughout the world hail China for having successfully exploded its first hydrogen bomb, US and British imperialism, modern revisionism, and all reactionaries mortally fear and deeply hate this great victory achieved by the Chinese people under the guidance of the invincible thought of Mao Tse-tung. With the connivance of the British government and incited by the official propaganda machine, a handful of anti-China elements, in the name of the "campaign for nuclear disarmament," created disorders and provocations in front of the Chinese Chargé d'Affaires Office in London on June 18 and 28. They were sternly rebuked by members of the office on both occasions.

A handful of ruffians, catering to the needs of US and British imperialism and the Soviet revisionist leading clique, carried out another provocation in front of the Chinese Chargé d'Affaires Office on the evening of July 4. Some of them went so far as to burn a copy of *Quotations from Chairman Mao Tse-tung*, which is most treasured by the revolutionary people of the world and regarded by them as a powerful weapon against imperialism, revisionism, and all reactionaries. Staff members of the Chinese Chargé d'Affaires Office, who have enormous love for the great leader Chairman Mao, immediately rushed out to stop the ruffians' shameless crime and managed to seize evidence of the crime on the spot.

The incident was a new and grave political provocation engineered by British imperialism against the great Chinese people. On July 5, Chinese chargé d'affaires ad interim Shen Ping lodged the most serious and most emphatic protest with the British Foreign Office.

26-2

"Protest against Ghanaian Authorities' Anti-Chinese Provocations," *PR* 9.41:38 (Oct. 7, 1966).

The embassy of the People's Republic of China in the Republic of Ghana handed a note to the Ghanaian Ministry of Foreign Affairs on October 1, lodging the most serious protest with the Ghanaian authorities against their anti-Chinese policy and the creation of an anti-Chinese incident. The note said:

> On September 23, 1966, B. A. Bentum, Secretary-General of the Ghana Trade Union Congress, went so far as to hold a press

conference on the pretext of an affair in which the Chiang Kai-shek clique's "Vice-Minister of Foreign Affairs" Yang Hsi-kun and his aide who stopped over in transit at Accra airport rudely obstructed the correspondent of the Hsinhua News Agency of China from performing his normal function, and at the conference B. A. Bentum concocted a story with ulterior motives that the Chinese embassy was "harbouring" Red Guards and wildly attacked the great cultural revolution in China.

The above-mentioned anti-Chinese incident constitutes yet another grave step of the Ghanaian authorities in pursuing their anti-Chinese policy. Since the Chinese people unfolded the great cultural revolution, the official press of Ghana has kept on making anti-Chinese outcries. In the period since August alone, the *Ghanaian Times*, the *Evening News*, and the *Daily Graphic* have printed a dozen or more articles venomously vilifying the great cultural revolution in China, making incitement and interfering in China's internal affairs. In particular, it must be pointed out with all gravity that these papers have even launched unscrupulous attacks on Chairman Mao Tse-tung, the most respected and beloved great leader of the Chinese people. This is what the 700 million Chinese people absolutely will not tolerate. The Chinese embassy hereby lodges the most serious protest with the Ghanaian authorities.

26-3

"Protest against Nepalese Government Connivance at Anti-China Outrage," *PR* 10.29:39 (July 14, 1967).

On the evening of July 1, a group of Nepalese hooligans, instigated and directed by US imperialism, Soviet revisionism, and the Indian reactionaries, and with the connivance of the Nepalese government, carried out anti-China activities in front of the Chinese photo exhibition hall in Kathmandu. They made several attempts to break into the exhibition hall, clamoring hysterically for removal of the portrait of the Chinese people's great leader Chairman Mao and of the Chinese national flag. They shouted anti-China slogans and viciously insulted Chairman Mao, the red sun that shines most brightly in the hearts of the Chinese people. Nepalese progressive students, who cherish boundless love for Chairman Mao, the great teacher of the world revolutionary people, and treasure the friendship between the Nepalese and Chinese peoples, rushed to the exhibition hall to defend Chairman Mao's portrait. They shouted: "We will defend Chairman Mao with our blood!" "We will always be loyal to Chairman Mao!" "We pledge to fight to the end against the US and Indian reactionaries!"

The second secretary of the Indian embassy in Nepal, Singh, who took part in plotting the anti-China outrage, came out into the open and beat the Nepalese who defended the friendship between the Nepalese and Chinese peoples, when he saw that the scheme was not fully realized.

The hooligans also hurled stones at the cars of the Chinese embassy, the Kathmandu branch of the Hsinhua News Agency and Chinese experts, and wounded one Chinese diplomat.

It was reported that US "peace corps" and military men were backing the anti-China hooligans from behind the scenes. The US embassy sent personnel to Nepalese universities to spread rumors against China and incite Nepalese students to oppose China. The Soviet embassy was also extremely busy those days. The TASS correspondent in Nepal openly incited Nepalese students and reporters to oppose China.

The Nepalese government approved and supported this anti-China outrage. In the past six months, the reactionary Nepalese press has continually carried articles slandering China. Reactionary forces in Nepal forbade Nepalese students to wear badges with a profile of Chairman Mao or carry *Quotations from Chairman Mao Tse-tung*. At the time of the outrage, the Chinese side repeatedly demanded that the Nepalese government stop it. However, this demand was ignored. When the hooligans were committing the outrage, the Nepalese commissioner in Bagmati was right on the spot.

On instructions from the Chinese government, Chinese Ambassador in Nepal Yang Kung-su lodged a serious protest with the Nepalese government on July 5 against the anti-China outrage. The ambassador stressed that the great socialist China was not to be bullied. In conducting anti-China activities, imperialism, revisionism, and all reactionaries would break their own skulls. Those who follow them in their anti-China campaign would suffer the consequences of their own actions.

NOTE

A leading Nepal newspaper published the official public response of its government:

> Kathmandu. July 10.
> A foreign office press note states:
>
> "The attention of the foreign office of His Majesty's Government has been drawn to the recent broadcast of Radio Peking and the publication of the People's Republic of China in Kathmandu regarding the recent incident that took place before the Chinese stall

in the Ramailo Mela alleging the association of HMG in the incident. A spokesman of the foreign office has characterised it as baseless and unrealistic. He further revealed that a strong protest has been lodged with the Chinese government in respect of such baseless broadcast and publications designed to affect the friendly relations so happily subsisting between the two countries."[143]

Peking's response was heated:

> In its July 10 note to the Chinese embassy, the Nepalese Ministry of Foreign Affairs made no mention of the truth about the anti-China outrage in an attempt to evade its responsibility, instead it unwarrantedly protested against the Hsinhua News Agency's report on the July 1 Kathmandu incident. In its July 21 note to the Nepalese Foreign Ministry, the Chinese embassy categorically rejected Nepal's protest and lodged the most serious protest with the Nepalese government against insulting the Chinese people and the deliberate sabotage of Sino-Nepalese friendship by the reactionary forces in Nepal.
>
> The note drew attention to the fact that the Nepalese government had allowed US imperialism, Soviet revisionism, and Indian reaction to carry out unchecked anti-China activities in Nepal. Since the launching of China's great proletarian Cultural Revolution, large quantities of foreign newspapers and periodicals containing anti-Chinese material had been distributed in Nepal. The Nepalese press had also published many anti-Chinese articles slandering China's great Cultural Revolution and even openly insulting Chairman Mao, the great leader of the Chinese people. In spite of the representations made by the Chinese embassy, the Nepalese government had not taken any effective measures to stop the anti-China activities. The note stressed that the Nepalese government's assertion about forbidding any country to oppose a third country in Nepal actually meant allowing blatant attacks on China by imperialism, revisionism, and reaction and by the reactionary forces in Nepal, while forbidding the Chinese side from making necessary and justified exposure and rebuttal.
>
> The note cited irrefutable facts to show that the anti-China incident on July 1 was engineered by US imperialism and Indian reaction and had the approval and support of the Nepalese government. The Nepalese press is still spreading rumours about China, vilifying and attacking it, and the Hsinhua News Agency is a particular target of such attacks. The Nepalese government has even intervened directly by restricting the sale of Chinese publica-

> tions, confiscating copies of *Quotations From Chairman Mao Tse-tung* and other writings by Chairman Mao, intimidating bookshops dealing in Chinese publications and the Nepal-China Friendship Association which has been upholding Sino-Nepalese friendship, while conniving at hooligans' tearing up pictures about China exhibited by the Nepal-China Friendship Association. The note said that recently the Nepalese government had repeatedly told the Chinese ambassador that it wished to safeguard the friendship between Nepal and China. If the Nepalese government is really sincere about this, then it must promptly annul all measures discriminating against China and stop all anti-Chinese statements and deeds on Nepalese territory. If the Nepalese side does not care for the friendship which took China and Nepal a long time to build, but allows imperialism, revisionism, and reaction to carry on their evil ways in Nepal or even follows them in opposing China, then the Nepalese government must bear full responsibility for all the serious consequences arising therefrom.[44]

The following year the sensitivity to publicity of the PRC's agents abroad produced another embarrassing incident in Nepal:

> The veteran editor of the *Indian Express,* Frank Moraes, had his own taste of a Chinese-type *gherao* while driving along the Nepalese stretch of the Kathmandu/Lhasa highway. Together with a Nepali editor, Manindra Raj Shreshta, and *Time/Life* photographer Marilyn Silverstone, Mr. Moraes stopped the car at the site of the Sunkosi hydroelectric project which Chinese technicians are setting up. Apparently the photographer annoyed the Chinese and, as the party was driving back, a truck full of Chinese technicians overtook it and forced it to stop, while another blocked it from the rear. For 2½ hours the Chinese shouted abuse, pounding the car and covering it with spittle, demanding the camera and negatives. The journalists refused, pointing out with some justice that they were on Nepalese territory. Finally the Chinese permitted the car to return to the project where the camera and film were handed to a Nepali officer, later to be returned—untampered with—after further argument with the Chinese. The Nepali told Mr. Moraes that the incident resulted from a "misunderstanding"—although the Chinese offered no such explanation.[145]

26-4

"Note Given by the Embassy of China in India to the Ministry of External Affairs, New Delhi, April 19, 1963," *White Paper*, no. 9:181–182.

The embassy of the People's Republic of China in India presents its compliments to the Ministry of External Affairs, government of India, and has the honour to state the following:

On February 20 this year the Chinese embassy verbally drew the attention of the Ministry of External Affairs to the screening in Bombay of a US anti-Chinese film "Satan Never Sleeps," and demanded that the screening of the film be immediately stopped. Now the film has again been shown in Delhi. In disregard of the proper demand of the embassy, the Indian authorities should have continued to allow the screening in India of this US film which insults the Chinese people, slanders and attacks the People's Republic of China. This is another unfriendly act towards the People's Republic of China. The embassy lodges a protest with the Indian Ministry of External Affairs against this, and once again demands that the Indian authorities take immediate measures to put an end to the screening of the said film.

The embassy of the People's Republic of China takes this opportunity to renew to the ministry the assurances of its highest consideration.

NOTE

The PRC has occasionally sought to protect its state property abroad by invoking the doctrine of foreign sovereign immunity, as item 26–5 illustrates; see also 27–12. The last item in this chapter suggests the PRC's interest in and perception of the recent evolution of this doctrine.

26-5

"Chairman of Kwangtung Provincial People's Government Yeh Chien-ying Issues Protest Against Seizure of Chinese Fishing Boat by British Authorities in Hong Kong," NCNA–Canton (Feb. 19, 1953), *SCMP*, no. 519:13 (Feb. 25–26, 1953).

Chairman of the Kwangtung Provincial People's Government Yeh Chien-ying has issued a protest against the open seizure of the Chinese fishing boat, "Yu Ch'iung", in Hong Kong, by the British government authorities. Text follows:

Of the five fishing boats left in Hong Kong of the Bureau of Marine Products of the Kwangtung Provincial People's Government, the "Yu Chin", "Yu Yang", "Yu Lien", and "Yu Pu" were seized by force by the British government authorities in Hong Kong in collusion with the American and Chiang Kai-shek bandits on June 12, 1950 and June 13, 1952 respectively. On January 31, 1953, the last fishing boat, "Yu Ch'iung", was also shamelessly seized by British government authorities in Hong Kong. On January 31, a tug-boat and a motor boat with armed personnel of the Marine Department of the British government in Hong Kong were dispatched to moor alongside the "Yu Ch'iung". Alltree, Head Bailiff of the British court in Hong Kong, led Mason and eight sailors to forcibly board the fishing boat, announcing the decree of the British court to tow away the fishing boat and force our crew to leave the boat. Refusing to leave the boat, Huang Chuang-wu, captain of the "Yu Ch'iung," solemnly announced that the boat was the government property of the People's Republic of China, and that the British government authorities in Hong Kong had positively no right to do anything. But Alltree was so barbarous and atrocious that he tore down the national flag on our boat, broke the chain of the anchor, forced the captain and a crew of three to leave, and ordered a tug-boat to unlawfully and forcibly tow away the fishing boat "Yu Ch'iung".

On April 5, 1951, I had issued a statement on [. . .] fishing boats, denouncing the unlawful and unreasonable action taken by the British government in Hong Kong to shield the American and Chiang Kai-shek bandits to seize [. . .] Chinese fishing boats, and pointing out that the British government in Hong Kong would be held responsible for all the consequences. The British government in Hong Kong, however, has continued to collude with the American and Chiang Kai-shek bandits, and seized all five Chinese fishing boats in Hong Kong. The Chinese people are very indignant at this series of barbarous actions taken by the British government authorities in Hong Kong in shamelessly colluding with the American and Chiang Kai-shek bandits to openly seize by force the property of the People's Republic of China. For this reason, I hereby especially lodge a protest with the British government authorities in Hong Kong, announcing that the series of actions taken by the British government authorities in Hong Kong in openly seizing the Chinese state property are unlawful and unreasonable, and that the responsibilities and consequences should be solely borne by the British government.

26-6

Chou Keng-sheng, *Hsien-tai ying-mei kuo-chi-fa ti ssu-hsiang tung-hsiang* (Trends in the thought of modern English and American international law; Peking, 1963), pp. 55, 61–62, 63–64.

(*6*) On the Question of A State's Judicial [Jurisdictional] Immunity

The so-called question of a state's judicial immunity refers to the [principle] that the acts and assets of a state are immune from the jurisdiction of foreign courts. Or, to explain it in another way, it is the question of the courts of one state refraining from the exercise of jurisdiction over the acts and assets of a foreign state. This is an old question in international law. Under the traditional theory of international law, the recognition of this principle of a state's judicial immunity, based upon state sovereignty, independence, equality, dignity, friendly relations and other reasons, is generally beyond question. The only problems have related to the concrete application of this principle, especially the limits of its application. Profound differences can be found among scholars of various states (generally reflecting the judicial practice of their own states). Generally speaking, Anglo-American scholars of international law have consistently adhered to the theory of absolute immunity; namely, all state acts or assets, regardless of their nature, are uniformly entitled to judicial immunity. This theory stands in contrast to that held by scholars on the European continent. The latter advocate the principle of restricted immunity; namely, a state's acts should be classified according to their nature as sovereign acts [jure imperii] or non-sovereign acts [jure gestionis] and only the former acts are entitled to judicial immunity. . . .

The so-called "Tate Letter" of 1952, an official letter sent by the then Acting Legal Advisor of the United States State Department [Jack B. Tate] to the Acting Attorney General [Philip B.] Perlman, represents an official expression of this new trend [toward accepting the theory of restricted immunity]. That official letter revealed the new policy of the United States State Department for dealing with the question of judicial immunity of foreign states. It obviously had the effect of greatly influencing the [above noted] trend in the theory of international law. Although the so-called "Tate Letter" of 1952 was sent by the Acting Legal Advisor of the State Department on behalf of the Secretary of State to the Attorney General, in reality it amounted to a kind of directive from the [United States executive branch] to the judicial branch. Therefore, the official letter itself possessed important political significance, and so immediately attracted wide attention within legal circles. The [Tate] letter began with the statement that the State Department had considered the question of judicial immunity of foreign states and had decided that immunity would no longer be granted in certain types of cases. The letter also noted the existence of two doctrines concerning the question of judicial immunity of states—the doctrine of absolute immunity and the doctrine of restricted immunity—and it affirmed that the State Department would henceforth adopt the doctrine of restricted immunity, that is to say, it would not recognize immunity for so-called non-sovereign acts [jure gestionis]. The letter also pointed out that even in states which had hitherto generally followed the doctrine of absolute immunity, a group of influential scholars had advocated the [adoption of] the doctrine of restricted immunity. It further noted that the contracting states of the 1926 Brussels Convention [a] gave up judicial immunity for state-owned commercial vessels. Moreover, the United States several years before had, by its own initiative, given up the right to demand immunity for commercial vessels operated by the United States government. Furthermore, it pointed out that even the United Kingdom, which hitherto supported the doctrine of absolute immunity, was now preparing to change its policy. Thus, with the exception of the Soviet Union and other states in the socialist camp, very few [states]

[a] On April 10, 1926, governments of Germany, Belgium, Brazil, Chile, Denmark, Spain, Estonia, France, Britain, Hungary, Italy, Japan, Latvia, Mexico, Norway, the Netherlands, Poland, Portugal, Serbia-Croatia-Slovenia [Yugoslavia], and Sweden sent their plenipotentiary representatives to Brussels and concluded "The Convention for the Unification of Certain Rules relating to the Immunities of State-Owned Vessels." [*LNTS* 176:199–219 (1937)] The said Convention provided that vessels owned or operated by a state or other vessels that at the time a cause of action arises are exclusively used on governmental and non-commercial service shall enjoy judicial immunity. Commercial vessels owned or operated by a state [and not used for governmental or non-commercial service], like privately owned vessels, cannot enjoy judicial immunity.

The Convention and the protocol annexed to it on May 24, 1934, did not enter into force until January 8, 1937. Up to the end of 1949, only 14 states had deposited their instruments of ratification of the Convention. The United States is not a signatory, Britain did not ratify the Convention, and France deposited its instrument of ratification in 1955.

supported the doctrine of absolute immunity. Barefacedly, the letter pointed out that the increased insistence on absolute immunity by state-trading countries made it indispensable for the United States to change its policy. In short, in cases where a foreign state requests absolute judicial immunity the United States would henceforth handle the matter in accordance with the doctrine of restricted immunity.[b]

The doctrine of restricted immunity laid down by this letter of the United States State Department received the support of United States scholars of international law. . . .

The above stated directive of the United States State Department was an even more barefaced manifestation and summation of the United States government's policy of attempting for many years to restrict the right of foreign states to claim judicial immunity. Its major purpose was obviously to cope with the growing external economic activities of the socialist states. Since there are no specific criteria to guide the concrete application of the so-called doctrine of restricted immunity and if everything is left to the United States alone to decide, there would be no safeguard whatsoever to insure that foreign states and assets of foreign states would enjoy [any] judicial immunity.

From the foregoing description, it is clear that on the question of judicial immunity [the views of] Anglo-American scholars of international law, reflecting the external policy of the states concerned, are more and more explicitly inclined toward abandoning the traditional doctrine of absolute immunity and are turning toward the adoption of the doctrine of restricted immunity. Lauterpacht and other like-minded scholars have even advocated the total abandonment of the principle of judicial immunity of states. This is a very important new trend in Anglo-American thought concerning international law.

[b] "Changed Policy Concerning the Granting of Sovereign Immunity to Foreign Governments," *Department of State Bulletin,* 26.678:984–985 (June 23, 1952).

Notes

Preface

1. *E.g.*, the Soviet Union stated in a note to the PRC dated February 9, 1967, that the PRC's anti-Soviet activities were "breaching the most elementary norms of international law and morality." *Pravda* (Feb. 10, 1967), p. 5; translated in "Further Soviet Complaints of Chinese Harassment," *CDSP* 19.6:6 (Mar. 1, 1967). In 1958 a US Department of State memorandum to its missions abroad charged China with having "shown no intention to honor its international obligations" and having, as "one of its first acts," abrogated "the treaties of the Republic of China, except those it chose to continue." See "US Policy on Nonrecognition of Communist China," in *Department of State Bulletin* 39.1002:388 (Sept. 8, 1958). The State Department in a 1963 study ("The Conduct of Communist China") charged China with four violations of specific agreements. See Luke T. Lee, *China and International Agreements* (Durham, N.C.: Rule of Law Press; Leiden: A. W. Sijthoff, 1969), p. 15, n. 3.

2. Letter to the *New York Times* by David N. Rowe, Joseph Kaplan, and fourteen other scholars (Nov. 12, 1970), p. 42.

3. *E.g.*, sometime French diplomat Jacques Guillermaz, who was stationed in Peking between 1964 and 1966, recalled: "One day when I was in an auto accident, I refused to sign a paper with a police letterhead because, according to international law, a diplomat cannot deal directly with the police. An official [of the PRC] said to me: 'The international law you talk about is the international law of foreigners. It is not ours.' " "Two Experts Explain China's Cultural Revolution, Trying to Comprehend the Incomprehensible," *New York Times Magazine* (Nov. 17, 1968), p. 178.

4. See Jerome Alan Cohen, ed., *China's Practice of International Law: Some Case Studies* (Cambridge, Mass.: Harvard University Press, 1972); Hungdah Chiu, *The People's Republic of China and the Law of Treaties* (Cambridge, Mass.: Harvard University Press, 1972); Luke T. Lee, *China and International Agreements;* James C. Hsiung, *Law and Policy in China's Foreign Relations* (New York: Columbia University Press, 1972); see also Shao-chuan Leng and Hungdah Chiu, eds., *Law in Chinese Foreign Policy: Communist China and Selected Problems of International Law* (Dobbs Ferry, N.Y.: Oceana, 1972); and Jean Beauté, *La République populaire de Chine et le droit international* (Paris: A. Pedone, 1964). For a survey of research in this field, see Lung-sheng Tao, "New Developments in Research," in Leng and Chiu, *Selected Problems*, pp. 281–295.

Introduction

1. See the essays in John K. Fairbank, ed., *The Chinese World Order: Traditional China's Foreign Relations* (Cambridge, Mass.: Harvard University Press, 1968), and works cited therein.

2. See Richard Louis Walker, *The Multi-State System of Ancient China* (Hamden, Conn.: Shoe String Press, 1953); and Benjamin I. Schwartz, "The Chinese Perception of World Order, Past and Present," in Fairbank, ed., *Chinese World Order*, p. 278.

3. Many ad hoc envoys were exchanged between the Northern and Southern dynasties. See Huang Pao-shih, *Chung-kuo li-tai hsing-jen k'ao* (A study of diplomatic agents in Chinese history; rev. ed., Taipei, 1969), pp. 156–188.

4. See Schwartz, p. 280, and Chi Chiao-sheng, "The Diplomacy of Appeasement in the Northern Sung Dynasty," in *Kuo-li cheng-chih ta-hsüeh hsüeh-pao* (Journal of National Chengchi University, Taipei) 21:85–86 (Taipei, 1970).

5. For the English translation of a treaty of peace that China concluded on an equal basis with Tibet in the first half of the eighth century, see Chanakya Sen [Bhahaai Sen Gupta], comp. and ed., *Tibet Disappears: A Documentary History of Tibet's International Status, the Great Rebellion and Its Aftermath* (London: Asia Publishing House, 1960), pp. 35–36.

6. See Joseph F. Fletcher, "China and Central Asia, 1368–1884," in Fairbank, ed., *Chinese World Order,* pp. 209–216.

7. See, generally, Schwartz, pp. 276–281.

8. See John E. Wills, Jr., "Ch'ing Relations with the Dutch, 1662–1690," in Fairbank, ed., *Chinese World Order,* p. 248.

9. Joseph Sebes, S.J., *The Jesuits and the Sino-Russian Treaty of Nerchinsk, 1689: The Diary of Thomas Pereira, S.J.* (Rome: Institutum Historicum, S.I., 1961), pp. 114–120. For an authoritative account of early diplomatic contacts between China and Russia, see Mark Mancall, *Russia and China: Their Diplomatic Relations to 1728* (Cambridge, Mass.: Harvard University Press, 1971).

10. See memorial to the K'angshi emperor, dated Aug. 3, 1676, in *Ta-Ch'ing sheng-tsu jen* (*K'ang-hsi*) *huang-ti shih-lu* (Veritable records of K'ang-hsi Emperor [1622–1723] of the Great Ch'ing [Empire]; Taipei, 1964), *chüan* 62:3a–b, English translation in Lo-shu Fu, *A Documentary Chronicle of Sino-Western Relations* (*1644–1820*) (Tucson: University of Arizona Press, 1966) I, 49–50; II, 455, n.91. A Soviet scholar has recently argued, however, that, despite being sent away for noncompliance with court protocol, Spathary, in fact, was quite successful in achieving a major goal of his mission—determining that the Ch'ing government had hostile intentions with respect to Russian settlements near the Amur River; see Joseph Fletcher, "V. A. Aleksandrov on Russo-Ch'ing Relations in the Seventeenth Century: Critique and Résumé," in *Kritika* (Cambridge, Mass.), 7.3:148 (Spring 1971).

11. John K. Fairbank, Edwin O. Reischauer, and Albert M. Craig, *East Asia: The Modern Transformation* (Boston: Houghton Mifflin, 1965), pp. 76–78.

12. Immanuel C. Y. Hsü, *China's Entrance into the Family of Nations: The Diplomatic Phase, 1858–1880* (Cambridge, Mass.: Harvard University Press, 1960), pp. 123–125.

13. For the texts of these treaties, see G. E. P. Hertslet, *Hertslet's China Treaties,* 3rd ed. (London: His Majesty's Stationery Office, 1908), I, 7–52 (Britain), 258–291 (France), 539–553 (United States).

14. *Ibid.;* John K. Fairbank, *Trade and Diplomacy on the China Coast: The Opening of the Treaty Ports, 1842–1854* (Cambridge, Mass.: Harvard University Press, 1964), pp. 96–98; Hsü, *China's Entrance,* pp. 31–35.

15. Hsü, *China's Entrance,* pp. 68–70, 98–105, 180–185.

16. *Ibid.,* p. 138.

17. *Ibid.,* pp. 136–138.

18. T. F. Tsiang, "Bismarck and the Introduction of International Law into China," *The Chinese Social and Political Science Review* 15.1:100 (April 1931). See also Hsü, *China's Entrance,* p. 132.

19. Hsü, *China's Entrance,* p. 125.

20. *Ibid.,* p. 135.

21. The quotation is from Ssu-yü Teng and John K. Fairbank, *China's Response to the West: A Documentary Survey 1839–1923* (New York: Atheneum, 1963), p. 98.

22. Memorial submitted by Li Hung-chang to the Emperor, dated April 24, 1873, in *Ch'ing-tai ch'ou-pan i-wu shih-mo* (History of the management of barbarian affairs of the Ch'ing dynasty; Peiping: Palace Museum, 1930), XC, 4; reprint ed. (Taipei: Kuo-feng ch'u-pan-she, 1963), VII, 2074. The authors are grateful to Mr. Thomas Huang, whose unpublished paper "The Relevance of

International Law to the Foreign Relations of Ch'ing China," called to our attention this and several other late Ch'ing experiences in adjusting to international law.

23. Memorial submitted by the Tsungli Yamen on the French minister's note with respect to entrusting the Russian minister to protect French nationals in China, dated Sept. 16, 1884, in *Ch'ing-chi wai-chiao shih-liao: kuang-hsü ch'ao* (Historical materials concerning foreign relations in the late Ch'ing period [1875–1908]; Peiping, Wang Hsi-yin, 1932), XLVI, 27–28.

24. See Li Hung-chang's memorial to the T'ung-chih Emperor on negotiating a commercial treaty with Peru, dated June 7, 1873, in *Ch'ing-mo tui-wai chiao-she t'iao-yüeh chi* (Treaties concluded [by China] during the late Ch'ing dynasty), Vol. I, *T'ung-chih t'iao-yüeh* (Treaties concluded during the T'ung-chih period [1862–1874]; Taipei: Kuo-feng ch'u-pan-she, 1963), p. 292–293. See also Special Agreement respecting Chinese Immigrants in Peru, signed on June 26, 1874 (together with the Commercial Treaty), in *Hertslet's China Treaties,* I, 420–422.

25. Article XVI of the Treaty of Friendship, Commerce, and Navigation between China and Peru, June 26, 1874, provides:

"The Contracting Parties agree that the Government, public officers, and citizens of the Republic of Peru shall fully and equally participate in all privileges, rights, immunities, jurisdiction, and advantages that may have been, or may be hereafter, granted by His Majesty the Emperor of China, to the Government, public officers, citizens or subjects of any other nation.

"In like manner, the Government, public officers, and subjects of the Empire of China shall enjoy in Peru all the rights, privileges, immunities and advantages of every kind which in Peru are enjoyed by the Government, public officers, citizens, or subjects of the most favored nation." (*Hertslet's China Treaties,* I, 419.)

26. See Sophia Su-fei Yen, *Taiwan in China's Foreign Relations, 1836–1874* (Hamden, Conn.: Shoe String Press, 1965), pp. 212–305; see also Chiang T'ing-fu [T. F. Tsiang], *Chin-tai chung-kuo wai-chiao shih-liao chi-yao* (Selected materials on modern Chinese diplomatic history; Taipei, 1959), II, 106–133, for excerpts of important Chinese documents and materials concerning the Sino-Japanese negotiation.

27. See minute of conversation between Li Hung-chang and the Japanese minister, Mori Arinori, annexed to the memorial submitted by the Tsungli Yamen to the Emperor on the Japanese intention to enter into friendly relations with Korea, dated Jan. 17, 1876, in *Ch'ing Kuang-hsü ch'ao Chung-Jih chiao-she shih-liao* (Historical materials relating to Sino-Japanese relations during the reign of the Kuang-hsü Emperor; Peiping, 1932), I, 8.

28. Dan Fenno Henderson, "Japanese Influences on Communist Chinese Legal Language," in Jerome Alan Cohen, ed., *Contemporary Chinese Law: Research Problems and Perspectives* (Cambridge, Mass.: Harvard University Press, 1970), p. 167.

29. *Papers Relating to the Foreign Relations of the United States, 1875* (Washington: Government Printing Office, 1875), I, 203–204, 235.

30. Kuo Sung-t'ao's memorial to the Emperor requesting a revised letter of credence, dated Apr. 11, 1877, in *Ch'ing-chi wai-chiao shih-liao: Kuang-hsü ch'ao,* IX, 22–23.

31. Liu Hsi-hung's memorial to the Emperor requesting to resign from the position of vice-minister to Britain, dated Apr. 11, 1877, in *Ch'ing-chi wai-chiao shih-liao: Kuang-hsü ch'ao,* IX, 23–24.

32. Mr. Chang Yen Hoon's letter to Mr. Blaine dated July 8, 1889, in *Papers Relating to the Foreign Relations of the United States, 1889* (Washington: Government Printing Office, 1890), p. 135.

33. See Bhek Pati Sinha, *Unilateral Denunciation of Treaty Because of Prior Violations of Obligations by Other Party* (The Hague: Martinus Nijhoff, 1966), p. 130.

34. Tsui Kuo-ying, *Ch'u-shih Mei-Jih-Pi-kuo jih-chi* (Diary of a mission to

the United States, Japan and Peru; n.p., 1895), VI, 38; Taipei reprint ed. (Taipei, n.d.), I, 586 (diary dated Apr. 12, 1891).

35. Fukuzawa Yukichi, *Tsūzoku kokkenron* (1878), reprinted in *Fukuzawa Zenshū* (Collected works of Fukuzawa Yukichi; Tokyo, 1926), p. 119.

36. See, *e.g.*, Wei Wen-han, "Discussing the Question of the Width of the Territorial Sea," *FH*, no. 3:23 (1957).

37. Compare the analogous argument in Hsü, *China's Entrance*, pp. 138–145, concerning why, in the decades following the introduction of international law in the early 1860's, Ch'ing statesmen did not make more positive use of their new knowledge of international law in order to abolish or revise the unjust treaties that the West had recently imposed.

38. The quotations are from Article XV of the Treaty between China and the United States Respecting Commercial Relations, signed Oct. 8, 1903, in *Hertslet's China Treaties*, I, 575.

39. Memorial submitted by the Tsungli Yamen to the Emperor on the French attempt to annex Vietnam in obvious violation of international law and on requesting financial support to purchase arms for resisting foreign aggression, dated Jan. 21, 1884. *Ch'ing-chi wai-chiao shih-liao*, XXXVIII, 25.

40. Telegram from Commissioner on Macao Boundary Delimitation Kao Erh-ch'ien to the Ministry of Foreign Affairs, dated Aug. 12, 1909, in *Ch'ing Hsüan-t'ung ch'ao wai-chiao shih-liao* (Historical materials on diplomacy during the reign of the Hsüan-t'ung Emperor of the Ch'ing dynasty; Peiping, 1933), VII, 5–6.

41. In June 1900 the Ch'ing government declared war on all foreign powers and ordered a siege of foreign legations at Peking. Boxer elements also killed one Japanese and one German diplomat. See Teng and Fairbank, *China's Response*, pp. 187–190. But when the allied forces of eight nations invaded Peking in August, their commanders openly allowed their forces to engage in pillaging and looting for three days. The commander of the allied forces, Von Waldersee, acknowledged that members of the forces also committed rape, homicide, arson, and other crimes. See Ch'en Kung-lu, *Chung-kuo chin-tai shih* (History of modern China; Shanghai, 1935), pp. 531–532. See also Von Waldersee's report, dated Oct. 22, 1900, in Yang Sung and Teng Li-ch'ün, *Chung-kuo chin-tai shih tzu-liao hsüan-chi* (Selected materials on history of modern China; Yung Meng-yüan, ed., Peking, 1954), pp. 520–523.

42. See Hungdah Chiu, "The Reception of Modern International Law in China," a paper prepared for the 28th International Congress of Orientalists, Canberra, Australia, Jan. 7–9, 1971, p. 10; A. Pearce Higgins, *The Hague Peace Conferences and Other International Conferences Concerning the Laws and Usages of War: Texts of Conventions with Commentaries* (Cambridge, Eng.: the University Press, 1909), pp. 95–179.

43. See L. Oppenheim, *International Law*, 7th ed., ed. H. Lauterpacht (London: Longmans, Green, 1952), II, 881; Hsieh Tien-tseng and Kuo Tzu-hsiung, *Chung-kuo ts'an-chia chih kuo-chi kung-yüeh hui-pien* (Collection of international conventions in which China participates; Shanghai, 1937), pp. 961–962, 976.

44. See *United States Statutes at Large* 30:1629–1655 (UPU) and 35:1918–1922 (IIA).

45. See Hsü, *China's Entrance*, pp. 206–207.

46. *Important Documents Relating to China's Revolution, 1912, with English Translations* (Shanghai: Commercial Press, Limited, 1912), pp. 67–68.

47. See, generally, William L. Tung, *China and the Foreign Powers: The Impact of and Reaction to Unequal Treaties* (Dobbs Ferry, N.Y.: Oceana Publications, Inc., 1970); Wesley R. Fishel, *The End of Extraterritoriality in China* (Berkeley and Los Angeles: University of California Press, 1952); Wang Shih-chieh and Hu Ching-yu, *Chung-kuo pu-p'ing-teng t'iao-yüeh chih fei-ch'u* (The abolition of China's unequal treaties; Taipei, 1967).

48. See, generally, [William] L. Tung, *China and Some Phases of Inter-*

national Law (London and New York: Oxford University Press, 1940); *China and the United Nations: Report of a Study Group Set up by the China Institute of International Affairs* (New York: Manhattan Publishing Co., 1959).

49. *China and the United Nations,* pp. 36–37.

50. For the text of the Chinese declaration on accepting the Court's compulsory jurisdiction, dated Oct. 26, 1946, see International Court of Justice, *Yearbook 1969–1970,* No. 24 (The Hague: I.C.J., 1970), p. 56.

51. See, generally, Franz Schurmann, *Ideology and Organization in Communist China* (Berkeley and Los Angeles: University of California Press, 1966); C. K. Yang, *A Chinese Village in Early Communist Transition* (Cambridge, Mass.: MIT Press, 1959); and Jerome Alan Cohen, *The Criminal Process in the People's Republic of China, 1949–1963: An Introduction* (Cambridge, Mass.: Harvard University Press, 1968), pp. 97–141.

52. Cohen, *Criminal Process,* pp. 9–14; Shao-chuan Leng, *Justice in Communist China: A Survey of the Judicial System of the Chinese People's Republic* (Dobbs Ferry, N.Y.: Oceana Publications, Inc., 1967), pp. 45–54.

53. Cohen, *Criminal Process,* pp. 14–18.

54. Jerome Alan Cohen, "The Chinese Communist Party and 'Judicial Independence,' 1949–1959," *Harvard Law Review* 82.5:993–994 (Mar. 1969).

55. Chang Wu-yün, "Smash Permanent Rules, Go 1,000 *Li* in One Day," *CFYC,* no. 5:60 (1958).

56. See Jerome Alan Cohen, "Chinese Mediation on the Eve of Modernization," *California Law Review* 54.2:1201–1226 (May 1966); Stanley Lubman, "Mao and Mediation: Politics and Dispute Resolution in Communist China," *California Law Review* 55.5:1284–1359 (Nov. 1967); and Jerome Alan Cohen, "Drafting People's Mediation Rules," in John Wilson Lewis, ed., *The City in Communist China* (Stanford, Calif.: Stanford University Press, 1971), pp. 30–33.

57. Richard M. Pfeffer, "Contracts in China Revisited, with a focus on Agriculture, 1949–63," *The China Quarterly,* no. 28:113–117, 125–128 (Oct.-Dec. 1966).

58. "Completely Smash the Feudal, Capitalist and Revisionist Legal Systems," in US Consulate General, Hong Kong, *Selections from China Mainland Magazines,* 625:23 (Sept. 3, 1968).

59. See, generally, *ibid.,* pp. 23–28.

60. For the Chinese text of the draft constitution, see "Revised Draft of the 'Constitution of the People's Republic of China,'" *Chung-kung yen-chiu* (Studies in Chinese Communism) 5.8:95–111 (August 1971). For commentary on the draft, see Jerome Alan Cohen, "Continuity and Change in China: Some 'Law Day' Thoughts," *South Carolina Law Review* 24.1:3–18 (1972), and John N. Hazard, "Communist Constitutionalism in a New Form," *Studies in Comparative Communism,* 4.1:107–116 (Jan. 1971).

61. Cohen, *Criminal Process,* pp. 5–7; Derk Bodde and Clarence Morris, *Law in Imperial China Exemplified by 190 Ch'ing Dynasty Cases (translated from the Hsing-an hui-lan with Historical, Social, and Juridical Commentaries,* (Cambridge, Mass.: Harvard University Press, 1967), chap. 1.

62. See Bodde and Morris, p. 502; and Shuzo Shiga, "Some Remarks on the Judicial System in China: Historical Development and Characteristics," in David C. Buxbaum, ed., *Traditional and Modern Legal Institutions in Asia and Africa* (Leiden: E. J. Brill, 1967), p. 47.

63. For excerpts of the provisions concerning human rights and freedoms in the 1947 ROC Constitution, see *Yearbook on Human Rights for 1947* (Lake Success, N.Y.: The United Nations, 1947), pp. 79–82. On May 19, 1949, martial law was applied to Taiwan by the Taiwan Garrison Headquarters. See *Chung-hua min-kuo liu-fa li-yu p'an-chieh ch'üan-pien* (Compilation of laws of the Republic of China, with interpretations and decisions; Taichung, 1964), IV, 1040–1041. Under Article 8 of the Martial Law (promulgated on Nov. 29, 1934, and amended on Jan. 14, 1949), certain serious offenses such as sedition, espionage, or

homicide may be tried by a military tribunal regardless of whether the person involved is on active military service (*ibid.*, pp. 1033–1034). Thus, Article 9 of the Constitution—which provides that no person, except those in active military service, shall be liable to military trial—was suspended. The manner of enforcement of the Martial Law has in fact suspended some other constitutional guarantees of the people under the 1947 Constitution.

64. This periodization draws heavily upon Peter Van Ness, *Revolution and Chinese Foreign Policy: Peking's Support for Wars of National Liberation* (Berkeley, Los Angeles, and London: University of California Press, 1970), pp. 10–18; and Harold C. Hinton, *Communist China in World Politics* (Boston: Houghton Mifflin Company, 1966), pp. 23–49.

65. Allen S. Whiting statement in US Congress, Senate, Committee on Foreign Relations, *United States Relations with the People's Republic of China: Hearings . . . on S.J. Res. 48, S. Res. 18, S. Res. 37, S. Res. 82, and S. Res. 139* (Washington, D.C.: Government Printing Office, 1972), pp. 183–185.

66. Seymour Topping, "Key Chinese Official Reported in Prison," *New York Times* (June 21, 1971), p. 1.

Part I. The Nature and Basis of International Law

1. See F. I. Kozhevnikov, ed., *International Law*, trans. Dennis Ogden (Moscow: Foreign Languages Publishing House [n.d.]), p. 7.

2. *Ibid.*, p. 11.

3. Bernard A. Ramundo, *Peaceful Coexistence: International Law and the Building of Communism* (Baltimore: Johns Hopkins Press, 1967), p. 25.

4. *Ibid.*

5. *Ibid.*, p. 26. For extended discussion of the twists and turns of Soviet scholarly efforts to define international law, see Kazimierz Grzybowski, *Soviet Public International Law: Doctrines and Diplomatic Practice* (Leiden: A. W. Sijthoff, 1970), pp. 4–22.

6. Reporter of Cheng-fa yen-chiu, "China Political Science and Law Association Held Fourth General Meeting," *CFYC*, no. 4:28 (1964).

7. The eighth edition of Oppenheim's *International Law*, I, 4–5, omits the adjective "civilized" before "states" in its definition of international law.

8. Chou Fu-lun, "On the Nature of Modern International Law—A Discussion with Comrade Lin Hsin," *CHYYC*, no. 3:55 (1958).

9. Chu Li-lu, "Refute Ch'en T'i-ch'iang's Absurd Theory Concerning International Law," *JMJP* (Sept. 18, 1957), p. 3.

10. Quotations appear in Chinese original; the sources of these passages are unknown.

11. The quotation appearing in the Chinese article is slightly different from what Jacques Maritain wrote. Maritain wrote: "As concerns the second main obstacle to the establishment of a lasting peace, namely the present state of political *inorganization* of the world, well, here we are getting to the core of the problem we have to discuss." (*Man and the State* [Chicago: University of Chicago Press, 1951] p. 196.)

12. "Toward a Strategy of Peace," (Address by President Kennedy), *Department of State Bulletin* 49.1253:5 (July 1, 1963).

13. E. A. Korovin, *Mezhdunarodnoe pravo perekhodnogo vremeni* (Moscow-Petrograd, 1923), pp. 15–16; English translation quoted from Mintauts Chakste, "Soviet Concepts of the State, International Law and Sovereignty," *AJIL* 43:27 (1949). But this group of jurists recognizes that certain rules of law could apply in areas of practical common interest, such as postal communication, health regulations, etc. According to Tunkin, Korovin himself afterward recognized such opinions as erroneous, and the overwhelming majority of Soviet jurists never shared the views expressed by Professor Korovin. G. I. Tunkin, "Coexistence and International Law," in Académie de Droit International, *Recueil des Cours*, (1958, Vol.

III), 95:5–6, 60 (Leiden: A. W. Sijthoff, 1959). For a criticism of Professor Korovin's view by Soviet jurists, see *SGP,* no. 7:67–77 (1952).

14. Kozhevnikov, ed., *International Law,* p. 11.

15. Ramundo, *Peaceful Coexistence,* pp. 18–24. For careful analyses of the Soviet literature, see *ibid.,* and Grzybowski, *Soviet Public International Law,* pp. 4–22.

16. *WCC 1956–1957,* IV (1958), p. 150; English translation in Noble Frankland, assisted by Vera King, *Documents on International Affairs 1956* (London: Oxford University Press, 1959), p. 465.

17. Yang was later purged as a rightist, and this article was severely criticized by other Communist Chinese writers, but none of the criticism was directed against the parts of the article dealing with international law.

18. Ch'iu Jih-ch'ing, "Further Discussion on the Systems of International Law at the Present Stage," *FH,* no. 3:43 (1958).

19. Hu Wen-chi, "On the Three Systems of International Law at the Present Stage," *FH,* no. 3:51 (1958).

Part II. Fundamental Principles of International Law

1. This paragraph is based on Te-hsu Ch'eng, "International Law in Early China (1122–249 B.C.)," *Chinese Social and Political Science Review* 11:44–46 (1927).

2. Truong Buu Lam, "Intervention Versus Tribute In Sino-Vietnamese Relations, 1788–1790," in John K. Fairbank, ed., *The Chinese World Order: Traditional China's Foreign Relations* (Cambridge, Mass.: Harvard University Press, 1968), pp. 165, 179.

3. *Ibid.,* p. 178.

4. For discussion of Soviet views on the sources of international law, see Kazimierz Grzybowski, *Soviet Public International Law* (Leiden, A. W. Sijthoff, 1970), pp. 25–32, and Bernard A. Ramundo, *Peaceful Coexistence: International Law in the Building of Communism* (Baltimore: Johns Hopkins Press, 1967), pp. 43–71.

5. See, *e.g.,* F. I. Kozhevnikov, ed., *International Law,* tr. Dennis Ogden. (Moscow: Foreign Languages Publishing House [n.d.]), pp. 12, 247–248.

6. Wei Liang, "On Post-World War II International Treaties," in *Kuo-chi t'iao-yüeh chi* (International treaty series), *1953–1955* (Peking: Shih-chieh chih-shih ch'u-pan-she, 1961), p. 660.

7. See, *e.g.,* Chou Keng-sheng, *Hsien-tai Ying-Mei kuo-chi-fa ti ssu-hsiang tung-hsiang* (Trends in the thought of modern English and American international law; Peking, 1963), p. 67.

8. Wai-chiao hsüeh-yüan kuo-chi-fa chiao-yen-shih pien (Office of Teaching and Research on International Law of the Institute of Diplomacy, ed.), *Kuo-chi kung-fa ts'an-k'ao wen-chien hüan-chi* (Selected reference documents on public international law; Peking, 1958), pp. 11–12.

9. See, *e.g.,* Ting Ku, "Firmly Maintain the Five Principles of Peaceful Coexistence," *KCWTYC,* no. 2:2 (1959). Another author writes: "In many important treaties concluded with . . . other countries, our country proposed a series of democratic principles which have produced great influence and become commonly observed principles among various countries." Chao Yüeh, "A Preliminary Criticism of Bourgeois International Law," *KCWTYC,* no. 3:8 (1959).

10. See, *e.g.,* G. I. Tunkin, "Remarks on the Juridical Nature of Customary Norms of International Law," *California Law Review* 49:428 (Aug. 1961).

11. Timothy A. Taracouzio, *The Soviet Union and International Law: A Study Based on the Legislation, Treaties and Foreign Relations of the Union of Socialist Soviet Republics* (New York: Macmillan Company, 1935), p. 13.

12. Kozhevnikov, ed., *International Law,* p. 12.

13. Tunkin, "Remarks," pp. 428–429.

14. See, *e.g.*, Chou Keng-sheng, "The Persecution of Chinese Personnel by the Brazilian Coup d'État Authority Is a Serious International Delinquency," *JMJP* (Apr. 24, 1964), p. 4.

15. Chiang Yang, "The Reactionary Thought of 'Universalism' in American Jurisprudence," *JMJP* (Dec. 17, 1963), p. 5.

16. "China Protests to Brazilian Authorities," *PR* 8.1:23 (Jan. 1, 1965).

17. "Chinese Embassy in Burundi Protests against Kidnapping of Staff Member by U.S. Embassy," NCNA–English, Bujumbura (June 9, 1964), in *SCMP*, no. 3238:28 (June 15, 1964).

18. Article II, Sino-Indonesian Friendship Treaty, April 1, 1961, *TYC 1961*, X:7 (pub. 1962). English translation in "Treaty of Friendship Between the People's Republic of China and the Republic of Indonesia," *PR* 4.24:11 (June 16, 1961). The Chinese text used the term "kuo-chi kuan-li," which should be translated as "international custom." But the PRC usually translates this term as "international practice."

19. "China Strongly Protests against Killing of Chinese Border Inhabitants by Burmese Troops," NCNA–English, Peking (Aug. 10, 1967), in *SCMP*, no. 4001:25 (Aug. 15, 1967).

20. "Japanese Government's Sabotage of China Trade Condemned," NCNA–English, Peking (Apr. 13, 1958), in *SCMP*, no. 1752:33 (Apr. 16, 1958).

21. "Chinese Foreign Ministry Strongly Protests Against Unreasonable Soviet Demand," *PR* 6.27:7 (July 5, 1963).

22. Ch'en T'i-ch'iang, "Taiwan—A Chinese Territory," *Law in the Service of Peace: International Association of Democratic Lawyers' Review* 5:43 (Dec. 1956).

23. Liu Tse-yung, "A Major Step to Protect China's Sovereign Rights," *PR* 1.29:13 (Sept. 16, 1958).

24. (Selected reference documents on public international law), pp. 11–12.

25. Kozhevnikov, ed., *International Law*, p. 13.

26. (Selected reference documents on public international law), pp. 11–12.

27. Chou Keng-sheng, (Trends in English and American International Law), p. 67.

28. Li Hao-p'ei, "Nationalization and International Law," *CFYC*, no. 2:10 (1958).

29. V. M. Shurshalov, review of N. M. Minasian, *Sushchnost' sovremennovo mezhdunarodnovo prava* (The essence of contemporary international law; Rostov: Publishing House of Rostov State University, 1962), *SGP*, no. 5:159 (1964), as quoted in Ramundo, *Peaceful Coexistence*, p. 69.

30. Kozhevnikov, ed., *International Law*, pp. 12–13.

31. V. M. Shurshalov, book review, *SGP*, no. 5:159 (1964), as quoted in Ramundo, *Peaceful Coexistence*, p. 69.

32. See Ramundo, *Peaceful Coexistence*, pp. 70–71, for representative Soviet views.

33. The resolution as it appears here was translated from the Chinese.

34. Edward McWhinney, "Soviet and Western International Law and the Cold War in the Era of Bipolarity," in *The Canadian Yearbook of International Law* (Vancouver: University of British Columbia, 1963), I, 42–43.

35. We are unable to locate the quoted passage in Philip C. Jessup's *Modern Law of Nations* (New York: Macmillan, 1948).

36. *Mezhdunarodnoe Pravo* (International law), ed. D. B. Levin and G. P. Kaliuzhnaia (Moscow: Publishing House "Legal Literature," 1964), p. 98, quoted in Ramundo, *Peaceful Coexistence*, p. 81.

37. B. B. Ganiushkin, book review. A. N. Talalaev, *Iuridicheskaia priroda mezhdunarodnogo dogovora* [The Legal Character of International Agreements] (Moscow: Publishing House of the Institute of International Relations, 1963). *SGP*, no. 7:167 (1964), cited in Ramundo, *Peaceful Coexistence*, p. 81.

38. G. I. Tunkin, *Voprosy Teorii Mezhdunarodnovo Prava* (Problems of the

theory of international law; Moscow: Gosizdat iurid. lit., 1962), p. 80, as cited in Ramundo, *Peaceful Coexistence,* p. 81.

39. Ramundo, *Peaceful Coexistence,* p. 81.

40. *Ibid.,* p. 86; see also Grzybowski, *Soviet Public International Law,* pp. 65–67.

41. M. I. Lazarev, "Mezhdunarodnopravovye Voprosy Dvizheniia Narodov za Mir," (International Legal Aspects of the People's Movement for Peace), *Sovetskii ezhegodnik, 1963* (Moscow: Publishing House "Science," 1965), pp. 45–69, esp. 63–66, discussed in Ramundo, *Peaceful Coexistence,* pp. 75–76.

42. The sources of these quotations are unknown.

43. See Article 14 of the Draft Declaration, found in UN General Assembly, *Official Records,* Fourth Session, suppl. 10 (A/925), 1949, p. 9.

44. Kozhevnikov, ed., *International Law,* pp. 14–15. For subsequent development of Soviet views on the relation of international law to domestic law, see Grzybowski, *Soviet Public International Law,* pp. 30–32.

45. See "Seventeen Japanese War Criminals Sentenced," NCNA-English, Peking (June 21, 1956), in *SCMP,* no. 1317:16–17 (June 26, 1956).

46. *FKHP 1960,* XI, 100–105.

47. Article 17, Act Regulating the Entry, Exit, Transit, Residence and Travel of Foreign Nationals, *JMJP* (Apr. 20, 1964), p. 2.

48. *WCC 1949–1950,* I (1957), 4; English translation in "Reds Proclaim a Republic in China, Chou Is Premier," *New York Times* (Oct. 2, 1949), p. 17.

49. Bandung, April 19, 1955, *WCC 1954–1955,* III (1958), 246. English translation in "Full Text of Premier Chou En-lai's Speech at Asian-African Conference," NCNA-English, Bandung (Apr. 19, 1955), in *SCMP,* no. 1031:3 (Apr. 20, 1955).

50. *WCC 1954–1955,* III (1958), 141; English translation in "Report on Foreign Affairs by Chou En-lai," NCNA-English, Peking (Aug. 13, 1954), in *CB,* no. 288:7 (Aug. 16, 1954).

51. For a detailed discussion of the Soviet attitude toward sovereignty, see Ramundo, *Peaceful Coexistence,* pp. 87–107.

52. See also, *e.g.,* Chien Yen of PLA Unit 4888, "Tear Off the Wrappings from Soviet Revisionists' Theory of 'Responsibility for Security,'" *PR* 12.36:20–22 (Sept. 3, 1969).

53. "Statement by the Spokesman of the Chinese Government—A Comment on the Soviet Government's Statement of August 21, 1963," (Sept. 1, 1963), in *PR* 6.36:15 (Sept. 6, 1963).

54. Quoted in G. I. Tunkin, "Socialist Internationalism and International Law," *New Times* 51:10 (Dec. 19, 1957).

55. The quotation is from *ibid.* It was cited with approval in Ch'iu Jih-ch'ing, "Further Discussion on the Systems of International Law at the Present Stage," *FH,* no. 3:40 (1958).

56. Ramundo, *Peaceful Coexistence,* p. 35; see also *ibid.,* pp. 32–36, for discussion of various Soviet formulations of socialist internationalism.

57. Tunkin, "Socialist Internationalism," p. 11.

58. The meeting was held in Moscow, Nov. 14–16, 1957. For the English text of the Declaration, see "Text of the Communique on Meeting in Moscow of Communist Party Leaders," *New York Times* (Nov. 22, 1957), p. 6.

59. The meeting was held in Moscow, Nov. 7–Dec. 1, 1960. For the English text of the statement, see "The 1960 Moscow Statement," *China Quarterly* 5: 25–52 (Jan.-Mar. 1961).

60. Yugoslav Ambassador to China Gives National Day Reception," *PR* 13.49:23 (Dec. 4, 1970). It is interesting that when the PRC and the Netherlands agreed to raise their diplomatic relations to the ambassadorial level, their joint communiqué included the following cryptic paragraph: "The Government of the Kingdom of the Netherlands holds that the principles of peaceful coexistence should imply noninterference in each other's internal affairs not only between

countries and groups of countries of different sociopolitical systems, but equally between countries belonging to an alliance and having identical or similar sociopolitical systems. The Government of the People's Republic of China appreciates this stand of the Government of the Kingdom of the Netherlands." ("China and Netherlands Raise Level of Diplomatic Relations," *PR* 15.21:20 [May 26, 1972].)

61. *FKHP 1956,* IV, 2–3.

62. We are unable to locate this passage from Khrushchev's statements in this period. In his July 19, 1958, message to President Eisenhower, Khrushchev stated that: "The Lebanese President's appeal to the United States was not supported by the Lebanese Parliament, and the Speaker of the Parliament has strongly protested against American armed intervention. Consequently, the 'invitation' sent by Chamoun has no constitutional validity." See "N. S. Khrushchev's Messages to President Eisenhower and Prime Ministers DeGaulle and Nehru," *Soviet News,* no. 3882:69 (July 22, 1958).

63. Frank Maloy Anderson, *The Constitutions and Other Select Documents Illustrative of the History of France, 1789–1907,* 2nd ed., rev. and enl. (Minneapolis: H. W. Wilson Company, 1908), pp. 133–134.

64. The Constitution of the Year I, adopted on June 24, 1793, provided in Article 119 that "[The French Republic] does not interfere in the government of other nations; it does not permit other nations to interfere in its own." *Ibid.,* p. 183.

65. No citation is given by the author.

66. No citation is given by the author.

67. Public Law, 86–90 (July 17, 1959), *US Statutes At Large,* vol. 73, p. 212. [S.J. Res. 111; July 17, 1959.]

68. Oppenheim, I, 7th ed., p. 280.

69. We cannot locate this passage from Oppenheim's text.

70. J. L. Brierly, *The Law of Nations,* 5th ed. (London: Oxford at the Clarendon Press, 1955), p. 309.

71. "Strengthening Friendship and Trust among the American Republics," *Department of State Bulletin,* 42.1080:353 (Mar. 7, 1960).

72. Translated from the Chinese. We have been unable to locate the source of this quotation.

73. Translated from the Chinese. We have been unable to locate the source of this quotation. An article by Tad Szulc mentioned that Latin American countries felt that IMF's funds had too many strings attached. The article also quoted President Kubitschek as saying that the Brazilian government "felt that the Fund's recommendations were invading the province of decision of the Brazilian Government." See Tad Szulc, "Latins May Join Rebellion on Aid," *New York Times* (June 15, 1959), p. 10.

74. We have been unable to locate the source of this quotation.

75. US Congress, House, Resolution 5113, Oct. 10, 1951, 82nd Cong., 1st Sess., *United States Statutes at Large,* Vol. 65, pp. 373–374.

76. Eisenhower's actual statement is as follows: "There is no sense [in] closing our eyes to some of the situations of the current time in Central America and in the Caribbean. But we do look primarily to the Organization of American States to take the initiative, otherwise we again would be called the dollar imperialists or something else of that kind." Reply made by President Eisenhower to a question asked at a news conference, July 1, 1959. US Department of State, Historical Office, *American Foreign Policy, Current Documents, 1959* (Washington, D.C.: US Government Printing Office, 1963), p. 348.

77. Commentator, "The Face of a Traitor," *JMJP* (Jan. 25, 1969) p. 6, translated in *PR* 12.8:14 (Feb. 21, 1969).

78. Commentator, "Most Absurd Logic, Flagrant Aggression," *JMJP,* Dec. 6, 1971, p. 1; translated in *PR* 14.50:6 (Dec. 10, 1971).

79. "Mao's Quotes in Kenya," *TASS*–English, Moscow (Aug. 4, 1967), in *FBIS,* no. 152/67:BB5 (Aug. 7, 1967).

80. "Ceylon Says Chinese Note 'Interference,'" English, Delhi (Aug. 19,

1967), in *FBIS*, no. 162/67:P2 (Aug. 21, 1967). Note on *FBIS* notation: "Words . . . enclosed in parentheses with a question mark were not clearly heard but have been supplied as appropriate to the context."

81. "Chinese Embassy in Ghana Refutes Ghana's Slander," NCNA–English, Peking (Mar. 19, 1966), in *SCMP*, no. 3663:23 (Mar. 23, 1966).

82. "Chinese Chargé d'Affaires a.i. in Uganda Lodges Protest," *PR* 14.31:29 (July 30, 1971).

83. For a review of PRC modes of intervention, see *e.g.*, Peter Van Ness, *Revolution and Chinese Foreign Policy: Peking's Support for Wars of National Liberation* (Berkeley, Los Angeles, and London: University of California Press, 1970); Thomas W. Robinson, "Peking's Revolutionary Strategy in the Developing World: The Failures of Success," *The Annals of the American Academy of Political and Social Science* 386:64–77 (Nov. 1969). For a case study of a Chinese Communist success, see J. J. Zasloff, *The Role of the Sanctuary in Insurgency: Communist China's Support to the Vietminh, 1946–1954* (Santa Monica, Calif.: Rand Corp., 1967).

84. See Eric Pace, "Iraq-Sponsored Arab Commando Group Emphasizes Ties with Chinese Reds," *New York Times* (Jan. 7, 1971), p. 12; and John W. Finney, "Arabs Said to Get Peking Arms Aid," *New York Times* (Sept. 26, 1966), pp. 1, 2.

85. "Sihanouk Says China Finances His Regime," *New York Times* (June 7, 1970), p. 3.

86. "Government of People's Republic of China and Royal Government of National Union of Cambodia Sign in Peking Agreement on Providing Gratuitous Military Aid by China to Cambodia," NCNA–English, Peking, Aug. 17, 1970, in *SCMP* 4726:79 (Aug. 26, 1970). The same NCNA news release reported also that in May 1970 the PRC signed another agreement with Sihanouk on providing a loan to his government.

87. "Chinese Government Formally Recognizes Royal Government of National Union of Cambodia," *PR* 13.20:14 (May 14, 1970); "Sihanouk in Peking, Still Termed Chief of State," *New York Times* (Mar. 20, 1970), p. 14.

88. See Harold C. Hinton, *Communist China in World Politics* (Boston: Houghton Mifflin Company, 1966), p. 195.

89. *Ibid.*, pp. 461–462.

90. *Ibid.*, p. 405.

91. For discussion of the legal aspects of Chinese attitudes toward the various applications of the principle of nonintervention, see Jerome Alan Cohen, "China and Intervention: Theory and Practice," *The University of Pennsylvania Law Review*, 121:471–505 (1973).

Part III. Participation in the International Community

1. Richard Louis Walker, *The Multi-State System of Ancient China* (Hamden, Conn.: Shoe String Press, 1953), p. 26.

2. Ch'en Ku-yüan, *Chung-kuo kuo-chi-fa so-yüan* (The origin of international law in China; Shanghai, 1934; reprint ed., Taipei, 1967), pp. 46–47.

3. Lan Wen-cheng, *Sui T'ang wu-tai shih* (History of the Sui, T'ang and the Five Dynasties; Taipei, 1970), pp. 114–115.

4. Truong Buu Lam, "Intervention versus Tribute in Sino-Vietnamese Relations, 1788–1790," in John King Fairbank, ed., *The Chinese World Order: Traditional China's Foreign Relations* (Cambridge, Mass.: Harvard University Press, 1968), pp. 167–172.

5. *Ibid.*, p. 174.

6. John K. Fairbank, "A Preliminary Framework," in *ibid.*, p. 10. For a fascinating description of the investiture missions sent to the Liu-ch'iu islands, see Ta-tuan Ch'en, "Investiture of Liu-Ch'iu Kings in the Ch'ing Period," in *ibid.*, pp. 135–164.

7. See "The Manifesto from the Provisional Government of the Republic of China to All Friendly Nations," Jan. 5, 1912, in *Important Documents Relating to China's Revolution, with English Translations* (Shanghai: Commercial Press, Limited, 1912), pp. 80, 81.

8. See Chang Chung-fu, *Chung-hua min-kuo wai-chiao-shih,* Vol. I, 3rd printing (Diplomatic history of the Republic of China; Taipei, 1961), pp. 44–45, 50.

9. Tang Tsou, *America's Failure in China, 1941–50* (Chicago: University of Chicago Press, 1963), p. 516. For an excellent summary of the political aspects of Sino-American recognition problems in this period, see *ibid.*, pp. 513–519.

10. See Article 18 of "Agreement on Internal Peace," in Mao Tse-tung, *Selected Works of Mao Tse-tung,* Vol. IV (Peking: Foreign Languages Press, 1961), p. 394.

11. For an English translation, see Albert P. Blaustein, ed., *Fundamental Legal Documents of Communist China* (South Hackensack, N.J.: Fred B. Rothman & Co., 1962), p. 53.

12. *Ibid.*

13. The court's judgment denied any interest to the Bank of China, which then appealed to the Court of Appeals for the Ninth Circuit. The Court of Appeals held that the Wells Fargo Bank and Union Trust Co. was liable for interest for the period up to the date of its deposit of money in court, except for the period from the date originally set for trial to the date of trial set pursuant to a continuance obtained by the Bank of China (209 F.2d 467).

14. 92 F. Supp. 920, 923–924 (1950).

15. On February 4, 1952, the US Court of Appeals for the Second Circuit handed down a procedural ruling in this case. *Republic of China* v. *American Express Co.,* 195 F.2d 230 (1952). The US District Court for the Southern District of New York subsequently held against the PRC on the merits in an unpublished opinion that appears to have been handed down on Feb. 9, 1953.

16. "US Won't Recognize China Claim to Assets," (AP), *Japan Times* (Mar. 15, 1972), p. 1.

17. "Statement by Spokesman of People's Bank of China Head Office," *PR* 15.11:3 (Mar. 17, 1972).

18. *Ibid.*

19. *Civil Air Transport Incorporated* v. *Claire Lee Chennault . . . and Others* (Central Air Transport Corporation), in Charles Loseby, ed., *The Hong Kong Law Reports* (Hong Kong: The Government Printer, [n.d.]), 34:386 (1950); and H. Lauterpacht, ed., *International Law Reports, 1950* (London: Butterworth & Co., Ltd., 1956), Case No. 45.

20. See H. Lauterpacht, ed., *International Law Reports, 1952,* pp. 86–87.

21. Excerpts from the relevant Order in Council and from the opinions of the judges in the trial and appellate proceedings may be found in *ibid.*, pp. 85 ff. "While the opinion of the Judicial Committee of the Privy Council is dated October 12, 1952, it appears that the result of its deliberations was announced earlier, namely, after the conclusion of the hearings [on] July 28." (*Ibid.*, p. 115, note 1.)

22. See Richard Harris, "Britain and China: Coexistence at Low Pressure," in A. M. Halpern, ed., *Policies toward China: Views from Six Continents* (New York: McGraw-Hill, 1965), pp. 17–20. For an interesting account of the similar experience of the Netherlands, see Ko Swan Sik, "The Establishment of Diplomatic Relations and the Scope of Diplomatic Immunity: The Dutch Experience with China," in Jerome A. Cohen, ed., *China's Practice of International Law: Some Case Studies,* (Cambridge, Mass.: Harvard University Press, 1972), pp. 57–85.

23. See "British Authorities in Hong Kong Seize Chinese Property," NCNA–English, Canton (May 14, 1955), in *SCMP,* no. 1048:47–48 (May 14–16, 1955).

24. "Chinese Note Exposes Indian Government's Hypocritical Maneuvers

in Support of 'Two Chinas' Plot," NCNA–English, Peking (Aug. 1, 1966), in *SCMP,* no. 3754–38 (Aug. 5, 1966).

25. *Ibid.*

26. Commentator, "Baring British Imperialism's Crafty Features," *JMJP* (Aug. 21, 1967), p. 2; translated under the same title in *PR* 10.35:22 (Aug. 25, 1967).

27. On March 22, 1967, the French government transferred control over the two buildings in dispute to the PRC Embassy in Paris. On March 23, the ROC lodged a strong protest, through the Director-General of the UNESCO, with the French government. It stated that the French seizure of these buildings "not only violated a French agreement with the UNESCO but also breached the protocol code long upheld by civilized nations." It further stated that the transfer of the two buildings to the PRC's embassy is "totally illegal" and "the Chinese government reserves all rights to the two buildings at issue." Hungdah Chiu, comp., "Chinese Contemporary Practices and Judicial Decisions Relating to International Law, February 1966 to March 1967," *Annals of the Chinese Society of International Law* (Taipei), 4:75 (Aug. 1967).

28. "Japan Denounced for Surrender of Embassy Building to Peiping," *Free China Weekly* 14.10:1 (Mar. 18, 1973).

29. "Protocol of People's Republic of China and Republic of San Marino on Establishment of Official Relations at Consular Level," *PR* 14.20:7 (May 14, 1971).

30. Seymour Topping, "Chou Says US Shield at Taiwan Is a Main Bar to Diplomatic Ties," *New York Times* (June 23, 1971), pp. 1, 2.

31. "Transcript of Nixon TV Address to Nation," *New York Times* (July 16, 1971), p. 3.

32. "Joint Communique," *PR* 15.9:5 (Mar. 9, 1972).

33. *E.g.,* compare Jerome Alan Cohen's remarks in "Comparative Approaches to Negotiations with the People's Republic of China," *AJIL* 66.4 (Proceedings of the American Society of International Law; Sept. 1972), pp. 108–114 with Earl C. Ravenal's "China Statement: Between the Lines," *Washington Post* (Mar. 5, 1972), p. D2. Some have argued that, regardless of verbiage, President Nixon's official visit to Peking constituted recognition by the United States of the PRC. See, *e.g.,* Arnold Fraleigh, "Recognition of Peking," (Letter to the Editor), *New York Times* (Jan. 23, 1972), Sec. 4, p. 12.

34. See, *e.g.,* "Transcript of ['Meet the Press'] TV Interview with [Marshall] Green," *Mainichi Daily News* (Mar. 29, 1972), p. 2.

34a. On February 28, 1973, Fu Tso-yi, Vice-Chairman of the Chinese People's Political Consultative Conference, claimed that "In the Shanghai Communique, the United States recognizes Taiwan as part of China's territory." See " 'February 28' Uprising in Taiwan Province Marked," *PR* 16.10:11 (Mar. 9, 1973).

35. "China and Britain to Exchange Ambassadors," *PR* 15.11:3 (Mar. 17, 1972).

36. See "London Announces," (AP, London, March 13, 1972), *China News* (Taipei, Mar. 14, 1972), p. 1.

37. "China and Netherlands Raise Level of Diplomatic Relations," *PR* 15.21:20 (May 26, 1972). Similarly, when Japan established diplomatic relations with the PRC on September 29, 1972, it announced in its joint communiqué with the PRC that it "fully understands and respects" the stand of the PRC that Taiwan is an inalienable part of the territory of the PRC and adhered "to its stand of complying with Article 8 of the Potsdam Proclamation" (i.e., Taiwan should be returned to China in accordance with the 1943 Cairo Declaration). "Text of the Chinese-Japanese Accord Signed by Chou and Tanaka," *New York Times* (Sept. 30, 1972), p. 12.

38. See James Hsiung, "China's Recognition Practice and Its Implications in International Law," in Cohen, ed., *China's Practice,* pp. 20–34, 51.

39. "Mujib Wants Recognition By China," (UPI) *Mainichi Daily News* (Jan. 16, 1972), p. 1.

40. "Communique on Establishment of Diplomatic Relations between China [and] Dahomey," NCNA-English, Peking (Nov. 13, 1964) in *SCMP*, no. 3339:30–31 (Nov. 18, 1964).

41. "Chinese Foreign Ministry's Statement on Dahomey Government's Unreasonable Decision to End Diplomatic Relations," NCNA-English, Peking (Jan. 5, 1966) in *SCMP*, no. 3613:27 (Jan. 10, 1966).

42. See Peter Van Ness, *Revolution and Chinese Foreign Policy: Peking's Support for Wars of National Liberation* (Berkeley and Los Angeles: University of California Press, 1970), pp. 4, 244.

43. See, *e.g.*, "Peking and Accra Expected to Sever Diplomatic Relations," *New York Times* (Oct. 26, 1966), p. 3; also Parts VI and VII of this book for PRC protests to Indonesia.

44. "P'ping, Burundi Resume Diplomatic Ties" (AP), *China News* (Oct. 15, 1971), p. 1; "Resumption of Diplomatic Relations Between China and Ghana," *PR* 15.9:3 (Mar. 9, 1972); "Chinese Embassy in Tunis To Resume Work," *PR* 14.42:19 (Oct. 15, 1971); "Jakarta Remains Wary of Chinese," *New York Times* (Aug. 13, 1972), p. 17.

45. "Ceylon Government's 'Two Chinas' Plot Protested," *PR* 10.40:38 (Sept. 29, 1967).

46. "Protest over Indonesian Government's 'Invitation' to Chiang Clique's 'Trade Delegation,'" *PR* 10.39:29 (Sept. 22, 1967).

47. "Strong Protest against Soviet Revisionist Clique's Crime of Collaborating with US Imperialism in 'Two Chinas' Plot," *PR* 11.13:9 (Mar. 29, 1968). 1968).

48. "Readers' Forum," *The Stamp Magazine* (United Kingdom), (Apr. 1968), p. 364.

49. "Strong Protest against Indian Government's New Crime in Creating 'Two Chinas,'" *PR* 11.35:30–31 (Aug. 30, 1968); see also "Strong Protest Over Indian Government's Scheme to Create 'Two Chinas,'" *PR* 11.42:30 (Oct. 18, 1968).

50. "French Parliamentary Delegation Sneaks into Taiwan for Collusion with Chiang Bandit Gang," *PR* 12.50:28 (Dec. 12, 1969).

51. "Chinese Embassy in Soviet Union Lodges Stern Protest with Soviet Foreign Ministry—Against Soviet Revisionists' Criminal Plot to Co-ordinate with US Imperialism in Creating 'Two Chinas,'" *PR* 13.3:3 (Jan. 16, 1970); see also "New Evidence of Criminal Collusion with Chiang Gang," *PR* 15.13:22 (Mar. 31, 1972).

52. "Strong Protest against the Bulgarian Government's Shameless Anti-China Activity," *PR* 12.23:4, 30 (June 6, 1969).

53. See, *e.g.*, Alvin Shuster, "London in Peking Accord: To Close Taiwan Offices," *New York Times* (Mar. 14, 1972), p. 1.

54. See Byron S. J. Weng, "Some Conditions of Peking's Participation in International Organizations," in Cohen, *China's Practice*, pp. 321–343.

55. "A Victory for World's People, Crushing Defeat for U.S. Imperialism," *PR* 14.44:6, 7–8 (Oct. 29, 1971).

56. "Japan No Longer to Accept New Trainees from Taiwan," *Asahi Evening News* (Mar. 18, 1972), p. 1.

57. "Taipei Denounces the UN For Erasing Taiwan Data," *New York Times* (City ed., Aug. 27, 1972), p. 2.

58. "UN Tentacles Extended to Cambodia—U Thant Flagrantly Recognizes Cambodian Rightist Clique." *PR* 13.16:25 (Apr. 17, 1970). In April 1973 the PRC, participating for the first time in the deliberations of the UN Economic Commission for Asia and the Far East (ECAFE), instructed its delegates to walk out of the meetings on three occasions in protest against representation decisions. Richard Halloran, "China's Protests Mark Tokyo Talk," *New York Times* (Apr.

15, 1973), p. 15. On April 12, PRC representative An Chih-yüan explained the action:

"ECAFE is an important regional body of the United Nations. At present, there are certain irrationalities in its composition. We must solemnly point out that the Royal Government of National Union of Cambodia under the leadership of Samdech Norodom Sihanouk, Head of State of Cambodia, is the sole legal government representing the Cambodian people, while the Lon Nol puppet clique is a handful of national scum, which is illegal from the very beginning and by no means qualified to represent the Cambodian people in ECAFE. The Paris agreement on Vietnam gives de facto recognition to the two administrations existing in south Vietnam, *i.e.*, the Provisional Revolutionary Government of the Republic of South Vietnam and the Saigon authorities. The Provisional Revolutionary Government of the Republic of South Vietnam is the genuine representative of the south Vietnamese people. In the present political situation, it is not appropriate to have the Saigon authorities unilaterally represented in ECAFE. In the circumstances in which agreement has been reached in Korea between the north and the south on the principles for the independent and peaceful reunification of Korea, it is unreasonable and abnormal for the south Korean authorities to be unilaterally represented in ECAFE." "Oppose Big Powers Seeking Hegemony," *PR* 16.16:15 (Apr. 20, 1973).

59. "UN Security Council Debates on 'Bangla Desh's' Application for UN Membership," *PR* 15.35:9 (Sept. 1, 1972).

60. "Government of 'Bangla Desh'—A 'Manchukuo' and Quisling Government," Speech by Ambassador Huang Hua, Dec. 6, 1971, in *PR* 14.51:15 (Dec. 17, 1971).

61. UN Doc. (S/3358) 1955, p. 3; *WCC 1954–1955*, III (1958), 230.

62. UN Security Council, *Official Records*, Fifth Year, 69:4 (Nov. 28, 1950).

63. "Premier Chou En-lai's Report on Asian-African Conference," NCNA–Peking (May 16, 1955), in *CB*, no. 328:8 (May 17, 1955).

64. "China Favours Increased Afro-Asian Representation in Principal UN Organs," *PR* 6.51:20–21 (Dec. 20, 1963).

65. UN General Assembly Resolution 1991A (XVIII) and 1991B (XVIII).

66. UN General Assembly, *Official Records*, 18th Session, Special Political Committee, 423rd Meeting (A/SPC/SR 423), Dec. 10, 1963, p. 257.

67. "China Favours Increased Afro-Asian Representation in Principal UN Organs," *PR* 6.51:21 (Dec. 20, 1963).

68. *Ibid.* Ch'en Yi's public statement of October 2, 1963, was made at the Guinean Embassy's National Day reception in Peking, "Guinean National Day Reception in Peking," NCNA–English (Oct. 2, 1963), in *SCMP*, no. 3074:36 (Oct. 7, 1963). Thus it is not surprising that the representative of Guinea, at the Special Political Committee meeting of December 10, 1963, expressed doubt at the Soviet explanation of the PRC's position. See UN General Assembly, *Official Records*, 18th Session, Special Political Committee, 423rd Meeting (A/SPC/SR. 423), Dec. 10, 1963, pp. 257–258.

69. See the Soviet statement in UN, General Assembly, *Official Records*, 18th Session, Special Political Committee, 427th meeting (A/SPC/SR.427), Dec. 14, 1963, p. 270; see also Albania's rebuttal of the Soviet statement in *ibid.*, 428th meeting (A/SPC/SR.428), Dec. 14, 1963, p. 277.

70. "Firmly Support the Just Demand of the Afro-Asian Countries for Increasing the Seats in the Principal Organs of the United Nations," editorial, *JMJP* (Dec. 18, 1963), p. 1; translated under the title "China Supports Broader Afro-Asian Representation in UN," in *PR* 6.52:15 (Dec. 27, 1963).

71. "Old UN Laws Do Not Bind Us, China," *Japan Times* (April 18, 1972), p. 4.

72. See "Text of Resolution of Albania, Algeria and 20 Other Countries and UN General Assembly Voting Results," *PR* 14.44:9 (Oct. 29, 1971).

73. See "Report on Representation of the People's Republic of China within the Organizations of the United Nations System," *International Legal Materials* 11.3:561 (May 1972).

74. *Ibid.*, pp. 567–568.

75. For an excellent summary of the situation with respect to the specialized agencies, see generally section entitled "Developments within the Organizations of the UN System Concerning Chinese Representation," in *ibid.*, pp. 561–570.

76. "News Briefs," *PR* 14.15:22 (Apr. 9, 1971). Similarly, the PRC refused to send observers to attend the 20th Olympic Games (1972). "China Will Not Send Observer Delegation to the Olympics," *PR* 15.35:23 (Sept. 1, 1972).

77. "China Still in Red Cross," *New York Times* (Sept. 5, 1967), p. 10.

78. "Red Cross Society of China Condemns International Red Cross Standing Commission for Serving US Imperialist Scheme to Create 'Two Chinas,'" *PR* 12.38:29–30 (Sept. 19, 1969).

79. "Peking 2nd Largest Donor to Peru Quake Victims," *New York Times* (Aug. 2, 1970), p. 8.

80. For an analysis of the first twenty years of the PRC's relations with the Red Cross, see G.I.A.D. Draper, "The People's Republic of China and the Red Cross," in Cohen, *China's Practice*, pp. 344–398.

81. "Chinese Red Cross Society Protests," *PR* 14.43:20 (Oct. 22, 1971).

Part IV. Claims to Territory

1. See Te-hsu Ch'eng, "International Law in Early China (1122–249 B.C.)," *Chinese Social and Political Science Review* 11.1:46–49 (Jan. 1927); Roswell S. Britton, "Chinese Interstate Intercourse Before 700 B.C.," *AJIL* 29:629–630 (1935); Richard Louis Walker, *The Multi-State System of Ancient China* (Hamden, Conn.: Shoe String Press, 1953), p. 29.

2. Francis Watson, *The Frontiers of China* (London: Chatto & Windus, 1966), p. 35.

3. See Fan Hao, *Sung shih* (History of the Sung Dynasty; Taipei, 1954), II, 24.

4. For the text of the treaty, see Chi Chiao-sheng, "The Diplomacy of Appeasement in the Northern Sung Dynasty," *Kuo-li cheng-chih ta-hsüeh hsüeh-pao*, 21:85–86 (Taipei, 1970).

5. C. P. Fitzgerald, "The Chinese View of Foreign Relations," *The World Today* 19.1:10–11 (Jan. 1963).

6. Immanuel C. Y. Hsü, *China's Entrance Into the Family of Nations: The Diplomatic Phase, 1858–1880* (Cambridge, Mass.: Harvard University Press, 1960), pp. 132–133; T. F. Tsiang, "Bismarck and the Introduction of International Law into China," *The Chinese Social and Political Science Review*, 15.1:98–101 (Apr. 1931).

7. John K. Fairbank, Edwin O. Reischauer, Albert M. Craig, *East Asia: The Modern Transformation* (Boston: Houghton Mifflin Company, 1965), p. 241; T. F. Tsiang, "Sino-Japanese Diplomatic Relations, 1870–1894," *Chinese Social and Political Science Review* 17.1:16–34 (Apr. 1933).

8. See minute of conversation between Li Hung-chang and the Japanese Minister Mori Arinori, in *Ch'ing Kuang-hsü ch'ao chung-jih chiao-she shih-liao* (Historical materials relating to Sino-Japanese relations during the reign of the Kuang-hsü Emperor; Peiping, 1932), I, 8.

9. The documents of protest from Taiwan are reproduced in T'ai-wan yin-hang ch'ing-chi yen-chiu shih, ed., *Ch'ing-chi wai-chiao shih-liao hsüan-chi* (Selections from historical materials relating to the diplomacy of the Ch'ing dynasty; Taipei: Chung-hua shu-chü, 1964), III, 278; and Tsai Erh-k'an and Chi Fu, eds., *Chung-tung chan-chi pen-mo* (History of Sino-Japanese War; Shanghai, 1897), IV, 58–60.

10. For the text of this Convention, see *LNTS* 11:174–208 (1922). The quotation is from Article 1, p. 190.

11. [William] L. Tung, *China and Some Phases of International Law* (London and New York: Oxford University Press, 1940), pp. 9, 15.

12. *Ibid.*, pp. 13–14.

13. *Ibid.*, pp. 16–17.

14. See, *e.g.*, Watson, *Frontiers*, pp. 21–29.

15. Chung-yang cheng-fa kan-pu hsüeh-hsiao hsing-fa chiao-yen-shih pien, *Chung-hua jen-min kung-ho-kuo hsing-fa tsung-tse chiang-i* (Lectures on the general principles of criminal law of the People's Republic of China; Peking, 1957, 4th printing, 1958), p. 36.

16. Translated from the Chinese. The entire Preamble to the Defense Agreement Pursuant to the North Atlantic Treaty between the United States of America and the Republic of Iceland, signed at Reykjavik, on May 5, 1951, reads as follows: "Having regard to the fact that the people of Iceland cannot themselves adequately secure their own defenses, and whereas experience has shown that a country's lack of defenses greatly endangers its security and that of its peaceful neighbors, the North Atlantic Treaty Organization has requested, because of the unsettled state of world affairs, that the United States and Iceland in view of the collective efforts of the parties to the North Atlantic Treaty to preserve peace and security in the North Atlantic Treaty area, make arrangements for the use of facilities in Iceland in defense of Iceland and thus also the North Atlantic Treaty area. In conformity with this proposal the following Agreement has been entered into." *UNTS* 205: 174 (1955).

17. Mao Tse-tung, "The Identity of Interests between the Soviet Union and All Mankind," September 28, 1939, in *Selected Works of Mao Tse-tung*, Vol. II (Peking, 1965), 279–280.

18. "Vice-Premier Ch'en Yi: China Backs Poland's Stand on its Western Frontier," *PR* 3.30:9 (July 26, 1960).

19. See "Chinese Foreign Ministry Statement on US Military Aircraft's Intrusion into China's Territorial Air," NCNA–English, Peking (May 13, 1960), in *SCMP*, no. 2261:31–32 (May 19, 1960); "*Jen-min jih-pao* on China's 100th Warning," NCNA–English, Peking (May 27, 1960), in *SCMP*, no. 2270:37–40 (June 2, 1960).

20. "Tiny Isles in Pacific Make Big Waves," *New York Times* (July 12, 1971), p. 2. The Shisha and Paracel Islands are different names for the same group of islands.

21. "China's Territory Nansha Islands Brooks No Violation," *PR* 14.30:19 (July 23, 1971).

22. Hungdah Chiu, assisted by Ming-shan Kuo and Ti-hung Liu, "A Study of the Tiaoyutai Islets Problem," *Cheng-ta fa-hsüeh p'ing-lun* (Chengchi Law Review, Taipei), 6:243 (June 1972).

23. *Ibid.*, p. 244.

24. *Ibid.*, p. 263.

25. *Tiao-yü-t'ai lieh-yü wen-t'i* (The problem of the Tiaoyutai Islets; Taipei, 1971), pp. 2–3, 28.

26. Takashi Oka, "Oil Under East China Sea is the Crux of 3-Nation Issue," *New York Times* (Jan. 30, 1971), p. 8.

27. "Tiaoyu and Other Islands Have Been China's Territory since Ancient Times," *PR* 15.1:13 (Jan. 7, 1972).

28. "The Position of the Government of Japan on the Senkaku Islands," Mar. 8, 1972, official text supplied by the Japanese government.

29. "Sato Government Tries to Annex China's Tiaoyu and Other Islands," *PR* 15.14:18 (Apr. 7, 1972).

30. See "An Chih-yüan Refutes Japanese Representative's Absurd Statement about Tiaoyu Island," *PR* 15.11:10 (Mar. 17, 1972).

31. "Huang Hua's Letter to UN Secretary-General and President of Security Council," *PR* 15.21:15 (May 26, 1972).

32. See, *e.g.*, Hungdah Chiu, "A Legal Analysis of Japan's Claim to Tiaoyutai Islets," *Cheng-ta fa-hsüeh p'ing-lun* (Chengchi Law Review), 5:1–25 (Dec. 1971); Toshio Okuhara, "The Territorial Sovereignty over the Senkaku Islands and Problems on the Surrounding Continental Shelf," *Japanese Annual of International Law*, 15:97–106 (1971); Kiyoshi Inoue, "The Tiaoyu Islands (Senkaku Islands) and Other Islands Are China's Territory," *PR* 15.19:18–22 (May 12, 1972); Senkaku Islands Study Committee, "Senkaku Islands and Japan's Territorial Rights," *Okinawa* (Tokyo) 56:8–15 (Mar. 1971); John Gittings, "Scramble for Oil in East China Sea," *Manchester Guardian*, Dec. 18, 1970.

33. See President Chiang Kai-shek's speech to the Provisional National Convention of the Kuomintang, April 1, 1938. Huang Shun-ch'ing, Lin Hsiung-hsiang and Kuo Hai-ming, eds., *T'ai-wan sheng t'ung-chih kao* (Draft history of Taiwan Province), Vol. 10, *Kuang-fu chih* (History of restoration; Taipei, 1952), p. 2.

34. Edgar Snow, *Red Star over China* (New York: Grove Press, Inc., 1968), p. 110.

35. United States Department of State, *United States Relations with China, with Special Reference to the Period 1944–1949* (Washington, D.C.: Government Printing Office, 1949), p. 308.

36. The English text of the agreement, entitled "Agreement Relating to the Status of United States Armed Forces in the Republic of China," signed at Taipei, Aug. 31, 1965, may be found in *UST* 17:373 (1966); *TIAS*, no. 5986.

37. For a collection of important Chinese and Western documents concerning the question of Taiwan, see Hungdah Chiu, ed., *China and the Question of Taiwan: Documents and Analysis* (New York: Praeger, 1973). See also Lung-chu Chen and W. M. Reisman, "Who Owns Taiwan: A Search for International Title," *The Yale Law Journal* 81.4:599–671 (March 1972) and Byron S. Weng, "The Legal Status of Taiwan," in Shao-chuan Leng and Hungdah Chiu, eds., *Law in Chinese Foreign Policy: Communist China and Selected Problems of International Law* (Dobbs Ferry, N.Y.: Oceana, 1972), pp. 123–177.

38. *Hertslet's China Treaties*, 3rd ed. (London: His Majesty's Stationery Office, 1908), I, 121.

39. "Anti-Imperialist Struggle of Chinese Compatriots in Macau—Another Brilliant Victory of Mao Tse-tung's Thought," NCNA–English, Hong Kong (Jan. 31, 1967), in *SCMP*, no. 3875:25 (Feb. 6, 1967).

40. The Portuguese authorities actually canceled plans to celebrate Macao's 400th anniversary as a result of the PRC's warnings. See "Macau Portuguese Call Off 'Celebrations,'" NCNA–English, Canton (Oct. 25, 1955), in *SCMP*, no. 1157: 30 (Oct. 26, 1955).

41. For subsequent developments, see Simon Head, "The Forgotten City," *FEER* 63.8:332–334 (Feb. 20, 1969); and "Kowloon Dispute with China Revived," *New York Times* (July 7, 1970), p. 2.

42. Quoted in "China Makes Claim in UN to Hong Kong, Macao," *International Herald Tribune* (Paris), Mar. 11–12, 1972, p. 1. The Special Committee decided to recommend to the General Assembly that Hong Kong and Macao be excluded from the list of territories to which the declaration on decolonization was applicable. "Special Committee on Decolonization," *UN Monthly Chronicle* 9.7:36 (July 1972).

43. O. Edmund Clubb, *Twentieth Century China* (New York: Columbia University Press, 1964), p. 323.

44. Chapter VI of the Common Programme, "Policy toward Nationalities," may be found in *The Important Documents of the First Plenary Session of the Chinese People's Political Consultative Conference* (Peking: Foreign Languages Press, 1949), pp. 18–19.

45. Harold C. Hinton, *Communist China in World Politics* (Boston: Houghton Mifflin Company, 1966), p. 285, n. 35, quoting from *White Paper No. I*,

p. 62, published by the Ministry of External Affairs of the government of India.

46. The quotation does not appear in Younghusband's book, but it was included in Younghusband's report to the British government. See *Accounts and Papers,* Cd. 2370 (1905) [*Further Papers Relating to Tibet, No. III,* Annexure to enclosure No. 362], pp. 274–275. See also Li Tieh-tseng, *Tibet, Today and Yesterday* [rev. ed. of *The Historical Status of Tibet*] (New York: Bookman Associates, 1960), p. 108.

47. *Accounts and Papers,* Cd. 1920 (1904) [*Papers Relating to Tibet,* No. 66], p. 154.

48. *Ibid.,* No. 78, p. 185.

49. *Accounts and Papers,* Cd. 2370 (1905) [No. 55], p. 18, cited in Li Tieh-tseng, "The Legal Position of Tibet," *AJIL* 50.2:399 (Apr. 1956).

50. We are unable to locate the source of the quoted passage.

51. For analysis of the complex questions relating to the status of Tibet and citations to relevant sources, see Alfred P. Rubin, "The Position of Tibet in International Law," *China Quarterly,* no. 35:110–154 (July-Sept. 1968).

52. See, *e.g.,* Alfred P. Rubin, "The Sino-Indian Border Disputes," *International and Comparative Law Quarterly* 9.1:96–125 (Jan. 1960); L. C. Green, "Legal Aspects of the Sino-Indian Border Dispute," *China Quarterly,* no. 3:42–58 (July-Sept. 1960); and K. Krishna Rao, "The Sino-Indian Boundary Question and International Law," *International and Comparative Law Quarterly,* 11.2:375–415 (Apr. 1962). For a valuable historical study, see Alistair Lamb, *The China-India Border: The Origins of the Disputed Boundaries* (London: Oxford University Press, 1964).

53. Arthur A. Stahnke, "The Place of International Law in Chinese Strategy and Tactics: The Case of the Sino-Indian Boundary Dispute," *Journal of Asian Studies* 30.1:118–119 (Nov. 1970).

54. See also the analysis of the negotiations in Neville Maxwell, *India's China War* (London: Jonathan Cape, 1970).

55. "Indian Concocted Stories about Chinese 'Intrusions' into Bhutan Refuted," *PR* 9.46:36 (Nov. 11, 1966).

56. "Fresh Aggression by Indian Troops Protested," *PR* 10.17:5 (Apr. 21, 1967).

57. Harold C. Hinton, *Communist China in World Politics* (Boston: Houghton Mifflin Company, 1966), p. 310, provides this translation from *Chung-hua jen-min kung-ho-kuo fen-sheng ti-t'u* (Provincial atlas of the People's Republic of China; Shanghai: Ti-t'u ch'u-pan-she, 1953), description to map 46 (Yünnan Province).

58. For the text of the final boundary treaty, see *TYC 1960,* IX (1961), 68. English text in "Boundary Treaty between the People's Republic of China and the Union of Burma," *PR* 3.40:29–34 (Oct. 4, 1960).

59. Hinton, *Communist China in World Politics,* pp. 321–322.

60. The English text of the Sino-Pakistani Agreement may be found in *AJIL* 57.3:713–716 (July 1963). The PRC rejected a protest by India against the settlement concluded with Pakistan. See "Chinese Foreign Ministry Note Refutes India's Anti-China Clamor," NCNA–English, Peking (May 20, 1965), in *SCMP,* no. 3464: 28–29 (May 25, 1965).

61. The English text of the treaty may be found in "Boundary Treaty between the People's Republic of China and the People's Republic of Mongolia," *CB,* no. 707:1–13 (Apr. 9, 1963).

62. The English text of the Sino-Afghan treaty may be found in "Boundary Treaty between the People's Republic of China and the Kingdom of Afghanistan," *PR* 6.48:7–8 (Nov. 29, 1963).

63. Hinton, *Communist China in World Politics,* p. 318, quoting from *Sino-Pakistan "Agreement," March 2, 1963: Some Facts* (New Delhi: Ministry of External Affairs, 1963), pp. 10–13.

64. See Karakhan's declarations of 1919 and 1920, in H. G. W. Woodhead, ed., *The China Year Book, 1924–25* (Tientsin, 1924), pp. 868–872.

65. *Ibid.*, Article V, p. 881; *LNTS* 37:178. There is a discrepancy concerning the date on which the agreement was signed. *The China Yearbook 1924–25* says it was signed on March 14, 1924; *LNTS* says May 1, 1924.

66. On March 12, 1936, the Soviet Union announced the conclusion of a "mutual assistance" protocol with Outer Mongolia. The Republic of China sent a strong note of protest to the Soviet government in April 1936. See Robert M. Slusser and Jan F. Triska, *A Calendar of Soviet Treaties, 1917–1957* (Stanford, Calif.: Stanford University Press, 1959), p. 109; Chiang Chung-cheng (Chiang Kai-shek), *Soviet Russia in China,* rev. enl. ed. (New York: Farrar, Straus and Cudahy, 1958), p. 74.

67. "Crimea (Yalta) Conference, 1945: Entry of Soviet Union into War against Japan," agreement signed at Yalta on Feb. 11, 1945, in Charles I. Bevans, comp., *Treaties and other International Agreements of the United States of America 1776–1949,* Vol. 3, *Multilateral, 1931–1945* (Washington, D.C.: Government Printing Office, 1969), p. 1022.

68. *Ibid.*

69. *UNTS* 10:300ff. (1947).

70. On February 1, 1952, the General Assembly of the United Nations adopted Resolution 505(VI) declaring, *inter alia,* "that the Union of Soviet Socialist Republics . . . has failed to carry out the Treaty of Friendship and Alliance between China and the Union of Soviet Socialist Republics of 14 August 1945." UN General Assembly, *Official Records,* Sixth Session, Supplement No. 20: Resolutions (A/2119), 1952, p. 4. On February 25, 1953, the Foreign Minister of the Republic of China declared "the Treaty of Friendship and Alliance between the Republic of China and the Union of Soviet Socialist Republics of August 14, 1945, and other Related Documents null and void." Ministry of Foreign Affairs, ed., *Treaties between the Republic of China and Foreign States, 1927–1957* (Taipei: Commercial Press, Ltd., 1958), p. 524. On March 1, 1967, the Ministry of Foreign Affairs of the Republic of China issued a statement opposing Australian recognition of Outer Mongolia. The statement argued that as of February 23, 1953, the date of annulment of the 1945 Sino-Soviet treaty, the legal position of Outer Mongolia should be restored to its original (pre-1945) status as a part of China. Hungdah Chiu, comp., "Chinese Contemporary Practices and Judicial Decisions Relating to International Law (February 1966 to March 1967)," *The Annals of the Chinese Society of International Law* (Taipei), 4:69–70 (Aug. 1967).

71. "On Agreement Establishing Two Sino-Soviet Stock Companies," *JMJP* (March 29, 1950), p. 1; "On Agreement Establishing Sino-Soviet Civil Aviation Joint Stock Company," *JMJP* (Apr. 2, 1950), p. 1.

72. Hinton, *Communist China in World Politics,* p. 29.

73. *Ibid.*, p. 325, quoting a Soviet government statement of September 20, 1963.

74. *Ibid.*, p. 326.

75. George Ginsburgs and Carl Pinkele, "The Genesis of the Territorial Issue in the Sino-Soviet Dialogue: Substantive Dispute or Ideological Pas de Deux?" in Jerome A. Cohen, ed., *China's Practice of International Law: Some Case Studies* (Cambridge, Mass.: Harvard University Press, 1972), pp. 237–238.

76. "Statement of the USSR Government," *Pravda* (June 14, 1969), pp. 1–2; English translation in *CDSP* 21.24:11 (July 9, 1969).

77. "Document of the Ministry of Foreign Affairs of the People's Republic of China—Refutation of the Soviet Government's Statement of June 13, 1969," Oct. 8, 1969, in *PR* 12.41:14–15 (Oct. 10, 1969).

78. *Ibid.*, p. 14.

79. *Ibid.*, pp. 13–14.

80. See "When Comrades Fall Out," *The Economist,* Vol. 234 (Jan. 24, 1970), p. 9.

81. "Peking Drops Claim to Korean Area," *New York Times* (Nov. 23, 1970), p. 5.

82. Hsü, *China's Entrance*, p. 133.

83. See n. 8, above.

84. Article 11 of the Sino-Mexican Treaty of Friendship, Commerce and Navigation, Dec. 14, 1899. *Hertslet's China Treaties*, I, 403–404.

85. Wei Wen-han, "Discussing the Question of the Width of the Territorial Sea," *FH*, no. 3:23 (1957).

86. See *AJIL*, supp. 24:25, 27, 234–235, 254 (1930).

87. Articles 10–12 of the Customs Preventive Law of June 19, 1934; English translation in *Laws and Regulations on the Regime of the Territorial Sea* (New York: The United Nations, 1957), pp. 113–114.

88. See UN Doc. (A/Conf. 13/SR.14), Apr. 25, 1958, reprinted in *United Nations Conference on the Law of the Sea*, Plenary Meeting, *Official Records*, II, 39 (New York: The United Nations, 1959).

89. See Wei Wen-han, "Discussing the Question," p. 23.

90. Commentator, "Sovereignty over Territorial Waters and 'Freedom of the Seas,'" *JMJP* (Dec. 28, 1957), p. 5.

91. For the PRC's reaction to Iceland's action, see Commentator, "Do Not Permit Interference with Iceland's Right to Decide the Scope of Its Territorial Sea," *JMJP* (Sept. 3, 1958), p. 4.

92. "Declaration on China's Territorial Sea [September 4, 1958]," *PR* 1.28:21 (Sept. 9, 1958).

93. For detailed references, see Tao Cheng, "Communist China and the Law of the Sea," *AJIL* 63.1:54ff. (Jan. 1969).

94. United States Department of State, *American Foreign Policy: Current Documents, 1958* (Washington, D.C.: Government Printing Office, 1962), p. 1198.

95. Translated from the Chinese. No reference was given by the author.

96. "Secretary Dulles' News Conference of September 9," *Department of State Bulletin*, 39.1005:488 (Sept. 29, 1958).

97. Translated from the Chinese. No reference was given by the author.

98. The relevant passages of Oppenheim's treatise are as follows: "Although Bynkershoek's rule that *terrae potestas finitur ubi finitur armorum vis* is now generally recognized by theory and practice, and consequently a belt of such breadth is considered under the sway of the littoral State as is within effective range of the shore batteries, there is still no unanimity on account of the fact that such range is day by day increasing." L. Oppenheim, *International Law*, 7th ed., by H. Lauterpacht (London: Longmans, Green, 1948), I, 444.

99. Oppenheim, *International Law*, 7th ed., by Lauterpacht, I, 445.

100. F. I. Kozhevnikov, ed., *Mezhdunarodnoe pravo*, Akademiia nauk SSSR, Institut prava (Moscow: Gos. izd-vo iurid. lit-ry, 1957), p. 208; English translation in F. I. Kozhevnikov, ed., *International Law*, tr. Dennis Ogden (Moscow: Foreign Languages Publishing House, [n. d.]), p. 212.

101. Fisheries Case (*United Kingdom* v. *Norway*), 1951 I.C.J. Rep. 116.

102. For a description of this case, see Ssu-yu Teng and John K. Fairbank, *China's Response to the West, A Documentary Survey 1839–1923* (New York: Atheneum, 1963), pp. 97–99.

103. "Unite to Oppose Despotic Powers," *PR* 14.26:13 (June 25, 1971).

104. "Peruvian Minister of Fisheries Visits China," *PR* 14.26:4 (June 25, 1971).

105. "Joint Communiqué on Establishment of Diplomatic Relations between China and Peru," Nov. 2, 1971, in *PR* 14.45:5 (Nov. 5, 1971).

106. "Diplomatic Relations Established between China and Argentina," Feb. 19, 1972, in *PR* 15.7–8:26–27 (Feb. 25, 1972).

107. "People's Republic of China Statement on the Law of the Sea," *International Legal Materials* 11.3:657, 660 (May 1972).

108. (*Lectures on the general principles of criminal law*), p. 36 (see n. 15, above).

109. See, *e.g.*, "Protest against Intrusions by Indian Military Aircraft," *PR* 10.32:54–55 (Aug. 4, 1967); "China Protests against Spy Flight of an American U-2 Plane," *PR* 5.38:7 (Sept. 21, 1962); and "Those American Balloons," *PC*, no. 7:20–21 (Apr. 1956).

110. See, *e.g.*, Neil Sheehan, "Chinese Down Straying US Plane near Hainan," *New York Times* (June 27, 1967), p. 4; and "Chinese Air Force Downs US Imperialist Unmanned Reconnaissance Plane," *PR* 11.4:5, 8 (Jan. 26, 1968).

111. "Law Expert Hsu Tun-chang on US Launching of Balloons," NCNA–English, Peking (Mar. 1, 1956), in *SCMP*, no. 1241:13 (Mar. 6, 1956); see also Ch'en T'i-ch'iang, "Launching of Military Reconnaissance Balloons over Other Countries Is a Violation of International Law," *JMJP* (Mar. 11, 1956), p. 4; translated in *SCMP*, no. 1254:23–25 (Mar. 23, 1956).

112. See "China Successfully Launches Its First Man-Made Earth Satellite," *PR* 13.18:4–5 (Apr. 30, 1970); "2nd Object in Orbit with China Satellite, US Aide Discloses," *New York Times* (May 20, 1970), p. 8.

113. "Another Fraud in US-Soviet Conspiracy, Says *Jen-min jih-pao*," NCNA–English, Peking (Jan. 28, 1967), in *SCMP*, no. 3872:33–34 (Feb. 1, 1967); "The Dilemma of American Jurists," *JMJP* (Oct. 19, 1957), p. 5.

114. E. A. Korovin *et al.*, "Discussions: The Mastering of Cosmos and Some Problems of International Relations" (in Russian), *Mezhdunarodnaia Zhizn'*, 11:116–125 (Moscow: [n.p.], 1959); translated into Chinese in *Kuo-chi wen-t'i i-ts'ung* (Collected translations on international problems), no. 1:44ff (1960).

115. For analysis of this article, see Hungdah Chiu, "Communist China and the Law of Outer Space," *International and Comparative Law Quarterly* 16.4: 1135–1138 (Oct. 1967).

Part V. The Exercise of Territorial Jurisdiction

1. Richard Louis Walker, *The Multi-State System of Ancient China* (Hamden, Conn.: Shoe String Press, 1953), pp. 24–25, 90.

2. This paragraph is based on Nien-tsu Tzou, "T'ang Laws Concerning Foreigners," *Annals of the Chinese Society of International Law* 5:68–77 (Aug. 1968).

3. R. Randle Edwards, "Ch'ing Control of Aliens Prior to the 'Treaty System,'" (unpublished paper, 1971). This paragraph of the text relies on Professor Edwards fascinating analysis. See also R. Randle Edwards, "Early Ch'ing Criminal Jurisdiction over European Merchants and Sailors," in Jerome Alan Cohen, R. Randle Edwards, and Fu-mei Chang Chen, eds., *China's Legal Tradition* (forthcoming).

4. See Immanuel C. Y. Hsü, *China's Entrance into the Family of Nations: The Diplomatic Phase, 1858–1880* (Cambridge, Mass.: Harvard University Press, 1960), pp. 123–125.

5. *Ibid.*, pp. 132–133.

6. See minute of conversation between Li Hung-chang and the Japanese Minister Mori Arinori annexed to the memorial submitted by the Tsungli Yamen to the Emperor on the Japanese intention to enter into friendly relations with Korea, dated Jan. 17, 1876, in *Ch'ing Kuang-hsü ch'ao chung-jih chiao-she shih-liao* (Historical materials relating to Sino-Japanese relations during the reign of the Kuang-hsü Emperor; Peiping: Palace Museum, 1932), I, 8.

7. Agreement between the High Commissioner Plenipotentiary of Japan and the Chinese Ministers [*sic*] of Foreign Affairs, Peking, Oct. 31, 1874. Inspector General of Customs, *Treaties, Conventions, etc. between China and Foreign States* (Shanghai: Statistical Department of the Inspectorate General of Customs, 1908), II, 1313–1315. For details, see Sophia Su-fei Yen, *Taiwan in China's Foreign Relations 1836–1874* (Hamden, Conn.: Shoe String Press, 1965), pp. 212–295.

8. For discussion of cases illustrating the extreme demands made by the United States representatives for protection and compensation for injury to American nationals, see *Papers Relating to the Foreign Relations of the United States, 1887* (Washington, D.C.: Government Printing Office, 1888), pp. 160–164; *Ch'ing-chi wai-chiao shih-liao: Kuang-hsü ch'ao,* LXVIII, 7–8; and Li Pao-hung, *Chung-Mei wai-chiao kuan-hsi* (Sino-American diplomatic relations; Changsha: Shang-wu yin-shu kuan, 1940), pp. 139–140. For cases illustrating the refusal of the United States to take adequate measures to protect Chinese nationals or to provide fair compensation for property loss or injury suffered by Chinese due to inadequate protection, see *Papers Relating to the Foreign Relations of the United States, 1881* (Washington, D.C.: Government Printing Office, 1882), pp. 319–320; Li Pao-hung's work cited earlier in this note (pp. 148–150); J. B. Moore, *A Digest of International Law* (Washington, D.C.: Government Printing Office, 1906), VI, 823–825, 835–836.

9. See, *e.g.*, William L. Tung, *China and the Foreign Powers: The Impact and Reaction to Unequal Treaties* (Dobbs Ferry, N.Y.: Oceana, 1970), pp. 146–345. For the exercise of territorial jurisdiction by the Republic of China prior to World War II, see [William] L. Tung, *China and Some Phases of International Law* (London: Oxford University Press, 1940), pp. 1–34.

10. Common Program of the CPPCC (passed at the 1st plenary session of the CPPCC, Sept. 29, 1949), *FLHP 1949–1950* (1952), p. 25.

11. Constitution of the PRC (passed at the 1st meeting of the 1st session of the NPC, Sept. 20, 1954; promulgated by the Presidium, Sept. 20, 1954), *FKHP 1954–1955*, I, 30.

12. Ch'ien Szu, "A Criticism of the Views of Bourgeois International Law on the Question of Population," *KCWTYC* 5:49 (1960).

13. See "Sedition Charges Dropped by US," *New York Times* (May 3, 1961), p. 19.

14. John Gittings, "A Phoenix Too Frequent," *FEER* 63.28:118 (July 10, 1969).

15. "Hong Kong Sends 5 Back to China," *New York Times* (Nov. 27, 1967), p. 26. See also, *e.g.*, "Chinese Free Hong Kong Briton; He Saw Three Missing Yachts," *New York Times* (Feb. 28, 1969), p. 3; "US Woman Spent 6 Mos. of Captivity in Hospital," *Japan Times* (Dec. 18, 1971), p. 3.

16. See, *e.g.*, "Swiss Say Taiwan Official Defected to Red China," *New York Times* (Mar. 9, 1971), p. 10; and "Foochow Armymen and Civilians Welcome Chou Chen-teh, Former Chiang Gang Platoon Leader, Who has Crossed Over," *PR* 12.38:30–31 (Sept. 19, 1969).

17. "Note given by the Ministry of Foreign Affairs, Peking, to the Embassy of India in China, 23 Sept. 1960," in *White Paper,* no. 4:74–75 (Mar.-Nov. 1960).

18. "Note given by the Ministry of Foreign Affairs of China to the Embassy of India in China, 31 Dec. 1959," in *White Paper,* no. 3:118–119 (Nov. 1959-Mar. 1960).

19. L. Oppenheim, *International Law,* 7th ed., by H. Lauterpacht (London: Longmans, Green, 1948), I, 448.

20. See William E. Butler, "The Legal Regime of Russian Territorial Waters," *AJIL* 62.1:65–69 (Jan. 1968).

21. Liu Tse-yung, "A Major Step to Protect China's Sovereign Rights," *PR* 1.29:13 (Sept. 16, 1958).

22. Butler, "The Legal Regime . . . ," p. 69.

23. Tao Cheng, "Communist China and the Law of the Sea," *AJIL* 63.1:61 (Jan. 1969).

24. Georg Schwarzenberger, *International Law,* 3d ed. (London: Steven & Sons Limited, 1957), I, 196.

25. F. I. Kozhevnikov, ed., *International Law,* tr. Dennis Ogden (Moscow: Foreign Languages Publishing House, [n.d.]), p. 228.

26. *UST* 15:1606, *TIAS,* no. 5639; *UNTS* 516:205 (1964).

27. See "Serious Warning to the US Aggressors," editorial, *JMJP* (Apr. 27, 1962), pp. 1–2; translated in NCNA–English, Peking (Apr. 27, 1962); in *SCMP*, no. 2733:27 (May 8, 1962).

28. Observer, "Johnson Administration's Act of Piracy," *JMJP* (May 2, 1965), p. 2; English translation in *PR* 8.19:23 (May 7, 1965).

29. "Chinese Government Statement Condemns US Imperialism's Crime of Aggression," *PR* 11.5:7 (Feb. 2, 1968).

30. See n. 28.

31. Editor, "Answers to Readers on Several Questions Concerning the Territorial Seas," *JMJP* (Sept. 7, 1958), p. 3.

32. "*Ta Kung Pao* Comment on US Insistence on Nuclear Tests on High Seas," Mar. 31, 1958; English summary, NCNA–English, Peking (Mar. 31, 1958), in *SCMP*, no. 1744:37 (Apr. 2, 1958).

33. See Tao Cheng, "Communist China and the Law of the Sea," p. 64, n. 91.

34. *Ibid.*, p. 65, n. 94, which cites the Annex to the "Temporary Regulations Concerning Motorized Trawler Fishing in East China Sea" issued by the Aquatic Products Control Board of the East China Military-Political Commission on December 16, 1950, in *Hua-tung ch'ü ts'ai-cheng ching-chi fa-ling hui-pien* (Collection of laws and decrees of the East China area regarding financial and economic matters), II, 1333–1337.

35. "State Council Issues Supplementary Regulations Concerning Order on Prohibited Fishing Zone," *JMJP* (Aug. 18, 1957), p. 4; see also Tao Cheng, "Communist China and the Law of the Sea," p. 65, n. 94.

36. See Luke T. Lee, "Treaty Relations of the People's Republic of China: A Study of Compliance," *University of Pennsylvania Law Review*, 116.2:276–277 (Dec. 1967).

37. "3 Yachts Believed Held by China," *New York Times* (Feb. 17, 1969), pp. 1, 6.

38. "Concern Voiced over Two Still Held by China," *New York Times* (Apr. 4, 1969), p. 6.

39. "2 Americans Released by Chinese Say They Were Forced to Sign Confessions," *New York Times* (Dec. 8, 1969), p. 5.

40. "47 Fishermen Returned to Hong Kong by China," *New York Times* (July 7, 1968), p. 10.

41. Nitchu Kokyo Kaifuku Sokushin Giin Renmei, Compiler, *Nitchu Kankei Shiryo 1945–1971* (Materials on Sino-Japanese Relations, Tokyo, 1971), pp. 166–167; English translation from Tao Cheng, "Communist China and the Law of the Sea," p. 67.

42. *FKHP 1959*, X, 331, 335. Port authorities are also authorized by Article 13 to deal with cases involving a foreign-flag ship at the request of the consul of the flag state.

43. Ni Cheng-ao, *Kuo-chi-fa chung ti ssu-fa kuan-hsia wen-t'i* (The question of judicial jurisdiction in international law; Peking, 1964), pp. 42–43.

44. "Sino-Soviet Treaty of Commerce and Navigation," *PR* 1.9:22 (Apr. 29, 1958).

45. Luke T. Lee, "Treaty Relations . . . ," p. 280.

46. Ni Cheng-ao, (*Question of Judicial Jurisdiction* . . .), pp. 43–44.

47. "Statement of the Soviet Maritime Ministry on 'S.S. Zagorsk,'" Tass–English, Moscow (Jan. 2, 1967), in *FBIS*, no. 2:BB1–2 (Jan. 4, 1967).

48. P. Demidov, "The Svirsk Arrives in Vladivostok," *Izvestia* (Aug. 19, 1967), pp. 1, 4; translated in *CDSP* 19.33:3–4 (Sept. 6, 1967).

49. "'Trial' of Captain; Svirsk Departure," broadcast, Vladivostok (Aug. 14, 1967); translated in *FBIS*, no. 157/67:BB3 (Aug. 14, 1967).

50. Shragin Commentary, "Hung Weiping (Red Guards) 'Savagery,'" broadcast, Moscow (Aug. 12, 1967); translated in *FBIS*, no. 157/67:BB4 (Aug. 14, 1967).

51. "Kosygin Telegram to Chou En-lai," broadcast, TASS–English, Moscow (Aug. 12, 1967), in *FBIS*, no. 157/67:BB1 (Aug. 14, 1967).

52. P. Demidov, "Disgraceful Provocation by Chinese Authorities," *Izvestia* (Apr. 13, 1968), p. 3; English translation in *CDSP* 20.15:28–29 (May 1, 1968).

53. "Strong Protest against Political Provocation by British Merchant Seamen," *PR* 10.22:53 (May 26, 1967).

54. "Political Provocation by British Sailors Will Not Be Tolerated," *PR* 10.31:29 (July 28, 1967).

55. See, *e.g.*, "Visiting Seamen Sentenced in China to Make Apology," *New York Times* (Mar. 31, 1967), p. 34.

56. Tillman Durdin, "Chinese Release Another Briton," *New York Times* (Oct. 25, 1970), p. 8.

57. See Jerome Alan Cohen, "Chinese Law and Sino-American Trade," in Alexander Eckstein, ed., *China Trade Prospects and United States Policy* (New York: Praeger, 1971), p. 146.

58. "Chinese Delegation to Sino-Soviet Joint Commission for Navigation on Boundary Rivers Returns to Harbin," *PR* 12.33:20 (Aug. 15, 1969).

59. "Soviet Renews China River Pact," *New York Times* (Dec. 21, 1970), p. 11.

60. See J. G. Starke, *Introduction to International Law,* 7th ed. (London: Butterworths, 1972), p. 185.

61. *Ibid.*, pp. 188–189.

62. "The United Nations Should Immediately Stop US Aggressive Action against China," editorial, *Kuang-ming jih-pao* (Oct. 19, 1954), p. 1; translated under the same title in NCNA–English, Peking (Oct. 19, 1954), in *SCMP,* no. 911:15 (Oct. 20, 1954).

63. "Serious Warning to the US Aggressors," [editorial, *JMJP* (Apr. 27, 1962), p. 1], translated under the same title in NCNA–English, Peking (Apr. 27, 1962), in *SCMP,* no. 2733:27 (May 8, 1962).

64. Ch'en T'i-ch'iang, "Launching of Military Reconnaissance Balloons over Other Countries Is a Violation of International Law," *JMJP* (Mar. 11, 1956), p. 4; translated under the same title in *SCMP,* no. 1254:23–24 (Mar. 23, 1956).

65. "Law Expert Hsu Tun-chang on US Launching of Balloons," NCNA–English, Peking (Mar. 1, 1956), in *SCMP,* no. 1241:13, 14 (Mar. 6, 1956).

66. Chen Wei, "Quibbling Does Not Change the Truth," *JMJP* (Feb. 11, 1956), p. 4; translated under the same title in *SCMP,* no. 1234:24 (Feb. 24, 1956).

67. *Ibid.*, p. 25.

68. See, *e.g.*, "Protest Against Hostile Action of the Chinese Authorities," *Izvestia* (Nov. 1, 1968), p. 3.

69. 49 Stat. 3000, T.S. No. 876; for the PRC's 1958 adherence, see *FKHP 1958,* VII, 338; *TYC 1958,* VII (1959), 195.

70. See PRC's cablegram to the ICAO dated May 30, 1950, *WCC 1949–1950,* I (1957), 126. But, when the ROC withdrew from the ICAO in 1953, the PRC failed to seize the opportunity to join that agency; nor did it register a public protest when the ROC rejoined the ICAO in 1956.

71. See "Air Transport Agreement between the Government of the People's Republic of China and Government of the Democratic Republic of Vietnam" (signed and entered into force on Nov. 8, 1955), in *Air Laws and Treaties of the World,* (Washington, D.C.: Government Printing Office, 1965), I, 443–444. For the text of another agreement concluded with a non-Communist state, see "Air Transport Agreement between the Government of Ceylon and the Government of the People's Republic of China" (signed Mar. 26, 1959), in *Ceylon Treaty Series No. 2* (1959). For a useful analysis of PRC activity in this area until late 1972, see John R. King and Susan C. Roosevelt, "Civil Aviation Agreements of the People's Republic of China," *Harvard International Law Journal* 14.2:316–344 (Spring 1973).

72. "It Was All an American Plot," *The Economist,* Vol. 237, 6632 (Oct. 3, 1970), p. 39.

73. "Hijacked Plane Back from China with 24," *New York Times* (Apr. 1, 1971), p. 12.

73a. "Hijacking of Aircraft," *UN Monthly Chronicle* 9.7:10 (July 1972).

73b. "Hijacking of Commercial Aircraft," *ibid.* 7.9:8 (Oct. 1970).

74. Luke T. Lee, "Treaty Relations . . . ," p. 274.

75. "Leading Chinese Jurist Demands Helou's Release by UAR," NCNA–English, Peking (Aug. 27, 1959), in *SCMP,* no. 2089:49 (Sept. 3, 1959); and "Chinese Jurists Condemn Persecution of Helou," NCNA–English, Peking (Aug. 28, 1959), in *ibid.,* p. 50.

76. Exchange of Notes Constituting an Agreement between the United States of America and China Relating to Mutual Defense Assistance, Taipei, January 30 and February 9, 1951, *UNTS* 132:275 (1952).

77. See *FLHP 1949–1950* (1952), p. 25.

78. Compare Articles 58 and 60 of the Common Program, *FLHP 1949–1950* (1952), p. 25, with Articles 98 and 99 of the Constitution, *FKHP 1954–1955,* I, 30.

79. *FLHP 1949–1950* (1952), pp. 3–5; English translation in Jerome A. Cohen, *The Criminal Process in the People's Republic of China, 1949–1963: An Introduction* (Cambridge, Mass.: Harvard University Press, 1968), pp. 299–302.

80. *FLHP 1952* (1954), pp. 25–28; English translation in Cohen, *Criminal Process,* pp. 308–311.

81. *FKHP* 1957, VI, 245–254; English translation in Cohen, *Criminal Process,* p. 205.

82. "*Jen Min Jih Pao* Article: Americans Expose United States Spying," NCNA–English, Peking (Dec. 5, 1954), in *SCMP,* no. 941:14–15 (Dec. 4–6, 1954). For discussion of this case, see Jerome Alan Cohen, "Chinese Attitudes toward International Law—and Our Own," in Jerome A. Cohen, ed., *Contemporary Chinese Law: Research Problems and Perspectives* (Cambridge, Mass.: Harvard University Press, 1970), pp. 289–290; Lung-sheng Tao, "Communist China's Criminal Jurisdiction over Aliens," *International and Comparative Law Quarterly* 19.4: 612–613 (Oct. 1970).

83. "Release for 11 US Spies Ordered," NCNA–English, Peking (Aug. 1, 1955), in *SCMP,* no. 1100:28 (July 30-Aug. 2, 1955).

84. For other examples, see, *e.g.,* "UN Resolution on US Spying Is Void, Says Chinese Legal Expert," NCNA–English, Peking (Dec. 16, 1954), in *SCMP,* no. 950:7–8 (Dec. 17, 1954); and "Judge Mei Ju-ao Denounces UN Resolution," NCNA–English, Peking (Dec. 19, 1954), in *SCMP,* no. 951:5–6 (Dec. 18–20, 1954).

85. "International Law Expert Tears to Shreds US Spy Denials," NCNA–English, Peking (Dec. 3, 1954), in *SCMP,* no. 941:14 (Dec. 4–6, 1954).

86. Tillman Durdin, "China Frees US Bishop; Says One Captive is Suicide," *New York Times* (July 11, 1970), p. 1.

86a. "China to Free Downey of the CIA Monday," (UPI), *New York Times* (Mar. 10, 1973), pp. 1, 10.

87. Lennart Petri, "Einige Betrachtungen über Recht und Rechtsprechung in der Volksrepublik China" (Some aspects of law and adjudication in the PRC), *Juristische Blätter* 93.1–2:29–30 (Jan. 16, 1971).

88. *Ibid.,* p. 30.

89. "Briton Held Three Years Is Free, Peking Says," *New York Times* (July 31, 1970), p. 5.

90. Tillman Durdin, "Peking Is Curbing Foreign Visitors," *New York Times* (June 28, 1968), p. 3.

90a. "Chinese Free German, Held as Spy for 5 Years," (Reuters), *New York Times* (Apr. 12, 1973), p. 8; "Freed Japanese Arrive in HK," *Mainichi Daily News* (Apr. 15, 1973), p. 1.

91. "Only Link to the Outside," *New York Times* (Nov. 27, 1969), city ed., p. 7.

92. *FKHP 1954–1955*, I, 30.
93. *FKHP 1954–1955*, I, 9.
94. *FLHP 1949–1950* (1952), p. 17.
95. *FKHP 1954–1955*, I, 4.
96. Nothing in the Economic Cooperation Agreement concluded between the United States and France on June 28, 1948, provides for such privileges. *UNTS* 19:9 (1948). But in the March 16 and 31, 1949, exchange of notes constituting an agreement between the United States and France relating to passport visa fees, France agreed that "United States citizens may, simply by presenting their national passport during the period of its validity, enter without a visa," while the United States merely "desires to grant as nearly as possible, consistent with statutory and other restrictions, similar concessions to citizens of France applying for non-immigrant passport visas." *UNTS* 84:283 (1951).
97. On January 4, 1951, Jen-min-pi (JMP) $24,900.00 was worth US $1 at the official Chinese exchange rate. Cheng Chu-yüan, *Chung-Kung ti chin-yung chih-tu* (The financial and monetary system of the Chinese Communists; Hong Kong: Yu-lien ch'u-pan-she, 1954), p. 118.
98. "Peking Municipal People's Council Bans Reactionary Franciscaines Missionaires de Marie," *PR* 9.37:37 (Sept. 9, 1966).
99. "Note given by the Ministry of Foreign Affairs, Peking, to the Embassy of India in China, Nov. 24, 1967," in *White Paper,* no. 14:78–79 (Feb. 1967-Apr. 1968). For the Indian protest, see *ibid.*, pp. 70–72.
100. Not printed in this book; for text of this note, see *Accounts and Papers*, Cmd. 8639 (1951–1952) [Correspondence on British Trade in China, No. 2], p. 3.
101. US Congress, House, Committee on Foreign Affairs, *Expropriation of American-Owned Property by Foreign Governments in the 20th Century,* 88th Cong., 1st sess., 1963, p. 16.
102. US Congress, House, Committee on Foreign Affairs, Subcommittee on the Far East and the Pacific, *Claims of Nationals of the United States Against the Chinese Communist Regime: Hearing on S.3675,* 89th Cong., 2nd sess., Sept. 29, 1966, pp. 14–15.
103. Statement of Fred B. Smith, General Counsel, Treasury Department, *ibid.*, p. 2.
104. Statement of Richard B. Kearney, *ibid.*, p. 8.
105. Statement of Kenneth B. Sprague, *ibid.*, p. 16.
106. See Jerome Alan Cohen, "Recognizing China," *Foreign Affairs* 50.1:42 (Oct. 1971); "US-China Dispute on Funds Reported Near a Settlement," (Reuters), *New York Times* (May 17, 1973), p. 16.
107. Great Britain, *Parliamentary Debates* (Lords), 5th ser., 189 (1953–1954), p. 503.
108. *FLHP 1954* (1955), p. 31.
109. See "Traveller's Tales," *FEER* 61.31:223 (Aug. 1, 1968); and "P'ping To Free Belgian Banker," *China News* (Taipei; Oct. 27, 1971), p. 1.
110. *Ibid.*
111. Derek Davies, "Twisting the Lions' Tails," *FEER* 61.31:230–233 (Aug. 1, 1968).
112. "Traveller's Tales"; *FEER* 61.31:223; see also Petri, "Recht und Rechtsprechung in China," p. 30.
113. Petri, "Recht," p. 30.
114. "7 Germans, Freed by China, Home," *New York Times* (Nov. 1, 1969), p. 12.
115. "Peking Frees Anthony Grey, British Newsman, Who Had Been Under House Arrest Since July, 1967," *ibid.* (Oct. 5, 1969), p. 24.
116. "Chinese Let Briton Visit Anthony Grey," *ibid.* (July 15, 1969), p. 3.
117. "Beating in Peking Described by Grey," *ibid.* (Oct. 14, 1969), p. 7.
118. "2d Briton Describes Jail," *ibid.* (Oct. 14, 1969), p. 7.

119. "Mao Faction in Minority, Japan Speculates," *Boston Globe* (Jan. 8, 1967), pp. 1, 10.

120. See, *e.g.*, Ling Ch'i-han, "It Is Entirely Legal for Egypt to Nationalize the Suez Canal Company," *Kuang-ming jih-pao* (Aug. 3, 1956), p. 4; English summary in "*Kuang Ming Jih Pao* Advises Western Powers to Keep Sober over Suez," NCNA–English, Peking (Aug. 3, 1956), in *SCMP*, no. 1346:40 (Aug. 9, 1956); and Wang Tieh-yai, "On the Illegality of the So-called Proposal for 'International Control' of the Suez Canal," *JMJP* (Aug. 15, 1956), p. 6; English summary under the title " 'International Control' over Suez against International Law, Says Expert," NCNA–English, Peking (Aug. 12, 1956), in *SCMP*, no. 1350: 24–25 (Aug. 15, 1956).

Part VI. The Exercise of Extraterritorial Jurisdiction

1. Background information for this introductory section has been obtained from Harley Farnsworth MacNair, *The Chinese Abroad, Their Position and Protection: A Study in International Law and Relations* (Shanghai: Commercial Press, Ltd., 1933); Victor Purcell, *The Chinese in Southeast Asia*, 2nd ed. (London: Oxford University Press, 1965); Donald E. Willmott, *The National Status of the Chinese in Indonesia: 1900–1958* (Ithaca, N.Y.: Cornell University, Department of Far Eastern Studies, Southeast Asia Program, 1961); Lea E. Williams, *The Future of the Overseas Chinese in Southeast Asia* (New York: McGraw-Hill, 1966); Mochtar Kusuma-atmadja, "The Sino-Indonesian Dual Nationality Treaty," an unpublished paper presented at a meeting of the panel on "China and World Order" of the American Society of International Law in Washington, D.C., Nov. 1969; and Stephen Fitzgerald, *China and the Overseas Chinese: A Study of Peking's Change in Policy 1949–1970* (Cambridge, Eng.: Cambridge University Press, 1972).

2. See, for example, the documents translated in Lo-shu Fu, *A Documentary Chronicle of Sino-Western Relations 1644–1820* (Tucson: University of Arizona Press, 1966), I, 157–159, 193.

3. See MacNair, *The Chinese Abroad*, pp. 13–16.

4. See, *e.g.*, Article V of the Convention of Peace and Friendship between Great Britain and China, signed October 24, 1860, in *Hertslet's China Treaties*, 3rd ed., (London: His Majesty's Stationery Office, 1908), I, 50.

5. Article V of the Additional Articles to the Treaty of Commerce between the United States and China of June 18, 1858, signed July 28, 1868, *ibid.*, p. 556.

6. Immanuel C. Y. Hsü, *China's Entrance into the Family of Nations: The Diplomatic Phase, 1858–1880* (Cambridge, Mass.: Harvard University Press, 1960), p. 172.

7. MacNair, *The Chinese Abroad*, p. 24.

8. Chu-tung Tsai, "The Chinese Nationality Law, 1909," *AJIL* 4.2:407 (Apr. 1910).

9. An English translation of the Law on the Acquisition and Loss of Chinese Nationality, promulgated March 28, 1909, may be found in *AJIL* 4 (supp.): 160–166 (1910).

10. Chu-tung Tsai, "Chinese Nationality Law," p. 407.

11. Articles III and VIII.

12. Article I. If the father was unknown or of indeterminate nationality, Article I provided that the child would be Chinese if the mother was Chinese.

13. Articles XI, XII, and XVIII.

14. An English translation of the Law of Nationality promulgated on February 5, 1929, may be found in *China Law Review* (Shanghai), 4.3:39–45 (Feb. 1930).

15. For an English translation of the Common Program, see A. P. Blaustein, ed., *Fundamental Legal Documents of Communist China* (South Hacken-

sack, N.J.: Fred B. Rothman & Co., 1962), pp. 34–53. Subsequent quotations are derived from this translation.

16. For an English translation of the Constitution, see *ibid.*, pp. 1–33. Article 98 of the Constitution was virtually identical with Article 58 of the Common Program, and Articles 100–103 of the former covered the duties mentioned in Article 8 of the latter.

17. Article 23, Electoral Law of the People's Republic of China for the All-China People's Congress and Local People's Congresses of All Levels, promulgated Mar. 1, 1953; *ibid.*, p. 200.

18. Article 141 of the Constitution of the Republic of China, promulgated on January 1, 1947, provides: "The foreign policy of the Republic of China, shall, in a spirit of independence and initiative and on the basis of the principles of equality and reciprocity, cultivate good-neighborliness with other nations and respect treaties and the Charter of the United Nations, in order to protect the rights and interests of Chinese citizens residing abroad. . . ." *China Yearbook 1963–64* (Taipei: China Publishing Co., 1964), p. 881.

19. See Article 26, paragraph 5; Article 64, paragraph 5; and Article 91, paragraph 5 of the Constitution of the Republic of China. *China Yearbook, 1963–64*, pp. 870, 874, and 876.

20. See Tao-tai Hsia, "Settlement of Dual Nationality between Communist China and Other Countries," *Östeuropa Recht* 11.1:28, n.2 (1965); Jerome A. Cohen, *The Criminal Process in the People's Republic of China, 1949–1963: An Introduction* (Cambridge, Mass.: Harvard University Press, 1968), p. 298.

21. See "Communiqué issued by the Bureau of National Statistics Concerning the Result of Investigation and Registration of National Population (November 1, 1954)," *FKHP 1954–1955*, I, 554.

22. See Chou En-lai, "Report on the Work of the Government," *PC*, no. 20:24 (Oct. 16, 1954).

23. Wang Chi-yuan, "Nationality of Overseas Chinese," *PC* no. 12:8–9 (June 16, 1955).

24. "What Is Dual Nationality?" *Shih-shih shou-ts'e* (Current affairs handbook), no. 9:39 (May 10, 1955).

25. See Willmott, *National Status*, p. 54.

26. *Ibid.*, pp. 54–61.

27. See Lea E. Williams, "Sino-Indonesian Diplomacy: A Study of Revolutionary International Politics," *China Quarterly*, no. 11:192–199 (July-Sept. 1962).

28. See, *e.g.*, "Foreign Minister Ch'en Yi's Letter on Dec. 24 to Indonesian Foreign Minister," NCNA–English, Peking (Dec. 25, 1959) in *SCMP*, no. 2167: 47–49 (Dec. 31, 1959).

29. See David Mozingo, "The Sino-Indonesian Dual Nationality Treaty," *Asian Survey* 1.10:25–26 (Dec. 1961).

30. *Ibid.*, p. 28.

31. See Justus M. van der Kroef, "The Sino-Indonesian Rupture," *China Quarterly*, no. 33:29 (Jan.-Mar. 1968).

32. *Ibid.*, pp. 25, 41.

33. Kusuma-atmadja, "Sino-Indonesian Dual Nationality Treaty," pp. 36–37.

34. *Ibid.*, p. 37.

35. Sino-Nepalese Exchange of Notes on Certain Matters Concerning Relations between China and Nepal, September 20, 1956, *TYC 1956*, V (1957), 7, 9; English translation by NCNA, Sept. 25, 1956, reprinted in *British and Foreign State Papers, 1955–1956*, 162:898–899 (London: Her Majesty's Stationery Office, 1965).

36. Hsia, "Settlement of Dual Nationality," p. 29.

37. "Chou En-lai's Talks to David Marshall on the Question of Nationality of Overseas Chinese in Singapore, Oct. 9, 1956," *WCC 1956–1957*, IV (1958), 136, 137; English translation under the title "Chou En-lai Receives David Marshall," Hsinhua News Agency Release, no. 2426:118 (Peking, Oct. 13, 1956).

38. Hsia, "Settlement of Dual Nationality," pp. 30–31.

39. George Ginsburgs, *Soviet Citizenship Law* (Leiden: A. W. Sijthoff, 1968), p. 184.

40. *Ibid.*, p. 196.

41. *Ibid.*, pp. 199–200.

42. See Hsia, "Settlement of Dual Nationality," p. 32, citing Ivan Sipkov, "Settlement of Dual Nationality in European Communist Countries," *AJIL* 56.4: 1016 (Oct. 1962).

43. Hsia, "Settlement of Dual Nationality," p. 34.

44. See Ginsburgs, *Soviet Citizenship Law,* pp. 199–217, for extensive analysis of the Soviet treaties.

45. See text at nn. 13, 14.

46. See text at n. 37.

47. Quoted in Hsia, "Settlement of Dual Nationality," p. 38, which is the source of this paragraph in the text.

48. Hecker, "Das Recht der Staatsangehörigkeit in China," in *Das Standesamt,* 12.11:303 (Nov. 10, 1959). We are grateful to Dr. Frank Münzel for having brought this article to our attention and translating it.

49. Recall text at n. 12 and item 23–2.

50. Hecker, "Das Recht," p. 303.

51. According to a national census report published by the PRC Bureau of National Statistics on November 1, 1954, the Han Chinese constitute 93.94 percent of China's population (including Taiwan). "Communiqué issued by the Bureau of National Statistics Concerning the Result of Investigation and Registration of National Population (November 1, 1954)," *FKHP 1954–1955,* I, 554. See also, *e.g.*, Amrit Lal, "Sinification of Ethnic Minorities in China," *Current Scene* 8.4:1 (Feb. 15, 1970).

52. Tuan-sheng Ch'ien, *The Government and Politics of China* (Cambridge, Mass.: Harvard University Press, 1950), p. 8.

53. *Ibid.*, pp. 8–9.

54. English translation in Blaustein, ed., *Fundamental Legal Documents,* p. 6.

55. À propos the relationship between "citizenship" and "nationality," a leading commentary on the Constitution stated: "Citizens are persons who possess a nationality and who enjoy the rights prescribed by the Constitution of that country and who assume the duties prescribed by the Constitution of that country. In our country, citizens are thus what we ordinarily speak of as nationals. All those who possess the nationality of the People's Republic of China and who enjoy rights and assume duties according to the Constitution are citizens of our country." Wu Te-feng *et al.*, eds., *Chung-hua jen-min kung-ho-kuo hsien-fa chiang-hua* (Lectures on the constitution of the People's Republic of China; Wuhan, 1956), p. 102.

56. Recall text at n. 35.

57. *White Paper,* no. 3:115–116 (Nov. 1959-Mar. 1960).

58. Basang Chulma appears to have been the wife of Dawa Thondup.

59. *White Paper,* no. 3:118–119.

60. Recall item 23–1 and text at n. 23.

61. Note given by the Ministry of External Affairs, New Delhi, to the Embassy of China in India, April 13, 1960, *White Paper,* no. 4:56–58 (Mar.-Nov. 1960).

62. Note given by the Ministry of Foreign Affairs, Peking, to the Embassy of India in China, Sept. 23, 1960, *White Paper,* no. 4:73.

63. Note given by the Ministry of External Affairs, New Delhi, to the Embassy of China in India, June 30, 1960, *White Paper,* no. 4:63.

64. Note given by the Ministry of Foreign Affairs, Peking, to the embassy of India in China, September 23, 1960, in *White Paper,* no. 4:74.

65. T. S. Rama Rao, "The Sino-Indian White Papers and Some Incidental

Questions of International Law," *Indian Year Book of International Affairs* 13.1: 264 (1964).

66. Liu Chia-chi, "On the Question of Dual Nationality," *FH*, no. 3:20, 22 (1957).

67. Chung-yang cheng-fa kang-pu hsüeh-hsiao hsing-fa chiao-yen-shih pien, ed., *Chung-hua jen-min kung-ho-kuo hsing-fa tsung-tse chiang-i* (Lectures on the general principles of criminal law of the People's Republic of China; Peking, 1957), p. 40.

68. "Chinese at Hong Kong Border Broadcast Demands to British," *New York Times,* City ed., (Aug. 26, 1967), p. 3.

69. See *Yin-tu hua-ch'iao chih* (Record of the overseas Chinese in India), compiled by the Commission for Compiling Overseas Chinese Records (Taipei, 1962), p. 112.

70. See "Chinese Compatriots in Macao Protest against Portuguese Authorities' Brutalities," *PR* 9.50:35 (Dec. 9, 1966).

71. See "Chinese People Armed with Mao Tse-tung's Thought Are Not to Be Trifled With," *PR* 9.51:17–18 (Dec. 16, 1966).

72. "Victory for the Patriotic Anti-Imperialist Struggle By Compatriots in Macao," *PR* 10.6:31 (Feb. 3, 1967).

73. See Charles Mohr, "Portuguese Blocking Refugees Seeking to Escape Via Macao," *New York Times* (Feb. 23, 1967), p. 6.

74. Letter dated Feb. 15, 1967, from Ambassador Liu Chieh to the Secretary General of the United Nations, quoted in Hungdah Chiu, compiler, "Chinese Contemporary Practices and Judicial Decisions Relating to International Law (February 1966 to March 1967)," *The Annals of the Chinese Society of International Law,* 4:72 (Aug. 1967).

75. See, e.g., (Record of the overseas Chinese in India), pp. 113, 117.

76. Note given by the Ministry of External Affairs, New Delhi, to the Embassy of China in India, Dec. 5, 1959, *White Paper,* no. 3:110.

77. "Rescued Chinese Guarded in Paris," *New York Times* (Apr. 30, 1971), p. 8.

78. "Paris Denies It Refused Asylum to Chinese Aide," *New York Times* (May 9, 1971), p. 19.

79. Article 58 of the Common Program, see text at n. 15, above.

80. At the time of writing the author was President of Wuhan University. He was removed from his post during the Cultural Revolution. See *Chung-kung jen-min lu* (Who's who in Communist China; Taipei, 1967), p. 144.

81. *FKHP 1959,* X, 335.

82. (Lectures on the criminal law), pp. 41–42.

83. "US Repatriates 48 Chinese Fishermen Rescued in Storm," *New York Times* (Jan. 10, 1967), p. 5.

84. "Victory for the Patriotic Anti-Imperialist Struggle By Compatriots in Macao," *PR* 10.6:31 (Feb. 3, 1967).

85. "Chinese People Denounce Soviet Revisionists' Fascist Atrocities," *PR* 10.6:25 (Feb. 3, 1967).

86. "In USSR Ministry of Foreign Affairs," *Pravda* (Jan. 26, 1967), p. 3; English translation in "Red Square Scuffle and Other Chinese Phenomena," *CDSP* 19.4:6 (Feb. 15, 1967).

87. "Soviet Revisionist Crime against Chinese Students in Iraq," *PR* 10.6:29 (Feb. 3, 1967).

88. "Protest against Unreasonable Persecution of Chinese Students in France," NCNA–English, Peking (Sept. 8, 1952), in *SCMP,* no. 411:1–2 (Sept. 9, 1952).

89. Lea E. Williams, *Future of the Overseas Chinese,* p. 29.

90. Van der Kroef, "Sino-Indonesian Rupture," pp. 28–29.

91. *Ibid.,* p. 26.

92. *Ibid.,* p. 34.

93. *JMJP* [People's Daily] Commentator, "British Imperialists Are Playing with Fire," *PR* 10.23:38–39 (June 2, 1967).

94. *JMJP* Commentator, " 'Gunboat Policy' Was Thrown into the Rubbish Heap Long Ago," *PR* 10.23:39–40 (June 2, 1967).

95. See, *e.g.*, "Vice-Foreign Minister Li Ke-nung Lodges Strong Protest with Thailand Government," NCNA–English, *Daily News Release*, no. 269:121 (Jan. 27, 1950); "Chinese People Cannot Tolerate Atrocities Perpetrated by French Army to [*sic*] Overseas Chinese," NCNA–English, *Daily News Release*, no. 262:84 (Jan. 20, 1950); and "F. O. [Foreign Office] Statement on British Persecution of Overseas Chinese," NCNA–English, *Daily News Release*, no. 586:207–208 (Dec. 30, 1950).

96. For another example, see "Strong Protest Over Burmese Government's Political Persecution of Overseas Chinese," *PR* 11.40:41–42 (Oct. 4, 1968).

97. "Overseas Chinese in Cuba Persecuted," NCNA–English, Peking (Apr. 2, 1951), in *SCMP*, no. 90:11–12 (Apr. 1–3, 1951).

98. "Chinese Vice Foreign Minister Lodges Strongest Protest with British Government," NCNA–English, Peking (May 22, 1967), in *SCMP*, no. 3946:29 (May 25, 1967).

99. "Chinese Walks Out on Briton," *New York Times* (May 24, 1967), p. 7.

100. "Hong Kong Widens Curfew as 2 Die in Rioting," *New York Times* (July 13, 1967), p. 13.

101. "Peking Rally Condemns British Authorities in Hong Kong," *PR* 10.33:30 (Aug. 11, 1967).

102. See, *e.g.*, "Hong Kong's Reds Step Up Pressure," *New York Times* (July 11, 1967), pp. 1, 14; and "Big 4-Day Joint Suspension of Trade in Hong Kong," *PR* 10.29:34 (July 14, 1967).

103. See the large quantity of correspondence between the PRC and India on this subject in *White Paper*, no. 3, pp. 141–151; no. 4, pp. 81–99; no. 5, pp. 100–142; no. 6, pp. 145–188, 227–232; no. 7, pp. 154–169.

104. The text of the Ordinance is in *The Current Indian Statutes, 1962*, ed. Anand Mohan Suri (Chandigarh: Punjab Law Reporter Press, [n.d.]), Pt. III, pp. 5–20; the text of the Defense Act is in *The Current Indian Statutes, 1963*, Pt. II, pp. 18–41; the text of the Defense Rules, G.S.R. 1465, published in *The Gazette of India, Extraordinary*, Pt. II, Sec. 3(1), dated Nov. 5, 1962.

105. Text in Amarendra Nath Sinha, *Law of Citizenship and Aliens in India* (New York and Bombay: Asia Publishing House, 1962), pp. 360–368.

106. The text of this Order is in *The Current Indian Statutes, 1962*, Pt. I, p. 122.

107. The text of this Order is in *The Current Indian Statutes, 1963*, Pt. I, pp. 113–114.

108. Text of 1939 Act in Sinha, *Law of Citizenship*, pp. 337–339.

109. The text of the October 30, 1962, Ordinance is in *The Current Indian Statutes, 1962*, Pt. III, pp. 20–21. This Ordinance was replaced by the Foreigners Law (Application and Amendment) Act (Nov. 24, 1962), in *Acts of Parliament, 1962*, pp. 231–232.

110. The text of this order, G.S.R. 1418, is in *The Current Indian Statutes, 1962*, Pt. I, p. 123.

111. See the Act of November 24, 1962, cited in n. 105.

112. The text of the Foreigners (Internment) Order of November 3, 1962, G.S.R. 1463 (amended by G.S.R. 1595 on November 16, 1962) is in *The Current Indian Statutes, 1962*, Pt. I, pp. 124–125.

113. India, Parliament, *Lok Sabha Debates*, 3rd Ser., 4th Sess. (1963), XIII, p. 1141.

114. See, *e.g.*, Joseph Lelyveld, "Curbs On Chinese Retained in India," *New York Times* (Sept. 4, 1967), p. 12. Personal interviews with former Chinese residents of India and with Indian officials have confirmed the information in the text.

115. Fu Chu, "The Persecution of Chinese Nationals by the Indian Government is a Serious Violation of International Law," *JMJP* (Nov. 30, 1962), p. 3. See also Ni Cheng-ao, "Introduction to the 1949 Geneva Convention Relating to the Protection of Civilian Persons in Time of War," *JMJP* (Jan. 22, 1963), p. 5. For analysis of the Chinese claims and supporting legal arguments, see Jerome Alan Cohen and Shao-chuan Leng, "The Sino-Indian Dispute over the Internment and Detention of Chinese in India," in Jerome Alan Cohen, ed., *China's Practice of International Law: Some Case Studies* (Cambridge, Mass.: Harvard University Press, 1972), pp. 268–320.

116. *E.g.*, Article 17, paragraph 1, of the Consular Convention between the Polish People's Republic and the Union of Soviet Socialist Republics, signed at Warsaw on January 21, 1958, merely provides: "A consul may protect the rights and interests of the sending State and its citizens and look after the welfare of such citizens. He may for that purpose apply direct to courts and authorities of his consular district." *UNTS* 319:318 (New York: The United Nations, 1960). Some of the conventions concluded among European Communist countries provided that the detaining authorities must notify the consul after detaining a national of his state. See Ivan Sipkov, "Consular Conventions of the European Communist Countries," *Östeuropa Recht* 13.3:180 (Sept. 1967).

117. "Foreign Ministry Raps Aid Stoppage by Burmese," broadcast, NCNA–English, Peking (Aug. 10, 1967), printed in *FBIS* 156/67:BBB5–6 (Aug. 11, 1967).

118. See "Chinese Embassy Protests against Ne Win Government's Attempt to Confiscate Chinese Relief for Victims," NCNA–English, Peking (Aug. 20, 1967), in *SCMP*, no. 4008:32–33 (Aug. 24, 1967).

119. See "Chinese Foreign Ministry's Note to Burmese Embassy," NCNA–English, Peking (Sept. 1, 1967), in *SCMP*, no. 4015:34 (Sept. 6, 1967); and "China Protests against Burma's Rejection of Chinese Demand," NCNA–English, Peking (Sept. 6, 1967), in *SCMP*, no. 4018:15–16 (Sept. 11, 1967).

120. Ping Chen, "We Oppose the Detention of Chinese Students by the United States Government," *Ta kung pao* (Tientsin; Dec. 18, 1954), English translation in *SCMP*, no. 956:11–13 (Dec. 29, 1954).

121. See, *e.g.*, William L. Ryan and Sam Summerlin, *The China Cloud: America's Tragic Blunder and China's Rise to Nuclear Power* (Boston: Little, Brown, 1968). Chien is written as Tsien Hsue-shen, or H. S. Tsien in *The China Cloud.*

122. "Peng Chen and Eikichi Kanbayashiyama Issue Joint Communiqué," NCNA–English, Peking (Oct. 17, 1955), in *SCMP*, no. 1151:57–58 (Oct. 15–18, 1955).

123. "*Kuang Ming Jih Pao* Demands Release of Chinese by Japanese Government," *NCNA*–English, Peking (Nov. 22, 1955), in *SCMP*, no. 1176:28 (Nov. 23, 1955).

124. "9,052 Overseas Chinese Deported from Malaya by British Government without Reason," NCNA–English, Canton (Dec. 3, 1951), in *SCMP*, no. 228:5 (Dec. 4, 1951).

125. "Chinese Students Studying in Hungary Return," *PR* 9.50:34 (Dec. 9, 1966).

126. "Strongest Protest against Mongolian Revisionist Clique's Anti-Chinese Atrocity," *PR* 10.23:36 (June 2, 1967).

127. "Chinese Foreign Ministry Protests against Bulgaria's Anti-China Action," *PR* 10.25:40 (June 16, 1967).

128. "Protest against Czechoslovak Revisionist Clique's Breach of Cultural Co-operation Agreement," *PR* 10.32:54 (Aug. 4, 1967).

129. Williams, *Future of the Overseas Chinese,* p. 66.

130. "Protest against Indonesian Government's Mass Expulsion of Chinese Nationals," *PR* 9.44:6 (Oct. 28, 1966); see also "China Warns Indonesian Government against Continued Persecution of Chinese Nationals," *PR* 10.29:39–40 (July 14, 1967).

131. On October 27, 1967, eighteen days after Jakarta announced an official suspension of its relations with Peking, the PRC reciprocated, holding Indonesia "fully responsible" for this development. "Chinese Government Statement: Strong Protest Against Reactionary Indonesian Government's Suspension of Diplomatic Relations between the Two Countries," *PR* 10.45:5–6 (Nov. 3, 1967).

132. "Foreign Minister Ch'en Yi's Letter to Subandrio" NCNA–English, Peking (Mar. 17, 1960), in *SCMP*, no. 2222:40 (Mar. 23, 1960).

133. Williams, "Sino-Indonesian Diplomacy," pp. 184, 196.

134. Also, see, *e.g.*, n. 132, above.

135. "Indonesian Government Condemned for Sabotaging China's Bringing Back Victimized Chinese," *PR* 10.15:37 (Apr. 7, 1967).

136. Van der Kroef, "Sino-Indonesian Rupture," p. 31.

137. "China Warns Indonesian Government against Continued Persecution of Chinese Nationals," *PR* 10.29:39–40 (July 14, 1967).

138. "Note Given by the Ministry of External Affairs, New Delhi, to the Embassy of China in India, 10 August 1963," *White Paper*, no. 10:59–60 (July 1963-Jan. 1964).

139. "China Decides to Send Civil Aircraft to Bring Seriously Wounded Overseas Chinese Back from Burma," NCNA–English, Peking (July 4, 1967), in *SCMP*, no. 3975:37 (July 7, 1967).

140. The Burmese reply of July 4, 1967, was mentioned in the Chinese note of July 5, 1967, to the Burmese ambassador to China. See "China Protests at Burma's Refusal to Let Wounded Chinese Come Back for Medical Treatment," NCNA–English, Peking (July 5, 1967) in *SCMP*, no. 3976:35 (July 10, 1967).

141. Williams, *Future of the Overseas Chinese*, p. 67.

142. See text at n. 82.

143. *The Commoner*, July 11, 1967.

144. "Nepalese Government Must Stop Anti-China Activities," *PR* 10.31:29 (July 28, 1967).

145. "Traveller's Tales," *FEER* 67.3:89 (Jan. 16, 1969).

GPSR Authorized Representative: Easy Access System Europe - Mustamäe tee 50, 10621 Tallinn, Estonia, gpsr.requests@easproject.com

www.ingramcontent.com/pod-product-compliance
Lightning Source LLC
LaVergne TN
LVHW052202200926
848481LV00001B/10
* 9 7 8 0 6 9 1 6 1 8 6 9 2 *